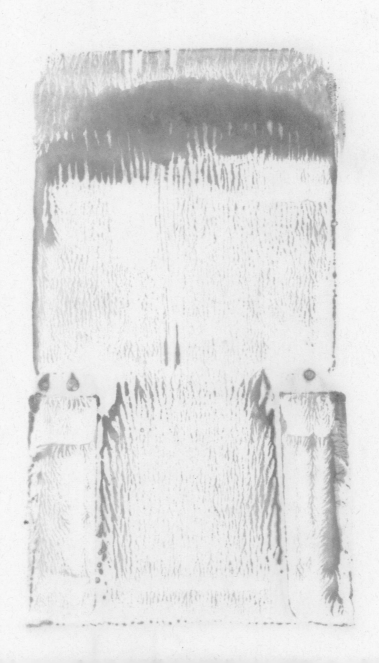

DAVID FELLMAN
Vilas Professor of Political Science, University of Wisconsin
ADVISORY EDITOR TO DODD, MEAD & COMPANY

THE CONSTITUTION AND THE SUPREME COURT

Second Edition

The CONSTITUTION *and* *the* SUPREME COURT

Second Edition

Wallace Mendelson

Professor of Government
The University of Texas

DODD, MEAD & COMPANY
New York · Toronto · 1970

For M. M.

My debt defies calculation.

Introduction

> In all societies the historical function of law has been to elaborate, rationalize, and protect the dominant institutions and accredited ways of life [whether "good" or "bad"], and the function of public law has been to apply ultimately the coercion of the state toward maintaining the outlines of those dominant institutions.
>
> MAX LERNER

This is a much enlarged and revised version of a volume that first appeared in 1959. Again the purpose is to offer a broad view of the governmental process called constitutional law. That, as I see it, involves three basic problems. One is judicial review—what belongs to the courts, and what to the political processes? This of course is merely a specialized aspect of the separation of powers. Another problem is federalism—what belongs to the nation, and what to the states? Finally the universal "conflict" between liberty and authority—what is Caesar's due, and from what must Caesar abstain?

For these basic problems each era provides its own answers according to its needs. Yet no age is ever quite independent of the others—even judges cannot escape history. The judicial process, then, necessarily involves more than logic. Without ignoring the claims of formal symmetry, it must synthesize established rules, pragmatic needs, and moral yearnings. It must honor reasonable expectations born of the past, yet allow *Lebensraum* for the present and the future. Ours, after all, is a "living Constitution." There are few fixed and final solutions in constitutional law.

In the unending search for workable solutions, the Supreme Court plays a crucial, but hardly an exclusive, role. Hence the effort to suggest, by incorporation of extra-judicial material, that judges are not the only agents of constitutional law—and that they too are responsive to the *Zeitgeist*.

On the bench as elsewhere, great artistry means *creative* response to the evolving processes of social life. Yet judges who go too far invite disaster. It is not for them to build a brave new world (or resurrect an old one)—the legislative function having been given to others. And so we are back again to the problem first mentioned: how far is too far for judges? This may be today's crucial issue.

For those who are not acquainted with the recording of Supreme Court decisions a few words of guidance may be useful. Prior to 1875, the Court's work was published by "authorized" reporters, as follows: Dallas (Dall.) 1789–1800;

Cranch (Cr.) 1801–1815; Wheaton (Wheat.) 1816–1827; Peters (Pet.) 1828–1842; Howard (How.) 1843–1860; Black (Bl.) 1861–1862; Wallace (Wall.) 1863–1874. The famous case of *Marbury* v. *Madison,* for example, is found in 1 Cr. 137 (1803). This reference, or citation, means that the case was decided in 1803 and is included in Vol. 1 of the Cranch reports at page 137. Since 1874 the work of the Supreme Court has been set out in the official *Supreme Court Reports* (United States Government Printing Office). In this series a case is cited, or referred to, by a volume number; the abbreviation, U. S.; a page number; and the date of the decision. Thus *Gitlow* v. *New York,* 268 U. S. 652 (1925), was decided in 1925 and will be found in vol. 268 of the *Supreme Court Reports* at page 652. The foregoing citation systems are used in this book. There are, however, two rival private reporting systems; namely, *The Supreme Court Reporter* (West Publishing Company) and *United States Supreme Court Reports, Lawyers Edition* (Lawyer's Cooperative Publishing Company). The former is identified by the abbreviation, S. Ct., the latter by the abbreviation, L. Ed. Volume and page numbers and decision dates are used with these identifying symbols just as they are used as indicated above with respect to the official *Supreme Court Reports.* Thus the *Gitlow* case will be found in 268 U. S. 652 (1925) and also in 45 S. Ct. 625 (1925) and 69 L.Ed. 1138 (1925). At the beginning of each volume of the two private reporter systems there is a conversion table which translates the official into the private citation and vice versa.

Cases referred to in the text without citation have been cited earlier, or are reproduced with citations at the end of the textual material in which they are mentioned. Footnotes have been eliminated from virtually all of the opinions represented herein.

Those who prefer a thoroughly historical approach will find the cases arranged in Appendix III in terms of major historic eras. Some may find this the proper order for student study and class discussion.

I gratefully acknowledge many helpful suggestions from Loren Beth, Alan Engel, David Fellman, and Robert McCloskey.

WALLACE MENDELSON

Austin, Texas
April, 1965

Contents

Part One | JUDICIAL REVIEW
What Belongs to the Judicial and
What to the Political Processes?

Congress and the President have all the force [of sword and purse], if they dare use it, . . . the Court has nothing but its power to persuade us.

CHARLES P. CURTIS

I. THE REVIEWING POWER AND ITS LIMITATIONS

The dispersion of power is a basic principle of government in the United States. Ultimate control is spread broadly among the people. This is the foundation of democracy. Governmental power is divided between nation and states. This is federalism. What is given to each is parceled out among three branches to accomplish the separation of powers. The purpose is not merely to avoid a tyrannical concentration of power. We seek as well the alignment of form to function and, above all, that unique democratic efficiency, the promise that governmental policies will be acceptable to those who must live with them.

But the principle of dispersion is only one foundation of American government. Familiarity obscures for us what to outside observers seems equally fundamental: our habit of dressing up the most intricate social, economic, and political problems in legal jargon and presenting them to the courts for "adjudication." "And so it happens, as one looks back over our history and the field of political discussions in the past, that he seems to see the whole region strewn with the wrecks of the Constitution—of what people have been imagining and putting forward as the Constitution. That it was unconstitutional to buy Louisiana and Florida; that it was unconstitutional to add new states to the Union from territory not belonging originally to it; that it was unconstitutional to govern the territories at all; that it was unconstitutional to charter a bank, to issue paper money, to make it a legal tender, to enact a protective tariff—that these and a hundred other things were a violation of the Constitution has been solemnly and passionately asserted by statesmen and lawyers."

Our practice suggests an inarticulate faith that within the four corners of the written Constitution are to be found the answers to all social problems, and that courts have special competence to read what is written there. Observing this a foreign visitor long ago concluded that, if asked where he found the American aristocracy (the governing class) he would reply "without hesitation . . . that it occupies the judicial bench and bar." Behind our open commitment to the fragmentation of power lurks a brooding remnant of distrust for popular government. This, perhaps, is the foundation of judicial review, or what its detractors call judicial supremacy. Whatever the terminology, the essence is clear: the power of a court in the name of the Constitution to disturb the results of the political processes.

Especially in eras when the Court is under heavy attack, as just before and during the Great Depression, it is argued that the judges "usurped" the power of review since it is not expressly conferred in the Constitution. But the fact is, our records of the Constitutional Convention indicate that most of the Founding Fathers understood and contemplated that the courts should have this power. Indeed, why else would they have provided in Article III that the federal courts should have jurisdiction in cases "arising under this Constitution"? Hamilton's well-known essay, *The Federalist*, No. 78, justified judicial review and used it as an argument in favor of ratification. The matter was discussed explicitly and apparently accepted in at least seven state ratifying assemblies. The first Congress wrote judicial review of state measures into Section 25 of the Judiciary Act of 1789 and the congressional debates on the Repeal Act of 1802 leave no doubt that judicial review of national legislation was generally contemplated before it was exercised by the Supreme Court in *Marbury* v. *Madison*. As Mr. Justice Holmes observed, "Although research has shown and practice has established the futility of the charge that it was a usurpation when this Court undertook to declare an Act of Congress unconstitutional, I suppose that we all agree that to do so is the gravest and most delicate duty that this Court is called on to perform."

Judicial review is "grave," "delicate," and controversial because it may be, and sometimes has been, used to frustrate the separation and division of powers. As though recognizing this risk, the Court has developed (parallel with *Marbury* v. *Madison*) principles of voluntary abstention. These corollaries of judicial review are designed to avoid unnecessary constitutional commitments (*Ashwander*, and *Spector*); advisory opinions (*Muskrat*); cases in which a litigant lacks a substantial, personal interest (*Tileston*); cases not ripe for adjudication (*Poe*); and cases presenting "political questions" in the sense that they raise issues as to which the Constitution provides no adequate guides for judicial decision, or as to which there is no adequate judicial remedy (*Coleman*, and compare *Baker*).

JAMES MADISON, *The Federalist*, NO. 44

If it be asked what is to be the consequence, in case the Congress shall misconstrue . . . the Constitution, and exercise powers not warranted by its true meaning, I answer, the same as if they should misconstrue or enlarge any other power vested in them; . . . the same, in short, as if the State legislatures should violate their respective constitutional authorities. In the first instance, the success of the usurpation will depend on the executive and judiciary departments, which are to expound and give effect to the legislative acts; and in the last resort a remedy must be obtained from the people, who can, by the election of more faithful representatives, annul the acts of the usurper.

JAMES MADISON, *The Federalist*, NO. 39

It is true that in controversies relating to the boundary between the two [state and federal] jurisdictions, the tribunal which is ultimately to decide, is to be established under the general government. But this does not change the principle of the case. The decision is to be impartially made, according to the rules of the Constitution; and all the usual and most effectual precautions are taken to secure this impartiality. Some such tribunal is clearly essential to prevent an appeal to the sword and a dissolution of the compact; and that it ought to be established under the general rather than under the local governments, or, to speak more properly, that it could be safely established under the first alone, is a position not likely to be combated.

JAMES MADISON, LETTER TO N. P. TRIST, DECEMBER, 1831

It will not escape notice that the Judicial authority of the U.S. when over-ruling that of a State, is complained of as subjecting a Sovereign State, with all its rights and duties, to the will of a Court composed of not more than seven individuals. This is far from a true state of the case. The question would be between a single State, and the authority of a tribunal representing as many States as compose the Union. . . .

The obvious necessity of a controul on the laws of the State, so far as they might violate the Constitution and laws of the U.S. left no option but as to the mode. The modes presenting themselves were 1. A [presidential] Veto on the passage of the State Laws. 2. A Congressional repeal of them. 3. A Judicial annulment of them. The first tho' extensively favored at the outset, was found on discussion liable to insuperable objections arising from the extent of Country and the multiplicity of State laws. The second was not free from such as gave a prefer-ence to the third as now provided by the Constitution. . . .

With respect to the supremacy of the Judicial power on questions occurring in the course of its functions, concerning the boundary of Jurisdiction between the U.S. and individual States, my opinion in favor of it was, as . . . the *Federalist* shews, of the earliest date; and I have never ceased to think that this supremacy was a vital principle of the Constitution as it is a prominent feature in its text. A supremacy of the Constitution and laws of the Union, without a supremacy in the exposition and execution of them, would be as much a mockery as a scabbard put into the hand of a Soldier without a sword in it. I have never been able to see that without such a view of the subject the Constitution itself could be the supreme law of the land; or that the *uniformity* of the Federal Authority throughout the parties to it could be preserved; or that without this *uniformity*, anarchy and disunion could be prevented.

JAMES MADISON, LETTER TO J. C. CABELL, APRIL 1, 1833

. . . the jurisdiction claimed for the federal judiciary is truly the only defen-sive armour of the federal government, or, rather, for the Constitution and laws of the United States. Strip it of that armour, and the door is wide open for nullification, anarchy, and convulsion. . . .

ALEXANDER HAMILTON, *The Federalist*, NO. 78

Some perplexity respecting the rights of the courts to pronounce legislative acts void, because contrary to the constitution, has arisen from an imagination that the doctrine would imply a superiority of the judiciary to the legislative power. It is urged that the authority which can declare the acts of another void, must necessarily be superior to the one whose acts may be declared void. As this doctrine is of great importance in all the American constitutions, a brief discussion of the ground on which it rests cannot be unacceptable.

There is no position which depends on clearer principles, than that every act of a delegated authority, contrary to the tenor of the commission under which it is exercised, is void. No legislative act, therefore, contrary to the Constitution, can be valid. To deny this, would be to affirm, that the deputy is greater than his principal; that the servant is above his master; that the representatives of the people are superior to the people themselves; that men acting by virtue of powers, may do not only what their powers do not authorize, but what they forbid.

If it be said that the legislative body are themselves the constitutional judges of their own powers, and that the construction they put upon them is conclusive upon the other departments, it may be answered, that this cannot be the natural presumption, where it is not to be collected from any particular provisions in the Constitution. It is not otherwise to be supposed, that the Constitution could intend to enable the representatives of the people to substitute their *will* to that of their constituents. It is far more rational to suppose, that the courts were designed to be an intermediate body between the people and the legislature, in order, among other things, to keep the latter within the limits assigned to their authority. The interpretation of the laws is the proper and peculiar province of the courts. A constitution is, in fact, and must be regarded by the judges, as a fundamental law. It therefore belongs to them to ascertain its meaning, as well as the meaning of any particular act proceeding from the legislative body. If there should happen to be an irreconcilable variance between the two, that which has the superior obligation and validity ought, of course, to be preferred; or, in other words, the Constitution ought to be preferred to the statute, the intention of the people to the intention of their agents.

Nor does this conclusion by any means suppose a superiority of the judicial to the legislative power. It only supposes that the power of the people is superior to both; and that where the will of the legislature, declared in its statutes, stands in opposition to that of the people, declared in the Constitution, the judges ought to be governed by the latter rather than the former. They ought to regulate their decisions by the fundamental laws, rather than by those which are not fundamental.

ALEXANDER HAMILTON, *The Federalist*, NO. 80

There ought always to be a constitutional method of giving efficacy to constitutional provisions. What, for instance, would avail restrictions on the authority of the State legislatures, without some constitutional mode of enforcing the observance of them? The States, by the plan of the convention, are prohibited from doing a variety of things, some of which are incompatible with the interests of the Union, and others with the principles of good government. The imposition of duties on imported articles, and the emission of paper money, are specimens of each kind. No man of sense will believe, that such prohibitions would be scrupulously regarded, without some effectual power in the government to restrain or correct the infractions of them. This power must either be a direct negative on the State laws, or an authority in the federal courts to overrule such as might be in manifest contravention of the articles of Union. There is no third course that I can imagine. The latter appears to have been thought by the convention preferable to the former, and, I presume, will be most agreeable to the States. . . . If there are such things as political axioms, the propriety of the judicial power of a government being coextensive with its legislative, may be ranked among the number. The mere necessity of uniformity in the interpretation of the national laws, decides the question. Thirteen independent courts of final jurisdiction over the same causes, arising upon the same laws, is a hydra in government from which nothing but contradiction and confusion can proceed.

THOMAS JEFFERSON, LETTERS TO JAMES MADISON, DECEMBER 20, 1787, AND MARCH 15, 1789

I like the negative [veto] given to the Executive, conjointly with a third of either House; though I should have liked it better, had the judiciary been associated for that purpose, or invested separately with a similar power.

[The above was written soon after Jefferson first saw the proposed new Constitution. Obviously he thought it did not provide for judicial review. Later Hamilton and Madison in *The Federalist* showed that the Constitution did contemplate judicial review. Thereafter (March 15, 1789) Jefferson wrote Madison as follows:]

In the arguments in favor of a declaration of rights, you omit one which has great weight with me: the legal check which it puts in the hands of the judiciary.

SECTION 25, JUDICIARY ACT OF 1789

The first Congress (19 members of which had been members of the Constitutional Convention) provided for Supreme Court review of state decisions which (1) invalidate any federal measure, or (2) uphold any state measure, challenged as repugnant to the federal Constitution. Obviously this Congress thought state courts would have the power of judicial review and that in such matters the Supreme Court should have the last word. The substance of these provisions of Section 25 has been re-enacted from time to time and has always been the law of the land. Its validity was challenged and upheld in *Martin v. Hunter's Lessee*, 1 Wheaton 304 (1816).

MARBURY v. *MADISON*
1 Cranch 137 (1803)

Near the end of the first Adams administration Congress authorized the President to appoint several justices of the peace for the District of Columbia. This was the occasion of the famous "midnight appointments," and the failure of Adams' Secretary of State to deliver the commissions of appointment. When the new administration took office, Secretary of State Madison, by direction of President Jefferson, refused delivery. Thereupon Marbury, one of the midnight appointees, went directly ("originally") to the Supreme Court requesting a judicial order (a writ of mandamus) to compel Madison to deliver his commission.

It will be noted that Article III, Section 2, of the Constitution gives the Supreme Court original jurisdiction only in cases "affecting Ambassadors, other public Ministers and Consuls, and those in which a State shall be a Party. . . ." Plainly Marbury's case did not fall in this category. Yet Marbury went originally to the Supreme Court, because in his view an act of Congress (Section 13 of the Judiciary Act of 1789) authorized him to do so. It was this apparent clash between the Constitution and the Act of Congress which became the crux of the Court's decision.

MR. CHIEF JUSTICE MARSHALL delivered the opinion of the Court. [First he observed that Marbury had a vested right to the office in question, and that a writ of mandamus was the proper remedy for securing such a right. Then he turned to the problem of whether that remedy "can issue from this Court".]

The act to establish the judicial courts of the United States authorizes the Supreme Court "to issue writs of mandamus, in cases warranted by the principles and usages of law, to any courts appointed, or persons holding office, under the authority of the United States." . . . The Constitution vests the whole judicial power of the United States in one Supreme Court, and such inferior courts as Congress shall, from time to time, ordain and establish. . . . In the distribution of this power, it is declared, that "the Supreme Court shall have original Jurisdiction, in all Cases affecting Ambassadors, other public Ministers and Consuls, and those in which a State shall be a Party. In all other cases, the Supreme Court shall have appellate jurisdiction." . . . If it had been intended to leave it in the discretion of the legislature, to apportion the judicial power between the Supreme and inferior courts, according to the will of that body, it would certainly have been useless to have proceeded further than to have defined the judicial power, and the tribunals in which it should be vested. The subsequent part of the section is mere surplusage—is entirely without meaning if such is to be the construction. . . . To enable this Court, then, to issue a mandamus, it must be shown to be an exercise of appellate jurisdiction, or to be necessary to enable them to exercise appellate jurisdiction. . . . It is the essential criterion of appellate jurisdiction, that it revises and corrects the proceedings in a cause already instituted, and does not create that cause. Although, therefore, a mandamus may be directed to courts, yet to issue such a writ to an officer, for the delivery of a paper, is, in effect, the same as to sustain an original action for that paper, and therefore, seems not to belong to appellate, but to original jurisdiction. Neither is it necessary in such a case as this, to enable the Court to exercise its appellate jurisdiction. The authority, therefore, given to the Supreme Court, by the act establishing the judicial courts of the United States, to issue writs of mandamus to public officers, appears not to be warranted by the Constitution; and it becomes necessary to inquire whether a jurisdiction so conferred can be exercised.

The question whether an act repugnant to the Constitution can become the law of the land, is a question deeply interesting to the United States; but, happily, not of an intricacy proportioned to its interest. It seems only necessary to recognize certain principles, supposed to have been long and well established, to decide it.

That the people have an original right to establish, for their future government, such principles as, in their opinion, shall most conduce to their own happiness, is the basis on which the whole American fabric has been erected. The exercise of this original right is a very great exertion; nor can it nor ought it to be frequently repeated. The principles, therefore, so established, are deemed fundamental. And as the authority from which they proceed is supreme, and can seldom act, they are designed to be permanent.

This original and supreme will organizes the government, and assigns to different departments their respective powers. It may either stop here, or establish certain limits not to be transcended by those departments.

The government of the United States is of the latter description. The powers of the legislature are defined and limited; and that those limits may not be mistaken, or forgotten, the Constitution is written. To what purpose are powers limited, and to what purpose is that limitation committed to writing, if these limits may, at any time, be passed by those intended to be restrained? The distinction between a government with limited and unlimited powers is abolished, if those limits do not confine the persons on whom they are imposed, and if acts prohibited and acts allowed are of equal obligation. It is a proposition too plain to be contested, that the Constitution controls any legislative act repugnant to it; or, that the legislation may alter the Constitution by an ordinary act.

Between these alternatives there is no middle ground. The Constitution is either a superior paramount law, unchangeable by ordinary means, or it is on a level with ordinary legislative acts, and, like other acts, is alterable when the legislature shall please to alter it.

If the former part of the alternative be true, then a legislative act contrary to the Constitution is not law; if the latter part be true, then written constitutions are absurd attempts, on the part of the people, to limit a power in its own nature illimitable.

Certainly all those who have framed written constitutions contemplate them as forming the fundamental and paramount law of the nation, and, consequently, the theory of every such government must be, that an act of the legislature, repugnant to the constitution, is void.

This theory is essentially attached to a written constitution, and is consequently to be considered, by this Court, as one of the fundamental principles of our society. It is not, therefore, to be lost sight of in the further consideration of this subject.

If an act of the legislature, repugnant to the Constitution, is void, does it, notwithstanding its invalidity, bind the courts, and oblige them to give it effect? Or, in other words, though it be not law, does it constitute a rule as operative as if it was a law? This would be to overthrow in fact what was established in theory; and would seem, at first view, an absurdity too gross to be insisted on. It shall, however, receive a more attentive consideration.

It is emphatically the province and duty of the judicial department to say what the law is. Those who apply the rule to particular cases, must of necessity expound and interpret that rule. If two laws conflict with each other, the courts must decide on the operation of each.

So if a law be in opposition to the Constitution; if both the law and the Constitution apply to a particular case, so that the court must either decide that case conformably to the law, disregarding the Constitution, or conformably to the Constitution, disregarding the law, the court must determine which of these conflicting rules governs the case. This is of the very essence of judicial duty.

If, then, the courts are to regard the Constitution, and the Constitution is superior to any ordinary act of the legislature, the Constitution, and not such ordinary act, must govern the case to which they both apply.

Those, then, who controvert the principle that the Constitution is to be considered, in court, as a paramount law, are reduced to the necessity of maintaining that court must close their eyes on the Constitution, and see only the law.

This doctrine would subvert the very foundation of all written constitutions. It would declare that an act which, according to the principles and theory of our government, is entirely void, is yet, in practice, completely obligatory. It would declare that if the legislature shall do what is expressly forbidden, such act, notwithstanding the express prohibition, is in reality effectual. It would be giving to the legislature a practical and real omnipotence, with the same breath which professes to restrict their powers within narrow limits. It is prescribing limits, and declaring that those limits may be passed at pleasure.

That it thus reduces to nothing what we have deemed the greatest improvement on political institutions, a written constitution, would of itself be sufficient, in America, where written constitutions have been viewed with so much reverence, for rejecting the construction. But the peculiar expressions of the Constitution of the United States furnish additional arguments in favor of its rejection.

The judicial power of the United States is extended to all cases arising under the Constitution.

Could it be the intention of those who gave this power, to say that in using it the Constitution should not be looked into? That a case arising under the Constitution should be decided without examining the instrument under which it arises?

This is too extravagant to be maintained.

In some cases, then, the Constitution must be looked into by the judges. And if they can open it at all, what part of it are they forbidden to read or to obey?

There are many other parts of the Constitution which serve to illustrate this subject.

It is declared that "No Tax or Duty shall be laid on Articles exported from any State." Suppose a duty on the export of cotton, of tobacco, or of flour; and a suit instituted to recover it. Ought judgment to be rendered in such a case? Ought the judges to close their eyes on the Constitution, and only see the law?

The Constitution declares that "No Bill of Attainder or ex post facto Law shall be passed."

If, however, such a bill should be passed, and a person should be prosecuted under it, must the court condemn to death those victims whom the Constitution endeavors to preserve?

"No Person," says the Constitution, "shall be convicted of Treason unless on the Testimony of two Witnesses to the same overt Act, or on Confession in open Court."

Here the language of the Constitution is addressed especially to the courts. It prescribes, directly for them, a rule of evidence not to be departed from. If the legislature should change that rule, and declare one witness, or a confession out of court, sufficient for conviction, must the constitutional principle yield to the legislative act?

From these, and many other selections which might be made, it is apparent that the framers of the Constitution contemplated that instrument as a rule for the government of courts, as well as of the legislature.

Why otherwise does it direct the judges to take an oath to support it? This oath certainly applies in an especial manner to their conduct in their official character. How immoral to impose it on them, if they were to be used as the instruments, and the knowing instruments, for violating what they swear to support!

The oath of office, too, imposed by the legislature, is completely demonstrative of the legislative opinion on this subject. It is in these words: "I do solemnly swear that I will administer justice without respect to persons, and do equal right to the poor and to the rich; and that I will faithfully and impartially discharge all the duties incumbent on me as ——, according to the best of my abilities and understanding, agreeably to the Constitution and laws of the United States."

Why does a judge swear to discharge his duties agreeably to the Constitution of the United States, if that Constitution forms no rule for his government? if it is closed upon him, and cannot be inspected by him?

If such be the real state of things, this is worse than solemn mockery. To prescribe, or to take this oath, becomes equally a crime.

It is also not entirely unworthy of observation, that in declaring what shall be the supreme law of the land, the Constitution itself is first mentioned; and not the laws of the United States generally, but those only which shall be made in pursuance of the Constitution, have that rank.

Thus, the particular phraseology of the Constitution of the United States confirms and strengthens the principle, supposed to be essential to all written constitutions, that a law repugnant to the Constitution is void; and that courts, as well as other departments, are bound by that instrument.

QUAERE: Was Section 13 of the Judiciary Act of 1789 in fact unconstitutional? It provided that "the Supreme Court shall also have appellate jurisdiction . . . in the cases hereinafter specially provided for; and shall have power to issue . . . writs of mandamus, in cases warranted by the principles and usages of law. . . ." Marshall and his associates read this to mean that the Court could issue writs of mandamus as a matter of original jurisdiction in cases which the Constitution allocates to its appellate jurisdiction only. So read, of course, the Act and the Constitution are in conflict.[1] But the Act may be read as authorizing such writs only in cases "warranted by the principles and usages of law," i.e., only when the Court properly has jurisdiction in an appropriate case. In short, interpreted one way, Section 13 raises a serious constitutional issue; read another way, it presents no such problem. In this situation, what should a court do? See the *Ashwander* rules, below.

ASHWANDER v. *TVA*
297 U.S. 288 (1936)

Excerpt from the concurring opinion of Mr. Justice Brandeis in which Justices Stone, Roberts, and Cardozo joined:

"Considerations of propriety, as well as long-established practice, demand that we refrain from passing upon the constitutionality of an act of Congress unless obliged to do so in the proper performance of our judicial function, when the question is raised by a party whose interests entitle him to raise it." *Blair* v. *United States*, 250 U.S. 273, 279. . . .

The Court has frequently called attention to the "great gravity and delicacy" of its function in passing upon the validity of an act of Congress; and has restricted exercise of this function by rigid insistence that the jurisdiction of federal courts is limited to actual cases and controversies; and that they have no power to give advisory opinions. On this ground it has in recent years ordered the dismissal of several suits challenging the constitutionality of important acts of Congress. . . .

The Court developed, for it own governance in the cases confessedly within its jurisdiction, a series of rules under which it has avoided passing upon a large part of all the constitutional questions pressed upon it for decision. They are:

1. The Court will not pass upon the constitutionality of legislation in a friendly, nonadversary, proceeding, declining because to decide such questions "is legitimate only in the last resort, and as a necessity in the determination of real, earnest, and vital controversy between individuals. It never was the thought that, by means of a friendly suit, a party beaten in the legislature could transfer to the courts an inquiry as to the constitutionality of the legislative act." . . .

2. The Court will not "anticipate a question of constitutional law in advance of the necessity of deciding it." . . . "It is not the

1. But see the exceptions clause at the end of Article III, Section 2, Paragraph 2.

habit of the court to decide questions of a constitutional nature unless absolutely necessary to a decision of the case." . . .

3. The Court will not "formulate a rule of constitutional law broader than is required by the precise facts to which it is to be applied." . . .

4. The Court will not pass upon a constitutional question although properly presented by the record, if there is also present some other ground upon which the case may be disposed of. This rule has found most varied application. Thus, if a case can be decided on either of two grounds, one involving a constitutional question, the other a question of statutory construction or general law, the Court will decide only the latter. . . . Appeals from the highest court of a state challenging its decision of a question under the federal Constitution are frequently dismissed because the judgment can be sustained on an independent state ground. . . .

5. The Court will not pass upon the validity of a statute upon complaint of one who fails to show that he is injured by its operation. . . . Among the many applica-

tions of this rule, none is more striking than the denial of the right of challenge to one who lacks a personal or property right. Thus, the challenge by a public official interested only in the performance of his official duty will not be entertained. . . . in *Fairchild* v. *Hughes*, 258 U.S. 126, the Court affirmed the dismissal of a suit brought by a citizen who sought to have the Nineteenth Amendment declared unconstitutional. In *Massachusetts* v. *Mellon*, 262 U.S. 447, the challenge of the federal Maternity Act was not entertained although made by the commonwealth on behalf of all its citizens.

6. The Court will not pass upon the constitutionality of a statute at the instance of one who has availed himself of its benefits. . . .

7. "When the validity of an act of Congress is drawn in question, and even if a serious doubt of constitutionality is raised, it is a cardinal principle that this Court will first ascertain whether a construction of the statute is fairly possible by which the question may be avoided." . . .

MUSKRAT v. UNITED STATES
219 U.S. 346 (1911)

In 1902 Congress provided for allocation of Cherokee tribal property to the Cherokees individually, and later in 1904 and 1906 increased the number of persons entitled to share in the final distribution. The effect of the later acts was to reduce the pro-rata share of those originally designated as allotees. To settle the resulting disputes Congress in 1907 authorized Muskrat to sue on behalf of the 1902 group to determine the validity of the 1904–1906 acts insofar as they sought to alter the original allotment.

MR. JUSTICE DAY delivered the opinion of the Court. . . .

It is therefore apparent that from its earliest history this court has consistently declined to exercise any powers other than those which are strictly judicial in their nature. . . .

As we have already seen, by the express terms of the Constitution, the exercise of the judicial power is limited to "cases" and

"controversies." Beyond this it does not extend, and unless it is asserted in a case or controversy within the meaning of the Constitution, the power to exercise it is nowhere conferred.

What, then, does the Constitution mean in conferring this judicial power with the right to determine "cases" and "controversies." . . . That question was dealt with by Mr. Justice Field, at the circuit, in the case of *Re Pacific R. Commission,* 32 Fed. 241, 255. Of these terms that learned justice said:

"The judicial article of the Constitution mentions cases and controversies. The term 'controversies,' if distinguishable at all from 'cases,' is so in that it is less comprehensive than the latter, and includes only suits of a civil nature. . . . By cases and controversies are intended the claims of litigants brought before the courts for determination by such regular proceedings as are established by law or custom for the protection or enforcement of rights, or the prevention, redress, or punishment of wrongs. Whenever the claim of a party under the Constitution, laws, or treaties of the United States takes such a form that the judicial power is capable of acting upon it, then it has become a case. The term implies the existence of present or possible adverse parties, whose contentions are submitted to the court for adjudication."

The power being thus limited to require an application of the judicial power to cases and controversies, is the act which undertook to authorize the present suits to determine the constitutional validity of certain legislation within the constitutional authority of the court? . . .

[T]he object and purpose of the suit [authorized by the act of Congress involved here] is wholly comprised in the determination of the constitutional validity of certain acts of Congress; and furthermore, in the last paragraph of the section, should a judgment be rendered in the court of claims, or this court, denying the constitutional validity of such acts, then the amount of compensation to be paid to attorneys employed for the purpose of testing the constitutionality of the law is to be paid out of funds in the Treasury of the United States belonging to the beneficiaries, the act having previously provided that the United States should be made a party, and the Attorney General be charged with the defense of the suits.

It is therefore evident that there is neither more nor less in this procedure than an attempt to provide for a judicial determination, final in this court, of the constitutional validity of an act of Congress. Is such a determination within the judicial power conferred by the Constitution, as the same has been interpreted and defined in the authoritative decisions to which we have referred? We think it is not. That judicial power, as we have seen, is the right to determine actual controversies arising between adverse litigants, duly instituted in courts of proper jurisdiction. The right to declare a law unconstitutional arises because an act of Congress relied upon by one or the other of such parties in determining their rights is in conflict with the fundamental law. The exercise of this, the most important and delicate duty of this court, is not given to it as a body with revisory power over the action of Congress, but because the rights of the litigants in justiciable controversies require the court to choose between the fundamental law and a law purporting to be enacted within constitutional authority, but in fact beyond the power delegated to the legislative branch of the government. This attempt to obtain a judicial declaration of the validity of the act of Congress is not presented in a "case" or "controversy," to which, under the Constitution of the United States, the judicial power alone extends. It is true the United States is made a defendant to this action, but it has no interest adverse to the claimants. The object is not to assert a property right as against the government, or to demand compensation for alleged wrongs because of action upon its part. The whole purpose of the law is to determine the constitutional validity of this class of legislation, in a suit not arising between parties concerning a property right necessarily involved in the decision in question, but in a proceeding against the government in its sovereign capacity, and concerning which the only judgment required is to settle the doubtful character of the legislation in question. Such judgment will not conclude private parties, when actual litigation brings to the court the question of the constitutionality of such legislation. In a legal sense the judgment could not be executed, and amounts in fact to no more than an expression of opinion upon the validity of the acts in question. Confining the jurisdiction of this court within the limitations conferred by the Constitution, which the court has hitherto been careful to observe, and whose boundaries it has refused to transcend, we think the Congress, in the act of March 1, 1907, exceeded the limitations of legislative authority, so far as it required of this court action not judicial in its nature within the meaning of the Constitution.

SPECTOR MOTOR SERVICE, INC. v. McLAUGHLIN
323 U.S. 101 (1944)

MR. JUSTICE FRANKFURTER delivered the opinion of the Court.

This is a suit brought in a United States district court to enjoin the enforcement of a State tax and for a declaratory judgment.

The Connecticut Corporation Business Tax Act of 1935, as amended, imposed on every corporation, not otherwise specially taxed, carrying on or having the right to carry on business within the State "a tax or excise upon its franchise for the privilege of carrying on or doing business within the state. . . ." Conn. Gen. Stat. Cum. Supp. 1935, § 418c, as amended by Conn. Gen. Stat. Supp. 1939, § 354e. Petitioner, a Missouri corporation with its principal place of business in Illinois, is engaged exclusively in the interstate trucking business. It is neither authorized by Connecticut to do intrastate trucking nor in fact does it engage in it. It maintains two leased terminals in Connecticut solely for the purpose of carrying on its interstate business. At the request of its lessor, it has filed with the Secretary of State in Connecticut a certificate of its incorporation in Missouri, has designated an agent in Connecticut for service of process, and has paid the statutory fee. On this state of facts the State Tax Commissioner determined that petitioner was subject to the Act of 1935, as amended, and assessed the tax against Spector for the years 1937 to 1940. Whereupon petitioner brought this suit in the United States District Court for the District of Connecticut to free itself from liability for the tax. Alleging appropriate grounds for equitable relief, petitioner claims that the "tax or excise" levied by the Act does not apply to it; and in the alternative that, if it should be deemed within the scope of the statute, the tax offends provisions of the Connecticut Constitution as well as the Commerce and Due Process Clauses of the United States Constitution.

The District Court construed the statute to be "a tax upon the exercise of a franchise to carry on intrastate commerce in the state" and therefore not applicable to petitioner. 47 F. Supp. 671, 675. On appeal the Circuit Court of Appeals for the Second Circuit construed the statute to reach all corporations having activity in Connecticut, whether doing or authorized to do intrastate business or, like the petitioner, engaged exclusively in interstate commerce. It further decided all contentions under the Connecticut Constitution against the petitioner. And so, the court below found itself compelled "to face directly the main issue whether the tax is in fact an unconstitutional burden on interstate commerce." 139 F.2d 809, 813. The dissenting judge thus phrased the issue: "we have before us in the barest possible form the effort of a state to levy an excise directly upon the privilege of carrying on an activity which is neither derived from the state, nor within its power to forbid." *Id.* at 822. It was conceded below that if the Connecticut tax was construed to cover petitioner it would run afoul the Commerce Clause, were this Court to adhere to what Judge Learned Hand called "an unbroken line of decisions." On the basis of what it deemed foreshadowing "trends," the majority ventured the prophecy that this Court would change its course, and accordingly sustained the tax. In view of the far-reaching import of such a disposition by the Circuit Court of Appeals we brought the case here. 322 U.S. 720.

Once doubts purely local to the Constitution and laws of Connecticut are resolved against the petitioner there are at stake in this case questions of moment touching the taxing powers of the States and their relation to the overriding national interests embodied in the Commerce Clause. This is so whether the issue be as broad and as bare as the District Court and Judge Learned Hand formulated it, or whether the Connecticut statute carries a more restricted meaning. If Connecticut in fact sought to tax the right to engage in interstate commerce, a long course of constitutional history and "an unbroken line of decisions" would indeed be brought into question. But even if Connecticut seeks merely to levy a tax on the net income of this interstate trucking business for activities attributed to Connecticut, questions under the Commerce Clause still remain if only because of what the court below called "ingenuous provisions as to allocation of net income in the case of business carried on partly without the state." 139 F.2d 809, 812.

We would not be called upon to decide any of these questions of constitutionality, with their varying degrees of difficulty, if, as the District Court held, the statute does not at all apply to one, like petitioner, not authorized to do intrastate business. Nor do they emerge until all other local Connecticut issues are decided against the petitioner. But even if the statute hits aspects of an exclusively interstate business, it is for Connecticut to decide from what aspect of interstate business she seeks an

exaction. It is for her to say what is the subject matter which she has sought to tax and what is the calculus of the tax she seeks. Every one of these questions must be answered before we reach the constitutional issues which divided the court below.

Answers to all these questions must precede consideration of the Commerce Clause. To none have we an authoritative answer. Nor can we give one. Only the Supreme Court of Errors of Connecticut can give such an answer. But this tax has not yet been considered or construed by the Connecticut courts. We have no authoritative pronouncements to guide us as to its nature and application. That the answers are not obvious is evidenced by the different conclusions as to the scope of the statute reached by the two lower courts. The Connecticut Supreme Court may disagree with the District Court and agree with the Circuit Court of Appeals as to the applicability of the statute. But this is an assumption and at best "a forecast rather than a determination." *Railroad Commission* v. *Pullman Co.*, 312 U.S. 496, 499. Equally are we without power to pass definitely on the other claims urged under Articles I and II of the Connecticut Constitution. If any should prevail, our constitutional issues would either fall or, in any event, may be formulated in an authoritative way very different from any speculative construction of how the Connecticut courts would view this law and its application. *Watson* v. *Buck*, 313 U.S. 387, 401–402.

If there is one doctrine more deeply rooted than any other in the process of constitutional adjudication, it is that we ought not to pass on questions of constitutionality —here the distribution of the taxing power as between the State and the Nation—unless such adjudication is unavoidable. And so, as questions of federal constitutional power have become more and more intertwined with preliminary doubts about local law, we have insisted that federal courts do not decide questions of constitutionality on the basis of preliminary guesses regarding local law. *Railroad Commission* v. *Pullman Co.*, *supra; Chicago* v. *Fieldcrest Dairies, 316 U.S. 168; In re Central R. Co. of New Jersey, 136 F.2d 633.* See also *Burford* v. *Sun Oil Co., 319 U.S. 315; Meredith* v. *Winter Haven, 320 U.S. 228, 235; Green* v. *Phillips Petroleum Co., 119 F.2d 466; Findley* v. *Odland, 127 F.2d 948; United States* v. *150.29 Acres of Land, 135 F.2d 878.* Avoidance of such guess-work, by holding the litigation in the federal courts until definite determinations on local law are made by the state courts, merely heeds this time-honored canon of constitutional adjudication.

We think this procedure should be followed in this case. The District Court had jurisdiction to entertain this bill and to give whatever relief is appropriate despite the Johnson Act and *Great Lakes Dredge Co.* v. *Huffman, 319 U.S. 293,* because of the uncertainty surrounding the adequacy of the Connecticut remedy. See *Waterbury Savings Bank* v. *Lawler, 46 Conn. 243; Wilcox* v. *Town of Madison, 106 Conn. 223, 137 A. 742.* But there is no doubt that Connecticut makes available an action for declaratory judgment for the determination of those issues of Connecticut law involved here. *Charter Oak Council, Inc.* v. *Town of New Hartford, 121 Conn. 466, 185 A. 575; Conzelman* v. *City of Bristol, 122 Conn. 218, 188 A. 659; Walsh* v. *City of Bridgeport, 2 Conn. Supp. 88.*

We therefore vacate the judgment of the Circuit Court of Appeals and remand the cause to the District Court with directions to retain the bill pending the determination of proceedings to be brought with reasonable promptitude in the State court in conformity with this opinion.

MR. JUSTICE DOUGLAS concurs in the result.

MR. JUSTICE BLACK dissents.

TILESTON v. ULLMAN

318 U.S. 44 (1943)

PER CURIAM.

This case comes here on appeal to review a declaratory judgment of the Supreme Court of Errors of Connecticut that §§ 6246 and 6562 of the General Statutes of Connecticut of 1930—prohibiting the use of drugs or instruments to prevent conception, and the giving of assistance or counsel in their use—are applicable to appellant, a registered physician, and as applied to him are constitutional. 129 Conn. 84, 26 A.2d 582, 588.

The suit was tried and judgment rendered on the allegations of the complaint which are stipulated to be true. Appellant alleged that the statute, if applicable to him, would prevent his giving professional advice concerning the use of contraceptives to three patients whose condition of health was such that their lives would be endangered by child-bearing, and that appellees,

law enforcement officers of the state, intend to prosecute any offense against the statute and "claim or may claim" that the proposed professional advice would constitute such an offense. The complaint set out in detail the danger to the lives of appellant's patients in the event that they should bear children, but contained no allegations asserting any claim under the Fourteenth Amendment of infringement of appellant's liberty or his property rights. The relief prayed was a declaratory judgment as to whether the statutes are applicable to appellant and if so whether they constitute a valid exercise of constitutional power "within the meaning and intent of Amendment XIV of the Constitution of the United States prohibiting a state from depriving any person of life without due process of law." On stipulation of the parties the state superior court ordered these questions of law reserved for the consideration and advice of the Supreme Court of Errors. That court, which assumed without deciding that the case was an appropriate one for a declaratory judgment, ruled that the statutes "prohibit the action proposed to be done" appellant and "are constitutional."

We are of the opinion that the proceeding in the state courts presents no constitutional question which appellant has standing to assert. The sole constitutional attack upon the statutes under the Fourteenth Amendment is confined to their deprivation of life—obviously not appellant's but his patients'. There is no allegation or proof that appellant's life is in danger. His patients are not parties to this proceeding and there is no basis on which we can say that he has standing to secure an adjudication of his patients' constitutional right to life, which they do not assert in their own behalf. *Cronin* v. *Adams*, 192 U.S. 108, 114; *Standard Stock Food Co.* v. *Wright*, 225 U.S. 540, 550; *Bosley* v. *McLaughlin*, 236 U.S. 385, 395; *Blair* v. *United States*, 250 U.S. 273; *The Winnebago*, 205 U.S. 354, 360; *Davis & Farnum Mfg. Co.* v. *Los An-*geles, 189 U.S. 207, 220. No question is raised in the record with respect to the deprivation of appellant's liberty or property in contravention of the Fourteenth Amendment nor is there anything in the opinion or judgment of the Supreme Court of Errors which indicates or would support a decision of any question other than those raised in the superior court and reserved by it for decision of the Supreme Court of Errors. That court's practice is to decline to answer questions not reserved. General Statutes § 5652; *Loomis Institute* v. *Healy*, 98 Conn. 102, 129, 119 A. 31; *John J. McCarthy Co.* v. *Alsop*, 122 Conn. 288, 298–99, 189 A. 464.

Since the appeal must be dismissed on the ground that appellant has no standing to litigate the constitutional question which the record presents, it is unnecessary to consider whether the record shows the existence of a genuine case or controversy essential to the exercise of the jurisdiction of this Court. *Cf. Nashville, C. & St. L. Ry. Co.* v. *Wallace*, 288 U.S. 249, 259.

Dismissed.

NOTE: In *Poe* v. *Ullman*, 367 U.S. 497 (1961), the plaintiffs asked the Court to declare unconstitutional Connecticut laws prohibiting the use of contraceptives. The action was dismissed on the ground that there was no justiciable *case or controversy* (see Constitution, Art III, Sec. 2) because the state had never tried to enforce them since their adoption in 1879: ". . . federal judicial power is to be exercised to strike down legislation . . . only at the instance of one who is himself immediately harmed, or immediately threatened with harm, by the challenged action. . . . This court cannot be umpire to debates concerning harmless, empty shadows. To find it necessary to pass on these statutes now, in order to protect appellants from the hazards of prosecution, would be to close our eyes to reality."

Justices Black, Douglas, Harlan, and Stewart dissented. The crux of the dissenting position perhaps is found in the Harlan opinion: ". . . the most substantial claim which these married persons press is their right to enjoy the privacy of their marital relations free of the enquiry of the criminal law. . . . And I cannot agree that their enjoyment of this privacy is not substantially impinged upon, when they are told that if they use contraceptives . . . the only thing that stands between them and being forced to render criminal account of their marital privacy is the whim of the prosecutor. . . ."

COLEMAN v. MILLER

307 U.S. 433 (1939)

Following the *Child Labor* cases (see Part Three, II) Congress in 1924 proposed a child labor amendment to the Constitution. In 1925 the Kansas legislature rejected and later, in 1937, approved this proposal. The validity of the approval was challenged in the state courts on the grounds (among others) that: (1) the prior rejection of the amendment was final, i.e., precluded any subsequent action by Kansas upon the same proposal; and (2) not having been approved by the prescribed number of states within a reasonable period, the proposed amendment had expired prior to 1937. These contentions were rejected by the state court. On review the Supreme Court disposed of some preliminary matters and then considered the two issues mentioned above:

Mr. Chief Justice Hughes delivered the opinion of the Court: . . .

The effect of the previous rejection of the amendment and of the lapse of time since its submission.

1. The state court adopted the view expressed by text-writers that a state legislature which has rejected an amendment proposed by the Congress may later ratify. The argument in support of that view is that Article V says nothing of rejection but speaks only of ratification and provides that a proposed amendment shall be valid as part of the Constitution when ratified by three-fourths of the states; that the power to ratify is thus conferred upon the state by the Constitution and, as a ratifying power, persists despite a previous rejection. The opposing view proceeds on an assumption that if ratification by "conventions" were prescribed by the Congress, a convention could not reject and, having adjourned sine, die, be reassembled and ratify. It is also premised, in accordance with views expressed by text-writers, that ratification if once given cannot afterwards be rescinded and the amendment rejected, and it is urged that the same effect in the exhaustion of the state's power to act should be ascribed to rejection; that a state can act "but once, either by convention or through its legislature."

Historic instances are cited. In 1865, the Thirteenth Amendment was rejected by the legislature of New Jersey which subsequently ratified it, but the question did not become important as ratification by the requisite number of states had already been proclaimed. The question did arise in connection with the adoption of the Fourteenth Amendment. The legislatures of Georgia, North Carolina and South Carolina had rejected the amendment in November and December, 1866. New governments were erected in those states (and in others) under the direction of Congress. The new legislatures ratified the amendment, that of North Carolina on July 4, 1868, that of South Carolina on July 9, 1868, and that of Georgia on July 21, 1868. Ohio and New Jersey first ratified and then passed resolutions withdrawing their consent. As there were then thirty-seven states, twenty-eight were needed to constitute the requisite three-fourths. On July 9, 1868, the Congress adopted a resolution requesting the Secretary of State to communicate "a list of the states of the Union whose legislatures have ratified the fourteenth article of amendment," and in Secretary Seward's report attention was called to the action of Ohio and New Jersey. On July 20 Secretary Seward issued a proclamation reciting the ratification by twenty-eight states, including North Carolina, South Carolina, Ohio and New Jersey, and stating that it appeared that Ohio and New Jersey had since passed resolutions withdrawing their consent and that "it is deemed a matter of doubt and uncertainty whether such resolutions are not irregular, invalid and therefore ineffectual." The Secretary certified that if the ratifying resolutions of Ohio and New Jersey were still in full force and effect, notwithstanding the attempted withdrawal, the amendment had become a part of the Constitution. On the following day the Congress adopted a concurrent resolution which, reciting that three-fourths of the states having ratified (the list including North Carolina, South Carolina, Ohio and New Jersey), declared the Fourteenth Amendment to be a part of the Constitution and that it should be duly promulgated as such by the Secretary of State. Accordingly, Secretary Seward, on July 28th, issued his proclamation embracing the states mentioned in the congressional resolution and adding Georgia.

Thus the political departments of the government dealt with the effect both of previous rejection and of attempted withdrawal and determined that both were ineffectual in the presence of an actual ratification. . . . This decision by the political departments of the government as to the validity of the adoption of the Fourteenth Amendment has been accepted.

We think that in accordance with this historic precedent the question of the efficacy of ratifications by state legislatures, in the light of previous rejection or attempted withdrawal, should be regarded as a political question pertaining to the political departments, with the ultimate authority in the Congress in the exercise of its control over the promulgation of the adoption of the amendment. . . .

2. The more serious question is whether the proposal by the Congress of the amendment had lost its vitality through lapse of time and hence it could not be ratified by the Kansas legislature in 1937. The argument of petitioners stresses the fact that nearly thirteen years elapsed between the proposal in 1924 and the ratification in question. It is said that when the amendment was proposed there was a definitely adverse popular sentiment and that at the

end of 1925 there had been rejection by both houses of the legislatures of sixteen states and ratification by only four states, and that it was not until about 1933 that an aggressive campaign was started in favor of the amendment. In reply, it is urged that Congress did not fix a limit of time for ratification and that an unreasonably long time had not elapsed since the submission; that the conditions which gave rise to the amendment had not been eliminated; that the prevalence of child labor, the diversity of state laws and the disparity in their administration, with the resulting competitive inequalities, continued to exist. Reference is also made to the fact that a number of the states have treated the amendment as still pending and that in the proceedings of the national government there have been indications of the same view. It is said that there were fourteen ratifications in 1933, four in 1935, one in 1936, and three in 1937.

We have held that the Congress in proposing an amendment may fix a reasonable time for ratification. *Dillon* v. *Gloss*, 256 U.S. 368. There we sustained the action of the Congress in providing in the proposed Eighteenth Amendment that it should be inoperative unless ratified within seven years. No limitation of time for ratification is provided in the instant case either in the proposed amendment or in the resolution of submission. But petitioners contend that, in the absence of a limitation by the Congress, the Court can and should decide what is a reasonable period within which ratification may be had. We are unable to agree with that contention.

It is true that in *Dillon* v. *Gloss* the Court said that nothing was found in Article V which suggested that an amendment once proposed was to be open to ratification for all time, or that ratification in some states might be separated from that in others by many years and yet be effective; that there was a strong suggestion to the contrary in that proposal and ratification were but succeeding steps in a single endeavor; that as amendments were deemed to be prompted by necessity, they should be considered and disposed of presently; and that there is a fair implication that ratification must be sufficiently contemporaneous in the required number of states to reflect the will of the people in all sections at relatively the same period; and hence that ratification must be within some reasonable time after the proposal. These considerations were cogent reasons for the decision in *Dillon* v. *Gloss*, that the Congress had the power to fix a reasonable time for ratification. But it does not follow that, whenever Congress has not exercised that power, the Court should take upon itself the responsibility of deciding what constitutes a reasonable time and determine accordingly the validity of ratifications. That question was not involved in *Dillon* v. *Gloss* and, in accordance with familiar principle, what was there said must be read in the light of the point decided.

Where are to be found the criteria for such a judicial determination? None are to be found in Constitution or statute. In their endeavor to answer this question petitioners' counsel have suggested that at least two years should be allowed; that six years would not seem to be unreasonably long; that seven years had been used by the Congress as a reasonable period; that one year, six months and thirteen days was the average time used in passing upon amendments which have been ratified since the first ten amendments; that three years, six months and twenty-five days has been the longest time used in ratifying. To this list of variables, counsel add that "the nature and extent of publicity and the activity of the public and of the legislatures of the several states in relation to any particular proposal should be taken into consideration." That statement is pertinent, but there are additional matters to be examined and weighed. When a proposed amendment springs from a conception of economic needs, it would be necessary, in determining whether a reasonable time had elapsed since its submission, to consider the economic conditions prevailing in the country, whether these had so far changed since

the submission as to make the proposal no longer responsive to the conception which inspired it or whether conditions were such as to intensify the feeling of need and the appropriateness of the proposed remedial action. In short, the question of a reasonable time in many cases would involve, as in this case it does involve, an appraisal of a great variety of relevant conditions, political, social and economic, which can hardly be said to be within the appropriate range of evidence receivable in a court of justice and as to which it would be an extravagant extension of judicial authority to assert judicial notice as the basis of deciding a controversy with respect to the validity of an amendment actually ratified. On the other hand, these conditions are appropriate for the consideration of the political departments of the government. The questions they involve are essentially political and not justiciable. They can be decided by the Congress with the full knowledge and appreciation ascribed to the national legislature of the political, social and economic conditions which have prevailed during the period since the submission of the amendment.

Our decision that the Congress has the power under Article V to fix a reasonable limit of time for ratification in proposing an amendment proceeds upon the assumption that the question, what is a reasonable time, lies within the congressional province. If it be deemed that such a question is an open one when the limit has not been fixed in advance, we think that it should also be regarded as an open one for the consideration of the Congress when, in the presence of certified ratifications by three-fourths of the states, the time arrives for the promulgation of the adoption of the amendment. The decision by the Congress, in its control of the action of the Secretary of State, of the question whether the amendment had been adopted within a reasonable time would not be subject to review by the courts. . . .

For the reasons we have stated . . . we think that the Congress in controlling the promulgation of the adoption of a constitutional amendment has the final determination of the question whether by lapse of time its proposal of the amendment had lost its vitality prior to the required ratifications. The state officials should not be restrained from certifying to the Secretary of State the adoption by the legislature of Kansas of the resolution of ratification.

As we find no reason for disturbing the decision of the Supreme Court of Kansas in denying the mandamus sought by petitioners, its judgment is affirmed but upon the grounds stated in this opinion.

[JUSTICES BLACK, FRANKFURTER, DOUGLAS, and ROBERTS thought the case should be dismissed on jurisdictional grounds. But since a majority held otherwise and had brought the case before the Court, the four Justices concurred in the result reached, but for these different reasons:]

Congress, possessing exclusive power over the amending process, cannot be bound by and is under no duty to accept the pronouncements upon that exclusive power by this Court or by the Kansas courts. Neither state nor federal courts can review that power. Therefore, any judicial expression amounting to more than mere acknowledgment of exclusive Congressional power over the political process of amendment is a mere admonition to the Congress in the nature of an advisory opinion, given wholly without constitutional authority.

[JUSTICES BUTLER and McREYNOLDS dissented on the ground that because more than a reasonable time had elapsed since the proposal of the amendment, it was no longer subject to approval by the states. That is, the dissenters considered this a legal, not a political, question.]

NOTE and QUAERE: Though it has been urged to do so many times, the Court has never interfered with the process of constitutional amendment. That is, no effort to have an amendment invalidated has been successful. Thus *Hollingsworth* v. *Virginia*, 3 Dallas 378 (1798), rejected the argument that a proposed amendment, like legislation, must be presented to the President for his approval or rejection. *Hawke* v. *Smith*, 253 U.S. 221 (1920), held that when a state legislature approves a proposed amendment pursuant to Article V of the federal Constitution, it acts in a federal capacity. Hence an amendment, otherwise properly adopted, is not invalid though not submitted to popular referendum as "required" by some state constitutions. *United States* v. *Sprague*, 282 U.S. 716 (1919), found no merit in the argument that since the Eighteenth Amendment restricted basic liberties and states' rights it should have been submitted to state conventions for ratification "by the people," rather than to the state legislatures. In *Leser* v. *Garnet*, 258 U.S. 130 (1922), the Court refused to look into the propriety of state ratifying resolutions on the ground that they had been accepted by the Secretary of State and that his promulgation of the amendment was not subject to question by the judiciary. Is this holding relevant to the argument, sometimes urged, that the Civil War Amendments are invalid because their ratification was obtained in part at least by military force during the Reconstruction? Is the Court's apparent reluctance to block the amending process a corollary of the principle of judicial review? Does it follow, in other words, that if the Court is to have the "last" word as to the meaning of the Constitution, it should leave the maximum freedom for the political processes of amendment?

BAKER v. CARR

369 U.S. 186 (1962)

In *Colegrove v. Green*, 328 U.S. 549 (1946), the Court (only seven judges sitting) was asked to block a district-type Illinois congressional election on the ground that the Illinois apportionment law was unconstitutional in that its districts were grossly unequal in population. Refusing relief on the ground that this was a non-judiciable political question, three judges stressed these elements: (1) this was a matter for the "exclusive authority" of Congress; (2) to consider it the Court would have to enter a "political thicket"; and (3) the Court at best could give only negative relief (invalidation of existing districts), a cure which it thought might be worse than the disease in view of an impending election. Three other judges rejected these views, holding that the issue was justiciable. The seventh judge agreed that the issue was justiciable, but voted to dismiss as a matter of equitable discretion in view of the "shortness of the time remaining" before the next election and the difficulties of an election at large.

Unlike *Colegrove,* the present case involves disproportionate state legislative districts; it arose under the equal protection clause of the Fourteenth Amendment. Relying on *Colegrove* and its progeny, a Federal District Court dismissed the case.

Mr. Justice Brennan delivered the opinion of the Court. . . .

IV

JUSTICIABILITY

In holding that the subject matter of this suit was not justiciable, the District Court relied on *Colegrove v. Green, supra,* and subsequent per curiam cases. The court stated: "From a review of these decisions there can be no doubt that the federal rule . . . is that the federal courts . . . will not intervene in cases of this type to compel legislative reapportionment." 179 F. Supp. at 826. We understand the District Court to have read the cited cases as compelling the conclusion that since the appellants sought to have a legislative apportionment held unconstitutional, their suit presented a "political question" and was therefore nonjusticiable. We hold that this challenge to an apportionment presents no nonjusticiable "political question." The cited cases do not hold the contrary.

Of course the mere fact that the suit seeks protection of a political right does not mean it presents a political question. Such an objection "is little more than a play upon words." *Nixon v. Cerndon,* 273 U.S. 536, 540. Rather, it is argued that apportionment cases, whatever the actual wording of the complaint, can involve no federal constitutional right except one resting on the guaranty of a republican form of government, and that complaints based on that clause have been held to present political questions which are nonjusticiable.

We hold that the claim pleaded here neither rests upon nor implicates the Guaranty Clause and that its justiciability is therefore not foreclosed by our decisions of cases involving that clause. The District Court misinterpreted *Colegrove v. Green* and other decisions of this Court on which it relied. Appellants' claim that they are being denied equal protection is justiciable, and if "discrimination is sufficiently shown, the right to relief under the equal protection clause is not diminished by the fact that the discrimination relates to political rights." *Snowden v. Hughes,* 321 U.S. 1, 11. To show why we reject the argument based on the Guaranty Clause, we must examine the authorities under it. But because there appears to be some uncertainty as to why those cases did present political questions, and specifically as to whether this apportionment case is like those cases, we deem it necessary first to consider the contours of the "political question" doctrine.

Our discussion, even at the price of extending this opinion, requires review of a number of political question cases, in order to expose the attributes of the doctrine—attributes which, in various settings, diverge, combine, appear, and disappear in seeming disorderliness. Since that review is undertaken solely to demonstrate that neither singly nor collectively do these cases support a conclusion that this apportionment case is nonjusticiable, we of course do not explore their implications in other contexts. That review reveals that in the Guaranty Clause cases and in the other "political question" cases, it is the relationship between the judiciary and the coordinate branches of the Federal Government, and not the federal judiciary's relationship to the States, which gives rise to the "political questions."

We have said that "in determining whether a question falls within [the political question] category, the appropriateness under our system of government of attributing finality to the action of the political departments and also the lack of satisfactory criteria for a judicial determination are dominant considerations." *Coleman* v. *Miller*, 307 U.S. 433, 454–455. The nonjusticiability of a political question is primarily a function of the separation of powers. Much confusion results from the capacity of the "political question" label to obscure the need for case-by-case inquiry. Deciding whether a matter has in any measure been committed by the Constitution to another branch of government, or whether the action of that branch exceeds whatever authority has been committed, is itself a delicate exercise in constitutional interpretation, and is a responsibility of this Court as ultimate interpreter of the Constitution. To demonstrate this requires no less than to analyze representative cases and to infer from them analytical threads that make up the political question doctrine. We shall then show that none of those threads catches this case.

Foreign relations: There are sweeping statements to the effect that all questions touching foreign relations are political questions. Not only does resolution of such issues frequently turn on standards that defy judicial application, or involve the exercise of a discretion demonstrably committed to the executive or legislature; but many such questions uniquely demand single-voiced statements of the Government's views. Yet it is error to suppose that every case or controversy which touches foreign relations lies beyond judicial cognizance. Our cases in this field seem invariably to show a discriminating analysis of the particular question posed, in terms of the history of its management by the political branches, of its susceptibility to judicial handling in the light of its nature and posture in the specific case, and of the possible consequences of judicial action. For example, though a court will not ordinarily inquire whether a treaty has been terminated, since on that question "governmental action . . . must be regarded as of controlling importance," if there has been no conclusive "governmental action" then a court can construe a treaty and may find it provides the answer. Compare *Terlinden* v. *Ames*, 184 U.S. 270, 285, with *Society for the Propagation of the Gospel in Foreign Parts* v. *New Haven*, 8 Wheat. 464, 492–495. Though a court will not undertake to construe a treaty in a manner inconsistent with a subsequent federal statute, no similar hesitancy obtains if the asserted clash is with state law. Compare *Whitney* v. *Robertson*, 124 U.S. 190, with *Kolovrat* v. *Oregon*, 366 U.S. 187. . . .

Dates of duration of hostilities: Though it has been stated broadly that "the power which declared the necessity is the power to declare its cessation, and what the cessation requires," *Commercial Trust Co.* v. *Miller*, 262 U.S. 51, 57, here too analysis reveals isolable reasons for the presence of political questions, underlying this Court's refusal to review the political departments' determination of when or whether a war has ended. Dominant is the need for finality in the political determination, for emergency's nature demands "a prompt and un-hesitating obedience," *Martin* v. *Mott*, 12 Wheat. 19, 30 (calling up of militia). . . .

Validity of enactments: In *Coleman* v. *Miller, supra,* this Court held that the questions of how long a proposed amendment to the Federal Constitution remained open to ratification and what effect a prior rejection had on a subsequent ratification, were committed to congressional resolution and involved criteria of decision that necessarily escaped the judicial grasp. Similar considerations apply to the enacting process: "the respect due to coequal and independent departments," and the need for finality and certainty about the status of a statute contribute to judicial reluctance to inquire whether, as passed, it complied with all requisite formalities. *Field* v. *Clark*, 143 U.S. 649, 672, 676–677; see *Leser* v. *Garnett*, 258 U.S. 130, 137. But it is not true that courts will never delve into a legislature's records upon such a quest: If the enrolled statute lacks an effective date, a court will not hesitate to seek it in the legislative journals in order to preserve the enactment. *Gardner* v. *Collector*, 6 Wall. 499. The political question doctrine, a tool for maintenance of governmental order, will not be so applied as to promote only disorder. . . .

It is apparent that several formulations which vary slightly according to the settings in which the questions arise may describe a political question, although each has one or more elements which identifies it as essentially a function of the separation of powers. Prominent on the surface of any case held to involve a political question is found a textually demonstrable constitutional commitment of the issue to a co-ordinate political department; or a lack of judicially discoverable and manageable standards for resolving it; or the impossibility of deciding without an initial policy determination of a kind clearly for nonjudicial discretion; or the impossibility of a court's undertaking independent resolution without expressing lack of the respect due coordinate branches of government; or an unusual need for unques-tioning adherence to a political decision already made; or the potentiality of embarrassment from multifarious pronouncements by various departments on one question.

Unless one of these formulations is inextricable from the case at bar, there should be no dismissal for nonjusticiability on the ground of a political question's presence. The doctrine of which we treat is one of "political questions," not one of "political cases." The courts cannot reject as "no law suit" a bona fide controversy as to whether some action denominated "political" exceeds constitutional authority. The cases we have reviewed show the necessity for discriminating inquiry into the precise facts and posture of the particular case, and the impossibility of resolution by any semantic cataloguing.

But it is argued that this case shares the characteristics of decisions that constitute a category not yet considered, cases concerning the Constitution's guaranty, in Art. IV, § 4, of a republican form of government. A conclusion as to whether the case at bar does present a political question cannot be confidently reached until we have considered those cases with special care. We shall discover that Guaranty Clause claims involve those elements which define a "political question," and for that reason and no other, they are nonjusticiable. In particular, we shall discover that the non-justiciability of such claims has nothing to do with their touching upon matters of state governmental organization.

Republican form of government: Luther v. *Borden*, 7 How. 1, 48 U.S. 1, though in form simply an action for damages for trespass was, as Daniel Webster said in opening the argument for the defense, "an unusual case." The defendants, admitting an otherwise tortious breaking and entering, sought to justify their action on the ground that they were agents of the established lawful government of Rhode Island, which State was then under martial law to defend itself from active insurrection; that the plaintiff was engaged in that insurrection; and that they entered under orders to arrest the plaintiff. The case arose "out of the unfortunate political differences which agitated the people of Rhode Island in 1841 and 1842," 48 U.S. at 34, which had resulted in a situation wherein two groups laid competing claims to recognition as the lawful government. The plaintiff's right to recover depended upon which of the two groups was entitled to such recognition; but the lower court's refusal to receive evidence or hear argument on that issue, its charge to the jury that the earlier established or "charter" government was lawful, and the verdict for the defendants, were affirmed upon appeal to this Court. . . .

Clearly, several factors were thought by the Court in *Luther* to make the question there "political": the commitment to the other branches of the decision as to which is the lawful state government; the unambiguous action by the President, in recognizing the charter government as the lawful authority; the need for finality in the executive's decision; and the lack of criteria by which a court could determine which form of government was republican.

But the only significance that *Luther* could have for our immediate purposes is in its holding that the Guaranty Clause is not a repository of judicially manageable standards which a court could utilize independently in order to identify a State's lawful government. The Court has since refused to resort to the Guaranty Clause—which alone had been invoked for the purpose—as the source of a constitutional standard for invalidating state action. . . .

Just as the Court has consistently held that a challenge to state action based on the Guaranty Clause presents no justiciable question so has it held, and for the same reasons, that challenges to congressional action on the ground of inconsistency with that clause present no justiciable question. . . .

We come, finally to the ultimate inquiry whether our precedents as to what constitutes a nonjusticiable "political question" bring the case before us under the umbrella of that doctrine. A natural beginning is to note whether any of the common characteristics which we have been able to identify and label descriptively are present. We find none: The question here is the consistency of state action with the Federal Constitution. We have no question decided, or to be decided, by a political branch of government coequal with this Court. Nor do we risk embarrassment of our government abroad, or grave disturbance at home if we take issue with Tennessee as to the constitutionality of her action here challenged. Nor need the appellants, in order to succeed in this action, ask the Court to enter upon policy determinations for which judicially manageable standards are lacking. Judicial standards under the Equal Protection Clause are well developed and familiar, and it has been open to courts since the enactment of the Fourteenth Amendment to determine, if on the particular facts they must, that a discrimination reflects *no* policy, but simply arbitrary and capricious action. . . .

We conclude then that the nonjusticiability of claims resting on the Guaranty Clause which arises from their embodiment of questions that were thought "political," can have no bearing upon the justiciability of the equal protection claim presented in this case. Finally, we emphasize that it is the involvement in Guaranty Clause claims of the elements thought to define "political questions," and no other feature, which could render them nonjusticiable. Specifically, we have said that such claims are not held nonjusticiable because they touch matters of state governmental organization. Brief examination of a few cases demonstrates this.

When challenges to state action respecting matters of "the administration of the affairs of the State and the officers through whom they are conducted" have rested on claims of constitutional deprivation which are amenable to judicial correction, this Court has acted upon its view of the merits of the claim. . . . And only last Term, in *Gomillion* v. *Lightfoot*, 364 U.S. 339, we applied the Fifteenth Amendment to strike down a redrafting of municipal boundaries which effected a discriminatory impairment of voting rights, in the face of what a majority of the Court of Appeals thought to be a sweeping commitment to state legislatures of the power to draw and redraw such boundaries.

Gomillion was brought by a Negro who had been a resident of the City of Tuskegee, Alabama, until the municipal boundaries were so recast by the State Legislature as to exclude practically all Negroes. The plaintiff claimed deprivation of the right to vote in municipal elections. The District Court's 167 F. Supp. 405, dismissal for want of jurisdiction and failure to state a claim upon which relief could be granted was affirmed by the Court of Appeals, 5 Cir., 270 F.2d 594. This Court unanimously reversed. This Court's answer to the argument that States enjoyed unrestricted control over municipal boundaries was:

"Legislative control of municipalities, no less than other state power, lies within the scope of relevant limitations imposed by the United States Constitution. . . . The opposite conclusion, urged upon us by respondents, would sanction the achievement by a State of any impairment of voting rights whatever so long as it was cloaked in the garb of the realignment of political subdivisions. 'It is inconceivable that guaranties embedded in the Constitution of the United States may thus be manipulated out of existence.'" 364 U.S. at 344–345.

To a second argument, that *Colegrove v. Green, supra,* was a barrier to hearing the merits of the case, the Court responded that Gomillion was lifted "out of the so-called 'political' arena and into the conventional sphere of constitutional litigation" because here was discriminatory treatment of a racial minority violating the Fifteenth Amendment.

"A statute which is alleged to have worked unconstitutional deprivations of petitioners' rights is not immune to attack simply because the mechanism employed by the legislature is a redefinition of municipal boundaries. . . . While in form this is merely an act redefining metes and

bounds, if the allegations are established, the inescapable human effect of this essay in geometry and geography is to despoil colored citizens, and only colored citizens, of their theretofore enjoyed voting rights. That was not *Colegrove v. Green.*

"When a State exercises power wholly within the domain of state interest, it is insulated from federal judicial review. But such insulation is not carried over when state power is used as an instrument for circumventing a federally protected right." 364 U.S. at 347.

We conclude that the complaint's allegations of a denial of equal protection present a justiciable constitutional cause of action upon which appellants are entitled to a trial and a decision. The right asserted is within the reach of judicial protection under the Fourteenth Amendment.

The judgment of the District Court is reversed and the cause is remanded for further proceedings consistent with this opinion.

Reversed and remanded.

MR. JUSTICE WHITTAKER did not participate in the decision of this case.

MR. JUSTICE DOUGLAS, concurring.

While I join the opinion of the Court and, like the Court, do not reach the merits, a word of explanation is necessary. I put to one side the problems of "political" questions involving the distribution of power between this Court, the Congress, and the Chief Executive. We have here a phase of the recurring problem of the relation of the federal courts to state agencies. More particularly, the question is the extent to which a State may weight one person's vote more heavily than it does another's. . . .

The traditional test under the Equal Protection Clause has been whether a State has made "an invidious discrimination," as it does when it selects "a particular race or nationality for oppressive treatment." See *Skinner v. Oklahoma,* 316 U.S. 535, 541. Universal equality is not the test; there is room for weighting. As we stated in *Williamson v. Lee Optical Co.,* 348 U.S. 483,

489, "The prohibition of the Equal Protection Clause goes no further than the invidious discrimination."

I agree with my Brother CLARK that if the allegations in the complaint can be sustained a case for relief is established. We are told that a single vote in Moore County, Tennessee, is worth 19 votes in Hamilton County, that one vote in Stewart or in Chester County is worth nearly eight times a single vote in Shelby or Knox County. The opportunity to prove that an "invidious discrimination" exists should therefore be given the appellants. . . .

With the exceptions of *Colegrove* v. *Green*, 328 U.S. 549; *MacDougall* v. *Green*, 335 U.S. 281; *South* v. *Peters*, 339 U.S. 276, and the decisions they spawned, the Court has never thought that protection of voting rights was beyond judicial cognizance. Today's treatment of those cases removes the only impediment to judicial cognizance of the claims stated in the present complaint.

The justiciability of the present claims being established, any relief accorded can be fashioned in the light of well-known principles of equity.

MR. JUSTICE CLARK, concurring. . . .

I believe it can be shown that this case is distinguishable from earlier cases dealing with the distribution of political power by a State, that a patent violation of the Equal Protection Clause of the United States Constitution has been shown, and that an appropriate remedy may be formulated. . . .

II

The controlling facts cannot be disputed. It appears from the record that 37% of the voters of Tennessee elect 20 of the 33 Senators while 40% of the voters elect 63 of the 99 members of the House. But this might not on its face be an "invidious discrimination," . . . for a "statutory discrimination will not be set aside if any state of facts reasonably may be conceived to justify it." *McGowan* v. *Maryland*, 366 U.S. 420, 426 (1961).

It is true that the apportionment policy incorporated in Tennessee's Constitution, i.e., state-wide numerical equality of representation with certain minor qualifications, is a rational one. . . . However, the root of the trouble is not in Tennessee's Constitution, for admittedly its policy has not been followed. The discrimination lies in the action of Tennessee's Assembly in allocating legislative seats to counties or districts created by it. Try as one may, Tennessee's apportionment just cannot be made to fit the pattern cut by its Constitution. This was the finding of the District Court. The policy of the Constitution referred to by the dissenters, therefore, is of no relevance here. We must examine what the Assembly has done. The frequency and magnitude of the inequalities in the present districting admit of no policy whatever. . . . The apportionment picture in Tennessee is a topsy-turvical of gigantic proportions. . . . Tennessee's apportionment is a crazy quilt without rational basis. . . .

No one contends that mathematical equality among voters is required by the Equal Protection Clause. But certainly there must be some rational design to a State's districting. The discrimination here does not fit any pattern. . . . My Brother HARLAN contends that other proposed apportionment plans contain disparities. Instead of chasing those rabbits he should first pause long enough to meet appellants' proof of discrimination by showing that in fact the present plan follows a rational policy. Not being able to do this, he merely counters with such generalities as "classic legislative judgment," no "significant discrepancy," and "de minimis departures." I submit that even a casual glance at the present apportionment picture shows these conclusions to be entirely fanciful. If present representation has a policy at all, it is to maintain the *status quo* of invidious discrimination at any cost. . . .

III

Although I find the Tennessee apportionment statute offends the Equal Protection Clause, I would not consider intervention by this Court into so delicate a field if there were any other relief available to the people of Tennessee. But the majority of the people of Tennessee have no "practical opportunities of exerting their political weight at the polls" to correct the existing "invidious discrimination." Tennessee has no initiative and referendum. I have searched diligently for other "practical opportunities" present under the law. I find none other than through the federal courts. The majority of the voters have been caught up in a legislative strait jacket. Tennessee has an "informed, civically militant electorate" and "an aroused popular conscience," but it does not sear "the conscience of the people's representatives." This is because the legislative policy has riveted the present seats in the Assembly to their respective constituencies, and by the votes of their incumbents a reapportionment of any kind is prevented. The people have been rebuffed at the hands of the Assembly; they have tried the constitutional convention route, but since the call must originate in the Assembly it, too, has been fruitless. They have tried Tennessee courts with the same result, and Governors have fought the tide only to flounder. It is said that there is recourse in Congress and perhaps that may be, but from a practical standpoint this is without substance. To date Congress has never undertaken such a task in any State. We therefore must conclude that the people of Tennessee are stymied and without judicial intervention will be saddled with the present discrimination in the affairs of their state government.

IV

Finally, we must consider if there are any appropriate modes of effective judicial relief. The federal courts are, of course, not forums for political debate, nor should they resolve themselves into state constitutional conventions or legislative assemblies. Nor should their jurisdiction be exercised in the hope that such a declaration, as is made today, may have the direct effect of bringing on legislative action and relieving the courts of the problem of fashioning relief. To my mind this would be nothing less than blackjacking the Assembly into re-

apportioning the State. If judicial competence were lacking to fashion an effective decree, I would dismiss this appeal. However . . . I see no such difficulty in the position of this case. One plan might be to start with the existing assembly districts, consolidate some of them, and award the seats thus released to those counties suffering the most egregious discrimination. Other possibilities are present and might be more effective. But the plan here suggested would at least release the strangle hold now on the Assembly and permit it to redistrict itself. . . .

MR. JUSTICE STEWART, concurring.

The separate writings of my dissenting and concurring Brothers stray so far from the subject of today's decision as to convey, I think, a distressingly inaccurate impression of what the Court decides. For that reason, I think it appropriate, in joining the opinion of the Court, to emphasize in a few words what the opinion does and does not say. . . .

I repeat, the Court today decides only: (1) that the District Court possessed jurisdiction of the subject matter; (2) that the complaint presents a justiciable controversy; (3) that the appellants have standing. My Brother CLARK has made a convincing prima facie showing that Tennessee's system of apportionment is in fact utterly arbitrary—without any possible justification in rationality. My Brother HARLAN has, with imagination and ingenuity, hypothesized possibly rational bases for Tennessee's system. But the merits of this case are not before us now. The defendants have not yet had an opportunity to be heard in defense of the State's system of apportionment; indeed, they have not yet even filed an answer to the complaint. As in other cases, the proper place for the trial is in the trial court, not here.

MR. JUSTICE FRANKFURTER, whom MR. JUSTICE HARLAN joins, dissenting.

The Court today reverses a uniform course of decision established by a dozen cases, including one by which the very claim now sustained was unanimously rejected only five years ago. The impressive body of rulings thus cast aside reflected the equally uniform course of our political history regarding the relationship between population and legislative representation— a wholly different matter from denial of the franchise to individuals because of race, color, religion or sex. Such a massive repudiation of the experience of our whole past in asserting destructively novel judicial power demands a detailed analysis of the role of this Court in our constitutional scheme. Disregard of inherent limits in the effective exercise of the Court's "judicial Power" not only presages the futility of judicial intervention in the essentially political conflict of forces by which the relation between population and representation has time out of mind been and now is determined. It may well impair the Court's position as the ultimate organ of "the supreme Law of the Land" in that vast range of legal problems, often strongly entangled in popular feeling, on which this Court must pronounce. The Court's authority—possessed neither of the purse nor the sword—ultimately rests on sustained public confidence in its moral sanction. Such feeling must be nourished by the Court's complete detachment, in fact and in appearance, from political entanglements and by abstention from injecting itself into the clash of political forces in political settlements.

A hypothetical claim resting on abstract assumptions is now for the first time made the basis for affording illusory relief for a particular evil even though it foreshadows deeper and more pervasive difficulties in consequence. The claim is hypothetical and the assumptions are abstract because the Court does not vouchsafe the lower courts—state and federal—guide-lines for formulating specific, definite, wholly unprecedented remedies for the inevitable litigations that today's umbrageous disposition is bound to stimulate in connection with politically motivated reapportionments in so many States. In such a setting, to promulgate jurisdiction in the abstract

is meaningless. It is devoid of reality as "a brooding omnipresence in the sky" for it conveys no intimation what relief, if any, a District Court is capable of affording that would not invite legislatures to play ducks and drakes with the judiciary. For this Court to direct the District Court to enforce a claim to which the Court has over the years consistently found itself required to deny legal enforcement and at the same time to find it necessary to withhold any guidance to the lower court how to enforce this turnabout, new legal claim, manifests an odd—indeed an esoteric—conception of judicial propriety. One of the Court's supporting opinions, as elucidated by commentary, unwittingly affords a disheartening preview of the mathematical quagmire (apart from divers judicially inappropriate and elusive determinants), into which this Court today catapults the lower courts of the country without so much as adumbrating the basis for a legal calculus as a means of extrication. Even assuming the indispensable intellectual disinterestedness on the part of judges in such matters, they do not have accepted legal standards or criteria or even reliable analogies to draw upon for making judicial judgments. To charge courts with the task of accommodating the incommensurable factors of policy that underlie these mathematical puzzles is to attribute, however flatteringly, omnicompetence to judges. The Framers of the Constitution persistently rejected a proposal that embodied this assumption and Thomas Jefferson never entertained it.

Recent legislation, creating a district appropriately described as "an atrocity of ingenuity," is not unique. Considering the gross inequality among legislative electoral units within almost every State, the Court naturally shrinks from asserting that in districting at least substantial equality is a constitutional requirement enforceable by courts. Room continues to be allowed for weighting. This of course implies that geography, economics, urban-rural conflict, and all the other non-legal factors which have throughout our history entered into political districting are to some extent not to be ruled out in the undefined vista now opened up by review in the federal courts of state reapportionments. To some extent —aye, there's the rub. In effect, today's decision empowers the courts of the country to devise what should constitute the proper composition of the legislatures of the fifty States. If state courts should for one reason or another find themselves unable to discharge this task, the duty of doing so is put on the federal courts or on this Court, if State views do not satisfy this Court's notion of what is proper districting.

We were soothingly told at the bar of this Court that we need not worry about the kind of remedy a court could effectively fashion once the abstract constitutional right to have courts pass on a state-wide system of electoral districting is recognized as a matter of judicial rhetoric, because legislatures would heed the Court's admonition. This is not only an euphoric hope. It implies a sorry confession of judicial impotence in place of a frank acknowledgment that there is not under our Constitution a judicial remedy for every political mischief, for every undesirable exercise of legislative power. The Framers carefully and with deliberate forethought refused so to enthrone the judiciary. In this situation, as in others of like nature, appeal for relief does not belong here. Appeal must be to an informed, civically militant electorate. In a democratic society like ours, relief must come through an aroused popular conscience that sears the conscience of the people's representatives. In any event there is nothing judicially more unseemly nor more self-defeating than for this Court to make *in terrorem* pronouncements, to indulge in merely empty rhetoric, sounding a word of promise to the ear, sure to be disappointing to the hope. . . .

I

In sustaining appellants' claim, based on the Fourteenth Amendment, that the District Court may entertain this suit, this Court's uniform course of decision over the years is overruled or disregarded. Explicitly it begins with *Colegrove* v. *Green, supra,* decided in 1946, but its roots run deep in the Court's historic adjudicatory process.

Colegrove held that a federal court should not entertain an action for declaratory and injunctive relief to adjudicate the constitutionality, under the Equal Protection Clause and other federal constitutional and statutory provisions, of a state statute establishing the respective districts for the State's election of Representatives to the Congress. Two opinions were written by the four Justices who composed the majority of the seven sitting members of the Court. Both opinions joining in the result in *Colegrove* v. *Green* agreed that considerations were controlling which dictated denial of jurisdiction though not in the strict sense of want of power. While the two opinions show a divergence of view regarding some of these considerations, there are important points of concurrence. Both opinions demonstrate a predominant concern, first, with avoiding federal judicial involvement in matters traditionally left to legislative policy-making; second, with respect to the difficulty—in view of the nature of the problems of apportionment and its history in this country—of drawing on or devising judicial standards for judgment, as opposed to legislative determinations, of the part which mere numerical equality among voters should play as a criterion for the allocation of political power; and, third, with problems of finding appropriate modes of relief—particularly, the problem of resolving the essentially political issue of the relative merits of at-large elections and elections held in districts of unequal population. . . .

II

The *Colegrove* doctrine, in the form in which repeated decisions have settled it, was not an innovation. It represents long judicial thought and experience. From its earliest opinions this Court has consistently recognized a class of controversies which do not lend themselves to judicial standards and judicial remedies. . . .

[Justice Frankfurter discusses the "political question" doctrine under the following headings: (1) war and foreign affairs; (2) structure and organization of state political institutions; (3) Negro disfranchisement; and (4) abstract questions of political power.]

5. The influence of these converging considerations—the caution not to undertake decision where standards meet for judicial judgment are lacking, the reluctance to interfere with matters of state government in the absence of an unquestionable and effectively enforceable mandate, the unwillingness to make courts arbiters of the broad issues of political organization historically committed to other institutions and for whose adjustment the judicial process is ill-adapted—has been decisive of the settled line of cases, reaching back more than a century, which holds that Art. IV, § 4, of the Constitution, guaranteeing to the States "a Republican Form of Government," is not enforceable through the courts. . . .

[Omitted here is a discussion of cases denying judicial responsibility for enforcing the republican form of government guaranty, particularly *Luther* v. *Borden,* 7 How. 1 (1849), and *Pacific States Telephone & Telegraph Co.* v. *Oregon,* 223 U.S. 118 (1912).]

III

The present case involves all of the elements that have made the Guarantee Clause cases nonjusticiable. It is, in effect, a Guarantee Clause claim masquerading under a different label. But it cannot make the case more fit for judicial action that appellants invoke the Fourteenth Amendment rather than Art. IV, § 4, where, in fact, the gist of their complaint is the same. . . .

What, then, is this question of legislative apportionment? Appellants invoke the right to vote and to have their votes counted. But they are permitted to vote and their votes are counted. They go to the polls, they cast their ballots, they send their representatives to the state councils. Their complaint is simply that the representatives are not sufficiently numerous or powerful —in short, that Tennessee has adopted a basis of representation with which they are dissatisfied. Talk of "debasement" or "dilution" is circular talk. One cannot speak of

"debasement" or "dilution" of the value of a vote until there is first defined a standard of reference as to what a vote should be worth. What is actually asked of the Court in this case is to choose among competing bases of representation—ultimately, really, among competing theories of political philosophy—in order to establish an appropriate frame of government for the State of Tennessee and thereby for all the States of the Union.

In such a matter, abstract analogies which ignore the facts of history deal in unrealities; they betray reason. This is not a case in which a State has, through a device however oblique and sophisticated, denied Negroes or Jews or redheaded persons a vote, or given them only a third or a sixth of a vote. That was *Gomillion* v. *Lightfoot.* . . . What Tennessee illustrates is an old and still widespread method of representation—representation by local geographical division, only in part respective of population—in preference to others, others, forsooth, more appealing. Appellants contest this choice and seek to make this Court the arbiter of the disagreement. They would make the Equal Protection Clause the charter of adjudication, asserting that the equality which it guarantees comports, if not the assurance of equal weight to every voter's vote, at least the basic conception that representation ought to be proportionate to population, a standard by reference to which the reasonableness of apportionment plans may be judged.

To find such a political conception legally enforceable in the broad and unspecific guarantee of equal protection is to rewrite the Constitution. . . . Certainly, "equal protection" is no more secure a foundation for judicial judgment of the permissibility of varying forms of representative government than is "Republican Form." Indeed since "equal protection of the laws" can only mean an equality of persons standing in the same relation to whatever governmental action is challenged, the determination whether treatment is equal presupposes a determination concerning the nature of the relationship. This, with respect to apportionment, means an inquiry into the theoretic base of representation in an acceptably republican state. For a court could not determine the equal-protection issue without in fact first determining the Republican-Form issue, simply because what is reasonable for equal protection purposes will depend upon what frame of government, basically, is allowed. To divorce "equal protection" from "Republican Form" is to talk about half a question.

The notion that representation proportioned to the geographic spread of population is so universally accepted as a necessary element of equality between man and man that it must be taken to be the standard of a political equality preserved by the Fourteenth Amendment—that it is, in appellants' words "the basic principle of representative government"—is, to put it bluntly, not true. However desirable and however desired by some among the great political thinkers and framers of our government, it has never been generally practiced, today or in the past. It was not the English system, it was not the colonial system, it was not the system chosen for the national government by the Constitution, it was not the system exclusively or even predominantly practiced by the States at the time of adoption of the Fourteenth Amendment, it is not predominantly practiced by the States today. Unless judges, the judges of this Court, are to make their private views of political wisdom the measure of the Constitution—views which in all honesty cannot but give the appearance, if not reflect the reality, of involvement with the business of partisan politics so inescapably a part of apportionment controversies—the Fourteenth Amendment provides no guide for judicial oversight of the representation problem. . . .

Manifestly, the Equal Protection Clause supplies no clearer guide for judicial examination of apportionment methods than would the Guarantee Clause itself. Apportionment, by its character, is a subject of extraordinary complexity, involving—even

after the fundamental theoretical issues concerning what is to be represented in a representative legislature have been fought out or compromised—considerations of geography, demography, electoral convenience, economic and social cohesions or divergencies among particular local groups, communications, the practical effects of political institutions like the lobby and the city machine, ancient traditions and ties of settled usage, respect for proven incumbents of long experience and senior status, mathematical mechanics, censuses compiling relevant data, and a host of others. Legislative responses throughout the country to the reapportionment demands of the 1960 Census have glaringly confirmed that these are not factors that lend themselves to evaluations of a nature that are the staple of judicial determinations or for which judges are equipped to adjudicate by legal training or experience or native wit. And this is the more so true because in every strand of this complicated, intricate web of values meet the contending forces of partisan politics. The practical significance of apportionment is that the next election results may differ because of it. Apportionment battles are overwhelmingly party or intra-party contests. It will add a virulent source of friction and tension in federal-state relations to embroil the federal judiciary in them. . . .

Although the District Court had jurisdiction in the very restricted sense of power to determine whether it could adjudicate the claim, the case is of that class of political controversy which, by the nature of its subject is unfit for federal judicial action. The judgment of the District Court, in dismissing the complaint for failure to state a claim on which relief can be granted, should therefore be affirmed.

Dissenting opinion of MR. JUSTICE HARLAN, whom MR. JUSTICE FRANKFURTER joins. . . .

It is at once essential to recognize this case for what it is. The issue here relates not to a method of state electoral apportionment by which seats in the *federal* House of Representatives are allocated, but solely to the right of a State to fix the basis of representation in its *own* legislature. Until it is first decided to what extent that right is limited by the Federal Constitution, and whether what Tennessee has done or failed to do in this instance runs afoul of any such limitation, we need not reach the issues of "justiciability" or "political question" or any of the other considerations which in such cases as *Colegrove* v. *Green* . . . led the Court to decline to adjudicate a challenge to a state apportionment affecting seats in the federal House of Representatives, in the absence of a controlling Act of Congress. . . .

I

I can find nothing in the Equal Protection Clause or elsewhere in the Federal Constitution which expressly or impliedly supports the view that state legislatures must be so structured as to reflect with approximate equality the voice of every voter. Not only is that proposition refuted by history . . . but it strikes deep into the heart of our federal system.

In the last analysis, what lies at the core of this controversy is a difference of opinion as to the function of representative government. It is surely beyond argument that those who have the responsibility for devising a system of representation may permissibly consider that factors other than bare numbers should be taken into account. The existence of the United States Senate is proof enough of that. . . . We must accept the present form of the Tennessee Legislature as the embodiment of the State's choice, or, more realistically, its compromise, between competing political philosophies. The federal courts have not been empowered by the Equal Protection Clause to judge whether this resolution to the State's internal political conflict is desirable or undesirable, wise or unwise. . . .

There is nothing in the Federal Constitution to prevent a State, acting not irrationally, from choosing any electoral legislative structure it thinks best suited to the interests, temper, and customs of its people. . . . A State's choice to distribute electoral strength among geographical units, rather than according to a census of population, is certainly no less a rational decision of policy than would be its choice to levy a tax on property rather than a tax on income. Both are legislative judgments entitled to equal respect from this Court.

II

The claim that Tennessee's system of apportionment is so unreasonable as to amount to a capricious classification of voting strength stands up no better under dispassionate analysis.

The Court has said time and again that the Equal Protection Clause does not demand of state enactments either mathematical identity or rigid equality. . . . All that is prohibited is "invidious discrimination" bearing no rational relation to any permissible policy of the State. . . .

What then is the basis for the claim made in this case that the distribution of state senators and representatives is the product of capriciousness or of some constitutionally prohibited policy? It is not that Tennessee has arranged its electoral districts with a deliberate purpose to dilute the voting strength of one race, cf. *Gomillion* v. *Lightfoot* . . . or that some religious group is intentionally underrepresented. . . . Rather, the claim is that the State Legislature has unreasonably retained substantially the same allocation of senators and representatives as was established by statute in 1901, refusing to recognize the great shift in the population balance between urban and rural communities that has occurred in the meantime. . . .

A Federal District Court is asked to say that the passage of time has rendered the 1901 apportionment obsolete to the point where its continuance becomes vulnerable under the Fourteenth Amendment. But is not this matter one that involves a classic legislative judgment? Surely it lies within the province of a state legislature to conclude that an existing allocation of senators and representatives constitutes a desirable balance of geographical and demographical representation, or that in the interest of stability of government it would be best to defer for some further time the redistribution of seats in the state legislature.

Indeed, I would hardly think it unconstitutional if a state legislature's expressed reason for establishing or maintaining an electoral imbalance between its rural and urban population were to protect the State's agricultural interests from the sheer weight of numbers of those residing in its cities. . . . These are matters of local policy, on the wisdom of which the federal judiciary is neither permitted nor qualified to sit in judgment. . . .

From a reading of the majority and concurring opinions one will not find it difficult to catch the premises that underlie this decision. The fact that the appellants have been unable to obtain political redress of their asserted grievances appears to be re-garded as a matter which should lead the Court to stretch to find some basis for judicial intervention. . . . The majority seems to have accepted the argument, pressed at the bar, that if this Court merely asserts authority in this field, Tennessee and other "malapportioning" States will quickly respond with appropriate political action, so that this Court need not be greatly concerned about the federal courts becoming further involved in these matters. At the same time the majority has wholly failed to reckon with what the future may hold in store if this optimistic prediction is not fulfilled. Thus, what the Court is doing reflects more an adventure in judicial experimentation than a solid piece of constitutional adjudication. . . .

II. JUDICIAL RESTRAINT

We turn now to cases accepted as appropriate for decision, i.e., cases in which the principles of abstention are deemed inapplicable. The difficulty here is that while the Constitution may give hints, it often provides less than obvious answers to crucial problems. In this impasse, an ancient tradition insists that constitutional doubt is to be resolved in favor of the view taken by the politically responsible organs of government. That is, if choice must be made between two or more reasonable interpretations, let it be made by those who are directly answerable to the people. This is how Mr. Justice Holmes expressed it in a famous dissent when the Court struck down a measure forbidding the teaching of German in public schools: "I think I appreciate the objection to the law but it appears to me to present a question upon which men reasonably might differ and therefore I am unable to say that the Constitution of the United States prevents the experiment being tried." *Meyer* v. *Nebraska*, 262 U.S. 390 (1923). By this rule a statute, like a jury verdict, must stand regardless of how mistaken it may seem to judges, unless they are prepared to hold that no reasonable man could have found as the legislature (or jury) did find. On this basis the two authentic voices of the people—jury and legislature—enjoy the same basic sanctity, the same immunity from judicial fiat. Of course, like other tools, this one too may be abused. But at its best it does suggest an external, objective standard for the guidance of a hard pressed court, a standard rooted in the only sound basis, according to Holmes, for any legal system—"the actual feelings and demands of the community, whether right or wrong." This, the so-called reasonable-man or rational-basis test, is also expressed in the proposition that legislation must be presumed to be constitutional unless the contrary can be demonstrated beyond all reasonable doubt. (See the excerpts from *Fletcher, Brown,* and *Ogden.*)

Only in recent years, and only with respect to the great First Amendment freedoms, have these principles of judicial self-restraint been questioned from the bench. (See for example the excerpts from *Carolene Products* and *Thomas* v. *Collins*.)

One thing seems clear: there is no completely convincing argument for the abolition or retention of judicial review in the abstract for it has many aspects. We have accepted it in principle along with a countervailing practice that subjects judges, when feeling runs deep, to irresistible political pressures. The Jeffersonian and New Deal assaults upon the Court, for example, failed in the sense that the Chase impeachment and the court reorganization plan were rejected in Congress. On the surface judicial independence was vindicated. But if Jefferson and Roosevelt lost as a matter of tactics, their strategy immediately prevailed. Perhaps in the end the problem of judicial review comes to this: is the accommodation of modern needs to ancient traditions (whether or not embodied in formal, written documents), is reconciliation of stability and change, essentially a judicial or a political function? Of course, we do not cling exclusively to one or the other. It is a matter of shifting tendency or degree on which the two great democratic peoples—the British and the American—lean in opposite directions. That they are committed to legislative, and we to judicial, supremacy may rest in part on differing political party structures. The British have "responsible" parties; we do not. In any case, as a matter of history under both systems the pressure of public opinion in the long run seems finally to prevail. Provided the run is not too long, surely this is as it should be in democratic countries. Perhaps our difficulty is that while we believe in democracy, we also fear it. If so, until this inner conflict is resolved we are not apt to find either judges or doctrines that will give more than partisan satisfaction.

CHIEF JUSTICE MARSHALL FOR THE COURT IN *Fletcher* v. *Peck*,
6 CRANCH 87 (1810)

The question, whether a law be void for repugnancy to the Constitution, is, at all times, a question of much delicacy, which ought seldom, if ever, to be decided in the affirmative, in a doubtful case. . . . The opposition between the Constitution and the law should be such that the judge feels a clear and strong conviction of their incompatibility with each other.

[This was the first case in which a state measure was held unconstitutional.]

CHIEF JUSTICE MARSHALL FOR THE COURT IN *Brown* v. *Maryland*,
12 WHEATON 419 (1827)

It has been truly said that the presumption is in favor of every legislative act, and that the whole burden of proof lies on him who denies its constitutionality.

MR. JUSTICE WASHINGTON FOR THE COURT IN *Ogden* v. *Saunders*,
12 WHEATON 213 (1827)

. . . the question which I have been examining is involved in difficulty and doubt. But if I could rest my opinion in favor of the constitutionality of the law . . . on no other ground than this doubt . . . that alone would . . . be a satisfactory vindication of it. It is but a decent respect due to the wisdom, the integrity, and the patriotism of the legislative body, by which any law is passed, to presume in favor of its validity, until its violation of the Constitution is proved beyond all reasonable doubt. This has always been the language of this Court . . . and I know that it expresses the honest sentiments of each and every member of this bench.

[This and the above quotations from Marshall are early statements of the "presumption of validity" of legislative acts, and the rule of "reasonable doubt."]

MR. JUSTICE STONE FOR THE COURT IN *United States* v. *Carolene Products Co.*, 304 U.S. 144, FOOTNOTE 4 (1938)

There may be narrower scope for operation of the presumption of constitutionality when legislation appears on its face to be within a specific prohibition of the Constitution, such as those of the first ten amendments, which are deemed equally specific when held to be embraced within the Fourteenth. . . .

It is unnecessary to consider now whether legislation which restricts those political processes which can ordinarily be expected to bring about repeal of undesirable legislation, is to be subjected to more exacting judicial scrutiny under the general prohibitions of the Fourteenth Amendment than are most other types of legislation. . . .

Nor need we enquire whether similar considerations enter into the review of statutes directed at particular religions . . . , or national . . . , or racial minorities . . . , whether prejudice against discrete and insular minorities may be a special condition, which tends seriously to curtail the operation of those political processes ordinarily to be relied upon to protect minorities, and which may call for a correspondingly more searching judicial inquiry.

[This is perhaps the first judicial language which openly questioned the presumption of validity, and the rule of reasonable doubt in civil liberty cases.]

MR. JUSTICE RUTLEDGE FOR THE COURT IN *Thomas* v. *Collins*, 323 U.S. 516 (1945)

The case confronts us again with the duty our system places on this Court to say where the individual's freedom ends and the State's power begins. Choice on that border, now as always delicate, is perhaps more so where the usual presumption supporting legislation is balanced by the preferred place given in our scheme to the great, the indispensable democratic freedoms secured by the First Amendment. . . . That priority gives these liberties a sanctity and a sanction not permitting dubious intrusions.

[This is an early statement of the "preferred place" rule.]

MR. JUSTICE STONE DISSENTING IN *United States* v. *Butler*, 297 U.S. 1 (1936)

The power of courts to declare a statute unconstitutional is subject to two guiding principles of decision which ought never to be absent from judicial consciousness. One is that courts are concerned only with the power to enact statutes, not with their wisdom. The other is that while unconstitutional exercise of power by the executive and legislative branches of the government is subject to judicial restraint, the only check upon our own exercise of power is our own sense of self-restraint. For the removal of unwise laws from the statute books appeal lies not to courts but to the ballot and to the processes of democratic government.

III. THE ROLE OF TEXT AND PRECEDENT

Surely the constitution of a growing, dynamic society must itself be a growing, dynamic thing. The Founders recognized this apparently in two ways: by authorizing formal amendments, and by writing for the most part in broad generalities which permit growth by "interpretation." To what extent should we accommodate changing circumstances by formal amendment—to what extent by judicial (or other) interpretation? Having once interpreted, is the judiciary bound thereby in future cases? The following excerpts indicate different responses to these questions.

CHIEF JUSTICE HUGHES FOR THE COURT IN *Home Building & Loan Assn. v. Blaisdell*, 290 U.S. 398 (1934)

It is no answer to say that this public need was not apprehended a century ago, or to insist that what the provisions of the Constitution meant to the vision of that day it must mean to the vision of our time. If by the statement that what the Constitution meant at the time of its adoption it means today, it is intended to say that the great clauses of the Constitution must be confined to the interpretation which the framers, with the considerations and outlook of their time, would have placed upon them, the statement carries its own refutation. It was to guard against such a narrow conception that Chief Justice Marshall uttered the memorable warning—"We must never forget that it is *a Constitution* we are expounding . . . a Constitution intended to endure for ages to come, and consequently, to be adapted to the various *crises* of human affairs."

MR. JUSTICE SUTHERLAND DISSENTING IN *West Coast Hotel Co. v. Parrish*, 300 U.S. 379 (1937)

It is urged that the question involved should now receive fresh consideration, among other reasons, because of "the economic conditions which have supervened"; but the meaning of the Constitution does not change with the ebb and flow of economic events. We frequently are told in more general words that the Constitution must be construed in the light of the present. If by that it is meant that the Constitution is made up of living words that apply to every new condition which they include, the statement is quite true. But to say, if that be intended, that the words of the Constitution mean today what they did not mean when written—that is, that they do not apply to a situation now to which they would have applied then—is to rob that instrument of the essential element which continues it in force as the people have made it until they, and not their official agents, have made it otherwise. . . .

The judicial function is that of interpretation; it does not include the power of amendment under the guise of interpretation. To miss the point of difference between the two is to miss all that the phrase "supreme law of the land" stands for and to convert what was intended as inescapable and enduring mandates into mere moral reflections.

If the Constitution, intelligently and reasonably construed in the light of these principles, stands in the way of desirable legislation, the blame must rest upon that instrument, and not upon the court for enforcing it according to its terms. The remedy in that situation—and the only true remedy—is to amend the Constitution. Judge Cooley, in the first volume of his *Constitutional Limitations* (8th Ed.), p. 124, very clearly pointed out that much of the benefit expected from written constitutions would be lost if their provisions were to be bent to circumstances or modified by public opinion. He pointed out that the common law, unlike a constitution, was subject to modification by public sentiment and action which the courts might recognize; but that "a court or legislature which should allow a change in public sentiment to influence it in giving to a written constitution a construction not warranted by the intention of its founders, would be justly chargeable with reckless disregard of official oath and public duty; and if its course could become a precedent, these instruments would be of little avail. . . . What a court is to do, therefore, is *to declare the law as written*, leaving it to the people themselves to make such changes as new circumstances may require. The meaning of the constitution is fixed when it is adopted, and it is not different at any subsequent time when a court has occasion to pass upon it."

MR. JUSTICE HOLMES FOR THE COURT IN *Gompers* v. *United States*, 233 U.S. 604 (1914)

The provisions of the Constitution are not mathematical formulas having their essence in their form; they are organic, living institutions transplanted from English soil. Their significance is vital, not formal; it is to be gathered not simply by taking the words and a dictionary, but by considering their origin and the line of their growth.

MR. JUSTICE HOLMES FOR THE COURT IN *Missouri* v. *Holland*, 252 U.S. 416 (1920)

The case before us must be considered in the light of our whole [national] experience and not merely in that of what was said a hundred years ago.

MR. JUSTICE BRANDEIS DISSENTING IN *Burnet* v. *Coronado Oil & Gas Co.*, 285 U.S. 393 (1932)

Stare decisis is not, like the rule of res adjudicata, a universal, inexorable command. . . . Stare decisis is usually the wise policy, because in most matters it is more important that the applicable rule of law be settled than that it be settled right. . . . This is commonly true even where the error is a matter of serious concern, provided correction can be had by legislation. But in cases involving the Federal Constitution, where correction through legislation is practically impossible, this Court has often overruled its earlier decisions. The Court bows to the lessons of experience and the force of better reasoning, recognizing that the process of trial and error, so fruitful in the physical sciences, is appropriate also in the judicial function.

IV. THE ORGANIZATION AND JURISDICTION OF THE FEDERAL COURTS

Article III of the Constitution provides for a Supreme Court and authorizes such lower federal courts as Congress may from time to time establish. Pursuant to this grant there are now from one to four federal trial courts (United States District Courts) in each state and the District of Columbia. Above them are eleven intermediate appellate tribunals (United States Courts of Appeals), each having jurisdiction to review decisions from district courts within a specified area or "circuit" and from various federal administrative agencies, such as the Federal Trade Commission. Most federal litigation gets no higher than this second judicial level. Only the very special case can go to the Supreme Court, as we shall see. It is crucial that the sole authority which that tribunal gets directly from the Constitution is a very limited original jurisdiction involving states, ambassadors, etc. All other federal court authority is to be distributed in such manner and among such courts as Congress may provide. The appellate authority of the Supreme Court with respect to "inferior" federal courts (and to state courts) is also subject to full congressional control.

Finally, the Constitution (Art. III, Sec. 2, Par. 1) provides that federal courts shall have jurisdiction (power to decide) only two categories of cases. One embraces those arising under the Constitution, federal statutes, and treaties. The reason for this is plain. If national law is to have uniform meaning throughout the nation, it cannot be left to the mutually independent judicial systems of the several states. However, the Constitution does not give this "federal question" jurisdiction, as it is called, exclusively to federal judges. Nor has Congress made it exclusive, except in a very limited field, e.g., federal bankruptcy. Thus cases involving federal law may arise and be decided in state courts. Beginning with Section 25 of the Judiciary Act of 1789 Congress has always provided for review of such cases by the Supreme Court of the United States, lest federal law have as many meanings as there are states. Madison, we have noted (Part One, I), argued in support of such jurisdiction. Nevertheless, it offended some in the early days that the decision of the highest court of a "sovereign state" should be reversible by an "outside" court. "The great Chief Justice" and his colleagues had something to say on this matter in *Cohens* v. *Virginia*. Since then the constitutional issue has been settled. But recently a famous States-righter has urged that Congress limit this and all appellate power of the Court—at least presumably in cases involving certain aspects of racial segregation. See the note on Byrnes, "The Supreme Court Must Be Curbed," page 44.

The other category of cases which federal courts may decide is that involving certain special parties *regardless of what law is involved*. For example, the ambassador of a foreign country may have his case involving a mere grocery bill tried in a federal court even though no federal law (Constitution, treaty, or act of Congress) is applicable. Obviously in such a case the federal court acts in effect as a special state tribunal. Recognizing this, Congress from the beginning has provided that in litigation of this type the federal courts shall apply state "laws."

By interpreting that word to mean only state legislative (not common) law the Supreme Court in effect authorized federal courts in "special party" cases to make and apply their own common law. *Swift* v. *Tyson*, 16 Peters 1 (1842). To this extent the states lost a large measure of control of their own admittedly local affairs. Admittedly local, because by hypothesis such cases do not arise under federal law.

If only cases involving ambassadors were involved, the problem would not be serious. Unfortunately, the "special party" jurisdiction of the federal courts is more extensive. Easily the most common and most troublesome part of it is that which rests on the fact that contending litigants come from different states. As Mr. Justice Frankfurter put it: "the stuff of diversity jurisdiction [as it is called] is state litigation. The availability of federal tribunals for controversies concerning matters which in themselves are outside of federal power and exclusively within state authority, is the essence of jurisdiction solely resting on the fact that a plaintiff and a defendant are citizens of different states. The power of Congress to confer such jurisdiction was based on the desire of the framers to assure out-of-state litigants courts free from susceptibility to potential local bias." However commendable the original motive, and whether or not that motive ever was, or is now, grounded in reality, it is clear that instead of "protecting out-of-state litigants against discrimination by state courts, the effect of diversity of jurisdiction was discrimination against citizens of the State in favor of litigants from without the State." *Lumbermen's Casualty Co.* v. *Elbert*, 348 U.S. 48, 54–55 (1954). This followed because, as a result of *Swift* v. *Tyson*, there arose within each state two common law legal systems. Which of the two would apply in a given case depended upon the "accident" of the citizenship of the litigants. Suppose, for example, a Texan were visiting his brother in Iowa. Riding together in an automobile, they were both hurt in a collision with a car driven by another Iowan. The Iowa brother could sue for damages only in a state court, because only state common law is involved and both litigants were citizens of the same state. The Texas brother, however, finding federal common law more favorable than that of the state, might choose to sue in a federal court. This he could do because he and the defendant were citizens of different states. Thus, while only one accident was involved, each lawsuit would be governed by a different legal system. Since in the supposed case the one had a lenient, the other a more stringent, test as to what constitutes negligence, one brother might win his case and the other might lose. The difficulties of this strange double legal regime for the same local problems were magnified by another early decision which recognized that, for diversity jurisdiction purposes, a corporation is a "citizen" of the state in which it is incorporated. A Delaware corporation, for example, may enjoy "diversity" privileges in every other state in which it operates.

Possibly the rule that permitted federal courts to create their own independent common law was an expression of Federalist nationalism. Doubtless it arose in the hope, or expectation, that state judges would follow the federal common law so created. Had they complied, the dual law system for nonnational matters would not have arisen. We might have had a single, uniform common law for the entire country. The plain fact is, state judges did not comply. The result was chaos that had a remarkable tendency to work to the advantage of corporate litigants. The crux of the difficulty is seen in the infamous *Black & White Taxi-*

cab case, 276 U.S. 518 (1928). Two Kentucky corporations wanted to make a contract for the monopolistic conduct of a Kentucky taxi business. Such a monopoly would have been illegal under Kentucky common law, so one of the companies reincorporated in a neighboring state, made the contract, and then by means of a federal injunction in a diversity case was able under federal common law to enforce in Kentucky a trade restriction which violated Kentucky law. A system that made such things possible invited its own doom. It died in *Erie Railroad Co. v. Tompkins*, 304 U.S. 64 (1938), shortly after the curtain fell on the old regime. One difficulty remains. The diversity jurisdiction imposes a tremendous burden upon the federal courts. Now that they enforce in such cases the same law that is enforced by state courts is there any reason to continue it? If prejudice against outsiders is a danger in state courts, why is it not equally a danger in federal courts? Like their state counterparts federal trial judges and juries come from the states in which they sit. Where there is in fact state discrimination against outsiders the equal protection clause of the Fourteenth Amendment affords a federal remedy. There was no such provision in the Constitution when diversity jurisdiction was established!

DISCRETIONARY REVIEW BY THE SUPREME COURT

Obviously one Supreme Court of nine judges cannot review all cases decided in state and lower federal courts. That some system of selection is necessary finds expression in the constitutional provision giving Congress the power to regulate the Court's appellate jurisdiction (Art. III, Sec. 2, Par. 2). Congress has exercised this power by giving a "right" to appeal in a very limited category of cases and by granting the Court discretionary authority to review or not in other situations. One whose claim under federal law is rejected by the highest state court in which the issue can be raised has a "right" of appeal to the Supreme Court of the nation. Such a rejection occurs when a litigant invokes federal law and its validity is denied, or when he challenges a state law as being in violation of the federal Constitution and its validity is upheld. Conversely, when a lower federal court holds a state law in conflict with the federal Constitution, and in certain circumstances when such a court finds an act of Congress invalid, appeal is a matter of "right." Generally speaking, other cases get to the Supreme Court only as a matter of grace. That is to say, the Court may grant or deny review in its discretion by granting or refusing applications for the writ of certiorari. The thought is that since the Justices obviously cannot review all cases, they can by this method spend their limited time and energy where, in their opinion, it will do the most *public* good. For let us be clear, it is the appellate responsibility of state supreme courts and the United States Courts of Appeals to protect the merely private rights of litigants. The Supreme Court's responsibility is larger. Chief Justice Vinson expressed the orthodox view in the following terms: [1]

The Supreme Court is not, and never has been, primarily concerned with the correction of errors in lower court decisions. . . . If we took every case in which an interesting legal question is raised, or our *prima facie* impression is that the decision below is erroneous, we could not fulfill the constitutional and statutory

1. 69 S. Ct. VI (1949). Address before American Bar Association, September 7, 1949.

responsibilities placed upon the Court. To remain effective the Supreme Court must continue to decide only those cases which present questions whose resolution will have immediate importance far beyond the particular facts and parties involved.

For example, a classic case for the exercise of the discretionary power to review is one which will permit the Supreme Court to settle the matter on which two United States Courts of Appeal are in disagreement. Here the desideratum is not the private interest of any of the litigants, but the public interest in uniformity in the law throughout the nation.

In fact, the distinction between appeals as of right and review via certiorari is somewhat illusory. For over the years there has developed a practice whereby the Court rejects the former when they present what the judges consider only "insubstantial federal questions." See Mr. Justice Frankfurter's remarks in *Daniels* v. *Allen*, 344 U.S. 433, 491 (1953); and "The Insubstantial Federal Question," 62 *Harvard Law Review* 488 (1949).

DIAGRAM SHOWING THE APPELLATE AUTHORITY OF THE SUPREME COURT

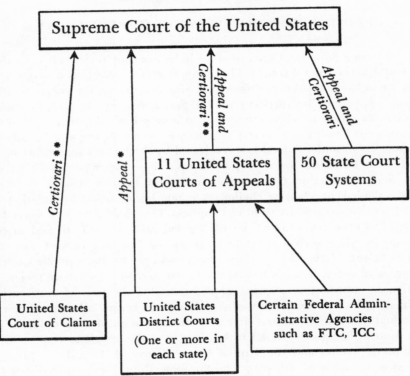

* Direct appeals from district courts are allowed only in very special circumstances to save time when time is crucial, as when a federal statute has been invalidated, or a federal injunction has blocked a vital process of state government.

** A Court of Appeals, like the Court of Claims, may certify to the Supreme Court "any question of law . . . as to which instructions are desired." This device is now seldom used because certified questions tend to raise hypothetical, rather than real, issues. These the Supreme Court shuns for the same reasons which have impelled it to avoid giving advisory opinions. *NLRB* v. *White Swan Co.*, 313 U.S. 23, 27 (1941).

COHENS v. *VIRGINIA*
6 Wheaton 264 (1821)

Cohens had been convicted in a state court for violating a Virginia anti-lottery statute. Having exhausted all state appeals, he sought review by the Supreme Court of the United States on "federal question" grounds; i.e., because of an alleged conflict between the state law and a federal law authorizing lotteries. Section 25 of the Judiciary Act of 1789 gave the Supreme Court reviewing authority in such cases. In exercising it, Marshall's Court sustained Cohens' conviction on the ground that the congressional lottery act applied only in the District of Columbia. The decision is important, not for that holding, but because of the Supreme Court's repudiation of Virginia's argument that the federal tribunal had no authority to review the judgment of a state court.

MR. CHIEF JUSTICE MARSHALL delivered the opinion of the Court: . . .

The questions presented to the court by the first two points made at the bar are of great magnitude, and may truly be said vitally to affect the Union. They exclude the inquiry whether the Constitution and laws of the United States have been violated by the judgment which the plaintiffs in error seek to review; and maintain that, admitting such violation, it is not in the power of the government to apply a corrective. They maintain that the nation does not possess a department capable of restraining, peaceably, and by authority of law, any attempts which may be made, by a part, against the legitimate powers of the whole; and that the government is reduced to the alternative of submitting to such attempts, or of resisting them by force. They maintain that the Constitution of the United States has provided no tribunal for the final construction of itself, or of the laws or treaties of the nation; but that this power may be exercised in the last resort by the courts of every state of the Union. That the Constitution, laws, and treaties may receive as many constructions as there are states; and that this is not a mischief, or, if a mischief is irremediable. . . .

1st. The first question to be considered is, whether the jurisdiction of this court is excluded by the character of the parties, one of them being a state, and the other a citizen of that state?

The 2d section of the third article of the Constitution defines the extent of the judicial power of the United States. Jurisdiction is given to the courts of the Union in two classes of cases. In the first, their jurisdiction depends on the character of the cause, whoever may be the parties. This class comprehends "all cases in law and equity arising under this Constitution, the laws of the United States, and treaties made, or which shall be made, under their authority." This clause extends the jurisdiction of the court to all the cases described, without making in its terms any exception whatever, and without any regard to the condition of the party. If there be any exception, it is to be implied against the express words of the article.

In the second class, the jurisdiction depends entirely on the character of the parties. In this are comprehended "controversies between two or more States, between a State and citizens of another State," "and between a State and foreign states, citizens, or subjects." If these be the parties, it is entirely unimportant what may be the subject of controversy. Be it what it may, these parties have a constitutional right to come into the courts of the Union. . . .

If . . . a case arising under the Constitution, or a law, must be one in which a party comes into court to demand something conferred on him by the Constitution or a law, we think the construction too narrow. A case in law or equity consists of the right of the one party, as well as of the other, and may truly be said to arise under the Constitution or a law of the United States, whenever its correct decision depends on the construction of either. . . .

The jurisdiction of the court, then, being extended by the letter of the Constitution to all cases arising under it, or under the laws of the United States, it follows that those who would withdraw any case of this description from that jurisdiction, must sustain the exemption they claim, on the spirit and true meaning of the Constitution, which spirit and true meaning must be so apparent as to overrule the words which its framers have employed. The counsel for the defendant in error have undertaken to do this; and have laid down the general proposition, that a sovereign independent state is not suable, except by its own consent.

This general proposition will not be controverted. But its consent is not requisite in each particular case. It may be given in a general law. And if a state has surrendered any portion of its sovereignty, the question whether a liability to suit be a part of this portion, depends on the instrument by which the surrender is made. If upon a just construction of that instrument, it shall appear that the state has submitted to be sued, then it has parted with this sovereign right of judging in every case on the justice of its own pretensions, and has entrusted that power to a tribunal in whose impartiality it confides.

The American states, as well as the American people, have believed a close and firm Union to be essential to their liberty and to their happiness. They have been taught by experience, that this Union cannot exist without a government for the whole; and they have been taught by the same experience that this government would be a mere shadow, that must disappoint all their hopes, unless invested with large portions of that sovereignty which belongs to independent states. Under the influence of this opinion, and thus instructed by experience, the American

people, in the conventions of their respective states, adopted the present Constitution.

If it could be doubted whether, from its nature, it were not supreme in all cases where it is empowered to act, that doubt would be removed by the declaration that "this Constitution, and the laws of the United States which shall be made in pursuance thereof and all treaties made, or which shall be made, under the authority of the United States, shall be the supreme law of the land; and the judges in every state shall be bound thereby, anything in the Constitution or laws of any state to the contrary notwithstanding."

This is the authoritative language of the American people; and, if gentlemen please, of the American states. It marks with lines too strong to be mistaken, the characteristic distinction between the government of the Union and those of the states. The general government, though limited as to its objects, is supreme with respect to those objects. This principle is a part of the Constitution; and if there be any who deny its necessity, none can deny its authority.

To this supreme government ample powers are confided; and if it were possible to doubt the great purposes for which they were so confided, the people of the United States have declared that they are given "in order to form a more perfect union, establish justice, insure domestic tranquillity, provide for the common defense, promote the general welfare, and secure the blessings of liberty to themselves and their posterity."

With the ample powers confided to this supreme government, for these interesting purposes, are connected many express and important limitations on the sovereignty of the states, which are made for the same purposes. The powers of the Union on the great subjects of war, peace, and commerce, and on many others, are in themselves limitations of the sovereignty of the states; but in addition to these, the sovereignty of the states is surrendered in many instances where the surrender can only operate to the benefit of the people, and where, perhaps, no other power is conferred on congress than a conservative power to maintain the principles established in the Constitution. The maintenance of these principles in their purity is certainly among the great duties of the government. One of the instruments by which this duty may be peaceably performed is the judicial department. It is authorized to decide all cases, of every description, arising under the Constitution or laws of the United States. From this general grant of jurisdiction, no exception is made of those cases in which a state may be a party. When we consider the situation of the government of the Union and of a state, in relation to each other; the nature of our Constitution; the subordination of the state governments to that Constitution; the great purpose for which jurisdiction over all cases arising under the Constitution and laws of the United States, is confided to the judicial department; are we at liberty to insert in this general grant, an exception of those cases in which a state may be a party? Will the spirit of the Constitution justify this attempt to control its words? We think it will not. We think a case arising under the Constitution or laws of the United States, is cognizable in the courts of the Union, whoever may be the parties to that case....

... If jurisdiction depended entirely on the character of the parties, and was not given where the parties have not an original right to come into court, that part of the 2d section of the 3rd article, which extends the judicial power to all cases arising under the Constitution and laws of the United States, would be surplusage. It is to give jurisdiction where the character of the parties would not give it, that this very important part of the clause was inserted. It may be true, that the partiality of the state tribunals, in ordinary controversies between a state and its citizens, was not apprehended, and therefore the judicial power of the Union was not extended to such cases; but this was not the sole nor the greatest object for which this department was created. A more important, a much more interesting object, was the pres-

ervation of the Constitution and laws of the United States, so far as they can be preserved by judicial authority; and therefore the jurisdiction of the courts of the Union was expressly extended to all cases arising under that Constitution and those laws. If the Constitution or laws may be violated by proceedings instituted by a state against its own citizens, and if that violation may be such as essentially to affect the Constitution and the laws, such as to arrest the progress of government in its constitutional course, why should these cases be excepted from that provision which expressly extends the judicial power of the Union to *all* cases arising under the Constitution and laws? . . .

2d. The second objection to the jurisdiction of the court is, that its appellate power cannot be exercised, in any case, over the judgment of a state court.

This objection is sustained chiefly by arguments drawn from the supposed total separation of the judiciary of a state from that of the Union, and their entire independence of each other. The argument considers the federal judiciary as completely foreign to that of a state; and as being no more connected with it, in any respect whatever, than the court of a foreign state. If this hypothesis be just, the argument founded on it is equally so; but if the hypothesis be not supported by the Constitution, the argument fails with it.

This hypothesis is not founded on any words in the Constitution, which might seem to countenance it, but on the unreasonableness of giving a contrary construction to words which seem to require it; and on the incompatibility of the application of the appellate jurisdiction to the judgments of state courts, with that constitutional relation which subsists between the government of the Union and the governments of those states which compose it.

Let this unreasonableness, this total incompatibility, be examined.

That the United States form, for many, and for most important purposes, a single nation, has not yet been denied. In war, we are one people. In making peace, we are one people. In all commercial regulations, we are one and the same people. In many other respects, the American people are one; and the government which is alone capable of controlling and managing their interests in all these respects, is the government of the Union. It is their government, and in that character, they have no other. America has chosen to be, in many respects, and to many purposes, a nation; and for all these purposes, her government is complete; to all these objects it is competent. The people have declared, that in the exercise of all powers given for these objects, it is supreme. It can, then, in effecting these objects, legitimately control all individuals or governments within the American territory. The constitution and laws of a state, so far as they are repugnant to the Constitution and laws of the United States, are absolutely void. These states are constituent parts of the United States; they are members of one great empire—for some purposes sovereign, for some purposes subordinate.

In a government so constituted, is it unreasonable, that the judicial power should be competent to give efficacy to the constitutional laws of the legislature? That department can decide on the validity of the constitution or law of a state, if it be repugnant to the Constitution or to a law of the United States. Is it unreasonable, that it should also be empowered to decide on the judgment of a state tribunal enforcing such unconstitutional law? Is it so very unreasonable, as to furnish a justification for controlling the words of the constitution?

We think it is not. We think that in a government acknowledgedly supreme, with respect to objects of vital interest to the nation, there is nothing inconsistent with sound reason, nothing incompatible with the nature of government, in making all its departments supreme, so far as respects those objects, and so far as is necessary to their attainment. The exercise of the appellate power over those judgments of the state tribunals which may contravene the Constitution or laws of the United States, is, we believe, essential to the attainment of those objects.

The propriety of entrusting the construction of the Constitution, and laws made in pursuance thereof, to the judiciary of the Union has not, we believe, as yet, been drawn into question. It seems to be a corollary from this political axiom, that the federal courts should either possess exclusive jurisdiction in such cases, or a power to revise the judgment rendered in them, by the state tribunals. If the federal and state courts have concurrent jurisdiction in all cases arising under the Constitution, laws, and treaties of the United States; and if a case of this description brought in a state court cannot be removed before judgment, nor revised after judgment, then the construction of the Constitution, laws, and treaties of the United States is not confided particularly to their judicial department, but is confided equally to that department and to the state courts, however they may be constituted. "Thirteen independent courts," says a very celebrated statesman (and we have now more than twenty such courts), "of final jurisdiction over the same causes, arising upon the same laws, is a hydra in government, from which nothing but contradiction and confusion can proceed."

. . . Let the nature and objects of our Union be considered; let the great fundamental principles, on which the fabric stands, be examined; and we think, the result must be, that there is nothing so extravagantly absurd, in giving to the court of the nation the power of revising the decisions of local tribunals, on questions which affect the nation, as to require that words which import this power should be restricted by a forced construction. . . .

Judgment affirmed.

NOTE: In a well-known article, "The Supreme Court Must Be Curbed," [1] former Justice James Byrnes was highly critical of the Court for holding invalid "the laws of 17 States under which segregated public school systems were established"

1. From a copyrighted article in *U.S. News & World Report,* May 18, 1956. Used by permission.

and for two subsequent decisions allegedly pleasing to Communists. Some of the cases in question came to the Supreme Court by virtue of its appellate jurisdiction to review state decisions resting upon federal law. Others involved review of lower federal court decisions. In part, Mr. Byrnes said:

> Power intoxicates men. It is never voluntarily surrendered. It must be taken from them. The Supreme Court must be curbed.
>
> The Constitution authorizes Congress to regulate the appellate jurisdiction of the Supreme Court. Loyal Americans who believe in constitutional government appeal to the court of public opinion in the hope that you will urge the Congress to act before it is too late.

The "intoxicating power" that Mr. Byrnes referred to would not be destroyed by the adoption of his proposal to restrict the appellate jurisdiction of the Supreme Court. It would merely be taken from a higher court and thus left to lower courts. If this were done, there would be potentially as many versions of national law as there are state supreme and federal appellate courts, some sixty-one. For, absent a supreme national reviewing tribunal, there would be no device for coordinating these completely separate and independent jurisdictions. National law, including the Constitution, would mean different things in different states—and even perhaps within the same state. To that extent the United States would cease to be a nation. What Mr. Byrnes sought via legislation is precisely what the State of Virginia tried to read into the Constitution, and Chief Justice Marshall rejected, in *Cohens* v. *Virginia*.

The Court was effectively "curbed" in the Byrnes manner to forestall Supreme Court review of the Reconstruction. *Ex parte McCardle*, 7 Wallace 506 (1869). There, too, as in the Chase impeachment and the court reorganization plan, powerful political forces frustrated judicial review.

ERIE RAILROAD COMPANY v. TOMPKINS

304 U.S. 64 (1938)

Tompkins was injured in an Erie Railroad accident in Pennsylvania. He sued for negligence in New York in a federal district court, the court's jurisdiction resting on "diversity of citizenship," not "federal question," grounds. Erie argued that Tompkins had been a trespasser and that under Pennsylvania law a railroad is not liable for mere negligence to trespassers. The lower federal courts held that Pennsylvania law was irrelevant because "general law," that is, federal common law, applied. On this basis Tompkins obtained a judgment. The Supreme Court reviewed on certiorari.

MR. JUSTICE BRANDEIS delivered the opinion of the Court:

The question for decision is whether the oft-challenged doctrine of *Swift* v. *Tyson* shall now be disapproved. . . .

First. *Swift* v. *Tyson*, 16 Pet. 1, 18, held that federal courts exercising jurisdiction on the ground of diversity of citizenship need not, in matters of general jurisprudence, apply the unwritten law of the state as declared by its highest court; that they are free to exercise an independent judgment as to what the common law of the state is—or should be; and that, as there stated by Mr. Justice Story, "the true interpretation of the 34th section [of the

Judiciary Act of 1789] limited its application to state laws strictly local, that is to say, to the positive statutes of the state, and the construction thereof adopted by the local tribunals, and to rights and titles to things having a permanent locality, such as the rights and titles to real estate, and other matters immovable and intraterritorial in their nature and character. It never has been supposed by us, that the section did apply, or was designed to apply, to questions of a more general nature, not at all dependent upon local statutes or local usages of a fixed and permanent operation, as, for example, to the construction of ordinary contracts or other written instruments, and especially to questions of general commercial law, where the state tribunals are called upon to perform the like functions as ourselves, that is, to ascertain, upon general reasoning and legal analogies, what is the true exposition of the contract or instrument, or what is the just rule furnished by the principles of commercial law to govern the case."

The Court in applying the rule of section 34 to equity cases, in *Mason* v. *United States*, 260 U.S. 545, 559, said: "The statute, however, is merely declarative of the rule which would exist in the absence of the statute." The federal courts assumed, in the broad field of "general law," the power to declare rules of decision which Congress was confessedly without power to enact as statutes. Doubt was repeatedly expressed as to the correctness of the construction given section 34, and as to the soundness of the rule which it introduced. But it was the more recent research of a competent scholar, who examined the original document, which established that the construction given to it by the Court was erroneous; and that the purpose of the section was merely to make certain that, in all matters except those in which some federal law is controlling, the federal courts exercising jurisdiction in diversity of citizenship cases would apply as their rules of decision the law of the state, unwritten as well as written. . . .

Experience in applying the doctrine of *Swift* v. *Tyson* had revealed its defects political and social; and the benefits expected to flow from the rule did not accrue. Persistence of state courts in their own opinions on questions of common law prevented uniformity; and the impossibility of discovering a satisfactory line of demarcation between the province of general law and that of local law developed a new well of uncertainties.

On the other hand, the mischievous results of the doctrine had become apparent. Diversity of citizenship jurisdiction was conferred in order to prevent apprehended discrimination in state courts against those not citizens of the state. *Swift* v. *Tyson* introduced grave discrimination by noncitizens against citizens. It made rights enjoyed under the unwritten "general law" vary according to whether enforcement was sought in the state or in the federal court; and the privilege of selecting the court in which the right should be determined was conferred upon the non-citizen. Thus, the doctrine rendered impossible equal protection of the law. In attempting to promote uniformity of law throughout the United States, the doctrine had prevented uniformity in the administration of the law of the state.

The discrimination resulting became in practice far-reaching. This resulted in part from the broad province accorded to the so-called "general law" as to which federal courts exercised an independent judgment. In addition to questions of purely commercial law, "general law" was held to include the obligations under contracts entered into and to be performed within the state; the extent to which a carrier operating within a state may stipulate for exemption from liability for his own negligence or that of his employee; the liability for torts committed within the state upon persons resident or property located there, even where the question of liability depended upon the scope of a property right conferred by the state; and the right to exemplary or punitive damages. Furthermore, state decisions construing local deeds, mineral conveyances, and even devises of real estate were disregarded.

In part the discrimination resulted from

the wide range of persons held entitled to avail themselves of the federal rule by resort to the diversity of citizenship jurisdiction. Through this jurisdiction individual citizens willing to remove from their own state and become citizens of another might avail themselves of the federal rule. And, without even change of residence, a corporate citizen of the state could avail itself of the federal rule by reincorporating under the laws of another state, as was done in the *Taxicab Case*.

The injustice and confusion incident to the doctrine of *Swift* v. *Tyson* have been repeatedly urged as reasons for abolishing or limiting diversity of citizenship jurisdiction. Other legislative relief has been proposed. If only a question of statutory construction were involved, we should not be prepared to abandon a doctrine so widely applied throughout nearly a century. But the unconstitutionality of the course pursued has now been made clear and compels us to do so.

Third. Except in matters governed by the federal Constitution or by acts of Congress, the law to be applied in any case is the law of the state. And whether the law of the state shall be declared by its legislature in a statute or by its highest court in a decision is not a matter of federal concern. There is no federal general common law. Congress has no power to declare substantive rules of common law applicable in a state whether they be local in their nature or "general," be they commercial law or a part of the law of torts. And no clause in the Constitution purports to confer such a power upon the federal courts. As stated by Mr. Justice Field when protesting in *Baltimore & Ohio R.R. Co.* v. *Baugh*, 149 U.S. 368, 401, against ignoring the Ohio common law of fellow-servant liability: "I am aware that what has been termed the general law of the country—which is often little less than what the judge advancing the doctrine thinks at the time should be the general law on a particular subject— has been often advanced in judicial opinions of this Court to control a conflicting law of a state. I admit that learned judges have fallen into the habit of repeating this

doctrine as a convenient mode of brushing aside the law of a state in conflict with their views. And I confess that, moved and governed by the authority of the great names of those judges, I have, myself, in many instances, unhesitatingly and confidently, but I think now erroneously, repeated the same doctrine. But, notwithstanding the great names which may be cited in favor of the doctrine, and notwithstanding the frequency with which the doctrine has been reiterated, there stands, as a perpetual protest against its repetition, the Constitution of the United States, which recognizes and preserves the autonomy and independence of the states—independence in their legislative and independence in their judicial departments. Supervision over either the legislative or the judicial action of the states is in no case permissible except as to matters by the Constitution specifically authorized or delegated to the United States. Any interference with either, except as thus permitted, is an invasion of the authority of the state and, to that extent, a denial of its independence."

The fallacy underlying the rule declared in *Swift* v. *Tyson* is made clear by Mr. Justice Holmes. . . .

"Books written about any branch of the common law treat it as a unit, cite cases from this Court, from the Circuit Courts of Appeals, from the state courts, from England and the Colonies of England indiscriminately, and criticise them as right or wrong according to the writer's notions of a single theory. It is very hard to resist the impression that there is one august corpus, to understand which clearly is the only task of any court concerned. If there were such a transcendental body of law outside of any particular state but obligatory within it unless and until changed by statute, the courts of the United States might be right in using their independent judgment as to what it was. But there is no such body of law. The fallacy and illusion that I think exist consist in supposing that there is this outside thing to be found. Law is a word used with different meanings, but law in the sense in which courts speak of it today does not exist without some definite authority behind it. The common law so far as it is enforced in a state, whether called common law or not, is not the common law generally but the law of that state existing by the authority of that state without regard to what it may have been in England or anywhere else. [*Black & White Taxi. Co.* v. *Brown & Yellow Taxi. Co.*, 276 U.S. 518, dissenting at 532, 533 (1928), Brandeis and Stone, JJ., concurring in the dissent.]"

Thus the doctrine of *Swift* v. *Tyson* is, as Mr. Justice Holmes said, "an unconstitutional assumption of powers by the courts of the United States which no lapse of time or respectable array of opinion should make us hesitate to correct." In disapproving that doctrine we do not hold unconstitutional section 34 of the Federal Judiciary Act of 1789 or any other act of Congress. We merely declare that in applying the doctrine this Court and the lower courts have invaded rights which in our opinion are reserved by the Constitution to the several states.

Fourth. The defendant contended that by the common law of Pennsylvania as declared by its highest court in *Falchetti* v. *Pennsylvania R. Co.*, 307 Pa. 203, 160 A. 859, the only duty owed to the plaintiff

was to refrain from willful or wanton injury. The plaintiff denied that such is the Pennsylvania law. In support of their respective contentions the parties discussed and cited many decisions of the supreme court of the state. The Circuit Court of Appeals ruled that the question of liability is one of general law; and on that ground declined to decide the issue of state law. As we hold this was error, the judgment is reversed and the case remanded to it for further proceedings in conformity with our opinion.

Reversed.

MR. JUSTICE BUTLER (MR. JUSTICE Mc-REYNOLDS concurring with him) dissented.

MR. JUSTICE REED, concurring. . . .

To decide the case now before us and to "disapprove" the doctrine of *Swift* v. *Tyson* requires only that we say that the words "the laws" include in their meaning the decisions of the local tribunals. As the majority opinion shows, by its reference to Mr. Warren's researches and the first quotation from Mr. Justice Holmes, that this Court is now of the view that "laws" includes "decisions," it is unnecessary to go further and declare that the "course pursued" was "unconstitutional," instead of merely erroneous. . . .

NOTE: The Court here explicitly holds its own prior conduct unconstitutional. If, as Mr. Justice Reed suggests, his brother Brandeis seems to have forgotten the rules which he himself had urged in *Ashwander's* case, the answer is simple. There Brandeis urged judicial self-restraint, lest the authority of the political branches of government be restricted gratuitously. *Erie* restricts the power of the federal judiciary to intrude upon state authority in purely local affairs. The two opinions are expressions in different contexts of a single principle—judicial self-restraint in deference to other agencies of government.

Just as *Cohens* insures uniformity in the application of federal law throughout the nation, *Erie* insures uniformity in the application of state substantive law throughout the state.

ACTS OF CONGRESS PROVIDING FOR THE APPELLATE JURISDICTION OF THE SUPREME COURT

Article III of the Constitution gives Congress control over the appellate (but not the original) jurisdictior of the Supreme Court. Following are the current basic statutory provisions. It is these, of course, that Mr. Byrnes thought should be modified (see Note p. 44).

REVIEW OF STATE COURT DECISIONS (SEC. 1257, TITLE 28, UNITED STATES CODE)

Final judgments or decrees rendered by the highest court of a State in which a decision could be had, may be reviewed by the Supreme Court as follows:

(1) By appeal, where is drawn in question the validity of a treaty or statute of the United States and the decision is against its validity.

(2) By appeal, where is drawn in question the validity of a statute of any state on the ground of its being repugnant to the Constitution, treaties or laws of the United States, and the decision is in favor of its validity.

(3) By writ of certiorari, where the validity of a treaty or statute of the United States is drawn in question or where the validity of a State statute is drawn in question on the ground of its being repugnant to the Constitution, treaties or laws of the United States, or where any title, right, privilege or immunity is specially set up or claimed under the Constitution, treaties or statutes of, or commission held or authority exercised under, the United States.

REVIEW OF LOWER FEDERAL COURT DECISIONS (SEC. 1254, TITLE 28, UNITED STATES CODE)

(1) By writ of certiorari granted upon the petition of any party to any civil or criminal case, before or after rendition of judgment or decree;

(2) By appeal by a party relying on a State statute held by a court of appeals to be invalid as repugnant to the Constitution, treaties or laws of the United States, but such appeal shall preclude review by writ of certiorari at the instance of such appellant, and the review on appeal shall be restricted to the Federal questions presented;

(3) By certification at any time by a court of appeals of any question of law in any civil or criminal case as to which instructions are desired, and upon such certification the Supreme Court may give binding instructions or require the entire record to be sent up for decision of the entire matter in controversy.

CONSIDERATIONS GOVERNING REVIEW ON CERTIORARI (RULE 19[1], REVISED RULES OF THE SUPREME COURT, 1954)

A review on writ of certiorari is not a matter of right, but of sound judicial discretion, and will be granted only where there are special and important reasons therefor. The following, while neither controlling nor fully measuring the court's discretion, indicate the character of reasons which will be considered.

(a) Where a state court has decided a federal question of substance not theretofore determined by this court, or has decided it in a way probably not in accord with applicable decisions of this court.

(b) Where a court of appeals has rendered a decision in conflict with the decision of another court of appeals on the same matter; or has decided an important state or territorial question in a way in conflict with applicable state or territorial law; or has decided an important question of federal law which has not been, but should be, settled by this court; or has decided a federal question in a way in conflict with applicable decisions of this court; or has so far departed from the accepted and usual course of judicial proceedings, or so far sanctioned such a departure by a lower court, as to call for an exercise of this court's power of supervision.

NOTE: By tradition any four Justices may grant a writ of certiorari and thus bring a case before the Court. Failure to grant a writ is not an adjudication of the issues in question. As Mr. Justice Frankfurter put it in *Maryland* v. *Baltimore Radio Show*, 338 U.S. 912 (1950): "The sole significance of . . . a denial of a petition for writ of certiorari [is] simply . . . that fewer than four members of the Court deemed it desirable to review a decision of a lower court as a matter of sound 'judicial discretion.'" Can five judges dismiss the writ as having been improvidently granted? See the discussion of this point by Justices Frankfurter and Harlan in *Rogers* v. *Missouri Pacific Rd.*, 352 U.S. 500 (1957).

THE WORK OF THE SUPREME COURT

The following tables [1] summarize the workload of the Court during the 1958–62 terms.

DISPOSITION OF CASES

	1958	1959	1960	1961	1962
Original Docket	**3**	**0**	**1**	**0**	**3**
With Full Opinion	*1*	*0*	*1*	*0*	*1*
By Memorandum Order	*2*	*0*	*0*	*0*	*2*
Appellate Docket	**886**	**860**	**887**	**860**	**972**
On Merits	240	206	244	191	280
With Full Opinion	*129*	*115*	*132*	*115*	*136*
On Petition for Certiorari	646	654	643	669	692
Denied	*635*	*644*	*626*	*659*	*675*
Dismissed	*11*	*10*	*17*	*10*	*17*
[Granted]	*116*	*122*	*89*	*103*	*115*
Miscellaneous Docket	**874**	**927**	**1,023**	**1,282**	**1,349**
On Merits	36	39	27	67	105
With Full Opinion	*2*	*0*	*0*	*1*	*0*
By Memorandum Order	*34*	*39*	*27*	*68*	*105*
On Petition for Certiorari	717	734	871	1,093	1,086
Denied	*712*	*742*	*863*	*1,086*	*1,077*
Dismissed	*5*	*1*	*8*	*7*	*9*
[Granted]	*24*	*55*	*22*	*38*	*92*
Other Applications Denied or Withdrawn	121	145	125	120	158
With Full Opinion	*1*	*0*	*0*	*0*	*0*
By Memorandum Order	*120*	*145*	*125*	*120*	*158*
[Granted]	*0*	*0*	*0*	*1*	*3*
By Memorandum Order	*111*	*91*	*112*	*76*	*144*
TOTAL	**1,763**	**1,787**	**1,911**	**2,142**	**2,324**
Remaining	281	356	385	428	473

1. From 77 *Harvard Law Review*, pp. 90–91 (1963). Copyright © 1963 by The Harvard Law Review Association.

SOURCES OF CASES DISPOSED OF ON MERITS AND ON PETITION FOR CERTIORARI

	1958	1959	1960	1961	1962
District Courts	**40**	**38**	**38**	**39**	**88**
Affirmed	14	20	22	18	38
Reversed	12	11	5	9	18
Vacated and Remanded	9	3	4	4	12
Dismissed	5	4	7	8	18
Denied	0	0	0	0	2
Courts of Appeals	**862**	**845**	**923**	**973**	**965**
Affirmed	32	33	36	15	18
Reversed	51	41	48	43	40
Vacated and Remanded	24	31	19	38	29
Dismissed	13	9	14	13	18
Denied	742	731	806	864	860
State Courts	**701**	**726**	**791**	**971**	**1,069**
Affirmed	17	6	10	11	4
Reversed	23	18	21	24	40
Vacated and Remanded	3	8	4	7	75
Dismissed	87	67	102	83	93
Denied	571	627	654	846	857
Specialized Federal Courts	**34**	**32**	**33**	**38**	**39**
Affirmed	0	0	2	2	0
Reversed	0	3	2	1	1
Vacated and Remanded	0	0	0	0	1
Dismissed	0	1	0	0	4
Denied	34	28	29	35	33
Total	**1,637**	**1,641**	**1,785**	**2,021**	**2,161**
Affirmed	63	59	70	46	60
Reversed	86	73	75	77	99
Vacated and Remanded	36	42	27	49	117
Dismissed	105	81	123	104	133
Denied	1,347	1,386	1,489	1,745	1,752
Total Percentages					
Affirmed	3.8%	3.6%	3.9%	2.3%	2.8%
Reversed	5.3%	4.4%	4.2%	3.8%	4.6%
Vacated and Remanded	2.2%	2.6%	1.5%	2.4%	5.4%
Dismissed	6.4%	4.9%	6.9%	5.2%	6.1%
Denied	82.3%	84.5%	83.5%	86.3%	81.1%

SELECTED READINGS

GENERAL

Association of American Law Schools, *Selected Essays on Constitutional Law* (1938 and 1963)

C. A. Beard, *The Supreme Court and the Constitution* (1912)

C. A. Beard, *An Economic Interpretation of the Constitution* (1913)

A. Bickel, *The Least Dangerous Branch* (1963)

C. L. Black, *The People and the Court* (1960)

L. Boudin, *Government by the Judiciary* (1932)

E. Cahn, *Supreme Court and Supreme Law* (1954)

R. K. Carr, *The Supreme Court and Judicial Review* (1942)

C. E. Clark, "The Dilemma of American Judges," 35 *American Bar Association Journal* 8 (1949)

E. S. Corwin, *Liberty Against Government* (1948)
C. P. Curtis, *Lions Under the Throne* (1947)
J. P. Frank, *The Marble Palace* (1958)
P. A. Freund, *The Supreme Court of the United States* (1961)
L. Hand, *The Bill of Rights* (1958)
R. H. Jackson, *The Struggle for Judicial Supremacy* (1941)
R. H. Jackson, *The Supreme Court in the American System of Government* (1955)
A. H. Kelly and W. Harbison, *The American Constitution* (1963)
R. G. McCloskey (ed.), *Essays in Constitutional Law* (1957)
R. G. McCloskey, *The American Supreme Court* (1960)
F. McDonald, *We the People: The Economic Origins of the Constitution* (1958)
A. C. McLaughlin, *A Constitutional History of the United States* (1935)
A. T. Mason and W. Beaney, *The Supreme Court in a Free Society* (1959)
W. F. Murphy, *Congress and the Court* (1962)
W. F. Murphy and C. H. Pritchett, *Judges and Politics* (1961)
T. R. Powell, *Vagaries and Varities in Constitutional Interpretation* (1956)
C. H. Pritchett, *The American Constitution* (1959)
E. V. Rostow, *The Sovereign Prerogative* (1962)
R. Scigliano, *The Courts: A Reader in the Judicial Process* (1962)
C. B. Swisher, *American Constitutional Development* (1943)
J. B. Thayer, "Origin and Scope of American Doctrine of Constitutional Law," 7
    Harvard Law Review 129 (1893)
C. Warren, *The Making of the Constitution* (1928)
C. Warren, *The Supreme Court in United States History* (1947)
H. Wechsler, *Principles, Politics and Fundamental Law* (1960)
A. Westin, *An Autobiography of the Supreme Court* (1963)
B. F. Wright, *The Growth of American Constitutional Law* (1942)

COURT ORGANIZATION AND AUTHORITY

C. Bunn, *United States Courts* (1949)
T. C. Clark, "Internal Operation of the United States Supreme Court," 43 *Journal of
    the American Judicature Society* 45 (1959)
S. D. Elliott, "Court Curbing Proposals in Congress," 33 *Notre Dame Lawyer* 597 (1958)
F. Frankfurter and J. Landis, *The Business of the Supreme Court* (1928)
H. M. Hart and H. Wechsler, *The Federal Courts and the Federal System* (1953)
J. M. Leiman, "The Rule of Four," 57 *Columbia Law Review* 975 (1957)
J. D. Lucas, "Legislative Apportionment and Representative Government: The Meaning
    of *Baker* v. *Carr*," 61 *Michigan Law Review* 711 (1963)
R. G. McCloskey, "The Reapportionment Case," 76 *Harvard Law Review* 54 (1962)
P. Neal, "*Baker* v. *Carr*: Politics in Search of Law," 1962 *Supreme Court Review* 252
C. G. Post, *The Supreme Court and Political Questions* (1936)
W. Wagner, *The Federal States and their Judiciary* (1959)
M. Wendell, *Relations Between Federal and State Courts* (1949)

THE SEPARATION OF POWERS

Part Two

What Belongs to the President and What to Congress?

THE Separation of Powers contemplates that each branch of government shall be primarily responsible for its own unique function. The check and balance system gives each some authority to impede the operation of the others. As Mr. Justice Brandeis observed, this system was designed not for efficiency, but for protection against tyrants.

We have dealt so far with the relationship of the judicial and political processes as though it presented a single facet. It is not that simple! In *Marbury* v. *Madison* the Court struck down a measure that had been approved by both houses of Congress and by the President. Surely judicial intervention in such a case is more difficult to defend than intervention calculated merely to determine where authority lies in case of conflict between the "separated" political branches, that is, between the legislature and the executive. In such an impasse judicial review is something of a substitute for the parliamentary system's "vote of no confidence" or "dissolution." The classic modern example of this is *Youngstown Sheet and Tube Co.* v. *Sawyer*. There all members of the Court recognized the power of the national government to seize the steel mills (by legislation, i.e., by joint action of Congress and the President; or by a measure passed over a presidential veto). The question was whether the President could do so without the concurrence of Congress, or more accurately, whether he could do so when Congress had already provided different means for dealing with the problem. The latter statement of the issue seems preferable for it is quite plain that few, if any, judges in the *Steel Seizure* case questioned our long established commitment to "inherent" executive authority in emergency situations not provided for by established legislative policy. The development of this "inherent" presidential power is broadly traced in Chief Justice Vinson's dissenting opinion in the *Steel Seizure* case. Other aspects of the judicial role as arbiter between Congress and the President are seen in the *Prize, Wiener, Myers, Humphrey,* and *Lovett* cases. *Merryman* and *General Electric* save courts from executive and legislative intrusion.

Just as there is a difference between judicial review which frustrates the whole political mechanism (*Marbury* v. *Madison*), and review merely to determine "where authority lies as between the democratic forces in our system of government" (the *Steel Seizure* case), so other distinctions must be recognized. Intrusion by federal judges upon the political processes of the national government is quite different from intrusion upon the states (Part Three). Finally review for the protection of civil liberty entails considerations not present when only economic interests are at stake, and surely in this context a distinction between procedural and substantive liberties must be recognized (Part Four).

I. THE DIVISION OF AUTHORITY

FEDERAL RADIO COMMISSION v. GENERAL ELECTRIC CO.
281 U.S. 464 (1930)

The Federal Radio Commission refused to renew a broadcasting license on the terms desired by General Electric. This determination was reversed by a Court of Appeals. The Commission then sought review by writ of certiorari.

MR. JUSTICE VAN DEVANTER delivered the opinion of the Court. . . .

The Act of 1927 . . . was enacted as a regulation of interstate and foreign radio communication; and it is in such activities that the company's broadcasting station is used. The act, as amended in 1928, c. 263, 45 Stat. 373, and 1929, c. 701, 45 Stat. 1559, directs that no broadcasting station be used in such communication except in accordance with the act and under a license granted for the purpose; authorizes the Radio Commission to grant station licenses and renewals thereof, both for periods not exceeding three months, and otherwise gives it wide powers in administering the act; restricts the granting of station licenses and renewals to instances "where public convenience, interest or necessity will be served thereby"; authorizes the commission to determine the question of public convenience, interest, or necessity; declares that decisions of the commission in all matters over which it has jurisdiction "shall be final, subject to the right of appeal" therein given; provides (section 16) that any applicant for a station license or the renewal of such a license, whose application is refused by the commission, may appeal from such decision to the Court of Appeals of the District of Columbia; directs that the grounds of the appeal be stated and the revision be confined to them; requires the commission, where an appeal is taken, to transmit to the court the originals or certified copies of all papers and evidence presented upon the application refused, together with a copy of the commission's decision and a statement of the facts and grounds of the decision; authorizes the court to take additional evidence upon such terms and conditions as it may deem proper; and provides that the court "shall hear, review and determine the appeal upon said record and evidence, and may alter or revise the decision appealed from and enter such judgment as to it may seem just."

We think it plain from this résumé of the pertinent parts of the act that the powers confided to the commission respecting the granting and renewal of station licenses are purely administrative, and that the provision for appeals to the Court of Appeals does no more than make that court a superior and revising agency in the same field. The court's province under that provision is essentially the same as its province under the legislation which up to a recent date permitted appeals to it from administrative decisions of the Commissioner of Patents. Indeed, the provision in the act of 1927 is patterned largely after that legislation. And while a few differences are found, there is none that is material here.

Referring to the provisions for patent appeals this court said in *Butterworth* v. *U.S.*, 112 U.S. 50, 60, that the function of the court thereunder was not that of exercising ordinary jurisdiction at law or in equity, but of taking a step in the statutory proceeding under the patent laws in aid of the Patent Office. And in *Postum Cereal Company* v. *California Fig Nut Company*, 272 U.S. 693, 698, which related to a provision for a like appeal in a trade-mark proceeding, this court held: "The decision of the Court of Appeals under section 9 of the act of 1905 is not a judicial judgment. It is a mere administrative decision. It is merely an instruction to the Commissioner of Patents by a court which is made part of the machinery of the Patent Office for administrative purposes." Another case in point is *Keller* v. *Potomac Electric Power Co.*, 261 U.S. 428, 442–444, which involved a statutory proceeding in the courts of the District of Columbia to revise an order of a commission fixing the valuation of the property of a public utility for future rate-making purposes. There this court held that the function assigned to the courts of the District in the statutory proceeding was not judicial in the sense of the Constitution, but was legislative and advisory, because it was that of instructing and aiding

the commission in the exertion of power which was essentially legislative.

In the cases just cited, as also in others, it is recognized that the courts of the District of Columbia are not created under the judiciary article of the Constitution but are legislative courts, and therefore that Congress may invest them with jurisdiction of appeals and proceedings such as have been just described.

But this court cannot be invested with jurisdiction of that character, whether for purposes of review or otherwise. It was brought into being by the judiciary article of the Constitution, is invested with judicial power only, and can have no jurisdiction other than of cases and controversies falling within the classes enumerated in that article. It cannot give decisions which are merely advisory; nor can it exercise or participate in the exercise of functions which are essentially legislative or administrative. *Keller* v. *Potomac Electric Power Co., supra*, page 444, of 261 U.S., and cases cited; *Postum Cereal Co.* v. *California Fig Nut Company, supra*, pages 700–701 of 272 U.S.; *Liberty Warehouse Co.* v. *Grannis*, 273 U.S. 70, 74; *Willing* v. *Chicago Auditorium Association*, 277 U.S. 274, 289; *Ex parte Bakelite Corporation*, 279 U.S. 438, 449. . . .

Writ of certiorari dismissed.

MR. CHIEF JUSTICE HUGHES did not participate in the consideration or decision of this case.

FEDERAL RADIO COMMISSION v. NELSON BROS. CO.

289 U.S. 266 (1933)

After the *General Electric* case, above, Congress amended Section 16 (d) of the Radio Act of 1927 to read as follows:

"At the earliest convenient time the court shall hear and determine the appeal upon the record before it, and shall have power, upon such record, to enter a judgment affirming or reversing the decision of the commission, and, in event the court shall render a decision and enter an order reversing the decision of the commission, it shall remand the case to the commission to carry out the judgment of the court: *Provided, however*, That the review by the court shall be limited to questions of law and that findings of fact by the commission, if supported by substantial evidence, shall be conclusive unless it shall clearly appear that the findings of the commission are arbitrary or capricious. The court's judgment shall be final, subject, however, to review by the

Supreme Court of the United States upon writ of certiorari on petition therefor under section 347 of title 28 of the Judicial Code by appellant, by the commission, or by any interested party intervening in the appeal."

In the present case the Commission terminated Nelson's broadcasting license and allocated the frequency to another applicant. A Court of Appeals set this order aside as "arbitrary and capricious." On review, Chief Justice Hughes made the following comments on behalf of the Court:

[Our] review is now expressly limited to "questions of law" and it is provided "that findings of fact by the commission, if supported by substantial evidence, shall be conclusive unless it shall clearly appear that the findings of the commission are arbitrary or capricious." This limitation is in sharp contrast with the previous grant of authority. No longer is the Court entitled to revise the Commission's decision and to enter such judgment as the Court may think just. The limitation manifestly demands judicial, as distinguished from administrative, review. Questions of law form the appropriate subject of judicial determinations. Dealing with activities admittedly within its regulatory power, the Congress established the Commission as its instrumentality to provide continuous and expert supervision and to exercise the administrative judgment essential in applying legislative standards to a host of instances. These standards the Congress prescribed. The powers of the Commission were defined, and definition is limitation. Whether the Commission applies the legislative standards validly set up, whether it acts within the authority conferred or goes beyond it, whether its proceedings satisfy the pertinent demands of due process, whether, in short, there is compliance with the legal requirements which fix the province of the Commission and govern its action, are appropriate questions for judicial decision. These are questions of law upon which the Court is to pass. The provision that the Commission's findings of fact, if supported by substantial evidence, shall be conclusive unless it clearly appears that the findings are arbitrary or capricious, cannot be regarded as an attempt to vest in the Court an authority to revise the action of the Commission from an administrative standpoint and make an administrative judgment. A finding without substantial evidence to support it—an arbitrary or capricious finding—does violence to the law. It is without the sanction of the authority conferred. And an inquiry into the facts before the Commission, in order to ascertain whether its findings are thus vitiated, belongs to the judicial province and does not trench upon, or involve the exercise of, administrative authority. Such an examination is not concerned with the weight of evidence or with the wisdom or expediency of the administrative action. . . .

If the questions of law thus presented were brought before the Court by suit to restrain the enforcement of an invalid administrative order, there could be no question as to the judicial character of the proceeding. But that character is not altered by the mere fact that remedy is afforded by appeal. The controlling question is whether the function to be exercised by the Court is a judicial function, and, if so, it may be exercised on an authorized appeal from the decision of an administrative body. We must not "be misled by a name, but look to the substance and intent of the proceeding." . . .

THE PRIZE CASES

67 U.S. 635 (1863)

In the absence of a state of war a blockade is illegal in international law. In 1861 President Lincoln declared a blockade of Southern ports—without a formal declaration of war by Congress. This case considers the validity of the blockade, and thus of the seizure of certain foreign and Southern vessels when they tried to run the blockade.

MR. JUSTICE GRIER. . . .

By the Constitution, Congress alone has the power to declare a national or foreign war. It cannot declare war against a State, or any number of States, by virtue of any clause in the Constitution. The Constitution confers on the President the whole Executive power. He is bound to take care that the laws be faithfully executed. He is Commander-in-chief of the Army and Navy of the United States, and of the militia of the several States when called into the actual service of the United States. He has no power to initiate or declare a war either against a foreign nation or a domestic State. But by the Acts of Congress of February 28th, 1795, and 3d of March, 1807, he is authorized to call out the militia and use the military and naval forces of the United States in case of invasion by foreign nations, and to suppress insurrection against the government of a State or of the United States.

If a war be made by invasion of a foreign nation, the President is not only authorized but bound to resist force by force. He does not initiate the war, but is bound to accept the challenge without waiting for any special legislative authority. And whether the hostile party be a foreign invader, or States organized in rebellion, it is none the less a war, although the declaration of it be *"unilateral."* Lord Stowell (1 Dodson, 247) observes, "It is not the less a war on *that account,* for war may exist without a declaration on either side. It is so laid down by the best writers on the law of nations. A declaration of war by one country only, is not a mere challenge to be accepted or refused at pleasure by the other."

The battles of Palo Alto and Resaca de la Palma had been fought before the passage of the Act of Congress of May 13th, 1846, which recognized *"a state of war as existing by the act of the Republic of Mexico."* This act not only provided for the future prosecution of the war, but was itself a vindication and ratification of the

Act of the President in accepting the challenge without a previous formal declaration of war by Congress.

This greatest of civil wars was not gradually developed by popular commotion, tumultuous assemblies, or local unorganized insurrections. However long may have been its previous conception, it nevertheless sprung forth suddenly from the parent brain, a Minerva in the full panoply of *war.* The President was bound to meet it in the shape it presented itself, without waiting for Congress to baptize it with a name; and no name given to it by him or them could change the fact. . . .

Whether the President in fulfilling his duties, as Commander-in-chief, in suppressing an insurrection, has met with such armed hostile resistance, and a civil war of such alarming proportions as will compel him to accord to them the character of belligerents, is a question to be decided *by him,* and this Court must be governed by the decisions and acts of the political department of the Government to which this power was entrusted. "He must determine what degree of force the crisis demands." The proclamation of blockade is itself official and conclusive evidence to the Court that a state of war existed which demanded and authorized a recourse to such a measure, under the circumstances peculiar to the case. . . .

Without admitting that such an act was necessary under the circumstances, it is plain that if the President had in any manner assumed powers which it was necessary should have the authority or sanction of Congress, that on the well known principle of law, *"omnis ratihabitio retrotrahitur et mandato equiparatur,"* this ratification has operated to perfectly cure the defect. In the case of *Brown* v. *United States,* (8 Cr., 131, 132, 133,) Mr. Justice Story treats of this subject, and cites numerous authorities to which we may refer to prove this position, and concludes, "I am perfectly satisfied that no subject can commence hostilities or capture property of an enemy, when the sovereign has prohibited it. But suppose he did, I would ask if the sovereign may not ratify his proceedings, and thus by a retroactive operation give validity to them?"

Although Mr. Justice Story dissented from the majority of the Court on the whole case, the doctrine stated by him on this point is correct and fully substantiated by authority.

The objection made to this act of ratification, that it is *ex post facto,* and therefore unconstitutional and void, might possibly have some weight on the trial of an indictment in a criminal Court. But precedents from that source cannot be received as authoritative in a tribunal administering public and international law.

On this first question therefore we are of the opinion that the President had a right, *jure belli,* to institute a blockade of ports in possession of the States in rebellion, which neutrals are bound to regard. . . .

Mr. Justice Nelson, dissenting. . . .

An idea seemed to be entertained that all that was necessary to constitute a war was organized hostility in the district or country in a state of rebellion—that conflicts on land and on sea—the taking of towns and capture of fleets—in fine, the magnitude and dimensions of the resistance against the Government—constituted war with all the belligerent rights belonging to civil war. With a view to enforce this idea, we had, during the argument, an imposing historical detail of the several measures adopted by the Confederate States to enable them to resist the authority of the general Government, and of many bold and daring acts of resistance and of conflict. It was said that war was to be ascertained by looking at the armies and navies or public force of the contending parties, and the battles lost and won—that in the language of one of the learned counsel, "Whenever the situation of opposing hostilities has assumed the proportions and pursued the methods of war, then peace is driven out, the ordinary authority and administration of law are suspended, and war in fact and by necessity is the *status* of the nation until peace is restored and the laws resumed their dominion."

Now, in one sense, no doubt this is war, and may be a war of the most extensive and threatening dimensions and effects, but it is a statement simply of its existence in a material sense, and has no relevancy or weight when the question is what constitutes war in a legal sense, in the sense of the law of nations, and of the Constitution of the United States? For it must be a war in this sense to attach to it all the consequences that belong to belligerent rights. Instead, therefore, of inquiring after armies and navies, and victories lost and won, or organized rebellion against the general Government, the inquiry should be into the law of nations and into the municipal fundamental laws of the Government. For we find there that to constitute a civil war in the sense in which we are speaking, before it can exist, in contemplation of law, it must be recognized or declared by the sovereign power of the State, and which sovereign power by our Constitution is lodged in the Congress of the United States —civil war, therefore, under our system of government, can exist only by an act of Congress, which requires the assent of two of the great departments of the Government, the Executive and Legislative.

[Chief Justice Taney and Justices Catron and Clifford joined in this dissent.]

YOUNGSTOWN SHEET AND TUBE CO. v. SAWYER

343 U.S. 579 (1952)

Mr. Justice Black delivered the opinion of the Court:

We are asked to decide whether the President was acting within his constitutional power when he issued an order directing the Secretary of Commerce to take possession of and operate most of the Nation's steel mills. The mill owners argue that the President's order amounts to lawmaking, a legislative function which the Constitution has expressly confided to the Congress and not to the President. The Government's position is that the order was made on findings of the President that his action was necessary to avert a national catastrophe which would inevitably result from a stoppage of steel production, and that in meeting this grave emergency the President was acting within the aggregate of his constitutional powers as the Nation's Chief Executive and the Commander in Chief of the Armed Forces of the United States. The issue emerges here from the following series of events:

In the latter part of 1951, a dispute arose between the steel companies and their employees over terms and conditions that should be included in new collective bargaining agreements. Long-continued conferences failed to resolve the dispute. On December 18, 1951, the employees' representative, United Steelworkers of America, C.I.O., gave notice of an intention to strike when the existing bargaining agreements expired on December 31. Thereupon the Federal Mediation and Conciliation Service intervened in an effort to get labor and management to agree. This failing, the President on December 22, 1951, referred the dispute to the Federal Wage Stabilization Board to investigate and make recommendations for fair and equitable terms of settlement. This Board's report resulted in no settlement. On April 4, 1952, the Union gave notice of a nationwide strike called to begin at 12:01 a.m. April 9. The indispensability of steel as a component of substantially all weapons and other war materials led the President to believe that the proposed work stoppage would immediately jeopardize our national defense and that governmental seizure of the steel mills was necessary in order to assure the continued availability of steel. Reciting these considerations for his action, the President, a few hours before the strike was to begin, issued Executive Order 10340 . . . The order directed the Secretary of Commerce

to take possession of most of the steel mills and keep them running. . . .

The President's power, if any, to issue the order must stem either from an act of Congress or from the Constitution itself. There is no statute that expressly authorizes the President to take possession of property as he did here. Nor is there any act of Congress to which our attention has been directed from which such a power can fairly be implied. Indeed, we do not understand the Government to rely on statutory authorization for this seizure. . . .

Moreover, the use of the seizure technique to solve labor disputes in order to prevent work stoppages was not only unauthorized by any congressional enactment; prior to this controversy, Congress had refused to adopt that method of settling labor disputes. When the Taft-Hartley Act was under consideration in 1947, Congress rejected an amendment which would have authorized such governmental seizures in cases of emergency. . . .

It is clear that if the President had authority to issue the order he did, it must be found in some provision of the Constitution. And it is not claimed that express constitutional language grants this power to the President. The contention is that presidential power should be implied from the aggregate of his powers under the Constitution. Particular reliance is placed on provisions in Article II which say that "the executive Power shall be vested in a President . . ."; that "he shall take Care that the Laws be faithfully executed"; and that he "shall be Commander in Chief of the Army and Navy of the United States."

The order cannot properly be sustained as an exercise of the President's military power as Commander in Chief of the Armed Forces. The Government attempts to do so by citing a number of cases upholding broad powers in military commanders engaged in day-to-day fighting in a theater of war. Such cases need not concern us here. Even though "theater of war" be an expanding concept, we cannot with faithfulness to our constitutional system hold that the Commander in Chief of the

Armed Forces has the ultimate power as such to take possession of private property in order to keep labor disputes from stopping production. This is a job for the Nation's lawmakers, not for its military authorities.

Nor can the seizure order be sustained because of the several constitutional provisions that grant executive power to the President. In the framework of our Constitution, the President's power to see that the laws are faithfully executed refutes the idea that he is to be a lawmaker. The Constitution limits his functions in the law-making process to the recommending of laws he thinks wise and the vetoing of laws he thinks bad. And the Constitution is neither silent nor equivocal about who shall make laws which the President is to execute. The first section of the first article says that "All legislative Powers herein granted shall be vested in a Congress of the United States. . . ." After granting many powers to the Congress, Article I goes on to provide that Congress may "make all Laws which shall be necessary and proper for carrying into Execution the foregoing Powers and all other Powers vested by this Constitution in the Government of the United States, or in any Department or Officer thereof." . . .

It is said that other Presidents without congressional authority have taken possession of private business enterprises in order to settle labor disputes. But even if this be true, Congress has not thereby lost its exclusive constitutional authority to make laws necessary and proper to carry out the powers vested by the Constitution "in the Government of the United States, or any Department or Officer thereof."

The Founders of this Nation entrusted the law-making power to the Congress alone in both good and bad times. It would do no good to recall the historical events, the fears of power and the hopes for freedom that lay behind their choice. Such a review would but confirm our holding that this seizure order cannot stand.

The judgment of the District Court is affirmed.

[MR. JUSTICE DOUGLAS concurred in the Court's opinion but added another reason for its conclusion; namely, that in view of the condemnation provision in the Fifth Amendment, the branch of government with "the power to pay compensation for a seizure is the only one able to authorize a seizure. . . ." JUSTICES FRANKFURTER, JACKSON, BURTON, and CLARK also wrote separate concurring opinions. Each emphasized that Congress had not only failed to authorize presidential seizure, but had provided quite different means for dealing in an emergency with labor-management disputes.

CHIEF JUSTICE VINSON, joined by JUSTICES REED and MINTON, dissented. After emphasizing the gravity of a steel strike in the context of the Korean War the dissenters argued in part as follows:]

II

The steel mills were seized for a public use. The power of eminent domain, invoked in this case, is an essential attribute of sovereignty and has long been recognized as a power of the Federal Government. *Kohl* v. *United States*, 91 U.S. 367 (1876). Plaintiffs cannot complain that any provision in the Constitution prohibits the exercise of the power of eminent domain in this case. The Fifth Amendment provides: "nor shall private property be taken for public use, without just compensation." It is no bar to this seizure for, if the taking is not otherwise unlawful, plaintiffs are assured of receiving the required just compensation. *United States* v. *Pewee Coal Co.*, 341 U.S. 114 (1951).

Admitting that the Government could seize the mills, plaintiffs claim that the implied power of eminent domain can be exercised only under an Act of Congress; under no circumstances, they say, can that power be exercised by the President unless he can point to an express provision in enabling legislation. This was the view adopted by the District Judge when he granted the preliminary injunction. Without an answer, without hearing evidence, he determined the issue on the basis of his "fixed conclusion . . . that defendant's acts are illegal" because the President's only course in the face of an emergency is to present the matter to Congress and await the final passage of legislation which will enable the Government to cope with threatened disaster.

Under this view, the President is left powerless at the very moment when the need for action may be most pressing and when no one, other than he, is immediately capable of action. Under this view, he is left powerless because a power not expressly given to Congress is nevertheless found to rest exclusively with Congress.

Consideration of this view of executive impotence calls for further examination of the nature of the separation of powers under our tripartite system of Government. . . .

This comprehensive grant of the executive power to a single person was bestowed soon after the country had thrown the yoke of monarchy. Only by instilling initiative and vigor in all of the three departments of Government, declared Madison, could tyranny in any form be avoided. Hamilton added: "Energy in the Executive is a leading character in the definition of good government. It is essential to the protection of the community against foreign attack; it is not less essential to the steady administration of the laws; to the protection of property against those irregular and high-handed combinations which sometimes interrupt the ordinary course of justice; to the security of liberty against the enterprises and assaults of ambition, of faction, and of anarchy." It is thus apparent that the Presidency was deliberately fashioned as an office of power and independence. Of course, the Framers created no autocrat capable of arrogating any power unto himself at any time. But neither did they create an automaton impotent to exercise the powers of Government at a time when the survival of the Republic itself may be at stake.

In passing upon the grave constitutional question presented in this case, we must never forget, as Chief Justice Marshall admonished, that the Constitution is "intended to endure for ages to come, and,

consequently, to be adapted to the various *crises* of human affairs," and that "[i]ts means are adequate to its ends." Cases do arise presenting questions which could not have been foreseen by the Framers. In such cases, the Constitution has been treated as a living document adaptable to new situations. But we are not called upon today to expand the Constitution to meet a new situation. For, in this case, we need only look to history and time-honored principles of constitutional law—principles that have been applied consistently by all branches of the Government throughout our history. It is those who assert the invalidity of the Executive Order who seek to amend the Constitution in this case.

III

A review of executive action demonstrates that our Presidents have on many occasions exhibited the leadership contemplated by the Framers when they made the President Commander in Chief, and imposed upon him the trust to "take Care that the Laws be faithfully executed." With or without explicit statutory authorization, Presidents have at such times dealt with national emergencies by acting promptly and resolutely to enforce legislative programs, at least to save those programs until Congress could act. Congress and the courts have responded to such executive initiative with consistent approval.

Our first President displayed at once the leadership contemplated by the Framers. When the national revenue laws were openly flouted in some sections of Pennsylvania, President Washington, without waiting for a call from the state government, summoned the militia and took decisive steps to secure the faithful execution of the laws. When international disputes engendered by the French revolution threatened to involve this country in war, and while congressional policy remained uncertain, Washington issued his Proclamation of Neutrality. Hamilton, whose defense of the Proclamation has endured the test of time, invoked the argument that the Executive has the duty to do that which will preserve peace until Congress acts and, in addition, pointed to the need for keeping the Nation informed of the requirements of existing laws and treaties as part of the faithful execution of the laws.

President John Adams issued a warrant for the arrest of Jonathan Robbins in order to execute the extradition provisions of a treaty. This action was challenged in Congress on the ground that no specific statute prescribed the method to be used in executing the treaty. John Marshall, then a member of the House of Representatives, made the following argument in support of the President's action:

"The treaty, which is a law, enjoins the performance of a particular object. The person who is to perform this object is marked out by the Constitution, since the person is named who conducts the foreign intercourse, and is to take care that the laws be faithfully executed. The means by which it is to be performed, the force of the nation, are in the hands of this person. Ought not this person to perform the object, although the particular mode of using the means has not been prescribed? Congress, unquestionably may prescribe the mode, and Congress may devolve on others the whole execution of the contract; but, till this be done, it seems the duty of the Executive department to execute the contract by any means it possesses." Efforts in Congress to discredit the President for his action failed. Almost a century later, this Court had occasion to give its express approval to "the masterly and conclusive argument of John Marshall."

Jefferson's initiative in the Louisiana Purchase, the Monroe Doctrine, and Jackson's removal of Government deposits from the Bank of the United States further serve to demonstrate by deed what the Framers described by word when they vested the whole of the executive power in the President.

Without declaration of war, President Lincoln took energetic action with the outbreak of the Civil War. He summoned troops and paid them out of the Treasury without appropriation therefor. He proclaimed a naval blockade of the Con-federacy and seized ships violating that blockade. Congress, far from denying the validity of these acts, gave them express approval. The most striking action of President Lincoln was the Emancipation Proclamation, issued in aid of the successful prosecution of the Civil War, but wholly without statutory authority.

In an action furnishing a most apt precedent for this case, President Lincoln directed the seizure of rail and telegraph lines leading to Washington without statutory authority. Many months later, Congress recognized and confirmed the power of the President to seize railroads and telegraph lines and provided criminal penalties for interference with Government operation. This Act did not confer on the President any additional powers of seizure. Congress plainly rejected the view that the President's acts had been without legal sanction until ratified by the legislature. Sponsors of the bill declared that its purpose was only to confirm the power which the President already possessed. Opponents insisted a statute authorizing seizure was unnecessary and might even be construed as limiting existing Presidential powers.

Other seizures of private property occurred during the Civil War, just as they had occurred during previous wars. In *United States* v. *Russell*, 13 Wall. 623 (1872), three river steamers were seized by Army Quartermasters on the ground of "imperative military necessity." This Court affirmed an award of compensation, stating:

"Extraordinary and unforeseen occasions arise, however, beyond all doubt, in cases of extreme necessity in time of war or of immediate and impending public danger, in which private property may be impressed into the public service, or may be seized and appropriated to the public use, or may even be destroyed without the consent of the owner." . . .

"Exigencies of the kind do arise in time of war or impending public danger, but it is the emergency, as was said by a great magistrate, that gives the right, and it is clear that the emergency must be shown to exist before the taking can be justified. Such a justification may be shown, and when shown the rule is well settled that the officer taking private property for such a purpose, if the emergency is fully proved, is not a trespasser, and that the government is bound to make full compensation to the owner."

In *In re Neagle,* 135 U.S. 1 (1890) this Court held that a federal officer had acted in line of duty when he was guarding a Justice of this Court riding circuit. It was conceded that there was no specific statute authorizing the President to assign such a guard. In holding that such a statute was not necessary, the Court broadly stated the question as follows:

"[The President] is enabled to fulfil the duty of his great department, expressed in the phrase that 'he shall take care that the laws be faithfully executed.'

"Is this duty limited to the enforcement of acts of Congress or of treaties of the United States according to their *express terms,* or does it include the rights, duties and obligations growing out of the Constitution itself, our international relations, and all the protection implied by the nature of the government under the Constitution?"

The latter approach was emphatically adopted by the Court.

President Hayes authorized the widespread use of federal troops during the Railroad Strike of 1877. President Cleveland also used the troops in the Pullman Strike of 1895 and his action is of special significance. No statute authorized this action. No call for help had issued from the Governor of Illinois; indeed Governor Altgeld disclaimed the need for supplemental forces. But the President's concern was that federal laws relating to the free flow of interstate commerce and the mails be continuously and faithfully executed without interruption. To further this aim his agents sought and obtained the injunction upheld by this Court in *In re Debs,* 158 U.S. 564 (1895). The Court scrutinized each of the steps taken by the President to insure execution of the "mass of legislation" dealing with commerce and the mails and gave his conduct full approval. Congress likewise took note of this use of Presidential power to forestall apparent obstacles to the faithful execution of the laws. By separate resolutions, both the Senate and the House commended the Executive's action.

President Theodore Roosevelt seriously contemplated seizure of Pennsylvania coal mines if a coal shortage necessitated such action. In his autobiography, President Roosevelt expounded the "Stewardship Theory" of Presidential power, stating that "the executive is subject only to the people, and, under the Constitution, bound to serve the people affirmatively in cases where the Constitution does not explicitly forbid him to render the service." Because the contemplated seizure of the coal mines was based on this theory, then ex-President Taft criticized President Roosevelt in a passage in his book relied upon by the District Court in this case. Taft, *Our Chief Magistrate and His Powers* (1915), 139–147. In the same book, however, President Taft agreed that such powers of the President as the duty "to take care that the laws be faithfully executed" could not be confined to "express Congressional statutes." *In re Neagle, supra,* and *In re Debs, supra,* were cited as conforming with Taft's concept of the office, id., at pp. 88–94, as they were later to be cited with approval in his opinion as Chief Justice in *Myers* v. *United States,* 272 U.S. 52, 133 (1926).

In 1909, President Taft was informed that government owned oil lands were being patented by private parties at such a rate that public oil lands would be depleted in a matter of months. Although Congress had explicitly provided that these lands were open to purchase by United States citizens, 29 Stat. 526 (1897), the President nevertheless ordered the lands withdrawn from sale "[i]n aid of proposed legislation." In *United States* v. *Midwest Oil Co.,* 236 U.S. 459 (1915), the President's action was sustained as consistent with executive practice throughout our history. An excellent brief was filed in the case by the Solicitor General, Mr. John W. Davis, together with Assistant Attorney General Knaebel, later Reporter for this Court. In this brief, the situation confronting President Taft was described as "an emergency; there was no time to wait for the action of Congress." The brief then discusses the powers of the President under the Constitution in such a case:

"Ours is a self-sufficient Government within its sphere. (*Ex parte Siebold,* 100 U.S. 371, 395; *In re Debs,* 158 U.S. 564, 578). 'Its means are adequate to its ends' (*McCulloch* v. *Maryland,* 4 Wheat. 316, 424), and it is rational to assume that its active forces will be found equal in most things to the emergencies that confront it. The function of making laws is peculiar to Congress, and the Executive can not exercise that function to any degree. But this is not to say that all of the subjects concerning which laws might be made are perforce removed from the possibility of Executive influence. The Executive may act upon things and upon men in many relations which have not, though they might have, been actually regulated by Congress. In other words, just as there are fields which are peculiar to Congress and fields which are peculiar to the Executive, so there are fields which are common to both, in the sense that the Executive may move within them until they shall have been occupied by legislative action. These are not the fields of legislative prerogative, but fields within which the lawmaking power may enter and dominate whenever it chooses. This situation results from the fact that the President is the active agent, not of Congress, but of the Nation. As such he performs the duties which the Constitution lays upon him immediately, and as such, also, he executes the laws and regulations adopted by Congress. He is the agent of the people of the United States, deriving all his powers from them and responsible directly to them. In no sense is he the agent of Congress. He obeys and executes the laws of Congress, not because Congress is enthroned in authority over him, but because the Constitution directs him to do so.

"Therefore it follows that in ways short of making laws or disobeying them, the Executive may be under a grave constitutional duty to act for the national protection in situations not covered by the acts of Congress, and in which, even, it may not be said that his action is the direct expression of any particular one of the independent powers which are granted to him specifically by the Constitution. Instances wherein the President has felt and fulfilled such a duty have not been rare in our history, though, being for the public benefit and approved by all, his acts have seldom been challenged in the courts. We are able, however, to present a number of apposite cases which were subjected to judicial inquiry." . . .

This brief is valuable not alone because of the caliber of its authors but because it lays bare in succinct reasoning the basis of the executive practice which this Court approved in the Midwest Oil case.

During World War I, President Wilson established a War Labor Board without awaiting specific direction by Congress. With William Howard Taft and Frank P. Walsh as co-chairmen, the Board had as its purpose the prevention of strikes and lockouts interfering with the production of goods needed to meet the emergency. Effectiveness of War Labor Board decision was accomplished by Presidential action, including seizure of industrial plants. Seizure of the Nation's railroads was also ordered by President Wilson.

Beginning with the Bank Holiday Proclamation and continuing through World War II, executive leadership and initiative were characteristic of President Franklin D. Roosevelt's administration. In 1939, upon the outbreak of war in Europe, the President proclaimed a limited national emergency for the purpose of strengthening our national defense. By May of 1941, the danger from the Axis belligerents having become clear, the President proclaimed "an unlimited national emergency" calling for mobilization of the Nation's defenses to repel aggression.

"The Constitution also places on the President the responsibility and vests in him the powers of Commander in Chief of the Army and of the Navy. These weapons for the protection of the continued existence of the Nation are placed in his sole command and the implication is clear that he should not allow them to become paralyzed by failure to obtain supplies for which Congress has appropriated the money and which it has directed the President to obtain." . . .

Meanwhile, and also prior to Pearl Harbor, the President ordered the seizure of a shipbuilding company and an aircraft parts plant. Following the declaration of war, but prior to the Smith-Connally Act of 1943, five additional industrial concerns were seized to avert interruption of needed production. During the same period, the President directed seizure of the Nation's coal mines to remove an obstruction to the effective prosecution of the war.

The procedures adopted by President Roosevelt closely resembled the methods employed by President Wilson. A National War Labor Board, like its predecessor of World War I, was created by Executive Order to deal effectively and fairly with disputes affecting defense production. Seizures were considered necessary, upon disobedience of War Labor Board orders, to assure that the mobilization effort remained a "going concern," and to enforce the economic stabilization program. . .

Following passage of the Smith-Connally Act [1943], seizures to assure continued production on the basis of terms recommended by the War Labor Board were based upon that Act as well as upon the President's power under the Constitution and the laws generally. A question did arise as to whether the statutory language relating to "any plant, mine, or facility equipped for the manufacture, production, or mining of any articles or materials" authorized the seizure of properties of Montgomery Ward & Co., a retail department store and mail order concern. The Attorney General (Biddle) issued an opin-ion that the President possessed the power to seize Montgomery Ward properties to prevent a work stoppage whether or not the terms of the Smith-Connally Act authorized such a seizure. This opinion was in line with the views on Presidential powers maintained by the Attorney General's predecessors (Murphy and Jackson) and his successor (Clark). Accordingly, the President ordered seizure of the Chicago properties of Montgomery Ward in April, 1944, when that company refused to obey a War Labor Board order concerning the bargaining representative of its employees in Chicago. In Congress, a Select Committee to Investigate Seizure of the Property of Montgomery Ward & Co., assuming that the terms of the Smith-Connally Act did not cover this seizure, concluded that the seizure "was not only within the Constitutional power but was the plain duty of the President." Thereafter, an election determined the bargaining representative for the Chicago employees and the properties were returned to Montgomery Ward & Co. In December, 1944, after continued defiance of a series of War Labor Board orders, President Roosevelt ordered the seizure of Montgomery Ward properties throughout the country. The Court of Appeals for the Seventh Circuit upheld this seizure on statutory grounds and also indicated its disapproval of a lower court's denial of seizure power apart from express statute.

More recently, President Truman acted to repel aggression by employing our armed forces in Korea. Upon the intervention of the Chinese Communists, the President proclaimed the existence of an unlimited national emergency requiring the speedy build-up of our defense establishment. Congress responded by providing for increased manpower and weapons for our own armed forces, by increasing military aid under the Mutual Security Program and by enacting economic stabilization measures, as previously described.

This is but a cursory summary of executive leadership but it amply demonstrates that Presidents have taken prompt action to enforce the laws and protect the country whether or not Congress happened to provide in advance for the particular method of execution. At the minimum, the executive actions reviewed herein sustain the action of the President in this case. And many of the cited examples of Presidential practice go far beyond the extent of power necessary to sustain the President's order to seize the steel mills. The fact that temporary executive seizures of industrial plants to meet an emergency have not been directly tested in this Court furnishes not the slightest suggestion that such actions have been illegal. Rather, the fact that Congress and the courts have consistently recognized and given their support to such

executive action indicates that such a power of seizure has been accepted throughout our history.

History bears out the genius of the Founding Fathers, who created a Government subject to law but not left subject to inertia when vigor and initiative are required.

Focusing now on the situation confronting the President on the night of April 8, 1952, we cannot but conclude that the President was performing his duty under the Constitution "to take care that the laws be faithfully executed"—a duty described by President Benjamin Harrison as "the central idea of the office." . . .

NOTE: In *Myers* v. *United States,* 272 U.S. 52 (1926), the Court speaking through Chief Justice (formerly President) Taft, held unconstitutional an act of Congress limiting the President's power to remove from office a member of the executive branch of the national government. The rationale of the Court's position was that the President, as Chief Executive, has full responsibility for "executing" the laws and so to avoid conflict must have power commensurate with that responsibility, i.e., power to "fire" those of his agents in the executive department in whom he lacks confidence. Justices Holmes, McReynolds, and Brandeis dissented. In the latter's words, the separation of powers was not calculated "to avoid friction, but, by means of the inevitable friction incident to the distribution of governmental powers among three departments, to save the people from autocracy." Later in *Humphrey's Executor (Rathbun)* v. *United States,* 295 U.S. 602 (1935), the Court unanimously modified the *Myers* decision by holding it applicable only to purely executive offices. Accordingly Congress may limit the President's power to discharge regulatory commissioners who in addition to executive, also perform quasi-legislative and quasi-judicial, functions. Thus an executive attempt to discharge a member of the Federal Trade Commission before the expiration of his term as fixed by Congress (and not upon any ground authorized by Congress) was held invalid.

In a converse situation Congress attempted by cutting off their pay (not by impeachment) to "fire" certain specified executive officials who had the support and confidence of the President. This effort was held invalid as a bill of attainder (Constitution, Art. I, Sec. 9). *United States* v. *Lovett,* 328 U.S. 303 (1946).

In cases of executive action which present no conflict between presidential and congressional policy, the Court virtually always defers to the President—frequently on the ground that his powers are political in nature and so not subject to judicial review. See cases referred to in the dissenting opinion in the *Steel Seizure* case.

WIENER v. UNITED STATES

357 U.S. 349 (1958)

MR. JUSTICE FRANKFURTER delivered the opinion of the court:

This is a suit for back pay, based on petitioner's alleged illegal removal as a member of the War Claims Commission. The facts are not in dispute. By the War Claims Act of 1948, 62 Stat. 1240, Congress established that Commission with "jurisdiction to receive and adjudicate according to law," § 3 claims for compensating internees, prisoners of war, and religious organizations, §§ 5, 6 and 7, who suffered personal injury or property damage at the hands of the enemy in connection with World War II. The Commission was to be composed of three persons, at least two of whom were to be members of the bar, to be appointed by the President, by and with the advice and consent of the Senate. The Commission was to wind up its affairs not later than three years after the expiration of the time for filing claims, originally limited to two years but extended by successive legislation first to March 1, 1951, 63 Stat. 112, and later to March 31, 1952, 65 Stat. 28. This limit on the Commission's life was the mode by which the tenure of the Commissioners was defined, and Congress made no provision for removal of a Commissioner.

Having been duly nominated by President Truman, the petitioner was confirmed on June 2, 1950, and took office on June 8, following. On his refusal to heed a request for his resignation, he was, on December 10, 1953, removed by President Eisenhower in the following terms: "I regard it as in the national interest to complete the administration of the War Claims Act of 1948, as amended, with personnel of my own selection." The following day, the President made recess appointments to the Commission, including petitioner's post.

After Congress assembled, the President, on February 15, 1954, sent the names of the new appointees to the Senate. The Senate had not confirmed these nominations when the Commission was abolished, July 1, 1954, by Reorganization Plan No. 1 of 1954, 68 Stat. 1279, issued pursuant to the Reorganization Act of 1949, 63 Stat. 203. Thereupon, petitioner brought this proceeding in the Court of Claims for recovery of his salary as a War Claims Commissioner from December 10, 1953, the day of his removal by the President, to June 30, 1954, the last day of the Commission's existence. A divided Court of Claims dismissed the petition, 135 Ct. Cl. 827, 142 F. Supp. 910. We brought the case here, 352 U.S. 980, because it presents a variant of the constitutional issue decided in *Humphrey's Executor* v. *United States*, 295 U.S. 602.

Controversy pertaining to the scope and limits of the President's power of removal fills a thick chapter of our political and judicial history. The long stretches of its history, beginning with the very first Congress, with early echoes in the Reports of this Court, were laboriously traversed in *Myers* v. *United States*, 272 U.S. 52, and need not be retraced. President Roosevelt's reliance upon the pronouncements of the Court in that case in removing a member of the Federal Trade Commission on the ground that "the aims and purposes of the Administration with respect to the work of the Commission can be carried out most effectively with personnel of my own selection" reflected contemporaneous professional opinion regarding the significance of the *Myers* decision. Speaking through a Chief Justice who himself had been President, the Court did not restrict itself to the immediate issue before it, the President's inherent power to remove a postmaster.

obviously an executive official. As of set purpose and not by way of parenthetic casualness, the Court announced that the President had inherent constitutional power of removal also of officials who have "duties of a quasi-judicial character . . . whose decisions after hearing affect interests of individuals, the discharge of which the President can not in a particular case properly influence or control." *Myers* v. *United States, supra,* at 135. This view of presidential power was deemed to flow from his "constitutional duty of seeing that the laws be faithfully executed." *Ibid.*

The assumption was short-lived that the *Myers* case recognized the President's inherent constitutonal power to remove officials, no matter what the relation of the executive to the discharge of their duties and no matter what restrictions Congress may have imposed regarding the nature of their tenure. The versatility of circumstances often mocks a natural desire for definitiveness. Within less than ten years a unanimous Court, in *Humphrey's Executor* v. *United States,* 295 U.S. 602, narrowly confined the scope of the *Myers* decision to include only "all purely executive officers." 295 U.S., at 628. The Court explicitly "disapproved" the expressions in *Myers* supporting the President's inherent constitutional power to remove members of quasi-judicial bodies. 295 U.S., at 626–627. Congress had given members of the Federal Trade Commission a seven-year term and also provided for the removal of a Commissioner by the President for inefficiency, neglect of duty or malfeasance in office. In the present case, Congress provided for a tenure defined by the relatively short period of time during which the War Claims Commission was to operate—that is, it was to wind up not later than three years after the expiration of the time for filing of claims. But nothing was said in the Act about removal.

This is another instance in which the most appropriate legal significance must be drawn from congressional failure of explicitness. Necessarily this is a problem in probabilities. We start with one certainty.

The problem of the President's power to remove members of agencies entrusted with duties of the kind with which the War Claims Commission was charged was within the lively knowledge of Congress. Few contests between Congress and the President have so recurringly had the attention of Congress as that pertaining to the power of removal. Not the least significant aspect of the *Myers* case is that on the Court's special invitation Senator George Wharton Pepper, of Pennsylvania, presented the position of Congress at the bar of this Court.

Humphrey's case was a *cause célèbre*— and not least in the halls of Congress. And what is the essence of the decision in Humphrey's case? It drew a sharp line of cleavage between officials who were part of the Executive establishment and were thus removable by virtue of the President's constitutional powers, and those who are members of a body "to exercise its judgment without the leave or hindrance of any other official or any department of the government," 295 U.S., at 625–626, as to whom a power of removal exists only if Congress may fairly be said to have conferred it. This sharp differentiation derives from the difference in functions between those who are part of the Executive establishment and those whose tasks require absolute freedom from Executive interference. "For it is quite evident," again to quote *Humphrey's Executor*, "that one who holds his office only during the pleasure of another, cannot be depended upon to maintain an attitude of independence against the latter's will." 295 U.S., at 629.

Thus, the most reliable factor for drawing an inference regarding the President's power of removal in our case is the nature of the function that Congress vested in the War Claims Commission. What were the duties that Congress confided to this Commission? And can the inference fairly be drawn from the failure of Congress to provide for removal that these Commissioners were to remain in office at the will of the President? For such is the assertion of power on which petitioner's removal must rest. The ground of President Eisenhower's removal of petitioner was precisely the same as President Roosevelt's removal of Humphrey. Both Presidents desired to have Commissioners, one on the Federal Trade Commission, the other on the War Claims Commission, "of my own selection." They wanted these Commissioners to be their men. The terms of removal in the two cases are identical and express the assumption that the agencies of which the two Commissioners were members were subject in the discharge of their duties to the control of the Executive. An analysis of the Federal Trade Commission Act left this Court in no doubt that such was not the conception of Congress in creating the Federal Trade Commission. The terms of the War Claims Act of 1948 leave no doubt that such was not the conception of Congress regarding the War Claims Commission.

The history of this legislation emphatically underlines this fact. The short of it is that the origin of the Act was a bill, H.R. 4044, 80th Cong., 1st Sess., passed by the House that placed the administration of a very limited class of claims by Americans against Japan in the hands of the Federal Security Administrator and provided for a Commission to inquire into and report upon other types of claims. See H.R. Rep. No. 976, 80th Cong., 1st Sess. The Federal Security Administrator was indubitably an arm of the President. When the House bill reached the Senate, it struck out all but the enacting clause, rewrote the bill, and established a Commission with "jurisdiction to receive and adjudicate according to law" three classes of claims, as defined by §§ 5, 6 and 7. The Commission was established as an adjudicating body with all the paraphernalia by which legal claims are put to the test of proof, with finality of determination "not subject to review by any other official of the United States or by any court, by mandamus or otherwise." § 11. Awards were to be paid out of a War Claims Fund in the hands of the Secretary of the Treasury, whereby such claims were given even more assured collectability than

adheres to judgments rendered in the Court of Claims. See S. Rep. No. 1742, 80th Cong., 2d Sess. With minor amendment, see H.R. Rep. No. 2439, 80th Cong., 2d Sess. 10–11 (Conference Report), this Senate bill became law.

When Congress has for distribution among American claimants funds derived from foreign sources, it may proceed in different ways. Congress may appropriate directly; it may utilize the Executive; it may resort to the adjudicatory process. See *La Abra Silver Mining Co.* v. *United States,* 175 U.S. 423. For Congress itself to have made appropriations for the claims with which it dealt under the War Claims Act was not practical in view of the large number of claimants and the diversity in the specific circumstances giving rise to the claims. The House bill in effect put the distribution of the narrow class of claims that it acknowledged into Executive hands, by vesting the procedure in the Federal Security Administrator. The final form of the legislation, as we have seen, left the widened range of claims to be determined by adjudication. Congress could, of course, have given jurisdiction over these claims to the District Courts or to the Court of Claims. The fact that it chose to establish a Commission to "adjudicate according to law" the classes of claims defined in the statute did not alter the intrinsic judicial character of the task with which the Commission was charged. The claims were to be "adjudicated according to law," that is, on the merits of each claim, supported by evidence and governing legal considerations, by a body that was "entirely free from the control or coercive influence, direct or indirect," *Humphrey's Executor* v. *United States, supra,* 295 U.S., at 629, of either the Executive or the Congress. If, as one must take for granted, the War Claims Act precluded the President from influencing the Commission in passing on a particular claim, *a fortiori* must it be inferred that Congress did not wish to have hang over the Commission the Damocles' sword of removal by the President for no reason other than that he preferred to have on that Commission men of his own choosing.

For such is this case. We have not a removal for cause involving the rectitude of a member of an adjudicatory body, nor even a suspensory removal until the Senate could act upon it by confirming the appointment of a new Commissioner or otherwise dealing with the matter. Judging the matter in all the nakedness in which it is presented, namely, the claim that the President could remove a member of an adjudicatory body like the War Claims Commission merely because he wanted his own appointees on such a Commission, we are compelled to conclude that no such power is given to the President directly by the Constitution, and none is impliedly conferred upon him by statute simply because Congress said nothing about it. The philosophy of *Humphrey's Executor,* in its explicit language as well as its implications, precludes such a claim.

The judgment is reversed.

EX PARTE MERRYMAN

17 Fed. Cas. 144, No. 9, 487 (1861)

On April 27, 1861, President Lincoln issued the following order suspending the writ of habeas corpus:

The Commanding General of the Army of the United States:

You are engaged in suppressing an insurrection against the laws of the United States. If at any point on or in the vicinity of any military line which is now or which shall be used between the city of Philadelphia and the city of Washington you find resistance which renders it necessary to suspend the writ of *habeas corpus* for the public safety, you personally or through the officer in command at the point where resistance occurs, are authorized to suspend that writ.

TANEY, Circuit Justice. The application in this case for a writ of habeas corpus is made to me under the 14th section of the judiciary act of 1789, which renders effectual for the citizen the constitutional privilege of the writ of habeas corpus. That act gives to the courts of the United States, as well as to each justice of the supreme court, and to every district judge, power to grant writs of habeas corpus for the purpose of an inquiry into the cause of commitment. The petition was presented to me, at Washington, under the impression that I would order the prisoner to be brought before me there, but as he was confined in Fort McHenry, in the city of Baltimore, which is in my circuit, I resolved to hear it in the latter city, as obedience to the writ, under such circumstances, would not withdraw General Cadwaladar, who had him in charge, from the limits of his military command.

The petition presents the following case: The petitioner resides in Maryland, in Baltimore county; while peaceably in his own house, with his family, it was at two o'clock on the morning of the 25th of May 1861, entered by an armed force, professing to act under military orders; he was then compelled to rise from his bed, taken into custody, and conveyed to Fort McHenry, where he is imprisoned by the commanding officer, without warrant from any lawful authority.

The commander of the fort, General George Cadwalader, by whom he is detained in confinement, in his return to the writ does not deny any of the facts alleged in the petition. He states that the prisoner was arrested by order of General Keim, of Pennsylvania, and conducted as aforesaid to Fort McHenry, by his order, and placed in his (General Cadwalader's) custody, to be there detained by him as a prisoner.

A copy of the warrant or order under which the prisoner was arrested was demanded by his counsel, and refused: and it is not alleged in the return, that any specific act, constituting any offence against the laws of the United States, has been charged against him upon oath, but he appears to have been arrested upon general charges of treason and rebellion, without proof, and without giving the names of the witnesses, or specifying the acts which, in the judgment of the military officer, constituted these crimes. Having the prisoner thus in custody upon these vague and unsupported accusations, he refuses to obey the writ of habeas corpus, upon the ground that he is duly authorized by the president to suspend it. . . .

As the case comes before me, therefore, I understand that the president not only claims the right to suspend the writ of habeas corpus himself, at his discretion, but to delegate that discretionary power to a military officer, and to leave it to him to determine whether he will or will not obey judicial process that may be served upon him. No official notice has been given to the courts of justice, or to the public, by proclamation or otherwise, that the president claimed this power, and had exercised it in the manner stated in the return. And I certainly listened to it with some surprise, for I had supposed it to be one of those points of constitutional law upon which there was no difference of opinion, and that it was admitted on all hands, that the privilege of the writ could not be suspended, except by act of congress. . . .

The clause of the constitution, which authorizes the suspension of the privilege of the writ of habeas corpus, is in the 9th section of the first article. This article is devoted to the legislative department of the United States, and has not the slightest reference to the executive department. It begins by providing "that all legislative powers therein granted, shall be vested in a congress of the United States, which shall consist of a senate and house of representatives." And after prescribing the manner in which these two branches of the legislative department shall be chosen, it proceeds to enumerate specifically the legislative powers which it thereby grants [and legislative powers which it expressly prohibits]; and at the conclusion of this specification, a clause is inserted giving congress "the power to make all laws which shall be necessary and proper for carrying into execution the foregoing powers, and all other powers vested by this constitution in the government of the United States, or in any department or officer thereof." . . .

It is the second article of the constitution that provides for the organization of the executive department, enumerates the powers conferred on it, and prescribes its duties. And if the high power over the liberty of the citizen now claimed, was intended to be conferred on the president, it would undoubtedly be found in plain words in this article; but there is not a word in it that can furnish the slightest ground to justify the exercise of the power. . . .

The right of the subject to the benefit of the writ of habeas corpus, it must be recollected, was one of the great points in controversy, during the long struggle in England between arbitrary government and free institutions, and must therefore have strongly attracted the attention of the statesmen engaged in framing a new and, as they supposed, a freer government than the one which they had thrown off by the revolution. From the earliest history of the common law, if a person were imprisoned, no matter by what authority, he had a right to the writ of habeas corpus, to bring his case before the king's bench; if no specific offence were charged against him in the warrant of commitment, he was entitled to be forthwith discharged; and if an offence were charged which was bailable in its character, the court was bound to set him at liberty on bail. The most exciting contests between the crown and the people of England, from the time of Magna Charta, were in relation to the privilege of this writ, and they continued until the passage of the statute of 31 Car. II., commonly known as the great habeas corpus act. . . .

If the president of the United States may suspend the writ, then the constitution of the United States has conferred upon him more regal and absolute power over the liberty of the citizen, than the people of England have thought it safe to entrust to the crown; a power which the queen of England cannot exercise at this day, and which could not have been lawfully exercised by the sovereign even in the reign of Charles the First.

LINCOLN RESPONDS TO THE MERRYMAN CASE, JULY 4, 1861

Soon after the first call for militia it was considered a duty to authorize the Commanding General in proper cases, according to his discretion, to suspend the privilege of the writ of *habeas corpus,* or, in other words, to arrest and detain without resort to the ordinary processes and forms of law such individuals as he might deem dangerous to the public safety. This authority has purposely been exercised but very sparingly. Nevertheless, the legality and propriety of what has been done under it are questioned, and the attention of the country has been called to the proposition that one who is sworn to "take care that the laws be faithfully executed" should not himself violate them. Of course some consideration was given to the questions of power and propriety before this matter was acted upon. The whole of the laws which were required to be faithfully executed were being resisted and failing of execution in nearly one-third of the States. Must they be allowed to finally fail of execution, even had it been perfectly clear that by the use of the means necessary to their execution some single law, made in such extreme tenderness of the citizen's liberty that practically it relieves more of the guilty than of the innocent, should to a very limited extent be violated? To state the question more directly, Are all the laws *but one* to go unexecuted, and the Government itself go to pieces lest that one be violated? Even in such a case, would not the official oath be broken if the Government should be overthrown when it was believed that disregarding the single law would tend to preserve it? But it was not believed that this question was presented. It was not believed that any law was violated. The provision of the Constitution that "the privilege of the writ of *habeas corpus* shall not be suspended unless when, in cases of rebellion or invasion, the public safety may require it" is equivalent to a provision—is a provision—that such privilege may be suspended when, in cases of rebellion or invasion, the public safety *does* require it. It was decided that we have a case of rebellion and that the public safety does require the qualified suspension of the privilege of the writ which was authorized to be made. Now it is insisted that Congress, and not the Executive, is vested with this power; but the Constitution itself is silent as to which or who is to exercise the power; and as the provision was plainly made for a dangerous emergency, it can not be believed the framers of the instrument intended that in every case the danger should run its course until Congress could be called together, the very assembling of which might be prevented, as was intended in this case, by the rebellion.

No more extended argument is now offered, as an opinion at some length will probably be presented by the Attorney-General. Whether there shall be any legislation upon the subject, and, if any, what, is submitted entirely to the better judgment of Congress.

II. THE DELEGATION OF POWERS

The *Steel Seizure, Wiener,* and related problems, like judicial review itself, are problems in the separation of powers. A corollary of the separation principle is the nondelegability of powers. Congress, for example, may not defeat separation by delegating legislative authority to the President. It is settled, however, that Congress may assign discretionary power to the executive (or others), provided the delegation is accompanied by adequate standards or norms to guide the delegee in the exercise thereof. The theory is that by such limitations Congress itself is doing the legislating, i.e., fixing the policy, and so legislative power is not being given improperly to others. The question in such cases then is whether the standards fixed by Congress are adequate. Not until *Panama Refining Co.* v. *Ryan*, 293 U.S. 388 (1934), *Schechter* v. *United States*, 295 U.S. 495 (1935), and *Carter* v. *Carter Coal Co.*, 298 U.S. 238 (1936), and not since, has any delegation been held invalid for vagueness in its guiding standards. The modern, and indeed the pre-1934, approach to this problem is found in the *Opp Cotton Mills* case.

Compare the separation of powers principles under which the Court refuses to accept even a constitutional "delegation" of unguided, or standardless, authority. See *Colegrove* v. *Green* and *Coleman* v. *Miller* (Part One, II). As to delegation of powers with respect to the conduct of foreign affairs, see *United States* v. *Curtiss-Wright Export Corp.* (Part Three, II).

OPP COTTON MILLS v. ADMINISTRATOR

312 U.S. 126 (1941)

The Fair Labor Standards Act sought to establish minimum wages in certain interstate businesses by authorizing an Administrator, with the aid of industry committees, to fix wage rates within the limits of 30 to 40 cents per hour for a standard work week. The purpose of the leeway, and the manner in which it should be used, were outlined in the act.

MR. JUSTICE STONE delivered the opinion of the court. . . .

There remains the question whether the Act is an unconstitutional delegation of the legislative power of Congress. Petitioner urges that the standards prescribed for fixing the authorized minimum wages between 30 and 40 cents per hour are too vague and indefinite to admit of any judicial determination whether they are within or without the standards prescribed by Congress. . . .

Section 8 defines, with precision, the policy of the Act to raise the minimum wage to the 40 cents per hour limit "as rapidly as economically feasible without substantially curtailing employment" in each industry, and the standards of the administrative action applicable to the Administrator are those made applicable to the committee which it is provided "shall recommend to the Administrator the highest minimum wage rates for the industry which it determines, having due regard to economic and competitive conditions, will not substantially curtail employment in the industry." But it is said that application of these standards in an industry is made contingent upon the determination whether the industry is to be classified and if so, whether it is to be subject to particular wage differentials, and that these determinations in turn depend upon factors so inadequately defined as to afford no standard of administrative action. . . .

The mandate of the Constitution that all legislative powers granted "shall be vested" in Congress has never been thought to preclude Congress from resorting to the aid of administrative officers or boards as fact-finding agencies whose findings, made in conformity to previously adopted legislative standards or definitions of congressional policy, have been made prerequisite to the operation of its statutory command. The adoption of the declared policy by Congress and its definition of the circumstances in which its command is to be effective, constitute the performance, in the constitutional sense, of the legislative function.

True, the appraisal of facts in the light of the declared policy and in conformity to prescribed legislative standards, and the inferences to be drawn by the administrative agency from the facts, so appraised, involve the exercise of judgment within the prescribed limits. But where, as in the present case, the standards set up for the guidance of the administrative agency, the procedure which it is directed to follow and the record of its action which is required by the statute to be kept or which is in fact preserved, are such that Congress, the courts and the public can ascertain whether the agency has conformed to the standards which Congress has prescribed, there is no failure of performance of the legislative function.

While fact finding may be and often is a step in the legislative process, the Constitution does not require that Congress should find for itself every fact upon which it bases legislation. "It is a *constitution* we are expounding" "intended to endure for ages to come, and, consequently, to be adapted to the various *crises* of human affairs." *McCulloch* v. *Maryland* . . . In an increasingly complex society Congress obviously could not perform its functions if it were obliged to find all the facts subsidiary to the basic conclusions which support the defined legislative policy in fixing, for example, a tariff rate, a railroad rate or the rate of wages to be applied in particular industries by a minimum wage law. The Constitution, viewed as a continuously operative charter of Government, is not to be interpreted as demanding the impossible or the impracticable. The essentials of the legislative function are the determination of the legislative policy and its formulation as a rule of conduct. Those essentials are preserved when Congress specifies the basic conclusions of fact upon ascertainment of which, from relevant data by a designated administrative agency, it ordains that its statutory command is to be effective.

The present statute satisfies those requirements. The basic facts to be ascertained administratively are whether the prescribed wage as applied to an industry will substantially curtail employment, and whether to attain the legislative end there is need for wage differentials applicable to classes in industry. The factors to be considered in arriving at these determinations, both those specified and "other relevant factors," are those which are relevant to or have a bearing on the statutory objective. The fact that Congress accepts the administrative judgment as to the relative weights to be given to these factors in each case when that judgment in other respects is arrived at in the manner prescribed by the statute, instead of attempting the impossible by prescribing their relative weight in advance for all cases, is no more an abandonment of the legislative function than when Congress accepts and acts legislatively upon the advice of experts as to social or economic conditions without re-examining for itself the data upon which that advice is based. . . .

Affirmed.

SELECTED READINGS

E. S. Corwin, *Total War and the Constitution* (1953)

E. S. Corwin, *The President: Office and Powers, 1787–1957* (1957)

P. Herring, *Presidential Leadership* (1940)

L. Jaffe, "An Essay on Delegation of Legislative Power," 47 *Columbia Law Review* 359, 561 (1947)

P. Kauper, "The Steel Seizure Case," 51 *Michigan Law Review* 141 (1952)

R. E. Neustadt, *Presidential Power* (1960)

R. Parker, "Separation of Powers Revisited," 49 *Michigan Law Review* 1009 (1951)

R. Parker, "Removal Power of the President and Independent Administrative Agencies," 36 *Indiana Law Journal* 63 (1960)

C. Rossiter, *The American Presidency* (1956)

G. Schubert, *The Presidency in the Courts* (1957)

M. P. Sharp, "The Classical American Doctrine of 'The Separation of Powers,'" 2 *University of Chicago Law Review* 385 (1935)

J. M. Smith and C. P. Cotter, *Powers of the President During Crisis* (1960)

A. T. Vanderbilt, *The Doctrine of the Separation of Powers and Its Present-Day Significance* (1953)

A. Westin, *The Anatomy of a Constitutional Law Case* (1958)

Part Three | FEDERALISM
What Belongs to the Nation and What to the States?

I. BACKGROUND

JAMES MADISON, "ORIGIN OF THE CONSTITUTIONAL CONVENTION" (1835)

At the date of the Convention, the aspect & retrospect of the pol. condition of the U.S. could not but fill the pub. mind with a gloom which was relieved only by a hope that so select a Body would devise an adequate remedy for the existing and prospective evils so impressively demanding it.

It was seen that the public debt rendered so sacred by the cause in which it had been incurred remained without any provision for its payment. The reiterated and elaborate efforts of Cong. to procure from the States a more adequate power to raise the means of payment had failed. The effect of the ordinary requisitions of Congress had only displayed the inefficiency of the auth^y making them; none of the States having duly complied with them, some having failed altogether or nearly so; and in one instance, that of N. Jersey, a compliance was *expressly* refused; nor was more yielded to the expostulations of members of Cong^s deputed to her Legislature, than a mere repeal of the law, without a compliance (see letter of Grayson to J.M.).

The want of Auth^y in Cong^s to regulate Commerce had produced in Foreign nations particularly G.B., a monopolizing policy injurious to the trade of the U.S., and destructive to their navigation; the imbecility and anticipated dissolution of the Confederacy extinguish^g all apprehensions of a Countervailing policy on the part of the U. States.

The same want of a general power over Commerce led to an exercise of the power separately, by the States, wch not only proved abortive, but engendered rival, conflicting and angry regulations. Besides the vain attempts to supply their respective treasuries by imposts, which turned their commerce into the neighbouring ports, and to coerce a relaxation of the British monopoly of the W. Ind^a navigation, which was attempted by Virginia, (see Journal of   ) the States having ports for foreign commerce, taxed & irritated the adjoining States, trading thro' them, as N.Y., Pen^a, Virg^a & S. Carolina. Some of the States, as Connecticut, taxed imports as from Mass^{ts}, higher than imports even from G.B. of wch Mass^{ts} complained to Virg^a and doubtless to other states (see letter of J.M.). In sundry instances as of N.Y., N.J., P^a & Maryl^d, (see   ). The navigation laws treated the Citizens of other States as aliens.

In certain cases the Auth^y of the Confederacy was disregarded, as in violation not only of the Treaty of peace; but of Treaties with France & Holland, which were complained of to Cong^s.

In other cases the Fed^l Auth^y was violated by Treaties & wars with Indians, as by Geo.; by troops raised & kept up with^t the consent of Cong^s, as by Mass^{ts}; by compacts with^t the consent of Cong^s, as between Pen^a and N. Jersey, and between Virg^a & Maryl^d. From the Legisl: Journals of Virg^a it appears, that a vote refusing to apply for a sanction of Cong^s was followed by a vote agst the communication of the Compact to Cong^s.

In the internal administration of the States a violation of Contracts had become familiar in the form of depreciated paper made a legal tender, of property substituted for money, of Instalment laws, and of the occlusions of the Courts of Justice; although evident that all such interferences affected the rights of other States, Relatively creditor, as well as Citizens Creditors within the State.

Among the defects which had been severely felt was that of a uniformity in cases requiring it, as laws of naturalization and bankruptcy, a Coercive authority operating on individuals and a guaranty of the internal tranquillity of the States.

As a natural consequence of this distracted and disheartening condition of the union, the Fed^l Auth^y had ceased to be respected abroad, and dispositions were shewn there, particularly in G.B., to take advantage of its imbecility, and to speculate on its approaching downfall: At home it had lost all confidence & credit; the unstable and unjust career of the States had also forfeited the respect & confidence essential to order and good Govt^t involving a general decay of confidence between Man & man. It was found moreover that those least partial to popular Gov^t, or most distrustful of its efficacy were yielding to anticipations, that from an increase of the confusion a Gov^t might result more congenial with their taste or their opinions. Whilst those most devoted to the principles and forms of Republics, were alarmed for the cause of liberty itself, at stake in the American Experiment, and anxious for a system that w^d avoid the inefficacy of a mere confederacy without passing into the opposite extreme of a consolidated gov^t It was known that there were individuals who had betrayed a bias towards Monarchy and there had always been some not unfavorable to a partition of the Union into several Confederacies; either from a better chance of figuring on a Sectional Theatre, or that the Sections would require stronger Gov^{ts}, or by their hostile conflicts lead to a monarchical consolidation. The idea of a dismemberment had recently made its appearance in the Newspapers.

Such were the defects, the deformities, the diseases and the ominous prospects, for which the Convention were to provide a remedy, and which ought never to be overlooked in expounding & appreciating the Constitutional Charter, the remedy that was provided.

GEORGE WASHINGTON, LETTERS TO DR. GORDON, JULY 8, 1783, AND TO JOHN JAY, AUGUST 1, 1786

To suppose that the general concerns of this country can be directed by thirteen heads, or one head without competent powers, is a solecism, the bad effects of which every man who has had the practical knowledge to judge from, that I have, is fully convinced of; tho' none perhaps has felt them in so forcible and distressing a degree. The People at large, and at a distance from the theatre of action, who only know that the machine was kept in motion, and that they are at last arrived at the first object of their wishes, are satisfied with the event, without investigating the causes of the slow progress to it, or of the expenses which have accrued, and which they have been unwilling to pay—great part of which has arisen from that want of energy in the Federal Constitution, which I am complaining of, and which I wish to see given to it by a Convention of the People, instead of hearing it remarked that, as we have worked through an arduous contest with the powers Congress already have (but which, by the by, have been gradually diminishing) why should they be invested with more? . . . For Heaven's sake, who are Congress? Are they not the creatures of the People, amenable to them for their conduct, and dependent from day to day on their breath? Where then can be the danger of giving them such powers as are adequate to the great ends of Government and to all the general purposes of the Confederation (I repeat the word general, because I am no advocate for their having to do with the particular policy of any State, further than it concerns the Union at large). . . .

Your sentiments, that our affairs are drawing rapidly to a crisis, accord with my own. What the event will be is also beyond the reach of my foresight. . . . I do not conceive we can exist long as a nation without having lodged somewhere a power which will pervade the whole Union in as energetic a manner, as the authority of the State Governments extends over the several States. . . . Requisitions are a perfect nullity, where thirteen sovereign, independent, disunited States are in the habit of discussing and refusing compliance with them at their option. Requisitions are actually little better than a jest and a byeword throughout the land. If you tell the Legislatures they have violated the treaty of peace and invaded the prerogatives of the Confederacy, they will laugh in your face. What then is to be done? Things cannot go on in the same train forever. It is much to be feared, as you observe, that the better kind of people, being disgusted with the circumstances, will have their minds prepared for any revolution whatever. We are apt to run from one extreme into another. To anticipate and prevent disastrous contingencies, would be the part of wisdom and patriotism.

THE VIRGINIA PLAN AND THE FOUNDING FATHERS

The main purpose of the Constitutional Convention of 1787 was to protect national interests from the states' rights anarchy described by Madison and Washington in the above selections. To this end, Hamilton wanted to abolish the states entirely, and substitute a unitary government. This radical approach was rejected in favor of a federal system in which a national government would have the power to protect national interests—all else being reserved to the states and the people. The following excerpt from Robert Stern, "The Scope of the Phrase Interstate Commerce," [1] considers the problem of the scope of national power.

Is the commerce clause now being construed too broadly, too narrowly, or neither? There doubtless have been many who in recent years have thought that the Court was interpreting the commerce power much too broadly in permitting

1. *American Bar Association Journal* 823, 871 (1955).

Congress to regulate almost every aspect of the nation's economic structure. The exhaustive work of Professor Crosskey appears to be alone in urging that the current doctrines are too narrow and that all commerce within the United States is comprehended by the phrase "commerce among the several states."

The Constitutional Convention itself furnishes the criterion by which the question may be answered. For almost two months after it first convened, the Convention devoted itself to consideration of the principles which should be followed in the new Constitution, prior to submission to the Committee on Detail for drafting. With respect to the powers to be granted the National Government, the Convention twice approved resolutions based on Randolph's Virginia Plan, which

"Resolved, that the national legislature ought to possess the legislative rights vested in Congress by the confederation: and

"moreover, to legislate in all cases for the general interests of the Union, and also in those to which the states are separately incompetent, or

"in which the harmony of the United States may be interrupted by the exercise of individual legislation." [2]

Twice, more restrictive proposals were defeated.[3] When the Committee on Detail reported a draft enumerating the powers of Congress, including the commerce clause, substantially in their present form, there was no objection—and no discussion of the commerce power as such.[4] It was obvious that the Convention believed that the enumeration conformed to the principles set forth for the guidance of the Committee in the resolution previously adopted.[5]

It is reasonable to interpret the provisions of a document drafted to achieve these expressed purposes in a manner which will best accomplish the stated objectives, even though it be recognized that developments during the ensuing one hundred and sixty-eight years have greatly enlarged the area which, under these principles, would fall within the federal sphere. Furthermore, these principles for determining the scope of the federal power would seem to be as sensible today as in 1787. What better reasons can there be for the exercise of the national authority than that the regulation is needed for the general interests of the Union, or that the states are separately incompetent, or that uniformity is needed rather than individual legislation?

Which of the suggested ways of defining the scope of the commerce power best conforms with the standards approved by the Convention?

The narrowest test seriously proposed in recent years, that applied by the Supreme Court in cases such as *Carter* v. *Carter Coal Co.*, would allow federal regulation of intrastate transactions "directly affecting" interstate commerce, but not when the activities were in fields, such as production or manufacture, which the Court thought were too "local" in nature. Experience has demonstrated, however, that production problems are national in character. Strikes do interrupt interstate commerce and thereby harm other states than those in which they occur. The amount of a commodity produced has a direct impact on the amount shipped as well as on interstate prices, and cannot be controlled except on a nation-wide basis. The forces of competition prevent individual states from

2. Madison's Debates, as reported in H.R. Doc. No. 398, 69th Cong. 1st Sess. (1927), entitled *Documents Illustrative of the Formation of the Union of the American States*, pages 466, 117, 129–130, 234–235, 389–390.

3. *Id.*, at 205, 211, 234, 388–389.

4. *Id.*, at 475, 555.

5. Abel, "The Commerce Clause in the Constitutional Convention and in Contemporary Comment," 25 *Minn. Law Rev.* 432, 440 (1941); Stern, "That Commerce Which Concerns More States Than One," 47 *Harv. Law Rev.* 1335, 1338–1340 (1934).

fixing minimum wages for employees working in factories which compete with factories in other states. Because the market is interstate, the states are "separately incompetent." The test which the Court has abandoned would have left such problems to the states which could not possibly have coped with them. Such a result is certainly not in harmony with the resolutions approved by the framers. Nor can the creation of an economic hiatus in which the National Government cannot act for "legal" reasons and the states for economic ones possibly be desirable. It is not in the public interest that government, that is the people acting as an entity, be impotent. Those who believe that no government should intermeddle in economic affairs are entitled to present their views to Congress, but not to assert that they find support for freezing them into our basic charter of government in the constitutional provision which affirmatively authorizes the regulation of commerce.

NOTE AND QUAERE: *Carter* v. *Carter Coal Co.,* 298 U.S. 238 (1936), recognizing part of the evidence referred to in the Stern article above, derives an opposite conclusion: "The convention, however, declined to confer upon Congress power in such general (i.e., Virginia Plan) terms; instead, . . . it carefully limited the powers which it thought wise to entrust to Congress by specifying them. . . ." See Abel, "The Commerce Clause in the Constitutional Convention and in Contemporary Comment," 25 *Minnesota Law Review* 432 (1941). Do you find as a matter of language that Article I, Section 8 "carefully limited" the powers of Congress? Does it seem designed to do so?

THOMAS JEFFERSON, LETTER TO GEORGE WYTHE, SEPTEMBER 16, 1787

My own general idea was, that the States should severally preserve their sovereignty in whatever concerns themselves alone, and that whatever may concern another State, or any foreign nation, should be made a part of the federal sovereignty; that the exercise of the federal sovereignty should be divided among three several bodies, legislative, excutive, and judiciary, as the State sovereignties are; and that some peaceable means should be contrived, for the federal head to force compliance on the part of the States.

JAMES MADISON, *The Federalist,* NO. 46

[According to Madison, the proposed new federal government need not be feared because] the first and most natural attachment of the people will be to the governments of their respective states. [But with uncanny insight he added] If . . . the people should in future become more partial to the federal than to the State governments, the change can only result from such manifest and irresistible proofs of a better administration as will overcome all their antecedent propensities. And in that case, the people ought not surely to be precluded from giving most of their confidence where they may discover it to be most due. . . .

The argument . . . may be put into a very concise form, which appears altogether conclusive. Either the mode in which the federal government is to be constructed will render it sufficiently dependent upon [i.e., accountable to] the people, or it will not. On the first assumption, it will be restrained by that dependence from forming schemes obnoxious to their [*sic*] constituents. On the other assumption, it will not possess the confidence of the people, and its schemes of usurpation will be easily defeated by the State governments, who will be supported by the people.

REPORT OF PRESIDENT EISENHOWER'S COMMISSION ON INTERGOVERNMENTAL RELATIONS (1955)

People in the United States, as elsewhere, have looked more and more to government for assistance in solving their social and economic problems. The National Government has sometimes responded more readily than have the State and local governments. The Commission does not deal with the issue of whether or not governments rather than individuals should satisfy these needs. What it faces is the fact that the National Government has gradually undertaken some new activities which are susceptible of a larger measure of State and local handling. The Commission does not essay a judgment as to whether unreadiness on the part of the States and localities or overzealousness onthe part of the National Government, or both, may have caused the existing division of activities. It merely emphasizes the fact that the more effectively our State and local government structures, procedures, and policies can be adapted to present-day governmental objectives, the less occasion there will be for bypassing State action in the future. . . .

Early in its study, the Commission was confronted with the fact that many State constitutions restrict the scope, effectiveness, and adaptability of State and local action. These self-imposed constitutional limitations make it difficult for many States to perform all of the services their citizens require, and consequently have frequently been the underlying cause of State and municipal pleas for Federal assistance.

It is significant that the Constitution prepared by the Founding Fathers, with its broad grants of authority and avoidance of legislative detail, has withstood the test of time far better than the constitutions later adopted by the States. A due regard for the need for stability in government requires adherence to basic constitutional principles until strong and persistent public policy requires a change. A dynamic society requires a constant review of legislative detail to meet changing conditions and circumstances.

The Commission finds a very real and pressing need for the States to improve their constitutions. A number of States recently have taken energetic action to rewrite outmoded charters. In these States this action has been regarded as a first step in the program to achieve the flexibility required to meet the modern needs of their citizens. . . .

In a majority of States, city dwellers outnumber the citizens of rural areas. Yet in most States the rural voters are overwhelmingly in control of one legislative house, and overweighted if not dominant in the other. . . .

The problem of reapportionment is important in the area of study of this Commission because legislative neglect of urban communities has led more and more people to look to Washington for more and more of the services and controls they desire. One of the study reports prepared for the Commission makes this very clear.

"If states do not give cities their rightful allocation of seats in the legislature, the tendency will be toward direct Federal-municipal dealings. These began in earnest in the early days of the depression. There is only one way to avoid this in the future. It is for the states to take an interest in urban problems, in metropolitan government, in city needs. If they do not do this, the cities will find a path to Washington as they did before, and this time it may be permanent, with the ultimate result that there may be a new government arrangement that will break down the constitutional pattern which has worked so well up to now."

In addition to reapportionment, there are a number of other measures that would enable State legislatures to become more effective instruments of policy formation. In this age of rapid change, legislative bodies are called upon to deal with an increasing number of complex and technical issues. Most State legislatures are not, however, in a position to give the time and study that many of these issues should have. Most of the States impose constitutional limitations on the frequency and length of sessions. Only ten State constitutions provide for annual sessions and several of those limit every other session to fiscal matters. The low pay of most legislators and their inadequate physical and staff arrangements accentuate the effect of limited sessions. . . .

In a number of States, the constitution earmarks so high a proportion of the tax revenues that the legislature's power to appropriate money applies to less than half of the State's expenditures. This tends to undermine the principle of responsible representative government and limits the ability of the legislators to adapt the spending policies of the State to changing needs and conditions. . . .

Today, few States have an adequate executive branch headed by a governor who can be held generally accountable for executing and administering the laws of the State. . . .

The objective of decentralization cannot be attained by a readjustment of National-State relations alone. It will be fully achieved only when carried through to the lowest levels of government, where every citizen has the opportunity to participate actively and directly. The strengthening of local governments requires that activities that can be handled by these units be allocated to them, together with the financial resources necessary for their support. . . .

By using their power to strengthen their own governments and those of their subdivisions, the States can relieve much of the pressure for, and generate a strong counterpressure against, improper expansion of National action. Thereby they can increase their chances of enjoying an enlarged participation in the total task of governing the Nation. . . .

The problem of preserving a fiscal balance among the governments comprising the federal system arises because of the unequal distribution of tax resources. The problem is actually threefold: (1) Some imbalance exists between the National Government and the States. The latter are handicapped, relative to the National Government, in tapping available resources. (2) There is an imbalance among States; the geographical distribution of resources is uneven and places some States in disadvantageous positions as compared with others. (3) Further imbalances arise within individual States as a result of concentration of resources in certain areas. . . .

NOTE: A far more outspoken criticism of state government will be found in R. S. Allen (ed.), *Our Sovereign States*, particularly at page vii (1949). Recently Dennis Brogan, a British observer of American affairs, noted the discrepancy between our professions and our practice. Judging by what we do, he said, and ignoring what we say, it is plain that Americans have less confidence in state than in national government. Why else would we turn so plainly from the one to the other when we want to get things done? After all, no one sits in Congress but representatives from the states. Madison's "prophecy" seems to have been fulfilled —presumably in part for the reasons indicated by the Eisenhower Commission on Intergovernmental Relations. Another reason, of course, is that the constantly increasing growth and centralization of private economic power have necessitated a countervailing power in government.

CHALMERS SHERWIN, "SCIENCE, SCIENTISTS, AND POLITICS" (1963)[1]

A common modern complaint is that while government has spread like an octopus, our problems have grown worse. It follows that the cure for our ills is less government. But government did not bloom spontaneously. It grew in response to the scientific revolution. As men have invented more gadgets and uncovered more knowledge about the world, an enormous expansion of government has been necessary, both to protect the public interest and to foster further scientific advance.

In 1800 the government of the United States played a modest role. It had an army, a postal department, a tax on whiskey, and some import duties; the Department of State kept track of the world. That was about it. But by 1830 railroad and steamboat traffic began to grow, and, to regulate it in the public interest, so did federal power. Later, internal combustion engines were invented, more was discovered about aeronautical science, and suddenly airways had to be regulated. Telegraph, radio, and television each generated complicated governmental problems. Modern chemistry and pharmaceuticals brought into being the whole field of food and drug control.

The economic disaster of agricultural overproduction, a triumph of applied science, is a prime example of the difficulties that technology has handed to government. The farm problem really began in 1862 when land-grant colleges were founded with federal support. By 1900 science was being applied to agriculture on a big scale, and by 1920 food production was beginning to be excessive. Hybrids, modern machinery, new methods of food processing, and new types of fertilizers were developed, and all at once America was producing too much food. Science and technology caused the surplus, but the federal government had to try to cope with it. Its efforts to do so, plus its efforts to make agriculture still more efficient, have spawned a giant bureaucratic structure.

The biggest surge of all in government growth was caused by the exploration of the atom. In 1939, when science suddenly found a major key to the secrets, no one but the government could afford to exploit it. Science has not stopped finding keys—those to space, for example—and the job of the federal government has not stopped getting bigger. Atomic and space research are unsuitable for private exploration, not only because the government alone can afford the massive costs, but also because the results require governmental control.

II. NATIONAL AUTHORITY

1. THE COMMERCE POWER

JAMES MADISON IN THE CONSTITUTIONAL CONVENTION,
SEPTEMBER 15, 1787

Whether the states are now restrained from laying tonnage duties depends on the extent of the power [of Congress] "to regulate commerce." These terms are

1. Center for the Study of Democratic Institutions.

vague, but they seem to exclude the power of the states. They may certainly be restrained by treaty. . . . He was more and more convinced that the regulation of commerce was in its nature indivisible and ought to be wholly under one authority.

[This is from Madison's notes where he always referred to himself in the third person.]

GIBBONS v. OGDEN
9 Wheaton 1 (1824)

To encourage development of steam navigation, New York granted Robert Fulton (the inventor of the steamboat) exclusive steamboat rights on the Hudson River *in New York* for a limited period of years. Thanks to this grant, Fulton was able to get financial backing and to build successful steamboats, one of which was operated for him under the New York grant by Ogden. Gibbons intruded by running a steamboat from New York to New Jersey in violation of the Fulton "patent." This case began as an action by the Fulton interests to stop the infringement.

MR. CHIEF JUSTICE MARSHALL delivered the opinion of the Court: . . .

The appellant contends that this decree [of the court below] is erroneous, because the laws which purport to give the exclusive privilege it sustains are repugnant to the Constitution and laws of the United States.

They are said to be repugnant—

1. To that clause in the Constitution which authorizes Congress to regulate commerce.

2. To that which authorizes Congress to promote the progress of science and useful arts. . . .

As preliminary to the very able discussions of the Constitution which we have heard from the bar, and as having some influence on its construction, reference has been made to the political situation of these states, anterior to its formation. It has been said that they were sovereign, were completely independent, and were connected with each other only by a league. This is true. But, when these allied sovereigns converted their league into a government, when they converted their congress of ambassadors, deputed to deliberate on their common concerns, and to recommend measures of general utility, into a legislature, empowered to enact laws on the

most interesting subjects, the whole character in which the states appear underwent a change, the extent of which must be determined by a fair consideration of the instrument by which that change was effected.

This instrument contains an enumeration of powers expressly granted by the people to their government. It has been said that these powers ought to be construed strictly. But why ought they to be so construed? Is there one sentence in the Constitution which gives countenance to this rule? In the last of the enumerated powers, that which grants, expressly, the means for carrying all others into execution, Congress is authorized "to make all laws which shall be necessary and proper" for the purpose. But this limitation on the means which may be used is not extended to the powers which are conferred; nor is there one sentence in the Constitution, which has been pointed out by the gentlemen of the bar, or which we have been able to discern, that prescribes this rule. We do not, therefore, think ourselves justified in adopting it. What do gentlemen mean by a strict construction? If they contend only against that enlarged construction, which would extend words beyond their natural and obvious import, we might question the application of the term, but should not controvert the principle. If they contend for that narrow construction which, in support of some theory not to be found in the Constitution, would deny to the government those powers which the words of the grant, as usually understood, import, and which are consistent with the general views and objects of the instrument; for that narrow construction, which would cripple the government, and render it unequal to the objects for which it is declared to be instituted, and to which the powers given, as fairly understood, render it competent; then we cannot perceive the propriety of this strict construction, nor adopt it as the rule by which the Constitution is to be expounded. As men whose intentions require no concealment generally employ the words which most directly and aptly express the ideas they intend to convey, the enlightened patriots who framed our Constitution, and the people who adopted it, must be understood to have employed words in their natural sense, and to have intended what they have said. If, from the imperfection of human language, there should be serious doubts respecting the extent of any given power, it is a well-settled rule that the objects for which it was given, especially when those objects are expressed in the instrument itself, should have great influence in the construction. We know of no reason for excluding this rule from the present case. The grant does not convey power which might be beneficial to the grantor, if retained by himself, or which can enure solely to the benefit of the grantee; but is an investment of power for the general advantage, in the hands of agents selected for that purpose; which power can never be exercised by the people themselves, but must be placed in the hands of agents, or lie dormant. We know of no rule for construing the extent of such powers, other than is given by the language of the instrument which confers them, taken in connection with the purposes for which they were conferred.

The words are: "Congress shall have Power . . . To regulate Commerce with foreign Nations, and among the several States, and with the Indian Tribes." The subject to be regulated is commerce; and our Constitution being, as was aptly said at the bar, one of enumeration, and not of definition, to ascertain the extent of the power, it becomes necessary to settle the meaning of the word. The counsel for the appellee would limit it to traffic, to buying and selling, or the interchange of commodities, and do not admit that it comprehends navigation. This would restrict a general term, applicable to many objects, to one of its significations. Commerce, undoubtedly, is traffic, but it is something more: it is intercourse. It describes the commercial intercourse between nations, and parts of nations, in all its branches, and is regulated by prescribing rules for carrying on that intercourse. The mind can scarcely conceive a system for regulating commerce between nations which shall exclude all laws concerning navigation, which shall be silent on the admission of the vessels of the one nation into the ports of the other, and be confined to prescribing rules for the conduct of individuals, in the actual employment of buying and selling, or of barter.

If commerce does not include navigation, the government of the Union has no direct power over that subject, and can make no law prescribing what shall constitute American vessels, or requiring that they shall be navigated by American seamen. Yet this power has been exercised from the commencement of the government, has been exercised with the consent of all, and has been understood by all to be a commercial regulation. All America understands, and has uniformly understood, the word "commerce" to comprehend navigation. It was so understood, and must have been so understood, when the Constitution was framed. The power over commerce, including navigation, was one of the primary objects for which the people of America adopted their government, and must have been contemplated in forming it. The Convention must have used the word in that sense, because all have understood it in that sense; and the attempt to restrict it comes too late. . . .

The word used in the Constitution, then, comprehends, and has been always understood to comprehend, navigation within its meaning; and a power to regulate navigation is as expressly granted as if that term had been added to the word "commerce."

To what commerce does this power extend? The Constitution informs us, to commerce "with foreign Nations, and among the several States, and with the Indian Tribes." It has, we believe, been universally admitted that these words comprehend every species of commercial intercourse between the United States and foreign nations. No sort of trade can be carried on between this country and any other to which this power does not extend. It has been truly said that commerce, as the word is used in the Constitution, is a unit, every part of which is indicated by the term. If this be the admitted meaning of the word, in its application to foreign nations, it must carry the same meaning throughout the sentence, and remain a unit, unless there be some plain intelligible cause which alters it.

The subject to which the power is next applied is to commerce "among the several States." The word "among" means intermingled with. A thing which is among others is intermingled with them. Commerce among the states cannot stop at the external boundary line of each state, but may be introduced into the interior.

It is not intended to say that these words comprehend that commerce which is completely internal, which is carried on between man and man in a state, or between different parts of the same state, and which does not extend to or affect other states. Such a power would be inconvenient and is certainly unnecessary.

Comprehensive as the word "among" is, it may very properly be restricted to that commerce which concerns more states than one. . . . The completely internal commerce of a state, then, may be considered as reserved for the state itself.

But, in regulating commerce with foreign nations, the power of Congress does not stop at the jurisdictional lines of the several states. It would be a very useless power if it could not pass those lines. The commerce of the United States with foreign nations is that of the whole United States. Every district has a right to participate in it. The deep streams which penetrate our country in every direction pass through the interior of almost every state in the Union, and furnish the means of exercising this right. If Congress has the power to regulate it, that power must be exercised whenever the subject exists. If it exists within the states, if a foreign voyage may commence or terminate at a port within a state, then the power of Congress may be exercised within a state.

This principle is, if possible, still more clear when applied to commerce "among the several States." They either join each other, in which case they are separated by a mathematical line, or they are remote from each other, in which case other states lie between them. What is commerce "among" them; and how is it to be conducted? Can a trading expedition between two adjoining states commence and terminate outside of each? And if the trading intercourse be between two states remote from each other, must it not commence in one, terminate in the other, and probably pass through a third? Commerce among the states must, of necessity, be commerce within the states. In the regulation of trade with the Indian tribes, the action of the law, especially when the Constitution was made, was chiefly within a state. The power of Congress, then, whatever it may be, must be exercised within the territorial jurisdiction of the several states. . . .

We are now arrived at the inquiry, what is this power?

It is the power to regulate; that is, to prescribe the rule by which commerce is to be governed. This power, like all others vested in Congress, is complete in itself, may be exercised to its utmost extent, and acknowledges no limitations other than are prescribed in the Constitution. These are expressed in plain terms, and do not affect the questions which arise in this case, or which have been discussed at the bar. If, as has always been understood, the sovereignty of Congress, though limited to specified objects, is plenary as to those objects, the power over commerce with foreign nations, and among the several states, is vested in Congress as absolutely as it would be in a single government, having in its constitution the same restrictions on the exercise of the power as are found in the Constitution of the United States. . . .

The power of Congress, then, comprehends navigation within the limits of every state in the Union, so far as that navigation may be, in any manner, connected with "commerce with foreign Nations, or among the several States, or with the Indian Tribes." It may, of consequence, pass the jurisdictional line of New York, and act upon the very waters to which the prohibition now under consideration applies.

But it has been urged with great earnestness that, although the power of Congress to regulate commerce with foreign nations, and among the several states, be co-extensive with the subject itself, and have no other limits than are prescribed in the Constitution, yet the states may severally exercise the same power within their respective jurisdictions. In support of this argument, it is said that they possessed it as an inseparable attribute of sovereignty before the formation of the Constitution, and still retain it, except so far as they have surrendered it by that instrument; that this principle results from the nature of the government, and is secured by the Tenth Amendment; that an affirmative grant of power is not exclusive, unless in its own nature it be such that the continued exercise of it by the former possessor is inconsistent with the grant, and that this is not of that description.

The appellate, conceding these postulates, except the last, contends that full power to regulate a particular subject implies the whole power, and leaves no residuum; that a grant of the whole is incompatible with the existence of a right in another to any part of it. . . .

In discussing the question whether this power is still in the states, in the case under consideration, we may dismiss from it the inquiry, whether it is surrendered by the mere grant to Congress, or is retained until Congress shall exercise the power. We may dismiss that inquiry because it has been exercised, and the regulations which Congress deemed it proper to make are now in full operation. The sole question is, Can a state regulate commerce with foreign nations and among the states while Congress is regulating it? . . .

The act passed in 1803, prohibiting the importation of slaves into any state which shall itself prohibit their importation, implies, it is said, an admission that the states possessed the power to exclude or admit them; from which it is inferred that they possess the same power with respect to other articles.

If this inference were correct; if this power was exercised, not under any particular clause in the Constitution, but in virtue of a general right over the subject of commerce, to exist as long as the Constitution itself, it might now be exercised. Any state might now import African slaves into its own territory. But it is obvious that the power of the states over this subject, previous to the year 1808, constitutes an exception to the power of Congress to regulate commerce, and the exception is expressed in such words as to manifest clearly the intention to continue the preexisting right of the states to admit or exclude for a limited period. The words are, "the migration or importation of such persons as any of the states now existing shall think proper to admit, shall not be prohibited by the Congress prior to the year 1808." The whole object of the exception is to preserve the power to those states which might be disposed to exercise it; and its language seems to the Court to convey this idea unequivocally. The possession of this particular power then, during the time limited in the Constitution, cannot be admitted to prove the possession of any other similar power.

It has been said that the act of August 7,

1789, acknowledges a concurrent power in the states to regulate the conduct of pilots, and hence is inferred an admission of their concurrent right with Congress to regulate commerce with foreign nations and amongst the states. But this inference is not, we think, justified by the fact. Although Congress cannot enable a state to legislate, Congress may adopt the provisions of a state on any subject. When the government of the Union was brought into existence, it found a system for the regulation of its pilots in full force in every state. The act which has been mentioned adopts this system, and gives it the same validity as if its provisions had been specially made by Congress. But the act, it may be said, is prospective also, and the adoption of laws to be made in future presupposes the right in the maker to legislate on the subject.

The act unquestionably manifests an intention to leave this subject entirely to the states until Congress should think proper to interpose; but the very enactment of such a law indicates an opinion that it was necessary; that the existing system would not be applicable to the new state of things unless expressly applied to it by Congress. . . .

These acts were cited at the bar for the purpose of showing an opinion in Congress that the states possess, concurrently with the legislature of the Union, the power to regulate commerce with foreign nations and among the states. Upon reviewing them, we think they do not establish the proposition they were intended to prove. They show the opinion that the states retain powers enabling them to pass the laws to which allusion has been made, not that those laws proceed from the particular power which has been delegated to Congress.

It has been contended by the counsel for the appellant that, as the word to "regulate" implies in its nature full power over the thing to be regulated, it excludes, necessarily, the action of all others that would perform the same operation on the same thing. That regulation is designed for the entire result, applying to those parts which

remain as they were, as well as to those which are altered. It produces a uniform whole, which is as much disturbed and deranged by changing what the regulating power designs to leave untouched, as that on which it has operated.

There is great force in this argument, and the Court is not satisfied that it has been refuted.

Since, however, in exercising the power of regulating their own purely internal affairs, whether of trading or police, the states may sometimes enact laws, the validity of which depends on their interfering with, and being contrary to, an act of Congress passed in pursuance of the Constitution, the Court will enter upon the inquiry whether the laws of New York, as expounded by the highest tribunal of that state, have, in their application to this case, come into collision with an act of Congress, and deprived a citizen of a right to which that act entitles him. Should this collision exist, it will be immaterial whether those laws were passed in virtue of a concurrent power "to regulate Commerce with foreign Nations and among the several States," or, in virtue of a power to regulate their domestic trade and police. In one case and the other, the acts of New York must yield to the law of Congress; and the decision sustaining the privilege they confer, against a right given by a law of the Union, must be erroneous. . . .

The questions . . . whether the conveyance of passengers be a part of the coasting trade, and whether a vessel can be protected in that occupation by a coasting license, are not, and cannot be, raised in this case. The real and sole question seems to be, whether a steam machine, in actual use, deprives a vessel of the privileges conferred by a license.

In considering this question, the first idea which presents itself, is that the laws of Congress for the regulation of commerce do not look to the principle by which vessels are moved. That subject is left entirely to individual discretion; and in that vast and complex system of legislative enactment concerning it, which embraces everything which the legislature thought it necessary to notice, there is not, we believe, one word respecting the peculiar principle by which vessels are propelled through the water, except what may be found in a single act, granting a particular privilege to steamboats. With this exception, every act, either prescribing duties, or granting privileges, applies to every vessel, whether navigated by the instrumentality of wind or fire, of sails or machinery. The whole weight of proof, then, is thrown upon him who would introduce a distinction to which the words of the law give no countenance.

If a real difference could be admitted to exist between vessels carrying passengers and others, it has already been observed that there is no fact in this case which can bring up that question. And, if the occupation of steamboats be a matter of such general notoriety that the Court may be presumed to know it, although not specially informed by the record, then we deny that the transportation of passengers is their exclusive occupation. It is a matter of general history, that, in our western waters, their principal employment is the transportation of merchandise; and all know that in the waters of the Atlantic they are frequently so employed.

But all inquiry into this subject seems to the Court to be put completely at rest, by the act already mentioned, entitled, "An Act for the Enrolling and Licensing of Steamboats."

This Act authorizes a steamboat employed, or intended to be employed, only in a river or bay of the United States, owned wholly or in part by an alien, resident within the United States, to be enrolled and licensed as if the same belonged to a citizen of the United States.

This Act demonstrates the opinion of Congress, that steamboats may be enrolled and licensed, in common with vessels using sails. They are, of course, entitled to the same privileges, and can no more be restrained from navigating waters, and entering ports which are free to such vessels, than if they were wafted on their voyage by the winds, instead of being propelled by the agency of fire. The one element may be as legitimately used as the other, for every commercial purpose authorized by the laws of the Union; and the act of a state inhibiting the use of either to any vessel having a license under the act of Congress, comes, we think, in direct collision with that act.

As this decides the cause, it is unnecessary to enter in an examination of that part of the Constitution which empowers Congress to promote the progress of science and the useful arts. . . .

Reversed.

Mr. Justice Johnson rendered a concurring opinion.

ALBERT J. BEVERIDGE, *The Life of John Marshall* [1]

But few events in our history have had a larger and more substantial effect on the well-being of the American people than this decision, and Marshall's opinion in the announcement of it. New York instantly became a free port for all America. Steamboat navigation of American rivers, relieved from the terror of possible and actual state-created monopolies, increased at an incredible rate; and, because of two decades of restraint and fear, at abnormal speed.

New England manufacturers were given a new life, since the transportation of anthracite coal—the fuel recently discovered and aggravatingly needed—was made cheap and easy. The owners of factories, the promoters of steamboat traffic, the innumerable builders of river craft on every navigable stream in the country, the farmer who wished to send his products to market, the manufacturer

1. Albert J. Beveridge, *The Life of John Marshall* (Boston: Houghton Mifflin Company, 1929), Vol. 4, pp. 446–447.

who sought quick and inexpensive transportation of his wares—all acclaimed Marshall's decision because all found in it a means to their own interests.

The possibilities of transportation by steam railways soon became a subject of discussion by enterprising men, and Marshall's opinion gave them tremendous encouragement. It was a guarantee that they might build railroads across State lines and be safe from local interference with interstate traffic. Could the Chief Justice have foreseen the development of the railway as an agency of Nationalism, he would have realized, in part, the permanent and ever-growing importance of his opinion—in part, but not wholly; for the telegraph, the telephone, the oil and gas pipe line were also to be affected for the general good by Marshall's statesmanship as set forth in his outgiving in *Gibbons* v. *Ogden*.

It is not immoderate to say that no other judicial pronouncement in history was so wedded to the inventive genius of man and so interwoven with the economic and social evolution of a nation and a people. After almost a century, Marshall's Nationalist theory of commerce is more potent than ever; and nothing human is more certain than that it will gather new strength as far into the future as forecast can penetrate.

At the time of its delivery, nobody complained of Marshall's opinion except the agents of the steamboat monopoly, the theorists of Localism, and the slave autocracy. All these influences beheld, in Marshall's statesmanship, their inevitable extinction. All correctly understood that the Nationalism expounded by Marshall, if truly carried out, sounded their doom.

THE DANIEL BALL
10 Wallace 557 (1871)

This case began as an action to penalize commercial steamboating on navigable waters of the United States without a federal license. The boat in question operated on the Grand River exclusively *in Michigan* between two Michigan cities.

MR. JUSTICE FIELD delivered the opinion of the Court: . . .

There is, undoubtedly an internal commerce which is subject to the control of the States. The power delegated to Congress is limited to commerce "among the several States," with foreign nations, and with the Indian tribes. This limitation necessarily excludes from federal control all commerce not thus designated and, of course, that commerce which is carried on entirely within the limits of a State, and does not extend to or affect other States. *Gibbons* v. *Ogden*, 9 Wheat. 194. In this case it is admitted that the steamer was engaged in shipping and transporting, down Grand River, goods destined and marked for other States than Michigan, and in receiving and transport-ing up the river goods brought within the State from without its limits; but inasmuch as her agency in the transportation was entirely within the limits of the State, and she did not run in connection with, or in continuation of, any line of vessels or railway leading to other States, it is contended that she was engaged entirely in domestic commerce. But this conclusion does not follow. So far as she was employed in transporting goods destined for other States, or goods brought from without the limits of Michigan and destined to places within that State, she was engaged in commerce between the States, and however limited that commerce may have been, she was, so far as it went, subject to the legislation of Congress. She was employed as an instrument of that commerce; for whenever a commodity has begun to move as an article of trade from one State to another, commerce in that commodity between the States has commenced. The fact that several different and independent agencies are employed in transporting the commodity, some acting entirely in one State, and some acting through two or more States, does in no respect affect the character of the transaction. To the extent in which each agency acts in that transportation, it is subject to the regulation of Congress.

It is said that if the position here asserted be sustained, there is no such thing as the domestic trade of a State; that Congress may take the entire control of the commerce of the country, and extend its regulations to the railroads within a State on which grain or fruit is transported to a distant market.

We answer that the present case relates to transportation on the navigable waters of the United States, and we are not called upon to express an opinion upon the power of Congress over interstate commerce when carried on by land transportation. And we answer further, that we are unable to draw any clear and distinct line between the authority of Congress to regulate an agency employed in commerce between the States, when that agency extends through two or more States, and when it is confined in its action entirely within the limits of a single State. If its authority does not extend to an agency in such commerce when that agency is confined within the limits of a State, its entire authority over interstate commerce may be defeated. Several agencies combining, each taking up the commodity transported at the boundary line at one end of a State, and leaving it at the boundary line at the other end, the federal jurisdiction would be entirely ousted, and the constitutional provision would become a dead letter.

We perceive no error in the record, and the decree of the Circuit Court must be affirmed.

PENSACOLA TELEGRAPH CO. v. *WESTERN UNION*

96 U.S. 1 (1878)

In 1866 Congress provided for a national telegraph system. A Florida law gave exclusive telegraph rights within certain of its counties to a local company in a manner that would frustrate the congressional program. This is an appeal from a Federal Circuit decision upholding the Act of Congress.

MR. CHIEF JUSTICE WAITE delivered the opinion of the court. . . .

Since the case of *Gibbons* v. *Ogden* (9 Wheat. 1), it has never been doubted that commercial intercourse is an element of commerce which comes within the regulating power of Congress. Post-offices and post-roads are established to facilitate the transmission of intelligence. Both commerce and the postal service are placed within the power of Congress, because, being national in their operation, they should be under the protecting care of the national government.

The powers thus granted are not confined to the instrumentalities of commerce, or the postal system known or in use when the Constitution was adopted, but they keep pace with the progress of the country, and adapt themselves to the new developments of times and circumstances. They extend from the horse with its rider to the stage-coach, from the sailing-vessel to the steamboat, from the coach and the steamboat to the railroad, and from the railroad to the telegraph, as these new agencies are successively brought into use to meet the demands of increasing population and wealth. They were intended for the government of the business to which they relate, at all times and under all circumstances. As they were entrusted to the general government for the good of the nation, it is not only the right, but the duty, of Congress to see to it that intercourse among the States and the transmission of intelligence are not obstructed or unnecessarily encumbered by State legislation.

The electric telegraph marks an epoch in the progress of time. In a little more than a quarter of a century it has changed the habits of business, and become one of the necessities of commerce. It is indispensable as a means of inter-communication, but especially is it so in commercial transactions. The statistics of the business before the recent reduction in rates show that more than eighty per cent of all the messages sent by telegraph related to commerce. Goods are sold and money paid upon telegraphic orders. Contracts are made by telegraphic correspondence, cargoes secured, and the movement of ships directed. The telegraphic announcement of the markets abroad regulates prices at home, and a prudent merchant rarely enters upon an important transaction without using the telegraph freely to secure information.

It is not only important to the people, but to the government. . . .

The government of the United States, within the scope of its powers, operates upon every foot of territory under its jurisdiction. It legislates for the whole nation, and is not embarrassed by State lines. Its peculiar duty is to protect one part of the country from encroachments by another upon the national rights which belong to all.

The State of Florida has attempted to confer upon a single corporation the exclusive right of transmitting intelligence by telegraph over a certain portion of its territory. . . . The legislation of Florida, if sustained, excludes all commercial intercourse by telegraph between the citizens of the other States and those residing upon this territory, except by the employment of this corporation. The United States cannot communicate with their own officers by telegraph except in the same way. The State, therefore, clearly has attempted to regulate commercial intercourse between its citizens and those of other States, and to control the transmission of all telegraphic correspondence within its own jurisdiction.

It is unnecessary to decide how far this might have been done if Congress had not acted upon the same subject, for it has acted. The statute of July 24, 1866, in effect, amounts to a prohibition of all State monopolies in this particular. It substantially declares, in the interest of commerce and the convenient transmission of intelligence from place to place by the government of the United States and its citizens, that the erection of telegraph lines shall, so far as State interference is concerned, be free to all who will submit to the conditions imposed by Congress, and that corporations organized under the laws of one State for constructing and operating telegraph lines shall not be excluded by another from prosecuting their business within its jurisdiction, if they accept the terms proposed by the national government for this national privilege. . . .

Decree affirmed.

MR. JUSTICE FIELD and MR. JUSTICE HUNT dissent. . . .

MR. JUSTICE HARLAN did not sit in this case, nor take any part in deciding it.

STATES' RIGHTS AND LAISSEZ-FAIRE

It will be seen that in the foregoing cases (as late as 1878) the commerce power of Congress was generously construed in the spirit of the Virginia Plan (see above) to escape the anarchical conditions that had prevailed under the Articles of Confederation. Then beginning in the 1890s (and continuing until 1937) laissez-faire set in (see the *Knight, Dagenhart, Schechter,* and *Carter* cases, below).

Of course, laissez-faire is an economic, not a constitutional, doctrine, but it found expression (as a restriction on national power) in states' rights and the Tenth Amendment.

Even in the laissez-faire era, however, the broad Virginia Plan conception of national power prevailed in cases not involving laissez-faire interests. This double standard is an aspect of what has been called "dual federalism." It meant that states' rights somehow limited even the *expressly delegated* national powers *for some, but not for all, purposes.* Thus dual federalism protected "reputable" business in its more modern transgressions (e.g., trusts and child labor), but not in such old-fashioned immoralities as prostitution, gambling, impure foods, liquor, narcotics, or "fraudulent" margarine (see cases referred to in *Hammer* v. *Dagenhart* and *Bailey* v. *Drexel Furniture Co.*, below).

It would be erroneous to suppose that the sudden new concern for states' rights in the 1890's brought the states new freedom to manage their own affairs. Quite the contrary! States' rights in this context was merely a device to hamstring national government. Contemporaneously with dual federalism, as we shall see, the courts developed the doctrine of "substantive due process" to save "reputable" business interests from the "sovereign states." Thus did laissez-faire economic doctrine find expression in the Constitution—for a time.

The intellectual underpinnings of the strange laissez-faire interval in American history between 1894 and 1937 had been laid earlier in the Gilded Age—the age of Hill and Fisk, Gould and Vanderbilt, Rockefeller, Sage, Carnegie, and all the others. Richard Hofstadter calls it the era of the Spoilsmen; Parrington called it the age of the Great Barbecue, an allusion to the vast natural resources that were served up in gluttonous portions for exploitation by the great captains of industry. In a brilliant chapter on "The Gospel of Wealth of the Gilded Age," Ralph Gabriel[1] describes the spirit of the times:

The gospel of wealth implied that the government of society in that most important of all areas, the economic, should be in the hands of a natural aristocracy. This leadership should be chosen in the hard school of competition. The rugged individualists assumed that the competitive struggle of the market selects out the weak and the incompetent and puts in positions of power those individuals who are distinguished for initiative, vision, judgment, and organizing ability. The prophets of the gospel of wealth believed that the best interests of society are furthered by putting the government of the economic area of society into the hands of these natural leaders. This ideal, of course, became the fact. . . .

The corollary of the doctrine of natural leadership was the philosophy of the police function of the State. The State exists, taught Porter, McCosh, and Carnegie, to maintain order and protect property. Its activities must be limited to these functions.

The gospel of wealth inevitably implied a philosophy of poverty. Poverty should be for the individual a temporary status. With initiative, industry, and ability he should rise above it. For the masses who do not rise, poverty must be a badge of failure proclaiming that the individual is defective in capacity, or morals, or both.

Of course the old frontier ideal of rugged individualism was cruelly out of place in the age of big business. John D. Rockefeller, founder of the first gargan-

1. Ralph Henry Gabriel, *The Course of American Democratic Thought.* (Copyright 1940 The Ronald Press Company.)

tuan trust—a model for many others—expressed it bluntly: "This movement [toward consolidation] . . . has revolutionized the way of doing business all over the world. The time was ripe for it. It had to come. . . . The day of combination is here to stay. Individualism has gone, never to return." Plainly the gospel of wealth was a smokescreen to hide ugly facts of economic life. By H. D. Lloyd's famous contemporary account, "In an incredible number of the necessaries and luxuries of life, from meat to tombstones, some inner circle of the 'fittest' has sought, and very often obtained, the sweet power which Judge Barrett found the sugar trust had: It 'can close every refinery at will, close some and open others, limit the purchase of raw material (thus jeopardizing, and in considerable degree controlling, its production), artificially limit the production of refined sugar, enhance the price to enrich themselves and their associates at the public expense, and depress the price when necessary to crush out and impoverish a foolhardy rival.'" When the Sherman Anti-Trust Act was passed in 1890 there were fewer than a dozen important trusts with a total capitalization of less than one billion. The great growth of "monopoly" came in the decade following emasculation of that act in the *Sugar Trust* case (*United States* v. *E. C. Knight*). By 1904 Moody could list 318 "greater" or "lesser" industrial combines representing a consolidation of almost 5,300 separate plants with a capitalization of some $7 billion. Worst of all was the "Money Trust." According to the Pujo Committee Report in 1912, the House of Morgan and its associates held 341 directorships in 112 corporations whose total resources were more than $22 billion, that is, more than the total assessed value of all property in the twenty-two states and territories west of the Mississippi and more than double the assessed value of all property in the thirteen southern states.

Of course as it turned out "the masses" were not long willing to accept such exploitation by the "fittest." Before the end of the century labor began to organize. The first upheavals came in the "Great Strike of '77," the Haymarket riot in 1886, and the Homestead and Pullman strikes of 1892 and 1894. As John Mitchell, a leader in the early labor movement, saw it in 1903: "The average wage earner has made up his mind that he must remain a wage earner. He has given up the hope of a kingdom to come, where he himself will be a capitalist, and he asks that the reward for his work be given to him as a working man. Singly, he has been too weak to enforce his just demands . . . he has sought strength in union and has associated himself into labor organizations." The broader implications of the problem were suggested by Washington Gladden in *The Labor Question* (1911): [2]

There is one department of our life, and this the largest interest of all, which has not been democratized. Our industries are still largely on an autocratic or feudalistic basis. We have been trying to correlate a political democracy with an industrial feudalism. They do not work well together. I do not think that they will endure together. . . . The workingmen will lose their political liberty, or they will gain their industrial liberty. I do not think that they will lose their votes; I think that they will gain their right to have a voice in determining what wages they shall receive and under what conditions they shall work. . . .

I am speaking, of course, of the large system of industry under which the world's work is now mainly done. . . . Under this system the capitalist manager

2. Washington Gladden, *The Labor Question.* (Copyright 1911 by the Pilgrim Press.)

assumes the exclusive right to fix the rate of wages, the hours of labor, the conditions under which the work is done. He cannot, of course, discuss these matters
with each of his one thousand or ten thousand workmen; there can, therefore,
be no semblance of a bargain in the case; it is an ultimatum; the employer
presents it, the workingman can take it or leave it. It would be absurd for a
single laborer to propose to chaffer about wages or hours of labor with the
American Steel Corporation or the Pennsylvania Railroad Company. Out of
these circumstances very naturally grows the assumption, on the part of the
employer, that the right as well as the power to fix the laborer's wages belongs
exclusively to him. When, therefore, any man or any body of men proposes to
have something to say about it, he indignantly resents the proposal; he calls it
interfering with his business. What he says to them is precisely this: "It is none
of your business what wages you shall receive; it is my business to tell you how
much you can have, and I cannot permit any one to dictate to me about my
business." . . .

Simultaneously the Granger, Alliance, Greenback, and Populist movements
reflected the farmer's dissatisfaction with the gospel of wealth and what lay
behind it. These political movements ultimately resulted in the Interstate Commerce Act (1887) to regulate the railroads, the Sherman Anti-Trust Act (1890)
and the income tax (1894). The Supreme Court's answer to the labor movement
was "government by injunction," a summary device for sending strike leaders
to jail. *In re Debs,* 158 U.S. 564 (1895). Its simultaneous response to legislative
reform was invalidation of the income tax, *Pollock* v. *Farmers' Loan & Trust Co.,*
and emasculation of the Sherman and Interstate Commerce Acts. *United States*
v. *E. C. Knight;* the *Social Circle* case 162 U.S. 184 (1896), the *Maximum Rate*
case, 167 U.S. 479 (1897). In short, by the end of the nineteenth century the legal
foundations of laissez-faire had been written into the Constitution. The planta-
tion economy had been destroyed forever. Labor had been throttled. Midwestern
agrarian efforts to check the worst abuses of the gilded age, after a brief period
of success prior to the 1890's (e.g. *Munn* v. *Illinois,* 94 U.S. 113 [1876]) had been
checkmated by judicial supremacy (see Part Four, I). Emasculation of the Interstate Commerce Commission left the railroads free to continue their old discriminatory practices without national or state interference.[3] Trusts had obtained
a large degree of immunity from prosecution and their ill-gotten income was tax
exempt. Destruction of the income tax as an alternate source of federal revenue
ended all hope of tariff reform. Thus the consumer—farmer and laborer—was
saddled with the cost of monopoly and the cost of government. Such were the
socioeconomic effects of laissez faire and the gospel of wealth as criteria of
judicial review.

Against this background William Jennings Bryan caught the imagination of
millions in his famous "Cross of Gold" address and crystallized opposition to the
"money power" in the great campaign of 1896. His efforts bore fruit in Teddy
Roosevelt's Square Deal, Wilson's New Freedom, and Franklin Roosevelt's New
Deal. Meanwhile, the gospel of wealth became a defensive mechanism to maintain the status quo. By familiar principles of cultural lag, it lived on in constitutional law long after it had been repudiated at the polls. The end came with the

---

3. National regulation had been undertaken a year after the Court held in the *Wabash* case,
118 U.S. 557 (1886), that interstate railroads could not be regulated by the states.

crisis of the great depression and what Professor Corwin called the "return to the Constitution."

If the wisdom of hindsight permits easy condemnation of the old Court, we must not forget that it lived in an era of revolutionary change. America was moving rapidly from the frontier to the city—from farm to factory. Old ways of life and old values were rudely damaged. Repair came slowly by a painful process of trial and error. In this disturbing flux the Court's fault at worst was adherence amidst uncertainty to old, familiar ideals—ideals which in the abstract at least were held long and persistently by most Americans. Is it not after all the judicial function to hold the consecrated ground until the probing political processes have obtained a secure footing on more promising shores?

UNITED STATES v. *E. C. KNIGHT*

156 U.S. 1 (1895)

MR. CHIEF JUSTICE FULLER . . . delivered the opinion of the court.

By the purchase of the stock of the four Philadelphia refineries, with shares of its own stock, the American Sugar Refining Company acquired nearly complete control of the manufacture of refined sugar within the United States. The bill charged that the contracts under which these purchases were made constituted combinations in restraint of trade, and that in entering into them the defendants combined and conspired to restrain the trade and commerce in refined sugar among the several States and with foreign nations, contrary to the act of Congress of July 2, 1890. . . .

The fundamental question is, whether conceding that the existence of a monopoly in manufacture is established by the evidence, that monopoly can be directly suppressed under the act of Congress in the mode attempted by this bill.

It cannot be denied that the power of the State to protect the lives, health, and property of its citizens, and to preserve good order and the public morals, "the power to govern men and things within the limits of its dominion," is a power originally and always belonging to the States, not surrendered by them to the general government, nor directly restrained by the Constitution of the United States,

and essentially exclusive. The relief of the citizens of each State from the burden of monopoly and the evils resulting from the restraint of trade among such citizens was left with the States to deal with, and this court has recognized their possession of that power even to the extent of holding that an employment or business carried on by private individuals, when it becomes a matter of such public interest and importance as to create a common charge or burden upon the citizen; in other words, when it becomes a practical monopoly, to which the citizen is compelled to resort and by means of which a tribute can be exacted from the community, is subject to regulation by state legislative power. On the other hand, the power of Congress to regulate commerce among the several States is also exclusive. The Constitution does not provide that interstate commerce shall be free, but, by the grant of this exclusive power to regulate it, it was left free except as Congress might impose restraints. Therefore it has been determined that the failure of Congress to exercise this exclusive power in any case is an expression of its will that the subject shall be free from restrictions or impositions upon it by the several States, and if a law passed by a State in the exercise of its acknowledged powers comes into conflict with that will, the Congress and the State cannot occupy the position of equal opposing sovereignties, because the Constitution declares its supremacy and that of the laws passed in pursuance thereof; and that which is not supreme must yield to that which is supreme. "Commerce, undoubtedly, is traffic," said Chief Justice Marshall, "but it is something more; it is intercourse. It describes the commercial intercourse between nations and parts of nations in all its branches, and is regulated by prescribing rules for carrying on that intercourse." That which belongs to commerce is within the jurisdiction of the United States, but that which does not belong to commerce is within the jurisdiction of the police power of the State. . . .

The argument is that the power to control the manufacture of refined sugar is a monopoly over a necessary of life, to the enjoyment of which by a large part of the population of the United States interstate commerce is indispensable, and that, therefore, the general government in the exercise of the power to regulate commerce may repress such monopoly directly and set aside the instruments which have created it. But this argument cannot be confined to necessaries of life merely, and must include all articles of general consumption. Doubtless the power to control the manufacture of a given thing involves in a certain sense the control of its disposition, but this is a secondary and not the primary sense; and although the exercise of that power may result in bringing the operation of commerce into play, it does not control it, and affects it only incidentally and indirectly. Commerce succeeds to manufacture, and is not a part of it. The power to regulate commerce is the power to prescribe the rule by which commerce shall be governed, and is a power independent of the power to suppress monopoly. But it may operate in repression of monopoly whenever that comes within the rules by which commerce is governed or whenever the transaction is itself a monopoly of commerce. . . .

It is vital that the independence of the commercial power and of the police power, and the delimitation between them, however sometimes perplexing, should always be recognized and observed, for while the one furnishes the strongest bond of union, the other is essential to the preservation of the autonomy of the States as required by our dual form of government; and acknowledged evils, however grave and urgent they may appear to be, had better be borne, than the risk be run, in the effort to suppress them, of more serious consequences by resort to expedients of even doubtful constitutionality. . . .

Contracts, combinations, or conspiracies to control domestic enterprise in manufacture, agriculture, mining, production in all its forms, or to raise or lower prices or wages, might unquestionably tend to restrain external as well as domestic trade, but the restraint would be an indirect result, however inevitable and whatever its extent, and such result would not necessarily determine the object of the contract, combination, or conspiracy.

Again, all the authorities agree that in order to vitiate a contract or combination it is not essential that its result should be a complete monopoly; it is sufficient if it really tends to that end and to deprive the public of the advantages which flow from free competition. Slight reflection will show that if the national power extends to all contracts and combinations in manufacture, agriculture, mining, and other productive industries, whose ultimate result may affect external commerce, comparatively little of business operations and affairs would be left for state control.

It was in the light of well-settled principles that the act of July 2, 1890, was framed. Congress did not attempt thereby to assert the power to deal with monopoly directly as such; or to limit and restrict the rights of corporations created by the States or the citizens of the States in the acquisition, control, or disposition of property; or to regulate or prescribe the price or prices at which such property or the products thereof should be sold; or to make criminal the acts of persons in the acquisition and control of property which the States of their residence or creation sanctioned or permitted. Aside from the provisions applicable where Congress might exercise municipal power, what the law struck at was combinations, contracts, and conspiracies to monopolize trade and commerce among the several States or with foreign nations; but the contracts and acts of the defendants related exclusively to the acquisition of the Philadelphia refineries and the business of sugar refining in Pennsylvania, and bore no direct relation to commerce between the States or with foreign nations. . . . There was nothing in the proofs to indicate any intention to put a restraint upon trade or commerce, and the fact, as we have seen, that trade or commerce might be indirectly affected was not enough to entitle complainants to a decree. . . .

Decree affirmed.

MR. JUSTICE HARLAN, dissenting. . . .

What is commerce among the States? The decisions of this court fully answer the question. "Commerce, undoubtedly, is traffic, but it is something more: it is intercourse." It does not embrace the completely interior traffic of the respective States—that which is "carried on between man and man in a State, or between different parts of the same State and which does not extend to or affect other States"—but it does embrace "every species of commercial intercourse" between the United States and foreign nations and among the States, and, therefore, it includes such traffic or trade, buying, selling, and interchange of commodities, as directly affects or necessarily involves the interests of the People of the United States. "Commerce, as the word is used in the Constitution, is a unit," and "cannot stop at the external boundary line of each State, but may be introduced into the interior." "The genius and character of the whole government seem to be, that its action is to be applied to all the external concerns of the nation, *and to those internal concerns which affect the States generally.*"

These principles were announced in *Gibbons* v. *Ogden*, and have often been approved. . . .

In the light of these principles, determining as well the scope of the power to regulate commerce among the States as the nature of such commerce, we are to inquire whether the act of Congress of July 2, 1890 . . . entitled "An act to protect trade and commerce against unlawful restraints and monopolies" . . . is repugnant to the Constitution. . . .

It would seem to be indisputable that no *combination* of corporations or individuals can, *of right*, impose unlawful restraints upon *interstate* trade, whether upon transportation or upon such interstate intercourse and traffic as precede transportation, any more than it can, *of right*, impose unreasonable restraints upon the completely internal traffic of a State. The supposition cannot be indulged that this general proposition will be disputed. If it be true that a *combination* of corporations or individuals may, so far as the power of Congress is concerned, subject interstate trade, in any of its stages, to unlawful restraints, the conclusion is inevitable that the Constitution has failed to accomplish one primary object of the Union, which was to place commerce *among the States* under the control of the common government of all the people, and thereby relieve or protect it against burdens or restrictions imposed, by whatever authority, for the benefit of particular localities or special interests. . . .

The power of Congress covers and protects the absolute freedom of such intercourse and trade among the States as may or must succeed manufacture and precede transportation from the place of purchase. This would seem to be conceded; for, the court in the present case expressly declares that "*contracts to buy*, sell, or exchange goods *to be transported among the several States*, the transportation and its instrumentalities, and articles bought, sold, or exchanged for the purpose of such transit among the States, or put in the way of transit, *may be regulated*, but this is *because they form part of interstate trade or commerce.*" Here is a direct admission—one which the settled doctrines of this court justify—that contracts to buy and the purchasing of goods *to be transported from one State to another,* and transportation, with its instrumentalities, are all *parts* of interstate trade or commerce. Each part of such trade is then under the protection of Congress. And yet, by the opinion and judgment in this case, if I do not misapprehend them, Congress is without power to protect the commercial intercourse that such purchasing necessarily involves against the restraints and burdens arising from the existence of *combinations* that meet purchasers, from whatever State they come, with the threat—for it is nothing more nor less than a threat—that they *shall not* purchase what they desire to purchase, *except at the prices fixed by such combinations.* . . .

In my judgment, the citizens of the several States composing the Union are entitled, of right, to buy goods in the State where they are manufactured, or in any other State, without being confronted by an illegal combination whose business extends throughout the whole country, which by the law everywhere is an enemy to the public interests, and which prevents such buying, except at prices arbitrarily fixed by it. I insist that the free course of trade among the States cannot coexist with such combinations. When I speak of trade I mean the buying and selling of articles of every kind that are recognized articles of interstate commerce. Whatever improperly obstructs the free course of interstate intercourse and trade, as involved in the buying and selling of articles to be carried from one State to another, may be reached by Congress, under its authority to regulate commerce among the States. The exercise of that authority so as to make trade among the States, in all recognized articles of commerce, absolutely free from unreasonable or illegal restrictions imposed by combinations, is justified by an express grant of power to Congress and would redound to the welfare of the whole country. I am unable to perceive that any such result would imperil the autonomy of the States, especially as that result cannot be attained through the action of any one State. . . .

THE SHREVEPORT CASE

234 U.S. 342 (1914)

MR. JUSTICE HUGHES delivered the opinion of the court. . . .

These suits were brought in the Commerce Court . . . to set aside an order of the Interstate Commerce Commission, dated March 11, 1912, upon the ground that it exceeded the Commission's authority. . . .

The gravamen of the complaint, said the Interstate Commerce Commission, was that the carriers made rates out of Dallas and other Texas points into eastern Texas which were much lower than those which they extended into Texas from Shreveport. The situation may be briefly described: Shreveport, Louisiana, is about 40 miles from the Texas state line, and 231 miles from Houston, Texas, on the line of the Houston, East & West Texas and Houston and Shreveport Companies . . . ; it is 189 miles from Dallas, Texas, on the line of the Texas & Pacific. Shreveport competes with both cities for the trade of the intervening territory. The rates on these lines from Dallas and Houston, respectively, eastward to intermediate points, in Texas, were much less, according to distance, than from Shreveport westward to the same points. It is undisputed that the difference was substantial, and injuriously affected the commerce of Shreveport. . . .

The Interstate Commerce Commission [in effect ordered an equalizing increase in the Texas local notes].

The point of the objection to the order is that, as the discrimination found by the Commission to be unjust arises out of the relation of intrastate rates, maintained under state authority, to interstate rates that have been upheld as reasonable, its correction was beyond the Commission's power. . . . The invalidity of the order is challenged upon two grounds:

(1.) That Congress is impotent to control the intrastate charges of an interstate carrier even to the extent necessary to prevent injurious discrimination against interstate traffic. . . .

Congress is empowered to regulate,—that is, to provide the law for the government of interstate commerce; to enact "all appropriate legislation" for its "protection and advancement." . . . As it is competent for Congress to legislate to these ends, unquestionably it may seek their attainment by requiring that the agencies of interstate commerce shall not be used in such manner as to cripple, retard, or destroy it. The fact that carriers are instruments of intrastate commerce, as well as of interstate commerce, does not derogate from the complete and paramount authority of Congress over the latter, or preclude the Federal power from being exerted to prevent the intrastate operations of such carriers from being made a means of injury to that which has been confided to Federal care. Wherever the interstate and intrastate transactions of carriers are so related that the government of the one involves the control of the other, it is Congress, and not the state, that is entitled to prescribe the final and dominant rule, for otherwise Congress would be denied the exercise of its constitutional authority, and the state, and not the nation, would be supreme within the national field. . . .

It is for Congress to supply the needed correction where the relation between intrastate and interstate rates presents the evil to be corrected, and this it may do completely by reason of its control over the interstate carrier in all matters having such a close and substantial relation to interstate commerce that it is necessary or appropriate to exercise the control for the effective government of that commerce.

It is also clear that, in removing the injurious discriminations against interstate traffic arising from the relation of intrastate to interstate rates, Congress is not bound to reduce the latter below what it may deem to be a proper standard fair to the carrier and to the public. Otherwise, it could prevent the injury to interstate commerce only by the sacrifice of its judgment as to interstate rates. Congress is entitled to maintain its own standard as to these rates, and to forbid any discriminatory action by interstate carriers which will obstruct the freedom of movement of interstate traffic over their lines in accordance with the terms it establishes.

Having this power, Congress could provide for its execution through the aid of a subordinate body; and we conclude that the order of the Commission now in question cannot be held invalid upon the ground that it exceeded the authority which Congress could lawfully confer. . . .

Mr. Justice Lurton and Mr. Justice Pitney dissent.

U.S. CHILDREN'S BUREAU, "CHILD LABOR AND THE WELFARE OF CHILDREN IN AN ANTHRACITE COAL-MINING DISTRICT" (1922) [1]

The life of the district revolves around the mines and for the boys more than for their fathers their place of employment was the mines. The canvass made by the Children's Bureau showed that for the district as a whole 90.4 per cent of

1. U.S. Children's Bureau, *Publication No. 116* (1922).

the boys doing full-time work were in mining as compared with 78 per cent of their fathers. . . . The fact that the breakers offered opportunities for profitable employment of young boys is the explanation of the large number of boys employed in connection with the mining of anthracite coal. . . .

These breakers which tower above the town . . . are great barnlike structures filled with chutes, sliding belts, and great crushing and sorting machines. Around these machines a scaffolding was built on which the workers stand or sit. The coal is raised from the mine to the top of the breaker and dumped down the chute into a crushing machine, which breaks it into somewhat smaller lumps. These are carried along a moving belt or gravity incline on each side of which men and boys stand or sit picking out pieces of slate and any coal which has slate mixed with it. . . .

Whatever the hazards and dangers of the breakers are, underground work is much more undesirable for young boys. . . . Young boys were working daily underground at the time this investigation was made. . . . Of the trapper boys, seventeen were only thirteen and three were only twelve years old when they began to do regular full-day duty at this work. . . .

The boys who turned by hand the ventilating fans frequently worked on the dangerous robbing sections where the last remaining coal is being cut away from pillars and walls and where, in consequence, the roof sometimes falls in or the section is filled with a waste material known as slush. The men interviewed told of the nervous strain they experienced when they worked at robbing. Turning the fans for these workers was the first underground work for twelve boys. . . . A few other boys were employed underground, as oilers and laborers doing a variety of work.

HAMMER v. DAGENHART

247 U.S. 251 (1918)

To discourage child labor, Congress in 1916 prohibited the shipment in interstate and foreign commerce of any product of mines or factories which employed children below specified ages, or employed other children in excess of specified hours.

MR. JUSTICE DAY delivered the opinion of the court: . . .

The attack upon the act rests upon three propositions: First: It is not a regulation of interstate and foreign commerce; second: It contravenes the Tenth Amendment to the Constitution; third: It conflicts with the Fifth Amendment to the Constitution.

The controlling question for decision is: Is it within the authority of Congress in regulating commerce among the states to prohibit the transportation in interstate commerce of manufactured goods, the product of a factory in which, within thirty days prior to their removal therefrom,

children under the age of fourteen have been employed or permitted to work, or children between the ages of fourteen and sixteen years have been employed or permitted to work more than eight hours in any day, or more than six days in any week, or after the hour of seven o'clock p.m., or before the hour of 6 o'clock a.m.? . . . But it is insisted that adjudged cases in this court establish the doctrine that the power to regulate given to Congress incidentally includes the authority to prohibit the movement of ordinary commodities and therefore that the subject is not open for discussion. The cases demonstrate the contrary. They rest upon the character of the particular subjects dealt with and the fact that the scope of governmental authority, state or national, possessed over them is such that the authority to prohibit is as to them but the exertion of the power to regulate.

The first of these cases is *Champion* v. *Ames*, 188 U.S. 321, the so-called *Lottery Case*, in which it was held that Congress might pass a law having the effect to keep the channels of commerce free from use in the transportation of tickets used in the promotion of lottery schemes. In *Hipolite Egg Co.* v. *United States*, 220 U.S. 45, this court sustained the power of Congress to pass the Pure Food and Drug Act which prohibited the introduction into the States by means of interstate commerce of impure foods and drugs. In *Hoke* v. *United States*, 227 U.S. 308, this court sustained the constitutionality of the so-called "White Slave Traffic Act" whereby the transportation of a woman in interstate commerce for the purpose of prostitution was forbidden. In that case we said, having reference to the authority of Congress, under the regulatory power, to protect the channels of interstate commerce: "If the facility of interstate transportation can be taken away from the demoralization of lotteries, the debasement of obscene literature, the contagion of diseased cattle or persons, the impurity of food and drugs, the like facility can be taken away from the systematic enticement to, and the enslavement in prostitution and debauchery of women, and, more insistently, of girls."

In *Caminetti* v. *United States*, 242 U.S. 470, we held that Congress might prohibit the transportation of women in interstate commerce for the purposes of debauchery and kindred purposes. In *Clark Distilling Co.* v. *Western Maryland Railway Co.*, 242 U.S. 311, the power of Congress over the transportation of intoxicating liquors was sustained. . . .

In each of these instances the use of interstate transportation was necessary to the accomplishment of harmful results. In other words, although the power over inter-

state transportation was to regulate, that could only be accomplished by prohibiting the use of the facilities of interstate commerce to effect the evil intended.

This element is wanting in the present case. The thing intended to be accomplished by this statute is the denial of the facilities of interstate commerce to those manufacturers in the States who employ children within the prohibited ages. The act in its effect does not regulate transportation among the states, but aims to standardize the ages at which children may be employed in mining and manufacturing within the states. The goods shipped are of themselves harmless. The act permits them to be freely shipped after thirty days from the time of their removal from the factory. When offered for shipment, and before transportation begins, the labor of their production is over, and the mere fact that they were intended for interstate commerce transportation does not make their production subject to federal control under the commerce power.

Commerce "consists of intercourse and traffic . . . and includes the transportation of persons and property, as well as the purchase, sale and exchange of commodities." The making of goods and the mining of coal are not commerce, nor does the fact that these things are to be afterwards shipped, or used in interstate commerce, make their production a part thereof. *Delaware, Lackawanna & Western R.R. Co.* v. *Yurkonis*, 238 U.S. 439.

Over interstate transportation, or its incidents, the regulatory power of Congress is ample, but the production of articles, intended for interstate commerce, is a matter of local regulation.

"When the commerce begins is determined, not by the character of the commodity, nor by the intention of the owner to transfer it to another state for sale, nor by his preparation of it for transportation, but by its actual delivery to a common carrier for transportation, or the actual commencement of its transfer to another state." (Mr. Justice Jackson in *In re Greene*, 52 F. 113). This principle has been recognized often in this court. *Coe* v. *Errol*, 116 U.S. 517; *Bacon* v. *Illinois*, 227 U.S. 504, and cases cited. If it were otherwise, all manufacture intended for interstate shipment would be brought under federal control to the practical exclusion of the authority of the States, a result certainly not contemplated by the framers of the Constitution when they vested in Congress the authority to regulate commerce among the States. *Kidd* v. *Pearson*, 128 U.S. 1, 21.

It is further contended that the authority of Congress may be exerted to control interstate commerce in the shipment of child-made goods because of the effect of the circulation of such goods in other states where the evil of this class of labor has been recognized by local legislation, and the right to thus employ child labor has been more rigorously restrained than in the State of production. In other words, that the unfair competition, thus engendered, may be controlled by closing the channels of interstate commerce to manufacturers in those States where the local laws do not meet what Congress deems to be the more just standard of other States.

There is no power vested in Congress to require the States to exercise their police power so as to prevent possible unfair competition. Many causes may co-operate to give one State, by reason of local laws or conditions, an economic advantage over others. The commerce clause was not intended to give to Congress a general authority to equalize such conditions. In some of the States laws have been passed fixing minimum wages for women, in others the local law regulates the hours of labor of women in various employments. Business done in such States may be at an economic disadvantage when compared with States which have no such regulations; surely, this fact does not give Congress the power to deny transportation in interstate commerce to those who carry on business where the hours of labor and the rate of compensation for women have not been fixed by a standard in use in other States and approved by Congress . . .

That there should be limitations upon the right to employ children in mines and factories in the interest of their own and the public welfare, all will admit. That such employment is generally deemed to require regulation is shown by the fact that the brief of counsel states that every State in the Union has a law upon the subject, limiting the right to thus employ children. In North Carolina, the State wherein is located the factory in which the employment was had in the present case, no child under twelve years of age is permitted to work.

It may be desirable that such laws be uniform, but our Federal Government is one of enumerated powers; "this principle," declared Chief Justice Marshall in *McCulloch* v. *Maryland*, 4 Wheat. 316, "is universally admitted."

A statute must be judged by its natural and reasonable effect. *Collins* v. *New Hampshire*, 171 U.S. 30, 33, 34. The control by Congress over interstate commerce cannot authorize the exercise of authority not entrusted to it by the Constitution. *Pipe Line Case*, 234 U.S. 548, 560. The maintenance of the authority of the States over matters purely local is as essential to the preservation of our institutions as is the conservation of the supremacy of the federal power in all matters entrusted to the Nation by the Federal Constitution.

In interpreting the Constitution it must never be forgotten that the nation is made up of States to which are entrusted the powers of local government. . . . To sustain this statute would not be in our judgment a recognition of the lawful exertion of congressional authority over interstate commerce, but would sanction an invasion by the federal power of the control of a matter purely local in its character, and over which no authority has been delegated to Congress in conferring the power to regulate commerce among the States.

We have neither authority nor disposition to question the motives of Congress in enacting this legislation. The purposes intended must be attained consistently with constitutional limitations and not by an invasion of the powers of the States. This court has no more important function than that which devolves upon it the obligation to preserve inviolate the constitutional limitations upon the exercise of authority federal and state to the end that each may continue to discharge, harmoniously with the other, the duties entrusted to it by the Constitution.

In our view the necessary effect of this act is, by means of a prohibition against the movement in interstate commerce of ordinary commercial commodities to regulate the hours of labor of children in factories and mines within the States, a purely state authority. Thus the act in a two-fold sense is repugnant to the Constitution. It not only transcends the authority delegated to Congress over commerce but also exerts a power as to a purely local matter to which the federal authority does not extend. The far reaching result of upholding the act cannot be more plainly indicated than by pointing out that if Congress can thus regulate matters entrusted to local authority by prohibition of the movement of commodities in interstate commerce, all freedom of commerce will be at an end, and the power of the States over local matters may be eliminated, and thus our system of government be practically destroyed.

For these reasons we hold that this law exceeds the constitutional authority of Congress. It follows that the decree of the District Court must be affirmed.

MR. JUSTICE HOLMES, dissenting: . . .

The first step in my argument is to make plain what no one is likely to dispute—that the statute in question is within the power expressly given to Congress if considered only as to its immediate effects and that if invalid it is so only upon some collateral ground. The statute confines itself to prohibiting the carriage of certain goods in interstate or foreign commerce. Congress is given power to regulate such commerce in unqualified terms. It would not be argued today that the power to regulate does not include the power to prohibit. Regulation means the prohibition of some-

thing, and when interstate commerce is the matter to be regulated I cannot doubt that the regulation may prohibit any part of such commerce that Congress sees fit to forbid. At all events it is established by the *Lottery Case* and others that have followed it that a law is not beyond the regulative power of Congress merely because it prohibits certain transportation out and out. *Champion* v. *Ames*, 188 U.S. 321, 355, 359, et seq. So I repeat that this statute in its immediate operation is clearly within the Congress's constitutional power.

The question then is narrowed to whether the exercise of its otherwise constitutional power by Congress can be pronounced unconstitutional because of its possible reaction upon the conduct of the States in a matter upon which I have admitted that they are free from direct control. I should have thought that that matter had been disposed of so fully as to leave no room for doubt. I should have thought that the most conspicuous decisions of this Court had made it clear that the power to regulate commerce and other constitutional powers could not be cut down or qualified by the fact that it might interfere with the carrying out of the domestic policy of any State. . . .

The Pure Food and Drug Act which was sustained in *Hipolite Egg Co.* v. *United States*, 220 U.S. 45, with the intimation that "no trade can be carried on between the States to which it [the power of Congress to regulate commerce] does not extend," 57, applies not merely to articles that the changing opinions of the time condemn as intrinsically harmful but to others innocent in themselves, simply on the ground that the order for them was induced by a preliminary fraud. *Weeks* v. *United States*, 245 U.S. 618. It does not matter whether the supposed evil precedes or follows the transportation. It is enough that in the opinion of Congress the transportation encourages the evil. . . .

The act does not meddle with anything belonging to the States. They may regulate their internal affairs and their domestic commerce as they like. But when they seek to send their products across the state line they are no longer within their rights. If there were no Constitution and no Congress their power to cross the line would depend upon their neighbors. Under the Constitution such commerce belongs not to the States but to Congress to regulate. It may carry out its views of public policy whatever indirect effect they may have upon the activities of the States. Instead of being encountered by a prohibitive tariff at her boundaries the State encounters the public policy of the United States which it is for Congress to express. The public policy of the United States is shaped with a view to the benefit of the nation as a whole. . . . The national welfare as understood by Congress may require a different attitude within its sphere from that of some self-seeking State. It seems to me entirely constitutional for Congress to enforce its understanding by all the means at its command.

MR. JUSTICE MCKENNA, MR. JUSTICE BRANDEIS, and MR. JUSTICE CLARKE concur in this opinion.

QUAERE: In the *Dagenhart* case the Court accepted as true counsel's proposition that every state in the Union had legislation limiting child labor. Why then did Congress twice find it desirable to pass such legislation? Under the circumstances, could the congressional measures be deemed intrusions upon state policy?

LOWELL MELLETT, "A THANKLESS CHILD" [2]

Some six years after the Court upheld young Reuben Dagenhart's "constitutional" right to work "more hours every day than a boy of fourteen ought to work," Lowell Mellett interviewed the "winner" of that famous litigation:

I found him at his home in Charlotte. He is about the size of the office boy— weighs a hundred and five pounds, he told me. But he is a married man with a child. He is twenty years old.

"What benefit," I asked him, "did you get out of the suit which you won in the United States Supreme Court?" . . .

"I don't see that I got any benefit. I guess I'd been a lot better off if they hadn't won it. Look at me! A hundred and five pounds, a grown man and no education. I may be mistaken, but I think the years I've put in in the cotton mills have stunted my growth. They kept me from getting any schooling. I had to stop school after the third grade and now I need the education I didn't get. . . . From twelve years old on, I was working twelve hours a day—from six in the morning till seven at night, with time out for meals. And sometimes I worked nights besides. Lifting a hundred pounds and I only weighed sixty-five pounds myself." . . .

"Just what did you and John get out of that suit, then?" was asked.

"Why, we got some automobile rides when them big lawyers from the North was down here. Oh, yes, and they bought both of us a coca-cola! That's all we got out of it."

"What did you tell the judge when you were in court?"

"Oh, John and me never was in court! Just Paw was there. John and me was just little kids in short pants. I guess we wouldn't have looked like much in court. We were working in the mill while the case was going on. But Paw went up to Washington." . . .

"It would have been a good thing for all the kids in this state if that law they

2. Lowell Mellett, "How Sharper than a Serpent's Tooth to Have a Thankless Child," in *Labor*, November 17, 1923. (By permission of the author.)

passed had been kept. Of course, they do better now than they used to. You don't see so many babies working in the factories, but you see a lot of them that ought to be going to school."

NOTE on the *Schechter* and *Carter* cases: *Schechter* v. *United States*, 295 U.S. 495 (1935), and *Carter* v. *Carter Coal Co.*, 298 U.S. 238 (1936), struck down respectively the National Industrial Recovery Act (1933) and the Bituminous Coal Act (1935). The one had been designed to control cutthroat competitive business practices and improve working conditions; the other to stabilize prices and improve labor standards in the especially hard-pressed soft coal industry. In both cases, the Court found the "flow" or "stream of commerce" concept inapplicable; i.e., the wholesaling of chickens in New York (*Schechter*), and coal mining (*Carter*), occurred in the one case after, in the other before, the flow of interstate commerce. Here the Court drew upon the old *E. C. Knight* case principle that "manufacturing is not commerce." But if mining and local wholesaling, like manufacturing, are not in themselves commerce, do they not affect commercial affairs in "more states than one"? Compare *Gibbons* v. *Ogden*. Recognizing of necessity that they did, the Court found that such affection was merely "indirect," however extensive; whereas only "direct" effects could bring such matters within the authority of Congress. In short, affection was considered a qualitative, not a quantitative, principle. As Mr. Justice Sutherland expressed it for the Court in *Carter's* case:

The distinction between a direct and an indirect effect turns, not upon the magnitude of either the cause or the effect, but entirely upon the manner in which the effect has been brought about. If the production by one man of a single ton of coal intended for interstate sale and shipment, and actually so sold and shipped, affects interstate commerce [only] indirectly, the effect does not become direct by multiplying the tonnage, or increasing the number of men employed. . . .

Of course, a major part of the coal produced in the coal-mining states is exported for use in other states. Ninety-six percent of the poultry marketed in New York City came from outside the state. Only a few months before *Schechter's* case the same New York City wholesale poultry industry had been found to be within the national commerce power for anti-trust purposes. *Local 167* v. *United States*, 291 U.S. 293 (1934).

THE GREAT DEPRESSION AND THE NEW DEAL

When the stock market crashed in the fall of 1929, the Great Depression was upon us. Within three years there were some 13 million unemployed out of a labor force of 52 million. This meant that one out of four wage-earners could not support himself or his family. The employed in many cases were not much better off. In a wide variety of industries, from steel and iron to textiles, earnings ranged from 20 to 30 cents an hour—and many workers had only part-time employment. One-fourth of the working women in Chicago were getting less than 10 cents an hour.

In 1932, total wages paid were 60 percent less than those of 1929. Dividends were 57 percent less, while American business as a whole operated at a net loss of over five billion dollars. General Motors common stock fell from 72¾ to 7⅝; Radio Corporation from 101 to 2½; United States Steel from 261¾ to 21¼. The rate of business failures was staggering.

Farmers suffered even more, because for them the depression had begun soon after World War I. As A. N. Schlesinger, Jr., wrote in *The Crisis of the Old Order:* [3]

The shadow fell over the cities and towns; it fell as heavily over the country-side. Farmers had already drawn extensively on their savings before 1929. The Wall Street explosion only made their situation worse by diminishing even more the demand for farm products. And, where industry could protect its price structure by meeting reduced demand with reduced output, farmers, unable to control output, saw no way to maintain income except to increase planting. Total crop acreage actually rose in 1930 and showed no significant decline in 1931.

The burden of agricultural adjustment thus fell not on production but on price. The figures were dramatic. Between 1929 and 1934 agricultural production declined 15 percent in volume, 40 percent in price; industrial production 42 percent in volume, 15 percent in price. The relative stability of industrial prices worsened the farmers' terms of trade; the ratio of the prices the farmer received to the prices he paid plunged from 109 in 1919 (in terms of 1910–14 prices) and 89 in 1929 to 64 in 1931. Corn slid down to 15 cents, cotton and wool to 5 cents, hogs and sugar to 3 cents, and beef to 2.5 cents. A farmer who chewed one thick plug of Drummond a day required almost a bushel of wheat a day to keep him in chewing tobacco. It took 16 bushels of wheat—more than the average yield of a whole acre—to buy one of his children a pair of $4 shoes. Net farm income in 1932 was $1.8 billion—less than one-third what it had been three years earlier. So appalling a slump left many farm families with little income, and many with no income at all.

The farmer's obligations—his taxes and his debts—had been calculated in terms of the much higher price levels of the twenties. A cotton farmer who borrowed $800 when cotton was 16 cents a pound, borrowed the equivalent of 5000 pounds of cotton; now, with cotton moving toward 5 cents, he must pay back the debt with over 15,000 pounds of cotton. And, while the farmer's income fell by 64 percent, his burden of indebtedness fell a mere 7 percent. In the meantime, fences were standing in disrepair, crops were rotting, livestock was not worth the freight to market, farm machinery was wearing out. Some found it cheaper to burn their corn than to sell it and buy coal. On every side, notices of mortgage foreclosures and tax sales were going up on gate posts and in country courthouses. William Allen White summed it up: "Every farmer, whether his farm is under mortgage or not, knows that with farm products priced as they are today, sooner or later he must go down."

In the face of such economic disaster, no government responsive to the wishes of its people could be quiescent. Congress and the executive responded with a "New Deal" immediately after the election of President Roosevelt in 1932. But what of laissez-faire and the Supreme Court?

The judicial age that began in 1895 with the emasculation of the Sherman Anti-Trust Act and the destruction of the income tax closed in 1936 with the

3. A. N. Schlesinger, Jr., *The Crisis of the Old Order,* pp. 175–175. Copyright 1957 by Houghton Mifflin Company.

invalidation of the first New Deal effort to solve the farm problem (see *United States* v. *Butler*, below). That decision was but one of seven (including *Schechter* and *Carter*) which together destroyed a major portion of the New Deal effort to alleviate the Great Depression. Then came the crucial election of 1936. Would the people support the New Deal, or would they repudiate it as a flagrant violator of the Constitution? As it turned out President Roosevelt carried all but two states. After this unmatched vindication at the polls he announced a court reorganization plan in February, 1937. It was essentially a device to pack, or unpack, the Supreme Court (according to one's bias). A few weeks later, without any change in its membership, the Court rendered opinions in the *Jones & Laughlin* and *Steward Machine Co.* cases. Note the position of each Justice in these two cases and compare his position in *United States* v. *Butler*. Doubtless this "switch in time" helped defeat the reorganization plan by making it unnecessary. In short, the Court as usual—if a little tardily—had responded to the deeply felt needs and wishes of the American people. Or to put it differently, we returned to the Virginia Plan concept of national power—after some forty-two years (1895–36) of laissez-faire. Thus again, as in crisis after crisis beginning with the one that arose under the Articles of Confederation, we turned to national government for help.

NLRB v. JONES & LAUGHLIN STEEL CORPORATION
301 U.S. 1 (1937)

To improve the purchasing power of labor and to implement the ideals expressed a generation earlier by Mitchell and Gladden (see above), Congress in 1935 passed the Wagner (National Labor Relations) Act. It outlawed employer "unfair labor practices" —i.e., management efforts to prevent unionization and collective bargaining. Finding that Jones & Laughlin had violated the Act, the National Labor Relations Board issued a cease and desist order. This case arose when, pursuant to the statute, the board sought judicial enforcement of its order.

MR. CHIEF JUSTICE HUGHES delivered the opinion of the Court: . . .

Contesting the ruling of the Board, the respondent argues (1) that the Act is in reality a regulation of labor relations and not of interstate commerce; (2) that the Act can have no application to the respondent's relations with its production employees because they are not subject to regulation by the federal government; and (3) that the provisions of the Act violate section 2 of Article III and the Fifth and Seventh Amendments of the Constitution of the United States.

The facts as to the nature and scope of the business of the Jones & Laughlin Steel Corporation have been found by the Labor Board, and, so far as they are essential to the determination of this controversy, they are not in dispute. . . .

Summarizing these operations, the Labor Board concluded that the works in Pittsburgh and Aliquippa "might be likened to the heart of a self-contained, highly integrated body. They draw in the raw materials from Michigan, Minnesota, West Virginia, Pennsylvania in part through arteries and by means controlled by the respondent; they transform the materials and then pump them out to all parts of the nation through the vast mechanism which the respondent has elaborated."

To carry on the activities of the entire steel industry, 33,000 men mine ore, 44,000 men mine coal, 4,000 men quarry limestone, 16,000 men manufacture coke, 343,000 men manufacture steel, and 83,000 men transport its product. Respondent has about 10,000 employees in its Aliquippa plant, which is located in a community of about 30,000 persons. . . .

First. *The scope of the Act.*—. . . The grant of authority to the Board does not purport to extend to the relationship between all industrial employees and employers. Its terms do not impose collective bargaining upon all industry regardless of effects upon interstate or foreign commerce. It purports to reach only what may be deemed to burden or obstruct that commerce and, thus qualified, it must be construed as contemplating the exercise of control within constitutional bounds. It is a familiar principle that acts which directly burden or obstruct interstate or foreign commerce, or its free flow, are within the reach of the congressional power. Acts having that effect are not rendered immune because they grow out of labor disputes. It is the effect upon commerce, not the source of the injury, which is the criterion. Whether or not particular action does affect commerce in such a close and intimate fashion as to be subject to federal control, and hence to lie within the authority conferred upon the Board, is left by the statute to be determined as individual cases arise. We are thus to inquire whether in the instant case the constitutional boundary has been passed.

Second. *The unfair labor practices in question.*—The unfair labor practices found by the Board are those defined in section 8, subdivisions (1) and (3). These provide:

"Sec. 8. It shall be an unfair labor practice for an employer—

"(1) To interfere with, restrain, or coerce employees in the exercise of the rights guaranteed in section 7." . . .

"(3) By discrimination in regard to hire

or tenure of employment or any term or condition of employment to encourage or discourage membership in any labor organization: . . ."

Section 8, subdivision (1), refers to section 7, which is as follows:

"Sec. 7. Employees shall have the right to self-organization, to form, join, or assist labor organizations, to bargain collectively through representatives of their own choosing, and to engage in concerted activities, for the purpose of collective bargaining or other mutual aid or protection."

Thus, in its present application, the statute goes no further than to safeguard the right of employees to self-organization and to select representatives of their own choosing for collective bargaining or other mutual protection without restraint or coercion by their employer.

That is a fundamental right. Employees have as clear a right to organize and select their representatives for lawful purposes as the respondent has to organize its business and select its own officers and agents. Discrimination and coercion to prevent the free exercise of the right of employees to self-organization and representation is a proper subject for condemnation by competent legislative authority. Long ago we stated the reason for labor organizations. We said that they were organized out of the necessities of the situation; that a single employee was helpless in dealing with an employer; that he was dependent ordinarily on his daily wage for the maintenance of himself and family; that if the employer refused to pay him the wages that he thought fair, he was nevertheless unable to leave the employ and resist arbitrary and unfair treatment; that union was essential to give laborers opportunity to deal on an equality with their employer. . . .

Third. *The application of the Act to employees engaged in production.*—*The principle involved.*—Respondent says that whatever may be said of employees engaged in interstate commerce, the industrial relations and activities in the manufacturing department of respondent's enterprise are not subject to federal regulation. The argu-

ment rests upon the proposition that manufacturing in itself is not commerce. [Cit-
ing several cases.]

The fundamental principle is that the
power to regulate commerce is the power
to enact "all appropriate legislation" for "its
protection and advancement" . . . ; to
adopt measures "to promote its growth and
insure its safety" . . . ; "to foster, protect,
control and restrain." . . . That power is
plenary and may be exerted to protect
interstate commerce "no matter what the
source of the dangers which threaten it."
. . . Although activities may be intrastate
in character when separately considered, if
they have such a close and substantial relation to interstate commerce that their control is essential or appropriate to protect
that commerce from burdens and obstructions, Congress cannot be denied the power
to exercise that control. Undoubtedly the
scope of this power must be considered in
the light of our dual system of government
and may not be extended so as to embrace
effects upon interstate commerce so indirect
and remote that to embrace them, in view
of our complex society, would effectually
obliterate the distinction between what is
national and what is local and create a
completely centralized government. The
question is necessarily one of degree. . . .

That intrastate activities, by reason of
close and intimate relation to interstate
commerce, may fall within federal control
is demonstrated in the case of carriers who
are engaged in both interstate and intrastate transportation. There federal control
has been found essential to secure the
freedom of interstate traffic from interference or unjust discrimination and to
promote the efficiency of the interstate
service. *Shreveport Case (Houston, E. &
W. T. R. Co.* v. *United States),* 234 U.S.
342; *Railroad Commission* v. *Chicago,
B. & Q. R. Co.,* 257 U.S. 563. It is manifest
that intrastate rates deal *primarily* with a
local activity. But in rate-making they bear
such a close relation to interstate rates that
effective control of the one must embrace
some control over the other. Under the
Transportation Act, 1920, Congress went

so far as to authorize the Interstate Commerce Commission to establish a state-wide
level of intrastate rates in order to prevent
an unjust discrimination against interstate
commerce. . . .

The close and intimate effect which
brings the subject within the reach of federal power may be due to activities in relation to productive industry although the
industry when separately viewed is local.
This has been abundantly illustrated in the
application of the Federal Anti-Trust Act.
In the *Standard Oil Co. Case,* 221 U.S. 1,
and *American Tobacco Co. Case,* 221 U.S.
106, that statute was applied to combinations of employers engaged in productive
industry. . . .

Upon the same principle, the Anti-Trust
Act has been applied to the conduct of
employees engaged in production. . . .

It is thus apparent that the fact that the
employees here concerned were engaged in
production is not determinative. The question remains as to the effect upon interstate commerce of the labor practice involved. In the *Schechter Case* we found
that the effect there was so remote as to be
beyond the federal power. To find "immediacy or directness" there was to find it
"almost everywhere," a result inconsistent
with the maintenance of our federal system. In the *Carter Case,* 298 U.S. 238, [in
which the Bituminous Coal Conservation
Act of 1935 was struck down] the Court
was of the opinion that the provisions of
the statute relating to production were invalid upon several grounds,—that there
was improper delegation of legislative
power, and that the requirements not only
went beyond any sustainable measure of
protection of interstate commerce but were
also inconsistent with due process. These
cases are not controlling here.

Fourth. *Effects of the unfair labor practice in respondent's enterprise.*—Giving full
weight to respondent's contention with respect to a break in the complete continuity
of the "stream of commerce" by reason of
respondent's manufacturing operations, the
fact remains that the stoppage of those
operations by industrial strife would have a

most serious effect upon interstate commerce. In view of respondent's far-flung activities, it is idle to say that the effect would be indirect or remote. It is obvious that it would be immediate and might be catastrophic. We are asked to shut our eyes to the plainest facts of our national life and to deal with the question of direct and indirect effects in an intellectual vacuum. Because there may be but indirect and remote effects upon interstate commerce in connection with a host of local enterprises throughout the country, it does not follow that other industrial activities do not have such a close and intimate relation to interstate commerce as to make the presence of industrial strife a matter of the most urgent national concern. When industries organize themselves on a national scale, making their relation to interstate commerce the dominant factor in their activities, how can it be maintained that their industrial labor relations constitute a forbidden field into which Congress may not enter when

it is necessary to protect interstate commerce from the paralyzing consequences of industrial war? We have often said that interstate commerce itself is a practical conception. It is equally true that interferences with that commerce must be appraised by a judgment that does not ignore actual experience.

Experience has abundantly demonstrated that the recognition of the right of employees to self-organization and to have representatives of their own choosing for the purpose of collective bargaining is often an essential condition of industrial peace. Refusal to confer and negotiate has been one of the most prolific causes of strife. This is such an outstanding fact in the history of labor disturbances that it is a proper subject of judicial notice and requires no citation of instances.

MR. JUSTICE McREYNOLDS (MR. JUSTICE VAN DEVANTER, MR. JUSTICE SUTHERLAND, and MR. JUSTICE BUTLER concurring with him) dissented.

UNITED STATES v. DARBY LUMBER CO.

312 U.S. 100 (1941)

> The Fair Labor Standards Act of 1938 provided for minimum wages for a forty-hour standard work week, overtime pay for work in excess of forty hours per week, and restrictions upon child labor in certain "interstate" businesses. This case began as a criminal prosecution for violation of the Act.

MR. JUSTICE STONE delivered the opinion of the Court:

The two principal questions raised by the record in this case are, first, whether Congress has constitutional power to prohibit the shipment in interstate commerce of lumber manufactured by employees whose wages are less than a prescribed minimum or whose weekly hours of labor at that wage are greater than a prescribed maximum, and, second, whether it has power to prohibit the employment of workmen in the production of goods "for interstate commerce" at other than prescribed wages and hours. A subsidiary question is

whether in connection with such prohibitions Congress can require the employer subject to them to keep records showing the hours worked each day and week by each of his employees including those engaged "in the production and manufacture of goods to wit, lumber for 'interstate commerce.'" . . .

The prohibition of shipment of the proscribed goods in interstate commerce. Section 15(*a*) (1) prohibits, and the indictment charges, the shipment in interstate commerce, of goods produced for interstate commerce by employees whose wages and hours of employment do not conform to the requirements of the Act. Since this section is not violated unless the commodity shipped has been produced under labor conditions prohibited by section 6 and section 7, the only question arising under the commerce clause with respect to such shipments is whether Congress has the constitutional power to prohibit them.

While manufacture is not of itself interstate commerce, the shipment of manufactured goods interstate is such commerce and the prohibition of such shipment by Congress is indubitably a regulation of the commerce. The power to regulate commerce is the power "to prescribe the rule by which commerce is to be governed." *Gibbons* v. *Ogden*, 9 Wheat. 1, 196. It extends not only to those regulations which aid, foster, and protect the commerce, but embraces those which prohibit it. It is conceded that the power of Congress to prohibit transportation in interstate commerce includes noxious articles, *Lottery Case*, 188 U.S. 321; stolen articles, *Brooks* v. *United States*, 267 U.S. 432; kidnapped persons, *Gooch* v. *United States*, 297 U.S. 124; and articles such as intoxicating liquor or convict made goods, traffic in which is forbidden or restricted by the laws of the state of destination. *Kentucky Whip & Collar Co.* v. *Illinois Central R. Co.*, 299 U.S. 334.

But it is said that the present prohibition falls within the scope of none of these categories; that while the prohibition is nominally a regulation of the commerce its motive or purpose is regulation of wages and hours of persons engaged in manufacture, the control of which has been reserved to the states and upon which Georgia and some of the states of destination have placed no restriction; that the effect of the present statute is not to exclude the prescribed articles from interstate commerce in aid of state regulations as in *Kentucky Whip & Collar Co.* v. *Illinois Central R. Co.*, *supra*, but instead under the guise of a regulation of interstate commerce, it undertakes to regulate wages and hours within the state contrary to the policy of the state which has elected to leave them unregulated.

The power of Congress over interstate commerce "is complete in itself, may be exercised to its utmost extent, and acknowledges no limitations other than are prescribed in the Constitution." *Gibbons* v. *Ogden*, *supra*. That power can neither be enlarged nor diminished by the exercise or non-exercise of state power. *Kentucky Whip & Collar Co.* v. *Illinois Central R. Co. supra*. Congress, following its own conception of public policy concerning the restrictions which may appropriately be imposed on interstate commerce, is free to exclude from the commerce articles whose use in the states for which they are destined it may conceive to be injurious to the public health, morals or welfare, even though the state has not sought to regulate their use.

Such regulation is not forbidden invasion of state power merely because either its motive or its consequence is to restrict the use of articles of commerce within the states of destination; and is not prohibited unless by other constitutional provisions. It is no objection to the assertion of the power to regulate interstate commerce that its exercise is attended by the same incidents which attend the exercise of the police power of the states.

The motive and purpose of the present regulation are plainly to make effective the congressional conception of public policy that interstate commerce should not be made the instrument of competition in the distribution of goods produced under substandard labor conditions, which competition is injurious to the commerce and to the states from and to which the commerce flows. The motive and purpose of a regulation of interstate commerce are matters for the legislative judgment upon the exercise of which the Constitution places no restriction and over which the Courts are given no control. *McCray* v. *United States*, 195 U.S. 27; *Sonzinsky* v. *United States*, 300 U.S. 506, 513. "The judicial cannot prescribe to the legislative department of the government limitations upon the exercise of its acknowledged power." *Veazie Bank* v. *Fenno*, 8 Wall. 533, 548. Whatever their motive and purpose, regulations of commerce which do not infringe some constitutional prohibition are within the plenary power conferred on Congress by the commerce clause. Subject only to that limitation, presently to be considered, we conclude that the prohibition of the shipment interstate of goods produced under the forbidden substandard labor conditions is within the constitutional authority of Congress.

In the more than a century which has elapsed since the decision of *Gibbons* v. *Ogden,* these principles of constitutional interpretation have been so long and repeatedly recognized by this Court as applicable to the commerce clause, that there would be little occasion for repeating them now were it not for the decision of this Court 22 years ago in *Hammer* v. *Dagenhart,* 247 U.S. 251. In that case it was held by a bare majority of the Court over the powerful and now classic dissent of Mr. Justice Holmes setting forth the fundamental issues involved, that Congress was without power to exclude the products of child labor from interstate commerce. The reasoning and conclusion of the Court's opinion there cannot be reconciled with the conclusion which we have reached, that the power of Congress under the commerce clause is plenary to exclude any article from interstate commerce subject only to the specific prohibitions of the Constitution.

Hammer v. *Dagenhart* has not been followed. The distinction on which the decision was rested that congressional power to prohibit interstate commerce is limited to articles which in themselves have some harmful or deleterious property—a distinction which was novel when made and unsupported by any provision of the Constitution—has long since been abandoned. *Brooks* v. *United States,* 267 U.S. 432; *Kentucky Whip & Collar Co.* v. *Illinois C. R. Co.,* 299 U.S. 334; *Mulford* v. *Smith,* 307 U.S. 38. The thesis of the opinion that the motive of the prohibition or its effect to control in some measure the use or pro-

duction within the states of the article thus excluded from the commerce can operate to deprive the regulation of its constitutional authority has long since ceased to have force. And finally we have declared "The authority of the federal government over interstate commerce does not differ in extent or character from that retained by the states over intrastate commerce." *United States* v. *Rock Royal Co-operative,* 307 U.S. 533, 569.

The conclusion is inescapable that *Hammer* v. *Dagenhart* was a departure from the principles which have prevailed in the interpretation of the commerce clause both before and since the decision and that such vitality, as a precedent, as it then had has long since been exhausted. It should be and now is overruled.

Validity of the wage and hour requirements. Section 15(a) (2) and sections 6 and 7 require employers to conform to the wage and hour provisions with respect to all employees engaged in the production of goods for interstate commerce. As appellee's employees are not alleged to be "engaged in interstate commerce" the validity of the prohibition turns on the question whether the employment, under other than the prescribed labor standards, of employees engaged in the production of goods for interstate commerce is so related to the commerce and so affects it as to be within the reach of the power of Congress to regulate it.

To answer this question we must at the outset determine whether the particular acts charged in the counts which are laid under section 15(a) (2) as they were construed below, constitute "production for commerce" within the meaning of the statute. As the government seeks to apply the statute in the indictment, and as the court below construed the phrase "produced for interstate commerce," it embraces at least the case where an employer engaged, as is appellee, in the manufacture and shipment of goods in filling orders of extrastate customers, manufactures his product with the intent or expectation that according to the normal course of his business all or some part of it will be selected for shipment to those customers.

Without attempting to define the precise limits of the phrase, we think the acts alleged in the indictment are within the sweep of the statute. The obvious purpose of the Act was not only to prevent the interstate transportation of the proscribed product, but to stop the initial step toward transportation, production with the purpose of so transporting it. Congress was not unaware that most manufacturing businesses shipping their product in interstate commerce make it in their shops without reference to its ultimate destination and then after manufacture select some of it for shipment interstate and some intrastate according to the daily demands of their business, and that it would be practically impossible, without disrupting manufacturing businesses, to restrict the prohibited kind of production to the particular pieces of lumber, cloth, furniture or the like which later move in interstate rather than intrastate commerce.

The recognized need of drafting a workable statute and the well-known circumstances in which it was to be applied are persuasive of the conclusion, which the legislative history supports, that the "production for commerce" intended includes at least production of goods, which, at the time of production, the employer, according to the normal course of his business, intends or expects to move in interstate commerce although, through the exigencies of the business, all of the goods may not thereafter actually enter interstate commerce.

There remains the question whether such restriction on the production of goods for commerce is a permissible exercise of the commerce power. The power of Congress over interstate commerce is not confined to the regulation of commerce among the states. It extends to those activities intrastate which so affect interstate commerce or the exercise of the power of Congress over it as to make regulation of them appropriate means to the attainment of a legitimate end, the exercise of the granted power of Congress to regulate interstate commerce. See *McCulloch* v. *Maryland,* 4 Wheat. 316, 421. . . .

Congress, having by the present Act adopted the policy of excluding from interstate commerce all goods produced for the commerce which do not conform to the specified labor standards, it may choose the means reasonably adapted to the attainment of the permitted end, even though they involve control of intrastate activities. . . . A familiar like exercise of power is the regulation of intrastate transactions which are so commingled with or related to interstate commerce that all must be regulated if the interstate commerce is to be effectively controlled. *Shreveport Case,* 234 U.S. 342. Similarly Congress may require inspection and preventive treatment of all cattle in a disease-infected area in order to prevent shipment in interstate commerce of some of the cattle without the treatment. *Thornton* v. *United States,* 271 U.S. 414. It may prohibit the removal, at destination, of labels required by the Pure Food & Drugs Act to be affixed to articles transported in interstate commerce. *McDermott* v. *Wisconsin,* 228 U.S. 115. And we have recently held that Congress in the exercise of its power to require inspection and grading of tobacco shipped in interstate commerce may compel such inspection and grading of all tobacco sold at local auction rooms from which a substantial part but not all of the tobacco sold is shipped in interstate commerce. *Currin* v. *Wallace,* 306 U.S. 11. . . .

We think also that section 15(a) (2), now under consideration, is sustainable independently of section 15(a) (1), which prohibits shipment or transportation of the proscribed goods. As we have said the evils aimed at by the Act are the spread of substandard labor conditions through the use of the facilities of interstate commerce for competition by the goods so produced with those produced under the prescribed or better labor conditions; and the consequent dislocation of the commerce itself caused by the impairment or destruction of local businesses by competition made effective through interstate commerce. The Act is thus directed at the suppression of a method or kind of competition in interstate commerce which it has in effect condemned as "unfair," as the Clayton Act, 38 Stat. 730, has condemned other "unfair methods of competition" made effective through interstate commerce.

The Sherman Act and the National Labor Relations Act are familiar examples of the exertion of the commerce power to prohibit or control activities wholly intrastate because of their effect on interstate commerce. . . .

The means adopted by section 15(a) (2) for the protection of interstate commerce by the suppression of the production of the condemned goods for interstate commerce is so related to the commerce and so affects it as to be within the reach of the commerce power. Congress, to attain its objective in the suppression of nation-wide competition in interstate commerce by goods produced under substandard labor conditions, has made no distinction as to the volume or amount of shipments in the commerce or of production for commerce by any particular shipper or producer. It recognized that in present day industry, competition by a small part may affect the whole and that the total effect of the competition of many small producers may be great. See H. Rept. No. 2182, 75th Cong. 1st Sess., p. 7. The legislation aimed at a whole embraces all its parts. Cf. *National Labor Relations Board* v. *Fainblatt*, 306 U.S. 601, 606. . . .

Our conclusion is unaffected by the Tenth Amendment which provides: "The powers not delegated to the United States by the Constitution, nor prohibited by it to the States, are reserved to the States respectively, or to the people." The Amendment states but a truism that all is retained which has not been surrendered. There is nothing in the history of its adoption to suggest that it was more than declaratory of the relationship between the national and state governments as it had been established by the Constitution before the Amendment or that its purpose was other than to allay fears that the new national government might seek to exercise powers not granted, and that the states might not be able to exercise fully their reserved powers.

From the beginning and for many years the Amendment has been construed as not depriving the national government of authority to resort to all means for the exercise of a granted power which are appropriate and plainly adapted to the permitted end. Whatever doubts may have arisen of the soundness of that conclusion they have been put at rest by the decisions under the Sherman Act and the National Labor Relations Act which we have cited.

Validity of the requirement of records of wages and hours. Section 15(a) (5) and section 11(c). These requirements are incidental to those for the prescribed wages and hours, and hence validity of the former turns on validity of the latter. Since, as we have held, Congress may require production for interstate commerce to conform to those conditions, it may require the employer, as a means of enforcing the valid law, to keep a record showing whether he has in fact complied with it. The requirement for records even of the intrastate transaction is an appropriate means to the legitimate end. . . .

Reversed.

WICKARD v. FILBURN

317 U.S. 111 (1942)

The second Agricultural Adjustment Act, i.e., the act of 1938, as amended, sought to stabilize the price of farm goods and adjust supply to market needs by establishing a marketing quota for each participating farm. Penalties were prescribed for violation of assigned quotas. The issue in this case was whether wheat grown by Filburn and consumed on his own farm could be counted in determining whether he had exceeded his quota. The contention, of course, was that such wheat, never shipped or intended for shipment in interstate commerce, was not within the regulatory power of Congress.

MR. JUSTICE JACKSON delivered the opinion of the Court: . . .

In July of 1940, pursuant to the Agricultural Adjustment Act of 1938, as then amended, there was established for the appellee's 1941 crop a wheat acreage allotment of 11.1 acres and a normal yield of 20.1 bushels of wheat an acre. He was given notice of such allotment in July of 1940 before the Fall planting of his 1941 crop of wheat, and again in July of 1941, before it was harvested. He sowed, however, 23 acres, and harvested from his 11.9 acres of excess acreage 239 bushels, which under the terms of the Act as amended on May 26, 1941, constituted farm marketing excess, subject to a penalty of 49 cents a bushel, or $117.11 in all. The appellee has not paid the penalty and he has not postponed or avoided it by storing the excess under regulations of the Secretary of Agriculture, or by delivering it up to the Secretary. The Committee, therefore, refused him a marketing card, which was, under the terms of regulations promulgated by the Secretary, necessary to protect a buyer from liability to the penalty and upon its protecting lien.

The general scheme of the Agricultural Adjustment Act of 1938 as related to wheat is to control the volume moving in interstate and foreign commerce in order to avoid surpluses and shortages and the consequent abnormally low or high wheat prices and obstructions to commerce. Within prescribed limits and by prescribed standards the Secretary of Agriculture is directed to ascertain and proclaim each year a national acreage allotment for the next crop of wheat, which is then apportioned to the states and their counties, and is eventually broken up into allotments for individual farms. Loans and payments to wheat farmers are authorized in stated circumstances.

The Act provides further that whenever it appears that the total supply of wheat as of the beginning of any marketing year, beginning July 1, will exceed a normal year's domestic consumption and export by more than 35 percent, the Secretary shall so proclaim not later than May 15 prior to the beginning of such marketing year; and that during the marketing year a compulsory national marketing quota shall be in effect with respect to the marketing of wheat. Between the issuance of the proclamation and June 10, the Secretary must, however, conduct a referendum of farmers who will be subject to the quota to determine whether they favor or oppose it; and if more than one third of the farmers voting in the referendum do oppose, the Secretary must prior to the effective date of the quota by proclamation suspend its operation. . . .

It is urged that under the commerce clause of the Constitution, Article I, section 8, clause 3, Congress does not possess the power it has in this instance sought to exercise. The question would merit little consideration since our decision in *United States* v. *Darby*, 312 U.S. 100, sustaining the federal power to regulate production of goods for commerce except for the fact that this Act extends federal regulation to production not intended in any part for commerce, but wholly for consumption on the farm. The Act includes a definition of "market" and its derivatives so that as related to wheat in addition to its conventional meaning it also means to dispose of "by feeding (in any form) to poultry or livestock which, or the products of which, are sold, bartered, or exchanged, or to be so disposed of." Hence, marketing quotas not only embrace all that may be sold without penalty but also what may be consumed on the premises. Wheat produced on excess acreage is designated as "available for marketing" as so defined and the penalty is imposed thereon. Penalties do not depend upon whether any part of the wheat either within or without the quota is sold or intended to be sold. The sum of this is that the federal government fixes a quota including all that the farmer may harvest for sale or for his own farm needs, and declares that wheat produced on excess acreage may neither be disposed of nor used except upon payment of the penalty or except it is stored as required by the Act or delivered to the Secretary of Agriculture.

Appellee says that this is a regulation of production and consumption of wheat. Such activities are, he urges, beyond the reach of congressional power under the commerce clause, since they are local in character, and their effects upon interstate commerce are at most "indirect." In answer the government argues that the statute regulates neither production nor consumption, but only marketing; and, in the alternative, that if the Act does go beyond the regulation of marketing it is sustainable as a "necessary and proper" implementation of the power of Congress over interstate commerce.

The government's concern lest the Act be held to be a regulation of production or consumption rather than of marketing is attributable to a few dicta and decisions of this Court which might be understood to lay it down that activities such as "production," "manufacturing," and "mining" are strictly "local" and, except in special circumstances which are not present here, cannot be regulated under the commerce power because their effects upon interstate commerce are, as matter of law, only "indirect." Even today, when this power has been held to have great latitude, there is no decision of this Court that such activities may be regulated where no part of the product is intended for interstate commerce or intermingled with the subjects thereof. We believe that a review of the course of decision under the commerce clause will make plain, however, that questions of the power of Congress are not to be decided by reference to any formula which would

give controlling force to nomenclature such as "production" and "indirect" and foreclose consideration of the actual effects of the activity in question upon interstate commerce.

At the beginning Chief Justice Marshall described the federal commerce power with a breadth never yet exceeded. *Gibbons* v. *Ogden*, 9 Wheat. 1, 194, 195. He made emphatic the embracing and penetrating nature of this power by warning that effective restraints on its exercise must proceed from political rather than from judicial processes. 9 Wheat. at page 197.

For nearly a century, however, decisions of this Court under the commerce clause dealt rarely with questions of what Congress might do in the exercise of its granted power under the clause and almost entirely with the permissibility of state activity which it was claimed discriminated against or burdened interstate commerce. During this period there was perhaps little occasion for the affirmative exercise of the commerce power, and the influence of the clause on American life and law was a negative one, resulting almost wholly from its operation as a restraint upon the powers of the states. In discussion and decision the point of reference instead of being what was "necessary and proper" to the exercise by Congress of its granted power, was often some concept of sovereignty thought to be implicit in the status of statehood. Certain activities such as "production," "manufacturing," and "mining" were occasionally said to be within the province of state governments and beyond the power of Congress under the commerce clause.

It was not until 1887 with the enactment of the Interstate Commerce Act that the interstate commerce power began to exert positive influence in American law and life. This first important federal resort to the commerce power was followed in 1890 by the Sherman Anti-Trust Act and, thereafter, mainly after 1903, by many others. These statutes ushered in new phases of adjudication, which required the Court to approach the interpretation of the commerce clause in the light of an actual exercise by Congress of its power thereunder.

When it first dealt with this new legislation, the Court adhered to its earlier pronouncements, and allowed but little scope to the power of Congress. *United States v. E. C. Knight Co.,* 156 U.S. 1. These earlier pronouncements also played an important part in several of the five cases in which this Court later held that acts of Congress under the commerce clause were in excess of its power.

Even while important opinions in this line of restrictive authority were being written, however, other cases called forth broader interpretations of the commerce clause destined to supersede the earlier ones, and to bring about a return to the principles first enunciated by Chief Justice Marshall in *Gibbons* v. *Ogden, supra.*

Not long after the decision of *United States* v. *E. C. Knight Co., supra,* Mr. Justice Holmes, in sustaining the exercise of national power over intrastate activity, stated for the Court that "commerce among the states is not a technical legal conception, but a practical one, drawn from the course of business." *Swift & Co.* v. *United States,* 196 U.S. 375, 398. It was soon demonstrated that the effects of many kinds of intrastate activity upon interstate commerce were such as to make them a proper subject of federal regulation. In some cases sustaining the exercise of federal power over intrastate matters the term "direct" was used for the purpose of stating, rather than of reaching, a result; in others it was treated as synonymous with "substantial" or "material"; and in others it was not used at all. Of late its use has been abandoned in cases dealing with questions of federal power under the commerce clause.

In the *Shreveport Rate Cases (Houston, E. & W. T. R. Co.* v. *United States),* 234 U.S. 342, the Court held that railroad rates of an admittedly intrastate character and fixed by authority of the state might, nevertheless, be revised by the federal government because of the economic effects which they had upon interstate commerce. The opinion of Mr. Justice Hughes found federal intervention constitutionally author-ized because of "matters having such a close and substantial relation to interstate traffic that the control is essential or appropriate to the security of that traffic, to the efficiency of the interstate service, and to the maintenance of the conditions under which interstate commerce may be conducted upon fair terms and without molestation or hindrance." 234 U.S. at page 351.

The Court's recognition of the relevance of the economic effects in the application of the commerce clause exemplified by this statement has made the mechanical application of legal formulas no longer feasible. Once an economic measure of the reach of the power granted to Congress in the commerce clause is accepted, questions of federal power cannot be decided simply by finding the activity in question to be "production" nor can consideration of its economic effects be foreclosed by calling them "indirect." The present Chief Justice has said in summary of the present state of the law: "The commerce power is not confined in its exercise to the regulation of commerce among the states. It extends to those activities intrastate which so affect interstate commerce, or the exertion of the power of Congress over it, as to make regulation of them appropriate means to the attainment of a legitimate end, the effective execution of the granted power to regulate interstate commerce. . . . The power of Congress over interstate commerce is plenary and complete in itself, may be exercised to its utmost extent, and acknowledges no limitations other than are prescribed in the Constitution. . . . It follows that no form of state activity can constitutionally thwart the regulatory power granted by the commerce clause to Congress. Hence the reach of that power extends to those intrastate activities which in a substantial way interfere with or obstruct the exercise of the granted power." *United States* v. *Wrightwood Dairy Co.,* 315 U.S. 110, 119.

Whether the subject of the regulation in question was "production," "consumption," or "marketing" is, therefore, not material for purposes of deciding the question of federal power before us. That an activity is of local character may help in a doubtful case to determine whether Congress intended to reach it. The same consideration might help in determining whether in the absence of congressional action it would be permissible for the state to exert its power on the subject matter, even though in so doing it to some degree affected interstate commerce. But even if appellant's activity be local and though it may not be regarded as commerce, it may still, whatever its nature, be reached by Congress if it exerts a substantial economic effect on interstate commerce and this irrespective of whether such effect is what might at some earlier time have been defined as "direct" or "indirect."

The parties have stipulated a summary of the economics of the wheat industry. Commerce among the states in wheat is large and important. Although wheat is raised in every state but one, production in most states is not equal to consumption. Sixteen states on average have had a surplus of wheat above their own requirements for feed, seed, and food. Thirty-two states and the District of Columbia, where production has been below consumption, have looked to these surplus-producing states for their supply as well as for wheat for export and carryover.

The wheat industry has been a problem industry for some years. Largely as a result of increased foreign production and import restrictions, annual exports of wheat and flour from the United States during the ten-year period ending in 1940 averaged less than 10 percent of total production, while during the 1920's they averaged more than 25 percent. The decline in the export trade has left a large surplus in production which in connection with an abnormally large supply of wheat and other grains in recent years caused congestion in a number of markets; tied up railroad cars; and caused elevators in some instances to turn away grains, and railroads to institute embargoes to prevent further congestion.

Many countries, both importing and ex-

porting, have sought to modify the impact of the world market conditions on their own economy. Importing countries have taken measures to stimulate production and self-sufficiency. The four large exporting countries of Argentina, Australia, Canada, and the United States have all undertaken various programs for the relief of growers. Such measures have been designed in part at least to protect the domestic price received by producers. Such plans have generally evolved towards control by the central government.

In the absence of regulation the price of wheat in the United States would be much affected by world conditions. During 1941 producers who cooperated with the Agricultural Adjustment program received an average price on the farm of about $1.16 a bushel as compared with the world market price of 40 cents a bushel.

Differences in farming conditions, however, make these benefits mean different things to different wheat growers. There are several large areas of specialization in wheat, and the concentration on this crop reaches 27 percent of the crop land, and the average harvest runs as high as 155 acres. Except for some use of wheat as stock feed and for seed, the practice is to sell the crop for cash. Wheat from such areas constitutes the bulk of the interstate commerce therein.

On the other hand, in some New England states less than 1 percent of the crop land is devoted to wheat, and the average harvest is less than five acres per farm. In 1940 the average percentage of the total wheat production that was sold in each state as measured by value ranged from 29 percent thereof in Wisconsin to 90 percent in Washington. Except in regions of large-scale production, wheat is usually grown in rotation with other crops; for a nurse crop for grass seeding; and as a cover crop to prevent soil erosion and leaching. Some is sold, some kept for seed, and a percentage of the total production much larger than in areas of specialization is consumed on the farm and grown for such purpose. Such farmers, while growing some wheat, may even find the balance of their interest on the consumer's side.

The effect of consumption of home-grown wheat on interstate commerce is due to the fact that it constitutes the most variable factor in the disappearance of the wheat crop. Consumption on the farm where grown appears to vary in an amount greater than 20 percent of average production. The total amount of wheat consumed as food varies but relatively little, and use as seed is relatively constant.

The maintenance by government regulation of a price for wheat undoubtedly can be accomplished as effectively by sustaining or increasing the demand as by limiting the supply. The effect of the statute before us is to restrict the amount which may be produced for market and the extent as well to which one may forestall resort to the market by producing to meet his own needs. That appellee's own contribution to the demand for wheat may be trivial by itself is not enough to remove him from the scope of federal regulation where, as here, his contribution, taken together with that of many others similarly situated, is far from trivial. *National Labor Relations Board* v. *Fainblatt*, 306 U.S. 601, 606, *et seq.*, 307 U.S. 609; *United States* v. *Darby*, *supra*, 312 U.S. at page 123.

It is well established by decisions of this Court that the power to regulate commerce includes the power to regulate the prices at which commodities in that commerce are dealt in and practices affecting such prices. One of the primary purposes of the Act in question was to increase the market price of wheat and to that end to limit the volume thereof that could affect the market. It can hardly be denied that a factor of such volume and variability as home-consumed wheat would have a substantial influence on price and market conditions. This may arise because being in marketable condition such wheat overhangs the market and, if induced by rising prices, tends to flow into the market and check price increases. But if we assume that it is never marketed, it supplies a need of the man who grew it which would otherwise be reflected by purchases in the open market. Home-grown wheat in this sense competes with wheat in commerce. The stimulation of commerce is a use of the regulatory function quite as definitely as prohibitions or restrictions thereon. This record leaves us in no doubt that Congress may properly have considered that wheat consumed on the farm where grown if wholly outside the scheme of regulation would have a substantial effect in defeating and obstructing its purpose to stimulate trade therein at increased prices. . . .

Reversed.

HEART OF ATLANTA MOTEL v. *UNITED STATES*
85 S. Ct. 348 (1964)

The motel involved here is located in Atlanta, Georgia, and is "readily accessible" to two interstate highways. It "solicits patronage from outside the State of Georgia through various national advertising media, including magazines of national circulation . . . ; it accepts convention trade from outside Georgia and approximately 75% of its registered guests are from out of state." Refusing to accept Negro patronage, it was charged with violating Title II of the Civil Rights Act of 1964, which prohibits racial discrimination in any business establishment if it "is a place of public accommodation" and "if its operations affect [interstate] commerce."

Admittedly the motel's operations brought it within the act. The question was: Is the act within the commerce power of Congress?

MR. JUSTICE CLARK delivered the opinion of the Court. . . .

While the Act as adopted carried no congressional findings the record of its passage through each house is replete with evidence of the burdens that discrimination by race or color places upon interstate commerce. See Hearings before Senate Committee on Commerce on S. 1732, 88th Cong., 1st Sess.; S. Rep. No. 872, *supra*; Hearings before Senate Committee on the Judiciary on S. 1731, 88th Cong., 1st Sess.; Hearings before House Subcommittee No. 5 on miscellaneous proposals regarding Civil Rights, 88th Cong., 1st Sess., ser. 4; H. R. Rep. No. 914, *supra*. This testimony included the fact that our people have become increasingly mobile with millions of all races traveling from State to State; that Negroes in particular have been the subject of discrimination in transient accommodations, having to travel great distances to secure the same; that often they have been unable to obtain accommodations and have had to call upon friends to put them up overnight, S. Rep. No. 872, at 14–22; and that these conditions had become so acute as to require the listing of available lodging for Negroes in a special guidebook which was itself "dramatic testimony of the difficulties" Negroes encounter in travel, Senate Commerce Hearings, at 692–694. These exclusionary practices were found to be nationwide, the Under Secretary of Commerce testifying that there is "no question that this discrimination in the North still exists to a large degree" and in the West and Midwest as well. Senate Commerce Hearings, at 735, 744. This testimony indicated a qualitative as well as quantitive effect on interstate travel by Negroes. The former was the obvious impairment of the Negro traveler's pleasure and convenience that resulted when he continually was uncertain of finding lodging. As for the latter, there was evidence that this uncertainty stemming from racial discrimination had the effect of discouraging travel on the part of a substantial portion of the Negro community.

Senate Commerce Hearings, at 744. This was the conclusion not only of the Under Secretary of Commerce but also of the Administrator of the Federal Aviation Agency who wrote the Chairman of the Senate Commerce Committee that it was his "belief that air commerce is adversely affected by the denial to a substantial segment of the traveling public of adequate and desegregated public accommodations." Senate Commerce Hearings, at 12–13. We shall not burden this opinion with further details since the voluminous testimony presents overwhelming evidence that discrimination by hotels and motels impedes interstate travel. . . .

[After quoting at length from Chief Justice Marshall's opinion in *Gibbons* v. *Ogden*, the opinion continued as follows:] In short, the determinative test of the exercise of power by the Congress under the Commerce Clause is simply whether the activity sought to be regulated is "commerce which concerns more than one state" and has a real and substantial relation to the national interest. Let us now turn to this facet of the problem.

That the "intercourse" of which the Chief Justice spoke included the movement of persons through more States than one was settled as early as 1849, in the *Passenger Cases,* 7 How. 283, where Mr. Justice McLean stated: "That the transportation of passengers is a part of commerce is not now an open question." At 401. Again in 1913 Mr. Justice McKenna, speaking for the Court, said: "Commerce among the States, as we have said, consists of intercourse and traffic between their citizens, and includes the transportation of persons and property." *Hoke* v. *United States,* 227 U.S. 308, 320. And only four years later in 1916 in *Caminetti* v. *United States,* 242 U.S. 470, Mr. Justice Day held for the Court:

"The transportation of passengers in interstate commerce, it has long been settled, is within the regulatory power of Congress, under the commerce clause of the Constitution, and the authority of Congress to keep the channels of interstate commerce free from immoral and injurious uses has been frequently sustained, and is no longer open to question. [At 491.]"

Nor does it make any difference whether the transportation is commercial in character. *Id.*, at 484–486. In *Morgan* v. *Virginia*, 328 U.S. 373 (1946), Mr. Justice Reed observed as to the modern movement of persons among the States:

"The recent changes in transportation brought about by the coming of automobiles does not seem of great significance in the problem. People of all races travel today more extensively than in 1878 when this Court first passed upon state regulation of racial segregation in commerce. [It but] emphasizes the soundness of this Court's early conclusion in *Hall* v. *DeCuir*, 95 U.S. 485. [At 383.]"

The same interest in protecting interstate commerce which led Congress to deal with segregation in interstate carriers and the white slave traffic has prompted it to extend the exercise of its power to gambling, *Lottery Case,* 188 U.S. 321 (1903); to criminal enterprises, *Brooks* v. *United States,* 267 U.S. 432 (1925); to deceptive practices in the sale of products, *Federal Trade Comm'n* v. *Mandel Bros., Inc.,* 359 U.S. 385 (1959); to fraudulent security transactions, *Securities & Exchange Comm'n* v. *Ralston Purina Co.,* 346 U.S. 119 (1953); to misbranding of drugs, *Weeks* v. *United States,* 245 U.S. 618 (1918); to wages and hours, *United States* v. *Darby,* 312 U.S. 100 (1941); to members of labor unions, *Labor Board* v. *Jones & Laughlin Steel Corp.,* 301 U.S. 1 (1937); to crop control, *Wickard* v. *Filburn,* 317 U.S. 111 (1942); to discrimination against shippers, *United States* v. *Baltimore & Ohio R. Co.,* 333 U.S. 169 (1948); to the protection of small business from injurious price cutting, *Moore* v. *Mead's Fine Bread Co.,* 348 U.S. 115 (1954); to resale price maintenance, *Hudson Distributors, Inc.* v. *Eli Lilly & Co.,* 377 U.S. 386 (1964); *Schwegmann* v. *Calvert Distillers Corp.,* 341 U.S. 384 (1951); to professional football, *Radovich* v. *National Football League,* 352 U.S. 445 (1957); and to racial discrimination by owners and managers of terminal restaurants, *Boynton* v. *Virginia,* 364 U.S. 454 (1960).

That Congress was legislating against moral wrongs in many of these areas rendered its enactments no less valid. In framing Title II of this Act Congress was also dealing with what it considered a moral problem. But that fact does not detract from the overwhelming evidence of the disruptive effect that racial discrimination has had on commercial intercourse. It was this burden which empowered Congress to enact appropriate legislation, and, given this basis for the exercise of its power, Congress was not restricted by the fact that the particular obstruction to interstate commerce with which it was dealing was also deemed a moral and social wrong.

It is said that the operation of the motel here is of a purely local character. But, assuming this to be true, "if it is interstate commerce that feels the pinch, it does not matter how local the operation that applies the squeeze." *United States* v. *Women's Sportswear Mfrs. Assn.,* 336 U.S. 460, 464 (1949). See *Labor Board* v. *Jones & Laughlin Steel Corp., supra.* As Chief Justice Stone put it in *United States* v. *Darby, supra:*

"The power of Congress over interstate commerce is not confined to the regulation of commerce among the states. It extends to those activities intrastate which so affect interstate commerce or the exercise of the power of Congress over it as to make regulation of them appropriate means to the attainment of a legitimate end, the exercise of the granted power of Congress to regulate interstate commerce. See *McCulloch* v. *Maryland,* 4 Wheat. 316, 421. [At 118.]"

Thus the power of Congress to promote interstate commerce also includes the power to regulate the local incidents thereof, including local activities in both the States of origin and destination, which might have a substantial and harmful effect upon that commerce. One need only examine the evidence which we have discussed above to see that Congress may—as it has—prohibit racial discrimination by motels serving travelers, however "local" their operations may appear. . . .

[JUSTICES BLACK, DOUGLAS, and GOLDBERG

wrote concurring opinions—the latter judges holding that Title II, as applied in this case, could also be justified by virtue of Sec. 5 of the Fourteenth Amendment per their opinions in *Bell* v. *Maryland*, below.]

KATZENBACH v. McCLUNG

85 S. Ct. 377 (1964)

> This case is substantially like *Heart of Atlanta Motel* except that the establishment here is "a family-owned restaurant in Birmingham, Alabama . . . with a seating capacity [for] 220 customers." Its only substantial relation to interstate commerce is its source of supplies. Thus in the 12 months preceding passage of the 1964 Civil Rights Act "the restaurant purchased locally approximately $150,000 worth of food . . . 46% of which was meat that it bought from a local supplier who had procured it from outside the State."

MR. JUSTICE CLARK delivered the opinion of the Court. . . .

As we noted in *Heart of Atlanta Motel* both Houses of Congress conducted prolonged hearings on the Act. And, as we said there, while no formal findings were made, which of course is not necessary, it is well that we make mention of the testimony at these hearings the better to understand the problem before Congress and determine whether the Act is a reasonable and appropriate means toward its solution. The record is replete with testimony of the burdens placed on interstate commerce by racial discrimination in restaurants. A comparison of per capita spending by Negroes in restaurants, theaters, and like establishments indicated less spending, after discounting income differences, in areas where discrimination is widely practiced. This condition, which was especially aggravated in the South, was attributed in the testimony of the Under Secretary of Commerce to racial segregation. See Hearings before the Senate Committee on Commerce on S. 1732, 88th Cong., 1st Sess., 695. This diminutive spending springing from a refusal to serve Negroes and their total loss as customers has, regardless of the absence of direct evidence, a close connection to interstate commerce. The fewer cus-

tomers a restaurant enjoys the less food it sells and consequently the less it buys. S. Rep. No. 872, at 19; Senate Commerce Hearings, at 207. In addition, the Attorney General testified that this type of discrimination imposed "an artificial restriction on the market" and interfered with the flow of merchandise. Senate Commerce Hearings, at 18–19; also, on this point, see testimony of Senator Magnuson, 110 Cong. Rec. 7174. In addition, there were many references to discriminatory situations causing wide unrest and having a depressant effect on general business conditions in the respective communities. See, *e.g.*, Senate Commerce Hearings, at 623–630, 695–700, 1384–1385.

Moreover there was an impressive array of testimony that discrimination in restaurants had a direct and highly restrictive effect upon interstate travel by Negroes. This resulted, it was said, because discrimination practices prevent Negroes from buying prepared food served on the premises while on a trip, except in isolated and unkempt restaurants and under most unsatisfactory and often unpleasant conditions. This obviously discourages travel and obstructs interstate commerce for one can hardly travel without eating. Likewise, it was said, that discrimination deterred professional, as well as skilled, people from moving into areas where such practices occurred and thereby caused industry to be reluctant to establish there. S. Rep. No. 872, at 18–19.

We believe that this testimony afforded ample basis for the conclusion that established restaurants in such areas sold less interstate goods because of the discrimination, that interstate travel was obstructed directly by it, that business in general suffered and that many new businesses refrained from establishing there as a result of it. Hence the District Court was in error in concluding that there was no connection between discrimination and the movement of interstate commerce. Rather than such connection being outside "common experience," as the court said, its conclusion flies in the face of stubborn fact.

It goes without saying that, viewed in isolation, the volume of food purchased by Ollie's Barbecue from sources supplied from out of state was insignificant when compared with the total foodstuffs moving in commerce. But, as our late Brother Jackson said for the Court in *Wickard* v. *Filburn*, 317 U.S. 111 (1942):

"That appellee's own contribution to the demand for wheat may be trivial by itself is not enough to remove him from the scope of federal regulation where, as here, his contribution, taken together with that of many others similarly situated, is far from trivial. [At 127–128.]"

We noted in *Heart of Atlanta Motel* that a number of witnesses attested the fact that racial discrimination was not merely a state or regional problem but was one of nation-wide scope. Against this background, we must conclude that while the focus of the legislation was on the individual restaurant's relation to interstate commerce, Congress appropriately considered the importance of that connection with the knowledge that the discrimination was but "representative of many others throughout the country, the total incidence of which if left unchecked may well become far-reaching in its harm to commerce." *Polish Alliance* v. *Labor Board*, 322 U.S. 643, 648 (1944).

With this situation spreading as the record shows, Congress was not required to await the total dislocation of commerce. As was said in *Consolidated Edison Co.* v. *Labor Board*, 305 U.S. 197 (1938):

"But it cannot be maintained that the exertion of federal power must await the disruption of that commerce. Congress was entitled to provide reasonable preventive measures and that was the object of the National Labor Relations Act. [At 222.]"

5. *The Power of Congress to Regulate Local Activities.*

Article I, § 8, cl. 3, confers upon Congress the power "to regulate commerce . . . among the several States" and Clause 18 of the same Article grants it the power "to make all Laws which shall be necessary and proper for carrying into Execution the foregoing Powers. . . ." This grant, as we have pointed out in *Heart of Atlanta Motel* "extends to those activities intrastate which so affect interstate commerce, or the exertion of the power of Congress over it, as to make regulation of them appropriate means to the attainment of a legitimate end, the effective execution of the granted power to regulate interstate commerce." *United States* v. *Wrightwood Dairy Co.*, 315 U.S. 110, 119 (1942). Much is said about a restaurant business being local but "even if appellee's activity be local and though it may not be regarded as commerce, it may still, whatever its nature, be reached by Congress if it exerts a substantial economic effect on interstate commerce. . . ." *Wickard* v. *Filburn, supra,* at 125. The activities that are beyond the reach of Congress are "those which are completely within a particular State, which do not affect other States, and with which it is not necessary to interfere, for the purpose of executing some of the general powers of the government." *Gibbons* v. *Ogden,* 9 Wheat. 1, 195 (1824). This rule is as good today as it was when Chief Justice Marshall laid it down almost a century and a half ago.

This Court has held time and again that this power extends to activities of retail establishments, including restaurants, which directly or indirectly burden or obstruct interstate commerce. We have detailed the cases in *Heart of Atlanta Motel, supra,* and will not repeat them here.

Nor are the cases holding that interstate commerce ends when goods come to rest in the state of destination apposite here. That line of cases has been applied with reference to state taxation or regulation but not in the field of federal regulation. . . .

Confronted as we are with the facts laid before Congress, we must conclude that it had a rational basis for finding that racial discrimination in restaurants had a direct and adverse effect on the free flow of interstate commerce. Insofar as the section of the Act here relevant is concerned, § 201 (b) (2) and (c), Congress prohibited discrimination

only in those establishments having a close tie to interstate commerce, i.e., those, like McClung's, serving food that has come from out of the State. We think in so doing that Congress acted well within its power to protect and foster commerce in extending the coverage of Title II only to those restaurants offering to serve interstate travelers or serving food, a substantial portion of which has moved in interstate commerce.

[JUSTICES BLACK, DOUGLAS, and GOLDBERG wrote concurring opinions—the latter judges holding that Title II could also be justified by virtue of Sec. 5 of the Fourteenth Amendment per their opinions in *Bell* v. *Maryland*, below.]

FEDERAL TRADE COMMISSION v. BUNTE BROTHERS, INC.

312 U.S. 349 (1941)

MR. JUSTICE FRANKFURTER delivered the opinion of the Court:

The Federal Trade Commission found that Bunte Brothers, candy manufacturers in Illinois, sold products there in what the trade calls "break and take" packages, which makes the amount the purchaser receives dependent upon chance; and that thereby it was enabled in the Illinois market to compete unfairly with manufacturers outside of Illinois who could not indulge in this device because the Trade Commission has barred "break and take" packages as an "unfair method of competition." . . . Deeming the "break and take" sales unfair methods of competition under § 5, even though the sales took place wholly within Illinois, the Commission forbade Bunte Brothers further use of the device. The circuit court of appeals set aside the order, 110 F.2d 412, and we brought the case here because the issue at stake presents an important aspect of the interplay of state and federal authority. 311 U.S. 624.

The scope of § 5 is in controversy. That section, the court below held, authorizes the Commission to proceed only against

business practices employed in interstate commerce. The Commission urges that its powers are not so restricted, that it may also proscribe unfair methods used in intrastate sales when these result in a handicap to interstate competitors.

While one may not end with the words of a disputed statute, one certainly begins there. "Unfair methods of competition in commerce" are the concern of § 5, and the Commission is "directed to prevent persons . . . from using unfair methods of competition in commerce . . ." The "commerce" in which these methods are barred is interstate commerce. Neither ordinary English speech nor the considered language of legislation would aptly describe the sales by Bunte Brothers of its "break and take" assortments in Illinois as "using unfair methods of competition in [interstate] commerce." When in order to protect interstate commerce Congress has regulated activities which in isolation are merely local, it has normally conveyed its purpose explicitly. See for example, National Labor Relations Act, § § 2 (7), 9 (c), 10 (a), 49 Stat. 450, 453, 29 U.S.C. § § 152 (7), 159 (c), 160 (a); Bitu-

Minous Coal Act, § 4–A, 50 Stat. 83, 15 U.S.C. § 834; Federal Employers' Liability Act, § 1, 35 Stat. 65, as amended, 53 Stat. 1404, 45 U.S.C. § 51. To be sure, the construction of every such statute presents a unique problem in which words derive vitality from the aim and nature of the specific legislation. But bearing in mind that in ascertaining the scope of congressional legislation a due regard for a proper adjustment of the local and national interests in our federal scheme must always be in the background, we ought not to find in § 5 radiations beyond the obvious meaning of language unless otherwise the purpose of the Act would be defeated. *Minnesota Rate Cases,* 230 U.S. 352, 398–412.

That for a quarter century the Commission has made no such claim is a powerful indication that effective enforcement of the Trade Commission Act is not dependent on control over intrastate transactions. Authority actually granted by Congress of course cannot evaporate through lack of administrative exercise. But just as established practice may shed light on the extent of power conveyed by general statutory language, so the want of assertion of power by those who presumably would be alert to exercise it, is equally significant in determining whether such power was actually conferred. See *Norwegian Nitrogen Co.* v. *United States,* 288 U.S. 294, 315. This practical construction of the Act by those entrusted with its administration is reinforced by the Commission's unsuccessful attempt in 1935 to secure from Congress an express grant of authority over transactions "affecting" commerce in addition to its control of practices in commerce. S. Rep. No. 46, 74th Cong., 1st Sess. These circumstances are all the more significant in that during the whole of the Commission's life the so-called *Shreveport* doctrine operated in the regulatory field committed to the Interstate Commerce Commission. And it is that doctrine which gives the contention of the Trade Commission its strongest support.

Translation of an implication drawn from the special aspects of one statute to a totally different statute is treacherous business. The Interstate Commerce Act and the Federal Trade Commission Act are widely disparate in their historic settings, in the enterprises which they affect, in the range of control they exercise, and in the relation of these controls to the functioning of the federal system. We need not at this late day rehearse the considerations that led to the *Shreveport* decision. *Houston E. & W. T. Ry. Co.* v. *United States,* 234 U.S. 342. The nub of it, in the language of Chief Justice Taft, lay in the relation between intrastate and interstate railroad traffic: "Effective control of the one must embrace some control over the other in view of the blending of both in actual operation. The same rails and the same cars carry both. The same men conduct them." *Wisconsin Railroad Commission* v. *Chicago, B. & Q. R. Co.,* 257 U.S. 563, 588. And so when the Interstate Commerce Commission found that the intrastate rates of a carrier subject to the Act in effect operated as a discrimination against its interstate traffic, this Court sustained the power of the Commission to bring the two rates into harmonious relation and thereby to terminate the unlawful discrimination. Congress in 1920 revised the Interstate Commerce Act and explicitly confirmed this power of the Commerce Commission. 41 Stat. 484, 49 U.S.C. § 13 (4).

There is the widest difference in practical operation between the control over local traffic intimately connected with interstate traffic and the regulatory authority here asserted. Unlike the relatively precise situation presented by rate discrimination, "unfair competition" was designed by Congress as a flexible concept with evolving content. . . . It touches the greatest variety of unrelated activities. The Trade Commission in its Report for 1939 lists as "unfair competition" thirty-one diverse types of business practices which run the gamut from bribing employees of prospective customers to selling below cost for hindering competition. The construction of § 5 urged by the Commission would thus give a federal agency pervasive control over myriads of local businesses in matters heretofore traditionally left to local custom or local law. Such control bears no resemblance to the strictly confined authority growing out of railroad rate discrimination. An inroad upon local conditions and local standards of such far-reaching import as is involved here, ought to await a clearer mandate from Congress. The problem now before us is very different from that which was recently presented by *United States* v. *Darby, ante,* p. 100. We had there to consider the full scope of the constitutional power of Congress under the Commerce Clause in relation to the subject matter of the Fair Labor Standards Act. This case presents the narrow question of what Congress did, not what it could do. And we merely hold that to read "unfair methods of competition in [interstate] commerce" as though it meant "unfair methods of competition in any way affecting interstate commerce," requires, in view of all the relevant considerations, much clearer manifestation of intention than Congress has furnished.

Affirmed.

MR. JUSTICE DOUGLAS, dissented.

NOTE: *Bunte* illustrates the difference between the constitutional issue of how much power Congress has, and the political problem of how much of its constitutional power it has used. Here the Court found that Congress had not used all of its available power. This left Congress free, of course, to use more, less, or none as it (subject to voter control) might find proper.

UNITED STATES v. CALIFORNIA
297 U.S. 175 (1936)

California owned and operated an "interstate" railroad. Is such an operation subject to federal safety regulations applicable generally to the interstate railroad industry? Notice that this case was decided before the *Graves* case.

MR. JUSTICE STONE delivered the opinion of the Court:

The state urges that it is not subject to the Federal Safety Appliance Act. It is not denied that the omission charged would be a violation if by a privately-owned rail carrier in interstate commerce. But it is said that as the state is operating the railroad without profit, for the purpose of facilitating the commerce of the port, and is using the net proceeds of operation for harbor improvement, see *Sherman* v. *United States,* [282 U.S. 25], *Denning* v. *State,* 123 Cal. 316, it is engaged in performing a public function in its sovereign capacity and for that reason cannot constitutionally be subjected to the provisions of the federal act. In any case it is argued that the statute is not to be construed as applying to the state acting in that capacity.

Despite reliance upon the point both by the government and the state, we think it unimportant to say whether the state conducts its railroad in its "sovereign" or in its "private" capacity. That in operating its railroad it is acting within a power reserved to the states cannot be doubted. See *Puget Sound Power & Light Co.* v. *Seattle,* 291 U.S. 619, 624; *Green* v. *Frazier,* 253 U.S. 233; *Jones* v. *Portland,* 245 U.S. 217. The only question we need consider, is whether the exercise of that power, in whatever capacity, must be in subordination to the power to regulate interstate commerce, which has been granted specifically to the national government. The sovereign power of the states is necessarily diminished to the extent of the grants of power to the federal government in the Constitution. The power of a state to fix intrastate railroad rates must yield to the power of the national government when their regulation is appropriate to the regulation of interstate commerce. . . .

The analogy of the constitutional immunity of state instrumentalities from federal taxation, on which respondent relies, is not illuminating. That immunity is implied from the nature of our federal system and the relationship within it of state and national governments, and is equally a restriction on taxation by either of the instrumentalities of the other. Its nature requires that it be so construed as to allow to each government reasonable scope for its taxing power, see *Metcalf & Eddy* v. *Mitchell*, 269 U.S. 514, 522–524, which would be unduly curtailed if either by extending its activities could withdraw from the taxing power of the other subjects of taxation traditionally within it. *Halvering* v. *Powers*, 293 U.S. 214, 225; *Ohio* v. *Helvering*, 292 U.S. 360; *South Carolina* v. *United States*, 199 U.S. 437; see *Murray* v. *Wilson Distilling Co.*, 213 U.S. 151, 173, explaining *South Carolina* v. *United States, supra.* Hence we look to the activities in which the states have traditionally engaged as marking the boundary of the restriction upon the federal taxing power. But there is no such limitation upon the plenary power to regulate commerce. The state can no more deny the power if its exercise has been authorized by Congress than can an individual.

California, by engaging in interstate commerce by rail, has subjected itself to the commerce power, and is liable for a violation of the Safety Appliance Act, as are other carriers, unless the statute is to be deemed inapplicable to state-owned railroads because it does not specifically mention them. The Federal Safety Appliance Act is remedial, to protect employees and the public from injury because of defective railway appliances, . . . and to safeguard interstate commerce itself from obstruction and injury due to defective appliances upon locomotives and cars used on the highways of interstate commerce, even though their individual use is wholly intrastate. . . . The danger to be apprehended is as great and commerce may be equally impeded whether the defective appliance is used on a railroad which is state-owned or privately-owned. No convincing reason is advanced why interstate commerce and persons and property concerned in it should not receive the protection of the act whenever a state, as well as a privately-owned carrier, brings itself within the sweep of the statute, or why its all-embracing language should not be deemed to afford that protection.

In *Ohio* v. *Helvering, supra*, it was held that a state, upon engaging in the business, became subject to a federal statute imposing a tax on those dealing in intoxicating liquors, although states were not specifically mentioned in the statute. The same conclusion was reached in *South Carolina* v. *United States, supra;* and see *Helvering* v. *Powers, supra.* Similarly the Interstate Commerce Commission has regarded this and other state-owned interstate rail carriers as subject to its jurisdiction, although the Interstate Commerce Act does not in terms apply to state-owned rail carriers. *See California Canneries Co.* v. *Southern P. Co.*, 51 I.C.C. 500, 502, 503; *United States* v. *Belt Line R. Co.*, 56 I.C.C. 121; *Texas State Railroad*, 34 I.C.C. Val. R. 276. . . .

Reversed.

2. THE TAXING POWER

POLLOCK v. *FARMERS' LOAN & TRUST COMPANY*
158 U.S. 601 (1895)

In the first decision in this case a few weeks earlier, the Court found two aspects of the 1894 income tax act invalid (as indicated in the following opinion), but the Court was evenly divided on other issues—one judge not participating. To resolve the problem, a rehearing was granted with the following result.

MR. CHIEF JUSTICE FULLER delivered the opinion of the court. . . .

. . . The Constitution divided Federal taxation into two great classes, the class of direct taxes and the class of duties, imposts, and excises, and prescribed two rules which qualify the grant of power as to each class.

The power to lay direct taxes, apportioned among the several States in proportion to their representation in the popular branch of Congress, a representation based on population as ascertained by the census, was plenary and absolute, but to lay direct taxes without apportionment was forbidden. The power to lay duties, imposts, and excises was subject to the qualification that the imposition must be uniform throughout the United States.

Our previous decision was confined to the consideration of the validity of the tax on the income from real estate, and on the income from municipal bonds. The question thus limited was whether such taxation was direct or not, in the meaning of the Constitution; and the court went no farther, as to the tax on the incomes from real estate, than to hold that it fell within the same class as the source whence the income was derived, that is, that a tax upon the realty and a tax upon the receipts therefrom were alike direct; while as to the income from municipal bonds, that could not be taxed because of want of power to tax the source, and no reference was made to the nature of the tax being direct or indirect.

We are now permitted to broaden the field of inquiry, and determine to which of the two great classes a tax upon a person's entire income, whether derived from rents, or products, or otherwise, of real estate, or from bonds, stocks or other forms of personal property, belongs; and we are unable to conclude that the enforced subtraction from the yield of all the owner's real or personal property, in the manner prescribed, is so different from a tax upon the property itself, that it is not a direct, but an indirect tax, in the meaning of the Constitution. . . .

We know of no reason for holding otherwise than that the words "direct taxes" on the one hand, and "duties, imposts, and excises" on the other, were used in the Constitution in their natural and obvious sense, nor, in arriving at what those terms embrace, do we perceive any ground for enlarging them beyond, or narrowing them within, their natural and obvious import at the time the Constitution was framed and ratified. . . .

In the light of the struggle in the convention as to whether or not the new Nation should be empowered to levy taxes directly on the individual until after the States had failed to respond to requisitions —a struggle which did not terminate until the amendment to that effect, proposed by Massachusetts and concurred in by South Carolina, New Hampshire, New York, and Rhode Island, had been rejected—it would seem beyond reasonable question that direct taxation, taking the place as it did of requisitions, was purposely restrained to apportionment according to representation, in order that the former system as to ratio might be retained, while the mode of collection was changed. . . .

The reasons for the clauses of the Constitution in respect of direct taxation are not far to seek. The States, respectively, possessed plenary powers of taxation. They could tax the property of their citizens in such manner and to such extent as they saw fit; they had unrestricted powers to impose duties or imposts on imports from abroad, and excises on manufactures, consumable commodities, or otherwise. They gave up the great sources of revenue derived from commerce; they retained the concurrent power of levying excises, and duties if covering anything other than excises; but in respect of them the range of taxation was narrowed by the power granted over interstate commerce, and by the danger of being put at disadvantage in dealing with excises on manufactures. They retained the power of direct taxation, and to that they looked as their chief resource; but even in respect of that, they granted the concurrent power, and if the tax were placed by both governments on the same subject, the claim of the United States had preference. Therefore, they did not grant the power of direct taxation without regard to their own condition and resources as States; but they granted the power of apportioned direct taxation, a power just as efficacious to serve the needs of the general government, but securing to the States the opportunity to pay the amount apportioned, and to recoup from their own citizens in the most feasible way, and in harmony with their systems of local self-government. If, in the changes of wealth and population in particular States, apportionment produced inequality, it was an inequality stipulated for, just as the equal representation . . . in the Senate, was stipulated for. The Constitution ordains affirmatively that each State shall have two members of that body, and negatively that no State shall by amendment be deprived of its equal suffrage in the Senate without its consent. The Constitution ordains affirmatively that representatives and direct taxes shall be apportioned among the several States according to numbers, and negatively that no direct tax shall be laid unless in proportion to the enumeration. . . .

It is said that a tax on the whole income of property is not a direct tax in the meaning of the Constitution, but a duty, and, as a duty, leviable without apportionment, whether direct or indirect. We do not think so. Direct taxation was not restricted in one breath, and the restriction blown to the winds in another. . . .

. . . Thus we find Mr. Hamilton, while writing to induce the adoption of the Constitution, *first,* dividing the power of taxation into *external* and *internal,* putting in to the former the power of imposing duties on imported articles and into the latter all remaining powers; and, *second,* dividing the latter into *direct* and *indirect,* putting into the latter, duties and excises on articles of consumption.

It seems to us to inevitably follow that in Mr. Hamilton's judgment at that time all internal taxes, except duties and excises on articles of consumption, fell into the category of direct taxes. . . .

. . . He gives, however, it appears to us, a definition which covers the question before us. A tax upon one's whole income is a tax upon the annual receipts from his whole property, and as such falls within the same class as a tax upon that property, and is a direct tax, in the meaning of the Constitution. And Mr. Hamilton in his report on the public credit, in referring to contracts with citizens of a foreign country, said: "This principle, which seems critically correct, would exempt as well the income as the capital of the property. It protects the use, as effectually as the thing. What, in fact, is property, but a fiction, without the beneficial use of it? In many cases, indeed, the *income* or *annuity* is the property itself." 3 Hamilton's Works, 34. . . .

The Constitution prohibits any direct tax, unless in proportion to numbers as ascertained by the census; and, in the light of the circumstances to which we have referred, is it not an evasion of that prohibition to hold that a general unapportioned tax, imposed upon all property owners as a body for or in respect of their property, is not direct, in the meaning of the Constitution, because confined to the income therefrom?

Whatever the speculative views of political economists or revenue reformers may be, can it be properly held that the Constitution, taken in its plain and obvious sense, and with due regard to the circumstances attending the formation of the government, authorizes a general unapportioned tax on the products of the farm and the rents of real estate, although imposed merely because of ownership and with no possible means of escape from payment, as belonging to a totally different class from that which includes the property from whence the income proceeds?

There can be only one answer, unless the constitutional restriction is to be treated as utterly illusory and futile, and the object of its framers defeated. We find it impossible to hold that a fundamental requisition, deemed so important as to be enforced by two provisions, one affirmative and one negative, can be refined away by forced distinctions between that which gives value to property and the property itself.

Nor can we perceive any ground why the same reasoning does not apply to capital in personalty held for the purpose of income or ordinarily yielding income, and to the income therefrom. All the real estate of the country, and all its invested personal property, are open to the direct operation of the taxing power if an apportionment be made according to the Constitution. The Constitution does not say that no direct tax shall be laid by apportionment on any other property than land; on the contrary, it forbids all unapportioned direct taxes; and we know of no warrant for excepting personal property from the exercise of the power, or any reason why an apportioned direct tax cannot be laid and assessed. . . .

We have considered the act only in respect of the tax on income derived from real estate, and from invested personal property, and have not commented on so much of it as bears on gains or profits from business, privileges, or employments, in view of the instances in which taxation on business, privileges, or employments has assumed the guise of an excise tax and been sustained as such.

Being of opinion that so much of the sections of this law as lays a tax on income from real and personal property is invalid, we are brought to the question of the effect of that conclusion upon these sections as a whole.

It is elementary that the same statute may be in part constitutional and in part unconstitutional, and if the parts are wholly independent of each other, that which is constitutional may stand while that which is unconstitutional will be rejected. And in the case before us there is no question as to validity of this act, except sections twenty-seven to thirty-seven,

inclusive, which relate to the subject which has been under discussion; and as to them we think that the rule laid down by Chief Justice Shaw in *Warren* v. *Charlestown*, 2 Gray, 84, is applicable, that if the different parts "are so mutually connected with and dependent on each other, as conditions, considerations or compensations for each other, as to warrant the belief that the legislature intended them as a whole, and that, if all could not be carried into effect, the legislature would not pass the residue independently, and some parts are unconstitutional, all the provisions which are thus dependent, conditional or connected, must fall with them." . . .

Our conclusions may, therefore, be summed up as follows:

First. We adhere to the opinion already announced, that, taxes on real estate being indisputably direct taxes, taxes on the rents or incomes of real estate are equally direct taxes.

Second. We are of opinion that taxes on personal property, or on the income of personal property, are likewise direct taxes.

Third. The tax imposed by sections twenty-seven to thirty-seven, inclusive, of the act of 1894, so far as it falls on the income of real estate and of personal property, being a direct tax within the meaning of the Constitution, and, therefore, unconstitutional and void because not apportioned according to representation, all those sections, constituting one entire scheme of taxation, are necessarily invalid.

The decrees hereinbefore entered in this court will be vacated; the decrees below will be reversed, and the case remanded, with instructions to grant the relief prayed.

Mr. Justice Harlan dissenting. . . .

In my judgment a tax on *income* derived from real property ought not to be, and until now has never been, regarded by any court as a direct tax on such property within the meaning of the Constitution. As the great mass of lands in most of the States do not bring any rents, and as incomes from rents vary in different States, such a tax cannot possibly be apportioned among the States on the basis merely of numbers with any approach to equality of right among taxpayers, any more than a tax on carriages or other personal property could be so apportioned. And, in view of former adjudications, beginning with the *Hylton* case and ending with the *Springer* case, a decision now that a tax on income from real property can be laid and collected only by apportioning the same among the States, on the basis of numbers, may, not improperly, be regarded as a judicial revolution, that may sow the seeds of hate and distrust among the people of different sections of our common country. . . .

In determining whether a tax on income from rents is a direct tax, within the meaning of the Constitution, the inquiry is not whether it may in some way indirectly affect the land or the land owner, but whether it is a *direct* tax *on the thing taxed, the land.* The circumstance that such a tax may possibly have the effect to diminish the value of the use of the land is neither decisive of the question nor important. While a tax *on the land* itself, whether at a fixed rate applicable to all lands without regard to their value, or by the acre or according to their market value, might be deemed a direct tax within the meaning of the Constitution as interpreted in the *Hylton* case, a duty on rents is a duty on something distinct and entirely separate from, although issuing out of, the land. . . .

In my judgment—to say nothing of the disregard of the former adjudications of this court, and of the settled practice of the government—this decision may well excite the gravest apprehensions. It strikes at the very foundations of national authority, in that it denies to the general government a power which is, or may become, vital to the very existence and preservation of the Union in a national emergency, such as that of war with a great commercial nation, during which the collection of all duties upon imports will cease or be materially diminished. It tends to reestablish that condition of helplessness in which Congress found itself during the period of the Articles of Confederation, when it was without authority by laws operating directly upon individuals, to lay and collect, through its own agents, taxes sufficient to pay the debts and defray the expenses of government, but was dependent, in all such matters, upon the good will of the States, and their promptness in meeting requisitions made upon them by Congress. . . .

I dissent from the opinion and judgment of the court.

[The separate dissenting opinions of JUSTICES BROWN, JACKSON, and WHITE have been omitted here.]

NOTE: The *Pollock* decision was circumvented by the Sixteenth Amendment in 1913. In *Graves* v. *New York ex rel O'Keefe,* below, the Court observed: "The theory, which once won a qualified approval, that a tax on income is legally or economically a tax on its source, is no longer tenable. . . ."

BAILEY v. *DREXEL FURNITURE COMPANY*
259 U.S. 20 (1922)

After the *Dagenhart* case Congress tried to discourage child labor by a special tax on the net income of mines, quarries, factories, and mills employing children under specified ages. Earlier the Court had sustained federal levies on state bank notes, *Veazie* v. *Fenno,* 8 Wallace 533 (1869), and yellow oleomargarine, *McCray* v. *United States,* 145 U.S. 27 (1904). The levy on state bank notes was designed to, and did, drive out state currency in favor of a single monetary system for the entire country. The yellow margarine tax, forty times higher than the corresponding tax on white margarine, was obviously intended not for revenue, but to protect butter from competition—one rationalization for this purpose being that it was somehow fraudulent to make margarine look like butter. The narcotics tax in *United States* v. *Doremus,* 249 U.S. 86 (1919), on the other hand, was so low (a dollar a year on narcotics dealers) that it could not possibly have been calculated to raise revenue. Indeed, it probably was not high enough to pay the costs of collection. Congress's obvious purpose, as disclosed in the elaborate system of records required for narcotics transactions, was to police the drug traffic. In upholding the bank note, margarine, and narcotics taxes the Court had emphasized that since Congress was exercising an acknowledged power, it was not for judges to examine the legislative motive. In such matters, said the *Veazie* opinion, "the responsibility of the legislature is not to the Courts, but to the people by whom its members are elected." On the basis of these cases Congress thought it could tax child labor out of existence.

MR. CHIEF JUSTICE TAFT delivered the opinion of the court:

This case presents the question of the constitutional validity of the Child Labor Tax Law. . . .

The law is attacked on the ground that it is a regulation of the employment of child labor in the States—an exclusively state function under the Federal Constitution and within the reservations of the Tenth Amendment. It is defended on the ground that it is a mere excise tax levied by the Congress of the United States under its broad power of taxation conferred by § 8, Article I, of the Federal Constitution. We must construe the law and interpret the intent and meaning of Congress from the language of the act. The words are to be given their ordinary meaning unless the context shows that they are differently used. Does this law impose a tax with only that incidental restraint and regulation which a tax must inevitably involve? Or does it regulate by the use of the so-called tax as a penalty? If a tax, it is clearly an excise. If it were an excise on a commodity or other thing of value we might not be permitted under previous decisions of this court to infer solely from its heavy burden that the act intends a prohibition instead of a tax. But this act is more. It provides a heavy exaction for a departure from a detailed and specified course of conduct in business. That course of business is that employers shall employ in mines and quar-

ries, children of an age greater than sixteen years; in mills and factories, children of an age greater than fourteen years, and shall prevent children of less than sixteen years in mills and factories from working more than eight hours a day or six days in the week. If an employer departs from this prescribed course of business, he is to pay the Government one-tenth of his entire net income in the business for a full year. The amount is not to be proportioned in any degree to the extent or frequency of the departures, but is to be paid by the employer in full measure whether he employs five hundred children for a year, or employs only one for a day. Moreover, if he does not know the child is within the named age limit, he is not to pay; that is to say, it is only where he knowingly departs from the prescribed course that payment is to be exacted. Scienter is associated with penalties not with taxes. The employer's factory is to be subject to inspection at any time not only by the taxing officers of the Treasury, the Department normally charged with the collection of taxes, but also by the Secretary of Labor and his subordinates whose normal function is the advancement and protection of the welfare of the workers. In the light of these features of the act, a court must be blind not to see that the so-called tax is imposed to stop the employment of children within the age limits prescribed. Its prohibitory and regulatory effect and purpose are palpable. All others can see and understand this. How can we properly shut our minds to it?

It is the high duty and function of this court in cases regularly brought to its bar to decline to recognize or enforce seeming laws of Congress, dealing with subjects not entrusted to Congress but left or committed by the supreme law of the land to the control of the States. We can not avoid the duty even though it requires us to refuse to give effect to legislation designed to promote the highest good. The good sought in unconstitutional legislation is an insidious feature because it leads citizens and legislators of good purpose to promote it without thought of the serious breach it will make in the ark of our covenant or the harm which will come from breaking down recognized standards. In the maintenance of local self government, on the one hand, and the national power, on the other, our country has been able to endure and prosper for near a century and a half.

Out of a proper respect for the acts of a coordinate branch of the Government, this court has gone far to sustain taxing acts as such, even though there has been ground for suspecting from the weight of the tax it was intended to destroy its subject. But, in the act before us, the presumption of validity cannot prevail, because the proof of the contrary is found on the very face of its provisions. Grant the validity of this law, and all that Congress would need to do, hereafter, in seeking to take over to its control any one of the great number of subjects of public interest, jurisdiction of which the States have never parted with, and which are reserved to them by the Tenth Amendment, would be to enact a detailed measure of complete regulation of the subject and enforce it by a so-called tax upon departures from it. To give such magic to the word "tax" would be to break down all constitutional limitation of the powers of Congress and completely wipe out the sovereignty of the States.

The difference between a tax and a penalty is sometimes difficult to define and yet the consequences of the distinction in the required method of their collection often are important. Where the sovereign enacting the law has power to impose both tax and penalty the difference between revenue production and mere regulation may be immaterial, but not so when one sovereign can impose a tax only, and the power of regulation rests in another. Taxes are occasionally imposed in the discretion of the legislature on proper subjects with the primary motive of obtaining revenue from them and with the incidental motive of discouraging them by making their continuance onerous. They do not lose their character as taxes because of the incidental motive. But there comes a time in the extension of the penalizing features of the so-called tax when it loses its character as such and becomes a mere penalty with the characteristics of regulation and punishment. Such is the case in the law before us. Although Congress does not invalidate the contract of employment or expressly declare that the employment within the mentioned ages is illegal, it does exhibit its intent practically to achieve the latter result by adopting the criteria of wrongdoing and imposing its principal consequence on those who transgress its standard.

The case before us can not be distinguished from that of *Hammer* v. *Dagenhart*. . . . Congress there enacted a law to prohibit transportation in interstate commerce of goods made at a factory in which there was employment of children with the same ages and for the same number of hours a day and days in a week as are penalized by the act in this case. This court held the law in that case to be void. It said:

"In our view the necessary effect of this act is, by means of prohibition against the movement in interstate commerce of ordinary commercial commodities, to regulate hours of labor of children in factories and mines within the States, a purely state authority."

In the case at the bar, Congress in the name of a tax which on the face of the act is a penalty seeks to do the same thing, and the effort must be equally futile. . . .

But it is pressed upon us that this court has gone so far in sustaining taxing measures the effect or tendency of which was to accomplish purposes not directly within congressional power that we are bound by authority to maintain this law.

The first of these is *Veazie Bank* v. *Fenno.* . . .

The next case is that of *McCray* v. *United States.* . . . In neither of these cases did the law objected to show on its face as does the law before us the detailed specifications of a regulation of a state concern and business with a heavy exaction to promote the efficacy of such regulation. . . .

United States v. *Doremus* . . . involved the validity of the Narcotic Drug Act, 38 Stat. 785, which imposed a special tax on the manufacture, importation and sale or gift of opium or coca leaves or their compounds or derivatives. . . .

The court said that the act could not be declared invalid just because another motive than taxation, not shown on the face of the act, might have contributed to its passage. This case does not militate against the conclusion we have reached in respect of the law now before us. The court, there, made manifest its view that the provisions of the so-called taxing act must be naturally and reasonably adapted to the collection of the tax and not solely to the achievement of some other purpose plainly within state power. . . .

For the reasons given, we must hold the Child Labor Tax Law invalid and the judgment of the District Court is affirmed.

MR. JUSTICE CLARKE dissented.

NOTE: On August 13, 1787, the Constitutional Convention considered the relation between taxation and regulation. Here is James Madison's view: "The word revenue [is] ambiguous. In many acts, particularly in the regulation of trade, the object would be twofold. The raising of revenue would be one of them. How could it be determined which was the primary or predominant one. . . . When the contest was first opened with Great Britain their power to regulate trade was admitted. Their power to raise revenue rejected. An accurate investigation of the subject afterward proved that no line could be drawn between the two cases." No one questioned the accuracy of this observation.

Shortly thereafter on May 13, 1789, in the House of Representatives, Madison argued in favor of a tax on the slave trade. "It is to be hoped," he said, "that by expressing a national disapprobation of this trade, *we may destroy it*, and save ourselves from reproaches, and our posterity the imbecility ever attendant on a country filled with slaves." In short, Madison wanted to destroy the slave trade by taxation, just as later Congressmen wanted to destroy child labor by the same approach.

UNITED STATES v. KAHRIGER

345 U.S. 22 (1953)

MR. JUSTICE REED delivered the opinion of the Court:

The issue raised by this appeal is the constitutionality of the occupational tax provisions of the Revenue Act of 1951, which levy a tax on persons engaged in the business of accepting wagers, and require such persons to register with the Collector of Internal Revenue. The unconstitutionality of the tax is asserted on two grounds.

First, it is said that Congress, under the pretense of exercising its power to tax has attempted to penalize illegal intrastate gambling through the regulatory features of the Act (26 U.S.C. (Supp. V) § 3291) and has thus infringed the police power which is reserved to the States. Secondly, it is urged that the registration provisions of the tax violate the privilege against self-incrimination and are arbitrary and vague, contrary to the guarantees of the Fifth Amendment.

The case comes here on appeal, in accordance with 18 U.S.C. § 3731, from the United States District Court for the Eastern District of Pennsylvania, where an information was filed against appellee alleging that he was in the business of accepting wagers and that he wilfully failed to register for and pay the occupational tax in question. Appellee moved to dismiss on the ground that the sections upon which the indictment was based were unconstitutional. The District Court sustained the motion on the authority of our opinion in *United States v. Constantine*, 296 U.S. 287. The court reasoned that "while the subject matter of this legislation so far as revenue purposes is concerned is within the scope of Federal authority," the tax was unconstitutional in that the information called for by the registration provisions was "peculiarly applicable to the applicant from the standpoint of law enforcement and vice control," and therefore the whole of the legislation was an infringement by the Federal Government on the police power reserved to the states by the Tenth Amendment. *United States v. Kahriger*, 105 F. Supp. 322, 323.

The result below is at odds with the position of the seven other district courts which have considered the matter, and, in our opinion, is erroneous.

In the term following the *Constantine* opinion, this Court pointed out in *Sonzinsky v. United States*, 300 U.S. 506, at 513 (a case involving a tax on a "limited class" of objectionable firearms alleged to be prohibitory in effect and "to disclose unmistakably the legislative purpose to regulate rather than to tax"), that the subject of the tax in *Constantine* was "described or treated as criminal by the taxing statute." The tax in the *Constantine* case was a special additional excise tax of $1,000, placed only on persons who carried on a liquor business in violation of state law. The wagering tax with which we are here concerned applied to all persons engaged in the business of receiving wagers regardless of whether such activity violates state law.

The substance of respondent's position with respect to the Tenth Amendment is that Congress has chosen to tax a specified business which is not within its power to regulate. The precedents are many upholding taxes similar to this wagering tax as a proper exercise of the federal taxing power. In the *License Tax Cases*, 5 Wall. 462, the controversy arose out of indictments for selling lottery tickets and retailing liquor in various states without having first obtained and paid for a license under the Internal Revenue Act of Congress. The objecting taxpayers urged that Congress could not constitutionally tax or regulate activities carried on within a state. P. 470. The Court pointed out that Congress had "no power of regulation nor any direct control" (5 Wall., at 471, 472) over the business there involved. The Court said if the licenses were to be regarded as by themselves giving authority to carry on the licensed business it might be impossible to reconcile the granting of them with the Constitution. P. 471.

"But it is not necessary to regard these laws as giving such authority. So far as they relate to trade within State limits, they give none, and can give none. They simply express the purpose of the government not to interfere by penal proceedings with the trade nominally licensed, if the required taxes are paid. The power to tax is not questioned, nor the power to impose penalties for nonpayment of taxes. The granting of a license, therefore, must be regarded as nothing more than a mere form of imposing a tax, and of implying nothing except that the licensee shall be subject to no penalties under national law, if he pays it. *Id.*, at 471."

Appellee would have us say that because there is legislative history indicating a congressional motive to suppress wagering, this tax is not a proper exercise of such taxing power. In the *License Cases, supra,* it was admitted that the federal license "discouraged" the activities. The intent to curtail and hinder, as well as tax, was also manifest in the following cases, and in each of them the tax was upheld: *Veazie Bank* v. *Fenno,* 8 Wall. 533 (tax on paper money issued by state banks); *McCray* v. *United States,* 195 U.S. 27, 59 (tax on colored oleomargarine); *United States* v. *Doremus,* 249 U.S. 86, and *Nigro* v. *United States,* 276 U.S. 332 (tax on narcotics); *Sonzinsky* v. *United States,* 300 U.S. 506 (tax on firearms); *United States* v. *Sanchez,* 340 U.S. 42 (tax on marijuana).

It is conceded that a federal excise tax does not cease to be valid merely because it discourages or deters the activities taxed. Nor is the tax invalid because the revenue obtained is negligible. Appellee, however, argues that the sole purpose of the statute is to penalize only illegal gambling in the states through the guise of a tax measure. As with the above excise taxes which we have held to be valid, the instant tax has a regulatory effect. But regardless of its regulatory effect, the wagering tax produces revenue. As such it surpasses both the narcotics and firearms taxes which we have found valid. . . .

Penalty provisions in tax statutes added for breach of a regulation concerning activities in themselves subject only to state regulation have caused this Court to declare the enactments invalid. Unless there are provisions, extraneous to any tax need, courts are without authority to limit the exercise of the taxing power. All the provisions of this excise are adapted to the collection of a valid tax.

Nor do we find the registration requirements of the wagering tax offensive. All that is required is the filing of names, addresses, and places of business. This is quite general in tax returns. Such data are directly and intimately related to the collection of the tax and are "obviously support-able as in aid of a revenue purpose." *Sonzinsky* v. *United States,* 300 U.S. 506, at 513. The registration provisions made the tax simpler to collect.

Appellee's second assertion is that the wagering tax is unconstitutional because it is a denial of the privilege against self-incrimination as guaranteed by the Fifth Amendment.

Since appellee failed to register for the wagering tax, it is difficult to see how he can now claim the privilege even assuming that the disclosure of violations of law are called for. In *United States* v. *Sullivan,* 274 U.S. 259, defendant was convicted of refusing to file an income tax return. It was assumed that his income "was derived from business in violation of the National Prohibition Act." *Id.,* at 263.

"As the defendant's income was taxed, the statute, of course, required a return. See *United States* v. *Sischo,* 262 U.S. 165. In the decision that this was contrary to the Constitution, we are of the opinion that the protection of the Fifth Amendment was pressed too far. If the form of return provided called for answers that the defendant was privileged from making he could have raised the objection in the return, but could not on that account refuse to make any return at all. (274 U.S., at 263.)"

Assuming that respondent can raise the self-incrimination issue, that privilege has relation only to past acts, not to future acts that may or may not be committed. 8 Wigmore (3d ed., 1940) § 2259(c). If respondent wishes to take wagers subject to excise taxes under § 3285, *supra,* he must pay an occupational tax and register. Under the registration provisions of the wagering tax, appellee is not compelled to confess to acts already committed, he is merely informed by the statute that in order to engage in the business of wagering in the future he must fulfill certain conditions.

Finally, we consider respondent's contention that the order of dismissal was correct because a conviction under the sections in question would violate the due process clause because the classification is arbitrary and the statutory definitions are vague.

The applicable definitions are 26 U.S.C. (Supp. V) § 3285(b), (d) and (e). The arbitrariness is said to arise from discrimination because some wagering activities are excluded. The Constitution does not require that a tax statute cover all phases of a taxed or licensed business. Respondent predicates vagueness of the statute upon the use, in defining the subject of the tax, of the description "engaged in the business" of wagering and "usually" in § 3285 (b) (2). We have no doubt the definitions make clear the activities covered and excluded.

Reversed.

Mr. Justice Jackson, concurring:

I concur in the judgment and opinion of the Court, but with such doubt that if the minority agreed upon an opinion which did not impair legitimate use of the taxing power I probably would join it. But we deal here with important and contrasting values in our scheme of government, and it is important that neither be allowed to destroy the other.

On the one hand, the Fifth Amendment provides that no person "shall be compelled in any criminal case to be a witness against himself." This has been broadly construed to confer immunity not only "in any criminal case" but in any federal inquiry where the information might be useful later to convict of a federal crime. Extension of the immunity doctrines to the federal power to inquire as to income derived from violation of state penal laws would create a large number of immunities from reporting which would vary from state to state. Moreover, the immunity can be claimed without being established, otherwise one would be required to prove guilt to avoid admitting it. Sweeping and undiscriminating application of the immunity doctrines to taxation would almost give the taxpayer an option to refuse to report, as it now gives witnesses a virtual option to refuse to testify. The Fifth Amendment should not be construed to impair the taxing power conferred by the original Constitution, and especially by the Sixteenth Amendment, further than is absolutely required.

Of course, all taxation has a tendency proportioned to its burdensomeness to discourage the activity taxed. One cannot formulate a revenue-raising plan that would not have economic and social consequences. Congress may and should place the burden of taxes where it will least handicap desirable activities and bear most heavily on useless or harmful ones. If Congress may tax one citizen to the point of discouragement for making an honest living, it is hard to say that it may not do the same to another just because he makes a sinister living. If the law-abiding must tell all to the tax collector, it is difficult to excuse one because his business is law-breaking. Strangely enough, Fifth Amendment protection against self-incrimination has been refused to business as against inquisition by the regulatory power, *Shapiro* v. *United States*, 335 U.S. 1, in what seemed to me a flagrant violation of it. See dissenting opinion, *id.*, at 70.

But here is a purported tax law which requires no reports and lays no tax except from specified gamblers whose calling in most states is illegal. It requires this group to step forward and identify themselves, not because they like others have income, but because of its source. This is difficult to regard as a rational or good-faith revenue measure, despite the deference that is due Congress. On the contrary, it seems to be a plan to tax out of existence the professional gambler whom it has been found impossible to prosecute out of existence. Few pursuits are entitled to less consideration at our hands than professional gambling, but the plain unwelcome fact is that it continues to survive because a large and influential part of our population patronizes and protects it.

The United States has a system of taxation by confession. That a people so numerous, scattered and individualistic annually assesses itself with a tax liability, often in highly burdensome amounts, is a reassuring sign of the stability and vitality of our system of self-government. What surprised me in once trying to help administer these laws was not to discover examples of recalcitrance, fraud or self-serving mistakes in reporting, but to discover that such derelictions were so few. It will be a sad day for the revenues if the good will of the people toward their taxing system is frittered away in efforts to accomplish by taxation moral reforms that cannot be accomplished by direct legislation. But the evil that can come from this statute will probably soon make itself manifest to Congress. The evil of a judicial decision impairing the legitimate taxing power by extreme constitutional interpretations might not be transient. Even though this statute approaches the fair limits of constitutionality, I join the decision of the Court.

MR. JUSTICE FRANKFURTER, dissenting:

The Court's opinion manifests a natural difficulty in reaching its conclusion. Constitutional issues are likely to arise whenever Congress draws on the taxing power not to raise revenue but to regulate conduct. This is so, of course, because of the distribution of legislative power as between the Congress and the State Legislatures in the regulation of conduct.

To review in detail the decisions of this Court, beginning with *Veazie Bank* v. *Fenno*, 8 Wall. 533, dealing with this ambivalent type of revenue enactment, would be to rehash the familiar. Two generalizations may, however, safely be drawn from this series of cases. Congress may make an oblique use of the taxing power in relation to activities with which Congress may deal directly, as for instance, commerce between the States. Thus, if the dissenting views of Mr. Justice Holmes in *Hammer* v. *Dagenhart*, 247, U.S. 251, 277, had been the decision of the Court, as they became in *United States* v. *Darby*, 312 U.S. 100, the effort to deal with the problem of child labor through an assertion of the taxing power in the statute considered in *Child Labor Tax Case*, 259 U.S. 20, would by the latter case have been sustained. However, when oblique use is made of the taxing power as to matters which substantively are

not within the powers delegated to Congress, the Court cannot shut its eyes to what is obviously, because designedly, an attempt to control conduct which the Constitution left to the responsibility of the States, merely because Congress wrapped the legislation in the verbal cellophane of a revenue measure.

Concededly the constitutional questions presented by such legislation are difficult. On the one hand, courts should scrupulously abstain from hobbling congressional choice of policies, particularly when the vast reach of the taxing power is concerned. On the other hand, to allow what otherwise is excluded from congressional authority to be brought within it by casting legislation in the form of a revenue measure could, as so significantly expounded in the *Child Labor Tax Case, supra,* offer an easy way for the legislative imagination to control "any one of the great number of subjects of public interest, jurisdiction of which the States have never parted with. . . ." *Child Labor Tax Case,* at 38. I say "significantly" because Mr. Justice Holmes and two of the Justices who had joined his dissent in *Hammer* v. *Dagenhart*, McKenna and Brandeis, J. J., agreed with the opinion in the *Child Labor Tax Case*. Issues of such gravity affecting the balance of powers within our federal system are not susceptible of comprehensive statement by smooth formulas such as that a tax is nonetheless a tax although it discourages the activities taxed, or, that a tax may be imposed although it may effect ulterior ends. No such phrase, however fine and well-worn, enables one to decide the concrete case.

What is relevant to judgment here is that, even if the history of this legislation as it went through Congress did not give one the libretto to the song, the context of the circumstances which brought forth this enactment—sensationally exploited disclosures regarding gambling in big cities and small, the relation of this gambling to corrupt politics, the impatient public response to these disclosures, the feeling of ineptitude or paralysis on the part of local law-enforcing agencies—emphatically supports what was revealed on the floor of Congress, namely, that what was formally a means of raising revenue for the Federal Government was essentially an effort to check if not to stamp out professional gambling.

A nominal taxing measure must be found an inadmissible intrusion into a domain of legislation reserved for the States not merely when Congress requires that such a measure is to be enforced through a detailed scheme of administration beyond the obvious fiscal needs, as in the *Child Labor Tax Case, supra.* That is one ground for holding that Congress was constitutionally disrespectful of what is reserved to the States. Another basis for deeming such a formal revenue measure inadmissible is presented by this case. In addition to the fact that Congress was concerned with activity beyond the authority of the Federal Government to deal with, the enforcing provision of this enactment is designed for the systematic confession of crimes with a view to prosecution for such crimes under State law.

It is one thing to hold that the exception, which the Fifth Amendment makes to the duty of a witness to give his testimony when relevant to a proceeding in a federal court, does not include the potential danger to that witness of possible prosecution in a State court, *Brown* v. *Walker,* 161 U.S. 591, 606, and, conversely, that the Fifth Amendment does not enable States to give immunity from use in federal courts of testimony given in a State court. *Feldman* v. *United States,* 322 U.S. 487. It is a wholly different thing to hold that Congress, which cannot constitutionally grapple directly with gambling in the States, may compel self-incriminating disclosures for the enforcement of State gambling laws, merely because it does so under the guise of a revenue measure obviously passed not for

revenue purposes. The motive of congressional legislation is not for our scrutiny, provided only that the ulterior purpose is not expressed in ways which negative what the revenue words on their face express and, as in this case, which do not seek enforcement of the formal revenue purpose through means that offend those standards of decency in our civilization against which due process is a barrier.

I would affirm this judgment.

MR. JUSTICE DOUGLAS, while not joining in the entire opinion, agrees with the views expressed herein that this tax is an attempt by the Congress to control conduct which the Constitution has left to the responsibility of the States.

MR. JUSTICE BLACK, with whom MR. JUSTICE DOUGLAS concurs, dissenting:

The Fifth Amendment declares that no person "shall be compelled in any criminal case to be a witness against himself." The Court nevertheless here sustains an Act which requires a man to register and confess that he is engaged in the business of gambling. I think this confession can provide a basis to convict him of a federal crime for having gambled before registration without paying a federal tax. 26 U.S.C. (Supp. V) §§ 3285, 3290, 3291, 3294. Whether or not the Act has this effect, I am sure that it creates a squeezing device contrived to put a man in federal prison if he refuses to confess himself into a state prison as a violator of state gambling laws. The coercion of confessions is a common but justly criticized practice of many countries that do not have or live up to a Bill of Rights. But we have a Bill of Rights that condemns coerced confessions, however refined or legalistic may be the technique of extortion. I would hold that this Act violates the Fifth Amendment. See my dissent in *Feldman* v. *United States,* 322 U.S. 487, 494–503.

NOTE AND QUAERE: See also Mr. Justice Frankfurter's precautionary language in *Polish National Alliance* v. *National Labor Relations Board,* 322 U.S. 643, 650 (1944):

The interpenetrations of modern society have not wiped out state lines. It is not for us to make inroads upon our federal system either by indifference to its maintenance or excessive regard for the unifying forces of modern technology. Scholastic reasoning may prove that no activity is isolated within the boundaries of a single state, but that cannot justify absorption of legislative power by the United States over every activity.

In what sense, if any, can the Federal gambling tax and the *Kahriger* decision be called interferences with states' rights? (See also quaere following *Hammer* v. *Dagenhart,* above.)

HELVERING v. GERHARDT
304 U.S. 405 (1938)

Collector v. *Day,* 11 Wallace 113 (1871), held that the salary of a state judge was immune from the federal income tax. This was based on Marshall's dictum in *McCulloch* v. *Maryland,* below, that the power to tax involves the power to destroy. The problem came up again in the present case when the federal government sought to tax the salary of an employee of a state agency, the New York Port Authority.

MR. JUSTICE STONE delivered the opinion of the Court. . . .

The Constitution contains no express limitation on the power of either a state or the national government to tax the other, or its instrumentalities. The doctrine that there is an implied limitation stems from *McCulloch* v. *Maryland,* 4 Wheat. 316, in which it was held that a state tax laid specifically upon the privilege of issuing bank notes, and in fact applicable alone to the notes of national banks, was invalid since it impeded the national government in the exercise of its power to establish and maintain a bank, implied as an incident to the borrowing, taxing, war and other powers specifically granted to the national government by Article I, § 8 of the Constitution. It was held that Congress, having power to establish a bank by laws which, when enacted under the Constitution, are supreme, also had power to protect the bank by striking down state action impeding its operations; and it was thought that the state tax in question was so inconsistent with Congress's constitutional action in establishing the bank as to compel the conclusion that Congress intended to forbid application of the tax to the federal bank notes. Cf. *Osborn* v. *Bank of United States,* 9 Wheat. 738, 865–868.

In sustaining the immunity from state taxation, the opinion of the Court, by Chief Justice Marshall, recognized a clear distinction between the extent of the power of a state to tax national banks and that of the national government to tax state instrumentalities. He was careful to point out not only that the taxing power of the national government is supreme, by reason of the constitutional grant, but that in laying a federal tax on state instrumentalities the people of the states, acting through their representatives, are laying a tax on their own institutions and consequently are subject to political restraints which can be counted on to prevent abuse. State taxation of national instrumentalities is subject to no such restraint, for the people outside the state have no representatives who participate in the legislation; and in a real sense, as to them, the taxation is without representation. The exercise of the national taxing power is thus subject to a safeguard which does not operate when a state undertakes to tax a national instrumentality.

It was perhaps enough to have supported

the conclusion that the tax was invalid, that it was aimed specifically at national banks and thus operated to discriminate against the exercise by the Congress of a national power. Such discrimination was later recognized to be in itself a sufficient ground for holding invalid any form of state taxation adversely affecting the use or enjoyment of federal instrumentalities. *Miller* v. *Milwaukee,* 272 U.S. 713; cf. *Pacific Co., Ltd.* v. *Johnson,* 285 U.S. 480, 493. But later cases have declared that federal instrumentalities are similarly immune from nondiscriminatory state taxation— from the taxation of obligations of the United States as an interference with the borrowing power, *Weston* v. *Charleston,* 2 Pet. 449; and from a tax on "offices" levied upon the office of a captain of a revenue cutter, *Dobbins* v. *Erie County,* 16 Pet. 435.

That the taxing power of the federal government is nevertheless subject to an implied restriction when applied to state instrumentalities was first decided in *Collector* v. *Day,* 11 Wall. 113, where the salary of a state officer, a probate judge, was held to be immune from federal income tax. The question there presented to the Court was not one of interference with a granted power in a field in which the federal government is supreme, but a limitation by implication upon the granted federal power to tax. In recognizing that implication for the first time, the Court was concerned with the continued existence of the states as governmental entities, and their preservation from destruction by the national taxing power. The immunity which it implied was sustained only because it was one deemed necessary to protect the states from destruction by the federal taxation of those governmental functions which they were exercising when the Constitution was adopted and which were essential to their continued existence. . . .

We need not stop to inquire how far, as indicated in *McCulloch* v. *Maryland, supra,* the immunity of federal instrumentalities from state taxation rests on a different basis from that of state instrumentalities;

or whether or to what degree it is more extensive. As to those questions, other considerations may be controlling which are not pertinent here. It is enough for present purposes that the state immunity from the national taxing power, when recognized in *Collector* v. *Day, supra,* was narrowly limited to a state judicial officer engaged in the performance of a function which pertained to state governments at the time the Constitution was adopted without which no state "could long preserve its existence."

There are cogent reasons why any constitutional restriction upon the taxing power granted to Congress, so far as it can be properly raised by implication, should be narrowly limited. One, as was pointed out by Chief Justice Marshall in *McCulloch* v. *Maryland,* . . . is that the people of all the states have created the national government and are represented in Congress. Through that representation they exercise the national taxing power. The very fact that when they are exercising it they are taxing themselves serves to guard against its abuse through the possibility of resort to the usual processes of political action which provides a readier and more adaptable means than any which courts can afford, for securing accommodation of the competing demands for national revenue, on the one hand, and for reasonable scope for the independence of state action, on the other.

Another reason rests upon the fact that any allowance of a tax immunity for the protection of state sovereignty is at the expense of the sovereign power of the nation to tax. Enlargement of the one involves diminution of the other. When enlargement proceeds beyond the necessity of protecting the state, the burden of the immunity is thrown upon the national government with benefit only to a privileged class of taxpayers. . . . With the steady expansion of the activity of state governments into new fields they have undertaken the performance of functions not known to the states when the Constitution was adopted, and have taken over the management of business enterprises once conducted exclusively by private individuals subject to the national taxing power. In a complex economic society tax burdens laid upon those who directly or indirectly have dealings with the states, tend, to some extent not capable of precise measurement, to be passed on economically and thus to burden the state government itself. But if every federal tax which is laid on some new form of state activity, or whose economic burden reaches in some measure the state or those who serve it, were to be set aside as an infringement of state sovereignty, it is evident that a restriction upon national power, devised only as a shield to protect the states from curtailment of the essential operations of government which they have exercised from the beginning, would become a ready means for striking down the taxing power of the nation. . . .

In a period marked by a constant expansion of government activities and the steady multiplication of the complexities of taxing systems, it is perhaps too much to expect that the judicial pronouncements marking the boundaries of state immunity should present a completely logical pattern. But they disclose no purposeful departure from, and indeed definitely establish, two guiding principles of limitation for holding the tax immunity of state instrumentalities to its proper function. The one, dependent upon the nature of the function being performed by the state or in its behalf, excludes from the immunity activities thought not to be essential to the preservation of state governments even though the tax be collected from the state treasury. The state itself was taxed for the privilege of carrying on the liquor business in *South Carolina* v. *United States*, 199 U.S. 437, and in *Ohio* v. *Helvering*, 292 U.S. 360; and a tax on the income of a state officer engaged in the management of a state-owned corporation operating a street railroad was sustained in *Helvering* v. *Powers*, 293 U.S. 214, because it was thought that the functions discouraged by these taxes were not indispensable to the maintenance of a state government. The other principle, exemplified by those cases where the tax laid upon individuals affects the state only as the burden is passed on to it by the taxpayer, forbids recognition of the immunity when the burden on the state is so speculative and uncertain that if allowed it would restrict the federal taxing power without affording any corresponding tangible protection to the state government; even though the function be thought important enough to demand immunity from a tax upon the state itself, it is not necessarily protected from a tax which well may be substantially or entirely absorbed by private persons. *Metcalf & Eddy* v. *Mitchell*, 269 U.S. 514. . . .

With these controlling principles in mind we turn to their application in the circumstances of the present case. The challenged taxes . . . are upon the net income of respondents, derived from their employment in common occupations not shown to be different in their methods or duties from those of similar employees in private industry. The taxpayers enjoy the benefits and protection of the laws of the United States. They are under a duty to support the government and are not beyond the reach of its taxing power. A nondiscriminatory tax laid on their net income, in common with that of all other members of the community, could by no reasonable probability be considered to preclude the performance of the function which New York and New Jersey have undertaken, or to obstruct it more than like private enterprises are obstructed by our taxing system. Even though, to some unascertainable extent, the tax deprives the state of the advantage of paying less than the standard rate for the services which they engage, it does not curtail any of those functions which have been thought hitherto to be essential to their continued existence as states. . . . The effect of the immunity if allowed would be to relieve respondents of their duty of financial support to the national government, in order to secure to the state a theoretical advantage so speculative in its character and measurement as to be unsubstantial. A tax immunity devised for protection of the states as government entities cannot be pressed so far. . . .

Expressing no opinion whether a federal tax may be imposed upon the Port Authority itself with respect to its receipt of income or its other activities, we decide only that the present tax neither precludes nor threatens unreasonably to obstruct any function essential to the continued existence of the state government. So much of the burden of the tax laid upon respondents' income as may reach the state is but a necessary incident to the coexistence within the same organized government of the two taxing sovereigns, and hence is a burden the existence of which the Constitution presupposes. The immunity, if allowed, would impose to an inadmissible extent a restriction upon the taxing power which the Constitution has granted to the federal government.

Reversed.

MR. JUSTICE CARDOZO and MR. JUSTICE REED took no part in the consideration or decision in this case.

MR. JUSTICE BLACK [concurred].

[MR. JUSTICE BUTLER wrote a dissenting opinion in which MR. JUSTICE McREYNOLDS concurred.]

NOTE: For the fate of *Collector* v. *Day*, see *Graves* v. *New York ex rel O'Keefe*, below. As to federal power to *regulate* state activities, see *United States* v. *California*, above.

NEW YORK v. *UNITED STATES*
326 U.S. 572 (1946)

A lower court held that the State of New York, like others engaged in the bottling and sale of mineral water, was subject to the federal tax on such operations. New York claimed exemption on the ground that this was a "usual, traditional and essential governmental function." The Supreme Court granted certiorari.

MR. JUSTICE FRANKFURTER announced the judgment of the Court and delivered an opinion in which MR. JUSTICE RUTLEDGE joined.

Section 615(a) (5) of the 1932 Revenue Act, 47 Stat. 169, 264, imposed a tax on mineral waters. The United States brought this suit to recover taxes assessed against the State of New York on the sale of mineral waters taken from Saratoga Springs, New York. The State claims immunity from this tax on the ground that "in the bottling and sale of the said waters the defendant State of New York was engaged in the exercise of a usual, traditional and essential governmental function." The claim was rejected by the District Court and judgment went for the United States.

48 F. Supp. 15. The judgment was affirmed by the Circuit Court of Appeals for the Second Circuit. 140 F.2d 608. The strong urging of New York for further clarification of the amenability of States to the taxing power of the United States led us to grant certiorari. 322 U.S. 724. After the case was argued at the 1944 Term, reargument was ordered.

On the basis of authority the case is quickly disposed of. When States sought to control the liquor traffic by going into the liquor business, they were denied immunity from federal taxes upon the liquor business. *South Carolina* v. *United States*, 199 U.S. 437; *Ohio* v. *Helvering*, 292 U.S. 360. And in rejecting a claim of immunity from federal taxation when Massachusetts took over the street railways of Boston, this Court a decade ago said: "We see no reason for putting the operation of a street railway [by a State] in a different category from the sale of liquors." *Helvering* v. *Powers*, 293 U.S. 214, 227. We certainly see no reason for putting soft drinks in a different constitutional category from hard drinks. See also *Allen* v. *Regents*, 304 U.S. 439.

But the fear that one government may cripple or obstruct the operations of the other early led to the assumption that there was a reciprocal immunity of the instrumentalities of each from taxation by the other. It was assumed that there was an equivalence in the implications of taxation by a State of the governmental activities of the National Government and the taxation by the National Government of State instrumentalities. The considerations bearing upon taxation by the States of activities or agencies of the federal government are not correlative with the considerations bearing upon federal taxation of State agencies or activities. The federal government is the government of all the States, and all the States share in the legislative process by which a tax of general applicability is laid.

In the older cases, the emphasis was on immunity from taxation. The whole tendency of recent cases reveals a shift in emphasis to that of limitation upon immunity. They also indicate an awareness of the limited rôle of courts in assessing the relative weight of the factors upon which immunity is based. Any implied limitation upon the supremacy of the federal power to levy a tax like that now before us, in the absence of discrimination against State activities, brings fiscal and political factors into play. The problem cannot escape issues that do not lend themselves to judgment by criteria and methods of reasoning that are within the professional training and special competence of judges. Indeed the claim of implied immunity by States from federal taxation raises questions not wholly unlike provisions of the Constitution, such as that of Art. IV, § 4, guaranteeing States a republican form of government, see *Pacific States Tel. & Tel. Co.* v. *Oregon*, 223 U.S. 118, which this Court has deemed not within its duty to adjudicate.

We have already held that by engaging in the railroad business a State cannot withdraw the railroad from the power of the federal government to regulate commerce. *United States* v. *California*, 297 U.S. 175. See also *University of Illinois* v. *United States*, 289 U.S. 48. Surely the power of Congress to lay taxes has impliedly no less a reach than the power of Congress to regulate commerce. There are, of course, State activities and State-owned property that partake of uniqueness from the point of view of intergovernmental relations. These inherently constitute a class by themselves. Only a State can own a State house; only a State can get income by taxing. These could not be included for purposes of federal taxation in any abstract category of taxpayers without taxing the State as a State. But so long as Congress generally taps a source of revenue by whomsoever earned and not uniquely capable of being earned only by a State, the Constitution of the United States does not forbid it merely because its incidence falls also on a State. . . .

The process of constitutional adjudication does not thrive on conjuring up horrible possibilities that never happen in the real world and devising doctrines sufficiently comprehensive in detail to cover the remotest contingency. Nor need we go beyond what is required for a reasoned disposition of the kind of controversy now before the Court. The restriction upon States not to make laws that discriminate against interstate commerce is a vital constitutional principle, even though "discrimination" is not a code of specifics but a continuous process of application. So we decide enough when we reject limitations upon the taxing power of Congress derived from such untenable criteria as "proprietary" against "governmental" activities of the States, or historically sanctioned activities of Government or activities conducted merely for profit, and find no restriction upon Congress to include the States in levying a tax exacted equally from private persons upon the same subject matter.

Judgment affirmed.

MR. JUSTICE JACKSON took no part in the consideration or decision of this case.

[The concurring opinion of MR. JUSTICE RUTLEDGE is omitted.]

MR. CHIEF JUSTICE STONE concurring:

MR. JUSTICE REED, MR. JUSTICE MURPHY, MR. JUSTICE BURTON, and I concur in the result. We are of the opinion that the tax here involved should be sustained and the judgment below affirmed.

In view of our decisions in *South Carolina* v. *United States*, 199 U.S. 437; *Ohio* v. *Helvering*, 292 U.S. 360; *Helvering* v. *Powers*, 293 U.S. 214; and *Allen* v. *Regents*, 304 U.S. 439, we would find it difficult not to sustain the tax in this case, even though we regard as untenable the distinction between "governmental" and "proprietary" interests on which those cases rest to some extent. But we are not prepared to say that the national government may constitutionally lay a nondiscriminatory tax on every class of property and activities of States and individuals alike.

Concededly a federal tax discriminating against a State would be an unconstitutional exertion of power over a coexisting sovereignty within the same framework of government. But our difficulty with the formula, now first suggested as offering a new solution for an old problem, is that a federal tax which is not discriminatory as to the subject matter may nevertheless so affect the State, merely because it is a State that is being taxed, as to interfere unduly with the State's performance of its sovereign functions of government. The counterpart of such undue interference has been recognized since Marshall's day as the implied immunity of each of the dual sovereignties of our constitutional system from taxation by the other. *McCulloch* v. *Maryland*, 4 Wheat. 316. We add nothing to this formula by saying, in a new form

of words, that a tax which Congress applies generally to the property and activities of private citizens may not be in some instances constitutionally extended to the States merely because the States are included among those who pay taxes on a like subject of taxation.

If the phrase "non-discriminatory tax" is to be taken in its long accepted meaning as referring to a tax laid on a like subject matter, without regard to the personality of the taxpayer, whether a State, a corporation or a private individual, it is plain that there may be nondiscriminatory taxes which, when laid on a State, would nevertheless impair the sovereign status of the State quite as much as a like tax imposed by a State on property or activities of the national government. *Mayo* v. *United States*, 319 U.S. 441, 447, 448. This is not because the tax can be regarded as discriminatory but because a sovereign government is the taxpayer, and the tax, even though non-discriminatory, may be regarded as infringing its sovereignty.

It is enough for present purposes that the immunity of the State from federal taxation would, in this case, accomplish a withdrawal from the taxing power of the nation a subject of taxation of a nature which has been traditionally within that power from the beginning. Its exercise now, by a non-discriminatory tax, does not curtail the business of the state government more than it does the like business of the citizen. It gives merely an accustomed and reasonable scope to the federal taxing power. Such a withdrawal from a non-discriminatory federal tax, and one which does not bear on the State any differently than on the citizen, is itself an impairment of the taxing power of the national government, and the activity taxed is such that its taxation does not unduly impair the State's functions of government. . . .

The problem is not one to be solved by a formula, but we may look to the structure of the Constitution as our guide to decision. "In a broad sense, the taxing power of either government, even when exercised in a manner admittedly necessary and proper, unavoidably has some effect upon the other. The burden of federal taxation necessarily sets an economic limit to the practical operation of the taxing power of the states, and vice versa. Taxation by either the state or the federal government affects in some measure the cost of operation of the other.

"But neither government may destroy the other nor curtail in any substantial manner the exercise of its powers. Hence the limitation upon the taxing power of each, so far as it affects the other, must receive a practical construction which permits both to function with the minimum of interference each with the other; and that limitation cannot be so varied or extended as seriously to impair either the taxing power of the government imposing the tax . . . or the appropriate exercise of the functions of the government affected by it." *Metcalf & Eddy* v. *Mitchell,* [269 U.S. 514] 523–524. . . .

Mr. Justice Douglas, with whom Mr. Justice Black concurs, dissenting: . . .

I do not believe *South Carolina* v. *United States* states the correct rule. A State's project is as much a legitimate governmental activity whether it is traditional, or akin to private enterprise, or conducted for profit. Cf. *Helvering* v. *Gerhardt,* 304 U.S. 405, 426, 427. A State may deem it as essential to its economy that it own and operate a railroad, a mill, or an irrigation system as it does to own and operate bridges, street lights, or a sewage disposal plant. What might have been viewed in an earlier day as an improvident or even dangerous extension of state activities may today be deemed indispensable. But as Mr. Justice White said in his dissent in *South Carolina* v. *United States,* any activity in which a State engages within the limits of its police power is a legitimate governmental activity. Here a State is disposing of some of its natural resources. Tomorrow it may issue securities, sell power from its public power project, or manufacture fertilizer. Each is an exercise of its power of sovereignty. Must it pay the federal government for the privilege of exercising that

inherent power? If the Constitution grants it immunity from a tax on the issuance of securities, on what grounds can it be forced to pay a tax when it sells power or disposes of other natural resources? . . .

Woodrow Wilson stated the starting point for me when he said that "the States of course possess every power that government has ever anywhere exercised, except only those powers which their own constitutions or the Constitution of the United States explicitly or by plain inference withhold. They are the ordinary governments of the country; the federal government is its instrument only for particular purposes." The supremacy clause, Article VI, clause 2, applies to federal laws within the powers delegated to Congress by the States. But it is antagonistic to the very implications of our federal system to say that the power of Congress to lay and collect taxes, Article I, § 8, includes the power to tax any state activity or function so long as the tax does not discriminate against the States. . . .

A tax is a powerful, regulatory instrument. Local government in this free land does not exist for itself. The fact that local government may enter the domain of private enterprise and operate a project for profit does not put it in the class of private business enterprise for tax purposes. Local government exists to provide for the welfare of its people, not for a limited group of stockholders. If the federal government can place the local governments on its tax collector's list, their capacity to serve the needs of their citizens is at once hampered or curtailed. The field of federal excise taxation alone is practically without limits. Many state activities are in marginal enterprises where private capital refuses to venture. Add to the cost of these projects a federal tax and the social program may be destroyed before it can be launched. In any case, the repercussions of such a fundamental change on the credit of the States and on their programs to take care of the needy and to build for the future would be considerable. To say the present tax will be sustained because it does not impair the State's functions of government is to conclude either that the sale by the State of its mineral water is not a function of government or that the present tax is so slight as to be no burden. The former obviously is not true. The latter overlooks the fact that the power to tax lightly is the power to tax severely. The power to tax is indeed one of the most effective forms of regulations. And no more powerful instrument for centralization of government could be devised. For with the federal government immune and the States subject to tax, the economic ability of the federal government to expand its activities at the expense of the States is at once apparent. That is the result whether the rule of *South Carolina* v. *United States* be perpetuated or a new rule of discrimination be adopted. . . .

3. THE SPENDING POWER

The next two cases should be read in the light of "The Great Depression and the New Deal," page 107.

UNITED STATES v. *BUTLER*
297 U.S. 1 (1936)

To raise farm income and relieve the pressure of unmarketable "surplus" crops Congress sought to restrict farm production by the Agricultural Adjustment Act of 1933. This was to be accomplished by "benefit payments" to those farmers who would follow an acreage reduction program. The scheme was financed by a special tax upon the processing of farm goods. In this case a cotton processor refused to pay the processing tax. The United States brought an action to collect it.

MR. JUSTICE ROBERTS delivered the opinion of the Court: . . .

First. At the outset the United States contends that the respondents have no standing to question the validity of the tax. The position is that the act is merely a revenue measure levying an excise upon the activity of processing cotton—a proper subject for the imposition of such a tax—the proceeds of which go into the federal treasury and thus become available for appropriation for any purpose. It is said that what the respondents are endeavoring to do is to challenge the intended use of the money pursuant to Congressional appropriation when, by confession, that money will have become the property of the government and the taxpayer will no longer have any interest in it. *Massachusetts* v. *Mellon*, 262 U.S. 447, is claimed to foreclose litigation by the respondents or other taxpayers, as such, looking to restraint of the expenditure of government funds. That case might be an authority in the petitioners' favor if we were here concerned merely with a suit by a taxpayer to restrain the expenditure of the public moneys. . . . But here the respondents who are called upon to pay moneys as taxes, resist the exaction as a step in an unauthorized plan. This circumstance clearly distinguishes the case. The government in substance and effect asks us to separate the Agricultural Adjustment Act into two statutes, the one levying an excise on processors of certain commodities; the other appropriating the public moneys independently of the first. Passing the novel suggestion that two statutes enacted as parts of a single scheme should be tested as if they were distinct and unrelated, we think the legislation now before us is not susceptible of such separation and treatment.

The tax can only be sustained by ignoring the avowed purpose and operation of the act, and holding it a measure merely laying an excise upon processors to raise revenue for the support of government. Beyond cavil the sole object of the legislation is to restore the purchasing power of agricultural products to a parity with that prevailing in an earlier day; to take money from the processor and bestow it upon farmers who will reduce their acreage for the accomplishment of the proposed end, and, meanwhile, to aid these farmers during the period required to bring the prices of their crops to the desired level. . . .

Second. The Government asserts that even if the respondents may question the propriety of the appropriation embodied in the statute, their attack must fail because Article I, § 8 of the Constitution, authorizes the contemplated expenditure of the funds raised by the tax. This contention presents the great and the controlling question in the case. . . .

The clause thought to authorize the legislation—the first—confers upon the Congress power "to lay and collect Taxes, Duties, Imposts and Excises, to pay the Debts and provide for the common Defence and general Welfare of the United States. . . ." It is not contended that this provision grants power to regulate agricultural production upon the theory that such legislation would promote the general welfare. The government concedes that the phrase "to provide for the general welfare" qualifies the power "to lay and collect taxes." The view that the clause grants power to provide for the general welfare, independently of the taxing power, has never been authoritatively accepted. Mr. Justice Story points out that, if it were adopted, "it is obvious that under color of the generality of the words, to 'provide for the common defence and general welfare,' the government of the United States is, in reality, a government of general and unlimited powers, notwithstanding the subsequent enumeration of specific powers."

The true construction undoubtedly is that the only thing granted is the power to tax for the purpose of providing funds for payment of the nation's debts and making provision for the general welfare.

Nevertheless, the Government asserts that warrant is found in this clause for the adoption of the Agricultural Adjustment Act. The argument is that Congress may appropriate and authorize the spending of moneys for the "general welfare"; that the phrase should be liberally construed to cover anything conducive to national welfare; that decision as to what will promote such welfare rests with Congress alone, and the courts may not review its determination; and, finally, that the appropriation under attack was in fact for the general welfare of the United States.

The Congress is expressly empowered to lay taxes to provide for the general welfare. Funds in the Treasury as a result of taxation may be expended only through appropriation. (Article I, § 9, cl. 7.) They can never accomplish the objects for which they were collected, unless the power to appropriate is as broad as the power to tax. The necessary implication from the terms of the grant is that the public funds may be appropriated "to provide for the general welfare of the United States." These words cannot be meaningless, else they would not have been used. The conclusion must be that they were intended to limit and define the granted power to raise and to expend money. How shall they be construed to effectuate the intent of the instrument?

Since the foundation of the nation, sharp differences of opinion have persisted as to the true interpretation of the phrase. Madison asserted it amounted to no more than a reference to the other powers enumerated in the subsequent clauses of the same section; that, as the United States is a government of limited and enumerated powers, the grant of power to tax and spend for the general national welfare must be confined to the enumerated legislative fields committed to the Congress. In this view the phrase is mere tautology, for taxation and appropriation are or may be necessary incidents of the exercise of any of the enumerated legislative powers. Hamilton, on the other hand, maintained the clause confers a power separate and distinct from those later enumerated, is not restricted in meaning by the grant of them, and Congress consequently has a substantive power to tax and to appropriate, limited only by the requirement that it shall be exercised to provide for the general welfare of the United States. Each contention has had the support of those whose views are entitled to weight. This court has noticed the question, but has never found it necessary to decide which is the true construction. Mr. Justice Story, in his Commentaries, espouses the Hamiltonian position. We shall not review the writings of public men and commentators or discuss the legislative practice. Study of all these leads us to conclude that the reading advocated by Mr. Justice Story is the correct one. While, therefore, the power to tax is not unlimited, its confines are set in the clause which confers it, and not in those of section 8 which bestow and define the legislative powers of the Congress. . . .

We are not now required to ascertain the scope of the phrase "general welfare of the United States" or to determine whether an appropriation in aid of agriculture falls within it. Wholly apart from that question, another principle embedded in our Constitution prohibits the enforcement of the Agricultural Adjustment Act. The act invades the reserved rights of the states. It is a statutory plan to regulate and control agricultural production, a matter beyond the powers delegated to the federal government. The tax, the appropriation of the funds raised, and the direction for their disbursement, are but parts of the plan. They are but means to an unconstitutional end. . . .

The power of taxation, which is expressly granted, may, of course, be adopted as a means to carry into operation another power also expressly granted. But resort to the taxing power to effectuate an end which is not legitimate, not within the scope of the Constitution, is obviously inadmissible. . . .

In the *Child Labor Tax Case,* 259 U.S. 20, and in *Hill* v. *Wallace,* 259 U.S. 44, this court had before it statutes which purported to be taxing measures. But their purpose was found to be to regulate the conduct of manufacturing and trading, not in interstate commerce, but in the states—matters not within any power conferred upon Congress by the Constitution—and the levy of the tax a means to force compliance. The court held this was not a constitutional use, but an unconstitutional abuse of the power to tax. In *Linder* v. *United States,* 268 U.S. 5, we held that the power to tax could not justify the regulation of the practice of a profession, under the pretext of raising revenue. In *United States* v. *Constantine,* 296 U.S. 287, we declared that Congress could not, in the guise of a tax, impose sanctions for violation of state law respecting the local sale of liquor. These decisions demonstrate that Congress could not, under the pretext of raising revenue, lay a tax on processors who refuse to pay a certain price for cotton and exempt those who agree so to do, with the purpose of benefiting producers.

Third. If the taxing power may not be used as the instrument to enforce a regulation of matters of state concern with respect to which the Congress has no authority to interfere, may it, as in the present case, be employed to raise the money necessary to purchase a compliance which the Congress is powerless to command? The Government asserts that whatever might be said against the validity of the plan, if compulsory, it is constitutionally sound because the end is accomplished by voluntary co-operation. There are two sufficient answers to the contention. The regulation is not in fact voluntary. The farmer, of course, may refuse to comply, but the price of such refusal is the loss of benefits. The amount offered is intended to be sufficient to exert pressure on him to agree to the proposed regulation. The power to confer or withhold unlimited benefits is the power to coerce or destroy. If the cotton grower elects not to accept the benefits, he will receive less for his crops; those who receive payments will be able to undersell him. The result may well be financial ruin. . . .

But if the plan were one for purely voluntary co-operation it would stand no better so far as federal power is concerned. At best, it is a scheme for purchasing with federal funds submission to federal regulation of a subject reserved to the states.

It is said that Congress has the undoubted right to appropriate money to executive officers for expenditure under contracts between the government and individuals; that much of the total expenditures is so made. But appropriations and expenditures under contracts for proper governmental purposes cannot justify contracts which are not within federal power. And contracts for the reduction of acreage and the control of production are outside the range of that power. An appropriation to be expended by the United States under contracts calling for violation of a state law clearly would offend the Constitution. Is a statute less objectionable which authorizes expenditure of federal moneys to induce action in a field in which the United States has no power to intermeddle? The Congress cannot invade state jurisdiction to compel individual action; no more can it purchase such action. . . .

We are not here concerned with a conditional appropriation of money, nor with a provision that if certain conditions are not complied with the appropriation shall no longer be available. By the Agricultural Adjustment Act the amount of the tax is appropriated to be expended only in payment under contracts whereby the parties bind themselves to regulation by the federal government. There is an obvious difference between a statute stating the conditions upon which moneys shall be expended and one effective only upon assumption of a contractual obligation to submit to a regulation which otherwise could not be enforced. Many examples pointing the distinction might be cited. We are referred to appropriations in aid of education, and it is said that no one has doubted the power of Congress to stipulate the sort of education for which money shall be expended.

But an appropriation to an educational institution which by its terms is to become available only if the beneficiary enters into a contract to teach doctrines subversive of the Constitution is clearly bad. An affirmance of the authority of Congress so to condition the expenditure of an appropriation would tend to nullify all constitutional limitations upon legislative power.

But it is said that there is a wide difference in another respect, between compulsory regulation of the local affairs of a state's citizens and the mere making of a contract relating to their conduct; that, if any state objects, it may declare the contract void and thus prevent those under the state's jurisdiction from complying with its terms. The argument is plainly fallacious. The United States can make the contract only if the federal power to tax and to appropriate reaches the subject-matter of the contract. If this does reach the subject-matter, its exertion cannot be displaced by state action. To say otherwise is to deny the supremacy of the laws of the United States; to make them subordinate to those of a state. This would reverse the cardinal principle embodied in the Constitution and substitute one which declares that Congress may only effectively legislate as to matters within federal competence when the states do not dissent.

Congress has no power to enforce its commands on the farmer to the ends sought by the Agricultural Adjustment Act. It must follow that it may not indirectly accomplish those ends by taxing and spending to purchase compliance. The Constitution and the entire plan of our government negative any such use of the power to tax and to spend as the act undertakes to authorize. It does not help to declare that local conditions throughout the nation have created a situation of national concern; for this is but to say that whenever there is a widespread similarity of local conditions, Congress may ignore constitutional limitations upon its own powers and usurp those reserved to the states. If, in lieu of compulsory regulation of subjects within the states' reserved jurisdiction, which is prohibited, the Congress could invoke the taxing and spending power as a means to accomplish the same end, clause 1 of § 8 of article 1 would become the instrument for total subversion of the governmental powers reserved to the individual states. . . .

Until recently no suggestion of the existence of any such power in the federal government has been advanced. The expressions of the framers of the Constitution, the decisions of this court interpreting that instrument and the writings of great commentators will be searched in vain for any suggestion that there exists in the clause under discussion or elsewhere in the Constitution, the authority whereby every provision and every fair implication from that instrument may be subverted, the independence of the individual states obliterated, and the United States converted into a central government exercising uncontrolled police power in every state of the Union, superseding all local control or regulation of the affairs or concerns of the states.

Hamilton himself, the leading advocate of broad interpretation of the power to tax and to appropriate for the general welfare, never suggested that any power granted by the Constitution could be used for the destruction of local self-government in the states. Story countenances no such doctrine. It seems never to have occurred to them, or to those who have agreed with them, that the general welfare of the United States (which has aptly been termed "an indestructible Union, composed of indestructible States,") might be served by obliterating the constituent members of the Union. But to this fatal conclusion the doctrine contended for would inevitably lead. And its sole premise is that, though the makers of the Constitution, in erecting the federal government, intended sedulously to limit and define its powers, so as to reserve to the states and the people sovereign power, to be wielded by the states and their citizens and not to be invaded by the United States, they nevertheless by a single clause gave power to the Congress to tear down the barriers, to invade the state's jurisdiction, and to become a parlia-

ment of the whole people, subject to no restrictions save such as are self-imposed. The argument, when seen in its true character and in the light of its inevitable results, must be rejected.

Since, as we have pointed out, there was no power in the Congress to impose the contested exaction, it could not lawfully ratify or confirm what an executive officer had done in that regard. Consequently the Act of 1935 does not affect the rights of the parties.

The judgment is affirmed.

MR. JUSTICE STONE, dissenting:

[The] pivot on which the decision of the Court is made to turn . . . is that a levy unquestionably within the taxing power of Congress may be treated as invalid because it is a step in a plan to regulate agricultural production and is thus a forbidden infringement of state power. The levy is not any the less an exercise of taxing power because it is intended to defray an expenditure for the general welfare rather than for some other support of government. Nor is the levy and collection of the tax pointed to as affecting the regulation. While all federal taxes inevitably have some influence on the internal economy of the states, it is not contended that the levy of a processing tax upon manufacturers using agricultural products as raw material has any perceptible regulatory effect upon either their production or manufacture. The tax is unlike the penalties which were held invalid in the *Child Labor Tax Case,* 259 U.S. 20, in *Hill* v. *Wallace,* 259 U.S. 44, in *Linder* v. *United States,* 268 U.S. 5, 17, and in *United States* v. *Constantine,* 296 U.S. 287, because they were themselves the instruments of regulation by virtue of their coercive effect on matters left to the control of the states. Here regulation, if any there be, is accomplished not by the tax, but by the method by which its proceeds are expended, and would equally be accomplished by any like use of public funds, regardless of their source.

The method may be simply stated. Out of the available fund payments are made to such farmers as are willing to curtail their productive acreage, who in fact do so and who in advance have filed their written undertaking to do so with the Secretary of Agriculture. In saying that this method of spending public moneys is an invasion of the reserved powers of the states, the Court does not assert that the expenditure of public funds to promote the general welfare is not a substantive power specifically delegated to the national government, as Hamilton and Story pronounced it to be. It does not deny that the expenditure of funds for the benefit of farmers and in aid of a program of curtailment of production of agricultural products, and thus of a supposedly better ordered national economy, is within the specifically granted power. But it is declared that state power is nevertheless infringed by the expenditure of the proceeds of the tax to compensate farmers for the curtailment of their cotton acreage. Although the farmer is placed under no legal compulsion to reduce acreage, it is said that the mere offer of compensation for so doing is a species of economic coercion which operates with the same legal force and effect as though the curtailment were made mandatory by act of Congress. In any event it is insisted that even though not coercive the expenditure of public funds to induce the recipients to curtail production is itself an infringement of state power, since the federal government cannot invade the domain of the states by the "purchase" of performance of acts which it has no power to compel.

Of the assertion that the payments to farmers are coercive, it is enough to say that no such contention is pressed by the taxpayer, and no such consequences were to be anticipated or appear to have resulted from the administration of the act. The suggestion of coercion finds no support in the record or in any data showing the actual operation of the act. Threat of loss, not hope of gain, is the essence of economic coercion. . . . The presumption of constitutionality of a statute is not to be overturned by an assertion of its coercive effect which rests on nothing more substantial than groundless speculation.

It is upon the contention that state power is infringed by purchased regulation of agricultural production that chief reliance is placed. It is insisted that, while the Constitution gives to Congress, in specific and unambiguous terms, the power to tax and spend, the power is subject to limitations which do not find their origin in any express provision of the Constitution and to which other expressly delegated powers are not subject.

The Constitution requires that public funds shall be spent for defined purpose, the promotion of the general welfare. Their expenditure usually involves payment on terms which will insure use by the selected recipients within the limits of the constitutional purpose. Expenditures would fail of their purpose and thus lose their constitutional sanction if the terms of payment were not such that by their influence on the action of the recipients the permitted end would be attained. The power of Congress to spend is inseparable from persuasion to action over which Congress has no legislative control. Congress may not command that the science of agriculture be taught in state universities. But if it would aid the teaching of that science by grants to state institutions, it is appropriate, if not necessary, that the grant be on the condition, incorporated in the Morrill Act, 12 Stat. 503, 26 Stat. 417, that it be used for the intended purpose. Similarly it would seem to be compliance with the Constitution, not violation of it, for the government to take and the university to give a contract that the grant would be so used. It makes no difference that there is a promise to do an act which the condition is calculated to induce. Condition and promise are alike valid since both are in furtherance of the national purpose for which the money is appropriated.

These effects upon individual action, which are but incidents of the authorized expenditure of government money, are pronounced to be themselves a limitation upon the granted power. . . .

Such a limitation is contradictory and destructive of the power to appropriate for the public welfare, and is incapable of practical application. The spending power of Congress is in addition to the legislative power and not subordinate to it. This independent grant of the power of the purse, and its very nature, involving in its exercise the duty to insure expenditure within the granted power, presuppose freedom of selection among divers ends and aims, and the capacity to impose such conditions as will render the choice effective. It is a contradiction in terms to say that there is power to spend for the national welfare, while rejecting any power to impose conditions reasonably adapted to the attainment of the end which alone would justify the expenditure.

The limitation now sanctioned must lead to absurd consequences. The government may give seeds to farmers, but may not condition the gift upon their being planted in places where they are most needed or even planted at all. The government may give money to the unemployed, but may not ask that those who get it shall give labor in return, or even use it to support their families. It may give money to sufferers from earthquake, fire, tornado, pestilence, or flood, but may not impose conditions, health precautions designed to prevent the spread of disease, or induce the movement of population to safer or more sanitary areas. All that, because it is purchased regulation infringing state powers, must be left for the states, who are unable or unwilling to supply the necessary relief. . . .

That the governmental power of the purse is a great one is not now for the first time announced. Every student of the history of government and economics is aware of its magnitude and of its existence in every civilized government. Both were well understood by the framers of the Constitution when they sanctioned the grant of the spending power to the federal government, and both were recognized by Hamilton and Story, whose views of the spending power as standing on a parity with the other powers specifically granted, have hitherto been generally accepted. . . . The power to tax and spend is not without constitutional restraints. One restriction is that the purpose must be truly national. Another is that it may not be used to coerce action left to state control. Another is the conscience and patriotism of Congress and the Executive. . . . Courts are not the only agency of government that must be assumed to have capacity to govern. Congress and the courts both unhappily may falter or be mistaken in the performance of their constitutional duty. But interpretation of our great charter of government which proceeds on any assumption that the responsibility for the preservation of our institutions is the exclusive concern of any one of the three branches of government, or that it alone can save them from destruction is far more likely, in the long run, "to obliterate the constituent members" of "an indestructible union of indestructible states" than the frank recognition that language, even of a constitution, may mean what it says: that the power to tax and spend includes the power to relieve a nationwide economic maladjustment by conditional gifts of money.

MR. JUSTICE BRANDEIS and MR. JUSTICE CARDOZO join in this opinion.

ALEXANDER HAMILTON, "REPORT ON MANUFACTURES" (1791)

[Referring to the General Welfare Clause, Hamilton observed:] The phrase is as comprehensive as any that could have been used, because it was not fit that the constitutional authority of the Union to appropriate its revenues should have been restricted within narrower limits than the "general welfare," and because this necessarily embraces a vast variety of particulars which are susceptible neither of specification nor of definition. It is therefore of necessity left to the discretion of the National Legislature to pronounce upon the objects which concern the general welfare, and for which, under that description, an appropriation of money is requisite and proper. And there seems to be no room for a doubt that whatever concerns the general interests of learning, of agriculture, of manufactures, and of commerce, are within the sphere of the national councils, as far as regards an application of money.

PRESIDENT WASHINGTON, EIGHTH ANNUAL MESSAGE TO CONGRESS

This message urged Congress to establish certain public "manufactures," a national university and, as the following excerpt indicates, funds for aid to agriculture.

It will not be doubted, that with reference either to individual, or National Welfare, Agriculture is of primary importance. In proportion as Nations advance in population, and other circumstances of maturity, this truth becomes more apparent; and renders the cultivation of the Soil more and more, an object of public patronage. Institutions for promoting it, grow up, supported by the public purse: and to what object can it be dedicated with greater propriety? Among the means which have been employed to this end, none have been attended with greater success than the establishment of Boards, composed of proper characters, charged with collecting and diffusing information, and enabled by premiums, and small pecuniary aids, to encourage and assist a spirit of discovery and improvement. This species of establishment contributes doubly to the increase of improvement; by stimulating to enterprise and experiment, and by drawing to a common centre, the results everywhere of individual skill and observation; and spreading them thence over the whole Nation. Experience accordingly has shewn, that they are very cheap Instruments, of immense National benefits.

STEWARD MACHINE CO. v. *DAVIS*

301 U.S. 548 (1937)

The unemployment aspect of the Social Security Act involves a federal excise (payroll) tax upon employers of eight or more workers. Tax-payers are allowed a credit against this tax (to the extent of 90 percent thereof) for any amount paid into a federally approved state unemployment compensation system. The purpose of the credit plainly was to encourage state unemployment insurance legislation. After paying the tax, the company here sued for a full refund.

MR. JUSTICE CARDOZO delivered the opinion of the Court: . . .

The assault on the statute proceeds on an extended front. Its assailants take the ground that the tax is not an excise; that it is not uniform throughout the United States as excises are required to be; that its exceptions are so many and arbitrary as to violate the Fifth Amendment; that its purpose was not revenue, but an unlawful invasion of the reserved powers of the states; and that the states in submitting to it have yielded to coercion and have abandoned governmental functions which they are not permitted to surrender.

The objections will be considered seriatim with such further explanation as may be necessary to make their meaning clear.

First. The tax, which is described in the statute as an excise, is laid with uniformity throughout the United States as a duty, an impost or an excise upon the relation of employment.

1. We are told that the relation of employment is one so essential to the pursuit of happiness that it may not be burdened with a tax. Appeal is made to history. From the precedents of colonial days we are supplied with illustrations of excises common in the colonies. They are said to have been bound up with the enjoyment of particular commodities. Appeal is also made to principle or the analysis of concepts. An excise, we are told, imports a tax upon a privilege; employment, it is said, is a right, not a privilege, from which it follows that employment is not subject to an excise. Neither the one appeal nor the other leads to the desired goal.

As to the argument from history: Doubtless there were many excises in colonial days and later that were associated, more or less intimately, with the enjoyment of the use of property. This would not prove, even if no others were then known, that the forms then accepted were not subject to enlargement. . . . But in truth other excises *were* known, and known since early times. . . . [Examples cited.] Our colonial forebears knew more about ways of taxing than some of their descendants seem to be willing to concede.

The historical prop failing, the prop or fancied prop of principle remains. We learn that employment for lawful gain is a "natural" in "inherent" or "inalienable" right, and not a "privilege" at all. But natural rights, so called, are as much subject to taxation as rights of less importance. An excise is not limited to vocations or activities that may be prohibited altogether. It is not limited to those that are the outcome of a franchise. It extends to vocations or activities pursued as of common right. What the individual does in the operation of a business is amenable to taxation just as much as what he owns, at all events if the classification is not tyrannical or arbitrary. "Business is as legitimate an object of the taxing powers as property."

. . . The statute books of the states are strewn with illustrations of taxes laid on occupations pursued of common right. We find no basis for a holding that the power in that regard which belongs by accepted practice to the legislatures of the states, has been denied by the Constitution to the Congress of the nation.

2. The tax being an excise, its imposition must conform to the canon of uniformity. There has been no departure from this requirement. According to the settled doctrine the uniformity exacted is geographical, not intrinsic. . . .

Second. The excise is not invalid under the provisions of the Fifth Amendment by force of its exemptions.

The statute does not apply, as we have seen, to employers of less than eight. It does not apply to agricultural labor, or domestic service in a private home, or to some other classes of less importance. Petitioner contends that the effect of these restrictions is an arbitrary discrimination vitiating the tax.

The Fifth Amendment unlike the Fourteenth has no equal protection clause. But even the states, though subject to such a clause, are not confined to a formula of rigid uniformity in framing measures of taxation. They may tax some kinds of property at one rate, and others at another, and exempt others altogether. They may lay an excise on the operations of a particular kind of business, and exempt some other kind of business closely akin thereto. If this latitude of judgment is lawful for the states, it is lawful, a fortiori, in legislation by the Congress, which is subject to restraints less narrow and confining.

The classifications and exemptions directed by the statute now in controversy have support in considerations of policy and practical convenience that cannot be condemned as arbitrary. The classifications and exemptions would therefore be upheld if they had been adopted by a state and the provisions of the Fourteenth Amendment were invoked to annul them. . . . The Act of Congress is therefore valid, so far at least as its system of exemptions is concerned, and this though we assume that discrimination, if gross enough, is equivalent to confiscation and subject under the Fifth Amendment to challenge and annulment.

Third. The excise is not void as involving the coercion of the states in contravention of the Tenth Amendment or of restrictions implicit in our federal form of government.

The proceeds of the excise when collected are paid into the Treasury at Washington, and thereafter are subject to appropriation like public moneys generally. No presumption can be indulged that they will be misapplied or wasted. Even if they were collected in the hope or expectation that some other and collateral good would be furthered as an incident, that without more would not make the Act invalid. This indeed is hardly questioned. The case for the petitioner is built on the contention that here an ulterior aim is wrought into the very structure of the Act, and what is even more important that the aim is not only ulterior, but essentially unlawful. In particular, the 90 per cent credit is relied upon as supporting that conclusion. But before the statute succumbs to an assault upon these lines, two propositions must be made out by the assailant. There must be a showing in the first place that separated from the credit the revenue provisions are incapable of standing by themselves. There must be a showing in the second place that the tax and the credit in combination are weapons of coercion, destroying or impairing the autonomy of the states. The truth of each proposition being essential to the success of the assault, we pass for convenience to a consideration of the second, without pausing to inquire whether there has been a demonstration of the first.

To draw the line intelligently between duress and inducement there is need to remind ourselves of facts as to the problem of unemployment that are now matters of common knowledge. The relevant statistics are gathered in the brief of counsel for the government. Of the many available figures a few only will be mentioned. During the years 1929 to 1936, when the country was passing through a cyclical depression, the

number of the unemployed mounted to unprecedented heights. Often the average was more than 10 million; at times a peak was attained of 16 million or more. Disaster to the breadwinner meant disaster to dependents. Accordingly the roll of the unemployed, itself formidable enough, was only a partial roll of the destitute or needy. The fact developed quickly that the states were unable to give the requisite relief. The problem had become national in area and dimensions. There was need of help from the nation if the people were not to starve. It is too late today for the argument to be heard with tolerance that in a crisis so extreme the use of the moneys of the nation to relieve the unemployed and their dependents is a use for any purpose narrower than the promotion of the general welfare. The nation responded to the call of the distressed. Between January 1, 1933, and July 1, 1936, the states (according to statistics submitted by the government) incurred obligations of $689,291,802 for emergency relief; local subdivisions an additional $775,675,366. In the same period the obligations for emergency relief incurred by the national government were $2,929,307,-125, or twice the obligations of states and local agencies combined. According to the President's budget message for the fiscal year 1938, the national government expended for public works and unemployment relief for the three fiscal years 1934, 1935, and 1936, the stupendous total of $8,681,000,000. The parens patriae has many reasons—fiscal and economic as well as social and moral—for planning to mitigate disasters that bring these burdens in their train.

In the presence of this urgent need for some remedial expedient, the question is to be answered whether the expedient adopted has overleapt the bounds of power. The assailants of the statute say that its dominant end and aim is to drive the state legislatures under the whip of economic pressure into the enactment of unemployment compensation laws at the bidding of the central government. Supporters of the statute say that its operation is not con-

straint, but the creation of a larger freedom, the states and the nation joining in
a cooperative endeavor to avert a common
evil. Before Congress acted, unemployment
compensation insurance was still, for the
most part, a project and no more. Wisconsin was the pioneer. Her statute was
adopted in 1931. At times bills for such
insurance were introduced elsewhere, but
they did not reach the stage of law. In
1935, four states (California, Massachusetts,
New Hampshire, and New York) passed unemployment laws on the eve of the adoption of the Social Security Act, and two
others did likewise after the federal act and
later in the year. The statutes differed to
some extent in type, but were directed to
a common end. In 1936, 28 other states fell
in line, and eight more the present year.
But if states had been holding back before
the passage of the federal law, inaction was
not owing, for the most part, to the lack
of sympathetic interest. Many held back
through alarm lest in laying such a toll
upon their industries, they would place
themselves in a position of economic disadvantage as compared with neighbors or
competitors. See House Report, No. 615,
74th Congress, 1st session, p. 8; Senate
Report, No. 628, 74th Congress, 1st session,
p. 11. Two consequences ensued. One was
that the freedom of a state to contribute
its fair share to the solution of a national
problem was paralyzed by fear. The other
was that in so far as there was failure by
the states to contribute relief according to
the measure of their capacity, a disproportionate burden, and a mountainous one,
was laid upon the resources of the government of the nation.

The Social Security Act is an attempt to
find a method by which all these public
agencies may work together to a common
end. Every dollar of the new taxes will
continue in all likelihood to be used and
needed by the nation as long as states are
unwilling, whether through timidity or for
other motives, to do what can be done at
home. At least the inference is permissible
that Congress so believed, though retaining
undiminished freedom to spend the money

as it pleased. On the other hand fulfillment
of the home duty will be lightened and
encouraged by crediting the taxpayer upon
his account with the Treasury of the nation to the extent that his contributions
under the laws of the locality have simplified or diminished the problem of relief
and the probable demand upon the resources of the fisc. Duplicated taxes, or burdens that approach them, are recognized
hardships that government, state or national, may properly avoid. If Congress
believed that the general welfare would
better be promoted by relief through local
units than by the system then in vogue,
the cooperating localities ought not in all
fairness to pay a second time.

Who then is coerced through the operation of this statute? Not the taxpayer. He
pays in fulfillment of the mandate of the
local legislature. Not the state. Even now
she does not offer a suggestion that in passing the unemployment law she was affected
by duress. For all that appears she is satisfied with her choice, and would be sorely
disappointed if it were now to be annulled.
The difficulty with the petitioner's contention is that it confuses motive with coercion. "Every tax is in some measure regulatory. To some extent it interposes an
economic impediment to the activity taxed
as compared with others not taxed." In like
manner every rebate from a tax when conditioned upon conduct is in some measure
a temptation. But to hold that motive or
temptation is equivalent to coercion is to
plunge the law in endless difficulties. The
outcome of such a doctrine is the acceptance of a philosophical determinism by
which choice becomes impossible. Till now
the law has been guided by a robust common sense which assumes the freedom of
the will as a working hypothesis in the solution of its problems. The wisdom of the
hypothesis has illustration in this case.
Nothing in the case suggests the exertion
of a power akin to undue influence, if we
assume that such a concept can ever be
applied with fitness to the relations between state and nation. Even on that assumption the location of the point at which

pressure turns into compulsion, and ceases to be inducement, would be a question of degree,—at times, perhaps, of fact. The point had not been reached when Alabama made her choice. We cannot say that she was acting, not of her unfettered will, but under the strain of a persuasion equivalent to undue influence, when she chose to have relief administered under laws of her own making, by agents of her own selection, instead of under federal laws, administered by federal officers, with all the ensuing evils, at least to many minds, of federal patronage and power. There would be a strange irony, indeed, if her choice were now to be annulled on the basis of an assumed duress in the enactment of a statute which her courts have accepted as a true expression of her will. We think the choice must stand.

JUSTICES MCREYNOLDS, SUTHERLAND, VAN DEVENTER, and BUTLER dissented.

4. THE POWER TO CONDUCT WAR AND OTHER INTERNATIONAL AFFAIRS

WOODS v. MILLER CO.

333 U.S. 138 (1948)

Appeal from the District Court of the United States for the Northern District of Ohio.

MR. JUSTICE DOUGLAS delivered the opinion of the Court.

The case is here on a direct appeal, Act of August 24, 1937, 50 Stat. 752, 28 U.S.C. § 349a, from a judgment of the District Court holding unconstitutional Title II of the Housing and Rent Act of 1947. 61 Stat. 193, 196.

The Act became effective on July 1, 1947, and the following day the appellee demanded of its tenants increases of 40% and 60% for rental accommodations in the Cleveland Defense-Rental Area, an admitted violation of the Act and regulations adopted pursuant thereto. Appellant thereupon instituted this proceeding under § 206 (b) of the Act to enjoin the violations. A preliminary injunction issued. After a hearing it was dissolved and a permanent injunction denied.

The District Court was of the view that the authority of Congress to regulate rents by virtue of the war power (see *Bowles* v. *Willingham*, 321 U.S. 503) ended with the Presidential Proclamation terminating hostilities on December 31, 1946, since that proclamation inaugurated "peace-in-fact" though it did not mark termination of the war. It also concluded that, even if the war power continues, Congress did not act under it because it did not say so, and only if Congress says so, or enacts provisions so implying, can it be held that Congress intended to exercise such power. . . . See 74 F. Supp. 546.

We conclude, in the first place, that the war power sustains this legislation. The Court said in *Hamilton* v. *Kentucky Distilleries Co.*, 251 U.S. 146, 161, that the war power includes the power "to remedy the evils which have arisen from its rise and progress" and continues for the duration of that emergency. Whatever may be the consequences when war is officially terminated, the war power does not necessarily end with the cessation of hostilities. We recently held that it is adequate to support the preservation of rights created by wartime legislation, *Fleming* v. *Mohawk Wrecking & Lumber Co.*, 331 U.S. 111. But it has a broader sweep. In *Hamilton* v. *Kentucky Distilleries Co., supra,* and *Rup-*

pert v. *Caffey*, 251 U.S. 264, prohibition laws which were enacted after the Armistice in World War I were sustained as exercises of the war power because they conserved manpower and increased efficiency of production in the critical days during the period of demobilization, and helped to husband the supply of grains and cereals depleted by the war effort. Those cases followed the reasoning of *Stewart* v. *Kahn*, 11 Wall. 493, which held that Congress had the power to toll the statute of limitations of the States during the period when the process of their courts was not available to litigants due to the conditions obtaining in the Civil War.

The constitutional validity of the present legislation follows *a fortiori* from those cases. The legislative history of the present Act makes abundantly clear that there has not yet been eliminated the deficit in housing which in considerable measure was caused by the heavy demobilization of veterans and by the cessation or reduction in residential construction during the period of hostilities due to the allocation of building materials to military projects. Since the war effort contributed heavily to that deficit, Congress has the power even after the cessation of hostilities to act to control the forces that a short supply of the needed article created. If that were not true, the Necessary and Proper Clause, Art. I, § 8, cl. 18, would be drastically limited in its application to the several war powers. The Court has declined to follow that course in the past. . . . We decline to take it today. The result would be paralyzing. It would render Congress powerless to remedy conditions the creation of which necessarily followed from the mobilization of men and materials for successful prosecution of the war. So to read the Constitution would be to make it self-defeating.

We recognize the force of the argument that the effects of war under modern conditions may be felt in the economy for years and years, and that if the war power can be used in days of peace to treat all the wounds which war inflicts on our society,

it may not only swallow up all other powers of Congress but largely obliterate the Ninth and the Tenth Amendments as well. There are no such implications in today's decision. We deal here with the consequences of a housing deficit greatly intensified during the period of hostilities by the war effort. Any power, of course, can be abused. But we cannot assume that Congress is not alert to its constitutional responsibilities. And the question whether the war power has been properly employed in cases such as this is open to judicial inquiry. *Hamilton* v. *Kentucky Distilleries Co., supra; Ruppert* v. *Caffey, supra*.

The question of the constitutionality of action taken by Congress does not depend on recitals of the power which it undertakes to exercise. Here it is plain from the legislative history that Congress was invoking its war power to cope with a current condition of which the war was a direct and immediate cause. . . .

Reversed.

Mr. Justice Frankfurter concurs in this opinion because it decides no more than was decided in *Hamilton* v. *Kentucky Distilleries Co.,* 251 U.S. 146, and *Jacob Ruppert* v. *Caffey,* 251 U.S. 264, and merely applies those decisions to the situation now before the Court.

Mr. Justice Jackson, concurring.

I agree with the result in this case, but the arguments that have been addressed to us lead me to utter more explicit misgivings about war powers than the Court has done. The Government asserts no constitutional basis for this legislation other than this vague, undefined and undefinable "war power."

No one will question that this power is the most dangerous one to free government in the whole catalogue of powers. It usually is invoked in haste and excitement when calm legislative consideration of constitutional limitation is difficult. It is executed in a time of patriotic fervor that makes moderation unpopular. And, worst of all, it is interpreted by judges under the influence of the same passions and pressures. . . .

I think we can hardly deny that the war power is as valid a ground for federal rent control now as it has been at any time. We still are technically in a state of war. I would not be willing to hold that war powers may be indefinitely prolonged merely by keeping legally alive a state of war that had in fact ended. I cannot accept the argument that war powers last as long as the effects and consequences of war, for if so they are permanent—as permanent as the war debts. But I find no reason to conclude that we could find fairly that the present state of war is merely technical. We have armies abroad exercising our war power and have made no peace terms with our allies, not to mention our principal enemies. I think the conclusion that the war power has been applicable during the lifetime of this legislation is unavoidable.

KOREMATSU v. UNITED STATES

323 U.S. 214 (1945)

MR. JUSTICE BLACK delivered the opinion of the Court. . . .

The petitioner, an American citizen of Japanese descent, was convicted in a federal district court for remaining in San Leandro, California, a "Military Area," contrary to Civilian Exclusion Order No. 34 of the Commanding General of the Western Command, U.S. Army, which directed that after May 9, 1942, all persons of Japanese ancestry should be excluded from that area. No question was raised as to petitioner's loyalty to the United States. The Circuit Court of Appeals affirmed, and the importance of the constitutional question involved caused us to grant certiorari.

It should be noted, to begin with, that all legal restrictions which curtail the civil rights of a single racial group are immediately suspect. That is not to say that all such restrictions are unconstitutional. It is to say that courts must subject them to the most rigid scrutiny. Pressing public necessity may sometimes justify the existence of such restrictions; racial antagonism never can. . . .

The 1942 Act was attacked in the *Hirabayashi* case as an unconstitutional delegation of power; it was contended that the curfew order and other orders on which it rested were beyond the war powers of the Congress, the military authorities and of the President, as Commander in Chief of the Army; and finally that to apply the curfew order against none but citizens of Japanese ancestry amounted to a constitutionally prohibited discrimination solely on account of race. To these questions, we gave the serious consideration which their importance justified. We upheld the curfew order as an exercise of the power of the government to take steps necessary to prevent espionage and sabotage in an area threatened by Japanese attack.

In the light of the principles we announced in the *Hirabayashi* case, we are unable to conclude that it was beyond the war power of Congress and the Executive to exclude those of Japanese ancestry from the West Coast war area at the time they did. True, exclusion from the area in which one's home is located is a far greater deprivation than constant confinement to the home from 8 P.M. to 6 A.M. Nothing short of apprehension by the proper military authorities of the gravest imminent danger to the public safety can constitutionally justify either. But exclusion from a threatened area, no less than curfew, had a definite and close relationship to the prevention of espionage and sabotage. The military authorities, charged with the primary responsibility of defending our shores, concluded that curfew provided inadequate protection and ordered exclusion. They did so, as pointed out in our *Hirabayashi* opinion, in accordance with Congressional authority to the military to say who should, and who should not, remain in the threatened areas. . . .

Like curfew, exclusion of those of Japanese origin was deemed necessary because of the presence of an unascertained number of disloyal members of the group, most of whom we have no doubt were loyal to this country. It was because we could not reject the finding of the military authorities that it was impossible to bring about an immediate segregation of the disloyal from the loyal that we sustained the validity of the curfew order as applying to the whole group. In the instant case, temporary exclusion of the entire group was rested by the military on the same ground. The judgment that exclusion of the whole group was for the same reason a military imperative answers the contention that the exclusion was in the nature of group punishment based on antagonism to those of Japanese origin. That there were members of the group who retained loyalties to Japan has been confirmed by investigations made subsequent to the exclusions. Approximately five thousand American citizens of Japanese ancestry refused to swear unqualified allegiance to the United States and to renounce allegiance to the Japanese Emperor, and several thousand evacuees requested repatriation to Japan.

We uphold the exclusion order as of the time it was made and when the petitioner violated it. . . . In doing so, we are not unmindful of the hardships imposed by it upon a large group of American citizens. . . . But hardships are part of war, and war is an aggregation of hardships. All citizens alike, both in and out of uniform, feel the impact of war in greater or lesser measure. Citizenship has its responsibilities as well as its privileges, and in time of war the burden is always heavier. Compulsory exclusion of large groups of citizens from their homes, except under circumstances of direst emergency and peril, is inconsistent with our basic governmental institutions. But

when under conditions of modern warfare our shores are threatened by hostile forces, the power to protect must be commensurate with the threatened danger. . . .

It is said that we are dealing here with the case of imprisonment of a citizen in a concentration camp solely because of his ancestry, without evidence or inquiry concerning his loyalty and good disposition towards the United States. Our task would be simple, our duty clear, were this a case involving the imprisonment of a loyal citizen in a concentration camp because of racial prejudice. Regardless of the true nature of the assembly and relocation centers—and we deem it unjustifiable to call them concentration camps with all the ugly connotations that term implies—we are dealing specifically with nothing but an exclusion order. To cast this case into outlines of racial prejudice, without reference to the real military dangers which were presented, merely confuses the issue. Korematsu was not excluded from the Military Area because of hostility to him or his race. He *was* excluded because we are at war with the Japanese Empire, because the properly constituted military authorities feared an invasion of our West Coast and felt constrained to take proper security measures, because they decided that the military urgency of the situation demanded that all citizens of Japanese ancestry be segregated from the West Coast temporarily, and finally because Congress, reposing its confidence in this time of war in our military leaders—as inevitably it must—determined that they should have the power to do just this. There was evidence of disloyalty on the part of some, the military authorities considered that the need for action was great, and time was short. We cannot—by availing ourselves of the calm perspective of hindsight—now say that at that time these actions were unjustified.

Affirmed.

MR. JUSTICE FRANKFURTER, concurring. . . .

The provisions of the Constitution which confer on the Congress and the President powers to enable this country to wage war are as much part of the Constitution as provisions looking to a nation at peace. And we have had recent occasion to quote approvingly the statement of former Chief Justice Hughes that the war power of the Government is "the power to wage war successfully." *Hirabayashi* v. *United States, supra* at 93; and see *Home Bldg. & L. Assn.* v. *Blaisdell.* . . . Therefore, the validity of action under the war power must be judged wholly in the context of war. That action is not to be stigmatized as lawless because like action in times of peace would be lawless. To talk about a military order that expresses an allowable judgment of war needs by those entrusted with the duty of conducting war as "an unconstitutional order" is to suffuse a part of the Constitution with an atmosphere of unconstitutionality. The respective spheres of action of military authority and of judges are of course very different. But within their sphere, military authorities are no more outside the bounds of obedience to the Constitution than are judges within theirs. "The war power of the United States, like its other powers . . . is subject to applicable constitutional limitations." *Hamilton* v. *Kentucky Distilleries Co.,* 251 U.S. 146, 156. To recognize that military orders are "reasonably expedient military precautions" in time of war and yet to deny them constitutional legitimacy makes of the Constitution an instrument for dialectic subtleties not reasonably to be attributed to the hard-headed Framers, of whom a majority had had actual participation in war. . . . To find that the Constitution does not forbid the military measures now complained of does not carry with it approval of that which Congress and the Executive did. That is their business, not ours.

MR. JUSTICE ROBERTS:

I dissent, because I think the indisputable facts exhibit a clear violation of Constitutional rights.

This is not a case of keeping people off the streets at night as was *Hirabayashi* v. *United States,* 320 U.S. 81, nor a case of temporary exclusion of a citizen from an area for his own safety or that of the community, nor a case of offering him an opportunity to go temporarily out of an area where his presence might cause danger to himself or to his fellows. On the contrary, it is the case of convicting a citizen as a punishment for not submitting to imprisonment in a concentration camp, based on his ancestry, and solely because of his ancestry, without evidence or inquiry concerning his loyalty and good disposition towards the United States. If this be a correct statement of the facts disclosed by this record, and facts of which we take judicial notice, I need hardly labor the conclusion that Constitutional rights have been violated. . . .

MR. JUSTICE MURPHY, dissenting.

The exclusion of "all persons of Japanese ancestry, both alien and non-alien," from the Pacific Coast area on a plea of military necessity in the absence of martial law ought not to be approved. Such exclusion goes over "the very brink of constitutional power" and falls into the ugly abyss of racism.

In dealing with matters relating to the prosecution and progress of war, we must accord great respect and consideration to the judgments of the military authorities who are on the scene and who have full knowledge of the military facts. The scope of their discretion must, as a matter of necessity and common sense, be wide. And their judgments ought not to be overruled lightly by those whose training and duties ill-equip them to deal intelligently with matters so vital to the physical security of the nation.

At the same time, however, it is essential that there be definite limits to military discretion, especially where martial law has not been declared. Individuals must not be left impoverished of their constitutional rights on a plea of military necessity that has neither substance nor support. Thus, like other claims conflicting with the asserted constitutional rights of the individual, the military claim must subject itself to the judicial process of having its reasonableness determined and its conflicts with other interests reconciled. "What are the allowable limits of military discretion, and whether or not they have been overstepped in a particular case, are judicial questions." *Sterling* v. *Constantin,* 287 U.S. 378, 401.

The judicial test of whether the Government, on a plea of military necessity, can validly deprive an individual of any of his constitutional rights is whether the deprivation is reasonably related to a public danger that is so "immediate, imminent, and impending" as not to admit of delay and not to permit the intervention of ordinary constitutional processes to alleviate the danger. *United States* v. *Russell,* 13 Wall. 623, 627–8; *Mitchell* v. *Harmony,* 13 How. 115, 134–5; *Raymond* v. *Thomas,* 91 U.S. 712, 716. Civilian Exclusion Order No. 34, banishing from a prescribed area of the Pacific Coast "all persons of Japanese ancestry, both alien and nonalien," clearly does not meet that test. Being an obvious racial discrimination, the order deprives all those within its scope of the equal protection of the laws as guaranteed by the Fifth Amendment. It further deprives these individuals of their constitutional rights to live and work where they will, to establish a home where they choose and to move about freely. In excommunicating them without benefit of hearings, this order also deprives them of all their constitutional rights to procedural due process. Yet no reasonable relation to an "immediate, imminent, and impending" public danger is evident to support this racial restriction which is one of the most sweeping and complete deprivations of constitutional rights in the history of this nation in the absence of martial law. . . .

I dissent, therefore, from this legalization of racism. Racial discrimination in any form and in any degree has no justifiable part whatever in our democratic way of life. It is unattractive in any setting but it is utterly revolting among a free people who have embraced the principles set forth in the Constitution of the United States. All residents of this nation are kin in some way by blood or culture to a foreign land. Yet they are primarily and necessarily a part of the new and distinct civilization of the United States. They must accordingly be treated at all times as the heirs of the American experiment and as entitled to all the rights and freedoms guaranteed by the Constitution.

Mr. Justice Jackson, dissenting. . . .

It would be impracticable and dangerous idealism to expect or insist that each specific military command in an area of probable operations will conform to conventional tests of constitutionality. When an area is so beset that it must be put under military control at all, the paramount consideration is that its measures be successful, rather than legal. The armed services must protect a society, not merely its Constitution. The very essence of the military job is to marshal physical force, to remove every obstacle to its effectiveness, to give it every strategic advantage. Defense measures will not, and often should not, be held within the limits that bind civil authority in peace. No court can require such a commander in such circumstances to act as a reasonable man; he may be unreasonably cautious and exacting. Perhaps he should be. But a commander in temporarily focusing the life of a community on defense is carrying out a military program; he is not making law in the sense the courts know the term. He issues orders, and they may have certain authority as military commands, although they may be very bad as constitutional law.

But if we cannot confine military expedients by the Constitution, neither would I distort the Constitution to approve all that the military may deem expedient. That is what the Court appears to be doing, whether consciously or not. I cannot say, from any evidence before me, that the orders of General DeWitt were not reasonably expedient military precautions, nor could I say that they were. But even if they were permissible military procedures, I deny that it follows that they are constitutional. If, as the Court holds, it does follow, then we may well say that any military order will be constitutional and have done with it. . . .

Much is said of the danger to liberty from the Army program for deporting and detaining these citizens of Japanese extraction. But a judicial construction of the due process clause that will sustain this order is a far more subtle blow to liberty than the promulgation of the order itself. A military order, however unconstitutional, is not apt to last longer than the military emergency. Even during that period a succeeding commander may revoke it all. But once a judicial opinion rationalizes such an order to show that it conforms to the Constitution, or rather rationalizes the Constitution to show that the Constitution sanctions such an order, the Court for all time has validated the principle of racial discrimination in criminal procedure and of transplanting American citizens. The principle then lies about like a loaded weapon ready for the hand of any authority that can bring forward a plausible claim of an urgent need. Every repetition imbeds that principle more deeply in our law and thinking and expands it to new purposes. All who observe the work of courts are familiar with what Judge Cardozo described as "the tendency of a principle to expand itself to the limit of its logic." A military commander may overstep the bounds of constitutionality, and it is an incident. But if we review and approve, that passing incident becomes the doctrine of the Constitution. There it has a generative power of its own, and all that it creates will be in its own image. Nothing better illustrates this danger than does the Court's opinion in this case. . . .

EX PARTE MILLIGAN
4 Wallace 2 (1866)

> Milligan, a Southern sympathizer who lived in the North, was tried by a military tribunal and found guilty of several efforts to damage Northern military efforts in the Civil War. This case arose on petition for a writ of habeas corpus to free Milligan from military control.

MR. JUSTICE DAVIS delivered the opinion of the court: . . .

The controlling question in the case is this: Upon the facts stated in Milligan's petition, and the exhibits filed, had the military commission mentioned in it jurisdiction, legally, to try and sentence him? Milligan, not a resident of one of the rebellious States, or a prisoner of war, but a citizen of Indiana for twenty years past, and never in the military or naval service, is, while at his home, arrested by the military power of the United States, imprisoned, and, on certain criminal charges preferred against him, tried, convicted, and sentenced to be hanged by a military commission, organized under the direction of the military commander of the military district of Indiana. Had this tribunal the legal power and authority to try and punish this man? . . .

The Constitution of the United States is a law for rulers and people, equally in war and in peace, and covers with the shield of its protection all classes of men, at all times, and under all circumstances. No doctrine involving more pernicious consequences was ever invented by the wit of man than that any of its provisions can be suspended during any of the great exigencies of government. Such a doctrine leads directly to anarchy or despotism, but the theory of necessity on which it is based is false; for the government, within the Constitution, has all the powers granted to it which are necessary to preserve its existence; as has been happily proved by the result of the great effort to throw off its just authority.

Have any of the rights guaranteed by the Constitution been violated in the case of Milligan? and if so, what are they?

Every trial involves the exercise of judicial power; and from what source did the military commission that tried him derive their authority? Certainly no part of the judicial power of the country was conferred on them; because the Constitution expressly vests it "in one supreme court and such inferior courts as the Congress may from time to time ordain and establish," and it is not pretended that the commission was a court ordained and established by Congress. They cannot justify on the mandate of the President, because he is controlled by law, and has his appropriate sphere of duty, which is to execute, not to make, the laws; and there is "no unwritten criminal code to which resort can be had as a source of jurisdiction."

But it is said that the jurisdiction is complete under the "laws and usages of war."

It can serve no useful purpose to inquire what those laws and usages are, whence they originated, where found, and on whom they operate; they can never be applied to citizens in States which have upheld the authority of the government, and where the courts are open and their process unobstructed. This court has judicial knowledge that in Indiana the Federal authority was always unopposed, and its courts always open to hear criminal accusations and redress grievances; and no usage of war could sanction a military trial there for any offense whatever of a citizen in civil life, in nowise connected with the military service. Congress could grant no such power; and to the honor of our national legislature be it said, it has never been provoked by the state of the country even to attempt its exercise. One of the plainest constitutional provisions was, therefore, infringed when Milligan was tried by a court not ordained and established by Congress, and not composed of judges appointed during good behavior.

Why was he not delivered to the Circuit Court of Indiana to be proceeded against according to law? No reason of necessity could be urged against it; because Congress had declared penalties against the offenses charged, provided for their punishment, and directed that court to hear and determine them. And soon after this military tribunal was ended, the Circuit Court met, peacefully transacted its business, and adjourned. It needed no bayonets to protect it, and required no military aid to execute its judgments. It was held in a State, eminently distinguished for patriotism, by judges commissioned during the Rebellion, who were provided with juries, upright, intelligent, and selected by a marshal appointed by the President. The government had no right to conclude that Milligan, if guilty, would not receive in that court merited punishment; for its records disclose that it was constantly engaged in the trial of similar offenses, and was never interrupted in its administration of criminal justice. If it was dangerous, in the distracted condition of affairs, to leave Milligan unrestrained of his liberty, because he "conspired against the government, afforded aid and comfort to rebels, and incited the people to insurrection," the law said, arrest him, confine him closely, render him powerless to do further mischief; and then present his case to the grand jury of the district, with proofs of his guilt, and, if indicted, try him according to the course of the common law. If this had been done, the Constitution would have been vindicated, the law of 1863 enforced, and the securities for personal liberty preserved and defended.

Another guarantee of freedom was broken when Milligan was denied a trial by jury. The great minds of the country have differed on the correct interpretation to be given to the various provisions of the Federal Constitution; and judicial decision has been often invoked to settle their true meaning; but until recently no one ever doubted that the right of trial by jury was fortified in the organic law against the power of attack. It is now assailed; but if ideas can be expressed in words, and language has any meaning, this right—one of the most valuable in a free country—is preserved to every one accused of crime who is not attached to the army, or navy, or militia in actual service. The sixth amendment affirms that "in all criminal prosecutions the accused shall enjoy the right to a speedy and public trial by an impartial jury,"— language broad enough to embrace all persons and cases; but the fifth, recognizing the necessity of an indictment, or presentment, before anyone can be held to answer for high crimes, "except cases arising in the land or naval forces, or in the militia, when in actual service, in time of war or public danger"; and the framers of the Constitution, doubtless meant to limit the right of trial by jury, in the sixth amendment, to those persons who were subject to indictment or presentment in the fifth.

The discipline necessary to the efficiency of the army and navy required other and swifter modes of trial than are furnished by the common-law courts; and, in pursuance of the power conferred by the Constitution, Congress has declared the kinds of trial, and the manner in which they shall be conducted, for offenses committed while the party is in the military or naval service. Every one connected with these branches of the public service is amenable to the jurisdiction which Congress has created for their government, and, while thus serving, surrenders his right to be tried by the civil courts. All other persons, citizens of States where the courts are open, if charged with crime, are guaranteed the inestimable privilege of trial by jury. . . .

It is claimed that martial law covers with its broad mantle the proceedings of this military commission. The proposition is this: that in a time of war the commander of an armed force (if, in his opinion, the exigencies of the country demand it, and of which he is the judge) has the power, within the lines of his military district, to suspend all civil rights and their remedies, and subject citizens as well as soldiers to the rule of his will; and in the exercise of his lawful authority cannot be restrained, except by his superior officer or the President of the United States.

If this position is sound to the extent claimed, then when war exists, foreign or domestic, and the country is subdivided into military departments for mere convenience, the commander of one of them can, if he chooses, within his limits, on the plea of necessity, with the approval of the Executive, substitute military force for, and to the exclusion of, the laws, and punish all persons, as he thinks right and proper, without fixed or certain rules.

The statement of this proposition shows its importance; for, if true, republican government is a failure, and there is an end of liberty regulated by law. Martial law, established on such a basis, destroys every guarantee of the Constitution, and effectually renders the "military independent of, and superior to, the civil power,"—the attempt to do which by the King of Great Britain was deemed by our fathers such an offense, that they assigned it to the world as one of the causes which impelled them to declare their independence. Civil liberty and this kind of martial law cannot endure together; the antagonism is irreconcilable; and, in the conflict, one or the other must perish. . . .

The two remaining questions in this case must be answered in the affirmative. The suspension of the privilege of the writ of *habeas corpus* does not suspend the writ itself. The writ issues as a matter of course; and on the return made to it the court decides whether the party applying is denied the right of proceeding any further with it.

If the military trial of Milligan was contrary to law, then he was entitled, on the facts stated in his petition, to be discharged from custody by the terms of the act of Congress of March 3, 1863. . . .

But it is insisted that Milligan was a prisoner of war, and, therefore, excluded from the privileges of the statute. It is not easy to see how he can be treated as a prisoner of war, when he lived in Indiana for the past twenty years, was arrested there, and has not been, during the late troubles, a resident of any of the states in rebellion. If in Indiana he conspired with bad men to assist the enemy, he is punishable for it in the courts of Indiana; but, when tried for the offense, he cannot plead the rights of war; for he was not engaged in legal acts of hostility against the government, and only such persons, when captured, are prisoners of war. If he cannot enjoy the immunities attaching to the character of a prisoner of war, how can he be subject to their pains and penalties? . . .

The CHIEF JUSTICE [CHASE] delivered the following opinion:

We agree in the proposition that no department of the government of the United States—neither President, nor Congress, nor the Courts—possesses any power not given by the Constitution. . . .

The Constitution itself provides for military government as well as for civil government. And we do not understand it to be claimed that the civil safeguards of the Constitution have application in cases within the proper sphere of the former.

What, then, is that proper sphere? Congress has power to raise and support armies; to provide and maintain a navy; to make rules for the government and regulation of the land and naval forces; and to provide for governing such part of the militia as may be in the service of the United States.

It is not denied that the power to make rules for the government of the army and navy is a power to provide for trial and punishment by military courts without a jury. It has been understood and exercised from the adoption of the Constitution to the present time. . . .

We think, therefore, that the power of Congress, in the government of the land and naval forces and of the militia, is not at all affected by the fifth or any other amendment. It is not necessary to attempt any precise definition of the boundaries of this power. But may it not be said that government includes protection and defence as well as the regulation of internal administration? And is it impossible to imagine cases in which citizens conspiring or attempting the destruction or great injury of the national forces may be subjected by Congress to military trial and punishment in the just exercise of this undoubted con-

stitutional power? Congress is but the agent of the nation, and does not the security of individuals against the abuse of this, as of every other power, depend on the intelligence and virtue of the people, on their zeal for public and private liberty, upon official responsibility secured by law, and upon the frequency of elections rather than upon doubtful constructions of legislative powers? . . .

In Indiana, for example, at the time of the arrest of Milligan and his co-conspirators, it is established by the papers in the record, that the state was a military district, was the theatre of military operations, had been actually invaded, and was constantly threatened with invasion. It appears, also, that a powerful secret association, composed of citizens and others, existed within the state, under military organization, conspiring against the draft, and plotting insurrection, the liberation of the prisoners of war at various depots, the seizure of the state and national arsenals, armed cooperation with the enemy, and war against the national government.

We cannot doubt that, in such a time of public danger, Congress had power, under the Constitution, to provide for the organization of a military commission, and for trial by that commission of persons engaged in this conspiracy. The fact that the Federal courts were open was regarded by Congress as a sufficient reason for not exercising the power; but that fact could not deprive Congress of the right to exercise it. Those courts might be open and undisturbed in the execution of their functions, and yet wholly incompetent to avert threatened danger, or to punish, with adequate promptitude and certainty, the guilty conspirators.

In Indiana, the judges and officers of the courts were loyal to the government. But it might have been otherwise. In times of rebellion and civil war it may often happen, indeed, that judges and marshals will be in active sympathy with the rebels, and courts their most efficient allies.

We have confined ourselves to the question of power. It was for Congress to determine the question of expediency. And Congress did determine it. That body did not see fit to authorize trials by military commission in Indiana, but by the strongest implication prohibited them. With that prohibition we are satisfied, and should have remained silent if the answers to the questions certified had been put on that ground, without denial of the existence of a power which we believe to be constitutional and important to the public safety,— a denial which, as we have already suggested, seems to draw in question the power of Congress to protect from prosecution the members of military commissions who acted in obedience to their superior officers, and whose action, whether warranted by law or not, was approved by that upright and patriotic President under whose administration the Republic was rescued from threatened destruction. . . .

We think that the power of Congress, in such times and in such localities, to authorize trials for crimes against the security and safety of the national forces, may be derived from its constitutional authority to raise and support armies and to declare war, if not from its constitutional authority to provide for governing the national forces.

We have no apprehension that this power, under our American system of government, in which all official authority is derived from the people, and exercised under direct responsibility to the people, is more likely to be abused than the power to regulate commerce, or the power to borrow money. And we are unwilling to give our assent by silence to expressions of opinion which seem to us calculated, though not intended, to cripple the constitutional powers of the government, and to augment the public dangers in times of invasion and rebellion.

MR. JUSTICE WAYNE, MR. JUSTICE SWAYNE and MR. JUSTICE MILLER, concur with me in these views.

NOTE: Toth, a civilian, was arrested by the military and taken to Korea for court-martial on charges of murder allegedly committed in Korea while he was a member of the armed forces of the United States. Toth's alleged connection with the offense had not been discovered until after his discharge from military service. Congress had authorized trial by court-martial in such circumstances lest discharged servicemen go unpunished. (Civil courts in the United States would have no authority to try such cases.) Toth was released through a writ of habeas corpus on the ground that as a civilian he could not be tried by court-martial. *United States ex rel. Toth* v. *Quarles,* 350 U.S. 11 (1955). In *Reid* v. *Covert* and *Kinsella* v. *Krueger,* 354 U.S. 1 (1957), the Court modified an old tradition that civilians accompanying the armed forces are subject to court-martial. The civilians in question—wives of servicemen on overseas duty—had been convicted of murdering their husbands. Reversing the convictions, the Court was divided. Mr. Justice Black, joined by Chief Justice Warren and Justices Douglas and Brennan, stood on a rigid rule that, "when the United States acts against citizens abroad it can [not] do so free of the Bill of Rights." Justice Frankfurter and Harlan, concurring in the result, took the more flexible, established view of the applicability of the Constitution abroad. In Mr. Justice Harlan's words, "I agree with my brother Frankfurter that, in view of *Ross* [140 U.S. 453 (1891)] and the *Insular Cases* [one of which is *Balzac* v. *Puerto Rico,* 258 U.S. 298 (1922)], we have before us a question analogous, ultimately, to issues of due process; one can say, in fact, that the question of which specific safeguards of the Constitution are appropriately to be applied in a particular context overseas can be reduced to the issue of what process is 'due' a defendant in the particular circumstances of a particular case." The concurring Justices thought that at least in capital cases the jury trial provisions of the Constitution were applicable to overseas civilian dependents of military personnel. Justices Clark and Burton dissented. Mr. Justice Whittaker did not participate in the decision of these cases.

In *Kinsella* v. *Singleton*, 361 U.S. 234 (1960), and *McElroy* v. *Guagliardo*, 361 U.S. 281 (1960), the *Covert-Kreuger* principle of trial by jury was extended to noncapital offenses committed by dependents of service personnel as well as by civilian employees of the armed forces at foreign bases.

EX PARTE QUIRIN
317 U.S. 1 (1942)

This is the famous *Nazi Saboteur* case. Quirin and several others admittedly landed secretly on the Florida coast from a German submarine. They were later picked up inland, tried by a special military commission (authorized by Congress), and found guilty of violating the laws of war. On petition for writs of habeas corpus, and on review of a District Court's refusal to issue such writs, the Supreme Court found that Quirin et al. were properly within military jurisdiction, that is, were not entitled to trial by jury.

[In a unanimous opinion (MR. JUSTICE MURPHY not participating) the Court through CHIEF JUSTICE STONE found Milligan's case inapplicable:]

We conclude that the Fifth and Sixth Amendments did not restrict whatever authority was conferred by the Constitution to try offenses against the law of war by military commission, and that petitioners, charged with such an offense not required to be tried by jury at common law, were lawfully placed on trial by the Commission without a jury.

Petitioners, and especially petitioner Haupt, stress the pronouncement of this Court in the *Milligan* case, 4 Wall. page 121, that the law of war "can never be applied to citizens in states which have upheld the authority of the government, and where the courts are open and their process unobstructed." Elsewhere in its

opinion, 4 Wall. at pages 118, 121, 122, and 131, the Court was at pains to point out that Milligan, a citizen twenty years resident in Indiana, who had never been a resident of any of the states in rebellion, was not an enemy belligerent either entitled to the status of a prisoner of war or subject to the penalties imposed upon unlawful belligerents. We construe the Court's statement as to the inapplicability of the law of war to Milligan's case as having particular reference to the facts before it. From them the Court concluded that Milligan, not being a part of or associated with the armed forces of the enemy, was a nonbelligerent, not subject to the law of war save as—in circumstances found not there to be present and not involved here— martial law might be constitutionally established.

NOTE: Habeas corpus is not a device for reviewing the merits of a decision by a military tribunal. Its limited purpose is to test the authority, or jurisdiction, of the deciding agency. In effect the Supreme Court in *Quirin's* case found that the laws of war were applicable and therefore the military commission had jurisdiction. But the laws of war were applicable only if Quirin et al. were invaders (belligerents). Who decided this crucial point? Apparently the commission's finding was treated by the Supreme Court as final. Of course the accused admitted that they had landed in partial uniform from an enemy vessel. But they claimed they had no intention of carrying out their sabotage orders, that they had gone on the mission only to escape from Nazi Germany. The Supreme Court specifically refused to *consider* this defense, that is, to review the finding of the military tribunal (317 U.S. at 25). Does this mean that any person in the United States who is merely charged with being an invader may be tried by the military and that its finding as to the fact of invasion will be conclusive?

General Yamashita was found guilty by an American military commission in the Philippines on charges of violating the law of war. This was before Philippine independence. On his petition for habeas corpus the Supreme Court held that "the order convening the commission was a lawful order, that the commission was lawfully constituted, that petitioner was charged with violation of the law of war and that the commission . . . did not violate any military, statutory or constitutional command." Moreover "it must be recognized," said the Court, ". . . that the military tribunals which Congress has sanctioned by the Articles of War are not courts whose rulings and judgments are made subject to review by this Court"; that the Court does "not appraise the evidence on which the petitioner was convicted"; and that "correction of . . . errors of decision is not for the courts but for the military authorities which are alone authorized to review. . . ." The petition was denied, two Justices dissenting on the ground that procedural errors in violation of the Fifth Amendment had been committed. *In re Yamashita*, 327 U.S. 1 (1946). Does citizenship matter in these cases, or does the Bill of Rights, if otherwise applicable, cover persons regardless of national allegiance? In *Quirin's* case the Court found the issue of citizenship *irrelevant;* the question was whether the accused were enemy belligerents regardless of citizenship.

As to the role of habeas corpus in nonmilitary proceedings, see Part Four, III, below.

PEREZ v. BROWNELL
356 U.S. 44 (1958)

Perez, a citizen of the United States by birth, remained outside this country from November 1944 to July 1947 for purposes of avoiding the draft. During that interval he voted in a political election in Mexico. The Nationality Act of 1940, as amended, provides that a person shall lose his citizenship by "voting in a political election in a foreign state. . . ." Perez brought suit in 1954 in a federal district court for a judgment declaring him to be a citizen of the United States. Relief was denied in two lower federal courts. The case reached the Supreme Court by certiorari.

Mr. Justice Frankfurter delivered the opinion of the Court. . . .

Our starting point is to ascertain whether the power of Congress to deal with foreign relations may reasonably be deemed to include a power to deal generally with the active participation, by way of voting, of American citizens in foreign political elections. Experience amply attests that in this day of extensive international travel, rapid communication and widespread use of propaganda, the activities of the citizens of one nation when in another country can easily cause serious embarrassments to the government of their own country as well as to their fellow citizens. We cannot deny to Congress the reasonable belief that these difficulties might well become acute, to the point of jeopardizing the successful conduct of international relations, when the citizen of one country chooses to participate in the political or governmental affairs of another country. The citizen may by his action unwittingly promote or encourage a course of conduct contrary to the interests of his own government; moreover, the people or government of the foreign country may regard his action to be the action of his government, or at least as a reflection if not an expression of its policy. Cf. Preuss, "International Responsibility for Hostile Propaganda Against Foreign States," 28 *Amer. Journal of Int'l Law* 649, 650.

It follows that such activity is regulable by Congress under its power to deal with foreign affairs. And it must be regulable on more than an ad hoc basis. The subtle influences and repercussions with which the government must deal make it reasonable for the generalized, although clearly limited, category of "political election" to be used in defining the area of regulation. That description carries with it the scope and meaning of its context and purpose; classes of elections—nonpolitical in the colloquial sense—as to which participation by Americans could not possibly have any effect on the relations of the United States with another country are excluded by any rational construction of the phrase. The classification that Congress has adopted

cannot be said to be inappropriate to the difficulties to be dealt with. Specific applications are of course open to judicial challenge, as are other general categories in the law, by a "gradual process of judicial inclusion and exclusion." *Davidson* v. *New Orleans*, 96 U.S. 97.

The question must finally be faced whether, given the power to attach some sort of consequence to voting in a foreign political election, Congress, acting under the necessary and proper clause, Art. I, § 8, cl. 18, could attach loss of nationality to it. Is the means, withdrawal of citizenship, reasonably calculated to effect the end that is within the power of Congress to achieve, the avoidance of embarrassment in the conduct of our foreign relations attributable to voting by American citizens in foreign political elections? The importance and extreme delicacy of the matters here sought to be regulated demand that Congress be permitted ample scope in selecting appropriate modes for accomplishing its purpose. The critical connection between this conduct and loss of citizenship is the fact that it is the possession of American citizenship by a person committing the act that makes the act potentially embarrassing to the American Government and pregnant with the possibility of embroiling this country in disputes with other nations. The termination of citizenship terminates the problem. Moreover, the fact is not without significance that Congress has interpreted this conduct, not irrationally, as importing not only something less than complete and unswerving allegiance to the United States but also elements of an allegiance to another country in some measure, at least, inconsistent with American citizenship.

Of course, Congress can attach loss of citizenship only as a consequence of conduct engaged in voluntarily. See *Mackenzie* v. *Hare*, 239 U.S. 299, 311–312. But it would be a mockery of this Court's decisions to suggest that a person, in order to lose his citizenship, must intend or desire to do so. The Court only a few years ago said of the person held to have lost her citizenship in *Mackenzie* v. *Hare, supra:* "The woman had not intended to give up her American citizenship." *Savorgnan* v. *United States*, 338 U.S. 491, 501. And the latter case sustained the denationalization of Mrs. Savorgnan although it was not disputed that she "had no intention of endangering her American citizenship or of renouncing her allegiance to the United States." 338 U.S., at page 495. What both women did do voluntarily was to engage in conduct to which acts of Congress attached the consequence of denationalization irrespective of—and, in those cases, absolutely contrary to—the intentions and desires of the individuals. Those two cases mean nothing—indeed, they are deceptive—if their essential significance is not rejection of the notion that the power of Congress to terminate citizenship depends upon the citizen's assent. It is a distortion of those cases to explain them away on a theory that a citizen's assent to denationalization may be inferred from his having engaged in conduct that amounts to an "abandonment of citizenship" or a "transfer of allegiance." Certainly an act of Congress cannot be invalidated by resting decisive precedents on a gross fiction —a fiction baseless in law and contradicted by the facts of the cases.

It cannot be said, then, that Congress acted without warrant when, pursuant to its power to regulate the relations of the United States with foreign countries, it provided that anyone who votes in a foreign election of significance politically in the life of another country shall lose his American citizenship. To deny the power of Congress to enact the legislation challenged here would be to disregard the constitutional allocation of governmental functions that it is this Court's solemn duty to guard. . . .

Judgment affirmed.

MR. CHIEF JUSTICE WARREN, with whom MR. JUSTICE BLACK and MR. JUSTICE DOUGLAS join, dissenting. . . .

The basic Constitutional provision crystallizing the right of citizenship is the first sentence of section one of the Fourteenth Amendment. It is there provided that "All persons born or naturalized in the United States, and subject to the jurisdiction thereof, are citizens of the United States and of the State wherein they reside." United States citizenship is thus the Constitutional birth-right of every person born in this country. This Court has declared that Congress is without power to alter this effect of birth in the United States. *United States* v. *Wong Kim Ark*, 169 U.S. 649, 703. The Constitution also provides that citizenship can be bestowed under a "uniform rule of naturalization," but there is no corresponding provision authorizing divestment. Of course, naturalization unlawfully procured can be set aside. But apart from this circumstance, the status of the naturalized citizen is secure. . . .

Twice before, this Court has recognized that certain voluntary conduct results in an impairment of the status of citizenship. In *Savorgnan* v. *United States*, 338 U.S. 491, an American citizen had renounced her citizenship and acquired that of a foreign state. This Court affirmed her loss of citizenship, recognizing that "From the beginning, one of the most obvious and effective forms of expatriation has been that of naturalization under the laws of another nation." 338 U.S. at page 498. *Mackenzie* v. *Hare*, 239 U.S. 299, involved an American woman who had married a British national. That decision sustained an act of Congress which provided that her citizenship was suspended for the duration of her marriage. . . . [This] case, like *Savorgnan*, simply acknowledges that United States citizenship can be abandoned, temporarily or permanently, by conduct showing a voluntary transfer of allegiance to another country.

The fatal defect in the statute before us is that its application is not limited to those situations that may rationally be said to constitute an abandonment of citizenship. In specifying that any act of voting in a foreign political election results in loss of citizenship, Congress has employed a classification so broad that it encompasses conduct that fails to show a voluntary abandonment of American citizenship. . . . The reach of this statute is best indicated by a decision of a former attorney general, holding that an American citizen lost her citizenship . . . by voting in an election in a Canadian town on the issue of whether beer and wine should be sold. Voting in a foreign election may be a most equivocal act, giving rise to no implication that allegiance has been compromised.

My conclusions are as follows. The government is without power to take citizenship away from a native-born or lawfully naturalized American. The Fourteenth Amendment recognizes that this priceless right is immune from the exercise of governmental powers. If the Government determines that certain conduct by United States citizens should be prohibited because of anticipated injurious consequences to the conduct of foreign affairs or to some other legitimate governmental interest, it may within the limits of the Constitution proscribe such activity and assess appropriate punishment. But every exercise of governmental power must find its source in the Constitution. The power to denationalize

is not within the letter or the spirit of the powers with which our Government was endowed. The citizen may elect to renounce his citizenship, and under some circumstances he may be found to have abandoned his status by voluntarily performing acts that compromise his undivided allegiance to his country. The mere act of voting in a foreign election, however, without regard to the circumstances attending the participation, is not sufficient to show a voluntary abandonment of citizenship. The record in this case does not disclose any of the circumstances under which this petitioner voted. We know only the bare fact that he cast a ballot. The basic right of American citizenship has been too dearly won to be so lightly lost.

[Mr. Justice Douglas wrote a separate dissenting opinion in which Mr. Justice Black joined.

Mr. Justice Whittaker filed a separate memorandum of dissent.]

TROP v. *DULLES*
356 U.S. 86 (1958)

In this case the Court held unconstitutional that part of the Nationality Act of 1940, as amended, which provides for loss of citizenship by reason of court-martial conviction and discharge from the armed forces for wartime desertion. The four judges who dissented in the *Perez* case used their arguments in that case on the majority side of this case. They also found that forfeiture of citizenship for desertion constituted a "cruel and unusual" punishment within the meaning of the Eighth Amendment. Justices Frankfurter, Burton, Clark, and Harlan who had been with the majority in *Perez*, dissented in *Trop*. For them the military power of Congress was sufficient in the one case, just as the foreign policy power was sufficient in the other, to support expatriation. The *Trop* decision thus turns essentially upon the views of Mr. Justice Brennan as seen in the following excerpt from his separate opinion:

Here, as in *Perez* v. *Brownell*, we must inquire whether there exists a relevant connection between the particular legislative enactment and the power granted to Congress by the Constitution. The Court there held that such a relevant connection exists between the power to maintain relations with other sovereign nations and the power to expatriate the American who votes in a

foreign election. (1) Within the power granted to Congress to regulate the conduct of foreign affairs lies the power to deal with evils which might obstruct or embarrass our diplomatic interests. Among these evils, Congress might believe, is that of voting by American citizens in political elections of other nations. Whatever the realities of the situation, many foreign nations may well view political activity on the part of Americans, even if lawful, as either expressions of official American positions or else as improper meddling in affairs not their own. In either event the reaction is liable to be detrimental to the interests of the United States. (2) Finding that this was an evil which Congress was empowered to prevent, the Court concluded that expatriation was a means reasonably calculated to achieve this end. . . .

But granting that Congress is authorized to deal with the evil of desertion, we must yet inquire whether expatriation is a means reasonably calculated to achieve this legitimate end and thereby designed to further the ultimate congressional objective —the successful waging of war. . . .

Admittedly Congress' belief that expatriation of the deserter might further the war effort may find some—though necessarily slender—support in reason. But here, any substantial achievement, by this device, of Congress' legitimate purposes under the war power seems fairly remote. It is at the same time abundantly clear that these ends could more fully be achieved by alternative methods not open to these objections. In the light of these factors, and conceding all that I possibly can in favor of the enactment, I can only conclude that the requisite rational relation between this statute and the war power does not appear—for in this relation the statute is not "really calculated to effect any of the objects entrusted to the government . . . ," *McCulloch* v. *Maryland*, 4 Wheat. 316, 423, 4 L.Ed. 579—and therefore that [this provision] falls beyond the domain of Congress.

NOTE: *Kennedy* v. *Mendoza-Martinez*, 372 U.S. 144 (1963), held unconstitutional those provisions of the Nationality Act of 1940 and the Immigration and Nationality Act of 1952 which impose loss of citizenship for "departing from or remaining outside of the . . . United States in time of war or . . . national emergency for the purpose of evading or avoiding [military] training and service." The Court's opinion by Mr. Justice Goldberg rested on a ground deemed not available in *Perez* and *Trop*, and which "obviates a choice here between the powers of Congress and the constitutional guarantee of citizenship." Thus the decision turned on the ground that "Congress has plainly imposed the sanction of deprivation of nationality as a punishment . . . without affording the procedural safeguards guaranteed by the Fifth and Sixth Amendments." Justices Stewart and White dissented on the basis of Perez.

UNITED STATES v. CURTISS-WRIGHT EXPORT CORP.

299 U.S. 304 (1936)

By joint resolution Congress authorized the President, if he found it conducive to peace, to impose an embargo on the shipment of arms to the countries at war in the Chaco. Under the terms of this resolution an embargo was proclaimed. Curtiss-Wright was prosecuted for shipping machine guns in violation of the proclamation.

MR. JUSTICE SUTHERLAND delivered the opinion of the Court: . . .

Whether, if the Joint Resolution had related solely to internal affairs it would be open to the challenge that it constituted an unlawful delegation of legislative power to the Executive, we find it unnecessary to determine. The whole aim of the resolution is to affect a situation entirely external to the United States, and falling within the category of foreign affairs. The determination which we are called to make, therefore, is whether the Joint Resolution, as applied to that situation, is vulnerable to attack under the rule that forbids a delegation of the law-making power. In other words, assuming (but not deciding) that the challenged delegation, if it were confined to internal affairs, would be invalid, may it nevertheless be sustained on the ground that its exclusive aim is to afford a remedy for a hurtful condition within foreign territory?

It will contribute to the elucidation of the question if we first consider the differences between the powers of the federal government in respect of foreign or external affairs and those in respect of domestic or internal affairs. That there are differences between them, and that these differences are fundamental may not be doubted.

The two classes of powers are different, both in respect of their origin and their nature. The broad statement that the federal government can exercise no powers except those specifically enumerated in the Constitution, and such implied powers as are necessary and proper to carry into effect the enumerated powers, is categorically true only in respect of our internal affairs. In that field, the primary purpose of the Constitution was to carve from the general mass of legislative powers *then possessed by the states* such portions as it was thought desirable to vest in the federal government, leaving those not included in the enumeration still in the states. *Carter* v. *Carter Coal Co.*, 298 U.S. 238, 294. That this doctrine applies only to powers which the states had, is self evident. And since the states severally never possessed international powers, such powers could not have been carved from the mass of state powers but obviously were transmitted to the United States from some other source. During the colonial period, those powers were possessed exclusively by and were entirely under the control of the Crown. By the Declaration of Independence, "the Representatives of the United States of America" declared the United [not the several] Colonies to be free and independent states, and as such to have "full Power to levy War, conclude Peace, contract Alliances, establish Commerce and to do all other Acts and Things which Independent States may of right do."

As a result of the separation from Great Britain by the colonies acting as a unit, the powers of external sovereignty passed from the Crown not to the colonies severally, but to the colonies in their collective and corporate capacity as the United States of America. Even before the Declaration, the colonies were a unit in foreign affairs, acting through a common agency—namely the Continental Congress, composed of delegates from the thirteen colonies. That agency exercised the powers of war and peace, raised an army, created a navy, and finally adopted the Declaration of Independence. Rulers come and go; governments end and forms of government change; but sovereignty survives. A political society cannot endure without a supreme will somewhere. Sovereignty is never held in suspense. When, therefore, the external sovereignty of Great Britain in respect of the colonies ceased, it immediately passed to the Union. See *Penhallow* v. *Doane*, 3 Dall. 54, 80–81. That fact was given practical application almost at once. The treaty of peace, made on September 23, 1783, was concluded between his Brittanic Majesty and the "United States of America." 8 Stat. —European Treaties—80.

The Union existed before the Constitution, which was ordained and established among other things to form "a more perfect Union." Prior to that event, it is clear that the Union, declared by the Articles of Confederation to be "perpetual," was the sole possessor of external sovereignty and in the Union it remained without change save in so far as the Constitution in express terms qualified its exercise. The Framers' Convention was called and exerted its power upon the irrefutable postulate that though the states were several their people in respect of foreign affairs were one. Compare *The Chinese Exclusion Case*, 130 U.S. 581,

604, 606. In that convention, the entire absence of state power to deal with those affairs was thus forcefully stated by Rufus King:

"The states were not 'sovereigns' in the sense contended for by some. They did not possess the peculiar features of sovereignty, —they could not make war, nor peace, nor alliances, nor treaties. Considering them as political beings, they were dumb, for they could not speak to any foreign sovereign whatever. They were deaf, for they could not hear any propositions from such sovereign. They had not even the organs or faculties of defence or offence, for they could not of themselves raise troops, or equip vessels, for war. 5 Elliott's *Debates* 212."

It results that the investment of the federal government with the powers of external sovereignty did not depend upon the affirmative grants of the Constitution. The powers to declare and wage war, to conclude peace, to make treaties, to maintain diplomatic relations with other sovereignties, if they had never been mentioned in the Constitution, would have vested in the federal government as necessary concomitants of nationality. Neither the Constitution nor the laws passed in pursuance of it have any force in foreign territory unless in respect of our own citizens (see *American Banana Co.* v. *United Fruit Co.,* 213 U.S. 347, 356); and operations of the nation in such territory must be governed by treaties, international understandings and compacts, and the principles of international law. As a member of the family of nations, the right and power of the United States in that field are equal to the right and power of the other members of the international family. Otherwise, the United States is not completely sovereign. The power to acquire territory by discovery and occupation (*Jones* v. *United States,* 137 U.S. 202, 212), the power to expel undesirable aliens (*Fong Yue Ting* v. *United States,* 149 U.S. 698, 705 et seq.), the power to make such international agreements as do not constitute treaties in the constitutional sense (*Altman & Co.* v. *United States,* 224

U.S. 583, 600–601; Crandall, *Treaties, Their Making and Enforcement,* 2d ed., p. 102 and note 1), none of which is expressly affirmed by the Constitution, nevertheless exist as inherently inseparable from the conception of nationality. This the court recognized, and in each of the cases cited found the warrant for its conclusions not in the provisions of the Constitution, but in the law of nations.

In *Burnet* v. *Brooks,* 288 U.S. 378, 396, we said, "As a nation with all the attributes of sovereignty, the United States is vested with all the powers of government necessary to maintain an effective control of international relations." Cf. *Carter* v. *Carter Coal Co., supra,* p. 295.

Not only, as we have shown, is the federal power over external affairs in origin and essential character different from that over internal affairs, but participation in the exercise of the power is significantly limited. In this vast external realm, with its important, complicated, delicate and manifold problems, the President alone has the power to speak or listen as a representative of the nation. He *makes* treaties with the advice and consent of the Senate; but he alone negotiates. Into the field of negotiation the Senate cannot intrude; and Congress itself is powerless to invade it. As Marshall said in his great argument of March 7, 1800, in the House of Representatives, "The President is the sole organ of the nation in its external relations, and its sole representative with foreign nations." Annals, 6th Cong., col. 613. . . .

It is important to bear in mind that we are here dealing not alone with an authority vested in the President by an exertion of legislative power, but with such an authority plus the very delicate, plenary and exclusive power of the President as the sole organ of the federal government in the field of international relations—a power which does not require as a basis for its exercise an act of Congress, but which, of course, like every other governmental power, must be exercised in subordination to the applicable provisions of the Constitution. It is quite apparent that if, in the maintenance of our international relations, embarrassment—perhaps serious embarrassment—is to be avoided and success for our aims achieved, congressional legislation which is to be made effective through negotiation and inquiry within the international field must often accord to the President a degree of discretion and freedom from statutory restriction which would not be admissible were domestic affairs alone involved. Moreover, he, not Congress, has the better opportunity of knowing the conditions which prevail in foreign countries, and especially is this true in time of war. He has his confidential sources of information. He has his agents in the form of diplomatic, consular and other officials. Secrecy in respect of information gathered by them may be highly necessary, and the premature disclosure of it productive of harmful results. Indeed, so clearly is this true that the first President refused to accede to a request to lay before the House of Representatives the instructions, correspondence and documents relating to the negotiation of the Jay Treaty—a refusal the wisdom of which was recognized by the House itself and has never since been doubted. In his reply to the request, President Washington said:

"The nature of foreign negotiations requires caution, and their success must often depend on secrecy; and even when brought to a conclusion a full disclosure of all the measures, demands, or eventual concessions which may have been proposed or contemplated would be extremely impolitic; for this might have a pernicious influence on future negotiations, or produce immediate inconveniences, perhaps danger and mischief, in relation to other powers. The necessity of such caution and secrecy was one cogent reason for vesting the power of making treaties in the President, with the advice and consent of the Senate, the principle on which that body was formed confining it to a small number of members. To admit, then, a right in the House of Representatives to demand and to have as a matter of course all the papers respecting a negotiation with a foreign power would be to establish a dangerous precedent. 1 *Messages and Papers of the Presidents,* p. 194. . . .'"

In the light of the foregoing observations, it is evident that this court should not be in haste to apply a general rule which will have the effect of condemning legislation like that under review as constituting an unlawful delegation of legislative power. The principles which justify such legislation find overwhelming support in the unbroken legislative practice which has prevailed almost from the inception of the national government to the present day. . . .

The judgment of the court below must be reversed and the cause remanded for further proceedings in accordance with the foregoing opinion.

Reversed.

MR. JUSTICE MCREYNOLDS does not agree. He is of opinion that the court below reached the right conclusion and its judgment ought to be affirmed.

MR. JUSTICE STONE took no part in the consideration or decision of this case.

QUAERE: Does the *Curtiss-Wright* decision mean that, like federalism, the separation and nondelegability of powers does not apply to the conduct of American foreign policy?

MISSOURI v. *HOLLAND*
252 U.S. 416 (1920)

By a treaty in 1916 the United States and Great Britain undertook to protect migratory birds in passage between Canada and their southern wintering quarters. An Act of

Congress implemented this treaty by various regulations including "closed seasons."
This was a suit by Missouri to prevent a federal game warden from enforcing the act.

MR. JUSTICE HOLMES delivered the opinion of the Court:

On December 8, 1916, a treaty between the United States and Great Britain was proclaimed by the President. It recited that many species of birds in their annual migrations traversed certain parts of the United States and of Canada, that they were of great value as a source of food and in destroying insects injurious to vegetation, but were in danger of extermination through lack of adequate protection. It therefore provided for specified closed seasons and protection in other forms, and agreed that the two powers would take or propose to their law-making bodies the necessary measures for carrying the treaty out. 39 Stat. 1702. The above mentioned Act of July 3, 1918, entitled an act to give effect to the convention, prohibited the killing, capturing, or selling of any of the migratory birds included in the terms of the treaty except as permitted by regulations compatible with those terms, to be made by the Secretary of Agriculture. Regulations were proclaimed on July 31, and October 25, 1918. 40 Stat. 1812; 1863. It is unnecessary to go into any details, because, as we have said, the question raised is the general one whether the treaty and statute are void as an interference with the rights reserved to the states.

To answer this question it is not enough to refer to the Tenth Amendment, reserving the powers not delegated to the United States, because by Article II, section 2, the power to make treaties is delegated expressly, and by Article VI treaties made under the authority of the United States, along with the Constitution and laws of the United States made in pursuance thereof, are declared the supreme law of the land. If the treaty is valid there can be no dispute about the validity of the statute under Article I, section 8, as a necessary and proper means to execute the powers of the government. The language of the Constitution as to the supremacy of treaties being general, the question before us is narrowed to an inquiry into the ground upon which the present supposed exception is placed.

It is said that a treaty cannot be valid if it infringes the Constitution, that there are limits, therefore, to the treaty-making power, and that one such limit is that what an act of Congress could not do unaided, in derogation of the powers reserved to the states, a treaty cannot do. An earlier act of Congress that attempted by itself and not in pursuance of a treaty to regulate the killing of migratory birds within the states had been held bad in the District Court. *United States* v. *Shauver,* 214 Fed. Rep. 154. *United States* v. *McCullagh,* 221 Fed. Rep. 288. Those decisions were supported by arguments that migratory birds were owned by the states in their sovereign capacity for the benefit of their people, and that under cases like *Geer* v. *Connecticut,* 161 U.S. 519, this control was one that Congress had no power to displace. The same argument is supposed to apply now with equal force.

Whether the two cases cited were decided rightly or not they cannot be accepted as a test of the treaty power. Acts of Congress are the supreme law of the land only when made in pursuance of the Constitution, while treaties are declared to be so when made under the authority of the United States. It is open to question whether the authority of the United States means more than the formal acts prescribed to make the convention. We do not mean to imply that there are no qualifications to the treaty-making power; but they must be ascertained in a different way. It is obvious that there may be matters of the sharpest exigency for the national well being that an act of Congress could not deal with but that a treaty followed by such an act could, and it is not lightly to be assumed that, in matters requiring national action, "a power which must belong to and somewhere reside in every civilized government" is not to be found. . . . We are not yet discussing the particular case before us but only are considering the validity of the test proposed. With regard to that we may add that when we are dealing with words that also are a constituent act, like the Constitution of the United States, we must realize that they have called into life a being the development of which could not have been foreseen completely by the most gifted of its begetters. It was enough for them to realize or to hope that they had created an organism; it has taken a century and has cost their successors much sweat and blood to prove that they created a nation. The case before us must be considered in the light of our whole experience and not merely in that of what was said a hundred years ago. The treaty in question does not contravene any prohibitory words to be found in the Constitution. The only question is whether it is forbidden by some invisible radiation from the general terms of the Tenth Amendment. We must consider what this country has become in deciding what that amendment has reserved.

The state as we have intimated founds its claim of exclusive authority upon an assertion of title to migratory birds, an assertion that is embodied in statute. No doubt it is true that as between a state and its inhabitants the state may regulate the killing and sale of such birds, but it does not follow that its authority is exclusive of paramount powers. To put the claim of the state upon title is to lean upon a slender reed. Wild birds are not in the possession of anyone; and possession is the beginning of ownership. The whole foundation of the state's rights is the presence within their jurisdiction of birds that yesterday had not arrived, tomorrow may be in another state and in a week a thousand miles away. If we are to be accurate we cannot put the case of the state upon higher ground than that the treaty deals with creatures that for the moment are within the state borders, that it must be carried out by officers of the United States within the same territory, and that but for the treaty the state would be free to regulate this subject itself.

As most of the laws of the United States are carried out within the states and as many of them deal with matters which in the silence of such laws the state might regulate, such general grounds are not enough to support Missouri's claim. Valid treaties of course "are as binding within the territorial limits of the states as they are elsewhere throughout the dominion of the United States." . . . No doubt the great body of private relations usually fall within the control of the state, but a treaty may override its power. . . .

Here a national interest of very nearly the first magnitude is involved. It can be protected only by national action in concert with that of another power. The subject matter is only transitorily within the state and has no permanent habitat therein. But for the treaty and the statute there soon might be no birds for any powers to deal with. We see nothing in the Constitution that compels the government to sit by while a food supply is cut off and the protectors of our forests and our crops are destroyed. It is not sufficient to rely upon the states. The reliance is vain, and were it otherwise, the question is whether the United States is forbidden to act. We are of the opinion that the treaty and statute must be upheld.

Decree affirmed.

Mr. Justice Van Devanter and Mr. Justice Pitney dissent.

QUAERE: If in view of the two preceding cases there are no states' rights vis-à-vis the national conduct of foreign affairs, what of civil rights in this context? In a per curiam opinion in *Wilson* v. *Girard*, 254 U.S. 524 (1957), the Court found nothing in the Constitution to invalidate a treaty authorizing a foreign country (Japan) to try an American soldier for an offense allegedly committed within its territory. Contrast the remarks of Mr. Justice Black, supported by three of his associates, in *Reid* v. *Covert*, 354 U.S. 1 (1957), referred to above.

NOTE: James Madison observed that "interference with the powers of the states is no constitutional criterion of the power of [the federal government]. If the power was not given, [the federal government] could not exercise it; if given, they might exercise it, although it should interfere with the laws or even the constitutions of the states." (II *Annals of Congress* 1897 [1st. Cong.])

EXECUTIVE AGREEMENTS

Soviet Russia nationalized the assets of a Russian insurance company. The New York judiciary held the act of nationalization, insofar as it related to property in New York, invalid under state law. Meanwhile, by *executive agreement,* the President of the United States in effect acknowledged the validity of the nationalization by agreeing to accept the property in question in partial discharge of Soviet debts to the United States. This executive (Litvinov) agreement was part of a general settlement between the Soviet Union and the United States as a prelude to resumption of diplomatic relations between the two nations. *United States* v. *Pink,* 315 U.S. 203 (1942), held that the agreement superseded state law. "The powers of the President in the conduct of foreign relations include the power, without the consent of the Senate, to determine the public policy of the United States with respect to the Russian nationalization decrees. . . . A treaty is a 'Law of the Land' under the supremacy clause . . . of the Constitution. Such international compacts and agreements as the Litvinov Assignment have a similar dignity. If the President had the power to determine the policy which was to govern the question of recognition [of Russia], then the Fifth Amendment does not stand in the way of giving full force and effect to the Litvinov Assignment."

Obviously, so-called "isolationist" circles found no comfort in *Pink, Fairfax, Missouri* v. *Holland,* and *Curtiss-Wright.* Under Senator Bricker's leadership the following proposed constitutional amendment was offered to the Senate in June, 1953:

Section 1. A provision of a treaty which conflicts with this Constitution shall not be of any force or effect.

Section 2. A treaty shall become effective as internal law in the United States only through legislation which would be valid in the absence of treaty.

Section 3. Congress shall have power to regulate all executive and other agreements with any foreign power or international organization. All such agreements shall be subject to the limitations imposed on treaties by this article.

Section 4. The Congress shall have power to enforce this article by appropriate legislation.

Section 5. This article shall be inoperative unless it shall have been ratified as an amendment to the Constitution by the legislatures of three-fourths of the several States within seven years from the date of its submission.

After debate early in 1954 the Senate voted to substitute the so-called George compromise, which provided:

Section 1. A provision of a treaty or other international agreement which conflicts with this Constitution shall not be of any force or effect.

Section 2. An international agreement other than a treaty shall become effective as internal law in the United States only by an act of Congress.

This was rejected by a vote of one less than the required two-thirds majority in the Senate on February 26, 1954.

5. IMPLIED POWERS

JAMES MADISON ON IMPLIED POWERS

In subsequent debate on the [proposed] tenth amendment, Madison successfully resisted an attempt to insert one word, to make it say that powers not *expressly* delegated to the United States are reserved to the states or to the people. No government, he contended, could be limited to express powers: "There must necessarily be admitted powers by implication." (I. Brant, "The Madison Heritage" in E. Cohn (ed.), *The Great Rights*, p. 34 [1963]).

THOMAS JEFFERSON'S OPINION ON THE
POWER OF CONGRESS TO CHARTER A BANK

Hamilton proposed, and Congress adopted, a plan to establish a national bank. President Washington had doubts as to the constitutionality of the measure. Before approving it he solicited opinions as to its validity. Hamilton's view was substantially that adopted by the Court in *McCulloch* v. *Maryland.* Attorney General Randolph and Secretary of State Jefferson thought the measure unconstitutional. Following is Jefferson's view, in part:

I consider the foundation of the Constitution as laid on this ground—that *all powers not delegated to the United States, by the Constitution, nor prohibited by it to the states, are reserved to the states, or to the people* (10th Amend.). To take a single step beyond the boundaries thus specially drawn around the powers of Congress, is to take possession of a boundless field of power, no longer susceptible of any definition.

The incorporation of a bank, and the powers assumed by this bill, have not, in my opinion, been delegated to the United States by the Constitution.

I. *They are not among the powers specially enumerated. For these are,*—

1. A power to *lay taxes* for the purpose of paying the debts of the United States. But no debt is paid by this bill, nor any tax laid. Were it a bill to raise money, its origination in the Senate would condemn it by the Constitution.

2. To "borrow money." But this bill neither borrows money nor insures the borrowing of it. The proprietors of the bank will be just as free as any other money-holders to lend, or not to lend, their money to the public. The operation proposed in the bill, first to lend them two millions, and then borrow them back again, cannot change the nature of the latter act, which will still be a payment, and not a loan, call it by what name you please.

3. "To regulate commerce with foreign nations, and among the states, and with the Indian tribes." To erect a bank, and to regulate commerce, are very different acts. He who erects a bank creates a subject of commerce in its bills; so does he who makes a bushel of wheat, or digs a dollar out of the mines; yet neither of these persons regulates commerce thereby. To make a thing which may be bought and sold, is not to prescribe regulations for buying and selling.

Besides, if this were an exercise of the power of regulating commerce, it would be void, as extending as much to the internal commerce of every state, as it is external. For the power given to Congress by the Constitution does not extend to the internal regulation of the commerce of a state . . . which remains exclusively with its own legislature; but to its external commerce only, that is to say, its commerce with another state, or with foreign nations, or with the Indian tribes. Accordingly, the bill does not propose the measure as a "regulation of trade," but as "productive of considerable advantage to trade."

Still less are these powers covered by any other of the special enumerations.

II. *Nor are they within either of the general phrases, which are the two following:—*

1. "To lay taxes to provide for the general welfare of the United States;" that is to say, "to lay taxes *for the purpose* of providing for the general welfare;" for the laying of taxes is the *power,* and the general welfare the *purpose* for which the power is to be exercised. Congress are not to lay taxes *ad libitum, for any purpose they please;* but only to *pay the debts, or provide for the welfare, of the Union.* In like manner, they are not *to do anything they please,* to provide for the general welfare, but only *to lay taxes* for that purpose. To consider the latter phrase, not as describing the purpose of the first, but as giving a distinct and independent power to do any act they please which might be for the good of the Union, would render all the preceding and subsequent enumerations of power completely useless. It would reduce the whole instrument to a single phrase—that of instituting a Congress with power to do whatever would be for the good of the United States; and, as they would be the sole judges of the good or evil, it would be also a power to do whatever evil they pleased. It is an established rule of construction, where a phrase will bear either of two meanings, to give it that which will allow some meaning to the other parts of the instrument, and not that which will render all the others useless. Certainly no such universal power was meant to be given them. It was intended to lace them up straitly within the enumerated powers, and those without which, as means, these powers could not be carried into effect. It is known that the very power now proposed *as a means,* was rejected *as an end by the Convention which formed the Constitution.* A proposition was made to them, to authorize Congress to open canals, and an amendatory one to empower them to incorporate. But the whole was rejected; and one of the reasons of objection urged in debate was, that they then would have a power to erect a bank, which would render great cities, where there were prejudices and jealousies on that subject, adverse to the reception of the Constitution.

2. The second general phrase is, "to make all laws *necessary* and proper for carrying into execution the enumerated powers." But they can all be carried into execution without a bank. A bank, therefore, is not *necessary,* and consequently not authorized by this phrase.

It has been much urged that a bank will give great facility or convenience in the collection of taxes. Suppose this were true; yet the Constitution allows only the means which are "necessary," not those which are merely "convenient," for effecting the enumerated powers. If such a latitude of construction be allowed to this phrase as to give any non-enumerated power, it will go to every one; for there is no one which ingenuity may not torture into a *convenience, in some way or other, to some one* of so long a list of enumerated powers. It would swallow up all the delegated powers, and reduce the whole to one phrase, as before observed. Therefore it was that the Constitution restrained them to the *necessary* means; that is to say, to those means without which the grant of the power would be nugatory. . . .

Perhaps bank bills may be a more *convenient* vehicle than treasury orders. But a little *difference* in the degree of convenience cannot constitute the necessity which the Constitution makes the ground for assuming any non-enumerated power. . . .

It must be added, however, that, unless the President's mind, on a view of everything which is urged for and against this bill, is tolerably clear that it is unauthorized by the Constitution, if the *pro* and the *con* hang so evenly as to balance his judgment, a just respect for the wisdom of the legislature would naturally decide the balance in favor of their opinion. It is chiefly for cases where they are clearly misled by error, ambition, or interest, that the Constitution has placed a check in the negative of the President.

McCULLOCH v. *MARYLAND*
4 Wheaton 316 (1819)

Jeffersonian hostility toward the National Bank found expression in state legislation. Maryland, for example, imposed a special tax on the issuance of notes in Maryland by institutions not chartered in that state. In the context of the times the tax could fall only on the Maryland branch of the National Bank. This case began as an action against the cashier of that bank to collect a penalty of $100 for issuing a note on which the tax had not been paid. We consider here only that part of the case dealing with congressional power to charter a bank. As to the validity of the state tax see Part Three, III).

MR. CHIEF JUSTICE MARSHALL delivered the opinion of the Court: . . .

The first question made in the cause is, Has Congress power to incorporate a bank? It has been truly said, that this can scarcely be considered as an open question, entirely unprejudiced by the former proceedings of the nation respecting it. The principle now contested was introduced at a very early period of our history, has been recognized by many successive legislatures, and has been acted upon by the judicial department, in cases of peculiar delicacy, as a law of undoubted obligation.

It will not be denied, that a bold and daring usurpation might be resisted, after an acquiescence still longer and more complete than this. But it is conceived that a doubtful question, one on which human reason may pause, and the human judgment be suspended, in the decision of which the great principles of liberty are not concerned, but the respective powers of those who are equally the representatives of the people, are to be adjusted, if not put at rest by the practice of the government, ought to receive a considerable impression from that practice. An exposition of the Constitution, deliberately established by legislative acts, on the faith of which an immense property has been advanced, ought not to be lightly disregarded.

The power now contested was exercised by the first Congress elected under the present Constitution. The bill for incorporating the Bank of the United States did not steal upon an unsuspecting legislature, and pass unobserved. Its principle was completely understood, and was opposed with equal zeal and ability. After being resisted, first in the fair and open field of debate, and afterwards in the executive cabinet, with as much persevering talent as any measure has ever experienced, and being supported by arguments which convinced minds as pure and as intelligent as this country can boast, it became a law. The original act was permitted to expire; but a short experience of the embarrassments to which the refusal to revive it exposed the government, convinced those who were most prejudiced against the measure of its necessity, and induced the passage of the present law. It would require no ordinary share of intrepidity to assert, that a measure adopted under these circumstances, was a bold and plain usurpation, to which the Constitution gave no countenance. These observations belong to the cause: but they are not made under the impression that, were the question entirely new, the law would be found irreconcilable with the Constitution.

In discussing this question, the counsel for the state of Maryland have deemed it of some importance, in the construction of the Constitution, to consider that instrument not as emanating from the people, but as the act of sovereign and independent states. The powers of the general government, it has been said, are delegated by the states, who alone are truly sovereign; and must be exercised in subordination to the states, who alone possess supreme dominion. It would be difficult to sustain this proposition. The convention which framed the Constitution was, indeed, elected by the state legislatures. But the instrument, when it came from their hands, was a mere proposal, without obligation, or pretensions to it. It was reported to the then existing Congress of the United States, with a request that it might "be submitted to a convention of delegates, chosen in each state by the people thereof, under the recommendation of its legislature, for their assent and ratification." This mode of proceeding was adopted; and by the convention, by Congress, and by the state legislatures, the instrument was submitted to the *people*. They acted upon it, in the only manner in which they can act safely, effectively, and wisely, on such a subject, by assembling in convention. It is true, they assembled in their several states; and where else should they have assembled? No political dreamer

was ever wild enough to think of breaking down the lines which separate the states, and of compounding the American people into one common mass. Of consequence, when they act, they act in their states. But the measures they adopt do not, on that account, cease to be the measures of the people themselves, or become the measures of the state governments.

From these conventions, the Constitution derives its whole authority. The government proceeds directly from the people; is "ordained and established" in the name of the people; and is declared to be ordained, "in Order to form a more perfect Union, establish Justice, insure domestic Tranquility, . . . and secure the Blessings of Liberty to themselves [ourselves] and to their [our] Posterity." The assent of the states, in their sovereign capacity, is implied, in calling a convention, and thus submitting that instrument to the people. But the people were at perfect liberty to accept or reject it; and their act was final. It required not the affirmance, and could not be negatived, by the state governments. The Constitution, when thus adopted, was of complete obligation, and bound the state sovereignties.

. . . The government of the Union, then (whatever may be the influence of this fact on the case), is, emphatically and truly, a government of the people. In form, and in substance, it emanates from them. Its powers are granted by them, and are to be exercised directly on them, and for their benefit.

This government is acknowledged by all, to be one of enumerated powers. The principle, that it can exercise only the powers granted to it, would seem too apparent, to have required to be enforced by all those arguments, which its enlightened friends, while it was pending before the people, found it necessary to urge; that principle is now universally admitted. But the question respecting the extent of the powers actually granted, is perpetually arising, and will probably continue to arise, as long as our system shall exist. In discussing these questions, the conflicting powers of the general and state governments must be brought into view, and the supremacy of their respective laws, when they are in opposition, must be settled.

If any one proposition could command the universal assent of mankind, we might expect that it would be this—that the government of the Union, though limited in its powers, is supreme within its sphere of action. This would seem to result, necessarily, from its nature. It is the government of all; its powers are delegated by all; it represents all, and acts for all. Though any one state may be willing to control its operations, no state is willing to allow others to control them. The nation, on those subjects on which it can act, must necessarily bind its component parts. But this question is not left to mere reason: the people have, in express terms, decided it, by saying, "this Constitution, and the Laws of the United States which shall be made in Pursuance thereof, . . . shall be the supreme Law of the Land," and by requiring that the members of the state legislatures, and the officers of the executive and judicial departments of the states, shall take the oath of fidelity to it. The government of the United States, then, though limited in its powers, is supreme; and its laws, when made in pursuance of the Constitution, form the supreme law of the land, "any Thing in the Constitution or Laws of any State to the Contrary notwithstanding."

Among the enumerated powers we do not find that of establishing a bank or creating a corporation. But there is no phrase in the instrument which, like the Articles of Confederation, excludes incidental or implied powers; and which requires that everything granted shall be expressly and minutely described. Even the Tenth Amendment, which was framed for the purpose of quieting the excessive jealousies which had been excited, omits the word "expressly," and declares only that the powers "not delegated to the United States [by the Constitution], nor prohibited [by it] to the States, are reserved to the States [respectively], or to the people"; thus leaving the question, whether the particular power which may become the subject of contest, has been delegated to the one government, or prohibited to the other, to depend on a fair construction of the whole instrument. The men who drew and adopted this Amendment had experienced the embarrassments resulting from the insertion of this word in the Articles of Confederation, and probably omitted it, to avoid those embarrassments. A constitution, to contain an accurate detail of all the subdivisions of which its great powers will admit, and of all the means by which they may be carried into execution, would partake of the prolixity of a legal code, and could scarcely be embraced by the human mind. It would, probably, never be understood by the public. Its nature, therefore, requires, that only its great outlines should be marked, its important objects designated, and the minor ingredients which compose those objects, be deduced from the nature of the objects themselves. That this idea was entertained by the framers of the American Constitution, is not only to be inferred from the nature of the instrument, but from the language. Why else were some of the limitations, found in the ninth section of the First Article, introduced? It is also, in some degree, warranted, by their having omitted to use any restrictive term which might prevent its receiving a fair and just interpretation. In considering this question, then, we must never forget, that it is a *constitution* we are expounding.

Although, among the enumerated powers of government, we do not find the word "bank," or "incorporation," we find the great powers, to lay and collect taxes; to borrow money; to regulate commerce; to declare and conduct a war; and to raise and support armies and navies. The sword and the purse, all the external relations, and no inconsiderable portion of the industry of the nation, are intrusted to its government. It can never be pretended, that these vast powers draw after them others of inferior importance, merely because they are inferior. Such an idea can never be advanced. But it may with great reason be contended, that a government, intrusted with such ample powers, on the due execution of which the happiness and prosperity of the nation so vitally depends, must also be intrusted with ample means for their execution. The power being given, it is the interest of the nation to facilitate its execution. It can never be their interest, and cannot be presumed to have been their intention, to clog and embarrass its execution, by withholding the most appropriate means. Throughout this vast republic, from the St. Croix to the Gulf of Mexico, from the Atlantic to the Pacific, revenue is to be collected and expended, armies are to be marched and supported. The exigencies of the nation may require, that the treasure raised in the north should be transported to the south, that raised in the east, conveyed to the west, or that this order should be reversed. Is that construction of the Constitution to be preferred, which would render these operations difficult, hazardous, and expensive? Can we adopt that construction (unless the words imperiously require it), which would impute to the framers of that instrument, when granting these powers for the public good, the intention of impeding their exercise by withholding a choice of means? If, indeed, such be the mandate of the Constitution, we have only to obey; but that instrument does not profess to enumerate the means by which the powers it confers may be executed; nor does it prohibit the creation of a corporation, if the existence of such a being be essential, to the beneficial exercise of those powers. It is, then, the subject of fair inquiry, how far such means may be employed.

It is not denied, that the powers given to the government imply the ordinary means of execution. That, for example, of raising revenue, and applying it to national purposes, is admitted to imply the power of conveying money from place to place, as the exigencies of the nation may require, and of employing the usual means of conveyance. But it is denied, that the government has its choice of means; or, that it may employ the most convenient means, if,

to employ them, it be necessary to erect a corporation. . . .

. . . The power of creating a corporation, though appertaining to sovereignty, is not, like the power of making war, or levying taxes, or of regulating commerce, a great substantive and independent power, which cannot be implied as incidental to other powers, or used as a means of executing them. It is never the end for which other powers are exercised, but a means by which other objects are accomplished. No contributions are made to charity for the sake of an incorporation, but a corporation is created to administer the charity; no seminary of learning is instituted in order to be incorporated, but the corporate character is conferred to subserve the purposes of education. No city was ever built with the sole object of being incorporated, but is incorporated as affording the best means of being well governed. The power of creating a corporation is never used for its own sake, but for the purpose of effecting something else. No sufficient reason is, therefore, perceived, why it may not pass as incidental to those powers which are expressly given, if it be a direct mode of executing them.

But the Constitution of the United States has not left the right of Congress to employ the necessary means, for the execution of the powers conferred on the government, to general reasoning. To its enumeration of powers is added that of making "all laws which shall be necessary and proper, for carrying into execution the foregoing powers, and all other powers vested by this Constitution, in the government of the United States, or in any department thereof."

The counsel for the state of Maryland have urged various arguments, to prove that this clause, though in terms a grant of power, is not so in effect; but is really restrictive of the general right, which might otherwise be implied, of selecting means for executing the enumerated powers.

In support of this proposition, they have found it necessary to contend, that this clause was inserted for the purpose of conferring on Congress the power of making laws. That, without it, doubts might be entertained, whether Congress could exercise its powers in the form of legislation.

But could this be the object for which it was inserted? . . . That a legislature, endowed with legislative powers, can legislate, is a proposition too self-evident to have been questioned.

But the argument on which most reliance is placed, is drawn from the peculiar language of this clause. Congress is not empowered by it to make all laws, which may have relation to the powers conferred on the government, but such only as may be "necessary and proper" for carrying them into execution. The word "necessary" is considered as controlling the whole sentence, and as limiting the right to pass laws for the execution of the granted powers, to such as are indispensable, and without which the power would be nugatory. That it excludes the choice of means, and leaves to Congress, in each case, that only which is most direct and simple.

Is it true, that this is the sense in which the word "necessary" is always used? Does it always import an absolute physical necessity, so strong, that one thing, to which another may be termed necessary, cannot exist without that other? We think it does not. If reference be had to its use, in the common affairs of the world, or in approved authors, we find that it frequently imports no more than that one thing is convenient, or useful, or essential to another. To employ the means necessary to an end, is generally understood as employing any means calculated to produce the end, and not as being confined to those single means, without which the end would be entirely unattainable. Such is the character of human language, that no word conveys to the mind, in all situations, one single definite idea; and nothing is more common than to use words in a figurative sense. Almost all compositions contain words, which, taken in their rigorous sense, would convey a meaning different from

that which is obviously intended. It is essential to just construction, that many words which import something excessive, should be understood in a more mitigated sense—in that sense which common usage justifies. The word "necessary" is of this description. It has not a fixed character peculiar to itself. It admits of all degrees of comparison; and is often connected with other words, which increase or diminish the impression the mind receives of the urgency it imports. A thing may be necessary, very necessary, absolutely or indispensably necessary. To no mind would the same idea be conveyed, by these several phrases. . . . This word, then, like others, is used in various senses; and, in its construction, the subject, the context, the intention of the person using them, are all to be taken into view.

Let this be done in the case under consideration. The subject is the execution of those great powers on which the welfare of a nation essentially depends. It must have been the intention of those who gave these powers, to insure, as far as human prudence could insure, their beneficial execution. This could not be done by confining the choice of means to such narrow limits as not to leave it in the power of Congress to adopt any which might be appropriate, and which were conducive to the end. This provision is made in a constitution intended to endure for ages to come, and, consequently, to be adapted to the various crises of human affairs. To have prescribed the means by which governments should, in all future time, execute its powers, would have been to change, entirely, the character of the instrument, and give it the properties of a legal code. It would have been an unwise attempt to provide, by immutable rules, for exigencies which, if foreseen at all, must have been seen dimly, and which can be best provided for as they occur. To have declared that the best means shall not be used, but those alone without which the power given would be nugatory, would have been to deprive the legislature of the capacity to avail itself of experience, to exercise its reason, and to accommodate its legislation to circumstances. . . .

But the argument which most conclusively demonstrates the error of the construction contended for by the counsel for the state of Maryland, is founded on the intention of the convention, as manifested in the whole clause. To waste time and argument in proving that, without it, Congress might carry its powers into execution, would be not much less idle than to hold a lighted taper to the sun. As little can it be required to prove, that in the absence of this clause, Congress would have some choice of means. That it might employ those which, in its judgment, would most advantageously effect the object to be accomplished. That any means adapted to the end, any means which tended directly to the execution of the constitutional powers of the government, were in themselves constitutional. This clause, as construed by the state of Maryland, would abridge and almost annihilate this useful and necessary right of the legislature to select its means. That this could not be intended, is, we should think, had it not been already controverted, too apparent for controversy. We think so for the following reasons:

1. The clause is placed among the powers of Congress, not among the limitations on those powers.

2. Its terms purport to enlarge, not to diminish the powers vested in the government. It purports to be an additional power, not a restriction on those already granted. No reason has been or can be assigned, for thus concealing an intention to narrow the discretion of the national legislature, under words which purport to enlarge it. The framers of the Constitution wished its adoption, and well knew that it would be endangered by its strength, not by its weakness. Had they been capable of using language which would convey to the eye one idea, and, after deep reflection, impress on the mind another, they would rather have disguised the grant of power, than its limitation. If, then, their intention

had been, by this clause, to restrain the free use of means which might otherwise have been implied, that intention would have been inserted in another place, and would have been expressed in terms resembling these: "In carrying into execution the foregoing powers, and all others," etc., "no laws shall be passed but such as are necessary and proper." Had the intention been to make this clause restrictive, it would unquestionably have been so in form as well as in effect.

The result of the most careful and attentive consideration bestowed upon this clause is, that if it does not enlarge, it cannot be construed to restrain the powers of Congress, or to impair the right of the legislature to exercise its best judgment in the selection of measures to carry into execution the constitutional powers of the government. If no other motive for its insertion can be suggested, a sufficient one is found in the desire to remove all doubts respecting the right to legislate on that vast mass of incidental powers which must be involved in the Constitution, if that instrument be not a splendid bauble.

We admit, as all must admit, that the powers of the government are limited, and that its limits are not to be transcended. But we think the sound construction of the Constitution must allow to the national legislature that discretion, with respect to the means by which the powers it confers are to be carried into execution, which will enable that body to perform the high duties assigned to it, in the manner most beneficial to the people. Let the end be legitimate, let it be within the scope of the Constitution, and all means which are appropriate, which are plainly adapted to that end, which are not prohibited, but consist with the letter and spirit of the Constitution, are constitutional. . . .

If a corporation may be employed indiscriminately with other means to carry into execution the powers of the government, no particular reason can be assigned for excluding the use of a bank, if required for its fiscal operations. To use one, must be within the discretion of Congress, if it be an appropriate mode of executing the powers of government. That it is a convenient, a useful, and essential instrument in the prosecution of its fiscal operations, is not now a subject of controversy. All those who have been concerned in the administration of our finances, have concurred in representing its importance and necessity; and so strongly have they been felt, that statesmen of the first class, whose previous opinions against it had been confirmed by every circumstance which can fix the human judgment, have yielded those opinions to the exigencies of the nation. . . .

After the most deliberate consideration, it is the unanimous and decided opinion of this Court, that the act to incorporate the Bank of the United States is a law made in pursuance of the Constitution, and is a part of the supreme law of the land. . . .

PRESIDENT JACKSON'S VETO OF THE BANK BILL (1832)

After *McCulloch* v. *Maryland* and shortly before the charter of the second National Bank was to expire, a bill to recharter it was passed by Congress. Following is a part of President Jackson's veto message.

The Congress, the Executive, and the Court must each for itself be guided by its own opinion of the Constitution. Each public officer who takes an oath to support the constitution swears that he will support it as he understands it, and not as it is understood by others. It is as much the duty of the House of Representatives, of the Senate, and of the President to decide upon the constitutionality of any bill or resolution which may be presented to them for passage or approval as it is of the supreme judges when it may be brought before them for judicial decision. The opinion of the judges has no more authority over Congress than the opinion of Congress has over the judges, and on that point the President is independent of both. The authority of the Supreme Court must not, therefore, be permitted to control the Congress or the Executive when acting in their legislative capacities, but to have only such influence as the force of their reasoning may deserve. . . .

NOTE: Three Congresses and two Presidents (Washington and Madison) had approved the creation of a national bank before President Jackson's veto message. Those who think of the Court as the primary interpreter of the Constitution should consider that a member of the executive branch, Hamilton, had sponsored the bank originally. Congress and the President had adopted it in 1791 and again in 1816 after considering the constitutional issue which later was settled in *McCulloch* v. *Maryland*. The Court thus merely approved an interpretation implicit in prior legislative and executive action.

JUILLIARD v. *GREENMAN*
110 U.S. 421 (1884)

The Legal Tender Acts (passed during the Civil War) made "greenbacks" legal tender for public and private debts. This "paper money" was held invalid as applied to antecedent debts in *Hepburn* v. *Griswold*, 8 Wallace 603 (1869). A few months later after a change in Court personnel, *Knox* v. *Lee*, 12 Wallace 457 (1870), upheld such legislation *as a war measure*. Thereafter the 1878 Legal Tender Act—a response to the agrarian Greenback Movement—raised the question of whether Congress could provide for "paper money" in peacetime.

MR. JUSTICE GRAY delivered the opinion of the court . . .

Congress, as the legislature of a sovereign nation, being expressly empowered by the constitution "to lay and collect taxes, to pay the debts and provide for the common defense and general welfare of the United States," and "to borrow money on the credit of the United States," and "to coin money and regulate the value thereof and of foreign coin;" and being clearly authorized, as incidental to the exercise of those great powers, to emit bills of credit, to charter national banks, and to provide a national currency for the whole people, in the form of coin, treasury notes, and national bank bills; and the power to make the notes of the government a legal tender in payment of private debts being one of the powers belonging to sovereignty in other civilized nations, and not expressly withheld from congress by the constitution; we are irresistibly impelled to the conclusion that the impressing upon the treasury notes of the United States the quality of being a legal tender in payment of private debts is an appropriate means, conducive and plainly adapted to the execution of the undoubted powers of congress, consistent with the letter and spirit of the constitution, and therefore within the meaning of that instrument, "necessary and proper for carrying into execution the powers vested by this constitution in the government of the United States."

Such being our conclusion in matter of law, the question whether at any particular time, in war or in peace, the exigency is such, by reason of unusual and pressing demands on the resources of the government, or of the inadequacy of the supply of gold and silver coin to furnish the currency needed for the uses of the government and of the people, that it is, as matter of fact, wise and expedient to resort to this means, is a political question, to be determined by congress when the question of exigency arises, and not a judicial question, to be afterwards passed upon by the courts. To quote once more from the judgment in *McCulloch* v. *Maryland:* "Where the law is not prohibited, and is really calculated to effect any of the objects intrusted to the government, to undertake here to inquire into the degree of its necessity would be to pass the line which circumscribes the judicial department, and to tread on legislative ground." 4 Wheat. 423.

It follows that the act of May 31, 1878, *c.* 146, is constitutional and valid, and that the circuit court rightly held that the tender in treasury notes, reissued and kept in circulation under that act, was a tender of lawful money in payment of the defendant's debt to the plaintiff.

Judgment affirmed.

FIELD, J., dissenting. . . .

If there be anything in the history of the Constitution which can be established with moral certainty, it is that the framers of that instrument intended to prohibit the issue of legal-tender notes both by the general government and by the states, and thus prevent interference with the contracts of private parties. . . .

For nearly three-quarters of a century after the adoption of the Constitution, and until the legislation during the recent civil war, no jurist and no statesman of any position in the country ever pretended that a power to impart the quality of legal tender to its notes was vested in the general government. There is no recorded word of even one in favor of its possessing the power. All conceded, as an axiom of constitutional law, that the power did not exist.

Mr. Webster, from his first entrance into public life in 1812, gave great consideration to the subject of the currency, and in an elaborate speech on that subject, made in the senate in 1836, then sitting in this room, he said: "Currency, in a large and perhaps just sense, includes not only gold and silver and bank bills, but bills of exchange also. It may include all that adjusts exchanges and settles balances in the operations of trade and business; but if we understand by currency the legal money of the country, and that which constitutes a legal tender for debts, and is the standard measure of value, then undoubtedly nothing is included but gold and silver. Most unquestionably there is no legal tender, and there can be no legal tender in this country, under the authority of this government or any other, but gold and silver, either the coinage of our own mints or foreign coins at rates regulated by congress. This is a constitutional principle, perfectly plain and of the highest importance. The states are expressly prohibited from making anything but gold and silver a legal tender in payment of debts; and although no such express prohibition is applied to congress, yet, as congress has no power granted to it in this respect but to coin money and to regulate the value of foreign coins, it clearly has no power to substitute paper or anything else for coin as a tender in payment of debts and in discharge of contracts. Congress has exercised this power fully in both its branches; it has coined money and still coins it; it has regulated the value of foreign coins, and still regulates their value. The legal tender, therefore, the constitutional standard of value, is established and cannot be overthrown. To overthrow it would shake the whole system." 4 Webster's Works, 271. . . .

Undoubtedly congress has power to alter the value of coins issued, either by increasing or diminishing the alloy they contain; so it may alter, at its pleasure, their denominations; it may hereafter call a dollar an eagle, and it may call an eagle a dollar. But if it be intended to assert that congress can make the coins changed the equivalent of those having a greater value in their previous condition, and compel parties contracting for the latter to receive coins with diminished value, I must be permitted to deny any such authority. Any such declaration on its part would be not only utterly inoperative in fact, but a shameful disregard of its constitutional duty. As I said on a former occasion: "The power to coin money, as declared by this court, is a great trust devolved upon congress, carrying with it the duty of creating and maintaining a uniform standard of value throughout the Union, and it would be a manifest abuse of this trust to give to the coins issued by its authority any other than their real value. By debasing the coins, when once the standard is fixed, is meant giving to the coins by their form and impress a certificate of their having a relation to that standard different from that which in truth they possess; in other words, giving to the coins a false certificate of their value. Arbitrary and profligate governments have often resorted to this miserable scheme of robbery, which Mill designates as a shallow and impudent artifice, the 'least covert of all modes of knavery, which consists in calling a shilling a pound, that a debt of one hundred pounds may be cancelled by the payment of one hundred shillings.' "

III. STATES' RIGHTS WITH RESPECT TO NATIONAL AFFAIRS

1. STATE REGULATION OF INTERSTATE COMMERCE

In 1785 Madison wrote Monroe that "it surely is necessary to lodge the power [of trade regulation] where trade can be regulated with effect; and experience has confirmed what reason foresaw, that it can never be so regulated by the States acting in their separate capacities." Later in his notes for the Constitutional Convention Madison observed that the "practice of many States in restricting the commercial intercourse with other States . . . is certainly adverse to the spirit of the Union, and tends to beget retaliatory regulations . . . destructive of the general harmony." The unfortunate experience under the Articles of Confederation which Madison refers to resulted in the Commerce Clause and the Court's broad construction of it in *Gibbons* v. *Ogden*. Did the states retain any power with respect to interstate commerce? In the *Steamboat Case,* Daniel Webster had argued that as the commerce clause "implied in its nature, full power over the thing to be regulated, it excludes, necessarily, the action of all others that would perform the same operation on the same thing." Marshall responded cryptically, "There is great force in this argument, and the Court is not satisfied that it has been refuted." But decision on the point was avoided. Later other Justices, particularly President Jackson's appointees, vigorously repudiated Marshall's suggestion of the exclusive nature of the national power. As Chief Justice Taney observed in *The License Cases,* 5 Howard 504, 579 (1847):

. . . it appears to me to be very clear, that the mere grant of power to the general government cannot, upon any just principles of construction, be construed to be an absolute prohibition to the exercise of any power over the same subject by the states. The controlling and supreme power over commerce with foreign nations and the several states is undoubtedly conferred upon Congress. Yet in my judgment, the State may nevertheless . . . make regulations for its own territory; and such regulations are valid unless they come in conflict with a law of Congress.

Whether the national power is exclusive as Marshall apparently thought, or concurrent as Taney clearly supposed, is one of the classic problems of constitutional law. The exclusive view in effect means that the affirmative grant of the commerce power to Congress implies a negative: a denial of such power to the states. The concurrent view admits no negative implications; that is, the commerce clause merely authorizes Congress to act—such negatives as the Founding Fathers saw fit to impose upon the states are to be found in Article I, Section 10 of the Constitution and no general denial of commercial powers for the states is included there.

The very existence of the supremacy clause (Art. VI, Par. 2 of the Constitution) gives support to Taney's view. For unless some national powers (those not denied the states in Art. 1, Sec. 10) are deemed concurrent, the supremacy clause would be surplusage. Only because the founders recognized that national and state authority overlap was it necessary to provide which should prevail in case of conflict. If the two were completely separated and mutually exclusive, each would be supreme in its own sphere. Precisely because of the overlap, or concurrency, of powers, as Madison pointed out (see Part Three, II), what is reserved to the states cannot be used as the criterion of what is delegated to the nation. Failure to recognize this is the inherent fallacy of dual federalism. Merely because the control of local real estate is a matter reserved to the states for some purposes does not mean that such matters do not come within federal authority for other purposes.

Traditionally the Federalist Marshall and his Jacksonian Democratic successor, Chief Justice Taney, have been depicted as contrasting advocates respectively of nationalism and localism. The supposed antithesis is misleading.

To be sure the Jacksonians, like their Jeffersonian predecessors, endorsed states' rights. But for them that was more an economic, than a political, concept. It was a weapon against "the jobbery and corruption and consolidation" to which in their view Hamilton's, and later Clay's, economic paternalism led. Calhoun blundered when he mistook Jacksonian anti-mercantilism for parochialism. Old Hickory's angry response rings down through the ages. "Our Federal Union—it must and shall be preserved." Jackson's forceful response to Carolinian nullification found judicial expression later in the Wisconsin case of *Ableman* v. *Booth,* 21 Howard 506 (1859). There Taney and his Court upheld the unqualified power of the central government to enforce national law without state interference. And surely *The Genessee Chief,* 12 Howard 443 (1851), greatly expanding the maritime authority of the federal government, does not bespeak an invidious localism. The essential difference between the Federalist Marshall and the Jacksonian Taney lay not in any difference in attitude as to the positive scope of national power, but in the effect of that power on state authority.[1] Marshall's nationalism implied restrictions upon the states which Taney's rejected. To put it simply, Marshall respected national authority; Taney respected *national and state* authority. Of course, in case of actual conflict between the part and the whole, Taney recognized the supremacy of the latter. The concurrent view of the commerce power simply means that the states are free to deal with interstate commerce as they see fit *in the absence of conflicting congressional legislation.* Marshall's exclusive view on the other hand meant that the states may never exercise the commerce power, regardless of whether Congress has done so, or not.

Which of the two conflicting views has prevailed? After years of conflict and uncertainty a compromise, silently acquiesced in by Taney, was reached in *Cooley* v. *Board of Wardens:* ". . . the power to regulate commerce embraces a vast field containing not only many, but exceedingly various subjects quite unlike in nature; some imperatively demanding a single uniform rule . . . ; and some . . . as imperatively demanding that diversity, which alone can meet the local necessities. . . ."

It followed that in the one category the commerce power was exclusively national, in the other it was concurrent. In either situation, of course, Congress may legislate, if it so desires! The point of the *Cooley* rule is that *state* regulation of interstate commerce is never permissible in the one category, but is permissible in the other, provided Congress has not exercised its power in a manner inconsistent with state regulation. *Cooley's* case involved a Pennsylvania regulation of pilotage in the Philadelphia harbor. Of course, the measure applied to interstate and foreign commerce. But in view of the great diversity of harbor conditions in the several ports throughout the country, and in the absence of any congressional effort to deal with the problem, state regulation was sustained. A modern application of the *Cooley* approach in a context amenable to local treatment is seen in *Thompson,* and in a context susceptible only of uniform, national treatment in *Southern Pacific* v. *Arizona.*

1. See Mendelson, "Dred Scott's Case—Reconsidered," 38 *Minn. Law Review* 16 (1953).

As a matter of history, the *Cooley* rule did not dispose of the problem. Even Marshall recognized, despite his nationalistic outlook, that some power must remain with the states to protect themselves from harmful interstate transactions. He never conceded them any part of the commerce power. He and his Court did, however, recognize that in the absence of a conflicting act of Congress a state could enact local "police" or "health" measures impinging upon at least some aspects of interstate commerce. Thus Delaware was permitted to safeguard health and property from marshland conditions by a dam which cut off all commerce on a small but navigable stream. *Willson* v. *Blackbird Creek Marsh Co.*, 2 Peters 245 (1829). This conceptualistic distinction between state commerce and police measures seems to have been essentially a retreat from the effect, without abandoning the principle, of the exclusiveness of the commerce power. In any event, it was immediately picked up by states' righters. In their hands the police power concept grew to include along with "health" also matters of "public safety, welfare, and morals." But local burdens upon national commerce are not less burdensome for being called police measures. And so the problem of interference by the part with the whole assumed a new verbal form. The old laissez-faire solution is seen in *Di Santo's* case; the more modern solution in *California* v. *Thompson* and *Southern Pacific*.

COOLEY v. BOARD OF WARDENS

12 Howard 299 (1851)

Writ of error to the Supreme Court of Pennsylvania.

An act of the Pennsylvania Legislature, passed in 1803, provided that every "ship arriving from or bound to any foreign port or place" must engage a local pilot, and that failure to do so would result in a fine equal to half the pilotage of the vessel so neglecting to employ a pilot, payable to the Board of Wardens of the Port of Philadelphia by the master, owner, or consignee, to a fund for superannuated pilots and their dependents.

MR. JUSTICE CURTIS delivered the opinion of the court: . . .

That the power to regulate commerce includes the regulation of navigation, we consider settled. And when we look to the nature of the service performed by pilots, to the relations which that service and its compensations bear to navigation between the several States, and between the ports of the United States and foreign countries, we are brought to the conclusion, that the regulation of the qualifications of pilots, of the modes and times of offering and rendering their services, of the responsibilities which shall rest upon them, of the powers they shall possess, of the compensation they may demand, and of the penalties by which their rights and duties may be enforced, do constitute regulations of navigation, and consequently of commerce, within the just meaning of this clause of the Constitution. . . .

If the law of Pennsylvania, now in question, had been in existence at the date of this Act of Congress (quoted below), we might hold it to have been adopted by Congress, and thus made a law of the United States, and so valid. Because this Act does, in effect, give the force of an Act of Congress, to the then existing State laws on this subject, so long as they should continue unrepealed by the State which enacted them.

But the law on which these actions were founded was not enacted till 1803. What effect, then, can be attributed to so much of the Act of 1789 as declares that pilots shall continue to be regulated in conformity "with such laws as the States may respectively hereafter enact for the purpose, until further legislative provision shall be made by Congress"?

If the States were divested of the power to legislate on this subject by the grant of the commercial power to Congress, it is plain this Act could not confer upon them power thus to legislate. If the Constitution excluded the States from making any law regulating commerce, certainly Congress cannot regrant, or in any manner reconvey to the States that power. And yet this Act of 1789 gives its sanction only to laws enacted by the States. This necessarily implies a constitutional power to legislate; for only a rule created by the sovereign power of a State acting in its legislative capacity, can be deemed a law, enacted by a State; and if the State has so limited its sovereign power that it no longer extends to a particular subject, manifestly it cannot, in any proper sense, be said to enact laws thereon. Entertaining these views we are brought directly and unavoidably to the consideration of the question, whether the grant of the commercial power to Congress, did *per se* deprive the States of all power to regulate pilots. This question has never been decided by this court, nor, in our judgment, has any case depending upon all the considerations which must govern this one, come before this court. The grant of commercial power to Congress does not contain any terms which expressly exclude the States from exercising an authority over its subject matter. If they are excluded it must be because the nature of the power, thus granted to Congress, requires that a similar authority should not exist in the States. . . .

The diversities of opinion, therefore, which have existed on this subject, have arisen from the different views taken of the nature of this power. But when the nature of a power like this is spoken of, when it is said that the nature of the power requires that it should be exercised exclusively by Congress, it must be intended to refer to the subjects of that power, and to say they are of such a nature as to require exclusive legislation by Congress. Now, the power to regulate commerce, embraces a vast field, containing not only many, but exceedingly various subjects, quite unlike in their nature; some imperatively demanding a single uniform rule, operating equally on the commerce of the United States in every port; and some, like the subject now in question, as imperatively demanding that diversity, which alone can meet the local necessities of navigation.

Either absolutely to affirm, or deny, that the nature of this power requires exclusive legislation by Congress, is to lose sight of the nature of the subjects of this power, and to assert concerning all of them, what is really applicable but to a part. Whatever subjects of this power are in their nature national, or admit only of one uniform system, or plan of regulation, may justly be said to be of such a nature as to require exclusive legislation by Congress. That this cannot be affirmed of laws for the regulation of pilots and pilotage is plain. The Act of 1789 contains a clear and authoritative declaration by the first Congress, that the nature of this subject is such, that until Congress should find it necessary to exert its power, it should be left to the legislation of the States; that it is local and not national; that it is likely to be the best provided for, not by one system, or plan of regulations, but by as many as the legislative discretion of the several States should deem applicable to the local peculiarities of the ports within their limits.

Viewed in this light, so much of this Act of 1789 as declares that pilots shall continue to be regulated "by such laws as the States may respectively hereafter enact for that purpose," instead of being held to be inoperative, as an attempt to confer on the States a power to legislate, of which the Constitution had deprived them, is allowed an appropriate and important signification. It manifests the understanding of Congress, at the outset of the government, that the nature of this subject is not such as to require its exclusive legislation. The practice of the States, and of the national government, has been in conformity with this declaration, from the origin of the national government to this time; and the nature of the subject, when examined, is such as to leave no doubt of the superior fitness and propriety, not to say the absolute necessity, of different systems of regulation, drawn from local knowledge and experience, and conformed to local wants. How, then, can we say, that by the mere grant of power to regulate commerce, the States are deprived of all the power to legislate on this subject, because from the nature of the power the legislation of Congress must be exclusive. . . .

It is the opinion of a majority of the court that the mere grant to Congress of the power to regulate commerce, did not deprive the States of power to regulate pilots, and that although Congress has legislated on this subject, its legislation manifests an intention, with a single exception, not to regulate this subject, but to leave its regulation to the several States. To these precise questions, which are all we are called on to decide, this opinion must be understood to be confined. It does not extend to the question what other subjects, under the commercial power, are within the exclusive control of Congress, or may be regulated by the States in the absence of all congressional legislation; nor to the general question how far any regulation of a subject by Congress may be deemed to operate as an exclusion of all legislation by the States upon the same subject. . . .

If the grant of commercial power in the Constitution has deprived the States of all power to legislate for the regulation of pilots, if their laws on this subject are mere usurpations upon the exclusive power of the general government, and utterly void, it may be doubted whether Congress could, with propriety, recognize them as laws, and adopt them as its own acts; and how are

the Legislatures of the States to proceed in the future, to watch over and amend these laws, as the progressive wants of a growing commerce will require, when the members of those legislatures are made aware that they cannot legislate on this subject without violating the oaths they have taken to support the Constitution of the United States?

We are of the opinion that this State law was enacted by virtue of a power, residing in the State to legislate; that it is not in conflict with any law of Congress; that it does not interfere with any system which Congress has established by making regulations, or by intentionally leaving individuals to their own unrestricted action; that this law is therefore valid and the judgment of the Supreme Court of Pennsylvania in each case must be affirmed.

Mr. Justice McLean and Mr. Justice Wayne dissented; and Mr. Justice Daniel, although he concurred in the judgment of of the Court, yet dissented from its reasoning.

Mr. Justice McLean: . . .

That a state may regulate foreign commerce, or commerce among the states, is a doctrine which has been advanced by individual judges of this Court; but never before, I believe, has such a power been sanctioned by the decision of this Court. In this case, the power to regulate pilots is admitted to belong to the commercial power of Congress; and yet it is held, that a state, by virtue of its inherent power, may regulate the subject, until such regulation shall be annulled by Congress. This is the principle established by this decision. Its language is guarded, in order to apply the decision only to the case before the Court. But such restrictions can never operate, so as to render the principle inapplicable to other cases. And it is in this light that the decision is chiefly to be regretted. . . .

From this race of legislation between Congress and the states, and between the states, if this principle be maintained, will arise a conflict similar to that which existed before the adoption of the Constitution. . . .

. . . Congress, to whom the subject peculiarly belongs, should have been applied to, and no doubt it would have adopted the act of the state.

MR. JUSTICE DANIEL: . . .

The true question here is, whether the power to enact pilot laws is appropriate and necessary, or rather more appropriate and necessary to the state or the federal governments. It being conceded that this power has been exercised by the states from their very dawn of existence; that it can be practically and beneficially applied by the local authorities only; it being conceded, as it must be, that the power to pass pilot laws, as such, has not been in any express terms delegated to Congress, and does not necessarily conflict with the right to establish commercial regulations, I am forced to conclude that this is an original and inherent power in the states, and not one to be merely tolerated, or held subject to the sanction of the federal government.

CALIFORNIA v. THOMPSON

313 U.S. 109 (1941)

California law requires the licensing and bonding of those who sell, or negotiate for, transportation over the public highways of the state. Thompson was convicted of violating this law with respect to interstate commerce.

MR. JUSTICE STONE delivered the opinion of the Court. . . .

As this Court has often had occasion to point out, the Commerce Clause, in conferring on Congress power to regulate commerce, did not wholly withdraw from the states the power to regulate matters of local concern with respect to which Congress has not exercised its power, even though the regulation affects interstate commerce. Ever since *Willson* v. *Blackbird Creek Marsh Co.*, 2 Pet. 245, and *Cooley* v. *Board of Port Wardens*, 12 How. 299, it has been recognized that there are matters of local concern, the regulation of which unavoidably involves some regulation of interstate commerce, but which because of their local character and their number and diversity may never be adequately dealt with by Congress. Because of their local character, also, there is wide scope for local regulation without impairing the uniformity of control of the national commerce in matters of national concern and without materially obstructing the free flow of commerce which were the principal objects sought to be secured by the Commerce Clause. Notwithstanding the Commerce Clause, such regulation in the absence of Congressional action has, for the most part, been left to the states by the decisions of this Court, subject only to other applicable constitutional restraints. See cases collected in *Di Santo* v. *Pennsylvania, supra,* 273 U.S. 40.

A state may license trainmen engaged in interstate commerce in order to insure their skill and fitness. *Smith* v. *Alabama,* 124 U.S. 465; *Nashville, Chattanooga & St. Louis Railroad* v. *Alabama,* 128 U.S. 96. It may define the size of crews manning interstate trains. *Chicago, R. I. & P. R. Co.* v. *Arkansas,* 219 U.S. 453; *Missouri Pacific R. Co.* v. *Norwood,* 283 U.S. 249, and prescribe regulations for payment of their wages. *Erie R. Co.* v. *Williams,* 233 U.S. 685. It may require interstate passenger cars to be heated and guard posts to be placed on bridges of an interstate railroad. *New York, New Haven & Hartford R. Co.* v. *New York,* 165 U.S. 628. It may limit the speed of interstate trains within city limits. *Erb* v. *Morasch,* 177 U.S. 584. It may require an interstate railroad to eliminate grade crossings. *Erie R. Co.* v. *Board of*

Public Utility Commissioners, 254 U.S. 394, 409, 412. It may pass local quarantine laws applicable to merchandise moving in interstate commerce as a means of protecting local health. *Morgan's etc., S. S. Co.* v. *Board of Health of State of Louisiana,* 118 U.S. 455; *Compagnie Française* v. *Board of Health,* 186 U.S. 380. It may regulate and protect the safe and convenient use of its harbors and navigable waterways unless there is conflict with some act of Congress. *Willson* v. *Blackbird Creek Marsh Co., supra;* see *Clyde Mallory Lines* v. *State of Alabama,* 296 U.S. 261. It may regulate pilots and pilotage in its harbors. *Cooley* v. *Board of Port Wardens, supra.* Where, as here, Congress has not entered the field, a state may pass inspection laws and regulations applicable to articles of interstate commerce designed to safeguard the inhabitants of the state from fraud, provided only that the regulation neither discriminates against nor substantially obstructs the commerce. *Turner* v. *Maryland,* 107 U.S. 38; *Plumley* v. *Massachusetts,* 155 U.S. 461; *Patapsco Guana Co.* v. *Board of Agriculture of North Carolina,* 171 U.S. 345, 357, 358; *Savage* v. *Jones,* 225 U.S. 501; see, also, *Minnesota Rate cases,* 230 U.S. 352 398–412, 33 S.Ct. 729, 739–745, and cases cited; *South Carolina State Highway Dept.* v. *Barnwell Bros.,* 303 U.S. 177, 185–191, and cases cited.

The present case is not one of prohibiting interstate commerce or licensing it on conditions which restrict or obstruct it. Cf. *Crutcher* v. *Kentucky,* 141 U.S. 47; *Dahnke-Walker Co.* v. *Bondurant,* 257 U.S. 282. For here the regulation is applied to one who is not himself engaged in the transportation but who acts only as broker or intermediary in negotiating a transportation contract between the passengers and the carrier. The license required of those engaged in such business is not conditioned upon any control or restriction of the movement of the traffic interstate but only on the good character and responsibility of those engaged locally as transportation brokers.

Fraudulent or unconscionable conduct of those so engaged which is injurious to their patrons, is peculiarly a subject of local concern and the appropriate subject of local regulation. In every practical sense regulation of such conduct is beyond the effective reach of Congressional action. Unless some measure of local control is permissible, it must go largely unregulated. In any case until Congress undertakes its regulation we can find no adequate basis for saying that the Constitution, interpreted as a working instrument of government, has foreclosed regulation, such as the present, by local authority.

In *Di Santo* v. *Pennsylvania,* this Court took a different view. Following what it conceived to be the reasoning of *McCall* v. *California,* 136 U.S. 104, it held that a Pennsylvania statute requiring others than railroad or steamship companies, who engage in the interstate sale of steamship tickets or of orders for transportation to and from foreign countries, to procure a license by giving proof of good moral character and filing a bond as security against fraud and misrepresentation to purchasers, was an infringement of the Commerce Clause. Since the decision in that case this Court has been repeatedly called upon to examine the constitutionality of numerous local regulations affecting interstate motor vehicle traffic. It has uniformly held that in the absence of pertinent Congressional legislation there is constitutional power in the states to regulate interstate commerce by motor vehicle wherever it affects the safety of the public or the safety and convenient use of its highways, provided only that the regulation does not in any other respect unnecessarily obstruct interstate commerce. *Continental Baking Co.* v. *Woodring,* 286 U.S. 352, 371; *Bradley* v. *Public Utilities Commission,* 289 U.S. 92, 95; see *South Carolina State Highway Dept.* v. *Barnwell Bros., supra,* and cases cited; *H. P. Welch Co.* v. *New Hampshire,* 306 U.S. 79, 83; *Eichholz* v. *Public Service Commission,* 306 U.S. 268; *Maurer* v. *Hamilton,* 309 U.S. 598, 603; and see *Ziffrin, Inc.* v. *Reeves,* 308 U.S. 132.

If there is authority in the state, in the

exercise of its police power, to adopt such regulations affecting interstate transportation, it must be deemed to possess the power to regulate the negotiations for such transportation where they affect matters of local concern which are in other respects within state regulatory power, and where the regulation does not infringe the national interest in maintaining the free flow of commerce and in preserving uniformity in the regulation of the commerce in matters of national concern. See *Hartford Accident & Indemnity Co.* v. *Illinois*, 298 U.S. 155.

The decision in the *Di Santo* case was a departure from this principle which has been recognized since *Cooley* v. *Board of Port Wardens, supra*. It cannot be reconciled with later decisions of this Court which have likewise recognized and applied the principle, and it can no longer be regarded as controlling authority.

Reversed.

SOUTHERN PACIFIC v. ARIZONA
325 U.S. 761 (1945)

An Arizona statute of 1912 prohibited trains in excess of 70 freight, or 14 passenger, cars within that state. The Southern Pacific was prosecuted for violating this limitation.

MR. CHIEF JUSTICE STONE delivered the opinion of the Court: . . .

Although the commerce clause conferred on the national government power to regulate commerce, its possession of the power does not exclude all state power of regulation. Ever since *Willson* v. *Black-Bird Creek Marsh Co.*, 2 Pet. 245, and *Cooley* v. *Board of Wardens*, 12 How. 299, it has been recognized that, in the absence of conflicting legislation by Congress, there is a residuum of power in the state to make laws governing matters of local concern which nevertheless in some measure affect interstate commerce or even, to some extent, regulate it. . . .

But ever since *Gibbons* v. *Ogden*, 9 Wheat. 1, the states have not been deemed to have authority to impede substantially the free flow of commerce from state to state, or to regulate those phases of the national commerce which, because of the need of national uniformity, demand that their regulation, if any, be prescribed by a single authority. *Cooley* v. *Board of Wardens, supra*, 319; *Leisy* v. *Hardin*, 135 U.S. 100, 108, 109; *Minnesota Rate Cases*, [230 U.S. 352] 399, 400; *Edwards* v. *California*, 314 U.S. 160, 176. Whether or not this long recognized distribution of power between the national and the state governments is predicated upon the implications of the commerce clause itself, *Brown* v. *State of Maryland*, 12 Wheat. 419, 447; *Minnesota Rate Cases, supra*, 399, 400; *Pennsylvania* v. *West Virginia*, 262 U.S. 553, 596; *Baldwin* v. *G. A. F. Seelig*, 294 U.S. 511, 522; *South Carolina State Highway Department* v. *Barnwell Bros.* [303 U.S. 177, 185], or upon the presumed intention of Congress, where Congress has not spoken, *Welton* v. *Missouri*, 91 U.S. 275, 282; *Hall* v. *De Cuir*, 95 U.S. 485, 490; *Brown* v. *Houston*, 114 U.S. 622, 631; *Bowman* v. *Chicago, etc., Ry.*, 125 U.S. 465, 481, 482; *Leisy* v. *Hardin, supra*; *In re Rahrer*, 140 U.S. 545, 559, 560; *Brennan* v. *City of Titusville*, 153 U.S. 289, 302; *Covington, etc., Bridge Co.* v. *Kentucky*, 154 U.S. 204, 212; *Graves* v. *New York ex rel. O'Keefe*, 306 U.S. 466, 479, note; Dowling, *Interstate Commerce and State Power*, 27 Va. Law Rev. 1, the result is the same.

For a hundred years it has been accepted constitutional doctrine that the commerce clause, without the aid of Congressional legislation, thus affords some protection from state legislation inimical to the national commerce, and that in such cases, where Congress has not acted, this Court, and not the state legislature, is under the commerce clause the final arbiter between the competing demands of state and national interests. . . .

Congress has undoubted power to redefine the distribution of power over interstate commerce. It may either permit the states to regulate the commerce in a manner which would otherwise not be permissible, *In re Rahrer, supra,* 561, 562; *Adams Express Co.* v. *Kentucky,* 238 U.S. 190, 198; *Rosenberger* v. *Pacific Express Co.,* 241 U.S. 48, 50, 51; *Clark Distilling Co.* v. *Western Maryland Ry. Co.,* 242 U.S. 311, 325, 326; *Whitfield* v. *Ohio,* 297 U.S. 431, 438–440; *Kentucky Whip & Collar Co.* v. *Illinois Cent. R. Co.,* 299 U.S. 334, 350–351; *Hooven & Allison* v. *Evatt,* 324 U.S. 652, 679, or exclude state regulation even of matters of peculiarly local concern which nevertheless affect interstate commerce. *Addyston Pipe & Steel Co.* v. *United States,* 175 U.S. 211, 230; *Louisville & N. R. Co.* v. *Mottley,* 219 U.S. 467; *Houston E. & W. T. Ry. Co.* v. *United States,* 234 U.S. 342; *American Express Co.* v. *South Dakota ex rel. Caldwell,* 244 U.S. 617, 626; *Illinois Cent. R. Co.* v. *Public Utilities Comm. of Illinois,* 254 U.S. 493, 506; *New York* v. *United States,* 257 U.S. 591, 601; *Louisiana Public Service Commission* v. *Texas & N. O. R. Co.,* 284 U.S. 125, 130; *Pennsylvania R. Co.* v. *Illinois Brick Co.,* 297 U.S. 447, 459.

But in general Congress has left it to the courts to formulate the rules thus interpreting the commerce clause in its application, doubtless because it has appreciated the destructive consequences to the commerce of the nation if their protection were withdrawn, *Gwin, etc., Inc.* v. *Henneford, supra,* 441, and has been aware that in their application state laws will not be invalidated without the support of relevant factual material which will "afford a sure basis" for an informed judgment. *Terminal R. Association* v. *Brotherhood of Railroad Trainmen, supra,* 8; *Southern R. Co.* v. *King,* 217 U.S. 524. Meanwhile, Congress has accommodated its legislation, as have the states, to these rules as an estab-

lished feature of our constitutional system. There has thus been left to the states wide scope for the regulation of matters of local state concern, even though it in some measure affects the commerce, provided it does not materially restrict the free flow of commerce across state lines, or interfere with it in matters with respect to which uniformity of regulation is of predominant national concern.

Hence the matters for ultimate determination here are the nature and extent of the burden which the state regulation of interstate trains, adopted as a safety measure, imposes on interstate commerce, and whether the relative weights of the state and national interests involved are such as to make inapplicable the rule, generally observed, that the free flow of interstate commerce and its freedom from local restraints in matters requiring uniformity of regulation are interests safeguarded by the commerce clause from state interference.

While this Court is not bound by the findings of the state court, and may determine for itself the facts of a case upon which an asserted federal right depends, *Hooven & Allison* v. *Evatt, supra,* p. 659, and cases cited, the facts found by the state trial court showing the nature of the interstate commerce involved, and the effect upon it of the train limit law, are not seriously questioned. Its findings with respect to the need for and effect of the statute as a safety measure, although challenged in some particulars which we do not regard as material to our decision, are likewise supported by evidence. Taken together the findings supply an adequate basis for decision of the constitutional issue.

The findings show that the operation of long trains, that is trains of more than fourteen passengers and more than seventy freight cars, is standard practice over the main lines of the railroads of the United States, and that, if the length of trains is to be regulated at all, national uniformity in the regulation adopted, such as only Congress can prescribe, is practically indispensable to the operation of an efficient and economical national railway system.

On many railroads passenger trains of more than fourteen cars and freight trains of more than seventy cars are operated, and on some systems freight trains are run ranging from one hundred and twenty-five to one hundred and sixty cars in length. Outside of Arizona, where the length of trains is not restricted, appellant runs a substantial proportion of long trains. In 1939 on its comparable route for through traffic through Utah and Nevada from 66 to 85% of its freight trains were over 70 cars in length and over 43% of its passenger trains included more than fourteen passenger cars.

In Arizona, approximately 93% of the freight traffic and 95% of the passenger traffic is interstate. Because of the Train Limit Law appellant is required to haul over 30% more trains in Arizona than would otherwise have been necessary. The record shows a definite relationship between operating costs and the length of trains, the increase in length resulting in a reduction of operating costs per car. The additional cost of operation of trains complying with the Train Limit Law in Arizona amounts for the two railroads traversing that state to about $1,000,000 a year. The reduction in train lengths also impedes efficient operation. More locomotives and more manpower are required; the necessary conversion and reconversion of train lengths at terminals and the delay caused by breaking up and remaking long trains upon entering and leaving the state in order to comply with the law, delays the traffic and diminishes its volume moved in a given time, especially when traffic is heavy. . . .

The unchallenged findings leave no doubt that the Arizona Train Limit Law imposes a serious burden on the interstate commerce conducted by appellant. It materially impedes the movement of appellant's interstate trains through that state and interposes a substantial obstruction to the national policy proclaimed by Congress, to promote adequate, economical and efficient railway transportation service. Interstate Commerce Act, preceding § 1, 54 Stat.

899. Enforcement of the law in Arizona, while train lengths remain unregulated or are regulated by varying standards in other states, must inevitably result in an impairment of uniformity of efficient railroad operation because the railroads are subjected to regulation which is not uniform in its application. Compliance with a state statute limiting train lengths requires interstate trains of a length lawful in other states to be broken up and reconstituted as they enter each state according as it may impose varying limitations upon train lengths. The alternative is for the carrier to conform to the lowest train limit restriction of any of the states through which its trains pass, whose laws thus control the carriers' operations both within and without the regulating state. . . .

At present the seventy freight car laws are enforced only in Arizona and Oklahoma, with a fourteen car passenger car limit in Arizona. The record here shows that the enforcement of the Arizona statute results in freight trains being broken up and reformed at the California border and in New Mexico, some distance from the Arizona line. Frequently it is not feasible to operate a newly assembled train from the New Mexico yard nearest to Arizona, with the result that the Arizona limitation governs the flow of traffic as far east as El Paso, Texas. For similar reasons the Arizona law often controls the length of passenger trains all the way from Los Angeles to El Paso.

If one state may regulate train lengths, so may all the others, and they need not prescribe the same maximum limitations. The practical effect of such regulations is to control train operations beyond the boundaries of the state exacting it because of the necessity of breaking up and reassembling long trains at the nearest terminal points before entering and after leaving the regulating state. The serious impediment to the free flow of commerce by the local regulation of train lengths and the practical necessity that such regulation, if any, must be prescribed by a single body having a nation-wide authority are apparent.

The trial court found that the Arizona law had no reasonable relation to safety, and made train operation more dangerous. Examination of the evidence and the detailed findings makes it clear that this conclusion was rested on facts found which indicate that such increased danger of accident and personal injury as may result from the greater length of trains is more than offset by the increase in the number of accidents resulting from the larger number of trains when train lengths are reduced. In considering the effect of the statute as a safety measure, therefore, the factor of controlling significance for present purposes is not whether there is basis for the conclusion of the Arizona Supreme Court that the increase in length of trains beyond the statutory maximum has an adverse effect upon safety of operation. The decisive question is whether in the circumstances the total effect of the law as a safety measure in reducing accidents and casualties is so slight or problematical as not to outweigh the national interest in keeping interstate commerce free from interferences which seriously impede it and subject it to local regulation which does not have a uniform effect on the interstate train journey which it interrupts.

The principal source of danger of accident from increased length of trains is the resulting increase of "slack action" of the train. Slack action is the amount of free movement of one car before it transmits its motion to an adjoining coupled car. This free movement results from the fact that in railroad practice cars are loosely coupled, and the coupling is often combined with a shock-absorbing device, a "draft gear," which, under stress, substantially increases the free movement as the train is started or stopped. . . .

On comparison of the number of slack action accidents in Arizona with those in Nevada, where the length of trains is now unregulated, the trial court found that with substantially the same amount of traffic in each state the number of accidents was relatively the same in long as in short train operations. While accidents from slack ac-

tion do occur in the operation of passenger trains, it does not appear that they are more frequent or the resulting shocks more severe on long than on short passenger trains. Nor does it appear that slack action accidents occurring on passenger trains, whatever their length, are of sufficient severity to cause serious injury or damage.

As the trial court found, reduction of the length of trains also tends to increase the number of accidents because of the increase in the number of trains. The application of the Arizona law compelled appellant to operate 30.08%, or 4,304, more freight trains in 1938 than would otherwise have been necessary. And the record amply supports the trial court's conclusion that the frequency of accidents is closely related to the number of trains run. The number of accidents due to grade crossing collisions between trains and motor vehicles and pedestrians, and to collisions between trains, which are usually far more serious than those due to slack action, and accidents due to locomotive failures, in general vary with the number of trains. Increase in the number of trains results in more starts and stops, more "meets" and "passes," and more switching movements, all tending to increase the number of accidents not only to train operatives and other railroad employees, but to passengers and members of the public exposed to danger by train operations.

Railroad statistics introduced into the record tend to show that this is the result of the application of the Arizona Train Limit Law to appellant, both with respect to all railroad casualties within the state and those affecting only trainmen whom the train limit law is supposed to protect. The accident rate in Arizona is much higher than on comparable lines elsewhere, where there is no regulation of length of trains. The record lends support to the trial court's conclusion that the train length limitation increased rather than diminished the number of accidents. This is shown by comparison of appellant's operations in Arizona with those in Nevada, and by comparison of operations of appellant and of the Santa Fe Railroad in Arizona with those of the same roads in New Mexico, and by like comparison between appellant's operations in Arizona and operations throughout the country.

Upon an examination of the whole case the trial court found that "if short-train operation may or should result in any decrease in the number or severity of the 'slack' or 'slack-surge' type of accidents or casualties, such decrease is substantially more than offset by the increased number of accidents and casualties from other causes that follow the arbitrary limitation of freight trains to 70 cars . . . and passenger trains to 14 cars."

We think, as the trial court found, that the Arizona Train Limit Law, viewed as a safety measure, affords at most slight and dubious advantage, if any, over unregulated train lengths, because it results in an increase in the number of trains and train operations and the consequent increase in train accidents of a character generally more severe than those due to slack action. Its undoubted effect on the commerce is the regulation, without securing uniformity, of the length of trains operated in interstate commerce, which lack is itself a primary cause of preventing the free flow of commerce by delaying it and by substantially increasing its cost and impairing its efficiency. In these respects the case differs from those where a state, by regulatory measures affecting the commerce, has removed or reduced safety hazards without substantial interference with the interstate movement of trains. Such are measures abolishing the car stove, *New York, N. H. & H. R. Co.* v. *New York,* 165 U.S. 628; requiring locomotives to be supplied with electric headlights, *Atlantic Coast Line R. Co.* v. *Georgia,* 234, U.S. 280; providing for full train crews, *Chicago, R. I. & P. Ry. Co.* v. *Arkansas,* 219 'J.S. 453; *St. Louis, I. M. & S. R. Co.* v. *Arkansas,* 240 U.S. 518; *Missouri Pac. R. Co.,* v. *Norwood,* 283 U.S. 249; and for the equipment of freight trains with cabooses, *Terminal Railroad Association* v. *Brotherhood, supra.*

The principle that, without controlling Congressional action, a state may not regulate interstate commerce so as substantially to affect its flow or deprive it of needed uniformity in its regulation is not to be avoided by "simply invoking the convenient apologetics of the police power," . . .

More recently in *Kelly* v. *State of Washington, ex rel. Foss Co.,* 302 U.S. 1, 15, we have pointed out that when a state goes beyond safety measures which are permissible because only local in their effect upon interstate commerce, and "attempts to impose particular standards as to structure, design, equipment, and operation [of vessels plying interstate], which in the judgment of its authorities may be desirable, but pass beyond what is plainly essential to safety and seaworthiness, the State will encounter the principle that such requirements, if imposed at all, must be through the action of Congress which can establish a uniform rule. Whether the State in a particular matter goes too far must be left to be determined when the precise question arises."

Here we conclude that the state does go too far. Its regulation of train lengths, admittedly obstructive to interstate train operation, and having a seriously adverse effect on transportation efficiency and economy, passes beyond what is plainly essential for safety since it does not appear that it will lessen rather than increase the danger of accident. Its attempted regulation of the operation of interstate trains cannot establish nation-wide control such as is essential to the maintenance of an efficient transportation system, which Congress alone can prescribe. The state interest cannot be preserved at the expense of the national interest by an enactment which regulates interstate train lengths without securing such control, which is a matter of national concern. To this the interest of the state here asserted is subordinate.

Appellees especially rely on the full train crew cases, *Chicago, R. I. & Pac. Ry. Co.* v. *State of Arkansas, supra; St. Louis, I. M. & S. R. Co.* v. *State of Arkansas, supra; Missouri Pacific R. Co.* v. *Norwood, supra,* and also on *South Carolina Highway Dept.* v. *Barnwell Bros.*, supra, as supporting the state's authority to regulate the length of interstate trains. While the full train crew laws undoubtedly placed an added financial burden on the railroads in order to serve a local interest, they did not obstruct interstate transportation or seriously impede it. They had no effects outside the state beyond those of picking up and setting down the extra employees at the state boundaries; they involve no wasted use of facilities or serious impairment of transportation efficiency, which are among the factors of controlling weight here. . . .

The contrast between the present regulation and the full train crew laws in point of their effects on commerce, and the like contrast with the highway safety regulations, in point of the nature of the subject of regulation and the state's interest in it, illustrate and emphasize the considerations which enter into a determination of the relative weights of state and national interests where state regulation affecting interstate commerce is attempted. Here examination of all the relevant factors makes it plain that the state interest is outweighed by the interest of the nation in an adequate, economical and efficient railway transportation service, which must prevail.

Reversed.

Mr. Justice Rutledge concurs in the result.

Mr. Justice Black, dissenting: . . .

For more than a quarter of a century, railroads and their employees have engaged in controversies over the relative virtues and dangers of long trains. . . . This controversy between the railroads and their employees, which was nationwide, was carried to Congress. Extensive hearings took place. . . . It is significant, however, that American railroads never once asked Congress to exercise its unquestioned power to enact uniform legislation on that subject, and thereby invalidate the Arizona law. That which for some unexplained reason they did not ask Congress to do when it had the very subject of train length limita-

tions under consideration, they shortly thereafter asked an Arizona state court to do.

In the state court a rather extraordinary "trial" took place. Charged with violating the law, the railroad admitted the charge. It alleged that the law was unconstitutional, however, and sought a trial of facts on that issue. The essence of its charge of unconstitutionality rested on one of these two grounds: (1) the legislature and people of Arizona erred in 1912 in determining that the running of long cars was dangerous; or (2) railroad conditions had so improved since 1912 that previous dangers did not exist to the same extent, and that the statute should be stricken down either because it cast an undue burden on interstate commerce by reason of the added cost, or because the changed conditions had rendered the Act "arbitrary and unreasonable." Thus, the issue which the court "tried" was not whether the railroad was guilty of violating the law, but whether the law was unconstitutional either because the legislature had been guilty of misjudging the facts concerning the degree of the danger of long trains, or because the 1912 conditions of danger no longer existed.

Before the state trial judge finally determined that the dangers found by the legislature in 1912 no longer existed, he heard evidence over a period of 5½ months which appears in about 3,000 pages of the printed record before us. It then adopted findings of fact submitted to it by the railroad, which cover 148 printed pages, and conclusions of law which cover 5 pages. We can best understand the nature of this "trial" by analogizing the same procedure to a defendant charged with violating a state or national safety appliance act, where the defendant comes into court and admits violation of the act. In such cases, the ordinary procedure would be for the court to pass upon the constitutionality of the act, and either discharge or convict the defendants. The procedure here, however, would justify quite a different trial method. Under it, a defendant is permitted to offer voluminous evidence to show that a legislative body has erroneously resolved disputed facts in finding a danger great enough to justify the passage of the law. This new pattern of trial procedure makes it necessary for a judge to hear all the evidence offered as to why a legislature passed a law and to make findings of fact as to the validity of those reasons. If under today's ruling a court does make findings, as to a danger contrary to the findings of the legislature, and the evidence heard "lends support" to those findings, a court can then invalidate the law. In this respect, the Arizona County Court acted, and this Court today is acting, as a "superlegislature."

Even if this method of invalidating legislative acts is a correct one, I still think that the "findings" of the state court do not authorize today's decision. That court did not find that there is no unusual danger from slack movements in long trains. It did decide on disputed evidence that the long train "slack movement" dangers were more than offset by prospective dangers as a result of running a larger number of short trains, since many people might be hurt at grade crossings. There was undoubtedly some evidence before the state court from which it could have reached such a conclusion. There was undoubtedly as much evidence before it which would have justified a different conclusion.

Under those circumstances, the determination of whether it is in the interest of society for the length of trains to be governmentally regulated is a matter of public policy. Someone must fix that policy —either the Congress, or the state, or the courts. A century and a half of constitutional history and government admonishes this Court to leave that choice to the elected legislative representatives of the people themselves, where it properly belongs both on democratic principles and

the requirements of efficient government. . . .

The Supreme Court of Arizona did not discuss the County Court's so-called findings of fact. It properly designated the Arizona statute as a safety measure, and finding that it bore a reasonable relation to its purpose declined to review the judgment of the legislature as to the necessity for the passage of the act. In so doing it was well fortified by a long line of decisions of this Court. Today's decision marks an abrupt departure from that line of cases. . . .

The history of congressional consideration of this problem leaves little if any room to doubt that the choice of Congress to leave the state free in this field was a deliberate choice, which was taken with a full knowledge of the complexities of the problems and the probable need for diverse regulations in different localities. I am therefore compelled to reach the conclusion that today's decision is the result of the belief of a majority of this Court that both the legislature of Arizona and the Congress made wrong policy decisions in permitting a law to stand which limits the length of railroad trains. . . .

Mr. Justice Douglas, dissenting:

I have expressed my doubts whether the courts should intervene in situations like the present and strike down state legislation on the grounds that it burdens interstate commerce. *McCarroll* v. *Dixie Greyhound Lines*, 309 U.S. 176, 183–189. My view has been that the courts should intervene only where the state legislation discriminated against interstate commerce or was out of harmony with laws which Congress had enacted. . . . Whether the question arises under the commerce clause or the Fourteenth Amendment, I think the legislation is entitled to a presumption of validity. . . .

NOTE AND QUAERE: Examine carefully the Court's answer to Mr. Justice Black's dissenting argument. For an application of the principle behind that answer, see *Prudential Insurance Co.* v. *Benjamin,* below.

Do you think the Arizona Train Limit Law was in fact adopted as a safety measure, or was the safety language merely a "sugar coating" for a labor "featherbedding" measure? Note how the Court—surely with tongue in cheek—respects the state's characterization of the act as safety legislation.

Those who find that the language of *Southern Pacific* does not precisely conform with that of the *Cooley* case may find a reconciliation in *California v. Zook*, 336 U.S. 725 (1949), where the Court said, ". . . if a case falls within an area in commerce thought to demand a uniform national rule, state activity is struck down. If the activity is one of predominantly local interest, state action is sustained. More accurately, the question is whether the state interest is outweighed by a national interest in the unhampered operation of interstate commerce."

DI SANTO v. *PENNSYLVANIA*

273 U.S. 34 (1927)

> For the reasons indicated in the opinion of Mr. Justice Brandeis, Pennsylvania sought by means of a licensing system to prevent fraud in the sale of steamship tickets for passage to and from foreign countries. Di Santo was prosecuted for violation of this legislation.

MR. JUSTICE BUTLER delivered the opinion of the Court: . . .

The soliciting of passengers and the sale of steamship tickets and orders for passage between the United States and Europe constitute a well-recognized part of foreign commerce. . . . A state statute which by its necessary operation directly interferes with or burdens foreign commerce is a prohibited regulation and invalid, regardless of the purpose with which it was passed. . . . Such legislation cannot be sustained as an exertion of the police power of the state to prevent possible fraud. . . . The Congress has complete and paramount authority to regulate foreign commerce and, by appropriate measures, to protect the public against the frauds of those who sell these tickets and orders. The sales here in question are related to foreign commerce as directly as are sales made in ticket offices maintained by the carriers and operated by their servants and employees. The license fee and other things imposed by the act on plaintiff in error, who initiates for his principals a transaction in foreign commerce, constitute a direct burden on that commerce. This case is controlled by *Texas Transport Co. v. New Orleans*, 264 U.S. 150, and *McCall v. California*, 136 U.S. 104. Judgment reversed.

MR. JUSTICE BRANDEIS, with whom MR. JUSTICE HOLMES concurs, dissenting:

The statute is an exertion of the police power of the state. Its evident purpose is to prevent a particular species of fraud and imposition found to have been practiced in Pennsylvania upon persons of small means, unfamiliar with our language and institutions. Much of the immigration into the United States is effected by arrangements made here for remittance of the means of travel. The individual immigrant is often an advance guard. After gaining a foothold here, he has his wife and children, aged parents, brothers, sisters or other relatives follow. To this end he remits steamship tickets or orders for transportation. The purchase of the tickets involves trust in the dealer. This is so not only because of the nature of the transaction, but also because a purchaser when unable to pay the whole price at one time makes successive deposits on account, the ticket or order not being delivered until full payment is made. The facilities for remitting both cash and steamship tickets are commonly furnished by private bankers of the same nationality as the immigrant. It was natural that the supervision of persons engaged in the business of supplying steamship tickets should be committed by the statute to the commissioner of banking.

Although the purchase made is of an ocean steamship ticket, the transaction regulated is wholly intrastate—as much so as if the purchase were of local real estate or of local theater tickets. There is no purpose on the part of the state to regulate foreign commerce. The statute is not an obstruction to foreign commerce. It does not discriminate against foreign commerce. It places no direct burden upon such commerce. It does not affect the commerce except indirectly. Congress could, of course, deal with the subject, because it is connected with foreign commerce. But it has not done so. Nor has it legislated on any allied subject. Thus, there can be no contention that Congress has occupied the field. And obviously, also, this is not a case in which the silence of Congress can be interpreted as a prohibition of state action—as a declaration that in the sale of ocean steamship tickets fraud

may be practiced without let or hindrance. If Pennsylvania must submit to seeing its citizens defrauded, it is not because Congress has so willed, but because the Constitution so commands. I cannot believe that it does. . . .

MR. JUSTICE STONE, dissenting: . . .

In this case the traditional test of the limit of state action by inquiring whether the interference with commerce is direct or indirect seems to me too mechanical, too uncertain in its application, and too remote from actualities, to be of value. In thus making use of the expressions, "direct" and "indirect interference" with commerce, we are doing little more than using labels to describe a result rather than any trustworthy formula by which it is reached.
. . .

I am not persuaded that the regulation here is more than local in character or that it interposes any barrier to commerce. Until Congress undertakes the protection of local communities from the dishonesty of the sellers of steamship tickets, it would seem that there is no adequate ground for holding that the regulation here involved is a prohibited interference with commerce.

MR. JUSTICE HOLMES and MR. JUSTICE BRANDEIS concur in this opinion.

NOTE: *Di Santo,* though overruled by *California* v. *Thompson,* above, is included here to emphasize the difference between the Court's old conceptual approach in the laissez-faire era and its modern pragmatic approach as seen in *Southern Pacific. Di Santo* also shows that "In the years preceding 1937, the Court without ever openly abandoning the *Cooley* test, used . . . other expressions—such as whether the state law was a 'burden,' or a 'substantial' or 'undue' burden, on commerce, whether the effect on commerce was 'direct' or 'indirect.' . . . It was difficult, if not impossible to tell . . . whether these expressions merely constituted different methods of stating the *Cooley* doctrine, or whether the Court was applying different tests." Stern, "The Problems of Yesteryear—Commerce and Due Process," 4 *Vanderbilt Law Review* 446 (1951).

Leisy v. *Hardin,* 135 U.S. 100 (1890), held that "inasmuch as interstate commerce, consisting in the transportation, purchase, sale and exchange of commodities, is national in character and must be governed [if at all] by a uniform system," a state "prohibition" act was invalid. The effect was to outlaw the kind of local restrictions upon the national market that had plagued us under the Articles of Confederation. By this principle obviously a state could not protect its labor standards by excluding child-made products of other states. Compare *Hammer* v. *Dagenhart* in which the Court invalidated a *congressional* effort to outlaw interstate shipment of child-made goods. In short such shipments could not be controlled by a state because they *do* constitute interstate commerce and could not be controlled by Congress because they *do not* constitute interstate commerce. Such is the essence of dual federalism as the servant of laissez-faire.

2. STATE TAXATION OF INTERSTATE AND FOREIGN COMMERCE

American experience under the Articles of Confederation demonstrated for all time the danger of leaving with the separate states a power to tax interstate trade. The effort of each to gain advantages for itself by discriminatory tax burdens doomed the welfare of all. Moreover, interstate commerce has peculiarly seductive charms for state legislatures always hard pressed by increasing needs for revenue. It is rich and it has special political appeal. To tap it is in large measure to impose burdens upon those outside the taxing state; that is, upon those who cannot vote the imposing legislators out of office. For these reasons state taxation of national commerce is a perennial problem raising more litigation than any other constitutional issue. Plainly it invokes considerations not present when merely police or commercial regulations are in issue. Because of this the *Cooley* rule has not been used extensively in state tax cases. Or to put it more accurately, there was once a long-established doctrine that all interstate commerce demands uniformity of treatment for tax purposes and so the states could not tax it at all. *The Passenger Cases,* 7 Howard 283 (1849); *State Freight Tax Case,* 15 Wallace 232 (1873). But if this cured one problem, it raised another. To give national trade full immunity means that competing, local business will have to pay an undue share of the cost of local government—whose benefits interstate trade also enjoys. The problem then is to protect the national market from strangulation by the states and yet make national commerce pay its fair share of the cost of local government. Surely there is no obvious solution.

On at least two items agreement has been all but universal. There is a point at which interstate and foreign commerce ends, i.e., becomes local (*Brown* v. *Maryland*); and states may not discriminate against national, in favor of local, commerce (*Best* v. *Maxwell*). But this does not take us far. For example, many a tax that is not in fact discriminatory may be too burdensome for healthy trade among the states. Many a levy that is verbally neutral may have highly selective economic consequences. Another difficulty is the elusive nature of tax-incidence economics. Can judges tread where economists step lightly? Judicial responses to these difficulties are seen in the cases which follow. Like so many others in this field, they should be read for instruction in the difficulties of the problem and not for thumb rules.

BROWN v. MARYLAND

12 Wheat. 419 (1827)

Mr. Chief Justice Marshall delivered the opinion of the Court. . . .

The cause depends entirely on the question, whether . . . a State can constitutionally require the importer of foreign articles to [pay a license tax] before he shall be permitted to sell a bale or package so imported. . . .

It has been truly said, that the presumption is in favor of every legislative act, and that the whole burden of proof lies on him who denies its constitutionality. The plaintiffs in error take the burden upon themselves, and insist, that the act under consideration is repugnant to two provisions in the constitution of the United States. 1. To that which declares that "no state shall, without the consent of Congress, lay any imposts or duties on imports or exports, except what may be absolutely necessary for executing its inspection laws." 2. To that which declares that congress shall have power "to regulate commerce with foreign nations, and among the several states, and with the Indian tribes."

1. The first inquiry is into the extent of the prohibition upon states "to lay any imposts or duties on imports or exports." The counsel for the State of Maryland would confine this prohibition to laws imposing duties on the act of importation or exportation. The counsel for the plaintiffs in error give them a much wider scope. In performing the delicate and important duty of construing clauses in the Constitution of our country, which involve conflicting powers of the government of the Union, and of the respective States, it is proper to take a view of the literal meaning of the words to be expounded, of their connection with other words, and of the general objects to be accomplished by the prohibitory clause, or by the grant of power. What, then, is the meaning of the words, "imposts, or duties on imports or exports"?

An impost, or duty on imports, is a custom or a tax levied on articles brought into a country, and is most usually secured before the importer is allowed to exercise his rights of ownership over them, because evasions of the law can be prevented more certainly by executing it while the articles are in its custody. It would not, however, be less an impost or duty on the articles, if it were to be levied on them after they were landed. The policy and consequent practice of levying or securing the duty before, or on entering the port, does not limit the power to that state of things, nor, consequently, the prohibition, unless the true meaning of the clause so confines it. What, then, are "imports"? The lexicons inform us, they are "things imported." If we appeal to usage for the meaning of the word, we shall receive the same answer. They are the articles themselves which are brought into the country. "A duty on imports," then, is not merely a duty on the act of importation, but is a duty on the thing imported. It is not, taken in its literal sense, confined to a duty levied while the article is entering the country, but extends to a duty levied after it has entered the country. The succeeding words of the sentence which limit the prohibition, show the extent in which it was understood. The limitation is, "except what may be absolutely necessary for executing its inspection laws." Now, the inspection laws, so far as they act upon articles for exportation, are generally executed on land, before the article is put on board the vessel; so far as they act upon importations, they are generally executed upon articles which are landed. The tax or duty of inspection, then, is a tax which is frequently, if not always paid for service performed on land, while the article is in the bosom of the country.

Yet this tax is an exception to the prohibition on the States to lay duties on imports or exports. The exception was made because the tax would otherwise have been within the prohibition. If it be a rule of interpretation to which all assent, that the exception of a particular thing from general words, proves that, in the opinion of the lawgiver, the thing excepted would be within the general clause, had the exception not been made, we know no reason why this general rule should not be as applicable to the constitution as to other instruments. If it be applicable, then, this exception in favor of duties for the support of inspection laws, goes far in proving that the framers of the constitution classed taxes of a similar character with those imposed for the purpose of inspection, with duties on imports and exports, and supposed them to be prohibited.

If we quit this narrow view of the subject, and passing from the literal interpretation of the words, look to the objects of the prohibition, we find no reason for withdrawing the act under consideration from its operation. From the vast inequality between the different states of the Confederacy, as to commercial advantages, few subjects were viewed with deeper interest, or excited more irritation, than the manner in which the several States exercised, or seemed disposed to exercise, the power of laying duties on imports. From motives which were deemed sufficient by the statesmen of that day, the general power of taxation, indispensably necessary as it was, and jealous as the States were of any encroachment on it, was so far abridged as to forbid them to touch imports or exports, with the single exception which has been noticed. Why are they restrained from imposing these duties? Plainly, because, in the general opinion, the interest of all would be best promoted by placing that whole subject under the control of Congress. Whether the prohibition to "lay imposts, or duties on imports or exports," proceeded from an apprehension that the power might be so exercised as to disturb that equality among the States which was generally advantageous, or that harmony between them which it was desirable to preserve, or to maintain unimpaired our commercial connections with foreign nations, or to confer this source of revenue on the government of the Union, or whatever other motive might have induced the prohibition, it is plain, that the object would be as completely defeated by a power to tax the article in the hands of the importer the instant it was landed, as by a power to tax it while entering the port. There is no difference, in effect, between a power to prohibit the sale of an article, and a power to prohibit its introduction into the country. The one would be a necessary consequence of the other. No goods would be imported if none could be sold. No object of any description can be accomplished by laying a duty on importation, which may not be accomplished with equal certainty by laying a duty on the thing imported in the hands of the importer. It is obvious, that the same power which imposes a light duty, can impose a very heavy one, one which amounts to a prohibition. Questions of power do not depend on the degree to which it may be exercised. If it may be exercised at all, it must be exercised at the will of those in whose hands it is placed. If the tax may be levied in this form by a State, it may be levied to an extent which will defeat the revenue by impost, so far as it is drawn from importations into the particular State. We are told, that such wild and irrational abuse of power is not to be apprehended, and is not to be taken into view when discussing its existence. All power may be abused; and if the fear of its abuse is to constitute an argument against its existence, it might be urged against the existence of that which is universally acknowledged, and which is indispensable as to the general safety. The States will never be so mad as to destroy their own commerce, or even to lessen it. . . .

The counsel for the state of Maryland insists, with great reason, that if the words of the prohibition be taken in their utmost latitude, they will abridge the power of taxation, which all admit to be essential to the states, to an extent which has never yet been suspected, and will deprive them of resources which are necessary to supply revenue, and which they have heretofore been admitted to possess. These words must, therefore, be construed with some limitation; and, if this be admitted, they insist that entering the country is the point of time when the prohibition ceases, and the power of the state to tax commences. It may be conceded, that the words of the prohibition ought not to be pressed to their utmost extent; that in our complex system, the object of the powers conferred on the government of the Union, and the nature of the often conflicting powers which remain in the states, must always be taken into view, and may aid in expounding the words of any particular clause. But, while we admit that sound principles of construction ought to restrain all courts from carrying the words of the prohibition beyond the object the constitution is intended to secure; that there must be a point of time when the prohibition ceases, and the power of the state to tax commences; we cannot admit that this point of time is the instant that the articles enter the country. It is, we think, obvious that this construction would defeat the prohibition.

The constitutional prohibition on the States to lay a duty on imports, a prohibition which a vast majority of them must feel an interest in preserving, may certainly come in conflict with their acknowledged power to tax persons and property within their territory. The power, and the restriction on it, though quite distinguishable when they do not approach each other, may yet, like the intervening colours between white and black, approach so nearly as to perplex the understanding, as colours perplex the vision in marking the distinction between them. Yet the distinction exists, and must be marked as the cases arise. Till they do arise, it might be premature to state any rule as being universal in its application. It is sufficient for the present to say, generally, that when the importer has so acted upon the thing imported, that it has become incorporated and mixed up

with the mass of property in the country, it has perhaps, lost its distinctive character as an import, and has become subject to the taxing power of the State; but while remaining the property of the importer, in his warehouse, in the original form or package in which it was imported, a tax upon it is too plainly a duty on imports to escape the prohibition in the constitution. . . .

This indictment is against the importer, for selling a package of dry goods in the form in which it was imported, without a license. This state of things is changed if he sells them, or otherwise mixes them with the general property of the State, by breaking up his packages, and travelling with them as an itinerant pedlar. In the first case, the tax intercepts the import, as an import, on its way to become incorporated with the general mass of property, and denies it the privilege of becoming so incorporated until it shall have contributed to the revenue of the State. It denies to the importer the right of using the privilege which he has purchased from the United States, until he shall have also purchased it from the State. In the last cases, the tax finds the article already incorporated with the mass of property, by the act of the importer. . . .

But if it should be proved, that a duty on the article itself would be repugnant to the Constitution, it is still argued that this is not a tax upon the article, but on the person. The State, it is said, may tax occupations, and this is nothing more. It is impossible to conceal from ourselves that this is varying the form without varying the substance. It is treating a prohibition which is general, as if it were confined to a particular mode of doing the forbidden thing. All must perceive that a tax on the sale of an article, imported only for sale, is a tax on the article itself. It is true the State may tax occupations generally, but this tax must be paid by those who employ the individual, or is a tax on his business. The lawyer, the physician, or the mechanic, must either charge more on the article in which he deals, or the thing itself is taxed through his person. This the State has a right to do, because no constitutional prohibition extends to it. So, a tax on the occupation of an importer is, in like manner, a tax on importation. It must add to the price of the article, and be paid by the consumer, or by the importer himself, in like manner as a direct duty on the article itself would be made. This the State has not a right to do, because it is prohibited by the constitution. . . .

We think, then, that the act under which the plaintiffs in error were indicted, is repugnant to that article of the constitution which declares, that "no state shall lay any impost or duties on imports or exports."

2. Is it also repugnant to that clause in the constitution which empowers "congress to regulate commerce with foreign nations, and among the several states, and with the Indian tribes"? The oppressed and degraded state of commerce, previous to the adoption of the constitution, can scarcely be forgotten. It was regulated by foreign nations, with a single view to their own interests; and our disunited efforts to counteract their restrictions, were rendered impotent by want of combination. Congress, indeed, possessed the power of making treaties; but the inability of the federal government to enforce them had become so apparent, as to render that power in a great degree useless. Those who felt the injury arising from this state of things, and those who were capable of estimating the influence of commerce on the prosperity of nations, perceived the necessity of giving the control over this important subject to a single government. It may be doubted, whether any of the evils proceeding from the feebleness of the federal government, contributed more to that great revolution which introduced the present system, than the deep and general conviction, that commerce ought to be regulated by congress. It is not, therefore, matter of surprise, that the grant should be as extensive as the mischief, and should comprehend all foreign commerce, and all commerce among the States. To construe the power so as to impair its effi-

cacy, would tend to defeat an object, in the attainment of which the American public took, and justly took, that strong interest which arose from a full conviction of its necessity.

What, then, is the just extent of a power to regulate commerce with foreign nations, and among the several States? This question was considered in the case of *Gibbons* v. *Ogden*, 9 Wheat. 1, in which it was declared to be complete in itself, and to acknowledge no limitations other than are prescribed by the Constitution. The power is co-extensive with the subject on which it acts, and cannot be stopped at the external boundary of a State, but must enter its interior. We deem it unnecessary now to reason in support of these propositions. Their truth is proved by facts continually before our eyes, and was, we think, demonstrated, if they could require demonstration, in the case already mentioned.

If this power reaches the interior of a State, and may be there exercised, it must be capable of authorizing the sale of those articles which it introduces. Commerce is intercourse—one of its most ordinary ingredients is traffic. It is inconceivable, that the power to authorize this traffic, when given in the most comprehensive terms, with the intent that its efficacy should be complete, should cease at the point when its continuance is indispensable to its value.

. . . Any penalty inflicted on the importer, for selling the article, in his character of importer, must be in opposition to the act of congress which authorizes importation. Any charge on the introduction and incorporation of the articles into and with the mass of property in the country, must be hostile to the power of congress to regulate commerce, since an essential part of that regulation, and principal object of it is, to prescribe the regular means for accomplishing that introduction and incorporation. The distinction between a tax on the thing imported, and on the person of the importer, can have no influence on this part of the subject. It is too obvious for controversy, that they interfere equally with the power to regulate commerce.

It has been contended, that this construction of the power to regulate commerce, as was contended in construing the prohibition to lay duties on imports, would abridge the acknowledged power of a State to tax its own citizens, or their property within its territory. We admit this power to be sacred; but cannot admit, that it may be used so as to obstruct the free course of a power given to congress. We cannot admit, that it may be used so as to obstruct or defeat the power to regulate commerce. It has been observed, that the powers remaining with the States may be so exercised as to come in conflict with those vested in congress. When this happens, that which is not supreme must yield to that which is supreme. This great and universal truth is inseparable from the nature of things, and the Constitution has applied it to the often interfering powers of the general and state governments, as a vital principle of perpetual operation. It results, necessarily, from this principle, that the taxing power of the States must have some limits. It cannot reach and restrain the action of the national government within its proper sphere. It cannot reach the administration of justice in the courts of the Union, or the collection of the taxes of the United States, or restrain the operation of any law which congress may constitutionally pass. It cannot interfere with any regulation of commerce. If the States may tax all persons and property found on their territory, what shall restrain them from taxing goods in their transit through the State from one part to another, for the purpose of re-exportation? The laws of trade authorize this operation, and general convenience requires it. Or what should restrain a State from taxing any article passing through it, from one State to another, for the purpose of traffic? or from taxing the transportation of articles passing from the State itself to another State for commercial purposes? These cases are all within the sovereign power of taxation, but would obviously derange the measures of congress to regulate commerce, and affect materially the purpose for which that power was given. We deem it unnecessary to press this argument further, or to give additional illustrations of it, because the subject was taken up and considered with great attention, in *McCulloch* v. *Maryland*, . . . the decision in which case is, we think, entirely applicable to this.

It may be proper to add, that we suppose the principles laid down in this case, to apply equally to importations from a sister State. . . .

. . . The judgment is to be reversed. . . .

[MR. JUSTICE THOMPSON delivered a dissenting opinion.]

NOTE: The "original package" doctrine has been followed in foreign commerce cases. With a few exceptions, it has been abandoned in interstate commerce cases in favor of the doctrines illustrated in the following cases.

BEST v. MAXWELL
311 U.S. 454 (1940)

MR. JUSTICE REED delivered the opinion of the Court:

Appellant, a New York retail merchandise establishment, rented a display room in a North Carolina hotel for several days during February, 1938, and took orders for goods corresponding to samples; it filled the orders by shipping direct to the customers from New York City. Before using the room appellant paid under protest the tax required by chapter 127 § 121 (e), of the North Carolina Laws of 1937, which levies an annual privilege tax of $250 on every person or corporation, not a regular retail merchant in the state, who displays samples in any hotel room rented or occupied temporarily for the purpose of securing retail orders. Appellant not being a regular retail merchant of North Carolina admittedly comes within the statute. Asserting, however, that the tax was unconstitutional, especially in view of the commerce clause, it brought this suit for a refund and succeeded in the trial court. The Supreme Court of North Carolina reversed and then, being evenly divided on rehearing, allowed the reversal to stand. The prevailing opinion characterized the tax as one on the commercial use of temporary quarters, which in its operation did not discriminate against interstate commerce and therefore did not come into conflict with the commerce clause.

The commerce clause forbids discrimination, whether forthright or ingenious. In each case it is our duty to determine whether the statute under attack, whatever its name may be, will in its practical operation work discrimination against interstate commerce. This standard we think condemns the tax at bar. Nominally the statute taxes all who are not regular retail merchants in North Carolina, regardless of whether they are residents or non-residents. We must assume, however, on this record that those North Carolina residents competing with appellant for the sale of similar merchandise will normally be regular retail merchants. The retail stores of the state are the natural outlets for merchandise, not those who sell only by sample. Some of these local shops may, like appellant, rent temporary display rooms in sections of North Carolina where they have no permanent store, but even these escape the tax at bar because the location of their central retail store somewhere within the state will qualify them as "regular retail merchants in the State of North Carolina." The only corresponding fixed-sum license tax to which appellant's real competitors are subject is a tax of $1 per annum for the privilege of doing business. Nonresidents wishing to display their wares must either establish themselves as regular North Carolina retail merchants at prohibitive expense, or else pay this $250 tax that bears no relation to actual or probable sales but must be paid in advance no matter how small the sales turn out to be. Interstate commerce can hardly survive in so hostile an atmosphere. A $250 investment in advance, required of out-of-state retailers but not of their real local competitors, can operate only to discourage and hinder the appearance of interstate commerce in the North Carolina retail market. Extra-state merchants would be compelled to turn over their North Carolina trade to regular local merchants selling by sample. North Carolina regular retail merchants would benefit, but to the same extent the commerce of the Nation would suffer discrimination.

The freedom of commerce which allows the merchants of each state a regional or national market for their goods is not to be fettered by legislation, the actual effect of which is to discriminate in favor of intrastate businesses, whatever may be the ostensible reach of the language.

Judgment reversed.

GALVESTON, HARRISBURG & SAN ANTONIO RAILWAY v. TEXAS

210 U.S. 217 (1908)

It has long been settled that goods being transported in interstate commerce are not subject to property taxes in the states through which they pass. *The State Freight Tax*

Case, 15 Wallace 232 (1873). But it is clear that a state may tax local property that is used for interstate commerce purposes—railroad tracks, for example.

It was also settled long ago that a state may not constitutionally tax the gross receipts of interstate business—such a tax was deemed too great a burden on interstate commerce. *Philadelphia & S. Mail S.S. Co. v. Pennsylvania,* 122 U.S. 326 (1887). Apparently in an effort to get around this prohibition, Texas levied on each railroad within its boundaries an annual tax, not "on," but "equal to 1 percent of its gross receipts." Of course, the Court was not fooled by the linguistic dodge; but was the tax in essence a prohibited gross receipts tax, or was it merely a tax on property the value of which was measured by its earning power?

MR. JUSTICE HOLMES delivered the opinion of the Court: . . .

The lines of the railroad concerned are wholly within the state, but they connect with other lines, and a part, in some instances much the larger part, of their gross receipts is derived from the carriage of passengers and freights coming from, or destined to, points without the state. In view of this portion of their business, the railroads contend that the case is governed by *Philadephia & S. Mail S. S. Co. v. Pennsylvania,* 122 U.S. 326. The counsel for the state rely upon *Maine v. Grand Trunk R. Co.,* 142 U.S. 217, and maintain, if necessary, that the later overrules the earlier case.

In *Philadelphia & S. Mail S. S. Co. v. Pennsylvania, supra,* it was decided that a tax upon the gross receipts of a steamship corporation of the state, when such receipts were derived from commerce between the states and with foreign countries, was unconstitutional. We regard this decision as unshaken and as stating established law. . . . In *Maine v. Grand Trunk R. Co., supra,* the authority of the *Philadelphia Steamship Company* case was accepted without question, and the decision was justified by the majority as not in any way qualifying or impairing it. The validity of the distinction was what divided the court.

It being once admitted, as of course it must be, that not every law that affects commerce among the states is a regulation of it in a constitutional sense, nice distinctions are to be expected. Regulation and commerce among the states both are practical rather than technical conceptions, and, naturally, their limits must be fixed by practical lines. As the property of companies engaged in such commerce may be taxed (*Pullman's Palace Car Co. v. Pennsylvania,* 141 U.S. 18) and may be taxed at its value as it is, in its organic relations, and not merely as a congeries of unrelated items, taxes on such property have been sustained that took account of the augmentation of value from the commerce in which it was engaged. *Adams Exp. Co. v. Ohio State Auditor,* 165 U.S. 194; *Adams Exp. Co. v. Kentucky,* 166 U.S. 171; *Fargo v. Hart,* 193 U.S. 490, 499. So it has been held that a tax on the property and business of a railroad operated within the state might be estimated prima facie by gross income, computed by adding to the income derived from business within the state the proportion of interstate business equal to the proportion between the road over which the business was carried within the state to the total length of the road over which it was carried. *Wisconsin & M. R. Co. v. Powers,* 191 U.S. 379.

Since the commercial value of property consists in the expectation of income from it, and since taxes ultimately, at least, in the long run, come out of income, obviously taxes called taxes on property, and those called taxes on income or receipts, tend to run into each other somewhat as fair value and anticipated profits run into each other in the law of damages. The difficulty of distinguishing them became greater when it was decided, not without much debate and difference of opinion, that interstate carriers' property might be taxed as a going concern. In *Wisconsin & M. R. Co. v. Powers, supra,* the measure of property by income purported only to be prima facie valid. But the extreme case came earlier. In *Maine* v. *Grand Trunk R. Co., supra,* "an annual excise tax for the privilege of exercising its franchise" was levied upon everyone operating a railroad in the state, fixed by percentages, varying up to a certain limit, upon the average gross receipts per mile multiplied by the number of miles within the state, when the road extended outside. This seems at first sight like a reaction from the *Philadelphia & Southern Mail Steamship Company* case. But it may not have been. The estimated gross receipts per mile may be said to have been made a measure of the value of the property per mile. That the effort of the state was to reach that value, and not to fasten on the receipts from transportation as such, was shown by the fact that the scheme of the statute was to establish a system. The buildings of the railroad and its lands and fixtures outside of its right of way were to be taxed locally, as other property was taxed, and this excise with the local tax were to be in lieu of all taxes. The language shows that the local tax was not expected to include the additional value gained by the property being part of a going concern. That idea came in later. The excise was an attempt to reach that additional value. The two taxes together fairly may be called a commutation tax. . . .

"By whatever name the exaction may be called, if it amounts to no more than the ordinary tax upon property or a just equivalent therefor, ascertained by reference thereto, it is not open to attack as inconsistent with the Constitution." *Postal Teleg. Cable Co.* v. *Adams, supra.* See *New York, L. E. & W. R. Co.* v. *Pennsylvania,* 158 U.S. 431, 438, 439. The question is whether this is such a tax. It appears sufficiently, perhaps from what has been said, that we are to look for a practical rather than a logical or philosophical distinction. The state must be allowed to tax the property, and to tax it at its actual value as a going concern. On the other hand, the state cannot tax the interstate business. The two necessities hardly admit of an absolute logical reconciliation.

Yet the distinction is not without sense. When a legislature is trying simply to value property, it is less likely to attempt or to effect injurious regulation than when it is aiming directly at the receipts from interstate commerce. A practical line can be drawn by taking the whole scheme of taxation into account. That must be done by this court as best it can. Neither the state courts nor the legislatures, by giving the tax a particular name or by the use of some form of words, can take away our duty to consider its nature and effect. If it bears upon commerce among the states so directly as to amount to a regulation in a relatively immediate way, it will not be saved by name or form. *Stockard* v. *Morgan,* 185 U.S. 27, 37, . . .

We are of opinion that the statute levying this tax does amount to an attempt to regulate commerce among the states. The distinction between a tax "equal to" 1 percent of gross receipts, and a tax of 1 percent of the same, seems to us nothing, except where the former phrase is the index of an actual attempt to reach the property and to let the interstate traffic and the receipts from it alone. We find no such attempt or anything to qualify the plain inference from the statute, taken by itself. On the contrary, we rather infer from the judgment of the state court and from the argument on behalf of the state that another tax on the property of the railroad is upon a valuation of that property, taken as a going concern. This is merely an effort to reach the gross receipts, not even disguised by the name of an occupation tax, and in no way helped by the words "equal to."

Of course, it does not matter that the plaintiffs in error are domestic corporations, or that the tax embraces indiscriminately gross receipts from commerce within as well as outside of the state. We are of opinion that the judgments should be reversed.

Judgment reversed.

MR. JUSTICE HARLAN wrote a dissenting opinion in which MR. JUSTICE WHITE and MR. JUSTICE FULLER joined.

NOTE on the sales tax: When the states were especially hard pressed for revenue in the Great Depression, many of them resorted to a general sales tax. But since this is merely a new name for the old gross receipts tax, it raised serious constitutional problems. For, as we have seen, such taxes could not be levied on interstate transactions. This meant that the sales tax could be "evaded" by buying one's goods in an interstate, rather than in a local, transaction. Thus the buyer's state would lose not only the tax but also the business. To avoid this difficulty the State of Washington developed the "use tax" on goods bought out-of-state for use in Washington. When that tax was upheld in *Henneford* v. *Silas Mason Co.*, 300 U.S. 577 (1937), it was an easy step to *McGoldrick* v. *Berwind-White Coal Co.*, 309 U.S. 33 (1940), which permitted New York to do directly what Washington had done indirectly; namely, to tax an interstate sale. But this raised another difficulty. If such sales could now be taxed, there was a risk that they would be taxed twice (once by the state of the buyer, and once by the state of the seller). This would put interstate sales at a competitive disadvantage vis-à-vis local sales which are subject at most to only one sales tax. To meet this problem the Court permitted only the buyer's state (not the seller's) to tax an interstate sale. See *Gwin, White & Prince* v. *Henneford*, 305 U.S. 434 (1939), and *Freeman* v. *Hewit*, 329 U.S. 249 (1947).

MICHIGAN-WISCONSIN P. L. CO. v. CALVERT

347 U.S. 157 (1954)

MR. JUSTICE CLARK delivered the opinion of the Court. . . .

The question presented is whether the Commerce Clause is infringed by a Texas tax on the occupation of "gathering gas," measured by the entire volume of gas "taken," as applied to an interstate natural gas pipeline company, where the taxable incidence is the taking of gas from the outlet of an independent gasoline plant within the State for the purpose of immediate interstate transmission. . . . It is now well settled that a tax imposed on a local activity related to interstate commerce is valid if, and only if, the local activity is not such an integral part of the interstate process, the flow of commerce, that it cannot realistically be separated from it. *Memphis Natural Gas Co.* v. *Stone*, 335 U.S. 80, 87 (1948). . . . This economic process is inherently unsusceptible of division into a distinct local activity capable of forming the basis for the tax here imposed, on the one hand, and a

separate movement in commerce, on the other. It is difficult to conceive of a factual situation where the incidence of taking or loading for transmission is more closely related to the transmission itself. This Court has held that much less integrated activity is "so closely related to interstate transportation as to be practically a part of it." We are therefore of the opinion that the taking of the gas here is essentially a part of interstate commerce itself.

Here it is perhaps sufficient that the privilege taxed, namely the taking of the gas, is not so separate and distinct from interstate transportation as to support the tax. But additional objection is present if the tax be upheld. It would "permit a multiple burden upon that commerce," *Joseph* v. *Carter & Weekes Stevedoring Co.* (330 U.S. at 429), for if Texas may impose this "first taking" tax measured by the total volume of gas so taken, then Michigan and the other recipient states have at least equal right to tax the first taking or "unloading" from the pipeline of the same gas when it arrives for distribution. Oklahoma might then seek to tax the first taking of the gas as it crossed into that State. The net effect would be substantially to resurrect the customs barriers which the Commerce Clause was designed to eliminate. "The very purpose of the Commerce Clause was to create an area of free trade among the several States. That clause vested the power of taxing a transaction forming an unbroken process of interstate commerce in the Congress, not in the States." *McLeod* v. *J. E. Dilworth Co.,* 322 U.S. 327, 330, 331.

NOTE: As to congressional power to control state taxation of interstate commerce, see the note following the *Prudential Insurance* case, below.

3. STATE INTERFERENCE WITH FEDERAL FUNCTIONS

McCULLOCH v. *MARYLAND*

4 Wheaton 316 (1819)

> After the Court found that Congress had implied power to charter a bank (see above), it considered whether a state could tax the bank so created.

MR. CHIEF JUSTICE MARSHALL delivered the opinion of the Court. . . .

That the power of taxation is one of vital importance; that it is retained by the states; that it is not abridged by the grant of a similar power to the government of the Union; that it is to be concurrently exercised by the two governments are truths which have never been denied. But such is the paramount character of the constitution, that its capacity to withdraw any subject from the action of even this power, is admitted. The states are expressly forbidden to lay any duties on imports or exports, except what may be absolutely necessary for executing their inspection laws. If the obligation of this prohibition must be conceded —if it may restrain a state from the exercising of its taxing power on imports and exports the same paramount character would seem to restrain, as it certainly may restrain, a state from such other exercise of this power, as is in its nature incompatible with, and repugnant to, the constitutional laws of the Union. A law, absolutely repugnant to another, as entirely repeals that other as if express terms of repeal were used.

On this ground, the counsel for the bank place its claim to be exempted from the power of a state to tax its operations. There is no express provision for the case, but the claim has been sustained on a principle which so entirely pervades the Constitution, is so intermixed with the materials which compose it, so interwoven with its web, so blended with its texture, as to be incapable of being separated from it, without rending it into shreds. This great principle is, that the Constitution and the laws made in pursuance thereof are supreme; that they control the constitution and laws of the respective states, and cannot be controlled by them. From this, which may be almost termed an axiom, other propositions are deduced as corollaries, on the truth or error of which, and on their application to this case, the case has been supposed to depend. These are, 1st. That a power to create implies a power to preserve: 2d. That a power to destroy, if wielded by a different hand, is hostile to, and incompatible with, these powers to create and preserve: 3d. That where this repugnancy exists, that authority which is supreme must control, not yield to that over which it is supreme. . . .

The power of Congress to create, and of course, to continue, the bank, was the subject of the preceding part of this opinion;

and is no longer to be considered as questionable. That the power of taxing it by the states may be exercised so as to destroy it, is too obvious to be denied. But taxation is said to be an absolute power, which acknowledges no other limits than those expressly prescribed in the Constitution, and like sovereign power of every other description, is trusted to the discretion of those who use it. But the very terms of this argument admit, that the sovereignty of the state, in the article of taxation itself, is subordinate to, and may be controlled by, the Constitution of the United States. How far it has been controlled by that instrument must be a question of construction. In making this construction, no principle not declared, can be admissible, which would defeat the legitimate operations of a supreme government. It is of the very essence of supremacy, to remove all obstacles to its action within its own sphere, and so to modify every power vested in subordinate governments, as to exempt its own operations from their own influence. This effect need not be stated in terms. It is so involved in the declaration of supremacy, so necessarily implied in it, that the expression of it could not make it more certain. We must, therefore, keep it in view, while construing the Constitution. . . .

The sovereignty of a state extends to everything which exists by its own authority, or is introduced by its permission; but does it extend to those means which are employed by Congress to carry into execution powers conferred on that body by the people of the United States? We think it demonstrable that it does not. Those powers are not given by the people of a single state. They are given by the people of the United States, to a government whose laws, made in pursuance of the Constitution, are declared to be supreme. Consequently, the people of a single state cannot confer a sovereignty which will extend over them.

If we measure the power of taxation residing in a state, by the extent of sovereignty which the people of a single state possess, and can confer on its government, we have an intelligible standard, applicable to every case to which the power may be applied. We have a principle which leaves the power of taxing the people and property of a state unimpaired; which leaves to a state the command of all its resources, and which places beyond its reach, all those powers which are conferred by the people of the United States on the government of the Union, and all those means which are given for the purpose of carrying those powers into execution. We have a principle which is safe for the states, and safe for the Union. We are relieved, as we ought to be, from clashing sovereignty; from interfering powers; from a repugnancy between a right in one government to pull down, what there is an acknowledged right in another to build up; from the incompatibility of a right in one government to destroy, what there is a right in another to preserve. We are not driven to the perplexing inquiry, so unfit for the judicial department, what degree of taxation is the legitimate use, and what degree may amount to the abuse of the power. The attempt to use it on the means employed by the government of the Union, in pursuance of the Constitution, is itself an abuse, because it is the usurpation of a power, which the people of a single state cannot give. We find, then, on just theory, a total failure of this original right to tax the means employed by the government of the Union, for the execution of its powers. The right never existed, and the question whether it has been surrendered, cannot arise.

But, waiving this theory for the present, let us resume the inquiry, whether this power can be exercised by the respective states, consistently with a fair construction of the Constitution? That the power to tax involves the power to destroy; that the power to destroy may defeat and render useless the power to create; that there is a plain repugnance in conferring on one government a power to control the constitutional measures of another, which other, with respect to those very measures, is declared to be supreme over that which exerts the control, are propositions not to be denied. But all inconsistencies are to be reconciled by the magic of the word *confidence*. Taxation, it is said, does not necessarily and unavoidably destroy. To carry it to the excess of destruction, would be an abuse, to presume which, would banish that confidence which is essential to all government. But is this a case of confidence? Would the people of any one state trust those of another with a power to control the most significant operations of their state government? We know they would not. Why, then, should we suppose, that the people of any one state should be willing to trust those of another with a power to control the operations of a government to which they have confided their most important and most valuable interests? In the legislature of the Union alone, are all represented. The legislature of the Union alone, therefore, can be trusted by the people with the power of controlling measures which concern all, in the confidence that it will not be abused. This, then, is not a case of confidence, and we must consider it as it really is.

If we apply the principle for which the state of Maryland contends, to the Constitution generally, we shall find it capable of changing totally the character of that instrument. We shall find it capable of arresting all the measures of the government, and of prostrating it at the foot of the states. The American people have declared their Constitution and the laws made in pursuance thereof, to be supreme; but this principle would transfer the supremacy, in fact, to the states. If the states may tax one instrument, employed by the government in the execution of its powers, they may tax any and every other instrument. They may tax the mail; they may tax the mint; they may tax patent rights; they may tax the papers of the customhouse; they may tax judicial process; they may tax all the means employed by the government, to an excess which would defeat all the ends of government. This was not intended by the American people. They did not design to make their government dependent on the states. . . .

. . . If the controlling power of the states be established; if their supremacy as to taxation be acknowledged; what is to restrain their exercising this control in any shape they may please to give it? Their sovereignty is not confined to taxation; that is not the only mode in which it might be displayed. The question is, in truth, a question of supremacy; and if the right of the states to tax the means employed by the general government be conceded, the declaration that the Constitution, and the laws made in pursuance thereof, shall be the supreme law of the land, is empty and unmeaning declamation. . . .

It has also been insisted, that, as the power of taxation in the general and state governments is acknowledged to be concurrent, every argument which would sustain the right of the general government to tax banks chartered by the states, will equally sustain the right of the states to tax banks chartered by the general government. But the two cases are not on the same reason. The people of all the states have created the general government, and have conferred upon it the general power of taxation. The people of all the states, and the states themselves, are represented in congress, and, by their representatives, exercise this power. When they tax the chartered institutions of the states, they tax their constituents; and these taxes must be uniform. But when a state taxes the operations of the government of the United States, it acts upon institutions created, not by their own constituents, but by people over whom they claim no control. It acts upon the measures of a government created by others as well as themselves, for the benefit of others in common with themselves. The difference is that which always exists, and always must exist, between the action of the whole on a part, and the action of a part on the whole—between the laws of a government declared to be supreme, and those of a government which, when in opposition to those laws, is not supreme.

But if the full application of this argument could be admitted, it might bring into question the right of congress to tax the state banks, and could not prove the right of the states to tax the Bank of the United States.

The court has bestowed on this subject its most deliberate consideration. The result is a conviction that the states have no power, by taxation or otherwise, to retard, impede, burden, or in any manner control, the operations of the constitutional laws enacted by congress to carry into execution the powers vested in the general government. This is, we think, the unavoidable consequence of that supremacy which the Constitution has declared. We are unanimously of opinion, that the law passed by the legislature of Maryland, imposing a tax on the Bank of the United States, is unconstitutional and void.

This opinion does not deprive the states of any resources which they originally possessed. It does not extend to a tax paid by the real property of the bank, in common with the other real property within the state, nor to a tax imposed on the interest which the citizens of Maryland may hold in this institution, in common with other property of the same description throughout the state. But this is a tax on the operations of the bank, and is, consequently, a tax on the operation of an instrument employed by the government of the Union to carry its powers into execution. Such a tax must be unconstitutional.

JAMES MADISON, *The Federalist*, NO. 44

[Speaking of the supremacy clause in Article VI, Madison observed] as the constitutions [and laws] of the States differ much from each other, it might happen that a treaty or national law, of great and equal importance to the States, would interfere with some and not with other constitutions [or laws], and would consequently be valid in some States, at the same time that it would have no effect in others.

In fine, the world would have seen, for the first time, a system of government founded on an inversion of the fundamental principles of all government; it would have seen the authority of the whole society everywhere subordinate to the authority of the parts; it would have seen a monster, in which the head was under the direction of the members.

GRAVES v. *NEW YORK EX REL. O'KEEFE*
306 U.S. 466 (1939)

O'Keefe, an employee of the Home Owners' Loan Corporation (a federal agency), did not report his salary for New York State income tax purposes. He thought himself immune on the basis of *McCulloch* as extended in *Collector* v. *Day* (see above). A New York court upheld this view. The Supreme Court granted certiorari.

MR. JUSTICE STONE delivered the opinion of the Court. . . .

For the purposes of this case we may assume that the creation of the Home Owners' Loan Corporation was a constitutional exercise of the powers of the federal government. Cf. *Kay* v. *United States*, 303 U.S. 1. As that government derives its authority wholly from powers delegated to it by the Constitution, its every action within its constitutional power is governmental action, and since Congress is made the sole judge of what powers within the constitutional grant are to be exercised, all activities of government constitutionally authorized by Congress must stand on a parity with respect to their constitutional immunity from taxation. *McCulloch* v. *Maryland*, 4 Wheat. 316, 432; *Van Brocklin* v. *Tennessee*, 117 U.S. 151, 158–159; *South Carolina* v. *United States*, 199 U.S. 437, 451, 452; *Helvering* v. *Gerhardt*, 304 U.S. 405, 412–415. And when the national government lawfully acts through a corporation which it owns and controls, those activities are governmental functions entitled to whatever tax immunity attaches to those functions when carried on by the government itself through its departments. . . .

. . . The constitutional immunity of either government from taxation by the other, where Congress is silent, has its source in an implied restriction upon the powers of the taxing government. So far as the implication rests upon the purpose to avoid interference with the functions of the taxed government or the imposition upon it of the economic burden of the tax, it is plain that there is no basis for implying a purpose of Congress to exempt the federal government or its agencies from tax burdens which are unsubstantial or which courts are unable to discern. Silence of Congress implies immunity no more than does the silence of the Constitution. It follows that when exemption from state taxation is claimed on the ground that the federal government is burdened by the tax, and Congress has disclosed no intention with respect to the claimed immunity, it is in order to consider the nature and effect of the alleged burden, and if it appears that there is no ground for implying a constitutional immunity, there is equally a want of any ground for assuming any purpose on the part of Congress to create an immunity. . . .

Assuming, as we do, that the Home Owners' Loan Corporation is clothed with the same immunity from state taxation as the government itself, we cannot say that the present tax on the income of its employees lays any unconstitutional burden upon it. All the reasons for refusing to imply a constitutional prohibition of federal income taxation of salaries of state employees, stated at length in the *Gerhardt* case, are of equal force when immunity is claimed from state income tax on salaries paid by the national government or its agencies. In this respect we perceive no basis for a difference in result whether the taxed income be salary or some other form of compensation, or whether the taxpayer be an employee or an officer of either a state or the national government, or of its instrumentalities. In no case is there basis for the assumption that any such tangible or certain economic burden is imposed on the government concerned as would justify a court's declaring that the taxpayer is clothed with the implied constitutional tax immunity of the government by which he is employed. That assumption, made in *Collector* v. *Day, supra,* and in *New York ex rel. Rogers* v. *Graves, supra,* is contrary to the reasoning and to the conclusions reached in the *Gerhardt* case and in *Metcalf & Eddy* v. *Mitchell, supra; Group No. 1 Oil Corporation* v. *Bass,* 283 U.S. 279; *James* v. *Dravo Contracting Co., supra; Helvering* v. *Mountain Producers Corp., supra; McLoughlin* v. *Commissioner,* 303 U.S. 218. In their light the assumption can no longer be made. *Collector* v. *Day, supra,* and *New York ex rel. Rogers* v. *Graves, supra,* are overruled so far as they recognize an implied constitutional immunity from income taxation of the salaries of officers or employees of the national or a state government or their instrumentalities.

So much of the burden of a nondiscriminatory general tax upon the incomes of employees of a government, state or national, as may be passed on economically to that government, through the effect of the tax on the price level of labor or materials, is but the normal incident of the organization within the same territory of two governments, each possessing the taxing power. The burden, so far as it can be said to exist or to affect the government in any indirect or incidental way, is one which the Constitution presupposes, and hence it cannot rightly be deemed to be within an implied restriction upon the taxing power of the national and state governments which the Constitution has expressly granted to one and has confirmed to the other. The immunity is not one to be implied from the Constitution, because if allowed it would impose to an inadmissible extent a restriction on the taxing power which the Constitution has reserved to the state governments.

Reversed.

MR. CHIEF JUSTICE HUGHES concurs in the result.

[A concurring opinion by MR. JUSTICE FRANKFURTER is here omitted.]

MR. JUSTICE BUTLER, dissenting.

MR. JUSTICE MCREYNOLDS and I are of opinion that the Home Owners' Loan Corporation, being an instrumentality of the United States heretofore deemed immune from state taxation, "it necessarily results,"

as held in *New York ex rel. Rogers* v. *Graves*, 299 U.S. 401, "that fixed salaries and compensation paid to its officers and employees in their capacity as such are likewise immune"; and that the judgment of the state court, unquestionably required by that decision, should be affirmed.

From the decision just announced, it is clear that the Court has overruled *Dobbins* v. *Commissioners of Erie County*, 16 Pet. 435, *Collector* v. *Day*, 11 Wall. 113, *New York ex rel. Rogers* v. *Graves*, *supra*, and *Brush* v. *Commissioner*, 300 U.S. 352. Thus now it appears that the United States has always had power to tax salaries of state officers and employees and that similarly free have been the States to tax salaries of officers and employees of the United States. The compensation for past as well as for future service to be taxed and the rates prescribed in the exertion of the newly disclosed power depend on legislative discretion not subject to judicial revision. . . .

NOTE AND QUAERE: The Court overruled *Collector* v. *Day* which was based on *McCulloch*, but it did not overrule *McCulloch*. How do you explain this?

In a modern case involving state taxation of federal banks, the Court observed that such state authority does "not stem from the powers 'reserved to the States' under the Tenth Amendment," but is "conferred by Congress which has under the Constitution exclusive authority to determine whether and to what extent its instrumentalities . . . should be immune from state taxation." *Maricopa County* v. *Valley Bank*, 318 U.S. 357, 361 (1943).

For converse cases (federal taxes on state operations) see *Helvering* v. *Gerhardt*, and *New York* v. *United States*, above.

JOHNSON v. *MARYLAND*

254 U.S. 51 (1920)

MR. JUSTICE HOLMES delivered the opinion of the court: . . .

The plaintiff in error was an employee of the Post Office Department of the United States, and while driving a government motor truck in the transportation of mail over a post road from Mt. Airy, Maryland, to Washington, was arrested in Maryland,

and was tried, convicted and fined for so driving without having obtained a license from the state. He saved his constitutional rights by motion to quash, by special pleas which were overruled upon demurrer and by motion in arrest of judgment. The facts were admitted and the naked question is whether the state has power to require such an employee to obtain a license by submitting to an examination concerning his competence and paying three dollars, before performing his official duty in obedience to superior command. . . .

Of course an employee of the United States does not secure a general immunity from state law while acting in the course of his employment. That was decided long ago by Mr. Justice Washington in *United States* v. *Hart*, Pet.C.C. 390, Fed.Cas.No.15, 316; 5 Op.Attys.Gen. 554. It very well may be that, when the United States has not spoken, the subjection to local law would extend to general rules that might affect incidentally the mode of carrying out the employment—as, for instance, a statute or ordinance regulating the mode of turning at the corners of streets. *Commonwealth* v. *Closson*, 229 Mass. 329, 118 N.E. 653, L.R.A. 1918c, 939. This might stand on much the same footing as liability under the common law of a state to a person injured by the driver's negligence. But even the most unquestionable and most universally applicable of state laws, such as those concerning murder, will not be allowed to control the

conduct of a marshal of the United States acting under and in pursuance of the laws of the United States. *Ex parte Neagle*, 135 U.S. 1.

It seems to us that the immunity of the instruments of the United States from state control in the performance of their duties extends to [and exempts them from] a requirement that they desist from performance until they satisfy a state officer upon examination that they are competent for a necessary part of them and pay a fee for permission to go on. Such a requirement does not merely touch the government servants remotely by a general rule of conduct; it lays hold of them in their specific attempt to obey orders and requires qualifications in addition to those that the government has pronounced sufficient. It is the duty of the department to employ persons competent for their work and that duty it must be presumed has been performed. *Keim* v. *United States*, 177 U.S. 290, 293.

Judgment reversed.

Mr. Justice Pitney and Mr. Justice McReynolds dissent.

NOTE: For a converse case of federal regulation of a state activity see *United States* v. *California*, above.

4. THE EFFECT OF FEDERAL LEGISLATION ON STATE AUTHORITY

McCulloch v. *Maryland* and *Gibbons* v. *Ogden* both demonstrate that when a valid federal and a valid state measure are in direct conflict, the former prevails by virtue of the supremacy clause (Art. VI). In some cases, however, the clash is not quite so clear and direct as it was for example in *McCulloch*. The problem then may have to be resolved in terms of whether Congress intended to "occupy the field" (and thus exclude state legislation), or to let state and federal law coexist. This is illustrated in *Pennsylvania* v. *Nelson*. There a state court, applying a state law, had found the defendant guilty of sedition against the United States. The Supreme Court on review found that by several security acts Congress had occupied the field—which is to say it had superseded state power to punish subversion *against the United States*. Later in *Uphaus* v. *Wyman*, 360 U.S. 72 (1959), the Court held that the federal security program does not preclude state investigation of subversive activity *against the state*.

Southern Pacific v. *Arizona*, above, illustrates the *Nelson* problem in a different context. The Interstate Commerce Act authorizes the Interstate Commerce Commission to regulate train lengths in emergencies. This administrative authority had not been exercised at the time the case arose. Does the Arizona act conflict with the congressional act; that is, did Congress preempt the whole matter of interstate train lengths when it authorized the Interstate Commerce Commission to regulate train lengths in certain circumstances? Or to put it differently, did Congress mean that there was to be no such regulation except by the Interstate Commerce Commission in emergencies? The Court answered these questions in the following language:

> We do not gain either from their words or from the legislative history any hint that Congress . . . intended, apart from Commission action, to supersede state laws, regulating train lengths. We can hardly suppose that Congress, merely by conferring authority on the Commission to regulate car service in an "emergency," intended to restrict the exercise, otherwise lawful, of state power to regulate train lengths before the Commission finds an "emergency" to exist.
> Congress, in enacting legislation within its constitutional authority over interstate commerce, will not be deemed to have intended to strike down a state statute designed to protect the health and safety of the public unless its purpose to do so is clearly manifested, . . . or unless the state law, in terms or in its practical administration, conflicts with the Act of Congress, or plainly and palpably infringes its policy. . . . Congress, although asked to do so, has declined to pass legislation specifically limiting trains to seventy cars. We are therefore brought to appellant's principal contention, that the state statute contravenes the commerce clause of the Federal Constitution.

In all cases of this type, of course, the Court's job is to determine how much of the problem-area Congress intended to preempt. If the Court "guesses" wrong, or if Congress changes its mind, new legislation can "reverse" the Court. Thus, for example, if Congress wants to permit the states to deal with subversion against the United States, it need only make that intention clear. Thereafter, the states would be free to act. Though invited to do so several times, Congress has not seen fit to "override" *Pennsylvania* v. *Nelson* in this manner.

If the Court had held in *Nelson* that Congress had not intended to preempt the whole area of subversion against the United States, the states could have operated in the unoccupied zone—until such time as Congress saw fit to take over.

The *Prudential* case deals with a more difficult problem: Can Congress "vacate" a field and permit states to occupy it—though the field in question is one from which the states would seem to be barred by the *Cooley*, and related, rules?

PENNSYLVANIA v. NELSON

350 U.S. 497 (1956)

A Pennsylvania court found Nelson guilty of advocating overthrow of the Government of the United States. The state Supreme Court overruled the conviction.

CHIEF JUSTICE WARREN delivered the opinion of the court. . . .

The precise holding of the [state Supreme Court], and all that is before us for review, is that the Smith Act of 1940, as amended in 1948, which prohibits the knowing advocacy of the overthrow of the Government of the United States by force and violence, supersedes the enforceability of the Pennsylvania Sedition Act which proscribes the same conduct. . . .

It should be said at the outset that the decision in this case does not affect the right of states to enforce their sedition laws at times when the Federal Government has not occupied the field and is not protecting the entire country from seditious conduct. The distinction between the two situations was clearly recognized by the court below. Nor does it limit the jurisdiction of the states where the Constitution and Congress have specifically given them concurrent jurisdiction. . . . Neither does it limit the right of the state to protect itself at any time against sabotage or attempted violence of all kinds. Nor does it prevent the state from prosecuting where the same act constitutes both a Federal offense and a state offense under the police power. . . .

Where, as in the instant case, Congress has not stated specifically whether a Federal statute has occupied a field in which the states are otherwise free to legislate, different criteria have furnished touchstones for decision. . . . In this case, we think that each of several tests of supersession is met.

First, "The scheme of Federal regulation [is] so pervasive as to make reasonable the inference that Congress left no room for the states to supplement it." . . . The Congress determined in 1940 that it was necessary for it to re-enter the field of anti-subversive legislation, which had been abandoned by it in 1921. In that year it enacted the Smith Act which proscribes advocacy of the overthrow of any government—federal, state or local—by force and violence and organization of and knowing membership in a group which so advocates. Conspiracy to commit any of these acts is punishable under the general criminal conspiracy provisions in 18 U.S.C. § 371. The Internal Security Act of 1950 is aimed more directly at Communist organizations. It distinguishes between "Communist-action organizations" and "Communist-front organizations," requiring such organizations to register and file annual reports with the Attorney General, giving complete details as to their officers and funds. Members of Communist-action organizations who have not been registered by their organization must register as individuals. . . . The Communist Control Act of 1954 declares "that the Communist party of the United States, although purportedly a political party is in fact an instrumentality of a conspiracy to overthrow the Government of the United States" and that "its role as the agency of a hostile foreign power renders its existence a clear, present and continuing danger to the security of the United States." . . .

We examine these Acts only to determine the Congressional plan. . . . Taken as a whole they evince a Congressional plan which makes it reasonable to determine that no room has been left for the states to supplement it. Therefore a state sedition statute is superseded regardless of whether it purports to supplement the federal law. . . .

Second, the federal statutes "touch a field in which the Federal interest is so dominant that the Federal system [must] be assumed to preclude enforcement of state laws on the same subject." . . . Congress has devised an all-embracing program for resistance to the various forms of totalitarian aggression. . . . It accordingly proscribed sedition against all government in the nation—national, state and local. . . . Congress having thus treated seditious conduct as a matter of vital national concern, it is in no sense a local enforcement problem. . . .

Third, enforcement of state sedition acts presents a serious danger of conflict with the administration of the federal program. Since 1939, in order to avoid a hampering of uniform enforcement of its program by sporadic local prosecutions, the Federal

Government has urged local authorities not to intervene in such matters, but to turn over to the federal authorities immediately and unevaluated all information concerning subversive activities. The President made such a request on Sept. 6, 1939, when he placed the Federal Bureau of Investigation in charge of investigation in this field. . . .

Since we find that Congress has occupied the field to the exclusion of parallel state legislation, that the dominant interest of the Federal Government precludes state intervention and that administration of state Acts would conflict with the operation of the Federal plan, we are convinced that the decision of the Supreme Court of Pennsylvania is unassailable.

MR. JUSTICE REED, with whom MR. JUSTICE BURTON and MR. JUSTICE MINTON join, dissenting. . . .

The "occupation of the field" argument has been developed by this Court for the Commerce Clause and legislation thereunder to prevent partitioning of this country by locally erected trade barriers. In those cases this Court has ruled that state legislation is superseded when it conflicts with the comprehensive regulatory scheme and purpose of a federal plan. . . . But the federal sedition laws are distinct criminal statutes that punish willful advocacy of the use of force against "the government of the United States or the government of any State." These criminal laws proscribe certain local activity without creating any statutory or administrative regulation. There is, consequently, no question as to whether some general congressional regulatory scheme might be upset by a coinciding state plan. In these circumstances the conflict should be clear and direct before this Court reads a congressional intent to void state legislation into the federal sedition acts.

We look upon the Smith Act as a provision for controlling incitements to overthrow by force and violence the Nation, or any State, or any political subdivision of either. Such an exercise of federal police power carries, we think, no such dominancy over similar state powers as might be attributed to continuing federal regulations concerning foreign affairs or coinage, for example. In the responsibility of national and local governments to protect themselves against sedition, there is no "dominant interest."

[The dissenters found no evidence that the state law was administered in such a way as to hamper enforcement of the Smith Act and stated that] mere fear by courts of possible difficulties does not seem to us in these circumstances a valid reason for ousting a State from exercise of its police power.

PRUDENTIAL INSURANCE CO. v. BENJAMIN
328 U.S. 408 (1946)

In *Paul* v. *Virginia*, 8 Wallace 168 (1869), it had been held that "insurance is not commerce." On this foundation the insurance industry has long been regulated and taxed by the states. In *United States* v. *South-Eastern Underwriters Association*, 322 U.S. 533 (1944), the *Paul* case was "abandoned," that is, it was held that insurance is commerce and thus, if it is interstate in character, comes within congressional power. Fearing that this might result in invalidation of many state laws with respect to insurance, Congress in the McCarran Act declared that the business of insurance shall be subject to regulation and taxation by the states. Congress obviously was not prepared to undertake the arduous task of replacing the states in the insurance regulatory field. This case arose in view of the *South-Eastern* case, as a challenge to the validity of a South Carolina tax on the premiums received by outside companies from business done in that state. No similar tax was imposed on local companies. Prudential argued that the tax was unconstitutional as a discriminatory burden on interstate commerce.

MR. JUSTICE RUTLEDGE delivered the opinion of the Court:

[The cases on which Prudential relies] from *Welton* v. *Missouri*, 91 U.S. 275, until now have outlawed state taxes found to discriminate against interstate commerce. No one of them involved a situation like that now here. In each the question of validity of the state taxing statute arose when Congress' power lay dormant. In none had Congress acted or purported to act, either by way of consenting to the state's tax or otherwise. Those cases therefore presented no question of the validity of such a tax where Congress had taken affirmative action consenting to it or purporting to give it validity. Nor, consequently, could they stand as controlling precedents for such a case.

This would seem so obvious as hardly to require further comment, except for the fact that Prudential has argued so earnestly to the contrary. Its position puts the McCarran Act to one side, either as not intended to have effect toward validating this sort of tax or, if construed otherwise, as constitutionally ineffective to do so. Those questions present the controlling issues in this case. But before we turn to them it will be helpful to note the exact effects of Prudential's argument.

Fundamentally it maintains that the commerce clause "of its own force" and without reference to any action by Congress, whether through its silence or otherwise, forbids discriminatory state taxation of interstate commerce. This is to say, in effect, that neither Congress acting affirmatively nor Congress and the states thus acting coordinately can validly impose any regulation which the Court has found or would find to be forbidden by the commerce clause, if laid only by state action taken while Congress' power lies dormant. In this view the limits of state power to regulate commerce in the absence of affirmative action by Congress are also the limits of Congress' permissible action in this respect, whether taken alone or in coordination with state legislation.

Merely to state the position in this way

compels its rejection. So conceived, Congress' power over commerce would be nullified to a very large extent. For in all the variations of commerce clause theory it has never been the law that what the states may do in the regulation of commerce, Congress being silent, is the full measure of its power. Much less has this boundary been thought to confine what Congress and the states acting together may accomplish. . . .

[The cases most important for the decision now] are the ones involving situations where the silence of Congress or the dormancy of its power has been taken judicially, on one view or another of its constitutional effects, as forbidding state action, only to have Congress later disclaim the prohibition or undertake to nullify it. Not yet has this Court held such a disclaimer invalid or that state action supported by it could not stand. On the contrary, in each instance it has given effect to the congressional judgment contradicting its own previous one. [See especially *Pennsylvania* v. *Wheeling Bridge Co.*, 18 Howard 421 (1855) and *Clark Distilling Co.* v. *Western Maryland Ry.*, 242 U.S. 311 (1917).]

It is true that rationalizations have differed concerning those decisions, indeed also that the judges participating in them differed in this respect. But the results have been lasting and are at least as important, for the direction given to the process of accommodating federal and state authority, as the reasons stated for reaching them. None of the decisions conceded, because none involved any question of, the power of Congress to make conclusive its own mandate concerning what is commerce. But apart from that function of defining the outer boundary of its power, whenever Congress' judgment has been uttered affirmatively to contradict the Court's previously expressed view that specific action taken by the states in Congress' silence was forbidden by the commerce clause, this body has accommodated its previous judgment to Congress' expressed approval.

Some part of this readjustment may be explained in ways acceptable on any theory of the commerce clause and the relations of Congress and the courts toward its functioning. Such explanations however, hardly go to the root of the matter. For the fact remains that, in these instances, the sustaining of Congress' overriding action has involved something beyond correction of erroneous factual judgment in deference to Congress' presumably better-informed view of the facts, and also beyond giving due deference to its conception of the scope of its powers, when it repudiates, just as when its silence is thought to support, the inference that it has forbidden state action.

Prudential has not squarely met this fact. Fixed with the sense of applicability of the *Welton* or *Shelby County* [145 U.S. 1 (1892)] line of cases, it rather has posed an enigma for the bearing of the bridge and liquor cases upon the decision to be made. It is, if the commerce clause "by its own force" forbids discriminatory state taxation, or other measures, how is it that Congress by expressly consenting can give that action validity?

The answer need not be labored. Prudential in this case makes no contention that commerce is not involved. Its argument is exactly the opposite. Its contention founded on the commerce clause is one wholly of implied prohibition within the field of commerce.

This it regards as operative not only in Congress' silence, but in the face of its positive expression by the McCarran Act that the continued regulation and taxation by the states of the business of insurance is in accord with Congress' policy. That expression raises questions concerning its own validity and also concerning whether the policy stated extends to the kind of state legislation which is immediately in issue. But those questions are not answered, as Prudential seeks to have them answered, by any conception that Congress' declaration of policy adds nothing to the validity of what the states have done within the area covered by the declaration or, in other words, that it is mere brutum fulmen. For to do this not only would produce intolerable consequences for restricting Congress' power. It would ignore the very basis on

which the second *Wheeling Bridge* case and indeed the *Clark Distilling* case have set the pattern of the law for governing situations like that now presented. Accordingly we turn to the issues which are more alive and significant for the future.

In considering the issues raised by the McCarran Act and the question of its applicability, ground may be cleared by putting aside some matters strenuously argued in the State Supreme Court and here. . . . And for present purposes we assume that the tax would be discriminatory in the sense of Prudential's contention and that all of its business done in South Carolina and affected by the tax is done "in" or as a part of interstate commerce. . . .

Two conclusions, corollary in character and important for this case, must be drawn from Congress' action and the circumstances in which it was taken. One is that Congress intended to declare, and in effect declared, that uniformity of regulation, and of state taxation, are not required in reference to the business of insurance by the national public interest, except in the specific respects otherwise expressly provided for. This necessarily was a determination by Congress that state taxes, which in its silence might be held invalid as discriminatory, do not place on interstate insurance business a burden which it is unable generally to bear or should not bear in the competition with local business. Such taxes were not uncommon among the states, and the statute clearly included South Carolina's tax now in issue.

That judgment was one of policy and reflected long and clear experience. For, notwithstanding the long incidence of the tax and its payment by Prudential without question prior to the *South-Eastern* decision, the record of Prudential's continuous success in South Carolina over decades refutes any idea that payment of the tax handicapped it in any way tending to exclude it from competition with local business or with domestic insurance companies. Indeed Prudential makes no contrary contention on any factual basis, nor could it well do so. For the *South-Eastern* decision did not, and could not, wipe out all this experience or its weight or bearing, as a matter of the practical consequences resulting from operation of the tax, upon that question. *Robertson* v. *United States, post,* p. 440.

Consequently Prudential's case for discrimination must rest upon the idea either that the commerce clause forbids the state to exact more from it in taxes than from purely local business; or that the tax is somehow technically of an inherently discriminatory character or possibly of a type which would exclude or seriously handicap new entrants seeking to establish themselves in South Carolina. As to each of these grounds, moreover, the argument subsumes that Congress' contrary judgment, as a matter of policy relating to the regulation of interstate commerce, cannot be effective, either "of its own force" alone or as operative in conjunction with and to sustain the state's policy.

In view of all these considerations, we would be going very far to rule that South Carolina no longer may collect her tax. To do so would flout the expressly declared policies of both Congress and the state. Moreover it would establish a ruling never heretofore made and in doing this would depart from the whole trend of decision in a great variety of situations most analogous to the one now presented. For, as we have already emphasized, the authorities most closely in point upon the problem are not, as appellant insists, those relating to discriminatory state taxes laid in the dormancy of Congress' power. They are rather the decisions which, in every instance thus far not later overturned, have sustained coordinated action taken by Congress and the states in the regulation of commerce.

The power of Congress over commerce exercised entirely without reference to coordinated action of the states is not restricted, except as the Constitution expressly provides, by any limitations which forbids it to discriminate against interstate commerce and in favor of local trade. Its plenary scope enables Congress not only to promote but also to prohibit interstate commerce, as it has done frequently and for a great variety of reasons. That power does not run down a one-way street or one of narrowly fixed dimensions. Congress may keep the way open, confine it broadly or closely, or close it entirely, subject only to the restrictions placed upon its authority by other constitutional provisions and the requirement that it shall not invade the domains of action reserved exclusively for the states.

This broad authority Congress may exercise alone, subject to those limitations, or in conjunction with coordinated action by the states, in which case limitations imposed for the preservation of their powers become inoperative and only those designed to forbid action altogether by any power or combination of powers in our governmental system remain effective. Here both Congress and South Carolina have acted, and in complete coordination, to sustain the tax. It is therefore reinforced by the exercise of all the power of government residing in our scheme. Clear and gross must be the evil which would nullify such an exertion, one which could arise only by exceeding beyond cavil some explicit and compelling limitation imposed by a constitutional provision or provisions designed and intended to outlaw the action taken entirely from our constitutional framework. . . . No conceivable violation of the commerce clause, in letter or spirit, is presented. Nor is contravention of any other limitation. . . . There are limitations applicable to each of these separately and some to their coordinated exercise. But neither the former nor the latter is to be found merely in the fact that the authority is thus divided. Such a conception would reduce the joint exercise of power by Congress and the states to achieve common ends in the regulation of our society below the effective range of either power separately exerted, without basis in specific constitutional limitation or otherwise than in the division itself. We know of no grounding, in either constitutional experience or spirit, for such a restriction. For great reasons of policy and history not now necessary to restate, these great powers were separated. They were not forbidden to cooperate or by doing so to achieve legislative consequences, particularly in the great fields of regulating commerce and taxation, which, to some extent at least, neither could accomplish in isolated exertion. . . .

Affirmed.

MR. JUSTICE BLACK concurs in the result.

MR. JUSTICE JACKSON took no part in the consideration or decision of this case.

QUAERE: Does Mr. Justice Rutledge really answer the basic difficulty? How can Congress authorize what the Constitution has been held to forbid? As the Court put it later with reference to the *Prudential* case, "There is no longer any question that Congress can redefine the areas of local and national predominance, . . . despite theoretical inconsistency with the rationale of the commerce clause . . . as a limitation in its own right." *California* v. *Zook,* 336 U.S. 725, 728 (1949). Is *Prudential* based upon the "consent of Congress" principle embedded in Article 1, Section 10 of the Constitution?

May it be said that in striking a balance between the commercial interests of nation and state the Court is not acting in its constitutional capacity, but only as a nonjudicial, mediatory body? The distinction would help to explain why some decisions of the judges may be overruled by Congress and some may not. Notice the language of Chief Justice Stone in the *Southern Pacific* case as to mediatory (nonjudicial?) functions of the Court.

NOTE: *Northwestern States Portland Cement Co.* v. *Minnesota,* 358 U.S. 450 (1959), upheld a state net income tax on a pro-rata share of the income of an out-of-state corporation doing part of its interstate business in the taxing state. Shortly thereafter Congress put severe limitations on state power to impose such taxes (15 U.S. Code, Sec. 381). It also ordered a congressional committee study of the whole problem of state taxation of income derived from interstate commerce (15 U.S. Code, Sec. 201) with a view toward possible future legislation.

IV. STATES' RIGHTS WITH RESPECT TO OTHER STATES

A sovereign state, France, for example, may or may not, at its pleasure: (1) respect (give "full faith and credit") to the public acts of another nation; (2) discriminate against foreigners within its boundaries; (3) extradite a fugitive from justice. Article IV of the Constitution literally denies such freedom to the states that constitute our federal union. Yet by judicial interpretation these provisions have been substantially modified. The constitutional duty to render up a fugitive is simply not enforceable by legal process. *Kentucky* v. *Dennison,* 24 Howard 66 (1861). Thus, despite the plain language of the Constitution, an American state, like a sovereign nation, may or may not, at its pleasure, grant extradition upon the request of a sister state; in other words this is a "political" question. This result, never overruled, apparently reflects the ante-bellum states'-rights attitude of the Court that achieved it.

The full faith and credit clause of Article IV was designed to compel recognition in every state of rights and relationships established by the official acts of a sister state. A valid Illinois marriage, for example, must be treated as valid in all other American states. A sovereign nation, of course, is under no similar obligation, though in practice it will often act as though it were. Within the United States the problem usually arises in respect to state court judgments. The general rule is, they must be honored by sister states. But again perhaps in deference to states' rights, state courts have been permitted to question outside judgments by questioning the jurisdiction of the tribunals which rendered them. The classic difficulty is the Nevada divorce decree. The problem arises in this manner. North Carolina law, for example, shuns the easy dissolution of marriages. A North Carolinian wife goes to Nevada for the sole purpose of getting a divorce, gets one, returns home, and then acquires another husband. North Carolina prosecutes for bigamy. Whether or not the "new marriage" is bigamous depends upon the validity of the Nevada divorce. *Williams* v. *North Carolina,* 325 U.S. 226 (1945), held in such a case that a court in the "home" state may disregard the out-of-state "divorce," if it reasonably finds that the person who obtained the decree had not established domicile in the divorcing state—the latter being an indispensable prerequisite to jurisdiction for divorce purposes. The point is, North Carolina did not have to give full faith and credit to the Nevada court's implicit finding as to domicile.

The privileges and immunities clause of Article IV, whatever the original purpose, has been interpreted to forbid any state to discriminate unduly against the citizens of sister states in favor of its own citizens. The qualifying term "unduly" is necessary because some forms of "discrimination" against outsiders have been upheld. For example, "A State may . . . require residence within its limits for a given time before a citizen of another state who becomes a resident thereof shall exercise the right of suffrage or become eligible to office." *Blake* v. *McClung,* 172 U.S. 239, 256 (1898). Moreover, it has been traditional that a state may give preference to its own citizens with respect to certain natural resources. Thus a state may prevent outsiders from exploiting its oyster beds on the theory that such resources are common property held in trust for state citizens. *McCready* v. *Virginia,* 94 U.S. 391 (1877). As the Court said in *Toomer* v. *Witsell,* 334 U.S. 385 (1948):

Like many other constitutional provisions, the privileges and immunities clause is not an absolute. It does bar discrimination against citizens of other states where there is no substantial reason for the discrimination beyond the mere fact that they are citizens of other states. But it does not preclude disparity of treatment in the many situations where there are perfectly valid independent reasons for it. Thus the inquiry in each case must be concerned with whether such reasons do exist and whether the degree of discrimination bears a close relation to them. The inquiry must also, of course, be conducted with due regard for the principle that the states should have considerable leeway in analyzing local evils and in prescribing appropriate cures.

It followed that, unlike the stationary oyster beds in inland water in the *McCready* case, migratory shrimp in coastal waters could not be reserved by a state for its own residents. Nor did it matter that the attempted reservation was effected not directly, but by a grossly disproportionate tax allegedly designed to compensate for the added cost of enforcing a game conservation law against outsiders. Neither may a state give resident, as against nonresident, creditors a priority in the distribution of a bankrupt's local assets. *Blake* v. *McClung,* 172 U.S. 239 (1898). So much for the privileges and immunities of state citizenship; those of United States citizenship are considered in Part Four, I and VII.

Two other constitutional provisions make relations between American states quite different from those between sovereign nations. Article III, Section 2, Paragraph 1, gives the Supreme Court compulsory jurisdiction of controversies between two or more states. This has been used extensively to settle boundary disputes and river pollution and diversion problems. Mr. Justice Holmes disclosed the essence of such jurisdiction when he remarked that usually it involves a case which must "be considered in the untechnical spirit proper for dealing with a quasi-international controversy, remembering that there is no municipal code governing the matter, and that this Court may be called on to adjust differences that cannot be dealt with by Congress or disposed of by the legislature of either state alone." *Virginia* v. *West Virginia,* 220 U.S. 1 (1911). That is, in such controversies the Court sits more as a mediatory, than as a law-enforcing, agency. It may be noted that the Justices will not entertain a suit brought in the name of a state, if the state is not in fact a real party in interest. Thus in *New York* v. *Louisiana* and *New Hampshire* v. *Louisiana,* 108 U.S. 76 (1883), actions on Louisiana's defaulted bonds were dismissed when it became clear that the plaintiff states were suing only in behalf of certain of their citizens. Finally, American states are quite unlike sovereign, national states in that Article I, Section 10, Paragraph 3, of the Constitution forbids agreements or compacts between states, or between a state and a foreign power, without the consent of a third party, namely, Congress.

SELECTED READINGS

William Anderson, *The Nation and the States: Rivals or Partners* (1955)
G. M. Bergman, "Federal Power to Tax and Spend, 31 *Minnesota Law Review* 328 (1947)
J. L. Call, "Limited Government and the Welfare Clause," 60 *Dickinson Law Review* 197 (1956)
E. S. Corwin, *The Commerce Power versus States Rights* (1936)
E. S. Corwin, *Total War and the Constitution* (1947)
N. T. Dowling, "Interstate Commerce and State Power—Revised Version," 27 *Virginia Law Review* 1 (1940)
"Federal Taxation as an Exercise of Federal Police Power," 28 *Notre Dame Lawyer* 127 (1952)
F. Frankfurter, *The Commerce Clause Under Marshall, Taney and Waite* (1937)
P. A. Freund, "Umpiring the Federal System," 54 *Columbia Law Review* 561 (1954)
P. J. Hartman, *State Taxation of Interstate Commerce* (1953)
J. J. Kilpatric, *The Sovereign States* (1957)
A. W. Macmahon, *Federalism, Mature and Emergent* (1955)

R. Pound, C. H. McIlwain, and R. F. Nichols, *Federalism as a Democratic Process* (1942)

T. R. Powell, *Vagaries and Varities in Constitutional Interpretation* (1956)

W. D. Ribble, *State and National Power over Commerce* (1937)

J. R. Schmidhauser, *The Supreme Court as Final Arbiter in Federal-State Relations, 1789–1957* (1958)

B. Schwartz, "War Power in Britain and America," 20 *New York University Law Quarterly Review* 325 (1945)

A. E. Sutherland, "Restricting the Treaty Power," 65 *Harvard Law Review* 1305 (1952)

"The War Power Extended," 17 *George Washington Law Review* 461 (1949)

H. Wechsler, "Political Safeguards of Federalism," 54 *Columbia Law Review* 543 (1954)

L. D. White, *The States and the Nation* (1953)

Part Four | LIBERTY AND AUTHORITY
What Belongs to Government and What to the Individual?

WE TURN now from the problems of federalism (the limitations upon each level of government which spring from the existence of the other level) to restraints upon government in favor of the liberties of the individual. These may be divided into two groups, procedural and substantive. The former limit the procedure or *manner* in which government may operate. The latter distinguish between what government may and may not do (assuming its procedure is impeccable in either case). While the complexities of federalism do not plague those who, like the French and English, have not adopted our dual system of government, the difficulty of reconciling liberty and authority is universal. Nevertheless, the two problems share a common foundation: how to have unity without uniformity, liberty without anarchy, order without stagnation.

I. PROPERTY AND PRIVATE ENTERPRISE

The Federalists were men of substance, or, in Hamilton's words, of "wealth and talents." Their well-known sense of insecurity in the face of state trade barriers, paper money, and stay laws prior to 1787 made them ardent nationalists. Thus just as Federalist fear found expression in Marshall's exclusive view of the national commerce power, it also found temporary expression in promiscuous use of the contract clause (Art. 1, Sec. 10) to insulate selected economic interests from states' rights *in local affairs*. Georgia, for example, could not revoke a grant of land obtained from it by fraud after the property in question had been sold by the defrauders to innocent third parties. *Fletcher* v. *Peck*, 6 Cranch 87 (1810). New Hampshire could not even alter the terms of a royal charter to make it more amenable to new-world needs. *Dartmouth College* v. *Woodward*. Such use of a constitutional provision designed to prevent states from relieving debtors of their obligations (the bankruptcy power having been given to Congress) seems plainly excessive. Apparently even Marshall recognized this. In *Dartmouth* he acknowledges that such cases were "not in the mind of the Convention when the [contract clause] was framed. . . ." His opinion in *Fletcher* v. *Peck* rests weakly on the contract clause and is fortified by an *alternate* proposition: the "general principles, which are common to our free institutions. . . ." In short, when the "great Chief Justice" found the Constitution wanting he was not above resorting to "natural law."

This exaggerated regard for private, at the expense of public, interests soon gave way to Jacksonian respect for democracy and states' rights. In the *Charles River Bridge* case, 11 Peters 420 (1837), Chief Justice Taney for the Court observed that "While the rights of property are sacredly guarded, we must not forget, that the community also have rights and the well-being of every citizen depends on their faithful preservation." Massachusetts had granted the Charles River Bridge Company the right to build a toll bridge between Boston and Charlestown. Some two generations later, in 1828, when one bridge was no longer adequate to serve the two thriving cities, the state authorized a competing bridge. This, it was argued, violated the obligations of the original grant. The Court avoided meeting the issue head-on. Whereas Marshall had resolved ambiguity in the Dartmouth charter against the state and in favor of the grantees, Taney took the opposite position with respect to the Charles River charter. Pointing out how disastrous it would be if, for example, the old turnpike charters by *Dartmouth* inviolability were permitted to strangulate the then infant railroad industry, Chief Justice Taney adopted the principle of the strict construction of state grants. Since the original bridge company's "contract" had not expressly provided for exclusive rights, none were to be implied, i.e., "nothing passes by implication" in a public grant to private persons. It is noteworthy that Marshall's old associate, Mr. Justice Story, dissenting, rejected the doctrine of strict construction—and tells us that Marshall, who had heard the case before his death, concurred in Story's views.

A little later further inroads were made upon the *Fletcher-Dartmouth* doctrine of vested interests when the Court held that a state could not by the grant of a charter, however *explicit,* be deemed to have bargained away its power to govern. Thus in *West River Bridge Co.* v. *Dix,* 6 Howard 507 (1848), the grant of an exclusive privilege to erect a toll bridge was held not to foreclose the state's power later to condemn the bridge in the interest of the public road system. Similarly in *Stone* v. *Mississippi,* 101 U.S. 814 (1880), a grant of lottery privileges was subsumed to the state's power to protect the public health, safety, morals, and welfare. So too, a corporate charter to manufacture intoxicants must give way to a later prohibition act. *Boston Beer Co.* v. *Mass.,* 97 U.S. 25 (1877). Finally it was even recognized that obligations of private contracts cannot stand in the way of the state's power to stay the foreclosure of mortgages for a reasonable period in the face of a serious depression. *Home Building & Loan Association* v. *Blaisdell,* 290 U.S. 398 (1934). Meanwhile the states discovered they need not grant irrevocable and unalterable charters. Thus did we at first follow, and soon abandon, Blackstone's Old-World rule that, "so great . . . is the regard of the law for private property . . . it will not authorize the least violation of it; no, not even for the general good of the whole community."

Not until laissez-faire engulfed the Court in the 1890's did vested interests again seriously impede the power to govern. While dual federalism was an effective brake upon Congress, the contract clause was too narrow (inherently and by then-established limitations) to hamstring state government. Thus he who would stifle the power of the states to manage their own economic affairs must find new constitutional weapons. Could the Civil War amendments be pressed into such service? Ironically, the effort began in that fortress of states' rights, the deep South. The great Alabama lawyer, John A. Campbell, who had resigned from the Supreme Court at the outbreak of the Civil War, first urged the Justices to impose laissez-faire upon the states in a highly imaginative argument based on the Thirteenth and Fourteenth Amendments. His effort was flatly rejected. The new constitutional provisions had not been adopted to make the national Government a supervisor of state economic policy! (*The Slaughter House Cases.*) Accordingly, when farmers first felt the pinch of big business—in unreasonably high and discriminatory freight rates—there was no constitutional impediment to relief by state legislation. Sustaining the famous Granger regulation of grain elevator rates in *Munn* v. *Illinois,* the Court observed that "businesses affected with a public interest" may be regulated for the protection of the public. "We know that this is a power which may be abused; but that is no argument against its existence. For protection against abuses by legislatures the people must resort to the polls, not to the Courts." This echo of Marshall's remark in *Gibbons* v. *Ogden* was doomed. Within a generation laissez-faire had set in. Campbell's argument had found expression in Mr. Justice Field's *Slaughter House* dissent—and Field was persistent. As new judges came to the bench imbued with the gospel of wealth, his dissenting view gradually became the law of the land. After casting about among the several improbable alternatives which Campbell had suggested, the Court finally settled in the 1890's upon the due process clause of the Fourteenth Amendment. No matter that this and the other Civil War amendments had been inspired by the cruel problems of the newly freed Negro, or that for over five hundred years due process had been essentially a procedural limitation! New wine gave the ancient vessel a substantive connotation congenial to laissez-faire doctrine. Thus a particular economic philosophy, entirely unrelated to the due process conception of a fair hearing or to the problems of slavery and its aftermath, became law. *Lochner* v. *New York.* Holmes protested that the Fourteenth Amendment had not enacted Herbert Spencer's *Social Statics,* the then latest literary expression of laissez-faire. Still, if a passing economic fancy was to be read into the Constitution, the due process clauses (the Fifth Amendment was eventually contaminated too) were as good a place as any to put it.

In accordance with the new spirit the *Munn* v. *Illinois* concept of "business affected with a public interest" was narrowed to include only "public utilities." And so, for example, state legislative efforts to prevent the scalping of theater tickets, *Tyson* v. *Banton,* 273 U.S. 418 (1927), and to protect the unemployed from exploitation by private employment agencies, *Ribnik* v. *McBride,* 277

U.S. 350 (1928), were invalidated. Moreover, even in the narrow public utility field where regulation was permitted, the Court undertook to "supervise" the rate-making process. *Smyth* v. *Ames,* 169 U.S. 466 (1898). If only because of the costs and slowness of the judicial process, the Court's intrusion in this area of finance and economics was somewhat less than brilliantly successful. Indeed judicial frustration of these state efforts to protect the consumer (where there is no competition to protect him) accounts in large measure for the advent of public ownership in the electric power industry.

The upshot of the Court's new approach beginning in the 1890's was that between dual federalism and the new version of due process a huge anarchic area was created in which no government had power to govern. The field was surrendered to the captains of industry all in accordance with principles laid down in Andrew Carnegie's gospel. Legislative power to protect *labor* was substantially impaired at the state level (*Lochner* v. *New York; Ribnik* v. *McBride*) and at the national level as well (*Hammer* v. *Dagenhart; Adair* v. *United States,* 208 U.S. 161 [1908]; see also *Schechter* and *Carter,* Part Three, II, above). Similarly the *consumer* forewent protection by the states (*Weaver* v. *Palmer Bros.; Tyson* v. *Branton; Smyth* v. *Ames*) and also by the nation (*United States* v. *E. C. Knight*).

That economic laissez-faire rather than the Constitution was the foundation of these decisions is suggested by the fact that, in contemporaneous cases not involving "reputable" business interests, dual federalism did not impede national legislation (see, for example, the cases referred to in *Hammer* v. *Dagenhart*) and due process did not limit the states. Thus a Virginia law authorizing sterilization of the mentally unfit, *Buck* v. *Bell,* 274 U.S. 200 (1927), and a compulsory vaccination measure, *Jacobson* v. *Massachusetts,* 197 U.S. 11 (1905), were upheld over strenuous objection in the name of personal liberty. Even prohibition of "wickedness" in the form of pool halls and the then radical cigarette was permissible. *Murphy* v. *California,* 225 U.S. 623 (1912); *Austin* v. *Tennessee,* 179 U.S. 343 (1900).

This double standard, too, passed away. In the spring of 1937 the change began when the power of a state to fix minimum wages for women and children was upheld. *West Coast Hotel Co.* v. *Parrish.* Only ten months earlier, in June, 1936, such power had been denied. *Morehead* v. *Tipaldo,* 298 U.S. 587. Similarly *Olson* v. *Nebraska,* 313 U.S. 236 (1941), expressly overruled *Ribnik* and with it the idea that only certain kinds of business—public utilities—are subject to public regulation:

The *Ribnik* case, freed from the ["business affected with a public interest"] test which it employed, can no longer survive. But respondents maintain that the statute here in question is invalid for other reasons. They insist that special circumstances must be shown to support the validity of such drastic legislation as price-fixing, that the executive, technical and professional workers which respondents serve have not been shown to be in need of special protection from exploitation, that legislative limitation of maximum fees for employment agencies is certain to react unfavorably upon those members of the community for whom it is most difficult to obtain jobs, that the increasing competition of public employment agencies and of charitable, labor-union, and employer association employment agencies have curbed excessive fees by private agencies, and that there is nothing in this record to overcome the presumption as to the result of the operation of such competitive, economic forces. And in the latter connection respondents urge that since no circumstances are shown which curb competition between the private agencies and the other types of agencies, there are no conditions which the legislature might reasonably believe would redound to the public injury unless corrected by such legislation.

We are not concerned, however, with the wisdom, need, or appropriateness of the legislation. Differences of opinion on that score suggest a choice which "should be left where . . . it was left by the Constitution—to the States and the Congress." There is no necessity for the state to demonstrate before us that evils persist despite the competition which attends the bargaining in this field. In final analysis, the only constitutional prohibitions or restraints which respondents have suggested for the invalidation of this legislation are those notions of public policy embedded in earlier decisions of this Court but which, as Mr. Justice Holmes long admonished, should not be read into the Constitution. . . . Since they do not find expression in the Constitution, we cannot give them continuing vitality as standards by which the constitutionality of the economic and social programs of the states is to be determined.

Smyth v. *Ames* was abandoned in *Federal Power Commission* v. *Hope Natural Gas Co.,* 320 U.S. 591 (1944). As Mr. Justice Frankfurter had said in *Driscoll* v. *Edison Light & Power Co.,* 307 U.S. 104, 122 (1939):

Experience has made it overwhelmingly clear that *Smyth* v. *Ames* and the uses to which it has been put [have been a failure]. The determination of utility rates—what may fairly be exacted from the public and what is adequate to enlist enterprise—does not present questions of an essentially legal nature in the sense that legal education and lawyer's learning afford peculiar competence for their adjustment. These are matters for the application of whatever knowledge economics and finance may bring to the practicalities of business enterprise. The only relevant function of law in dealing with this intersection of government and enterprise is to secure observance of those procedural safeguards in the exercise of legislative powers which are the historic foundations of due process.

In short the problem of rate regulation was returned insofar as federal courts are concerned to the utility commissions established for that purpose by state and federal legislation. But see Mendelson, "*Smyth* v. *Ames* in State Courts, 1942 to 1952," 37 *Minnesota Law Review* 159 (1953).

Was the Court, as reconstituted in the years after 1937, to be merely "pro-labor" or "pro-consumer," as the old had been "pro-business"? Was it a matter merely of rival economic dogmas or was something deeper involved? A test came when the New Deal Court met face to face an old-dealish "anti-labor" law in *Lincoln Federal Labor Union* v. *Northwestern Iron Company.* The elaborate and somewhat apologetic opinions in this case suggest how much the new Justices were troubled. Yet they held to their basic principle of respect for democratic government. Obviously substantive due process as the embodiment of laissez-faire or any other economic dogma is dead and has been since 1936. The police power of the states to deal with local economic affairs has been restored. Here is a reflection of the same new respect for state competence that found expression in the overruling of *Swift* v. *Tyson* (see Part One, IV) and in the earlier rejection of Marshall's exclusive view of the commerce power (see Part Three, III). Was the "expansion" (restoration) of federal power after 1936 at the expense of state authority? Or is it rather that the "Constitutional Revolution, Limited" of 1937 freed *both state and national power* from laissez-faire restrictions that had developed between the 1880's and 1937? It is deeply significant for those who are interested in the nature of the judicial process that the "revolution" was not grounded on any radically new constitutional principle. Judicial review has not been repudiated! Substantive due process has not been rejected in principle! As the *Lincoln Federal Union* case makes clear, the Court has simply returned to the old "reasonable-man" test when in the context of modern economic life the Constitution speaks with less than crystal clarity. The result is that no regulation by a state of its own economy has run afoul of substantive due process since 1936. Of course state measures which affect other states (Part Three, III)—or which interfere with basic personal liberty such as free speech (Part Four, IV)—raise quite different constitutional problems. That is why quite different tests have been deemed relevant for their solution.

DARTMOUTH COLLEGE v. WOODWARD
4 Wheaton 518 (1819)

A royal charter of 1769 established Dartmouth College and authorized a self-perpetuating board of trustees to manage it. After the American Revolution the State of New Hampshire enacted legislation to convert the college into a state university by placing it under a Board of Overseers appointed by the state governor. The trustees brought suit to test the validity of the new arrangement.

The opinion of the Court was delivered by MR. CHIEF JUSTICE MARSHALL: . . .

It can require no argument to prove, that the circumstances of this case constitute a contract. An application is made to the crown for a charter to incorporate a religious and literary institution. In the application, it is stated that large contributions have been made for the object, which will be conferred on the corporation, as soon as it shall be created. The charter is granted, and on its faith the property is conveyed. Surely in this transaction every ingredient of a complete and legitimate contract is to be found.

The points for consideration are,

1. Is this contract protected by the Constitution of the United States?

2. Is it impaired by the [legislative] acts under which the defendant holds?

1. On the first point it has been argued, that the word "contract," in its broadest sense, would comprehend the political relations between the government and its citizens, would extend to offices held within a State for State purposes, and to many of those laws concerning civil institutions, which must change with circumstances, and be modified by ordinary legislation; which deeply concern the public, and which, to preserve good government, the public judgment must control. That even marriage is a contract, and its obligations are affected by the laws respecting divorces. That the clause in the Constitution, if construed in its greatest latitude, would prohibit these laws. Taken in its broad unlimited sense, the clause would be an unprofitable and vexatious interference with the internal concerns of a State, would unnecessarily and

unwisely embarrass its legislation, and render immutable those civil institutions, which are established for purposes of internal government, and which, to subserve those purposes, ought to vary with varying circumstances. That as the framers of the Constitution could never have intended to insert in that instrument a provision so unnecessary, so mischievous, and so repugnant to its general spirit, the term "contract" must be understood in a more limited sense. That it must be understood as intended to guard against a power of at least doubtful utility, the abuse of which had been extensively felt; and to restrain the legislature in future from violating the right to property. That anterior to the formation of the Constitution, a course of legislation had prevailed in many, if not in all, of the States, which weakened the confidence of man in man, and embarrassed all transactions between individuals, by dispensing with a faithful performance of engagements. To correct this mischief, by restraining the power which produced it, the State legislatures were forbidden "to pass any law impairing the obligation of contracts," that is, of contracts respecting property, under which some individual could claim a right to something beneficial to himself; and that since the clause in the Constitution must in construction receive some limitation, it may be confined, and ought to be confined, to cases of this description; to cases within the mischief it was intended to remedy.

The general correctness of these observations cannot be controverted. That the framers of the Constitution did not intend to restrain the States in the regulation of their civil institutions, adopted for internal government, and that the instrument they have given us, is not to be so construed, may be admitted. The provision of the Constitution never has been understood to embrace other contracts, than those which respect property, or some object of value, and confer rights which may be asserted in a court of justice. It never has been understood to restrict the general right of the legislature to legislate on the subject of divorces. Those acts enable some tribunal,

not to impair a marriage contract, but to liberate one of the parties because it has been broken by the other. When any State legislature shall pass an act annulling all marriage contracts, or allowing either party to annul it without the consent of the other, it will be time enough to inquire, whether such an act be constitutional. . . .

This is plainly a contract to which the donors, the trustees, and the crown (to whose rights and obligations New Hampshire succeeds) were the original parties. It is a contract made on a valuable consideration. It is a contract for the security and disposition of property. It is a contract on the faith of which real and personal estate has been conveyed to the corporation. It is then a contract within the letter of the Constitution, and within its spirit also, unless the fact that the property is invested by the donors in trustees, for the promotion of religion and education, for the benefit of persons who are perpetually changing, though the objects remain the same, shall create a particular exception, taking this case out of the prohibition contained in the Constitution.

It is more than possible that the preservation of rights of this description was not particularly in the view of the framers of the Constitution, when the clause under consideration was introduced into that instrument. It is probable that interferences of more frequent recurrence, to which the temptation was stronger, and of which the mischief was more extensive, constituted the great motive for imposing this restriction on the State legislatures. But although a particular and a rare case may not, in itself, be of sufficient magnitude to induce a rule, yet it must be governed by the rule, when established, unless some plain and strong reason for excluding it can be given. It is not enough to say, that this particular case was not in the mind of the Convention when the article was framed, nor of the American people when it was adopted. It is necessary to go further, and to say that, had this particular case been suggested, the language would have been so varied as to exclude it, or it would have been made a special exception. The case being within the words of the rule, must be within its operation likewise, unless there be something in the literal construction so obviously absurd or mischievous, or repugnant to the general spirit of the instrument, as to justify those who expound the Constitution in making it an exception. . . .

The opinion of the Court, after mature deliberation, is, that this is a contract, the obligation of which cannot be impaired, without violating the Constitution of the United States. This opinion appears to us to be equally supported by reason, and by the former decisions of this Court.

2. We next proceed to the inquiry, whether its obligation has been impaired by those acts of the legislature of New Hampshire, to which the special verdict refers.

From the review of this charter, which has been taken, it appears, that the whole power of governing the college, of appointing and removing tutors, of fixing their salaries, of directing the course of study to be pursued by the students, and of filling up vacancies created in their own body, was vested in the trustees. On the part of the crown it was expressly stipulated, that this corporation, thus constituted, should continue forever; and that the number of trustees should forever consist of twelve, and no more. By this contract the crown was bound, and could have made no violent alteration in its essential terms, without impairing its obligation.

By the revolution, the duties, as well as the powers, of government devolved on the people of New Hampshire. It is admitted, that among the latter was comprehended the transcendent power of parliament, as well as that of the executive department. It is too clear to require the support of argument, that all contracts, and rights, respecting property, remained unchanged by the revolution. The obligations then, which were created by the charter to Dartmouth College, were the same in the new, that they had been in the old government. The power of the government was also the same. A repeal of this charter at any time prior to the adoption of the present Con-

stitution of the United States, would have been an extraordinary and unprecedented act of power, but one which could have been contested only by the restrictions upon the legislature, to be found in the constitution of the State. But the Constitution of the United States has imposed this additional limitation, that the legislature of a State shall pass no act "impairing the obligation of contracts."

It has been already stated, that the act "to amend the charter, and enlarge and improve the corporation of Dartmouth College," increases the number of trustees to twenty-one, gives the appointment of the additional members to the executive of the State, and creates a board of overseers, to consist of twenty-five persons, of whom twenty-one are also appointed by the executive of New Hampshire, who have power to inspect and control the most important acts of the trustees.

On the effect of this law [of 1816], two opinions cannot be entertained. Between acting directly, and acting through the agency of trustees and overseers, no essential difference is perceived. The whole power of governing the college is transferred from trustees appointed according to the will of the founder, expressed in the charter to the executive of New Hampshire. The management and application of the funds of this eleemosynary institution, which are placed by the donors in the hands of trustees named in the charter, and empowered to perpetuate themselves, are placed by this act under the control of the government of the State. The will of the State is substituted for the will of the donors, in every essential operation of the college. This is not an immaterial change. The founders of the college contracted not merely for the perpetual application of the funds which they gave to the object for which those funds were given; they contracted, also, to secure that application by the constitution of the corporation. They contracted for a system which should, as far as human foresight can provide, retain forever the government of the literary institution they had formed, in the hands of persons approved by themselves. This system is totally changed. The charter of 1769 exists no longer. It is reorganized; and reorganized in such a manner as to convert a literary institution, moulded according to the will of its founders, and placed under the control of private literary men, into a machine entirely subservient to the will of government. This may be for the advantage of this college in particular, and may be for the advantage of literature in general; but it is not according to the will of the donors, and is subversive of that contract on the faith of which their property was given. . . .

It results from this opinion, that the acts of the legislature of New Hampshire, which are stated in the special verdict found in this cause, are repugnant to the Constitution of the United States; and that the judgment on this special verdict ought to have been for the plaintiffs. The judgment of the State Court must, therefore, be reversed.

[JUSTICES WASHINGTON and STORY concurred in separate opinions. MR. JUSTICE DUVALL dissented without discussion.]

SLAUGHTER HOUSE CASES

16 Wallace 36 (1873)

"To protect the health of the City of New Orleans" Louisiana's legislature chartered (compare the Dartmouth charter) a slaughter-house company and gave it for twenty-five years exclusive slaughtering privileges in the city. Other butchers in the area could slaughter only at the company's abattoir and only by paying a fee for the privilege. One purpose of the legislation plainly was to restrict slaughtering to specified localities. These cases came up from the state courts in an effort by the nonfavored butchers to enjoin the "monopoly."

MR. JUSTICE MILLER delivered the opinion of the Court: . . .

It is not, and cannot be successfully controverted, that it is both the right and the duty of the legislative body—the supreme power of the State or municipality—to prescribe and determine the localities where the business of slaughtering for a great city may be conducted. To do this effectively it is indispensable that all persons who slaughter animals for food shall do it in those places *and nowhere else.*

The statute under consideration defines these localities and forbids slaughtering in any other. It does not, as has been asserted, prevent the butcher from doing his own slaughtering. On the contrary, the Slaughter-House Company is required, under a heavy penalty, to permit any person who wishes to do so, to slaughter in their houses; and they are bound to make ample provision for the convenience of all slaughtering for

the entire city. The butcher then is still permitted to slaughter, to prepare, and to sell his own meats; but he is required to slaughter at a specified place and to pay reasonable compensation for the use of the accommodations furnished him at that place.

The wisdom of the monopoly granted by the legislature may be open to question, but it is difficult to see a justification for the assertion that the butchers are deprived of the right to labor in their occupation, or the people of their daily service in preparing food, or how this statute, with the duties and guards imposed upon the company, can be said to destroy the business of the butcher, or seriously interfere with its pursuit.

The power here exercised by the legislature of Louisiana is, in its essential nature, one which has been, up to the present period in the constitutional history of this country, always conceded to belong to the States, however it may *now* be questioned in some of its details. . . .

Unless, therefore, it can be maintained that the exclusive privilege granted by this charter to the corporation is beyond the power of the legislature of Louisiana, there can be no just exception to the validity of the statute. And in this respect we are not able to see that these privileges are especially odious or objectionable. The duty imposed as a consideration for the privilege is well defined, and its enforcement well guarded. The prices or charges to be made by the company are limited by the statute, and we are not advised that they are on the whole exorbitant or unjust.

The proposition is, therefore, reduced to these terms: Can any exclusive privileges be granted to any of its citizens, or to a corporation, by the legislature of a State? . . .

The plaintiffs in error accepting this issue, allege that the statute is a violation of the Constitution of the United States in these several particulars:

That it creates an involuntary servitude forbidden by the thirteenth article of amendment;

That it abridges the privileges and immunities of citizens of the United States;

That it denies to the plaintiffs the equal protection of the laws; and,

That it deprives them of their property without due process of law; contrary to the provisions of the first section of the fourteenth article of amendment.

This court is thus called upon for the first time to give construction to these articles.

We do not conceal from ourselves the great responsibility which this duty devolves upon us. No questions so far-reaching and pervading in their consequences, so profoundly interesting to the people of this country, and so important in their bearing upon the relations of the United States, and of the several States to each other and to the citizens of the States and of the United States, have been before this court during the official life of any of its present members. We have given every opportunity for a full hearing at the bar; we have discussed it freely and compared views among ourselves; we have taken ample time for careful deliberation, and we now propose to announce the judgments which we have formed in the construction of those articles, so far as we have found them necessary to the decision of the cases before us, and beyond that we have neither the inclination nor the right to go. . . . .

On the most casual examination of the language of these [Civil War] amendments, no one can fail to be impressed with the one pervading purpose found in them all, lying at the foundation of each, and without which none of them would have been even suggested; we mean the freedom of the slave race, the security and firm establishment of that freedom, and the protection of the newly-made freeman and citizen from the oppressions of those who had formerly exercised unlimited dominion over him. It is true that only the fifteenth amendment, in terms, mentions the Negro by speaking of his color and his slavery. But it is just as true that each of the other articles was addressed to the grievances of that race, and designed to remedy them as the fifteenth.

We do not say that no one else but the Negro can share in this protection. Both the language and spirit of these articles are to have their fair and just weight in any question of construction. Undoubtedly while Negro slavery alone was in the mind of the Congress which proposed the thirteenth article, it forbids any other kind of slavery, now or hereafter. If Mexican peonage or the Chinese cooly labor system shall develop slavery of the Mexican or Chinese race within our territory, this amendment may safely be trusted to make it void. And so if other rights are assailed by the States which properly and necessarily fall within the protection of these articles, that protection will apply, though the party interested may not be of African descent. But what we do say, and what we wish to be understood is, that in any fair and just construction of any section or phrase of these amendments, it is necessary to look to the purpose which we have said was the pervading spirit of them all, the evil which they were designed to remedy, and the process of continued addition to the Constitution, until that purpose was supposed to be accomplished, as far as constitutional law can accomplish it. . . . [The Court held that the Thirteenth Amendment had nothing whatsoever to do with the Louisiana butchering law.]

The next observation is more important in view of the arguments of counsel in the present case. It is, that the distinction between citizenship of the United States and citizenship of a State is clearly recognized and established. Not only may a man be a citizen of the United States without being a citizen of a State, but an important element is necessary to convert the former into the latter. He must reside within the State to make him a citizen of it, but it is only necessary that he should be born or naturalized in the United States to be a citizen of the Union.

It is quite clear, then, that there is a citizenship of the United States, and a citizenship of a State, which are distinct from each other, and which depend upon different characteristics or circumstances in the individual.

We think this distinction and its explicit recognition in this [the Fourteenth] amendment of great weight in this argument, because the next paragraph of this same section, which is the one mainly relied on by the plaintiffs in error, speaks only of privileges and immunities of citizens of the United States, and does not speak of those of citizens of the several States. The argument, however, in favor of the plaintiffs rests wholly on the assumption that the citizenship is the same, and the privileges and immunities guaranteed by the clause are the same.

The language is, "No State shall make or enforce any law which shall abridge the privileges or immunities of citizens of *the United States.*" It is a little remarkable, if this clause was intended as a protection to the citizens of a State against the legislative power of his own State, that the word citizen of the State should be left out when it

is so carefully used, and used in contradistinction to citizens of the United States, in the very sentence which precedes it. It is too clear for argument that the change in phraseology was adopted understandingly and with a purpose.

Of the privileges and immunities of the citizen of the United States, and of the privileges and immunities of the citizen of the State, and what they respectively are, we will presently consider; but we wish to state here that it is only the former which are placed by this clause under the protection of the Federal Constitution, and that the latter, whatever they may be, are not intended to have any additional protection by this paragraph of the amendment.

If, then, there is a difference between the privileges and immunities belonging to a citizen of the United States as such, and those belonging to the citizen of the State as such the latter must rest for their security and protection where they have heretofore rested; for they are not embraced by this paragraph of the amendment. . . .

Fortunately we are not without judicial construction of [the state citizenship clause in Art. 4, Sec. 2] of the Constitution. The first and the leading case on the subject is that of *Corfield* v. *Coryell,* 6 Fed. Cas. 3230, decided by Mr. Justice Washington in the Circuit Court for the District of Pennsylvania in 1823.

"The inquiry," he says, "is, what are the privileges and immunities of citizens of the several States? We feel no hesitation in confining these expressions to those privileges and immunities which are fundamental; which belong of right to the citizens of all free governments, and which have at all times been enjoyed by citizens of the several States which compose this Union, from the time of their becoming free, independent, and sovereign. What these fundamental principles are, it would be more tedious than difficult to enumerate. They may all, however, be comprehended under the following general heads: protection by the government, with the right to acquire and possess property of every kind, and to pursue and obtain happiness and safety, subject, nevertheless, to such restraints as the government may prescribe for the general good of the whole." . . .

It would be the vainest show of learning to attempt to prove by citations of authority, that up to the adoption of the recent amendments, no claim or pretense was set up that those rights depended on the Federal government for their existence or protection, beyond the very few express limitations which the Federal Constitution imposed upon the States—such, for instance, as the prohibition against ex post facto laws, bills of attainder, and laws impairing the obligation of contracts. But with the exception of these and a few other restrictions, the entire domain of the privileges and immunities of citizens of the States, as above defined, lay within the constitutional and legislative power of the States, and without that of the Federal government. Was it the purpose of the fourteenth amendment, by the simple declaration that no State should make or enforce any law which shall abridge the privileges and immunities of *citizens of the United States,* to transfer the security and protection of all the civil rights which we have mentioned, from the States to the Federal government? And where it is declared that Congress shall have the power to enforce that article, was it intended to bring within the power of Congress the entire domain of civil rights heretofore belonging exclusively to the States?

All this and more must follow, if the proposition of the plaintiffs in error be sound. For not only are these rights subject to the control of Congress whenever in its discretion any of them are supposed to be abridged by State legislation, but that body may also pass laws in advance, limiting and restricting the exercise of legislative power by the States, in their most ordinary and usual functions, as in its judgment it may think proper on all such subjects. And still further, such a construction followed by the reversal of the judgments of the Supreme Court of Louisiana in these cases, would constitute this court a perpetual censor upon all legislation of the States, on the

civil rights of their own citizens, with authority to nullify such as it did not approve as consistent with those rights, as they existed at the time of the adoption of this amendment. The argument we admit is not always the most conclusive which is drawn from the consequences urged against the adoption of a particular construction of an instrument. But when, as in the case before us, these consequences are so serious, so far-reaching and pervading, so great a departure from the structure and spirit of our institutions; when the effect is to fetter and degrade the State governments by subjecting them to the control of Congress, in the exercise of powers heretofore universally conceded to them of the most ordinary and fundamental character; when in fact it radically changes the whole theory of the relations of the State and Federal governments to each other and of both these governments to the people; the argument has a force that is irresistible, in the absence of language which expresses such a purpose too clearly to admit of doubt.

We are convinced that no such results were intended by the Congress which proposed these amendments, nor by the legislatures of the States which ratified them.

Having shown that the privileges and immunities relied on in the argument are those which belong to citizens of the States as such, and that they are left to the State governments for security and protection, and not by this article placed under the special care of the Federal government, we may hold ourselves excused from defining the privileges and immunities of citizens of the United States which no State can abridge, until some case involving those privileges may make it necessary to do so.

But lest it be said that no such privileges and immunities are to be found if those we have been considering are excluded, we venture to suggest some which owe their existence to the Federal government, its National character, its Constitution, or its laws.

One of these is well described in the case of *Crandall* v. *Nevada,* 6 Wall. 35. It is said to be the right of the citizens of this great country, protected by implied guarantees of its Constitution, "to come to the seat of government to assert any claim he may have upon that government, to transact any business he may have with it, to seek its protection, to share its offices, to engage in administering its functions. He has the right of free access to its seaports, through which all operations of foreign commerce are conducted, to the sub-treasuries, land offices, and courts of justice in the several States." And quoting from the language of Chief Justice Taney in another case, it is said "that for all the great purposes for which the Federal government was established, we are one people, with one common country, we are all citizens of the United States;" and it is, as such citizens, that their rights are supported in this court in *Crandall* v. *Nevada*.

Another privilege of a citizen of the United States is to demand the care and protection of the Federal government over his life, liberty, and property when on the high seas or within the jurisdiction of a foreign government. Of this there can be no doubt, nor that the right depends upon his character as a citizen of the United States. The right to peaceably assemble and petition for redress of grievances, the privilege of the writ of habeas corpus, are rights of the citizen guaranteed by the Federal Constitution. The right to use the navigable waters of the United States, however they may penetrate the territory of the several States, all rights secured to our citizens by treaties with foreign nations, are dependent upon citizenship of the United States, and not citizenship of a State. One of these privileges is conferred by the very article under consideration. It is that a citizen of the United States can, of his own volition, become a citizen of any State of the Union by a bona fide residence therein, with the same rights as other citizens of that State. To these may be added the rights secured by the thirteenth and fifteenth articles of amendment, and by the other clause of the fourteenth, next to be considered.

But it is useless to pursue this branch of the inquiry, since we are of opinion that the rights claimed by these plantiffs in error, if they have any existence, are not privileges and immunities of citizens of the United States within the meaning of the clause of the fourteenth amendment under consideration. . . .

The argument has not been much pressed in these cases that the defendant's charter deprives the plaintiffs of their property without due process of law, or that it denies to them the equal protection of the law. The first of these paragraphs has been in the Constitution since the adoption of the fifth amendment, as a restraint upon the federal power. It is also to be found in some form of expression in the constitutions of nearly all the States, as a restraint upon the power of the States. This law, then, has practically been the same as it now is during the existence of the government, except so far as the present amendment may place the restraining power over the States in this matter in the hands of the Federal government.

We are not without judicial interpretation, therefore, both State and National, of the meaning of this clause. And it is sufficient to say that under no construction of that provision that we have ever seen, or any that we deem admissible, can the restraint imposed by the State of Louisiana upon the exercise of their trade by the butchers of New Orleans be held to be a deprivation of property within the meaning of that provision.

"Nor shall any State deny to any person within its jurisdiction the equal protection of the laws."

In the light of the history of these amendments, and the pervading purpose of them, which we have already discussed, it is not difficult to give a meaning to this clause. The existence of laws in the States where the newly emancipated Negroes resided, which discriminated with gross injustice and hardship against them as a class, was the evil to be remedied by this clause, and by it such laws are forbidden.

If, however, the States did not conform their laws to its requirements, then by the

fifth section of the article of amendment
Congress was authorized to enforce it by
suitable legislation. We doubt very much
whether any action of a State not directed by way of discrimination against the
Negroes as a class, or on account of their
race, will ever be held to come within the
purview of this provision. It is so clearly a
provision for that race and that emergency,
that a strong case would be necessary for its
application to any other. But as it is a State
that is to be dealt with, and not alone the
validity of its laws, we may safely leave
that matter until Congress shall have
exercised its power, or some case of State
oppression, by denial of equal justice in its
courts, shall have claimed a decision at our
hands. We find no such case in the one
before us, and do not deem it necessary to
go over the argument again, as it may have
relation to this particular clause of the
amendment. . . .

The judgments of the Supreme Court of
Louisiana in these cases are affirmed.

MR. JUSTICE FIELD, dissenting: . . .

The question presented is . . . one of the
gravest importance, not merely to the parties here, but to the whole country. It is
nothing less than the question whether the
recent amendments to the Federal Constitution protect the citizens of the United States
against the deprivation of their common
rights by State legislation. In my judgment
the fourteenth amendment does afford such
protection, and was so intended by the Congress which framed and the States which
adopted it.

The amendment does not attempt to confer any new privileges or immunities upon
citizens, or to enumerate or define those already existing. It assumes that there are
such privileges and immunities which belong of right to citizens as such, and ordains
that they shall not be abridged by State
legislation. If this inhibition has no reference to privileges and immunities of this
character, but only refers, as held by the
majority of the court in their opinion, to
such privileges and immunities as were before its adoption specially designated in the

Constitution or necessarily implied as belonging to citizens of the United States, it
was a vain and idle enactment, which accomplished nothing, and most unnecessarily
excited Congress and the people on its passage. With privileges and immunities thus
designated or implied no State could ever
have interfered by its laws, and no new constitutional provision was required to inhibit
such interference. The supremacy of the
Constitution and the laws of the United
States always controlled any State legislation of that character. But if the amendment
refers to the natural and inalienable rights
which belong to all citizens, the inhibition
has a profound significance and consequence.

What, then, are the privileges and immunities which are secured against abridgment by State legislation? . . .

The terms, privileges and immunities, are
not new in the Amendment; they were in
the Constitution before the Amendment
was adopted. They are found in the Second
Section of the Fourth Article, which declares that "the citizens of each State shall
be entitled to all privileges and immunities
of citizens in the several States," and they
have been the subject of frequent consideration in judicial decisions. In *Corfield
v. Coryell*, Mr. Justice Washington said he
had "no hesitation in confining these expressions to those privileges and immunities
which were, in their nature, fundamental;
which belong of right to citizens of all free
governments, and which have at all times
been enjoyed by the citizens of the several
States which composed the Union, from the
time of their becoming free, independent,
and sovereign;" and, in considering what
those fundamental privileges were, he said
that perhaps it would be more tedious than
difficult to enumerate them, but that they
might be "all comprehended under the following general heads: protection by the government; the enjoyment of life and liberty,
with the right to acquire and possess property of every kind, and to pursue and obtain happiness and safety, subject, nevertheless, to such restraints as the government
may justly prescribe for the general good

of the whole." This appears to me to be a sound construction of the clause in question. The privileges and immunities designated are those *which of right belong to the citizens of all free governments.* Clearly among these must be placed the right to pursue a lawful employment in a lawful manner, without other restraint than such as equally affects all persons. In the discussions in Congress upon the passage of the Civil Rights Act repeated reference was made to this language of Mr. Justice Washington. It was cited by Senator Trumbull with the observation that it enumerated the very rights belonging to a citizen of the United States set forth in the first section of the act, and with the statement that all persons born in the United States, being declared by the act citizens of the United States, would thenceforth be entitled to the rights of citizens, and that these were the great fundamental rights set forth in the act; and that they were set forth "as appertaining to every freeman." . . .

This equality of right, with exemption from all disparaging and partial enactments, in the lawful pursuits of life, throughout the whole country, is the distinguishing privilege of citizens of the United States. To them, everywhere, all pursuits, all professions, all avocations are open without other restrictions than such as are imposed equally upon all others of the same age, sex, and condition. The State may prescribe such regulations for every pursuit and calling of life as will promote the public health, secure the good order and advance the general prosperity of society, but when once prescribed, the pursuit or calling must be free to be followed by every citizen who is within the conditions designated, and will conform to the regulations. This is the fundamental idea upon which our institutions rest, and unless adhered to in the legislation of the country our government will be a republic only in name. The fourteenth amendment, in my judgment, makes it essential to the validity of the legislation of every State that this equality of right should be respected. How widely this equality has been departed from, how entirely rejected and trampled upon by the act of Louisiana, I have already shown. And it is to me a matter of profound regret that its validity is recognized by a majority of this court, for by it the right of free labor, one of the most sacred and imprescriptible rights of man, is violated. . . .

I am authorized by the CHIEF JUSTICE [CHASE], MR. JUSTICE SWAYNE, and MR. JUSTICE BRADLEY, to state that they concur with me in this dissenting opinion.

JUSTICES BRADLEY and SWAYNE delivered separate dissenting opinions.

NOTE: The *Slaughter House* interpretation of the privileges and immunities of United States citizenship has remained essentially as outlined by Mr. Justice Miller. Like the Tenth Amendment it seems tautological; that is, apparently it protects only interests which would be protected in any event by other constitutional provisions. To put it differently, such meaning as the Court has found in the general provisions of the Fourteenth Amendment, it has found in the due process and equal protection clauses. The net effect was hardly restrictive, however, for as Holmes observed apropos the laissez-faire Court, only the sky was the limit to what could be found in due process. Putting the eggs in the equal protection-due process basket (which protects "persons") at least had the effect of encompassing aliens. Such protection would not have been possible if the Court had relied chiefly on the privileges and immunities clause (which covers only citizens). But was this the crucial consideration? Or was it that the laissez-faire Justices settled upon equal protection-due process rather than privileges and immunities because business corporations could more plausibly be treated as "persons" under the former, than as "citizens" under the latter?

It will be noted that in the *Slaughter House Cases* there was no interstate commerce problem. There was one in *Munn* v. *Illinois*, but the Court found it susceptible of state treatment under the *Cooley* rule. In the *Wabash* case (Part Three, II) the Court later invalidated state regulation of railroad rates on commerce clause grounds. Compare *Di Santo's* case (Part Three, III).

MUNN v. ILLINOIS

94 U.S. 113 (1877)

This is one of the six famous *Granger Cases* which together tested the validity of state laws fixing maximum charges for grain warehousing and for rail transportation.

MR. CHIEF JUSTICE WAITE delivered the opinion of the court. . . .

. . . Every statute is presumed to be constitutional. The courts ought not to declare one to be unconstitutional, unless it is clearly so. If there is doubt, the expressed will of the legislature should be sustained.

The Constitution contains no definition of the word "deprive," as used in the Fourteenth Amendment. To determine its signification, therefore, it is necessary to ascertain the effect which usage has given it, when employed in the same or a like connection.

While this provision of the amendment is new in the Constitution of the United States, as a limitation upon the powers of the states, it is old as a principle of civilized government. It is found in Magna Charta, and, in substance if not in form, in nearly or quite all the constitutions that have been from time to time adopted by the several states of the Union. By the Fifth Amendment, it was introduced into the Constitution of the United States as a limitation upon the powers of the national government, and by the Fourteenth, as a guaranty against any encroachment upon an acknowledged right of citizenship by the legislatures of the states. . . .

When one becomes a member of society, he necessarily parts with some rights or privileges which, as an individual not affected by his relations to others, he might retain. "A body politic," as aptly defined in the preamble of the constitution of Massachusetts, "is a social compact by which the whole people covenants with each citizen, and each citizen with the whole people, that all shall be governed by certain laws for the common good." This does not confer power upon the whole people to control rights which are purely and exclusively private, *Thorpe* v. *R. & B. Railroad Co.*, 27 Vt. 140; but it does authorize the establishment of laws requiring each citizen to so conduct himself, and so use his own property, as not unnecessarily to injure another. This is the very essence of government, and has found expression in the maxim, *sic utere tuo ut alienum non laedas*. From this source come the police powers, which . . . "are nothing more or less than the powers of government inherent in every sovereignty, . . . that is to say, . . . the power to govern men and things." Under these powers the government regulates the conduct of its citizens one towards another, and the manner in which each shall use his own property, when such regulation becomes necessary for the public good. In their exercise it has been customary in England from time immemorial, and in this country from its first colonization, to regulate ferries, common carriers, hackmen, bakers, millers, wharfingers, innkeepers, etc., and in so doing to fix a maximum of charge to be made for services rendered, accommodations furnished, and articles sold. To this day, statutes are to be found in many of the states upon some or all these subjects; and we think it has never yet been successfully contended that such legislation came within any of the constitutional prohibitions against interference with private property. . . .

From this it is apparent that, down to the time of the adoption of the Fourteenth Amendment, it was not supposed that statutes regulating the use, or even the price of the use, of private property necessarily deprived an owner of his property without due process of law. Under some circumstances they may, but not under all. The amendment does not change the law in this particular: it simply prevents the states from doing that which will operate as such a deprivation.

This brings us to inquire as to the principles upon which this power of regulation rests, in order that we may determine what is within and what without its operative effect. Looking, then, to the common law, from whence came the right which the Constitution protects, we find that when private property is "affected with a public interest, it ceases to be *juris privati* only." This was said by Lord Chief Justice Hale more than two hundred years ago. . . . Property does become clothed with a public interest when used in a manner to make it of public consequence, and affect the community at large. When, therefore, one devotes his property to a use in which the public has an interest, he, in effect, grants to the public an interest in that use, and must submit to be controlled by the public for the common good, to the extent of the interest he has thus created. He may withdraw his grant by discontinuing the use; but, so long as he maintains the use, he must submit to the control. . . .

And the same has been held as to warehouses and warehousemen. . . .

From the same source comes the power to regulate the charges of common carriers, which was done in England as long ago as the third year of the reign of William and Mary, and continued until within a comparatively recent period. . . .

Common carriers exercise a sort of public office, and have duties to perform in which the public is interested. . . . Their business is, therefore, "affected with a public interest," within the meaning of the doctrine which Lord Hale has so forcibly stated.

But we need not go further. Enough has already been said to show that, when private property is devoted to a public use, it is subject to public regulation. It remains only to ascertain whether the warehouses of these plaintiffs in error, and the business which is carried on there, come within the operation of this principle.

For this purpose we accept as true the statements of fact contained in the elaborate brief of one of the counsel of the plaintiffs in error. From these it appears that ". . . The quantity [of grain] received in Chicago has made it the greatest grain market in the world. This business has created a demand for means by which the immense quantity of grain can be handled or stored, and these have been found in grain warehouses. . . . In this way the largest traffic between the citizens of the country north and west of Chicago and the citizens of the country lying on the Atlantic coast north of Washington is in grain which passes through the elevators of Chicago. In this way the trade in grain is carried on by the inhabitants of seven or eight of the great states of the west with four or five of the states lying on the seashore, and forms the largest part of interstate commerce in these states. The grain warehouses or elevators in Chicago are immense structures, holding from 300,000 to 1,000,000 bushels at one time, according to size. . . . It has been found impossible to preserve each owner's grain separate, and this has given rise to a system of inspection and grading, by which the grain of different owners is mixed, and receipts issued for the number of bushels, which are negotiable, and redeemable in like kind, upon demand.

This mode of conducting the business was inaugurated more than twenty years ago, and has grown to immense proportions. The railways have found it impracticable to own such elevators, and public policy forbids the transaction of such business by the carrier; the ownership has, therefore, been by private individuals, who have embarked their capital and devoted their industry to such business as a private pursuit."

In this connection it must also be borne in mind that, although in 1874 there were in Chicago fourteen warehouses adapted to this particular business, and owned by about thirty persons, nine business firms controlled them, and that the prices charged and received for storage were such "as have been from year to year agreed upon and established by the different elevators or warehouses in the city of Chicago, and which rates have been annually published in one or more newspapers printed in said city, in the month of January in each year, as the established rates for the year then next ensuing such publication." Thus it is apparent that all the elevating facilities through which these vast productions "of seven or eight great states of the west" must pass on the way "to four or five of the states on the seashore" may be a "virtual" monopoly.

Under such circumstances it is difficult to see why, if the common carrier, or the miller, or the ferryman, or the innkeeper, or the wharfinger, or the baker, or the cartman, or the hackney-coachman, pursues a public employment and exercises "a sort of public office," these plaintiffs in error do not. They stand, to use again the language of their counsel, in the very "gateway of commerce," and take toll from all who pass. Their business most certainly "tends to a common charge, and is become a thing of public interest and use." . . . Certainly, if any business can be clothed "with a public interest and cease to be *juris privati* only," this has been. It may not be made so by the operation of the constitution of Illinois or this statute, but it is by the facts.

We also are not permitted to overlook the fact that, for some reason, the people of Illinois, when they revised their constitution in 1870, saw fit to make it the duty of the general assembly to pass laws "for the protection of producers, shippers, and receivers of grain and produce," article 13, section 7; and by section 5 of the same article, to require all railroad companies receiving and transporting grain in bulk or otherwise to deliver the same at any elevator to which it might be consigned, that could be reached by any track that was or could be used by such company, and that all railroad companies should permit connections to be made with their tracks, so that any public warehouse, etc., might be reached by the cars on their railroads. This indicates very clearly that during the twenty years in which this peculiar business had been assuming its present "immense proportions," something had occurred which led the whole body of the people to suppose that remedies such as are usually employed to prevent abuses by virtual monopolies might not be inappropriate here. For our purposes we must assume that, if a state of facts could exist that would justify such legislation, it actually did exist when the statute now under consideration was passed. For us the question is one of power, not of expediency. If no state of circumstances could exist to justify such a statute, then we may declare this one void, because in excess of the legislative power of the state. But if it could, we must presume it did. Of the propriety of legislative interference within the scope of legislative power, the legislature is the exclusive judge. . . .

We know that this is a power which may be abused; but that is no argument against its existence. For protection against abuses by legislatures the people must resort to the polls, not to the courts. . . .

We come now to consider the effect upon this statute of the power of Congress to regulate commerce.

It was very properly said in the case of the *State Tax on Railway Gross Receipts*, 15 Wallace 284, that "it is not everything that affects commerce that amounts to a regulation of it, within the meaning of the Constitution." The warehouses of these plaintiffs in error are situated and their business carried on exclusively within the limits of the State of Illinois. They are used as instruments by those engaged in state as well as those engaged in interstate commerce, but they are no more necessarily a part of commerce itself than the dray or the cart by which, but for them, grain would be transferred from one railroad station to another. Incidentally they may become connected with interstate commerce, but not necessarily so. Their regulation is a thing of domestic concern, and, certainly, until Congress acts in reference to their interstate relations, the state may exercise all the powers of government over them, even though in so doing it may indirectly operate upon commerce outside its immediate jurisdiction. We do not say that a case may not arise in which it will be found that a state, under the form of regulating its own affairs, has encroached upon the exclusive domain of Congress in respect to interstate commerce, but we do say that, upon the facts as they are represented to us in this record, that has not been done. . . .

We conclude, therefore, that the statute in question is not repugnant to the Constitution of the United States, and that there is no error in the judgment. . . .

Judgment affirmed.

MR. JUSTICE FIELD and MR. JUSTICE STRONG dissented.

MR. JUSTICE FIELD. . . . I am compelled to dissent from the decision of the court in this case, and from the reasons upon which that decision is founded. The principle upon which the opinion of the majority proceeds is, in my judgment, subversive of the rights of private property, heretofore believed to be protected by constitutional guaranties against legislative interference, and is in conflict with the authorities cited in its support. . . .

If this be sound law, if there be no protection, either in the principles upon which our republican government is founded, or in the prohibitions of the Constitution against such invasion of private rights, all property and all business in the State are held at the mercy of a majority of its legislature. The public has no greater interest in the use of buildings for the storage of grain than it has in the use of buildings for the residences of families, nor, indeed, anything like so great an interest; and, according to the doctrine announced, the legislature may fix the rent of all tenements used for residences, without reference to the cost of their erection. If the owner does not like the rates prescribed, he may cease renting his houses. He has granted to the public, says the court, an interest in the use of the buildings, and "he may withdraw his grant by discontinuing the use; but, so long as he maintains the use, he must submit to the control." The public is interested in the manufacture of cotton, woollen, and silken fabrics, in the construction of machinery, in the printing and publication of books and periodicals, and in the making of utensils of every variety, useful and ornamental; indeed, there is hardly an enterprise or business engaging the attention and labor of any considerable portion of the community, in which the public has not an interest in the sense in which that term is used by the court in its opinion; and the doctrine which allows the legislature to interfere with and regulate the charges which the owners of property thus employed shall make for its use, that is, the rates at which all these different kinds of business shall be carried on, has never before been asserted, so far as I am aware, by any judicial tribunal in the United States. . . .

No State "shall deprive any person of life, liberty, or property without due process of law," says the Fourteenth Amendment to the Constitution. By the term "life," as here used, something more is meant than mere animal existence. The inhibition against its deprivation extends to all those limbs and faculties by which life is enjoyed. The provision equally prohibits the mutilation of the body by the amputation of an arm or leg, or the putting out of an eye, or the destruction of any other organ of the body through which the soul communicates with the outer world. The deprivation not only of life, but of whatever God has given to every one with life, for its growth and enjoyment, is prohibited by the provision in question, if its efficacy be not frittered away by judicial decision.

By the term "liberty," as used in the provision, something more is meant than mere freedom from physical restraint or the bounds of a prison. It means freedom to go where one may choose, and to act in such manner, not inconsistent with the equal rights of others, as his judgment may dictate for the promotion of his happiness; that is, to pursue such callings and avocations as may be most suitable to develop his capacities, and give to them their highest enjoyment.

The same liberal construction which is required for the protection of life and liberty, in all particulars in which life and liberty are of any value, should be applied to the protection of private property. If the legislature of a State, under pretense of providing for the public good, or for any other reason, can determine, against the consent of the owner, the uses to which private property shall be devoted, or the prices which the owner shall receive for its uses, it can deprive him of the property as completely as by a special act for its confiscation or destruction. If, for instance, the owner is prohibited from using his building for the purposes for which it was designed, it is of little consequence that he is permitted to retain the title and possession; or, if he is compelled to take as compensation for its use less than the expenses to which he is subjected by its ownership, he is, for all practical purposes, deprived of the property, as effectually as if the legislature had ordered his forcible dispossession. If it be admitted that the legislature has any control over the compensation, the extent of that compensation becomes a mere matter of legislative discretion. The amount fixed will operate as a partial destruction of the value of the property, if it fall below the amount which the owner would obtain by contract, and, practically, as a complete destruction, if it be less than the cost of retaining its possession. There is, indeed, no protection of any value under the constitutional provision, which does not extend to the use and income of the property, as well as to its title and possession. . . .

1. ECONOMIC DUE PROCESS

LOCHNER v. *NEW YORK*

198 U.S. 45 (1905)

> This case held invalid, as a deprivation of liberty without due process, a state law limiting employment in bakeries to a maximum of sixty hours per week and ten hours per day. The law apparently had been enacted as a precaution against lung disease caused by excessive inhalation of flour.

Mr. Justice Peckham delivered the opinion of the Court: . . .

The statute necessarily interferes with the right of contract between the employer and employees, concerning the number of hours in which the latter may labor in the bakery of the employer. The general right to make a contract in relation to his business is part of the liberty of the individual protected by the Fourteenth Amendment of the federal Constitution. Under that provision no state can deprive any person of life, liberty, or property without due process of law. The right to purchase or to sell labor is part of the liberty protected by this amendment, unless there are circumstances which exclude the right. There are, however, certain powers, existing in the sovereignty of each state in the Union, somewhat vaguely termed police powers, the exact description and limitation of which have not been attempted by the courts. Those powers, broadly stated, and without, at present, any attempt at a more specific limitation, relate to the safety, health, morals, and general welfare of the public. Both property and liberty are held on such reasonable conditions as may be imposed by the governing power of the state in the exercise of those powers, and with such conditions the Fourteenth Amendment was not designed to interfere.

The state, therefore, has power to prevent the individual from making certain kinds of contracts, and in regard to them the federal Constitution offers no protection. If the contract be one which the state, in the legitimate exercise of its police power, has the right to prohibit, it is not prevented from prohibiting it by the Fourteenth Amendment. Contracts in violation of a statute, either of the federal or state government, or a contract to let one's property for immoral purposes, or to do any other unlawful act, could obtain no protection from the federal Constitution, as coming under the liberty of person or of free contract. Therefore, when the state, by its legislature, in the assumed exercise of its police powers, has passed an act which seriously limits the right to labor or the right of contract in regard to their means of livelihood between persons who are *sui juris* (both employer and employee), it becomes of great importance to determine which shall prevail,—the right of the individual to labor for such time as he may choose, or the right of the state to prevent the individual from laboring, or from entering into any contract to labor, beyond a certain time prescribed by the state. . . .

It must, of course, be conceded that there is a limit to the valid exercise of the police power by the state. There is no dispute concerning this general proposition. Otherwise the Fourteenth Amendment would have no efficacy and the legislatures of the states would have unbounded power, and it would be enough to say that any piece of legislation was enacted to conserve the morals, the health, or the safety of the people; such legislation would be valid, no matter how absolutely without foundation the claim might be. The claim of the police power would be a mere pretext—become another and delusive name for the supreme sovereignty of the state to be exercised free from constitutional restraint. This is not contended for. In every case that comes before this Court, therefore, where legislation of this character is concerned, and where the protection of the federal Constitution is sought, the question necessarily arises: Is this a fair, reasonable, and appropriate exercise of the police power of the state, or is it an unreasonable, unnecessary, and arbitrary interference with the right of the individual to his personal liberty, or to enter into those contracts in relation to labor which may seem to him appropriate or necessary for the support of himself and his family? Of course the liberty of contract relating to labor includes both parties to it. The one has as much right to purchase as the other to sell labor.

This is not a question of substituting the judgment of the court for that of the legislature. If the Act be within the power of the state it is valid, although the judgment of the court might be totally opposed to the enactment of such a law. But the question would still remain: Is it within the police power of the state? and that question must be answered by the court.

The question whether this Act is valid as a labor law, pure and simple, may be dismissed in a few words. There is no reasonable ground for interfering with the liberty of persons or the right of free contract, by determining the hours of labor, in the occupation of a baker. There is no contention that bakers as a class are not equal in intelligence and capacity to men in other trades or manual occupations, or that they are not able to assert their rights and care for themselves without the protecting arm of the state, interfering with their independence of judgment and of action. They are in no sense wards of the state. Viewed in the light of a purely labor law, with no reference whatever to the question of health, we think that a law like the one before us involves neither the safety, the morals, nor the welfare of the public, and that the interest of the public is not in the slightest degree affected by such an act. The law must be upheld, if at all, as a law pertaining to the health of the individual engaged in the occupation of a baker. It does not affect any other portion of the public than those who are engaged in that occupation. Clean and wholesome bread does not depend upon whether the baker works but 10 hours per day or only 60 hours a week. The limitation of the hours of labor does not come within the police power on that ground.

It is a question of which of two powers or rights shall prevail,—the power of the state to legislate or the right of the individual to liberty of person and freedom of contract. The mere assertion that the subject relates, though but in a remote degree, to the public health, does not necessarily render the enactment valid. The act must have a more direct relation, as a means to an end, and the end itself must be appropriate and legitimate, before an act can be held to be valid which interferes with the general right of an individual to be free in his person and in his power to contract in relation to his own labor. . . .

We think the limit of the police power has been reached and passed in this case. There is, in our judgment, no reasonable foundation for holding this to be necessary or appropriate as a health law to safeguard the public health, or the health of the individuals who are following the trade of a baker. If this statute be valid, and if, therefore, a proper case is made out in which to deny the right of an individual, *sui juris,* as employer or employee, to make contracts for the labor of the latter under the protection of the provisions of the federal Constitution, there would seem to be no length to which legislation of this nature might not go.

We think that there can be no fair doubt that the trade of a baker, in and of itself, is not an unhealthy one to that degree which would authorize the legislature to interfere with the right to labor, and with the right of free contract on the part of the individual, either as employer or employee. In looking through statistics regarding all trades and occupations, it may be true that the trade of a baker does not appear to be as healthy as some other trades, and is also vastly more healthy than still others. To the common understanding the trade of a baker has never been regarded as an unhealthy one. Very likely physicians would not recommend the exercise of that or of any other trade as a remedy for ill health. Some occupations are more healthy than others, but we think there are none which might not come under the power of the legislature to supervise and control the hours of working therein, if the mere fact that the occupation is not absolutely and perfectly healthy is to confer that right upon the legislative department of the government. It might be safely affirmed that almost all occupations more or less affect the health. There must be more than the mere fact of the possible existence of some small amount of unhealthiness to warrant legislative interference with liberty. It is unfortunately true that labor, even in any department, may possibly carry with it the seeds of unhealthiness. But are we all, on that account, at the mercy of legislative majorities? A printer, a tinsmith, a locksmith, a carpenter, a cabinetmaker, a drygoods clerk, a bank's, a lawyer's or a physician's clerk, or a clerk in almost any kind of business, would all come under the power of the legislature, on this assumption. No trade, no occupation, no mode of earning one's living, could escape this all-pervading power, and the acts of the legislature in limiting the hours of labor in all employments would be valid, although such limitation might seriously cripple the ability of the laborer to support himself and his family.

In our large cities there are many buildings into which the sun penetrates for but a short time in each day, and these buildings are occupied by people carrying on the business of bankers, brokers, lawyers, real estate, and many other kinds of business, aided by many clerks, messengers, and other employees. Upon the assumption of the validity of this Act under review, it is not possible to say that an act, prohibiting lawyer's or bank clerks, or others, from contracting to labor for their employers more than 8 hours a day would be invalid. It might be said that it is unhealthy to work more than that number of hours in an apartment lighted by artificial light during the working hours of the day; that the occupation of the bank clerk, the lawyer's clerk, the real-estate clerk, or the broker's clerk, in such offices is therefore unhealthy, and the legislature in its paternal wisdom must, therefore, have the right to legislate on the subject of, and to limit, the hours for such labor, and, if it exercises that power, and its validity be questioned, it is sufficient to say, it has reference to the public health; it has reference to the health of the employees condemned to labor day after day in buildings where the sun never shines; it is a health law, and therefore it is valid, and cannot be questioned by the courts.

It is also urged, pursuing the same line of argument, that it is to the interest of the state that its population should be strong and robust, and therefore any legislation which may be said to tend to make people healthy must be valid as health laws, enacted under the police power. If this be a valid argument and a justification for this kind of legislation, it follows that the protection of the federal Constitution from undue interference with liberty of person and freedom of contract is visionary, wherever the law is sought to be justified as a valid exercise of the police power. Scarcely any law but might find shelter under such assumptions, and conduct, properly so called, as well as contract, would come under the restrictive sway of the legislature. Not only the hours of employees, but the hours of employers, could be regulated, and doctors, lawyers, scientists, all professional men, as well as athletes and artisans, could be forbidden to fatigue their brains and bodies by prolonged hours of exercise, lest the fighting strength of the state be impaired. We mention these extreme cases because the contention is extreme.

We do not believe in the soundness of the views which uphold this law. On the contrary, we think that such a law as this, although passed in the assumed exercise of the police power, and as relating to the public health, or the health of the employees named, is not within that power, and is invalid. The Act is not, within any fair meaning of the term, a health law, but is an illegal interference with the rights of individuals, both employers and employees, to make contracts regarding labor upon such terms as they may think best, or which they may agree upon with the other parties to such contracts. Statutes of the nature of that under review, limiting the hours in which grown and intelligent men may labor to earn their living, are mere meddlesome interferences with the rights of the individual, and they are not saved from condemnation by the claim that they are passed in the exercise of the police power and upon the subject of the health of the individual whose rights are interfered with, unless there be some fair ground, reasonable in and of itself, to say that there is material danger to the public health, or to the health of the employees, if the hours of labor are not curtailed. . . .

It was further urged on the argument that restricting the hours of labor in the case of bakers was valid because it tended to cleanliness on the part of the workers, as a man was more apt to be cleanly when not overworked, and if cleanly then his "output" was also more likely to be so. . . . The connection, if any exist, is too shadowy and thin to build any argument for the interference of the legislature. If the man works 10 hours a day it is all right, but if $10\frac{1}{2}$ or 11 his health is in danger and his bread may be unhealthful, and, therefore, he shall not be permitted to do it. This, we think, is unreasonable and entirely arbitrary. . . .

It is impossible for us to shut our eyes

to the fact that many of the laws of this character, while passed under what is claimed to be the police power for the purpose of protecting the public health or welfare, are, in reality, passed from other motives. . . .

. . . It seems to us that the real object and purpose were simply to regulate the hours of labor between the master and his employees (all being men, *sui juris*), in a private business, not dangerous in any degree to morals, or in any real and substantial degree to the health of the employees. Under such circumstances the freedom of master and employee to contract with each other in relation to their employment, and in defining the same, cannot be prohibited or interfered with, without violating the federal Constitution.

The judgment of the Court of Appeals of New York as well as that of the Supreme Court and of the County Court of Oneida County must be reversed and the case remanded to the County Court for further proceedings not inconsistent with this opinion.

MR. JUSTICE HARLAN with whom MR. JUSTICE WHITE and MR. JUSTICE DAY concurred, dissenting: . . .

I find it impossible, in view of common experience, to say that there is here no real or substantial relation between the means employed by the state and the end sought to be accomplished by its legislation. . . .

MR. JUSTICE HOLMES, dissenting:

I regret sincerely that I am unable to agree with the judgment in this case, and I think it my duty to express my dissent.

This case is decided upon an economic theory which a large part of the country does not entertain. If it were a question whether I agreed with that theory, I should desire to study it further and long before making up my mind. But I do not conceive that to be my duty, because I strongly believe that my agreement or disagreement has nothing to do with the right of a majority to embody their opinions in law.

It is settled by various decisions of this Court that state constitutions and state laws may regulate life in many ways which we as legislators might think as injudicious or if you like as tyrannical as this, and which equally with this interfere with the liberty to contract. Sunday laws and usury laws are ancient examples. A more modern one is the prohibition of lotteries. The liberty of the citizen to do as he likes so long as he does not interfere with the liberty of others to do the same, which has been a shibboleth for some well-known writers, is interfered with by school laws, by the post office, by every state or municipal institution which takes his money for purposes thought desirable, whether he likes it or not.

The Fourteenth Amendment does not enact Mr. Herbert Spencer's Social Statics. The other day we sustained the Massachusetts vaccination law. *Jacobson* v. *Massachusetts*, 197 U.S. 11. United States and state statutes and decisions cutting down the liberty to contract by way of combination are familiar to this Court. *Northern Securities Co.* v. *United States*, 193 U.S. 197. Two years ago we upheld the prohibition of sales of stock on margins, or for future delivery, in the constitution of California. *Otis* v. *Parker*, 187 U.S. 606. The decision sustaining an 8-hour law for miners is still recent. *Holden* v. *Hardy*, 169 U.S. 366. Some of these laws embody convictions or prejudices which judges are likely to share. Some may not. But a constitution is not intended to embody a particular economic theory, whether of paternalism and the organic relation of the citizen to the state or of laissez faire. It is made for people of fundamentally differing views, and the accident of our finding certain opinions natural and familiar or novel and even shocking ought not to conclude our judgment upon the question whether statutes embodying them conflict with the Constitution of the United States.

General propositions do not decide concrete cases. The decision will depend on a judgment or intuition more subtle than any articulate major premise. But I think that the proposition just stated, if it is accepted, will carry us far toward the end. Every opinion tends to become a law. I think that the word "liberty" in the Fourteenth Amendment is perverted when it is held to prevent the natural outcome of a dominant opinion, unless it can be said that a rational and fair man necessarily would admit that the statute proposed would infringe fundamental principles as they have been understood by the traditions of our people and our law. It does not need research to show that no such sweeping condemnation can be passed upon the statute before us. A reasonable man might think it a proper measure on the score of health. Men whom I certainly could not pronounce unreasonable would uphold it as a first installment of a general regulation of the hours of work. Whether in the latter aspect it would be open to the charge of inequality I think it unnecessary to discuss.

WEAVER v. PALMER BROS. CO.
270 U.S. 402 (1926)

In an effort to prevent the spread of disease, Pennsylvania prohibited the use of shoddy in the manufacturing of comfortables. Arguing that steam sterilization adequately foreclosed the problem of disease, a manufacturer here succeeded in having the law held invalid. Of the company's evidence, the Court, via Mr. Justice Butler observed: . . .

This . . . tends strongly to show that in the absence of sterilization or disinfection there would be little, if any, danger to the health of the users of comfortables filled with shoddy, new or secondhand; and confirms the conclusion that all danger from the use of shoddy may be eliminated by sterilization. . . . As against that fact, the provision in question cannot be sustained as a measure to protect health; and the fact that the act permits the use of numerous materials, prescribing sterilization if they are secondhand, also serves to show that the prohibition of the use of shoddy, new or old, even when sterilized, is unreasonable and arbitrary. The business here involved is legitimate and useful; and, while it is subject to all reasonable regulation, the absolute prohibition of the use of shoddy in the manufacture of comfortables is purely arbitrary and violates the due process clause of the Fourteenth Amendment.

MR. JUSTICE HOLMES, dissenting:

If the Legislature of Pennsylvania was of opinion that disease is likely to be spread by the use of unsterilized shoddy in comfortables I do not suppose that this Court would pronounce the opinion so manifestly absurd that it could not be acted upon. If we should not, then I think that we ought to assume the opinion to be right for the purpose of testing the law. The Legislature may have been of opinion further that the actual practice of filling comfortables with unsterilized shoddy gathered from filthy floors was wide spread, and this again we must assume to be true. It is admitted to be impossible to distinguish the innocent from the infected product in any practicable way, when it is made up into the comfortables. On these premises, if the Legislature regarded the danger as very great and inspection and tagging as inadequate remedies, it seems to me that in order to prevent the spread of disease it constitutionally could forbid any use of shoddy for bedding and upholstery. . . .

MR. JUSTICE BRANDEIS and MR. JUSTICE STONE concur in this opinion.

NEBBIA v. NEW YORK
291 U.S. 502 (1934)

> Pursuant to state law, the Milk Control Board fixed the store price of milk at nine cents a quart. A grocer was found guilty of undercutting this price. On appeal he challenged the law on due process and equal protection grounds. The conviction was upheld over the dissent of Justices McReynolds, Van Devanter, Sutherland, and Butler.
> Speaking for the court, Mr. Justice Roberts observed in part:

We may as well say at once that the dairy industry is not in the accepted sense of the phrase, a public utility. We think the appellant is also right in asserting that there is in this case no suggestion of any monopoly or monopolistic practice. It goes without saying that those engaged in the business are in no way dependent upon public grants or franchises for the privilege of conducting their activities. But if, as must be conceded, the industry is subject to regulation in the public interest, what constitutional principle bars the state from correcting existing maladjustments by legislation touching prices? We think there is no such principle. The due process clause makes no mention of sales or prices any more than it speaks of business or contracts or buildings or other incidents of property. The thought seems nevertheless to have persisted that there is something peculiarly sacrosanct about the price one may charge for what he makes or sells, and that, however able to regulate other elements of manufacture or trade, with incidental effect upon price, the state is incapable of directly controlling the price itself. This view was negatived many years ago. *Munn* v. *Illinois*, 94 U.S. 113. . . .

It is clear that there is no closed class or category of businesses affected with a public interest, and the function of courts in the application of the Fifth and Fourteenth Amendments is to determine in each case whether circumstances vindicate the challenged regulation as a reasonable exertion of governmental authority or condemn it as arbitrary or discriminatory. *Wolff Packing Co.* v. *Industrial Court.* . . . The phrase "affected with a public interest" can, in the nature of things, mean no more than that an industry, for adequate reason, is subject to control for the public good. In several of the decisions of this court wherein the expressions "affected with a public interest," and "clothed with a public use," have been brought forward as the criteria of the validity of price control, it has been admitted that they are not susceptible of definition and form an unsatisfactory test of the constitutionality of legislation directed at business practices or prices. These decisions must rest, finally, upon the basis that the requirements of due process were not met because the laws were found arbitrary in their operation and effect. But there can be no doubt that upon proper occasion and by appropriate measures the state may regulate a business in any of its aspects, including the prices to be charged for the products or commodities it sells.

So far as the requirement of due process is concerned, and in the absence of other constitutional restriction, a state is free to adopt whatever economic policy may reasonably be deemed to promote public welfare, and to enforce that policy by legislation adapted to its purpose. The courts are without authority either to declare such policy, or, when it is declared by the legislative arm, to override it. If the laws passed are seen to have a reasonable relation to a proper legislative purpose, and are neither arbitrary nor discriminatory, the requirements of due process are satisfied, and judicial determination to that effect renders a court *functus officio.* "Whether the free operation of the normal laws of competition is a wise and wholesome rule for trade and commerce is an economic question which this court need not consider or determine." *Northern Securities Co.* v. *United States,* 193 U.S. 197, 337–8. And it is equally clear that if the legislative policy be to curb unrestrained and harmful competition by measures which are not arbitrary or discriminatory it does not lie with the courts to determine that the rule is unwise. With the wisdom of the policy adopted, with the adequacy or practicability of the law enacted to forward it, the courts are both incompetent and unauthorized to deal. . . .

Price control, like any other form of regulation, is unconstitutional only if arbitrary, discriminatory, or demonstrably irrelevant to the policy the legislature is free to adopt, and hence an unnecessary and unwarranted interference with individual liberty.

WEST COAST HOTEL COMPANY v. PARRISH
300 U.S. 379 (1937)

> A hotel company violated a Washington minimum wage regulation by paying a chambermaid less than $14.50 for 48 hours of work. The company appealed, resting its case on *Adkins* v. *Children's Hospital,* 261 U.S. 525 (1923), and the *Tipaldo* case (1936).

MR. CHIEF JUSTICE HUGHES delivered the opinion of the court. . . .

The recent case of *Morehead* v. *New York ex rel. Tipaldo,* 298 U.S. 587, came here on certiorari to the New York court which had held the New York minimum wage act for women to be invalid. A minority of this Court thought that the New York statute was distinguishable in a material feature from that involved in the Adkins case, and that for that and other reasons the New York statute should be sustained. But the Court of Appeals of New York had said that it found no material difference between the two statutes and this Court held that the "meaning of the statute" as fixed by the decision of the state court "must be accepted here as if the meaning had been specifically expressed in the enactment." . . . That view led to the affirmance by this Court of the judgment in the Morehead case, as the Court considered that the only question before it was whether the Adkins case was distinguishable and that reconsideration of that decision had not been sought. . . .

We think that the question which was not deemed to be open in the Morehead Case is open and is necessarily presented here. The Supreme Court of Washington has upheld the minimum wage statute of that state. It has decided that the statute is a reasonable exercise of the police power of the state. In reaching that conclusion, the state court has invoked principles long established by this Court in the application of the Fourteenth Amendment. The state court has refused to regard the decision in the Adkins Case as determinative and has pointed to our decisions both before and since that case as justifying its position. We are of the opinion that this ruling of the state court demands on our part a re-examination of the Adkins Case. The importance of the question, in which many states having similar laws are concerned, the close division by which the decision in the Adkins case was reached, and the economic conditions which have supervened, and in the light of which the reasonableness of the exercise of the protective power of the state must be considered, make it not only appropriate, but we think imperative, that in deciding the present case the subject should receive fresh consideration. . . .

The principle which must control our decision is not in doubt. The constitutional provision invoked is the due process clause of the Fourteenth Amendment governing the states, as the due process clause invoked in the Adkins case governed Congress. In each case the violation alleged by those attacking minimum wage regulation for women is deprivation of freedom of contract. What is this freedom? The Constitution does not speak of freedom of contract. It speaks of liberty and prohibits the deprivation of liberty without due process of law. In prohibiting that deprivation the Constitution does not recognize an absolute and uncontrollable liberty. Liberty in each of its phases has its history and connotation. But the liberty safeguarded is liberty in a social organization which requires the protection of law against the evils which menace the health, safety, morals and welfare of the people. Liberty under the Constitution is thus necessarily subject to the restraints of due process, and regulation which is reasonable in relation to its subject and is adopted in the interests of the community is due process. . . .

The minimum wage to be paid under the Washington statute is fixed after full consideration by representatives of employers, employees and the public. It may be assumed that the minimum wage is fixed in consideration of the services that are performed in the particular occupations under normal conditions. Provision is made for special licenses at less wages in the case of women who are incapable of full service. The statement of Mr. Justice Holmes in the Adkins case is pertinent: "This statute does not compel anybody to pay anything. It simply forbids employment at rates below those fixed as the minimum requirement of health and right living. It is safe to assume that women will not be employed at even the lowest wages allowed unless they earn them, or unless the employer's business can sustain the burden. In short the law in its character and operation is like hundreds of so-called police laws that have been upheld." And Chief Justice Taft forcibly pointed out the consideration which is basic in a statute of this character: "Legislatures which adopt a requirement of maximum hours or minimum wages may be presumed to believe that when sweating employers are prevented from paying unduly low wages by positive law they will continue their business, abating that part of their profits, which were wrung from the necessities of their employees, and will concede the better terms required by the law, and that while in individual cases, hardship may result, the restriction will enure to the benefit of the general class of employees in whose interest the law is passed and so to that of the community at large." . . .

We think that the views thus expressed are sound and that the decision in the Adkins case was a departure from the true application of the principles governing the regulation by the state of the relation of employer and employed. . . .

. . . What can be closer to the public interest than the health of women and their protection from unscrupulous and overreaching employers? And if the protection of women is a legitimate end of the exercise of state power, how can it be said that the requirement of the payment of a minimum wage fairly fixed in order to meet the very necessities of existence is not an admissible means to that end? The legislature of the state was clearly entitled to consider the situation of women in employment, the fact that they are in the class receiving the least pay, that their bargaining power is relatively weak, and that they are the ready victims of those who would take advantage of their necessitous circumstances. The legislature was entitled to adopt measures to reduce the evils of the "sweating system," the exploiting of workers at wages so low as to be insufficient to meet the bare cost of living thus making their very helplessness the occasion of a most injurious competition. The legislature had the right to consider that its minimum wage requirements would be an important aid in carrying out its policy of protection. The adoption of similar requirements by many states evidences a deep-seated conviction both as to the presence of the evil and as to the means adapted to check it. Legislative response to that conviction cannot be regarded as arbitrary or capricious and that is all we have to decide. Even if the wisdom of the policy be regarded as debatable and its effects uncertain, still the legislature is entitled to its judgment. . . .

. . . We may take judicial notice of the unparalleled demands for relief which arose during the recent period of depression and still continue to an alarming extent despite the degree of economic recovery which has been achieved. It is unnecessary to cite official statistics to establish what is of common knowledge through the length and breadth of the land. While in the instant case no factual brief has been presented, there is no reason to doubt that the state of Washington has encountered the same social problem that is present elsewhere. The community is not bound to provide what is in effect a subsidy for unconscionable employers. The community may direct its law-making power to correct the abuse which springs from their selfish disregard of the public interest. . . .

Our conclusion is that the case of *Adkins* v. *Children's Hospital* should be, and it is, overruled. The judgment of the Supreme Court of the State of Washington is Affirmed.

MR. JUSTICE SUTHERLAND, dissenting.

MR. JUSTICE VAN DEVANTER, MR. JUSTICE MCREYNOLDS, MR. JUSTICE BUTLER and I think the judgment of the court below should be reversed.

The principles and authorities relied upon to sustain the judgment, were considered in *Adkins* v. *Children's Hospital* and *Morehead* v. *New York ex rel. Tipaldo, supra;* and their lack of application to cases like the one in hand was pointed out. A sufficient answer to all that is now said will be found in the opinions of the court in those cases. . . .

LINCOLN FEDERAL LABOR UNION v. *NORTHWESTERN IRON CO.*
335 U.S. 525 (1949)

Appeal from the Supreme Court of Nebraska.

MR. JUSTICE BLACK delivered the opinion of the Court:

Under employment practices in the United States, employers have sometimes limited work opportunities to members of unions, sometimes to non-union members, and at other times have employed and kept their workers without regard to whether they were or were not members of a union. Employers are commanded to follow this latter employment practice in the states of North Carolina and Nebraska. A North Carolina statute and a Nebraska constitutional amendment provide that no person in those states shall be denied an opportunity to obtain or retain employment because he is or is not a member of a labor organization. To enforce this policy North Carolina and Nebraska employers are also forbidden to enter into contracts or agreements obligating themselves to exclude persons from employment because they are or are not labor union members. . . .

Fourth. It is contended that these state laws deprive appellants of their liberty without due process of law in violation of the Fourteenth Amendment. Appellants argue that the laws are specifically designed to deprive all persons within the two states of "liberty" (1) to refuse to hire or retain any person in employment because he is or is not a union member, and (2) to make a contract or agreement to engage in such employment discrimination against union or non-union members.

Much of appellants' argument here seeks to establish that due process of law is denied employees and union men by that part of these state laws that forbids them to make contracts with the employer obligating him to refuse to hire or retain non-union workers. But that part of these laws does no more than provide a method to aid enforcement of the heart of the laws, namely, their command that employers must not discriminate against either union or non-union members because they are such. If the states have constitutional power to ban such discrimination by law, they also have power to ban contracts which if performed would bring about the prohibited discrimination. *Chicago, B. & Q. R. Co.* v. *McGuire,* 219 U.S. 549, 570, 571.

Many cases are cited by appellants in which this Court has said that in some instances the due process clause protects the liberty of persons to make contracts. But none of these cases, even those according the broadest constitutional protection to the making of contracts, ever went so far as to indicate that the due process clause bars a state from prohibiting contracts to engage in conduct banned by a valid state law. So here, if the provisions in the state laws against employer discrimination are valid, it follows that the contract prohibition also is valid. *Bayside Fish Flour Co.* v. *Gentry,* 297 U.S. 422, 427. And see *Sage* v. *Hampe,* 235 U.S. 99, 104–105. We therefore turn to the decisive question under the due process contention, which is: Does the due process clause forbid a state to pass laws clearly designed to safeguard the opportunity of non-union workers to get and hold jobs, free from discrimination against them because they are non-union workers?

There was a period in which labor union members who wanted to get and hold jobs were the victims of widespread employer discrimination practices. Contracts between employers and their employees were used by employers to accomplish this anti-union employment discrimination. Before hiring workers, employers required them to sign agreements stating that the workers were not and would not become labor union members. Such anti-union practices were so obnoxious to workers that they gave these

required agreements the name of "yellow dog contracts." This hostility of workers also prompted passage of state and federal laws to ban employer discrimination against union members and to outlaw yellow dog contracts.

In 1907 this Court in *Adair* v. *United States,* 208 U.S. 161, considered the federal law which prohibited discrimination against union workers. Adair, an agent of the Louisville & Nashville Railroad Company, had been indicted and convicted for having discharged Coppage, an employee of the railroad, because Coppage was a member of the Order of Locomotive Firemen. This Court there held, over the dissents of Justices McKenna and Holmes, that the railroad, because of the due process clause of the Fifth Amendment, had a constitutional right to discriminate against union members and could therefore do so through use of yellow dog contracts. The chief reliance for this holding was *Lochner* v. *New York,* 198 U.S. 45, which had invalidated a New York law prescribing maximum hours for work in bakeries. This Court had found support for its *Lochner* holding in what had been said in *Allgeyer* v. *Louisiana,* 165 U.S. 578, a case on which appellants here strongly rely. There were strong dissents in the *Adair* and *Lochner* cases.

In 1914 this Court reaffirmed the principles of the *Adair* case in *Coppage* v. *Kansas,* 236 U.S. 1, again over strong dissents, and held that a Kansas statute outlawing yellow dog contracts denied employers and employees a liberty to fix terms of employment. For this reason the law was held invalid under the due process clause.

The *Allgeyer-Lochner-Adair-Coppage* constitutional doctrine was for some years followed by this Court. It was used to strike down laws fixing minimum wages and maximum hours in employment, laws fixing prices, and laws regulating business activities. . . .

This Court beginning at least as early as 1934, when the *Nebbia* case was decided, has steadily rejected the due process philosophy enunciated in the *Adair-Coppage* line of cases. In doing so it has consciously returned closer and closer to the earlier constitutional principle that states have power to legislate against what are found to be injurious practices in their internal commercial and business affairs, so long as their laws do not run afoul of some specific federal constitutional prohibition, or of some valid federal law. See *Nebbia* v. *United States, supra* at 523–524, and *West Coast Hotel Co.* v. *Parrish, supra* at 392–395, and cases cited. Under this constitutional doctrine the due process clause is no longer to be so broadly construed that the congress and state legislatures are put in a strait jacket when they attempt to suppress business and industrial conditions which they regard as offensive to the public welfare.

Appellants now ask us to return, at least in part, to the due process philosophy that has been deliberately discarded. Claiming that the Federal Constitution itself affords protection for union members against discrimination, they nevertheless assert that the same Constitution forbids a state from providing the same protection for non-union members. Just as we have held that the due process clause erects no obstacle to block legislative protection of union members, we now hold that legislative protection can be afforded non-union workers.

Affirmed.

MR. JUSTICE FRANKFURTER concurred in a separate opinion.

MR. JUSTICE RUTLEDGE and MR. JUSTICE MURPHY concurred in a separate opinion.

NOTE: In upholding a state regulation of business against various objections, Mr. Justice Frankfurter for the Court in *Osborn* v. *Ozlin,* 310 U.S. 53, 62 (1940), observed, "It is equally immaterial that . . . state action may run counter to the economic wisdom of Adam Smith or of J. Maynard Keynes, or may be ultimately mischievous even from the point of view of the avowed state policy. Our inquiry must be narrower." But see Paulsen, "The Persistence of Substantive Due Process in the States," 34 *Minn. Law Review* 92 (1950); Hetherington, "State Economic Regulation and Substantive Due Process of Law," 53 *Northwestern University Law Review* 13, 226 (1958).

DAY-BRITE LIGHTING v. MISSOURI

342 U.S. 421 (1952)

MR. JUSTICE DOUGLAS delivered the opinion of the Court.

Missouri has a statute, Mo. Rev. Stat., 1949, § 129.060, first enacted in 1897, which was designed to end the coercion of employees by employers in the exercise of the franchise. It provides that an employee may absent himself from his employment for four hours between the opening and closing of the polls without penalty, and that any employer who among other things deducts wages for that absence is guilty of a misdemeanor.

Appellant is a Missouri corporation doing business in St. Louis. November 5, 1946, was a day for general elections in Missouri, the polls being open from 6 a.m. to 7 p.m. One Grotemeyer, an employee of appellant, was on a shift that worked from 8 a.m. to 4:30 p.m. each day, with thirty minutes for lunch. His rate of pay was $1.60 an hour. He requested four hours from the scheduled work day to vote on November 5, 1946. That request was refused; but Grotemeyer and all other employees on his shift were allowed to leave at 3 p.m. that day, which gave them four consecutive hours to vote before the polls closed.

Grotemeyer left his work at 3 p.m. in order to vote and did not return to work that day. He was not paid for the hour and a half between 3 p.m. and 4:30 p.m. Appellant was found guilty and fined for penalizing Grotemeyer in violation of the statute. The judgment was affirmed by the Missouri Supreme Court, 362 Mo. 299, 240 S.W.2d 886, over the objection that the statute violated the Due Process and the Equal Protection Clauses of the Fourteenth Amendment and the Contract Clause of Art. I, § 10.

The liberty of contract argument pressed on us is reminiscent of the philosophy of *Lochner* v. *State of New York*, 198 U.S. 45, . . . *Coppage* v. *State of Kansas*, 236 U.S. 1; . . . *Adkins* v. *Children's Hospital of District of Columbia*, 261 U.S. 525, . . . and others of that vintage. Our recent decisions make plain that we do not sit as a superlegislature to weigh the wisdom of legislation nor to decide whether the policy which it expresses offends the public welfare. The legislative power has limits, as *Tot* v. *United States*, 319 U.S. 463, holds. But the state legislatures have constitutional authority to experiment with new techniques; they are entitled to their own standard of the public welfare; they may within extremely broad limits control practices in the business-labor field, so long as specific constitutional prohibitions are not violated and so long as conflicts with valid and controlling federal laws are avoided. . . .

West Coast Hotel Co. v. *Parrish, supra,* overruling *Adkins* v. *Children's Hospital, supra,* held constitutional a state law fixing minimum wages for women. The present statute contains in form a minimum wage requirement. There is a difference in the purpose of the legislation. Here it is not the protection of the health and morals of the citizen. Missouri by this legislation has sought to safeguard the right of suffrage by taking from employers the incentive and power to use their leverage over employees to influence the vote. But the police power is not confined to a narrow category; it extends, as stated in *Noble State Bank* v. *Haskell*, 219 U.S. 104, 111, to all the great public needs. The protection of the right of suffrage under our scheme of things is basic and fundamental.

The only semblance of substance in the constitutional objection to Missouri's law is that the employer must pay wages for a period in which the employee performs no services. Of course many forms of regulation reduce the net return of the enterprise; yet that gives rise to no constitutional infirmity. . . . Most regulations of business necessarily impose financial burdens on the enterprise for which no compensation is paid. Those are part of the costs of our civilization. Extreme cases are conjured up where an employer is required to pay wages for a period that has no relation to the legitimate end. Those cases can await decision as and when they arise. The present law has no such infirmity. It is designed to eliminate any penalty for exercising the right of suffrage and to remove a practical obstacle to getting out the vote. The public welfare is a broad and inclusive concept. The moral, social, economic, and physical well-being of the community is one part of it; the political well-being, another. The police power which is adequate to fix the financial burden for one is adequate for the other. The judgment of the legislature that time out for voting should cost the employee nothing may be a debatable one. It is indeed conceded by the opposition to be such. But if our recent cases mean anything, they leave debatable issues as respects business, economic, and social affairs to legislative decision. We could strike down this law only if we returned to the philosophy of the Lochner, Coppage, and Adkins cases.

The classification of voters so as to free employees from the domination of employers is an attempt to deal with an evil to which the one group has been exposed. The need for that classification is a matter for legislative judgment, . . . and does not amount to a denial of equal protection under the laws.

Affirmed.

MR. JUSTICE FRANKFURTER concurs in the result.

MR. JUSTICE JACKSON, dissenting. . . .

To sustain this statute by resort to the analogy of minimum wage laws seems so farfetched and unconvincing as to demonstrate its weakness rather than its strength. Because a State may require payment of a minimum wage for hours that are worked it does not follow that it may compel payment for time that is not worked. To overlook a distinction so fundamental is to confuse the point in issue. . . .

I suppose a State itself has considerable latitude to offer inducements to voters who do not value their franchise enough to vote on their own time, even if they seem to me corrupting or discriminating ones. Perhaps my difficulty with today's decision is that I cannot rise above an old-fashioned valuation of American citizenship which makes a state-imposed pay-for-voting system appear to be a confession of failure of popular representative government.

It undoubtedly is the right of every union negotiating with an employer to bargain for voting time without loss of pay. It is equally the right of any individual employee to make that part of his hire. I have no reason to doubt that a large number of voters already have voluntary arrangements which make their absence for voting without cost. But a constitutional philosophy which sanctions intervention by the State to fix terms of pay without work may be available tomorrow to give constitutional sanction to state-imposed terms of employment less benevolent.

BERMAN v. PARKER

348 U.S. 26 (1954)

MR. JUSTICE DOUGLAS delivered the opinion of the Court:

This is an appeal . . . from the judgment of a three-judge District Court which dismissed a complaint seeking to enjoin the condemnation of appellants' property under the District of Columbia Redevelopment Act of 1945. . . .

We deal, in other words, with what traditionally has been known as the police power. An attempt to define its reach or trace its outer limits is fruitless, for each case must turn on its own facts. The definition is essentially the product of legislative determinations addressed to the purposes of government, purposes neither abstractly nor historically capable of complete definition. Subject to specific constitutional limitations, when the legislature has spoken, the public interest has been declared in terms well-nigh conclusive. In such cases the legislature, not the judiciary, is the main guardian of the public needs to be served by social legislation, whether it be Congress legislating concerning the District of Columbia, see *Block* v. *Hirsh*, 256 U.S. 135, or the State legislating concerning local affairs.

See *Olsen* v. *State of Nebraska*, 313 U.S. 236; *Lincoln Federal Labor Union No. 19129, A.F. of L.* v. *Northwestern Co.*, 335 U.S. 525; *California State Ass'n Inter-Ins. Bureau* v. *Maloney*, 341 U.S. 105. This principle admits of no exception merely because the power of eminent domain is involved. The role of the judiciary in determining whether that power is being exercised for a public purpose is an extremely narrow one. See *Old Dominion Land Co.* v. *United States*, 269 U.S. 55, 66; *United States ex rel. Tennessee Valley Authority* v. *Welch*, 327 U.S. 546, 552.

Public safety, public health, morality, peace and quiet, law and order—these are some of the more conspicuous examples of the traditional application of the police power to municipal affairs. Yet they merely illustrate the scope of the power and do not delimit it. See *Noble State Bank* v. *Haskell*, 219 U.S. 104, 111. Miserable and disreputable housing conditions may do more than spread disease and crime and immorality. They may also suffocate the spirit by reducing the people who live there to the status of cattle. They may indeed make living an almost insufferable burden. They may also be an ugly sore, a blight on the community which robs it of charm, which makes it a place from which men turn. The misery of housing may despoil a community as an open sewer may ruin a river.

We do not sit to determine whether a particular housing project is or is not desirable. The concept of the public welfare is broad and inclusive. See *Day-Brite Lighting, Inc.* v. *State of Missouri*, 342 U.S. 421, 424. The values it represents are spiritual as well as physical, aesthetic as well as monetary. It is within the power of the legislature to determine that the community should be beautiful as well as healthy, spacious as well as clean, well-balanced as well as carefully patrolled. In the present case, the Congress and its authorized agencies have made determinations that take into account a wide variety of values. It is not for us to reappraise them. If those who govern the District of Columbia decide that the Nation's capital should be beautiful as well as sanitary, there is nothing in the Fifth Amendment that stands in the way.

Once the object is within the authority of Congress, the right to realize it through the exercise of eminent domain is clear. For the power of eminent domain is merely the means to the end. See *Luxton* v. *North River Bridge Co.*, 153 U.S. 525, 529–530; *United States* v. *Gettysburg Electric R. Co.*, 160 U.S. 668, 679. Once the object is within the authority of Congress, the means by which it will be attained is also for Congress to determine. Here one of the means chosen is the use of private enterprise for redevelopment of the area. Appellants argue that this makes the project a taking from one businessman for the benefit of another businessman. But the means of executing the project are for Congress and Congress alone to determine, once the public purpose has been established. See *Luxton* v. *North River Bridge Co.*, *supra;* cf. *Highland* v. *Russell Car Co.*, 279 U.S. 253. The public end may be as well or better served through an agency of private enterprise than through a department of government—or so the Congress might conclude.

We cannot say that public ownership is the sole method of promoting the public purposes of community redevelopment projects. What we have said also disposes of any contention concerning the fact that certain property owners in the area may be permitted to repurchase their properties for redevelopment in harmony with the overall plan. That, too, is a legitimate means which Congress and its agencies may adopt, if they choose.

In the present case, Congress and its authorized agencies attack the problem of the blighted parts of the community on an area rather than on a structure-by-structure basis. That, too, is opposed by appellants. They maintain that since their building does not imperil health or safety nor contribute to the making of a slum or a blighted area, it cannot be swept into a redevelopment plan by the mere dictum of the Planning Commission or the Commissioners. The particular uses to be made of the land in the project were determined with regard to the needs of the particular community. The experts concluded that if the community were to be healthy, if it were not to revert again to a blighted or slum area, as though possessed by a congenital disease, the area must be planned as a whole. It was not enough, they believed, to remove existing buildings that were insanitary or unsightly. It was important to redesign the whole area so as to eliminate the conditions that cause slums—the overcrowding of dwellings, the lack of parks, the lack of adequate streets and alleys, the absence of recreational areas, the lack of light and air, the presence of outmoded street patterns. It was believed that the piecemeal approach, the removal of individual structures that were offensive, would be only a palliative. The entire area needed redesigning so that a balanced, integrated plan could be developed for the region, including not only new homes but also schools, churches, parks, streets, and shopping centers. In this way it was hoped that the cycle of decay of the area could be controlled and the birth of future slums prevented. Cf. *Gohld Realty Co.* v. *City of*

Hartford, 141 Conn. 135, 141–144, 104 A.2d 365, 368–370; *Hunter v. Norfolk Redevelopment Authority,* 195 Va. 326, 338–339, 78 S.E.2d 893, 900–901. Such diversification in future use is plainly relevant to the maintenance of the desired housing standards and therefore within congressional power.

If owner after owner were permitted to resist these redevelopment programs on the ground that his particular property was not being used against the public interest, integrated plans for redevelopment would suffer greatly. The argument pressed on us is, indeed, a plea to substitute the landowner's standard of the public need for the standard prescribed by Congress. But as we have already stated, community redevelop-

ment programs need not, by force of the Constitution, be on a piecemeal basis—lot by lot, building by building.

It is not for the courts to oversee the choice of the boundary line nor to sit in review on the size of a particular project area. Once the question of the public purpose has been decided, the amount and character of land to be taken for the project and the need for a particular tract to complete the integrated plan rests in the discretion of the legislative branch. See *Shoemaker* v. *United States,* 147 U.S. 282, 298; *United States ex rel. Tennessee Valley Authority* v. *Welch, supra,* 327 U.S. at page 554; *United States* v. *Carmack,* 329 U.S. 230, 247. . . .

UNITED STATES v. CAUSBY

328 U.S. 256 (1946)

MR. JUSTICE DOUGLAS delivered the opinion of the Court.

This is a case of first impression. The problem presented is whether respondents' property was taken within the meaning of the Fifth Amendment by frequent and regular flights of army and navy aircraft over respondents' land at low altitudes. The Court of Claims held that there was a taking and entered judgment for respondent, one judge dissenting. 104 Ct. Cls. 342, 60 F. Supp. 751. The case is here on a petition for a writ of certiorari which we granted because of the importance of the question presented. . . .

The airplane is part of the modern environment of life, and the inconveniences which it causes are normally not compensable under the Fifth Amendment. The airspace, apart from the immediate reaches above the land, is part of the public domain. We need not determine at this time what those precise limits are. Flights over private land are not a taking, unless they are so low and so frequent as to be a direct and immediate interference with the enjoyment and use of the land. We need

not speculate on that phase of the present case. For the findings of the Court of Claims plainly establish that there was a diminution in value of the property and that the frequent, low-level flights were the direct and immediate cause. We agree with the Court of Claims that a servitude has been imposed upon the land. . . .

Since on this record it is not clear whether the easement taken is a permanent or a temporary one, it would be premature for us to consider whether the amount of the award made by the Court of Claims was proper.

The judgment is reversed and the cause is remanded to the Court of Claims so that it may make the necessary findings in conformity with this opinion.

Reversed.

MR. JUSTICE JACKSON took no part in the consideration or decision of this case.

MR. JUSTICE BLACK, dissenting.

The Fifth Amendment provides that "private property" shall not "be taken for public use, without just compensation." The Court holds today that the Government has "taken" respondents' property by repeatedly flying Army bombers directly above respondents' land at a height of eighty-three feet where the light and noise from these planes caused respondents to lose sleep and their chickens to be killed. Since the effect of the Court's decision is to limit, by the imposition of relatively absolute constitutional barriers, possible future adjustments through legislation and regulation which might become necessary with the growth of air transportation, and since in my view the Constitution does not contain such barriers, I dissent. . . .

No greater confusion could be brought about in the coming age of air transportation than that which would result were courts by constitutional interpretation to hamper Congress in its efforts to keep the air free. Old concepts of private ownership of land should not be introduced into the field of air regulation. I have no doubt that Congress will, if not handicapped by judicial interpretations of the Constitution, preserve the freedom of the air, and at the same time, satisfy the just claims of aggrieved persons. The noise of newer, larger, and more powerful planes may grow louder and louder and disturb people more and more. But the solution of the problems precipitated by these technological advances and new ways of living cannot come about through the application of rigid Constitutional restraints formulated and enforced by the courts. What adjustments may have to be made, only the future can reveal. It seems certain, however, that courts do not possess the techniques or the personnel to consider and act upon the complex combinations of factors entering into the problems. The contribution of courts must be made through the awarding of damages for injuries suffered from the flying of planes, or by the granting of injunctions to prohibit their flying. When these two simple remedial devices are elevated to a Constitutional level under the Fifth Amendment, as the Court today seems to have done, they can stand as obstacles to better adapted techniques that might be offered by experienced experts and accepted by Congress. Today's opinion is, I fear, an opening wedge for an unwarranted judicial interference with the power of Congress to develop solutions for new and vital and national problems. In my opinion this case should be reversed on the ground that there has been no "taking" in the Constitutional sense.

MR. JUSTICE BURTON joins in this dissent.

2. ECONOMIC EQUAL PROTECTION

The equal protection clause of the Fourteenth Amendment, along with due process, for a while was also pressed into the service of laissez-faire. In *Connolly* v. *Union Sewer Pipe Co.*, 184 U.S. 540 (1902), for example, a state anti-trust act was held invalid because it covered businessmen, but not farmers. This was overruled in *Tigner* v. *Texas*, 310 U.S. 141 (1940). The new approach to equal protection, as well as to due process, is set out in the following cases.

WILLIAMSON v. LEE OPTICAL

348 U.S. 483 (1955)

An Oklahoma statute prohibited opticians from fitting or duplicating eyeglass lenses without a prescription from an ophthalmologist or optometrist (Sec. 2); advertisement of eyeglasses, etc. (Sec. 3); and retail stores from furnishing space therein to any person purporting to perform eye examinations and visual care (Sec. 4). Sections 2 and 4 were challenged as violations of due process; Section 3 was challenged as a violation of equal protection in that it applied to opticians, etc., but not to the sellers of ready-to-wear eyeglasses.

MR. JUSTICE DOUGLAS delivered the opinion of the Court: . . .

[As to Sec. 2, the] Oklahoma law may exact a needless, wasteful requirement in many cases. But it is for the legislature, not the courts, to balance the advantages and disadvantages of the new requirement. It appears that in many cases the optician can easily supply the new frames or new lenses without reference to the old written prescription. It also appears that many written prescriptions contain no directive data in regard to fitting spectacles to the face. But in some cases the directions contained in the prescription are essential, if the glasses are to be fitted so as to correct the particular defects of vision or alleviate the eye condition. The legislature might have concluded that the frequency of occasions when a prescription is necessary was sufficient to justify this regulation of the fitting of eyeglasses. Likewise, when it is necessary to duplicate a lens, a written prescription may or may not be necessary. But the legislature might have concluded that one was needed often enough to require one in every case. Or the legislature may have concluded that eye examinations were so critical, not only for correction of vision but also for detection of latent ailments or diseases, that every change in frames and every duplication of a lens should be accompanied by a prescription from a medical expert. To be sure, the present law does not require a new examination of the eyes every time the frames are changed or the lenses duplicated. For if the old prescription is on file with the optician, he can go ahead and make the new fitting or duplicate the lenses. But the law need not be in every respect logically consistent with its aims to be constitutional. It is enough that there is an evil at hand for correction, and that it might be thought that the particular legislative measure was a rational way to correct it.

The day is gone when this Court uses the due process clause of the Fourteenth Amendment to strike down state laws, regulatory of business and industrial conditions, because they may be unwise, improvident or out of harmony with a particular school of thought. See *Nebbia* v. *New York,* 291 U.S. 502; *West Coast Hotel Co.* v. *Parrish,* 300 U.S. 379; *Olsen v. Nebraska,* 313 U.S. 236; *Lincoln Federal Labor Union, A. F. L.* v. *Northwestern Iron & Metal Co.,* 335 U.S. 525; *Daniel* v. *Family Secur. Life Ins. Co.,* 336 U.S. 220; *Day-Brite Lighting, Inc.* v. *Missouri,* 342 U.S. 421. We emphasize again what Chief Justice Waite said in *Munn* v. *Illinois,* 94 U.S. 113, "For protection against abuses by legislatures, the people must resort to the polls, not to the courts."

[As to Sec. 3, the] problem of legislative classification is a perennial one, admitting of no doctrinaire definition. Evils in the same field may be of different dimensions and proportions, requiring different remedies. Or so the legislature may think. *Tigner* v. *Texas,* 310 U.S. 141. Or the reform may take one step at a time, addressing itself to the phase of the problem which seems most acute to the legislative mind. . . . The legislature may select one phase of one field and apply a remedy there, neglecting the others. . . . The prohibition of the equal protection clause goes no further than the invidious discrimination. We cannot say that that point has been reached here. For all this record shows, the ready-to-wear branch of this business may not loom large in Oklahoma or may present problems of regulation distinct from the other branch.

[As to Sec. 4, it] seems to us that this regulation distinct from the other branch. footing as the denial to corporations of the right to practice dentistry. *Semler* v. *Oregon State Dental Examiners, supra* (294 U.S. 611). It is an attempt to free the profession, to as great an extent as possible, from all taints of commercialism. It certainly might be easy for an optometrist with space in a retail store to be merely a front for the retail establishment. In any case, the opportunity for that nexus may be too great for safety, if the eye doctor is allowed inside the retail store. Moreover, it may be deemed important to effective regulation that the eye doctor be restricted to geographical locations that reduce the temptations of commercialism. Geographical location may be an important consideration in a legislative program which aims to raise the treatment of the human eye to a strictly professional level. We cannot say that the regulation has no rational relation to that objective and therefore is beyond constitutional bounds.

[The judgment of the lower court was reversed insofar as it held the Oklahoma law invalid.]

MR. JUSTICE HARLAN took no part in the consideration or decision of these cases.

RAILWAY EXPRESS AGENCY v. NEW YORK

336 U.S. 106 (1949)

MR. JUSTICE DOUGLAS delivered the opinion of the Court.

Section 124 of the Traffic Regulations of the City of New York promulgated by the Police Commissioner provides:

"No person shall operate, or cause to be operated, in or upon any street an advertising vehicle; provided that nothing herein contained shall prevent the putting of business notices upon business delivery vehicles, so long as such vehicles are engaged in the usual business or regular work of the owner and not used merely or mainly for advertising."

Appellant is engaged in a nation-wide express business. It operates about 1,900 trucks in New York City and sells the space on the exterior sides of these trucks for advertising. That advertising is for the most part unconnected with its own business. It was convicted in the magistrates court and fined. The judgment of conviction was sustained in the Court of Special Sessions. . . . The Court of Appeals affirmed without opinion by a divided vote. . . . The case is here on appeal . . .

The Court of Special Sessions concluded that advertising on vehicles using the streets of New York City constitutes a distraction to vehicle drivers and to pedestrians alike and therefore affects the safety of the public in the use of the street. We do not sit to weigh evidence on the due process issue in order to determine whether the regulation is sound or appropriate; nor is it our function to pass judgment on its wisdom. See *Olsen* v. *State of Nebraska*, 313 U.S. 236. We would be trespassing on one of the most intensely local and specialized of all municipal problems if we held that this regulation had no relation to the traffic problem of New York City. It is the judgment of the local authorities that it does have such a relation. And nothing has been advanced which shows that to be palpably false.

The question of equal protection of the laws is pressed more strenuously on us. It is pointed out that the regulation draws the line between advertisements of products sold by the owner of the truck and general advertisements. It is argued that unequal treatment on the basis of such a distinction is not justified by the aim and purpose of the regulation. It is said, for example, that one of appellant's trucks carrying the advertisement of a commercial house would not cause any greater distraction of pedestrians and vehicles drivers than if the commercial house carried the same advertisement on its own truck. Yet the regulation allows the latter to do what the former is forbidden from doing. It is therefore contended that the classification which the regulation makes has no relation to the traffic problems since a violation turns not on what kind of advertisements are carried on trucks but on whose trucks they are carried.

That, however, is a superficial way of analyzing the problem, even if we assume that it is premised on the correct construction of the regulation. The local authorities may well have concluded that those who advertise their own wares on their trucks do not present the same traffic problem in view of the nature or extent of the advertising which they use. It would take a degree of omniscience which we lack to say that such is not the case. If that judgment is correct, the advertising displays that are exempt have less incidence on traffic than those of appellants.

We cannot say that that judgment is not an allowable one. Yet if it is, the classification has relation to the purpose for which it is made and does not contain the kind of discrimination against which the Equal Protection Clause affords protection. It is by such practical considerations based on experience rather than by theoretical inconsistencies that the question of equal protection is to be answered. *Patsone* v. *Commonwealth of Pennsylvania*, 232 U.S. 138, 144. . . . And the fact that New York City sees fit to eliminate from traffic this kind of distraction but does not touch what may be even greater ones in a different category, such as the vivid displays on Times Square, is immaterial. It is no requirement of equal protection that all evils of the same genus be eradicated or none at all. . . .

Affirmed.

MR. JUSTICE RUTLEDGE acquiesces in the Court's opinion and judgment, *dubitante* on the question of equal protection of the laws.

MR. JUSTICE JACKSON, concurring.

There are two clauses of the Fourteenth Amendment which this Court may invoke to invalidate ordinances by which municipal governments seek to solve their local problems. One says that no state shall "deprive any person of life, liberty, or property, without due process of law." The other declares that no state shall "deny to any person within its jurisdiction the equal protection of the laws."

My philosophy as to the relative readiness with which we should resort to these two clauses is almost diametrically opposed to the philosophy which prevails on this Court. While claims of denial of equal protection are frequently asserted, they are rarely sustained. But the Court frequently uses the due process clause to strike down measures taken by municipalities to deal with activities in their streets and public places which the local authorities consider to create hazards, annoyances or discomforts to their inhabitants. . . .

The burden should rest heavily upon one who would persuade us to use the due process clause to strike down a substantive law or ordinance. Even its provident use against municipal regulations frequently disables all government—state, municipal and federal—from dealing with the conduct in question because the requirement of due process is also applicable to State and Federal Governments. Invalidation of a statute or an ordinance on due process grounds leaves ungoverned and ungovernable conduct which many people find objectionable.

Invocation of the equal protection clause, on the other hand, does not disable any governmental body from dealing with the subject at hand. It merely means that the prohibition or regulation must have a broader impact. I regard it as a salutary doctrine that cities, states and the Federal Government must exercise their powers so as not to discriminate between their inhabitants except upon some reasonable differentiation fairly related to the object of regulation. This equality is not merely abstract justice. The framers of the Constitution knew, and we should not forget today, that there is no more effective practical guaranty against arbitrary and unreasonable government than to require that the principles of law which officials would impose upon a minority must be imposed generally. Conversely, nothing opens the door to arbitrary action so effectively as to allow those officials to pick and choose only a few to whom they will apply legislation and thus to escape the political retribution that might be visited upon them if larger numbers were affected. Courts can take no better measure to assure that laws will be just than to require that laws be equal in operation. . . .

NOTE: In *Morey* v. *Doud,* 354 U.S. 457 (1957), the Court found that Illinois had reached the point of invidious discrimination in exempting the American Express Company from the requirement that any firm selling or issuing money orders in that state must secure a license and submit to state regulation. Justices Black, Frankfurter, and Harlan dissented. As Mr. Justice Frankfurter put it, "I regretfully find myself unable to appreciate why the State . . . may not choose to allow small units to carry on a business so fraught with public interests [only] under the regulations devised by the statute . . . while at the same time it finds such measures of control needless in a case of (as the Court admitted) 'a world-wide enterprise of unquestioned solvency and high financial standing.' "

It is crucial that after a decision like that in *Morey* v. *Doud,* the state is free to continue its policy of protecting the consumer from fly-by-night money-order dealers: it need only eliminate the "discrimination" in favor of the American Express Company. Consider the position of the state if the law had been invalidated on due process laissez-faire grounds.

As to application of the equal protection clause in the context of race relations, see Part Four, V.

II. THE BILL OF RIGHTS AND THE CIVIL WAR AMENDMENTS

The markedly Federalist (mercantile) orientation of the Founding Fathers is starkly revealed in their careful safeguards for commercial interests (see, for example, Art. I, Secs. 9 and 10) and their contrasting failure to provide a Bill of Rights. Of course the Federalist leader, Hamilton, explained the omission in seemingly sympathetic terms, ". . . why declare that things shall not be done which there is no power to do? Why, for instance, should it be said that the liberty of the press shall not be restrained, when no power is given by which restrictions may be imposed . . . ?" The argument is hardly convincing in view of Hamilton's own doctrine of implied powers—a doctrine which he developed to support his projected national bank and which the Court embraced in *McCulloch* v. *Maryland.* In any event the omission and Hamilton's rationalization of it were not acceptable to Thomas Jefferson and those of his persuasion. "A bill of rights is what the people are entitled to against every government on earth . . . and what no just government should refuse. . . ." To obtain ratification of the Constitution, its sponsors were compelled to concede the point. A compromise was achieved by ratification with the understanding that amendments would be considered at once. Accordingly Madison introduced in the first Congress a series of proposals, ten of which (the first ten amendments) were adopted within two years and are commonly called the Bill of Rights. Of these the first three deal essentially with substantive, and the next five with procedural, matters. The last two are concerned, not with specific rights but with general principles. It is crucial that the first eight amendments apply only to the national government—they do not protect the rights of the individual from *state* intrusion! As Marshall's Court held long ago, "In almost every convention by which the Constitution was adopted, amendments to guard against the abuse of power were recommended. The amendments demanded security against the apprehended encroachments of the general government—not against those of the local governments. In compliance with a sentiment thus generally expressed, to quiet fears thus extensively entertained, amendments [the Bill of Rights] were . . . adopted. These amendments contain no expression indicating an intention to apply them to the state governments. This Court cannot so apply them." *Barron* v. *Baltimore*, 7 Peters 243, 250 (1833). This has always been the accepted interpretation.

Later experience resulted in the so-called Civil War Amendments—the Thirteenth, Fourteenth, and Fifteenth. These in a sense are an extension of the Bill of Rights plainly directed against intrusion *by the states* upon basic procedural and substantive liberties of the individual. Apart from the very concrete provisions as to slavery, citizenship, and voting, the interests protected are expressed in general, abstract terms. (See the privileges and immunities, due process, and equal protection clauses of the Fourteenth Amendment.) To obviate the vagueness—to supply standards for adjudication—it has been suggested from time to time that what is written in the Bill of Rights (and no more) should be read into the broad generalities of the Fourteenth Amendment. This in effect would make the Bill of Rights applicable to the states. As a practical matter, though not in theory, *Barron* v. *Baltimore* would be destroyed. The *Palko* answer to this suggestion (building upon the earlier *Hurtado* approach) is orthodox, but in recent years it has been vigorously challenged by Justices Black and Douglas. Their views, and Mr. Justice Frankfurter's defense of the established position, are found in *Adamson* v. *California*. The dissenters' position presumably is designed to enlarge states' rights with respect to economic affairs and restrict them with respect to civil liberty—a reaction no doubt to the old laissez-faire perversion of the Fourteenth Amendment. (See Part Four, I.)

Obviously all this has federalistic implications. The broader the shield of the Fourteenth Amendment for the protection of the individual, the less that is left for states' rights. Conversely the narrower the liberties of the individual, the greater the power of the states. Viewed in this light the *Palko* rule is a compromise between extreme parochialism and extreme libertarianism. It gives the states the greatest possible freedom compatible with full federal protection for the minimum, basic essentials of human liberty. This compromise is especially significant when it is recalled that the Civil War Amendments do not merely restrain the states; they also delegate power to the national government.

For in view of judicial failure to protect the Negro in *Dred Scott's* case, 19 Howard 393 (1857), these amendments authorize Congress by appropriate legislation to enforce the newly created civil rights. Of course this does not preclude the more traditional forms of judicial enforcement of constitutional provisions.

HURTADO v. *CALIFORNIA*

110 U.S. 516 (1884)

The California Constitution of 1879 authorized criminal charges to be brought by information rather than by grand jury indictment. Hurtado was found guilty of murder in a proceeding initiated by an information.

MR. JUSTICE MATHEWS delivered the opinion of the court. . . .

The proposition of law we are asked to affirm is that an indictment or presentment by a grand jury, as known to the common law of England, is essential to that "due process of law," when applied to prosecutions for felonies, which is secured and guaranteed by this provision of the Constitution of the United States, and which accordingly it is forbidden to the States respectively to dispense with in the administration of criminal law. . . .

It is maintained on behalf of the plaintiff in error that the phrase "due process of law" is equivalent to "law of the land," as found in the 29th chapter of Magna Charta; that by immemorial usage it has acquired a fixed, definite, and technical meaning; that it refers to and includes, not only the general principles of public liberty and private right, which lie at the foundation of all free government, but the very institutions which, venerable by time and custom, have been tried by experience and found fit and necessary for the preservation of those principles, and which, having been the birthright and inheritance of every English subject, crossed the Atlantic with the colonists and were transplanted and established in the fundamental laws of the State; that, having been originally introduced into the Constitution of the United States as a limitation upon the powers of the government, brought into being by that instrument, it has now been added as an additional security to the individual against oppression by the States themselves; that one of these institutions is that of the grand jury, an indictment or presentment by which against the accused in cases of alleged felonies is an essential part of due process of law, in order that he may not be harassed or destroyed by prosecutions founded only upon private malice or popular fury. . . .

The Constitution of the United States was ordained . . . by descendants of Englishmen, who inherited the traditions of English law and history; but it was made for an undefined and expanding future, and for a people gathered and to be gathered from many nations and of many tongues. And while we take just pride in the principles and institutions of the common law, we are not to forget that in lands where other systems of jurisprudence prevail, the ideas and processes of civil justice are also not unknown. Due process of law, in spite of the absolutism of continental governments, is not alien to that code which survived the Roman Empire as the foundation of modern civilization in Europe. . . . There is nothing in Magna Charta, rightly construed as a broad charter of public right and law, which ought to exclude the best ideas of all systems and of every age; and as it was the characteristic principle of the common law to draw its inspiration from every fountain of justice, we are not to assume that the sources of its supply have been exhausted. On the contrary, we should expect that the new and various experiences of our own situation and system will mould and shape it into new and not less useful forms. . . .

In this country written constitutions were deemed essential to protect the rights and liberties of the people against the encroachments of power delegated to their governments, and the provisions of Magna Charta were incorporated into Bills of Rights. They were limitations upon all the powers of government, legislative as well as executive and judicial.

It necessarily happened, therefore, that as these broad and general maxims of liberty and justice held in our system a different place and performed a different function from their position and office in English constitutional history and law, they would receive and justify a corresponding and more comprehensive interpretation. Applied in England only as guards against executive usurpation and tyranny, here they have become bulwarks also against arbitrary legislation; but, in that application, as it would be incongruous to measure and restrict them by the ancient customary English law, they must be held to guarantee not particular forms of procedure, but the very substance of individual rights to life, liberty, and property. . . .

We are to construe this phrase in the Fourteenth Amendment by the *usus loquendi* of the Constitution itself. The same words are contained in the Fifth Amendment. That article makes specific and express provision for perpetuating the institution of the grand jury, so far as relates to prosecutions for the more aggravated crimes under the laws of the United States. It declares that:

"No person shall be held to answer for a capital or otherwise infamous crime, unless on a presentment or indictment of a grand jury, except in cases arising in the land or naval forces, or in the militia when in actual service in time of war or public danger; nor shall any person be subject for the same offence to be twice put in jeopardy of life or limb; nor shall he be compelled in any criminal case to be witness against himself." [It then immediately adds]: "Nor

be deprived of life, liberty, or property, without due process of law."

According to a recognized canon of interpretation, especially applicable to formal and solemn instruments of constitutional law, we are forbidden to assume, without clear reason to the contrary, that any part of this most important amendment is superfluous. The natural and obvious inference is, that in the sense of the Constitution "due process of law" was not meant or intended to include, *ex vi termini*, the institution and procedure of a grand jury in any case. The conclusion is equally irresistible, that when the same phrase was employed in the Fourteenth Amendment to restrain the action of the States, it was used in the same sense and with no greater extent; and that if in the adoption of that amendment it had been part of its purpose to perpetuate the institution of the grand jury in all the States, it would have embodied, as did the Fifth Amendment, express declarations to that effect. Due process of law in the latter refers to that law of the land which derives its authority from the legislative powers conferred upon congress by the Constitution of the United States, exercised within the limits therein prescribed, and interpreted according to the principles of the common law. In the Fourteenth Amendment, by parity of reason, it refers to that law of the land in each State, which derives its authority from the inherent and reserved powers of the State, exerted within the limits of those fundamental principles of liberty and justice which lie at the base of all our civil and political institutions, and the greatest security for which resides in the right of the people to make their own laws, and alter them at their pleasure. . . . Affirmed.

MR. JUSTICE HARLAN dissenting. . . .

I omit further citations of authorities, which are numerous, to prove that, according to the settled usages and modes of proceeding existing under the common and statute law of England at the settlement of this country, information in capital cases was not consistent with the "law of the land," or with "due process of law." Such was the understanding of the patriotic men who established free institutions upon this continent. Almost the identical words of Magna Charta were incorporated into most of the State Constitutions before the adoption of our national Constitution. When they declared, in substance, that no person should be deprived of life, liberty, or property, except by the judgment of his peers or the law of the land, they intended to assert his right to the same guaranties that were given in the mother country by the great charter and the laws passed in furtherance of its fundamental principles. . . .

But it is said that the framers of the Constitution did not suppose that due process of law necessarily required for a capital offence the institution and procedure of a grand jury, else they would not in the same amendment prohibiting the deprivation of life, liberty, or property, without due process of law, have made specific and express provision for a grand jury where the crime is capital or otherwise infamous; therefore, it is argued, the requirement by the Fourteenth Amendment of due process of law in all proceedings involving life, liberty, and property, without specific reference to grand juries in any case whatever, was not intended as a restriction upon the power which it is claimed the States previously had, so far as the express restrictions of the national Constitution are concerned, to dispense altogether with grand juries.

This line of argument, it seems to me, would lead to results which are inconsistent with the vital principles of republican government. If the presence in the Fifth Amendment of a specific provision for grand juries in capital cases, alongside the provision for due process of law in proceedings involving life, liberty, or property, is held to prove that "due process of law" did not, in the judgment of the framers of the Constitution, necessarily require a grand jury in capital cases, inexorable logic would require it to be, likewise, held that the right not to be put twice in jeopardy of life and limb for the same

offence, nor compelled in a criminal case to testify against one's self—rights and immunities also specifically recognized in the Fifth Amendment—were not protected by that due process of law required by the settled usages and proceedings existing under the common and statute law of England at the settlement of this country. More than that, other amendments of the Constitution proposed at the same time, expressly recognize the right of persons to just compensation for private property taken for public use; their right, when accused of crime, to be informed of the nature and cause of the accusation against them, and to a speedy and public trial, by an impartial jury of the State and district wherein the crime was committed; to be confronted by the witnesses against them; and to have compulsory process for obtaining witnesses in their favor. Will it be claimed that these rights were not secured by the "law of the land" or by "due process of law," as declared and established at the foundation of our government? Are they to be excluded from the enumeration of the fundamental principles of liberty and justice, and, therefore, not embraced by "due process of law?" If the argument of my brethren be sound, those rights—although universally recognized at the establishment of our institutions as secured by that due process of law which for centuries had been the foundation of Anglo-Saxon liberty—were not deemed by our fathers as essential in the due process of law prescribed by our Constitution; because,—such seems to be the argument—had they been regarded as involved in due process of law they would not have been specifically and expressly provided for, but left to the protection given by the general clause forbidding the deprivation of life, liberty, or property without due process of law. Further, the reasoning of the opinion indubitably leads to the conclusion that but for the specific provisions made in the Constitution for the security of the personal rights enumerated the general inhibition against deprivation of life, liberty, and property without due process of law would not have prevented congress from enacting a statute in derogation of each of them. . . .

Now, it is a fact of momentous interest in this discussion, that, when the Fourteenth Amendment was submitted and adopted, the Bill of Rights and the constitutions of twenty-seven States expressly forbade criminal prosecutions, by information, for capital cases; while, in the remaining ten states, they were impliedly forbidden by a general clause declaring that no person should be deprived of life otherwise than by "the judgment of his peers or the law of the land," or "without due process of law." It may be safely affirmed that, when that Amendment was adopted, a criminal prosecution, by information, for a crime involving life, was not permitted in any one of the States composing the Union. So that the court, in this case, while conceding that

the requirement of due process of law protects the fundamental principles of liberty and justice, adjudges, in effect, that an immunity or right, recognized at the common law to be essential to personal security, jealously guarded by our national Constitution against violation by any tribunal or body exercising authority under the general government, and expressly or impliedly recognized, *when the Fourteenth Amendment was adopted,* in the Bill of Rights or Constitution of every State in the Union, is, yet, not a fundamental principle in governments established, as those of the States of the Union are, to secure to the citizen liberty and justice, and, therefore, is not involved in that due process of law required in proceedings conducted under the sanction of a State.

MR. JUSTICE FIELD did not take part in the decision of this case.

PALKO v. CONNECTICUT

302 U.S. 319 (1937)

> In a state trial court Palko was found guilty of second-degree murder and sentenced to life imprisonment. Believing that the trial court had committed errors to Palko's advantage, the state appealed as authorized by state legislation. A new trial resulted, notwithstanding Palko's plea of double jeopardy. The second trial brought a conviction of first-degree murder and a death sentence. Palko appealed.

Appeal from the Supreme Court of Errors of Connecticut.

MR. JUSTICE CARDOZO delivered the opinion of the Court:

A statute of Connecticut permitting appeals in criminal cases to be taken by the state is challenged by appellant as an infringement of the Fourteenth Amendment. . . .

1. The execution of the sentence will not deprive appellant of his life without the process of law assured to him by the Fourteenth Amendment of the Federal Constitution.

The argument for appellant is that what-

ever is forbidden by the Fifth Amendment is forbidden by the Fourteenth also. The Fifth Amendment, which is not directed to the states, but solely to the federal government, creates immunity from double jeopardy. No person shall be "subject for the same offense to be twice put in jeopardy of life or limb." The Fourteenth Amendment ordains, "nor shall any State deprive any person of life, liberty, or property, without due process of law." To retry a defendant, though under one indictment and only one, subjects him, it is said, to double jeopardy in violation of the Fifth Amendment, if the prosecution is one on behalf of the United States. From this the consequence is said to follow that there is a denial of life or liberty without due process of law, if the prosecution is one on behalf of the People of a State. Thirty-five years ago a like argument was made to this court in *Dreyer* v. *Illinois,* 187 U.S. 71, 85, and was passed without consideration of its merits as unnecessary to a decision. The question is now here.

We do not find it profitable to mark the precise limits of the prohibition of double jeopardy in federal prosecutions. The subject was much considered in *Kepner* v. *United States,* 195 U.S. 100, decided in 1904 by a closely divided court. The view was there expressed for a majority of the court that the prohibition was not confined to jeopardy in a new and independent case. It forbade jeopardy in the same case if the new trial was at the instance of the government and not upon defendant's motion. Cf. *Trono* v. *United States,* 199 U.S. 521. All this may be assumed for the purpose of the case at hand, though the dissenting opinions (195 U.S. 100, 134, 137) show how much was to be said in favor of a different ruling. Right-minded men, as we learn from those opinions, could reasonably, even if mistakenly, believe that a second trial was lawful in prosecutions subject to the Fifth Amendment, if it was all in the same case. Even more plainly, right-minded men could reasonably believe that in espousing that conclusion they were not favoring a practice repugnant to the conscience of mankind. Is double jeopardy in such circumstances, if double jeopardy it must be called, a denial of due process forbidden to the States? The tyranny of labels, *Snyder* v. *Massachusetts,* 291 U.S. 97, 114, must not lead us to leap to a conclusion that a word which in one set of facts may stand for oppression or enormity is of like effect in every other.

We have said that in appellant's view the Fourteenth Amendment is to be taken as embodying the prohibitions of the Fifth. His thesis is even broader. Whatever would be a violation of the original bill of rights (Amendments I to VIII) if done by the federal government is now equally unlawful by force of the Fourteenth Amendment if

done by a state. There is no such general rule.

The Fifth Amendment provides, among other things, that no person shall be held to answer for a capital or otherwise infamous crime unless on presentment or indictment of a grand jury. This court has held that, in prosecutions by a state, presentment or indictment by a grand jury may give way to informations at the instance of a public officer. *Hurtado* v. *California,* 110 U.S. 516; *Gaines* v. *Washington,* 277 U.S. 81, 86. The Fifth Amendment provides also that no person shall be compelled in any criminal case to be a witness against himself. This court has said that, in prosecutions by a state, the exemption will fail if the state elects to end it. *Twining* v. *New Jersey,* 211 U.S. 78, 106, 111, 112. Cf. *Snyder* v. *Massachusetts, supra,* p. 105; *Brown* v. *Mississippi,* 297 U.S. 278, 285. The Sixth Amendment calls for a jury trial in criminal cases and the Seventh for a jury trial in civil cases at common law where the value in controversy shall exceed twenty dollars. This court has ruled that consistently with those amendments trial by jury may be modified by a state or abolished altogether. *Walker* v. *Sauvinet,* 92 U.S. 90; *Maxwell* v. *Dow,* 176 U.S. 581; *New York Central R. Co.* v. *White,* 243 U.S. 188, 208; *Wagner Electric Co.* v. *Lyndon,* 262 U.S. 226, 232. As to the Fourth Amendment, one should refer to *Weeks* v. *United States,* 232 U.S. 383, 398, and as to other provisions of the Sixth, to *West* v. *Louisiana,* 194 U.S. 258.

On the other hand, the due process clause of the Fourteenth Amendment may make it unlawful for a state to abridge by its statutes the freedom of speech which the First Amendment safeguards against encroachment by the Congress, *De Jonge* v. *Oregon,* 299 U.S. 353, 364; *Herndon* v. *Lowry,* 301 U.S. 242, 259; or the like freedom of the press, *Grosjean* v. *American Press Co.,* 297 U.S. 233; *Near* v. *Minnesota,* 283, U.S. 697, 707; or the free exercise of religion, *Hamilton* v. *Regents of University,* 293 U.S. 245, 262; Cf. *Grosjean* v. *American Press Co., supra; Pierce* v. *Society of Sisters,* 268 U.S. 510; or the right of peaceable assembly, without which speech would be unduly trammeled, *De Jonge* v. *Oregon, supra; Herndon* v. *Lowry, supra;* or the right of one accused of crime to the benefit of counsel. *Powell* v. *Alabama,* 287 U.S. 45. In these and other situations immunities that are valid as against the federal government by force of the specific pledges of particular amendments have been found to be implicit in the concept of ordered liberty, and thus, through the Fourteenth Amendment, become valid as against the states.

The line of division may seem to be wavering and broken if there is a hasty catalogue of the cases on the one side and the other. Reflection and analysis will induce a different view. There emerges the perception of a rationalizing principle which gives to discrete instances a proper order and coherence. The right to trial by jury and the immunity from prosecution except as the result of an indictment may have value and importance. Even so, they are not of the very essence of a scheme of ordered liberty. To abolish them is not to violate a "principle of justice so rooted in the traditions and conscience of our people as to be ranked as fundamental." *Snyder* v. *Massachusetts, supra,* p. 105; *Brown* v. *Mississippi, supra,* p. 285; *Herbert* v. *Louisiana,* 272 U.S. 312, 316. Few would be so narrow or provincial as to maintain that a fair and enlightened system of justice would be impossible without them. What is true of jury trials and indictments is true also, as the cases show, of the immunity from compulsory self-incrimination. *Twining* v. *New Jersey, supra.* This too might be lost, and justice still be done. Indeed, today as in the past there are students of our penal system who look upon the immunity as a mischief rather than a benefit, and who would limit its scope, or destroy it altogether. No doubt there would remain the need to give protection against torture, physical or mental. *Brown* v. *Mississippi, supra.* Justice, however, would not perish if the accused were subject to a duty to respond to orderly inquiry. The exclusion of these immunities and privileges from the privileges and im-

munities protected against the action of the states has not been arbitrary or casual. It has been dictated by a study and appreciation of the meaning, the essential implications, of liberty itself.

We reach a different plane of social and moral values when we pass to the privileges and immunities that have been taken over from the earlier articles of the federal bill of rights and brought within the Fourteenth Amendment by a process of absorption. These in their origin were effective against the federal government alone. If the Fourteenth Amendment has absorbed them, the process of absorption has had its source in the belief that neither liberty nor justice would exist if they were sacrificed. *Twining* v. *New Jersey, supra,* p. 99. This is true, for illustration, of freedom of thought and speech. Of that freedom one may say that it is the matrix, the indispensable condition, of nearly every other form of freedom. With rare aberrations a pervasive recognition of that truth can be traced in our history, political and legal. So it has come about that the domain of liberty, withdrawn by the Fourteenth Amendment from encroachment by the states, has been enlarged by latter-day judgments to include liberty of the mind as well as liberty of action. . . . Fundamental too in the concept of due process, and so in that of liberty, is the thought that condemnation shall be rendered only after trial. *Scott* v. *McNeal,* 154 U.S. 34; *Blackmer* v. *United States,* 284 U.S. 421. The hearing, moreover, must be a real one, not a sham or a pretense. *Moore* v. *Dempsey,* 261, U.S. 86; *Mooney* v. *Holohan,* 294 U.S. 103. For that reason, ignorant defendants in a capital case were held to have been condemned unlawfully when in truth, though not in form, they were refused the aid of counsel. *Powell* v. *Alabama, supra,* pp. 67, 68. The decision did not turn upon the fact that the benefit of counsel would have been guaranteed to the defendants by the provisions of the Sixth Amendment if they had been prosecuted in a federal court. The decision turned upon the fact that in the particular situation laid before us in the evidence the benefit of counsel was essential to the substance of a hearing.

Our survey of the cases serves, we think, to justify the statement that the dividing line between them, if not unfaltering throughout its course, has been true for the most part to a unifying principle. On which side of the line the case made out by the appellant has appropriate location must be the next inquiry and the final one. Is that kind of double jeopardy to which the statute has subjected him a hardship so acute and shocking that our polity will not endure it? Does it violate those "fundamental principles of liberty and justice which lie at the base of all our civil and political institutions"? *Herbert* v. *Louisiana, supra.* The answer surely must be "no." What the answer would have to be if the state were permitted after a trial free from error to try the accused over again or to bring another case against him, we have no occasion to consider. We deal with the statute before us and no other. The state is not attempting to wear the accused out by a multitude of cases with accumulated trials. It asks no more than this, that the case against him shall go on until there shall

be a trial free from the corrosion of substantial legal error. *State* v. *Felch,* 92 Vt. 477; *State* v. *Lee, supra.* This is not cruelty at all, nor even vexation in any immoderate degree. If the trial had been infected with error adverse to the accused, there might have been review at his instance, and, as often as necessary to purge the vicious taint. A reciprocal privilege, subject at all times to the discretion of the presiding judge (*State* v. *Carabetta,* 106 Conn. 114; 137 Atl. 394), has now been granted to the state. There is here no seismic innovation. The edifice of justice stands, its symmetry, to many, greater than before.

2. The conviction of appellant is not in derogation of any privileges or immunities that belong to him as a citizen of the United States.

There is argument in his behalf that the privileges and immunities clause of the Fourteenth Amendment as well as the due process clause has been flouted by the judgment.

Maxwell v. *Dow, supra,* p. 584, gives all the answer that is necessary.

The judgment is affirmed.

Mr. Justice Butler dissents.

ADAMSON v. CALIFORNIA

332 U.S. 46 (1947)

Adamson's conviction of murder was upheld by the highest court of California. This appeal sprang from a state law which permitted the prosecution to comment to the jury upon the failure of the accused to take the witness stand. Adamson's contention was that such comment in effect converted his silence into a confession of guilt and so constituted involuntary self-incrimination. This argument is accepted as valid in federal trials.

Appeal from the Supreme Court of California.

Mr. Justice Reed delivered the opinion of the Court: . . .

In the first place, appellant urges that the provision of the Fifth Amendment that no person "shall be compelled in any criminal case to be a witness against himself" is a fundamental national privilege or immu-

nity protected against state abridgement by the Fourteenth Amendment or a privilege or immunity secured, through the Fourteenth Amendment, against deprivation by state action because it is a personal right, enumerated in the federal Bill of Rights.

Secondly, appellant relies upon the due process of law clause of the Fourteenth Amendment to invalidate the provisions of the California law, . . . and as applied (a) because comment on failure to testify is permitted, (b) because appellant was forced to forego testimony in person because of danger of disclosure of his past convictions through cross-examination. . . .

We shall assume, but without any intention thereby of ruling upon the issue, that permission by law to the court, counsel and jury to comment upon and consider the failure of defendant "to explain or to deny by his testimony any evidence or facts in the case against him" would infringe defendant's privilege against self-incrimination under the Fifth Amendment if this were a trial in a court of the United States under a similar law. Such an assumption does not determine appellant's rights under the Fourteenth Amendment. It is settled law that the clause of the Fifth Amendment, protecting a person against being compelled to be a witness against himself, is not made effective by the Fourteenth Amendment as a protection against state action on the ground that freedom from testimonial compulsion is a right of national citizenship, or because it is a personal privilege or immunity secured by the Federal Constitution as one of the rights of man that are listed in the Bill of Rights.

The reasoning that leads to those conclusions starts with the unquestioned premise that the Bill of Rights, when adopted, was for the protection of the individual against the federal government and its provisions were inapplicable to similar actions done by the states. *Barron* v. *Baltimore,* 7 Pet. 243; *Feldman* v. *United States,* 322 U.S. 487, 490. With the adoption of the Fourteenth Amendment, it was suggested that the dual citizenship recognized by its first sentence secured for citizens federal protection for their elemental privileges and immunities of state citizenship. The *Slaughter-House Cases* [16 Wall. 36] decided, contrary to the suggestion, that these rights, as privileges and immunities of state citizenship, remained under the sole protection of the state governments. This Court, without the expression of a contrary view upon that phase of the issues before the Court, has approved this determination.

Maxwell v. *Bugbee,* 250 U.S. 525, 537; *Hamilton* v. *Regents,* 293 U.S. 245, 261. The power to free defendants in state trials from self-incrimination was specifically determined to be beyond the scope of the privileges and immunities clause of the Fourteenth Amendment in *Twining* v. *New Jersey,* 211 U.S. 78, 91–98. "The privilege against self-incrimination may be withdrawn and the accused put upon the stand as a witness for the state." The *Twining* case likewise disposed of the contention that freedom from testimonial compulsion, being specifically granted by the Bill of Rights, is a federal privilege or immunity that is protected by the Fourteenth Amendment against state invasion. This Court held that the inclusion in the Bill of Rights of this protection against the power of the national government did not make the privilege a federal privilege or immunity secured to citizens by the Constitution against state action. *Twining* v. *New Jersey, supra,* at 98–99; *Palko* v. *Connecticut, supra,* at 328. . . . We reaffirm the conclusion of the *Twining* and *Palko* cases that protection against self-incrimination is not a privilege or immunity of national citizenship.

Appellant secondly contends that if the privilege against self-incrimination is not a right protected by the privileges and immunities clause of the Fourteenth Amendment against state action, this privilege, to its full scope under the Fifth Amendment, inheres in the right to a fair trial. A right to a fair trial is a right admittedly protected by the due process clause of the Fourteenth Amendment. Therefore, appellant argues, the due process clause of the Fourteenth Amendment protects his privilege against self-incrimination. The due process clause of the Fourteenth Amendment, however, does not draw all the rights of the federal Bill of Rights under its protection. That contention was made and rejected in *Palko* v. *Connecticut,* 302 U.S. 319, 323. It was rejected with citation of the cases excluding several of the rights, protected by the Bill of Rights, against infringement by the National Government.

Nothing has been called to our attention that either the framers of the Fourteenth Amendment or the states that adopted it intended its due process clause to draw within its scope the earlier amendments to the Constitution. *Palko* held that such provisions of the Bill of Rights as were "implicit in the concept of ordered liberty," p. 325, became secure from state interference by the clause. But it held nothing more.

Specifically, the due process clause does not protect, by virtue of its mere existence, the accused's freedom from giving testimony by compulsion in state trials that is secured to him against federal interference by the Fifth Amendment. *Twining* v. *New Jersey,* 211 U.S. 78, 99–114; *Palko* v. *Connecticut, supra,* p. 323. For a state to require testimony from an accused is not necessarily a breach of a state's obligation to give a fair trial. Therefore, we must examine the effect of the California law applied in this trial to see whether the comment on failure to testify violates the protection against state action that the due process clause does grant to an accused. The due process clause forbids compulsion to testify by fear of hurt, torture or exhaustion. It forbids any other type of coercion that falls within the scope of due process. California follows Anglo-American legal tradition in excusing defendants in criminal prosecutions from compulsory testimony. Cf. VIII *Wigmore on evidence* (3d ed.) § 2252. That is a matter of legal policy and not because of the requirements of due process under the Fourteenth Amendment. So our inquiry is directed, not at the broad question of the constitutionality of compulsory testimony from the accused under the due process clause, but to the constitutionality of the provision of the California law that permits comment upon his failure to testify. It is, of course, logically possible that while an accused might be required, under appropriate penalties, to submit himself as a witness without a violation of due process, comments by judge or jury on inferences to be drawn from his failure to testify, in jurisdictions where an accused's privilege

against self-incrimination is protected, might deny due process. For example, a statute might declare that a permitted refusal to testify would compel an acceptance of the truth of the prosecution's evidence.

Generally, comment on the failure of an accused to testify is forbidden in American jurisdictions. This arises from state constitutional or statutory provisions similar in character to the federal provisions. Fifth Amendment and 28 U.S.C. § 632. California, however, is one of a few states that permit limited comment upon a defendant's failure to testify. That permission is narrow. The California law . . . authorizes comment by court and counsel upon the "failure of the defendant to explain or to deny by his testimony any evidence or facts in the case against him." This does not involve any presumption, rebuttable or irrebuttable, either of guilt or of the truth of any fact, that is offered in evidence. Compare *Tot* v. *United States,* 319, U.S. 463, 470. It allows inferences to be drawn from proven facts. Because of this clause, the court can direct the jury's attention to whatever evidence there may be that a defendant could deny and the prosecution can argue as to inferences that may be drawn from the accused's failure to testify. Compare *Caminetti* v. *United States,* 242 U.S. 470, 492–95; *Raffel* v. *United States,* 271 U.S. 494, 497. There is here no lack of power in the trial court to adjudge and no denial of a hearing. California has prescribed a method for advising the jury in the search for truth. However sound may be the legislative conclusion that an accused should not be compelled in any criminal case to be a witness against himself, we see no reason why comment should not be made upon his silence. It seems quite natural that when a defendant has opportunity to deny or explain facts and determines not to do so, the prosecution should bring out the strength of the evidence by commenting upon defendant's failure to explain or deny it. The prosecution evidence may be of facts that may be beyond the knowledge of the accused. If so, his failure to testify would have little if any weight. But the facts may be such as are necessarily in the knowledge of the accused. In that case a failure to explain would point to an inability to explain.

Appellant sets out the circumstances of this case, however, to show coercion and unfairness in permitting comment. The guilty person was not seen at the place and time of the crime. There was evidence, however, that entrance to the place or room where the crime was committed might have been obtained through a small door. It was freshly broken. Evidence showed that six fingerprints on the door were petitioner's. Certain diamond rings were missed from the deceased's possession. There was evidence that appellant, sometime after the crime, asked an unidentified person whether the latter would be interested in purchasing a diamond ring. As has been stated, the information charged other crimes to appellant and he admitted them. His argument here is that he could not take the stand to deny the evidence against him because he would be subjected to a cross-examination as to former crimes to impeach his veracity and the evidence so produced might well bring about his conviction. Such cross-examination is allowable in California. *People v. Adamson*, 27 Cal. 2d 478, 494, 165 P.2d 3, 11. Therefore, appellant contends the California statute permitting comment denies him due process.

It is true that if comment were forbidden, an accused in this situation could remain silent and avoid evidence of former crimes and comment upon his failure to testify. We are of the view, however, that a state may control such a situation in accordance with its own ideas of the most efficient administration of criminal justice. The purpose of due process is not to protect an accused against a proper conviction but against an unfair conviction. When evidence is before a jury that threatens conviction, it does not seem unfair to require him to choose between leaving the adverse evidence unexplained and subjecting himself to impeachment through disclosure of former crimes. Indeed, this is a dilemma with which any defendant may be faced. If facts, adverse

to the defendant, are proven by the prosecution, there may be no way to explain them favorably to the accused except by a witness who may be vulnerable to impeachment on cross-examination. The defendant must then decide whether or not to use such a witness. The fact that the witness may also be the defendant makes the choice more difficult but a denial of due process does not emerge from the circumstances. . . .

We find no other error that gives ground for our intervention in California's administration of criminal justice.

Affirmed.

MR. JUSTICE FRANKFURTER, concurring:

Less than ten years ago, Mr. Justice Cardozo announced as settled constitutional law that while the Fifth Amendment, "which is not directed to the states, but solely to the federal government," provides that no person shall be compelled in any criminal case to be a witness against himself, the process of law assured by the Fourteenth Amendment does not require such immunity from self-crimination: "in prosecutions by a state, the exemption will fail if the state elects to end it." *Palko* v. *Connecticut*, 302 U.S. 319, 322, 324. Mr. Justice Cardozo spoke for the Court, consisting of Mr. Chief Justice Hughes, and McReynolds, Brandeis, Sutherland, Stone, Roberts, Black, JJ. (Mr. Justice Butler dissented.) The matter no longer called for discussion; a reference to *Twining* v. *New Jersey*, 211 U.S. 78, decided thirty years before the *Palko* case, sufficed. . . . After enjoying unquestioned prestige for forty years, the *Twining* case should not now be diluted, even unwittingly, either in its judicial philosophy or in its particulars. As the surest way of keeping the *Twining* case intact, I would affirm this case on its authority. . . .

The short answer to the suggestion that the provision of the Fourteenth Amendment, which ordains "nor shall any State deprive any person of life, liberty, or property, without due process of law," was a way of saying that every State must thereafter initiate prosecutions through indictment by a grand jury, must have a trial by a jury of twelve in criminal cases, and must have trial by such a jury in common law suits where the amount in controversy exceeds twenty dollars, is that it is a strange way of saying it. It would be extraordinarily strange for a Constitution to convey such specific commands in such a roundabout and inexplicit way. . . . The notion that the Fourteenth Amendment was a covert way of imposing upon the States all the rules which it seemed important to Eighteenth Century statesmen to write into the Federal Amendments, was rejected by judges who were themselves witnesses of the process by which the Fourteenth Amendment became part of the Constitution. Arguments that may now be adduced to prove that the first eight Amendments were concealed within the historic phrasing of the Fourteenth Amendment were not unknown at the time of its adoption. A surer estimate of their bearing was possible for judges at the time than distorting distance is likely to vouchsafe. Any evidence of design or purpose not contemporaneously known could hardly have influenced those who ratified the Amendment. Remarks of a particular proponent of the Amendment, no matter how influential, are not to be deemed part of the Amendment. What was submitted for ratification was his proposal, not his speech. . . . There is suggested merely a selective incorporation of the first eight Amendments into the Fourteenth Amendment. Some are in and some are out, but we are left in the dark as to which are in and which are out. Nor are we given the calculus for determining which go in and which stay out. If the basis of selection is merely that those provisions of the first eight Amendments are incorporated which commend themselves to individual justices as indispensable to the dignity and happiness of a free man, we are thrown back to a merely subjective test. The protection against unreasonable search and seizure might have primacy for one judge, while trial by a jury of twelve for every claim above twenty dollars might appear to another as an ultimate need in a free society.

In the history of thought "natural law" has a much longer and much better founded meaning and justification than such subjective selection of the first eight Amendments for incorporation into the Fourteenth. . . .

And so, when, as in a case like the present, a conviction in a State court is here for review under a claim that a right protected by the due process clause of the Fourteenth Amendment has been denied, the issue is not whether an infraction of one of the specific provisions of the first eight Amendments is disclosed by the record. The relevant question is whether the criminal proceedings which resulted in conviction deprived the accused of the due process of law to which the United States Constitution entitled him. Judicial review of that guaranty of the Fourteenth Amendment inescapably imposes upon this Court an exercise of judgment upon the whole course of the proceedings in order to ascertain whether they offend those canons of decency and fairness which express the notions of justice of English-speaking peoples even toward those charged with the most heinous offenses. These standards of justice are not authoritatively formulated anywhere as though they were prescriptions in a pharmacopoeia. But neither does the application of the due process clause imply that judges are wholly at large. The judicial judgment in applying the due process clause must move within the limits of accepted notions of justice and is not to be based upon the idiosyncrasies of a merely personal judgment. The fact that judges among them-selves may differ whether in a particular case a trial offends accepted notions of justice is not disproof that general rather than idiosyncratic standards are applied. An important safeguard against such merely individual judgment is an alert deference to the judgment of the State court under review.

MR. JUSTICE BLACK, dissenting: . . .

The Court refuses to meet and decide the appellant's first contention. But while the Court's opinion, as I read it, strongly implies that the Fifth Amendment does not, of itself, bar comment upon failure to testify in federal courts, the Court nevertheless assumes that it does in order to reach the second constitutional question involved in appellant's case. I must consider the case on the same assumption that the Court does. For the discussion of the second contention turns out to be a decision which reaches far beyond the relatively narrow issues on which this case might have turned.

This decision reasserts a constitutional theory spelled out in *Twining* v. *New Jersey*, 211 U.S. 78, that this Court is endowed by the Constitution with boundless power under "natural law" periodically to expand and contract constitutional standards to conform to the Court's conception of what at a particular time constitutes "civilized decency" and "fundamental liberty and justice." Invoking this *Twining* rule, the Court concludes that although comment upon testimony in a federal court would violate the Fifth Amendment, identical comment in a state court does not violate today's fashion in civilized decency and fundamentals and is therefore not prohibited by the Federal Constitution as amended.

The *Twining* case was the first, as it is the only, decision of this Court which has squarely held that states were free, notwithstanding the Fifth and Fourteenth Amendments, to extort evidence from one accused of crime. I agree that if *Twining* be reaffirmed, the result reached might appropriately follow. But I would not reaffirm the *Twining* decision. I think that decision and the "natural law" theory of the Constitution upon which it relies degrade the constitutional safeguards of the Bill of Rights and simultaneously appropriate for this Court a broad power which we are not authorized by the Constitution to exercise. . . . My reasons for believing that the *Twining* decision should not be revitalized can best be understood by reference to the constitutional, judicial, and general history that preceded and followed the case. That reference must be abbreviated far more than

is justified but for the necessary limitations of opinion-writing.

My study of the historical events that culminated in the Fourteenth Amendment, and the expressions of those who sponsored and favored, as well as those who opposed its submission and passage, persuades me that one of the chief objects that the provisions of the Amendment's first section, separately, and as a whole, were intended to accomplish was to make the Bill of Rights applicable to the states. With full knowledge of the import of the *Baron* [7 Pet. 243] decision, the framers and backers of the Fourteenth Amendment proclaimed its purpose to be to overturn the constitutional rule that case had announced. This historical purpose has never received full consideration or exposition in any opinion of this Court interpreting the Amendment. [An extensive discussion of the *Slaughter House* and subsequent cases is omitted.]

I cannot consider the Bill of Rights to be an outworn 18th Century "strait jacket" as the *Twining* opinion did. Its provisions may be thought outdated abstractions by some. And it is true that they were designed to meet ancient evils. But they are the same kind of human evils that have emerged from century to century wherever excessive power is sought by the few at the expense of the many. In my judgment the people of no nation can lose their liberty so long as a Bill of Rights like ours survives and its basic purposes are conscientiously interpreted, enforced and respected so as to afford continuous protection against old, as well as new, devices and practices which might thwart those purposes. I fear to see the consequences of the Court's practice of substituting its own concepts of decency and fundamental justice for the language of the Bill of Rights as its point of departure in interpreting and enforcing that Bill of Rights. If the choice must be between the selective process of the *Palko* decision applying some of the Bill of Rights to the States, or the *Twining* rule applying none of them, I would choose the *Palko* selective process. But rather than accept either of these choices, I would follow what

I believe was the original purpose of the Fourteenth Amendment—to extend to all the people of the nation the complete protection of the Bill of Rights. To hold that this Court can determine what, if any, provisions of the Bill of Rights will be enforced, and if so to what degree, is to frustrate the great design of a written Constitution. . . .

Since *Marbury* v. *Madison*, 1 Cranch 137, was decided, the practice has been firmly established, for better or worse, that courts can strike down legislative enactments which violate the Constitution. This process, of course, involves interpretation, and since words can have many meanings, interpretation obviously may result in contraction or extension of the original purpose of a constitutional provision, thereby affecting policy. But to pass upon the constitutionality of statutes by looking to the particular standards enumerated in the Bill of Rights and other parts of the Constitution is one thing; to invalidate statutes because of application of "natural law" deemed to be above and undefined by the Constitution is another. "In the one instance, courts proceeding within clearly marked constitutional boundaries seek to execute policies

written into the Constitution; in the other, they roam at will in the limitless area of their own beliefs as to reasonableness and actually select policies, a responsibility which the Constitution entrusts to the legislative representatives of the people." *Federal Power Commission* v. *Pipeline Co.*, 315 U.S. 575, 599, 601, n. 4.

Mr. Justice Douglas joins in this opinion.

Mr. Justice Murphy, with whom Mr. Justice Rutledge concurs, dissenting:

While in substantial agreement with the views of Mr. Justice Black, I have one reservation and one addition to make.

I agree that the specific guarantees of the Bill of Rights should be carried over intact into the first section of the Fourteenth Amendment. But I am not prepared to say that the latter is entirely and necessarily limited by the Bill of Rights. Occasions may arise where a proceeding falls so far short of conforming to fundamental standards of procedure as to warrant constitutional condemnation in terms of a lack of due process despite the absence of a specific provision in the Bill of Rights. . . .

NOTE: Mr. Justice Black had joined in the Court's decision in the *Palko* case. Whatever the merits of the end he seeks in *Adamson*, the historical foundation for his position is highly questionable. See Fairman and Morrison, "Does the Fourteenth Amendment Incorporate the Bill of Rights?" 2 *Stanford Law Review* 5 and 140 (1949). Justices Black and Douglas also failed in their effort to upset the established view that corporations are "persons" within the meaning of the Fourteenth Amendment. *Connecticut General Life Insurance Co.* v. *Johnson*, 303 U.S. 77, 83 (1938); *Wheeling Steel Corp.* v. *Glander*, 337 U.S. 562, 576 (1949). This position, like their stand in the *Adamson* case, is calculated to emphasize the libertarian, as against the economic, coverage of the amendment. But corporations sometimes publish newspapers and may be threatened by state laws impinging upon freedom of the press. In such a case, Justices Black and Douglas seem to have abandoned their *Connecticut General-Glander* arguments. See *Times-Mirror Co.* v. *Superior Court of California*, 314 U.S. 252 (1941). Similarly in *Poe* v. *Ullman*, below, Justice Douglas (and perhaps Justice Black) abandoned the *Adamson* dissenting view that the Fourteenth Amendment is limited by the Bill of Rights: "Though I believe that 'due process' as used in the Fourteenth

Amendment includes all of the first eight amendments, I do not think it is restricted and confined to them." Thus Mr. Justice Douglas, at least, while still clinging to part of the *Adamson* dissent, had switched over to the Court's view of due process as a growing conception of fairness capable of combating new forms of evil unknown to those who gave us the Bill of Rights.

III. PROCEDURAL RIGHTS OF THE INDIVIDUAL— THE FAIR HEARING

Possibly the oldest element of liberty in the Anglo-American tradition is one that springs from Magna Charta. The King shall not "go against," or harm, any of his subjects except by "the law of the land," or in more modern terminology, no person shall be deprived of "life, liberty, or property without due process of law." See the Fifth and Fourteenth Amendments. The purpose of the prohibition, reflecting its ancient origin, was elemental—to limit means, not ends; tactics, not strategy. For example, a man was not to be punished summarily for failure to pay a tax. He must be given a fair trial, including among other things an opportunity to show that he had paid the tax in question, or that in fact the tax was not due. This is not a limitation on the power to impose taxes. It is merely a limitation on the *manner* of collecting them.

Obviously procedural due process cannot be fully defined in a neat catch-all rule. Perhaps Judge Learned Hand expressed it best when he said that it embodies the English sporting sense of fair play. Its viable nature is illustrated in the cases that follow. Is it too vague, too lacking in standards, for judicial enforcement? Does it give the judiciary a roving commission to govern? Part of the answer is that here the concern is not with the making of policy, but simply with the fair enforcement of it. Mr. Justice Brandeis made the point when he said, "One can never be sure of ends—political, social, economic. There must always be doubt and difference of opinion; one can be 51 percent sure." But as to means, or procedures, there is more certainty. Here "fundamentals do not change; centuries of thought have established standards." In short, whether an income tax or a tariff is better for a given place and time is highly debatable. Different people and different generations will have disparate answers, as our history demonstrates. On the other hand, that a tax of whatever kind should be fairly collected, and what constitutes fairness in this context, are relatively clear and unchanging. Essentially the due process requirement is this: when a person is charged with an offense he must be given a FAIR HEARING, a decent opportunity to defend himself. This perhaps is the major foundation in the Anglo-American tradition of personal liberty. It is a cushion between the individual and government, relevant at least in some degree to all the capacities in which government operates—judicial, legislative, executive, and administrative. Of course it is most highly developed in the oldest form of public action, the criminal prosecution. Precisely because the principle of the fair hearing is so old and so basic some of its elements have crystallized and found more concrete expression in various parts of the Bill of Rights. But the latter contains other things, too, and the ancient, yet living, concept of procedural fairness is hardly exhausted by concrete expression of a few of its elements; hence the *Palko* rule.

1. NOTICE AND ARREST

LANZETTA v. NEW JERSEY

306 U.S. 451 (1939)

MR. JUSTICE BUTLER delivered the opinion of the Court.

By this appeal we are called on to decide whether, by reason of vagueness and uncertainty, a recent enactment of New Jersey, § 4, R.S.N.J.1937, 2:136–4, c. 155, Laws 1934, is repugnant to the due process clause of the Fourteenth Amendment, U.S.C.A. Const. It is as follows: "Any person not engaged in any lawful occupation, known to be a member of any gang consisting of two or more persons, who has been convicted at least three times of being a disorderly person, or who has been convicted of any crime, in this or in any other State, is declared to be a gangster. . . ." Every violation is punishable by fine not exceeding $10,000 or imprisonment not exceeding 20 years, or both. . . .

The phrase "consisting of two or more persons" is all that purports to define "gang." The meanings of that word indicated in dictionaries and in historical and sociological writings are numerous and varied. Nor is the meaning derivable from the common law, for neither in that field nor anywhere in the language of the law is there definition of the word. Our attention has not been called to, and we are unable to find, any other statute attempting to make it criminal to be a member of a "gang." . . .

The lack of certainty of the challenged provision is not limited to the word "gang" or to its dependent "gangster." Without resolving the serious doubts arising from the generality of the language, we assume that the clause "any person not engaged in any lawful occupation" is sufficient to identify a class to which must belong all capable of becoming gangsters within the terms of the provision. The enactment employs the expression, "known to be a member." It is ambiguous. There immediately arises the doubt whether actual or putative association is meant. If actual membership is required, that status must be established as a fact, and the word "known" would be without significance. If reputed membership is enough, there is uncertainty whether that reputation must be general or extend only to some persons. And the statute fails to indicate what constitutes membership or how one may join a "gang."

The challenged provision condemns no act or omission; the terms it employs to indicate what it purports to denounce are so vague, indefinite and uncertain that it must be condemned as repugnant to the due process clause of the Fourteenth Amendment.

Reversed.

NOTE: The indictment or charge by which a prosecution is initiated is invalid if it does not give the accused fair notice of the alleged crime. Similarly no conviction is valid if it does not conform with the indictment or charge. See *Cole* v. *Arkansas*, 333 U.S. 196 (1948).

HENRY v. UNITED STATES

361 U.S. 98 (1959)

MR. JUSTICE DOUGLAS delivered the opinion of the Court.

Petitioner stands convicted of unlawfully possessing three cartons of radios valued at more than $100 which had been stolen from an interstate shipment. See 18 U.S.C. § 659. The issue in the case is whether there was probable cause for the arrest leading to the search that produced the evidence on which the conviction rests. A timely motion to suppress the evidence was made by petitioner and overruled by the District Court; and the judgment of conviction was affirmed by the Court of Appeals on a divided vote. 259 F.2d 725. The case is here on a petition for a writ of certiorari, 359 U.S. 904.

There was a theft from an interstate shipment of whisky at a terminal in Chicago. The next day two FBI agents were in the neighborhood investigating it. They saw petitioner and one Pierotti walk across a street from a tavern and get into an automobile. The agents had been given, by the employer of Pierotti, information of an undisclosed nature "concerning the implication of the defendant Pierotti with interstate shipments." But, so far as the record shows, he never went so far as to tell the agents he suspected Pierotti of any such thefts. The agents followed the car and saw it enter an alley and stop. Petitioner got out of the car, entered a gangway leading to residential premises and returned in a few minutes with some cartons. He placed them in the car and he and Pierotti drove off. The agents were unable to follow the car. But later they found it parked at the same place near the tavern. Shortly they saw petitioner and Pierotti leave the tavern, get into the car, and drive off. The car stopped in the same alley as before; petitioner entered the same gangway and returned with more cartons. The agents observed this transaction from a distance of some 300

feet and could not determine the size, number or contents of the cartons. As the car drove off the agents followed it and finally, when they met it, waved it to a stop. As he got out of the car, petitioner was heard to say, "Hold it; it is the G's." This was followed by, "Tell him he [you] just picked me up." The agents searched the car, placed the cartons (which bore the name "Admiral" and were addressed to an out-of-state company) in their car, took the merchandise and petitioner and Pierotti to their office and held them for about two hours when the agents learned that the cartons contained stolen radios. They then placed the men under formal arrest.

The statutory authority of FBI officers and agents to make felony arrests without a warrant is restricted to offenses committed "in their presence" or to instances where they have "reasonable grounds to believe that the person to be arrested has committed or is committing" a felony. 18 U.S.C. § 3052. The statute states the constitutional standard, for it is the command of the Fourth Amendment that no warrants for either searches or arrests shall issue except "upon probable cause, supported by oath or affirmation, and particularly describing the place to be searched, and the persons or things to be seized."

The requirement of probable cause has roots that are deep in our history. The general warrant, in which the name of the person to be arrested was left blank, and the writs of assistance, against which James Otis inveighed, both perpetuated the oppressive practice of allowing the police to arrest and search on suspicion. Police control took the place of judicial control, since no showing of "probable cause" before a magistrate was required. The Virginia Declaration of Rights, adopted June 12, 1776, rebelled against that practice:

"That general warrants, whereby any

officer or messenger may be commanded to
search suspected places without evidence of
a fact committed, or to seize any person or
persons not named, or whose offence is not
particularly described and supported by
evidence, are grievous and oppressive, and
ought not to be granted."

The Maryland Declaration of Rights
(1776), Art. XXIII, was equally emphatic:

"That all warrants, without oath or
affirmation, to search suspected places, or to
seize any person or property, are grievous
and oppressive; and all general warrants—
to search suspected places, or to apprehend
suspected persons, without naming or describing the place, or the person in special
—are illegal, and ought not to be granted."

And see North Carolina Declaration of
Rights (1776), Art. XI; Pennsylvania Constitution (1776), Art. X; Massachusetts Constitution (1780), Pt. I, Art. XIV.

That philosophy later was reflected in
the Fourth Amendment. And as the early
American decisions both before and immediately after its adoption show, common
rumor or report, suspicion, or even "strong
reason to suspect" was not adequate to support a warrant for arrest. And that principle
has survived to this day. See *United States
v. Di Re,* 332 U.S. 581, 593–595; *Johnson v.
United States,* 333 U.S. 10, 13–15; *Giordenello v. United States,* 357 U.S. 480, 486.
Its high water was *Johnson v. United States,
supra,* where the smell of opium coming
from a closed room was not enough to support an arrest and search without a warrant.
It was against this background that two
scholars recently wrote, "Arrest on mere
suspicion collides violently with the basic
human right of liberty."

Evidence required to establish guilt is
not necessary. *Brinegar v. United States,*
338 U.S. 160; *Draper v. United States,* 358
U.S. 307. On the other hand, good faith on
the part of the arresting officers is not
enough. Probable cause exists if the facts
and circumstances known to the officer warrant a prudent man in believing that the
offense has been committed. *Stacey v.
Emery,* 97 U.S. 642, 645. And see *Director
General v. Kastenbaum,* 263 U.S. 25, 28;

United States v. *Di Re, supra,* at 592;
Giordenello v. *United States, supra,* at 486.
It is important, we think, that this requirement be strictly enforced, for the standard
set by the Constitution protects both the
officer and the citizen. If the officer acts with
probable cause, he is protected even though
it turns out that the citizen is innocent.
Carroll v. United States, 267 U.S. 132, 156.
And while a search without a warrant is,
within limits, permissible if incident to a
lawful arrest, if an arrest without a warrant
is to support an incidental search, it must
be made with probable cause. *Carroll v.
United States, supra,* at 155–156. This immunity of officers cannot fairly be enlarged
without jeopardizing the privacy or security
of the citizen. We turn then to the question
whether prudent men in the shoes of these
officers (*Brinegar v. United States, supra,* at
175) would have seen enough to permit
them to believe that petitioner was violating
or had violated the law. We think not.

The prosecution conceded below, and adheres to the concession here, that the arrest
took place when the federal agent stopped
the car. That is our view on the facts of
this particular case. When the officers interrupted the two men and restricted their liberty of movement, the arrest, for purposes
of this case, was complete. It is, therefore,
necessary to determine whether at or before
that time they had reasonable cause to believe that a crime had been committed. The
fact that afterwards contraband was discovered is not enough. An arrest is not
justified by what the subsequent search discloses, as *Johnson v. United States, supra,*
holds.

It is true that a federal crime had been
committed at a terminal in the neighborhood, whisky having been stolen from an
interstate shipment. Petitioner's friend,
Pierotti, had been suspected of some implication in some interstate shipments, as
we have said. But as this record stands, what
those shipments were and the manner in
which he was implicated remain unexplained and undefined. The rumor about
him is therefore practically meaningless. On
the record there was far from enough evi-

dence against him to justify a magistrate in issuing a warrant. So far as the record shows, petitioner had not even been suspected of criminal activity prior to this time. Riding in the car, stopping in an alley, picking up packages, driving away— these were all acts that were outwardly innocent. Their movements in the car had no mark of fleeing men or men acting furtively. The case might be different if the packages had been taken from a terminal or from an interstate trucking platform. But they were not. As we have said, the alley where the packages were picked up was in a residential section. The fact that packages have been stolen does not make every man who carries a package subject to arrest nor the package subject to seizure. The police must have reasonable grounds to believe that the particular package carried by the citizen is contraband. Its shape and design might at times be adequate. The weight of it and the manner in which it is carried might at times be enough. But there was nothing to indicate that the cartons here in issue probably contained liquor. The fact that they contained other contraband appeared only some hours after the arrest. What transpired at or after the time the car was stopped by the officers is, as we have said, irrelevant to the narrow issue before us. To repeat, an arrest is not justified by what the subsequent search discloses. Under our system suspicion is not enough for an officer to lay hands on a citizen. It is better, so the Fourth Amendment teaches, that the guilty sometimes go free than that citizens be subject to easy arrest.

The fact that the suspects were in an automobile is not enough. *Carroll* v. *United States, supra,* liberalized the rule governing searches when a moving vehicle is involved. But that decision merely relaxed the requirements for a warrant on grounds of practicality. It did not dispense with the need for probable cause.

Reversed.

Mr. Justice Black concurs in the result.

Mr. Justice Clark, whom The Chief Justice joins, dissenting.

The Court decides this case on the narrow ground that the arrest took place at the moment the Federal Bureau of Investigation agents stopped the car in which petitioner was riding and at that time probable cause for it did not exist. While the Government, unnecessarily it seems to me, conceded that the arrest was made at the time the car was stopped, this Court is not bound by the Government's mistakes.

The record shows beyond dispute that the agents had received information from co-defendant Pierotti's employer implicating Pierotti with interstate shipments. The agents began a surveillance of petitioner and Pierotti after recognizing them as they came out of a bar. Later the agents observed them loading cartons into an automobile from a gangway up an alley in Chicago. The agents had been trailing them, and after it appeared that they had delivered the first load of cartons, the suspects returned to the same platform by a circuitous route through streets and alleys. The agents then saw petitioner load another set of cartons into the car and drive off with the same. A few minutes later the agents stopped the car, alighted from their own car, and approached the petitioner. As they did so, petitioner was overheard to say: "Hold it; it is the G's," and "Tell him he [you] just picked me up." Since the agents had actually seen the two suspects together for several hours, it was apparent to them that the statement was untrue. Upon being questioned, the defendants stated that they had borrowed the car from a friend. During the questioning and after petitioner had stepped out of the car one of the agents happened to look through the door of the car which petitioner had left open and saw three cartons stacked up inside which resembled those petitioner had just loaded into the car from the gangway. The agent saw that the cartons bore Admiral shipping labels and were addressed to a company in Cincinnati, Ohio. Upon further questioning, the agent was told that the cartons were in the car when the defendants borrowed it. Knowing this to be untrue, the agents then searched the car, arrested petitioner and his companion, and seized the cartons.

The Court seems to say that the mere stopping of the car amounted to an arrest of the petitioner. I cannot agree. The suspicious activities of the petitioner during the somewhat prolonged surveillance by the agents warranted the stopping of the car. The sighting of the cartons with their interstate labels in the car gave the agents reasonable ground to believe that a crime was in the course of its commission in their very presence. The search of the car and the subsequent arrest were therefore lawful and the motion to suppress was properly overruled.

In my view, the time at which the agents were required to have reasonable grounds to believe that petitioner was committing a felony was when they began the search of the automobile, which was after they had seen the cartons with interstate labels in the car. The earlier events certainly disclosed ample grounds to justify the following of the car, the subsequent stopping thereof, and the questioning of petitioner by the agents. This interrogation, together with the sighting of the cartons and the labels, gave the agents indisputable probable cause for the search and arrest.

When an investigation proceeds to the point where an agent has reasonable grounds to believe that an offense is being committed in his presence, he is obligated to proceed to make such searches, seizures, and arrests as the circumstances require. It is only by such alertness that crime is discovered, interrupted, prevented, and punished. We should not place additional burdens on law enforcement agencies.

I would affirm the judgments on the rationale of *Brinegar* v. *United States*, 338 U.S. 160 (1949), and *Carroll* v. *United States*, 267 U.S. 132 (1925).

2. BAIL

Carlson v. *Landon*, 342 U.S. 524 (1952), held that "the Eighth Amendment has not prevented Congress from defining the class of cases in which bail shall be allowed. . . . Thus in criminal cases it is not compulsory where the punishment may be death." Justices Black, Frankfurter, Douglas, and Burton dissented—two of them holding that the Amendment prohibited the unreasonable denial of bail.

Stack v. *Boyle*, 342 U.S. 1 (1951), held that in a Smith Act prosecution, bail of $50,000 was excessive, since there was no showing of justification for higher bail than in other cases with similar penalties. Whether the Fourteenth Amendment limits state authority with respect to bail was considered but not decided in *New York* v. *O'Neill*, 359 U.S. 1 (1959).

ADDRESS BY ATTORNEY GENERAL ROBERT F. KENNEDY TO THE ACADEMY OF TRIAL LAWYERS OF ALLEGHENY COUNTY, PITTSBURGH, PENNSYLVANIA, JUNE 1, 1964

The theory of the bail system—the *only* justification recognized for it by the courts—is that a bail bond is necessary to insure the appearance of the defendant at trial.

In actual practice, the bail system measures human freedom by financial ability. In the words of a recent report:

"Those who go free on bail are released not because they are innocent but because they can buy their liberty. The balance are detained not because they are guilty but because they are poor. Though the accused be harmless, and has a home, family and job which make it likely that—if released—he would show up for trial, he may still be held. Conversely, the habitual offender who may be dangerous to the safety of the community may gain his release."

As citizens in an age of reason, this may be offensive to us. As members of a profession concerned with the protection of human rights we may be shocked. But a close examination of the bail system reveals that it is shot through with other illogical and inconsistent features.

It is one of the basic premises of the bail system, for example, that the higher the bail, the greater the likelihood that the defendant will appear in court. But since almost all bail requirements are met by a commercial bail transaction, it is the bondsman rather than the defendant who bears the risk in most cases.

The defendant's stake in appearing is limited to the collateral—if any—which the bondsman may have required him to put up in order to get the bond. If the bondsman does not require collateral, the defendant ordinarily has *no* financial stake in complying with the terms of the bond. And this is a matter which the court does not decide or even know in most instances.

Whenever there is a commercial bail transaction, of course, it is the bondsman who assumes the paramount role in determining the defendant's freedom. The bondsman is an independent businessman who is free to reject a prospective client for any reason without regard to the consequences to the defendant.

As Judge Skelly Wright said in a recent opinion: "Professional bondsmen hold the keys to the jail in their pockets. . . . The court and the commissioner are relegated to the relatively unimportant chore of fixing the amount of bail."

There are many examples of how the bondsman's right to reject any application may conflict with the interests of a defendant. Bail in a "nominal" amount may be too small for a bondsman to bother with. As a business judgment, the bondsman may prefer professional criminals who know the rules over amateur offenders who may panic. The professional criminal rarely has the difficulty of making bail that many poor people experience.

Here in Pittsburgh you might be familiar with the recent charges that jail officials have received a cut on bond premiums. It may not be great consolation to you to know that similar charges have been made in most major cities.

There are other abuses of the bail system every bit as flagrant as this petty graft. Far too often bail is used to give defendants "a taste of jail" or to coerce them in some other way. Too often simple mistakes have resulted in gross unfairness. . . .

Last year alone Federal prisoners spent 600,000 man days in jails awaiting trial at a cost of $2 million to the Federal Government. In the city of New York in 1962, nearly 60,000 prisoners spent an average of 30 days each in pretrial detention. At $6.25 per man per day that cost the city more than $10,000,000 for that one year.

There are comparable figures for every large city. A substantial part of their facilities and budget are devoted to the detention in jails of prisoners who are presumably innocent and awaiting trial. And beyond that their welfare budgets are paid to the families of wage earners that they have thus imprisoned.

But the cost in human resources, the tragic loss in the lives of many individuals is far greater. The man who goes to jail for failure to make bond is treated in almost every jurisdiction just like the convicted criminal serving a sentence. His home may be disrupted, his family humiliated and his chance of making a living permanently taken away.

Recently in Los Angeles a man accused of a minor crime waited 207 days in jail because he did not have the money to get out. At his trial a jury found him not guilty.

Here in Pennsylvania a defendant accused of driving without a license and unable to raise a $300 bond spent 54 days in jail awaiting trial. The maximum penalty for the offense with which he was charged was 5 days.

In Glen Cove, N.Y., Daniel Walker was arrested on suspicion of robbery of a delicatessen. He couldn't raise the $10,000 bail or the bondsman's fee. He spent 55 days in jail. His wife had to move in with her parents, his car was repossessed, his credit destroyed. Later, he was found to be the victim of mistaken identity. When freed, it took him four months to find another job.

And remaining in jail may have substantial effect on any defendant's ability to make a proper defense. He is severely restricted in the contribution he can make to the pretrial investigation and in conferences with his attorney. The experience in jail may affect his demeanor and attitude in the courtroom and as a witness.

If he is convicted the defendant who has lost his job and been removed from his family will have much less chance for probation than one who has kept his job, earned money and maintained his family ties.

All available data indicated that the defendant held in jail until his trial is severely disadvantaged when compared with the defendant who is released. The jailed defendant is far more likely to be convicted and far less likely to receive probation if he is convicted.

In a Philadelphia study only 52% of bailed defendants were convicted compared with 82% of those jailed. Among the convicted, only 22% of the bailed defendants got prison sentences compared with 59%—almost three times the rate—from the group that had been jailed. In the District of Columbia another study of those convicted revealed that 25% of those who had been on bail were released on probation against only 6% of those who had been kept in jail. . . .

Some of the proposed alternatives to bail are still in the idea stage; others have been tried for long periods with remarkably satisfactory results. I would like to tell you about one of the most notable experiments: the Vera Foundation's Manhattan Bail Project.

This project was begun in the fall of 1961 with a grant of $115,000 from the Ford Foundation. It was staffed by law students from New York University. The staff interviewed felony defendants paying particularly close attention to those factors which would make the defendant a good parole risk.

Currently it has been found that 65% of the defendants interviewed can be recommended for release on their own recognizance before trial. The project has been so successful to date that 70% of its recommendations are accepted by the court and almost 80% are agreed to by the District Attorney's office.

Of the 2,195 defendants paroled in this way through April 8, 1964, only 15 failed to show up in court. This is a rate of $7/10$ of 1%, well below the no-show rate for those out on bail and impressive enough to make the project an unqualified success. The point was proved.

In the Department of Justice we are making a wholesale reevaluation of bail practices. We began a little over a year ago by instructing all U.S. Attorneys to recommend the release of defendants on their own recognizance in every practicable case.

With this one step we have tripled—from 6% to 18%—the rate of release of defendants without bail. In four judicial districts more than 65% of the defendants are so released. And we have found that the percentage of those who failed to appear has remained just about the same—about 2½%—as those required to post bail.

We are also undertaking an experimental study of other approaches. I hope within the next year we can expand in the U.S. Attorney's offices the experimental use of a summons in lieu of arrest, a procedure now the subject of an extensive study in New York City.

3. RIGHT TO COUNSEL

GIDEON v. *WAINWRIGHT*

372 U.S. 335 (1963)

MR. JUSTICE BLACK delivered the opinion of the Court.

Petitioner was charged in a Florida state court with having broken and entered a poolroom with intent to commit a misdemeanor. This offense is a felony under Florida law. Appearing in court without funds and without a lawyer, petitioner asked the court to appoint counsel for him, whereupon the following colloquy took place:

"The COURT: Mr. Gideon, I am sorry, but I cannot appoint Counsel to represent you in this case. Under the laws of the State of Florida, the only time the Court can appoint Counsel to represent a Defendant is when that person is charged with a capital offense. I am sorry, but I will have to deny your request to appoint Counsel to defend you in this case.

"The DEFENDANT: The United States Supreme Court says I am entitled to be represented by Counsel."

Put to trial before a jury, Gideon conducted his defense about as well as could be expected from a layman. He made an opening statement to the jury, cross-examined the State's witnesses, presented witnesses in his own defense, declined to testify himself, and made a short argument "emphasizing his innocence to the charge contained in the Information filed in this case." The jury returned a verdict of guilty, and petitioner was sentenced to serve five years in the state prison. Later, petitioner filed in the Florida Supreme Court this habeas corpus petition attacking his conviction and sentence on the ground that the trial court's refusal to appoint counsel for him denied him rights "guaranteed by the Constitution and the Bill of Rights by the United States Government." Treating the petition for habeas corpus as properly before it, the State Supreme Court, "upon consideration thereof" but without an opinion, denied all relief. Since 1942, when *Betts* v. *Brady*, 316 U.S. 455, was decided by a divided Court, the problem of a defendant's federal constitutional right to counsel in a state court has been a continuing source of controversy and litigation in both state and federal courts. To give this problem another review here, we granted certiorari. 370 U.S. 908. Since Gideon was proceeding *in forma pauperis*, we appointed counsel to represent him and requested both sides to discuss in their briefs and oral arguments the following: "Should this Court's holding in *Betts* v. *Brady*, 316 U.S. 455, be reconsidered?"

I

The facts upon which Betts claimed that he had been unconstitutionally denied the right to have counsel appointed to assist him are strikingly like the facts upon which Gideon here bases his federal constitutional claim. Betts was indicted for robbery in a Maryland state court. On arraignment, he told the trial judge of his lack of funds to hire a lawyer and asked the court to appoint one for him. Betts was advised that it was not the practice in that county to appoint counsel for indigent defendants except in murder and rape cases. He then pleaded not guilty, had witnesses summoned, cross-examined the State's witnesses, examined his own, and chose not to testify himself. He was found guilty by the judge, sitting without a jury, and sentenced to eight years in prison. Like Gideon, Betts sought release by habeas corpus, alleging that he had been denied the right to assistance of counsel in violation of the Fourteenth Amendment. Betts was denied any relief, and on review this Court affirmed. It was held that a refusal to appoint counsel for an indigent defendant charged with a felony did not necessarily violate the Due Process Clause of the Fourteenth Amendment, which for reasons given the Court deemed to be the only applicable federal constitutional provision. The Court said:

"Asserted denial [of due process] is to be tested by an appraisal of the totality of facts in a given case. That which may, in one setting, constitute a denial of fundamental fairness, shocking to the universal sense of justice, may, in other circumstances, and in the light of other considerations, fall short of such denial." 316 U.S., at 462.

Treating due process as "a concept less rigid and more fluid than those envisaged in other specific and particular provisions of the Bill of Rights," the Court held that refusal to appoint counsel under the particular facts and circumstances in the Betts case was not so "offensive to the common and fundamental ideas of fairness" as to amount to a denial of due process. Since the facts and circumstances of the two cases are so nearly indistinguishable, we think the *Betts* v. *Brady* holding if left standing would require us to reject Gideon's claim that the Constitution guarantees him the assistance of counsel. Upon full reconsideration we conclude that *Betts* v. *Brady* should be overruled.

II

The Sixth Amendment provides, "In all criminal prosecutions, the accused shall enjoy the right . . . to have the Assistance of Counsel for his defence." We have con-

strued this to mean that in federal courts counsel must be provided for defendants unable to employ counsel unless the right is competently and intelligently waived. Betts argued that this right is extended to indigent defendants in state courts by the Fourteenth Amendment. In response the Court stated that, while the Sixth Amendment laid down "no rule for the conduct of the states, the question recurs whether the constraint laid by the amendment upon the national courts expresses a rule so fundamental and essential to a fair trial, and so, to due process of law, that it is made obligatory upon the states by the Fourteenth Amendment." 316 U.S., at 465. In order to decide whether the Sixth Amendment's guarantee of counsel is of this fundamental nature, the Court in Betts set out and considered "[r]elevant data on the subject . . . afforded by constitutional and statutory provisions subsisting in the colonies and the states prior to the inclusion of the Bill of Rights in the national Constitution, and in the constitutional, legislative, and judicial history of the states to the present date." 316 U.S., at 465. On the basis of this historical data the Court concluded that "appointment of counsel is not a fundamental right, essential to a fair trial." . . .

We accept *Betts* v. *Brady's* assumption, based as it was on our prior cases, that a provision of the Bill of Rights which is "fundamental and essential to a fair trial" is made obligatory upon the States by the Fourteenth Amendment. We think the Court in Betts was wrong, however, in concluding that the Sixth Amendment's guarantee of counsel is not one of these fundamental rights. Ten years before *Betts* v. *Brady,* this Court, after full consideration of all the historical data examined in Betts, had unequivocally declared that "the right to the aid of counsel is of this fundamental character." *Powell* v. *Alabama,* 287 U.S. 45, 68 (1932). While the Court at the close of its Powell opinion did by its language, as this Court frequently does, limit its holding to the particular facts and circumstances of that case, its conclusions about the fundamental nature of the right to counsel are unmistakable. . . . The fact is that in deciding as it did—that "appointment of counsel is not a fundamental right, essential to a fair trial"—the Court in *Betts* v. *Brady* made an abrupt break with its own well-considered precedents. In returning to these old precedents, sounder we believe than the new, we but restore constitutional principles established to achieve a fair system of justice. Not only these precedents but also reason and reflection require us to recognize that in our adversary system of criminal justice, any person haled into court, who is too poor to hire a lawyer, cannot be assured a fair trial unless counsel is provided for him. This seems to us to be an obvious truth. Governments, both state and federal, quite properly spend vast sums of money to establish machinery to try defendants accused of crime. Lawyers to prosecute are everywhere deemed essential to protect the public's interest in an orderly society. Similarly, there are few defendants charged with crime, few indeed, who fail to hire the best lawyers they can get to prepare and present their defenses. The government hires lawyers to prosecute and defendants who have the money hire lawyers to defend are the strongest indications of the widespread belief that lawyers in criminal courts are necessities, not luxuries. The right of one charged with crime to counsel may not be deemed fundamental and essential to fair trials in some countries, but it is in ours. From the very beginning, our state and national constitutions and laws have laid great emphasis on procedural and substantive safeguards designed to assure fair trials before impartial tribunals in which every defendant stands equal before the law. This noble ideal cannot be realized if the poor man charged with crime has to face his accusers without a lawyer to assist him. . . . The Court in *Betts* v. *Brady* departed from the sound wisdom upon which the Court's holding in *Powell* v. *Alabama* rested. Florida, supported by two other States, has asked that *Betts* v. *Brady* be left intact. Twenty-two States, as friends of the Court, argue that *Betts* was "an anach-ronism when handed down" and that it should now be overruled. We agree.

The judgment is reversed and the cause is remanded to the Supreme Court of Florida for further action not inconsistent with this opinion.

Reversed.

MR. JUSTICE DOUGLAS.

While I join the opinion of the Court a brief historical résumé of the relation between the Bill of Rights and the first section of the Fourteenth Amendment seems pertinent. Since the adoption of that Amendment, ten Justices have felt that it protects from infringement by the States the privileges, protections, and safeguards granted by the Bill of Rights.

Justice Field, the first Justice Harlan, and probably Justice Brewer, took that position in *O'Neil* v. *Vermont,* 144 U.S. 323, 362–363, 370–371, as did Justices Black, Douglas, Murphy and Rutledge in *Adamson* v. *California,* 332 U.S. 46, 71–72, 124. And see *Poe* v. *Ullman,* 367 U.S. 497, 515–522 (dissenting opinion). That view was also expressed by Justices Bradley and Swayne in the *Slaughter-House Cases,* 16 Wall. 36, 118–119, 122, and seemingly was accepted by Justice Clifford when he dissented with Justice Field in *Walker* v. *Sauvinet,* 92 U.S. 90, 92. Unfortunately it has never commanded a Court. Yet, happily, all constitutional questions are always open. *Erie R. Co.* v. *Tompkins,* 304 U.S. 64. And what we do today does not foreclose the matter.

My BROTHER HARLAN is of the view that a guarantee of the Bill of Rights that is made applicable to the States by reason of the Fourteenth Amendment is a lesser version of that same guarantee as applied to the Federal Government. Mr. Justice Jackson shared that view. But that view has not prevailed and rights protected against state invasion by the Due Process Clause of the Fourteenth Amendment are not watered-down versions of what the Bill of Rights guarantees.

MR. JUSTICE CLARK, concurring in the result. . . .

MR. JUSTICE HARLAN, concurring.

I agree that *Betts* v. *Brady* should be overruled, but consider it entitled to a more respectful burial than has been accorded, at least on the part of those of us who were not on the Court when that case was decided.

I cannot subscribe to the view that *Betts* v. *Brady* represented "an abrupt break with its own well-considered precedents." Ante, p. 344. In 1932, in *Powell* v. *Alabama*, 287 U.S. 45, a capital case, this Court declared that under the particular facts there presented—"the ignorance and illiteracy of the defendants, their youth, the circumstances of public hostility . . . and above all that they stood in deadly peril of their lives" (287 U.S., at 71)—the state court had a duty to assign counsel for the trial as a necessary requisite of due process of law. It is evident that these limiting facts were not added to the opinion as an afterthought; they were repeatedly emphasized, see 287 U.S., at 52, 57–58, 71, and were clearly regarded as important to the result.

Thus when this Court, a decade later, decided *Betts* v. *Brady*, it did no more than to admit of the possible existence of special circumstances in noncapital as well as capital trials, while at the same time insisting that such circumstances be shown in order to establish a denial of due process. The right to appointed counsel had been recognized as being considerably broader in federal prosecutions, see *Johnson* v. *Zerbst*, 304 U.S. 458, but to have imposed these requirements on the States would indeed have been "an abrupt break" with the almost immediate past. The declaration that the right to appointed counsel in state prosecutions, as established in *Powell* v. *Alabama*, was not limited to capital cases was in truth not a departure from, but an extension of, existing precedent.

The principles declared in Powell and in Betts, however, have had a troubled journey throughout the years that have followed first the one case and then the other. Even by the time of the Betts decision, dictum in at least one of the Court's opinions had indicated that there was an absolute right to the services of counsel in the trial of state capital cases. Such dicta continued to appear in subsequent decisions, and any lingering doubts were finally eliminated by the holding of *Hamilton* v. *Alabama*, 368 U.S. 52.

In noncapital cases, the "special circumstances" rule has continued to exist in form while its substance has been substantially and steadily eroded. In the first decade after Betts, there were cases in which the Court found special circumstances to be lacking, but usually by a sharply divided vote. However, no such decision has been cited to us, and I have found none, after *Quicksall* v. *Michigan*, 339 U.S. 660, decided in 1950. At the same time, there have been not a few cases in which special circumstances were found in little or nothing more than the "complexity" of the legal questions presented, although those questions were often of only routine difficulty. The Court has come to recognize, in other words, that the mere existence of a serious criminal charge constituted in itself special circumstances requiring the services of counsel at trial. In truth the *Betts* v. *Brady* rule is no longer a reality.

This evolution, however, appears not to have been fully recognized by many state courts, in this instance charged with the frontline responsibility for the enforcement of constitutional rights. To continue a rule which is honored by this Court only with lip service is not a healthy thing and in the long run will do disservice to the federal system.

The special circumstances rule has been formally abandoned in capital cases, and the time has now come when it should be similarly abandoned in noncapital cases, at least as to offenses which, as the one involved here, carry the possibility of a substantial prison sentence. (Whether the rule should extend to *all* criminal cases need not now be decided.) This indeed does no more than to make explicit something that has long since been foreshadowed in our decisions.

In agreeing with the Court that the right to counsel in a case such as this should now be expressly recognized as a fundamental right embraced in the Fourteenth Amendment, I wish to make a further observation. When we hold a right or immunity, valid against the Federal Government, to be "implicit in the concept of ordered liberty" and thus valid against the States, I do not read our past decisions to suggest that by so holding, we automatically carry over an entire body of federal law and apply it in full sweep to the States. Any such concept would disregard the frequently wide disparity between the legitimate interests of the States and of the Federal Government, the divergent problems that they face, and the significantly different consequences of their actions. Cf. *Roth* v. *United States*, 354 U.S. 476, 496–508 (separate opinion of this writer). In what is done today I do not understand the Court to depart from the principles laid down in *Palko* v. *Connecticut*, 302 U.S. 319, or to embrace the concept that the Fourteenth Amendment "incorporates" the Sixth Amendment as such.

On these premises I join in the judgment of the Court.

NOTE: *Escobedo* v. *Illinois*, 84 S. Ct. 1758 (1964), held that where a preindictment "investigation is no longer a general inquiry into an unsolved crime but has begun to focus on a particular suspect, the suspect has been taken into custody, the police carry out a process of interrogations that lends itself to eliciting incriminating statements, the suspect has requested and been denied an opportunity to consult with his lawyer, and the police have not effectively warned him of his constitutional right to remain silent, the accused has been denied" the assistance of counsel—and no statement elicited by the police during the interrogation may be used against him at a criminal trial.

Justices Clark, Stewart, Harlan and White dissented—three of them observing *inter alia* that "It is incongruous to assume that the provision for counsel in the Sixth Amendment was meant to amend or supersede the self-incrimination provision of the Fifth Amendment. . . . That amendment addresses itself to the very issue of incriminating admissions . . . and resolves it by proscribing only compelled statements."

Does *Escobedo* mean, as some believe, that the right to counsel begins when a preindictment, police investigation ceases to be general and begins to focus on a particular suspect?

Douglas v. *California*, 372 U.S. 353 (1963), recognized an indigent's right to appointed counsel for at least one appellate review of a criminal conviction where such review is otherwise available as a matter of right.

About one out of three criminal case defendants in the federal courts is a pauper. For some state courts the proportion runs as high as 60 percent. In the light of these figures and the *Gideon* decision, consider the following comment of a young lawyer:

I was appointed to represent in the federal court a defendant charged with narcotics addiction who did not have funds to hire an attorney. After several consultations with my client and one or more trips to the court for arraignment purposes, the actual trial of this case lasted twenty-one days. At the time of the trial, I had been engaged in general law practice for slightly more than five years, was 32 years of age, married, and the father of three children.

Under the circumstances, I lost substantial sums of money and contact with other clients. It became necessary for me to borrow funds to continue my law practice. I received no remuneration whatsoever from my client or the court.

Courts, of course, have no money to pay counsel fees in these cases. Since the late 1930's the Judicial Conference, numerous Attorneys General, and the American Bar Association have urged Congress to provide funds, but none were forthcoming until the Criminal Justice Act of August, 1964. This measure authorizes modest counsel and related fees for federal cases. The states have done little or nothing to provide paid counsel for indigents in state and local cases.

Another aspect of the meaning of *Gideon* is revealed in the following excerpt from *Time Magazine* (p. 53, October 18, 1963):

Florida law officials, even those who felt that the decision was constitutionally sound, were dismayed by its practical consequences. Of the 8,000 prisoners in Florida penal institutions, 4,542 were convicted without benefit of counsel. Already more than 3,000 have petitioned for review of their convictions. Court calendars are jammed; distraught prosecutors are working overtime searching petitioners' records and drawing up answering briefs; county budget directors are hunting desperately for funds to pay for retrials. The only hope for straightening things out, says the clerk of Escambia County's court of records, is to give some "Gideonite" a new trial and reconvict him. "If we give him a heavier sentence than he got the first time, maybe that will serve as a lesson to the others."

That lesson will not be easy to teach. In many cases where the courts have granted a new trial, it is virtually impossible for the prosecutor to rebuild the case—records and evidence are gone, witnesses have disappeared. Judge Joseph McNulty points to the pending case of a man sentenced to life imprisonment in 1938 for second-degree murder after being tried without a lawyer. "He's pleading not guilty, and it will be impossible to try him. The witnesses are dead or gone, and I'm not sure they can even prove there was a corpse. They'll probably have to let him go."

Improving Justice. While the Gideon decision will undoubtedly lead to the freeing of many prisoners who were guilty as charged, it has also improved the processes of justice in new criminal cases in Florida. After the Supreme Court ruling, Florida speedily passed a public-defender law requiring courts to appoint counsel in criminal cases unless the defendant explicitly waives his right to counsel. And courts have begun to keep fuller, more careful records in all criminal prosecutions.

At the time of the Gideon decision, four states in addition to Florida— Alabama, Mississippi and the two Carolinas—had no laws requiring counsel for indigent defendants except in capital cases. Since then, the legislatures in Alabama and North Carolina have passed measures to provide counsel for lawyer-less defendants in all felony cases. Mississippi courts have adopted a policy of appointing counsel for defendants charged with felonies, and South Carolina judges no longer permit defendants without counsel to plead guilty. In all four states, prisoners have petitioned for review of their cases.

And what of Clarence Gideon himself? He was retried in a state court, acquitted and freed. He is now living in Gainesville, Fla., lawfully employed as an electrician.

Ellis MacDougall, Director of the Department of Corrections of South Carolina, reported that in his state sixty-seven of the first sixty-eight cases retried on the basis of *Gideon* went against the accused who received their original sentences *without credit for time already served.*

4. A FAIR TRIBUNAL AND PROSECUTOR

TUMEY v. *OHIO*
273 U.S. 510 (1927)

State legislation, supplemented by a municipal ordinance, authorized the mayor of an Ohio city to try bootlegging cases. Half the fines he collected were to go to the city. In addition to his salary the mayor was to receive his costs from the accused, but only in case of conviction. The Supreme Court, through Chief Justice Taft, held this procedure invalid as follows:

All questions of judicial qualification may not involve constitutional validity. Thus matters of kinship, personal bias, state policy, remoteness of interest would seem generally to be matters merely of legislative discretion. *Wheeling* v. *Black*, 25 W. Va. 266,270. But it certainly violates the Fourteenth Amendment and deprives a defendant in a criminal case of due process of law to subject his liberty or property to the judgment of a court, the judge of which has a direct, personal, substantial pecuniary interest in reaching a conclusion against him in his case. . . .

We have been referred to no cases at common law in England, prior to the separation of the colonies from the mother country, showing a practice that inferior judicial officers were dependent upon the conviction of the defendant for receiving their compensation. Indeed, in analogous cases it is very clear that the slightest pecuniary interest of an officer, judicial or quasi-judicial, in the resolving of the subject-matter which he was to decide, rendered the decision voidable. *Bonham's Case*, 8 Coke, 118a [holding a fine imposed by the Royal College of Physicians invalid, partly because the College was to receive one-half the fine]. . . . From this review we con-

clude that a system by which an inferior judge is paid for his service only when he convicts the defendant has not become so embedded by custom in the general practice, either at common law or in this country, that it can be regarded as due process of law, unless the costs usually imposed are so small that they may be properly ignored as within the maxim *de minimis non curat lex*. . . .

It is . . . argued that the evidence shows clearly that the defendant was guilty and that he was only fined $100, which was the minimum amount, and therefore that he can not complain of a lack of due process either in his conviction or in the amount of the judgment. The plea was not guilty and he was convicted. No matter what the evidence was against him, he had the right to have an impartial judge. He seasonably raised the objection and was entitled to halt the trial because of the disqualification of the judge, which existed both because of his direct pecuniary interest in the outcome, and because of his official motive to convict and to graduate the fine to help the financial needs of the village. There were thus presented at the outset both features of the disqualification.

MOORE v. DEMPSEY

261 U.S. 86 (1923)

MR. JUSTICE HOLMES delivered the opinion of the Court. . . .

The appellants are five Negroes who were convicted of murder in the first degree and sentenced to death by the Court of the State of Arkansas. The ground of the petition for the writ is that the proceedings in the State Court, although a trial in form, were only a form, and that the appellants were hurried to conviction under the pressure of a mob, without any regard for their rights, and without according to them due process of law.

The case stated by the petition is as follows, and it will be understood that while we put it in narrative form, we are not affirming the facts to be as stated, but only what we must take them to be, as they are admitted by the demurrer: On the night of September 30, 1919, a number of colored people, assembled in their church, were attacked and fired upon by a body of white men, and, in the disturbance that followed a white man was killed. The report of the killing caused great excitement and was followed by the hunting down and shooting of many Negroes, and also by the killing, on October 1, of one Clinton Lee, a white man, for whose murder the petitioners were indicted. They seem to have been arrested with many others on the same day. The petitioners say that Lee must have been killed by other whites, but that we leave on one side, as what we have to deal with is not the petitioners' innocence or guilt, but solely the question whether their constitutional rights have been preserved. They say that their meeting was to employ counsel for protection against extortions practised upon them by the landowners, and that the landowners tried to prevent their effort; but that again we pass by as not directly bearing upon the trial. It should be mentioned, however, that O. S. Bratton, a son

of the counsel who is said to have been contemplated, and who took part in the argument here, arriving for consultation on October 1, is said to have barely escaped being mobbed; that he was arrested and confined during the month on a charge of murder, and on October 31 was indicted for barratry, but, later in the day, was told that he would be discharged, but that he must leave secretly by a closed automobile to take the train at West Helena, four miles away, to avoid being mobbed. It is alleged that the judge of the Court in which the petitioners were tried facilitated the departure, and went with Bratton to see him safely off.

A Committee of Seven was appointed by the Governor in regard to what the committee called the "insurrection" in the county. The newspapers daily published inflammatory articles. On the seventh a statement by one of the committee was made public, to the effect that the present trouble was "a deliberately planned insurrection of the Negroes against the whites, directed by an organization known as the 'Progressive Farmers and Household Union of America,' established for the purpose of banding Negroes together for the killing of white people." According to the statement, the organization was started by a swindler, to get money from the blacks.

Shortly after the arrest of the petitioners a mob marched to the jail for the purpose of lynching them, but were prevented by the presence of United States troops and the promise of some of the Committee of Seven and other leading officials that, if the mob would refrain, as the petition puts it, they would execute those found guilty in the form of law. The Committee's own statement was that the reason that the people refrained from mob violence was "that this Committee gave our citizens their solemn promise that the law would be carried out." According to affidavits of two white men and the colored witnesses on whose testimony the petitioners were convicted, produced by the petitioners since the last decision of the Supreme Court, hereafter mentioned, the Committee made good their promise by calling colored witnesses and having them whipped and tortured until they would say what was wanted, among them being the two relied on to prove the petitioners' guilt. However this may be, a grand jury of white men was organized on October 27, with one of the Committee of Seven, and, it is alleged, with many of a posse organized to fight the blacks, upon it, and, on the morning of the 29th, the indictment was returned. On November 3 the petitioners were brought into Court, informed that a certain lawyer was appointed their counsel, and were placed on trial before a white jury,—blacks being systematically excluded from both grand and petit juries. The Court and neighborhood were thronged with an adverse crowd that threatened the most dangerous consequences to anyone interfering with the desired result. The counsel did not venture to demand delay or a change of venue, to challenge a juryman, or to ask for separate trials. He had no preliminary consultation with the accused, called no witnesses for the defense, although they could have been produced, and did not put the defendants on the stand. The trial lasted about three quarters of an hour, and in less than five minutes the jury brought in a verdict of guilty of murder in the first degree. According to the allegations and affidavits there never was a chance for the petitioners to be acquitted; no juryman could have voted for an acquittal and continued to live in Phillips County, and if any prisoner, by any chance, had been acquitted by a jury, he could not have escaped the mob. . . .

In *Frank* v. *Mangum*, 237 U.S. 309, 335, it was recognized, of course, that if in fact a trial is dominated by a mob, so that there is an actual interference with the course of justice, there is a departure from due process of law; and that "if the State, sup-

plying no corrective process, carries into execution a judgment of death or imprisonment based upon a verdict thus produced by mob domination, the State deprives the accused of his life or liberty without due process of law." We assume, in accordance with that case, that the corrective process supplied by the State may be so adequate that interference by habeas corpus ought not be allowed. It certainly is true that mere mistakes of law in the course of a trial are not to be corrected in that way. But if the case is that the whole proceeding is a mask,—that counsel, jury, and judge were swept to the fatal end by an irresistible wave of public passion, and that the State Courts failed to correct the wrong,—neither perfection in the machinery for the correction nor the possibility that the trial court and counsel saw no other way of avoiding an immediate outbreak of the mob can prevent this Court from securing to the petitioners their constitutional rights.

In this case a motion for a new trial on the ground alleged in this petition was overruled, and, upon exceptions and appeal to the Supreme Court, the judgment was affirmed. The Supreme Court said that the complaint of discrimination against petitioners by the exclusion of colored men from the jury came too late, and, by way of answer to the objection that no fair trial could be had in the circumstances, stated that it could not say "that this must necessarily have been the case"; that eminent counsel was appointed to defend the petitioners, that the trial was had according to law, the jury correctly charged, and the testimony legally sufficient. On June 8, 1921, two days before the date fixed for their execution, a petition for habeas corpus was presented to the Chancellor, and he issued the writ and an injunction against the execution of the petitioners; but the Supreme Court of the State held the Chancellor had no jurisdiction under the state law, whatever might be the law of the United States. The present petition, perhaps, was suggested by the language of the Court: "What the result would be of an application to a Federal Court we need not inquire." It was presented to the District Court on September 21. We shall not say more concerning the corrective process afforded to the petitioners than that it does not seem to us sufficient to allow a Judge of the United States to escape the duty of examining the facts for himself, when, if true, as alleged, they make the trial absolutely void. We have confined the statement to facts admitted by the demurrer. We will not say that they cannot be met, but it appears to us unavoidable that the District Judge should find whether the facts alleged are true, and whether they can be explained so far as to leave the state proceedings undisturbed.

Order reversed. The case to stand for hearing before the District Court.

MR. JUSTICE MCREYNOLDS [with whom MR. JUSTICE SUTHERLAND concurred] dissenting: . . .

The Supreme Court of the State twice reversed the conviction of other Negroes charged with committing murder during the disorders of September, 1919. The first opinion came down on the very day upon which the judgment against petitioners was affirmed, and held the verdict so defective that no judgment could be entered upon it. The second directed a reversal because the trial court had refused to hear evidence on the motion to set aside the regular panel of the petit jury. *Banks* v. *State*, 143 Ark. 154; *Ware* v. *State*, 146 Ark. 321. The Supreme Court, as well as the trial court, considered the claims of petitioners, set forth by trusted counsel in the motion for a new trial. This Court denied a petition for certiorari wherein the facts and circumstances now relied upon were set out with great detail. . . .

With all those things before him, I am unable to say that the District Judge, acquainted with local conditions, erred when he held the petition for the writ of habeas corpus insufficient. His duty was to consider the whole case and decide whether there appeared to be substantial reason for further proceedings. . . .

IRVIN v. DOWD

366 U.S. 717 (1961)

MR. JUSTICE CLARK delivered the opinion of the Court.

This is a habeas corpus proceeding, brought to test the validity of petitioner's conviction for murder and sentence of death in the Circuit Court of Gibson County, Indiana. The Indiana Supreme Court affirmed the conviction in *Irvin* v. *State*, 236 Ind. 384, 139 N.E.2d 898, and we denied direct review by certiorari "without prejudice to filing for federal habeas corpus after exhausting state remedies." 353 U.S. 948. Petitioner immediately sought a writ of habeas corpus, under 28 U.S.C. § 2241, in the District Court for the Northern District of Indiana, claiming that his conviction had been obtained in violation of the Fourteenth Amendment in that he did not receive a fair trial. That court dismissed the proceeding on the ground that petitioner had failed to exhaust his state remedies. 153 F. Supp. 531. On appeal, the Court of Appeals for the Seventh Circuit affirmed the dismissal. 251 F.2d 548. We granted certiorari, 356 U.S. 948, and remanded to the Court of Appeals for decision on the merits or remand to the District Court for reconsideration. 359 U.S. 394. The Court of Appeals retained jurisdiction and decided the claim adversely to petitioner. 271 F.2d 552. We granted certiorari, 361 U.S. 959.

As stated in the former opinion, 359 U.S. at pages 396–397:

"The constitutional claim arises in this way. Six murders were committed in the vicinity of Evansville, Indiana, two in December 1954, and four in March 1955. The crimes, extensively covered by news media in the locality, aroused great excitement and indignation throughout Vanderburgh County, where Evansville is located, and adjoining Gibson County, a rural county of approximately 30,000 inhabitants. The petitioner was arrested on April 8, 1955. Shortly thereafter, the Prosecutor of Vanderburgh County and Evansville police officials issued press releases, which were intensively publicized, stating that the petitioner had confessed to the six murders. The Vanderburgh County Grand Jury soon indicted the petitioner for the murder which resulted in his conviction. This was the murder of Whitney Wesley Kerr allegedly committed in Vanderburgh County on December 23, 1954. Counsel appointed to defend petitioner immediately sought a change of venue from Vanderburgh County, which was granted, but to adjoining Gibson County. Alleging that the widespread and inflammatory publicity had also highly prejudiced the inhabitants of Gibson County against the petitioner, counsel, on October 29, 1955, sought another change of venue, from Gibson County to a county sufficiently removed from the Evansville locality that a fair trial would not be prejudiced. The motion was denied, apparently because the pertinent Indiana statute allows only a single change of venue."

During the course of the *voir dire* examination, which lasted some four weeks, petitioner filed two more motions for a change of venue and eight motions for continuances. All were denied. . . .

England, from whom the Western World has largely taken its concepts of individual liberty and of the dignity and worth of every man, has bequeathed to us safeguards for their preservation, the most priceless of which is that of trial by jury. This right has become as much American as it was once the most English. Although this Court has said that the Fourteenth Amendment does not demand the use of jury trials in a State's criminal procedure, *Fay* v. *New York*, 332 U.S. 261; *Palko* v. *State of Connecticut*, 302 U.S. 319, every State has constitutionally

provided trial by jury. See Columbia University Legislative Drafting Research Fund, *Index Digest of State Constitutions* 578–579 (1959). In essence, the right to jury trial guarantees to the criminally accused a fair trial by a panel of impartial, "indifferent" jurors. The failure to accord an accused a fair hearing violates even the minimal standards of due process. *In re Oliver*, 333 U.S. 257; *Tumey* v. *Ohio*, 273 U.S. 510. "A fair trial in a fair tribunal is a basic requirement of due process." *In re Murchison*, 349 U.S. 133, 136. In the ultimate analysis, only the jury can strip a man of his liberty or of his life. In the language of Lord Coke, a juror must be as "indifferent as he stands unsworn." Co. Litt. 155b. His verdict must be based upon the evidence developed at the trial. Cf. *Thompson* v. *City of Louisville*, 362 U.S. 199. This is true, regardless of the heinousness of the crime charged, the apparent guilt of the offender or the station in life which he occupies. It was so written into our law as early as 1807 by Chief Justice Marshall in 1 *Burr's Trial* 416 (1807). "The theory of the law is that a juror who has formed an opinion cannot be impartial." *Reynolds* v. *United States*, 98 U.S. 145, 155.

It is not required, however, that the jurors be totally ignorant of the facts and issues involved. In these days of swift, widespread and diverse methods of communication, an important case can be expected to arouse the interest of the public in the vicinity, and scarcely any of those best qualified to serve as jurors will not have formed some impression or opinion as to the merits of the case. This is particularly true in criminal cases. To hold that the mere existence of any preconceived notion as to the guilt or innocence of an accused, without more, is sufficient to rebut the presumption of a prospective juror's impartiality would be to establish an impossible standard. It is sufficient if the juror can lay aside his impression or opinion and render a verdict based on the evidence presented in court. . . .

Here the buildup of prejudice is clear and convincing. An examination of the then current community pattern of thought as indicated by the popular news media is singularly revealing. For example, petitioner's first motion for a change of venue from Gibson County alleged that the awaited trial of petitioner had become the *cause célèbre* of this small community—so much so that curbstone opinions, not only as to petitioner's guilt but even as to what punishment he should receive, were solicited and recorded on the public streets by a roving reporter, and later were broadcast over the local stations. A reading of the 46 exhibits which petitioner attached to his motion indicates that a barrage of newspaper headlines, articles, cartoons and pictures was unleashed against him during the six or seven months preceding his trial. The motion further alleged that the newspapers in which the stories appeared were delivered regularly to approximately 95% of the dwellings in Gibson County and that, in addition, the Evansville radio and TV stations, which likewise blanketed that county, also carried extensive newscasts covering the same incidents. These stories revealed the details of his background, including a reference to crimes committed when a juvenile, his convictions for arson almost 20 years previously, for burglary and by a court-martial on AWOL charges during the war. He was accused of being a parole violator. The headlines announced his police line-up identification, that he faced a lie detector test, had been placed at the scene of the crime and that the six murders were solved but petitioner refused to confess. Finally, they announced his confession to the six murders and the fact of his indictment for four of them in Indiana. They reported petitioner's offer to plead guilty if promised a 99-year sentence, but also the determination, on the other hand, of the prosecutor to secure the death penalty, and that petitioner had confessed to 24 burglaries (the *modus operandi* of these robberies was compared to that of the murders and the similarity noted). One story dramatically relayed the promise of a sheriff to devote his life to securing petitioner's execution by the State of Kentucky, where petitioner is alleged to have committed one of the six murders, if Indiana failed to do so. Another characterized petitioner as remorseless and without conscience but also as having been found sane by a court-appointed panel of doctors. In many of the stories petitioner was described as the "confessed slayer of six," a parole violator and fraudulent-check artist. Petitioner's court-appointed counsel was quoted as having received "much criticism over being Irvin's counsel" and it was pointed out, by way of excusing the attorney, that he would be subject to disbarment should he refuse to represent Irvin. On the day before the trial the newspapers carried the story that Irvin had orally admitted the murder of Kerr (the victim in this case) as well as "the robbery-murder of Mrs. Mary Holland; the murder of Mrs. Wilhemina Sailer in Posey County, and the slaughter of three members of the Duncan family in Henderson County, Ky."

It cannot be gainsaid that the force of this continued adverse publicity caused a sustained excitement and fostered a strong prejudice among the people of Gibson County. In fact, on the second day devoted to the selection of the jury, the newspapers reported that "strong feelings, often bitter and angry, rumbled to the surface," and that "the extent to which the multiple murders—three in one family—have aroused feelings throughout the area was emphasized Friday when 27 of the 35 prospective jurors questioned were excused for holding biased pretrial opinions. . . ." A few days later the feeling was described as "a pattern of deep and bitter prejudice against the former pipe-fitter." Spectator comments, as printed by the newspapers, were "my mind is made up"; "I think he is guilty"; and "he should be hanged."

Finally, and with remarkable understatement, the headlines reported that "impartial jurors are hard to find." The panel consisted of 430 persons. The court itself excused 268 of those on challenges for cause as having fixed opinions as to the guilt of petitioner; 103 were excused because of conscientious objection to the imposition of the death penalty; 20, the maximum allowed, were peremptorily challenged by petitioner and 10 by the State; 12 persons and two alternates were selected as jurors and the rest were excused on personal grounds, e.g., deafness, doctor's orders, etc. An examination of the 2,783-page *voir dire* record shows that 370 prospective jurors or almost 90% of those examined on the point (10 members of the panel were never asked whether or not they had any opinion) entertained some opinion as to guilt—ranging in intensity from mere suspicion to absolute certainty. A number admitted that, if they were in the accused's place in the dock and he in theirs on the jury with their opinions, they would not want him on a jury.

Here the "pattern of deep and bitter prejudice" shown to be present throughout the community, cf. *Stroble* v. *State of California*, 343 U.S. 181, was clearly reflected in the sum total of the *voir dire* examination of a majority of the jurors finally placed in the jury box. Eight out of the 12 thought petitioner was guilty. With such an opinion permeating their minds, it would be difficult to say that each could exclude this preconception of guilt from his deliberations. The influence that lurks in an opinion once formed is so persistent that it unconsciously fights detachment from the mental processes of the average man. See *Delaney* v. *United States*, 1 Cir., 199 F.2d 107, 39 A.L.R.2d 1300. Where one's life is at stake—and accounting for the frailties of human nature—we can only say that under the light of the circumstances here the finding of impartiality does not meet constitutional standards. Two-thirds of the jurors had an opinion that petitioner was guilty and were familiar with the material facts and circumstances involved, including the fact that other murders were attributed to him, some going so far as to say that it would take evidence to overcome their belief. One said that he "could not . . . give the defendant the benefit of the doubt that he is innocent." Another stated that he had a "somewhat" certain fixed opinion as to petitioner's guilt. No doubt each juror

was sincere when he said that he would be fair and impartial to petitioner, but psychological impact requiring such a declaration before one's fellows is often its father. Where so many, so many times, admitted prejudice, such a statement of impartiality can be given little weight. As one of the jurors put it, "You can't forget what you hear and see." With his life at stake, it is not requiring too much that petitioner be tried in an atmosphere undisturbed by so huge a wave of public passion and by a jury other than one in which two-thirds of the members admit, before hearing any testimony, to possessing a belief in his guilt. . . .

Petitioner's detention and sentence of death pursuant to the void judgment is in violation of the Constitution of the United States and he is therefore entitled to be freed therefrom. The judgments of the Court of Appeals and the District Court are vacated and the case remanded to the latter. However, petitioner is still subject to custody under the indictment filed by the State of Indiana in the Circuit Court of Gibson County charging him with murder in the first degree and may be tried on this or another indictment. . . . Therefore, on remand, the District Court should enter such orders as are appropriate and consistent with this opinion, cf. *Grandsinger* v. *Bovey*, D.C., 153 F. Supp. 201, 240, which allowed the State a reasonable time in which to retry petitioner. . . .

Vacated and remanded.

MR. JUSTICE FRANKFURTER, concurring.

Of course I agree with the Court's opinion. But this is, unfortunately, not an isolated case that happened in Evansville, Indiana, nor an atypical miscarriage of justice due to anticipatory trial by newspapers instead of trial in court before a jury. . . .

But, again and again, such disregard of fundamental fairness is so flagrant that the Court is compelled, as it was only a week ago, to reverse a conviction in which prejudicial newspaper intrusion has poisoned the outcome. *Janko* v. *United States*, 81

S.Ct. 1662. . . . This Court has not yet decided that the fair administration of criminal justice must be subordinated to another safeguard of our constitutional system—freedom of the press, properly conceived. The Court has not yet decided that, while convictions must be reversed and miscarriages of justice result because the minds of jurors or potential jurors were poisoned, the poisoner is constitutionally protected in plying his trade.

NOTE: In *Rideau* v. *Louisiana,* 373 U.S. 73 (1963), petitioner's jail confession was filmed and broadcast three times by a local television station. ". . . Without pausing to examine a particularized transcript of the *voir dire* examination of the members of the jury," the Court held that a motion for change of venue should have been granted. "For anyone who has ever watched television, the conclusion cannot be avoided that this spectacle . . . in a very real sense *was* Rideau's trial—at which he pleaded guilty to murder. Any subsequent court proceeding in a community so pervasively exposed to such a spectacle could be but a hollow formality."

Mr. Justice Clark, joined by his Brother Harlan, objected because there had been no showing of a "substantial nexus between the televised 'interview' and petitioner's trial. . . ."

HERNANDEZ v. TEXAS

347 U.S. 475 (1954)

MR. CHIEF JUSTICE WARREN delivered the opinion of the Court.

The petitioner, Pete Hernandez, was indicted for the murder of one Joe Espinosa by a grand jury in Jackson County, Texas. He was convicted and sentenced to life imprisonment. The Texas Court of Criminal Appeals affirmed the judgment of the trial court. 251 S.W.2d 531. Prior to the trial, the petitioner, by his counsel, offered timely motions to quash the indictment and the jury panel. He alleged that persons of Mexican descent were systematically excluded from service as jury commissioners, grand jurors, and petit jurors, although there were such persons fully qualified to serve residing in Jackson County. The petitioner asserted that exclusion of this class deprived him, as a member of the class, of the equal protection of the laws guaranteed by the Fourteenth Amendment of the Constitution. After a hearing, the trial court denied the motions. At the trial, the motions were renewed, further evidence taken, and the motions again denied. An allegation that the trial court erred in denying the motions was the sole basis of petitioner's appeal. . . .

In numerous decisions, this Court has held that it is a denial of the equal protection of the laws to try a defendant of a particular race or color under an indictment issued by a grand jury, or before a petit jury, from which all persons of his race or color have, solely because of that race or color, been excluded by the State, whether acting through its legislature, its courts, or its executive or administrative officers. Although the Court has had little occasion to rule on the question directly, it has been recognized since *Strauder* v. *State of West Virginia,* 100 U.S. 303, 25 L.Ed. 664, that the exclusion of a class of persons from jury service on grounds other than race or color may also deprive a defendant who is a member of that class of the constitutional guarantee of equal protection of the laws. The State of Texas would have us hold that there are only two classes—white and Negro—within the contemplation of the Fourteenth Amendment. The decisions of this Court do not support that view. And, except where the question presented involves the exclusion of persons of Mexican descent from juries, Texas courts have taken a broader view of the scope of the equal protection clause.

Throughout our history differences in race and color have defined easily identifiable groups which have at times required the aid of the courts in securing equal treatment under the laws. But community prejudices are not static, and from time to time other differences from the community norm may define other groups which need the same protection. Whether such a group exists within a community is a question of fact. When the existence of a distinct class is demonstrated, and it is further shown that the laws, as written or as supplied, single out that class for different treatment not based on some reasonable classification, the guarantees of the Constitution have been violated. The Fourteenth Amendment is not directed solely against discrimination due to a "two-class theory"—that is, based upon differences between "white" and Negro.

As the petitioner acknowledges, the Texas system of selecting grand and petit jurors by the use of jury commissions is fair on its face and capable of being utilized without discrimination. But as this Court has held, the system is susceptible to abuse and can be employed in a discriminatory manner. The exclusion of otherwise eligible persons from jury service solely because of their ancestry or national origin is discrimination prohibited by the Fourteenth Amendment. The Texas statute makes no such discrimination, but the petitioner alleges that those administering the law do.

The petitioner's initial burden in substantiating his charge of group discrimina-tion was to prove that persons of Mexican descent constitute a separate class in Jackson County, distinct from "whites." One method by which this may be demonstrated is by showing the attitude of the community. Here the testimony of responsible officials and citizens contained the admission that residents of the community distinguished between "white" and "Mexican." The participation of persons of Mexican descent in business and community groups was shown to be slight. Until very recent times, children of Mexican descent were required to attend a segregated school for the first four grades. At least one restaurant in town prominently displayed a sign announcing "No Mexicans Served." On the courthouse grounds at the time of the hearing, there were two men's toilets, one unmarked, and the other marked "Colored Men" and "Hombres Aqui" ("Men Here"). No substantial evidence was offered to rebut the logical inference to be drawn from these facts, and it must be concluded that petitioner succeeded in his proof.

Having established the existence of a class, petitioner was then charged with the burden of proving discrimination. To do so, he relied on the pattern of proof established by *Norris* v. *State of Alabama*, 294 U.S. 587. In that case, proof that Negroes constituted a substantial segment of the population of the jurisdiction, that some Negroes were qualified to serve as jurors, and that none had been called for jury service over an extended period of time, was held to constitute prima facie proof of the systematic exclusion of Negroes from jury service. This holding, sometimes called the "rule of exclusion," has been applied in other cases, and it is available in supplying proof of discrimination against any delineated class.

The petitioner established that 14% of the population of Jackson County were persons with Mexican or Latin American surnames, and that 11% of the males over 21 bore such names. The County Tax Assessor testified that 6 or 7 percent of the freeholders on the tax rolls of the County were persons of Mexican descent. The State of Texas stipulated that "for the last twenty-five years there is no record of any person with a Mexican or Latin American name having served on a jury commission, grand jury or petit jury in Jackson County." The parties also stipulated that "there are some male persons of Mexican or Latin American descent in Jackson County who, by virtue of being citizens, freeholders, and having all other legal prerequisites to jury service, are eligible to serve as members of a jury commission, grand jury and/or petit jury."

The petitioner met the burden of proof imposed in *Norris* v. *Alabama, supra.* To rebut the strong prima facie case of the denial of the equal protection of the laws guaranteed by the Constitution thus established, the State offered the testimony of five jury commissioners that they had not discriminated against persons of Mexican or Latin American descent in selecting jurors. They stated that their only objective had been to select those whom they thought were best qualified. This testimony is not enough to overcome the petitioner's case. As the Court said in *Norris* v. *Alabama*:

"That showing as to the long-continued exclusion of Negroes from jury service, and as to the many Negroes qualified for that service, could not be met by mere generalities. If, in the presence of such testimony as defendant adduced, the mere general assertions by officials of their performance of duty were to be accepted as an adequate justification for the complete exclusion of Negroes from jury service, the constitutional provision . . . would be but a vain and illusory requirement."

The same reasoning is applicable to these facts.

Circumstances or chance may well dictate that no persons in a certain class will serve on a particular jury or during some particular period. But it taxes our credulity to say that mere chance resulted in there being no members of this class among the over six thousand jurors called in the past 25 years. The result bespeaks discrimination, whether or not it was a conscious decision on the part of any individual jury commissioner. The judgment of conviction must be reversed.

To say that this decision revives the rejected contention that the Fourteenth Amendment requires proportional representation of all the component ethnic groups of the community on every jury ignores the facts. The petitioner did not seek proportional representation, nor did he claim a right to have persons of Mexican descent sit on the particular juries which he faced. His only claim is the right to be indicted and tried by juries from which all members of his class are not systematically excluded—juries selected from among all qualified persons regardless of national origin or descent. To this much, he is entitled by the Constitution.

Reversed.

NOTE: According to Federal Judge Richard Rives of Alabama, "lawyers residing in many Southern jurisdictions rarely, almost to the point of never, raise the issue of systematic exclusion of Negroes from juries"—and the few who do so do it "at the risk of personal sacrifice which may extend to loss of practice and social ostracism."

Under the *Palko* principle the states, unlike the federal government under the Sixth Amendment, are not required to provide jury trials. It is enough that they provide fair trials. *Maxwell* v. *Dow*, 176 U.S. 581 (1900). If juries are used, they must conform to the principles indicated in *Irvin* and *Hernandez*.

In July, 1962, Judge A. J. Bowe reported that requests for jury trials in Chicago's municipal court dropped 70 percent after the fee for a six-man jury trial was raised from $6 to $50, and for a 12-man jury from $12 to $100.

ALCORTA v. *TEXAS*

355 U.S. 28 (1957)

PER CURIAM.

Petitioner, Alvaro Alcorta, was indicted for murder in a Texas state court for stabbing his wife to death. Vernon's Tex. Pen. Code, 1948, Art. 1256. He admitted the killing but claimed it occurred in a fit of passion when he discovered his wife, whom he had already suspected of marital infidelity, kissing one Castilleja late at night in a parked car. Petitioner relied on Texas statutes which treat killing under the influence of a "sudden passion arising from an adequate cause . . . as would commonly produce a degree of anger, rage, resentment, or terror in a person of ordinary temper sufficient to render the mind incapable of cool reflection" as murder without malice punishable by a maximum sentence of five years imprisonment. Vernon'sTex.Pen. Code, 1948, Arts. 1257a, 1257b, 1257c. The jury, however, found him guilty of murder with malice and, acting under broad statutory authority to determine the extent of punishment, sentenced him to death. The judgment and sentence were affirmed by the Texas Court of Criminal Appeals. 294 S.W.2d 112.

Castilleja, the only eye witness to the killing, testified for the state at petitioner's trial. In response to inquiries by the prosecutor about his relationship with the petitioner's wife, Castilleja said that he had simply driven her home from work a couple of times, and in substance testified that his relationship with her had been nothing more than a casual friendship. He stated that he had given her a ride on the night she was killed and was parked in front of her home with his car lights out at two o'clock in the morning because of engine trouble. The prosecutor then asked what had transpired between Castilleja and petitioner's wife in the parked car:

"Q. Did you have a conversation with Herlinda? A. Yes; she opened the door. She was going to get off [*sic*] and, then, she told me to tell my sister to come and pick her up in the morning so she could go to church.

"Q. To tell your sister, Delfina Cabrera, to come pick her up in the morning so she could go to church? A. Yes."

At the conclusion of Castilleja's testimony the following colloquy took place between him and the prosecutor:

"Q. Natividad [Castilleja], were you in love with Herlinda? A. No.

"Q. Was she in love with you? A. No.

"Q. Had you ever talked about love? A. No.

"Q. Had you ever had any dates with her other than to take her home? A. No. Well, just when I brought her from there.

"Q. Just when you brought her from work? A. Yes."

All this testimony was quite plainly inconsistent with petitioner's claim that he had come upon his wife kissing Castilleja in the parked car.

Some time after petitioner's conviction had been affirmed Castilleja issued a sworn statement in which he declared that he had given false testimony at the trial. Relying on this statement petitioner asked the trial court to issue a writ of habeas corpus. He contended that he had been denied a fair trial in violation of State and Federal Constitutions because Castilleja had testified falsely, with the knowledge of the prosecutor, that his relationship with petitioner's wife had been only "that of a friend and neighbor, and that he had had no 'dates,' nor other relations with her, when in truth and in fact the witness had been her lover and paramour, and had had sexual intercourse with her on many occasions. . . ." Petitioner further alleged that he had no knowledge of this illicit intercourse at the time of his trial.

A hearing was held on the petition for habeas corpus. Castilleja was called as a witness. He confessed having sexual intercourse with petitioner's wife on five or six occasions within a relatively brief period before her death. He testified that he had informed the prosecutor of this before trial and the prosecutor had told him he should not volunteer any information about such intercourse but if specifically asked about it to answer truthfully. The prosecutor took the stand and admitted that these statements were true. He conceded that he had not told petitioner about Castilleja's illicit intercourse with his wife. He also admitted that he had not included this information in a written statement taken from Castilleja prior to the trial but instead had noted it in a separate record. At the conclusion of the hearing the trial judge denied the petition for habeas corpus. Petitioner then applied to the Texas Court of Criminal Appeals for a writ of habeas corpus but that court, acting on the record made at the hearing before the trial court, also refused to issue the writ. We granted certiorari, 353 U.S. 972. Texas concedes that petitioner has exhausted all remedies available to him under state law.

Under the general principles laid down by this Court in *Mooney* v. *Holohan,* 294 U.S. 103, and *Pyle* v. *State of Kansas,* 317 U.S. 213, petitioner was not accorded due process of law. It cannot seriously be disputed that Castilleja's testimony, taken as a whole, gave the jury the false impression that his relationship with petitioner's wife was nothing more than that of casual friendship. This testimony was elicited by the prosecutor who knew of the illicit intercourse between Castilleja and petitioner's wife. Undoubtedly Castilleja's testimony was seriously prejudicial to petitioner. It tended squarely to refute his claim that he had adequate cause for a surge of "sudden passion" in which he killed his wife. If Castilleja's relationship with petitioner's wife had been truthfully portrayed to the jury, it would have, apart from impeaching his credibility, tended to corroborate petitioner's contention that he had found his wife embracing Castilleja. If petitioner's defense had been accepted by the jury, as it might well have been if Castilleja had not been allowed to testify falsely, to the knowledge of the prosecutor, his offense would have been reduced to "murder without malice" precluding the death penalty now imposed upon him.

The judgment is reversed and the cause is remanded to the Court of Criminal Appeals of the State of Texas for further proceedings not inconsistent with this opinion.

It is so ordered.

Reversed and remanded.

NOTE: In *Jencks* v. *United States,* 355 U.S. 657 (1957), it was held that a "criminal action must be dismissed when the Government [refuses to release for use by the accused] relevant statements or reports . . . of Government witnesses touching the subject matter of their testimony at the trial." The purpose of such release, of course, is to enable the accused to explore any discrepancy between what an "informer" says behind closed doors and what he is willing to say under oath in open court where he is subject to cross-examination. The decision in this case is not a matter of constitutional law, but of judicial administration (compare the *Weeks* rule), a discharge of the Court's responsibility for the fair administration of justice in the federal courts. It is simply a special application of the principle of discovery which has long found expression in the federal rules with respect both to civil (Rule 34) and criminal (Rule 16) procedure. The thought is that the outcome of a lawsuit should not depend upon the ability of one side to suppress evidence which might be of value to the other side. The background of the *Jencks* case of course is the "revolving informer" whose information apparently varies with the needs of the moment.[1]

5. SEARCH AND SEIZURE

AGUILAR v. TEXAS
84 S. Ct. 1509 (1964)

MR. JUSTICE GOLDBERG delivered the opinion of the Court.

This case presents questions concerning the constitutional requirements for obtaining a state search warrant.

Two Houston police officers applied to a local Justice of the Peace for a warrant to search for narcotics in petitioner's home. In support of their application, the officers submitted an affidavit which, in relevant part, recited that:

"Affiants have received reliable information from a credible person and do believe that heroin, marijuana, barbiturates, and other narcotics and narcotic paraphernalia are being kept at the above described premises for the purpose of sale and use contrary to the provisions of the law."

The search warrant was issued.

In executing the warrant, the local police, along with federal officers, announced at petitioner's door that they were police with a warrant. Upon hearing a commotion within the house, the officers forced their way into the house and seized petitioner in the act of attempting to dispose of a packet of narcotics.

At his trial in the state court, petitioner, through his attorney, objected to the introduction of evidence obtained as a result of the execution of the warrant. The objections were overruled and the evidence admitted. Petitioner was convicted of illegal possession of heroin and sentenced to serve 20 years in the state penitentiary. On appeal to the Texas Court of Criminal Appeals, the conviction was affirmed, 172 Tex. Crim. 629, 362 S. W. 2d 111, affirmance upheld on rehearsing, 172 Tex. Crim. 631, 362 S. W. 2d 112. We granted a writ of certiorari to consider the important constitutional questions involved. 375 U.S. 812.

In *Ker* v. *California,* 374 U.S. 23, we held that the Fourth "Amendment's proscriptions are enforced against the States through the Fourteenth Amendment," and that "the standard of reasonableness is the same under the Fourth and Fourteenth Amendments." *Id.,* at 33. Although *Ker* involved a search without a warrant, that case must certainly be read as holding that the standard for obtaining a search warrant is likewise "the same under the Fourth and Fourteenth Amendments."

An evaluation of the constitutionality of a search warrant should begin with the rule that "the informed and deliberate determinations of magistrates empowered to issue warrants . . . are to be preferred over the hurried action of officers . . . who may happen to make arrests." *United States* v. *Lefkowitz,* 285 U.S. 452, 464. The reasons for this rule go to the foundations of the Fourth Amendment. A contrary rule "that evidence sufficient to support a magistrate's disinterested determination to issue a search warrant will justify the officers in making a search without a warrant would reduce the Amendment to a nullity and leave the people's homes secure only in the discretion of police officers." *Johnson* v. *United States,* 333 U.S. 10, 14. Under such a rule

1. See Matusow's confession of perjury in this case (*New York Times,* Jan. 29, 1955, p. 3, col. 6) and in his book *False Witness* (1955). See also Richard Rovere, "The Kept Witness" (*Harper's Magazine,* vol. 210, pp. 25–34, May, 1955.).

"resort to [warrants] would ultimately be discouraged." *Jones* v. *United States*, 362 U.S. 257, 270. Thus, when a search is based upon a magistrate's rather than a police officer's, determination of probable cause, the reviewing courts will accept evidence of a less "judicially competent or persuasive character than would have justified an officer in acting on his own without a warrant," *ibid.*, and will sustain the judicial determination so long as "there was substantial basis for [the magistrate] to conclude that the narcotics were probably present. . . ." *Id.*, at 271. As so well stated by Mr. Justice Jackson:

"The point of the Fourth Amendment, which often is not grasped by zealous officers, is not that it denies law enforcement the support of the usual inferences which reasonable men draw from evidence. Its protection consists in requiring that those inferences be drawn by a neutral and detached magistrate instead of being judged by the officer engaged in the often competitive enterprise of ferreting out crime." *Johnson* v. *United States, supra,* at 13–14.

Although the reviewing court will pay substantial deference to judicial determinations of probable cause, the court must still insist that the magistrate perform his "neutral and detached" function and not serve merely as a rubber stamp for the police.

In *Nathanson* v. *United States*, 290 U.S. 41, a warrant was issued upon the sworn allegation that the affiant "has cause to suspect and does believe" that certain merchandise was in a specified location. *Id.*, at 44. The Court, noting that the affidavit "went upon a mere affirmation of suspicion and belief *without any statement of adequate supporting facts*," id., at 46 (emphasis added), announced the following rule:

"Under the Fourth Amendment, an officer may not properly issue a warrant to search a private dwelling unless he can find probable cause therefor from *facts or circumstances* presented to him under oath or affirmation. Mere affirmance of belief or suspicion is not enough." *Id.*, at 47. (Emphasis added.)

The Court, in *Giordenello* v. *United States*, 357 U.S. 480, applied this rule to an affidavit similar to that relied upon here. Affiant in that case, swore that petitioner "did receive, conceal, etc., narcotic drugs . . . with knowledge of unlawful importation. . . ." *Id.*, at 481. The Court announced the guiding principles to be:

"that the inferences from the facts which lead to the complaint '[must] be drawn by a neutral and detached magistrate instead of being judged by the officer engaged in the often competitive enterprise of ferreting out crime.' *Johnson* v. *United States*, 333 U.S. 10, 14. The purpose of the complaint, then, is to enable the appropriate magistrate . . . to determine whether the 'probable cause' required to support a warrant exists. The Commissioner must judge for himself the persuasiveness of the facts relied on by a complaining officer to show probable cause. He should not accept without question the complainant's mere conclusion . . ." 357 U.S., at 486.

The Court, applying these principles to the complaint in that case, stated that:

"it is clear that it does not pass muster because it does not provide any basis for the Commissioner's determination . . . that probable cause existed. The complaint contains no affirmative allegation that affiant spoke with personal knowledge of the matters contained therein; it does not indicate any sources for the complainant's belief; and it does not set forth any other sufficient basis upon which a finding of probable cause could be made." *Ibid.*

The vice in the present affidavit is at least as great as in *Nathanson* and *Giordenello*. Here the "mere conclusion" that petitioner possessed narcotics was not even that of the affiant himself; it was that of an unidentified informant. The affidavit here not only "contains no affirmative allegation that the affiant spoke with personal knowledge of the matters contained therein," it does not even contain an "affirmative allegation" that the affiant's unidentified source "spoke with personal knowledge." For all that appears, the source here merely suspected, believed or concluded that there were narcotics in petitioner's possession. The magistrate here certainly could not "judge for himself the persuasiveness of the facts relied on . . . to show probable cause." He necessarily accepted "without question" the informant's "suspicion," "belief" or "mere conclusion."

Although an affidavit may be based on hearsay information and need not reflect the direct personal observations of the affiant, *Jones* v. *United States,* 362 U.S. 257, the magistrate must be informed of some of the underlying circumstances from which the informant concluded that the narcotics were where he claimed they were, and some of the underlying circumstances from which the officer concluded that the informant, whose identity need not be disclosed, see *Rugendorf* v. *United States,* 376 U.S. 528, was "credible" or his information "reliable." Otherwise, "the inferences from the facts which lead to the complaint" will be drawn not "by a neutral and detached magistrate," as the Constitution requires, but instead, by a police officer "engaged in the often competitive enterprise of ferreting out crime." *Giordenello* v. *United States, supra,* at 486; *Johnson* v. *United States, supra,* at 14, or, as in this case, by an unidentified informant.

We conclude, therefore, that the search warrant should not have been issued because the affidavit did not provide a sufficient basis for a finding of probable cause and that the evidence obtained as a result of the search warrant was inadmissible in petitioner's trial.

The judgment of the Texas Court of Criminal Appeal is reversed and the case remanded for proceedings not inconsistent with this opinion.

Reversed and remanded.

MR. JUSTICE HARLAN, concurring.

But for *Ker* v. *California,* 374 U.S. 23, I would have voted to affirm the judgment of the Texas court. Given *Ker,* I cannot escape the conclusion that to do so would tend to "relax Fourth Amendment standards . . . in derogation of law enforcement standards in the federal system . . ." (my

concurring opinion in *Ker, supra,* at 45–46). Contrary to what is suggested in the dissenting opinion of my Brother CLARK in the present case (*post,* p. 3, note 1), the standards laid down in *Giordenello* v. *United States,* 357 U.S. 480, did in my view reflect constitutional requirements. Being unwilling to relax those standards for federal prosecutions, I concur in the opinion of the Court.

MR. JUSTICE CLARK, whom MR. JUSTICE BLACK and MR. JUSTICE STEWART join, dissenting.

First, it is well to point out the information upon which the search warrant in question was based: About January 1, 1960, Officers Strickland and Rogers from the narcotics division of the Houston Police Department received reliable information from a credible person that petitioner Aguilar had heroin and other narcotic drugs and narcotic paraphernalia in his possession at his residence, 509 Pinckney Street, Houston, Texas; after receiving this information the officers, the record indicates, kept the premises of petitioner under surveillance for about a week.

On January 8, 1960, the two officers applied for a search warrant and executed an affidavit before a justice of the peace in which they alleged under oath that petitioner's residence at 509 Pinckney Street "is a place where we each have reason to believe and do believe that [Aguilar] . . . has in his possession therein narcotic drugs . . . for the purpose of the unlawful sale thereof, and where such narcotic drugs are unlawfully sold." In addition and in support of their belief, the officers included in the affidavit the further allegation that they "have received reliable information from a credible person and do believe that heroin . . . and other narcotics and narcotic paraphernalia are being kept at . . . [petitioner's] premises for the purpose of sale and use contrary to the provisions of the law."

Upon executing the warrant issued on the strength of this affidavit, the officers knocked on the door of Aguilar's house. Someone inside asked who was there and the officers replied that they were police and that they had a search warrant. At this they heard someone "scuffle and start to run inside of the house." The officers entered and pursued the petitioner, who ran into a back bathroom. Petitioner threw a packet of heroin into the commode, but an officer retrieved the packet before it could be flushed down the drain.

I

At trial petitioner objected to the introduction into evidence of the heroin obtained through execution of the search warrant on the ground that the affidavit was "nothing more than hearsay." The Court holds the affidavit insufficient and sets aside the conviction on the basis of two cases, neither of which is controlling.

First is *Nathanson* v. *United States,* 290 U.S. 41 (1933). In that case the affidavit stated that the affiant had "cause to suspect and [did] believe that certain merchandise" was in the premises described. There was nothing in *Nathanson,* either in the affidavit or in the other proof introduced at trial, to suggest that any facts had been brought out to support a reasonable belief or even a suspicion. Accordingly, the Court held that "[m]ere affirmance of belief or suspicion is not enough." At 47. But in Fourth Amendment cases findings of reasonableness or of probable cause necessarily rest on the facts and circumstances of each particular case. In *Aguilar,* the affidavit was based not only on "affirmance of belief" but in addition upon *"reliable information from a credible person"* plus a week's surveillance by the affiants. *Nathanson* is, therefore, *not* apposite.

The second case the Court relies on is *Giordenello* v. *United States,* 357 U.S. 480 (1958). There the affidavit alleged that "Giordenello did receive, conceal, etc., narcotic drugs, to-wit: heroin hydrochloride with knowledge of unlawful importation. . . ." The opinion of the Court, by MR. JUSTICE HARLAN, after discussing Rules 3 and 4 of the Federal Rules of Criminal Procedure, held that the defect in the complaint was that it "does not provide any basis for the Commissioner's determination

under Rule 4 that probable cause existed." At 486. The dissent in the case, in commenting on the Court's holding that the complaint was invalid, said: "The Court does not strike down this complaint directly on the Fourth Amendment, but merely on an extension of Rule 4." At 491. Indeed, the holding could not have been made on the requirements of the Fourth Amendment because at that time (1958) the decisions of this Court consistently held that the exclusionary rule was not a Fourth Amendment requirement but one of evidence under our supervisory powers. See *Wolf* v. *Colorado,* 338 U.S. 25, 28, 39–40 (1949); *Mapp* v. *Ohio,* 367 U.S. 643, 678 (1961) (dissent of MR. JUSTICE HARLAN). It was not until *Mapp* (1961) that the federal rule was held to be a constitutional mandate and was, accordingly, applied to the States. Since *Giordenello* was a federal case, decided under our supervisory powers (Rules 3 and 4 of the Federal Rules of Criminal Procedure), it does not control here. As we said in *Ker* v. *California,* 374 U.S. 23, 33 (1963), "the demands of our federal system compel us to distinguish between evidence held inadmissible because of our supervisory powers over federal courts and that held inadmissible because prohibited by the United States Constitution."

Even if *Giordenello* was rested on the Constitution, it would not be controlling here because of the significant differences in the facts of the two cases. In *Giordenello* the Court said: "The complaint . . . does not indicate any sources for the complainant's belief; and it does not set forth any *other* sufficient basis upon which a finding of probable cause could be made." 357 U.S., at 486. (Emphasis supplied.) Here, in Aguilar's case, the affidavit did allege a "source for the complainant's belief," *i.e.,* "reliable information from a credible person . . . that heroin . . . and other narcotics . . . are being kept" in petitioner's premises "for the purpose of sale and use contrary to the provisions of the law." This takes the affidavit here entirely outside the *Giordenello* holding. In *Giordenello* no source of information was stated, whereas here there was a reliable one. The affidavit thus shows "probable cause" within the meaning of the Fourth Amendment, as that Amendment was interpreted by this Court in *Draper* v. *United States*, 358 U.S. 307 (1959), where it was contended that the information given by an informant to an officer was inadmissible because it was hearsay. The Court in *Draper* held that petitioner was "entirely in error. *Brinegar* v. *United States* . . . has settled the question the other way." At 311. In the following year this was reaffirmed in *Jones* v. *United States*, 362 U.S. 257, 271 (1960): "We conclude therefore that hearsay may be the basis for a warrant." Furthermore, in the case of *Rugendorf* v. *United States*, decided only this Term, we held an affidavit good based on information that an informer had seen certain furs in Rugendorf's basement. 376 U.S. 528. In the Aguilar affidavit the informer told the officers that narcotics were actually "kept at the above described premises for the purpose of sale. . . ." The Court seems to hold that what the informer says is the test of his reliability. I submit that this has nothing to do with it. The officer's experience with the informer is the test and here the two officers swore the informer to be credible and the information reliable. At the hearing on the motion to suppress, Officer Strickland testified that he delayed getting the search warrant for a week in order to "set up a surveillance on the house." The informant's statement, Officer Strickland said, was "the first information" received and was only "some of" that which supported the application for the warrant. The totality of the circumstances upon which the officer relied is certainly pertinent to the validity of the warrant. See the use of such testimony in *Giordenello, supra*, at 485, 486. And, just as in that case, there is nothing in the record here to show what the officers verbally told the magistrate. The surveillance of Aguilar's house, which is confirmed by the State's brief, apparently gave the officers further evidence upon which they based their personal belief. Hence the affidavit here is a far cry from "suspicion" or "af-

firmance of belief." It was based on reliable information from a credible informant plus personal surveillance by the officers.

Furthermore, the Courts of Appeals have often approved affidavits similar to the one here. See, e.g., *United States* v. *Eisner*, 297 F.2d 595 (C.A. 6th Cir.); *Evans* v. *United States*, 242 F.2d 534 (C.A. 6th Cir.); *United States* v. *Ramirez*, 279 F.2d 712, 715 (C.A. 2d Cir.); (dictum); and *United States* v. *Meeks*, 313 F.2d 464 (C.A. 6th Cir.). We denied certiorari in *Eisner*, 369 U.S. 859, although the affidavit there stated only that "[i]nformation has been obtained by S. A. Clifford Anderson . . . which he believes to be reliable . . . ," 297 F.2d, at 596, and in *Evans*, 353 U.S. 976, where the affiant was a man who "came to the headquarters of the federal liquor law enforcement officers and stated that he wished to give information . . . ," 242 F.2d, at 535.

In summary, the information must be more than mere wholly unsupported suspicion but less than "would justify condemnation," as Chief Justice Marshall said in *Locke* v. *United States*, 7 Cranch 339, 348 (1813). As Chief Justice Taft said in *Carroll* v. *United States*, 267 U.S. 132, 162 (1925): Probable cause exists where "the facts and circumstances within their [the officers'] knowledge and of which they had reasonably trustworthy information [are] . . . sufficient in themselves to warrant a man of reasonable caution in the belief that" an offense has been or is being committed. And as Mr. Justice Rutledge so well stated in *Brinegar* v. *United States*, 338 U.S. 160, 176 (1949):

"These long-prevailing standards seek to safeguard citizens from rash and unreasonable interferences with privacy and from unfounded charges of crime. They also seek to give fair leeway for enforcing the law in the community's protection. Because many situations which confront officers in the course of executing their duties are more or less ambiguous, room must be allowed for some mistakes on their part. But the mistakes must be those of reasonable men, acting on facts leading sensibly to their conclusions of probability. The rule of probable cause is a practical, nontechnical conception affording the best compromise that has been found for accommodating these often opposing interests. Requiring more would unduly hamper law enforcement. To allow less would be to leave law-abiding citizens at the mercy of the officers' whim or caprice."

Believing that the Court has substituted a rigid, academic formula for the unrigid standards of reasonableness and "probable cause" laid down by the Fourth Amendment itself—a substitution of technicality for practicality—and believing that the Court's holding will tend to obstruct the administration of criminal justice throughout the country, I respectfully dissent.

UNITED STATES v. RABINOWITZ

339 U.S. 56 (1950)

It is settled that in some circumstances a search incidental to a valid arrest is not unreasonable within the meaning of the Fourth Amendment. In *Harris* v. *United States,* 331 U.S. 445 (1947), a closely divided Court accepted a warrantless search of the accused's five-room apartment in conjunction with his legal arrest therein. A few months later a similarly divided Court seemed to go to the other extreme by repudiating the search of a distillery at which a valid arrest was made *when there had been ample opportunity to get a search warrant,* but one had not been obtained. *Trupiano* v. *United States,* 334 U.S. 699 (1948). A compromise between these two extremes seems to have been reached in *United States* v. *Rabinowitz.*

Mr. Justice Minton delivered the opinion of the Court: . . .

The question presented here [on certiorari] is the reasonableness of a search without a search warrant of a place of business consisting of a one-room office, incident to a valid arrest. . . .

The Fourth Amendment provides: "The right of the people to be secure in their persons, houses, papers, and effects, against unreasonable searches and seizures, shall not be violated, and no Warrants shall issue, but upon probable cause, supported by Oath or affirmation, and particularly describing the place to be searched, and the persons or things to be seized."

It is unreasonable searches that are prohibited by the Fourth Amendment. *Carroll* v. *United States,* 267 U.S. 132. It was recognized by the framers of the Constitution that there were reasonable searches for which no warrant was required. The right of the "people to be secure in their persons" was certainly of as much concern to the framers of the Constitution as the property of the person. Yet no one questions the right, without a search warrant, to search the person after a valid arrest. The right to search the person incident to arrest always has been recognized in this country and in England. *Weeks* v. *United States,* 232 U.S. 383. Where one had been placed in the custody of the law by valid action of officers, it was not unreasonable to search him.

Of course, a search without warrant incident to an arrest is dependent initially on a valid arrest. Here the officers had a warrant for respondent's arrest which was, as far as can be ascertained, broad enough to cover the crime of possession charged in the second count, and consequently respondent was properly arrested. Even if the warrant of arrest were not sufficient to authorize the arrest for possession of the stamps, the arrest therefor was valid because the officers had probable cause to believe that a felony was being committed in their very presence. *Carroll* v. *United States,* 267 U.S. 132.

The arrest was therefore valid in any event, and respondent's person could be lawfully searched. Could the officers search his desk, safe and file cabinets, all within plain sight of the parties, and all located under respondent's immediate control in his one-room office open to the public?

. . . In the instant case the search was not general or exploratory for whatever might be turned up. Specificity was the mark of the search and seizure here. There was probable cause to believe that respondent was conducting his business illegally. The search was for stamps overprinted illegally, which were thought upon the most reliable information to be in the possession of and concealed by respondent in the very room where he was arrested, over which room he had immediate control and in which he had been selling such stamps unlawfully. *Harris* v. *United States*, 331 U.S. 145, which has not been overruled, is ample authority for the more limited search here considered. In all the years of our nation's existence, with special attention to the prohibition era, it seems never to have been questioned seriously that a limited search such as here conducted as incident to a lawful arrest was a reasonable search and therefore valid. It has been considered in the same pattern as search of the person after lawful arrest.

What is a reasonable search is not to be determined by any fixed formula. The Constitution does not define what are "unreasonable" searches and, regrettably, in our discipline we have no ready litmus-paper test. The recurring questions of the reasonableness of searches must find resolution in the facts and circumstances of each case. *Go-Bart Co.* v. *United States*, 282 U.S. 344, 357. Reasonableness is in the first instance for the District Court to determine. We think the District Court's conclusion that here the search and seizure were reasonable should be sustained because: (1) the search and seizure were incident to a valid arrest; (2) the place of the search was a business room to which the public, including the officers, was invited; (3) the room was small and under the immediate and complete control of respondent; (4) the search did not extend beyond the room used for unlawful

purposes; (5) the possession of the forged and altered stamps was a crime, just as it is a crime to possess burglars' tools, lottery tickets or counterfeit money.

Assuming that the officers had time to procure a search warrant, were they bound to do so? We think not, because the search was otherwise reasonable, as previously concluded. . . .

A rule of thumb requiring that a search warrant always be procured whenever practicable may be appealing from the vantage point of easy administration. But we cannot agree that this requirement should be crystallized into a sine qua non to the reasonableness of a search. It is fallacious to judge events retrospectively and thus to determine, considering the time element alone, that there was time to procure a search warrant. Whether there was time may well be dependent upon considerations other than the ticking off of minutes or hours. The judgment of the officers as to when to close the trap on a criminal committing a crime in their presence or who they have reasonable cause to believe is committing a felony is not determined solely upon whether there was time to procure a search warrant. Some flexibility will be accorded law officers engaged in daily battle with criminals for whose restraint criminal laws are essential. . . .

The mandate of the Fourth Amendment is that the people shall be secure against *unreasonable* searches. It is not disputed that there may be reasonable searches, incident to an arrest, without a search warrant. Upon acceptance of this established rule that some authority to search follows from lawfully taking the person into custody, it becomes apparent that such searches turn upon the reasonableness under all the circumstances and not upon the practicability of procuring a search warrant, for the warrant is not required. To the extent that *Trupiano* v. *United States*, 334, U.S. 699, requires a search warrant solely upon the basis of the practicability of procuring it rather than upon the reasonableness of the search after a lawful arrest, that case is overruled. The relevant test is not whether it is reasonable to procure a search warrant, but whether the search was reasonable. . . .

Reversed.

MR. JUSTICE DOUGLAS took no part in the consideration or decision of this case.

MR. JUSTICE BLACK, dissenting:

Trupiano v. *United States,* 334 U.S. 699, was decided on the unarticulated premise that the Fourth Amendment of itself barred the use of evidence obtained by what the Court considered an "unreasonable" search. . . . The present case comes within that rule: the trial court admitted certain evidence procured by a search and seizure without a search warrant although the officers had ample time and opportunity to get one. Whether this Court should adhere to the *Trupiano* principle making evidence so obtained inadmissible in federal courts now presents no more than a question of what is wise judicial policy. Although the rule does not in all respects conform to my own ideas, I think that the reasons for changing it are outweighed by reasons against its change.

In recent years, the scope of the rule has been a subject of almost constant judicial controversy both in trial and appellate courts. In no other field has the law's uncertainty been more clearly manifested. To some extent that uncertainty may be unavoidable. The *Trupiano* case itself added new confusions "in a field already replete with complexities." . . . But overruling that decision merely aggravates existing uncertainty. For as Mr. Justice Frankfurter points out, today's holding casts doubt on other cases recently decided. And I do not understand how trial judges can be expected to foresee what further shifts may occur. In my judgment it would be wiser judicial policy to adhere to the *Trupiano* rule of evidence, at least long enough to see how it works. . . .

. . . Unquestionably its application will now and then permit a guilty person to escape without conviction because of hasty or ill-advised action on the part of enforcement officers. But the same may be said of the requirements of the Fourth Amendment which the exclusionary rule was fashioned to implement. The framers of the Fourth Amendment must have concluded that reasonably strict search and seizure requirements were not too costly a price to pay for protection against the dangers incident to invasion of private premises and papers by officers, some of whom might be overzealous and oppressive. . . .

I would affirm the judgment of the Court of Appeals.

MR. JUSTICE FRANKFURTER, whom MR. JUSTICE JACKSON joins, dissenting:

The clear-cut issue before us is this: in making a lawful arrest, may arresting officers search without a search warrant not merely the person under arrest or things under his immediate physical control, but the premises where the arrest is made, although there was ample time to secure such a warrant and no danger that the "papers and effects" for which a search warrant could be issued would be despoiled or destroyed?

The old saw that hard cases make bad law has its basis in experience. But petty cases are even more calculated to make bad law. The impact of a sordid little case is apt to obscure the implications of the generalization to which the case gives rise. Only thus can I account for a disregard of the history embedded in the Fourth Amendment and the great place which belongs to that Amendment in the body of our liberties as recognized and applied by unanimous decisions over a long stretch of the Court's history.

It is a fair summary of history to say that the safeguards of liberty have frequently been forged in controversies involving not very nice people. And so, while we are concerned here with a shabby defrauder, we must deal with his case in the context of what are really the great themes expressed by the Fourth Amendment. A disregard of the historic materials underlying the Amendment does not answer them. . . .

To tear "unreasonable" from the context and history and purpose of the Fourth Amendment in applying the narrow exception of search as an incident to an arrest is to disregard *the* reason to which reference must be made when a question arises under the Fourth Amendment. It is to make the arrest an incident to an unwarranted search instead of a warrantless search an incident to an arrest. The test by which searches and seizures must be judged is whether conduct is consonant with the main aim of the Fourth Amendment. The main aim of the Fourth Amendment is against invasion of the right of privacy as to one's effects and papers without regard to the result of such invasion. The purpose of the Fourth Amendment was to assure that the existence of probable cause as the legal basis for making a search was to be determined by a judicial officer before arrest and not after, subject only to what is necessarily to be expected from such requirement. The exceptions cannot be enthroned into the rule. The justification for intrusion into a man's privacy was to be determined by a magistrate uninfluenced by what may turn out to be a successful search for papers, the desire to search for which might be the very reason for the Fourth Amendment's prohibition. The framers did not regard judicial authorization as a formal requirement for a piece of paper. They deemed a man's belongings part of his personality and his life. . . .

. . . It is suggested that we cannot afford the luxury of [the British standard of] subordination of the police to law because greater obedience to law is part of English life generally. I do not think that acceptance of lower standards than those prevailing in England should be written by us into law. That only serves to encourage low standards, not to elevate them. It is unfair to our people to suggest that they cannot attain as high standards as do the British in guarding against police excesses without impairing effective means for combatting crime. Experience proves that it is a counsel of despair to assume that the police cannot be kept within the bounds of the principles which the Fourth and Fifth Amendments embody except at the cost of impotence in preventing crime and dealing sternly with its commission. . . .

It is most relevant that the officers had "no excuse for not getting a search warrant," 176 F.2d, 732, 735, for that is precisely what the Fourth Amendment was directed against—that some magistrate and not the police officer should determine, if such determination is not precluded by necessity, who shall be rummaging around in my room, whether it be a small room or a very large room, whether it be one room, or two rooms, or three rooms, or four rooms.

It is not as though we are asked to extend a mischievous doctrine that has been shown to hamper law enforcers. We are asked to overrule decisions based on a long course of prior unanimous decisions, drawn from history and legislative experience. In overruling *Trupiano* we overrule the underlying principle of a whole series of recent cases: *United States* v. *Di Re*, 332 U.S. 581; *Johnson* v. *United States*, 333 U.S. 10; *Mc-Donald* v. *United States*, 335 U.S. 451, based on the earlier cases. For these cases ought not to be allowed to remain as derelicts on the stream of the law, if we overrule *Trupiano*. These are not outmoded decisions eroded by time. Even under normal circumstances, the Court ought not to overrule such a series of decisions where no mischief flowing from them has been made manifest. Respect for continuity in law, where reasons for change are wanting, alone requires adherence to *Trupiano* and the other decisions. Especially ought the Court not needlessly reenforce the instabilities of our day by giving fair ground for the belief that Law is the expression of chance—for instance, of unexpected changes in the Court's composition and the contingencies in the choice of successors.

MAPP v. OHIO
367 U.S. 643 (1961)

The Fifth Amendment prohibits *the use in court* of compulsory self-incrimination. The Fourth Amendment outlaws "unreasonable searches and seizures," but says nothing about the use of improperly seized evidence. *Weeks* v. *United States,* 232 U.S. 383 (1914), held that such evidence could not be used in federal courts. Is the *Weeks* exclusionary rule so basic as to be included in the Fourteenth Amendment via the *Palko* principle?

MR. JUSTICE CLARK delivered the opinion of the Court.

Appellant stands convicted of knowingly having had in her possession and under her control certain lewd and lascivious books, pictures, and photographs in violation of § 2905.34 of Ohio's Revised Code. As officially stated in the syllabus to its opinion, the Supreme Court of Ohio found that her conviction was valid though "based primarily upon the introduction in evidence of lewd and lascivious books and pictures unlawfully seized during an unlawful search of defendant's home. . . ." 170 Ohio St. 427–428, 166 N.E.2d 387, 388. . . .

The state says that even if the search were made without authority, or otherwise unreasonably, it is not prevented from using the unconstitutionally seized evidence at trial, citing *Wolf* v. *People of State of Colorado,* 1949, 338 U.S. 25, at page 33, in which this Court did indeed hold "that in a prosecution in a State court for a State crime the Fourteenth Amendment does not forbid the admission of evidence obtained by an unreasonable search and seizure." On this appeal, of which we have noted probable jurisdiction, 364 U.S. 868, it is urged once again that we review that holding. . . .

II

In 1949, 35 years after Weeks was announced, this Court, in *Wolf* v. *People of State of Colorado, supra,* again for the first time, discussed the effect of the Fourth Amendment upon the States through the operation of the Due Process Clause of the Fourteenth Amendment. It said:

"[W]e have no hesitation in saying that were a State affirmatively to sanction such police incursion into privacy it would run counter to the guaranty of the Fourteenth Amendment." At page 28 of 338 U.S.

Nevertheless, after declaring that the "security of one's privacy against arbitrary intrusion by the police" is "implicit in the 'concept of ordered liberty' and as such enforceable against the States through the Due Process Clause," cf. *Palko* v. *State of Connecticut,* 1937, 302 U.S. 319, and announcing that it "stoutly adhere[d]" to the Weeks decision, the Court decided that the Weeks exclusionary rule would not then be imposed upon the States as "an essential ingredient of the right." 338 U.S. at pages 27–29. The Court's reasons for not considering essential to the right to privacy, as a curb imposed upon the States by the Due Process Clause, that which decades before had been posited as part and parcel of the Fourth Amendment's limitation upon federal encroachment of individual privacy, were bottomed on factual considerations.

While they are not basically relevant to a decision that the exclusionary rule is an essential ingredient of the Fourth Amendment as the right it embodies is vouchsafed against the States by the Due Process Clause, we will consider the current validity of the factual grounds upon which Wolf was based.

The Court in Wolf first stated that "[t]he contrariety of views of the States" on the adoption of the exclusionary rule of Weeks was "particularly impressive" (338 U.S. at page 29), and, in this connection, that it could not "brush aside the experience of States which deem the incidence of such conduct by the police too slight to call for a deterrent remedy . . . by overriding the [States'] relevant rules of evidence." At pages 31–32 of 338 U.S. While in 1949, prior to the Wolf case, almost two-thirds of the States were opposed to the use of the exclusionary rule, now, despite the Wolf case, more than half of those since passing upon it, by their own legislative or judicial decision, have wholly or partly adopted or adhered to the Weeks rule. See *Elkins* v. *United States,* 1960, 364 U.S. 206, Appendix, at pages 224–232. Significantly, among those now following the rule is California which, according to its highest court, was "compelled to reach that conclusion because other remedies have completely failed to secure compliance with the constitutional provisions. . . ." *People* v. *Cahan,* 1955, 44 Cal.2d 434, 445, 282 P.2d 905, 911, 50 A.L.R.2d 513. In connection with this California case, we note that the second basis elaborated in Wolf in support of its failure to enforce the exclusionary doctrine against the States was that "other means of protection" have been afforded "the right to privacy." 338 U.S. at page 30. The experience of California that such other remedies have been worthless and futile is buttressed by the experience of other States. The obvious futility of relegating the Fourth Amendment to the protection of other remedies has, moreover, been recognized by this Court since Wolf. See *Irvine* v. *People of State of California,* 1954, 347 U.S. 128, 137.

Likewise, time has set its face against what Wolf called the "weighty testimony" of *People* v. *Defore,* 1926, 242 N.Y. 13, 150 N.E. 585. There Justice (then Judge) Cardozo, rejecting adoption of the Weeks exclusionary rule in New York, had said that "[t]he Federal rule as it stands is either too strict or too lax." 242 N.Y. at page 22, 150 N.E. at page 588. However, the force of that reasoning has been largely vitiated by later decisions of this Court. These include the recent discarding of the "silver platter" doctrine which allowed federal

judicial use of evidence seized in violation of the Constitution by state agents, *Elkins* v. *United States, supra;* the relaxation of the formerly strict requirements as to standing to challenge the use of evidence thus seized, so that now the procedure of exclusion, "ultimately referable to constitutional safeguards," is available to anyone even "legitimately on [the] premises" unlawfully searched, *Jones* v. *United States,* 1960, 362 U.S. 257, 266–267; and finally, the formulation of a method to prevent state use of evidence unconstitutionally seized by federal agents, *Rea* v. *United States,* 1956, 350 U.S. 214. Because there can be no fixed formula, we are admittedly met with "recurring questions of the reasonableness of searches," but less is not to be expected when dealing with a Constitution, and, at any rate, "[r]easonableness is in the first instance for the [trial court] to determine." *United States* v. *Rabinowitz,* 1950, 339 U.S. 56, 63.

It, therefore, plainly appears that the factual considerations supporting the failure of the Wolf Court to include the Weeks exclusionary rule when it recognized the enforceability of the right to privacy against the States in 1949, while not basically relevant to the constitutional consideration, could not, in any analysis, now be deemed controlling.

III

Some five years after Wolf, in answer to a plea made here Term after Term that we overturn its doctrine on applicability of the Weeks exclusionary rule, this Court indicated that such should not be done until the States had "adequate opportunity to adopt or reject the [Weeks] rule." *Irvine* v. *People of State of California, supra,* 347 U.S. at page 134, 74 S.Ct. at page 384. There again it was said:

"Never until June of 1949 did this Court hold the basic search-and-seizure prohibition in any way applicable to the states under the Fourteenth Amendment." *Ibid.*

And only last Term, after again carefully re-examining the Wolf doctrine in *Elkins* v. *United States, supra,* the Court pointed out that "the controlling principles" as to search and seizure and the problem of admissibility "seemed clear" (364 U.S. at page 212, 1441 of 80 S. Ct.) until the announcement in Wolf "that the Due Process Clause of the Fourteenth Amendment does not itself require state courts to adopt the exclusionary rule" of the Weeks case. At page 213 of 364 U.S., at page 1442 of 80 S. Ct. At the same time the Court pointed out, "the underlying constitutional doctrine which Wolf established . . . that the Federal Constitution . . . prohibits unreasonable searches and seizures by state officers" had undermined the "foundation upon which the admissibility of state-seized evidence in a federal trial originally rested. . . ." *Ibid.* The Court concluded that it was therefore obliged to hold, although it chose the narrower ground on which to do so, that all evidence obtained by an unconstitutional search and seizure was inadmissible in a federal court regardless of its source. Today we once again examine Wolf's constitutional documentation of the right to privacy free from unreasonable state intrusion, and, after its dozen years on our books, are led by it to close the only courtroom door remaining open to evidence secured by official lawlessness in flagrant abuse of that basic right, reserved to all persons as a specific guarantee against that very same unlawful conduct. We hold that all evidence obtained by searches and seizures in violation of the Constitution is, by that same authority, inadmissible in a state court.

IV

Since the Fourth Amendment's right of privacy has been declared enforceable against the States through the Due Process Clause of the Fourteenth, it is enforceable against them by the same sanction of exclusion as is used against the Federal Government. Were it otherwise, then just as without the Weeks rule the assurance against unreasonable federal searches and seizures would be "a form of words," valueless and undeserving of mention in a perpetual charter of inestimable human liberties, so too, without that rule the freedom from state invasions of privacy would be so ephemeral and so neatly severed from its conceptual nexus with the freedom from all brutish means of coercing evidence as not to merit this Court's high regard as a freedom "implicit in 'the concept of ordered liberty.' " At the time that the Court held in Wolf that the Amendment was applicable to the States through the Due Process Clause, the cases of this Court, as we have seen, had steadfastly held that as to federal officers the Fourth Amendment included the exclusion of the evidence seized in violation of its provisions. Even Wolf "stoutly adhered" to that proposition. The right to privacy, when conceded operatively enforceable against the States, was not susceptible of destruction by evulsion of the sanction upon which its protection and enjoyment had always been deemed dependent under the Boyd, Weeks and Silverthorne cases. Therefore, in extending the substantive protections of due process to all constitutionally unreasonable searches—state or federal—it was logically and constitutionally necessary that the exclusion doctrine—an essential part of the right to privacy—be also insisted upon as an essential ingredient of the right newly recognized by the Wolf case. In short, the admission of the new constitutional right by Wolf could not consistently tolerate denial of its most important constitutional privilege, namely, the exclusion of the evidence which an accused had been forced to give by reason of the unlawful seizure. To hold otherwise is to grant the right but in reality to withhold its privilege and enjoyment. Only last year the Court itself recognized that the purpose of the exclusionary rule "is to deter—to compel respect for the constitutional guaranty in the only effectively available way—by removing the incentive to disregard it." *Elkind* v. *United States, supra,* 364 U.S. at page 217.

Indeed, we are aware of no restraint, similar to that rejected today, conditioning the enforcement of any other basic constitutional right. The right to privacy, no less important than any other right carefully and particularly reserved to the people, would stand in marked contrast to all other rights declared as "basic to a free society." *Wolf* v. *People of State of Colo-*

rado, supra, 338 U.S. at page 27. This Court has not hesitated to enforce as strictly against the States as it does against the Federal Government the rights of free speech and of a free press, the rights to notice and to a fair, public trial, including, as it does, the right not to be convicted by use of a coerced confession, however logically relevant it be, and without regard to its reliability. *Rogers* v. *Richmond,* 1961, 365 U.S. 534. And nothing could be more certain than that when a coerced confession is involved, "the relevant rules of evidence" are overriden without regard to "the incidence of such conduct by the police," slight or frequent. Why should not the same rule apply to what is tantamount to coerced testimony by way of unconstitutional seizure of goods, papers, effects, documents, etc.? We find that, as to the Federal Government, the Fourth and Fifth Amendments and, as to the States, the freedom from unconscionable invasions of privacy and the freedom from convictions based upon coerced confessions do enjoy an "intimate relation" in their perpetuation of "principles of humanity and civil liberty [secured] . . . only after years of struggle." *Bram* v. *United States,* 1897, 168 U.S. 532, 543–544. They express "supplementing phases of the same constitutional purpose— to maintain inviolate large areas of personal privacy." *Feldman* v. *United States,* 1944, 322 U.S. 487, 489–490. The philosophy of each Amendment and of each freedom is complementary to, although not dependent upon, that of the other in its sphere of influence—the very least that together they assure in either sphere is that no man is to be convicted on unconstitutional evidence. Cf. *Rochin* v. *People of State of California,* 1952, 342 U.S. 165.

V

Moreover, our holding that the exclusionary rule is an essential part of both the Fourth and Fourteenth Amendments is not only the logical dictate of prior cases, but it also makes very good sense. There is no war between the Constitution and common sense. Presently, a federal prosecutor may make no use of evidence illegally seized, but a State's attorney across the street may,

although he supposedly is operating under the enforceable prohibitions of the same Amendment. Thus the State, by admitting evidence unlawfully seized, serves to encourage disobedience to the Federal Constitution which it is bound to uphold. Moreover, as was said in Elkins, "[t]he very essence of a healthy federalism depends upon the avoidance of needless conflict between state and federal courts." 364 U.S. at page 221. Such a conflict, hereafter needless, arose this very Term, in *Wilson* v. *Schnettler,* 1961, 365 U.S. 381, in which, and in spite of the promise made by Rea, we gave full recognition to our practice in this regard by refusing to restrain a federal officer from testifying in a state court as to evidence unconstitutionally seized by him in the performance of his duties. Yet the double standard recognized until today hardly put such a thesis into practice. In non-exclusionary States, federal officers, being human, were by it invited to and did, as our cases indicate, step across the street to the State's attorney with their unconstitutionally seized evidence. Prosecution on the basis of that evidence was then had in a state court in utter disregard of the enforceable Fourth Amendment. If the fruits of an unconstitutional search had been inadmissible in both state and federal courts, this inducement to evasion would have been sooner eliminated. There would be no need to reconcile such cases as Rea and Schnettler, each pointing up the hazardous uncertainties of our heretofore ambivalent approach.

Federal-state cooperation in the solution of crime under constitutional standards will be promoted, if only by recognition of their now mutual obligation to respect the same fundamental criteria in their approaches. "However much in a particular case insistence upon such rules may appear as a technicality that inures to the benefit of a guilty person, the history of the criminal law proves that tolerance of shortcut methods in law enforcement impairs its enduring effectiveness." *Miller* v. *United States,* 1958, 357 U.S. 301, 313. Denying shortcuts to only one of two cooperating law enforcement agencies tends naturally to breed legitimate suspicion of "working arrangements" whose results are equally tainted. *Byars* v. *United States,* 1927, 273 U.S. 28; *Lustig* v. *United States,* 1949, 338 U.S. 74.

There are those who say, as did Justice (then Judge) Cardozo, that under our constitutional exclusionary doctrine "[t]he criminal is to go free because the constable has blundered." *People* v. *DeFore,* 242 N.Y. at page 21, 150 N.E. at page 587. In some cases this will undoubtedly be the result. But, as was said in Elkins, "there is another consideration—the imperative of judicial integrity." 364 U.S. at page 222. The criminal goes free, if he must, but it is the law that sets him free. Nothing can destroy a government more quickly than its failure to observe its own laws, or worse, its disregard of the charter of its own existence. As Mr. Justice Brandeis, dissenting, said in *Olmstead* v. *United States,* 1928, 277 U.S. 438, 485: "Our government is the potent, the omnipresent teacher. For good or for ill, it teaches the whole people by its example. . . . If the government becomes a lawbreaker, it breeds contempt for law; it invites every man to become a law unto himself; it invites anarchy." Nor can it lightly be assumed that, as a practical matter, adoption of the exclusionary rule fetters law enforcement. Only last year this Court expressly considered that contention and found that "pragmatic evidence of a sort" to the contrary was not wanting. *Elkins* v. *United States, supra,* 364 U.S. at page 218. The Court noted that "The federal courts themselves have operated under the exclusionary rule of Weeks for almost half a century; yet it has not been suggested either that the Federal Bureau of Investigation has thereby been rendered ineffective, or that the administration of criminal justice in the federal courts has thereby been disrupted. Moreover, the experience of the states is impressive. . . . The movement toward the rule of exclusion has been halting but seemingly inexorable." *Id.,* 364 U.S. at pages 218–219.

The ignoble shortcut to conviction left open to the State tends to destroy the entire system of constitutional restraints on which the liberties of the people rest. Having once recognized that the right to privacy embodied in the Fourth Amendment is enforceable against the States, and that the right to be secure against rude invasions of privacy by state officers is, therefore, constitutional in origin, we can no longer permit that right to remain an empty promise. Because it is enforceable in the same manner and to like effect as other basic rights secured by the Due Process Clause, we can no longer permit it to be revocable at the whim of any police officer who, in the name of law enforcement itself, chooses to suspend its enjoyment. Our decision, founded on reason and truth, gives to the individual no more than that which the Constitution guarantees him, to the police officer no less than that to which honest law enforcement is entitled, and, to the courts, that judicial integrity so necessary in the true administration of justice.

The judgment of the Supreme Court of Ohio is reversed and the cause remanded for further proceedings not inconsistent with this opinion.

Reversed and remanded.

[Concurring opinions by JUSTICES BLACK and DOUGLAS, as well as a memorandum by MR. JUSTICE STEWART, are omitted here.]

MR. JUSTICE HARLAN, whom MR. JUSTICE FRANKFURTER and MR. JUSTICE WHITTAKER join, dissenting.

In overruling the Wolf case the Court, in my opinion, has forgotten the sense of judicial restraint which, with due regard for *stare decisis,* is one element that should enter into deciding whether a past decision of this Court should be overruled. Apart from that I also believe that the Wolf rule represents sounder Constitutional doctrine than the new rule which now replaces it. . . .

I would not impose upon the States this federal exclusionary remedy. The reasons given by the majority for now suddenly turning its back on Wolf seem to me notably unconvincing.

First, it is said that "the factual grounds

upon which Wolf was based" have since changed, in that more States now follow the Weeks exclusionary rule than was so at the time Wolf was decided. While that is true, a recent survey indicates that at present one half of the States still adhere to the common-law non-exclusionary rule, and one, Maryland, retains the rule as to felonies. Berman and Oberst, "Admissibility of Evidence by an Unconstitutional Search and Seizure," 55 N.W.L.Rev. 525, 532–533. But in any case surely all this is beside the point, as the majority itself indeed seems to recognize. Our concern here, as it was in Wolf, is not with the desirability of that rule but only with the question whether the States are Constitutionally free to follow it or not as they may themselves determine, and the relevance of the disparity of views among the States on this point lies simply in the fact that the judgment involved is a debatable one. Moreover, the very fact on which the majority relies, instead of lending support to what is now being done, points away from the need of replacing voluntary state action with federal compulsion.

The preservation of a proper balance between state and federal responsibility in the administration of criminal justice demands patience on the part of those who might like to see things move faster among the States in this respect. Problems of criminal law enforcement vary widely from State to State. One State, in considering the totality of its legal picture, may conclude that the need for embracing the Weeks rule is pressing because other remedies are unavailable or inadequate to secure compliance with the substantive Constitutional principle involved. Another, though equally solicitous of Constitutional rights, may choose to pursue one purpose at a time, allowing all evidence relevant to guilt to be brought into a criminal trial, and dealing with Constitutional infractions by other means. Still another may consider the exclusionary rule too rough and ready a remedy, in that it reaches only unconstitutional intrusions which eventuate in criminal prosecution of the victims. Further, a State after experimenting with the Weeks rule for a time may, because of unsatisfactory experience with it, decide to revert to a nonexclusionary rule. And so on. From the standpoint of Constitutional permissibility in pointing a State in one direction or another, I do not see at all why "time has set its face against" the considerations which led Mr. Justice Cardozo, then chief judge of the New York Court of Appeals, to reject for New York in *People* v. *Defore,* 242 N.Y. 13, 150 N.E. 585, the Weeks exclusionary rule. For us the question remains, as it has always been, one of state power, not one of passing judgment on the wisdom of one state course or another. In my view this Court should continue to forbear from fettering the States with an adamant rule which may embarrass them in coping with their own peculiar problems in criminal law enforcement. . . .

I regret that I find so unwise in principle and so inexpedient in policy a decision motivated by the high purpose of increasing respect for Constitutional rights. But in the last analysis I think this Court can increase respect for the Constitution only if it rigidly respects the limitations which the Constitution places upon it, and respects as well the principles inherent in its own processes. In the present case I think we exceed both, and that our voice becomes only a voice of power, not of reason. . . .

FRANK v. MARYLAND

359 U.S. 360 (1959)

A health inspector found evidence of serious rodent infection in Frank's yard. Without a warrant, the inspector requested permission to inspect the house. Frank refused and was prosecuted for violating a statute requiring him to open his house for daytime inspection on demand by an inspector having grounds for suspecting a health nuisance. On review the Supreme Court upheld a conviction after the following discussion of the historical basis of the Fourth Amendment by Mr. Justice Frankfurter:

The history of the constitutional protection against official invasion of the citizen's home makes explicit the human concerns which it was meant to respect. In years prior to the Revolution leading voices in England and the Colonies protested against the ransacking by Crown officers of the homes of citizens in search of evidence of crime or of illegally imported goods. The vivid memory by the newly independent Americans of these abuses produced the Fourth Amendment as a safeguard against such arbitrary official action by officers of the new Union, as like provisions had already found their way into State Constitutions.

In 1765, in England, what is properly called the great case of *Entick* v. *Carrington*, 19 Howell's State Trials, Col. 1029, announced the principle of English law which became part of the Bill of Rights and whose basic protection has become imbedded in the concept of due process of law. It was there decided that English law did not allow officers of the Crown to break into a citizen's home, under cover of a general executive warrant, to search for evidence of the utterance of libel. Among the reasons given for that decision were these:

"It is very certain, that the law obligeth no man to accuse himself; because the necessary means of compelling self-accusation, falling upon the innocent as well as the guilty, would be both cruel and unjust; and it should seem, that search for evidence is disallowed upon the same principle. There too the innocent would be confounded with the guilty." *Id.*, at col. 1073.

These were not novel pronouncements to the colonists. A few years earlier, in Boston, revenue officers had been authorized to use Writs of Assistance, empowering them to search suspected places, including private houses, for smuggled goods. In 1761 the validity of the use of the Writs was contested in the historic proceedings in Boston. James Otis attacked the Writ of Assistance

because its use placed "the liberty of every man in the hands of every petty officer." His powerful argument so impressed itself first on his audience and later on the people of all the Colonies that President Adams was in retrospect moved to say that "American Independence was then and there born." Many years later this Court, in *Boyd* v. *United States,* 116 U.S. 616, carefully reviewed this history and pointed out, as did Lord Camden in *Entick* v. *Carrington,* that

". . . the 'unreasonable searches and seizures' condemned in the fourth amendment are almost always made for the purpose of compelling a man to give evidence against himself, which in criminal cases is condemned in the fifth amendment; and compelling a man 'in a criminal case to be a witness against himself,' which is condemned in the fifth amendment, throws light on the question as to what is an 'unreasonable search and seizure' within the meaning of the fourth amendment." 116 U.S. at page 633.

Against this background two protections emerge from the broad constitutional proscription of official invasion. The first of these is the right to be secure from intrusion into personal privacy, the right to shut the door on officials of the state unless their entry is under proper authority of law. The second, and intimately related protection, is self-protection: the right to resist unauthorized entry which has as its design the securing of information to fortify the coercive power of the state against the individual, information which may be used to effect a further deprivation of life or liberty or property. Thus, evidence of criminal action may not, save in very limited and closely confined situations, be seized without a judicially issued search warrant. It is this aspect of the constitutional protection to which the quoted passages from *Entick* v. *Carrington* and *Boyd* v. *United States* refer. Certainly it is not necessary to accept any particular theory of the interrelationship of the Fourth and Fifth Amendments to realize what history makes plain, that it was on the issue of the right to be secure from searches for evidence to be used in criminal prosecutions or for forfeitures that the great battle for fundamental liberty was fought. While these concerns for individual rights were the historic impulses behind the Fourth Amendment and its analogues in state constitutions, the application of the Fourth Amendment and the extent to which the essential right of privacy is protected by the Due Process Clause of the Fourteenth Amendment are of course not restricted within these historic bounds.

But giving the fullest scope to this constitutional right to privacy, its protection cannot be here invoked. The attempted inspection of appellant's home is merely to determine whether conditions exist which the Baltimore Health Code proscribes. If they do appellant is notified to remedy the infringing conditions. No evidence for criminal prosecution is sought to be seized. Appellant is simply directed to do what he could have been ordered to do without any inspection, and what he cannot properly resist, namely, act in a manner consistent with the maintenance of minimum community standards of health and well-being, including his own. Appellant's resistance can only be based, not on admissible self-protection, but on a rarely voiced denial of any official justification for seeking to enter his home. The constitutional "liberty" that is asserted is the absolute right to refuse consent for an inspection designed and pursued solely for the protection of the community's health, even when the inspection is conducted with due regard for every convenience of time and place.

[Mr. Justice Douglas, dissenting, joined by the Chief Justice and Justices Black and Brennan, responded as follows:]

The Court misreads history when it relates the Fourth Amendment primarily to searches for evidence to be used in criminal prosecutions. That certainly is not the

teaching of *Entick* v. *Carrington*, 19 Howell's St.Tr. col. 1029. At that time—1765—it was the search for the nonconformist that led British officials to ransack private homes. The commands of our First Amendment (as well as the prohibitions of the Fourth and the Fifth) reflect the teachings of *Entick* v. *Carrington, supra.* These three amendments are indeed closely related, safeguarding not only privacy and protection against self-incrimination but "conscience and human dignity and freedom of expression as well." See *Ullmann* v. *United States,* 350 U.S. 422, 445 et seq., (dissent); *Feldman* v. *United States,* 322 U.S. 487, 499. It is only in that setting that *Entick* v. *Carrington, supra,* can be understood, as evidenced by Lord Camden's long review of the oppressive practices directed at the press by the Star Chamber, the Long Parliament, and the Licensing Acts. 19 Howell's St.Tr. cols. 1069–1072. It was in the setting of freedom of expression that Lord Camden denounced the general warrants. Taylor, *The American Constitution* (1911), p. 234, gives the correct interpretation of that historical episode:

"In the effort to destroy the freedom of the press, by a strained exercise of the prerogative a general warrant was issued in 1763 for the discovery and apprehension of the authors and printers (not named) of the obnoxious No. 45 of the North Briton, which commented in severe and offensive terms on the King's Speech at the prorogation of Parliament and upon the unpopular Peace of Paris recently (February 10, 1763) concluded. Forty-nine persons, including Wilkes, were arrested under the general warrant; and when it was ascertained that Wilkes was the author, an information for libel was filed against him on which a verdict was obtained. In suits afterward brought against the Under-Secretary of State who had issued the general warrant, Wilkes, and Dryden Leach, one of the printers arrested on suspicion, obtained verdicts for damages. When the matter came before the King's Bench in 1765, Lord Mansfield and the other three judges pronounced the general warrant illegal, declaring that 'no degree of antiquity could give sanction to a usage bad in itself.' " And see 2 Paterson, *Liberty of the Subject* (1877), pp. 129–132.

This history, also recounted in *Boyd* v. *United States*, 116 U.S. 616, 625–626, was, in the words of Mr. Justice Bradley, "fresh in the memories of those who achieved our independence and established our form of government." The Fourth Amendment thus has a much wider frame of reference than mere criminal prosecutions.

The fallacy in maintaining that the Fourth Amendment was designed to protect criminals only was emphasized by Judge Prettyman in *District of Columbia* v. *Little*, 85 U.S. App. D.C. 242, 178 F.2d 13, 16–17, 13 A.L.R.2d 954, affirmed on other grounds, 339 U.S. 1.

"The argument is wholly without merit, preposterous in fact. The basic premise of the prohibition against searches was not protection against self-incrimination; it was the common-law right of a man to privacy in his home, a right which is one of the indispensable ultimate essentials of our concept of civilization. It was firmly established in the common law as one of the bright features of the Anglo-Saxon contributions to human progress. It was not related to crime or to suspicion of crime. It belonged to all men, not merely to criminals, real or suspected. So much is clear from any examination of history, whether slight or exhaustive. The argument made to us has not the slightest basis in history. It has no greater justification in reason. To say that a man suspected of crime has a right to protection against search of his home without a warrant, but that a man not suspected of crime has no such protection, is a fantastic absurdity." . . .

The well-known protests of the elder Pitt against invasion of the home by the police, had nothing to do with criminal proceedings.

"The poorest man may in his cottage bid defiance to all the force of the Crown. It may be frail—its roof may shake—the wind may blow through it—the storm may enter, the rain may enter—but the King of England cannot enter—all his force dares not cross the threshold of the ruined tenement!"

While this statement did not specifically refer to the general warrant, it was said in reference to the danger of excise officers entering private homes to levy the "Cyder Tax." 15 Hansard, *Parliamentary History of England* (1753–1765) p. 1307.

Some of the statutes which James Otis denounced did not involve criminal proceedings. They in the main regulated customs and allowed forfeitures of goods shipped into the Colonies in violation of English shipping regulations. The twenty-dollar forfeiture involved here is no different in substance from the ones that Otis and the colonists found so objectionable. For their objection went not to the amount or size of the forfeiture but to the lawless manner in which it was collected. "Every man prompted by revenge, ill humour, or wantonness to inspect the inside of his neighbor's house, may get a writ of assistance." Tudor, *Life of James Otis* (1823), p. 68. It was not the search that was vicious. It was the *absence of a warrant issued on a showing of probable cause* that Otis denounced—the precise situation we have here:

"Now one of the most essential branches of English liberty is the freedom of one's house. A man's house is his castle; and whilst he is quiet, he is as well guarded as a prince in his castle. This writ, if it should be declared legal, would totally annihilate this privilege. Customhouse officers may enter our houses when they please; we are commanded to permit their entry. Their menial servants may enter, may break locks, bars, and every thing in their way: and whether they break through malice or revenge, no man, no court, can inquire. Bare suspicion without oath is sufficient." *Id.*, at 66–67.

6. SELF-INCRIMINATION

HOFFMAN v. *UNITED STATES*
341 U.S. 479 (1951)

MR. JUSTICE CLARK delivered the opinion of the Court.

Petitioner has been convicted of criminal contempt for refusing to obey a federal court order requiring him to answer certain questions asked in a grand jury investigation. He raises here important issues as to the application of the privilege against self-incrimination under the Fifth Amendment, claimed to justify his refusal.

A special federal grand jury was convened at Philadelphia on September 14, 1950, to investigate frauds upon the Federal Government, including violations of the customs, narcotics and internal revenue liquor laws of the United States, the White Slave Traffic Act, perjury, bribery, and other federal criminal laws, and conspiracy to commit all such offenses. In response to subpoena petitioner appeared to testify on the day the grand jury was empaneled, and was examined on October 3. The pertinent interrogation, in which he refused to answer, follows:

"Q. What do you do now, Mr. Hoffman? A. I refuse to answer.

"Q. Have you been in the same undertaking since the first of the year? A. I don't understand the question.

"Q. Have you been doing the same thing you are doing now since the first of the year? A. I refuse to answer.

"Q. Do you know Mr. William Weisberg? A. I do.

"Q. How long have you known him? A. Practically twenty years, I guess.

"Q. When did you last see him? A. I refuse to answer.

"Q. Have you seen him this week? A. I refuse to answer.

"Q. Do you know that a subpoena has been issued for Mr. Weisberg? A. I heard about it in Court.

"Q. Have you talked with him on the telephone this week? A. I refuse to answer.

"Q. Do you know where Mr. William Weisberg is now? A. I refuse to answer."

It was stipulated that petitioner declined to answer on the ground that his answers might tend to incriminate him of a federal offense. . . .

The Fifth Amendment declares in part that "No person . . . shall be compelled in any Criminal Case to be a witness against himself." This guarantee against testimonial compulsion, like other provisions of the Bill of Rights, "was added to the original Constitution in the conviction that too high a price may be paid even for the unhampered enforcement of the criminal law and that, in its attainment, other social objects of a free society should not be sacrificed." *Feldman* v. *United States*, 1944, 322 U.S. 487, 489. This provision of the Amendment must be accorded liberal construction in favor of the right it was intended to secure. *Counselman* v. *Hitchcock*, 1892, 142 U.S. 547, 562; *Arndstein* v. *McCarthy*, 1920, 254 U.S. 71, 72–73.

The privilege afforded not only extends to answers that would in themselves support a conviction under a federal criminal statute but likewise embraces those which would furnish a link in the chain of evidence needed to prosecute the claimant for a federal crime. *(Patricia) Blau* v. *United States*, 1950, 340 U.S. 159. But this protection must be confined to instances where the witness has reasonable cause to apprehend danger from a direct answer.

Mason v. *United States*, 1917, 244 U.S. 362, 365, and cases cited. The witness is not exonerated from answering merely because he declares that in so doing he would incriminate himself—his say-so does not of itself establish the hazard of incrimination. It is for the court to say whether his silence is justified, *Rogers* v. *United States*, 1951, 340 U.S. 367, and to require him to answer if "it clearly appears to the court that he is mistaken." *Temple* v. *Commonwealth*, 1880, 75 Va. 892, 899. However, if the witness, upon interposing his claim, were required to prove the hazard in the sense in which a claim is usually required to be established in court, he would be compelled to surrender the very protection which the privilege is designed to guarantee. To sustain the privilege, it need only be evident from the implications of the question, in the setting in which it is asked, that a responsive answer to the question or an explanation of why it cannot be answered might be dangerous because injurious disclosure could result. The trial judge in appraising the claim "must be governed as much by his personal perception of the peculiarities of the case as by the facts actually in evidence." See Taft, J., in *Ex parte Irvine*, C.C.S.D. Ohio, 1896, 74 F. 954, 960. . . .

The court should have considered, in connection with the business questions, that the chief occupation of some persons involves evasion of federal criminal laws, and that a truthful answer by petitioner to these questions might have disclosed that he was engaged in such proscribed activity.

Also, the court should have recognized, in considering the Weisberg questions, that one person with a police record summoned to testify before a grand jury investigating the rackets might be hiding or helping to hide another person of questionable repute sought as a witness. To be sure, the Government may inquire of witnesses before the grand jury as to the whereabouts of unlocated witnesses; ordinarily the answers to such questions are harmless if not fruitless. But of the seven questions relating to Weisberg (of which three were answered), three were designed to draw information as to petitioner's contacts and connection with the fugitive witness; and the final question, perhaps an afterthought of the prosecutor, inquired of Weisberg's whereabouts at the time. All of them could easily have required answers that would forge links in a chain of facts imperiling petitioner with conviction of a federal crime. The three questions, if answered affirmatively, would establish contacts between petitioner and Weisberg during the crucial period when the latter was eluding the grand jury; and in the context of these inquiries the last question might well have called for disclosure that Weisberg was hiding away on petitioner's premises or with his assistance. Petitioner could reasonably have sensed the peril of prosecution for federal offenses ranging from obstruction to conspiracy.

In this setting it was not "perfectly clear, from a careful consideration of all the circumstances in the case, that the witness is mistaken, and that the answer[s] cannot possibly have such tendency" to incriminate. *Temple* v. *Commonwealth*, 1880, 75 Va. 892, 898, cited with approval in *Counselman* v. *Hitchcock*, 1892, 142 U.S. 547. See also, *Arndstein* v. *McCarthy*, 1920, 254 U.S. 71. . . .

Reversed.

MR. JUSTICE REED dissents. He agrees with the conclusions reached by Judges Goodrich and Kalodner as expressed in the opinion below.

ADAMSON v. CALIFORNIA

(This case, also involving self-incrimination, appears on page 284.)

MALLOY v. HOGAN

84 S. Ct. 1489 (1964)

MR. JUSTICE BRENNAN delivered the opinion of the Court.

In this case we are asked to reconsider prior decisions holding that the privilege against self-incrimination is not safeguarded against state action by the Fourteenth Amendment. *Twining v. New Jersey*, 211 U.S. 78; *Adamson v. California*, 332 U.S. 46.

The petitioner was arrested during a gambling raid in 1959 by Hartford, Connecticut, police. He pleaded guilty to the crime of pool-selling, a misdemeanor, and was sentenced to one year in jail and fined $500. The sentence was ordered to be suspended after 90 days, at which time he was to be placed on probation for two years. About 16 months after his guilty plea, petitioner was ordered to testify before a referee appointed by the Superior Court of Hartford County to conduct an inquiry into alleged gambling and other criminal activities in the county. The petitioner was asked a number of questions related to events surrounding his arrest and conviction. He refused to answer any question "on the grounds it may tend to incriminate me." The Superior Court adjudged him in contempt, and committed him to prison until he was willing to answer the questions. Petitioner's application for a writ of habeas corpus was denied by the Superior Court, and the Connecticut Supreme Court of Errors affirmed. 150 Conn. 220; 187 A.2d 744. The latter court held that the Fifth Amendment's privilege against self-incrimination was not available to a witness in a state proceeding, that the Fourteenth Amendment extended no privilege to him, and that the petitioner had not properly invoked the privilege available under the Connecticut Constitution. We granted certiorari. 373 U.S. 948. We reverse. We hold that the Fourteenth Amendment guaranteed the petitioner the protection of the Fifth Amendment's privilege against self-incrimination, and that under the applicable federal standard, the Connecticut Supreme Court of Errors erred in holding that the privilege was not properly invoked.

The extent to which the Fourteenth Amendment prevents state invasion of rights enumerated in the first eight Amendments has been considered in numerous cases in this Court since the Amendment's adoption in 1868. Although many Justices have deemed the Amendment to incorporate all eight of the Amendments, the view which has thus far prevailed dates from the decision in 1897 in *Chicago, B. & Q.R. Co. v. Chicago*, 166 U.S. 226, which held that the Due Process Clause requires the States to pay just compensation for private property taken for public use. It was on the authority of that decision that the Court said in 1908 in *Twining v. New Jersey, supra,* that "it is possible that some of the personal rights safeguarded by the first eight Amendments against National action may also be safeguarded against state action, because a denial of them would be a denial of due process of law." 211 U.S., at 99.

The Court has not hesitated to re-examine past decisions according the Fourteenth Amendment a less central role in the preservation of basic liberties than that which was contemplated by its Framers when they added the Amendment to our constitutional scheme. Thus, although the Court as late as 1922 said that "neither the Fourteenth Amendment nor any other provision of the Constitution of the United States imposes upon the States any restrictions about 'freedom of speech'. . . ," *Prudential Ins. Co. v. Cheek*, 259 U.S. 530, 543, three years later *Gitlow v. New York*, 268 U.S. 652, initiated a series of decisions which today holds immune from state invasion every First Amendment protection for the cherished rights of mind and spirit —the freedoms of speech, press, religion, assembly, association, and petition for redress of grievances.

Similarly, *Palko* v. *Connecticut*, 302 U.S. 319, decided in 1938, suggested that the rights secured by the Fourth Amendment, were not protected against state action, citing at 302 U.S. 324, the statement of the Court in 1914 in *Weeks* v. *United States*, 232 U.S. 383, 398, that "the Fourth Amendment is not directed to individual misconduct of [state] officials." In 1961, however, the Court held that in the light of later decisions, it was taken as settled that ". . . the Fourth Amendment's right of privacy has been declared enforceable against the States through the Due Process Clause of the Fourteenth. . . ." *Mapp* v. *Ohio*, 367 U.S. 643, 655. Again, although the Court held in 1942 that in a state prosecution for a noncapital offense, "appointment of counsel is not a fundamental right," *Betts* v. *Brady*, 316 U.S. 455, 471; cf. *Powell* v. *Alabama*, 287 U.S. 45, only last Term this decision was re-examined and it was held that provision of counsel in all criminal cases was "a fundamental right essential to a fair trial," and thus was made obligatory on the States by the Fourteenth Amendment. *Gideon* v. *Wainwright*, 372 U.S. 335, 344–345.

We hold today that the Fifth Amendment's exception from compulsory self-incrimination is also protected by the Fourteenth Amendment against abridgment by the States. Decisions of the Court since *Twining* and *Adamson* have departed from the contrary view expressed in those cases. We discuss first the decisions which forbid the use of coerced confessions in state criminal prosecutions.

Brown v. *Mississippi*, 297 U.S. 278, was the first case in which the Court held that the Due Process Clause prohibited the States from using the accused's coerced confessions against him. The Court in *Brown* felt impelled, in light of *Twining*, to say that its conclusion did not involve the privilege against self-incrimination. "Compulsion by torture to extort a confession is a different matter." 297 U.S. 285. But this distinction was soon abandoned, and today the admissibility of a confession in a state criminal prosecution is tested by the same standard applied in federal prosecutions since 1897, when, in *Bram* v. *United States*, 168 U.S. 532, the Court held that "In criminal trials, in the courts of the United States, wherever a question arises whether a confession is incompetent because not voluntary, the issue is controlled by that portion of the Fifth Amendment to the Constitution of the United States, commanding that no person 'shall be compelled in any criminal case to be a witness against himself.' " *Id.*, at 542. Under this test, the constitutional inquiry is not whether the conduct of state officers in obtaining the confession was shocking, but whether the confession is "free and voluntary: that is, [it] must not be extracted by any sort of threats or violence, nor obtained by any direct or implied promises, however slight, nor by the exertion of any improper influence. . . ." *Id.*, at 542–543; see also *Hardy* v. *United States*, 186 U.S. 224, 229; *Wan* v. *United States*, 266 U.S. 1, 14; *Smith* v. *United States*, 348 U.S. 147, 150. In other words the person must not have been compelled to incriminate himself. We have held inadmissible even a confession secured by so mild a whip as the refusal, under certain circumstances, to allow a suspect to call his wife until he confessed. *Haynes* v. *Washington*, 373 U.S. 503.

The marked shift to the federal standard in state cases began with *Lisenba* v. *California*, 314 U.S. 219, where the Court spoke of accused's "free choice to admit, to deny, or to refuse to answer." *Id.*, at 241. See *Ashcraft* v. *Tennessee*, 322 U.S. 143; *Malinski* v. *New York*, 324 U.S. 401; *Spano* v. *New York*, 360 U.S. 315; *Lynumn* v. *Illinois*, 372 U.S. 528; *Haynes* v. *Washington*, 373 U.S. 503. The shift reflects recognition that the American system of criminal prosecution is accusatorial, not inquisitorial, and that the Fifth Amendment privilege is its essential mainstay. *Rogers* v. *Richmond*, 365 U.S. 534, 541. Governments, state and federal, are thus constitutionally compelled to establish guilt by evidence independently and freely secured, and may not by coercion prove a charge against an accused out of his own mouth. Since the Fourteenth Amendment prohibits the States from inducing a person to confess through "sympathy falsely aroused," *Spano* v. *New York, supra,* at p. 323, or other like inducement far short of "compulsion by torture," *Haynes* v. *Washington, supra,* it follows *a fortiori* that it also forbids the States to resort to imprisonment, as here, to compel him to answer questions that might incriminate him. The Fourteenth Amendment secures against state invasion the same privilege that the Fifth Amendment guarantees against federal infringement—the right of a person to remain silent unless he chooses to speak in the unfettered exercise of his own will, and to suffer no penalty, as held in *Twining,* for such silence.

This conclusion is fortified by our recent decision in *Mapp* v. *Ohio,* 367 U.S. 643, overruling *Wolf* v. *Colorado, supra,* which had held "that in a prosecution in a state court for a state crime the Fourteenth Amendment does not forbid the admission of evidence obtained by an unreasonable search and seizure," 338 U.S., at 33. *Mapp* held that the Fifth Amendment privilege against self-incrimination implemented the Fourth Amendment in such cases, and that the two guarantees of personal security conjoined in the Fourteenth Amendment to make the exclusionary rule obligatory upon the States. We relied upon the great case of *Boyd* v. *United States,* 116 U.S. 616, decided in 1886, which, considering the Fourth and Fifth Amendments as running "almost into each other," *id.,* at 630, held that "Breaking into a house and opening boxes and drawers are circumstances of aggravation; but any forceable and compulsory extortion of a man's own testimony or of his private papers to be used as evidence to convict him of crime or to forfeit his goods, is within the condemnation of [those Amendments]. . . ." At 630. We said in *Mapp:*

"We find that, as to the Federal Government, the Fourth and Fifth Amendments,

and as to the States, the freedom from unconscionable invasions of privacy and the freedom from convictions based upon coerced confessions do enjoy an 'intimate relation' in their perpetuation of 'principles of humanity and civil liberty [secured] . . . only after years of struggle,' *Bram* v. *United States,* 168 U.S. 532, 543–544. . . . The philosophy of each amendment and of each freedom is complementary to, although not dependent upon, that of the other in its sphere of influence—the very least that together they assure in either sphere is that no man is to be convicted on unconstitutional evidence." 367 U.S. 656–657.

In thus returning to the *Boyd* view that the privilege is one of the "principles of a free government," 116 U.S., at 632, *Mapp* necessarily repudiated the *Twining* concept of the privilege as a mere rule of evidence, "best defended not as an unchangeable principle of universal justice but as a law proved by experience to be expedient." 211 U.S., at 113.

The respondent State of Connecticut concedes in its brief that under our decisions, particularly those involving coerced confessions, "the accusatorial system has become a fundamental part of the fabric of our society and, hence, is enforceable against the States." The State urges, however, that the availability of the federal privilege to a witness in a state inquiry is to be determined according to a less stringent standard than is applicable in a federal proceeding. We disagree. We have held that the guarantees of the First Amendment, *Gitlow* v. *New York, supra; Cantwell* v. *Connecticut, supra; Louisiana ex rel. Gremillion* v. *NAACP, supra,* the prohibition of unreasonable searches and seizures of the Fourth Amendment, *Ker* v. *California, supra,* and the right to counsel guaranteed by the Sixth Amendment, *Gideon* v. *Wainwright, supra,* are all to be enforced against the States under the Fourteenth Amendment according to the same standards that protect those personal rights against federal encroachment. In the coerced confession cases, involving the policies of the privilege itself, there has been no suggestion that a confession might be considered coerced if used in a federal but not a state tribunal. The Court thus has rejected the notion that the Fourteenth Amendment applies to the states only a "watered-down, subjective version of the Bill of Rights," *Ohio ex rel. Eaton* v. *Price,* 364 U.S. 263, 275 (dissenting opinion). If *Cohen* v. *Hurley,* 366 U.S. 117, and *Adamson* v. *California, supra,* suggest such an application of the privilege against self-incrimination, that suggestion cannot survive recognition of the degree to which the *Twining* view of the privilege has been eroded. What is accorded is a privilege of refusing to incriminate one's self, and the feared prosecution may be by either federal or state authorities. *Murphy* v. *Waterfront Comm'n, infra.* It would be incongruous to have different standards determine the validity of a claim of privilege based on the same feared prosecution, depending on whether the claim was asserted in a state or federal court. Therefore, the same standards must determine whether an accused's silence in either a federal or state proceeding is justified.

We turn to the petitioner's claim that the State of Connecticut denied him the protection of his federal privilege. It must be considered irrelevant that the petitioner was a witness in a statutory inquiry and not a defendant in a criminal prosecution, for it has long been settled that the privilege protects witnesses in similar federal inquiries. *Counselman* v. *Hitchcock,* 142 U.S. 547; *McCarthy* v. *Arndstein,* 266 U.S. 34; *Hoffman* v. *United States,* 341 U.S. 479. We recently elaborated the content of the federal standard in *Hoffman:*

"The privilege afforded not only extends to answers that would in themselves support a conviction . . . but likewise embraces those which would furnish a link in the chain of evidence needed to prosecute . . . if the witness, upon interposing his claim, were required to prove the hazard . . . he would be compelled to surrender the very protection which the privilege is designed to guarantee. To sustain the privilege, it need only be evident from the im-

plication of the question, in the setting in which it is asked, that a responsive answer to the question or an explanation of why it cannot be answered might be dangerous because injurious disclosure would result." 341 U.S., at 486–487.

We also said that, in applying that test, the judge must be "*'perfectly clear,* from a careful consideration of all the circumstances in the case, that the witness is mistaken, and that the answer[s] *cannot possibly* have such tendency' to incriminate." 341 U.S., at 488. The State of Connecticut argues that the Connecticut courts properly applied the federal standards to the facts of this case. We disagree.

The investigation in the course of which petitioner was questioned began when the Superior Court in Hartford County appointed the Honorable Ernest A. Inglis, formerly Chief Justice of Connecticut, to conduct an inquiry into whether there was reasonable cause to believe that crimes, including gambling, were being committed in Hartford County. Petitioner appeared on January 16 and 25, 1961, and in both instances he was asked substantially the same questions about the circumstances surrounding his arrest and conviction for pool-selling in late 1959. The questions which petitioner refused to answer may be summarized as follows: (1) for whom did he work on September 11, 1959; (2) who selected and paid his counsel in connection with his arrest on that date and subsequent conviction; (3) who selected and paid his bondsman; (4) who paid his fine; (5) what was the name of the tenant in the apartment in which he was arrested; and (6) did he know John Bergoti. The Connecticut Supreme Court of Errors ruled that the answers to these questions could not tend to incriminate him because the defenses of double jeopardy and the running of the one-year statute of limitations on misdemeanors would defeat any prosecution growing out of his answers to the first five questions. As for the sixth question, the court held that petitioner's failure to explain how a revelation of his relationship with Bergoti would incriminate him vitiated his claim to the protection of the privilege afforded by state law.

The conclusions of the Court of Errors, tested by the federal standard, fails to take sufficient account of the setting in which the questions were asked. The interrogation was part of a wide-ranging inquiry into crime, including gambling, in Hartford. It was admitted on behalf of the State at oral argument—and indeed it is obvious from the questions themselves—that the State desired to elicit from the petitioner the identity of the person who ran the pool-selling operation in connection with which he had been arrested in 1959. It was apparent that petitioner might apprehend that if this person were still engaged in unlawful activity, disclosure of his name might furnish a link in a chain of evidence sufficient to connect the petitioner with a more recent crime for which he might still be prosecuted.

Analysis of the sixth question, concerning whether petitioner knew John Bergoti, yields a similar conclusion. In the context of the inquiry, it should have been apparent to the referee that Bergoti was suspected by the State to be involved in some way in the subject matter of the investigation. An affirmative answer to the question might well have either connected petitioner with a more recent crime, or at least have operated as a waiver of his privilege with reference to his relationship with a possible criminal. See *Rogers* v. *United States*, 340 U.S. 367. We conclude, therefore, that as to each of the questions, it was "evident from the implication of the question, in the setting in which it [was] asked, that a responsive answer to the question or an explanation of why it [could not] be answered might be dangerous because injurious disclosure could result," *Hoffman* v. *United States, supra*, 341 U.S. 486–487; see *Singleton* v. *United States*, 343 U.S. 944.

Reversed.

While MR. JUSTICE DOUGLAS joins the opinion of the Court, he also adheres to his concurrence in *Gideon* v. *Wainwright*, 372 U.S. 335, 345.

MR. JUSTICE WHITE, with whom MR. JUSTICE STEWART joins, dissenting.

I

The Fifth Amendment safeguards an important complex of values, but it is difficult for me to perceive how these values are served by the Court's holding that the privilege was properly invoked in this case. While purporting to apply the prevailing federal standard of incrimination—the same standard of incrimination that the Connecticut courts applied—the Court has all but stated that a witness' invocation of the privilege to any question is to be automatically, and without more, accepted. With deference, I prefer the rule permitting the judge rather than the witness to determine when an answer sought is incriminating.

The established rule has been that the witness' claim of the privilege is not final, for the privilege qualifies a citizen's general duty of disclosure only when his answers would subject him to danger from the criminal law. The privilege against self-incrimination or any other evidentiary privilege does not protect silence which is solely an expression of political protest, a desire not to inform, a fear of social obloquy or economic disadvantage or fear of prosecution for future crimes. *Smith* v. *United States*, 337 U.S. 137, 147; *Brown* v. *Walker*, 161 U.S. 591, 605, 631. If the general duty to testify when subpoenaed is to remain and the privilege is to be retained as a protection against compelled incriminating answers, the trial judge must be permitted to make a meaningful determination of when answers tend to incriminate. See *The Queen* v. *Boyes*, 1 B & S 311, 329–330 (1861); *Mason* v. *United States*, 244 U.S. 362. I do not think today's decision permits such a determination.

Answers which would furnish a lead to other evidence needed to prosecute or convict a claimant of a crime—clue evidence—cannot be compelled, but "this protection must be confined to instances where the witness has reasonable cause to apprehend danger from a direct answer." *Hoffman* v. *United States,* 371 U.S. 479, at 486; *Mason* v. *United States,* 244 U.S. 362. Of course the witness is not required to disclose so much of the danger as to render his privilege nugatory. But that does not justify a flat rule of no inquiry and automatic acceptance of the claim of privilege. In determining whether the witness has a reasonable apprehension, the test in the federal courts has been that the judge is to decide from the circumstances of the case, his knowledge of matters surrounding the inquiry and the nature of the evidence which is demanded from the witness. *Hoffman* v. *United States,* 341 U.S. 479; *Mason* v. *United States,* 244 U.S. 362. Cf. *Rogers* v. *United States,* 340 U.S. 367. This rule seeks and achieves a workable accommodation between what are obviously important competing interests. As Mr. Chief Justice Marshall said: "The principle which entitles the United States to the testimony of every citizen, and the principle by which every witness is privileged not to accuse himself, can neither of them be entirely disregarded. . . . When a question is propounded, it belongs to the court to consider and to decide whether any direct answer to it can implicate the witness." *In re Willie,* 25 Fed. Cas. No. 14,692e, at 38–39. I would not only retain this rule but apply it in its present form. Under this test, Malloy's refusals to answer some, if not all, of the questions put to him were clearly not privileged.

II

In November 1959, Malloy was arrested in a gambling raid in Hartford and was convicted of pool-selling, an offense defined as occupying and keeping a building containing gambling apparatus. After a 90-day jail term, his one-year sentence was suspended and Malloy was placed on probation for two years. In early 1961, Malloy was summoned to appear in an investigation into whether crimes, including gambling, had been committed in Hartford County, and was asked various questions obviously and solely designed to ascertain who Malloy's associates were in connection

with his pool-selling activities in Hartford in 1959. Malloy initially refused to answer virtually all the questions put to him, including such innocuous ones as whether he was the William Malloy arrested and convicted of pool-selling in 1959. After he was advised to consult with counsel and did so, he declined to answer each one of the following questions on the ground that it would tend to incriminate him:

"Q. Now, on September 11, 1959, when you were arrested at 600 Asylum Street, and the same arrest for which you were convicted in the Superior Court on November 5, 1959, for whom were you working?

"Q. On September 11, 1959, when you were arrested, and the same arrest for which you were convicted in the Superior Court on November 5, 1959, who furnished the money to pay your fine when you were convicted in the Superior Court?

. . . . .

"Q. After your arrest on September 11, 1959, and the same arrest for which you were convicted on November 5, 1959, who selected your bondsman?

"Q. As a result of your arrest on September 11, 1959, and the same arrest for which you were convicted on November 5, 1959, who furnished the money to pay your fine?

"Q. Do you know whose apartment it was [that you were arrested in on September 11, 1959]?

"Q. Do you know John Bergoti?

. . . . .

"Q. I ask you again, Mr. Malloy, now, so there will be no misunderstanding of what I want to know. When you were arrested on September 11, 1959, at 600 Asylum Street in Hartford, and the same arrest for which you were convicted in Superior Court on November 5, 1959, for whom were you working?"

It was for refusing to answer these questions that Malloy was cited for contempt, the Connecticut courts noting that the privilege does not protect one against informing on friends or associates.

These were not wholly innocuous questions on their face, but they clearly were in light of the finding, of which Malloy was told, that he was immune from prosecution for any pool-selling activities in 1959. As the Connecticut Supreme Court of Errors found, the State bore its burden of proving that the statute of limitation barred any prosecution for any type of violation of the state pool-selling statute in 1959. Malloy advanced the claim before the Connecticut courts, and again before this Court, that he could perhaps be prosecuted for a conspiracy and that the statute of limitation on a felony was five years. But the Connecticut courts were unable to find any state statute which Malloy's gambling activities in 1959 in Hartford, the subject of the inquiry, could have violated and Malloy has not yet pointed to one. Beyond this Malloy declined to offer any explanation or hint at how the answers sought could have incriminated him. In these circumstances it is wholly speculative to find that the questions about others, not Malloy, posed a substantial hazard of criminal prosecution to Malloy. Theoretically, under some unknown but perhaps possible conditions any fact is potentially incriminating. But if this be the rule, there obviously is no reason for the judge, rather than the witness, to pass on the claim of privilege. The privilege becomes a general one against answering distasteful questions.

The Court finds that the questions were incriminating because petitioner "might apprehend that if [his associates in 1959] were still engaged in unlawful activity, disclosure of [their] name might furnish a link in a chain of evidence sufficient to connect the petitioner with a more recent crime for which he might still be prosecuted." *Ante,* p. 12. The assumption necessary to the above reasoning is that all persons, or all who have committed a misdemeanor, are continuously engaged in crime. This is but another way of making the claim of privilege automatic. It is not only unrealistic generally but peculiarly inappropriate in this case. Unlike cases relied on by the Court, like *Hoffman v. United States, supra,* where the claimant was known to be involved in rackets in the area, which were the subject of the inquiry, and had a

"broadly published police record," Malloy had no record as a felon. He had engaged once in an unlawful activity—pool-selling— a misdemeanor and was given a suspended sentence. He had been on probation since that time and was on probation at the time of the inquiry. Again, unlike *Hoffman,* nothing in these questions indicates petitioner was called because he was suspected of criminal activities after 1959. There is no support at all in this record for the cynical assumption that he had committed criminal acts after his release in 1960.

Even on the Court's assumption that persons convicted of a disdemeanor are necessarily suspect criminals, sustaining the privilege in these circumstances is unwarranted, for Malloy placed no reliance on this theory in the courts below or in this Court. In order to allow the judge passing on the claim to understand how the answers sought are incriminating, I would at least require the claimant to state his grounds for asserting the privilege to questions seemingly irrelevant to any incriminating matters.

Adherence to the federal standard of incrimination stated in *Mason* and *Hoffman, supra,* in form only, while its content is eroded in application, is hardly an auspicious beginning for application of the privilege to the States. As was well stated in a closely analogous situation, "[t]o continue a rule which is honored by this Court only with lip service is not a healthy thing and in the long run will do disservice to the federal system," *Gideon v. Wainwright,* 372 U.S. 335, at 351 (Harlan, J., concurring).

I would affirm.

Mr. Justice Harlan, whom Mr. Justice Clark joins, dissenting.

Connecticut has adjudged this petitioner in contempt for refusing to answer questions in a state inquiry. The courts of the State, whose laws embody a privilege against self-incrimination, refused to recognize the petitioner's claim of privilege, finding that the questions asked him were not incriminatory. This Court now holds the contempt adjudication unconstitutional because, it is decided: (1) the Fourteenth Amendment makes the Fifth Amendment privilege against self-incrimination applicable to the States; (2) the federal standard justifying a claim of this privilege likewise applies to the States; and (3) judged by that standard the petitioner's claim of privilege should have been upheld.

Believing that the reasoning behind the Court's decision carries extremely mischievous, if not dangerous consequences for our federal system in the realm of criminal law enforcement, I must dissent. The importance of the issue presented and the serious incursion which the Court makes on time-honored, basic constitutional principles justifies a full exposition of my reasons.

I

I can only read the Court's opinion as accepting in fact what it rejects in theory: the application to the States, via the Fourteenth Amendment, of the forms of federal criminal procedure embodied within the first eight Amendments to the Constitution. While it is true that the Court deals today with only one aspect of state criminal procedure, and rejects the wholesale "incorporation" of such federal constitutional requirements, the logical gap between the Court's premises and its novel constitutional conclusion can, I submit, be bridged only by the additional premise that the Due Process Clause of the Fourteenth Amendment is a shorthand directive to this Court to pick and choose among the provisions of the first eight Amendments and apply those chosen, freighted with their entire accompanying body of federal doctrine, to law enforcement in the States.

I accept and agree with the proposition that continuing re-examination of the constitutional conception of Fourteenth Amendment "due process" of law is required, and that development of the community's sense of justice may in time lead to expansion of the protection which due process affords. In particular in this case, I agree that principles of justice to which due process gives expression, as reflected in decisions of this Court, prohibit a State, as

the Fifth Amendment prohibits the Federal Government, from imprisoning a person *solely* because he refuses to give evidence which may incriminate him under the laws of the State. I do not understand, however, how this process of re-examination, which must refer always to the guiding standard of due process of law, including, of course, reference to the particular guarantees of the Bill of Rights, can be short-circuited by the simple device of incorporating into due process, without critical examination, the whole body of law which surrounds a specific prohibition directed against the Federal Government. The consequence of such an approach to due process as it pertains to the States is inevitably disregard of all relevant differences which may exist between state and federal criminal law and its enforcement. The ultimate result is compelled uniformity, which is inconsistent with the purpose of our federal system and which is achieved either by encroachment on the States' sovereign powers or by dilution in federal law enforcement of the specific protections found in the Bill of Rights. . . .

III

The previous discussion shows that this Court's decisions do not dictate the "incorporation" of the Fifth Amendment's privilege against self-incrimination into the Fourteenth Amendment. Approaching the question more broadly, it is equally plain that the line of cases exemplified by *Palko* v. *Connecticut, supra,* in which this Court has reconsidered the requirements which the Due Process Clause imposes on the States in the light of current standards, furnishes no general theoretical framework for what the Court does today.

The view of the Due Process Clause of the Fourteenth Amendment which this Court has consistently accepted and which has "thus far prevailed," *ante,* p. 3, is that its requirements are as "old as a principle of civilized government," *Munn* v. *Illinois,* 94 U.S. 113, 123, the specific applications of which must be ascertained "by the gradual process of judicial inclusion and exclusion . . . ," *Davidson* v. *New Orleans,*

96 U.S. 97, 104. Due Process requires "observance of those general rules established in our system of jurisprudence for the security of private rights." *Hagar* v. *Reclamation District No. 108,* 111 U.S. 701, 708. See *Hurtado* v. *California,* 110 U.S. 516, 537.

"This Court has never attempted to define with precision the words 'due process of law'. . . . It is sufficient to say that there are certain immutable principles of justice which inhere in the very idea of free government which no member of the Union may disregard. . . ." *Holden* v. *Hardy,* 169 U.S. 366, 389.

It followed from this recognition that due process encompassed the fundamental safeguards of the individual against the abusive exercise of governmental power that some of the restraints on the Federal Government which were specifically enumerated in the Bill of Rights applied also against the States. But, while inclusion of a particular provision in the Bill of Rights might provide historical evidence that the right involved was traditionally regarded as fundamental, inclusion of the right in due process was otherwise entirely independent of the first eight Amendments:

". . . [I]t is possible that some of the personal rights safeguarded by the first eight Amendments against National action may also be safeguarded against state action, because a denial of them would be a denial of due process of law. . . . *If this is so, it is not because those rights are enumerated in the first eight Amendments, but because they are of such a nature that they are included in the conception of due process of law.*" *Twining, supra,* at 99. (Emphasis supplied.) . . .

The Court's approach in the present case is in fact nothing more or less than "incorporation" in snatches. If, however, the Due Process Clause *is* something more than a reference to the Bill of Rights and protects only those rights which derive from fundamental principles, as the majority purports to believe, it is just as contrary to precedent and just as illogical to incorporate the provisions of the Bill of Rights

one at a time as it is to incorporate them all at once.

IV

The Court's undiscriminating approach to the Due Process Clause carries serious implications for the sound working of our federal system in the field of criminal law.

The Court concludes, almost without discussion, that "the same standards must determine whether an accused's silence in either a federal or state proceeding is justified.". . . . About all that the Court offers in explanation of this conclusion is the observation that it would be "incongruous" if different standards governed the assertion of a privilege to remain silent in state and federal tribunals. Such "incongruity," however, is at the heart of our federal system. The powers and responsibilities of the state and federal governments are not congruent; under our Constitution, they are not intended to be. Why should it be thought, as an *a priori* matter, that limitations on the investigative powers of the States are in all respects identical with limitations on the investigative power of the Federal Government? This certainly does not follow from the fact that we deal here with constitutional requirements; for the provisions of the Constitution which are construed are different.

As the Court pointed out in *Abbate* v. *United States,* 359 U.S. 187, 195, "the States under our federal system have the principal responsibility for defining and prosecuting crimes." The Court endangers this allocation of responsibility for the prevention of crime when it applies to the States doctrines developed in the context of federal law enforcement, without any attention to the special problems which the States as a group or particular States may face. If the power of the States to deal with local crime is unduly restricted, the likely consequence is a shift of responsibility in this area to the Federal Government, with its vastly greater resources. Such a shift, if it occurs, may in the end serve to weaken the very liberties which the Fourteenth Amendment safeguards by bringing us closer to the monolithic society which our federalism rejects.

Equally dangerous to our liberties is the alternative of watering down protections against the Federal Government embodied in the Bill of Rights so as not unduly to restrict the powers of the States. The dissenting opinion in *Aguilar* v. *Texas, supra,* evidences that this danger is not imaginary. See my concurring opinion in *Aguilar, id.,* at —.

Rather than insisting, almost by rote, that the Connecticut court, in considering the petitioner's claim of privilege, was required to apply the "federal standard," the Court should have fulfilled its responsibility under the Due Process Clause by inquiring whether the proceedings below met the demands of fundamental fairness which due process embodies. Such an approach may not satisfy those who see in the Fourteenth Amendment a set of easily applied "absolutes" which can afford a haven from unsettling doubt. It is, however, truer to the spirit which requires this Court constantly to re-examine fundamental principles and at the same time enjoins it from reading its own preferences into the Constitution.

The Connecticut Supreme Court of Errors gave full and careful consideration to the petitioner's claim that he would incriminate himself if he answered the questions put to him. It noted that its decisions "from a time antedating the adoption of . . . [the Connecticut] constitution in 1818" had upheld a privilege to refuse to answer incriminating questions. 150 Conn. 220, 223. Stating that federal cases treating the Fifth Amendment privilege had "persuasive force" in interpreting its own constitutional provisions, and citing *Hoffman* v. *United States,* 341 U.S. 479, in particular, the Supreme Court of Errors described the requirements for assertion of the privilege by quoting from one of its own cases, *id.,* at 225:

"[A] witness . . . has the right to refuse to answer any question which would tend to incriminate him. But a mere claim on his part that the evidence will tend to incriminate him is not sufficient. . . . [He

having] made his claim, it is then . . . [necessary for the judge] to determine in the exercise of a legal discretion whether, from the circumstances of the case and the nature of the evidence which the witness is called upon to give, there is reasonable ground to apprehend danger of criminal liability from his being compelled to answer. That danger 'must be real and appreciable, with reference to the ordinary operation of law in the ordinary course of things—not a danger of an imaginary and unsubstantial character, having reference to some extraordinary and barely possible contingency, so improbable that no reasonable man would suffer it to influence his conduct. We think that a merely remote and naked possibility, out of the ordinary course of law and such as no reasonable man would be affected by, should not be suffered to obstruct the administration of justice. The object of the law is to afford to a party, called upon to give evidence in a proceeding *inter alios,* protection against being brought by means of his own evidence within the penalties of the law. But it would be to convert a salutary protection into a means of abuse if it were to be held that a mere imaginary possibility of danger, however, remote and improbable, was sufficient to justify the withholding of evidence essential to the ends of justice.' Cockburn, C. J., in *Regina* v. *Boyes,* 1 B. & S. 311, 330. . . ." *McCarthy* v. *Clancy,* 110 Conn. 482, 488–489.

The court carefully applied the above standard to each question which the petitioner was asked. It dealt first with the question whether he knew John Bergoti. The court said:

"Bergoti is nowhere described or in any way identified, either as to his occupation, actual or reputed, or as to any criminal record he may have had. . . . Malloy made no attempt even to suggest to the court how an answer to the question whether he knew Bergoti could possibly incriminate him. . . . On this state of the record the question was proper, and Malloy's claim of privilege, made without explanation, was correctly overruled. Malloy 'chose to keep the door tightly closed and to deny the court the smallest glimpse of the danger he apprehended. He cannot then complain that we see none.' *In re Pillo,* 11 N.J. 8, 22, 93 A.2d 176. . . ." 150 Conn., at 226–227.

The remaining questions are summarized in the majority's opinion, *ante,* p. 11. All of them deal with the circumstances surrounding the petitioner's conviction on a gambling charge in 1959. The court declined to decide "whether, on their face and apart from any consideration of Malloy's immunity from prosecution, the questions should or should not have been answered in the light of his failure to give any hint of explanation as to how answers to them could incriminate him." 150 Conn., at 227. The court considered the State's claim that the petitioner's prior conviction was sufficient to clothe him with immunity from prosecution for other crimes to which the questions might pertain, but declined to rest its decision on that basis. *Id.,* at 227–229. The court concluded, however, that the running of the statute of limitations on misdemeanors committed in 1959 and the absence of any indication that Malloy had engaged in any crime other than a misdemeanor removed all appearance of danger of incrimination from the questions propounded concerning the petitioner's activities in 1959. The court summarized this conclusion as follows:

"In all this, Malloy confounds vague and improbable possibilities of prosecution with reasonably appreciable ones. Under claims like his, it would always be possible to work out some finespun and improbable theory from which an outside chance of prosecution could be envisioned. Such claims are not enough to support a claim of privilege, at least where, as here, a witness suggests no rational explanation of his fears of incrimination, and the questions themselves, under all the circumstances, suggest none." *Id.,* at 230–231.

Peremptorily rejecting all of the careful analysis of the Connecticut court, this Court creates its own "finespun and improbable theory" about how these questions might have incriminated the petitioner. With respect to his acquaintance with Bergoti, this Court says only:

"In the context of the inquiry, it should have been apparent to the referee that Bergoti was suspected by the State to be involved in some way in the subject matter of the investigation. An affirmative answer to the question might well have either connected petitioner with a more recent crime, or at least have operated as a waiver of his privilege with reference to his relationship with a possible criminal." *Ante,* pp. 12–13.

The other five questions, treated at length in the Connecticut court's opinion, got equally short shrift from this Court; it takes the majority, unfamiliar with Connecticut law and far removed from the proceedings below, only a dozen lines to consider the questions and conclude that they were incriminating:

"The interrogation was part of a wide-ranging inquiry into crime, including gambling, in Hartford. It was admitted on behalf of the State at oral argument—and indeed it is obvious from the questions themselves—that the State desired to elicit from the petitioner the identity of the person who ran the pool-selling operation in connection with which he had been arrested in 1959. It was apparent that petitioner might apprehend that if this person were still engaged in unlawful activity, disclosure of his name might furnish a link in a chain of evidence sufficient to connect the petitioner with a more recent crime for which he might still be prosecuted." (Footnote omitted.) . . . .

I do not understand how anyone could read the opinion of the Connecticut court and conclude that the state law which was the basis of its decision or the decision itself was lacking in fundamental fairness. The truth of the matter is that under any standard—state or federal—the commitment for contempt was proper. Indeed, as indicated above, there is every reason to believe that the Connecticut court did apply the *Hoffman* standard quoted approvingly in the majority's opinion. I entirely agree with my Brother White, *post*, pp. 4–5, that if the matter is viewed only from the standpoint of the federal standard, such standard was fully satisfied. The Court's reference to a federal standard is, to put it bluntly, simply an excuse for the Court to substitute its own superficial assessment of the facts and state law for the careful and better informed conclusions of the state court. No one who scans the two opinions with an objective eye will, I think, reach any other conclusion.

I would affirm.

MURPHY v. NEW YORK HARBOR WATERFRONT COMMISSION

84 S. Ct. 1594 (1964)

MR. JUSTICE GOLDBERG delivered the opinion of the Court.

We have held today that the Fifth Amendment privilege against self-incrimination must be deemed fully applicable to the States through the Fourteenth Amendment. *Malloy* v. *Hogan, ante*, at —. This case presents a related issue: whether one jurisdiction within our federal structure may compel a witness, whom it has immunized from prosecution under its laws, to give testimony which might then be used to convict him of a crime against another such jurisdiction.

Petitioners were subpoenaed to testify at a hearing conducted by the Waterfront Commission of New York Harbor concerning a work stoppage at the Hoboken, New Jersey, piers. After refusing to respond to certain questions about the stoppage on the ground that the answers might tend to incriminate them, petitioners were granted immunity from prosecution under the laws of New Jersey and New York. Notwithstanding this grant of immunity, they still refused to respond to the questions on the ground that the answers might tend to incriminate them under *federal* law, to which the grant of immunity did not purport to extend. Petitioners were thereupon held in civil and criminal contempt of court. The New Jersey Supreme Court reversed the criminal contempt conviction on procedural grounds but, relying on this Court's decisions in *Knapp* v. *Schweitzer*, 357 U.S. 371; *Feldman* v. *United States*, 322 U.S. 487; and *United States* v. *Murdock*, 284 U.S. 141, affirmed the civil contempt judgments on the merits. The court held that a State may constitutionally compel a witness to give testimony which might be used in a federal prosecution against him. 39 N.J. 436, 452–458.

Since a grant of immunity is valid only if it is coextensive with the scope of the privilege against self-incrimination, *Counselman* v. *Hitchcock*, 142 U.S. 547, we must now decide the fundamental constitutional question of whether, absent an immunity provision, one jurisdiction in our federal structure may compel a witness to give testimony which might incriminate him under the laws of another jurisdiction. The answer to this question must depend, of course, on whether such an application of the privilege promotes or defeats its policies and purposes.

I

THE POLICIES OF THE PRIVILEGE

The privilege against self-incrimination "registers an important advance in the development of our liberty—'one of the great landmarks in man's struggle to make himself civilized.'" *Ullmann* v. *United States*, 350 U.S. 422, 426. It reflects many of our fundamental values and most noble aspirations: our unwillingness to subject those suspected of crime to the cruel trilemma of self-accusation, perjury or contempt; our preference for an accusatorial rather than an inquisitorial system of criminal justice; our fear that self-incriminating statements will be elicited by inhumane treatment and abuses; our sense of fair play which dictates "a fair state-individual balance by requiring the government to leave the individual alone until good cause is shown for disturbing him and by requiring the government in its contest with the individual to shoulder the entire load," 8 Wigmore, Evidence (McNaughton rev., 1961), 317; our respect for the inviolability of the human personality and of the right of each individual "to a private enclave where he may lead a private life," *United States* v. *Grunewald,* 233 F.2d 556, 581–582 (Frank, J., dissenting), rev'd 353 U.S. 391; our distrust of self-deprecatory statements; and our realization that the privilege, while sometimes "a shelter to the guilty," is often "a protection to the innocent." *Quinn* v. *United States,* 349 U.S. 155, 162.

Most, if not all, of these policies and purposes are defeated when a witness "can be whipsawed into incriminating himself under both state and federal law even though" the constitutional privilege against self-incrimination is applicable to each. Cf. *Knapp* v. *Schweitzer,* 357 U.S. 371, 385 (dissenting opinion of Mr. Justice Black). This has become especially true in our age of "cooperative federalism," where the federal and state governments are waging a united front against many types of criminal activity.

Respondent contends, however, that we should adhere to the "established rule" that the constitutional privilege against self-incrimination does not protect a witness in one jurisdiction against being compelled to give testimony which could be used to convict him in another jurisdiction. This "rule" has three decisional facets: *United States* v. *Murdock,* 284 U.S. 141, held that the Federal Government could compel a witness to give testimony which might incriminate him under state law; *Knapp* v. *Schweitzer,* 357 U.S. 371, held that a State could compel a witness to give testimony

which might incriminate him under federal law; and *Feldman* v. *United States,* 322 U.S. 487, held that testimony thus compelled by a State could be introduced into evidence in the federal courts.

Our decision today in *Malloy* v. *Hogan, supra,* necessitates a reconsideration of this rule. Our review of the pertinent cases in this Court and of their English antecedents reveals that *Murdock* did not adequately consider the relevant authorities and has been significantly weakened by subsequent decisions of this Court, and, further, that the legal premises underlying *Feldman* and *Knapp* have since been rejected. . . .

IV
CONCLUSIONS

In light of the history, policies and purposes of the privilege against self-incrimination, we now accept as correct the construction given the privilege by the English courts and by Chief Justice Marshall and Justice Holmes. See *United States* v. *The Saline Bank of Virginia, supra; Ballmann* v. *Fagin, supra.* We reject—as unsupported by history or policy—the deviation from that construction only recently adopted by this Court in *United States* v. *Murdock, supra,* and *Feldman* v. *United States, supra.* We hold that the constitutional privilege against self-incrimination protects a state witness against incrimination under federal as well as state law and a federal witness against incrimination under state as well as federal law.

We must now decide what effect this holding has on existing state immunity legislation. In *Counselman* v. *Hitchcock,* 142 U.S. 547, this Court considered a federal statute which provided that no "evidence obtained from a party or witness by means of a judicial proceeding . . . shall be given in evidence, or in any manner used against him . . . in any Court of the United States. . . ." *Id.,* at 560. Notwithstanding this statute, appellant, claiming his privilege against self-incrimination, refused to answer certain questions before a federal grand jury. The Court said "that legislation cannot abridge a constitutional privilege, and that it cannot replace or supply one, at least unless it is so broad as to have the same extent in scope and effect." *Id.,* at 585. Applying this principle to the facts of that case, the Court upheld appellant's refusal to answer on the ground that the statute: "could not, and would not, prevent the use of his testimony to search out other testimony to be used in evidence against him or his property, in a criminal proceeding in such court . . . ," *id.,* at 564, that it: "could not prevent the obtaining and the use of witnesses and evidence which should be attributable directly to the testimony he might give under compulsion, and on which he might be convicted, when otherwise, and if he had refused to answer, he could not possibly have been convicted . . . ," *ibid.,* and that it: "affords no protection against that use of compelled testimony which consists in gaining therefrom a knowledge of the details of a crime, and of sources of information which may supply other means of convicting the witness or party." *Id.,* at 586.

Applying the holding of that case to our holdings today that the privilege against self-incrimination protects a state witness against federal prosecution, *ante,* at 25–26, and that "the same standards must determine whether [a witness'] silence in either a federal or state proceeding is justified," *Malloy* v. *Hogan, ante,* at —, we hold the constitutional rule to be that a state witness may not be compelled to give testimony which may be incriminating under federal law unless the compelled testimony and its fruits cannot be used in any manner by federal officials in connection with a criminal prosecution against him. We conclude, moreover, that in order to implement this constitutional rule and accommodate the interests of the State and Federal Governments in investigating and prosecuting crime, the Federal Government must be prohibited from making any such use of compelled testimony and its fruits. This exclusionary rule, while permitting the States to secure information necessary for effective law enforcement, leaves the witness and the Federal Government in

substantially the same position as if the witness had claimed his privilege in the absence of a state grant of immunity.

It follows that petitioners here may now be compelled to answer the questions propounded to them. At the time they refused to answer, however, petitioners had a reasonable fear, based on this Court's decision in *Feldman* v. *United States, supra,* that the federal authorities might use the answers against them in connection with a federal prosecution. We have now overruled *Feldman* and held that the Federal Government may make no such use of the answers. Fairness dictates that petitioners should now be afforded an opportunity, in light of this development, to answer the questions. Cf. *Raley* v. *Ohio,* 360 U.S. 423. Accordingly, the judgment of the New Jersey courts ordering petitioners to answer the questions may remain undisturbed. But the judgment of contempt is vacated and the cause remanded to the New Jersey Supreme Court for proceedings not inconsistent with this opinion.

It is so ordered.

Mr. Justice Black concurs in the judgment and opinion of the Court for the reasons stated in that opinion and for the reasons stated in *Feldman* v. *United States,* 322 U.S. 487, 494 (dissenting opinion), as well as *Adamson* v. *California,* 332 U.S. 46, 68 (dissenting opinion); *Speiser* v. *Randall,* 357, U.S. 513, 529 (concurring opinion); *Bartkus* v. *Illinois,* 359 U.S. 121, 150 (dissenting opinion); and *Abbate* v. *United States,* 359 U.S. 187, 201 (dissenting opinion).

Mr. Justice Harlan, whom Mr. Justice Clark joins, concurring.

Unless I wholly misapprehend the Court's opinion, its holding that testimony compelled in a state proceeding over a witness' claim that such testimony will incriminate him may not be used against the witness in a federal criminal prosecution rests on *constitutional* grounds. On that basis, the contrary conclusion of *Feldman* v. *United States,* 322 U.S. 487, is overruled.

I believe that the constitutional holding of *Feldman* was correct, and would not overrule it. To the extent, however, that the decision in that case may have rested also on a refusal to exercise this Court's "supervisory power" over the administration of justice in federal courts, I think that it can no longer be considered good law, in light of this Court's subsequent decision in *Elkins* v. *United States,* 364 U.S. 206. In *Elkins,* this Court, exercising its supervisory power, did away with the "silver platter" doctrine and prohibited the use of evidence unconstitutionally seized by state authorities in a federal criminal trial involving the person suffering such a seizure. I believe that a similar supervisory rule of exclusion should follow in a case of the kind now before us, and solely on that basis concur in this judgment.

I

The Court's constitutional conclusions are thought by it to follow from what it terms the "policies" of the privilege against self-incrimination and a re-examination of various cases in this Court, particularly in the context of early English law. Almost entirely absent from the statement of "policies" is any reference to the particular problem of this case; at best, the statement suggests the set of values which are on one side of the issue. The discussion of precedent is scarcely more helpful. It intertwines decisions of this Court with decisions in English courts, which *perhaps* follow a different rule, and casts doubt for one reason or another on every American case which does not accord with the result now reached. When the skein is untangled, however, and the line of cases is spread out, two facts clearly emerge:

(1) With two early and somewhat doubtful exceptions, this Court has consistently rejected the proposition that the danger of incrimination in the court of another jurisdiction is a sufficient basis for invoking a privilege against self-incrimination;

(2) Without any exception, in every case involving an immunity statute in which the Court has treated the question now before

us, it has rejected the present majority's views. . . .

II

Part I of this opinion shows, I believe, that the Court's analysis of prior cases hardly furnishes an adequate basis for a new departure in constitutional law. Even if the Court's analysis were sound, however, it would not support reversal of the *Feldman* rule on *constitutional* grounds.

If the Court were correct in asserting that the "separate sovereignty" theory of self-incrimination should be discarded, that would, as the Court says, lead to the conclusion that "a state witness [is protected] against incrimination under federal as well as state law and a federal witness against incrimination under state as well as federal law." *Ante,* p. 26. However, dealing strictly with the situation presented by this case, that conclusion does *not* in turn lead to a constitutional rule that the testimony of a state witness (or evidence to which his testimony leads) who is compelled to testify in state proceedings may not be used against him in a federal prosecution. Protection which the Due Process Clause affords against the *States* is quite obviously not any basis for a constitutional rule regulating the conduct of *federal* authorities in *federal* proceedings.

The Court avoids this problem by mixing together the Fifth Amendment and the Fourteenth and talking about "the constitutional privilege against self-incrimination," *ante,* pp. 25–26. Such an approach, which deals with "constitutional" rights at large, unrelated either to particular provisions of the Constitution or to relevant differences between the States and the Federal Government warns of the dangers for our federalism to which the "incorporation" theory of the Fourteenth Amendment leads. See my dissenting opinion in *Malloy* v. *Hogan, ante,* p. —.

The Court's reasons for overruling *Feldman* thus rest on an entirely new conception of the *Fifth Amendment,* namely that it applies to federal use of state compelled incriminating testimony. The opinion, however, contains nothing at all to contradict the traditional, well-understood conception of the Fifth Amendment, to which, therefore, I continue to adhere:

"The sole—although deeply valuable—purpose of the Fifth Amendment privilege against self-incrimination is the security of the individual against the exertion of the power of the Federal Government to compel incriminating testimony with a view to enabling that same Government to convict a man out of his own mouth." *Knapp v. Schweitzer, supra,* at 380.

It is no service to our constitutional liberties to encumber the particular provisions which safeguard them with a gloss for which neither the text nor history provides any support.

Accordingly, I cannot accept the majority's conclusion that a rule prohibiting federal authorities from using in aid of a federal prosecution incriminating testimony compelled in state proceedings is constitutionally required.

III

I would, however, adopt such a rule in the exercise of our supervisory power over the administration of federal criminal justice. See *McNabb* v. *United States,* 318 U.S. 332, 340–341. The rule seems to me to follow from the Court's rejection, in the exercise of its supervisory power, of the "silver platter" doctrine as applied to the use in federal courts of evidence unconstitutionally seized by state officers. *Elkins* v. *United States,* 364 U.S. 206.

Since I reject the majority's argument that the "separate sovereignty" theory of self-incrimination is historically unfounded,

I do not base my conclusion on the holding in *Malloy, ante,* that due process prohibits a State from compelling a witness to testify. My conclusion is based rather on the ground that such a rule is protective of the values which the federal privilege against self-incrimination expresses, without in any way interfering with the independent action of the States and the Federal Government in their respective spheres. Increasing interaction between the state and federal governments speaks strongly against permitting federal officials to make prosecutorial use of testimony which a State has compelled when that same testimony could not constitutionally have been compelled by the Federal Government and then used against the witness. Prohibiting such use in no way limits federal power to investigate and prosecute for federal crime, which power will be as full after a State has completed an investigation as before. This adjustment between state investigations of local crime and federal prosecutions for federal crime seems particularly desirable in view of the increasing, productive cooperation between federal and state authorities in the prevention of crime. By insulating intergovernmental cooperation from the danger of any encroachment on the federal privilege against self-incrimination, such a rule in the long run will probably make joint programs for crime prevention more effective.

On this basis, I concur in the judgment of the Court.

MR. JUSTICE WHITE, with whom MR. JUSTICE STEWART joins, concurring. . . .

FIKES v. ALABAMA

352 U.S. 191 (1957)

MR. CHIEF JUSTICE WARREN delivered the opinion of the Court:

Petitioner is under sentence of death for the crime of burglary with intent to commit rape. He seeks reversal of the judgment through a writ of certiorari to the Supreme

Court of Alabama, which sustained the conviction. 263 Ala. 89. Petitioner raised three issues in support of his position that he had been denied due process of law. He alleged:

1. Admission into evidence of two con-

fessions extracted from him under circumstances demonstrating that the statements were coerced or involuntary.

2. Denial by the trial judge of petitioner's request to testify about the manner in which the confessions were obtained without subjecting himself to unlimited cross-examination as to the facts of the crime charged.

3. Selection of the grand jury which indicted him by a method that systematically discriminated against members of his race.

We granted certiorari to determine whether the requirements of due process under the Fourteenth Amendment had been satisfied in these aspects of petitioner's conviction. 350 U.S. 993. The judgment must be reversed because of the admission of the confessions. Therefore, it is unnecessary at this time to decide or discuss the other two issues raised by petitioner.

The facts essential to the present decision are as follows:

During the early months of 1953, a number of housebreakings, some involving rape or attempted rape, were committed in the City of Selma, Alabama. The present trial concerned one of these crimes. On the night of April 24, 1953, an intruder broke into the apartment of the daughter of the city's mayor. She awoke to find a Negro man sitting on her with a knife at her throat. A struggle ensued which carried the woman and her assailant through the bedroom, hall, and living room, where she finally was able to seize the knife, at which point he fled. These rooms were all lighted. The victim testified that the attacker "had a towel draped over his head" throughout the incident; she did not identify petitioner as the attacker in her testimony at the trial. However, two other women testified to similar housebreakings (one of which resulted in rape), and they each identified petitioner as the burglar. This testimony was admitted at the present trial "solely on the question of intent and identity of defendant and his motive on the occasion then on trial." 263 Ala., at 99. This, with the challenged confessions, was substan-

tially all the evidence concerning the crime at the trial.

About midnight on May 16, 1953, petitioner was apprehended in an alley in a white neighborhood in Selma by private persons, who called the police. The officers jailed him "on an open charge of investigation." The next day, a Sunday, the questioning that led to the challenged confessions began. It is, of course, highly material to the question before this Court to ascertain petitioner's character and background. He is a Negro, 27 years old in 1953, who started school at age eight and left at 16 while still in the third grade. There was testimony by three psychiatrists at the trial, in connection with a pleaded defense of insanity, to the effect that petitioner is a schizophrenic and highly suggestible. His mother testified that he had always been "thick-headed." Petitioner worked in a gas station in his home town of Marion, some 30 miles from Selma. So far as appears, his only prior involvement with the law was a conviction for burglary of a store in November 1949; he was released on parole in January 1951.

The questioning of petitioner was conducted principally by Captain Baker of the Selma police. His testimony that he repeatedly advised petitioner "that he was entitled to counsel and his various rights" must be viewed in the light of the facts concerning petitioner's mentality and experience just outlined.

The interrogation began on Sunday, May 17, with a two-hour session in the morning in Captain Baker's office. That afternoon, petitioner was questioned for two and a half or three hours, during part of which time he was driven around the city to some of the locations of the unsolved burglaries. During this ride, petitioner also talked to the sheriff of his home county, who had been called to Selma at petitioner's request, according to Captain Baker's testimony.

On Monday, petitioner talked with his employer. Captain Baker continued questioning for two hours in the morning. He testified that a warrant was served on petitioner in jail, but that petitioner did not request a preliminary hearing. In fact, he was not taken before any judicial officer prior to the confessions. That afternoon, petitioner was driven to Kilby State Prison, which is located in another county, about 55 miles from Selma and some 80 miles from petitioner's home in Marion. The testimony of the responsible officers was that this removal was done for petitioner's protection, although no specific threat against him had been made.

At Kilby Prison, petitioner was kept in the "segregation unit," out of contact with other prisoners. He saw only the jailers and Selma officers who drove over to question him. Petitioner was interrogated in an office in the prison. On Monday, there was questioning there for "several hours" in the afternoon and "a little while" after supper. The next interrogation was on Wednesday. It lasted "several hours" in the afternoon and into the evening. The following day petitioner was questioned for two hours in the afternoon and about an hour and a half in the evening. That day his father came to the prison to see him, but was refused admittance.

On Thursday evening, the first confession occurred. It was introduced at the trial through a tape recording. The confession consists of an interrogation by Captain Baker. Petitioner responded chiefly in yes-or-no answers to his questions, some of which were quite leading or suggestive.

Petitioner was questioned again for three hours on Saturday, May 23. That day, a lawyer who came to the prison to see him was turned away. On Sunday, petitioner's father was allowed to visit his son. This was the only contact petitioner had during the entire period in question with family or friend, or for that matter with anyone he knew, except the talks at the beginning of the week with the sheriff of his own county, in the presence of Selma officers, and with his employer.

In the second week of his incarceration, on Tuesday afternoon, petitioner was questioned for about two and a half hours. At this time, the second confession was made. Like the other, it consists of responses to

questions. The second confession was taken down by a prison stenographer and signed by petitioner after it was read to him.

This outline of the facts surrounding the taking of the confessions comes entirely from the testimony of the State witnesses, who under the circumstances were the only ones who could testify at the trial on this subject other than the prisoner himself. He did not testify, because of the trial judge's ruling that he would be subject to unlimited cross-examination concerning the offense charged against him. Standing alone, the State's evidence establishes that the confessions in the present case were not voluntary within the meaning of the decisions of this Court.

Here the prisoner was an uneducated Negro, certainly of low mentality, if not mentally ill. He was first arrested by civilians, lodged in jail, and then removed to a state prison far from his home. We do not criticize the decision to remove the prisoner before any possibility of violence might mature, but petitioner's location and the conditions of his incarceration are facts to be weighed in connection with the issue before us. For a period of a week, he was kept in isolation, except for sessions of questioning. He saw no friend or relative. Both his father and a lawyer were barred in attempts to see him. The protections to be afforded to a prisoner upon preliminary hearing were denied him, contrary to the law of Alabama. He was questioned for several hours at a time over the course of five days preceding the first confession, and again interrogated at length before the written confession was secured.

There is no evidence of physical brutality, and particular elements that were present in other cases in which this Court ruled that a confession was coerced do not appear here. On the other hand, some of the elements in this case were not present in all of the prior cases. The objective facts in the present case are very much like those that were before the Court in *Turner v. Pennsylvania*, 338 U.S. 62, while the present petitioner was a weaker and more susceptible subject than the record in that case reveals Turner to have been. And cf. *Johnson* v. *Pennsylvania,* 340 U.S. 881. The totality of the circumstances that preceded the confessions in this case goes beyond the allowable limits. The use of the confessions secured in this setting was a denial of due process.

Neither *Stein* v. *New York,* 346 U.S. 156, nor any of the other cases relied on by respondent stands in the way of this conclusion. In *Stein,* the Court said:

"The limits in any case depend upon a weighing of the circumstances of pressure against the power of resistance of the person confessing. What would be overpowering to the weak of will or mind might be utterly ineffective against an experienced criminal." 346 U.S. at 185.

That is the same standard that has been utilized in each case, according to its total facts. Cf., e.g., *Watts* v. *Indiana,* 338 U.S. 49, 53; *Lyons* v. *Oklahoma,* 322 U.S. 596, 602–605. We hold that the circumstances of pressure applied against the power of resistance of this petitioner, who cannot be deemed other than weak of will or mind, deprived him of due process of law. So viewed, the judgment of conviction in this case cannot stand.

Reversed.

Mr. Justice Frankfurter, whom Mr. Justice Brennan joins, concurring. . . .

Mr. Justice Harlan, whom Mr. Justice Reed and Mr. Justice Burton join, dissenting:

The setting aside of this conviction, in my opinion, oversteps the boundary between this Court's function under the Fourteenth Amendment and that of the state courts in the administration of state criminal justice. I recognize that particularly in "coerced confession" cases the boundary line is frequently difficult to draw. But this Court has recognized that its corrective power over state courts in criminal cases is narrower than that which it exercises over the lower federal courts. *Watts* v. *Indiana,* 338 U.S. 49, 50.

In this instance I do not think it can be said that the procedures followed in obtaining petitioner's confessions violated constitutional due process. The elements usually associated with cases in which this Court has been constrained to act are, in my opinion, not present here in constitutional proportions, separately or in combination. Concededly, there was no brutality or physical coercion. And psychological coercion is by no means manifest. While the total period of interrogation was substantial, the questioning was intermittent; it never exceeded two or three hours at a time, and all of it took place during normal hours; "relay" tactics, such as were condemned in *Turner* v. *Pennsylvania,* 338 U.S. 62, and other cases, were not employed. True, petitioner's mental equilibrium appears to have been less than normal, but these facts were before the trial judge and the jury. The absence of arraignment, much as that practice is to be deprecated, loses in significance in light of the State's representation at the oral argument that this was not an unusual thing in Alabama. As this Court recognizes, it did not of itself make the confessions inadmissible. Petitioner's removal to Kilby Prison, after authorization by a state circuit judge, stands on quite a different footing from the episode in *Ward* v. *Texas,* 316 U.S. 547. And I am not satisfied that there was any deliberate purpose to keep the petitioner incommunicado, such as existed in *Watts* v. *Indiana, Turner* v. *Pennsylvania,* and *Harris* v. *South Carolina* (U.S.) all *supra.* Before the first confession, petitioner, at his own request, was permitted to see the sheriff of his home county, and his employer. His father, although not permitted to see petitioner on the day of the first confession, was allowed to see him before the second confession. The lawyer who sought to see petitioner was refused permission because, having no authority from petitioner or his family to represent him, the prison authorities evidently thought he was trying to solicit business.

The Supreme Court of Alabama, after reviewing the record, has sustained the conviction. 263 Ala. 89, 81 So2d 203. I find nothing here beyond a state of facts upon which reasonable men might differ in their conclusions as to whether the confessions had been coerced. In the absence of anything in the conduct of the state authorities which "shocks the conscience" or does "more than offend some fastidious squeamishness or private sentimentalism about combatting crime too energetically," *Rochin* v. *California*, 342 U.S. 165, 172, I think that due regard for the division between state and federal functions in the administration of criminal justice requires that we let Alabama's judgment stand.

NOTE AND QUAERE: "The net effect of the decision was to return the *Fikes* case to the Alabama courts for retrial—this time without use of the tainted confessions. More important was the over-all effect; once again, and this time by a split decision, the court had inflamed the suspicions of critics who hold that too many of its recent decisions are anchored more in sociology than in the solid substance of the law." [1]

Do you find "solid substance" in the law of due process? Does the *Fikes* case turn on a legal, or a factual, issue?

JACKSON v. DENNO
84 S. Ct. 1774 (1964)

This case is important for the light it gives on procedure at the trial level for determining whether a confession is, or is not, voluntary.

As to the status of such a determination on review, Mr. Justice Jackson expressed the orthodox view when he observed: "Of course, this Court cannot allow itself to be completely bound by state court determination of any issue essential to decision of a claim of federal right, or else federal law could be frustrated by distorted fact finding. But that does not mean that we give no weight to the decision below, or approach the record de novo or with the latitude of choice open to some state appellate courts, such as the New York Court of Appeals."

For a more thorough exploration of the problem see part IV of Mr. Justice Frankfurter's opinion in *Culombe* v. *Connecticut*, 367 U.S. 568 (1961).

MR. JUSTICE WHITE delivered the opinion of the Court. . . .

It is now axiomatic that a defendant in a criminal case is deprived of due process of law if his conviction is founded, in whole or in part, upon an involuntary confession, without regard for the truth or falsity of the confession. *Rogers* v. *Richmond*, 365 U.S. 534, and even though there is ample evidence aside from the confession to support the conviction. *Malinski* v. *New York*, 324 U.S. 401; *Stroble* v. *California*, 343 U.S. 181; *Payne* v. *Arkansas*, 356 U.S. 560.

Equally clear is the defendant's constitutional right at some stage in the proceedings to object to the use of the confession and to have a fair hearing and a reliable determination on the issue of voluntariness, a determination uninfluenced by the truth or falsity of the confession. *Rogers* v. *Richmond, supra*. In our view, the New York procedure employed in this case did not afford a reliable determination of the voluntariness of the confession offered in evidence at the trial, did not adequately protect Jackson's right to be free of a con-

1. Courtesy *Time*. (Copyright, Time Inc., 1957.)

viction based upon a coerced confession and therefore cannot withstand constitutional attack under the Due Process Clause of the Fourteenth Amendment. We therefore reverse the judgment below denying the writ of habeas corpus.

III

Under the New York rule, the trial judge must make a preliminary determination regarding a confession offered by the prosecution and exclude it if in no circumstances could the confession be deemed voluntary. But if the evidence presents a fair question as to its voluntariness, as where certain facts bearing on the issue are in dispute or where reasonable men could differ over the inferences to be drawn from undisputed facts, the judge "must receive the confession and leave to the jury, under proper instructions, the ultimate determination of its voluntary character and also its truthfulness." *Stein* v. *New York*, 346 U.S. 156, 172. If an issue of coercion is presented, the judge may not resolve conflicting evidence or arrive at his independent appraisal of the voluntariness of the confession, one way or the other. These matters he must leave to the jury.

This procedure has a significant impact upon the defendant's Fourteenth Amendment rights. In jurisdictions following the orthodox rule, under which the judge himself solely and finally determines the voluntariness of the confession, or those following the Massachusetts procedure, under which the jury passes on voluntariness only after the judge has fully and independently resolved the issue against the accused, the judge's conclusions are clearly evident from the record since he either admits the confession into evidence if it is voluntary or rejects it if involuntary. Moreover, his findings upon disputed issues of fact are expressly stated or may be ascertainable from the record. In contrast, the New York jury returns only a general verdict upon the ultimate question of guilt or innocence. It is impossible to discover whether the jury found the confession voluntary and relied upon it, or involuntary and supposedly ignored it. Nor is there any indication of how the jury resolved disputes in the evidence concerning the critical facts underlying the coercion issue. Indeed, there is nothing to show that these matters were resolved at all, one way or the other.

These uncertainties inherent in the New York procedure were aptly described by the Court in *Stein* v. *New York*, 346 U.S. 156, 177–178:

"Petitioners suffer a disadvantage inseparable from the issues they raise in that this procedure does not produce any definite, open and separate decision of the confession issue. Being cloaked by the general verdict, petitioners do not know what result they really are attacking here. . . . This method of trying the coercion issue to a jury is not informative as to its disposition. Sometimes the record permits a guess or inference, but where other evidence of guilt is strong a reviewing court cannot learn whether the final result was to receive or to reject the confessions as evidence of guilt. Perhaps a more serious, practical cause of dissatisfaction is the absence of any assurance that the confessions did not serve as make-weights in a compromise verdict, some jurors accepting the confessions to overcome lingering doubt of guilt, others rejecting them but finding their doubts satisfied by other evidence, and yet others or perhaps all never reaching a separate and definite conclusion as to the confessions but returning an unanalytical and impressionistic verdict based on all they had heard."

[JUSTICES BLACK, CLARK, STEWART and HARLAN dissented as to the invalidation of New York's procedure.]

QUAERE: Would the Massachusetts procedure be permissible in the light of *Denno?*

THE WATTS, TURNER, AND HARRIS CASES
338 U.S. 49, 62, 68 (1949)

Concurring in *Watts,* and dissenting in the two other cases, Mr. Justice Jackson raised an important *practical* problem in criminal law enforcement:

These three cases, from widely separated states, present essentially the same problem. Its recurrence suggests that it has roots in some condition fundamental and general to our criminal system.

In each case police were confronted with one or more brutal murders which the authorities were under the highest duty to solve. Each of these murders was unwitnessed, and the only positive knowledge on which a solution could be based was possessed by the killer. In each there was reasonable ground to *suspect* an individual but not enough legal evidence to *charge* him with guilt. In each the police attempted to meet the situation by taking the suspect into custody and interrogating him. This extended over varying periods. In each, confessions were made and received in evidence at the trial. Checked with external evidence, they are inherently believable, and were not shaken as to truth by anything that occurred at the trial. Each confessor was convicted by a jury and state courts affirmed. This Court sets all three convictions aside.

The seriousness of the Court's judgment is that no one suggests that any course held promise of solution of these murders other than to take the suspect into custody for questioning. The alternative was to close the books on the crime and forget it, with the suspect at large. This is a grave choice for a society in which two-thirds of the murders already are closed out as insoluble.

A concurring opinion, however, goes to the very limit and seems to declare for outlawing any confession, however freely given, if obtained during a period of custody between arrest and arraignment—which, in practice, means all of them.

Others would strike down these confessions because of conditions which they say make them "involuntary." In this, on only a printed record, they pit their judgment against that of the trial judge and the jury. Both, with the great advantage of hearing and seeing the confessor and also the officers whose conduct and bearing toward him is in question, have found that the confessions were voluntary. In addition, the majority overrule in each case one or more state appellate courts, which have the same limited opportunity to know the truth that we do.

Amid much that is irrelevant or trivial, one serious situation seems to me to stand out in these cases. The suspect neither had nor was advised of his right to get counsel. This presents a real dilemma in a free society. To subject one without counsel to questioning which may and is intended to convict him, is a real peril to individual freedom. To bring in a lawyer means a real peril to solution of the crime, because, under our adversary system, he deems that his sole duty is to protect his client—guilty or innocent—and that in such a capacity he owes no duty whatever to help society solve its crime problem. Under this conception of criminal procedure, any lawyer worth his salt will tell the suspect in no uncertain terms to make no statement to police under any circumstances.

If the State may arrest on suspicion and interrogate without counsel, there is no denying the fact that it largely negates the benefits of the constitutional guaranty of the right to assistance of counsel. Any lawyer who has ever been called into a case after his client has "told all" and turned any evidence he has over to the Government, knows how helpless he is to protect his client against the facts thus disclosed.

I suppose the view one takes will turn on what one thinks should be the right of an accused person against the State. Is it his right to have the judgment on the facts? Or is it his right to have a judgment based on only such evidence as he cannot conceal from the authorities, who cannot compel him to testify in court and also cannot question him before? Our system comes close to the latter by any interpretation, for the defendant is shielded by such safeguards as no system of law except the Anglo-American concedes to him.

Of course, no confession that has been obtained by any form of physical violence to the person is reliable and hence no conviction should rest upon one obtained in that manner. Such treatment not only breaks the will to conceal or lie, but may even break the will to stand by the truth. Nor is it questioned that the same result can sometimes be achieved by threats, promises, or inducements, which torture the mind but put no scar on the body. . . . But if ultimate quest in a criminal trial is the truth and if the circumstances indicate no violence or threats of it, should society be deprived of the suspect's help in solving a crime merely because he was confined and questioned when uncounseled?

We must not overlook that, in these as in some previous cases, once a confession is obtained it supplies ways of verifying its trustworthiness. In these cases before us the verification is sufficient to leave me in no doubt that the admissions of guilt were genuine and truthful. Such corroboration consists in one case of finding a weapon where the accused has said he hid it, and in others that conditions which could only have been known to one who was implicated correspond with his story. It is possible, but it is rare, that a confession, if repudiated on the trial, standing alone will convict unless there is external proof of its verity.

In all such cases, along with other conditions criticized, the continuity and duration of the questioning is invoked and it is called an "inquiry," "inquest" or "inquisition," depending mainly on the emotional state of the writer. But as in some of the cases here, if interrogation is permissible at all, there are sound reasons for prolonging it—which the opinions here ignore. The suspect at first perhaps makes an effort to exculpate himself by alibis or other statements. These are verified, found false, and he is then confronted with his falsehood. Sometimes (though such cases do not reach us) verification proves them true or credible and the suspect is released. Sometimes, as here, more than one crime is involved. The duration of an interrogation may well depend on the temperament, shrewdness and cunning of the accused and the competence of the examiner. But, assuming a right to examine at all, the right must include what is made reasonably necessary by the facts of the particular case.

If the right of interrogation be admitted, then it seems to me that we must leave it to trial judges and juries and state appellate courts to decide individual cases, unless they show some want of proper standards of decision. I find nothing to indicate that any of the courts below in these cases did not have a correct understanding of the Fourteenth Amendment, unless this Court thinks it means absolute prohibition of interrogation while in custody before arraignment.

I suppose no one would doubt that our Constitution and Bill of Rights, grounded in revolt against the arbitrary measures of George III and in the philosophy of the French Revolution, represent the maximum restrictions upon the power of organized society over the individual that are compatible with the maintenance of organized society itself. They were so intended and should be so interpreted. It cannot be denied that, even if construed as these provisions traditionally have been, they contain an aggregate of restrictions which seriously limit the power of society to solve such crimes as confront us in these cases. Those restrictions we should not for that reason cast aside, but that is good reason for indulging in no unnecessary expansion of them.

I doubt very much if they require us to hold that the State may not take into custody and question one suspected reasonably of an unwitnessed murder. If it does, the people of this country must discipline themselves to seeing their police stand by helplessly while those suspected of murder prowl about unmolested. Is it a necessary price to pay for the fairness which we know as "due process of law"? And if not a necessary one, should it be demanded by this Court? I do not know the ultimate answer to these questions; but, for the present, I should not increase the handicap on society.

MALLORY v. UNITED STATES

354 U.S. 449 (1957)

> The *Watts, Turner,* and *Harris* cases, above, and *Breihaupt,* below, involve state proceedings and constitutional requirements. The present case involves a federal trial and the Federal Rules of Criminal Procedure. Reversing a conviction for rape, the Court per Mr. Justice Frankfurter said in part:

In *McNabb* v. *United States,* 318 U.S. 332, 343–344, . . . the Court held that police detention of defendants beyond the time when a committing magistrate was readily accessible constituted "wilful disobedience of law." In order adequately to enforce the congressional requirement of prompt arraignment, it was deemed necessary to render inadmissible incriminating statements elicited from defendants during a period of unlawful detention.

In *Upshaw* v. *United States,* 335 U.S. 410, which came here after the Federal Rules of Criminal Procedure had been in operation, the Court made it clear that Rule 5(a)'s standard of "without unnecessary delay" implied no relaxation of the McNabb doctrine.

The requirement of Rule 5(a) is part of the procedure devised by Congress for safeguarding individual rights without hampering effective and intelligent law enforcement. Provisions related to Rule 5(a) contemplate a procedure that allows arresting officers little more leeway than the interval between arrest and the ordinary administrative steps required to bring a suspect before the nearest available magistrate. . . .

The scheme for initiating a federal prosecution is plainly defined. The police may not arrest upon mere suspicion but only on "probable cause." The next step in the proceeding is to arraign the arrested person before a judicial officer as quickly as possible so that he may be advised of his rights and so that the issue of probable cause may be promptly determined. The arrested person may, of course, be "booked" by the police. But he is not to be taken to police headquarters in order to carry out a process of inquiry that lends itself, even if not so designed, to eliciting damaging statements to support the arrest and ultimately his guilt.

The duty enjoined upon arresting officers to arraign "without unnecessary delay" indicates that the command does not call for mechanical or automatic obedience. Circumstances may justify a brief delay between arrest and arraignment, as for instance, where the story volunteered by the accused is susceptible of quick verification through third parties. But the delay must not be of a nature to give opportunity for the extraction of a confession.

The circumstances of this case preclude a holding that arraignment was "without unnecessary delay." Petitioner was arrested in the early afternoon and was detained at headquarters within the vicinity of numerous committing magistrates. Even though the police had ample evidence from other sources than the petitioner for regarding the petitioner as the chief suspect, they first questioned him for approximately a half hour. When this inquiry of a nineteen-year-old lad of limited intelligence produced no confession, the police asked him to submit to a "lie-detector" test. He was not told of his rights to counsel or to a preliminary examination before a magistrate, nor was he warned that he might keep silent and "that any statement made by him may be used against him." After four hours of further detention at headquarters, during which arraignment could easily have been made in the same building in which the police headquarters were housed, petitioner was examined by the lie-detector operator for another hour and a half before his story began to waver. Not until he had confessed, when any judicial caution had lost its purpose, did the police arraign him.

We cannot sanction this extended delay, resulting in confession, without subordinat-

ing the general rule of prompt arraignment to the discretion of arresting officers in finding exceptional circumstances for its disregard. In every case where the police resort to interrogation of an arrested person and secure a confession, they may well claim, and quite sincerely, that they were merely trying to check on the information given by him. Against such a claim and the evil potentialities of the practice for which it is urged stands Rule 5(a) as a barrier. Nor is there an escape from the constraint laid upon the police by that Rule in that two other suspects were involved for the same crime. Presumably, whomever the police arrest they must arrest on "probable cause." It is not the function of the police to arrest, as it were, at large and to use an interrogating process at police headquarters in order to determine whom they should charge before a committing magistrate on "probable cause."

A POLICE CHIEF'S VIEW OF MAPP AND MALLORY [1]

In the following interview W. H. Parker, Chief of Police of Los Angeles, expressed his views as to the effect of *Mapp* v. *Ohio* and *Mallory* v. *United States,* both above.

Q. Is it getting harder for police to find and arrest a criminal?

A. Yes. The difficulty that we face is in search and seizure of evidence that might lead us to the solution of a case.

Q. How is that?

A. For a recent example: Two of our men were shot to death in a large store in Los Angeles when questioning a couple—a man and woman—who had aroused suspicion when they tried to cash a check. I think this exemplifies the difference in our problem today, as compared to 10 years ago.

Under past situations, our detectives would have immediately ascertained if there was any evidence in the possession of these people, then taken the couple into custody. But because of the "exclusionary evidence" rule, which requires that there must be probable cause for an arrest before the evidence is searched for and seized, these officers refrained from search. This gave the suspects an opportunity to shoot the officers. So because of their reticence to conduct the search, they both died.

Q. Is the "exclusionary evidence" rule a California law?

A. Yes. It goes back to 1955. But I have very good reason to believe that its adoption was prompted by a U.S. Supreme Court decision in which State

1. Part of a copyrighted interview which appeared in *U.S. News and World Report,* April 20, 1964, pp. 70–71.

courts were admonished to re-examine their position in relation to the "exclu-sionary evidence" rule of the federal courts.

Our State Supreme Court feared that, if it did not take some action, the Federal Government would impose its will upon the State. This fear was cer-tainly justified, because about two and a half years ago the Supreme Court of the United States, in an Ohio case, imposed the federal "exclusionary evidence" rule upon all the courts of all the States in the United States, and did so under the guise of due process of law.

Q. So it is now more difficult for a police officer to arrest a criminal—

A. That's right. Now, one of the things the U.S. Supreme Court did, in impos-ing its rule upon the State courts, is to raise the question: What constitutes "probable cause" for an arrest? This question is yet unanswered, which means that our police officers, attempting to cope with the crime problem, are at sea as to precisely when they do have "probable cause" for a valid arrest.

Now, this begets something else in turn—both on the court level and in police operations. The lower courts, not wishing to be reversed, are tending to protect the criminal's rights—bluntly—at the expense of protecting society's rights. And the police officer is inclined to be more conservative about any action that might be overruled by the courts.

So, all the way down the line, the tendency is to debilitate the administration of criminal justice at great expense to the general community.

. . . Q. Is it your feeling, then, that much of this general trend is originating with decisions of the Supreme Court?

A. Yes. May I give you an example? In the Mallory rule, limiting the elapsed time between a suspect's arrest and his arraignment in federal courts, I believe the direct quote out of the Supreme Court's decision is that the "police should not be given an opportunity in which to extract a confession."

Now, this all sounds very noble. It indicates that this rule will, in some way, prevent the police from using the rack and the screw in attempting to extort admissions of guilt from people who may be innocent. But what it actually means is that, as a general rule, confessions obtained before arraignment will not be admitted into evidence, even though valid and even though they may be the difference between success or failure in administering criminal justice.

We may throw out a thousand valid confessions with the hope that in doing so we may strike off some confession that was not properly obtained. This is a very expensive way to operate.

The States probably will get the Mallory rule, too, some day—if present trends continue. In fact, in a recent 5-to-4 decision by the U.S. Supreme Court, we barely escaped having the Mallory rule applied to California courts.

Q. What is the effect of all this on crime? Are criminals more free to operate than in the past?

A. Yes, indeed. Our criminals are at large to a far greater extent than they normally would have been under our previous methods of operation. They're committing far more crime than they normally would have, because they have the opportunity to engage in a greater amount of criminal activity.

Result is, we find ourselves overworked because of the additional crimes that are reported to us. The courts find themselves somewhat overworked because, with this great volume of crime, we are prosecuting far more people than we were. So, instead of fostering obedience to law on the theory that a human being will respond to kindness, we find that the criminal element has accepted leniency as sort of a license to continue its criminal activity. . . .

NOTE: *Ullman* v. *United States,* 350 U.S. 422 (1956), held that when the federal government gives a witness full immunity from prosecution (state and federal) for certain conduct, he cannot be prosecuted for such conduct—and to that extent can claim no privilege against self-incrimination under the Fifth Amendment. Justices Black and Douglas dissented on the ground that a witness in such circumstances might have to subject himself to various noncriminal "penalties," as well as social and economic reprisals. Compare the *Frank* case, above, where the Court held that the Fourth Amendment gives protection only in the context of criminal prosecution.

7. OTHER QUESTIONABLY OBTAINED EVIDENCE

BREITHAUPT v. *ABRAM*

352 U.S. 432 (1957)

MR. JUSTICE CLARK delivered the opinion of the Court.

Petitioner, while driving a pickup truck on the highways of New Mexico, was involved in a collision with a passenger car. Three occupants of the car were killed and petitioner was seriously injured. A pint whisky bottle, almost empty, was found in the glove compartment of the pickup truck. Petitioner was taken to a hospital and while lying unconscious in the emergency room the smell of liquor was detected on his breath. A state patrolman requested that a sample of petitioner's blood be taken. An attending physician, while petitioner was unconscious, withdrew a sample of about 20 cubic centimeters of blood by use of a hypodermic needle. This sample was delivered to the patrolman and subsequent laboratory analysis showed this blood to contain about .17% alcohol.

Petitioner was thereafter charged with involuntary manslaughter. Testimony regarding the blood test and its result was admitted into evidence at trial over petitioner's objection. This included testimony of an expert that a person with .17% alcohol in his blood was under the influence of intoxicating liquor. Petitioner was convicted and sentenced for involuntary manslaughter. He did not appeal the conviction. Subsequently, however, he sought release from his imprisonment by a petition for a writ of habeas corpus to the Supreme Court of New Mexico. That court, after argument, denied the writ. 58 N.M. 385, 271 P2d 827 (1954). Petitioner contends that his conviction, based on the result of the involuntary blood test, deprived him of his liberty without that due process of law guaranteed him by the Fourteenth Amendment to the Constitution. We granted certiorari, 351 U.S. 906, to determine whether the requirements of the due process clause, as it concerns state criminal proceedings, necessitate the invalidation of the conviction.

It has been clear since *Weeks* v. *United States,* 232 U.S. 383, that evidence obtained in violation of rights protected by the Fourth Amendment to the Federal Constitution must be excluded in federal criminal prosecutions. There is argument on behalf of petitioner that the evidence used here, the result of the blood test, was obtained in violation of the due process clause of the Fourteenth Amendment in that the taking was the result of an unreasonable search and seizure violative of the Fourth Amendment. Likewise, he argues that by way of the Fourteenth Amendment there has been a violation of the Fifth Amendment in that introduction of the test result compelled him to be a witness against himself. Petitioner relies on the proposition that "the generative principles" of the Bill of

Rights should extend the protections of the Fourth and Fifth Amendments to his case through the due process clause of the Fourteenth Amendment. But *Wolf* v. *Colorado*, 338 U.S. 25, answers this contention in the negative. See also *Twining* v. *New Jersey*, 211 U.S. 78; *Palko* v. *Connecticut*, 302 U.S. 319; *Irvine* v. *California*, 347 U.S. 128. New Mexico has rejected, as it may, the exclusionary rule set forth in *Weeks*, 232 U.S. 383, *supra*. *State* v. *Dillon*, 34 N.M. 366, 281 P 474. Therefore, the rights petitioner claims afford no aid to him here for the fruits of the violations, if any, are admissible in the State's prosecution.

Petitioner's remaining and primary assault on his conviction is not so easily unhorsed. He urges that the conduct of the state officers here offends that "sense of justice" of which we spoke in *Rochin* v. *California*, 342 U.S. 165. In that case state officers broke into the home of the accused and observed him place something in his mouth. The officers forced open his mouth after considerable struggle in an unsuccessful attempt to retrieve whatever was put there. A stomach pump was later forcibly used and among the matter extracted from his stomach were found narcotic pills. As we said there, "this course of proceeding by agents of government to obtain evidence is bound to offend even hardened sensibilities." Id. 342 U.S. at 172. We set aside the conviction because such conduct "shocked the conscience," and was so "brutal" and "offensive" that it did not comport with traditional ideas of fair play and decency. We therefore found that the conduct was offensive to due process. But we see nothing comparable here to the facts in *Rochin*.

Basically the distinction rests on the fact that there is nothing "brutal" or "offensive" in the taking of a sample of blood when done, as in this case, under the protective eye of a physician. To be sure, the driver here was unconscious when the blood was taken, but the absence of conscious consent, without more, does not necessarily render the taking a violation of a constitutional right; and certainly the test as ad-ministered here would not be considered offensive by even the most delicate. Furthermore, due process is not measured by the yardstick of personal reaction or the sphygmogram of the most sensitive person, but by that whole community sense of "decency and fairness" that has been woven by common experience into the fabric of acceptable conduct. It is on this bedrock that this Court has established the concept of due process. The blood test procedure has become routine in our everyday life. It is a ritual for those going into the military service as well as those applying for marriage licenses. Many colleges require such tests before permitting entrance and literally millions of us have voluntarily gone through the same, though a longer routine, in becoming blood donors. Likewise, we note that a majority of our States have either enacted statutes in some form authorizing tests of this nature or permit findings so obtained to be admitted in evidence. We therefore conclude that a blood test taken by a skilled technician is not such "conduct that shocks the conscience," *Rochin, supra*, (342 U.S. at 172), nor such a method of obtaining evidence that it offends a "sense of justice," *Brown* v. *Mississippi*, 297 U.S. 278, 285, 286. This is not to say that the indiscriminate taking of blood under different conditions, or by those not competent to do so may not amount to such "brutality" as would come under the *Rochin* rule. The chief law-enforcement officer of New Mexico, while at the Bar of this Court, assured us that every proper medical precaution is afforded an accused from whom the blood is taken.

The test upheld here is not attacked on the ground of any basic deficiency or of injudicious application, but admittedly is a scientifically accurate method of detecting alcoholic content in the blood, thus furnishing an exact measure upon which to base a decision as to intoxication. Modern community living requires modern scientific methods of crime detection lest the public go unprotected. The increasing slaughter on our highways, most of which should be avoidable, now reaches the astounding figures only heard of on the battlefield. The States, through safety measures, modern scientific methods, and strict enforcement of traffic laws, are using all reasonable means to make automobile driving less dangerous.

As against the right of an individual that his person be held inviolable, even against so slight an intrusion as is involved in applying a blood test of the kind to which millions of Americans submit as a matter of course nearly every day, must be set the interests of society in the scientific determination of intoxication, one of the great causes of the mortal hazards of the road. And the more so since the test likewise may establish innocence, thus affording protection against the treachery of judgment based on one or more of the senses. Furthermore, since our criminal law is to no small extent justified by the assumption of deterrence, the individual's right to immunity from such invasion of the body as is involved in a properly safeguarded blood test is far outweighed by the value of its deterrent effect due to public realization that the issue of driving while under the influence of alcohol can often by this method be taken out of the confusion of conflicting contentions.

For these reasons the judgment is affirmed.

MR. CHIEF JUSTICE WARREN, with whom MR. JUSTICE BLACK and MR. JUSTICE DOUGLAS join, dissenting:

The judgment in this case should be reversed if *Rochin* v. *California,* 342 U.S. 165, is to retain its vitality and stand as more than an instance of personal revulsion against particular police methods. I cannot agree with the Court when it says, "we see nothing comparable here to the facts in *Rochin.*" It seems to me the essential elements of the cases are the same and the same result should follow.

There is much in the Court's opinion concerning the hazards on our nation's highways, the efforts of the States to enforce the traffic laws and the necessity for the use of modern scientific methods in the detec-

tion of crime. Everybody can agree with these sentiments, and yet they do not help us particularly in determining whether this case can be distinguished from *Rochin.* That case grew out of police efforts to curb the narcotics traffic, in which there is surely a state interest of at least as great magnitude as the interest in highway law enforcement. Nor does the fact that many States sanction the use of blood test evidence differentiate the cases. At the time *Rochin* was decided illegally obtained evidence was admissible in the vast majority of States. In both *Rochin* and this case the officers had probable cause to suspect the defendant of the offense of which they sought evidence. In *Rochin* the defendant was known as a narcotics law violator, was arrested under suspicious circumstances and was seen by the officers to swallow narcotics. In neither case, of course, are we concerned with the defendant's guilt or innocence. The sole problem is whether the proceeding was tainted by a violation of the defendant's constitutional rights.

In reaching its conclusion that in this case, unlike *Rochin,* there is nothing "brutal" or "offensive" the Court has not kept separate the component parts of the problem. Essentially there are two: the character of the invasion of the body and the expression of the victim's will; the latter may be manifested by physical resistance. Of course, one may consent to having his blood extracted or his stomach pumped and thereby waive any due process objection. In that limited sense the expression of the will is significant. But where there is no affirmative consent, I cannot see that it should make any difference whether one states unequivocally that he objects or resorts to physical violence in protest or is in such condition that he is unable to protest. The Court, however, states that "the absence of conscious consent, without more, does not necessarily render the taking a violation of a constitutional right." This implies that a different result might follow if petitioner had been conscious and had voiced his objection. I reject the distinction. Since there clearly was no consent to the blood test, it is the nature of the invasion of the body that should be determinative of the due process question here presented. The Court's opinion suggests that an invasion is "brutal" or "offensive" only if the police use force to overcome a suspect's resistance. By its recital of the facts in *Rochin*—the references to a "considerable struggle" and the fact that the stomach pump was "forcibly used"—the Court finds *Rochin* distinguishable from this case. I cannot accept an analysis that would make physical resistance by a prisoner a prerequisite to the existence of his constitutional rights.

Apart from the irrelevant factor of physical resistance, the techniques used in this case and in *Rochin* are comparable. In each the operation was performed by a doctor in a hospital. In each there was an extraction of body fluids. Neither operation normally causes any lasting ill effects. The Court denominates a blood test as a scientific method for detecting crime and cites the frequency of such tests in our everyday life. The stomach pump too is a common and accepted way of making tests and relieving distress. But it does not follow from the fact that a technique is a product of science or is in common, consensual use for other purposes that it can be used to extract evidence from a criminal defendant without his consent. Would the taking of spinal fluid from an unconscious person be condoned because such tests are commonly made and might be used as a scientific aid to law enforcement?

Only personal reaction to the stomach pump and the blood test can distinguish them. To base the restriction which the due process clause imposes on state criminal procedures upon such reactions is to build on shifting sands. We should, in my opinion, hold that due process means at least that law-enforcement officers in their efforts to obtain evidence from persons suspected of crime must stop short of bruising the body, breaking skin, puncturing tissue or extracting body fluids, whether they contemplate doing it by force or by stealth.

Viewed according to this standard the judgment should be reversed.

MR. JUSTICE DOUGLAS, with whom MR. JUSTICE BLACK joins, dissenting:

The court seems to sanction in the name of law enforcement the assault made by the police on this unconscious man. If law enforcement were the chief value in our constitutional scheme, then due process would shrivel and become of little value in protecting the rights of the citizen. But those who fashioned the Constitution put certain rights out of the reach of the police and preferred other rights over law enforcement.

One source of protection of the citizen against state action is the due process clause of the Fourteenth Amendment. Our decisions hold that the police violate due process when they use brutal methods to obtain evidence against a man and use it to convict him. *Rochin* v. *California*, 342 U.S. 165; *Chambers* v. *Florida*, 309 U.S. 227. But the conception of due process is not limited to a prohibition of the use of force and violence against an accused. In *Leyra* v. *Denno*, 347 U.S. 556, we set aside a conviction where subtle, nonviolent methods had been used to exact a confession from a prisoner. For it was obvious that coercion might be the product of subtlety as well as of violence. We should take the same libertarian approach here.

As I understood today's decision there would be a violation of due process if the blood had been withdrawn from the accused after a struggle with the police. But the sanctity of the person is equally violated and his body assaulted where the prisoner is incapable of offering resistance as it would be if force were used to overcome his resistance. In both cases evidence is used to convict a man which had been obtained from him on an involuntary basis. I would not draw a line between the use of force on the one hand and trickery, subterfuge, or any police technique which takes advantage of the inability of the prisoner to resist on the other. Nor would I draw a line between involuntary extraction of words from his lips, the involuntary extraction of the contents of his stomach, and the involuntary extraction of fluids of his body when the evidence obtained is used to convict him. Under our system of government, police cannot compel people to furnish the evidence necessary to send them to prison. Yet there is compulsion here, following the violation by the police of the sanctity of the body of an unconscious man.

And if the decencies of a civilized state are the test, it is repulsive to me for the police to insert needles into an unconscious person in order to get the evidence necessary to convict him, whether they find the person unconscious, give him a pill which puts him to sleep, or use force to subdue him. The indignity to the individual is the same in one case as in the other, for in each is his body invaded and assaulted by the police who are supposed to be the citizen's protector.

I would reverse this judgment of conviction.

NOTE: In *Olmstead* v. *United States*, 277 U.S. 478 (1928), "listening in" on a telephone conversation via "wire-tapping" was held not to be a search and seizure within the meaning of the Fourth Amendment. The dissenting views of Justices Holmes and Brandeis were adopted by an act of Congress which in effect forbade the use in federal courts of wire-tap evidence. *Nardone* v. *United States*, 302 U.S. 379 (1937); *Benanti* v. *United States*, 78 S. Ct. 155 (1957). In *On Lee* v. *United States*, 343 U.S. 747 (1952), the *Olmstead* principle sustained use of damaging evidence obtained by an undercover agent in a conversation with a suspect. The agent was equipped with a concealed radio transmitter which broadcast the conversation to a government recording device. The Court held that neither the Constitution nor the act of Congress was applicable. Justices Black, Frankfurter, Douglas, and Burton dissented. See also *Lopez* v. *United States*, 373 U.S. 427 (1963).

8. PROOF OF THE CHARGE

THOMPSON v. *CITY OF LOUISVILLE*
362 U.S. 199 (1960)

MR. JUSTICE BLACK delivered the opinion of the Court.

Petitioner was found guilty in the Police Court of Louisville, Kentucky, of two offenses—loitering and disorderly conduct. The ultimate question presented to us is whether the charges against petitioner were so totally devoid of evidentiary support as to render his conviction unconstitutional under the Due Process Clause of the Fourteenth Amendment. Decision of this question turns not on the sufficiency of the evidence, but on whether this conviction rests upon any evidence at all.

The facts as shown by the record are short and simple. Petitioner, a long-time resident of the Louisville area, went into the Liberty End Cafe about 6:20 on a Saturday evening, January 24, 1959. In addition to selling food, the cafe was licensed to sell beer to the public and some 12 to 30 patrons were present during the time petitioner was there. When petitioner had been in the cafe about half an hour, two Louisville police officers came in on a "routine check." Upon seeing petitioner "out there on the floor dancing by himself," one of the officers, according to his testimony, went up to the manager who was sitting on a stool nearby and asked him how long petitioner had been in there and if he had bought anything. The officer testified that upon being told by the manager that petitioner had been there "a little over a half-hour and that he had not bought anything," he accosted Thompson and "asked him what was his reason for being in there and he said he was waiting on a bus." The officer then informed petitioner that he was under arrest and took him outside. This was the arrest for loitering. After going outside, the officer testified, petitioner "was very argumentative—he argued with us back and forth and so then we placed a disorderly conduct charge on him." Admittedly the disorderly conduct conviction rests solely on this one sentence description of petitioner's conduct after he left the cafe.

The foregoing evidence includes all that the city offered against him, except a record purportedly showing a total of 54 previous arrests of petitioner. Before putting on his defense, petitioner moved for a dismissal of the charges against him on the ground that a judgment of conviction on this record would deprive him of property and liberty without due process of law under the Fourteenth Amendment in that (1) there was no evidence to support findings of guilt and (2) the two arrests and prosecutions were reprisals against him because petitioner had employed counsel and demanded a judicial hearing to defend himself against prior and allegedly baseless charges by the police. This motion was denied.

Petitioner then put in evidence on his own behalf, none of which in any way strengthened the city's case. He testified that he bought, and one of the cafe employees served him, a dish of macaroni and a glass of beer and that he remained in the cafe waiting for a bus to go home. Further

evidence showed without dispute that at the time of his arrest petitioner gave the officers his home address; that he had money with him, and a bus schedule showing that a bus to his home would stop within half a block of the cafe at about 7:30; that he owned two unimproved lots of land; that in addition to work he had done for others, he had regularly worked one day or more a week for the same family for 30 years; that he paid no rent in the home where he lived and that his meager income was sufficient to meet his needs. The cafe manager testified that petitioner had frequently patronized the cafe, and that he had never told petitioner that he was unwelcome there. The manager further testified that on this very occasion he saw petitioner "standing there in the middle of the floor and patting his foot," and that he did not at any time during petitioner's stay there object to anything he was doing. There is no evidence that anyone else in the cafe objected to petitioner's shuffling his feet in rhythm with the music of the juke box or that his conduct was boisterous or offensive to anyone present. At the close of his evidence, petitioner repeated his motion for dismissal of the charges on the ground that a conviction on the foregoing evidence would deprive him of liberty and property without due process under the Fourteenth Amendment. The court denied the motion, convicted him of both offenses, and fined him $10 on each charge. . . .

The city correctly assumes here that if there is no support for these convictions in the record they are void as denials of due process. The pertinent portion of the city ordinance under which petitioner was convicted of loitering reads as follows: "It shall be unlawful for any person . . . , without visible means of support, or who cannot give a satisfactory account of himself, . . . to sleep, lie, loaf, or trespass in or about any premises, building, or other structure in the City of Louisville, without first having obtained the consent of the owner or controller of said premises, structure, or building; . . ." § 85-12, Ordinance of the City of Louisville. In addition to the fact that petitioner proved he had "visible means of support," the prosecutor at trial said "This is a loitering charge here. There is no charge of no visible means of support." Moreover, there is no suggestion that petitioner was sleeping, lying or trespassing in or about this cafe. Accordingly he could only have been convicted for being unable to give a satisfactory account of himself while loitering in the cafe, without the consent of the manager. Under the words of the ordinance itself, if the evidence fails to prove all three elements of this loitering charge, the conviction is not supported by evidence, in which event it does not comport with due process of law. The record is entirely lacking in evidence to support any of the charges.

Here, petitioner spent about half an hour on a Saturday evening in January in a public cafe which sold food and beer to the public. When asked to account for his presence there, he said he was waiting for a bus. The city concedes that there is no law making it an offense for a person in such a cafe to "dance," "shuffle" or "pat" his feet in time to music. The undisputed testimony of the manager, who did not know whether petitioner had bought macaroni and beer or not but who did see the patting, shuffling or dancing, was that petitioner was welcome there. The manager testified that he did not, at any time during petitioner's stay in the cafe, object to anything petitioner was doing and that he never saw petitioner do anything that would cause any objection. Surely this implied consent, which the city admitted in oral argument satisfies the ordinance. The arresting officer admitted that there was nothing in any way "vulgar" about what he called petitioner's "ordinary dance," whatever relevance, if any, vulgarity might have to a charge of loitering. There simply is no semblance of evidence from which any person could reasonably infer that peti-

tioner could not give a satisfactory account of himself or that he was loitering or loafing there (in the ordinary sense of the words) without "the consent of the owner or controller" of the cafe.

Petitioner's conviction for disorderly conduct was under § 85-8 of the city ordinance which, without definition, provides that "whoever shall be found guilty of disorderly conduct in the City of Louisville shall be fined . . ." etc. The only evidence of "disorderly conduct" was the single statement of the policeman that after petitioner was arrested and taken out of the cafe he was very argumentative. There is no testimony that petitioner raised his voice, used offensive language, resisted the officers or engaged in any conduct of any kind likely in any way to adversely affect the good order and tranquility of the City of Louisville. The only information the record contains on what the petitioner was "argumentative" about is his statement that he asked the officers "what they arrested me for." We assume, for we are justified in assuming, that merely "arguing" with a policeman is not, because it could not be, "disorderly conduct" as a matter of the substantive law of Kentucky. . . . Moreover, Kentucky law itself seems to provide that if a man wrongfully arrested fails to object to the arresting officer, he waives any right to complain later that the arrest was unlawful. *Nickell v. Commonwealth*, 285 S.W.2d 495, 496.

Thus we find no evidence whatever in the record to support these convictions. Just as "Conviction upon a charge not made would be sheer denial of due process," so is it a violation of due process to convict and punish a man without evidence of his guilt.

The judgments are reversed and the cause is remanded to the Police Court of the City of Louisville for proceedings not inconsistent with this opinion.

Reversed and remanded.

NOTE: *Garner* v. *Louisiana*, 368 U.S. 157 (1962), reversed the convictions of Negroes for disturbing the peace by sitting at lunch counters reserved for whites.

In this first sit-in case to reach the Supreme Court the decision turned, as in *Thompson,* upon the absence of evidence to support the charge.

9. DOUBLE JEOPARDY

GREEN v. *UNITED STATES*

355 U.S. 184 (1957)

Opinion of the Court by Mr. Justice Black. . . .

This case presents a serious question concerning the meaning and application of that provision of the Fifth Amendment to the Constitution which declares that no person shall ". . . be subject for the same offense to be twice put in jeopardy of life or limb. . . ."

The petitioner, Everett Green, was indicted by a District of Columbia grand jury in two counts. The first charged that he had committed arson by maliciously setting fire to a house. The second accused him of causing the death of a woman by this alleged arson which if true amounted to murder in the first degree punishable by death. Green entered a plea of not guilty to both counts and the case was tried by a jury. After each side had presented its evidence the trial judge instructed the jury that it could find Green guilty of arson under the first count and of either (1) first degree murder or (2) second degree murder under the second count. The trial judge treated second degree murder, which is defined by the District Code as the killing of another with malice aforethought and is punishable by imprisonment for a term of years or for life, as an offense included within the language charging first degree murder in the second count of the indictment.

The jury found Green guilty of arson and of second degree murder but did not find him guilty on the charge of murder in the first degree. Its verdict was silent on that charge. The trial judge accepted the verdict, entered the proper judgments and dismissed the jury. Green was sentenced to one to three years' imprisonment for arson and five to twenty years' imprisonment for murder in the second degree. He appealed the conviction of second degree murder. The Court of Appeals reversed that conviction because it was not supported by evidence and remanded the case for a new trial. 95 U.S. App. D.C. 45, 218 F.2d 856.

On remand Green was tried again for first degree murder under the original indictment. At the outset of this second trial he raised the defense of former jeopardy but the court overruled his plea. This time a new jury found him guilty of first degree murder and he was given the mandatory death sentence. Again he appealed. Sitting *en banc,* the Court of Appeals rejected his defense of former jeopardy, relying on *Trono* v. *United States,* 199 U.S. 521, and affirmed the conviction. 98 U.S. App. D.C. 413, 236 F.2d 708. One judge concurred in the result, and three judges dissented expressing the view that Green had twice been placed in jeopardy in violation of the Constitution. We granted certiorari, 352 U.S. 915. Although Green raises a number of other contentions here we find it necessary to consider only his claim of former jeopardy.

The constitutional prohibition against "double jeopardy" was designed to protect an individual from being subjected to the hazards of trial and possible conviction more than once for an alleged offense. In his *Commentaries,* which greatly influenced the generation that adopted the Constitution, Blackstone recorded:

". . . the plea of *auterfoits acquit,* or a former acquittal, is grounded on this universal maxim of the common law of England, that no man is to be brought into jeopardy of his life more than once for the same offence."

Substantially the same view was taken by this Court in *Ex parte Lange*, 18 Wall. 163, at page 169:

"The common law not only prohibited a second punishment for the same offence, but it went further and forbid a second trial for the same offence, whether the accused had suffered punishment or not, and whether in the former trial he had been acquitted or convicted."

The underlying idea, one that is deeply ingrained in at least the Anglo-American system of jurisprudence, is that the State with all its resources and power should not be allowed to make repeated attempts to convict an individual for an alleged offense, thereby subjecting him to embarrassment, expense and ordeal and compelling him to live in a continuing state of anxiety and insecurity, as well as enhancing the possibility that even though innocent he may be found guilty.

In accordance with this philosophy it has long been settled under the Fifth Amendment that a verdict of acquittal is final, ending a defendant's jeopardy, and even when "not followed by any judgment, is a bar to a subsequent prosecution for the same offence." *United States* v. *Ball*, 163 U.S. 662, 671. Thus it is one of the elemental principles of our criminal law that the Government cannot secure a new trial by means of an appeal even though an acquittal may appear to be erroneous. . . .

Moreover it is not even essential that a verdict of guilt or innocence be returned for a defendant to have once been placed in jeopardy so as to bar a second trial on the same charge. This Court, as well as most others, has taken the position that a defendant is placed in jeopardy once he is put to trial before a jury so that if the jury is discharged without his consent he cannot be tried again. *Wade* v. *Hunter*, 336 U.S. 684; 93 L. Ed. 974; *Kepner* v. *United States*, 195 U.S. 100, 128. In general see American Law Institute, *Administration of the Criminal Law: Double Jeopardy* 61–72

(1935). This prevents a prosecutor or judge from subjecting a defendant to a second prosecution by discontinuing the trial when it appears that the jury might not convict. At the same time jeopardy is not regarded as having come to an end so as to bar a second trial in those cases where "unforeseeable circumstances . . . arise during [the first] trial making its completion impossible, such as the failure of a jury to agree on a verdict." *Wade* v. *Hunter*, 336 U.S. 684, 689.

At common law a convicted person could not obtain a new trial by appeal except in certain narrow instances. As this harsh rule was discarded courts and legislatures provided that if a defendant obtained the reversal of a conviction by his own appeal he could be tried again for the same offense. Most courts regarded the new trial as a second jeopardy but justified this on the ground that the appellant had "waived" his plea of former jeopardy by asking that the conviction be set aside. Other courts viewed the second trial as continuing the same jeopardy which had attached at the first trial by reasoning that jeopardy did not come to an end until the accused was acquitted or his conviction became final. But whatever the rationalization, this Court has also held that a defendant can be tried a second time for an offense when his prior conviction for the same offense had been set aside on appeal. *United States* v. *Ball*, 163 U.S. 662.

In this case, however, we have a much different question. At Green's first trial the jury was authorized to find him guilty of either first degree murder (killing while perpetrating a felony) or, alternatively, of second degree murder (killing with malice aforethought). The jury found him guilty of second degree murder, but on his appeal that conviction was reversed and the case remanded for a new trial. At this new trial Green was tried again, not for second degree murder, but for first degree murder, even though the original jury had refused to find him guilty on that charge and it was in no way involved in his appeal. For the reasons stated hereafter, we conclude that this second trial for first degree murder placed Green in jeopardy twice for the same offense in violation of the Constitution.

. . . [T]he Government contends that Green "waived" his constitutional defense of former jeopardy to a second prosecution on the first degree murder charge by making a *successful* appeal of his improper conviction of second degree murder. We cannot accept this paradoxical contention. "Waiver" is a vague term used for a great variety of purposes, good and bad, in the law. In any normal sense, however, it connotes some kind of voluntary knowing relinquishment of a right. Cf. *Johnson* v. *Zerbst,* 304 U.S. 458. When a man has been convicted of second degree murder and given a long term of imprisonment it is wholly fictional to say that he "chooses" to forego his constitutional defense of former jeopardy on a charge of murder in the first degree in order to secure a reversal of an erroneous conviction of the lesser offense. In short, he has no meaningful choice. And as Mr. Justice Holmes observed, with regard to this same matter in *Kepner* v. *United States,* 195 U.S. 100, at page 135: "Usually no such waiver is expressed or thought of. Moreover, it cannot be imagined that the law would deny to a prisoner the correction of a fatal error unless he should waive other rights so important as to be saved by an express clause in the Constitution of the United States."

It is true that in Kepner, a case arising in the Philippine Islands under a statutory prohibition against double jeopardy, Mr. Justice Holmes dissented from the Court's holding that the Government could not appeal an acquittal in a criminal prosecution. He argued that there was only one continuing jeopardy until the "case" had finally been settled, appeal and all, without regard to how many times the defendant was tried, but that view was rejected by the Court. The position taken by the majority in Kepner is completely in accord with the deeply entrenched principle of our criminal law that once a person has been acquitted of an offense he cannot be

prosecuted again on the same charge. This Court has uniformly adhered to that basic premise. . . .

Reversed.

Mr. Justice Frankfurter, whom Mr. Justice Burton, Mr. Justice Clark and Mr. Justice Harlan join, dissenting. . . .

Even, if the question were here for the first time, we would not be justified in erecting the holding of the present case as a constitutional rule. Yet the opinion of the Court treats the question, not as one within our supervisory jurisdiction over federal criminal procedure, but as a question answered by the Fifth Amendment itself, and which therefore even Congress cannot undertake to affect.

Such an approach misconceives the purposes of the double jeopardy provision, and without warrant from the Constitution makes an absolute of the interests of the accused in disregard of the interests of society. In *Palko* v. *State of Connecticut,* 302 U.S. 319, we held that a State could permit the prosecution to appeal a conviction of second degree murder and on retrial secure a conviction of first degree murder without violating any "fundamental principles of liberty and justice." Since the State's interest in obtaining a trial "free from the corrosion of substantial legal error" was sufficient to sustain the conviction of the greater offense after an appeal by the State, it would of course sustain such a conviction if the defendant had himself appealed. Although this case defined conduct permissible under the Due Process Clause of the Fourteenth Amendment, it cannot wisely be ignored in tracing the constitutional limits imposed on the Federal Government. Nor should we ignore the fact that a substantial body of opinion in the States permits what today the Court condemns as violative of a "vital safeguard in our society [19 of the 36 which have considered the problem]."

Undeniably the framers of the Bill of Rights were concerned to protect defendants from oppression, and from efforts to secure, through the callousness of repeated prosecutions, convictions for whose justice no man could vouch. On the other hand, they were also aware of the countervailing interest in the vindication of criminal justice, which sets outer limits to the protections for those accused of crimes. . . . In

the circumstances of the present case, . . . the reversal of petitioner's conviction was a sufficient reason to justify a complete new trial in order that both parties might have one free from errors claimed to be prejudicial. . . .

CIUCCI v. ILLINOIS
356 U.S. 571 (1958)

PER CURIAM.

Petitioner was charged in four separate indictments with murdering his wife and three children, all of whom, with bullet wounds in their heads, were found dead in a burning building during the early hours of December 5, 1953. In three successive trials, petitioner was found guilty of the first degree murder of his wife and two of his children. At each of the trials the prosecution introduced into evidence details of all four deaths. Under Illinois law the jury is charged with the responsibility of fixing the penalty for first degree murder from 14 years' imprisonment to death. Ill. Rev. Stat. 1957, c. 38, § 360. At the first two trials, involving the death of the wife and one of the children, the jury fixed the penalty at 20 and 45 years' imprisonment respectively. At the third trial, involving the death of a second child, the penalty was fixed at death. On appeal the Supreme Court of Illinois affirmed the conviction, 8 Ill. 2d 619, and we granted certiorari to consider petitioner's claim that this third trial violated the due process clause of the Fourteenth Amendment to the Constitution of the United States. 353 U.S. 982.

It is conceded that under Illinois law each of the murders, although apparently taking place at the same time, constituted a separate crime and it is undisputed that evidence of the entire occurrence was relevant in each of the three prosecutions. In his brief in this Court petitioner has appended a number of articles which had ap-

peared in Chicago newspapers after the first and second trials attributing to the prosecution certain statements expressing extreme dissatisfaction with the prison sentences fixed by the jury and announcing a determined purpose to prosecute petitioner until a death sentence was obtained. Neither these articles nor their subject matter is included in the record certified to this Court from the Supreme Court of Illinois.

The five members of the Court who join in this opinion are in agreement that upon the record as it stands no violation of due process has been shown. The state was constitutionally entitled to prosecute these individual offenses singly at separate trials, and to utilize therein all relevant evidence, in the absence of proof establishing that such a course of action entailed fundamental unfairness. *Hoag* v. *New Jersey,* 356 U.S. ——; see *Palko* v. *Connecticut,* 302 U.S. 319, 328. . . .

MR. JUSTICE DOUGLAS, with whom the CHIEF JUSTICE and MR. JUSTICE BRENNAN concur, dissenting.

This case presents an instance of the prosecution being allowed to harass the accused with repeated trials and convictions on the same evidence, until it achieves its desired result of a capital verdict.

Petitioner's wife and three children were found dead in a burning building. It was later established that death was due both to the fire and to bullet wounds each had received in the head. Petitioner was first tried on an indictment charging that he had murdered his wife. At that trial the evidence was not limited to the wife's death. The deaths of the three children were also introduced, and testimony as to the cause of death of all of the victims was received. This trial was in effect a trial for the murder of all four victims for the gruesome details of each of the four deaths were introduced into evidence. Petitioner was found guilty. Under Illinois law the jury determines the sentence in a murder case between a minimum of 14 years' imprisonment and a maximum of death. Ill. Rev. Stat., 1957, c. 38, § 360. At that first trial the jury fixed the penalty at 20 years' imprisonment.

The prosecutor demanded another trial. Accordingly petitioner was next tried on a charge of murdering one of his daughters.

At the second trial the same evidence was introduced as in the first trial. Evidence concerning the four deaths once more was used. Once more all the gruesome details of the four crimes were presented to the jury. Once more the accused was tried in form for one murder, in substance for four. This time a different jury again found petitioner guilty and sentenced him to 45 years' imprisonment.

The prosecutor was still not satisfied with the result. And so a third trial was had, the one involved here.

In this third trial, petitioner was charged with murdering his son. This time petitioner objected before trial that he was being subjected to double jeopardy. He also moved to exclude testimony concerning the other deaths and after verdict he protested that he had been denied a fair trial guaranteed by the due process clause of the Fourteenth Amendment. The trial court overruled those objections. At the trial complete evidence of all of the deaths and their causes was again introduced. Once more the gruesome details of four murders were presented to a jury—the gathering of the family in their home, the fire at 2 a.m., the .22 caliber bullets in the bodies of the four victims, the borrowing by the accused of a .22 rifle, the arrival of the firemen, the autopsies at the morgue. This time a third jury sentenced petitioner to death.

In my view the due process clause of the Fourteenth Amendment prevents this effort by a state to obtain the death penalty. No constitutional problem would have arisen if petitioner had been prosecuted in one trial for as many murders as there were victims. But by using the same evidence in multiple trials the state continued its relentless prosecutions until it got the result it wanted. It in effect tried the accused for four murders three consecutive times, massing in each trial the horrible details of each of the four deaths. This is an unseemly and oppressive use of a criminal trial that violates the concept of due process contained in the Fourteenth Amendment, whatever its ultimate scope is taken to be.

Mr. Justice Black concurs in this dissent on the ground that the Fourteenth Amendment bars a state from placing a defendant twice in jeopardy for the same offense.

MEMORANDUM TO THE UNITED STATES ATTORNEYS,
FROM ATTORNEY GENERAL WILLIAM P. ROGERS, APRIL 6, 1959

Bartkus v. *Illinois,* 359 U.S. 121 (1959), upheld a federal conviction for robbery of a federal savings and loan association bank in Illinois, after the defendant had been acquitted in an Illinois court for the same robbery. *Abbate* v. *United States,* 359 U.S. 187 (1959), upheld a federal conviction for conspiracy to damage a federally owned communications system, after the defendant had been convicted in a state court for a conspiracy based on the same factual situation.

In two decisions on March 30, 1959, the Supreme Court of the United States reaffirmed the existence of a power to prosecute a defendant under both federal and state law for the same act or acts. That power, which the Court held is inherent in our federal system, has been used sparingly by the Department of Justice in the past. The purpose of this memorandum is to insure that in the future we continue that policy. After a state prosecution there should be no federal trial for the same act or acts unless the reasons are compelling.

In *Abbate* v. *United States* and *Bartkus* v. *Illinois* the Supreme Court held that there is no violation of the double jeopardy prohibition or of the due process clause of our federal Constitution where there are prosecutions of the defendant, both in the state and in the federal court, based upon the same act or acts.

This ruling reaffirmed the holding in *United States* v. *Lanza,* 260 U.S. 377, decided by the Supreme Court in 1922. In that case Chief Justice Taft, speaking for a unanimous Court, said:

"We have here two sovereignties, deriving power from different sources, capable of dealing with the same subject matter within the same territory. . . . Each government in determining what shall be an offense against its peace and dignity is exercising its own sovereignty, not that of the other.

"It follows that an act denounced as a crime by both national and state sovereignties is an offense against the peace and dignity of both and may be punished by each."

But the mere existence of a power, of course, does not mean that it should necessarily be exercised. In the *Bartkus* case the Court said:

"The men who wrote the Constitution as well as the citizens of the member states of the Confederation were fearful of the power of centralized government and sought to limit its power. Mr. Justice Brandeis has written that separation of power was adopted in the Constitution 'not to promote efficiency but to preclude the exercise of arbitrary power.' Time has not lessened the concern of the Founders in devising a federal system which would likewise be a safeguard against arbitrary government. The greatest self-restraint is necessary *when that federal system yields results with which a court is in little sympathy.*" (Emphasis added.)

The Court held then that precedent, experience and reason supported the conclusion of separate federal and state offenses.

It is our duty to observe not only the rulings of the Court but the spirit of the rulings as well. In effect, the Court said that although the rule of the *Lanza* case is sound law, enforcement officers should use care in applying it.

Applied indiscriminately and with bad judgment it, like most rules of law, could cause considerable hardship. Applied wisely it is a rule that is in the public interest. Consequently—as the Court clearly indicated—those of us charged with law enforcement responsibilities have a particular duty to act wisely and with self-restraint in this area.

Cooperation between federal and state prosecutive officers is essential if the gears of the federal and state systems are to mesh properly. We should continue to make every effort to cooperate with state and local authorities to the end that the trial occur in the jurisdiction, whether it be state or federal, where the public interest is best served. If this be determined accurately, and is followed by efficient and intelligent cooperation of state and federal law enforcement authorities, then consideration of a second prosecution very seldom should arise.

In such event I doubt that it is wise or practical to attempt to formulate detailed rules to deal with the complex situation which might develop, particularly because a series of related acts are often involved. However, no federal case should be tried when there has already been a state prosecution for substantially the same act or acts without the United States Attorney first submitting a recommendation to the appropriate Assistant Attorney General in the Department. No such recommendation should be approved by the Assistant Attorney General in charge of the Division without having it first brought to my attention.

10. REVIEW OF CONVICTIONS

GRIFFIN v. ILLINOIS

351 U.S. 12 (1956)

MR. JUSTICE BLACK announced the judgment of the Court and an opinion in which the CHIEF JUSTICE, MR. JUSTICE DOUGLAS, and MR. JUSTICE CLARK joined.

Illinois law provides that "Writs of error in all criminal cases are writs of right and shall be issued of course." The question presented here is whether Illinois may, consistent with the due process and equal protection clauses of the Fourteenth Amendment, administer this statute so as to deny adequate appellate review to the poor while granting such review to all others.

The petitioners Griffin and Crenshaw were tried together and convicted of armed robbery in the Criminal Court of Cook County, Illinois. Immediately after their conviction they filed a motion in the trial court asking that a certified copy of the entire record, including a stenographic transcript of the proceedings, be furnished them without cost. They alleged they were "poor persons with no means of paying the necessary fees to acquire the Transcript and Court Records needed to prosecute an appeal. . . ." These allegations were not denied. Under Illinois law in order to get full direct appellate review of alleged errors by a writ of error it is necessary for the defendant to furnish the appellate court with a bill of exceptions or report of proceedings at the trial certified by the trial judge. As Illinois concedes, it is sometimes impossible to prepare such bills of exceptions or reports without a stenographic transcript of the trial proceedings. Indigent defendants sentenced to death are provided with a free transcript at the expense of the

county where convicted. In all other criminal cases defendants needing a transcript, whether indigent or not, must themselves buy it. The petitioners contended in their motion before the trial court that failure to provide them with the needed transcript would violate the due process and equal protection clauses of the Fourteenth Amendment. The trial court denied the motion without a hearing.

Griffin and Crenshaw then filed a petition under the Illinois Post-Conviction Hearing Act. Only questions arising under the Illinois or Federal Constitution may be raised in proceedings under this Act. A companion state act provides that indigent petitioners under the Post-Conviction Act may, under some circumstances, obtain a free transcript. The effect is that indigents may obtain a free transcript to obtain appellate review of constitutional questions but not of other alleged trial errors such as admissibility and sufficiency of evidence. In their Post-Conviction proceeding petitioners alleged that there were manifest non-constitutional errors in the trial which entitled them to have their convictions set aside on appeal and that the only impediment to full appellate review was their lack of funds to buy a transcript. These allegations have not been denied. Petitioners repeated their charge that refusal to afford full appellate review solely because of poverty was a denial of due process and equal protection. This petition like the first was dismissed without hearing any evidence. The Illinois Supreme Court affirmed the dismissal solely on the ground that the charges raised no substantial state or federal constitutional questions—the only kind of questions which may be raised in Post-Conviction proceedings. We granted certiorari. 349 U.S. 937.

Counsel for Illinois concedes that these petitioners needed a transcript in order to get adequate appellate review of their alleged trial errors. There is no contention that petitioners were dilatory in their efforts to get appellate review, or that the Illinois Supreme Court denied review on the ground that the allegations of trial error were insufficient. We must therefore assume for purposes of this decision that errors were committed in the trial which would merit reversal, but that the petitioners could not get appellate review of those errors solely because they were too poor to buy a stenographic transcript. Counsel for Illinois denies that this violates either the due process or the equal protection clause, but states that if it does, the Illinois Post-Conviction statute entitles petitioners to a free transcript. The sole question for us to decide, therefore, is whether due process or equal protection has been violated.

Providing equal justice for poor and rich, weak and powerful alike is an age-old problem. People have never ceased to hope and strive to move closer to that goal. This hope, at least in part, brought about in 1215 the royal concessions of Magna Charta: "To no one will we sell, to no one will we refuse, or delay, right or justice. . . . No free man shall be taken or imprisoned, or disseised, or outlawed, or exiled, or anywise destroyed; nor shall we go upon him nor send upon him, but by the lawful judgment of his peers or by the law of the land." These pledges were unquestionably steps toward a fairer and more nearly equal application of criminal justice. In this tradition, our own constitutional guaranties of due process and equal protection both call for procedures in criminal trials which allow no invidious discriminations between persons and different groups of persons. Both equal protection and due process emphasize the central aim of our entire judicial system—all people charged with crime must, so far as the law is concerned, "stand on an equality before the bar of justice in every American court." *Chambers* v. *Florida*, 309 U.S. 227, 241. See also *Yick Wo* v. *Hopkins*, 118 U.S. 356, 369.

Surely no one would contend that either a State or the Federal Government could constitutionally provide that defendants unable to pay court costs in advance should be denied the right to plead not guilty or to defend themselves in court. Such a law would make the constitutional promise of a fair trial a worthless thing. Notice, the right to be heard, and the right to counsel would under such circumstances be meaningless promises to the poor. In criminal trials a State can no more discriminate on account of poverty than on account of religion, race, or color. Plainly the ability to pay costs in advance bears no rational relationship to a defendant's guilt or innocence and could not be used as an excuse to deprive a defendant of a fair trial. Indeed, a provision in the Constitution of Illinois of 1818 provided that every person in Illinois "ought to obtain right and justice freely, and without being obliged to purchase it, completely and without denial, promptly and without delay, conformably to the laws."

There is no meaningful distinction between a rule which would deny the poor the right to defend themselves in a trial court and one which effectively denies the poor an adequate appellate review accorded to all who have money enough to pay the costs in advance. It is true that a State is not required by the Federal Constitution to provide appellate courts or a right to appellate review at all. See, e.g., *McKane* v. *Durston*, 153 U.S. 684, 687–688. But that is not to say that a State that does grant appellate review can do so in a way that discriminates against some convicted defendants on account of their poverty. Appellate review has now become an integral part of the Illinois trial system for finally adjudicating the guilt or innocence of a defendant. Consequently at all stages of the proceedings the due process and equal protection clauses protect persons like petitioners from invidious discriminations. See *Cole* v. *Arkansas*, 333 U.S. 196, 201; *Dowd* v. *United States ex rel Cook*, 340 U.S. 206, 208; *Cochran* v. *Kansas*, 316 U.S. 255, 257; *Frank* v. *Mangum*, 237 U.S. 309, 327.

All of the States now provide some method of appeal from criminal convictions, recognizing the importance of appellate review to a correct adjudication of guilt or innocence. Statistics show that a substantial proportion of criminal convictions are reversed by state appellate courts. Thus to deny adequate review to the poor means that many of them may lose their life, liberty or property because of unjust convictions which appellate courts would set aside. Many States have recognized this and provided aid for convicted defendants who have a right to appeal and need a transcript but are unable to pay for it. A few have not. Such a denial is a misfit in a country dedicated to affording equal justice to all and special privileges to none in the administration of its criminal law. There can be no equal justice where the kind of trial a man gets depends on the amount of money he has. Destitute defendants must be afforded as adequate appellate review as defendants who have money enough to buy transcripts.

The Illinois Supreme Court denied these petitioners relief under the Post-Conviction Act because of its holding that no constitutional rights were violated. In view of our holding to the contrary the State Supreme Court may decide that petitioners are now entitled to a transcript, as the State's brief suggests. See *Ill. Rev. Stat.*, 1955, c. 37, § 163f. Cf. *Dowd* v. *United States ex rel. Cook*, 340 U.S. at 209–210. We do not hold, however, that Illinois must purchase a stenographer's transcript in every case where a defendant cannot buy it. The Supreme Court may find other means of affording adequate and effective appellate review to indigent defendants. For example, it may be that bystanders' bills of exceptions or other methods of reporting trial proceedings could be used in some cases. The Illinois Supreme Court appears to have broad power to promulgate rules of pro-

cedure and appellate practice. We are confident that the State will provide corrective rules to meet the problem which this case lays bare.

The judgment of the Supreme Court of Illinois is vacated and the cause is remanded to that court for further action not inconsistent with the foregoing paragraph. MR. JUSTICE FRANKFURTER joins in this disposition of the case.

Vacated and remanded.

MR. JUSTICE FRANKFURTER, concurring in this judgment: . . .

We should not indulge in the fiction that the law now announced has always been the law and, therefore, that those who did not avail themselves of it waived their rights. It is much more conducive to law's self-respect to recognize candidly the considerations that give prospective content to a new pronouncement of law. That this is consonant with the spirit of our law and justified by those considerations of reason which should dominate the law, has been luminously expounded by Mr. Justice Cardozo, shortly before he came here and in an opinion which he wrote for the Court. See Address of Chief Judge Cardozo, 55 *Report of New York State Bar Ass'n*, 263, 294 et seq., and *Great Northern R. Co.* v. *Sunburst Oil & Refining Co.*, 287 U.S. 358, 363–366. Such a molding of law, by way of adjudication, is peculiarly applicable to the problem at hand. The rule of law announced this day should be delimited as indicated.

MR. JUSTICE BURTON and MR. JUSTICE MINTON, whom MR. JUSTICE REED and MR. JUSTICE HARLAN join, dissenting:

While we do not disagree with the desirability of the policy of supplying an indigent defendant with a free transcript of testimony in a case like this, we do not agree that the Constitution of the United States compels each State to do so with the consequence that, regardless of the State's legislation and practice to the contrary, this Court must hold invalid state appellate proceedings wherever a required transcript has not been provided without cost to an indigent litigant who has requested that it be so provided. It is one thing for Congress and this Court to prescribe such procedure for the federal courts. It is quite another for this Court to hold that the Constitution of the United States has prescribed it for all state courts.

In the administration of local law the Constitution has been interpreted as permitting the several States generally to follow their own familiar procedure and practice. In so doing this Court has recognized the widely differing but locally approved procedures of the several States. Whether approving of the particular procedures or not, this Court has treated them largely as matters reserved to the States and within the broad range of permissible "due process" in a constitutional sense.

Illinois, as the majority admit, could thus deny an appeal altogether in a criminal case without denying due process of law. *McKane* v. *Durston*, 153 U.S. 684. To allow an appeal at all, but with some difference among convicted persons as to the terms upon which an appeal is exercised, does not deny due process. It may present a question of equal protection. The petitioners urge that point here.

Whether the Illinois statute denies equal protection depends upon whether, first, it is an arbitrary and unreasonable distinction for the legislature to make, between those convicted of a capital offense and those convicted of a lesser offense, as to their right to a free transcript. It seems to us the whole practice of criminal law teaches that there are valid distinctions between the ways in which criminal cases may be looked upon and treated without violating the Constitution. Very often we have cases where the convicted seek only to avoid the death penalty. As all practicing lawyers know, who have defended persons charged with capital offenses, often the only goal possible is to avoid the death penalty. There is something pretty final about a death sentence.

If the actual practice of law recognizes this distinction between capital and noncapital cases, we see no reason why the legislature of a State may not extend the full benefit of appeal to those convicted of capital offenses and deny it to those convicted of lesser offenses. It is the universal experience in the administration of criminal justice that those charged with capital offenses are granted special considerations. Examples of such will readily occur. All States allow a larger number of peremptory challenges of juror in capital cases than in other cases. Most States permit changes of venue in capital cases on different terms than in other criminal cases. Some States require a verdict of 12 jurors for conviction in a capital case but allow less than 12 jurors to convict in noncapital cases. On the other side of the coin, most States provide no statute of limitations in capital cases. We think the distinction here made by the Illinois statute between capital cases and noncapital cases is a reasonable and valid one.

Secondly, certainly Illinois does not deny equal protection to convicted defendants when the terms of appeal are open to all, although some may not be able to avail themselves of the full appeal because of their poverty. Illinois is not bound to make the defendants economically equal before its bar of justice. For a State to do so may be a desirable social policy, but what may be a good legislative policy for a State is not necessarily required by the Constitution of the United States. Persons charged with crimes stand before the law with varying degrees of economic and social advantage. Some can afford better lawyers and better investigations of their cases. Some can afford bail, some cannot. Why fix bail at any reasonable sum if a poor man can't make it?

The Constitution requires the equal protection of the law, but it does not require the States to provide equal financial means for all defendants to avail themselves of such laws. . . .

MR. JUSTICE HARLAN dissented in a separate opinion.

MOONEY v. HOLOHAN

294 U.S. 103 (1935)

Motion for leave to file petition for writ of *habeas corpus.*

PER CURIAM. Thomas J. Mooney asks leave to file petition for an original writ of *habeas corpus.* He states that he is unlawfully restrained of his liberty by the State of California under a commitment pursuant to a conviction, in February, 1917, of murder in the first degree and sentence of death subsequently commuted to life imprisonment. He submits the record of proceedings set forth in his petition for a writ of *habeas corpus* presented to the District Court of the United States for the Northern District of California and dismissed upon the ground that the petitioner had not exhausted his legal remedies in the state court. Applications to the Judges of the Circuit Court of Appeals for the Ninth Circuit for allowance of an appeal to that Court from the judgment of dismissal have severally been denied.

Petitioner charges that the State holds him in confinement without due process of law in violation of the Fourteenth Amendment of the Constitution of the United States. The grounds of his charge are, in substance, that the sole basis of his conviction was perjured testimony, which was knowingly used by the prosecuting authorities in order to obtain that conviction, and also that these authorities deliberately suppressed evidence which would have impeached and refuted the testimony thus given against him. He alleges that he could not by reasonable diligence have discovered prior to the denial of his motion for a new trial, and his appeal to the Supreme Court of the State, the evidence which was subsequently developed and which proved the testimony against him to have been perjured. Petitioner urges that the "knowing use" by the State of perjured testimony to

obtain the conviction and the deliberate suppression of evidence to impeach that testimony constituted a denial of due process of law. Petitioner further contends that the State deprives him of his liberty without due process of law by its failure, in the circumstances set forth, to provide any corrective judicial process by which a conviction so obtained may be set aside. . . .

The return does not put in issue any of the facts alleged in the petition. The return is in the nature of a demurrer. It submits that the petitioner "has failed to raise a Federal question and that, consequently, leave to file the petition should be denied." Reviewing decisions relating to due process, the Attorney General insists that the petitioner's argument is vitiated by the fallacy "that the acts or omissions of a prosecuting attorney can ever, *in and by themselves,* amount either to due process of law or to a denial of due process of law." The Attorney General states that if the acts or omissions of a prosecuting attorney "have the effect of withholding from a defendant the notice which must be accorded him under the due process clause, or if they have the effect of preventing a defendant from presenting such evidence as he possesses in defense of the accusation against him, then such acts or omissions of the prosecuting attorney may be regarded as *resulting* in a denial of due process of law." And, "conversely," the Attorney General contends that "it is only where an act or omission operates so as to deprive a defendant of notice or so as to deprive him of an opportunity to present such evidence as he has, that it can be said that due process of law has been denied."

Without attempting at this time to deal with the question at length, we deem it sufficient for the present purpose to say that we are unable to approve this narrow view of the requirement of due process. . . .

Reasoning from the premise that the petitioner has failed to show a denial of due process in the circumstances set forth in his petition, the Attorney General urges that the State was not required to afford any corrective judicial process to remedy the alleged wrong. The argument falls with the premise. *Frank* v. *Mangum*, 237 U.S. 309, 335; *Moore* v. *Dempsey*, 261 U.S. 86, 90, 91.

We are not satisfied, however, that the State of California has failed to provide such corrective judicial process. The prerogative writ of *habeas corpus* is available in that State. Constitution of California, Art. I, § 5; Art. VI, § 4. No decision of the Supreme Court of California has been brought to our attention holding that the state court is without power to issue this historic remedial process when it appears that one is deprived of his liberty without due process of law in violation of the Constitution of the United States. Upon the state courts, equally with the courts of the Union, rests the obligation to guard and enforce every right secured by that Constitution. *Robb* v. *Connolly*, 111 U.S. 624, 637. In view of the dominant requirement of the Fourteenth Amendment, we are not at liberty to assume that the State has denied to its court jurisdiction to redress the prohibited wrong upon a proper showing and in an appropriate proceeding for that purpose.

The decisions of the Supreme Court of California in relation to petitioner's conviction have dealt with the questions presented to that Court within the limitations of particular appellate procedure. When there was submitted to that Court the consent of the Attorney General to the reversal of the judgment against petitioner and to the granting of a new trial, the Court pointed out that no motion had been made by the defendant and that his appeal was awaiting hearing. *People* v. *Mooney*, 175 Cal. 666, 166 Pac. 999. When, again in advance of the hearing of his appeal, the defendant made his motion solely upon the ground of the Attorney General's consent, the Court held that its jurisdiction on appeal was limited to a determination whether there had been any error of law in the proceedings of the trial court and that the Court was confined to the record sent to it by the court below. *People* v. *Mooney*, 176 Cal. 105, 167 Pac. 696. On the appeal, the Court thus dealing with the record before it, found that the verdict was supported by the testimony presented and that no ground appeared for reversal. *People* v. *Mooney*, 177 Cal. 642, 171 P. 690. When, later, the defendant moved to set aside the judgment, and sought a certificate of probable cause on his appeal from an order denying his motion, the Court held that the general averments against the fairness of the trial were insufficient, but the Court did not place its denial of the application entirely upon that ground. The Court concluded that the proceeding by way of motion to set aside the judgment after it had become final and a motion for a new trial had been denied, and the time therefor had expired, was "in the nature of an application for a writ of *coram nobis,* at common law." The Court thought that such a writ did not lie to correct any error in the judgment of the Court nor to contradict or put in issue any fact directly passed upon and affirmed by the judgment itself. The Court, adopting the opinion of the court below, concluded that the judgment could not be set aside because it was predicated upon perjured testimony or because material evidence was concealed or suppressed; that the fraud in such a case was not such fraud as was "extrinsic to the record" and that it was only in cases of extrinsic fraud that the relief sought could be had. It was apparently in relation to such an application that the Court said that the injured party was "without remedy." *People* v. *Mooney*, 178 Cal. 525, 174 Pac. 325. And it was with respect to that proceeding, that the writ of certiorari was denied by this Court. *Mooney* v. *California*, 248 U.S. 579. The subsequent communications from the Justices of the Supreme Court in connection with applications for executive clemency were of an advisory character and were not judicial judgments under the requirements of the Constitution of the United States.

We do not find that petitioner has applied to the state court for a writ of *habeas corpus* upon the grounds stated in his petition here. That corrective judicial process has not been invoked and it is not shown to be unavailable. Despite the many proceedings taken on behalf of the petitioner, an application for the prerogative writ now asserted to be peculiarly suited to the circumstances disclosed by his petition has not been made to the state court. Orderly

procedure, governed by principles we have repeatedly announced, requires that before this Court is asked to issue a writ of *habeas corpus,* in the case of a person held under a state commitment, recourse should be had to whatever judicial remedy afforded by the State may still remain open. *Davis* v. *Burke,* 179 U.S. 399, 402; *Urquhart* v. *Brown,* 205 U.S. 179, 181, 182; *U.S. ex rel. Kennedy* v. *Tyler,* 269 U.S. 13, 17. See, also, *Bryant* v. *Zimmerman,* 278 U.S. 63, 70.

Accordingly, leave to file the petition is denied, but without prejudice.

Leave denied.

NOTE: If in the *Mooney* situation the state considers the petitioner's claim on the merits and denies relief, he may seek direct Supreme Court review of the decision of the highest state court. *Carnley* v. *Cochran,* 369 U.S. 506 (1962). But what if the Supreme Court denies certiorari, for example? May a person in this situation raise his problem in a petition for habeas corpus in a federal district court? In effect he will be asking the lowest federal court to "review" the decision of the highest state court—a position not calculated to please state judges. Nevertheless the answer is plainly yes. *Brown* v. *Allen,* 344 U.S. 443 (1953); *Fay* v. *Noia,* 372 U.S. 391 (1963). See also *Townsend* v. *Sain,* 372 U.S. 293 (1963).

EX PARTE MERRYMAN

(For more on habeas corpus, see this case and related materials in Part II, above.)

11. CRUEL AND UNUSUAL PUNISHMENT

FRANK LEE RUDOLPH, PETITIONER v. *ALABAMA*
84 S. Ct. 155 (1963)

Facts and opinion, 275 Ala. 115, 152 So. 2d 662.

Petition for writ of certiorari to the Supreme Court of Alabama.

Oct. 21, 1963. Denied.

MR. JUSTICE GOLDBERG, with whom MR. JUSTICE DOUGLAS and MR. JUSTICE BRENNAN join, dissenting:

I would grant certiorari in this case and

in *Snider* v. *Cunningham,* 84 S. Ct. 154, to consider whether the Eighth and Fourteenth Amendments to the United States Constitution permit the imposition of the death penalty on a convicted rapist who has neither taken nor endangered human life.

The following questions, *inter alia,* seem relevant and worthy of argument and consideration:

(1) In light of the trend both in this country and throughout the world against punishing rape by death, does the imposition of the death penalty by those States which retain it for rape violate "evolving standards of decency that mark the progress of [our] maturing society," or "standards of decency more or less universally accepted?"

(2) Is the taking of human life to protect a value other than human life consistent with the constitutional proscription against "punishments which by their excessive . . . severity are greatly disproportioned to the offenses charged?"

(3) Can the permissible aims of punishment (e.g., deterrence, isolation, rehabilitation) be achieved as effectively by punishing rape less severely than by death (e.g., by life imprisonment); if so, does the imposition of the death penalty for rape constitute "unnecessary cruelty?"

TROP v. *DULLES*

(This case, involving cruel and unusual punishment issues, appears on page 175.)

NOTE: According to the FBI "Uniform Crime Reports—1962" (p. 87) covering 1,655 cities with an estimated population of 54,396,000, there were 1,359,820 known offenses in 1962. Only 25.5 percent of them were "cleared," as follows: 306,826 persons were arrested—of these 84.5 were ultimately charged with crime. Of those charged, 93,381 (30.4 percent of arrests) were found guilty as charged; 21,479 (7 percent of arrests) were found guilty of a lesser offense; 107,092 (34.9 percent of arrests) were referred to juvenile courts; 37,510 cases (12.2 percent of arrests) were cleared by acquittal or dismissal.

12. THE FAIR HEARING AND THE ADMINISTRATIVE PROCESS—SECURITY CASES

Administrative handling of "security cases" in the Cold War raises old problems of fair procedure in a new context. Can a federal employee, for example, be discharged by his superiors on security grounds without an opportunity to see a full report of the case against him, or to confront and cross-examine his accusers? The Court of Appeals for the District of Columbia responded affirmatively on the ground that due process did not require a hearing with respect to "mere" dismissal from government service, that is, where no criminal penalty is involved. On appeal the Supreme Court was evenly divided, Mr. Justice Clark not participating. The decision of the lower court accordingly could not be disturbed. *Bailey* v. *Richardson*, 341 U.S. 918 (1951). But in *Joint Anti-Fascist Committee* v. *McGrath*, 341 U.S. 123 (1951), five Justices (including Mr. Justice Clark) agreed that due process required notice and an opportunity to be heard before the Attorney General could list an organization as subversive. A sixth judge found this implicit in the executive order under which the Attorney General had acted. Chief Justice Vinson and Justices Reed and Minton, dissenting, argued that no constitutional rights were infringed by the "mere" designation of an organization as subversive.

Most other cases of this type have been disposed of on procedural, but non-constitutional, grounds. Thus in *Communist Party* v. *Subversive Activities Control Board,* 351 U.S. 115 (1956), a subversive listing was returned to the Board for reconsideration, i.e., "to make certain that [it] bases its findings on untainted evidence." The difficulty was that three of the witnesses before the Board had subsequently discredited themselves and their testimony. *Peters* v. *Hobby,* 349 U.S. 331 (1955), again raised the issue of whether a federal employee could be discharged for security reasons where the adverse findings were based on statements of "secret" or "faceless informers" (persons whom the accused was not permitted to confront and cross-examine). See the Sixth Amendment. The issue was avoided by a finding that the Loyalty Review Board had had no authority to review the case because there had been no "appeal" for review. Accordingly its disloyalty finding was invalid for jurisdictional reasons. In *Cole* v. *Young,* 351 U.S. 536 (1956), a summary dismissal of a federal employee was upset on the ground that the act of Congress authorizing such dismissals without hearing applied only to employees in "sensitive" positions; and that the dismissal in question had been made without consideration as to the nature of Mr. Cole's employment. Dismissal of a principal target of the McCarthy fury was invalidated in *Service* v. *Dulles,* 354 U.S. 363 (1957), on the ground that the dismissing agency had violated its own relevant regulations. In *Harmon* v. *Brucker,* 355 U.S. 579 (1958), it was held that the Secretary of the Army exceeded his statutory authority in giving a less than honorable discharge based on *preinduction* political conduct of the dischargee. Similarly, *Kent* v. *Dulles,* 357 U.S. 116 (1958) held that Congress had not authorized the Secretary of State to deny passports to Communists or to persons who refused to take a "non-Communist" oath.

Green v. *McElroy,* 360 U.S. 474 (1959), invalidated the revocation of plaintiff's access to classified information—neither Congress nor the President having authorized revocation without a fair hearing. The revocation had led to the loss of plaintiff's job in a defense plant. In the course of its opinion the Court observed:

Certain principles have remained relatively immutable in our jurisprudence. One of these is that where governmental action seriously injures an individual, and the reasonableness of the action depends on fact findings, the evidence used to prove the Government's case must be disclosed to the individual so that he has an opportunity to show that it is untrue.

IV. FREEDOM OF UTTERANCE

1. BACKGROUND

WILLIAM BLACKSTONE, *Commentaries on the Laws of England* (1769)

The liberty of the press is indeed essential to the nature of a free state; but this consists in laying no *previous* restraints upon publications, and not in freedom from censure for criminal matter when published. Every freeman has an undoubted right to lay what sentiments he pleases before the public: to forbid this is to destroy the freedom of the press, but if he publishes what is improper, mischievous, or illegal, he must take the consequences of his own temerity. To subject the press to the restrictive power of a licenser, as was formerly done, both before and since the Revolution, is to subject all freedom of sentiment to the prejudices of one man, and make him the arbitrary and infallible judge of all controverted points in learning, religion, and government. But to punish (as the law does at present) any dangerous or offensive writings which, when published, shall on a fair and impartial trial be ajudged of a pernicious tendency, is necessary for the preservation of peace and good order, of government and religion,—the only solid foundations of civil liberty. Thus the will of individuals is still left free; the abuse only of that free will is the object of legal punishment. . . . (Book IV, p. 151)

THE FOX LIBEL ACT OF 1792

This famous English measure left the Blackstonian conception of freedom of the press unchanged, but it made a significant procedural change by providing that the jury "may give a general verdict of guilty or not guilty upon the whole matter. . . ." The result, as Dicey said, was that it was safe to publish anything which a jury of 12 shopkeepers would find permissible. Prior to the Fox Libel Act the jury's function was merely to determine whether the defendant had published the words in question, leaving the court to determine whether the publication was libelous.

The premise of the Fox measure presumably was that a jury would be apt to share, or sympathize with, the defendant's criticism of the royal government. Would this premise be valid today with respect to radical left- or right-wing criticisms?

LEONARD LEVY, *Legacy of Suppression* [1]

There is every reason to believe that the Bill of Rights was more the chance product of political expediency on all sides than of principled commitment to personal liberties. A broad libertarian theory of freedom of speech and press did not emerge in the United States until the Jeffersonians, when a minority party, were forced to defend themselves against the Federalist Sedition Act of 1798. In power, however, the Jeffersonians were not much more tolerant of their political critics than the Federalists had been.

. . . was it the intention of the generation from the Revolution to the First Amendment to supersede the common law by repudiating the Blackstonian concept that freedom of the press meant freedom from prior restraint?

Dean Levy's answer is that the intention was to incorporate into the First Amendment the common law rule against "prior restraint," with its corollary the "pernicious tendency" rule, and perhaps the Fox Libel Act principle. Those who gave us the Sedition Act of 1798 evidently shared Dean Levy's view on this point.

1. Leonard W. Levy, *Legacy of Suppression* (Cambridge, Mass.: Harvard University Press, 1960), pp. vii, x.

THE SEDITION ACT OF 1798

Section 2 provided in part that it was a crime for any person to write, print, or publish "any false, scandalous and malicious writing" against the Government of the United States, the Houses of Congress, or the President "with intent to defame" or to bring them "into contempt or disrepute." The punishment was a fine not exceeding $2,000 and imprisonment not exceeding two years.

It is noteworthy that this measure incorporates the two then most advanced liberal principles; namely, the Fox jury provision and the conception of truth as a defense. The latter was not accepted in England until Lord Campbell's Act in 1843.

MR. JUSTICE IREDELL'S CHARGE TO THE GRAND JURY IN THE CASE OF THE NORTHAMPTON INSURGENTS, PHILADELPHIA, APRIL 11, 1799

4. That objection is, that the [Sedition] act is in violation of this amendment of the Constitution.

"Congress shall make no law respecting an establishment of religion, or prohibiting the free exercise thereof; or abridging the freedom of speech, or of the press, or the right of the people peaceably to assemble, and to petition the government for a redress of grievances."

The question then is, whether this law has abridged the freedom of the press?

Here is a remarkable difference in expressions as to the different objects in the same clause. They are to make no law *respecting* an establishment of religion, or prohibiting the free exercise thereof, or *abridging* the freedom of speech, or of the press. When, as to one object, they entirely prohibit any act whatever, and, as to another object, only limit the exercise of the power, they must, in reason, be supposed to mean different things. I presume, therefore, that Congress may make a law *respecting* the press, provided the law be such as not to *abridge its freedom*. What might be deemed the freedom of the press, if it had been a new subject, and never before in discussion, might indeed admit of some controversy. But, so far as precedent, habit, laws, and practices are concerned, there can scarcely be a more definite meaning than that which all these have affixed to the term in question.

It is believed that, in every State in the Union, the common law principles concerning libels apply; and in some of the States words similar to the words of the Amendment are used in the Constitution itself, or a contemporary Bill of Rights, of equal authority, without ever being supposed to exclude any law being passed on the subject. So that there is the strongest proof that can be of a universal concurrence in America on this point, that the freedom of the press does not require that libellers shall be protected from punishment.

ALEXANDER MEIKLEJOHN, *Free Speech and Its Relation to Self-Government* [2]

. . . the vital point, as stated negatively, is that no suggestion of policy shall be denied a hearing because it is on one side of the issue rather than another. And this means that though citizens may, on other grounds, be barred from speaking,

2. Alexander Meiklejohn, *Free Speech and Its Relation to Self-Government* (New York: Harper & Brothers, 1948), pp. 26–27.

they may not be barred because their views are thought to be false or dangerous. No plan of action shall be outlawed because someone in control thinks it unwise, unfair, un-American. No speaker may be declared "out of order" because we disagree with what he intends to say. And the reason for this equality of status in the field of ideas lies deep in the very foundations of the self-governing process. When men govern themselves, it is they—and no one else—who must pass judgment upon unwisdom and unfairness and danger. And that means that unwise ideas must have a hearing as well as wise ones, unfair as well as fair, dangerous as well as safe, un-American as well as American. Just so far as, at any point, the citizens who are to decide an issue are denied acquaintance with information or opinion or doubt or disbelief or criticism which is relevant to that issue, just so far the result must be ill-considered, ill-balanced planning for the general good. *It is that mutilation of the thinking process of the community against which the First Amendment to the Constitution is directed.* The principle of the freedom of speech springs from the necessities of the program of self-government. It is not a Law of Nature or of Reason in the abstract. It is a deduction from the basic American agreement that public issues shall be decided by universal suffrage.

If, then, on any occasion in the United States it is allowable to say that the Constitution is a good document it is equally allowable, in that situation, to say that the Constitution is a bad document. If a public building may be used in which to say, in time of war, that the war is justified, then the same building may be used in which to say that it is not justified. If it be publicly argued that conscription for armed service is moral and necessary, it may likewise be publicly argued that it is immoral and unnecessary. If it may be said that American political institutions are superior to those of England or Russia or Germany, it may, with equal freedom, be said that those of England or Russia or Germany are superior to ours. These conflicting views may be expressed, must be expressed, not because they are valid, but because they are relevant. If they are responsibly entertained by anyone, we, the voters, need to hear them. When a question of policy is "before the house," free men choose to meet it not with their eyes shut, but with their eyes open. To be afraid of ideas, any idea, is to be unfit for self-government. Any such suppression of ideas about the common good, the First Amendment condemns with its absolute disapproval. The freedom of ideas shall not be abridged.

2. POLITICAL UTTERANCE—INCITEMENT OR DISCUSSION?

MASSES PUBLISHING COMPANY v. *PATTEN*
244 Fed. 535 (1917)

The court here enjoined the New York Postmaster from excluding an issue of a left-wing publication from the mails. (The decision was reversed on appeal—246 Fed. 24.) Holding that the Espionage Act could not be construed to outlaw the statements involved, Judge Learned Hand distinguished between protected and unprotected speech as follows:

One may not counsel or advise others to violate the law as it stands. Words are not only the keys of persuasion, but the triggers of action, and those which have no purport but to counsel the violation of law cannot by any latitude of interpretation be a part of that public opinion which is the final source of government in a democratic state.

. . . Political agitation, by the passions it arouses or the convictions it engenders, may in fact stimulate men to the violation of law. Detestation of existing policies is easily transformed into forcible resistance of the authority which puts them in execution, and it would be folly to disregard the causal relation between the two. Yet to assimilate agitation, legitimate as such, with direct incitement to violent resistance, is to disregard the tolerance of all methods of political agitation which in normal times is a safeguard of free government. The distinction is not a scholastic subterfuge, but a hard-bought acquisition in the fight for freedom, and the purpose to disregard it must be evident when the power exists. If one stops short of urging upon others that it is their duty or their interest to resist the law, it seems to me one should not be held to have attempted to cause its violation. If that be not the test, I can see no escape from the conclusion that under this section every political agitation which can be shown to be apt to create a seditious temper is illegal. I am confident that by such language Congress had no such revolutionary purpose in view.

SCHENCK v. UNITED STATES

249 U.S. 47 (1919)

MR. JUSTICE HOLMES delivered the opinion of the Court.

This is an indictment in three counts. The first charges a conspiracy to violate the Espionage Act of June 15, 1917, c. 30, tit. 1, § 3, 40 Stat. 217, 219 (Comp. St. 1918, § 10212c), by causing and attempting to cause insubordination, &c., in the military and naval forces of the United States, and to obstruct the recruiting and enlistment service of the United States, when the United States was at war with the German Empire, to-wit, that the defendant wilfully conspired to have printed and circulated to men who had been called and accepted for military service under the Act of May 18, 1917, c. 15, 40 Stat. 76 (Comp. St. 1918, §§ 2044a–2044k), a document set forth and alleged to be calculated to cause such insubordination and obstruction. The count alleges overt acts in pursuance of the conspiracy, ending in the distribution of the document set forth. The second count alleges a conspiracy to commit an offense against the United States, to-wit, to use the mails for the transmission of matter declared to be non-mailable by title 12, § 2, of the Act of June 15, 1917 (Comp. St. 1918, § 10401b), to-wit, the above mentioned document, with an averment of the same overt acts. The third count charges an unlawful use of the mails for the transmission of the same matter and otherwise as above. The defendants were found guilty on all the counts. They set up the First Amendment to the Constitution forbidding Congress to make any law abridging the freedom of speech, or of the press, and bringing the case here on that ground have argued some other points also of which we must dispose. . . .

The document in question upon its first printed side recited the first section of the Thirteenth Amendment, said that the idea embodied in it was violated by the conscription act and that a conscript is little better than a convict. In impassioned language it intimated that conscription was despotism in its worst form and a monstrous wrong against humanity in the interest of Wall Street's chosen few. It said, "Do not submit to intimidation," but in form at least confined itself to peaceful measures such as a petition for the repeal of the act. The other and later printed side of the sheet was headed "Assert Your Rights." It stated reasons for alleging that any one violated the Constitution when he refused to recognize "your right to assert your opposition to the draft," and went on, "If you do not assert and support your rights, you are helping to deny or disparage rights which it is the solemn duty of all citizens and residents of the United States to retain." It described the arguments on the other side as coming from cunning politicians and a mercenary capitalist press, and even silent consent to the conscription law as helping to support an infamous conspiracy. It denied the power to send our citizens away to foreign shores to shoot up the people of other lands, and added that words could not express the condemnation such cold-blooded ruthlessness deserves, &c., &c., winding up, "You must do your share to maintain, support and uphold the rights of the people of this country." Of course the document would not have been sent unless it had been intended to have some effect, and we do not see what effect it could be expected to have upon persons subject to the draft except to influence them to obstruct the carrying of it out. The defendants do not deny that the jury might find against them on this point.

But it is said, suppose that that was the tendency of this circular, it is protected by the First Amendment to the Constitution. Two of the strongest expressions are said to be quoted respectively from well-known public men. It well may be that the prohibition of laws abridging the freedom of speech is not confined to previous restraints, although to prevent them may have been the main purpose, as intimated in *Patterson* v. *Colorado,* 205 U.S. 454, 462. We admit that in many places and in ordinary times the defendants in saying all that was said in the circular would have been within their constitutional rights. But the character of every act depends upon the circum-

stances in which it is done. *Aikens* v. *Wisconsin,* 195 U.S. 194, 205, 206. The most stringent protection of free speech would not protect a man in falsely shouting fire in a theatre and causing a panic. It does not even protect a man from an injunction against uttering words that may have all the effect of force. *Gompers* v. *Buck's Stove & Range Co.,* 221 U.S. 418, 439. The question in every case is whether the words used are in such circumstances and are of such a nature as to create a clear and present danger that they will bring about the substantive evils that Congress has a right to prevent. It is a question of proximity and degree. When a nation is at war many things that might be said in time of peace are such a hindrance to its effort that their utterance will not be endured so long as men fight and that no Court could regard them as protected by any constitutional right. It seems to be admitted that if an actual obstruction of the recruiting service were proved, liability for words that produced that effect might be enforced. The statute of 1917 in section 4 (Comp. St. 1918, § 10212d) punishes conspiracies to obstruct as well as actual obstruction. If the act (speaking, or circulating a paper), its tendency and the intent with which it is done are the same, we perceive no ground for saying that success alone warrants making the act a crime. *Goldman* v. *United States,* 245 U.S. 474, 477. Indeed that case might be said to dispose of the present contention if the precedent covers all media concludendi. But as the right to free speech was not referred to specially, we have thought fit to add a few words. . . .

Judgments affirmed.

NOTE AND QUAERE: Concurring in *Whitney* v. *California,* below, Justice Brandeis (joined by Holmes) observed: "It is only the present danger of immediate evil or an intent to bring it about that warrants Congress in setting a limit to the expression of opinion. . . ." Which element was decisive in the *Schenck* case? Observe that in *Whitney* Justices Holmes and Brandeis felt they could not dissent on clear and present danger grounds because that issue had not been raised as a defense at the trial (and there had been some evidence of such a danger). Schenck of course could not have raised this issue at his trial for at that time the clear and present danger test had not yet been born.

WHITNEY v. *CALIFORNIA*

274 U.S. 357 (1927)

> Miss Whitney, heiress of a famous fortune, was convicted of violating a state criminal syndicalism law by organizing, and being a member of, a group advocating unlawful force as a political weapon. The conviction was sustained on appeal on grounds similar to those laid out in *Gitlow*.

Following is the concurring opinion of MR. JUSTICE BRANDEIS in which MR. JUSTICE HOLMES joined: . . .

The felony which the statute created is a crime very unlike the old felony of conspiracy or the old misdemeanor of unlawful assembly. The mere act of assisting in forming a society for teaching syndicalism, of becoming a member of it, or assembling with others for that purpose is given the dynamic quality of crime. There is guilt although the society may not contemplate immediate promulgation of the doctrine. Thus the accused is to be punished, not for attempt, incitement, or conspiracy, but for a step in preparation, which, if it threatens the public order at all, does so only remotely. The novelty in the prohibition introduced is that the statute aims, not at the practice of criminal syndicalism, nor even directly at the preaching of it, but at association with those who propose to preach it.

Despite arguments to the contrary which had seemed to me persuasive, it is settled that the due process clause of the Fourteenth Amendment applies to matters of substantive law as well as to matters of procedure. Thus all fundamental rights comprised within the term liberty are protected by the federal Constitution from invasion by the states. The right of free speech, the right to teach and the right of assembly are, of course, fundamental rights. . . . These may not be denied or abridged. But, although the rights of free speech and assembly are fundamental, they are not in their nature absolute. Their exercise is subject to restriction, if the particular restriction proposed is required in order to protect the state from destruction or from serious injury, political, economic or moral. That the necessity which is essential to a valid restriction does not exist unless speech would produce, or is intended to produce, a clear and imminent danger of some substantive evil which the state constitutionally may seek to prevent has been settled. See *Schenck* v. *United States*, 249 U.S. 47, 52.

It is said to be the function of the Legislature to determine whether at a particular time and under the particular circumstances the formation of, or assembly with, a society organized to advocate criminal syndicalism constitutes a clear and present danger of substantive evil; and that by enacting the law here in question the Legislature of California determined that question in the affirmative. Compare *Gitlow* v. *New York*. . . . The Legislature must obviously decide, in the first instance, whether a danger exists which calls for a particular protective measure. But where a statute is valid only in case certain conditions exist, the enactment of the statute cannot alone establish the facts which are essential to its validity. Prohibitory legislation has repeatedly been held invalid, because unnecessary, where the denial of liberty involved was that of engaging in a particular business. The powers of the courts to strike down an offending law are no less when the interests involved are not property rights, but the fundamental personal rights of free speech and assembly.

This court has not yet fixed the standard by which to determine when a danger shall be deemed clear; how remote the danger may be and yet be deemed present; and what degree of evil shall be deemed sufficiently substantial to justify resort to abridgment of free speech and assembly as the means of protection. To reach sound conclusions on these matters, we must bear in mind why a state is, ordinarily, denied the power to prohibit dissemination of social, economic and political doctrine which a vast majority of its citizens believes to be false and fraught with evil consequence.

Those who won our independence believed that the final end of the state was to make men free to develop their faculties, and that in its government the deliberative forces should prevail over the arbitrary. They valued liberty both as an end and as a means. They believed liberty to be the secret of happiness and courage to be the secret of liberty. They believed that freedom to think as you will and to speak as you think are means indispensable to the discovery and spread of political truth; that without free speech and assembly discussion would be futile; that with them, discussion affords ordinarily adequate protection against the dissemination of noxious doctrine; that the greatest menace to freedom is an inert people; that public discussion is a political duty; and that this should be a fundamental principle of the American government. They recognized the risks to which all human institutions are subject. But they knew that order cannot be secured merely through fear of punishment for its infraction; that it is hazardous to discourage thought, hope and imagination; that fear breeds repression; that repression breeds hate; that hate menaces stable government; that the path of safety lies in the opportunity to discuss freely supposed grievances and proposed remedies; and that the fitting remedy for evil counsels is good ones. Believing in the

power of reason as applied through public discussion, they eschewed silence coerced by law—the argument of force in its worst form. Recognizing the occasional tyrannies of governing majorities, they amended the Constitution so that free speech and assembly should be guaranteed.

Fear of serious injury cannot alone justify suppression of free speech and assembly. Men feared witches and burnt women. It is the function of speech to free men from the bondage of irrational fears. To justify suppression of free speech there must be reasonable ground to fear that serious evil will result if free speech is practiced. There must be reasonable ground to believe that the danger apprehended is imminent. There must be reasonable ground to believe that the evil to be prevented is a serious one. . . . The wide difference between advocacy and incitement, between preparation and attempt, between assembling and conspiracy, must be borne in mind. In order to support a finding of clear and present danger it must be shown either that immediate serious violence was to be expected or was advocated, or that the past conduct furnished reason to believe that such advocacy was then contemplated.

Those who won our independence by revolution were not cowards. They did not fear political change. They did not exalt order at the cost of liberty. To courageous, self-reliant men, with confidence in the power of free and fearless reasoning applied through the processes of popular government, no danger flowing from speech can be deemed clear and present, unless the incidence of the evil apprehended is so imminent that it may befall before there is opportunity for full discussion. If there be time to expose through discussion the falsehood and fallacies, to avert the evil by the process of education, the remedy to be applied is more speech, not enforced silence. Only an emergency can justify repression. Such must be the rule if authority is to be reconciled with freedom. Such, in my opinion, is the command of the Constitution. It is therefore always open to Americans to challenge a law abridging free speech and assembly by showing that there was no emergency justifying it.

Moreover, even imminent danger cannot justify resort to prohibition of these functions essential to effective democracy, unless the evil apprehended is relatively serious. Prohibition of free speech and assembly is a measure so stringent that it would be inappropriate as the means for averting a relatively trivial harm to society. A police measure may be unconstitutional merely because the remedy, although effective as means of protection, is unduly harsh or oppressive. . . . The fact that speech is likely to result in some violence or in destruction of property is not enough to justify its suppression. There must be the probability of serious injury to the State. Among free men, the deterrents ordinarily to be applied to prevent crime are education and punishment for violations of the law, not abridgment of the rights of free speech and assembly. . . .

Whether in 1919, when Miss Whitney did the things complained of, there was in California such clear and present danger of serious evil, might have been made the important issue in this case. She might have required that the issue be determined either by the court or by the jury. She claimed below that the statute as applied to her violated the federal Constitution; but she did not claim that it was void because there was no clear and present danger of serious evil, nor did she request that the existence of these conditions of a valid measure thus restricting the rights of free speech and assembly be passed upon by the court or a jury. On the other hand, there was evidence on which the court or jury might have found that such danger existed. [We are] unable to assent to the suggestion in the opinion of the court that assembling with a political party, formed to advocate the desirability of a proletarian revolution by mass action at some date necessarily far in the future, is not a right within the protection of the Fourteenth Amendment. In the present case, however, there was other testimony which tended to establish the existence of a conspiracy, on the part of members of the International Workers of the World, to commit present serious crimes, and likewise to show that such a conspiracy would be furthered by the activity of the society of which Miss Whitney was a member. Under these circumstances the judgment of the State court cannot be disturbed. . . .

GITLOW v. NEW YORK

268 U.S. 652 (1925)

> Gitlow was found guilty of "criminal anarchy" in that he had "advocated, advised and taught the duty, necessity, and propriety of overthrowing . . . government by force [in] certain writings" [namely, "The Left Wing Manifesto" and "The Revolutionary Age"]. His defense was that there was no evidence of any concrete result flowing from such publications, or of the likelihood of such result, and that therefore the statute under which he was charged was unconstitutional as applied to mere utterance of doctrine in such circumstances.

Mr. Justice Sanford delivered the opinion of the Court: . . .

The precise question presented, and the only question which we can consider under this writ of error, then, is whether the statute, as construed and applied in this case by the state courts, deprived the defendant of his liberty of expression in violation of the due process clause of the Fourteenth Amendment.

The statute does not penalize the utterance or publication of abstract "doctrine" or academic discussion having no quality of incitement to any concrete action. It is not aimed against mere historical or philosophical essays. It does not restrain the advocacy of changes in the form of government by constitutional and lawful means. What it prohibits is language advocating, advising, or teaching the overthrow of organized government by unlawful means. These words imply urging to action. Advocacy is defined in the Century Dictionary as: "1. The act of pleading for, supporting, or recommending; active espousal." It is not the abstract "doctrine" of overthrowing organized government by unlawful means which is denounced by the statute, but the advocacy of action for the accomplishment of that purpose. It was so construed and applied by the trial judge, who specifically charged the jury that: "A mere grouping of historical events and a prophetic deduction from them would neither constitute advocacy, advice or teaching of a doctrine for the overthrow of government by force, violence or unlawful means. [And] if it were a mere essay on the subject, as suggested by counsel, based upon deductions from alleged historical events, with no teaching, advice or advocacy of action, it would not constitute a violation of the statute. . . ."

The Manifesto, plainly, is neither the statement of abstract doctrine nor, as suggested by counsel, mere prediction that industrial disturbances and revolutionary mass strikes will result spontaneously in an inevitable process of evolution in the economic system. It advocates and urges in fervent language mass action which shall progressively foment industrial disturbances and through political mass strikes and revolutionary mass action overthrow and destroy organized parliamentary government. It concludes with a call to action in these words: "The proletariat revolution and the Communist reconstruction of society—*the struggle for these*—is now indispensable. . . . The Communist International calls the proletariat of the world to the final struggle!" This is not the expression of philosophical abstractions, the mere

prediction of future events; it is the language of direct incitement. . . .

. . . That the jury were warranted in finding that the Manifesto advocated not merely the abstract doctrine of overthrowing organized government by force, violence and unlawful means, but action to that end is clear.

For present purposes we may and do assume that freedom of speech and of the press—which are protected by the First Amendment from abridgment by Congress—are among the fundamental personal rights and "liberties" protected by the due process clause of the Fourteenth Amendment from impairment by the states. . . .

It is a fundamental principle, long established, that the freedom of speech and of the press which is secured by the Constitution, does not confer an absolute right to speak or publish, without responsibility, whatever one may choose, or an unrestricted and unbridled license that gives immunity for every possible use of language and prevents the punishment of those who abuse this freedom. . . .

That a State in the exercise of its police power may punish those who abuse this freedom by utterances inimical to the public welfare, tending to corrupt public morals, incite to crime, or disturb the public peace, is not open to question. . . .

And, for yet more imperative reasons, a State may punish utterances endangering the foundations of organized government and threatening its overthrow by unlawful means. These imperil its own existence as a constitutional State. Freedom of speech and press, said Story, does not protect disturbances to the public peace or the attempt to subvert the government. It does not protect publications or teachings which tend to subvert or imperil the government or to impede or hinder it in the performance of its governmental duties. *State* v. *Holm*, 139 Minn. 267. It does not protect publications prompting the overthrow of government by force; the punishment of those who publish articles which tend to destroy organized society being essential to the security of freedom and the stability of

the State. *People* v. *Most,* 171 N.Y. 423.
And a State may penalize utterances which
openly advocate the overthrow of the
representative and constitutional form of
government of the United States and the
several States, by violence or other unlawful means. . . .

By enacting the present statute the State
has determined, through its legislative
body, that utterances advocating the overthrow of organized government by force,
violence and unlawful means, are so inimical to the general welfare and involve
such danger of substantive evil that they
may be penalized in the exercise of its
police power. That determination must
be given great weight. Every presumption
is to be indulged in favor of the validity
of the statute. . . . That utterances inciting to the overthrow of organized government by unlawful means, present a sufficient danger of substantive evil to bring
their punishment within the range of legislative discretion, is clear. Such utterances,
by their very nature, involve danger to
the public peace and to the security of the
State. They threaten breaches of the peace
and ultimate revolution. And the immediate danger is none the less real and
substantial, because the effect of a given
utterance cannot be accurately foreseen.
The State cannot reasonably be required
to measure the danger from every such
utterance in the nice balance of a jeweler's
scale. A single revolutionary spark may
kindle a fire that, smouldering for a time,
may burst into a sweeping and destructive
conflagration. It cannot be said that the
State is acting arbitrarily or unreasonably
when in the exercise of its judgment as to
the measures necessary to protect the public peace and safety, it seeks to extinguish
the spark without waiting until it has en-
kindled the flame or blazed into the conflagration. It cannot reasonably be required
to defer the adoption of measures for its
own peace and safety until the revolutionary utterances lead to actual disturbances
of the public peace or imminent and immediate danger of its own destruction; but
it may, in the exercise of its judgment,

suppress the threatened danger in its in-
cipiency. . . .

We cannot hold that the present statute
is an arbitrary or unreasonable exercise of
the police power of the State unwarran-
tably infringing the freedom of speech or
press; and we must and do sustain its constitutionality.

This being so it may be applied to every
utterance—not too trivial to be beneath
the notice of the law—which is of such a
character and used with such intent and
purpose as to bring it within the prohibition of the statute. . . .

It is clear that the question in such cases
is entirely different from that involved in
those cases where the statute merely prohibits certain acts involving the danger of
substantive evil, without any reference to
language itself, and it is sought to apply
its provisions to language used by the defendant for the purpose of bringing about
the prohibited results. There, if it be contended that the statute cannot be applied
to the language used by the defendant because of its protection by the freedom of
speech or press, it must necessarily be
found, as an original question, without any
previous determination by the legislative
body, whether the specific language used
involved such likelihood of bringing about
the substantive evil as to deprive it of the
constitutional protection. In such cases it
has been held that the general provisions
of the statute may be constitutionally applied to the specific utterance of the defendant if its natural tendency and probable
effect was to bring about the substantive
evil which the legislative body might prevent. *Schenck* v. *United States,* 249 U.S.
47; *Debs* v. *United States,* 249 U.S. 211.
And the general statement in the Schenck
case that the "question in every case is
whether the words used are used in such
circumstances and are of such a nature as
to create a clear and present danger that
they will bring about the substantive evils,"
—upon which great reliance is placed in
the defendant's argument—was manifestly
intended, as shown by the context, to apply
only in cases of this class, and has no

application to those like the present, where the legislative body itself has previously determined the danger of substantive evil arising from utterances of a specified character. . . .

Affirmed.

MR. JUSTICE HOLMES, dissenting.

MR. JUSTICE BRANDEIS and I are of opinion that this judgment should be reversed. The general principle of free speech, it seems to me, must be taken to be included in the Fourteenth Amendment, in view of the scope that has been given to the word "liberty" as there used, although perhaps it may be accepted with a somewhat larger latitude of interpretation than is allowed to Congress by the sweeping language that governs or ought to govern the laws of the United States. If I am right, then I think that the criterion sanctioned by the full court in *Schenck* v. *United States, supra,* applies. "The question in every case is whether the words used are used in such circumstances and are of such a nature as to create a clear and present danger that they will bring about the substantive evils that [the state] has a right to prevent." It is true that in my opinion this criterion was departed from in *Abrams* v. *United States,* 250 U.S. 616, but the convictions that I expressed in that case are too deep for it to be possible for me as yet to believe that it and *Schaefer* v. *United States,* 251 U.S. 466, have settled the law. If what I think the correct test is applied, it is mani-

fest that there was no present danger of an attempt to overthrow the government by force on the part of the admittedly small minority who shared the defendant's views. It is said that this manifesto was more than a theory, that it was an incitement. Every idea is an incitement. It offers itself for belief and if believed it is acted on unless some other belief outweighs it or some failure of energy stifles the movement at its birth. The only difference between the expression of an opinion and an incitement in the narrower sense is the speaker's enthusiasm for the result. Eloquence may set fire to reason. But whatever may be thought of the redundant discourse before us it had no chance of starting a present conflagration. If in the long run the beliefs expressed in proletarian dictatorship are destined to be accepted by the dominant forces of the community, the only meaning of free speech is that they should be given their chance and have their way.

If the publication of this document had been laid as an attempt to induce an uprising against government at once and not at some indefinite time in the future it would have presented a different question. The object would have been one with which the law might deal, subject to the doubt whether there was any danger that the publication could produce any result, or in other words, whether it was not futile and too remote from possible consequences. But the indictment alleges the publication and nothing more.

DE JONGE v. *OREGON*
299 U.S. 353 (1937)

The defendant was convicted under an Oregon Criminal Syndicalism Law for presiding over and assisting in the conduct of a meeting of the Communist Party, an organization advocating criminal syndicalism (physical violence, sabotage, or other unlawful acts to accomplish industrial or political revolution). The evidence showed that De Jonge was a Communist, that the meeting was held under the auspices of the Communist Party, but that at the meeting no unlawful acts were done or advocated—and that its only purpose was to protest against certain allegedly illegal anti-labor raids and shootings.

Reversing the conviction, a unanimous Court, per CHIEF JUSTICE HUGHES, said in part:

Conviction upon a charge not made would be sheer denial of due process. It thus appears that, while defendant was a member of the Communist Party, he was not indicted for participating in its organization, or for joining it, or for soliciting members or for distributing its literature. He was not charged with teaching or advocating criminal syndicalism or sabotage or any unlawful acts, either at the meeting or elsewhere. He was accordingly deprived of the benefit of evidence as to the orderly and lawful conduct of the meeting and that it was not called or used for the advocacy of criminal syndicalism or sabotage or any unlawful action. His sole offense as charged, and for which he was convicted and sentenced to imprisonment for seven years, was that he had assisted in the conduct of a public meeting, albeit otherwise lawful, which was held under the auspices of the Communist Party. . . .

While the States are entitled to protect themselves from the abuse of the privileges of our institutions through an attempted substitution of force and violence in the place of peaceful political action in order to effect revolutionary changes in government, none of our decisions go to the length of sustaining such a curtailment of the right of free speech and assembly as the Oregon statute demands in its present application. In *Gitlow* v. *New York*, 268 U.S. 652, under the New York statute defining criminal anarchy, the defendant was found to be responsible for a "manifesto" advocating the overthrow of the government by violence and unlawful means. Id., 268 U.S. 652, at pages 656, 662, 663. In *Whitney* v. *California*, 274 U.S. 357, under the California statute relating to criminal syndicalism, the defendant was found guilty of willfully and deliberately assisting in the forming of an organization for the purpose of carrying on a revolutionary class struggle by criminal methods. The defendant was convicted of participation in what amounted to a conspiracy to commit serious crimes. Id., 274 U.S. 357, at pages 363, 364, 367, 379. . . .

Freedom of speech and of the press are fundamental rights which are safeguarded by the due process clause of the Fourteenth Amendment of the Federal Constitution. . . . The right of peaceable assembly is a right cognate to those of free speech and free press and is equally fundamental. As this Court said in *United States* v. *Cruikshank,* 92 U.S. 542, 552: "The very idea of a government, republican in form, implies a right on the part of its citizens to meet peaceably for consultation in respect to public affairs and to petition for a redress of grievances." The First Amendment of the Federal Constitution expressly guarantees that right against abridgement by Congress. But explicit mention there does not argue exclusion elsewhere. For the right is one that cannot be denied without violating those fundamental principles of liberty and justice which lie at the base of all civil and political institutions—principles which the Fourteenth Amendment embodies in the general terms of its due process clause. . . .

These rights may be abused by using speech or press or assembly in order to incite to violence and crime. The people through their Legislatures may protect themselves against that abuse. But the legislative intervention can find constitutional justification only by dealing with the abuse. The rights themselves must not be curtailed. The greater the importance of safeguarding the community from incitements to the overthrow of our institutions by force and violence, the more imperative is the need to preserve inviolate the constitutional rights of free speech, free press and free assembly in order to maintain the opportunity for free political discussion, to the end that government may be responsive to the will of the people and that changes, if desired, may be obtained by peaceful means. Therein lies the security of the Republic, the very foundation of constitutional government.

It follows from these considerations that, consistently with the Federal Constitution, peaceable assembly for lawful discussion cannot be made a crime. The holding of meetings for peaceable political action cannot be proscribed. Those who assist in the conduct of such meetings cannot be branded as criminals on that score. The question, if the rights of free speech and peaceable assembly are to be preserved, is not as to the auspices under which the meeting is held but as to its purpose; not as to the relations of the speakers, but whether their utterances transcend the bounds of the freedom of speech which the Constitution protects. If the persons assembling have committed crimes elsewhere, if they have formed or are engaged in a conspiracy against the public peace and order they may be prosecuted for their conspiracy or other violation of valid laws. But it is a different matter when the State, instead of prosecuting them for such offenses, seizes upon mere participation in a peaceable assembly and a lawful public discussion as the basis for a criminal charge.

We are not called upon to review the findings of the state court as to the objectives of the Communist Party. Notwithstanding those objectives, the defendant still enjoyed his personal right of free speech and to take part in a peaceable assembly having a lawful purpose, although called by that party. The defendant was none the less entitled to discuss the public issues of the day and thus in a lawful manner, without incitement to violence or crime, to seek redress of alleged grievances. That was of the essence of his guaranteed personal liberty.

We hold that the Oregon statute as applied to the particular charge as defined by the state court is repugnant to the due process clause of the Fourteenth Amendment. The judgment of conviction is reversed and the cause is remanded for further proceedings not inconsistent with this opinion.

DENNIS v. UNITED STATES

341 U.S. 494 (1951)

This is the 1949 case of the eleven top leaders of the Communist Party of the United States. The Supreme Court, accepting the factual findings of the trial court as approved by the Court of Appeals, granted certiorari only to consider whether relevant parts of the Smith Act were compatible with the First and Fifth Amendments.

MR. CHIEF JUSTICE VINSON announced the judgment of the Court and an opinion in which MR. JUSTICE REED, MR. JUSTICE BURTON, and MR. JUSTICE MINTON joined. . . .

The indictment [under the Smith Act] charged the petitioners with wilfully and knowingly conspiring (1) to organize as the Communist Party of the United States of America a society, group and assembly of persons who teach and advocate the overthrow and destruction of the Government of the United States by force and violence, and (2) knowingly and wilfully to advocate and teach the duty and necessity of overthrowing and destroying the Government of the United States by force and violence. The indictment further alleged that § 2 of the Smith Act proscribes these acts and that any conspiracy to take such action is a violation of § 3 of the Act. . . .

The obvious purpose of the statute is to protect existing Government, not from change by peaceable, lawful, and constitutional means, but from change by violence, revolution, and terrorism. That it is within the *power* of the Congress to protect the Government of the United States from armed rebellion is a proposition which requires little discussion. Whatever theoretical merit there may be to the argument that there is a "right" to rebellion against dictatorial governments is without force where the existing structure of the government provides for peaceful and orderly change. We reject any principle of governmental helplessness in the face of preparation for revolution, which principle, carried to its logical conclusion, must lead to anarchy. No one could conceive that it is not within the power of Congress to prohibit acts intended to overthrow the Government by force and violence. The question with which we are concerned here is not whether Congress has such *power*, but whether the *means* which it has employed conflict with the First and Fifth Amendments to the Constitution.

One of the bases for the contention that the means which Congress has employed are invalid takes the form of an attack on the face of the statute on the grounds that by its terms it prohibits academic discussion of the merits of Marxism-Leninism, that it stifles ideas and is contrary to all concepts of a free speech and a free press. . . .

The very language of the Smith Act negates the interpretation which petitioners would have us impose on that Act. It is directed at advocacy, not discussion. Thus, the trial judge properly charged the jury that they could not convict if they found that petitioners did "no more than pursue peaceful studies and discussions or teaching and advocacy in the realm of ideas." He further charged that it was not unlawful "to conduct in an American college or university a course explaining the philosophical theories set forth in the books which have been placed in evidence." Such a charge is in strict accord with the statutory language, and illustrates the meaning to be placed on those words. Congress did not intend to eradicate the free discussion of political theories, to destroy the traditional rights of Americans to discuss and evaluate ideas without fear of governmental sanction. Rather Congress was concerned with the very kind of activity in which the evidence showed these petitioners engaged. . . .

We pointed out in Douds, [339 U.S. 382: 1950], that the basis of the First Amend-

ment is the hypothesis that speech can rebut speech, propaganda will answer propaganda, free debate of ideas will result in the wisest governmental policies. It is for this reason that this Court has recognized the inherent value of free discourse. An analysis of the leading cases in this Court which have involved direct limitations on speech, however, will demonstrate that both the majority of the Court and the dissenters in particular cases have recognized that this is not an unlimited, unqualified right, but that the societal value of speech must, on occasion, be subordinated to other values and considerations.

No important case involving free speech was decided by this Court prior to *Schenck* v. *United States*, 249 U.S. 47 (1919). Indeed, the summary treatment accorded an argument based upon an individual's claim that the First Amendment protected certain utterances indicates that the Court at earlier dates placed no unique emphasis upon that right. It was not until the classic dictum of Justice Holmes in the *Schenck* case that speech *per se* received that emphasis in a majority opinion. That case involved a conviction under the Criminal Espionage Act, 40 Stat. 217. The question the Court faced was whether the evidence was sufficient to sustain the conviction. Writing for a unanimous Court, Justice Holmes stated that the "question in every case is whether the words used are used in such circumstances and are of such a nature as to create a clear and present danger that they will bring about the substantive evils that Congress has a right to prevent." 249 U.S. at 52. But the force of even this expression is considerably weakened by the reference at the end of the opinion to *Goldman* v. *United States*, 245 U.S. 474 (1918), a prosecution under the same statute. Said Justice Holmes, "Indeed [*Goldman*] might be said to dispose of the present contention if the precedent covers all *media concludendi*, but as the right to free speech was not referred to specially, we have thought fit to add a few words." 249 U.S. at 52. The fact is inescapable, too, that the phrase bore no connotation that the danger was to be any threat to the safety of the Republic. The charge was causing and attempting to cause insubordination in the military forces and obstruct recruiting. The objectionable document denounced conscription and its most inciting sentence was, "You must do your share to maintain, support and uphold the rights of the people of this country." 249 U.S. at 51. Fifteen thousand copies were printed and some circulated. This insubstantial gesture toward insubordination in 1917 during war was held to be a clear and present danger of bringing about the evil of military insubordination.

In several later cases involving convictions under the Criminal Espionage Act, the nub of the evidence the Court held sufficient to meet "clear and present danger" test enunciated in *Schenck* was as follows: *Frohwerk* v. *United States,* 249 U.S. 204 (1919)—publication of twelve newspaper articles attacking the war; *Debs* v. *United States,* 249 U.S. 211 (1919)—one speech attacking United States' participation in the war; *Abrams* v. *United States,* 250 U.S. 616 (1920)—circulation of copies of two different socialist circulars attacking the war; *Schaefer* v. *United States,* 251 U.S. 466 (1920)—publication of a German-language newspaper with allegedly false articles, critical of capitalism and the war; *Pierce* v. *United States,* 252 U.S. 239 (1920) —circulation of copies of a four-page pamphlet written by a clergyman, attacking the purpose of the war and United States' participation therein. Justice Holmes wrote the opinions for a unanimous Court in *Schenck, Frohwerk* and *Debs.* He and Justice Brandeis dissented in *Abrams, Schaefer* and *Pierce.* The basis of these dissents was that, because of the protection which the First Amendment gives to speech, the evidence in each case was insufficient to show that the defendants had created the requisite danger under *Schenck.* But these dissents did not mark a change of principle. The dissenters doubted only the probable effectiveness of the puny efforts toward subversion. In *Abrams,* they wrote, "I do not

doubt for a moment that by the same reasoning that would justify punishing persuasion to murder, the United States constitutionally may punish speech that produces or is intended to produce a clear and imminent danger that it will bring about forthwith certain substantive evils that the United States constitutionally may seek to prevent." 250 U.S. at 627. And in *Schaefer* the test was said to be "one of degree," 251 U.S. at 482, although it is not clear whether "degree" refers to clear and present danger or evil. Perhaps both were meant.

The rule we deduce from these cases is that where an offense is specified by a statute in nonspeech or nonpress terms, a conviction relying upon speech or press as evidence of violation may be sustained only when the speech or publication created a "clear and present danger" of attempting or accomplishing the prohibited crime, e.g., interference with enlistment. The dissents, we repeat, in emphasizing the value of speech, were addressed to the argument of the sufficiency of the evidence.

The next important case before the Court in which free speech was the crux of the conflict was *Gitlow* v. *New York* . . . (1925). There New York had made it a crime to "advocate . . . the necessity or propriety of overthrowing . . . the government by force. . . ." The evidence of violation of the statute was that the defendant had published a Manifesto attacking the Government and capitalism. The convictions were sustained, Justices Holmes and Brandeis dissenting. The majority refused to apply the "clear and present danger" test to the specific utterance. Its reasoning was as follows: The "clear and present danger" test was applied to the utterance itself in Schenck because the question was merely one of sufficiency of evidence under an admittedly constitutional statute. Gitlow, however, presented a different question. There a legislature had found that a certain kind of speech was, itself, harmful and unlawful. The constitutionality of such a state statute had to be adjudged by this Court just as it determined the constitutionality of any state statute, namely, whether the statute was "reasonable." Since it was entirely reasonable for a state to attempt to protect itself from violent overthrow the statute was perforce reasonable. The only question remaining in the case became whether there was evidence to support the conviction, a question which gave the majority no difficulty. Justices Holmes and Brandeis refused to accept this approach, but insisted that wherever speech was the evidence of the violation, it was necessary to show that the speech created the "clear and present danger" of the substantive evil which the legislature had the right to prevent. Justices Holmes and Brandeis, then, made no distinction between a federal statute which made certain acts unlawful, the evidence to support the conviction being speech, and a statute which made speech itself the crime. This approach was emphasized in *Whitney* v. *California*, 274 U.S. 357 (1927), where the Court was confronted with a conviction under the California Criminal Syndicalist statute. The Court sustained the conviction, Justices Brandeis and Holmes concurring in the result. In their concurrence they repeated that even though the legislature had designated certain speech as criminal, this could not prevent the defendant from showing that there was no danger that the substantive evil would be brought about.

Although no case subsequent to *Whitney* and *Gitlow* has expressly overruled the majority opinions in those cases, there is little doubt that subsequent opinions have inclined toward the Holmes-Brandeis rationale. And in *American Communications Assn.* v. *Douds, supra,* we were called upon to decide the validity of § 9 (h) of the Labor-Management Relations Act of 1947. That section required officials of unions which desired to avail themselves of the facilities of the National Labor Relations Board to take oaths that they did not belong to the Communist Party and that they did not believe in the overthrow of the Government by force and violence. We pointed out that Congress did not intend to punish belief, but rather intended to regulate the conduct of union affairs. We therefore held that any indirect sanction on speech which might arise from the oath requirement did not present a proper case for the "clear and present danger" test, for the regulation was aimed at conduct rather than speech. In discussing the proper measure of evaluation of this kind of legislation, we suggested that the Holmes-Brandeis philosophy insisted that where there was a direct restriction upon speech, a "clear and present danger" that the substantive evil would be caused was necessary before the statute in question could be constitutionally applied. And we stated, "[The First] Amendment requires that one be permitted to believe what he will. It requires that one be permitted to advocate what he will unless there is a clear and present danger that a substantial public evil will result therefrom." 339 U.S. at 412. But we further suggested that neither Justice Holmes nor Justice Brandeis ever envisioned that a shorthand phrase should be crystallized into a rigid rule to be applied inflexibly without regard to the circumstances of each case. Speech is not an absolute, above and beyond control by the legislature when its judgment, subject to review here, is that certain kinds of speech are so undesirable as to warrant criminal sanction. Nothing is more certain in modern society than the principle that there are no absolutes, that a name, a phrase, a standard has meaning only when associated with the considerations which gave birth to the nomenclature. See *American Communications Assn.* v. *Douds,* 339 U.S. at 397. To those who would paralyze our Government in the face of impending threat by encasing it in a semantic straitjacket we must reply that all concepts are relative.

In this case we are squarely presented with the application of the "clear and present danger" test, and must decide what that phrase imports. We first note that many of the cases in which this Court has reversed convictions by use of this or similar tests have been based on the fact that the interest which the State was attempting to protect was itself too insubstantial to warrant restriction of speech. In this category we may put such cases as *Schneider* v. *State,* 308 U.S. 147 (1939); *Cantwell* v. *Connecticut,* 310 U.S. 296 (1940); *Martin* v. *Struthers,* 319 U.S. 141 (1943); *West Virginia State Board of Education* v. *Barnette,* 319 U.S. 624 (1943); *Thomas* v. *Collins,* 323 U.S. 516 (1945); *Marsh* v. *Alabama,* 326 U.S. 501 (1946); but cf. *Prince* v. *Massachusetts,* 321 U.S. 158 (1944); *Cox* v. *New Hampshire,* 312 U.S. 569 (1941). Overthrow of the Government by force and violence is certainly a substantial enough interest for the Government to limit speech. Indeed, this is the ultimate value of any society, for if a society cannot protect its very structure from armed internal attack, it must follow that no subordinate value can be protected. If, then, this interest may be protected, the literal problem which is presented is what has been meant by the use of the phrase "clear and present danger" of the utterances bringing about the evil within the power of Congress to punish.

Obviously, the words cannot mean that before the Government may act, it must wait until the Putsch is about to be executed, the plans have been laid and the signal is awaited. If Government is aware that a group aiming at its overthrow is attempting to indoctrinate its members and to commit them to a course whereby they will strike when the leaders feel the circumstances permit, action by the Government is required. The argument that there is no need for Government to concern itself, for Government is strong, it possesses ample powers to put down a rebellion, it may defeat the revolution with ease needs no answer. For that is not the question. Certainly an attempt to overthrow the Government by force, even though doomed from the outset because of inadequate numbers or power of the revolutionists, is a sufficient evil for Congress to prevent. The damage which such attempts create both physically and politically to a nation makes it impossible to measure the validity

in terms of the probability of success, or the immediacy of a successful attempt. In the instant case the trial judge charged the jury that they could not convict unless they found that petitioners intended to overthrow the Government "as speedily as circumstances would permit." This does not mean, and could not properly mean, that they would not strike until there was certainty of success. What was meant was that the revolutionists would strike when they thought the time was ripe. We must therefore reject the contention that success or probability of success is the criterion.

The situation with which Justices Holmes and Brandeis were concerned in *Gitlow* was a comparatively isolated event, bearing little relation in their minds to any substantial threat to the safety of the community. Such also is true of cases like *Fiske* v. *Kansas,* 274 U.S. 380 . . . (1927), and *De Jonge* v. *Oregon,* 299, U.S. 353 . . . (1937); but cf. *Lazar* v. *Pennsylvania,* 286 U.S. 532 . . . (1932). They were not confronted with any situation comparable to the instant one—the development of an apparatus designed and dedicated to the overthrow of the Government, in the context of world crisis after crisis.

Chief Judge Learned Hand, writing for the majority below, interpreted the phrase as follows: "In each case [courts] must ask whether the gravity of the 'evil,' discounted by its improbability, justifies such invasion of free speech as is necessary to avoid the danger." 183 F2d at 212. We adopt this statement of the rule. As articulated by Chief Judge Hand, it is as succinct and inclusive as any other we might devise at this time. It takes into consideration those factors which we deem relevant, and relates their significances. More we cannot expect from words.

Likewise, we are in accord with the court below, which affirmed the trial court's finding that the requisite danger existed. The mere fact that from the period 1945 to 1948 petitioners' activities did not result in an attempt to overthrow the Government by force and violence is of course no answer to the fact that there was a group that was ready to make the attempt. The formation by petitioners of such a highly organized conspiracy, with rigidly disciplined members subject to call when the leaders, these petitioners, felt that the time had come for action, coupled with the inflammable nature of world conditions, similar uprisings in other countries, and the touch-and-go nature of our relations with countries with whom petitioners were in the very least ideologically attuned, convince us that their convictions were justified on this score. And this analysis disposes of the contention that a conspiracy to advocate, as distinguished from the advocacy itself, cannot be constitutionally restrained, because it comprises only the preparation. It is the existence of the conspiracy which creates the danger. . . . If the ingredients of the reaction are present, we cannot bind the Government to wait until the catalyst is added.

Although we have concluded that the finding that there was a sufficient danger to warrant the application of the statute was justified on the merits, there remains the problem of whether the trial judge's treatment of the issue was correct. He charged the jury, in relevant part, as follows:

"In further construction and interpretation of the statute I charge you that it is not the abstract doctrine of overthrowing or destroying organized government by unlawful means which is denounced by this law, but the teaching and advocacy of action for the accomplishment of that purpose, by language reasonably and ordinarily calculated to incite persons to such action. . . .

"If you are satisfied that the evidence establishes beyond a reasonable doubt that the defendants, or any of them, are guilty of a violation of the statute, as I have interpreted it to you, I find as a matter of law that there is sufficient danger of a substantive evil that the Congress has a right to prevent to justify the application of the statute under the First Amendment of the Constitution.

"This is matter of law about which you

have no concern. It is a finding on a matter of law which I deem essential to support my ruling that the case should be submitted to you to pass upon the guilt or innocence of the defendants. . . ."

It is thus clear that he reserved the question of the existence of the danger for his own determination, and the question becomes whether the issue is of such a nature that it should have been submitted to the jury. . . .

. . . The argument that the action of the trial court is erroneous, in declaring as a matter of law that such violation shows sufficient danger to justify the punishment despite the First Amendment, rests on the theory that a jury must decide a question of the application of the First Amendment. We do not agree.

When facts are found that establish the violation of a statute the protection against conviction afforded by the First Amendment is a matter of law. The doctrine that there must be a clear and present danger of a substantive evil that Congress has a right to prevent is a judicial rule to be applied as a matter of law by the courts. The guilt is established by proof of facts. Whether the First Amendment protects the activity which constitutes the violation of the statute must depend upon a judicial determination of the scope of the First Amendment applied to the circumstances of the case. . . .

Affirmed.

Mr. Justice Clark took no part in the consideration or decision of this case.

Mr. Justice Frankfurter, concurring in affirmance of the judgment: . . .

The language of the First Amendment is to be read not as barren words found in a dictionary but as symbols of historic experience illumined by the pressuppositions of those who employed them. Not what words did Madison and Hamilton use, but what was it in their minds which they conveyed? Free speech is subject to prohibition of those abuses of expression which a civilized society may forbid. As in the case of every other provision of the

Constitution that is not crystallized by the nature of its technical concepts, the fact that the First Amendment is not self-defining and self-enforcing neither impairs its usefulness nor compels its paralysis as a living instrument. . . .

. . . The demands of free speech in a democratic society as well as the interest in national security are better served by candid and informed weighing of the competing interests, within the confines of the judicial process, than by announcing dogmas too inflexible for the non-Euclidian problems to be solved.

But how are competing interests to be assessed? Since they are not subject to quantitative ascertainment, the issue necessarily resolves itself into asking, who is to make the adjustment?—who is to balance the relevant factors and ascertain which interest is in the circumstances to prevail? Full responsibility for the choice cannot be given to the courts. Courts are not representative bodies. They are not designed to be a good reflex of a democratic society. Their judgment is best informed, and therefore most dependable, within narrow limits. Their essential quality is detachment, founded on independence. History teaches that the independence of the judiciary is jeopardized when courts become embroiled in the passions of the day and assume primary responsibility in choosing between competing political, economic and social pressures.

Primary responsibility for adjusting the interests which compete in the situation before us of necessity belongs to the Congress. The nature of the power to be exercised by this Court has been delineated in decisions not charged with the emotional appeal of situations such as that now before us. . . .

A survey of the relevant decisions indicates that the results which we have reached are on the whole those that would ensue from careful weighing of conflicting interests. The complex issues presented by regulation of speech in public places, by picketing, and by legislation prohibiting advocacy of crime have been resolved by scrutiny of many factors besides the imminence and gravity of the evil threatened. The matter has been well summarized by a reflective student of the Court's work. "The truth is that the clear-and-present-danger test is an oversimplified judgment unless it takes account also of a number of other factors: the relative seriousness of the danger in comparison with the value of the occasion for speech or political activity; the availability of more moderate controls than those which the state has imposed; and perhaps the specific intent with which the speech or activity is launched. No matter how rapidly we utter the phrase 'clear and present danger,' or how closely we hyphenate the words, they are not a substitute for the weighing of values. They tend to convey a delusion of certitude when what is most certain is the complexity of the strands in the web of freedoms which the judge must disentangle." Freund, *On Understanding the Supreme Court*, 27–28. . . .

Bearing in mind that Mr. Justice Holmes regarded questions under the First Amendment as questions of "proximity and degree," *Schenk* v. *United States*, 249 U.S. at 52, it would be a distortion, indeed a mockery, of his reasoning to compare the "puny anonymities," 250 U.S. at 629, to which he was addressing himself in the Abrams case in 1919 or the publication that was "futile and too remote from possible consequences," 268 U.S. at 673, in the Gitlow case in 1925 with the setting of events in this case of 1950. . . .

Throughout our decisions there has recurred a distinction between the statement of an idea which may prompt its hearers to take unlawful action, and advocacy that such action be taken. . . .

It is true that there is no divining rod by which we may locate "advocacy." Exposition of ideas readily merges into advocacy. The same Justice who gave currency to application of the incitement doctrine in this field dissented four times from what he thought was its misapplication. As he said in the Gitlow dissent, "Every idea is an incitement." 268 U.S. at 673. . . . Even though advocacy of overthrow deserves little protection, we should hesitate to prohibit it if we thereby inhibit the interchange of rational ideas so essential to representative government and free society.

But there is underlying validity in the distinction between advocacy and the interchange of ideas, and we do not discard a useful tool because it may be misused. That such a distinction could be used unreasonably by those in power against hostile or unorthodox views does not negate the fact that it may be used reasonably against an organization wielding the power of the centrally controlled international Communist movement. The object of the conspiracy before us is clear enough that the chance of error in saying that the defendants conspired to advocate rather than to express ideas is slight. Mr. Justice Douglas quite properly points out that the conspiracy before us is not a conspiracy to overthrow the Government. But it would be equally wrong to treat it as a seminar in political theory. . . .

It is not for us to decide how we would adjust the clash of interests which this case presents were the primary responsibility for reconciling it ours. Congress has determined that the danger created by advocacy of overthrow justifies the ensuing restriction on freedom of speech. The determination was made after due deliberation, and the seriousness of the congressional purpose is attested by the volume of legislation passed to effectuate the same ends.

Can we then say that the judgment Congress exercised was denied it by the Constitution? Can we establish a constitutional doctrine which forbids the elected representatives of the people to make this choice? Can we hold that the First Amendment deprives Congress of what it deemed necessary for the Government's protection?

To make validity of legislation depends on judicial reading of events still in the womb of time—a forecast, that is, of the outcome of forces at best appreciated only with knowledge of the topmost secrets of nations—is to charge the judiciary with duties beyond its equipment. We do not

expect courts to pronounce historic verdicts on bygone events. Even historians have conflicting views to this day on the origin and conduct of the French Revolution. It is as absurd to be confident that we can measure the present clash of forces and their outcome as to ask us to read history still enveloped in clouds of controversy. . . .

MR. JUSTICE JACKSON, concurring. . . .

If we must decide that this Act and its application are constitutional only if we are convinced that petitioner's conduct creates a "clear and present danger" of violent overthrow, we must appraise imponderables, including international and national phenomena which baffle the best informed foreign offices and our most experienced politicians. We would have to foresee and predict the effectiveness of Communist propaganda, opportunities for infiltration, whether, and when, a time will come that they consider propitious for action, and whether and how fast our existing government will deteriorate. And we would have to speculate as to whether an approaching Communist coup would not be anticipated by a nationalistic fascist movement. No doctrine can be sound whose application requires us to make a prophecy of that sort in the guise of a legal decision. The judicial process simply is not adequate to a trial of such far-flung issues. The answers given would reflect our own political predilections and nothing more.

The authors of the clear and present danger test never applied it to a case like this, nor would I. If applied as it is proposed here, it means that the Communist plotting is protected during its period of incubation; its preliminary stages of organization and preparation are immune from the law; the Government can move only after imminent action is manifest, when it would, of course, be too late. . . .

What really is under review here is a conviction of conspiracy, after a trial for conspiracy, on an indictment charging conspiracy, brought under a statute outlawing conspiracy. With due respect to my colleagues, they seem to me to discuss anything under the sun except the law of conspiracy. One of the dissenting opinions even appears to chide me for "invoking the law of conspiracy." As that is the case before us, it may be more amazing that its reversal can be proposed without even considering the law of conspiracy. . . .

I do not suggest that Congress could punish conspiracy to advocate something, the doing of which it may not punish. Advocacy or exposition of the doctrine of communal property ownership, or any political philosophy unassociated with advocacy of its imposition by force or seizure of government by unlawful means could not be reached through conspiracy prosecution. But it is not forbidden to put down force or violence, it is not forbidden to punish its teaching or advocacy, and the end being punishable, there is no doubt of the power to punish conspiracy for the purpose. . . .

The law of conspiracy has been the chief means at the Government's disposal to deal with the growing problems created by such organizations. I happen to think it is an awkward and inept remedy, but I find no constitutional authority for taking this weapon from the Government. There is no constitutional right to "gang up" on the Government.

While I think there was power in Congress to enact this statute and that, as applied in this case, it cannot be held unconstitutional, I add that I have little faith in the long-range effectiveness of this conviction to stop the rise of the Communist movement. Communism will not go to jail with these Communists. No decision by this Court can forestall revolution whenever the existing government fails to command the respect and loyalty of the people and sufficient distress and discontent is allowed to grow up among the masses. Many failures by fallen govenments attest that no government can long prevent revolution by outlawry. Corruption, ineptitude, inflation, oppressive taxation, militarization, injustice, and loss of leadership capable of intellectual initiative in domestic

or foreign affairs are allies on which the Communists count to bring opportunity knocking to their door. Sometimes I think they may be mistaken. But the Communists are not building just for today—the rest of us might profit by their example.

Mr. Justice Black, dissenting. . . .

At the outset I want to emphasize what the crime involved in this case is, and what it is not. These petitioners were not charged with an attempt to overthrow the Government. They were not charged with overt acts of any kind designed to overthrow the Government. They were not even charged with saying anything or writing anything designed to overthrow the Government. The charge was that they agreed to assemble and to talk and publish certain ideas at a later date: The indictment is that they conspired to organize the Communist Party and to use speech or newspapers and other publications in the future to teach and advocate the forcible overthrow of the Government. No matter how it is worded, this is a virulent form of prior censorship of speech and press, which I believe the First Amendment forbids. I would hold § 3 of the Smith Act authorizing this prior restraint unconstitutional on its face and as applied. . . .

So long as this court exercises the power of judicial review of legislation, I cannot agree that the First Amendment permits us to sustain laws suppressing freedom of speech and press on the basis of Congress' or our own notions of mere "reasonableness." Such a doctrine waters down the First Amendment so that it amounts to little more than an admonition to Congress. The Amendment as so construed is not likely to protect any but those "safe" or orthodox views which rarely need its protection. I must also express my objection to the holding because as Mr. Justice Douglas' dissent shows, it sanctions the determination of a crucial issue of fact by the judge rather than by the jury. . . .

Public opinion being what it now is, few will protest the conviction of these Communist petitioners. There is hope, however, that in calmer times, when present pressures, passions and fears subside, this or some later Court will restore the First Amendment liberties to the high preferred place where they belong in a free society.

MR. JUSTICE DOUGLAS, dissenting:

If this were a case where those who claimed protection under the First Amendment were teaching the techniques of sabotage, the assassination of the President, the filching of documents from public files, the planting of bombs, the art of street warfare, and the like, I would have no doubts. The freedom to speak is not absolute; the teaching of methods of terror and other seditious conduct should be beyond the pale along with obscenity and immorality. This case was argued as if those were the facts. The argument imported much seditious conduct into the record. That is easy and it has popular appeal, for the activities of Communists in plotting and scheming against the free world are common knowledge. But the fact is that no such evidence was introduced at the trial. There is a statute which makes a seditious conspiracy unlawful. Petitioners, however, were not charged with a "conspiracy to overthrow" the Government. They were charged with a conspiracy to form a party and groups and assemblies of people who teach and advocate the overthrow of our Government by force or violence and with a conspiracy to advocate and teach its overthrow by force and violence. It may well be that indoctrination in the techniques of terror to destroy the Government would be indictable under either statute. But the teaching which is condemned here is of a different character. . . .

The vice of treating speech as the equivalent of overt acts of a treasonable or seditious character is emphasized by a concurring opinion, which by invoking the law of conspiracy makes speech do service for deeds which are dangerous to society. The doctrine of conspiracy has served divers and oppressive purposes and in its broad reach can be made to do great evil. But never until today has anyone seriously thought that the ancient law of conspiracy could constitutionally be used to turn speech into seditious conduct. Yet that is precisely what is suggested. I repeat that we deal here with speech alone, not with speech *plus* acts of sabotage or unlawful conduct. Not a single seditious act is charged in the indictment. To make a lawful speech unlawful because two men conceive it is to raise the law of conspiracy to appalling proportions. That course is to make a radical break with the past and to violate one of the cardinal principles of our constitutional scheme. . . .

There comes a time when even speech loses its constitutional immunity. Speech innocuous one year may at another time fan such destructive flames that it must be halted in the interests of the safety of the Republic. That is the meaning of the clear and present danger test. When conditions are so critical that there will be no time to avoid the evil that the speech threatens, it is time to call a halt. Otherwise, free speech which is the strength of the Nation will be the cause of its destruction. . . .

I had assumed that the question of the clear and present danger, being so critical an issue in the case, would be a matter for submission to the jury. It was squarely held in *Pierce* v. *United States*, 252 U.S. 239, 244, to be a jury question. . . .

Yet, whether the question is one for the Court or the jury, there should be evidence of record on the issue. This record, however, contains no evidence whatsoever showing that the acts charged, viz., the teaching of the Soviet theory of revolution with the hope that it will be realized, have created any clear and present danger to the Nation. The Court, however, rules to the contrary. It says, "The formation by petitioners of such a highly organized conspiracy, with rigidly disciplined members subject to call when the leaders, these petitioners, felt that the time had come for action, coupled with the inflammable nature of world conditions, similar uprisings in other countries, and the touch-and-go nature of our relations with countries with whom petitioners were in the very least ideologically attuned, convince us that their convictions were justified on this score."

That ruling is in my view not responsive to the issue in the case. We might as well say that the speech of petitioners is outlawed because Soviet Russia and her Red Army are a threat to world peace. . . .

The First Amendment provides that "Congress shall make no law . . . abridging the freedom of speech." The Constitution provides no exception. This does not mean, however, that the Nation need hold its hand until it is in such weakened condition that there is no time to protect itself from incitement to revolution. Seditious conduct can always be punished. But the command of the First Amendment is so clear that we should not allow Congress to call a halt to free speech except in the extreme case of peril from the speech itself. The First Amendment makes confidence in the common sense of our people and in their maturity of judgment the great postulate of our democracy. Its philosophy is that violence is rarely, if ever, stopped by denying civil liberties to those advocating resort to force. The First Amendment reflects the philosophy of Jefferson "that it is time enough for the rightful purposes of civil government for its officers to interfere when principles break out into overt acts against peace and good order. . . ."

YATES v. UNITED STATES
354 U.S. 298 (1957)

> Fourteen alleged leaders of the Communist Party were found guilty under the Smith Act of conspiring (1) to teach and advocate the duty and necessity of overthrowing the Government by force and violence, and (2) to organize the Communist Party, a society of persons who so teach and advocate. On review the Supreme Court held that the term "organize" as used in the Smith Act referred to the creation of the party, not to the later carrying on of its activities. Accordingly the convictions on the second charge could not be upheld because prosecution was barred by a statute of limitations. Two crucial items under the advocacy charge are considered in the following excerpts from the opinions.

MR. JUSTICE HARLAN delivered the opinion of the Court. . . .

II
INSTRUCTIONS TO THE JURY

Petitioners contend that the instructions to the jury were fatally defective in that the trial court refused to charge that, in order to convict, the jury must find that the advocacy which the defendants conspired to promote was of a kind calculated to "incite" persons to action for the forcible overthrow of the Government. It is argued that advocacy of forcible overthrow as mere *abstract doctrine* is within the free speech protection of the First Amendment; that the Smith Act, consistently with that constitutional provision, must be taken as proscribing only the sort of advocacy which incites to illegal *action*; and that the trial court's charge, by permitting conviction for mere advocacy, unrelated to its tendency to produce forcible action, resulted in an unconstitutional application of the Smith Act. The Government, which at the trial also requested the court to charge in terms of "incitement," now takes the position, however, that the true constitutional dividing line is not between inciting and abstract advocacy of forcible overthrow, but rather between advocacy as such, irrespective of its inciting qualities, and the mere discussion or exposition of violent overthrow as an abstract theory.

We print in the margin the pertinent parts of the trial court's instructions. [here omitted] After telling the jury that it could not convict the defendants for holding or expressing mere opinions, beliefs, or predictions relating to violent overthrow, the trial court defined the content of the proscribed advocacy or teaching in the following terms, which are crucial here:

"Any advocacy or teaching which does not include the urging of force and violence as the means of overthrowing and destroying the Government of the United States is not within the issue of the indictment here and can constitute no basis for any finding against the defendants.

"The kind of advocacy and teaching which is charged and upon which your verdict must be reached is not merely a desirability but a necessity that the Government of the United States be overthrown and destroyed by force and violence and not merely a propriety but a duty to overthrow and destroy the Government of the United States by force and violence."

There can be no doubt from the record that in so instructing the jury the court regarded as immaterial, and intended to withdraw from the jury's consideration, any issue as to the character of the advocacy in terms of its capacity to stir listeners to forcible action. Both the petitioners and the Government submitted proposed instructions which would have required the jury to find that the proscribed advocacy was not of a mere abstract doctrine of forcible overthrow, but of action to that end, by the use of language reasonably and ordinarily calculated to incite persons to such action. The trial court rejected these proposed instructions on the ground that any necessity for giving them which may have existed at the time the Dennis case was tried was removed by this Court's subsequent decision in that case. The court made it clear in colloquy with counsel that in its view the illegal advocacy was made out simply by showing that what was said dealt with forcible overthrow and that it was uttered with a specific intent to

accomplish that purpose, insisting that all such advocacy was punishable "whether in language of incitement or not." The Court of Appeals affirmed on a different theory, as we shall see later on.

We are thus faced with the question whether the Smith Act prohibits advocacy and teaching of forcible overthrow as an abstract principle, divorced from any effort to instigate action to that end, so long as such advocacy or teaching is engaged in with evil intent. We hold that it does not.

The distinction between advocacy of abstract doctrine and advocacy directed at promoting unlawful action is one that has been consistently recognized in the opinions of this Court, beginning with *Fox* v. *State of Washington*, 236 U.S. 273; *Schenck* v. *United States*, 249 U.S. 47. This distinction was heavily underscored in *Gitlow* v. *People of State of New York*, 268 U.S. 652, in which the statute involved was nearly identical with the one now before us, and where the Court, despite the narrow view there taken of the First Amendment, said:

"The statute does not penalize the utterance or publication of abstract 'doctrine' or academic discussion having no quality of incitement to any concrete action. . . . It is not the abstract 'doctrine' of overthrowing organized government by unlawful means which is denounced by the statute, but the advocacy of action for the accomplishment of that purpose. . . . This [Manifesto] . . . is [in] the language of direct incitement. . . . That the jury were warranted in finding that the Manifesto advocated not merely the abstract doctrine of overthrowing organized government by force, violence and unlawful means, but action to that end, is clear. . . . That utterances inciting to the overthrow of organized government by unlawful means, present a sufficient danger of substantive evil to bring their punishment within the range of legislative discretion, is clear." Id., 268 U.S. at pages 664–669.

We need not, however, decide the issue before us in terms of constitutional compulsion, for our first duty is to construe this statute. In doing so we should not assume that Congress chose to disregard a constitutional danger zone so clearly marked, or that it used the words "advocate" and "teach" in their ordinary dictionary meanings when they had already been construed as terms of art carrying a special and limited connotation. See *Willis* v. *Eastern Trust & Banking Co., supra; Joines* v. *Patterson, supra; James* v. *Appel,* 192 U.S. 129, 135. The Gitlow case and the New York Criminal Anarchy Act there involved, which furnished the prototype for the Smith Act, were both known and adverted to by Congress in the course of the legislative proceedings. Cf. *Carolene Products Co.* v. *United States, supra.* The legislative history of the Smith Act and related bills shows beyond all question that Congress was aware of the distinction between the advocacy or teaching of abstract doctrine and the advocacy or teaching of action, and that it did not intend to disregard it. The statute was aimed at the advocacy and teaching of concrete action for the forcible overthrow of the Government, and not of principles divorced from action.

The Government's reliance on this Court's decision in Dennis is misplaced. The jury instructions which were refused here were given there, and were referred to by this Court as requiring "the jury to find the facts *essential* to establish the substantive crime." 341 U.S. at page 512 (emphasis added). It is true that at one point in the late Chief Justice's opinion it is stated that the Smith Act "is directed at advocacy, not discussion," id., 341 U.S. at page 502, but it is clear that the reference was to advocacy of action, not ideas, for in the very next sentence the opinion emphasizes that the jury was properly instructed that there could be no conviction for "advocacy in the realm of ideas." The two concurring opinions in that case likewise emphasize the distinction with which we are concerned. Id., 341 U.S. at pages 518, 534, 536, 545, 546, 547, 571, 572.

In failing to distinguish between advocacy of forcible overthrow as an abstract doctrine and advocacy of action to that end, the District Court appears to have been led astray by the holding in Dennis that advocacy of violent action to be taken at some future time was enough. It seems to have considered that, since "inciting" speech is usually thought of as calculated to induce immediate action, and since Dennis held advocacy of action for future overthrow sufficient, this meant that advocacy, irrespective of its tendency to generate action, is punishable, provided only that it is uttered with a specific intent to accomplish overthrow. In other words, the District Court apparently thought that Dennis obliterated the traditional dividing line between advocacy of abstract doctrine and advocacy of action.

This misconceives the situation confronting the Court in Dennis and what was held there. Although the jury's verdict, interpreted in light of the trial court's instructions, did not justify the conclusion that the defendants' advocacy was directed at, or created any danger of, immediate overthrow, it did establish that the advocacy was aimed at building up a seditious group and maintaining it in readiness for action at a propitious time. In such circumstances, said Chief Justice Vinson, the Government need not hold its hand "until the putsch is about to be executed, the plans have been laid and the signal is awaited. If Government is aware that a group aiming at its overthrow is attempting to indoctrinate its members and to commit them to a course whereby they will strike when the leaders feel the circumstances permit, action by the Government is required." 341 U.S. at page 509. The essence of the Dennis holding was that indoctrination of a group in preparation for future violent action, as well as exhortation to immediate action, by advocacy found to be directed to "action for the accomplishment" of forcible overthrow, to violence as "a rule or principle of action," and employing "language of incitement," id., 341 U.S. at pages 511–512, is not constitutionally protected when the group is of sufficient size and cohesiveness, is sufficiently oriented towards action, and other circumstances are such as reasonably to justify apprehension that action will occur. This is quite a different thing from the view of the District Court here that mere doctrinal justification of forcible overthrow, if engaged in with the intent to accomplish overthrow, is punishable *per se* under the Smith Act. That sort of advocacy, even though uttered with the hope that it may ultimately lead to violent revolution, is too remote from concrete action to be regarded as the kind of indoctrination preparatory to action which was condemned in Dennis. As one of the concurring opinions in Dennis put it: "Throughout our decisions there has recurred a distinction between the statement of an idea which may prompt its hearers to take unlawful action, and advocacy that such action be taken." Id., 341 U.S. at page 545. There is nothing in Dennis which makes that historic distinction obsolete.

[The Court reviewed the record and concluded that some of the defendants should be retried but that others should be acquitted.]

Since there must be a new trial, we have not found it necessary to deal with the contentions of the petitioners as to the fairness of the trial already held. The judgment of the Court of Appeals is reversed, and the case remanded to the District Court for further proceedings consistent with this opinion.

It is so ordered.

Judgment of Court of Appeals reversed and case remanded to District Court with instructions.

[MR. JUSTICE BURTON concurred in the result. JUSTICES BRENNAN and WHITTAKER did not participate in the decision.]

MR. JUSTICE BLACK, with whom MR. JUSTICE DOUGLAS joins, concurring in part and dissenting in part.

I

I would reverse every one of these convictions and direct that all the defendants be acquitted. In my judgment the statutory provisions on which these prosecutions are based abridge freedom of speech, press and assembly in violation of the First Amendment to the United States Constitution. See my dissent and that of Mr. Justice Douglas in *Dennis* v. *United States*, 341 U.S. 494, 579, 581, 71 S. Ct. 857, 902, 903, 95 L. Ed. 1137. Also see my opinion in *American Communications Ass'n, C. I. O.* v. *Douds*, 339 U.S. 382, 445, 70 S. Ct. 674, 707, 94 L. Ed. 925.

The kind of trials conducted here are wholly dissimilar to normal criminal trials. Ordinarily these "Smith Act" trials are prolonged affairs lasting for months. In part this is attributable to the routine introduction in evidence of massive collections of books, tracts, pamphlets, newspapers, and manifestoes discussing Communism, Socialism, Capitalism, Feudalism and governmental institutions in general, which, it is not too much to say, are turgid, diffuse, abstruse, and just plain dull. Of course, no juror can or is expected to plow his way through this jungle of verbiage. The testimony of witnesses is comparatively insignificant. Guilt or innocence may turn on what Marx or Engels or someone else wrote or advocated as much as a hundred or more years ago. Elaborate, refined distinctions are drawn between "Communism," "Marxism," "Leninism," "Trotskyism," and "Stalinism." When the propriety of obnoxious or unorthodox views about government is in reality made the crucial issue, as it must be in cases of this kind, prejudice makes conviction inevitable except in the rarest circumstances.

II

Since the Court proceeds on the assumption that the statutory provisions involved are valid, however, I feel free to express my views about the issues it considers.

First.—I agree with Part I of the Court's opinion that deals with the statutory term, "organize," and holds that the organizing charge in the indictment was barred by the three-year statute of limitations.

Second.—I also agree with the Court insofar as it holds that the trial judge erred in instructing that persons could be punished under the Smith Act for teaching and advocating forceful overthrow as an abstract principle. But on the other hand,

I cannot agree that the instruction which the Court indicates it might approve is constitutionally permissible. The Court says that persons can be punished for advocating action to overthrow the Government by force and violence, where those to whom the advocacy is addressed are urged "to *do* something, now or in the future, rather than merely to *believe* in something." Under the Court's approach, defendants could still be convicted simply for agreeing to talk as distinguished from agreeing to act. I believe that the First Amendment forbids Congress to punish people for talking about public affairs, whether or not such discussion incites to action, legal or illegal. See Meiklejohn, *Free Speech and Its Relation to Self-Government.* Cf. Chafee, Book Review, 62 *Harv. L. Rev.* 891. As the Virginia Assembly said in 1785, in its "Statute for Religious Liberty," written by Thomas Jefferson, "it is time enough for the rightful purposes of civil government, for its officers to interfere when principles break out into overt acts against peace and good order. . . ."

Mr. Justice Clark, dissenting. . . .

The conspiracy charged here is the same as in Dennis, except that here it is geared to California conditions, and brought, for the period 1948 to 1951, under the general conspiracy statute, 18 U.S.C. § 371, 18 U.S.C.A. § 371, rather than the old conspiracy section of the Smith Act. The indictment charges petitioners with a conspiracy to violate two sections of the Smith Act, as recodified in 18 U.S.C. § 2385, 18 U.S.C.A. § 2385, by knowingly and wilfully (1) teaching and advocating the violent overthrow of the Government of the United States, and (2) organizing in California through the creation of groups, cells, schools, assemblies of persons, and the like, the Communist Party, a society which teaches or advocates violent overthrow of the Government.

The conspiracy includes the same group of defendants as in the Dennis case though petitioners here occupied a lower echelon in the party hierarchy. They, nevertheless, served in the same army and were engaged in the same mission. The convictions here were based upon evidence closely paralleling that adduced in Dennis and in *United States* v. *Flynn,* 2 Cir., 1954, 216 F.2d 354, both of which resulted in convictions. This Court laid down in Dennis the principles governing such prosecutions and they were closely adhered to here, although the nature of the two cases did not permit identical handling.

I would affirm the convictions. However, the Court has freed five of the convicted petitioners and ordered new trials for the remaining nine. As to the five, it says that the evidence is "clearly insufficient." I agree with the Court of Appeals, the District Court, and the jury that the evidence showed guilt beyond a reasonable doubt. It paralleled that in Dennis and Flynn and was equally as strong. In any event, this Court should not acquit anyone here. In its long history I find no case in which an acquittal has been ordered by this Court solely on the *facts.* It is somewhat late to start in now usurping the function of the jury, especially where new trials are to be held covering the same charges. It may be —although after today's opinion it is somewhat doubtful—that under the new theories announced by the Court for Smith Act prosecutions sufficient evidence might be available on remand. To say the least, the Government should have an opportunity to present its evidence under these changed conditions.

I cannot agree that half of the indictment against the remaining nine petitioners should be quashed as barred by the statute of limitations. I agree with my Brother Burton that the Court has incorrectly interpreted the term "organize" as used in the Smith Act. The Court concludes that the plain words of the Act, "Whoever organizes or *helps* or *attempts* to organize any society, group, or assembly of persons" (emphasis added) embodies only those "acts entering into the creation of a new organization." As applied to the Communist Party, the Court holds that it refers only to the reconstitution of the Party in 1945 and a part of the prosecution here is, therefore, barred by the three-year statute of limitations. This construction frustrates the purpose of the Congress for the Act was passed in 1940 primarily to curb the growing strength and activity of the Party. Under such an interpretation all prosecution would have been barred at the very time of the adoption of the Act for the Party was formed in 1919. If the Congress had been concerned with the initial establishment of the Party it would not have used the words "helps or attempts," nor the phrase "group, or assembly of persons." It was concerned with the new Communist fronts, cells, schools, and other groups, as well as assemblies of persons, which were being created nearly every day under the aegis of the Party to carry on its purposes. This is what the indictment here charges and the proof shows beyond doubt was in fact done. The decision today prevents for all time any prosecution of Party members under this subparagraph of the Act.

While the holding of the Court requires a reversal of the case and a retrial, the Court very properly considers the instructions given by the trial judge. I do not agree with the conclusion of the Court regarding the instructions, but I am highly pleased to see that it disposes of this problem so that on the new trial instructions will be given that will at least meet the views of the Court. I have studied the section of the opinion concerning the instructions and frankly its "artillery of words" leaves me confused as to why the majority concludes that the charge as given was insufficient. I thought that Dennis merely held that a charge was sufficient where it requires a finding that "the Party advocates the theory that there is a duty and necessity to overthrow the Government by force and violence . . . not as a prophetic insight or as a bit of . . . speculation, but as a program for winning adherents and as a policy to be translated into action" as soon as the circumstances permit. 341 U.S.

at pages 546–547 (concurring opinion). I notice however that to the majority

"The essence of the Dennis holding was that indoctrination of a group in preparation for future violent action, as well as exhortation to immediate action, by advocacy found to be directed to 'action for the accomplishment' of forcible overthrow, to violence as 'a rule or principle of action,' and employing 'language of incitement,' id., 341 U.S. at pages 511–512, is not constitutionality protected when the group is of sufficient size and cohesiveness, is sufficiently oriented towards action, and other circumstances are such as reasonably to justify apprehension that action will occur."

I have read this statement over and over but do not seem to grasp its meaning for I see no resemblance between it and what the respected Chief Justice wrote in Dennis, nor did I find any such theory in the concurring opinions. As I see it, the trial judge charged in essence all that was required under the Dennis opinions, whether one takes the view of the Chief Justice or of those concurring in the judgment. Apparently what disturbs the Court now is that the trial judge here did not give the Dennis charge although both the prosecution and the defense asked that it be given. Since he refused to grant these requests I suppose the majority feels that there must be some difference between the two charges, else the one that was given in Dennis would have been followed here. While there may be some distinctions between the charges, as I view them they are without material difference. I find, as the majority intimates, that the distinctions are too "subtle and difficult to grasp."

However, in view of the fact that the case must be retried, regardless of the disposition made here on the charges, I see no reason to engage in what becomes nothing more than an exercise in semantics with the majority about this phase of the case. Certainly if I had been sitting at the trial I would have given the Dennis charge, not because I consider it any more correct, but simply because it had the stamp of approval of this Court. Perhaps this approach is too practical. But I am sure the trial judge realizes now that practicality often pays.

I should perhaps add that I am in agreement with the Court in its holding that petitioner Schneiderman can find no aid from the doctrine of collateral estoppel.

NOTE: On remand the lower court dismissed all charges at the request of the Department of Justice. That request was made because "The comprehensive review conducted by department attorneys . . . establishes that we cannot satisfy the evidentiary requirements laid down by the Supreme Court in its opinion reversing the convictions in this matter."

3. POLITICAL UTTERANCE—DEFAMATION

NEAR v. *MINNESOTA*
283 U.S. 697 (1931)

A state law authorized injunctions to prohibit the "nuisance" of "malicious, scandalous and defamatory" periodicals. Near was found guilty of the nuisance and enjoined from publishing improper material, but not from "operating a newspaper in harmony with the public welfare." The newspaper in question had been violently anti-Semitic, and had made serious charges against city law-enforcing officials. The Chief of Police, for example, was charged with gross neglect of duty, illicit relations with gangsters, and with participation in graft.

MR. CHIEF JUSTICE HUGHES delivered the opinion of the Court. . . .

Fourth. The statute not only operates to suppress the offending newspaper or periodical but to put the publisher under an effective censorship. When a newspaper or periodical is found to be "malicious, scandalous and defamatory," and is suppressed as such, resumption of publication is punishable as a contempt of court by fine or imprisonment.

Thus, where a newspaper or periodical has been suppressed because of the circulation of charges against public officers of official misconduct, it would seem to be clear that the renewal of the publication of such charges would constitute a contempt and that the judgment would lay a permanent restraint upon the publisher, to escape which he must satisfy the court as to the character of a new publication.

Whether he would be permitted again to publish matter deemed to be derogatory to the same or other public officers would depend upon the court's ruling. In the present instance the judgment restrained the defendants from "publishing, circulating, having in their possession, selling or giving away any publication whatsoever which is a malicious, scandalous or defamatory newspaper, as defined by law." The law gives no definition except that covered by the words "scandalous and defamatory," and publications charging official misconduct are of that class. While the court, answering the objection that the judgment was too broad, saw no reason for construing it as restraining the defendants "from operating a newspaper in harmony with the public welfare to which all must yield," and said that the defendants had not indicated "any desire to conduct their business in the usual and legitimate manner," the manifest inference is that, at least with respect to a new publication directed against official misconduct, the defendant would be held, under penalty of punishment for contempt as provided in the statute, to a manner of publication which the court considered to be "usual and legitimate" and consistent with the public welfare.

If we cut through mere details of procedure, the operation and effect of the statute in substance is that public authorities may bring the owner or publisher of a newspaper or periodical before a judge upon a charge of conducting a business of publishing scandalous and defamatory matter—in particular that the matter consists of charges against public officers of official dereliction—and unless the owner or publisher is able and disposed to bring competent evidence to satisfy the judge that the charges are true and are published with good motives and for justifiable ends, his newspaper or periodical is suppressed and further publication is made punishable as a contempt. This is of the essence of censorship.

The question is whether a statute authorizing such proceedings in restraint of publication is consistent with the conception of the liberty of the press as historically conceived and guaranteed. In determining the extent of the constitutional protection, it has been generally, if not universally, considered that it is the chief purpose of the guaranty to prevent previous restraints upon publication. The struggle in England, directed against the legislative power of the licenser, resulted in renunciation of the censorship of the press. The liberty deemed to be established was thus described by Blackstone: "The liberty of the press is indeed essential to the nature of a free state; but this consists in laying no *previous* restraints upon publications, and not in freedom from censure for criminal matter when published. Every freeman has an undoubted right to lay what sentiments he pleases before the public; to forbid this, is to destroy the freedom

of the press; but if he publishes what is improper, mischievous or illegal, he must take the consequence of his own temerity." 4 *Bl. Com.* 151, 152; see Story on the Constitution, §§ 1884, 1889. . . .

The criticism upon Blackstone's statement has not been because immunity from previous restraint upon publication has not been regarded as deserving of special emphasis, but chiefly because that immunity cannot be deemed to exhaust the conception of the liberty guaranteed by state and federal constitutions. The point of criticism has been "that the mere exemption from previous restraints cannot be all that is secured by the constitutional provisions"; and that "the liberty of the press might be rendered a mockery and a delusion, and the phrase itself a by-word, if, while every man was at liberty to publish what he pleased, the public authorities might nevertheless punish him for harmless publications." 2 Cooley, Const. Lim., 8th ed., p. 885. But it is recognized that punishment for the abuse of the liberty accorded to the press is essential to the protection of the public, and that the common-law rules that subject the libeler to responsibility for the public offense, as well as for the private injury, are not abolished by the protection extended in our constitutions. Id., pp. 883, 884. The law of criminal libel rests upon that secure foundation. There is also the conceded authority of courts to punish for contempt when publications directly tend to prevent the proper discharge of judicial functions. . . . In the present case, we have no occasion to inquire as to the permissible scope of subsequent punishment. For whatever wrong the appellant has committed or may commit, by his publications, the State appropriately affords both public and private redress by its libel laws. As has been noted, the statute in question does not deal with punishments; it provides for no punishment, except in case of contempt for violation of the court's order, but for suppression and injunction, that is, for restraint upon publication.

The objection has also been made that

the principle as to immunity from previous restraint is stated too broadly, if every such restraint is deemed to be prohibited. That is undoubtedly true; the protection even as to previous restraint is not absolutely unlimited. But the limitation has been recognized only in exceptional cases. . . .

The statute in question cannot be justified by reason of the fact that the publisher is permitted to show, before injunction issues, that the matter published is true and is published with good motives and for justifiable ends. If such a statute, authorizing suppression and injunction on such a basis, is constitutionally valid, it would be equally permissible for the legislature to provide that at any time the publisher of any newspaper could be brought before a court, or even an administrative officer (as the constitutional protection may not be regarded as resting on more procedural details) and required to produce proof of the truth of his publication, or of what he intended to publish, and of his motives, or stand enjoined. If this can be done, the legislature may provide machinery for determining in the complete exercise of its discretion what are justifiable ends and restrain publication accordingly. And it would be but a step to a complete system of censorship. The recognition of authority to impose previous restraint upon publication in order to protect the community against the circulation of charges of misconduct, and especially of official misconduct necessarily would carry with it the admission of the authority of the censor against which the constitutional barrier was erected. The preliminary freedom, by virtue of the very reason for its existence, does not depend, as this Court has said, on proof of truth. *Patterson* v. *Colorado, supra.*

Equally unavailing is the insistence that the statute is designed to prevent the circulation of scandal which tends to disturb the public peace and to provoke assaults and the commission of crime. Charges of reprehensible conduct, and in particular of official malfeasance, unquestionably create a public scandal, but the theory of the constitutional guaranty is that even a more serious public evil would be caused by authority to prevent publication. . . .

For these reasons we hold the statute, so far as it authorized the proceedings in this action under clause (b) of section one, to be an infringement of the liberty of the press guaranteed by the Fourteenth Amendment. . . .

Judgment reversed.

MR. JUSTICE BUTLER, dissenting.

The decision of the Court in this case declares Minnesota and every other State powerless to restrain by injunction the business of publishing and circulating among the people malicious, scandalous and defamatory periodicals that in due course of judicial procedure has been adjudged to be a public nuisance. It gives to freedom of the press a meaning and a scope not heretofore recognized and construes "liberty" in the due process clause of the Fourteenth Amendment to put upon the States a federal restriction that is without precedent. . . .

The record shows, and it is conceded, that defendants' regular business was the publication of malicious, scandalous and defamatory articles concerning the principal public officers, leading newspapers of the city, many private persons and the Jewish race. It also shows that it was their purpose at all hazards to continue to carry on the business. In every edition slanderous and defamatory matter predominates to the practical exclusion of all else. Many of the statements are so highly improbable as to compel a finding that they are false. The articles themselves show malice. . . .

Defendant concedes that the editions of the newspaper complained of are "defamatory *per se.*" And he says: "It has been asserted that the constitution was never intended to be a shield for malice, scandal, and defamation when untrue, or published with bad motives, or for unjustifiable ends. . . . The contrary is true; every person *does* have a constitutional right to publish malicious, scandalous, and defamatory matter though untrue, and with bad motives, and for unjustifiable ends, *in the first instance*, though he is subject to responsibility therefor *afterwards.*" The record, when the substance of the articles is regarded, requires that concession here. And this Court is required to pass on the validity of the state law on that basis. . . .

The Minnesota statute does not operate as a *previous* restraint on publication within the proper meaning of that phrase. It does not authorize administrative control in advance such as was formerly exercised by the licensers and censors but prescribes a remedy to be enforced by a suit in equity. In this case there was previous publication made in the course of the business of regularly producing malicious, scandalous and defamatory periodicals. The business and publications unquestionably constitute an abuse of the right of free press. The statute denounces the things done as a nuisance on the ground, as stated by the state supreme court, that they threaten morals, peace and good order. There is no question of the power of the State to denounce such trans-

gressions. The restraint authorized is only in respect of continuing to do what has been duly adjudged to constitute a nuisance. . . .

It is well known, as found by the state supreme court, that existing libel laws are inadequate effectively to suppress evils resulting from the kind of business and publications that are shown in this case. The doctrine that measures such as the one before us are invalid because they operate as previous restraints to infringe freedom of press exposes the peace and good order of every community and the business and private affairs of every individual to the constant and protracted false and malicious assaults of any insolvent publisher who may have purpose and sufficient capacity to contrive and put into effect a scheme or program for oppression, blackmail or extortion.

The judgment should be affirmed.

Mr. Justice Van Devanter, Mr. Justice McReynolds, and Mr. Justice Sutherland concur in this opinion.

BEAUHARNAIS v. ILLINOIS

343 U.S. 250 (1952)

Mr. Justice Frankfurter delivered the opinion of the Court.

The petitioner was convicted upon information in the Municipal Court of Chicago of violating § 224a of Division 1 of the Illinois Criminal Code, Ill.Rev. Stat. 1949, c. 38, § 471. He was fined $200. The section provides:

"It shall be unlawful for any person, firm or corporation to manufacture, sell, or offer for sale, advertise or publish, present or exhibit in any public place in this state any lithograph, moving picture, play, drama, or sketch, which publication or exhibition portrays depravity, criminality, unchastity, or lack of virtue of a class of citizens, of any race, color, creed

or religion which said publication or exhibition exposes the citizens of any race, color, creed or religion to contempt, derision, or obloquy or which is productive of breach of the peace or riots. . . ."

Beauharnais challenged the statute as violating the liberty of speech and of the press guaranteed as against the States by the Due Process Clause of the Fourteenth Amendment, and as too vague, under the restrictions implicit in the same Clause, to support conviction for crime. The Illinois courts rejected these contentions and sustained defendant's conviction. . . .

The information, cast generally in the terms of the statute, charged that Beauharnais "did unlawfully . . . exhibit in public places lithographs, which publications portray depravity, criminality, unchastity or lack of virtue of citizens of Negro race and color and which exposes [*sic*] citizens of Illinois of the Negro race and color to contempt, derision, or obloquy. . . ." The lithograph complained of was a leaflet setting forth a petition calling on the Mayor and City Council of Chicago "to halt the further encroachment, harassment and invasion of white people, their property, neighborhoods and persons, by the Negro. . . ." Below was a call for "One million self respecting white people in Chicago to unite . . ." with the statement added that "If persuasion and the need to prevent the white race from becoming mongrelized by the Negro will not unite us, then the aggressions . . . rapes, robberies, knives, guns and marijuana of the Negro, surely will." This, with more language, similar if not so violent, concluded with an attached application for membership in the White Circle League of America, Inc. . . .

No one will gainsay that it is libelous falsely to charge another with being a rapist, robber, carrier of knives and guns, and user of marijuana. The precise question before us, then, is whether the protection of "liberty" in the Due Process Clause of the Fourteenth Amendment prevents a State from punishing such libels— as criminal libel has been defined, limited and constitutionally recognized time out of mind—directed at designated collectivities and flagrantly disseminated. . . .

Illinois did not have to look beyond her own borders or await the tragic experience of the last three decades to conclude that wilful purveyors of falsehood concerning racial and religious groups promote strife and tend powerfully to obstruct the manifold adjustments required for free, ordered life in a metropolitan, polyglot community. . . .

[The court here reviews the history of racial strife in Illinois.]

In the face of this history and its frequent obligato of extreme racial and religious propaganda, we would deny experience to say that the Illinois legislature was without reason in seeking ways to curb false or malicious defamation of racial and religious groups, made in public places and by means calculated to have a powerful emotional impact on those to whom it was presented. "There are limits to the exercise of these liberties [of speech and of the press]. The danger in these times from the coercive activities of those who in the delusion of racial or religious conceit would incite violence and breaches of the peace in order to deprive others of their equal right to the exercise of their liberties, is emphasized by events familiar to all. These and other transgressions of those limits the states appropriately may punish." This was the conclusion, again of a unanimous Court, in 1940. *Cantwell* v. *State of Connecticut, supra,* 310 U.S. at page 310. . . .

Libelous utterances not being within the area of constitutionally protected speech, it is unnecessary, either for us or for the State courts, to consider the issues behind the phrase "clear and present danger." Certainly no one would contend that obscene speech, for example, may be punished only upon a showing of such circumstances. Libel, as we have seen, is in the same class.

We find no warrant in the Constitution for denying to Illinois the power to pass the law here under attack. . . .

MR. JUSTICE BLACK, with whom MR. JUSTICE DOUGLAS concurs, dissenting. . . .

In view of . . . prior holdings, how does the Court justify its holding today that states can punish people for exercising the vital freedoms intended to be safeguarded from suppression by the First Amendment? The prior holdings are not referred to; the Court simply acts on the bland assumption that the First Amendment is wholly irrelevant. It is not even accorded the respect of a passing mention. This follows logically, I suppose, from recent constitutional doctrine which appears to measure state laws solely by this Court's notion of civilized "canons of decency," reasonableness, etc. . . . Under this "reasonableness" test, state laws abridging First Amendment freedoms are sustained if found to have a "rational basis. . . ."

Today's case degrades First Amendment freedoms to the "rational basis" level. . . .

This statute imposes state censorship over the theater, moving pictures, radio, television, leaflets, magazines, books and newspapers. No doubt the statute is broad enough to make criminal the "publication, sale, presentation or exhibition" of many of the world's great classics, both secular and religious.

The Court condones this expansive state censorship by painstakingly analogizing it to the law of criminal libel. As a result of this refined analysis, the Illinois statute emerges labeled a "group libel law." This label may make the Court's holding more palatable for those who sustain it, but the sugar-coating does not make the censorship less deadly. However tagged, the Illinois law is not that criminal libel which has been "defined, limited and constitutionally recognized time out of mind." For as "constitutionally recognized" that crime has provided for punishment of false, malicious, scurrilous charges against individuals, not against huge groups. . . .

[MR. JUSTICE REED, joined by his brother DOUGLAS, dissented in a separate opinion.]

MR. JUSTICE JACKSON, dissenting. . . .

Rulings of the trial court precluded the effort to justify statements of fact by proving their truth. The majority opinion concedes the unvarying recognition by the States that truth plus good motives is a defense in a prosecution for criminal libel. But here the trial court repeatedly refused defendant's offer of proof as to the truth of the matter published. Where an offer to prove the dominant element of a defense is rejected as immaterial, we can hardly refuse to consider defendant's constitutional question because he did not go through the useless ceremony of offering proof of a subsidiary element of the defense. If the court would not let him try to prove he spoke truth, how could he show that he spoke truth for good ends? Furthermore, the record indicates that defendant was asked to state what he had meant by the use of certain phrases, and the reason for forming the White Circle League— statements which apparently bore on the issue of motive and ends. But the trial court sustained a sweeping objection "to this whole line of examination."

NEW YORK TIMES v. SULLIVAN

84 S. Ct. 710 (1964)

Here for the first time the Court considered "the extent to which the constitutional protection for speech and press limits a State's power to award damages in a libel action brought by a public official against critics of his official conduct." The alleged libel occurred in a paid "editorial" advertisement which was critical of the police handling of certain race problems in Montgomery, Alabama. The ad contained some inaccurate statements respecting "factual" circumstances out of which the criticisms grew. The plaintiff was the city commissioner in charge of police. Neither he nor his office was directly referred to in the offending ad.

MR. JUSTICE BRENNAN delivered the opinion of the Court. . . .

II

Under Alabama law as applied in this case, a publication is "libelous per se" if the words "tend to injure a person . . . in his reputation" or to "bring [him] into public contempt"; the trial court stated that the standard was met if the words are such as to "injure him in his public office, or impute misconduct to him in his office, or want of official integrity, or want of fidelity to a public trust. . . ." The jury must find that the words were published "of and concerning" the plaintiff, but where the plaintiff is a public official his place in the governmental hierarchy is sufficient evidence to support a finding that his reputation has been affected by statements that reflect upon the agency of which he is in charge. Once "libel per se" has been established, the defendant has no defense as to stated facts unless he can persuade the jury that they were true in all their particulars. *Alabama Ride Co.* v. *Vance*, 235 Ala. 263, 178 So. 438 (1938); *Johnson Publishing Co.* v. *Davis*, 271 Ala. 474, 494–495, 124 So.2d 441, 457–458 (1960). His privilege of "fair comment" for expressions of opinion depends on the truth of the facts upon which the comment is based. *Parsons* v. *Age-Herald Publishing Co.*, 181 Ala. 439, 450, 61 So. 345, 350 (1913). Unless he can discharge the burden of proving truth, general damages are presumed, and may be awarded without proof of pecuniary injury. A showing of actual malice is apparently a prerequisite to recovery of punitive damages, and the defendant may in any event forestall these by a retraction meeting the statutory requirements. Good motives and belief in truth do not negate an inference of malice, but are relevant only in mitigation of punitive damages if the jury chooses to accord them weight. *Johnson Publishing Co.* v. *Davis, supra,* 271 Ala., at 495, 124 So.2d, at 458. . . . The state rule of law is not saved by its allowance of the defense of truth. A defense for erroneous statements honestly made is no less essential here than was the requirement of proof of guilty knowledge which, in *Smith* v. *California*, 361 U.S. 147, we held indispensable to a valid conviction of a bookseller for possessing obscene writings for sale. We said:

"For if the bookseller is criminally liable without knowledge of the contents, . . . he will tend to restrict the books he sells to those he has inspected; and thus the State will have imposed a restriction upon the distribution of constitutionally protected as well as obscene literature. . . . And the bookseller's burden would become the public's burden, for by restricting him the public's access to reading matter would be restricted. . . . [H]is timidity in the face of his absolute criminal liability, thus would tend to restrict the public's access to forms of the printed word which the State could not constitutionally suppress directly. The bookseller's self-censorship, compelled by the State, would be a censorship affecting the whole public, hardly less virulent for being privately administered. Through it, the distribution of all books, both obscene and not obscene, would be impelled." (361 U.S. 147, 153–154.)

A rule compelling the critic of official conduct to guarantee the truth of all his factual assertions—and to do so on pain of libel judgments virtually unlimited in amount—leads to a comparable "self-censorship." Allowance of the defense of truth, with the burden of proving it on the defendant, does not mean that only false speech will be deterred. Even courts accepting this defense as an adequate safeguard have recognized the difficulties of adducing legal proofs that the alleged libel was true in all its factual particulars. See e.g., *Post Publishing Co.* v. *Hallam*, 59 F. 530, 540 (6th Cir. 1893); see also *Noel*, 49 Col. L. Rev. 875, 892 (1949). Under such a rule, would-be critics of official conduct may be deterred from voicing their criticism, even though it is believed to be true and even though it is in fact true, because of doubt whether it can be proved in court or fear of the expense of having to do so. They tend to make only statements which "steer far wider of the unlawful zone." *Speiser* v. *Randall, supra,* 357 U.S. at 526. The rule thus dampens the vigor and limits the variety of public debate. It is inconsistent with the First and Fourteenth Amendments.

The constitutional guarantees require, we think, a federal rule that prohibits a public official from recovering damages for a defamatory falsehood relating to his official conduct unless he proves that the statement was made with "actual malice"—

that is, with knowledge that it was false or with reckless disregard of whether it was false or not. An oft-cited statement of a like rule, which has been adopted by a number of state courts, is found in the Kansas case of *Coleman* v. *MacLennan,* 78 Kan. 711, 98 P. 281 (1908). The State Attorney General, a candidate for re-election and a member of the commission charged with the management and control of the state school fund, sued a newspaper publisher for alleged libel in an article purporting to state facts relating to his official conduct in connection with a school-fund transaction. The defendant pleaded privilege and the trial judge, over the plaintiff's objection, instructed the jury that

"where an article is published and circulated among voters for the sole purpose of giving what the defendant believes to be truthful information concerning a candidate for public office and for the purpose of enabling such voters to cast their ballot more intelligently, and the whole thing is done in good faith and without malice, the article is privileged, although the principal matters contained in the article may be untrue in fact and derogatory to the character of the plaintiff; and in such a case the burden is on the plaintiff to show actual malice in the publication of the article."

In answer to a special question, the jury found that the plaintiff had not proved actual malice, and a general verdict was returned for the defendant. On appeal the Supreme Court of Kansas, in an opinion by Justice Burch, reasoned as follows (78 Kan., at 724, 98 P., at 286):

"[I]t is of the utmost consequence that the people should discuss the character and qualifications of candidates for their suffrages. The importance to the state and to society of such discussions is so vast, and the advantages derived are so great that they more than counter-balance the inconvenience of private persons whose conduct may be involved, and occasional injury to the reputations of individuals must yield to the public welfare, although at times such injury may be great. The public bene-fit from publicity is so great and the chance of injury to private character so small that such discussion must be privileged."

The court thus sustained the trial court's instruction as a correct statement of the law, saying:

"In such a case the occasion gives rise to a privilege qualified to this extent. Any one claiming to be defamed by the communication must show actual malice, or go remediless. This privilege extends to a great variety of subjects and includes matters of public concern, public men, and candidates for office." 78 Kan., at 723, 98 P., at 285.

Such a privilege for criticism of official conduct is appropriately analogous to the protection accorded a public official when *he* is sued for libel by a private citizen. In *Barr* v. *Matteo,* 360 U.S. 564, 575, this Court held the utterances of a federal official to be absolutely privileged if made "within the outer perimeter" of his duties. The States accord the same immunity to statements of their highest officers, although some differentiate their lesser officials and qualify the privilege they enjoy. But all hold that all officials are protected unless actual malice can be proved. The reason for the official privilege is said to be that the threat of damage suits would otherwise "inhibit the fearless, vigorous, and effective administration of policies of government" and "dampen the ardor of all but the most resolute, or the most irresponsible, in the unflinching discharge of their duties." *Barr* v. *Matteo, supra,* 360 U.S. at 571. Analogous considerations support the privilege for the citizen-critic of government. It is as much his duty to criticize as it is the official's duty to administer. See *Whitney* v. *California,* 274 U.S. 357, 375 (concurring opinion of Mr. Justice Brandeis), quoted *ante.* . . . As Madison said, see *ante,* . . . "the censorial power is in the people over the Government, and not in the Government over the people." It would give public servants an unjustified preference over the public they serve, if critics of official conduct did not have a fair equivalent of the immunity granted to the officials themselves.

We conclude that such a privilege is required by the First and Fourteenth Amendments.

III

We hold today that the Constitution delimits a State's power to award damages for libel in actions brought by public officials against critics of their official conduct. Since this is such an action, the rule requiring proof of actual malice is applicable. While Alabama law apparently requires proof of actual malice for an award of punitive damages, where general damages are concerned malice is "presumed." Such a presumption is inconsistent with the federal rule. "The power to create presumptions is not a means of escape from constitutional restrictions," *Bailey* v. *Alabama*, 219 U.S. 219, 239; "[t]he showing of malice required for the forfeiture of the privilege is not presumed but is a matter for proof by the plaintiff. . . ." *Lawrence* v. *Fox*, 357 Mich. 134, 146, 97 N.W.2d 719, 725 (1959). Since the trial judge did not instruct the jury to differentiate between general and punitive damages, it may be that the verdict was wholly an award of one or the other. But it is impossible to know, in view of the general verdict returned. Because of this uncertainty, the judgment must be reversed and the case remanded. *Stromberg* v. *California*, 283 U.S. 359, 367–368; *Williams* v. *North Carolina*, 317 U.S. 287, 291–292; see *Yates* v. *United States*, 354 U.S. 298, 311–312; *Cramer* v. *United States*, 325 U.S. 1, 36, n. 45.

Since respondent may seek a new trial, we deem that considerations of effective judicial administration require us to review the evidence in the present record to determine whether it could constitutionally support a judgment for respondent. This Court's duty is not limited to the elaboration of constitutional principles; we must also in proper cases review the evidence to make certain that those principles have been constitutionally applied. This is such a case, particularly since the question is one of alleged trespass across "the line between speech unconditionally guaranteed and speech which may legitimately be regulated." *Speiser* v. *Randall*, 357 U.S. 513, 525. In cases where that line must be drawn, the rule is that we "examine for ourselves the statements in issue and the circumstances under which they were made to see . . . whether they are of a character which the principles of the First Amendment, as adopted by the Due Process Clause of the Fourteenth Amendment, protect." *Pennekamp* v. *Florida*, 328 U.S. 331, 335; see also *One, Inc.*, v. *Olesen*, 355 U.S. 371; *Sunshine Book Co.* v. *Summerfield*, 355 U.S. 372. We must "make an independent examination of the whole record," *Edwards* v. *South Carolina*, 372 U.S. 229, 235, so as to assure ourselves that the judgment does not constitute a forbidden intrusion on the field of free expression.

Applying these standards, we consider that the proof presented to show actual malice lacks the convincing clarity which the constitutional standard demands, and hence that it would not constitutionally sustain the judgment for respondent under the proper rule of law. The case of the individual petitioners requires little discussion. Even assuming that they could constitutionally be found to have authorized the use of their names on the advertisement, there was no evidence whatever that they were aware of any erroneous statements or were in any way reckless in that regard. The judgment against them is thus without constitutional support.

As to the *Times*, we similarly conclude that the facts do not support a finding of actual malice. The statement by the *Times'* Secretary that, apart from the padlocking allegation, he thought the advertisement was "substantially correct," affords no constitutional warrant for the Alabama Supreme Court's conclusion that it was a "cavalier ignoring of the falsity of the advertisement [from which], the jury could not have been impressed with the bad faith of the *Times*, and its maliciousness inferable therefrom." The statement does not indicate malice at the time of the publication; even if the advertisement was not "substantially correct"—although respondent's own proofs tend to show that it was—

that opinion was at least a reasonable one, and there was no evidence to impeach the witness' good faith in holding it. The *Times'* failure to retract upon respondent's demand, although it later retracted upon the demand of Governor Patterson, is likewise not adequate evidence of malice for constitutional purposes. Whether or not a failure to retract may ever constitute such evidence, there are two reasons why it does not here. *First,* the letter written by the *Times* reflected a reasonable doubt on its part as to whether the advertisement could reasonably be taken to refer to respondent at all. *Second,* it was not a final refusal, since it asked for an explanation on this point—a request that respondent chose to ignore. Nor does the retraction upon the demand of the Governor supply the necessary proof. It may be doubted that a failure to retract which is not itself evidence of malice can retroactively become such by virtue of a retraction subsequently made to another party. But in any event that did not happen here, since the explanation given by the *Times'* Secretary for the distinction drawn between respondent and the Governor was a reasonable one, the good faith of which was not impeached.

Finally, there is evidence that the *Times* published the advertisement without checking its accuracy against the news stories in the *Times'* own files. The mere presence of the stories in the files does not, of course, establish that the *Times* "knew" the advertisement was false, since the state of mind required for actual malice would have to be brought home to the persons in the *Times'* organization having responsibility for the publication of the advertisement. With respect to the failure of those persons to make the check, the record shows that they relied upon their knowledge of the good reputation of many of those whose names were listed as sponsors of the advertisement, and upon the letter from A. Philip Randolph, known to them as a responsible individual, certifying that the use of the names was authorized. There was testimony that the persons handling the advertisement saw nothing in it that

would render it unacceptable under the *Times'* policy of rejecting advertisements containing "attacks of a personal character"; their failure to reject it on this ground was not unreasonable. We think the evidence against the *Times* supports at most a finding of negligence in failing to discover the misstatements, and is constitutionally insufficient to show the recklessness that is required for a finding of actual malice. Cf. *Charles Parker Co.* v. *Silver City Crystal Co.,* 142 Conn. 605, 618, 116 A.2d 440, 446 (1955); *Phoenix Newspapers, Inc.* v. *Choisser,* 82 Ariz. 271, 277–278, 312 P.2d 150, 154–155 (1957).

We also think the evidence was constitutionally defective in another respect: it was incapable of supporting the jury's finding that the allegedly libelous statements were made "of and concerning" respondent. Respondent relies on the words of the advertisement and the testimony of six witnesses to establish a connection between it and himself. Thus, in his brief to this Court, he states:

"The reference to respondent as police commissioner is clear from the ad. In addition, the jury heard the testimony of a newspaper editor . . . ; a real estate and insurance man . . . ; the sales manager of a men's clothing store . . . ; a food equipment man . . . ; a service station operator . . . ; and the operator of a truck line for whom respondent had formerly worked. . . . Each of these witnesses stated that he associated the statements with respondent. . . ." (Citations to record omitted.)

There was no reference to respondent in the advertisement, either by name or official position. A number of the allegedly libelous statements—the charges that the dining hall was padlocked and that Dr. King's home was bombed, his person assaulted, and a perjury prosecution instituted against him—did not even concern the police; despite the ingenuity of the arguments which would attach this significance to the word "They," it is plain that these statements could not reasonably be read as accusing respondent of personal involvement in the acts in question. The statements upon which respondent principally relies as referring to him are the two allegations that did concern the police or police functions: that "truckloads of police . . . ringed the Alabama State College Campus" after the demonstration on the State Capitol steps, and that Dr. King had been "arrested . . . seven times." These statements were false only in that the police had been "deployed near" the campus but had not actually "ringed" it and had not gone there in connection with the State Capitol demonstration, and in that Dr. King had been arrested only four times. The ruling that these discrepancies between what was true and what was asserted were sufficient to injure respondent's reputation may itself raise constitutional problems, but we need not consider them here. Although the statements may be taken as referring to the police, they did not on their face make even an oblique reference to respondent as an individual. Support for the asserted reference must, therefore, be sought in the testimony of respondent's witnesses. But none of them suggested any basis for the belief that respondent himself was attacked in the advertisement beyond the bare fact that he was in overall charge of the Police Department and thus bore official responsibility for police conduct; to the extent that some of the witnesses thought respondent to have been charged with ordering or approving the conduct or otherwise being personally involved in it, they based this notion not on any statements in the advertisement, and not on any evidence that he had in fact been so involved, but solely on the unsupported assumption that, because of his official position, he must have been. This reliance on the bare fact of respondent's official position was made explicit by the Supreme Court of Alabama. That court, in holding that the trial court "did not err in overruling the demurrer [of the *Times*] in the aspect that the libelous matter was not of and concerning the plaintiffs," based its ruling on the proposition that:

"We think it common knowledge that the average person knows that municipal agents, such as police and firemen, and others, are under the control and direction of the city governing body, and more particularly under the direction and control of a single commissioner. In measuring the performance or deficiencies of such groups, praise or criticism is usually attached to the official in complete control of the body." 273 Ala., at 674–675, 144 So.2d, at 39.

This proposition has disquieting implications for criticism of governmental conduct. For good reason, "no court of last resort in this country has ever held, or even suggested, that prosecutions for libel on government have any place in the American system of jurisprudence." *City of Chicago* v. *Tribune Co.*, 307 Ill. 595, 601, 139 N.E. 86, 88 (1923). The present proposition would sidestep this obstacle by transmuting criticism of government, however impersonal it may seem on its face, into personal criticism, and hence potential libel, of the officials of whom the government is composed. There is no legal alchemy by which a State may thus create the cause of action that would otherwise be denied for a publication which, as respondent himself said of the advertisement, "reflects not only on me but on the other Commissioners and the community." Raising as it does the possibility that a good-faith critic of government will be penalized for his criticism, the proposition relied on by the Alabama courts strikes at the very center of the constitutionally protected area of free expression. We hold that such a proposition may not constitutionally be utilized to establish that an otherwise impersonal attack on governmental operations was a libel of an official responsible for those operations. Since it was relied on exclusively here, and there was no other evidence to connect the statements with respondent, the evidence was constitutionally insufficient to support a finding that the statements referred to respondent.

The judgment of the Supreme Court of Alabama is reversed and the case is remanded to that court for further proceedings not inconsistent with this opinion.

Reversed and remanded.

MR. JUSTICE BLACK, with whom MR. JUS-
TICE DOUGLAS joins (concurring). . . .

In my opinion the Federal Constitution
has dealt with this deadly danger to the
press in the only way possible without leaving the free press open to destruction—by
granting the press an absolute immunity
for criticism of the way public officials do
their public duty. Compare *Barr* v. *Matteo,*
360 U.S. 564. Stopgap measures like those
the Court adopts are in my judgment not
enough. This record certainly does not indicate that any different verdict would have
been rendered here whatever the Court
had charged the jury about "malice,"
"truth," "good motives," "justifiable ends,"
or any other legal formulas which in theory
would protect the press. Nor does the
record indicate that any of these legalistic
words would have caused the courts below
to set aside or to reduce the half-million-
dollar verdict in any amount. . . .

MR. JUSTICE GOLDBERG, with whom MR.
JUSTICE DOUGLAS joins (concurring in the
result).

The Court today announces a constitutional standard which prohibits "a public
official from recovering damages for a defamatory falsehood relating to his official
conduct unless he proves that the statement
was made with 'actual malice'—that is,
with knowledge that it was false or with
reckless disregard of whether it was false
or not." . . . The Court thus rules that
the Constitution gives citizens and newspapers a "conditional privilege" immuniz-
ing nonmalicious misstatements of fact
regarding the official conduct of a government officer. The impressive array of history and precedent marshaled by the Court,
however, confirms my belief that the Constitution affords greater protection than that
provided by the Court's standard to citizen
and press in exercising the right of public
criticism.

In my view, the First and Fourteenth
Amendments to the Constitution afford to
the citizen and to the press an absolute,
unconditional privilege to criticize official
conduct despite the harm which may flow

from excesses and abuses. The prized
American right "to speak one's mind," cf.
Bridges v. *California,* 314 U.S. 252, 270,
about public officials and affairs needs
"breathing space to survive," *NAACP* v.
Button, 371 U.S. 415, 433. The right should
not depend upon a probing by the jury of
the motivation of the citizen or press. The
theory of our Constitution is that every
citizen may speak his mind and every newspaper express its view on matters of public
concern and may not be barred from
speaking or publishing because those in
control of government think that what is
said or written is unwise, unfair, false, or
malicious. In a democratic society, one who
assumes to act for the citizens in an executive, legislative, or judicial capacity
must expect that his official acts will be
commented upon and criticized. Such criticism cannot, in my opinion, be muzzled or
deterred by the courts at the instance of
public officials under the label of libel.

It has been recognized that "prosecutions for libel on government have [no]
place in the American system of jurisprudence." *City of Chicago* v. *Tribune Co.,*
307 Ill. 595, 601, 139 N.E. 86, 88. I fully
agree. Government, however, is not an abstraction; it is made up of individuals—of
governors responsible to the governed. In
a democratic society where men are free by
ballots to remove those in power, any
statement critical of governmental action
is necessarily "of and concerning" the governors and any statement critical of the
governors' official conduct is necessarily "of
and concerning" the government. If the
rule that libel on government has no place
in our Constitution is to have real meaning, then libel on the official conduct of the
governors likewise can have no place in
our Constitution.

We must recognize that we are writing
upon a clean slate. As the Court notes, although there have been "statements of this
Court to the effect that the Constitution
does not protect libelous publications . . .
[n]one of the cases sustained the use of
libel laws to impose sanctions upon expression critical of the official conduct of public

officials." . . . We should be particularly careful, therefore, adequately to protect the liberties which are embodied in the First and Fourteenth Amendments. It may be urged that deliberately and maliciously false statements have no conceivable value as free speech. That argument, however, is not responsive to the real issue presented by this case, which is whether that freedom of speech which all agree is constitutionally protected can be effectively safeguarded by a rule allowing the imposition of liability upon a jury's evaluation of the speaker's state of mind. If individual citizens may be held liable in damages for strong words, which a jury finds false and maliciously motivated, there can be little doubt that public debate and advocacy will be constrained. And if newspapers, publishing advertisements dealing with public issues, thereby risk liability, there can also be little doubt that the ability of minority groups to secure publication of their views on public affairs and to seek support for their causes will be greatly diminished. Cf. *Farmers Educational & Coop. Union* v. *WDAY, Inc.*, 360 U.S. 525, 530. The opinion of the Court conclusively demonstrates the chilling effect of the Alabama libel laws on First Amendment freedoms in the area of race relations. The American Colonists were not willing, nor should we be, to take the risk that "[m]en who injure and oppress the people under their administration [and] provoke them to cry out and complain" will also be empowered to "make that very complaint the foundation for new oppressions and prosecutions." The *Trial of John Peter Zenger*, 17 Howell's St. Tr. 675, 721–722 (1735) (argument of counsel to the jury.) To impose liability for critical, albeit erroneous or even malicious, comments on official conduct would effectively resurrect "the obsolete doctrine that the governed must not criticize their governors." Cf. *Sweeney* v. *Patterson*, 76 U.S. App. D.C. 23, 128 F.2d 457, 458.

Our national experience teaches that repressions breed hate and "that hate menaces stable government." *Whitney* v. *California*, 274 U.S. 357, 375 (Brandeis, J.,

concurring). We should be ever mindful of the wise counsel of Chief Justice Hughes:

"[I]mperative is the need to preserve inviolate the constitutional rights of free speech, free press and free assembly in order to maintain the opportunity for free political discussion, to the end that government may be responsive to the will of the people and that changes, if desired, may be obtained by peaceful means. Therein lies the security of the Republic, the very foundation of constitutional government." *De Jonge* v. *Oregon*, 299 U.S. 353, 365.

This is not to say that the Constitution protects defamatory statements directed against the private conduct of a public official or private citizen. Freedom of press and of speech insure that government will respond to the will of the people and that changes may be obtained by peaceful means. Purely private defamation has little to do with the political ends of a self-governing society. The imposition of liability for private defamation does not abridge the freedom of public speech. This, of course, cannot be said "where public officials are concerned or where public matters are involved. . . . [O]ne main function of the First Amendment is to ensure ample opportunity for the people to determine and resolve public issues. Where public matters are involved, the doubts should be resolved in favor of freedom of expression rather than against it." Douglas, *The Right of the People* (1958), p. 41.

In many jurisdictions, legislators, judges and executive officers are clothed with absolute immunity against liability for defamatory words uttered in the discharge of their public duties. See e.g., *Barr* v. *Matteo*, 360 U.S. 564; *City of Chicago* v. *Tribune Co.*, 307 Ill., at 610; 139 N.E., at 91. Judge Learned Hand ably summarized the policies underlying the rule:

"It does indeed go without saying that an official, who is in fact guilty of using his powers to vent his spleen upon others, or for any other personal motive not connected with the public good, should not escape liability for the injuries he may so cause; and, if it were possible in practice to confine such complaints to the guilty, it would be monstrous to deny recovery. The justification for doing so is that it is impossible to know whether the claim is well founded until the case has been tried, and that to submit all officials, the innocent as well as the guilty, to the burden of a trial and to the inevitable danger of its outcome, would dampen the ardor of all but the most resolute, or the most irresponsible, in the unflinching discharge of their duties. Again and again the public interest calls for action which may turn out to be founded on a mistake, in the face of which an official may later find himself hard put to it to satisfy a jury of his good faith. There must indeed be means of punishing public officers who have been truant to their duties; but that is quite another matter from exposing such as have been honestly mistaken to suit by anyone who has suffered from their errors. As is so often the case, the answer must be found in a balance between the evils inevitable in either alternative. In this instance it has been thought in the end better to leave unredressed the wrongs done by dishonest officers than to subject those who try to do their duty to the constant dread of retaliation. . . .

"The decisions have, indeed, always imposed as a limitation upon the immunity that the official's act must have been within the scope of his powers; and it can be argued that official powers, since they exist only for the public good, never cover occasions where the public good is not their aim, and hence that to exercise a power dishonestly is necessarily to overstep its bounds. A moment's reflection shows, however, that that cannot be the meaning of the limitation without defeating the whole doctrine. What is meant by saying that the officer must be acting within his power cannot be more than that the occasion must be such as would have justified the act, if he had been using his power for any of the purposes on whose account it was vested in him. . . ." *Gregoire* v. *Biddle,* 2 Cir., 177 F.2d 579, 581.

If the government official should be immune from libel actions so that his ardor to serve the public will not be dampened and "fearless, vigorous, and effective administration of policies of government" not be inhibited, *Barr* v. *Matteo, supra,* 360 U.S. at 571, then the citizen and the press should likewise be immune from libel actions for their criticism of official conduct. Their ardor as citizens will thus not be dampened and they will be free "to applaud or to criticize the way public employees do their jobs, from the least to the most important." If liability can attach to political criticism because it damages the reputation of a public official as a public official, then no critical citizen can safely utter anything but faint praise about the government or its officials. The vigorous criticism by press and citizen of the conduct of the government of the day by the officials of the day will soon yield to silence if officials in control of government agencies, instead of answering criticisms, can resort to friendly juries to forestall criticism of their official conduct.

The conclusion that the Constitution affords the citizen and the press an absolute privilege for criticism of official conduct does not leave the public official without defenses against unsubstantiated opinions or deliberate misstatements. "Under our system of government, counter argument and education are the weapons available to expose these matters, not abridgement . . . of free speech. . . ." *Wood* v. *Georgia,* 370 U.S. 375, 389. The public official certainly has equal if not greater access than most private citizens to media of communication. In any event, despite the possibility that some excesses and abuses may go unremedied, we must recognize that "the people of this nation have ordained in the light of history, that, in spite of the probability of excesses and abuses, [certain] liberties are, in the long view, essential to enlightened opinion and right conduct on the part of the citizens of a democracy." *Cantwell* v. *Connecticut,* 310 U.S. 296, 310. As Mr. Justice Brandeis correctly observed, "sunlight is the most powerful of all disinfectants."

For these reasons, I strongly believe that

the Constitution accords citizens and press an unconditional freedom to criticize official conduct. It necessarily follows that in a case such as this, where all agree that the allegedly defamatory statements related to official conduct, the judgments for libel cannot constitutionally be sustained.

4. COMPULSORY UTTERANCE—INVESTIGATIONS

McGRAIN v. *DAUGHERTY*
273 U.S. 135 (1927)

M. S. Daugherty refused to obey a Senate subpoena to testify in an investigation of his brother's administration of the Department of Justice. He was thereupon arrested by McGrain, a deputy of the Senate's Sergeant at Arms—and then released by a Federal District Court in a habeas corpus proceeding. McGrain appealed.

MR. JUSTICE VAN DEVANTER delivered the opinion of the court. . . .

Harry M. Daugherty became the Attorney General March 5, 1921, and held that office until March 28, 1924, when he resigned. Late in that period various charges of misfeasance and nonfeasance in the Department of Justice after he became its supervising head were brought to the attention of the Senate by individual senators and made the basis of an insistent demand that the department be investigated to the end that the practices and deficiencies which, according to the charges, were operating to prevent or impair its right administration might be definitely ascertained and that appropriate and effective measures might be taken to remedy or eliminate the evil. The Senate regarded the charges as grave and requiring legislative attention and action. Accordingly it formulated, passed and invited the House of Representatives to pass (and the body did pass) two measures taking important litigation then in immediate contemplation out of the control of the Department of Justice and placing the same in charge of special counsel to be appointed by the President; and also adopted a resolution authorizing and directing a select committee of five senators "to investigate circumstances and facts, to report the same to the Senate, concerning the alleged failure of Harry M. Daugherty, Attorney General of

the United States, to prosecute properly violators of the Sherman Anti-trust Act and the Clayton Act against monopolies and unlawful restraint of trade; the alleged neglect and failure of the said Harry M. Daugherty, Attorney General of the United States, to arrest and prosecute Albert B. Fall, Harry F. Sinclair, E. L. Doheny, C. R. Forbes, and their co-conspirators in defrauding the Government, as well as the alleged neglect and failure of the said Attorney General to arrest and prosecute many others for violations of Federal statutes, and his alleged failure to prosecute properly, efficiently, and promptly, and to defend, all manner of civil and criminal actions wherein the Government of the United States is interested as a party plaintiff or defendant. . . ."

The first of the principal questions, the one which the witness particularly presses on our attention, is . . . whether the Senate—or the House of Representatives, both being on the same plane in this regard—has power, through its own process, to compel a private individual to appear before it or one of its committees and give testimony needed to enable it efficiently to exercise a legislative function belonging to it under the Constitution.

The Constitution provides for a Congress, consisting of a Senate and House of Representatives, and invests it with "all legislative powers" granted to the United

States, and with power "to make all laws which shall be necessary and proper" for carrying into execution these powers and "all other powers" vested by the Constitution in the United States or in any department or officer thereof. . . . Other provisions show that, while bills can become laws only after being considered and passed by both houses of Congress, each house is to be distinct from the other, to have its own officers and rules, and to exercise its legislative function independently. . . . But there is no provision expressly investing either house with power to make investigations and exact testimony, to the end that it may exercise its legislative function advisedly and effectively. So the question arises whether this power is so far incidental to the legislative function as to be implied.

In actual legislative practice, power to secure needed information by such means has long been treated as an attribute of the power to legislate. It was so regarded in the British Parliament and in the colonial Legislatures before the American Revolution, and a like view has prevailed and been carried into effect in both houses of Congress and in most of the state Legislatures.

This power was both asserted and exerted by the House of Representatives in 1792, when it appointed a select committee to inquire into the St. Clair expedition and authorized the committee to send for necessary persons, papers and records. Mr. Madison, who had taken an important part in framing the Constitution only five years before, and four of his associates in that work, were members of the House of Representatives at the time, and all voted for the inquiry. . . . Other exertions of the power by the House of Representatives, as also by the Senate, are shown in the citations already made. Among those by the Senate, the inquiry ordered in 1859 respecting the raid by John Brown and his adherents on the armory and arsenal of the United States at Harper's Ferry is of special significance. The resolution directing the inquiry authorized the committee to send for persons and papers, to inquire into the facts pertaining to the raid and the means by which it was organized and supported, and to report what legislation, if any, was necessary to preserve the peace of the country and protect the public property. The resolution was briefly discussed and adopted without opposition. . . .

The state courts quite generally have held that the power to legislate carries with it by necessary implication ample authority to obtain information needed in the rightful exercise of that power, and to employ compulsory process for the purpose. . . .

Four decisions of this Court are cited and more or less relied on, and we now turn to them.

The first decision was in *Anderson* v. *Dunn*, 6 Wheat. 204 [1821]. The question there was whether, under the Constitution, the House of Representatives has power to attach and punish a person other than a member for contempt of its authority—in fact, an attempt to bribe one of its members. The Court regarded the powers as essential to the effective exertion of other powers expressly granted, and therefore as implied. . . .

The next decision was in *Kilbourn* v. *Thompson*, 103 U.S. 169 [1880]. The question there was whether the House of Representatives had exceeded its power in directing one of its committees to make a particular investigation. The decision was that it had. The principles announced and applied in the case are—that neither house of Congress possesses a "general power of making inquiry into the private affairs of the citizen"; that the power actually possessed is limited to inquiries relating to matters of which the particular house "has jurisdiction" and in respect of which it rightfully may take other action; that if the inquiry relates to "a matter wherein relief or redress could be had only by a judicial proceeding" it is not within the range of this power, but must be left to the courts, conformably to the constitutional separation of governmental powers; and that for the purpose of determining the essential character of the inquiry recourse may be had to the resolution or order under which it is made. [The Court found no hint of contemplated legislation, and evidently assumed the inquiry was designed to protect the United States as a creditor of a bankrupt firm—a matter then pending before a federal court, and concerning which Congress could not legislate.]

Next in order is *In re Chapman*, 166 U.S. 661 [1896]. The inquiry there in question was conducted under a resolution of the Senate and related to charges, published in the press, that Senators were yielding to corrupt influences. . . . Chapman appeared before the committee in response to a subpoena, but refused to answer questions pertinent to the inquiry, and was indicted and convicted under the act of 1857 for his refusal. The court sustained the constitutional validity of the act of 1857, and, . . . held that the inquiry related to the integrity and fidelity of Senators in the discharge of their duties, and therefore to a matter "within the range of the constitutional powers of the Senate" and in respect of which it could compel witnesses to appear and testify. . . .

The latest case is *Marshall* v. *Gordon*, 243 U.S. 521 [1916]. The question there was whether the House of Representatives exceeded its power in punishing, as for a contempt of its authority, a person—not a member—who had written, published, and sent to the chairman of one of its committees an ill-tempered and irritating letter respecting the action and purposes of the committee. Power to make inquiries and obtain evidence by compulsory process was not involved. The court recognized distinctly that the House of Representatives has implied power to punish a person not a member for contempt [but blocked punishment, since the offending letter was not apt to hinder congressional operations].

While these cases are not decisive of the question we are considering, they definitely settle two propositions which we recognize as entirely sound and having a bearing on its solution: One, that the two houses of Congress, in their separate relations, possess, not only such powers as are expressly

granted to them by the Constitution, but such auxiliary powers as are necessary and appropriate to make the express powers effective; and the other, that neither house is invested with "general" power to inquire into private affairs and compel disclosures, but only with such limited power of inquiry as is shown to exist when the rule of constitutional interpretation just stated is rightly applied. . . . And it is a necessary deduction from the decisions in *Kilbourn* v. *Thompson* and *In re Chapman* that a witness rightfully may refuse to answer where the bounds of the power are exceeded or the questions are not pertinent to the matter under inquiry.

We come now to the question whether it sufficiently appears that the purpose for which the witness's testimony was sought was to obtain information in aid of the legislative function. The court below answered the question in the negative and put its decision largely on this ground [that the Senate's alleged legislative purpose was not avowed until after the inquiry had been challenged; that the real purpose was to condemn H. S. Daugherty].

We are of opinion that the court's ruling on this question was wrong, and that it sufficiently appears, when the proceedings are rightly interpreted, that the object of the investigation and of the effort to secure the witness's testimony was to obtain information for legislative purposes.

It is quite true that the resolution directing the investigation does not in terms avow that it is intended to be in aid of legislation; but it does show that the subject to be investigated was the administration of the Department of Justice—whether its functions were being properly discharged or were being neglected or misdirected, and particularly whether the Attorney General and his assistants were performing or neglecting their duties in respect of the institution and prosecution of proceedings to punish crimes and enforce appropriate remedies against the wrongdoers; specific instances of alleged neglect being recited. Plainly the subject was one on which legislation could be had and would be materially aided by the information which the investigation was calculated to elicit. This becomes manifest when it is reflected that the functions of the Department of Justice, the powers and duties of the Attorney General, and the duties of his assistants are all subject to regulation by congressional legislation, and that the department is maintained and its activities are carried on under such appropriations as in the judgment of Congress are needed from year to year.

The only legitimate object the Senate could have in ordering the investigation was to aid it in legislating, and we think the subject-matter was such that the presumption should be indulged that this was the real object. An express avowal of the object would have been better; but in view of the particular subject-matter was not indispensable. . . .

We conclude that the investigation was ordered for a legitimate object; that the witness wrongfully refused to appear and testify before the committee and was lawfully attached; that the Senate is entitled to have him give testimony pertinent to the inquiry, either at its bar or before the committee; and that the district court erred in discharging him from custody under the attachment. . . .

What has been said requires that the final order in the district court discharging the witness from custody be reversed.

Final order reversed.

MR. JUSTICE STONE did not participate in the consideration or decision of the case.

WATKINS v. UNITED STATES

354 U.S. 178 (1957)

Witnesses before the House Un-American Activities Committee had implicated Watkins as a Communist. The Committee then questioned Watkins who testified freely as to his co-operation with the Communist Party for some five years prior to 1948. He was willing to answer any questions about his own activities and about persons he knew were, and believed still to be, Communists. He refused to answer questions about persons "who to my best knowledge and belief have long since removed themselves from the Communist movement." The essence of his refusal was expressed in the following language, "I am not going to plead the Fifth Amendment, but I refuse to answer certain questions that I believe are outside the proper scope of your committee's activities." Watkins was convicted of contempt of Congress. The case reached the Supreme Court via certiorari.

MR. CHIEF JUSTICE WARREN delivered the opinion of the Court.

[After recognizing the importance and breadth of legislative investigating power and the duty of "all citizens to cooperate with Congress in its efforts to obtain the facts needed for intelligent legislative action," the Chief Justice proceeded as follows:]

There was very little use of the power of compulsory process in early years to enable the Congress to obtain facts pertinent to the enactment of new statutes or the administration of existing laws. The first occasion for such an investigation arose in 1827 when the House of Representatives was considering a revision of the tariff laws. In the Senate, there was no use of a fact-finding investigation in aid of legislation until 1859. In the Legislative Reorganization Act, the Committee on Un-American Activities is the only standing committee of the House of Representatives that was given the power to compel disclosures.

It is not surprising, from the fact that the Houses of Congress so sparingly employed the power to conduct investigations, that there have been few cases requiring judicial review of the power. The nation was almost one hundred years old before the first case reached this Court to challenge the use of compulsory process as a legislative device, rather than in inquiries concerning the elections or privileges of Congressmen. In *Kilbourn* v. *Thompson*, 103 U.S. 168, decided in 1881, an investigation had been authorized by the House of Representatives to learn the circumstances surrounding the bankruptcy of Jay Cooke & Company, in which the United States had deposited funds. The committee became particularly interested in a private real estate pool that was a part of the financial structure. The Court found that the subject matter of the inquiry was "in its nature clearly judicial and therefore one in respect to which no valid legislation could be enacted." The House had thereby exceeded the limits of its own authority.

Subsequent to the decision in *Kilbourn*, until recent times, there were very few cases dealing with the investigative power. The matter came to the fore again when the Senate undertook to study the corruption in handling of oil leases in the 1920's. In *McGrain* v. *Dougherty*, 273 U.S. 135, and *Sinclair* v. *United States*, 279 U.S. 263, the Court applied the precepts of *Kilbourn* to uphold the authority of the Congress to conduct the challenged investigations. The Court recognized the danger to effective and honest conduct of the Government if the legislature's power to probe corruption in the executive branch were unduly hampered.

Following these important decisions, there was another lull in judicial review of investigations. The absence of challenge, however, was not indicative of the absence of inquiries. To the contrary, there was vigorous use of the investigative process by a Congress bent upon harnessing and directing the vast economic and social forces of the times. Only one case came before this Court, and the authority of the Congress was affirmed.

In the decade following World War II,

there appeared a new kind of congressional inquiry unknown in prior periods of American history. Principally this was the result of the various investigations into the threat of subversion of the United States Government, but other subjects of congressional interest also contributed to the changed scene. This new phase of legislative inquiry involved a broad-scale intrusion into the lives and affairs of private citizens. It brought before the courts novel questions of the appropriate limits of congressional inquiry. Prior cases, like *Kilbourn, McGrain* and *Sinclair,* had defined the scope of investigative power in terms of the inherent limitations of the sources of that power. In the more recent cases, the emphasis shifted to problems of accommodating the interest of the Government with the rights and privileges of individuals. The central theme was the application of the Bill of Rights as a restraint upon the assertion of governmental power in this form.

It was during this period that the Fifth Amendment privilege against self-incrimination was frequently invoked and recognized as a legal limit upon the authority of a committee to require that a witness answer its questions. Some early doubts as to the applicability of that privilege before a legislative committee never matured. When the matter reached this Court, the Government did not challenge in any way that the Fifth Amendment protection was available to the witness, and such a challenge could not have prevailed. It confined its argument to the character of the answers sought and to the adequacy of the claim of privilege. *Quinn* v. *United States*, 349 U.S. 155; *Emspak* v. *United States*, 349 U.S. 190; *Bart* v. *United States*, 349 U.S. 219.

A far more difficult task evolved from the claim by witnesses that the committees' interrogations were infringements upon the freedoms of the First Amendment. Clearly, an investigation is subject to the command that the Congress shall make no law abridging freedom of speech or press or assembly. While it is true that there is no statute to be reviewed, and that an investigation is not a law, nevertheless an investigation is part of law-making. It is justified solely as an adjunct to the legislative process. The First Amendment may be invoked against infringement of the protected freedoms by law or by law-making.

Abuses of the investigative process may imperceptibly lead to abridgement of protected freedoms. The mere summoning of a witness and compelling him to testify, against his will, about his beliefs, expressions or associations is a measure of governmental interference. And when those forced revelations concern matters that are unorthodox, unpopular, or even hateful to the general public, the reaction in the life of the witness may be disastrous. This effect is even more harsh when it is past beliefs, expressions or associations that are disclosed and judged by current standards rather than those contemporary with the matters exposed. Nor does the witness alone suffer the consequences. Those who are identified by witnesses and thereby placed in the same glare of publicity are equally subject to public stigma, scorn and obloquy. Beyond that, there is the more subtle and immeasurable effect upon those who tend to adhere to the most orthodox and uncontroversial views and associations in order to avoid a similar fate at some future time. That this impact is partly the result of non-governmental activity by private persons cannot relieve the investigators of their responsibility for initiating the reaction.

The Court recognized the restraints of the Bill of Rights upon congressional investigations in *United States* v. *Rumely*, 345 U.S. 41. The magnitude and complexity of the problem of applying the First Amendment to that case led the Court to construe narrowly the resolution describing the committee's authority. It was concluded that, when First Amendment rights are threatened, the delegation of power to the committee must be clearly revealed in its charter.

Accommodation of the congressional need for particular information with the individual and personal interest in privacy is an arduous and delicate task for any court. We do not underestimate the difficulties that would attend such an undertaking. It is manifest that despite the adverse effects which follow upon compelled disclosure of private matters, not all such inquiries are barred. *Kilbourn* v. *Thompson* teaches that such an investigation into individual affairs is invalid if unrelated to any legislative purpose. That is beyond the powers conferred upon the Congress in the Constitution. *United States* v. *Rumley* makes it plain that the mere semblance of legislative purpose would not justify an inquiry in the face of the Bill of Rights. The critical element is the existence of, and the weight to be ascribed to, the interest of the Congress in demanding disclosures from an unwilling witness. We cannot simply assume, however, that every congressional investigation is justified by a public need that overbalances any private rights affected. To do so would be to abdicate the responsibility placed by the Constitution upon the judiciary to insure that the Congress does not unjustifiably encroach upon an individual's right to privacy nor abridge his liberty of speech, press, religion or assembly.

Petitioner has earnestly suggested that the difficult questions of protecting these rights from infringement by legislative inquiries can be surmounted in this case because there was no public purpose served in his interrogation. His conclusion is based upon the thesis that the Subcommittee was engaged in a program of exposure for the sake of exposure. The sole purpose of the inquiry, he contends, was to bring down upon himself and others the violence of public reaction because of their past beliefs, expressions and associations. In support of this argument, petitioner has marshalled an impressive array of evidence that some Congressmen have believed that such was their duty, or part of it.

We have no doubt that there is no congressional power to expose for the sake of exposure. The public is, of course, entitled to be informed concerning the workings of its government. That cannot be inflated into a general power to expose where the predominant result can only be an invasion of the private rights of individuals. But a solution to our problem is not to be found in testing the motives of committee members for this purpose. Such is not our function. Their motives alone would not vitiate an investigation which had been instituted by a House of Congress if that assembly's legislative purpose is being served.

Petitioner's contentions do point to a situation of particular significance from the standpoint of the constitutional limitations upon congressional investigations. The theory of a committee inquiry is that the committee members are serving as the representatives of the parent assembly in collecting information for a legislative purpose. Their function is to act as the eyes and ears of the Congress in obtaining facts upon which the full legislature can act. To carry out this mission, committees and subcommittees, sometimes one Congressman, are endowed with the full power of the Congress to compel testimony. In this case, only two men exercised that authority in demanding information over petitioner's protest.

An essential premise in this situation is that the House or Senate shall have instructed the committee members on what they are to do with the power delegated to them. It is the responsibility of the Congress, in the first instance, to insure that compulsory process is used only in furtherance of a legislative purpose. That requires that the instructions to an investigating committee spell out that group's jurisdiction and purpose with sufficient particularity. Those instructions are embodied in the authorizing resolution. That document is the committee's charter. Broadly drafted and loosely worded, however, such resolutions can leave tremendous latitude to the discretion of the investigators. The more vague the committee's charter is, the greater becomes the possibility that the committee's specific actions are not in conformity with the will of the parent House of Congress.

The authorizing resolution of the Un-American Activities Committee was adopted in 1938 when a select committee, under the chairmanship of Representative Dies, was created. Several years later, the Committee was made a standing organ of the House with the same mandate. It defines the Committee's authority as follows:

"The Committee on Un-American Activities, as a whole or by subcommittee, is authorized to make from time to time investigations of (1) the extent, character, and objects of un-American propaganda activities in the United States, (2) the diffusion within the United States of subversive and un-American propaganda that is instigated from foreign countries or of a domestic origin and attacks the principle of the form of government as guaranteed by our Constitution, and (3) all other questions in relation thereto that would aid Congress in any necessary remedial legislation."

It would be difficult to imagine a less explicit authorizing resolution. Who can define the meaning of "un-American"? What is that single, solitary "principle of the form of government as guaranteed by our Constitution"? There is no need to dwell upon the language, however. At one time, perhaps, the resolution might have been read narrowly to confine the Committee to the subject of propaganda. The events that have transpired in the fifteen years before the interrogation of petitioner make such a construction impossible at this date. . . .

The members of the Committee have clearly demonstrated that they did not feel themselves restricted in any way to propaganda in the narrow sense of the word. Unquestionably the Committee conceived of its task in the grand view of its name. Un-American activities were its target, no matter how or where manifested. Notwithstanding the broad purview of the Committee's experience, the House of Representatives repeatedly approved its continuation. Five times it extended the life of the special committee. Then it made the group a standing committee of the House. A year later, the Committee's charter was em-

434 Liberty and Authority

bodied in the Legislative Reorganization Act. On five occasions, at the beginning of sessions of Congress, it has made the authorizing resolution part of the rules of the House. On innumerable occasions, it has passed appropriation bills to allow the Committee to continue its efforts.

Combining the language of the resolution with the construction it has been given, it is evident that the preliminary control of the Committee exercised by the House of Representatives is slight or nonexistent. No one could reasonably deduce from the charter the kind of investigation that the Committee was directed to make. As a result, we are asked to engage in a process of retroactive rationalization. Looking backward from the events that transpired, we are asked to uphold the Committee's actions unless it appears that they were clearly not authorized by the charter. As a corollary to this inverse approach, the Government urges that we must view the matter hospitably to the power of the Congress—that if there is any legislative purpose which might have been furthered by the kind of disclosure sought, the witness must be punished for withholding it. No doubt every reasonable indulgence of legality must be accorded to the actions of a coordinate branch of our Government. But such deference cannot yield to an unnecessary and unreasonable dissipation of precious constitutional freedoms.

The Government contends that the public interest at the core of the investigations of the Un-American Activities Committee is the need by the Congress to be informed of efforts to overthrow the Government by force and violence so that adequate legislative safeguards can be erected. From this core, however, the Committee can radiate outward infinitely to any topic thought to be related in some way to armed insurrection. The outer reaches of this domain are known only by the content of "un-American activities." Remoteness of subject can be aggravated by a probe for a depth of detail even farther removed from any basis of legislative action. A third dimension is added when the investigators turn their attention to the past to collect minutiae on remote topics, on the hypothesis that the past may reflect upon the present.

The consequences that flow from this situation are manifold. In the first place, a reviewing court is unable to make the kind of judgment made by the Court in *United States* v. *Rumley, supra.* The Committee is allowed, in essence, to define its own authority, to choose the direction and focus of its activities. In deciding what to do with the power that has been conferred upon them, members of the Committee may act pursuant to motives that seem to them to be the highest. Their decisions, nevertheless, can lead to ruthless exposure of private lives in order to gather data that is neither desired by the Congress nor useful to it. Yet it is impossible in this circumstance, with constitutional freedoms in jeopardy, to declare that the Committee has ranged beyond the area committed to it by its parent assembly because the boundaries are so nebulous.

More important and more fundamental than that, however, it insulates the House that has authorized the investigation from the witnesses who are subjected to the sanctions of compulsory process. There is a wide gulf between the responsibility for the use of investigative power and the actual exercise of that power. This is an especially vital consideration in assuring respect for constitutional liberties. Protected freedoms should not be placed in danger in the absence of a clear determination by the House or the Senate that a particular inquiry is justified by a specific legislative need.

It is, of course, not the function of this Court to prescribe rigid rules for the Congress to follow in drafting resolutions establishing investigating committees. That is a matter peculiarly within the realm of the legislature, and its decisions will be accepted by the courts up to the point where their own duty to enforce the constitutionally protected rights of individuals is affected. An excessively broad charter, like that of the House Un-American Activities Committee, places the courts in an untenable position if they are to strike a balance between the public need for a particular interrogation and the right of citizens to carry on their affairs free from unnecessary governmental interference. It is impossible in such a situation to ascertain whether any legislative purpose justifies the disclosures sought and, if so, the importance of that information to the Congress in furtherance of its legislative function. The reason no court can make this critical judgment is that the House of Representatives itself has never made it. Only the legislative assembly initiating an investigation can assay the relative necessity of specific disclosures.

Absence of the qualitative consideration of petitioner's questioning by the House of Representatives aggravates a serious problem, revealed in this case, in the relationship of congressional investigating committees and the witnesses who appear before them. Plainly these committees are restricted to the missions delegated to them, i.e., to acquire certain data to be used by the House or the Senate in coping with a problem that falls within its legislative sphere. No witness can be compelled to make disclosures on matters outside that area. This is a jurisdictional concept of pertinency drawn from the nature of a congressional committee's source of authority. It is not wholly different from nor unrelated to the element of pertinency embodied in the criminal statute under which petitioner was prosecuted. When the definition of jurisdictional pertinency is as uncertain and wavering as in the case of the Un-American Activities Committee, it becomes extremely difficult for the Committee to limit its inquiries to statutory pertinency.

Since World War II, the Congress has practically abandoned its original practice of utilizing the coercive sanction of contempt proceedings at the bar of the House. The sanction there imposed is imprisonment by the House until the recalcitrant witness agrees to testify or disclose the matters sought, provided that the incarceration does not extend beyond adjournment. The Congress has instead invoked the aid of the federal judicial system in protecting itself against contumacious conduct. It has become customary to refer these matters to the United States Attorneys for prosecution under criminal law.

The appropriate statute is found in 2 U.S.C. § 192. It provides:

"Every person who having been summoned as a witness by the authority of either House of Congress to give testimony or to produce papers upon any matter under inquiry before either House, or any joint committee established by a joint or concurrent resolution of the two Houses of Congress, or any committee of either House of Congress, willfully makes default, or who, having appeared, refuses to answer any question pertinent to the question under inquiry, shall be deemed guilty of a misdemeanor, punishable by a fine of not more than $1,000 nor less than $100 and imprisonment in a common jail for not less than one month nor more than twelve months."

In fulfillment of their obligation under this statute, the courts must accord to the defendants every right which is guaranteed to defendants in all other criminal cases. Among these is the right to have available, through a sufficiently precise statute, information revealing the standard of criminality before the commission of the alleged offense. Applied to persons prosecuted under § 192, this raises a special problem in that the statute defines the crime as refusal to answer "any question pertinent to the question under inquiry." Part of the standard of criminality, therefore, is the pertinency of the questions propounded to the witness.

The problem attains proportion when viewed from the standpoint of the witness who appears before a congressional committee. He must decide at the time the questions are propounded whether or not to answer. As the Court said in *Sinclair* v. *United States,* 279 U.S. 263, the witness acts at his peril. He is ". . . bound rightly to construe the statute." *Id.* 279 U.S. at 299. An erroneous determination on his part, even if made in the utmost good faith, does not exculpate him if the court should later rule that the questions were pertinent to the question under inquiry.

It is obvious that a person compelled to make this choice is entitled to have knowledge of the subject to which the interrogation is deemed pertinent. That knowledge must be available with the same degree of explicitness and clarity that the due process clause requires in the expression of any element of a criminal offense. The "vice of vagueness" must be avoided here as in all other crimes. There are several sources that can outline the "question under inquiry" in such a way that the rules against vagueness are satisfied. The authorizing resolution, the remarks of the chairman or members of the committee, or even the nature of the proceedings themselves might sometimes make the topic clear. This case demonstrates, however, that these sources often leave the matter in grave doubt.

The first possibility is that the authorizing resolution itself will so clearly declare the "question under inquiry" that a witness can understand the pertinency of questions asked him. The Government does not contend that the authorizing resolution of the Un-American Activities Committee could serve such a purpose. Its confusing breadth is amply illustrated by the innumerable and diverse questions into which the Committee has inquired under this charter since 1938. If the "question under inquiry" were stated with such sweeping and uncertain scope, we doubt that it would withstand an attack on the ground of vagueness.

That issue is not before us, however, in light of the Government's position that the immediate subject under inquiry before the Subcommittee interviewing petitioner was only one aspect of the Committee's authority to investigate un-American activities. Distilling that single topic from the broad field is an extremely difficult task upon the record before us. There was an opening statement by the Committee Chairman at the outset of the hearing, but this gives us no guidance. In this statement, the Chairman did no more than paraphrase the authorizing resolution and give a very general sketch of the past efforts of the Committee.

No aid is given as to the "question under inquiry" in the action of the full Committee that authorized the creation of the Subcommittee before which petitioner appeared. The Committee adopted a formal resolution giving the Chairman the power to appoint subcommittees ". . . for the purpose of performing any and all acts which the Committee as a whole is authorized to do." In effect, this was a device to enable the investigations to proceed with a quorum of one or two members and sheds no light on the relevancy of the questions asked of petitioner.

The Government believes that the topic of inquiry before the Subcommittee concerned Communist infiltration in labor. In his introductory remarks, the Chairman made reference to a bill, then pending before the Committee, which would have penalized labor unions controlled or dominated by persons who were, or had been, members of a "Communist-action" organization, as defined in the Internal Security Act of 1950. The Subcommittee, it is contended, might have been endeavoring to determine the extent of such a problem.

This view is corroborated somewhat by the witnesses who preceded and followed petitioner before the Subcommittee. Looking at the entire hearings, however, there is strong reason to doubt that the subject revolved about labor matters. The published transcript is entitled: Investigation of Communist Activities in the Chicago Area, and six of the nine witnesses had no connection with labor at all.

The most serious doubts as to the Subcommittee's "questions under inquiry," however, stem from the precise questions that petitioner has been charged with refusing to answer. Under the terms of the statute, after all, it is these which must be proved pertinent. Petitioner is charged with refusing to tell the Subcommittee whether or not he knew that certain named persons had been members of the Communist Party in the past. The Subcommittee's counsel read the list from the testimony of a previous witness who had identified them as Communists. Although this former witness was identified with labor, he had not stated that the persons he named were involved in union affairs. Of the thirty names propounded to petitioner, seven were completely unconnected with organized labor. One operated a beauty parlor. Another was a watchmaker. Several were identified as "just citizens" or "only Communists." When almost a quarter of the persons on the list are not labor people, the inference becomes strong that the subject before the Subcommittee was not defined in terms of Communism in labor.

The final source of evidence as to the "question under inquiry" is the chairman's response when petitioner objected to the questions on the grounds of lack of pertinency. The Chairman then announced that the Subcommittee was investigating "subversion and subversive propaganda." This is a subject at least as broad and indefinite as the authorizing resolution of the Committee, if not more so.

Having exhausted the several possible indicia of the "question under inquiry," we remain unenlightened as to the subject to which the questions asked petitioner were pertinent. Certainly, if the point is that obscure after trial and appeal, it was not adequately revealed to petitioner when he had to decide at his peril whether or not to answer. Fundamental fairness demands that no witness be compelled to make such a determination with so little guidance. Unless the subject matter has been made to appear with undisputable clarity, it is the duty of the investigative body, upon objection of the witness on grounds of pertinency, to state for the record the subject under inquiry at that time and the manner in which the propounded questions are pertinent thereto. To be meaningful, the explanation must describe what the topic under inquiry is and the connective reasoning whereby the precise questions asked relate to it.

The statement of the Committee Chairman in this case, in response to petitioner's protest, was woefully inadequate to convey sufficient information as to the pertinency of the questions to the subject under inquiry. Petitioner was thus not accorded a fair opportunity to determine whether he was within his rights in refusing to answer, and his conviction is necessarily invalid under the due process clause of the Fifth Amendment.

We are mindful of the complexities of modern government and the ample scope that must be left to the Congress as the sole constitutional depository of legislative power. Equally mindful are we of the indispensable function, in the exercise of that power, of congressional investigations. The conclusions we have reached in this case will not prevent the Congress, through its committees, from obtaining any information it needs for the proper fulfillment of its role in our scheme of government. The legislature is free to determine the kinds of data that should be collected. It is only those investigations that are conducted by use of compulsory process that give rise to a need to protect the rights of individuals against illegal encroachment. That protection can be readily achieved through procedures which prevent the separation of power from responsibility and which provide the constitutional requisites of fairness for witnesses. A measure of added care on the part of the House and the Senate in authorizing the use of compulsory process and by their committees in exercising that power would suffice. That is a small price to pay if it serves to uphold the principles of limited, constitutional government without constricting the power of the Congress to inform itself.

The judgment of the Court of Appeals is reversed, and the case is remanded to the District Court with instructions to dismiss the indictment.

It is so ordered.

MR. JUSTICE BURTON and MR. JUSTICE WHITTAKER took no part in the consideration or decision of this case.

MR. JUSTICE FRANKFURTER, concurring. . . .

MR. JUSTICE CLARK, dissenting:

As I see it the chief fault in the majority opinion is its mischievous curbing of the informing function of the Congress. While I am not versed in its procedures, my experience in the executive branch of the Government leads me to believe that the requirements laid down in the opinion for the operation of the committee system of inquiry are both unnecessary and unworkable. . . .

BARENBLATT v. UNITED STATES

360 U.S. 109 (1959)

MR. JUSTICE HARLAN delivered the opinion of the Court. . . .

We here review petitioner's conviction under 2 U.S.C. § 192 for contempt of Congress, arising from his refusal to answer certain questions put to him by a Subcommittee of the House Committee on Un-American Activities during the course of an inquiry concerning alleged Communist infiltration into the field of education. . . .

Petitioner's various contentions resolve themselves into three propositions: First, the compelling of testimony by the Subcommittee was neither legislatively authorized nor constitutionally permissible because of the vagueness of Rule XI of the House of Representatives, Eighty-third Congress, the charter of authority of the parent Committee. Second, petitioner was not adequately apprised of the pertinency of the Subcommittee's questions to the subject matter of the inquiry. Third, the questions petitioner refused to answer infringed rights protected by the First Amendment.

SUBCOMMITTEE'S AUTHORITY TO COMPEL TESTIMONY

At the outset it should be noted that Rule XI authorized this Subcommittee to compel testimony within the framework of the investigative authority conferred on the Un-American Activities Committee. Petitioner contends that *Watkins* v. *United States,* . . . nevertheless held the grant of this power in all circumstances ineffective because of the vagueness of Rule XI in delineating the Committee jurisdiction to which its exercise was to be appurtenant. This view of Watkins was accepted by two of the dissenting judges below. 252 F.2d at page 136.

The Watkins case cannot properly be read as standing for such a proposition. A principal contention in Watkins was that the refusals to answer were justified because the requirement of 2 U.S.C. § 192 that the questions asked be "pertinent to the question under inquiry" had not been satisfied. . . .This Court reversed the conviction solely on that ground, holding that Watkins had not been adequately apprised of the subject matter of the Subcommittee's investigation or the pertinency thereto of the questions he refused to answer, id., 354 U.S. at pages 206–209, 214–215; and see the concurring opinion in that case, id., 354 U.S. at page 216. In so deciding the Court drew upon Rule XI only as one of the facets in the total *mise en scène* in its search for the "question under inquiry" in that particular investigation. Id., 354 U.S. at pages 209–215. The Court, in other words, was not dealing with Rule XI at large, and indeed in effect stated that no such issue was before it, id., 354 U.S. at page 209. That the vagueness of Rule XI was not alone determinative is also shown by the Court's further statement that aside from the Rule "the remarks of the chairman or members of the committee, or even the nature of the proceedings themselves, might sometimes make the topic [under inquiry] clear." Ibid. In short, while Watkins was critical of Rule XI, it did not involve the broad and inflexible holding petitioner now attributes to it. . . .

We are urged, however, to construe

Rule XI so as at least to exclude the field of education from the Committee's compulsory authority. Two of the four dissenting judges below relied entirely, the other two alternatively, on this ground. 252 F.2d at pages 136, 138. The contention is premised on the course we took in *United States* v. *Rumely,* 345 U.S. 41, where in order to avoid constitutional issues we construed narrowly the authority of the congressional committee there involved. We cannot follow that route here for this is not a case where Rule XI has to "speak for itself, since Congress put no gloss upon it at the time of its passage," nor one where the subsequent history of the Rule has the "infirmity of *post litem motam,* self-serving declarations." See *United States* v. *Rumely, supra,* 345 U.S. at pages 44–45, 48.

To the contrary, the legislative gloss on Rule XI is again compelling. Not only is there no indication that the House ever viewed the field of education as being outside the Committee's authority under Rule XI, but the legislative history affirmatively evinces House approval of this phase of the Committee's work. . . .

PERTINENCY CLAIM

Undeniably a conviction for contempt under 2 U.S.C. § 192, 2 U.S.C.A. § 192 cannot stand unless the questions asked are pertinent to the subject matter of the investigation. *Watkins* v. *United States, supra,* 354 U.S. at pages 214–215, 77 S. Ct. at pages 1193–1194. But the factors which led us to rest decision on this ground in Watkins were very different from those involved here.

In Watkins the petitioner had made specific objection to the Subcommittee's questions on the ground of pertinency; the question under inquiry had not been disclosed in any illuminating manner; and the questions asked the petitioner were not only amorphous on their face, but in some instances clearly foreign to the alleged subject matter of the investigation—"Communism in labor." Id., 354 U.S. at pages 185, 209–215.

In contrast, petitioner in the case before us raised no objections on the ground of pertinency at the time any of the questions were put to him. . . . We need not, however, rest decision on petitioner's failure to object on this score, for here "pertinency" was made to appear "with undisputable clarity" [the Subcommittee having clearly indicated that the subject under inquiry was Communist infiltration into the field of education].

CONSTITUTIONAL CONTENTIONS

Our function, at this point, is purely one of constitutional adjudication in the particular case and upon the particular record before us, not to pass judgment upon the general wisdom or efficacy of the activities of this Committee in a vexing and complicated field.

The precise constitutional issue confronting us is whether the Subcommittee's inquiry into petitioner's past or present membership in the Communist Party transgressed the provisions of the First Amendment, which of course reach and limit congressional investigations. *Watkins, supra,* 354 U.S. at page 197.

The Court's past cases establish sure guides to decision. Undeniably, the First Amendment in some circumstances protects an individual from being compelled to disclose his associational relationships. However, the protections of the First Amendment, unlike a proper claim of the privilege against self-incrimination under the Fifth Amendment, do not afford a witness the right to resist inquiry in all circumstances. Where the First Amendment rights are asserted to bar governmental interrogation resolution of the issue always involves a balancing by the courts of the competing private and public interests at stake in the particular circumstances shown. . . .

The first question is whether this investigation was related to a valid legislative purpose, for Congress may not constitutionally require an individual to disclose his political relationships or other private affairs except in relation to such a purpose. See *Watkins* v. *United States, supra,* 354 U.S. at page 198.

That Congress has wide power to legislate in the field of Communist activity in this Country, and to conduct appropriate investigations in aid thereof, is hardly debatable. The existence of such power has never been questioned by this Court, and it is sufficient to say, without particularization, that Congress has enacted or considered in this field a wide range of legislative measures, not a few of which have stemmed from recommendations of the very Committee whose actions have been drawn in question here. In the last analysis this power rests on the right of self-preservation, "the ultimate value of any society," *Dennis* v. *United States,* 341 U.S. 494, 509. Justification for its exercise in turn rests on the long and widely accepted view that the tenets of the Communist Party include the ultimate overthrow of the Government of the United States by force and violence, a view which has been given formal expression by the Congress.

On these premises, this Court in its constitutional adjudications has consistently refused to view the Communist Party as an ordinary political party, and has upheld federal legislation aimed at the Communist problem which in a different context would certainly have raised constitutional issues of the gravest character. . . .

[W]e do not understand petitioner here to suggest that Congress in no circumstances may inquire into Communist activity in the field of education. Rather, his position is in effect that this particular investigation was aimed not at the revolutionary aspects but at the theoretical classroom discussion of communism.

In our opinion this position rests on a too constricted view of the nature of the investigatory process, and is not supported by a fair assessment of the record before us. An investigation of advocacy of or preparation for overthrow certainly embraces the right to identify a witness as a member of the Communist Party, see *Barsky* v. *United States,* 167 F.2d 241, and to inquire into the various manifestations of the Party's tenets. The strict require-

ments of a prosecution under the Smith Act, see *Dennis* v. *United States, supra,* and *Yates* v. *United States,* 354 U.S. 298, are not the measure of the permissible scope of a congressional investigation into "overthrow," for of necessity the investigatory process must proceed step by step. Nor can it fairly be concluded that this investigation was directed at controlling what is being taught at our universities rather than at overthrow. The statement of the Subcommittee Chairman at the opening of the investigation evinces no such intention, and so far as this record reveals nothing thereafter transpired which would justify our holding that the thrust of the investigation later changed. The record discloses considerable testimony concerning the foreign domination and revolutionary purposes and efforts of the Communist Party. That there was also testimony on the abstract philosophical level does not detract from the dominant theme of this investigation—Communist infiltration furthering the alleged ultimate purpose of overthrow. And certainly the conclusion would not be justified that the questioning of petitioner would have exceeded permissible bounds had he not shut off the Subcommittee at the threshold.

Nor can we accept the further contention that this investigation should not be deemed to have been in furtherance of a legislative purpose because the true objective of the Committee and of the Congress was purely "exposure." So long as Congress acts in pursuance of its constitutional power, the judiciary lacks authority to intervene on the basis of the motives which spurred the exercise of that power. *State of Arizona* v. *State of California,* 283 U.S. 423, 455, and cases there cited. "It is, of course, true," as was said in *McCray* v. *United States,* 195 U.S. 27, 55, "that if there be no authority in the judiciary to restrain a lawful exercise of power by another department of the government, where a wrong motive or purpose has impelled to the exertion of the power, that abuses of a power conferred may be temporarily effectual. The remedy for this, however, lies, not in abuse by the judicial authority of its functions, but in the people, upon whom, after all, under our institutions, reliance must be placed for the correction of abuses committed in the exercise of a lawful power." These principles of course apply as well to committee investigations into the need for legislation as to the enactments which such investigations may produce. Cf. *Tenney* v. *Brandhove*, 341 U.S. 367, 377–378. Thus, in stating in the Watkins case, 354 U.S. at page 200, that "there is no congressional power to expose for the sake of exposure," we at the same time declined to inquire into the "motives of committee members," and recognized that their "motives alone would not vitiate an investigation which had been instituted by a House of Congress if that assembly's legislative purpose is being served." Having scrutinized this record we cannot say that the unanimous panel of the Court of Appeals which first considered this case was wrong in concluding that "the primary purposes of the inquiry were in aid of legislative processes." 240 F.2d at page 881. Certainly this is not a case like *Kilbourn* v. *Thompson*, 103 U.S. 168, 192, where "the House of Representatives not only exceeded the limit of its own authority, but assumed a power which could only be properly exercised by another branch of the government, because it was in its nature clearly judicial." See *McGrain* v. *Daugherty*, 273 U.S. 135, 171. The constitutional legislative power of Congress in this instance is beyond question. . . .

We conclude that the balance between the individual and the governmental interests here at stake must be struck in favor of the latter, and that therefore the provisions of the First Amendment have not been offended.

We hold that petitioner's conviction for contempt of Congress discloses no infirmity, and that the judgment of the Court of Appeals must be affirmed.

Affirmed.

MR. JUSTICE BLACK, with whom THE CHIEF JUSTICE, and MR. JUSTICE DOUGLAS concur, dissenting. . . .

I do not agree that laws directly abridging First Amendment freedoms can be justified by a congressional or judicial balancing process. There are, of course, cases suggesting that a law which primarily regulates conduct but which might also indirectly affect speech can be upheld if the effect on speech is minor in relation to the need for control of the conduct. With these cases I agree. Typical of them are *Cantwell* v. *State of Connecticut*, 310 U.S. 296, and *Schneider* v. *State of New Jersey, Town of Irvington*, 308 U.S. 147. Both of these involved the right of a city to control its streets. . . . But we did not in Schneider, any more than in Cantwell, even remotely suggest that a law directly aimed at curtailing speech and political persuasion could be saved through a balancing process. Neither these cases, nor any others, can be read as allowing legislative bodies to pass laws abridging freedom of speech, press and association merely because of hostility to views peacefully expressed in a place where the speaker had a right to be. Rule XI, on its face and as here applied, since it attempts inquiry into beliefs, not action —ideas and associations, not conduct, does just that.

To apply the Court's balancing test under such circumstances is to read the First Amendment to say "Congress shall pass no law abridging freedom of speech, press, assembly and petition, unless Congress and the Supreme Court reach the joint conclusion that on balance the interests of the Government in stifling these freedoms is greater than the interest of the people in having them exercised." This is closely akin to the notion that neither the First Amendment nor any other provision of the Bill of Rights should be enforced unless the Court believes it is *reasonable* to do so. Not only does this violate the genius of our *written* Constitution, but it runs expressly counter to the injunction to Court and Congress made by Madison when he introduced the Bill of Rights. "If they [the first ten amendments] are incorporated into the Constitution, independent tribunals of justice will consider themselves in a peculiar manner the guardians of those rights; they will be an impenetrable bulwark against *every* assumption of power in the Legislative or Executive; they will be naturally led to resist *every* encroachment upon rights expressly stipulated for in the Constitution by the declaration of rights." Unless we return to this view of our judicial function, unless we once again accept the notion that the Bill of Rights means what it says and that this Court must enforce that meaning, I am of the opinion that our great charter of liberty will be more honored in the breach than in the observance.

But even assuming what I cannot assume, that some balancing is proper in this case, I feel that the Court after stating the test ignores it completely. At most it balances the right of the Government to preserve itself, against Barenblatt's right to refrain from revealing Communist affiliations. Such a balance, however, mistakes the factors to be weighed. In the first place, it completely leaves out the real interest in Barenblatt's silence, the interest of the people as a whole in being able to join organizations, advocate causes and make political "mistakes" without later being subjected to governmental penalties for having dared to think for themselves. It is this right, the right to err politically, which keeps us strong as a Nation. For no number of laws against communism can have as much effect as the personal conviction which comes from having heard its arguments and rejected them, or from having once accepted its tenets and later recognized their worthlessness. Instead, the obloquy which results from investigations such as this not only stifles "mistakes" but prevents all but the most courageous from hazarding any views which might at some later time become disfavored. This result, whose importance cannot be overestimated, is doubly crucial when it affects the universities, on which we must largely rely for the experimentation and development of new ideas essential to our country's welfare. It is these interests of society, rather than Barenblatt's own right to silence, which I think the Court should put on the balance against the demands of the Government, if any balancing process is to be tolerated. Instead they are not mentioned, while on the other side the demands of the Government are vastly overstated and called "self preservation." It is admitted that this Committee can only seek information for the purpose of suggesting laws, and that Congress' power to make laws in the realm of speech and association is quite limited, even on the Court's test. Its interest in making such laws in the field of education, primarily a state function, is clearly narrower still. Yet the Court styles this attenuated interest self-preservation and allows it to overcome the need our country has to let us all think, speak, and associate politically as we like and without fear of reprisal. . . .

Finally, I think Barenblatt's conviction violates the Constitution because the chief aim, purpose and practice of the House Un-American Activities Committee, as disclosed by its many reports, is to try witnesses and punish them because they are or have been Communists or because they refuse to admit or deny Communist affiliations. The punishment imposed is generally punishment by humiliation and public shame. There is nothing strange or novel about this kind of punishment. It is in fact one of the oldest forms of governmental punishment known to mankind; branding, the pillory, ostracism and subjection to public hatred being but a few examples of it. . . .

MR. JUSTICE BRENNAN, dissenting.

I would reverse this conviction. It is sufficient that I state my complete agreement with my Brother Black that no purpose for the investigation of Barenblatt is revealed by the record except exposure purely for the sake of exposure. This is not a purpose to which Barenblatt's rights under the First Amendment can validly be subordinated. An investigation in which the processes of law-making and law-evaluating are submerged entirely in exposure of individual behavior—in adjudication, of a sort, through the exposure process—is outside the constitutional pale of congressional inquiry.

NOTE: *Deutch* v. *United States*, 367 U.S. 456 (1961), reversed a contempt conviction of one who refused to testify before the House Un-American Activities Committee on the ground that he did not want to be an informer. The Court held that the prosecution had failed to prove the pertinency of the quesions. Due process, it was said, requires that the witness be made aware of the pertinency of the question at the time of the questioning (this the witness had waived by failing to raise the issue before the committee), and that the prosecution prove at the trial that the questions were pertinent to the matter "under inquiry." Justices Frankfurter, Clark, Harlan, and Whittaker, dissenting, thought the government had met the burden of proving pertinency.

UPHAUS v. *WYMAN*

360 U.S. 72 (1959)

Appeal from the Supreme Court of New Hampshire.

MR. JUSTICE CLARK delivered the opinion of the Court. . . .

As in Sweezy, the Attorney General of New Hampshire, who had been constituted a one-man legislative investigating committee by Joint Resolution of the Legislature, was conducting a probe of subversive activities in the State. In the course of his investigation the Attorney General called appellant, Executive Director of World Fellowship, Inc., a voluntary corporation organized under the laws of New Hampshire and maintaining a summer camp in the State. Appellant testified concerning his own activities, but refused to comply with two subpoenas *duces tecum* which called for the production of certain corporate records. . . . We now pass to a consideration of the sole question before us, namely, the validity of the order of contempt for refusal to produce the list of guests at World Fellowship, Inc., during the summer seasons of 1954 and 1955. . . .
Appellant vigorously contends that the New Hampshire Subversive Activities Act

of 1951 and the resolution creating the committee have been superseded by the Smith Act, as amended. In support of this position appellant cites *Pennsylvania* v. *Nelson, supra*. The argument is that Nelson, which involved a prosecution under a state sedition law, held that "Congress has intended to occupy the field of sedition." . . . In Nelson itself we said that the "precise holding of the court . . . is that the Smith Act . . . which prohibits the knowing advocacy of the overthrow of the Government of the United States by force and violence, supersedes the enforceability of the Pennsylvania Sedition Act which proscribed the *same conduct*." (Italics supplied.) 350 U.S., at 499. The basis of Nelson thus rejects the notion that it stripped the States of the right to protect themselves. All the opinion proscribed was a race between federal and state prosecutors to the courthouse door. The opinion made clear that a State could proceed with prosecutions for sedition against the State itself; that it can legitimately investigate in this area follows *a fortiori*. In *Sweezy* v. *New Hampshire, supra*, where the same contention was made as to the identical state Act, it was denied *sub silentio*. . . .

Appellant's other objections can be capsuled into the single question of whether New Hampshire, under the facts here, is precluded from compelling the production of the documents by the Due Process Clause of the Fourteenth Amendment. . . . The interest of the guests at World Fellowship in their associational privacy having been asserted, we have for decision the federal question of whether the public interests overbalance these conflicting private ones. Whether there was "justification" for the production order turns on the "substantiality" of New Hampshire's interests in obtaining the identity of the guests when weighed against the individual interests which the appellant asserts. *National Association for the Advancement of Colored People* v. *Alabama*, 357 U.S. 449.

What was the interest of the State? The Attorney General was commissioned to determine if there were any subversive persons within New Hampshire. The obvious starting point of such an inquiry was to learn what persons were within the State. It is therefore clear that the requests relate directly to the Legislature's area of interest, i.e., the presence of subversives in the State, as announced in its resolution. . . .

Moreover, the Attorney General had valid reason to believe that the speakers and guests at World Fellowship might be subversive persons within the meaning of the New Hampshire Act. . . . Although the evidence as to the nexus between World Fellowship and subversive activities may not be conclusive, we believe it sufficiently relevant to support the Attorney General's action. . . . The record reveals that appellant had participated in "Communist front" activities and that "[n]ot less than nineteen speakers invited by Uphaus to talk at World Fellowship had either been members of the Communist Party or had connections or affiliations with it or with one or more of the organizations cited as subversive or Communist controlled in the United States Attorney General's list." . . . While the Attorney General's list is designed for the limited

purpose of determining fitness for federal employment, *Wieman* v. *Updegraff*, 344 U.S. 183 (1952), and guilt by association remains a thoroughly discredited doctrine, it is with a legislative investigation—not a criminal prosecution—that we deal here. Certainly the investigatory power of the State need not be constricted until sufficient evidence of subversion is gathered to justify the institution of criminal proceedings.

The nexus between World Fellowship and subversive activities disclosed by the record furnished adequate justification for the investigation we here review. . . . The investigation was . . . undertaken in the interest of self-preservation, "the ultimate value of any society," *Dennis* v. *United States*, 341 U.S. 494, 509 (1951). This governmental interest outweighs individual rights in an associational privacy which, however real in other circumstances, cf. *National Association for the Advancement of Colored People* v. *Alabama, supra,* were here tenuous at best. The camp was operating as a public one, furnishing both board and lodging to persons applying therefor. As to them, New Hampshire law requires that World Fellowship, Inc., maintain a register, open to inspection of sheriffs and police officers. . . . We recognize, of course, that compliance with the subpoena will result in exposing the fact that the persons therein named were guests at World Fellowship. But so long as a committee must report to its legislative parent, exposure—in the sense of disclosure—is an inescapable incident of an investigation into the presence of subversive persons within a State. And the governmental interest in self-preservation is sufficiently compelling to subordinate the interest in associational privacy of persons who, at least to the extent of the guest registration statute, made public at the inception the association they now wish to keep private. . . .

Affirmed.

MR. JUSTICE BRENNAN, with whom THE CHIEF JUSTICE, MR. JUSTICE BLACK and MR. JUSTICE DOUGLAS join, dissenting.

. . . With due respect for my Brothers' views, I do not agree that a showing of any requisite legislative purpose or other state interest that constitutionally can subordinate appellant's rights is to be found in this record. Exposure purely for the sake of exposure is not such a valid subordinating purpose. . . . This record, I think, not only fails to reveal any interest of the State sufficient to subordinate appellant's constitutionally protected rights, but affirmatively shows that the investigatory objective was the impermissible one of exposure for exposure's sake. I therefore dissent from the judgment of the Court. . . .

Of course, the considerations entering into the weighing of the interests concerned is different where the problem is one of state exposure in the area of assembly and expression from where the problem is that of evaluating a state criminal or regulatory statute in these areas. Government must have freedom to make an appropriate investigation where there appears a rational connection with the law-making process, the processes of adjudication, or other essential governmental functions. In the investigatory stage of the legislative process, for example, the specific interest of the state and the final legislative means to be chosen to implement it are almost by definition not precisely defined at the start of the inquiry, and due allowance must accordingly be made. Also, when exposure is evaluated judicially as a governmental sanction, there should be taken into account the differences between it and the more traditional state-inflicted pains and penalties. True it is, therefore, that any line other than a universal subordination of free expression and association to the asserted interests of the state in investigation and exposure will be difficult of definition; but this Court has rightly turned its back on the alternative of universal subordination of protected interests, and we must define rights in this area the best we can. The problem is one in its nature calling for traditional case-by-case development of principles in the various permutations of circumstances where the conflict may appear. But guide lines must be marked out by the courts. . . . On the facts of this case I think that New Hampshire's investigation, as applied to the appellant, was demonstrably and clearly outside the wide limits of the power which must be conceded to the State even though it be attended by some exposure. In demonstration of this I turn to the detailed examination of the facts which this case requires. . . .

The investigation, as revealed by the report, was overwhelmingly and predominantly a roving, self-contained investigation of individual and group behavior, and behavior in a constitutionally protected area. Its whole approach was to name names, disclose information about those named, and observe that "facts are facts." . . . The report discloses an investigation in which the processes of law-making and law-evaluating were submerged entirely in exposure of individual behavior—in adjudication, of a sort, however much disclaimed, through the exposure process. If an investigation or trial, conducted by any organ of the State, which is aimed at the application of sanctions to individual behavior is to be upheld, it must meet the traditional standards that the common law in this country has established for the application of sanctions to the individual, or a constitutionally permissible modification of them. Cf. *Kilbourn* v. *Thompson*, 103 U.S. 168, 195. As a bare minimum there must be general standards of conduct, substantively constitutionally proper, applied to the individual in a fair proceeding with defined issues resulting in a binding, final determination. I had not supposed that a legislative investigation of the sort practiced here provided such a framework under the Constitution. . . .

This Court's approach to a very similar problem in *NAACP* v. *Alabama, supra,* should furnish a guide to the proper course of decision here. . . .

The Court describes the inquiry we must make in this matter as a balancing of interests. I think I have indicated that there has been no valid legislative interest of the

State actually defined and shown in the investigation as it operated, so that there is really nothing against which the appellant's rights of association and expression can be balanced. But if some proper legislative end of the inquiry can be surmised, through what must be a process of speculation, I think it is patent that there is really no subordinating interest in it demonstrated on the part of the State. . . . Here we must demand some initial showing by the State sufficient to counterbalance the interest in privacy as it relates to freedom of speech and assembly. On any basis that has practical meaning, New Hampshire has not made such a showing here. I would reverse the judgment of the New Hampshire Supreme Court.

MR. JUSTICE BLACK and MR. JUSTICE

DOUGLAS would decide this case on the ground that appellant is being deprived of rights under the First and Fourteenth Amendments, for the reasons developed in *Adler* v. *Board of Education*, 342 U.S. 485, 508 (dissenting opinion); *Beauharnais* v. *Illinois*, 343 U.S. 250, 267, 284 (dissenting opinions). But they join MR. JUSTICE BRENNAN's dissent because he makes clear to them that New Hampshire's legislative program resulting in the incarceration of appellant for contempt violates Art. I, § 10 of the Constitution which provides that "No State shall . . . pass any Bill of Attainder." See *United States* v. *Lovett*, 328 U.S. 303, 315–318, and cases cited; *Joint Anti-Fascist Refugee Committee* v. *McGrath*, 341 U.S. 123, 142–149 (concurring opinion).

GIBSON v. *FLORIDA LEGISLATIVE INVESTIGATING COMMITTEE*
372 U.S. 539 (1963)

Florida tried to rely on the *Barenblatt-Uphaus* line of cases to compel an NAACP officer to tell whether certain alleged Communists were members of NAACP. Reversing a contempt conviction, the Supreme Court observed:

. . . regardless of the label applied, be it "nexus," "foundation," or whatever . . . it is an essential prerequisite to the validity of an investigation which intrudes into the area of constitutionally protected rights . . . that the State convincingly show a substantial relation between the information sought and a subject of overriding and compelling state interest. . . . It is apparent that the result in [*Barenblatt*] was founded on the holding that the Communist Party is not an ordinary or legitimate political party . . . and that, because of its particular nature, membership therein is *itself* a permissible subject of regulation and legislative scrutiny. Assuming the correctness of the premises on which [*Barenblatt* and related] cases were decided, no further demonstration of com-

pelling governmental interest was deemed necessary. . . . [The] record in this case is insufficient to show a substantial connection between the Miami Branch of the NAACP and Communist activities. . . . In essence, there is here merely indirect, less than equivocal, and mostly hearsay, testimony that in years past some 14 people who were asserted to be or to have been Communists, or members of Communist front or "affiliated organizations," attended occasional meetings of the Miami Branch of the NAACP "and/or" were members of that Branch, which had a total membership of about 1,000. . . . The respondent Committee has laid no adequate foundation for its direct demands. [We] hold simply that groups which themselves are neither engaged in subversive or other illegal or improper activities, nor demonstrated to have any substantial connections with such activities, are to be protected in their rights of free and private association.

Mr. Justice Harlan, joined by his brothers Clark, Stewart and White dissented:

. . . until today, I had never supposed that any of our decisions . . . could possibly be taken as suggesting any difference in the degree of governmental investigatory interest as between Communist infiltration *of* organizations and Communist activity *by* organizations. . . . Given the unsoundness of the basic premise underlying the Court's holding as to the absence of "nexus," this decision surely falls of its own weight. For unless "nexus" requires an investigating agency to prove in advance the very things it is trying to find out, I do not understand how it can be said that the information preliminarily developed by the Committee's investigator was not sufficient to satisfy, under any reasonable tests, the requirement of "nexus."

NAACP v. *ALABAMA*
357 U.S. 449 (1958)

An Alabama statute similar to those in many other states required certain out-of-state corporations, before doing business in the State, to file the corporate charter and designate a place of business and an agent to receive service of process. NAACP, a New York, nonprofit corporation, thought itself exempt from the statute and operated in Alabama without complying therewith. In 1956 the Attorney General of Alabama brought an equity suit to enjoin any further NAACP activities within, and to oust the Association from, the state. Before trial, upon a motion by the Attorney General, the trial court ordered NAACP to submit certain papers including a list of all its Alabama members and agents. NAACP, still disclaiming the applicability of the statute, offered to comply with its requirements, but refused to produce the membership lists. For this refusal it was fined $100,000 for contempt of court. This judgment reached the Supreme Court via certiorari.

Mr. Justice Harlan delivered the opinion of the court. . . .

III

We thus reach petitioner's claim that the production order in the state litigation trespasses upon fundamental freedoms protected by the due process clause of the Fourteenth Amendment. Petitioner argues that in view of the facts and circumstances shown in the record, the effect of compelled disclosure of the membership lists will be to abridge the rights of its rank-and-file members to engage in lawful association in support of their common beliefs. It contends that governmental action which, although not directly suppressing association, nevertheless carries this consequence, can be justified only upon some overriding valid interest of the State.

Effective advocacy of both public and private points of view, particularly controversial ones, is undeniably enhanced by group association, as this Court has more than once recognized by remarking upon the close nexus between the freedoms of speech and assembly. *De Jonge* v. *Oregon*, 299 U.S. 353, 364; *Thomas* v. *Collins*, 323 U.S. 516, 530. It is beyond debate that freedom to engage in association for the advancement of beliefs and ideas is an inseparable aspect of the "liberty" assured by the due process clause of the Fourteenth Amendment, which embraces freedom of speech. See *Gitlow* v. *New York*, 268 U.S. 652, 666; *Palko* v. *Connecticut*, 302 U.S. 319, 324; *Cantwell* v. *Connecticut*, 310 U.S. 296, 303; *Staub* v. *City of Baxley*, 355 U.S. 313, 321. Of course, it is immaterial whether the beliefs sought to be advanced by association pertain to political, economic, religious, or cultural matters, and state action which may have the effect of curtailing the freedom to associate is subject to the closest scrutiny.

The fact that Alabama, so far as is relevant to the validity of the contempt judgment presently under review, has taken no direct action, cf. *De Jonge* v. *Oregon, supra; Near* v. *Minnesota*, 283 U.S. 697, to restrict the right of petitioner's members to associate freely, does not end inquiry into the effect of the production order. See *American Communications Assn.* v. *Douds*, 339 U.S. 382, 402. In the domain of these indispensable liberties, whether of speech, press, or association, the decisions of this Court recognize that abridgment of such rights, even though unintended, may inevitably follow from varied forms of governmental action. Thus in *Douds*, the Court stressed that the legislation there challenged, which on its face sought to regulate labor unions and to secure stability in interstate commerce, would have the practical effect "of discouraging" the exercise of constitutionally protected political rights, 339 U.S., at 393, and it upheld the statute only after concluding that the reasons advanced for its enactment were constitutionally sufficient to justify its possible deterrent effect upon such freedoms. Similar recognition of possible unconstitutional intimidation of the free exercise of the right to advocate underlay this Court's narrow construction of the authority of a congressional committee investigating lobbying and of an Act regulating lobbying, although in neither case was there an effort to suppress speech. *United States* v. *Rumely*, 345 U.S. 41, 46–47; *United States* v. *Harriss*, 347 U.S. 612, 625–626. The governmental action challenged may appear to be totally unrelated to protected liberties. Statutes imposing taxes upon rather than prohibiting particular activity have been struck down when perceived to have the consequence of unduly curtailing the liberty of freedom of press assured under the Fourteenth Amendment. *Grosjean* v. *American Press Co.*, 297 U.S. 233; *Murdock* v. *Pennsylvania*, 319 U.S. 105.

It is hardly a novel perception that compelled disclosure of affiliation with groups engaged in advocacy may constitute as effective a restraint on freedom of association as the forms of governmental action in the cases above were thought likely to produce upon the particular constitutional rights there involved. This court has recognized the vital relationship between freedom to associate and privacy in one's associations. When referring to the varied forms of governmental action which might interfere with freedom of assembly, it said in *American Communications Assn.* v. *Douds, supra.* at 402: "A requirement that adherents of particular religious faiths or political parties wear identifying armbands, for example, is obviously of this nature." Compelled disclosure of membership in an organization engaged in advocacy of particular beliefs is of the same order. Inviolability of privacy in group association may in many circumstances be indispensable to preservation of freedom of association, particularly where a group espouses dissident beliefs. Cf. *United States* v. *Rumely, supra,* at 56–58 (concurring opinion).

We think that the production order, in the respects here drawn in question, must be regarded as entailing the likelihood of a substantial restraint upon the exercise by petitioner's members of their right to freedom of association. Petitioner has made an uncontroverted showing that on past occasions revelation of the identity of its rank-and-file members has exposed these members to economic reprisal, loss of employment, threat of physical coercion, and other manifestations of public hostility. . . .

We turn to the final question whether Alabama has demonstrated an interest in obtaining the disclosures it seeks from petitioner which is sufficient to justify the deterrent effect which we have concluded these disclosures may well have on the free exercise by petitioner's members of their constitutionally protected right of association. See *American Communications Assn.* v. *Douds, supra,* at 400; *Schneider* v. *State,* 308 U.S. 147, 161. Such a ". . . subordinating interest of the state must be compelling," *Sweezy* v. *New Hampshire,* 354 U.S. 234, 265 (concurring opinion). It is not of moment that the state has here acted solely through its judicial branch, for whether legislative or judicial, it is still the application of state power which we are asked to scrutinize.

It is important to bear in mind that petitioner asserts no right to absolute immunity from state investigation, and no right to disregard Alabama's laws. As shown by its substantial compliance with the production order, petitioner does not deny Alabama's right to obtain from it such information as the state desires concerning the purposes of the Association and its activities within the state. Petitioner has not objected to divulging the identity of its members who are employed by or hold official positions with it. It has urged the rights solely of its ordinary rank-and-file members. This is therefore not analogous to a case involving the interest of a state in protecting its citizens in their dealings with paid solicitors or agents of foreign corporations by requiring identification. See *Cantwell* v. *Connecticut, supra,* at 306; *Thomas* v. *Collins, supra,* at 538.

Whether there was "justification" in this instance turns solely on the substantiality of Alabama's interest in obtaining the membership lists. During the course of a hearing before the Alabama Circuit Court on a motion of petitioner to set aside the production order, the State Attorney General presented at length, under examination by petitioner, the state's reason for requesting the membership lists. The exclusive purpose was to determine whether petitioner was conducting intrastate business in violation of the Alabama foreign corporation registration statute, and the membership lists were expected to help

resolve this question. The issues in the litigation commenced by Alabama by its bill in equity were whether the character of petitioner and its activities in Alabama had been such as to make petitioner subject to the registration statute, and whether the extent of petitioner's activities without qualifying suggested its permanent ouster from the state. Without intimating the slightest view upon the merits of these issues, we are unable to perceive that the disclosure of the names of petitioner's rank-and-file members has a substantial bearing on either of them. . . .

From what has already been said, we think it apparent that *Bryant* v. *Zimmerman,* 278 U.S. 63, cannot be relied on in support of the state's position, for that case involved markedly different considerations in terms of the interest of the state in obtaining disclosure. There, this Court upheld, as applied to a member of a local chapter of the Ku Klux Klan, a New York statute requiring any unincorporated association which demanded an oath as a condition to membership to file with state officials copies of its ". . . constitution, by-laws, rules, regulations and oath of membership, together with a roster of its membership and a list of its officers for the current year." N.Y. Laws 1923, c. 664, §§ 53, 56. In its opinion, the Court took care to emphasize the nature of the organization which New York sought to regulate. The decision was based on the particular character of the Klan's activities, involving acts of unlawful intimidation and violence, which the Court assumed was before the state legislature when it enacted the statute, and of which the Court itself took judicial notice. Furthermore, the situation before us is significantly different from that in *Bryant,* because the organization there had made no effort to comply with any of the requirements of New York's statute but rather had refused to furnish the state with *any* information as to its local activities. . . .

Reversed.

5. UTTERANCE OR UNEMPLOYMENT

WIEMAN v. *UPDEGRAFF*

344 U.S. 183 (1952)

MR. JUSTICE CLARK delivered the opinion of the Court.

This is an appeal from a decision of the Supreme Court of Oklahoma . . . upholding the validity of a loyalty oath prescribed by Oklahoma statute for all state officers and employees. . . . Appellants, employed by the state as members of the faculty and staff of Oklahoma Agricultural and Mechanical College, failed, within the thirty days permitted, to take the oath required by the Act. Appellee Updegraff, as a citizen and taxpayer, thereupon brought this suit in the District Court of Oklahoma County to enjoin the necessary state officials from paying further compensation to employees who had not subscribed to the oath. The appellants, who were permitted to intervene, attacked the validity of the Act on the grounds, among others, that it was a bill of attainder; an *ex post facto* law; impaired the obligation of their contracts with the State and violated the Due Process Clause of the Fourteenth Amendment. They also sought a mandatory injunction directing the state officers to pay their salaries regardless of their failure to take the oath. Their objections centered largely on the following clauses of the oath:

". . . That I am not affiliated directly or indirectly . . . with any foreign political agency, party, organization or Government, or with any agency, party, organization, association, or group whatever which has been officially determined by the United States Attorney General or other authorized agency of the United States to be a communist front or subversive organization; . . . that I will take up arms in the defense of the United States in time of War, or National Emergency, if necessary; that within the five (5) years immediately pre-

ceding the taking of this oath (or affirmation) I have not been a member of . . . any agency, party, organization, association, or group whatever which has been officially determined by the United States Attorney General or other authorized public agency of the United States to be a communist front or subversive organization. . . ."

The court upheld the Act and enjoined the state officers from making further salary payments to appellants. The Supreme Court of Oklahoma affirmed. . . .

The purpose of the Act, we are told, "was to make loyalty a qualification to hold public office or be employed by the State." 205 Okl. at page 305, 237 P.2d at page 136. During periods of international stress, the extent of legislation with such objectives accentuates our traditional concern about the relation of government to the individual in a free society. The perennial problem of defining that relationship becomes acute when disloyalty is screened by ideological patterns and techniques of disguise that make it difficult to identify. Democratic government is not powerless to meet this threat, but it must do so without infringing the freedoms that are the ultimate values of all democratic living. In the adoption of such means as it believes effective, the legislature is therefore confronted with the problem of balancing its interest in national security with the often conflicting constitutional rights of the individual.

In a series of cases coming here in recent years, we have had occasion to consider legislation aimed at safeguarding the public service from disloyalty. *Garner* v. *Board of Public Works*, 1951, 341 U.S. 716; *Adler* v. *Board of Education*, 1952, 342 U.S. 485; *Gerende* v. *Board of Supervisors*, 1951, 341

U.S. 56. It is in the context of these decisions that we determine the validity of the oath before us.

Garner involved a Los Angeles ordinance requiring all city employees to swear that they did not advocate the overthrow of the government by unlawful means or belong to organizations with such objectives. The ordinance implemented an earlier charter amendment which disqualified from municipal employment all persons unable to take such an oath truthfully. One of the attacks made on the oath in that case was that it violated due process because its negation was not limited to organizations known by the employee to be within the proscribed class. This argument was rejected because we felt justified in assuming that *scienter* was implicit in each clause of the oath.

Adler also indicated the importance of determining whether a rule of exclusion based on association applies to innocent as well as knowing activity. New York had sought to bar from employment in the public schools persons who advocate, or belong to organizations which advocate, the overthrow of the government by unlawful means. The Feinberg Law directed the New York Board of Regents to make a listing, after notice and hearing, of organizations of the type described. Under § 3022 of the statute, Education Law, McK. Consol. Laws, c. 16, the Regents provided by regulation that membership in a listed organization should be *prima facie* evidence of disqualification for office in the New York public schools. In upholding this legislation, we expressly noted that the New York courts had construed the statute to require knowledge of organizational purpose before the regulation could apply. 342 U.S. at page 494. Cf. *American Communications Ass'n v. Douds,* 1950, 339 U.S. 382, 413.

The oath in Gerende was required of candidates for public office who sought places on a Maryland ballot. On oral argument in that case, the Maryland Attorney General assured us that he would advise the proper state authorities to accept, as

complying with the statute, an affidavit stating that the affiant was not engaged in an attempt to overthrow the government by force or violence or knowingly a member of an organization engaged in such an attempt. Because we read an earlier Maryland Court of Appeals' decision as interpreting the statute so that such an affidavit would satisfy its requirements, we affirmed on the basis of this assurance.

We assumed in Garner, that if our interpretation of the oath as containing an implicit *scienter* requirement was correct, Los Angeles would give the petitioners who had refused to sign the oath an opportunity to take it as interpreted and resume their employment. But here, with our decision in Garner before it, the Oklahoma Supreme Court refused to extend to appellants an opportunity to take the oath. In addition, a petition for rehearing which urged that failure to permit appellants to take the oath as interpreted deprived them of due process was denied. This must be viewed as a holding that knowledge is not a factor under the Oklahoma statute. We are thus brought to the question touched on in Garner, Adler, and Gerende: whether the due process clause permits a state in attempting to bar disloyal individuals from its employ to exclude persons solely on the basis of organizational membership, regardless of their knowledge concerning the organizations to which they had belonged. For, under the statute before us, the fact of membership alone disqualifies. If the rule be expressed as a presumption of disloyalty, it is a conclusive one.

But membership may be innocent. A state servant may have joined a proscribed organization unaware of its activities and purposes. In recent years, many completely loyal persons have severed organizational ties after learning for the first time of the character of groups to which they had belonged. "They had joined, [but] did not know what it was; they were good, fine young men and women, loyal Americans, but they had been trapped into it—because one of the great weaknesses of all Americans, whether adult or youth, is to join something." At the time of affiliation, a group itself may be innocent, only later coming under the influence of those who would turn it toward illegitimate ends. Conversely, an organization formerly subversive and therefore designated as such may have subsequently freed itself from the influences which originally led to its listing.

There can be no dispute about the consequences visited upon a person excluded from public employment on disloyalty grounds. In the view of the community, the stain is a deep one; indeed, it has become a badge of infamy. Especially is this so in time of cold war and hot emotions when "each man begins to eye his neighbor as a possible enemy." Yet under the Oklahoma Act, the fact of association alone determines disloyalty and disqualification; it matters not whether association existed innocently or knowingly. To thus inhibit individual freedom of movement is to stifle the flow of democratic expression and controversy at one of its chief sources. We hold that the distinction observed between the case at bar and Garner, Adler and Gerende is decisive. Indiscriminate classification of innocent with knowing activity must fall as an assertion of arbitrary power. The oath offends due process. . . .

Reversed.

MR. JUSTICE JACKSON, not having heard the argument, took no part in the consideration or decision of this case.

MR. JUSTICE BURTON concurs in the result.

[JUSTICES BLACK and FRANKFURTER wrote concurring opinions in which MR. JUSTICE DOUGLAS joined.]

NOTE: In *Baggett v. Bullitt,* 84 S. Ct. 1316 (1964), the Court held a state loyalty oath invalid for vagueness in its use of such terms as "subversive persons" and "subversive organization." Justices Clark and Harlan dissented. Compare the *Lanzetta* case, above.

SHELTON v. TUCKER

364 U.S. 479 (1960)

This case held unconstitutional, because it was too broad, an Arkansas statute requiring public school teachers to file annually affidavits listing every organization to which they had belonged or regularly contributed during the preceding five years. Mr. Justice Stewart observed for the Court:

In a series of decisions this Court has held that, even though the governmental purpose be legitimate and substantial, that purpose cannot be pursued by means that broadly stifle fundamental personal liberties when the end can be more narrowly achieved. The breath of legislative abridgment must be viewed in the light of less drastic means for achieving the same basic purpose. . . .

The unlimited and indiscriminate sweep of the statute now before us brings it within the ban of our prior cases. The statute's comprehensive interference with associational freedom goes far beyond what might be justified in the exercise of the State's legitimate inquiry into the fitness and competency of its teachers. The judgments in both cases must be reversed.

JUSTICE FRANKFURTER, joined by JUSTICES CLARK, WHITTAKER, and HARLAN, dissented:

. . . I believe it impossible to determine *a priori* the place where the line should be drawn between what would be permissible inquiry and over-broad inquiry in a situation like this. Certainly the Court does not point that place out. There can be little doubt that much of the associational information called for by the statute will be of little or no use whatever to the school authorities, but I do not understand how those authorities can be expected to fix in advance the terms of their enquiry so that it will yield only relevant information.

I do not mean to say that alternatives such as an enquiry limited to the names of organizations of whose character the State is presently aware, or to a class of

organizations defined by their purposes, would not be more consonant with a decent respect for the privacy of the teacher, nor that such alternatives would be utterly unworkable. I do see, however, that these alternatives suffer from deficiencies so obvious where a State is bent upon discovering everything which would be relevant to its proper purposes, that I cannot say that it must, as a matter of constitutional compulsion, adopt some means instead of those which have been chosen here. . . .

NELSON v. *COUNTY OF LOS ANGELES*

362 U.S. 1 (1960)

MR. JUSTICE CLARK delivered the opinion of the Court.

Petitioners, when employees of the County of Los Angeles, California, were subpoenaed by and appeared before a Subcommittee of the House Un-American Activities Committee, but refused to answer certain questions concerning subversion. Previously, each petitioner, had been ordered by the County Board of Supervisors to answer any questions asked by the Subcommittee relating to his subversive activity, and § 1028.1 of the Government Code of the State of California made it the duty of any public employee to give testimony relating to such activity on pain of discharge "in the manner provided by law." Thereafter the County discharged petitioners on the ground of insubordination and violation of § 1028.1 of the Code. Nelson, a permanent social worker employed by the County's Department of Charities, was, upon his request, given a Civil Service Commission hearing which resulted in a confirmation of his discharge. Globe was a temporary employee of the same department and was denied a hearing on his discharge on the ground that, as such, he was not entitled to a hearing under the Civil Service Rules adopted pursuant to the County Charter. Petitioners

then filed these petitions for mandates seeking reinstatement, contending that the California statute and their discharges violated the Due Process Clause of the Fourteenth Amendment. Nelson's discharge was affirmed by the District Court of Appeal, 163 Cal. App. 2d 607, 329 P.2d 978, and Globe's summary dismissal was likewise affirmed, 163 Cal. App. 2d 595, 329 P.2d 971. A petition for review in each of the cases was denied without opinion by the Supreme Court of California, three judges dissenting. 163 Cal. App. 2d 614, 329 P.2d 983; 163 Cal. App. 2d 606, 329 P.2d 978. We granted certiorari. 360 U.S. 928. The judgment in Nelson's case is affirmed by an equally divided Court and will not be discussed. We conclude that Globe's dismissal was valid.

On April 6, 1956, Globe was served with a subpoena to appear before the Subcommittee at Los Angeles. On the same date, he was served with a copy of an order of the County Board of Supervisors, originally issued February 19, 1952, concerning appearances before the Subcommittee. This order provided, among other things, that it was the duty of any employee to appear before the Subcommittee when so ordered or subpoenaed, and to answer questions concerning subversion. The order specifically stated that any "employee who disobeys the declaration of this duty and order will be considered to have been insubordinate . . . and that such insubordination shall constitute grounds for discharge. . . ." At the appointed time, Globe appeared before the Subcommittee and was interrogated by its counsel concerning his familiarity with the John Reid Club. He claimed that this was a matter which was entirely his "own business," and, upon being pressed for an answer, he stated that the question was "completely out of line as far as my rights as a citizen are concerned, [and] I refuse to answer this question under the First and Fifth Amendments of the Constitution of the United States." On the same grounds he refused to answer further questions concerning the Club, including one relating to his own membership. Upon being asked if he had observed any Communist activities on the part of members of the Club, Globe refused to answer, and suggested to committee counsel "that you get one of your trained seals up here and ask them." He refused to testify whether he was "a member of the Communist Party now" "on the same grounds" and "as previously stated for previous reasons." On May 2, by letter, Globe was discharged, "without further notice," on "the grounds that [he had] been guilty of insubordination and of violation of Section 1028.1 of the Government Code of the State of California. . . ." The letter recited the fact that Globe had been served with a copy of the Board order relating to his "duty to testify as a County employee . . . before said Committee" and that, although appearing as directed, he had refused to answer the question, "Are you a member of the Communist Party now?" Thereafter Globe requested a hearing before the Los Angeles County Civil Service Commission, but it found that, as a temporary employee, he was not entitled to a hearing under the Civil Service Rules. This the petitioner does not dispute.

However, Globe contends that, despite his temporary status, his summary discharge was arbitrary and unreasonable and, therefore, violative of due process. He rea-

sons that his discharge was based on his invocation before the Subcommittee of his rights under the First and Fifth Amendments. But the record does not support even an inference in this regard, and both the order and the statute upon which the discharge was based avoided it. In fact, California's court has held to the contrary, saying, "At no time has the cause of petitioner's discharge been alleged to be anything but insubordination and a violation of section 1028.1, nor indeed under the record before us could it be." 163 Cal. App. 2d at pages 599, 329 P.2d at page 974. Moreover, this finding is buttressed by the language of the order and of California's statute. Both require the employee to answer any interrogation in the field outlined. Failure to answer "on any ground whatsoever any such questions" renders the employee "guilty of insubordination" and requires that he "be suspended and dismissed from his employment in the manner provided by law." California law in this regard, as declared by its court, is that Globe "has no vested right to county employment and may therefore be discharged summarily." We take this interpretation of California law as binding upon us.

We, therefore, reach Globe's contention that his summary discharge was nevertheless arbitrary and unreasonable. In this regard he places his reliance on *Slochower* v. *Board of Higher Education,* 350 U.S. 551 (1956). However, the New York statute under which Slochower was discharged specifically operated "to discharge every city employee who invokes the Fifth Amendment. In practical effect the questions asked are taken as confessed and made the basis of the discharge." Id., 350 U.S. at page 558. This "built-in" inference of guilt, derived solely from a Fifth Amendment claim, we held to be arbitrary and unreasonable. But the test here, rather than being the invocation of any constitutional privilege, is the failure of the employee to answer. California has not predicated discharge on any "built-in" inference of guilt in its statute, but solely on employee insubordination for failure to give information which we have held that the State has a legitimate interest in securing. See *Garner* v. *Board of Public Works of City of Los Angeles,* 341 U.S. 716 (1951); *Adler* v. *Board of Education,* 342 U.S. 485 (1952). Moreover it must be remembered that here—unlike Slochower—the Board had specifically ordered its employees to appear and answer.

We conclude that the case is controlled by *Beilan* v. *Board of Public Education, School Dist. of Philadelphia,* 357 U.S. 399 (1958), and *Lerner* v. *Casey,* 357 U.S. 468 (1958). It is not determinative that the interrogation here was by a federal body rather than a state one, as it was in those cases. Globe had been ordered by his employer as well as by California's law to appear and answer questions before the federal Subcommittee. These mandates made no reference to Fifth Amendment privileges. If Globe had simply refused, without more, to answer the Subcommittee's questions, we think that under the principles of Beilan and Lerner California could certainly have discharged him. The fact that he chose to place his refusal on a Fifth Amendment claim puts the matter in no different posture, for as in *Lerner, supra,* 357 U.S. at page 477, California did not employ that claim as the basis for drawing an inference of guilt. Nor do we think that this discharge is vitiated by any deterrent effect that California's law might have had on Globe's exercise of his federal claim of privilege. The State may nevertheless legitimately predicate discharge on refusal to give information touching on the field of security. See *Garner* and *Adler, supra.* Likewise, we cannot say as a matter of due process that the State's choice of securing such information by means of testimony before a federal body can be denied. Finally, we do not believe that California's grounds for discharge constituted an arbitrary classification. See *Lerner,* 357 U.S. at page 478. We conclude that the order of the County Board was not invalid under the Due Process Clause of the Fourteenth Amendment.

Affirmed.

MR. CHIEF JUSTICE WARREN took no part in the consideration or decision of this case.

MR. JUSTICE BLACK, whom MR. JUSTICE DOUGLAS joins, dissenting.

Section 1028.1 of the California Code, as here applied, provides that any California employee who refuses to incriminate himself when asked to do so by a Congressional Committee "shall be suspended and dismissed from his employment in the manner provided by law." The Fifth Amendment, which is a part of the Bill of Rights, provides that no person shall be compelled to incriminate ("to be a witness against") himself. . . .

Here, then, is a plain conflict between the Federal Constitution and § 1028.1 of the California Code. The Federal Constitution told Globe he could, without penalty, refuse to incriminate himself before any arm of the Federal Government; California, however, has deprived him of his job solely because he exercised this federal constitutional privilege. In giving supremacy to the California law, I think the Court approves a plain violation of Article VI of the Constitution of the United States which makes that Constitution "the supreme Law of the Land . . . any Thing in the Constitution or Laws of any State to the Contrary notwithstanding." I also think that this discharge under state law is a violation of the Due Process Clause of the Fourteenth Amendment in its authentic historical sense: that a State may not encroach upon the individual rights of people except for violation of a law that is valid under the "Law of the Land." "Law of the Land" of necessity includes the supreme law, the Constitution itself. . . .

MR. JUSTICE BRENNAN, with whom MR. JUSTICE DOUGLAS joins, dissenting.

This is another in the series of cases involving discharges of state and local employees from their positions after they claim their constitutional privilege against self-incrimination before investigating committees. See *Slochower* v. *Board of Higher Education,* 350 U.S. 551; *Beilan* v. *Board of Public Education,* 357 U.S. 399; *Lerner*

v. *Casey*, 357 U.S. 468. While I adhere on
this matter of constitutional law to the
views I expressed in dissent in the latter
two cases, 357 U.S. at page 417, it is
enough to say here that I believe this case
to be governed squarely by Slochower, and
on that basis I put my dissent. Of course
this opinion is limited solely to Globe's
discharge. . . .

In Slochower, this Court had a substantially identical situation before it. There
a local law which made a claim of the constitutional privilege "equivalent to a resignation" was struck down as violative of
the Due Process Clause of the Fourteenth
Amendment. Only one word is necessary
to add here to the Court's statement there
of its reason for voiding the provision: "As
interpreted and applied by the state courts,
it operates to discharge every [temporary]
employee who invokes the Fifth Amendment. In practical effect the questions
asked are taken as confessed and made the
basis of the discharge. No consideration is
given to such factors as the subject matter
of the questions, remoteness of the period
to which they are directed, or justification
for exercise of the privilege. It matters not
whether the plea resulted from mistake,
inadvertence or legal advice conscientiously
given, whether wisely or unwisely. The
heavy hand of the statute falls alike on all
who exercise their constitutional privilege,
the full enjoyment of which every person
is entitled to receive." 350 U.S. at page 558.
The Court distinguished instances in which
the employing government itself might be
conducting an investigation into the "fitness" of the employee.

As applied, then, to temporary or proba-
tionary employees, the California statute
contains the identical vice of automatic
discharge for a Fifth Amendment plea
made before another body, not concerned
with investigating the "fitness" of the employee involved. It is sought here to equate
Globe's case with those of Beilan and Lerner. But in the latter cases the Court took
the view that the state discharges were sustainable because the employees' pleas of
self-incrimination before local administra-

tive agency investigations of their competence and reliability prevented those employing bodies from having an adequate
record on which to reach an affirmative conclusion as to their competence and reliability. This failure to cooperate fully
(styled lack of candor) within the framework of the employer's own proceeding to
determine fitness, was said to be a constitutional basis for discharge. 357 U.S. at
pages 405–408; 357 U.S. at pages 475–479,
and see 357 U.S. at page 410 (concurring
opinion). But here there was not the
vaguest semblance of any local administrative procedure designed to determine the
fitness of Globe for further employment.
It has not been hitherto suggested that the
authorizing resolutions of the Un-American Activities Committee extend to enabling it to perform these functions on a
grant-in-aid basis to the States. Accordingly
there is presented here the very same arbitrary action—the drawing of an inference
of unfitness for employment from exercise
of the privilege before another body, without opportunity to explain on the part of
the employee, or duty on the part of the
employing body to attempt to relate the
employee's conduct specifically to his fitness for employment—as was involved in
Slochower. There is the same announced
abdication of the local administrative
body's own function of determining the fitness of its employees, in favor of an arbitrary and *per se* rule dependent on the
behavior of the employee before another
body not charged with determining his fitness.

It is said that this case differs from
Slochower because that case involved a
determination, based on his invocation of
the privilege, that the employee was guilty
of substantive misconduct, while this one
simply involves a case of "insubordination"
in the employee's failure to answer questions asked by the Congressional Committee which the employing agency has
ordered be answered. In the first place,
Slochower did not involve any finding by
the New York authorities that the employee was guilty of the matters as to which

he claimed the privilege. The claim of the privilege was treated by the State as equivalent to a resignation, 350 U.S. at page 554, and it was only "in practical effect," id., 350 U.S. at page 558, that the questions asked were taken as confessed; that is, the State claimed the power to take the same action, discharge of the employee from employment, upon a plea of the privilege, as it could have taken upon a confession of the matters charged. The case involved an inference of unfitness for office, then, drawn arbitrarily and without opportunity to explain, from the assertion of the privilege. The same is involved here, and the thin patina of "insubordination" that the statute encrusts on the exercise of the privilege does not change the matter. . . .

KONIGSBERG v. *STATE BAR OF CALIFORNIA*
366 U.S. 36 (1961)

MR. JUSTICE HARLAN delivered the opinion of the Court.

This case, involving California's second rejection of petitioner's application for admission to the state bar, is a sequel to *Konigsberg* v. *State Bar of California,* 353 U.S. 252, in which this Court reversed the State's initial refusal of his application.

Under California law the State Supreme Court may admit to the practice of law any applicant whose qualifications have been certified to it by the California Committee of Bar Examiners. Cal. Bus. & Prof. Code § 6064. To qualify for certification an applicant must, among other things, be of "good moral character," id., § 6060(c), and no person may be certified "who advocates the overthrow of the Government of the United States or of this State by force, violence, or other unconstitutional means. . . ." Id., § 6064.1. The Committee is empowered and required to ascertain the qualifications of all candidates. Id., § 6046. Under rules prescribed by the Board of Governors of the State Bar, an applicant before the Committee has "the burden of proving that he is possessed of good moral character, of removing any and all reasonable suspicion of moral unfitness, and that he is entitled to the high regard and confidence of the public." Id., Div. 3, c. 4, Rule X, § 101. Any applicant denied certification may have the Committee's action reviewed by the State Supreme Court. Id., § 6066.

In 1953 petitioner, having successfully passed the California bar examinations, applied for certification for bar membership. The Committee, after interrogating Konigsberg and receiving considerable evidence as to his qualifications, declined to certify him on the ground that he had failed to meet the burden of proving his eligibility under the two statutory requirements relating to good moral character and nonadvocacy of violent overthrow. That determination centered largely around Konigsberg's repeated refusals to answer Committee questions as to his present or past membership in the Communist Party. The California Supreme Court denied review without opinion. See 52 Cal. 2d 769, 770, 344 P.2d 777.

On certiorari this Court, after reviewing the record, held the state determination to have been without rational support in the evidence and therefore offensive to the Due Process Clause of the Fourteenth Amendment. *Konigsberg* v. *State Bar of California, supra.* At the same time the Court declined to decide whether Konigsberg's refusals to answer could constitutionally afford "an independent ground for exclusion from the Bar," considering that such an issue was not before it. Id., 353 U.S. 259–262. The case was remanded to the State Supreme Court "for further proceedings not inconsistent with this opinion." Id., 353 U.S. 274.

On remand petitioner moved the California Supreme Court for immediate admission to the bar. The court vacated its previous order denying review and referred the matter to the Bar Committee for further consideration. At the ensuing Committee hearings Konigsberg introduced further evidence as to his good moral character (none of which was rebutted), reiterated unequivocally his disbelief in violent overthrow, and stated that he had never knowingly been a member of any organization which advocated such action. He persisted, however, in his refusals to answer any questions relating to his membership in the Communist Party. The Committee again declined to certify him, this time on the ground that his refusals to answer had obstructed a full investigation into his qualifications. The California Supreme Court, by a divided vote, refused review, and also denied Konigsberg's motion for direct admission to practice. 52 Cal. 2d 769, 344 P.2d 777. We again brought the case here. 362 U.S. 910.

Petitioner's contentions in this Court in support of reversal of the California Supreme Court's order are reducible to three propositions: (1) the State's action was inconsistent with this Court's decision in the earlier Konigsberg case; (2) assuming the Committee's inquiries into Konigsberg's possible Communist Party membership were permissible, it was unconstitutionally arbitrary for the State to deny him admission because of his refusals to answer; and (3) in any event, Konigsberg was constitutionally justified in refusing to answer these questions.

I

[The discussion rejecting the first contention is here omitted.]

II

We think it clear that the Fourteenth Amendment's protection against arbitrary state action does not forbid a State from denying admission to a bar applicant so long as he refuses to provide unprivileged answers to questions having a substantial relevance to his qualifications. . . .

. . . [A]ll that California has in effect said is that in cases where, on matters material to an applicant's qualifications, there are gaps in the evidence presented by him which the agency charged with certification considers should be filled in the appropriate exercise of its responsibilities, an applicant will not be admitted to practice unless and until he cooperates with the agency's efforts to fill those gaps. . . .

In the context of the entire record of these proceedings, the application of the California rule in this instance cannot be said to be arbitrary or discriminatory. In the first Konigsberg case this Court held that neither the somewhat weak, but uncontradicted testimony, that petitioner had been a Communist Party member in 1941, nor his refusal to answer questions relating to Party membership, could rationally support any substantive adverse inferences as to petitioner's character qualifications, 353 U.S. 266–274. That was not to say, however, that these factors, singly or together, could not be regarded as leaving the investigatory record in sufficient uncertainty as constitutionally to permit application of the procedural rule which the State has now invoked, provided that Konigsberg had been first given due warning of the consequences of his continuing refusal to respond to the Committee's questions. Cf. 353 U.S. at page 261. . . .

III

Finally, petitioner argues that, in any event, he was privileged not to respond to questions dealing with Communist Party membership because they unconstitutionally impinged upon rights of free speech and association protected by the Fourteenth Amendment.

At the outset we reject the view that freedom of speech and association (*NAACP v. Alabama,* 357 U.S. 449, 460), as protected by the First and Fourteenth Amendments, are "absolutes," not only in the undoubted sense that where the constitutional protection exists it must prevail, but also in the sense that the scope of that protection must be gathered solely from literal reading of the First Amendment. Throughout its history this Court has consistently recognized at least two ways in which constitutionally protected freedom of speech is narrower than an unlimited license to talk. On the one hand certain forms of speech, or speech in certain contexts, have been considered outside the scope of constitutional protection. See, e.g., *Schenck* v. *United States*, 249 U.S. 47; *Chaplinsky* v. *New Hampshire*, 315 U.S. 568; *Dennis* v. *United States*, 341 U.S. 494; *Beauharnais* v. *Illinois*, 343 U.S. 250; *Yates* v. *United States*, 354 U.S. 298; *Roth* v. *United States*, 354 U.S. 476. On the other hand, general regulatory statutes, not intended to control the content of speech but incidentally limiting its unfettered exercise, have not been regarded as the type of law the First or Fourteenth Amendments forbade Congress or the States to pass, when they have been found justified by subordinating valid governmental interests, a prerequisite to constitutionality which has necessarily involved a weighing of the governmental interest involved. See e.g., *Schneider* v. *State*, 308 U.S. 147, 161; *Cox* v. *New Hampshire*, 312 U.S. 569; *Prince* v. *Massachusetts*, 321 U.S. 158; *Kovacs* v. *Cooper*, 336 U.S. 77; *American Communications Assn.* v. *Douds*, 339 U.S. 382; *Breard* v. *Alexandria*, 341 U.S. 622. It is in the latter class of cases that this Court has always placed rules compelling disclosure of prior association as an incident of the informed exercise of a valid governmental function. *Bates* v. *Little Rock*, 361 U.S. 516, 524. Whenever, in such a context, these constitutional protections are asserted against the exercise of valid governmental powers a reconciliation must be effected, and that perforce requires an appropriate weighing of the respective interests involved. . . . With more particular reference to the present context of a state decision as to character qualifications, it is difficult, indeed, to imagine a view of the constitutional protections of speech and association which would automatically and without consideration of the extent of the deterrence of speech and association and of the importance of the state function, exclude all reference to prior speech or association on such issues as character, purpose, credibility, or intent. On the basis of these considerations we now judge petitioner's contentions in the present case.

Petitioner does not challenge the constitutionality of § 6064.1 of the California Business and Professions Code forbidding certification for admission to practice of those advocating the violent overthrow of government. It would indeed be difficult to argue that a belief, firm enough to be carried over into advocacy, in the use of illegal means to change the form of the State or Federal Government is an unimportant consideration in determining the fitness of applicants for membership in a profession in whose hands so largely lies the safekeeping of this country's legal and political institutions. . . . Nor is the state interest in this respect insubstantially related to the right which California claims to inquire about Communist Party membership. This Court has long since recognized the legitimacy of a statutory finding that membership in the Communist Party is not unrelated to the danger of use for such illegal ends of powers given for limited purposes. See *American Communications Assn.* v. *Douds*, 339 U.S. 382; see also *Barenblatt* v. *United States*, 360 U.S. 109, 128–129; . . .

As regards the questioning of public employees relative to Communist Party membership it has already been held that the interest in not subjecting speech and association to the deterrence of subsequent disclosure is outweighed by the State's interest in ascertaining the fitness of the employee for the post he holds, and hence that such questioning does not infringe constitutional protections. *Beilan* v. *Board of Public Education*, 357 U.S. 399; *Garner* v. *Board of Public Works*, 341 U.S. 716. With respect to this same question of Communist Party membership, we regard the State's interest in having lawyers who are devoted to the law in its broadest sense, including not only its substantive provisions, but also its procedures for orderly changes, as clearly sufficient to outweigh the minimal effect upon free association occasioned by compulsory disclosure in the circumstances here presented.

There is here no likelihood that deterrence of association may result from foreseeable private action, see *NAACP* v. *Alabama, supra,* at 462, for bar committee interrogations such as this are conducted in private. . . . Nor is there the possibility that the State may be afforded the opportunity for imposing undetectable arbitrary consequences upon protected association, see *Shelton* v. *Tucker,* 364 U.S. 479, 486, for a bar applicant's exclusion by reason of Communist Party membership is subject to judicial review, including ultimate review by this Court, should it appear that such exclusion has rested on substantive or procedural factors that do not comport with the Federal Constitution. . . . In these circumstances it is difficult indeed to perceive any solid basis for a claim of unconstitutional intrusion into rights assured by the Fourteenth Amendment. . . .

The judgment of the Supreme Court of California is affirmed.

Affirmed.

MR. JUSTICE BLACK, with whom THE CHIEF JUSTICE and MR. JUSTICE DOUGLAS concur, dissenting. . . .

. . . [W]e have been pointed to no . . . California statutes, rules, regulations or court decisions which require or even permit rejection of a lawyer's application for admission solely because he refuses to answer questions. In this situation, it seems to me that Konigsberg has been rejected on a ground that is not supported by any authoritatively declared rule of law for the State of California. This alone would be enough for me to vote to reverse the judgment. There are other reasons, however.

Konigsberg's objection to answering questions as to whether he is or was a member of the Communist Party has, from the very beginning, been based upon the contention that the guarantees of free speech and association of the First Amendment as made controlling upon the States by the Fourteenth Amendment preclude California from denying him admission to its Bar for refusing to answer such questions. In this I think Konigsberg has been

correct. California has apparently not even attempted to make actual present membership in the Communist Party a bar to the practice of law, and even if it had, I assume it would not be contended that such a law could be applied to conduct that took place before the law was passed. For such an application would, I think, not only be a clear violation of the *ex post facto* provision of the Federal Constitution, but would also constitute a bill of attainder squarely within this Court's holdings in *Cummings* v. *State of Missouri* and *Ex parte Garland.* And yet it seems to me that this record shows, beyond any shadow of a doubt, that the reason Konigsberg has been rejected is because the Committee suspects that he was at one time a member of the Communist Party. I agree with the implication of the majority opinion that this is not an adequate ground to reject Konigsberg and that it could not be constitutionally defended.

The majority avoids the otherwise unavoidable necessity of reversing the judgment below on that ground by simply refusing to look beyond the reason given by the Committee to justify Konigsberg's rejection. . . .

The Court attempts to justify its refusal to apply the plain mandate of the First Amendment in part by reference to the so-called "clear and present danger test" forcefully used by Mr. Justice Holmes and Mr. Justice Brandeis, not to narrow but to broaden the then prevailing interpretation of First Amendment freedoms. I think very little can be found in anything they ever said that would provide support for the "balancing test" presently in use. . . . Thus here, where there is not a semblance of a "clear and present danger," and where there is more than ample time in which to combat by discussion any idea which may be involved, the majority permits the State of California to adopt measures calculated to suppress the advocacy of views about governmental affairs. . . .

. . . The interest of the Committee in satisfying its curiosity with respect to Konigsberg's "possible" membership in the

Communist Party two decades ago has been inflated out of all proportion to its real value—the vast interest of the public in maintaining unabridged the basic freedoms of speech, press and assembly has been paid little if anything more than lip service— and important constitutional rights have once again been "balanced" away. This of course, is an ever-present danger of the "balancing test" for the application of such a test is necessarily tied to the emphasis particular judges give to competing societal values. . . .

Mr. Justice Brennan, with whom The Chief Justice joins, dissenting.

. . . The Committee did not come forward . . . with evidence to show that Konigsberg unlawfully advocated the overthrow of the government. Under our decision in *Speiser* v. *Randall*, 357 U.S. 513, the Fourteenth Amendment therefore protects Konigsberg from being denied admission to the Bar for his refusal to answer the questions. . . .

6. UTTERANCE THREATENING MUNICIPAL ORDER

KOVACS v. *COOPER*
336 U.S. 77 (1949)

> In 1948 the Court had considered a Lockport, New York, ordinance permitting loudspeakers to be used for public communication only "under permission obtained from the chief of police." This was held invalid as a "previous restraint" without "standards prescribed" for its exercise. *Saia* v. *New York*, 334 U.S. 558 (1948)
> In *Kovacs'* case the Court, on appeal from a state conviction, upheld a Trenton, New Jersey, ordinance prohibiting emission of "loud and raucous noises" by sound trucks. "The preferred position of freedom of speech in a society that cherishes liberty for all does not," said Mr. Justice Reed (joined by his brothers Vinson and Burton), "require legislators to be insensible to claims by citizens to comfort and convenience."

Mr. Justice Frankfurter, concurring: . . .

To dispose of this case on the assumption that the *Saia* case, 334 U.S. 558, decided only the other day, was rightly decided, would be for me to start with an unreality. While I am not unaware of the circumstances that differentiate this case from what was ruled in *Saia*, further reflection has only served to reinforce the dissenting views I expressed in that case. . . .

The opinions in this case prompt me to make some additional observations. My brother Reed speaks of "the preferred position of freedom of speech," though, to be sure, he finds that the Trenton ordinance does not disregard it. This is a phrase that has uncritically crept into some recent opinions of this Court. I deem it a mischievous phrase, if it carries the thought,

which it may subtly imply, that any law touching communication is infected with presumptive invalidity. [A "chronological account of the evolution of talk about 'preferred position'" is here omitted.]

Behind the notion sought to be expressed by the formula as to "the preferred position of freedom of speech" lies a relevant consideration in determining whether an enactment relating to the liberties protected by the due process clause of the Fourteenth Amendment is violative of it. In law also, doctrine is illuminated by history. The ideas now governing the constitutional protection of freedom of speech derive essentially from the opinions of Mr. Justice Holmes.

The philosophy of his opinions on that subject arose from a deep awareness of the extent to which sociological conclusions are conditioned by time and circumstance. Because of this awareness Mr. Justice Holmes seldom felt justified in opposing his own opinion to economic views which the legislature embodied in law. But since he also realized that the progress of civilization is to a considerable extent the displacement of error which once held sway as official truth by beliefs which in turn have yielded to other beliefs, for him the right to search for truth was of a different order than some transient economic dogma. And without freedom of expression, thought becomes checked and atrophied. Therefore, in considering what interests are so fundamental as to be enshrined in the due process clause, those liberties of the individual which history has attested as the indispensable conditions of an open as against a closed society come to this Court with a momentum for respect lacking when appeal is made to liberties which derive merely from shifting economic arrangements. Accordingly, Mr. Justice Holmes was far more ready to find legislative invasion where free inquiry was involved than in the debatable area of economics. . . . The objection to summarizing this line of thought by the phrase "the preferred position of freedom of speech" is that it expresses a complicated process of constitutional adjudication by a deceptive formula. And it was Mr. Justice Holmes who admonished us that "To rest upon a formula is a slumber that, prolonged, means death." Such a formula makes for mechanical jurisprudence. . . .

Only a disregard of vital differences between natural speech, even of the loudest spellbinders, and the noise of sound trucks would give sound trucks the constitutional rights accorded to the unaided human voice. Nor is it for this Court to devise the terms on which sound trucks should be allowed to operate, if at all. These are matters for the legislative judgment controlled by public opinion. So long as a legislature does not prescribe what ideas may be noisily expressed and what may not be, nor discriminate among those who would make inroads upon the public peace, it is not for us to supervise the limits the legislature may impose in safeguarding the steadily narrowing opportunities for serenity and reflection. Without such opportunities freedom of thought becomes a mocking phrase, and without freedom of thought there can be no free society.

MR. JUSTICE JACKSON, concurring: . . .

I join the judgment sustaining the Trenton ordinance because I believe that operation of mechanical sound-amplifying devices conflicts with quiet enjoyment of home and park and with safe and legitimate use of street and market place, and that it is constitutionally subject to regulation or prohibition by the state or municipal authority. No violation of the due process clause of the Fourteenth Amendment by reason of infringement of free speech arises unless such regulation or prohibition undertakes to censor the contents of the broadcasting. Freedom of speech for Kovacs does not, in my view, include freedom to use sound amplifiers to drown out the natural speech of others.

I do not agree that, if we sustain regulations or prohibitions of sound trucks, they must therefore be valid if applied to other methods of "communication of ideas." The moving picture screen, the radio, the newspaper, the handbill, the sound truck and the street corner orator have differing natures, values, abuses and dangers. Each, in my view, is a law unto itself, and all we are dealing with now is the sound truck.

But I agree with Mr. Justice Black that this decision is a repudiation of that in *Saia* v. *New York,* 334 U.S. 558. Like him, I am unable to find anything in this record to warrant a distinction because of "loud and raucous" tones of this machine. The *Saia* decision struck down a more moderate exercise of the state's police power than the one now sustained. Trenton, as the ordinance reads to me, unconditionally bans all sound trucks from the city streets. Lockport relaxed its prohibition with a proviso to allow their use, even in areas set aside for public recreation, when and where the Chief of Police saw no objection. Comparison of this our 1949 decision with our

1948 decision, I think, will pretty hopelessly confuse municipal authorities as to what they may or may not do.

I concur in the present result only for the reasons stated in dissent in *Saia* v. *New York*, 334 U.S. 558, 566.

MR. JUSTICE BLACK, with whom MR. JUSTICE DOUGLAS and MR. JUSTICE RUTLEDGE concur, dissenting:

The question in this case is not whether appellant may constitutionally be convicted of operating a sound truck that emits "loud and raucous noises." The appellant was neither charged with nor convicted of operating a sound truck that emitted "loud and raucous noises." The charge against him in the police court was that he violated the city ordinance "in that he did, on South Stockton Street, in said City, play, use and operate a device known as a sound truck." The record reflects not even a shadow of evidence to prove that the noise was either "loud or raucous," unless these words of the ordinance refer to any noise coming from an amplifier, whatever its volume or tone. . . .

The New Jersey ordinance is on its face, and as construed and applied in this case by that state's courts, an absolute and unqualified prohibition of amplifying devices on any of Trenton's streets at any time, at any place, for any purpose, and without regard to how noisy they may be.

In *Saia* v. *New York*, 334 U.S. 558, we . . . placed use of loud speakers in public streets and parks on the same constitutional level as freedom to speak on streets without such devices, freedom to speak over radio, and freedom to distribute literature.

In this case the Court denies speech amplifiers the constitutional shelter recognized by our decisions and holding in the *Saia* case. This is true because the Trenton, New Jersey, ordinance here sustained goes beyond a mere prior censorship of all loud speakers with authority in the censor to prohibit some of them. This Trenton ordinance wholly bars the use of all loud speakers mounted upon any vehicle in any of the city's public streets.

In my view this repudiation of the prior *Saia* opinion makes a dangerous and unjustifiable breach in the constitutional barriers designed to insure freedom of expression. Ideas and beliefs are today chiefly disseminated to the masses of people through the press, radio, moving pictures, and public address systems. To some extent at least there is competition of ideas between and within these groups. The basic premise of the First Amendment is that all present instruments of communication, as well as others that inventive genius may bring into being, shall be free from governmental censorship or prohibition. Laws which hamper the free use of some instruments of communication thereby favor competing channels. Thus, unless constitutionally prohibited, laws like this Trenton ordinance can give an overpowering influence to views of owners of legally favored instruments of communication. . . . And it is an obvious fact that public speaking today without sound amplifiers is a wholly inadequate way to reach the people on a large scale. . . . But ordinances can be drawn which adequately protect a community from unreasonable use of public speaking devices without absolutely denying to the community's citizens all information that may be disseminated or received through this new avenue for trade in ideas. I would agree without reservation to the sentiment that "unrestrained use throughout a municipality of all sound amplifying devices would be intolerable." And of course cities may restrict or absolutely ban the use of amplifiers on busy streets in the business area. A city ordinance that reasonably restricts the volume of sound, or the hours during which an amplifier may be used, does not, in my mind, infringe the constitutionally protected area of free speech. It is because this ordinance does none of these things, but is instead an absolute prohibition of all uses of an amplifier on any of the streets of Trenton at any time that I must dissent.

I would reverse the judgment.

MR. JUSTICE RUTLEDGE, dissenting: . . .

What the effect of this decision may be

I cannot foretell except that *Kovacs* will stand convicted and the division among the majority voting to affirm leaves open for future determination whether absolute and total state prohibition of sound trucks in public places can stand consistently with the First Amendment. For myself, I have no doubt of state power to regulate their abuse in reasonable accommodation, by narrowly drawn statutes, to other interests concerned in use of the streets and in free-dom from public nuisance. But that the First Amendment limited its protections of speech to the natural range of the human voice as it existed in 1790 would be, for me, like saying that the commerce power remains limited to navigation by sail and travel by the use of horses and oxen in accordance with the principal modes of carrying on commerce in 1789. . . .

MR. JUSTICE MURPHY dissents.

FEINER v. NEW YORK

340 U.S. 315 (1951)

Certiorari to the Court of Appeals of New York.

MR. CHIEF JUSTICE VINSON delivered the opinion of the Court.

Petitioner was convicted of the offense of disorderly conduct, a misdemeanor under the New York penal laws, in the Court of Special Sessions of the City of Syracuse and was sentenced to thirty days in the county penitentiary. The conviction was affirmed by the Onondaga County Court and the New York Court of Appeals, 300 N.Y. 391, 91 N.E.2d 316 (1950). The case is here on certiorari, 339 U.S. 962 (1950), petitioner having claimed that the conviction is in violation of his right of free speech under the Fourteenth Amendment.

In the review of state decisions where First Amendment rights are drawn in question, we of course make an examination of the evidence to ascertain independently whether the right has been violated. Here, the trial judge, who heard the case without jury, rendered an oral decision at the end of the trial, setting forth his determination of the facts upon which he found the petitioner guilty. His decision indicated generally that he believed the state's witnesses, and his summation of the testimony was used by the two New York Courts on review in stating the facts. Our appraisal of the facts is, therefore, based upon the uncontroverted facts and, where controversy ex-ists, upon that testimony which the trial judge did reasonably conclude to be true.

On the evening of March 8, 1949, petitioner Irving Feiner was addressing an open-air meeting at the corner of South McBride and Harrison Streets in the City of Syracuse. At approximately 6:30 p.m., the police received a telephone complaint concerning the meeting, and two officers were detailed to investigate. One of these officers went to the scene immediately, the other arriving some twelve minutes later. They found a crowd of about seventy-five or eighty people, both Negro and white, filling the sidewalk and spreading out into the street. Petitioner, standing on a large wooden box on the sidewalk, was addressing the crowd through a loud-speaker system attached to an automobile. Although the purpose of his speech was to urge his listeners to attend a meeting to be held that night in the Syracuse Hotel, in its course he was making derogatory remarks concerning President Truman, the American Legion, the Mayor of Syracuse, and other local political officials.

The police officers made no effort to interfere with petitioner's speech, but were first concerned with the effect of the crowd on both pedestrian and vehicular traffic. They observed the situation from the opposite side of the street, noting that some pedestrians were forced to walk in the street to avoid the crowd. Since traffic was passing at the time, the officers attempted to get the people listening to petitioner back on the sidewalk. The crowd was restless and there was some pushing, shoving and milling around. One of the officers telephoned the police station from a nearby store, and then both policemen crossed the street and mingled with the crowd without any intention of arresting the speaker.

At this time, petitioner was speaking in a "loud, high-pitched voice." He gave the impression that he was endeavoring to arouse the Negro people against the whites, urging that they rise up in arms and fight for equal rights. The statements before such a mixed audience "stirred up a little excitement." Some of the onlookers made remarks to the police about their inability to handle the crowd and at least one threatened violence if the police did not act. There were others who appeared to be favoring petitioner's arguments. Because of the feeling that existed in the crowd both for and against the speaker, the officers finally "stepped in to prevent it from resulting in a fight." One of the officers approached the petitioner, not for the purpose of arresting him, but to get him to break up the crowd. He asked petitioner to get down off the box, but the latter refused to accede to his request and continued talking. The officer waited for a minute and then demanded that he cease talking. Although the officer had thus twice requested petitioner to stop over the course of several minutes, petitioner not only ignored him but continued talking. During all this time, the crowd was pressing closer around petitioner and the officer. Finally, the officer told petitioner he was under arrest and ordered him to get down from the box, reaching up to grab him. Petitioner stepped down, announcing over the microphone that "the law has arrived, and I suppose they will take over now." In all, the officer had asked petitioner to get down off the box three times over a space of four or five minutes. Petitioner had been speaking for over a half hour.

On these facts, petitioner was specifically charged with violation of § 722 of the Penal Law of New York, the pertinent part of which is set out in the margin. The bill of particulars, demanded by petitioner and furnished by the State, gave in detail the facts upon which the prosecution relied to support the charge of disorderly conduct. Paragraph C is particularly pertinent here: "By ignoring and refusing to heed and obey reasonable police orders issued at the time and place metioned in the Information to regulate and control said crowd and to prevent a breach or breaches of the peace and to prevent injury to pedestrians attempting to use said walk, and being forced into the highway adjacent to the place in question, and prevent injury to the public generally."

We are not faced here with blind condonation by a state court of arbitrary police action. Petitioner was accorded a full, fair trial. The trial judge heard testimony supporting and contradicting the judgment of the police officers that a clear danger of disorder was threatened. After weighing this contradictory evidence, the trial judge reached the conclusion that the police officers were justified in taking action to prevent a breach of the peace. The exercise of the police officers' proper discretionary power to prevent a breach of the peace was thus approved by the trial court and later by two courts on review. The courts below recognized petitioner's right to hold a street meeting at this locality, to make use of loud-speaking equipment in giving his speech, and to make derogatory remarks concerning public officials and the American Legion. They found that the officers in making the arrest were motivated solely by a proper concern for the preservation of order and protection of the general welfare, and that there was no evidence which could lend color to a claim that the acts of the police were a cover for suppression of petitioner's views and opinions. Petitioner was thus neither arrested nor convicted for the making or the content of his speech. Rather, it was the reaction which it actually engendered.

The language of *Cantwell* v. *Connecticut,* 310 U.S. 296 (1940), is appropriate here.

"The offense known as breach of the peace embraces a great variety of conduct destroying or menacing public order and tranquility. It includes not only violent acts but acts and words likely to produce violence in others. No one would have the hardihood to suggest that the principle of freedom of speech sanctions incitement to riot or that religious liberty connotes the privilege to exhort others to physical attack upon those belonging to another sect. When clear and present danger of riot, disorder, interference with traffic upon the public streets, or other immediate threat to public safety, peace, or order appears, the power of the State to prevent or punish is obvious. (310 U.S. at 308.)"

The findings of New York courts as to the condition of the crowd and the refusal of petitioner to obey the police requests, supported as they are by the record of this case, are persuasive that the conviction of petitioner for violation of public peace, order and authority does not exceed the bounds of proper state police action. This Court respects, as it must, the interest of the community in maintaining peace and order on its streets. *Schneider* v. *State*, 308 U.S. 147, 160 (1939); *Kovacs* v. *Cooper*, 336 U.S. 77, 82 (1949). We cannot say that the preservation of that interest here encroaches on the constitutional rights of this petitioner.

We are well aware that the ordinary murmurings and objections of a hostile audience cannot be allowed to silence a speaker, and are also mindful of the possible danger of giving overzealous police officials complete discretion to break up otherwise lawful public meetings. "A State may not unduly suppress free communication of views, religious or other, under the guise of conserving desirable conditions."

Cantwell v. *Connecticut, supra,* at 308. But we are not faced here with such a situation. It is one thing to say that the police cannot be used as an instrument for the suppression of unpopular views, and another to say that, when as here, the speaker passes the bounds of argument or persuasion and undertakes incitement to riot, they are powerless to prevent a breach of the peace. Nor in this case can we condemn the considered judgment of three New York courts approving the means which the police, faced with a crisis, used in the exercise of their power and duty to preserve peace and order. The findings of the state courts as to the existing situation and the imminence of greater disorder coupled with petitioner's deliberate defiance of the police officers convince us that we should not reverse this conviction in the name of free speech.

Affirmed.

[MR. JUSTICE FRANKFURTER concurred in a separate opinion emphasizing the unanimity of the highest court of New York in accepting the trial court's finding that Feiner was stopped because the police honestly believed that a breach of the peace was imminent. "It is not," said the Justice, "a constitutional principle that, in acting to preserve order, the police must proceed against the crowd, whatever its size and temper, and not against the speaker."

JUSTICES BLACK, DOUGLAS, and MINTON dissented on the ground that the evidence showed no serious threat of immediate disorder and that the police, if they were to intervene at all, should have thrown their weight on the side of the speaker, not of the unsympathetic crowd.]

EDWARDS v. SOUTH CAROLINA

372 U.S. 229 (1963)

MR. JUSTICE STEWART delivered the opinion of the Court.

The petitioners, 187 in number, were convicted in a magistrate's court in Columbia, South Carolina, of the common-law crime of breach of the peace. Their convictions were ultimately affirmed by the South Carolina Supreme Court, 239 S.C. 339, 123 S.E.2d 247. We granted certiorari, 369 U.S. 870, to consider the claim that these convictions cannot be squared with the Fourteenth Amendment of the United States Constitution.

There was no substantial conflict in the trial evidence. Late in the morning of March 2, 1961, the petitioners, high school and college students of the Negro race, met at the Zion Baptist Church in Columbia. From there, at about noon, they walked in separate groups of about 15 to the South Carolina State House grounds, an area of two city blocks open to the general public. Their purpose was "to submit a protest to the citizens of South Carolina, along with the Legislative Bodies of South Carolina, our feelings and our dissatisfaction with the present condition of discriminatory action against Negroes, in general, and to let them know that we were dissatisfied and that we would like for the laws which prohibited Negro privileges in this State to be removed."

Already on the State House grounds when the petitioners arrived were 30 or more law enforcement officers, who had advance knowledge that the petitioners were coming. Each group of petitioners entered the grounds through a driveway and parking area known in the record as the "horseshoe." As they entered, they were told by the law enforcement officials that "they had a right, as a citizen, to go through the State House grounds, as any other citizen has, as long as they were peaceful." During the next half hour or 45 minutes, the petitioners, in the same small groups, walked single file or two abreast in an orderly way through the grounds, each group carrying placards bearing such messages as "I am proud to be a Negro," and "Down with segregation."

During this time a crowd of some 200 to 300 onlookers had collected in the horseshoe area and on the adjacent sidewalks. There was no evidence to suggest that these onlookers were anything but curious, and no evidence at all of any threatening remarks, hostile gestures, or offensive language on the part of any member of the crowd. The City Manager testified that he recognized some of the onlookers, whom he did not identify, as "possible trouble makers," but his subsequent testimony made clear that nobody among the crowd actually caused or threatened any trouble. There was no obstruction of pedestrian or vehicular traffic within the State House grounds. No vehicle was prevented from entering or leaving the horseshoe area. Although vehicular traffic at a nearby street intersection was slowed down somewhat, an officer was dispatched to keep traffic moving. There were a number of bystanders on the public sidewalks adjacent to the State House grounds, but they all moved on when asked to do so, and there was no impediment of pedestrian traffic. Police protection at the scene was at all times sufficient to meet any foreseeable possibility of disorder.

In the situation and under the circumstances thus described, the police authorities advised the petitioners that they would be arrested if they did not disperse within 15 minutes. Instead of dispersing, the petitioners engaged in what the City Manager described as "boisterous," "loud," and "flamboyant" conduct, which, as his later testimony made clear, consisted of listening to a "religious harangue" by one of their leaders, and loudly singing "The Star Spangled Banner" and other patriotic and religious songs, while stamping their feet and clapping their hands. After 15 minutes had passed, the police arrested the petitioners and marched them off to jail.

Upon this evidence the state trial court convicted the petitioners of breach of the peace, and imposed sentences ranging from a $10 fine or five days in jail, to a $100 fine or 30 days in jail. In affirming the judgments, the Supreme Court of South Carolina said that under the law of that State the offense of breach of the peace "is not susceptible of exact definition," but that the "general definition of the offense" is as follows:

"In general terms, a breach of the peace is a violation of public order, a disturbance of the public tranquility, by any act or conduct inciting to violence . . . , it includes any violation of any law enacted to preserve peace and good order. It may consist of an act of violence or an act likely to produce violence. It is not necessary that the peace be actually broken to lay the foundation for a prosecution for this offense. If what is done is unjustifiable and unlawful, tending with sufficient directness to break the peace, no more is required. Nor is actual personal violence an essential element in the offense. . . .

"By 'peace,' as used in the law in this connection, is meant the tranquility enjoyed by citizens of a municipality or community where good order reigns among its members, which is the natural right of all persons in political society." 239 S.C., at 343–344, 123 S.E.2d, at 249. . . .

The state courts have held that the petitioners' conduct constituted breach of the peace under state law, and we may accept their decision as binding upon us to that extent. But it nevertheless remains our duty in a case such as this to make an independent examination of the whole record. *Blackburn* v. *Alabama*, 361 U.S. 199, 205 n. 5; *Pennekamp* v. *Florida*, 328 U.S. 331, 335; *Fiske* v. *Kansas*, 274 U.S. 380, 385–386. And it is clear to us that in arresting, convicting, and punishing the petitioners under the circumstances disclosed by this record, South Carolina infringed the petitioners' constitutionally protected rights of free speech, free assembly, and freedom to petition for redress of their grievances.

It has long been established that these First Amendment freedoms are protected by the Fourteenth Amendment from invasion by the States. *Gitlow* v. *New York*, 268 U.S. 652; *Whitney* v. *California*, 274 U.S. 357; *Stromberg* v. *California*, 283 U.S. 359; *DeJonge* v. *Oregon*, 299 U.S. 353; *Cantwell* v. *Connecticut*, 310 U.S. 296. The circumstances in this case reflect an ex-

ercise of these basic constitutional rights in their most pristine and classic form. The petitioners felt aggrieved by laws of South Carolina which allegedly "prohibited Negro privileges in this State." They peaceably assembled at the site of the State Government and there peaceably expressed their grievances "to the citizens of South Carolina, along with the Legislative Bodies of South Carolina." Not until they were told by police officials that they must disperse on pain of arrest did they do more. Even then, they but sang patriotic and religious songs after one of their leaders had delivered a "religious harangue." There was no violence or threat of violence on their part, or on the part of any member of the crowd watching them. Police protection was "ample."

This, therefore, was a far cry from the situation in *Feiner* v. *New York*, 340 U.S. 315, where two policemen were faced with a crowd which was "pushing, shoving, and milling around," id., at 317, where at least one member of the crowd "threatened violence if the police did not act," id., at 317, where "the crowd was pressing closer around petitioner and the officer," id., at 318, and where "the speaker passes the bounds of argument or persuasion and undertakes incitement to riot." Id., at 321. And the record is barren of any evidence of "fighting words." See *Chaplinsky* v. *New Hampshire*, 315 U.S. 568. . . .

The Fourteenth Amendment does not permit a State to make criminal the peaceful expression of unpopular views. "[A] function of free speech under our system of government is to invite dispute. It may indeed best serve its high purpose when it induces a condition of unrest, creates dissatisfaction with conditions as they are, or even stirs people to anger. Speech is often provocative and challenging. It may strike at prejudices and preconceptions and have profound unsettling effects as it presses for acceptance of an idea. That is why freedom of speech, . . . is . . . protected against censorship or punishment, unless shown likely to produce a clear and present danger of a serious substantive evil that rises far above public inconvenience, annoyance, or unrest. . . . There is no room under our Constitution for a more restrictive view. For the alternative would lead to standardization of ideas either by legislatures, courts, or dominant political or community groups." *Terminiello* v. *Chicago*, 337 U.S. 1, 4–5. As in the Terminiello case, the courts of South Carolina have defined a criminal offense so as to permit conviction of the petitioners if their speech "stirred people to anger, invited public dispute, or brought about a condition of unrest. A conviction resting on any of those grounds may not stand." Id., at 5.

For these reasons we conclude that these criminal convictions cannot stand.

Reversed.

MR. JUSTICE CLARK, dissenting.

The convictions of the petitioners, Negro high school and college students, for breach of the peace under South Carolina law are accepted by the Court "as binding upon us to that extent" but are held violative of "petitioners' constitutionally protected rights of free speech, free assembly, and freedom to petition for redress of their grievances." Petitioners, of course, had a right to peaceable assembly, to espouse their cause and to petition, but in my view the manner in which they exercised those rights was by no means the passive demonstration which this Court relates; rather, as the City Manager of Columbia testified, "a dangerous situation was really building up" which South Carolina's courts expressly found had created "an actual interference with traffic and an imminently threatened disturbance of the peace of the community." Since the Court does not attack the state courts' findings and accepts the convictions as "binding" to the extent that the petitioners' conduct constituted a breach of the peace, it is difficult for me to understand its understatement of the facts and reversal of the convictions.

The priceless character of First Amendment freedoms cannot be gainsaid, but it does not follow that they are absolutes immune from necessary state action reasonably designed for the protection of society. See *Cantwell* v. *Connecticut*, 310 U.S. 296, 304 (1940); *Schneider* v. *State*, 308 U.S. 147, 160 (1939). For that reason it is our duty to consider the context in which the arrests here were made. Certainly the city officials would be constitutionally prohibited from refusing petitioners access to the State House grounds merely because they disagreed with their views. See *Niemotko* v. *Maryland*, 340 U.S. 268 (1951). But here South Carolina's courts have found: "There is no indication whatever in this case that the acts of the police officers were taken as a subterfuge or excuse for the suppression of appellants' views and opinions." It is undisputed that the city officials specifically granted petitioners permission to assemble, imposing only the requirement that they be "peaceful." Petitioners then gathered on the State House grounds, during a General Assembly session, in a large number of almost 200, marching and carrying placards with slogans such as "Down with segregation" and "You may jail our bodies but not our souls." Some of them were singing.

The activity continued for approximately 45 minutes, during the busy noon-hour period, while a crowd of some 300 persons congregated in front of the State House and around the area directly in front of its entrance, known as the "horse-shoe," which was used for vehicular as well as pedestrian ingress and egress. During this time there were no efforts made by the city officials to hinder the petitioners in their rights of free speech and assembly; rather, the police directed their efforts to the traffic problems resulting from petitioners' activities. It was only after the large crowd had gathered, among which the City Manager and Chief of Police recognized potential troublemakers, and which together with the students had become massed on and around the "horse-shoe" so closely that vehicular and pedestrian traffic was materially impeded, that any action against the petitioners was taken. Then the City Manager, in what both the state intermediate and Supreme Court found to be the utmost good faith, decided that danger to peace and safety was imminent. Even at this juncture no orders were issued by the City Manager for the police to break up the crowd, now about 500 persons, and no arrests were made. Instead, he approached the recognized leader of the petitioners and requested him to tell the various groups of petitioners to disperse within 15 minutes, failing which they would be arrested. Even though the City Manager might have been honestly mistaken as to the imminence of danger this was certainly a reasonable request by the city's top executive officer in an effort to avoid a public brawl. But the response of petitioners and their leader was defiance rather than cooperation. The leader immediately moved from group to group among the students, delivering a "harangue" which, according to testimony in the record, "aroused [them] to a fever pitch causing this boisterousness, this singing and stomping."

For the next 15 minutes the petitioners sang "I shall not be moved" and various religious songs, stamped their feet, clapped their hands, and conducted what the South Carolina Supreme Court found to be a "noisy demonstration in defiance of [the dispersal] orders." 239 S.C. 339, 345, 123 S.E.2d 247, 250. Ultimately the petitioners were arrested, as they apparently planned from the beginning, and convicted on evidence the sufficiency of which the Court does not challenge. The question thus seems to me whether a State is constitutionally prohibited from enforcing laws to prevent breach of the peace in a situation where city officials in good faith believe, and the record shows, that disorder and violence are imminent, merely because the activities constituting that breach contain claimed elements of constitutionally protected speech and assembly. To me the answer under our cases is clearly in the negative.

Beginning, as did the South Carolina courts, with the premise that the petitioners were entitled to assemble and voice their dissatisfaction with segregation, the enlargement of constitutional protection for the conduct here is as fallacious as would be the conclusion that free speech necessarily includes the right to broadcast from a sound truck in the public streets. *Kovacs* v. *Cooper*, 336 U.S. 77 (1949). This Court said in *Thornhill* v. *Alabama*, 310 U.S. 88, 105 (1940), that "[t]he power and the duty of the state to take adequate steps to preserve the peace and to protect the privacy, the lives, and the property of its residents cannot be doubted." Significantly, in holding that the petitioner's picketing was constitutionally protected in that case the Court took pains to differentiate it from "picketing *en masse* or otherwise conducted which might occasion . . . imminent and aggravated danger. . . ." Ibid. Here the petitioners were permitted without hindrance to exercise their rights of free speech and assembly. Their arrests occurred only after a situation arose in which the law-enforcement officials on the scene considered that a dangerous disturbance was imminent. The County Court found that "[t]he evidence is clear that the officers were motivated solely by a proper concern for the preservation of order and the protection of the general welfare in the face of an actual interference with traffic and an imminently threatened disturbance of the peace of the community." In affirming, the South Carolina Supreme Court said the action of the police was "reasonable and motivated solely by a proper concern for the preservation of order and prevention of further interference with traffic upon the public streets and sidewalks." 239 S.C., at 345, 123 S.E.2d, at 249–250.

In *Cantwell* v. *Connecticut, supra,* at 308 this Court recognized that "[w]hen clear and present danger of riot, disorder, interference with traffic upon the public streets, or other immediate threat to public safety, peace, or order, appears, the power of the State to prevent or punish is obvious." And in *Feiner* v. *New York*, 340 U.S. 315 (1951), we upheld a conviction for breach of the peace in a situation no more dangerous than that found here. There the demonstration was conducted by only one person and the crowd was limited to approximately 80, as compared with the present lineup of some 200 demonstrators and 300 onlookers. There the petitioner was "endeavoring to arouse the Negro people against the whites, urging that they rise up in arms and fight for equal rights." Id., at 317. Only one person—in a city having an entirely different historical background—was exhorting adults. Here 200 youthful Negro demonstrators were being aroused to a "fever pitch" before a crowd of some 300 people who undoubtedly were hostile. Perhaps their speech was not so animated but in this setting their actions, their placards reading "You may jail our bodies but not our souls" and their chanting of "I shall not be moved," accompanied by stamping feet and clapping hands, created a much greater danger of riot and disorder. It is my belief that anyone conversant with the almost spontaneous combustion in some Southern communities in such a situation will agree that the City Manager's action may well have averted a major catastrophe.

The gravity of the danger here surely needs no further explication. The imminence of that danger has been emphasized at every stage of this proceeding, from the complaints charging that the demonstrations "tended directly to immediate violence" to the State Supreme Court's affirmance on the authority of *Feiner, supra.* This record, then, shows no steps backward from a standard of "clear and present danger." But to say that the police may not intervene until the riot has occurred is like keeping out the doctor until the patient dies. I cannot subscribe to such a doctrine. . . .

NOTE: For a review of the law with respect to expression that impinges upon municipal order, see Mr. Justice Frankfurter's concurring opinion in *Feiner* and related cases, 340 U.S. 315 (1951).

Talley v. *California,* 362 U.S. 60 (1960), involved a conviction for violating a Los Angeles ordinance against distribution of any handbill "in any place under any circumstances" unless the handbill identified the person who prepared, distributed, or sponsored it. The ordinance was held invalid on its face. Observing that the identification requirement "would tend to restrict freedom to distribute information and thereby freedom of expression," the Court added, "We have recently had occasion to hold in two cases that there are times and circumstances when States may not compel members of groups engaged in the dissemination of ideas to be publicly identified. *Bates* v. *City of Little Rock,* 361 U.S. 516; *NAACP* v. *State of Alabama,* 357 U.S. 449. The reason for those holdings was that identification and fear of reprisal might deter perfectly peaceful discussions of public matters of importance. This broad . . . ordinance is subject to the same infirmity."

Mr. Justice Clark, joined by his brothers Frankfurter and Whittaker, dissented on the ground that there was no claim or proof that Talley might suffer any injury whatever by identifying his handbills with his name—which made his situation quite unlike that of the complaining parties in the *Bates* and *NAACP* cases cited by the majority. On the other hand, the dissenters thought the community had a substantial interest in preventing "fraud, false advertising and libel."

Valentine v. *Chrestensen*, 316 U.S. 52 (1942) held that commercial advertising is not protected by the free utterance provisions of the Constitution.

7. FORCE WORDS—UTTERANCE PLUS

CRAIG v. *HARNEY*

331 U.S. 367 (1947)

Certiorari to the Court of Criminal Appeals of Texas.

Opinion of the Court by MR. JUSTICE DOUGLAS, announced by MR. JUSTICE REED.

Petitioners were adjudged guilty of constructive criminal contempt by the County Court of Nueces County, Texas, and sentenced to jail for three days. They sought to challenge the legality of their confinement by applying to the Court of Criminal Appeals for a writ of habeas corpus. That court by a divided vote denied the writ and remanded petitioners to the custody of the county sheriff. 149 Tex. Cr.—, 193 S.W.2d. 178. The case is here on a petition for a writ of certiorari which we granted because of the importance of the problem and because the ruling of the Texas court raised doubts whether it conformed to the principles, announced in *Bridges* v. *California*, 314 U.S. 252, and *Pennekamp* v. *Florida*, 328 U.S. 331.

Petitioners are a publisher, an editorial writer, and a news reporter of newspapers published in Corpus Christi, Texas. The County Court had before it a forcible detainer case, *Jackson* v. *Mayes*, whereby Jackson sought to regain possession from Mayes of a business building in Corpus Christi which Mayes (who was at the time in the armed services and whose affairs were being handled by an agent, one Burchard) claimed under a lease. That case turned on whether Mayes' lease was forfeited because of non-payment of rent. At the close of the testimony each side moved for an instructed verdict. The judge instructed the jury to return a verdict for Jackson. That was on May 26, 1945. The jury returned with a verdict for Mayes.

The judge refused to accept it and again instructed the jury to return a verdict for Jackson. The jury returned a second time with a verdict for Mayes. Once more the judge refused to accept it and repeated his prior instruction. It being the evening of May 26th and the jury not having complied, the judge recessed the court until the morning of May 27. Again the jury balked at returning the instructed verdict. But finally it complied, stating that it acted under coercion of the court and against its conscience.

On May 29th Mayes moved for a new trial. That motion was denied on June 6th. On June 4th an officer of the County Court filed with that court a complaint charging petitioners with contempt by publication. The publications referred to were an editorial and news stories published on May 26, 27, 28, 30, and 31 in the newspapers with which petitioners are connected. We have set forth the relevant parts of the publications in the appendix to this opinion. Browning, the judge, who is a layman and who holds an elective office, was criticised for taking the case from the jury. That ruling was called "arbitrary action" and a "travesty on justice." It was deplored that a layman, rather than a lawyer, sat as judge. Groups of local citizens were reported as petitioning the judge to grant Mayes a new trial and it was said that one group had labeled the judge's ruling as a "gross miscarriage of justice." It was also said that the judge's behavior had properly brought down "the wrath of public opinion upon his head," that the people were aroused because a serviceman "seems to be getting a raw deal," and that there was "no way of knowing whether justice was done, because the first rule of justice, giving both sides an opportunity to be heard, was repudiated." And the fact that there could be no appeal from the judge's ruling to a court "familiar with proper procedure and able to interpret and weigh motions and arguments by opposing counsel" was deplored.

The trial judge concluded that the reports and editorial were designed falsely to represent to the public the nature of the proceedings and to prejudice and influence the court in its ruling on the motion for a new trial then pending. Petitioners contended at the hearing that all that was reported did no more than to create the same impression that would have been created upon the mind of an average intelligent layman who sat through the trial. They disclaimed any purpose to impute unworthy motives to the judge or to advise him how the case should be decided or to bring the court into disrepute. The purpose was to "quicken the conscience of the judge" and to "make him more careful in discharging his duty."

The Court of Criminal Appeals, in denying the writ of habeas corpus, stated that the "issue before us" is "whether the publications . . . were reasonably calculated to interfere with the due administration of justice" in the pending case. 193 S.W.2d p. 186. It held that "there is no escape from the conclusion that it was the purpose and intent of the publishers . . . to force, compel, and coerce Judge Browning to grant Mayes a new trial. The only reason or motive for so doing was because the publishers did not agree with Judge Browning's decision or conduct of the case. According to their viewpoint, Judge Browning was wrong and they took it upon themselves to make him change his decision." *Id.* pp. 188–189. The court went on to say that "It is hard to conceive how the public press could have been more forcibly or substantially used or applied to make, force, and compel a judge to change a ruling or decision in a case pending before him than was here done." *Id.*, p. 189. The court distinguished the *Bridges* case, noting

that there the published statements carried threats of future adverse criticism and action on the part of the publisher if the pending matter was not disposed of in accordance with the views of the publisher, that the views of the publisher in the matter were already well known, and that the *Bridges* case was not private litigation but a suit in the outcome of which the public had an interest. *Id.*, p. 188. It concluded that the facts of this case satisfied the "clear and present danger" rule of the *Bridges* case. The test was, in the view of the court, satisfied "because the publications and their purpose were to impress upon Judge Browning (a) that unless he granted the motion for a new trial he would be subjected to suspicion as to his integrity and fairness and to odium and hatred in the public mind; (b) that the safe and secure course to avoid the criticism of the press and public opinion would be to grant the motion and disqualify himself from again presiding at the trial of the case; and (c) that if he overruled the motion for a new trial, there would be produced in the public mind such a disregard for the court over which he presided as to give rise to a purpose in practice to refuse to respect and obey any order, judgment, or decree which he might render in conflict with the views of the public press. (*Id.*, p. 189.)"

The court's statement of the issue before it and the reasons it gave for holding that the "clear and present danger" test was satisfied have a striking resemblance to the findings which the Court in *Toledo Newspaper Co.* v. *United States*, 247 U.S. 402, held adequate to sustain an adjudication of contempt by publication. That case held that comment on a pending case in a federal court was punishable by contempt if it had a "reasonable tendency" to obstruct the administration of justice. We revisited that case in *Nye* v. *United States*, 313 U.S. 33, 52, and disapproved it. And in *Bridges* v. *California, supra,* we held that the compulsion of the First Amendment, made applicable to the States by the Fourteenth (*Schneider* v. *Irvington*, 308 U.S. 147;

Murdock v. *Pennsylvania,* 319 U.S. 105, 108) forbade the punishment by contempt for comment on pending cases in absence of a showing that the utterances created a "clear and present danger" to the administration of justice. 314 U.S. pp. 260–264. We reaffirmed and reapplied that standard in *Pennekamp* v. *Florida, supra,* which also involved comment on matters pending before the court. We stated, p. 347:

"Courts must have power to protect the interests of prisoners and litigants before them from unseemly efforts to pervert judicial action. In the borderline instances where it is difficult to say upon which side the alleged offense falls, we think the specific freedom of public comment should weigh heavily against a possible tendency to influence pending cases. Freedom of discussion should be given the widest range compatible with the essential requirement of the fair and orderly administration of justice."

Neither those cases nor the present one raises questions concerning the full reach of the power of the state to protect the administration of justice by its courts. The problem presented is only a narrow, albeit important, phase of that problem—the power of a court promptly and without a jury trial to punish for comment on cases pending before it and awaiting disposition. The history of the power to punish for contempt (see *Nye* v. *United States, supra; Bridges* v. *California, supra*) and the unequivocal command of the First Amendment serve as constant reminders that freedom of speech and of the press should not be impaired through the exercise of that power, unless there is no doubt that the utterances in question are a serious and imminent threat to the administration of justice.

In a case where it is asserted that a person has been deprived by a state court of a fundamental right secured by the Constitution, an independent examination of the facts by this Court is often required to be made. . . .

We start with the news articles. A trial is a public event. What transpires in the court room is public property. If a transcript of the court proceedings had been published, we suppose none would claim that the judge could punish the publisher for contempt. And we can see no difference though the conduct of the attorneys, of the jury, or even of the judge himself, may have reflected on the court. Those who see and hear what transpired can report it with impunity. There is no special prerequisite of the judiciary which enables it, as distinguished from other institutions of democratic government, to suppress, edit, or censor events which transpire in proceedings before it.

The articles of May 26, 27, and 28 were partial reports of what transpired at the trial. They did not reflect good reporting, for they failed to reveal the precise issue before the judge. They said that Mayes, the tenant, had tendered a rental check. They did not disclose that the rental check was post-dated and hence, in the opinion of the judge, not a valid tender. In that sense the news articles were by any standard an unfair report of what transpired. But inaccuracies in reporting are commonplace. Certainly a reporter could not be laid by the heels for contempt because he missed the essential point in a trial or failed to summarize the issues to accord with the views of the judge who sat on the case. Conceivably, a plan of reporting on a case could be so designed and executed as to poison the public mind, to cause a march on the court house, or otherwise so disturb the delicate balance in a highly wrought situation as to imperil the fair and orderly functioning of the judicial process. But it takes more imagination than we possess to find in this rather sketchy and one-sided report of a case any imminent or serious threat to a judge of reasonable fortitude. See *Pennekamp* v. *Florida, supra.*

The accounts of May 30 and 31 dealt with the news of what certain groups of citizens proposed to do about the judge's ruling in the case. So far as we are advised, it was a fact that they planned to take the proposed action. The episodes were community events of legitimate interest. Whatever might be the responsibility of the group which took the action, those who reported it stand in a different position. Even if the former were guilty of contempt, freedom of the press may not be denied a newspaper which brings their conduct to the public eye.

The only substantial question raised pertains to the editorial. It called the judge's refusal to hear both sides "high-handed," a "travesty on justice," and the reason that public opinion was "outraged." It said that his ruling properly "brought down the wrath of public opinion upon his head" since a serviceman "seems to be getting a raw deal." The fact that there was no appeal from his decision to a "judge who is familiar with proper procedure and able to interpret and weigh motions and arguments by opposing counsel and to make his decisions accordingly" was a "tragedy." It deplored the fact that the judge was a "layman" and not a "competent attorney." It concluded that the "first rule of justice" was to give both sides an opportunity to be heard and when that rule was "repudiated," there was "no way of knowing whether justice was done."

This was strong language, intemperate language, and, we assume, an unfair criticism. But a judge may not hold in contempt one "who ventures to publish anything that tends to make him unpopular or to belittle him. . . ." See *Craig* v. *Hecht*, 263 U.S. 255, 281. Mr. Justice Holmes dissenting. The vehemence of the language used is not alone the measure of the power to punish for contempt. The fires which it kindles must constitute an imminent, not merely a likely, threat to the administration of justice. The danger must not be remote or even probable; it must immediately imperil.

We agree with the court below that the editorial must be appraised in the setting of the news articles which both preceded and followed it. It must also be appraised in light of the community environment which prevailed at that time. The fact that the jury was recalcitrant and balked, the fact that it acted under coercion and con-

trary to its conscience and said so were some index of popular opinion. A judge who is part of such a dramatic episode can hardly help but know that his decision is apt to be unpopular. But the law of contempt is not made for the protection of judges who may be sensitive to the winds of public opinion. Judges are supposed to be men of fortitude, able to thrive in a hardy climate. Conceivably a campaign could be so managed and so aimed at the sensibilities of a particular judge and the matter pending before him as to cross the forbidden line. But the episodes we have here do not fall in that category. Nor can we assume that the trial judge was not a man of fortitude.

The editorial's complaint was two-fold. One objection or criticism was that a layman rather than a lawyer sat on the bench. That is legitimate comment; and its relevancy could hardly be denied at least where judges are elected. In the circumstances of the present case, it amounts at the very most to an intimation that come the next election the newspaper in question will not support the incumbent. But it contained no threat to oppose him in the campaign if the decision on the merits was not overruled, nor any implied reward if it was changed. Judges who stand for reelection run on their records. That may be a rugged environment. Criticism is expected. Discussion of their conduct is appropriate, if not necessary. The fact that the discussion at this particular point of time was not in good taste falls far short of meeting the clear and present danger test.

The other complaint of the editorial was directed at the court's procedure—its failure to hear both sides before the case was decided. There was no attempt to pass on the merits of the case. The editorial, indeed, stated that there was no way of knowing whether justice was done. That criticism of the court's procedure—that it decided the case without giving both sides a chance to be heard—reduces the salient point of the case to a narrow issue. If the point had been made in a petition for rehearing, and reduced to lawyer's language,

it would be of trifling consequence. The
fact that it was put in layman's language,
colorfully phrased for popular consumption, and printed in a newspaper does not
seem to us to elevate it to the criminal
level. It might well have a tendency to
lower the standing of the judge in the public eye. But it is hard to see on these facts
how it could obstruct the course of justice
in the case before the court. The only demand was for a hearing. There was no demand that the judge reverse his position—
or else.

"Legal trials are not like elections, to be
won through the use of the meeting-hall,
the radio, and the newspaper." *Bridges* v.
California, supra, p. 271. But there was
here no threat or menace to the integrity
of the trial. The editorial challenged the
propriety of the court's procedure, not the
merits of its ruling. Any such challenge,
whether made prior or subsequent to the
final disposition of a case, would likely
reflect on the competence of the judge in
handling cases. But as we have said, the
power to punish for contempt depends on
a more substantial showing. Giving the
editorial all of the vehemence which the
court below found in it we fail to see how
it could in any realistic sense create an
imminent and serious threat to the ability
of the court to give fair consideration to
the motion for rehearing.

There is a suggestion that the case is
different from *Bridges* v. *California supra,*
in that we have here only private litigation,
while in the *Bridges* case labor controversies were involved, some of them being
criminal cases. The thought apparently is
that the range of permissible comment is
greater where the pending case generates
a public concern. The nature of the case
may, of course, be relevant in determining
whether the clear and present danger test
is satisfied. But, the rule of the *Bridges* and
Pennekamp cases is fashioned to serve the
needs of all litigation, not merely select
types of pending cases.

Reversed.

MR. JUSTICE MURPHY concurred in a
separate opinion.

MR. JUSTICE FRANKFURTER, joined by
CHIEF JUSTICE VINSON, dissented.

[He emphasized that the effect of the
Court's position was to destroy a theretofore unquestioned state power. And he
observed that the *Toledo, Nye,* and *Hecht*
cases on which the Court relied were not
relevant because they dealt not with the
constitutional authority of the states, but
merely with the interpretation of federal
legislation narrowly restricting the contempt power of federal courts. He then
continued as follows:]

We are not dealing here with criticisms,
whether temperate or unbridled, of action
in a case after a judge is through with it,
or of his judicial qualifications, or of his
conduct in general. Comment on what a
judge has done—criticism of the judicial
process in a particular case after it has exhausted itself—no matter how ill-informed
or irresponsible or misrepresentative, is
part of the precious right of the free play
of opinion. Whatever violence there may
be to truth in such utterances must be left
to the correction of truth.

The publications now in question did
not constitute merely a narrative of a
judge's conduct in a particular case nor a
general commentary upon his competence
or his philosophy. Nor were they a plea
for reform of the Texas legal system to the
end that county court judges should be
learned in the law and that a judgment in
a suit of forcible detainer may be appealable. The thrust of the articles was directed
to what the judge should do on a matter
immediately before him, namely to grant
a motion for a new trial. So the Texas
Court found. And it found this not in the
abstract but on the particular stage of the
happenings and in the circumstances disclosed by the record. The Texas Court
made its findings with reference to the
locality where the events took place and in
circumstances which may easily impart significance to the Texas Court but may
elude full appreciation here.

Corpus Christi, the locale of the drama,
had a population of less than 60,000 at the
last census, and Nueces County about

92,000. The three papers which published the articles complained of are under common control and are the only papers of general circulation in the area. It can hardly be a compelling presumption that such papers so controlled had no influence, at a time when patriotic fervor was running high, in stirring up sentiment of powerful groups in a small community in favor of a veteran to whom, it was charged, a great wrong had been done. It would seem a natural inference, as the court below in effect found, that these newspapers whipped up public opinion against the judge to secure reversal of his action and then professed merely to report public opinion. We cannot say that the Texas Court could not properly find that these newspapers asked of the judge, and instigated powerful sections of the community to ask of the judge, that which no one has any business to ask of a judge, except the parties and their counsel in open court, namely, that he should decide one way rather than another. Only if we can say that the Texas Court had no basis in reason to find what it did find, can we deny that the purpose of the articles in their setting was to induce the judge to grant a new trial. Surely a jury could reach such a conclusion on these facts. We ought not to allow less leeway to the Texas Court in drawing inferences than we would to a jury. Because it is a question of degree, the field in which a court, like a jury, may "exercise its judgment is, necessarily, a wide one." Mr. Justice Brandeis in *Schafer* v. *United States,* 251 U.S. 466, 483. Of course, the findings by a State court of what are usually deemed facts cannot foreclose our scrutiny of them if a constitutional right depends on a fair appraisal of those facts. But it would be novel doctrine indeed to say that we may consider the record as it comes before us from a State court as though it were our duty or right to ascertain the facts in the first instance. A State cannot by torturing facts preclude us from considering whether it has thereby denied a constitutional right. Neither can this Court find a violation of a constitutional right by denying to a State

its right to a fair appraisal of facts and circumstances peculiarly its concern. Otherwise, in every case coming here from a State court this Court might make independent examination of the facts, because every right claimed under the Constitution is a fundamental right. The "most respectful attention" which we have been told is due to a State would then be merely an empty profession. See *Pennekamp* v. *Florida,* 328 U.S. 331, 335.

If under all the circumstances the Texas Court here was not justified in finding that these publications created "a clear and present danger" of the substantive evil that Texas had a right to prevent, namely the purposeful exertion of extraneous influence in having the motion for a new trial granted, "clear and present danger" becomes merely a phrase for covering up a novel, iron constitutional doctrine. Hereafter the States cannot deal with direct attempts to influence the disposition of a pending controversy by a summary proceeding, except when the misbehavior physically prevents proceedings from going on in court, or occurs in its immediate proximity. Only the pungent pen of Mr. Justice Holmes could adequately comment on such a perversion of his phrase. . . .

MR. JUSTICE JACKSON, dissenting.

This is one of those cases in which the reasons we give for our decision are more important to the development of the law than the decision itself.

It seems to me that the Court is assigning two untenable, if not harmful, reasons for its action. The first is that this newspaper publisher has done no wrong. I take it that we could not deny the right of the state to punish him if he had done wrong and I do not suppose we could say that the traditional remedy was an unconstitutional one.

The right of the people to have a free press is a vital one, but so is the right to have a calm and fair trial free from outside pressures and influences. Every other right, including the right of a free press itself, may depend on the ability to get a judicial hearing as dispassionate and impartial as the weakness inherent in men will permit. I think this publisher passed beyond the legitimate use of press freedom and infringed the citizen's right to a calm and impartial trial. I do not think we can say that it is beyond the power of the state to exert safeguards against such interference with the course of trial as we have here.

This was a private lawsuit between individuals. It involved an issue of no greater public importance than which of two claimants should be the tenant of the "Playboy Cafe." The public interest in the litigation was that dispassionate justice be done by the court and that it appear to be done. . . .

For this Court to imply that this kind of attack during a pending case is all right seems to me to compound the wrong. The press of the country may rightfully take the decision of this Court to mean indifference toward, if not approval of, such attacks upon courts during pending cases. I think this opinion conveys a wrong impression of the responsibilities of a free press for the calm and dispassionate administration of justice and that we should not hesitate to condemn what has been done here.

But even worse is that this Court appears to sponsor the myth that judges are not as other men are, and that therefore newspaper attacks on them are negligible because they do not penetrate the judicial armor. Says the opinion: "But the law of contempt is not made for the protection of judges who may be sensitive to the winds of public opinion. Judges are supposed to be men of fortitude, able to thrive in a hardy climate." With due respect to those who think otherwise, to me this is an ill-founded opinion, and to inform the press that it may be irresponsible in attacking judges because they have so much fortitude is ill-advised, or worse. I do not know whether it is the view of the Court that a judge must be thick-skinned or just thick-headed, but nothing in my experience or observation confirms the idea that he is insensitive to publicity. Who does not prefer good to ill report of his work? And if fame—a good public name—is, as Milton said, the "last infirmity of noble mind," it is frequently the first infirmity of a mediocre one.

From our sheltered position, fortified by life tenure and other defenses to judicial independence, it is easy to say that this local judge ought to have shown more fortitude in the face of criticism. But he had no such protection. He was an elective judge, who held for a short term. I do not take it that an ambition of a judge to remain a judge is either unusual or dishonorable. Moreover, he was not a lawyer, and I regard this as a matter of some consequence. A lawyer may gain courage to render a decision that temporarily is unpopular because he has confidence that his profession over the years will approve it, despite its unpopular reception, as has been the case with many great decisions. But this judge had no anchor in professional opinion. Of course, the blasts of these little papers in this small community do not jolt us, but I am not so confident that we would be indifferent if a news monopoly in our entire jurisdiction should perpetrate this kind of an attack on us. . . .

QUAERE: Were those who interfered with the judicial process in *Irvin* v. *Dowd* and *Rideau* v. *Louisiana,* above, guilty of contempt of court? Would *Craig* (and cases cited therein) shield them? Is invalidation of a judgment tainted by improper outside interference—and immunity for the taintor—required by the Constitution? For a more recent contempt case, see *Wood* v. *Georgia,* 370 U.S. 375 (1962).

INTERNATIONAL BROTHERHOOD OF TEAMSTERS v. VOGT

354 U.S. 284 (1957)

Certiorari to the Supreme Court of Wisconsin.

MR. JUSTICE FRANKFURTER delivered the opinion of the Court.

This is one more in the long series of cases in which this Court has been required to consider the limits imposed by the Fourteenth Amendment on the power of a State to enjoin picketing. The case was heard below on the pleadings and affidavits, the parties stipulating that the record contained "all of the facts and evidence that would be adduced upon a trial on the merits. . . ." Respondent owns and operates a gravel pit in Ocononowoc, Wisconsin, where it employs 15 to 20 men. Petitioner unions sought unsuccessfully to induce some of respondent's employees to join the unions and commenced to picket the entrance to respondent's business with signs reading, "The men on this job are not 100% affiliated with the A.F.L." In consequence, drivers of several trucking companies refused to deliver and haul goods to and from respondent's plant, causing substantial damage to respondent. Respondent thereupon sought an injunction to restrain the picketing.

[The state Supreme Court] held that "One would be credulous, indeed, to believe under the circumstances that the union had no thought of coercing the employer to interfere with his employees in their right to join or refuse to join the defendant union." Such picketing, the court held, was for "an unlawful purpose," since Wis. Stat. § 111.06(2)(b) made it an unfair labor practice for an employee individually or in concert with others to "coerce, intimidate or induce any employer to interfere with any of his employes in the enjoyment of their legal rights . . . or to engage in any practice with regard to his employes which would constitute an unfair labor practice if undertaken by him on his own initiative." Relying on *Building Service Employees International Union v. Gazzam,* 339 U.S. 532, and *Pappas v. Stacey,* 151 Me. 36, 116 A2d 497, the Wisconsin Supreme Court therefore affirmed the granting of the injunction on this . . . ground. 270 Wis. 321a.

We are asked to reverse the judgment of the Wisconsin Supreme Court, which to a large extent rested its decision on that of the Supreme Judicial Court of Maine in *Pappas v. Stacey (Me.) supra.* When an appeal from that decision was filed here, this Court granted appellee's motion to dismiss for lack of a substantial federal question. 350 U.S. 870. Since the present case presents a similar question, we might well have denied certiorari on the strength of our decision in that case. In view of the recurrence of the question, we thought it advisable to grant certiorari, 352 U.S. 817, and to restate the principles governing this type of case. . . .

The series begins with *Truax v. Corrigan,* 257 U.S. 312, in which a closely divided Court found it to be violative of the equal protection clause—not of the due process clause—for a State to deny use of the injunction in the special class of cases arising out of labor conflicts. The considerations that underlay that case soon had to yield, through legislation and later through litigation, to the persuasiveness of undermining facts. Thus, to remedy the abusive use of the injunction in the federal courts (see Frankfurter and Greene, *The Labor Injunction*), the *Norris-LaGuardia Act,* 47 State. 70, 29 U.S.C. § 101, withdrew, subject to qualifications, jurisdiction from the federal courts to issue injunctions in labor disputes to prohibit certain acts. Its example was widely followed by state enactments.

Apart from remedying the abuses of the injunction in this general type of litigation, legislatures and courts began to find in one of the aims of picketing an aspect of communication. This view came to the fore in *Senn* v. *Tile Layers Protective Union*, 301 U.S. 468, where the Court held that the Fourteenth Amendment did not prohibit Wisconsin from authorizing peaceful stranger picketing by a union that was attempting to unionize a shop and to induce an employer to refrain from working in his business as a laborer.

Although the Court had been closely divided in the *Senn* case, three years later, in passing on a restrictive instead of a permissive state statute, the Court made sweeping pronouncements about the right to picket in holding unconstitutional a statute that had been applied to ban all picketing, with "no exceptions based upon either the number of persons engaged in the proscribed activity, the peaceful character of their demeanor, the nature of their dispute with an employer, or the restrained character and the accurateness of the terminology used in notifying the public of the facts of the dispute." *Thornhill* v. *Alabama*, 310 U.S. 88, 99. As the statute dealt at large with all picketing, so the Court broadly assimilated peaceful picketing in general to freedom of speech, and as such protected against abridgment by the Fourteenth Amendment.

These principles were applied by the Court in *A.F. of L.* v. *Swing*, 312 U.S. 321, to hold unconstitutional an injunction against peaceful picketing, based on a State's common-law policy against picketing when there was no immediate dispute between employer and employee. On the same day, however, the Court upheld a generalized injunction against picketing where there had been violence because "it could justifiably be concluded that the momentum of fear generated by past violence would survive even though future picketing might be wholly peaceful." *Milk*

Wagon Drivers Union v. *Meadowmoor Dairies*, 312 U.S. 287, 294.

Soon, however, the Court came to realize that the broad pronouncements, but not the specific holding, of *Thornhill* had to yield "to the impact of facts unforeseen," or at least not sufficiently appreciated. Cf. *People* v. *Charles Schweinler Press*, 214 N.Y. 395, 108 N.E. 639. See 28 *Harv. L. Rev.* 790. Cases reached the Court in which a state had designed a remedy to meet a specific situation or to accomplish a particular social policy. These cases made manifest that picketing, even though "peaceful," involved more than just communication of ideas and could not be immune from all state regulation. "Picketing by an organized group is more than free speech, since it involves patrol of a particular locality and since the very presence of a picket line may induce action of one kind or another, quite irrespective of the nature of the ideas which are being disseminated." *Bakery & P. Drivers & Helpers, I. B. T.* v. *Wohl*, 315 U.S. 769, 776 (concur. op.); see *Carpenters & J. Union* v. *Ritter's Cafe*, 315 U.S. 722, 725–728.

These latter two cases required the Court to review a choice made by two States between the competing interests of unions, employers, their employees, and the public at large. In the *Ritter's Cafe* case, Texas had enjoined as a violation of its antitrust law picketing of a restaurant by unions to bring pressure on its owner with respect to the use of nonunion labor by a contractor of the restaurant owner in the construction of a building having nothing to do with the restaurant. The Court held that Texas could, consistent with the Fourteenth Amendment, insulate from the dispute a neutral establishment that industrially had no connection with it. This type of picketing certainly involved little, if any, "communication."

In *Bakery & P. Drivers & Helpers, I. B. T.* v. *Wohl* (U.S.) *supra*, in a very narrowly restricted decision, the Court held that because of the impossibility of otherwise publicizing a legitimate grievance and because of the slight effect on "strangers" to the dispute, a State could not constitutionally prohibit a union from picketing bakeries in its efforts to have independent peddlers, buying from bakers and selling to small stores, conform to certain union requests. Although the Court in *Ritter's Cafe* and *Wohl* did not question the holding of *Thornhill,* the strong reliance on the particular facts in each case demonstrated a growing awareness that these cases involved not so much questions of free speech as review of the balance struck by a State between picketing that involved more than "publicity" and competing interests of state policy. (See also *Cafeteria Employees Union* v. *Angelos,* 320 U.S. 293, where the Court reviewed a New York injunction against picketing by a union of a restaurant that was run by the owners without employees. The New York court appeared to have justified an injunction on the alternate grounds that there was no "labor dispute" under the New York statute or that use of untruthful placards justified the injunction. We held, in a brief opinion, that the abuses alleged did not justify an injunction against all picketing and that *A.F. of L.* v. *Swing* governed the alternate ground for decision.)

The implied reassessments of the broad language of the *Thornhill* case were finally generalized in a series of cases sustaining injunctions against peaceful picketing, even when arising in the course of a labor controversy, when such picketing was counter to valid state policy in a domain open to state regulation. The decisive reconsideration came in *Giboney* v. *Empire Storage & Ice Co.* 336 U.S. 490. A union, seeking to organize peddlers, picketed a wholesale dealer to induce it to refrain from selling to nonunion peddlers. The state courts, finding that such an agreement would constitute a conspiracy in restraint of trade in violation of the state antitrust laws, enjoined the picketing. This Court affirmed unanimously.

"It is contended that the injunction against picketing adjacent to Empire's place of business is an unconstitutional abridgment of free speech because the picketers were attempting peacefully to publicize truthful facts about a labor dispute. . . . But the record here does not permit this publicizing to be treated in isolation. For according to the pleadings, the evidence, the findings, and the argument of the appellants, the sole immediate object of the publicizing adjacent to the premises of Empire, as well as the other activities of the appellants and their allies, was to compel Empire to agree to stop selling ice to nonunion peddlers. Thus all of appellants' activities . . . constituted a single and integrated course of conduct, which was in violation of Missouri's valid law. In this situation, the injunction did no more than enjoin an offense against Missouri Law, a felony." *Id.* 336 U.S. at 497, 498.

The Court therefore concluded that it was "clear that appellants were doing more than exercising a right of free speech or press. . . . They were exercising their economic power together with that of their allies to compel Empire to abide by union rather than by state regulation of trade." *Id.* 336 U.S. at 503.

The following Term, the Court decided a group of cases applying and elaborating on the theory of *Giboney*. In *Hughes* v. *Superior Court of California,* 339 U.S. 460, the Court held that the Fourteenth Amendment did not bar use of the injunction to prohibit picketing of a place of business solely to secure compliance with a demand that its employees be hired in percentage to the racial origin of its customers. "We cannot construe the due process clause as prohibiting California from securing respect for its policy against involuntary employment on racial lines by prohibiting systematic picketing that would subvert such policy." *Id.* 339 U.S. at 466. The Court also found it immaterial that the state policy had been expressed by the judiciary rather than by the legislature.

On the same day, the Court decided *International Brotherhood of Teamsters C. W. & H. Union* v. *Hanke,* 339 U.S. 470, holding that a State was not restrained by the Fourteenth Amendment from enjoining picketing of a business, conducted by the owner himself without employees, in order to secure compliance with a demand to become a union shop. Although there was no one opinion for the Court, its decision was another instance of the affirmance of an injunction against picketing because directed against a valid public policy of the State.

A third case, *Building Service Employees International Union* v. *Gazzam,* 339 U.S. 532, was decided the same day. Following an unsuccessful attempt at unionization of a small hotel and refusal by the owner to sign a contract with the union as bargaining agent, the union began to picket the hotel with signs stating that the owner was unfair to organized labor. The State, finding that the object of the picketing was in violation of its statutory policy against employer coercion of employees' choice of bargaining representative, enjoined picketing for such purpose. This Court affirmed, rejecting the argument that "the *Swing* case, 312 U.S. 321, *supra,* is controlling. . . . In that case this Court struck down the State's restraint of picketing based solely on the absence of an employer-employee relationship. An adequate basis for the instant decree is the unlawful objective of the picketing, namely, coercion by the employer of the employees' selection of a bargaining representative. Peaceful picketing for any lawful purpose is not prohibited by the decree under review." *Id.* 339 U.S. at 539.

A similar problem was involved in *United Assoc. J. P. & S.* v. *Graham,* 345 U.S. 192, where a state court had enjoined, as a violation of its "Right to Work" law, picketing that advertised that nonunion men were being employed on a building job. This Court found that there was evidence in the record supporting a conclusion that a substantial purpose of the picketing was to put pressure on the general contractor to eliminate nonunion men from the job and, on the reasoning of the cases that we have just discussed, held that the injunction was not in conflict with the Fourteenth Amendment.

This series of cases, then, established a broad field in which a State, in enforcing some public policy, whether of its criminal or its civil law, and whether announced by its legislature or its courts, could constitutionally enjoin peaceful picketing aimed at preventing effectuation of that policy.

In the light of this background, the Maine Supreme Judicial Court in 1955 decided, on an agreed statement of facts, the case of *Pappas* v. *Stacey,* 151 Me. 36. From the statement, it appeared that three union employees went on strike and picketed a restaurant peacefully "for the sole purpose of seeking to organize other employees of the Plaintiff, ultimately to have the Plaintiff enter into collective bargaining and negotiations with the Union. . . ." Maine had a statute providing that workers should have full liberty of self-organization, free from restraint by employers or other persons. The Maine Supreme Judicial Court drew the inference from the agreed statement of facts that "there is a steady and exacting pressure upon the employer to interfere with the free choice of the employees in the matter of organization. To say that the picketing is not designed to bring about such action is to forget an obvious purpose of the picketing—to cause economic loss to the business during noncompliance by the employees with the requests of the union." It therefore enjoined the picketing, and an appeal was taken to this Court.

The whole series of cases discussed above allowing, as they did, wide discretion to a State in the formulation of domestic policy, and not involving a curtailment of free speech in its obvious and accepted scope, led this Court, without the need of further argument, to grant appellee's motion to dismiss the appeal in that it no longer presented a substantial federal question. 350 U.S. 870.

The *Stacey* case is this case. As in *Stacey,* the present case was tried without oral testimony. As in *Stacey,* the highest state court drew the inference from the facts that the picketing was to coerce the employer to put pressure on his employees to join the union, in violation of the declared policy of the State. (For a declaration of similar congressional policy, see § 8 of the Taft-Hartley Act, 61 Stat. 140, 29 U.S.C. § 158.) The cases discussed above all hold that, consistent with the Fourteenth Amendment, a State may enjoin such conduct.

Of course, the mere fact that there is "picketing" does not automatically justify its restraint without an investigation into its conduct and purposes. State courts, no more than state legislatures, can enact blanket prohibitions against picketing. *Thornhill* v. *Alabama,* 310 U.S. 88, 84 L. ed. 1093, and *A.F. of L.* v. *Swing,* 312 U.S. 321, both *supra.* The series of cases following *Thornhill* and *Swing* demonstrate that the policy of Wisconsin enforced by the prohibition of this picketing is a valid one. In this case, the circumstances set forth in the opinion of the Wisconsin Supreme Court afford a rational basis for the inference it drew concerning the purpose of the picketing. No question was raised here concerning the breadth of the injunction, but of course its terms must be read in the light of the opinion of the Wisconsin Supreme Court, which justified it on the ground that the picketing was for the purpose of coercing the employer to coerce his employees. "If astuteness may discover argumentative excess in the scope of the [injunction] beyond what we constitutionally justify by this opinion, it will be open to petitioners to raise the matter, which they have not raised here, when the [case] on remand [reaches] the [Wisconsin] court." *International Brotherhood of Teamsters, C. W. & H. Union* v. *Hanke,* 339 U.S. at 480, 481.

Therefore, having deemed it appropriate to elaborate on the issues in the case, we affirm.

Mr. Justice Whittaker took no part in the consideration or decision of this case.

Mr. Justice Douglas, with whom The Chief Justice and Mr. Justice Black concur, dissenting:

The Court has now come full circle. In *Thornhill* v. *Alabama,* 310 U.S. 88, 102, we struck down a state ban on picketing on the ground that "the dissemination of information concerning the facts of a labor dispute must be regarded as within that area of free discussion that is guaranteed by the Constitution." Less than one year later, we held that the First Amendment protected organizational picketing on a factual record which cannot be distinguished from the one now before us. *A.F. of L.* v. *Swing,* 312 U.S. 321. Of course, we have always recognized that picketing has aspects which make it more than speech. *Bakery & P. Drivers & Helpers, I. B. T.* v. *Wohl,* 315 U.S. 769, 776, 777 (concurring opinion). That difference underlies our decision in *Giboney* v. *Empire Storage & Ice Co.* 336 U.S. 490. There, picketing was an essential part of "a single and integrated course of conduct, which was in violation of Missouri's valid law." *Id.* 336 U.S. at 498. And see *N.L.R.B.* v. *Virginia Electric & P. Co.* 314 U.S. 469, 477, 478. We emphasized that "there was clear danger, imminent and immediate, that unless restrained, appellants would succeed in making [the state] policy a dead letter. . . ." 336 U.S. at 503. Speech there was enjoined because it was an inseparable part of conduct which the State constitutionally could and did regulate.

But where, as here, there is no rioting, no mass picketing, no violence, no disorder, no fisticuffs, no coercion—indeed nothing but speech—the principles announced in *Thornhill* and *Swing* should give the advocacy of one side of a dispute First Amendment protection.

The retreat began when, in *International Brotherhood of Teamsters, C. W. & H. Union* v. *Hanke,* 339 U.S. 470, four members of the Court announced that all picketing could be prohibited if a state court decided that that picketing violated the State's public policy. The retreat became a rout in *United Assoc. J. P. & S.* v. *Graham,* 345 U.S. 192. It was only the "purpose" of the picketing which was relevant. The state court's characterization of the picketers' "purpose" had been made well-nigh conclusive. Considerations of the proximity of picketing to conduct which the State could control or prevent were abandoned, and no longer was it necessary for the state court's decree to be narrowly drawn to prescribe a specific evil. *Id.* 345 U.S. at 201–205 (dissenting opinion).

Today, the Court signs the formal surrender. State courts and state legislatures cannot fashion blanket prohibitions on all picketing. But, for practical purposes, the situation now is as it was when *Senn* v. *Tile Layers Protective Union,* 301 U.S. 468, was decided. State courts and state legislatures

are free to decide whether to permit or suppress any particular picket line for any reason other than a blanket policy against all picketing. I would adhere to the principle announced in *Thornhill.* I would adhere to the result reached in *Swing.* I would return to the test enunciated in *Giboney*— that this form of expression can be regulated or prohibited only to the extent that it forms an essential part of a course of conduct which the State can regulate or prohibit.

I would reverse the judgment below.

NOTE: *Chaplinsky* v. *New Hampshire,* 315 U.S. 568 (1942), involved a state law providing that: "No person shall address any offensive, derisive or annoying word to any other person who is lawfully in any street or other public place, nor call him by any offensive or derisive name, nor make any noise or exclamation in his presence and hearing with intent to deride, offend or annoy him, or to prevent him from pursuing his lawful business or occupation."

The defendant got into an argument on a public sidewalk and allegedly called his opponent a "Goddamned racketeer" and a "damned Fascist." The Court sustained the conviction with these comments:

> There are certain well-defined and narrowly limited classes of speech, the prevention and punishment of which have never been thought to raise any Constitutional problem. These include the lewd and obscene, the profane, the libelous, and the insulting or "fighting" words—those which by their very utterance inflict injury or tend to incite an immediate breach of the peace. It has been well observed that such utterances are no essential part of any exposition of ideas and are of such slight social value as a step to truth that any benefit that may be derived from them is clearly outweighed by the social interest in order and morality.

8. POLITICAL ASSOCIATION

SCALES v. *UNITED STATES*
367 U.S. 203 (1961)

Certiorari to the United States Court of Appeals for the Fourth Circuit.

MR. JUSTICE HARLAN delivered the opinion of the Court.

Our writ issued in this case (358 U.S. 917) to review a judgment of the Court of

Appeals (260 F.2d 21) affirming petitioner's conviction under the so-called membership clause of the Smith Act. 18 U.S.C. § 2385. The Act, among other things, makes a felony the acquisition or holding of knowing membership in any organization which advocates the overthrow of the Government of the United States by force or violence. The indictment charged that from January 1946 to the date of its filing (November 18, 1954) the Communist Party of the United States was such an organization, and that petitioner throughout that period was a member thereof, with knowledge of the Party's illegal purpose and a specific intent to accomplish overthrow "as speedily as circumstances would permit." . . .

It will bring the constitutional issues into clearer focus to notice first the premises on which the case was submitted to the jury. The jury was instructed that in order to convict it must find that within the three-year limitations period (1) the Communist Party advocated the violent overthrow of the Government, in the sense of present "advocacy of action" to accomplish that end as soon as circumstances were propitious; and (2) petitioner was an "active" member of the Party, and not merely "a nominal, passive, inactive or purely technical" member, with knowledge of the Party's illegal advocacy and a specific intent to bring about violent overthrow "as speedily as circumstances would permit."

The constitutional attack upon the membership clause, as thus construed, is that the statute offends (1) the Fifth Amendment, in that it impermissibly imputes guilt to an individual merely on the basis of his associations and sympathies, rather than because of some concrete personal involvement in criminal conduct; and (2) the First Amendment, in that it infringes free political expression and association. . . .

2. FIFTH AMENDMENT

In our jurisprudence guilt is personal, and when the imposition of punishment on a status or on conduct can only be justified by reference to the relationship of that status or conduct to other concededly criminal activity (here advocacy of violent overthrow), that relationship must be sufficiently substantial to satisfy the concept of personal guilt in order to withstand attack under the Due Process Clause of the Fifth Amendment. Membership, without more,

in an organization engaged in illegal advocacy, it is now said, has not heretofore been recognized by this Court to be such a relationship. This claim stands and we shall examine it, independently of that made under the First Amendment.

Any thought that due process puts beyond the reach of the criminal law all individual associational relationships, unless accompanied by the commission of specific acts of criminality, is dispelled by familiar concepts of the law of conspiracy and complicity. While both are commonplace in the landscape of the criminal law, they are not natural features. Rather they are particular legal concepts manifesting the more general principle that society, having the power to punish dangerous behavior, cannot be powerless against those who work to bring about that behavior. The fact that Congress has not resorted to either of these familiar concepts means only that the enquiry here must direct itself to an analysis of the relationship between the fact of membership and the underlying substantive illegal conduct, in order to determine whether that relationship is indeed too tenuous to permit its use as the basis of criminal liability. In this instance it is an organization which engages in criminal activity, and we can perceive no reason why one who actively and knowingly works in the ranks of that organization, intending to contribute to the success of those specifically illegal activities, should be any more immune from prosecution than he to whom the organization has assigned the task of carrying out the substantive criminal act. . . .

What must be met, then, is the argument that membership, even when accompanied by the elements of knowledge and specific intent, affords an insufficient quantum of participation in the organization's alleged criminal activity, that is, an insufficiently significant form of aid and encouragement to permit the imposition of criminal sanctions on that basis. It must indeed be recognized that a person who merely becomes a member of an illegal organization, by that "act" alone need be

doing nothing more than signifying his
assent to its purposes and activities on one
hand, and providing, on the other, only
the sort of moral encouragement which
comes from the knowledge that others believe in what the organization is doing. It
may indeed be argued that such assent and
encouragement do fall short of the concrete, practical impetus given to a criminal
enterprise which is lent for instance by a
commitment on the part of a conspirator
to act in furtherance of that enterprise. A
member, as distinguished from a conspirator, may indicate his approval of a criminal
enterprise by the very fact of his membership without thereby necessarily committing himself to further it by any act or
course of conduct whatever.

In an area of the criminal law which this
Court has indicated more than once demands its watchful scrutiny . . . these factors have weight and must be found to be
overborne in a total constitutional assessment of the statute. We think, however, they
are duly met when the statute is found to
reach only "active" members having also a
guilty knowledge and intent, and which
therefore prevents a conviction on what
otherwise might be regarded as merely an expression of sympathy with the alleged
criminal enterprise, unaccompanied by any
significant action in its support or any
commitment to undertake such action.

Thus, given the construction of the membership clause already discussed, we think
the factors called for in rendering members criminally responsible for the illegal
advocacy of the organization fall within
established, and therefore presumably constitutional standards of criminal imputa-
bility.

3. FIRST AMENDMENT

Little remains to be said concerning the
claim that the statute infringes First
Amendment freedoms. It was settled in
Dennis that the advocacy with which we
are here concerned is not constitutionally
protected speech, and it was further established that a combination to promote such
advocacy, albeit under the aegis of what
purports to be a political party, is not such

association as is protected by the First
Amendment. We can discern no reason
why membership, when it constitutes a
purposeful form of complicity in a group
engaging in this same forbidden advocacy,
should receive any greater degree of protection from the guarantees of that Amendment.

If it is said that the mere existence of
such an enactment tends to inhibit the
exercise of constitutionally protected rights,
in that it engenders an unhealthy fear that
one may find himself unwittingly embroiled
in criminal liability, the answer surely is
that the statute provides that a defendant
must be proven to have knowledge of the
proscribed advocacy before he may be convicted. It is, of course, true that quasi-
political parties or other groups that may
embrace both legal and illegal aims differ
from a technical conspiracy, which is defined by its criminal purpose, so that *all*
knowing association with the conspiracy is
a proper subject for criminal proscription
as far as First Amendment liberties are concerned. If there were a similar blanket
prohibition of association with a group having both legal and illegal aims, there would
indeed be a real danger that legitimate
political expression or association would be
impaired, but the membership clause, as
here construed, does not cut deeper into
the freedom of association than is necessary to deal with "the substantive evils that
Congress has a right to prevent." *Schenck*
v. *United States,* 249 U.S. 47, 52. The clause
does not make criminal all association with
an organization, which has been shown to
engage in illegal advocacy. There must be
clear proof that a defendant "specifically
intend[s] to accomplish [the aims of the
organization] by resort to violence." *Notto*
v. *United States,* post, . . . Thus the member for whom the organization is a vehicle
for the advancement of legitimate aims and
policies does not fall within the ban of
the statute: he lacks the requisite specific
intent "to bring about the overthrow of
the government as speedily as circumstances
would permit." Such a person may be
foolish, deluded, or perhaps merely opti-

mistic, but he is not by this statute made a criminal.

We conclude that petitioner's constitutional challenge must be overruled.

The judgment of the Court of Appeals must be

Affirmed.

MR. JUSTICE BLACK, dissenting. . . .

MR. JUSTICE DOUGLAS, dissenting. . . .

Even the Alien and Sedition Laws—shameful reminders of an early chapter in intolerance—never went so far as we go today. . . . There is here no charge of conspiracy, no charge of any overt act to overthrow the Government by force and violence, no charge of any other criminal act. . . .

We legalize today guilt by association, sending a man to prison when he committed no unlawful act. Today's break with tradition is a serious one. It borrows from the totalitarian philosophy. . . .

MR. JUSTICE BRENNAN, with whom THE CHIEF JUSTICE [WARREN] and MR. JUSTICE DOUGLAS join, dissenting. . . .

COMMUNIST PARTY v. SACB
367 U.S. 1 (1961)

MR. JUSTICE FRANKFURTER delivered the opinion of the Court.

This is a proceeding pursuant to § 14(a) of the Subversive Activities Control Act of 1950 to review an order of the Subversive Activities Control Board requiring the Communist Party of the United States to register as a Communist-action organization under § 7 of the Act. The Court of Appeals for the District of Columbia has affirmed the Board's registration order. . . .

[The Court here ruled that many constitutional issues, including Fifth Amendment self incrimination issues, were premature.]

B. *The Freedoms of Expression and Association Protected by the First Amendment.* The Communist Party would have us hold that the First Amendment prohibits Congress from requiring the registration and filing of information, including membership lists, by organizations substantially dominated or controlled by the foreign powers controlling the world Communist movement and which operate primarily to advance the objectives of that movement: the overthrow of existing government by any means necessary and the establishment in its place of a Communist totalitarian dictatorship (§§ 3(3), 2(1) (6)).

We cannot find such a prohibition in the First Amendment. So to find would make a travesty of that Amendment and the great ends for the well-being of our democracy that it serves.

No doubt, a governmental regulation which requires registration as a condition upon the exercise of speech may in some circumstances affront the constitutional guarantee of free expression. *Thomas* v. *Collins,* 323 U.S. 516. . . . The present statute does not, of course, attach the registration requirement to the incident of speech, but to the incidents of foreign domination and of operation to advance the objectives of the world Communist movement—operation which, the Board has found here, includes extensive, long-continuing organizational, as well as "speech" activity. Thus the Thomas case is applicable here only insofar as it establishes that subjection to registration requirements may be a sufficient restraint upon the exercise of liberties protected by the First Amendment to merit that it be weighed in the constitutional balance.

Similarly, we agree that compulsory disclosure of the names of an organization's members may in certain instances infringe constitutionally protected rights of association. *NAACP* v. *State of Alabama,* 357 U.S. 449; *Bates* v. *City of Little Rock,* 361 U.S. 516; *Shelton* v. *Tucker,* 364 U.S. 479. But to say this much is only to recognize one of the points of reference from which analysis must begin. To state that individual liberties may be affected is to establish the condition for, not to arrive at the conclusion of, constitutional decision. Against the impediments which particular governmental regulation causes to entire freedom of individual action, there must be weighed the value to the public of the ends which the regulation may achieve. *Schenck* v. *United States,* 249 U.S. 47; *Dennis* v. *United States,* 341 U.S. 494; *American Communications Ass'n, C.I.O.* v. *Douds,* 339 U.S. 382.

In the NAACP and Bates cases, this Court examined the circumstances under which disclosure was demanded, and concluded that "whatever interest the State may have in obtaining names of ordinary members has not been shown to be sufficient to overcome [the] constitutional objections to the production order." *NAACP* v. *State of Alabama,* 357 U.S. at page 465.

Thus, these cases hold that where the required making public of an organization's membership lists bears no rational relation to the interest which is asserted by the State to justify disclosure, and where because of community temper publication might prejudice members whose names were revealed, disclosure cannot constitutionally be compelled. . . .

The present case differs from *Thomas* v. *Collins* and from NAACP, Bates, and Shelton in the magnitude of the public interests which the registration and disclosure provisions are designed to protect and in the pertinence which registration and disclosure bear to the protection of those interests. Congress itself has expressed in § 2 of the Act both what those interests are and what, in its view, threatens them. On the basis of its detailed investigations Congress has found that there exists a world Communist movement, foreign-controlled, whose purpose it is by whatever means necessary to establish Communist totalitar-

ian dictatorship in the countries throughout the world, and which has already succeeded in supplanting governments in other countries. Congress has found that in furthering these purposes, the foreign government controlling the world Communist movement establishes in various countries action organizations which, dominated from abroad, endeavor to bring about the overthrow of existing governments, by force if need be, and to establish totalitarian dictatorships subservient to that foreign government. And Congress has found that these action organizations employ methods of infiltration and secretive and coercive tactics; that by operating in concealment and through Communist-front organizations they are able to obtain the support of persons who would not extend such support knowing of their true nature; that a Communist network exists in the United States; and that the agents of communism have devised methods of sabotage and espionage carried out in successful evasion of existing law. The purpose of the Subversive Activities Control Act is said to be to prevent the world-wide Communist conspiracy from accomplishing its purpose in this country.

It is not for the courts to re-examine the validity of these legislative findings and reject them. See *Harisiades* v. *Shaughnessy,* 342 U.S. 580, 590. They are the product of extensive investigation by Committees of Congress over more than a decade and a half. Cf. *Nebbia* v. *People of State of New York,* 291 U.S. 502, 516, 530. We certainly cannot dismiss them as unfounded or irrational imaginings. See *Galvan* v. *Press,* 347 U.S. 522, 529; *American Communications Ass'n, C.I.O.* v. *Douds,* 339 U.S. 382, 388–389. And if we accept them, as we must, as a not unentertainable appraisal by Congress of the threat which Communist organizations pose not only to existing government in the United States, but to the United States as a sovereign, independent nation—if we accept as not wholly unsupportable the conclusion that those organizations "are not free and independent organizations, but are sections of a world-wide Communist organization and are controlled, directed, and subject to the discipline of the Communist dictatorship of [a] foreign country," § 2(5)—we must recognize that the power of Congress to regulate Communist organizations of this nature is extensive. "Security against foreign danger is one of the primitive objects of civil society," James Madison wrote in *The Federalist* (No. 41). "It is an avowed and essential object of the American Union. The powers requisite for attaining it must be effectually confined to the federal councils." *The Federalist* (Wright ed. 1961) 295. See also *The Federalist* (Nos. 2–5), id., at 93 et seq. Means for effective resistance against foreign incursion—whether in the form of organizations which function, in some technical sense, as "agents" of a foreign power, or in the form of organizations which, by complete dedication and obedience to foreign directives, make themselves the instruments of a foreign power—may not be denied to the national legislature. "To preserve its independence, and give security against foreign aggression and encroachment, is the highest duty of every nation, and to attain these ends nearly all other considerations are to be subordinated. It matters not in what form such aggression and encroachment come. . . ." The Chinese Exclusion Case (*Chae Chan Ping* v. *United States*), 130 U.S. 581. . . .

Of course congressional power in this sphere, as in all spheres, is limited by the First Amendment. Individual liberties fundamental to American institutions are not to be destroyed under pretext of preserving those institutions, even from the gravest external dangers. But where the problems of accommodating the exigencies of self-preservation and the values of liberty are as complex and intricate as they are in the situation described in the findings of § 2 of the Subversive Activities Control Act—when existing government is menaced by a world-wide integrated movement which employs every combination of possible means, peaceful and violent, domestic and foreign, overt and clandestine, to destroy the government itself—the legislative judgment as to how that threat may best be met consistently with the safeguarding of personal freedom is not to be set aside merely because the judgment of judges would, in the first instance, have chosen other methods. Especially where Congress, in seeking to reconcile competing and urgently demanding values within our social institutions, legislates not to prohibit individuals from organizing for the effectuation of ends found to be menacing to the very existence of those institutions, but only to prescribe the conditions under which such organization is permitted, the legislative determination must be respected. *United Public Workers of America (C. I. O.)* v. *Mitchell*, 330 U.S. 75; *American Communications Ass'n, C. I. O.* v. *Douds, supra.* . . .

It is argued that if Congress may constitutionally enact legislation requiring the Communist Party to register, to list its members, to file financial statements, and to identify its printing presses, Congress may impose similar requirements upon any group which pursues unpopular political objectives or which expresses an unpopular political ideology. Nothing which we decide here remotely carries such an implication. The Subversive Activities Control Act applies only to *foreign-dominated* organizations which work primarily to advance the objectives of a world movement controlled by the government of a *foreign* country. See §§ 3(3), 2(4). It applies only to organizations directed, dominated, or controlled by a *particular* foreign country, the leader of a movement which, Congress has found, is "in its origins, its development, and its present practice, . . . a world-wide revolutionary movement whose purpose it is, by treachery, deceit, infiltration into other groups . . . , espionage, sabotage, terrorism, and any other means deemed necessary, to establish a Communist totalitarian dictatorship in the countries throughout the world through the medium of a world-wide Communist organization." § 2(1). This is the full purported reach of the statute, and its fullest effect. There is no attempt here to impose stifling obligations upon the proponents of a particular political creed as such, or even to check the importation of particular political ideas from abroad for propagation here. The Act compels the registration of organized groups which have been made the instruments of a long-continued, systematic, disciplined activity directed by a foreign power and purposing to overthrow existing government in this country. Organizations are subject to it only when shown, after administrative hearing subject to judicial review, to be dominated by the foreign power or its organs and to operate primarily to advance its purposes. That a portion of the evidence upon which such a showing is made may consist in the expression of political views by the organization does not alter the character of the Act or of the incidents to which it attaches. Such expressions are relevant only as probative of foreign control and of the purposes to which the organization's actions are directed. The Board, in the present proceeding, so understood the Act. The resignation requirement of § 7, on its face and as here applied, does not violate the First Amendment. . . .

Affirmed.

MR. CHIEF JUSTICE WARREN dissenting. . . .

V

In my view, the Court today strays from the well-trod path of our prior decisions by reaching out to decide constitutional issues prematurely. If the Court would remand on any one of the four errors which I have discussed, and I think each warrants a remand, the resolution of the difficult constitutional issues presented by this case would certainly be postponed, and perhaps made totally unnecessary. . . .

I think it is unwise for the Court to brush aside the non-constitutional errors disclosed by this record. However, since the Court insists upon doing so, I feel constrained to express my views on a dispositive constitutional issue which now confronts us by virtue of the Court's holding on the non-constitutional questions. I agree with Mr. Justice Brennan that,

once having entered the area of constitutional adjudication, the Court must decide now whether the Act violates the Fifth Amendment privilege against self-incrimination by requiring the petitioner's officers to submit a registration statement on behalf of the petitioner. For the reasons set forth in his opinion, which I join, I believe that the Act does constitute a violation of the Fifth Amendment.

MR. JUSTICE BLACK, dissenting.

I do not believe that it can be too often repeated that the freedoms of speech, press, petition and assembly guaranteed by the First Amendment must be accorded to the ideas we hate or sooner or later they will be denied to the ideas we cherish. The first banning of an association because it advocates hated ideas—whether that association be called a political party or not—marks a fateful moment in the history of a free country. That moment seems to have arrived for this country.

The Subversive Activities Control Act of 1950 here involved defines "Communist action" organizations and requires them to register with the Attorney General giving much information of every kind with regard to their property, income, activities and members. The Communist Party has been ordered to register under the Act by the Subversive Activities Control Board and has challenged the validity of that order on the ground, among others, that the Act is unconstitutional in that it amounts to a complete outlawry of the Communist Party. The contention is that this Act, considered as a whole and in its relation to existing laws which affect members of the Party, imposes such overhanging threats of disgrace, humiliation, fines, forfeitures and lengthy imprisonments upon registered organizations and their members, most of which burdens become effective automatically upon registration, that it will be impossible for the Party to continue to function if the registration order is upheld. . . .

In addition to these burdens imposed directly by the Act itself, the registration requirement must also be considered in the context of the other laws now existing which affect the Communist Party. The Act requires that the information obtained upon registration be given wide publicity thus insuring that those identified as members of the Party will be subjected to all the civil disabilities, criminal prosecutions and public harassments that have become common in recent years. I agree with Mr. Justice Douglas that this aspect of the Act is alone sufficient to establish its invalidity under the self-incrimination provision of the Fifth Amendment. But I think the interrelationship between the present Act and these other laws goes deeper than that, for I think that interrelationship establishes all but conclusively that the present Act cannot be upheld as a mere registration statute. The information elicited by the Act must be considered, not, as in the Viereck case, an aid to the exercise of individual judgment by the people, but rather a part of a pattern of suppression by the Government, for that is certainly the inevitable effect of any system that requires registration on the one hand and imposes pains and penalties upon those registering on the other. . . .

I think also that this outlawry of the Communist Party and imprisonment of its members violates the First Amendment. The question under that Amendment is whether Congress has power to outlaw an association, group or party either on the ground that it advocates a policy of violent overthrow of the existing government at some time in the distant future or on the ground that it is ideologically subservient to some foreign country. In my judgment, neither of these factors justifies an invasion of rights protected by the First Amendment. Talk about the desirability of revolution has a long and honorable history, not only in other parts of the world, but in our own country. This kind of talk, like any other, can be used at the wrong time and for the wrong purpose. But, under our system of Government, the remedy for this danger must be the same remedy that is applied to the danger that comes from any

other erroneous talk—education and contrary argument. If that remedy is not sufficient, the only meaning of free speech must be that the revolutionary ideas will be allowed to prevail.

This conclusion is not affected by the fact that those advocating a policy of revolution are in sympathy with a foreign government. If there is one thing certain about the First Amendment it is that this Amendment was designed to guarantee the freest interchange of ideas about all public matters and that, of course, means the interchange of *all* ideas, however such ideas may be viewed in other countries and whatever change in the existing structure of government it may be hoped that these ideas will bring about. Now, when this country is trying to spread the high ideals of democracy all over the world—ideals that are revolutionary in many countries—seems to be a particularly inappropriate time to stifle First Amendment freedoms in this country. The same arguments that are used to justify the outlawry of Communist ideas here could be used to justify an outlawry of the ideas of democracy in other countries. . . .

I am compelled to say in closing that I fear that all the arguments and urgings the Communists and their sympathizers can use in trying to convert Americans to an ideology wholly foreign to our habits and our instincts are far less dangerous to the security of this Nation than laws which embark us upon a policy of repression by the outlawry of minority parties because they advocate radical changes in the structure of Government. This widespread program for punishing ideas on the ground that they might impair the internal security of the Nation not only sadly fails to protect that security but also diverts our energies and thoughts from the many far more important problems that face us as a Nation in this troubled world.

I would reverse this case and leave the Communists free to advocate their beliefs in proletarian dictatorship publicly and openly among the people of this country with full confidence that the people will remain loyal to any democratic Government truly dedicated to freedom and justice—the kind of Government which some of us still think of as being "the last best hope of earth."

MR. JUSTICE DOUGLAS, dissenting.

I

The Subversive Activities Control Board found, and the Court of Appeals sustained the finding, that petitioner, the Communist Party of the United States, is "a disciplined organization" operating in this nation "under Soviet Union control" to install "a Soviet style dictatorship in the United States." Those findings are based, I think, on facts; and I would not disturb them. . . .

Freedom of association is included in the bundle of First Amendment rights. *NAACP* v. *State of Alabama*, 357 U.S. 449, 460. So if we had only the question whether those who band together to espouse a political, educational, literary, civic, or ideological cause could be made to register, I would protest. The late Zachariah Chafee spoke of the danger in limiting our freedoms under political pressures. "Universities," he wrote, "should not be transformed, as in Nazi Germany, into loud-speakers for the men who wield political power." *The Blessings of Liberty* (1956) 241. There have been attempts here to interfere by law in a myriad of ways with the shaping of public opinion through many groups, attacked because they were non-conformists of one kind or another. As we said recently, the identification of members of groups and fear of reprisal "might deter . . . peaceful discussions of public matters of importance." *Talley* v. *State of California*, 362 U.S. 60, 65. There is, in my view, a disability on the part of government to probe the intimacies of relationships in the myriad of lawful societies and groups in this country. See, for example, *United States* v. *Rumley,* 345 U.S. 41, 48, 56–58 (concurring opinion); *Bates* v. *City of Little Rock*, 361 U.S. 516, 527 (concurring opinion); *Uphaus* v. *Wyman*, 364 U.S. 388, 401, 405–408 (dissenting opinion). From those precedents I

would hopefully deduce two principles. First, no individual may be required to register before he makes a speech, for the First Amendment rights are not subject to any prior restraint. Second, a group engaged in lawful conduct may not be required to file with the Government a list of its members, no matter how unpopular it may be. For the disclosure of membership lists may cause harassment of members and seriously hamper their exercise of First Amendment rights. The more unpopular the group, the greater the likelihood of harassment. In logic then it might seem that the Communist Party, being at the low tide of popularity, might better make out a case of harassment than almost any other group on the contemporary scene.

We have, however, as I have said, findings that the Communist Party of the United States is "a disciplined organization" operating in this Nation "under Soviet Union control" with the aim of installing "a Soviet style dictatorship" here. These findings establish that more than debate, discourse, argumentation, propaganda, and other aspects of free speech and association are involved. An additional element enters, viz., espionage, business activities, and the formation of cells for subversion, as well as the use of speech, press, and association by a foreign power to produce on this continent a Soviet satellite.

Picketing is free speech *plus* (*Bakery and Pastry Drivers and Helpers Local, etc.* v. *Wohl*, 315 U.S. 769, 776–777, concurring opinion; *Giboney* v. *Empire Storage & Ice Co.,* 336 U.S. 490, 497–503) and hence can be restricted in all instances and banned in some. Registration of those who disseminate propaganda of foreign origin (see *Viereck* v. *United States*, 318 U.S. 236, 251) has been thought to fall in the same category as barring speech in places that will create traffic conditions (*Schneider* v. *State,* 308 U.S. 147, 160; *Cox* v. *State of New Hampshire*, 312 U.S. 569) or provoke breaches of the peace. *Chaplinsky* v. *State of New Hampshire*, 315 U.S. 568. Though the activities themselves are under the First

Amendment, the manner of their exercise or their collateral aspects fall without it.

Like reasons underlie our decisions which sustain laws that require various groups to register before engaging in specified activities. Thus lobbyists who receive fees for attempting to influence the passage or defeat of legislation in Congress may be required to register. *United States* v. *Harriss*, 347 U.S. 612, 74 S. Ct. 808, 98 L. Ed. 989. Criminal sanctions for failure to report and to disclose all contributions made to political parties are permitted. *Burroughs* v. *United States,* 290 U.S. 534, 54 S. Ct. 287, 78 L. Ed. 484. Publishers of newspapers, desiring reduced postal rates, have long been required to file with the Postmaster General and with the local post-office certain data concerning ownership and circulation; and those disclosure requirements have been sustained. *Lewis Publishing Co.* v. *Morgan,* 229 U.S. 288, 33 S. Ct. 867, 57 L. Ed. 1190. In short, the exercise of First Amendment rights often involves business or commercial implications which Congress in its wisdom may desire to be disclosed, just as it did in strictly financial matters under the Public Utility Holding Company Act of 1935, 15 U.S.C.A. § 79 et seq. See *Electric Bond & Share Co.* v. *Securities & Exchange Comm.,* 303 U.S. 419, 58 S. Ct. 678, 82 L. Ed. 936.

If lobbyists can be required to register, if political parties can be required to make disclosure of the sources of their funds, if the owners of newspapers and periodicals must disclose their affiliates, so may a group operating under the control of a foreign power.

The Bill of Rights was designed to give fullest play to the exchange and dissemination of ideas that touch the politics, culture, and other aspects of our life. When an organization is used by a foreign power to make advances here, questions of security are raised beyond the ken of disputation and debate between the people resident here. Espionage, business activities, formation of cells for subversion, as well as the exercise of First Amendment rights, are then used to pry open our society and

make intrusion of a foreign power easy. These machinations of a foreign power add additional elements to free speech just as marching up and down adds something to picketing that goes beyond free speech.

These are the reasons why, in my view, the bare requirement that the Communist Party register and disclose the names of its officers and directors is in line with the most exacting adjudications touching First Amendment activities.

II

While the Act is pregnant with constitutional questions, I deal now with only one, viz., whether § 7 of the Act is unconstitutional and void as conflicting with the provision against self-incrimination accorded by the Fifth Amendment. . . .

VII

My conclusion is that while the Communist Party can be compelled to register, no one acting for it can be compelled to sign a statement that he is an officer or director nor to disclose the names of its officers, directors, or members—unless the required immunity is granted. Why then, one may ask, do we have a registration law? Congress (past or present) is attempting to have its cake and eat it too. In my view Congress can require full disclosure of all the paraphernalia through which a foreign dominated and controlled organization spreads propaganda, engages in agitation, or promotes politics in this country. But the Fifth Amendment bars Congress from requiring full disclosure by one Act and by another Act making the facts admitted or disclosed *under compulsion* the ingredients of a crime.

There is a giving of evidence by the filing of a registration. Its filing is the equivalent of officials testifying in investigations conducted by the Executive or Legislative Branch. It is compulsory disclosure of evidence which links officers, directors, and members of the group with a crime. Force and compulsion are outlawed techniques for federal law enforcement. Coerced confessions are taboo because of the long bitter experience of minorities in trying to maintain their freedom under hostile regimes.

Our Constitution protects all minorities, no matter how despised they are.

Accordingly, I dissent.

Mr. Justice Brennan with whom The Chief Justice joins dissenting in part.

I agree with the Court and with Mr. Justice Douglas that the order requiring that the Party register and disclose its officers and members is not constitutionally invalid as an invasion of the rights of freedom of advocacy and association guaranteed by the First Amendment to Communists as well as to all others.

I also share the Court's view that we are not called upon in this case to decide the constitutionality of the various duties and sanctions attaching to the Party, and to individual members, once orders to register become final. We are required by this case to decide only the validity of the order requiring the petitioner to register in accordance with § 7 of the Act as implemented by the regulations and Form ISA–1 of the Attorney General. We should properly reach at this time only such constitutional questions as necessarily relate to the requirements governing registration.

The questions in addition to those under the First Amendment which seem to me most nearly within the sphere of permissible constitutional adjudication in this proceeding arise from the interaction of the registration requirements with the criminal statutes under which Communist Party membership is implicated. This interplay poses the question whether the registration requirements violate the Fifth Amendment privilege against self-incrimination. . . .

As to the merits of the Fifth Amendment claim, I believe that officials cannot be compelled to complete, sign and file the registration statement without abridging their privilege against self-incrimination. . . .

NOTE: In *Communist Party* v. *United States*, 331 F.2d 807 (December 17, 1963) a United States Court of Appeals said, "We do not hold that an organization may claim the privilege against self-incrimination, nor that an individual may claim the privilege on behalf of an organization or its members. We express no opinion concerning the Communist Party's duty to submit the data demanded. We hold only that the availability of someone to sign the [registration] forms was an element of the offense; that the officers, who should otherwise have signed, were unavailable by reason of their valid claim of the privilege against self-incrimination; that the government had the burden of showing that a volunteer was available; and that its failure to discharge this burden requires reversal of this conviction." The Supreme Court denied certiorari on June 8, 1964.

Aptheker v. *Secretary of State*, 84 S. Ct. 1659 (1964), held invalid as a deprivation of liberty guaranteed by the Fifth Amendment that part of the Subversive Activities Control Act which disqualifies all members of Communist organizations (as defined) from obtaining passports. Justices Clark and Harlan dissented. Mr. Justice White dissented in part.

For other aspects of freedom of association see *NAACP* v. *Alabama, Gibson* v. *Florida Legislative Investigating Committee, Shelton* v. *Tucker, Uphaus* v. *Wyman,* and *Nelson* v. *County of Los Angeles,* above.

9. ARTISTIC UTTERANCE—OBSCENITY AND RELATED MATTERS

JACOBELLIS v. *OHIO*

84 S. Ct. 1676 (1964)

MR. JUSTICE BRENNAN announced the judgment of the Court and delivered an opinion in which MR. JUSTICE GOLDBERG joins.

Appellant, Nico Jacobellis, manager of a motion picture theater in Cleveland Heights, Ohio, was convicted on two counts for possessing and exhibiting an obscene film in violation of Ohio Revised Code § 2905.34. He was fined $500 on the first count and $2,000 on the second, and was sentenced to the workhouse if the fines were not paid. His conviction, by a court of three judges upon waiver of trial by jury, was affirmed by an intermediate appellate court, 175 N.E.2d 123, and by the Supreme Court of Ohio, 173 Ohio St. 22, 179 N.E.2d 777. We noted probable jurisdiction of the appeal, 371 U.S. 808, and subsequently restored the case to the calendar for reargument, 373 U.S. 901. The dispositive question is whether the state courts properly found that the motion picture involved, a French film called *"Les Amants"* ("The Lovers"), was obscene and hence not entitled to the protection for free expression that is guaranteed by the First and Fourteenth Amendments. We conclude that the film is not obscene and that the judgment must accordingly be reversed.

Motion pictures are within the ambit of the constitutional guarantees of freedom of speech and of the press. *Joseph Burstyn, Inc.*, v. *Wilson*, 343 U.S. 495. But in *Roth* v. *United States*, and *Alberts* v. *California*, 354 U.S. 476, we held that obscenity is not subject to those guarantees. Application of an obscenity law to suppress a motion picture thus requires ascertainment of the "dim and uncertain line" that often separates obscenity from constitutionally protected expression. *Bantam Books, Inc.* v. *Sullivan*, 372 U.S. 58, 66; see *Speiser* v. *Randall*, 357 U.S. 513, 525. It has been suggested that this is a task in which our Court need not involve itself. We are told that the determination whether a particular motion picture, book, or other work of expression is obscene can be treated as a purely factual judgment on which a jury's verdict is all but conclusive, or that in any event the decision can be left essentially to state and lower federal courts, with this Court exercising only a limited review such as that needed to determine whether the ruling below is supported by "sufficient evidence." The suggestion is appealing, since it would lift from our shoulders a difficult, recurring, and unpleasant task. But we cannot accept it. Such an abnegation of judicial supervision in this field would be inconsistent with our duty to uphold the constitutional guarantees. Since it is only "obscenity" that is excluded from the constitutional protection, the question whether a particular work is obscene necessarily implicates an issue of constitutional law. See *Roth* v. *United States, supra,* 354 U.S., at 497–498 (separate opinion). Such an issue, we think, must ultimately be decided by this Court. Our duty admits of no "substitute for facing up to the tough individual problems of constitutional judgment involved in every obscenity case." *Id.,* at 498; see *Manual Enterprises, Inc.,* v. *Day,* 370 U.S. 478, 488 (separate opinion).

In other areas involving constitutional rights under the Due Process Clause, the Court has consistently recognized its duty to apply the applicable rules of law upon the basis of an independent review of the facts of each case. E.g., *Watts* v. *Indiana,* 338 U.S. 49, 51; *Norris* v. *Alabama,* 294 U.S. 587, 590. And this has been particularly true where rights have been asserted under the First Amendment guarantees of free expression. Thus in *Pennekamp* v. *Florida,* 328 U.S. 331, 335, the Court stated:

"The Constitution has imposed upon this Court final authority to determine the meaning and application of those words of that instrument which require interpretation to resolve judicial issues. With that responsibility, we are compelled to examine for ourselves the statements in issue and the circumstances under which they were made to see whether or not they . . . are of a character which the principles of the First Amendment, as adopted by the Due Process Clause of the Fourteenth Amendment, protect."

We cannot understand why the Court's duty should be any different in the present case, where Jacobellis has been subjected to a criminal conviction for disseminating a work of expression and is challenging that conviction as a deprivation of rights guaranteed by the First and Fourteenth Amendments. Nor can we understand why the Court's performance of its constitutional and judicial function in this sort of case should be denigrated by such epithets as "censor" or "super-censor." In judging alleged obscenity the Court is no more "censoring" expression than it has in other cases "censored" criticism of judges and public officials, advocacy of governmental overthrow, or speech alleged to constitute a breach of the peace. Use of an opprobrious label can neither obscure nor impugn the Court's performance of its obligation to test challenged judgments against the guarantees of the First and Fourteenth Amendments and, in doing so, to delineate the scope of constitutionally protected speech. Hence we reaffirm the principle that, in "obscenity" cases as in all others involving rights derived from the First Amendment guarantees of free expression, this Court cannot avoid making an independent constitutional judgment on the

facts of the case as to whether the material involved is constitutionally protected.

The question of the proper standard for making this determination has been the subject of much discussion and controversy since our decision in *Roth-Alberts* seven years ago. Recognizing that the test for obscenity enunciated there—"whether to the average person, applying contemporary community standards, the dominant theme of the material taken as a whole appeals to prurient interest," 354 U.S., at 489—is not perfect, we think any substitute would raise equally difficult problems, and we therefore adhere to that standard. We would reiterate, however, our recognition in *Roth* that obscenity is excluded from the constitutional protection only because it is "utterly without redeeming social importance," and that "the portrayal of sex, e.g., in art, literature, and scientific works, is not itself sufficient reason to deny material the constitutional protection of freedom of speech and press." *Id.,* at 484, 487. It follows that material dealing with sex in a manner that advocates ideas, *Kingsley Int'l Pictures Corp.* v. *Regents,* 360 U.S. 684, or that has literary or scientific or artistic value or any other form of social importance, may not be branded as obscenity and denied the constitutional protection. Nor may the constitutional status of the material be made to turn on a "weighing" of its social importance against its prurient appeal, for a work cannot be proscribed unless it is "utterly" without social importance. See *Zeitlin* v. *Arnebergh,* 59 Cal.2d 901, 920, 383 P.2d 152, 165, 31 Cal. Rptr. 800, 813 (1963). It should also be recognized that the *Roth* standard requires in the first instance a finding that the material "goes substantially beyond customary limits of candor in description or representation of such matters." This was a requirement of the Model Penal Code test that we approved in *Roth,* 354 U.S., at 487, n. 20, and it is explicitly reaffirmed in the more recent "Proposed Official Draft" of the Code. In the absence of such a deviation from society's standards of decency, we do not see how any official inquiry into the allegedly prurient appeal of a work of expression can be squared with the guarantees of the First and Fourteenth Amendments. See *Manual Enterprises, Inc.,* v. *Day,* 370 U.S. 478, 482–488 (separate opinion).

It has been suggested that the "contemporary community standards" aspect of the *Roth* test implies a determination of the constitutional question of obscenity in each case by the standards of the particular local community from which the case arises. This is an incorrect reading of *Roth.* The concept of "contemporary community standards" was first expressed by Judge Learned Hand in *United States* v. *Kennerley,* 209 F.2d 119, 121 (D.C.S.D.N.Y. 1913), where he said:

"Yet, if the time is not yet when men think innocent all that which is honestly germane to a pure subject, however little it may mince its words, still I scarcely think that they would forbid all which might corrupt the most corruptible, or that society is prepared to accept for its own limitations those which may perhaps be necessary to the weakest of its members. If there be no abstract definition, such as I have suggested, should not the word 'obscene' be allowed to indicate the present critical point in the compromise between candor and shame at which *the community may have arrived here and now?* . . . To put thought in leash to the *average conscience of the time* is perhaps tolerable, but to fetter it by the necessities of the lowest and least capable seems a fatal policy. . . .

"Nor is it an objection, I think, that such an interpretation gives to the words of the statute a varying meaning from time to time. Such words as these do not embalm the precise morals of an age or place; while they presuppose that some things will always be shocking to the public taste, the vague subject-matter is left to the gradual development of general notions about what is decent. . . ." (Italics added.)

It seems clear that in this passage Judge Hand was referring not to state and local "communities," but rather to "the community" in the sense of "society at large; . . . the public, or people in general." Thus, he recognized that under his standard the concept of obscenity would have "a varying meaning from time to time"— not from county to county, or town to town.

We do not see how any "local" definition of the "community" could properly be employed in delineating the area of expression that is protected by the Federal Constitution. MR. JUSTICE HARLAN pointed out in *Manual Enterprises, Inc.,* v. *Day, supra,* 370 U.S., at 488, that a standard based on a particular local community would have "the intolerable consequence of denying some sections of the country access to material, there deemed acceptable, which in others might be considered offensive to prevailing community standards of decency. Cf. *Butler* v. *Michigan,* 352 U.S. 380." It is true that *Manual Enterprises* dealt with the federal statute banning obscenity from the mails. But the mails are not the only means by which works of expression cross local-community lines in this country. It can hardly be assumed that all the patrons of a particular library, bookstand, or motion picture theater are residents of the smallest local "community" that can be drawn around that establishment. Furthermore, to sustain the suppression of a particular book or film in one locality would deter its dissemination in other localities where it might be held not obscene, since sellers and exhibitors would be reluctant to risk criminal conviction in testing the variation between the two places. It would be a hardy person who would sell a book or exhibit a film anywhere in the land after this Court had sustained the judgment of one "community" holding it to be outside the constitutional protection. The result would thus be "to restrict the public's access to forms of the printed word which the State could not constitutionally suppress directly." *Smith* v. *California,* 361 U.S. 147, 154.

It is true that local communities throughout the land are in fact diverse, and that in cases such as this one the Court is confronted with the task of reconciling the rights of such communities with the rights of individuals. Communities vary, however, in many respects other than their toleration of alleged obscenity, and such variances have never been considered to require or justify a varying standard for application of the Federal Constitution. The Court has regularly been compelled, in reviewing criminal convictions challenged under the Due Process Clause of the Fourteenth Amendment, to reconcile the conflicting rights of the local community which brought the prosecution and of the individual defendant. Such a task is admittedly difficult and delicate, but it is inherent in the Court's duty of determining whether a particular conviction worked a deprivation of rights guaranteed by the Federal Constitution. The Court has not shrunk from discharging that duty in other areas, and we see no reason why it should do so here. The Court has explicitly refused to tolerate a result whereby "the constitutional limits of free expression in the Nation would vary with state lines," *Pennekamp* v. *Florida, supra,* 328 U.S., at 335; we see even less justification for allowing such limits to vary with town or county lines. We thus reaffirm the position taken in *Roth* to the effect that the constitutional status of an allegedly obscene work must be determined on the basis of a national standard. It is, after all, a national Constitution we are expounding.

We recognize the legitimate and indeed exigent interest of States and localities throughout the Nation in preventing the dissemination of material deemed harmful to children. But that interest does not justify a total suppression of such material, the effect of which would be to "reduce the adult population . . . to reading only what is fit for children." *Butler* v. *Michigan,* 352 U.S. 380, 383. State and local authorities might well consider whether their objectives in this area would be better served by laws aimed specifically at preventing distribution of objectionable material to children, rather than at totally prohibiting its dissemination. Since the present conviction is based upon exhibition of the film to the public at large and not upon its exhibition to children, the judgment must be reviewed under the strict standard applicable in determining the scope of the expression that is protected by the Constitution.

We have applied that standard to the motion picture in question. "The Lovers" involves a woman bored with her life and marriage who abandons her husband and family for a young archaeologist with whom she has suddenly fallen in love. There is an explicit love scene in the last reel of the film, and the State's objections are based almost entirely upon that scene. The film was favorably reviewed in a number of national publications, although disparaged in others, and was rated by at least two critics of national stature among the best films of the year in which it was produced. It was shown in approximately 100 of the larger cities in the United States, including Columbus and Toledo, Ohio. We have viewed the film, in the light of the record made in the trial court, and we conclude that it is not obscene within the standards enunciated in *Alberts* v. *California* and *Roth* v. *United States,* which we reaffirm here.

Reversed.

MR. JUSTICE WHITE concurs in the judgment.

Opinion of MR. JUSTICE BLACK, with whom MR. JUSTICE DOUGLAS joins.

I concur in the reversal of this judgment. My belief, as stated in *Kingsley International Pictures Corp.* v. *Regents,* 360 U.S. 684, 690, is that "If despite the Constitution . . . this Nation is to embark on the dangerous road of censorship, my belief is that this Court is about the most inappropriate Supreme Board of Censors that could be found." My reason for reversing is that I think the conviction of appellant or anyone else for exhibiting a motion picture abridges freedom of the press as safeguarded by the First Amendment, which is made obligatory on the States by the Fourteenth. See my concurring opinions in *Quantity of Copies of Books* v. *Kansas, post*, p. —; *Smith* v. *California*, 361 U.S. 147, 155; *Kingsley International Pictures Corp.* v. *Regents*, *supra*. See also the dissenting opinion of MR. JUSTICE DOUGLAS in *Roth* v. *United States*, 354 U.S. 476, 508, and his concurring opinion in *Superior Films, Inc.*, v. *Department of Education*, 346 U.S. 587, 588, in both of which I joined.

MR. JUSTICE STEWART, concurring.

It is possible to read the Court's opinion in *Alberts* v. *California* and *Roth* v. *United States*, 354 U.S. 476, in a variety of ways. In saying this, I imply no criticism of the Court, which in those cases was faced with the task of trying to define what may be indefinable. I have reached the conclusion, which I think is confirmed at least by negative implication in the Court's decisions since *Roth* and *Alberts*, that under the First and Fourteenth Amendments criminal laws in this area are constitutionally limited to hard-core pornography. I shall not today attempt further to define the kinds of material I understand to be embraced within that short-hand description; and perhaps I could never succeed in intelligibly doing so. But I know it when I see it, and the motion picture involved in this case is not that.

MR. JUSTICE GOLDBERG, concurring.

The question presented is whether the First and Fourteenth Amendments permit the imposition of criminal punishment for exhibiting the motion picture entitled "The Lovers." I have viewed the film and I wish merely to add to my Brother BRENNAN's description that the love scene deemed objectionable is so fragmentary and fleeting that only a censor's alert would make an audience conscious that something "questionable" is being portrayed. Except for this rapid sequence, the film concerns itself with the history of an ill-matched and unhappy marriage—a familiar subject in old and new novels and in current television soap operas.

Although I fully agree with what my Brother BRENNAN has written, I am also of the view that adherence to the principles stated in *Joseph Burstyn, Inc.*, v. *Wilson*, 343 U.S. 495, requires reversal. In *Burstyn* MR. JUSTICE CLARK, delivering the unanimous judgment of the Court, said:

"[E]xpression by means of motion pictures is included within the free speech and free press guaranty of the First and Fourteenth Amendments. . . .

"To hold that liberty of expression by means of motion pictures is guaranteed by the First and Fourteenth Amendments, however, is not the end of our problem. It does not follow that the Constitution requires absolute freedom to exhibit every motion picture of every kind at all times and all places. . . . Nor does it follow that motion pictures are necessarily subject to the precise rules governing any other particular method of expression. Each method tends to present its own peculiar problems. But the basic principles of freedom of speech and the press, like the First Amendment's command, do not vary. Those principles, as they have frequently been enunciated by this Court, make freedom of expression the rule." *Id.*, at 502–503.

As in *Burstyn* "[t]here is no justification in this case for making an exception to that rule," *id.*, at 503, for by any arguable standard and criteria the exhibitors of this motion picture may not be criminally prosecuted unless the exaggerated character of the advertising rather than the obscenity of the film is to be the constitutional criterion.

THE CHIEF JUSTICE, with whom MR. JUSTICE CLARK joins, dissenting.

In this and other cases in this area of the law, which are coming to us in ever-increasing numbers, we are faced with the resolution of rights basic both to individuals and to society as a whole. Specifically, we are called upon to reconcile the right of the Nation and of the States to maintain a decent society and, on the other hand, the right of individuals to express themselves freely in accordance with the guarantees of the First and Fourteenth Amendments. Although the Federal Government and virtually every State has had laws proscribing obscenity since the Union was formed, and although this Court has recently decided that obscenity is not within the protection of the First Amendment, neither courts nor legislatures have been able to evolve a truly satisfactory definition of obscenity. In other areas of the law, terms like "negligence," although in common use for centuries, have been difficult to define except in the most general manner. Yet the courts have been able to function in such areas with a reasonable degree of efficiency. The obscenity problem, however, is aggravated by the fact that it involves the area of public expression, an area in which a broad range of freedom is vital to our society and is constitutionally protected.

Recently this Court put its hand to the task of defining the term "obscenity" in *Roth* v. *United States*, 354 U.S. 476. The definition enunciated in that case has generated much legal speculation as well as further judicial interpretation by state and federal courts. It has also been relied upon by legislatures. Yet obscenity cases continue to come to this Court, and it becomes increasingly apparent that we must settle as well as we can the question of what constitutes "obscenity" and the question of what standards are permissible in enforcing proscriptions against obscene matter. This Court hears cases such as the instant one not merely to rule upon the alleged obscenity of a specific film or book but to establish principles for the guidance of lower courts and legislatures. Yet most of our decisions since *Roth* have been given without opinion and have thus failed to furnish such guidance. Nor does the Court in the instant case—which has now been twice argued before us—shed any greater light on the problem. Therefore, I consider it appropriate to state my views at this time.

For all the sound and fury that the *Roth* test has generated, it has not been proved unsound, and I believe that we should try to live with it—at least until a more satisfactory definition is evolved. No government—be it federal, state, or local—should be forced to choose between repressing all material, including that within the realm of decency, and allowing unrestrained license to publish any material, no matter how vile. There must be a rule of reason in this as in other areas of the law, and we have attempted in the *Roth* case to provide such a rule.

It is my belief that when the Court said in *Roth* that obscenity is to be defined by reference to "community standards," it meant community standards—not a national standard, as is sometimes argued. I believe that there is no provable "national standard," and perhaps there should be none. At all events, this Court has not been able to enunciate one, and it would be unreasonable to expect local courts to divine one. It is said that such a "community" approach may well result in material being proscribed as obscene in one community but not in another, and, in all probability, that is true. But communities throughout the Nation are in fact diverse, and it must be remembered that, in cases such as this one, the Court is confronted with the task of reconciling conflicting rights of the diverse communities within our society and of individuals.

We are told that only "hard core pornography" should be denied the protection of the First Amendment. But who can define "hard core pornography" with any greater clarity than "obscenity"? And even if we were to retreat to that position, we would soon be faced with the need to define that term just as we now are faced with the need to define "obscenity." Meanwhile, those who profit from the commercial exploitation of obscenity would continue to ply their trade unmolested.

In my opinion, the use to which various materials are put—not just the words and pictures themselves—must be considered in determining whether or not the materials are obscene. A technical or legal treatise on pornography may well be inoffensive under most circumstances but, at the same time, "obscene" in the extreme when sold or displayed to children.

Finally, material which is in fact obscene

under the *Roth* test may be proscribed in a number of ways—for instance, by confiscation of the material or by prosecution of those who disseminate it—provided always that the proscription, whatever it may be, is imposed in accordance with constitutional standards. If the proceeding involved is criminal, there must be a right to a jury trial, a right to counsel, and all the other safeguards necessary to assure due process of law. If the proceeding is civil in nature, the constitutional requirements applicable in such a case must also be observed. There has been some tendency in dealing with this area of the law for enforcement agencies to do only that which is easy to do—for instance, to seize and destroy books with only a minimum of protection. As a result, courts are often presented with procedurely bad cases and, in dealing with them, appear to be acquiescing in the dissemination of obscenity. But if cases were well prepared and were conducted with the appropriate concern for constitutional safeguards, courts would not hesitate to enforce the laws against obscenity. Thus, enforcement agencies must realize that there is no royal road to enforcement; hard and conscientious work is required.

In light of the foregoing, I would reiterate my acceptance of the rule of the *Roth* case: Material is obscene and not constitutionally protected against regulation and proscription if "to the average person, applying contemporary community standards, the dominant theme of the material taken as a whole appeals to prurient interest." 354 U.S., at 489. I would commit the enforcement of this rule to the appropriate state and federal courts, and I would accept their judgments made pursuant to the *Roth* rule, limiting myself to a consideration only of whether there is sufficient evidence in the record upon which a finding of obscenity could be made. If there is no evidence in the record upon which such a finding could be made, obviously the material involved cannot be held obscene. Cf. *Thompson* v. *City of Louisville*, 362 U.S. 199. But since a mere modicum of evidence

may satisfy a "no evidence" standard, I am unwilling to give the important constitutional right of free expression such limited protection. However, protection of society's right to maintain its moral fiber and the effective administration of justice require that this Court not establish itself as an ultimate censor, in each case reading the entire record, viewing the accused material, and making an independent *de novo* judgment on the question of obscenity. Therefore, once a finding of obscenity has been made below under a proper application of the *Roth* test, I would apply a "sufficient evidence" standard of review—requiring something more than merely any evidence but something less than "substantial evidence on the record [including the allegedly obscene material] as a whole." Cf. *Universal Camera Corp.* v. *Labor Board*, 340 U.S. 474. This is the only reasonable way I can see to obviate the necessity of this Court's sitting as the Super Censor of all the obscenity purveyed throughout the Nation.

While in this case, I do not subscribe to some of the State's extravagant contentions, neither can I say that the courts below acted with intemperance or without sufficient evidence in finding the moving picture obscene within the meaning of the *Roth* test. Therefore, I would affirm the judgment.

MR. JUSTICE HARLAN, dissenting.

While agreeing with my Brother BRENNAN's opinion that the responsibilities of the Court in this area are no different than those which attend the adjudication of kindred constitutional questions, I have heretofore expressed the view that the States are constitutionally permitted greater latitude in determining what is bannable on the score of obscenity than is so with the Federal Government. See my opinion in *Roth* v. *United States*, 354 U.S. 476, 496; cf. my opinion in *Manual Enterprises, Inc.*, v. *Day*, 370 U.S. 478. While, as correctly said in MR. JUSTICE BRENNAN's opinion, the Court has not accepted that view, I nonetheless feel free to adhere to it in this developing aspect of constitutional law.

The more I see of these obscenity cases the more convinced I become that in permitting the States wide, but not federally unrestricted, scope in this field, while holding the Federal Government with a tight rein, lies the best promise for achieving a sensible accommodation between the public interest sought to be served by obscenity laws (cf. my dissenting opinion in *Bantam Books, Inc., v. Sullivan,* 372 U.S. 58, 76, 77) and protection of genuine rights of free expression.

I experience no greater ease than do other members of the Court in attempting to verbalize generally the respective constitutional tests, for in truth the matter in the last analysis depends on how particular challenged material happens to strike the minds of jurors or judges and ultimately those of a majority of the members of this Court. The application of any general constitutional tests must thus necessarily be pricked out on a case-by-case basis, but as a point of departure I would apply to the Federal Government the *Roth* standards as amplified in my opinion in *Manual Enterprises, supra.* As to the States, I would make the federal test one of rationality. I would not prohibit them from banning any material which, taken as a whole, has been reasonably found in state judicial proceedings to treat with sex in a fundamentally offensive manner, under rationally established criteria for judging such material.

On this basis, having viewed the motion picture in question, I think the State acted within permissible limits in condemning the film and would affirm the judgment of the Ohio Supreme Court.

NOTE: *Manual Enterprises, Inc.* v. *Day,* 370 U.S. 478 (1962), struck down an order of the Postmaster General which made certain magazines nonmailable for obscenity reasons, and also because they carried advertising as to where obscene matters could be obtained. Mr. Justice Harlan delivered the judgment of the court. His opinion, joined by Mr. Justice Stewart, rested on the ground that for material to be obscene it must not only appeal to the prurient interests of the reader or observer but must also be patently offensive so as to affront the current community standards of decency. In this case the magazines complained of featured photographs of nude or nearly nude males and were designed to appeal to the interests of the male homosexual. However, according to Mr. Justice Harlan, these portrayals of the male nude were not any more objectionable than the many portrayals of the female nude which society tolerates. In regard to the allegedly objectionable advertising, Mr. Justice Harlan stated that the government had not maintained its burden to prove that the publishers knew its advertisers were selling obscene materials. Mr. Justice Black concurred in the result. Mr. Justice Brennan, joined by Mr. Chief Justice Warren and Mr. Justice Douglas, concurred in the reversal in a separate opinion on the ground that the Postmaster General's order lacked legal authority since Congress had not vested him with power to bar obscene materials from the mails.

In *Mutual Films Corp.* v. *Industrial Commission of Ohio,* 236 U.S. 230 (1915), it was held that "the exhibition of moving pictures is a business, pure and simple, . . . conducted for profit, like other spectacles, not to be regarded . . . as part of the press, or as organs of public opinion." In *Joseph Burstyn, Inc.* v. *Wilson,* 315 U.S. 495 (1952), that view was abandoned: "motion pictures are a significant medium for the communication of ideas." It follows that movies are protected by the First and Fourteenth Amendments.

Burstyn arose under a New York law authorizing denial of a license for exhibition of any movie found by the licensing agency to be "obscure, indecent, immoral, inhuman, sacrilegious, or . . . of such a character that its exhibition would tend to corrupt morals or incite to crime. . . ." Burstyn was denied a license for "The Miracle" on the ground that it was "sacrilegious." The Court found the denial invalid because the statutory standard—"sacrilegious"—was so imprecise that it set the censor "adrift upon a boundless sea amid a myriad of conflicting currents of religious views, with no charts but those provided by the most vocal and powerful orthodoxies. New York cannot vest such unlimited restraining control over motion pictures in a censor. . . ."

KINGSLEY INT. PICTURES v. REGENTS
360 U.S. 684 (1959)

Appeal from the Court of Appeals of New York.

MR. JUSTICE STEWART delivered the opinion of the Court.

Once again the Court is required to consider the impact of New York's motion picture licensing law upon First Amendment liberties, protected by the Fourteenth Amendment from infringement by the States. Cf. *Joseph Burstyn, Inc.,* v. *Wilson,* 343 U.S. 495.

The New York statute makes it unlawful "to exhibit, or to sell, lease or lend for exhibition at any place of amusement for pay or in connection with any business in the state of New York, any motion picture film or reel [with certain exceptions not relevant here], unless there is at the time in full force and effect a valid license or permit therefor of the education department. . . ." The law provides that a license shall issue "unless such film or a part thereof is obscene, indecent, immoral, inhuman, sacrilegious, or is of such a character that its exhibition would tend to corrupt morals or incite to crime. . . ." A recent statutory amendment provides that "the term 'immoral' and the phrase 'of such a character that its exhibition would tend to corrupt morals' shall denote a motion picture film or part thereof, the dominant purpose or effect of which is

erotic or pornographic; or which portrays acts of sexual immorality, perversion, or lewdness, or which expressly or impliedly presents such acts as desirable, acceptable or proper patterns of behavior."

As the distributor of a motion picture entitled "Lady Chatterley's Lover," the appellant Kingsley submitted that film to the Motion Picture Division of the New York Education Department for a license. Finding three isolated scenes in the film " 'immoral' within the intent of our law," the Division refused to issue a license until the scenes in question were deleted. The distributor petitioned the Regents of the State of New York for a review of that ruling. The Regents upheld the denial of a license, but on the broader ground that "the whole theme of this motion picture is immoral under said law, for that theme is the presentation of adultery as a desirable, acceptable and proper pattern of behavior."

. . . A sharply divided Court of Appeals . . . reversed the Appellate Division and upheld the Regents' refusal to license the film for exhibition.

The Court of Appeals unanimously and explicitly rejected any notion that the film is obscene. See *Roth* v. *United States,* 354 U.S. 476. Rather, the court found that the picture as a whole "alluringly portrays adultery as proper behavior." As Chief

Judge Conway's prevailing opinion emphasized, therefore, the only portion of
the statute involved in this case is that
part of §§ 122 and 122(a) of the Education
Law requiring the denial of a license to
motion pictures "which are immoral in
that they portray 'acts of sexual immorality
. . . as desirable, acceptable, or proper
patterns of behavior.'" A majority of the
Court of Appeals ascribed to that language
a precise purpose of the New York Legislature to require the denial of a license to
a motion picture "because its subject
matter is adultery presented as being right
and desirable for certain people under certain circumstances."

We accept the premise that the motion
picture here in question can be so characterized. We accept too, as we must, the
construction of the New York Legislature's
language which the Court of Appeals has
put upon it. . . . That construction, we
emphasize, gives to the term "sexual immorality" a concept entirely different from
the concept embraced in words like "obscenity" or "pornography." Moreover, it is
not suggested that the film would itself
operate as an incitement to illegal action.
Rather, the New York Court of Appeals
tells us that the relevant portion of the
New York Education Law requires the
denial of a license to any motion picture
which approvingly portrays an adulterous
relationship, quite without reference to the
manner of its portrayal.

What New York has done, therefore, is
to prevent the exhibition of a motion picture because that picture advocates an idea
—that adultery under certain circumstances may be proper behavior. Yet the
First Amendment's basic guarantee is of
freedom to advocate ideas. The State, quite
simply, has thus struck at the very heart of
constitutionally protected liberty.

It is contended that the State's action was
justified because the motion picture attrac-
tively portrays a relationship which is contrary to the moral standards, the religious
precepts, and the legal code of its citizenry.
This argument misconceives what it is that
the Constitution protects. Its guarantee is

not confined to the expression of ideas that
are conventional or shared by a majority.
It protects advocacy of the opinion that
adultery may sometimes be proper, no less
than advocacy of socialism or the single
tax. And in the realm of ideas it protects
expression which is eloquent no less than
that which is unconvincing.

Advocacy of conduct proscribed by law
is not, as Mr. Justice Brandeis long ago
pointed out, "a justification for denying free
speech where the advocacy falls short of
incitement and there is nothing to indicate
that the advocacy would be immediately
acted on." *Whitney* v. *California*, 274 U.S.
357, at 376 (concurring opinion). . . .
Reversed.

MR. JUSTICE BLACK, concurring.

I concur in the Court's opinion and
judgment but add a few words because of
concurring opinions by several Justices who
rely on their appraisal of the movie Lady
Chatterley's Lover for holding that New
York cannot constitutionally bar it. Unlike
them, I have not seen the picture. My view
is that stated by MR. JUSTICE DOUGLAS,
that prior censorship of moving pictures
like prior censorship of newspapers and
books violates the First and Fourteenth
Amendments. If despite the Constitution,
however, this Nation is to embark on the
dangerous road of censorship, my belief is
that this Court is about the most inappropriate Supreme Board of Censors that
could be found. . . .

MR. JUSTICE FRANKFURTER, concurring
in the result.

As one whose taste in art and literature
hardly qualifies him for the *avant-garde*, I
am more than surprised, after viewing the
picture, that the New York authorities
should have banned "Lady Chatterley's
Lover." To assume that this motion picture
would have offended Victorian moral
sensibilities is to rely only on the stuffiest
of Victorian conventions. Whatever one's
personal preferences may be about such
matters, the refusal to license the exhibition of this picture, on the basis of the

1954 amendment to the New York State Education Law, can only mean that that enactment forbids the public showing of any film that deals with adultery except by way of sermonizing condemnation or depicts any physical manifestation of an illicit amorous relation. Since the denial of a license by the Board of Regents was confirmed by the highest court of the State, I have no choice but to agree with this Court's judgment in holding that the State exceeded the bounds of free expression protected by the "liberty" of the Fourteenth Amendment. But I also believe that the Court's opinion takes ground that exceeds the appropriate limits for decision. By way of reinforcing my brother HARLAN's objections to the scope of the Court's opinion, I add the following.

Even the author of "Lady Chatterley's Lover" did not altogether rule out censorship, nor was his passionate zeal on behalf of society's profound interest in the endeavors of true artists so doctrinaire as to be unmindful of the facts of life regarding the sordid exploitation of man's nature and impulses. He knew there was such a thing as pornography, dirt for dirt's sake, or, to be more accurate, dirt for money's sake. . . . In the course of the recent debate in both Houses of Parliament on the Obscene Publications Bill, now on its way to passage, designed to free British authors from the hazards of too rigorous application in our day of Lord Cockburn's ruling, in 1868, in *Regina* v. *Hicklin*, L.R. 3 Q.B. 360, weighty experience was adduced regarding the extensive dissemination of pornographic materials. . . . Nor is there any reason to believe that on this side of the ocean there has been a diminution in the pornographic business which years ago sought a flourishing market in some of the leading secondary schools for boys, who presumably had more means than boys in the public high schools. . . .

In short, there is an evil against which a State may constitutionally protect itself, whatever we may think about the questions of policy involved. The real problem is the formulation of constitutionally allowable safeguards which society may take against evil without impinging upon the necessary dependence of a free society upon the fullest scope of free expression. . . .

It is not our province to meet these recalcitrant problems of legislative drafting. Ours is the vital but very limited task of scrutinizing the work of the draftsmen in order to determine whether they have kept within the narrow limits of the kind of censorship which even D. H. Lawrence deemed necessary. The legislation must not be so vague, the language so loose, as to leave to those who have to apply it too wide a discretion for sweeping within its condemnation what is permissible expression as well as what society may permissibly prohibit. Always remembering that the widest scope of freedom is to be given to the adventurous and imaginative exercise of the human spirit, we have struck down legislation phrased in language intrinsically vague, unless it be responsive to the common understanding of men even though not susceptible of explicit definition. The ultimate reason for invalidating such laws is that they lead to timidity and inertia and thereby discourage the boldness of expression indispensable for a progressive society.

The New York legislation of 1954 was the product of careful lawyers who sought to meet decisions of this Court which had left no doubt that a motion-picture licensing law is not inherently outside the scope of the regulatory powers of a State under the Fourteenth Amendment. The Court does not strike the law down because of vagueness, as we struck down prior New York legislation. Nor does it reverse the judgment of the New York Court of Appeals, as I would, because in applying the New York law to "Lady Chatterley's Lover" it applied it to a picture to which it cannot constitutionally be applied without invading the area of constitutionally free expression. The difficulty which the Court finds seems to derive from some expressions culled here and there from the opinion of the Chief Judge of the New York Court of Appeals. . . .

Unless I misread the opinion of the Court, it strikes down the New York legislation in order to escape the task of deciding whether a particular picture is entitled to the protection of expression under the Fourteenth Amendment. Such an exercise of the judicial function, however onerous or ungrateful, inheres in the very nature of the judicial enforcement of the Due Process Clause. We cannot escape such instance-by-instance, case-by-case application of that clause in all the variety of situations that come before this Court. . . .

MR. JUSTICE DOUGLAS, with whom MR. JUSTICE BLACK joins, concurring.

While I join in the opinion of the Court, I adhere to the views I expressed in *Superior Films* v. *Department of Education,* 346 U.S. 587, 588–589, that censorship of movies is unconstitutional. . . . I can find in the First Amendment no room for any censor whether he is scanning an editorial, reading a news broadcast, editing a novel or a play, or previewing a movie. . . .

MR. JUSTICE CLARK, concurring in the result.

I can take the words of the majority of the New York Court of Appeals only in their clear, unsophisticated and common meaning. . . .

The minority of my brothers here, however, twist this holding into one that New York's Act requires "obscenity or incitement, not just mere abstract expressions of opinion." But I cannot so obliterate the repeated declarations above-mentioned that were made not only 15 times by the Court of Appeals but which were the basis of the Board of Regents' decision as well. Such a construction would raise many problems, not the least of which would be our failure to accept New York's interpretation of the scope of its own Act. I feel, as does the majority here, bound by their holding.

In this context, the Act comes within the ban of *Burstyn* v. *Wilson,* 343 U.S. 495 (1952). . . . The only limits on the censor's discretion is his understanding of what

is included within the term "desirable, acceptable or proper." This is nothing less than a roving commission in which individual impressions become the yardstick of action, and results in regulation in accordance with the beliefs of the individual censor rather than regulation by law. . . .

MR. JUSTICE HARLAN, whom MR. JUSTICE FRANKFURTER and MR. JUSTICE WHITTAKER join, concurring in the result.

I think the Court has moved too swiftly in striking down a statute which is the product of a deliberate and conscientious effort on the part of New York to meet constitutional objections raised by this Court's decisions respecting predecessor statutes in this field. But although I disagree with the Court that the parts of §§ 122 and 122-a of the New York Education Law . . . here particularly involved are unconstitutional on their face, I believe that in their application to this film constitutional bounds were exceeded. . . .

I do not understand that the Court would question the constitutionality of the particular portions of the statute with which we are here concerned if the Court read, as I do, the majority opinions in the Court of Appeals as construing these provisions to require obscenity or incitement, not just mere abstract expressions of opinion. It is difficult to understand why the Court should strain to read those opinions as it has. Our usual course in constitutional adjudication is precisely the opposite.

The application of the statute to this film is quite a different matter. . . .

Giving descriptive expression to what in matters of this kind are in the last analysis bound to be but individual subjective impressions, objectively as one may try to discharge his duty as a judge, is not apt to be repaying. I shall therefore content myself with saying that, according full respect to, and with, I hope, sympathetic consideration for, the views and characterizations expressed by others, I cannot regard this film as depicting anything more than a somewhat unusual, and rather pathetic, "love triangle," lacking in anything that could properly be termed obscene or corruptive of the public morals by inciting the commission of adultery. I therefore think that in banning this film New York has exceeded constitutional limits. . . .

NOTE: The implication of *Burstyn* and *Kingsley* is that licensing would be permissible under a statute which gave the "censor" proper guiding standards. To challenge this proposition, an exhibitor showed a movie without a license. This raised the censorship issue unincumbered by the standards problem. Emphasizing that "we are dealing only with motion pictures," the Court refused to invalidate the licensing requirement "on its face" as an improper prior restraint. Chief Justice Warren and Justices Black, Douglas, and Brennan dissented. *Times Film Corp.* v. *Chicago*, 365 U.S. 43 (1961).

KINGSLEY BOOKS v. BROWN

354 U.S. 436 (1957)

Appeal from the New York Court of Appeals.

MR. JUSTICE FRANKFURTER delivered the opinion of the Court:

This is a proceeding under § 22–a of the New York Code of Criminal Procedure (L. 1941, ch. 925), as amended in 1954 (L. 1954, ch. 702). This section supplements the existing conventional criminal provision dealing with pornography by authorizing the chief executive, or legal officer, of a municipality to invoke a "limited injunctive remedy," under closely defined procedural safeguards, against the sale and distribution of written and printed matter found after due trial to be obscene, and to obtain an order for the seizure, in default of surrender, of the condemned publications.

A complaint dated September 10, 1954, charged appellants with displaying for sale paper-covered obscene booklets, fourteen of which were annexed, under the general title of "Nights of Horror." The complaint prayed that appellants be enjoined from further distribution of the booklets, that they be required to surrender to the sheriff for destruction all copies in their possession, and, upon failure to do so, that the sheriff be commanded to seize and destroy those copies. The same day the appellants were ordered to show cause within four days why they should not be enjoined pendente lite from distributing the booklets. Appellants consented to the granting of an injunction pendente lite and did not bring the matter to issue promptly, as was their right under subdivision 2 of the challenged section, which provides that the persons sought to be enjoined "shall be entitled to a trial of the issues within one day after joinder of issue and a decision shall be rendered by the court within two days of the conclusion of the trial." After the case came to trial, the judge, sitting in equity, found that the booklets annexed to the complaint and introduced in evidence were clearly obscene—were "dirt for dirt's sake"; he enjoined their further distribution and ordered their destruction. He refused to enjoin "the sale and distribution of later issues" on the ground that "to rule against a volume not offered in evidence would . . . impose an unreasonable prior restraint upon freedom of the press." 208 Misc. 150, 167, 142 N.Y.S.2d 735.

Not challenging the construction of the statute or the finding of obscenity, appellants took a direct appeal to the New York Court of Appeals, a proceeding in which the constitutionality of the statute was the sole question open to them. That court (one judge not sitting) found no constitutional infirmity: three judges supported the unanimous conclusion by detailed discussion, the other three deemed a brief disposition justified by "ample outhority." 1 N.Y.2d 177, 151 N.Y.S.2d 639. A claim under the due process clause of the Fourteenth Amendment made throughout the state litigation brought the case here on appeal. 352 U.S. 962.

Neither in the New York Court of Appeals, nor here, did appellants assail the legislation insofar as it outlaws obscenity. The claim they make lies within a very narrow compass. Their attack is upon the power of New York to employ the remedial scheme of § 22–a. Authorization of an injunction pendente lite, as part of this scheme, during the period within which the issue of obscenity must be promptly tried and adjudicated in an adversary proceeding for which "[a]dequate notice, judicial hearing, [and] fair determination" are assured, 208 Misc. 150, 164, 142 N.Y.S.2d 735, is a safeguard against frustration of the public interest in effectuating judicial condemnation of obscene matter. It is a brake on the temptation to exploit a filthy business offered by the limited hazards of piecemeal prosecutions, sale by sale, of a publication already condemned as obscene. New York enacted this procedure on the basis of study by a joint legislative committee. Resort to this injunctive remedy, it is claimed, is beyond the constitutional power of New York in that it amounts to a prior censorship of literary product and as such is violative of that "freedom of thought, and speech" which has been "withdrawn by the Fourteenth Amendment from encroachment by the states." *Palko* v. *Connecticut,* 302 U.S. 319, 326, 327. Reliance is particularly placed upon *Near* v. *Minnesota,* 283 U.S. 697.

In an unbroken series of cases extending over a long stretch of this Court's history, it has been accepted as a postulate that "the primary requirements of decency may be enforced against obscene publications." *Id.* 283 U.S. at 716. And so our starting point is that New York can constitutionally convict appellants of keeping for sale the booklets incontestably found to be obscene. *Alberts* v. *California,* decided this day. The immediate problem then is whether New York can adopt as an auxiliary means of dealing with such obscene merchandising the procedure of § 22–a.

We need not linger over the suggestion that something can be drawn out of the due process clause of the Fourteenth Amendment that restricts New York to the criminal process in seeking to protect its people against the dissemination of pornography. It is not for this Court thus to limit the State in resorting to various weapons in the armory of the law. Whether proscribed conduct is to be visited by a criminal prosecution or by a qui tam action or by an injunction or by some or all of these remedies in combination, is a matter within the legislature's range of choice. See *Tigner* v. *Texas,* 310 U.S. 141, 148. If New York chooses to subject persons who disseminate obscene "literature" to criminal prosecution and also to deal with such books as deodands of old, or both, with due regard, of course, to appropriate opportunities for the trial of the underlying issue, it is not for us to gainsay its selection of remedies. Just as *Near* v. *Minnesota,* 283 U.S. 697, *supra,* one of the landmark opinions in shaping the constitutional protection of freedom of speech and of the press, left no doubts that "Liberty of speech, and of the press, is also not an absolute right," 283 U.S. at 708, it likewise made clear that "the protection even as to previous restraint is not absolutely unlimited." *Id.* 283 U.S. at 716. To be sure, the limitation is the exception; it is to be closely confined so as to preclude what may fairly be deemed licensing or censorship.

The judicial angle of vision in testing the validity of a statute like § 22–a is "the operation and effect of the statute in substance." *Id.* 283 U.S. at 713. The phrase "prior restraint" is not a self-wielding sword. Nor can it serve as a talismanic test. The duty of closer analysis and critical judgment in applying the thought behind the phrase has thus been authoritatively put by one who brings weighty learning to his support of constitutionally protected liberties: "What is needed," writes Professor Paul Freund, "is a pragmatic assessment of its operation in the particular circumstances. The generalization that prior restraint is particularly obnoxious in civil liberties cases must yield to more particularistic analysis." "The Supreme Court and Civil Liberties," 4 *Vand. L. Rev.* 533, 539.

Wherein does § 22–a differ in its effective operation from the type of statute upheld in *Alberts?* Section 311 of California's Penal Code provides that "Every person who wilfully and lewdly . . . keeps for sale . . . any obscene book . . . is guilty of a misdemeanor. . . ." Section 1141 of New York's Penal Law is similar. One would be bold to assert that the in terrorem effect of such statutes less restrains booksellers in the period before the law strikes than does § 22–a. Instead of requiring the bookseller to dread that the offer for sale of a book may without prior warning subject him to a criminal prosecution with the hazard of imprisonment, the civil procedure assures him that such consequences cannot follow unless he ignores a court order specifically directed to him for a prompt and carefully circumscribed determination of the issue of obscenity. Until then, he may keep the book for sale and sell it on his own judgment rather than "steer . . . nervously among the treacherous shoals." Warburg, "Onward, and Upward with the Arts," *The New Yorker*, April 20, 1957, p. 101, in connection with *R. v. Martin Secker Warburg, Ltd.*, [1954] 2 All. Eng. 683 (CCC).

Criminal enforcement and the proceeding under § 22–a interfere with a book's solicitation of the public precisely at the same stage. In each situation the law moves after publication; the book need not in either case have yet passed into the hands of the public. The *Alberts* record does not show that the matter there found to be obscene had reached the public at the time that the criminal charge of keeping such matter for sale was lodged, while here as a matter of fact copies of the booklets whose distribution was enjoined had been on sale

for several weeks when process was served. In each case the bookseller is put on notice by the complaint that sale of the publication charged with obscenity in the period before trial may subject him to penal consequences. In the one case he may suffer fine and imprisonment for violation of the criminal statute, in the other, for disobedience of the temporary injunction. The bookseller may of course stand his ground and confidently believe that in any judicial proceeding the book could not be condemned as obscene, but both modes of procedure provide an effective deterrent against distribution prior to adjudication of the book's content—the threat of subsequent penalization.

The method devised by New York in § 22–a for determining whether a publication is obscene does not differ in essential procedural safeguards from that provided under many state statutes making the distribution of obscene publications a misdemeanor. For example, while the New York criminal provision brings the State's criminal procedure into operation, a defendant is not thereby entitled to a jury trial. In each case a judge is the conventional trier of fact; in each, a jury may as a matter of discretion be summoned. Compare N.Y. City Criminal Courts Act § 31, Sub. 1(c) and Sub. 4, with N.Y. Civil Practice Act § 430. (Appellants, as a matter of fact, did not request a jury trial, they did not attack the statute in the courts below for failure to require a jury, and they did not bring that issue to this Court.) Of course, the due process clause does not subject the State to the necessity of having trial by jury in misdemeanor prosecutions.

Nor are the consequences of a judicial condemnation for obscenity under § 22–a more restrictive of freedom of expression than the result of conviction for a misdemeanor. In *Alberts*, the defendant was fined $500, sentenced to sixty days in prison, and put on probation for two years on condition that he not violate the obscenity statute. Not only was he completely separated from society for two months but he was also seriously restrained from trafficking in all obscene publications for a considerable time. Appellants, on the other hand, were enjoined from displaying for sale or distributing only the particular booklets theretofore published and adjudged to be obscene. Thus, the restraint upon appellants as merchants in obscenity was narrower than that imposed on *Alberts*.

Section 22–a's provision for the seizure and destruction of the instruments of ascertained wrongdoing expresses resort to a legal remedy sanctioned by the long history of the Anglo-American law. See Holmes, *The Common Law*, 24–26; *Van Oster* v. *Kansas*, 272 U.S. 465; *J. W. Goldsmith-Grant Co.* v. *United States*, 254 U.S. 505, 510–511; *Lawton* v. *Steele*, 152 U.S. 133; and see *United States* v. *Urbuteit*, 335 U.S. 355, dealing with misbranded articles under §304(a) of the Food, Drug, and Cosmetic Act, 52 Stat. 1044. It is worth noting that although the *Alberts* record does not reveal whether the publications found to be obscene were destroyed, provision is made for that by §§ 313 and 314 of the California Penal Code. Similarly, § 1144 of New York's Penal Law provides for destruction of obscene matter following conviction for its dissemination.

It only remains to say that the difference between *Near* v. *Minnesota*, 283 U.S. 697, *supra*, and this case is glaring in fact. The two cases are no less glaringly different when judged by the appropriate criteria of constitutional law. Minnesota empowered its courts to enjoin the dissemination of future issues of a publication because its past issues had been found offensive. In the language of Mr. Chief Justice Hughes, "This is of the essence of censorship." 283 U.S. at 713. As such, it was found unconstitutional. This was enough to condemn the statute wholly apart from the fact that the proceeding in *Near* involved not obscenity but matters deemed to be derogatory to a public officer. Unlike *Near*, § 22–a is concerned solely with obscenity and, as authoritatively construed, it studiously withholds restraint upon matters not already published and not yet found to be offensive.

The judgment is affirmed.

MR. CHIEF JUSTICE WARREN, dissenting:

My views on the rights of a State to protect its people against the purveyance of obscenity were expressed in *Alberts* v. *California,* also decided today. Here we have an entirely different situation.

This is not a criminal obscenity case. Nor is it a case ordering the destruction of materials disseminated by a person who has been convicted of an offense for doing so, as would be authorized under provisions in the laws of New York and other States. It is a case wherein the New York police, under a different state statute, summarily seized books which, in their opinion, were unfit for public use because of obscenity and then obtained a court order for their condemnation and destruction.

The majority opinion sanctions this proceeding. I would not. Unlike the criminal cases decided today, this New York law places the book on trial. There is totally lacking any standard in the statute for judging the book in context. The personal element basic to the criminal laws is entirely absent. In my judgment, the same object may have wholly different impact depending upon the setting in which it is placed. Under this statute, the setting is irrelevant.

It is the manner of use that should determine obscenity. It is the conduct of the individual that should be judged, not the quality of art or literature. To do otherwise is to impose a prior restraint and hence to violate the Constitution. Certainly in the absence of a prior judicial determination of illegal use, books, pictures and other objects of expression should not be destroyed. It savors too much of book burning.

I would reverse.

MR. JUSTICE DOUGLAS, with whom MR. JUSTICE BLACK concurs, dissenting:

There are two reasons why I think this restraining order should be dissolved.

First, the provision for an injunction pendente lite gives the State the paralyzing power of a censor. A decree can issue ex parte—without a hearing and without any ruling or finding on the issue of obscenity. This provision is defended on the ground that it is only a little encroachment, that a hearing must be promptly given and a finding of obscenity promptly made. But every publisher knows what awful effect a decree issued in secret can have. We tread here on First Amendment grounds. And nothing is more devastating to the rights that it guarantees than the power to restrain publication before even a hearing is held. This is prior restraint and censorship at its worst.

Second, the procedure for restraining by equity decree the distribution of all the condemned literature does violence to the First Amendment. The judge or jury which finds the publisher guilty in New York City acts on evidence that may be quite different from evidence before the judge or jury that finds the publisher not guilty in Rochester. In New York City the publisher may have been selling his tracts to juveniles, while in Rochester he may have sold to professional people. The nature of the group among whom the tracts are distributed may have an important bearing on the issue of guilt in any obscenity prosecution. Yet the present statute makes one criminal conviction conclusive and authorizes a statewide decree that subjects the distributor to the contempt power. I think every publication is a separate offense which entitles the accused to a separate trial. Juries or judges may differ in their opinions, community by community, case by case. The publisher is entitled to that leeway under our constitutional system. One is entitled to defend every utterance on its merits and not to suffer today for what he uttered yesterday. Free speech is not to be regulated like diseased cattle and impure butter. The audience (in this case the judge or the jury) that hissed yesterday may applaud today, even for the same performance.

The regime approved by the Court goes far toward making the censor supreme. It also substitutes punishment by contempt for punishment by jury trial. In both re-

spects it transgresses constitutional guarantees.

I would reverse this judgment and direct the restraining order to be dissolved.

MR. JUSTICE BRENNAN, dissenting:

I believe the absence in this New York obscenity statute of a right to jury trial is a fatal defect. Provision for jury trials in equity causes is made by § 430 of the New York Civil Practice Act, but only for discretionary jury trials, and advisory verdicts, to be followed or rejected by the trial judge as he deems fit and proper.

In *Alberts* v. *California,* and *Roth* v. *United States,* decided today, the Court held to be constitutional the following standard for judging obscenity—whether to the average person, applying contemporary community standards, the dominant theme of the material taken as a whole appeals to prurient interest. The statutes there involved allowed a jury trial of right, and we did not reach the question whether the safeguards necessary for securing the freedoms of speech and press for material not obscene included a jury determination of obscenity.

The jury represents a cross-section of the community and has a special aptitude for reflecting the view of the average person. Jury trial of obscenity therefore provides a peculiarly competent application of the standard for judging obscenity which, by its definition, calls for an appraisal of material according to the average person's application of contemporary community standards. A statute which does not afford the defendant, of right, a jury determination of obscenity falls short, in my view, of giving proper effect to the standard fashioned as the necessary safeguard demanded by the freedoms of speech and press for material which is not obscene. Of course, as with jury questions generally, the trial judge must initially determine that there is a jury question, i.e., that reasonable men may differ whether the material is obscene.

I would reverse the judgment and direct the restraining order to be dissolved.

BUTLER v. *MICHIGAN*

352 U.S. 380 (1957)

> Butler was convicted of selling a book in violation of a state obscenity statute which defined as obscene any publication tending to "incite minors to violent or depraved or immoral acts," or which tended "to the corruption of the morals of youth." The statute and conviction were held invalid on review. The crux of the decision appears in the following remarks from Mr. Justice Frankfurter's opinion for a unanimous Court:

The State insists that, by thus quarantining the general reading public against books not too rugged for grown men and women in order to shield juvenile innocence, it is exercising its powers to promote the general welfare. Surely, this is to burn the house to roast the pig. . . . We have before us legislation not reasonably restricted to the evil with which it is said to deal. The incidence of this enactment is to reduce the adult population of Michigan to reading only what is fit for children. It thereby arbitrarily curtails one of those liberties of the individual, now enshrined in the due process clause of the Fourteenth Amendment, that history has attested as the indispensable conditions for the maintenance and progress of a free society.

NOTE AND QUAERE: Obviously obscenity may be forbidden, but the problem of punishments or sanctions is difficult. May a bookseller be penalized for offering to sell an obscene book though he may be unaware that the book is in fact obscene? See *Smith* v. *California,* 361 U.S. 147 (1959).

Pursuant to Missouri law, a judge upon the sworn complaint of a police officer issued a warrant to seize any obscene material at six named places of business. Numerous copies of 280 publications were seized and a hearing was held about two weeks later. Some seven weeks thereafter, the judge ruled that 100 of the publications were obscene, and ordered them destroyed. The rest were returned to their owners. Is this procedure permissible? See *Marcus* v. *Property Search Warrants,* 367 U.S. 717 (1961), and *A Quantity of Copies of Books* v. *Kansas,* 84 S. Ct. 1723 (1964).

Suppose a state tries to "encourage morality in youth" by "listing" objectionable publications (with no other form of penalty). Is this procedure permissible? See *Bantam Books, Inc.* v. *Sullivan,* 372 U.S. 58 (1963).

10. PRIVATE RESTRAINTS ON UTTERANCE

MORRIS L. ERNST, *The First Freedom* [1]

Government is not the sole enemy of freedom. Concentrated economic power also acts as a restraint on thought. Monopolies of the mind have calmly entered

1. *The First Freedom.* Copyright 1946 by The Macmillan Company. Used by permission.

our folkways. We in the United States have forsaken free enterprise in the fields of communication. Competition is at a minimum.

Our press is fast evaporating. Ten states have not a single city with competing daily papers. Twenty-two states are without Sunday newspaper competition. Fourteen companies owning eighteen papers control about one quarter of our total daily circulation. Three hundred and seventy chain newspapers own about one fifth of all our circulation. More than a quarter of our daily circulation is absentee owned. We have a thousand less owners than a few decades ago. Thirty-two hundred weeklies—the backbone of local democracy—have disappeared. One company dominates more than 3,000 weeklies. There are only 117 cities left, in our entire nation, where competing dailies still exist.

We talk about the value of a competitive press but our treatment of this basic commodity—news and opinion—denies what we say.

One third of all regular radio stations are interlocked with newspapers. The bottleneck gets narrower. Four networks before the war had 95 percent of all nighttime broadcasting power. One hundred and forty-four advertisers account for 97 percent of all the network income. Eleven advertisers contribute about 50 percent of all the network income. A dozen advertising agents create the radio programs which bring to the networks one half of their income. Independent radio stations are the stepchildren of the mike. In more than 100 areas the only newspaper left owns the only radio station. What price competition!

The weekly attendance at movies amounts to more than 100 million people. But five companies control the 2,800 key theaters of the nation. These five companies—called the Big Five—pick up more than three quarters of all the nickels and dimes paid by the American movie audience for its screen entertainment. All other producers of films enter the market place by grace of these companies. We have allowed five giants to destroy our market place of free competition for movies. Moreover, two companies produce about 90 percent of all our raw film stock.

Such are a few of the startling facts that call for a national debate on the values of concentrated control by all too few people over the minds of 138 million people.

NOTE: See also *Report of the Commission on Freedom of the Press*, especially pages 37, 50–51, 67–68 (1947). It must be recognized that the Bill of Rights, like the Civil War amendments, blocks only governmental—not private or even social—interference with civil liberty. (Cf. Part Four, V.) As John Stuart Mill observed in his great essay on Liberty,

when society is itself the tyrant-society collectively over the separate individuals who compose it, . . . it practices a social tyranny more formidable than many kinds of political oppression, since, though not usually upheld by such extreme penalties, it leaves fewer means of escape, penetrating much more deeply into the details of life, and enslaving the soul itself. Protection, therefore, against the tyranny of the magistrate is not enough: there needs protection also against the tyranny of the prevailing opinion and feeling; against the tendency of society to impose, by other means than civil penalties, its own ideas and practices as rules of conduct on those who dissent from them. . . .

V. FREEDOM FROM RACIAL DISCRIMINATION

1. BACKGROUND

In response to the *Dred Scott* fiasco, the Thirteenth Amendment abolished slavery in the United States. But, if the old system was destroyed as a legal institution, many of its social, economic, and political incidents inevitably survived. To limit at least some of these was the purpose of the Fourteenth and Fifteenth Amendments. A Court whose members had lived through the ordeal of the Civil War and the resulting amendments explained the latter in *Strauder v. W. Virginia,* 100 U.S. 303 (1880):

This [Fourteenth Amendment] is one of a series of constitutional provisions having a common purpose; namely, securing to a race recently emancipated, a race that through many generations had been held in slavery, all the civil rights that the [white] race enjoy. It was designed to assure to the colored race the enjoyment of all the civil rights that under the law are enjoyed by white persons, and to give to that race the protection of the general government, in that enjoyment, whenever it should be denied by the States. It not only gave citizenship and the privileges of citizenship to persons of color, but it denied to any State the power to withhold from them the equal protection of the laws, and authorized Congress to enforce its provisions by appropriate legislation. . . . What is this but declaring that the law in the States shall be the same for the black as for the white; that all persons, whether colored or white, shall stand equal before the laws of the States, and, in regard to the colored race, for whose protection the amendment was primarily designed, that no discrimination shall be made against them by law because of their color? The words of the amendment, it is true, are prohibitory, but they contain a necessary implication of a positive immunity, or right, most valuable to the colored race,—the right to exemption from unfriendly legislation against them distinctively as colored,—exemption from legal discriminations, implying inferiority in civil society, lessening the security of their enjoyment of the rights which others enjoy, and discriminations which are steps towards reducing them to the condition of a subject race. [See also the *Slaughter House Cases,* Part Four, I.]

Less than twenty years later, after the judicial counterrevolution of 1895, the history and idealism of the Civil War amendments were abandoned. A Court which only a few months earlier had destroyed the income tax and emasculated the Sherman Anti-Trust Act could find nothing in the Constitution to save Negroes from the humiliation of racial segregation. Certainly it is significant that all but one of the judges who had joined in the Court's opinion in *Strauder* were no longer on the bench when *Plessy* was decided. The one exception, Mr. Justice Harlan, dissented in the later case.

Here, too, the constitutional "revolution" that began in 1937 brought a return to first principles. Separate-but-equal, like dual federalism and substantive due process of the same vintage, died with the "return to the Constitution." The change came gradually. At first the Court emphasized real equality, and rejected the traditional mock equality. It would not suffice for a state to provide a law school at home for whites and mere fiscal aid to qualified Negroes to help them attend law schools away from home, that is, in other states. *Missouri ex rel Gaines* v. *Canada*, 305 U.S. 337 (1938). Qualified Negroes must be furnished equivalent legal training within the state, if they are not admitted to the state law school. *Sipuel* v. *University of Oklahoma*, 332 U.S. 631 (1948). When admitted to a regular state university they may not be "segregated" for purposes of scholastic activity. *McLaurin* v. *Oklahoma State Regents*, 339 U.S. 637 (1950). In *Sweatt* v. *Painter*, 339 U.S. 629 (1950), the requirement of real equality was so far stressed as to suggest that at least in professional education nothing short of identical treatment would satisfy the Constitution. As a practical matter separate-but-equal was doomed:

Whether the University of Texas Law School is compared with the original or the new law school for Negroes, we cannot find substantial equality in the educational opportunities offered white and Negro law students by the State. In terms of number of the faculty, variety of courses and opportunity for specialization, size of the student body, scope of the library, availability of law review and similar activities, the University of Texas Law School is superior. What is more important, the University of Texas Law School possesses to a far greater degree those qualities which are incapable of objective measurement but which make for greatness in a law school. Such qualities, to name but a few, include reputation of the faculty, experience of the administration, position and influence of the alumni, standing in the community, traditions and prestige. It is difficult to believe that one who had a free choice between these law schools would consider the question close.

Moreover, although the law is a highly learned profession, we are well aware that it is an intensely practical one. The law school, the proving ground for legal learning and practice, cannot be effective in isolation from the individuals and institutions with which the law interacts. Few students and no one who has practiced law would choose to study in an academic vacuum, removed from the interplay of ideas and the exchange of views with which the law is concerned. The law school to which Texas is willing to admit petitioner excludes from its student body members of the racial groups which number 85 percent of the population of the State and include most of the lawyers, witnesses, jurors, judges, and other officials with whom petitioner will inevitably be dealing when he becomes a member of the Texas Bar. With such a substantial and significant segment of society excluded, we cannot conclude that the education offered petitioner is substantially equal to that which he would receive if admitted to the University of Texas Law School.

Of course the Civil War amendments are not the only constitutional impediment to racialism. The commerce clause is available and has been used by Congress to prevent railroads from subjecting "any particular person . . . to any undue or unreasonable prejudice or disadvantage in any respect whatsoever. . . ." Interstate Commerce Act, 49 U.S.C.A., Sec. 3 (1). This was interpreted in *Henderson* v. *United States*, 339 U.S. 816 (1950), to outlaw segregation in the dining car of an interstate train. Moreover, the dormant commerce clause by virtue of the *Cooley* rule has been held to forbid segregation on interstate buses. *Morgan* v. *Virginia,* 328 U.S. 373 (1946). See Part Three, III.

DRED SCOTT v. *SANDFORD*
19 Howard 393 (1857)

> Dred Scott, a slave in Missouri, was taken by his master to live in territory made free by the Missouri Compromise. Thereafter Scott returned to Missouri and sued his new master for his freedom on the theory that residence in free territory had made him free. This action began in a Federal Court which, per Article III of the Constitution, had jurisdiction of cases between *citizens* of different states. (Scott claimed to be a Missouri citizen, while his "master" was a citizen of New York.)

CHIEF JUSTICE TANEY delivered the opinion of the court. . . .

[The Court observed first that persons of African descent "were not intended to be included" as citizens of the United States, but were considered by the Founding Fathers "as a subordinate and inferior class of beings, who . . . had no rights or privileges but such as those who held the power and the government might choose to grant them."]

Now if the removal [to free territory] did not give [Scott and his family] their freedom, then by his own admission he is still a slave; and whatever opinions may be entertained in favor of a free person of the African race, no one supposes that a slave is a citizen of the State or of the United States. If, therefore, the acts done by his owner did not make them free persons, he is still a slave, and certainly incapable of suing in the character of a citizen. . . .

The Act of Congress, upon which the plaintiff relies, [the Missouri compromise] declares that slavery and involuntary servitude, except as a punishment for crime, shall be forever prohibited in all that part of the territory ceded by France, under the name of Louisiana, which lies north of thirty-six degrees thirty minutes north latitude, and not included within the limits of Missouri. And the difficulty which meets us at the threshold of this part of the inquiry is, whether Congress was authorized to pass this law under any of the powers granted to it by the Constitution; for if the authority is not given by that instrument, it is the duty of this court to declare it void and inoperative, and incapable of conferring freedom upon any one who is held as a slave under the laws of any one of the States.

The counsel for the plaintiff has laid much stress upon that article in the Constitution which confers on Congress the power "to dispose of and make all needful rules and regulations respecting the territory or other property belonging to the United States;" but, in the judgment of the court, that provision has no bearing on the present controversy, and the power there given, whatever it may be, is confined, and was intended to be confined, to the territory which at that time belonged to, or was claimed by, the United States, and was within their boundaries as settled by the treaty with Great Britain, and can have no influence upon a territory afterwards acquired from a foreign Government. It was a special provision for a known and particular territory, and to meet a present emergency, and nothing more. . . .

If this clause is construed to extend to territory acquired by the present Government from a foreign nation, outside of the limits of any charter from the British Government to a colony, it would be difficult to say, why it was deemed necessary to give the Government the power to sell any vacant lands belonging to the sovereignty which might be found within it; and if this was necessary, why the grant of this power should precede the power to legislate over it and establish a Government there; and still more difficult to say, why it was deemed necessary so specially and particularly to grant the power to make needful rules and regulations in relation to any personal or movable property it might acquire there. For the words, *other property* necessarily, by every known rule of interpretation, must mean property of a different description from territory or land. And the difficulty would perhaps be insurmountable in endeavoring to account for the last member of the sentence, which provides that "nothing in this Constitution shall be so construed as to prejudice any claims of the United States or any particular State," or to say how any particular State could have claims in or to a territory ceded by a foreign Government, or to account for associating this provision with the preceding provisions of the clause, with which it would appear to have no connection.

But the power of Congress over the person or property of a citizen can never be a mere discretionary power under our Constitution and form of Government. The powers of the Government and the rights and privileges of the citizen are regulated and plainly defined by the Constitution itself. And when the Territory becomes a part of the United States, the Federal Government enters into possession in the character impressed upon it by those who created it. It enters upon it with its powers over the citizen strictly defined, and limited by the Constitution, from which it derives its own existence, and by virtue of which alone it continues to exist and act as a Government and sovereignty. It has no power of any kind beyond it; and it cannot, when it enters a Territory of the United States, put off its character, and assume discretionary or despotic powers which the Constitution has denied to it. It cannot create for itself a new character separated from the

citizens of the United States, and the duties it owes them under the provisions of the Constitution. The Territory being a part of the United States, the Government and the citizen both enter it under the authority of the Constitution, with their respective rights defined and marked out; and the Federal Government can exercise no power over his person or property, beyond what that instrument confers, nor lawfully deny any right which it has reserved. . . .

The rights of private property have been guarded with equal care. Thus the rights of property are united with the rights of person, and placed on the same ground by the fifth amendment to the Constitution. . . . An Act of Congress which deprives a person of the United States of his liberty or property merely because he came himself or brought his property into a particular Territory of the United States, and who had committed no offense against the laws, could hardly be dignified with the name of due process of law. . . .

And this prohibition is not confined to the States, but the words are general, and extend to the whole territory over which the Constitution gives it power to legislate, including those portions of it remaining under territorial government, as well as that covered by States. It is a total absence of power everywhere within the dominion of the United States, and places the citizens of a territory, so far as these rights are concerned, on the same footing with citizens of the States, and guards them as firmly and plainly against any inroads which the general government might attempt, under the plea of implied or incidental powers. And if Congress itself cannot do this—if it is beyond the powers conferred on the Federal Government—it will be admitted, we presume, that it could not authorize a territorial government to exercise them. It could confer no power on any local government, established by its authority, to violate the provisions of the Constitution.

It seems, however, to be supposed, that there is a difference between property in a slave and other property, and that different rules may be applied to it in expounding the Constitution of the United States. And the laws and usages of nations, and the writings of eminent jurists upon the relation of master and slave and their mutual rights and duties, and the powers which governments may exercise over it, have been dwelt upon in the argument.

But . . . if the Constitution recognizes the right of property of the master in a slave, and makes no distinction between that description of property and other property owned by a citizen, no tribunal, acting under the authority of the United States, whether it be legislative, executive, or judicial, has a right to draw such a distinction, or deny to it the benefit of the provisions and guarantees which have been provided for the protection of private property against the encroachments of the Government.

Now . . . the right of property in a slave is distinctly and expressly affirmed in the Constitution. The right to traffic in it, like an ordinary article of merchandise and property, was guaranteed to the citizens of the United States, in every State that might desire it, for twenty years. And the Government in express terms is pledged to protect it in all future time, if the slave escapes from his owner. . . . And no word can be found in the Constitution which gives Congress a greater power over slave property, or which entitles property of that kind to less protection than property of any other description. The only power conferred is the power coupled with the duty of guarding and protecting the owner in his rights.

Upon these considerations, it is the opinion of the court that the Act of Congress [the Missouri compromise] which prohibited a citizen from holding and owning property of this kind in the territory of the United States north of the line therein mentioned, is not warranted by the Constitution, and is therefore void; and that neither Dred Scott himself, nor any of his family, were made free by being carried into this territory; even if they had been carried there

by the owner, with the intention of becoming a permanent resident. . . .

Upon the whole, therefore, it is the judgment of this court, that it appears by the record before us that the plaintiff in error is not a citizen of Missouri, in the sense in which that word is used in the Constitution; and that the Circuit Court of the United States, for that reason, had no jurisdiction in the case, and could give no judgment in it.

Its judgment for the defendant must, consequently, be reversed, and a mandate issued directing the suit to be dismissed for want of jurisdiction.

[JUSTICES WAYNE, NELSON, DANIEL, CAMPBELL, and CATRON delivered concurring opinions. MR. JUSTICE GRIER concurred in the opinions of CHIEF JUSTICE TANEY and MR. JUSTICE NELSON.]

MR. JUSTICE McLEAN dissenting. . . .

MR. JUSTICE CURTIS dissenting. . . .

The conclusions at which I have arrived on this part of the case are:

First. That the free native-born citizens of each State are citizens of the United States.

Second. That as free colored persons born within some of the States are citizens of those States, such persons are also citizens of the United States.

Third. That every such citizen, residing in any State, has the right to sue and is liable to be sued in the federal courts, as a citizen of that State in which he resides.

Fourth. That as the plea to the jurisdiction in this case shows no facts, except that the plaintiff was of African descent, and his ancestors were sold as slaves, and as these facts are not inconsistent with his citizenship of the United States, and his residence in the State of Missouri, the plea to the jurisdiction was bad, and the judgment of the Circuit Court overruling it, was correct.

I dissent, therefore, from that part of the opinion of the majority of the court, in which it is held that a person of African descent cannot be a citizen of the United States; . . .

Nor, in my judgment, will the position, that a prohibition to bring slaves into a Territory deprives any one of his property without due process of law, bear examination.

It must be remembered that this restriction on the legislative power is not peculiar to the Constitution of the United States; it was borrowed from Magna Charta; was brought to America by our ancestors, as part of their inherited liberties, and has existed in all the States, usually in the very words of the great charter. It existed in every political community in America in 1787, when the ordinance prohibiting slavery north and west of the Ohio was passed.

And if a prohibition of slavery in a Territory in 1820 violated this principle of Magna Charta, the ordinance of 1787 also violated it; and what power had, I do not say the Congress of the Confederation alone, but the Legislature of Virginia, or the Legislature of any or all the States of the Confederacy, to consent to such a violation? The people of the States had conferred no such power. I think I may at least say, if the Congress did then violate Magna Charta by the ordinance, no one discovered that violation. Besides, if the prohibition upon all persons, citizens as well as others, to bring slaves into a Ter-

ritory, and a declaration that if brought they shall be free, deprives citizens of their property without due process of law, what shall we say of the legislation of many of the slaveholding States which have enacted the same prohibition? As early as October, 1778, a law was passed in Virginia, that thereafter no slave should be imported into that Commonwealth by sea or by land, and that every slave who should be imported should become free. . . . I am not aware that such laws, though they exist in many States, were ever supposed to be in conflict with the principle of Magna Charta incorporated into the State Constitution. It was certainly understood by the Convention which framed the Constitution, and has been so understood ever since, that, under the power to regulate commerce, Congress could prohibit the importation of slaves; and the exercise of the power was restrained till 1808. A citizen of the United States owns slaves in Cuba, and brings them to the United States, where they are set free by the legislation of Congress. Does this legislation deprive him of his property without due process of law? If so, what becomes of the laws prohibiting the slave trade? If not, how can a similar regulation respecting a Territory violate the fifth amendment of the Constitution? . . .

2. THE CONCEPT OF EQUAL PROTECTION

PLESSY v. *FERGUSON*

163 U.S. 537 (1896)

MR. JUSTICE BROWN . . . delivered the opinion of the court.

This case turns upon the constitutionality of [a Louisiana statute providing that] "all railway companies carrying passengers . . . in this State, shall provide equal but separate accommodations for white, and colored, races . . ."

The constitutionality of this act is attacked upon the ground that it conflicts both with the Thirteenth Amendment of

the Constitution, abolishing slavery, and the Fourteenth Amendment, which prohibits certain restrictive legislation on the part of the states.

1. That it does not conflict with the Thirteenth Amendment, which abolished slavery and involuntary servitude, except as a punishment for crime, is too clear for argument. . . .

2. By the Fourteenth Amendment, all persons born or naturalized in the United

States, and subject to the jurisdiction thereof, are made citizens of the United States and of the state wherein they reside; and the states are forbidden from making or enforcing any law which shall abridge the privileges or immunities of citizens of the United States, or shall deprive any person of life, liberty or property without due process of law, or deny to any person within their jurisdiction the equal protection of the laws. . . .

The object of the amendment was undoubtedly to enforce the absolute equality of the two races before the law, but in the nature of things it could not have been intended to abolish distinctions based upon color, or to enforce social, as distinguished from political, equality, or a commingling of the two races upon terms unsatisfactory to either. Laws permitting, and even requiring, their separation in places where they are liable to be brought into contact do not necessarily imply the inferiority of either race to the other, and have been generally, if not universally, recognized as within the competency of the state legislatures in the exercise of their police power. The most common instance of this is connected with the establishment of separate schools for white and colored children, which has been held to be a valid exercise of the legislative power even by courts of states where the political rights of the colored race have been longest and most earnestly enforced.

One of the earliest of these cases is that of *Roberts* v. *City of Boston,* 5 Cush. 198 (1849), in which the Supreme Judicial Court of Massachusetts held that the general school committee of Boston had power to make provision for the instruction of colored children in separate schools established exclusively for them, and to prohibit their attendance upon the other schools. "The great principle," said Chief Justice Shaw, p. 206, "advanced by the learned and eloquent advocate for the plaintiff" (Mr. Charles Sumner), "is, that by the constitution and laws of Massachusetts, all persons without distinction of age or sex, birth or color, origin or condition, are equal before the law. . . . But, when this great prin-

ciple comes to be applied to the actual and various conditions of persons in society, it will not warrant the assertion, that men and women are legally clothed with the same civil and political powers, and that children and adults are legally to have the same functions and be subject to the same treatment; but only that the rights of all, as they are settled and regulated by law, are equally entitled to the paternal consideration and protection of the law for their maintenance and security." It was held that the powers of the committee extended to the establishment of separate schools for children of different ages, sexes and colors, and that they might also establish special schools for poor and neglected children, who have become too old to attend the primary school, and yet have not acquired the rudiments of learning, to enable them to enter the ordinary schools. Similar laws have been enacted by Congress under its general power of legislation over the District of Columbia . . . as well as by the legislatures of many of the states, and have been generally, if not uniformly, sustained by the courts. . . .

The distinction between laws interfering with the political equality of the Negro and those requiring the separation of the two races in schools, theatres, and railway carriages has been frequently drawn by this court. Thus in *Strauder* v. *West Virginia,* 100 U.S. 303, it was held that a law of West Virginia limiting to white male persons, 21 years of age and citizens of the state, the right to sit upon juries, was a discrimination which implied a legal inferiority in civil society, which lessened the security of the right of the colored race, and was a step toward reducing them to a condition of servility. Indeed, the right of a colored man that, in the selection of jurors to pass upon his life, liberty and property, there shall be no exclusion of his race, and no discrimination against them because of color, has been asserted in a number of cases. . . .

So far, then, as a conflict with the Fourteenth Amendment is concerned, the case reduces itself to the question whether the statute of Louisiana is a reasonable regulation, and with respect to this there must necessarily be a large discretion on the part of the legislature. In determining the question of reasonableness it is at liberty to act with reference to the established usages, customs and traditions of the people, and with a view to the promotion of their comfort, and the preservation of the public peace and good order. Gauged by this standard, we cannot say that a law which authorizes or even requires the separation of the two races in public conveyances is unreasonable or more obnoxious to the Fourteenth Amendment than the acts of Congress requiring separate schools for colored children in the District of Columbia, the constitutionality of which does not seem to have been questioned, or the corresponding acts of state legislatures.

We consider the underlying fallacy of the plaintiff's argument to consist in the assumption that the enforced separation of the two races stamps the colored race with a badge of inferiority. If this be so, it is not by reason of anything found in the act, but solely because the colored race chooses to put that construction upon it. The argument necessarily assumes that if, as has been more than once the case, and is not unlikely to be so again, the colored race should become the dominant power in the state legislature, and should enact a law in precisely similar terms, it would thereby relegate the white race to an inferior position. We imagine that the white race, at least, would not acquiesce in this assumption. The argument also assumes that social prejudices may be overcome by legislation and that equal rights cannot be secured to the Negro except by an enforced commingling of the two races. We cannot accept this proposition. If the two races are to meet upon terms of social equality, it must be the result of natural affinities, a mutual appreciation of each other's merits, and a voluntary consent of individuals. As was said by the Court of Appeals of New York in *People* v. *Gallagher,* 93 N.Y. 438, 448,

"this end can neither be accomplished nor prompted by laws which conflict with the general sentiment of the community upon whom they are designed to operate.

"When the government, therefore, has secured to each of its citizens equal rights before the law and equal opportunities for improvement and progress, it has accomplished the end for which it was organized and performed all of the functions respecting social advantages with which it is endowed."

Legislation.. is powerless to eradicate racial instincts or to abolish distinctions based upon physical differences, and the attempt to do so can only result in accentuating the difficulties of the present situation. If the civil and political rights of both races be equal, one cannot be inferior to the other civilly or politically. If one race be inferior to the other socially, the Constitution of the United States cannot put them upon the same plane. . . .

The judgment of the court below is, therefore, affirmed.

MR. JUSTICE HARLAN, dissenting:

In respect of civil rights, common to all citizens, the Constitution of the United States does not, I think, permit any public authority to know the race of those entitled to be protected in the enjoyment of such rights. Every true man has pride of race, and under appropriate circumstances when the rights of others, his equals before the law, are not to be affected, it is his privilege to express such pride and to take such action based upon it as to him seems proper. But I deny that any legislative body or judicial tribunal may have regard to the race of citizens when the civil rights of those citizens are involved. Indeed, such legislation as that here in question is inconsistent not only with that equality of rights which pertains to citizenship, national and state, but with the personal liberty enjoyed by everyone within the United States. . . .

It was said in argument that the statute of Louisiana does not discriminate against either race but prescribes a rule applicable alike to white and colored citizens. But this argument does not meet the difficulty.

Everyone knows that the statute in question had its origin in the purpose, not so much to exclude white persons from railroad cars occupied by blacks, as to exclude colored people from coaches occupied by or assigned to white persons. Railroad corporations of Louisiana did not make discrimination among whites in the matter of accommodation for travellers. The thing to accomplish was, under the guise of giving equal accommodations for whites and blacks, to compel the latter to keep to themselves while travelling in railroad passenger coaches. No one would be so wanting in candor as to assert the contrary. The fundamental objection, therefore, to the statute is that it interferes with the personal freedom of citizens. . . . If a white man and a black man choose to occupy the same public conveyance on a public highway, it is their right to do so, and no government, proceeding alone on grounds of race, can prevent it without infringing the personal liberty of each. . . .

The white race deems itself to be the dominant race in this country. And so it is, in prestige, in achievements, in education, in wealth, and in power. So, I doubt not, it will continue to be for all time, if it remains true to its great heritage and holds fast to the principles of constitutional liberty. But in the view of the Constitution, in the eye of the law, there is in this country no superior, dominant, ruling class of citizens. There is no caste here. Our Constitution is color-blind and neither knows nor tolerates classes among citizens. In respect of civil rights, all citizens are equal before the law. The humblest is the peer of the most powerful. The law regards man as man and takes no account of his surroundings or of his color when his civil rights as guaranteed by the supreme law of the land are involved. . . .

The arbitrary separation of citizens, on the basis of race, while they are on a public highway, is a badge of servitude wholly inconsistent with the civil freedom and the equality before the law established by the Constitution. It cannot be justified upon any legal grounds.

If evils will result from the commingling of the two races upon public highways established for the benefit of all, they will be infinitely less than those that will surely come from state legislation regulating the enjoyment of civil rights upon the basis of race. We boast of the freedom enjoyed by our people above all other peoples. But it is difficult to reconcile that boast with a state of the law which, practically, puts the brand of servitude and degradation upon a large class of our fellow citizens, our equals before the law. The thin disguise of "equal" accommodations for passengers in railroad coaches will not mislead anyone, nor atone for the wrong this day done. . . .

BROWN v. *TOPEKA*

347 U.S. 483 (1954)

Appeal from the United States District Court for the District of Kansas.

MR. CHIEF JUSTICE WARREN delivered the opinion of the Court:

These cases come to us from the States of Kansas, South Carolina, Virginia, and Delaware. They are premised on different facts and different local conditions, but a common legal question justifies their consideration together in this consolidated opinion.

In each of the cases, minors of the Negro race, through their legal representatives, seek the aid of the courts in obtaining admission to the public schools of their community on a nonsegregated basis. In each instance, they had been denied admission to schools attended by white children under laws requiring or permitting segregation according to race. This segregation was alleged to deprive the plaintiffs of the equal protection of the laws under the Fourteenth Amendment. In each of the cases other than the Delaware case, a three-judge federal district court denied relief to the plaintiffs on the so-called "separate but equal" doctrine announced by this Court in *Plessy* v. *Ferguson*, 163 U.S. 537. Under that doctrine, equality of treatment is accorded when the races are provided substantially equal facilities, even though these facilities be separate. In the Delaware case, the Supreme Court of Delaware adhered to that doctrine, but ordered that the plaintiffs be admitted to the white schools because of their superiority to the Negro schools.

The plaintiffs contend that segregated public schools are not "equal" and cannot be made "equal," and that hence they are deprived of the equal protection of the laws. Because of the obvious importance of the question presented, the Court took jurisdiction. Argument was heard in the 1952 Term, and reargument was heard this Term on certain questions propounded by the Court.

Reargument was largely devoted to the circumstances surrounding the adoption of the Fourteenth Amendment in 1868. It covered exhaustively consideration of the Amendment in Congress, ratification by the states, then existing practices in racial segregation, and the views of proponents and opponents of the Amendment. This discussion and our own investigation convince us that, although these sources cast some light, it is not enough to resolve the problem with which we are faced. At best, they are inconclusive. The most avid proponents of the post-War Amendments undoubtedly intended them to remove all legal distinctions among "all persons born or naturalized in the United States." Their opponents, just as certainly, were antagonistic to both the letter and the spirit of the Amendments and wished them to have the most limited effect. What others in Congress and the state legislatures had in mind cannot be determined with any degree of certainty.

An additional reason for the inconclusive nature of the Amendment's history, with respect to segregated schools, is the status of public education at that time. In the South, the movement toward free common schools, supported by general taxation, had not yet taken hold. Education of white children was largely in the hands of private groups. Education of Negroes was almost nonexistent, and practically all of the race were illiterate. In fact, any education of Negroes was forbidden by law in some states. Today, in contrast, many Negroes have achieved outstanding success in the arts and sciences as well as in the business and professional world. It is true that public education had already advanced further in the North, but the effect of the Amendment on Northern States was generally ignored in the congressional debates. Even in the North, the conditions of public education did not approximate those existing today. The curriculum was usually rudimentary; ungraded schools were common in rural areas; the school term was but three months a year in many states; and compulsory school attendance was virtually unknown. As a consequence, it is not surprising that there should be so little in the history of the Fourteenth Amendment relating to its intended effect on public education.

In the first cases in this Court construing the Fourteenth Amendment, decided shortly after its adoption, the Court interpreted it as proscribing all state-imposed discriminations against the Negro race. The doctrine of "separate but equal" did not make its appearance in this Court until 1896 in the case of *Plessy* v. *Ferguson, supra,* involving not education but transportation. American courts have since labored with the doctrine for over half a century. In this Court, there have been six cases involving the "separate but equal" doctrine in the field of public education. In *Cumming* v. *County Board of Education*, 175 U.S. 528, and *Gong Lum* v. *Rice,*

275 U.S. 78, the validity of the doctrine itself was not challenged. In more recent cases, all on the graduate school level, inequality was found in that specific benefits enjoyed by white students were denied to Negro students of the same educational qualifications. *Missouri ex rel. Gaines* v. *Canada,* 305 U.S. 337; *Sipuel* v. *Oklahoma,* 332 U.S. 631; *Sweatt* v. *Painter,* 339 U.S. 629; *McLaurin* v. *Oklahoma State Regents,* 339 U.S. 637. In none of these cases was it necessary to reexamine the doctrine to grant relief to the Negro plaintiff. And in *Sweatt* v. *Painter, supra,* the Court expressly reserved decision on the question whether *Plessy* v. *Ferguson* should be held inapplicable to public education.

In the instant cases, that question is directly presented. Here, unlike *Sweatt* v. *Painter,* there are findings below that the Negro and white schools involved have been equalized, or are being equalized, with respect to buildings, curricula, qualifications and salaries of teachers, and other "tangible" factors. Our decision, therefore, cannot turn on merely a comparison of these tangible factors in the Negro and white schools involved in each of the cases. We must look instead to the effect of segregation itself on public education.

In approaching this problem, we cannot turn the clock back to 1868 when the Amendment was adopted, or even to 1896 when *Plessy* v. *Ferguson* was written. We must consider public education in the light of its full development and its present place in American life throughout the Nation. Only in this way can it be determined if segregation in public schools deprives these plaintiffs of the equal protection of the laws.

Today, education is perhaps the most important function of state and local governments. Compulsory school attendance laws and the great expenditures for education both demonstrate our recognition of the importance of education to our democratic society. It is required in the performance of our most basic public responsibilities, even service in the armed forces. It is the very foundation of good citizenship. Today it is a principal instrument in awakening the child to cultural values, in preparing him for later professional training, and in helping him to adjust normally to his environment. In these days, it is doubtful that any child may reasonably be expected to succeed in life if he is denied the opportunity of an education. Such an opportunity, where the state has undertaken to provide it, is a right which must be made available to all on equal terms.

We come then to the question presented: Does segregation of children in public schools solely on the basis of race, even though the physical facilities and other "tangible" factors may be equal, deprive the children of the minority group of equal educational opportunities? We believe that it does.

In *Sweatt* v. *Painter, supra,* in finding that a segregated law school for Negroes could not provide them equal educational opportunities, this Court relied in large part on "those qualities which are incapable of objective measurement but which make for greatness in a law school." In *McLaurin* v. *Oklahoma State Regents, supra,* the Court, in requiring that a Negro admitted to a white graduate school be treated like all other students, again resorted to intangible considerations: ". . . his ability to study, to engage in discussions and exchange views with other students, and, in general, to learn his profession." Such considerations apply with added force to children in grade and high schools. To separate them from others of similar age and qualifications solely because of their race generates a feeling of inferiority as to their status in the community that may affect their hearts and minds in a way unlikely ever to be undone. The effect of this separation on their educational opportunities was well stated by a finding in the Kansas case by a court which nevertheless felt compelled to rule against the Negro plaintiffs:

"Segregation of white and colored children in public schools has a detrimental effect upon the colored children. The impact is greater when it has the sanction of the law; for the policy of separating the races is usually interpreted as denoting the inferiority of the Negro group. A sense of inferiority affects the motivation of a child to learn. Segregation with the sanction of law, therefore, has a tendency to retard the educational and mental development of Negro children and to deprive them of some of the benefits they would receive in a racially integrated school system."

Whatever may have been the extent of psychological knowledge at the time of *Plessy* v. *Ferguson,* this finding is amply supported by modern authority. Any language in *Plessy* v. *Ferguson* contrary to this finding is rejected.

We conclude that in the field of public education the doctrine of "separate but equal" has no place. Separate educational facilities are inherently unequal. Therefore, we hold that the plaintiffs and others similarly situated for whom the actions have been brought are, by reason of the segregation complained of, deprived of the equal protection of the laws guaranteed by the Fourteenth Amendment. This disposition makes unnecessary any discussion whether such segregation also violates the due process clause of the Fourteenth Amendment.

Because these are class actions, because of the wide applicability of this decision, and because of the great variety of local conditions, the formulation of decrees in these cases presents problems of considerable complexity. On reargument, the consideration of appropriate relief was necessarily subordinated to the primary question —the constitutionality of segregation in public education. We have now announced that such segregation is a denial of the equal protection of the laws. In order that we may have the full assistance of the parties in formulating decrees, the cases will be restored to the docket, and the parties are requested to present further argument on Questions 4 and 5 previously propounded by the Court for the reargument this Term. The Attorney General of the United States is again invited to participate. The Attorneys General of the states requiring or permitting segregation in public education will also be permitted to appear as amici curiae upon request to do so by September 15, 1954, and submission of briefs by October 1, 1954.

It is so ordered.

NOTE: In *Bolling* v. *Sharp,* 347 U.S. 497 (1954), relating to segregation in District of Columbia public schools, the Court observed that:

The Fifth Amendment, which is applicable to the District of Columbia, does not contain an equal protection clause as does the Fourteenth Amendment which applies only to the states. But the concepts of equal protection and due process, both stemming from the American ideal of fairness, are not mutually exclusive. The "equal protection of the laws" is a more explicit safeguard of prohibited unfairness than "due process of law," and, therefore, we do not imply that the two are always interchangeable phrases. But, as this Court has recognized, discrimination may be so unjustifiable as to be violative of due process.

BROWN v. TOPEKA

349 U.S. 294 (1955) [Second Decision]

MR. CHIEF JUSTICE WARREN delivered the opinion of the Court:

These cases were decided on May 17, 1954. The opinions of that date, declaring the fundamental principle that racial discrimination in public education is unconstitutional, are incorporated herein by reference. All provisions of federal, state, or local law requiring or permitting such discrimination must yield to this principle. There remains for consideration the manner in which relief is to be accorded.

Because these cases arose under different local conditions and their disposition will involve a variety of local problems, we requested further argument on the question of relief. In view of the nation-wide importance of the decision, we invited the Attorney General of the United States and the Attorneys General of all states requiring or permitting racial discrimination in public education to present their views on that question. The parties, the United States, and the States of Florida, North Carolina, Arkansas, Oklahoma, Maryland, and Texas filed briefs and participated in the oral argument.

These presentations were informative and helpful to the Court in its consideration of the complexities arising from the transition to a system of public education freed of racial discrimination. The presentations also demonstrated that substantial steps to eliminate racial discrimination in public schools have already been taken, not only in some of the communities in which these cases arose, but in some of the states appearing as amici curiae, and in other states as well. Substantial progress has been made in the District of Columbia and in the communities in Kansas and Delaware involved in this litigation. The defendants in the cases coming to us from South Carolina and Virginia are awaiting the decision of this Court concerning relief.

Full implementation of these constitutional principles may require solution of varied local school problems. School authorities have the primary responsibility for elucidating, assessing, and solving these problems; courts will have to consider whether the action of school authorities constitutes good faith implementation of the governing constitutional principles. Because of their proximity to local conditions and the possible need for further hearings, the courts which originally heard these cases can best perform this judicial appraisal. Accordingly, we believe it appropriate to remand the cases to those courts.

In fashioning and effectuating the decrees, the courts will be guided by equitable principles. Traditionally, equity has been characterized by a practical flexibility in shaping its remedies and by a facility for adjusting and reconciling public and private needs. These cases call for the exercise of these traditional attributes of equity power. At stake is the personal interest of the plaintiffs in admission to public schools as soon as practicable on a nondiscriminatory basis. To effectuate this interest may call for elimination of a variety of obstacles in making the transition to school systems operated in accordance with the constitutional principles set forth in our May 17, 1954, decision. Courts of equity may properly take into account the public interest in the elimination of such obstacles in a systematic and effective manner. But it should go without saying that the vitality of these constitutional principles cannot be allowed to yield simply because of disagreement with them.

While giving weight to these public and private considerations, the courts will require that the defendants make a prompt and reasonable start toward full compliance with our May 17, 1954, ruling. Once such a start has been made, the courts may find that additional time is necessary to carry out the ruling in an effective manner. The burden rests upon the defendants to establish that such time is necessary in the public interest and is consistent with good faith compliance at the earliest practicable date. To that end, the courts may consider problems related to administration, arising from the physical condition of the school plant, the school transportation system, personnel, revision of school districts and attendance areas into compact units to achieve a system of determining admission to the public schools on a nonracial basis, and revision of local laws and regulations which may be necessary in solving the foregoing problems. They will also consider the adequacy of any plans the defendants may propose to meet these problems and to effectuate a transition to a racially non-discriminatory school system. During this period of transition, the courts will retain jurisdiction of these cases.

The judgments below, except that in the *Delaware* case, are accordingly reversed and remanded to the District Courts to take such proceedings and enter such orders and decrees consistent with this opinion as are necessary and proper to admit to public schools on a racially nondiscriminatory basis with all deliberate speed the parties to these cases. The judgment in the *Delaware* case—ordering the immediate admission of the plaintiffs to schools previously attended only by white children—is affirmed on the basis of the principles stated in our May 17, 1954, opinion, but the case is remanded to the Supreme Court of Delaware for such further proceedings as that court may deem necessary in light of this opinion.

It is so ordered.

COOPER v. AARON
358 U.S. 1 (1958)

Opinion of the Court by THE CHIEF JUSTICE, MR. JUSTICE BLACK, MR. JUSTICE FRANKFURTER, MR. JUSTICE DOUGLAS, MR. JUSTICE BURTON, MR. JUSTICE CLARK, MR. JUSTICE HARLAN, MR. JUSTICE BRENNAN and MR. JUSTICE WHITTAKER.

As this case reaches us it raises questions of the highest importance to the maintenance of our federal system of government. It necessarily involves a claim by the Governor and Legislature of a State that there is no duty on state officials to obey federal court orders resting on this Court's considered interpretation of the United States Constitution. Specifically it involves actions by the Governor and Legislature of Arkansas upon the premise that they are not bound by our holding in *Brown* v. *Board of Education*, 347 U.S. 483. That holding was that the Fourteenth Amendment forbids States to use their governmental powers to bar children on racial grounds from attending schools where there is state participation through any arrangement, management, funds or property. We are urged to uphold a suspension of the Little Rock School Board's plan to do away with segregated public schools in Little Rock until state laws and efforts to upset and nullify our holding in *Brown* v. *Board of Education* have been further challenged and tested in the courts. We reject these contentions.

The case was argued before us on September 11, 1958. On the following day we unanimously affirmed the judgment of the Court of Appeals for the Eighth Circuit, 257 F.2d 33, which had reversed a judgment of the District Court for the Eastern District of Arkansas, 163 F. Supp. 13. The District Court had granted the application to the petitioners, the Little Rock School Board and School Superintendent, to suspend for two and one-half years the operation of the School Board's court-approved desegregation program. In order that the School Board might know, without doubt, its duty in this regard before the opening of school, which had been set for the following Monday, September 15, 1958, we immediately issued the judgment, reserving the expression of our supporting views to a later date. This opinion of all of the members of the Court embodies those views. . . .

[Here the Court reviewed in detail the school board's efforts to desegregate the Little Rock High School in the face of interference by state officers including the governor who had called out the state militia to prevent Negro students from entering the school.]

In affirming the judgment of the Court of Appeals which reversed the District Court we have accepted without reservation the position of the School Board, the Superintendent of Schools, and their counsel that they displayed entire good faith in the conduct of these proceedings and in dealing with the unfortunate and distressing sequence of events which has been outlined. We likewise have accepted the findings of the District Court as to the conditions at Central High School during the 1957–1958 school year, and also the findings that the educational progress of all the students, white and colored, of that school has suffered and will continue to suffer if the conditions which prevailed last year are permitted to continue.

The significance of these findings, however, is to be considered in the light of the fact, indisputably revealed by the record before us, that the conditions they depict are directly traceable to the actions of legislators and executive officials of the State of Arkansas, taken in their official capacities, which reflect their own determination to resist this Court's decision in the Brown case and which have brought about violent resistance to that decision in Arkansas. In its petition for certiorari filed in this Court, the School Board itself describes the situation in this language: "The legislative, executive, and judicial departments of the state government opposed the desegregation of Little Rock schools by enacting laws, calling out troops, making statements villifying federal law and federal courts, and failing to utilize state law enforcement agencies and judicial processes to maintain public peace."

One may well sympathize with the position of the Board in the face of the frustrating conditions which have confronted it, but, regardless of the Board's good faith, the actions of the other state agencies responsible for those conditions compel us to reject the Board's legal position. Had Central High School been under the direct management of the State itself, it could hardly be suggested that those immediately in charge of the school should be heard to assert their own good faith as a legal excuse for delay in implementing the constitutional rights of these respondents, when vindication of those rights was rendered difficult or impossible by the actions of other state officials. The situation here is in no different posture because the members of the School Board and the Superintendent of Schools are local officials; from the point of view of the Fourteenth Amendment, they stand in this litigation as the agents of the State.

The constitutional rights of respondents are not to be sacrificed or yielded to the violence and disorder which have followed upon the actions of the Governor and Legislature. As this Court said some 41 years ago in a unanimous opinion in a case involving another aspect of racial segregation: "It is urged that this proposed segregation will promote the public peace by preventing race conflicts. Desirable as this is, and important as is the preservation of the public peace, this aim cannot be accomplished by laws or ordinances which deny rights created or protected by the Federal Constitution." *Buchanan* v. *Warley*, 245 U.S. 60, 81. Thus law and order are not here to be preserved by depriving the Negro children of their constitutional rights. The record before us clearly establishes that the growth of the Board's difficulties to a magnitude beyond its unaided power to control is the product of state action. Those difficulties, as counsel for the Board forthrightly conceded on the oral argument in this Court, can also be brought under control by state action.

The controlling legal principles are plain. The command of the Fourteenth Amendment is that no "State" shall deny to any person within its jurisdiction the equal protection of the laws. "A State acts by its legislative, its executive, or its judicial authorities. It can act in no other way. The constitutional provision, therefore, must mean that no agency of the State, or of the officers or agents by whom its powers are exerted, shall deny to any person within its jurisdiction the equal protection of the laws. Whoever, by virtue of public position under a State government . . . denies or takes away the equal protection of the laws, violates the constitutional inhibition; and as he acts in the name and for the State, and is clothed with the State's power, his act is that of the State. This must be so, or the constitutional prohibition has no meaning." *Ex parte Virginia*, 100 U.S. 339, 347. Thus the prohibitions of the Fourteenth Amendment extend to all action of the State denying equal protection of the laws; whatever the agency of the State taking action, see *Virginia* v. *Rives*, 100 U.S. 313; *Pennsylvania* v. *Board of Directors of City Trusts of Philadelphia*, 353 U.S. 230; *Shelley* v. *Kraemer*, 334 U.S. 1; or whatever the guise in which it is taken, see *Derrington* v. *Plummer*, 240 F.2d 922; *Department of Conservation and Development* v. *Tate*, 231 F.2d 615. In short, the constitutional rights of children not to be discriminated against in school admission on grounds of race or color declared by this Court in the Brown case can neither be nullified openly and directly by state legislators or state executives or judicial officers, nor nullified indirectly by them through evasive schemes for segregation whether attempted "ingeniously or ingenuously." *Smith* v. *Texas*, 311 U.S. 128, 132.

What has been said, in the light of the facts developed, is enough to dispose of the case. However, we should answer the premise of the actions of the Governor and Legislature that they are not bound by our holding in the Brown case. It is necessary only to recall some basic constitutional propositions which are settled doctrine.

Article VI of the Constitution makes the Constitution the "supreme Law of the Land." In 1803, Chief Justice Marshall speaking for a unanimous Court, referring to the Constitution as "the fundamental and paramount law of the nation," declared in the notable case of *Marbury* v. *Madison*, 1 Cranch 137, 177, that "It is emphatically the province and duty of the judicial department to say what the law is." This decision declared the basic principle that the federal judiciary is supreme in the exposition of the law of the Constitution, and that principle has ever since been respected by this Court and the Country as a permanent and indispensable feature of our constitutional system. It follows that the interpretation of the Fourteenth Amendment enunciated by this Court in the Brown case is the supreme law of the land, and Art. VI of the Constitution makes it of binding effect on the States "any Thing in the Constitution or Laws of any State to the Contrary notwithstanding." Every state legislator and executive and judicial officer is solemnly committed by oath taken pursuant to Art. VI, p. 3, "to support this Constitution." Chief Justice Taney, speaking for a unanimous Court in 1859, said that this requirement reflected the framers' "anxiety to preserve it [the Constitution] in full force, in all its powers, and to guard against resistance to or evasion of its authority, on the part of a State. . . ." *Ableman* v. *Booth*, 21 How. 506, 524.

No state legislator or executive or judicial officer can war against the Constitution without violating his undertaking to support it. Chief Justice Marshall spoke for a unanimous Court in saying that: "If the legislatures of the several states may, at will, annul the judgments of the courts of the United States, and destroy the rights acquired under those judgments, the constitution itself becomes a solemn mockery. . . ." *United States* v. *Peters*, 5 Cranch 115, 136. A Governor who asserts a power to nullify a federal court order is similarly restrained. If he had such power, said Chief Justice Hughes, in 1932, also for a unanimous Court, "it is manifest that the fiat of a state Governor, and not the Constitution of the United States, would be the supreme law of the land; that the restrictions of the Federal Constitution upon the exercise of state power would be but impotent phrases. . . ." *Sterling* v. *Constantin*, 287 U.S. 378, 397–398.

It is, of course, quite true that the responsibility for public education is primarily the concern of the States, but it is equally true that such responsibilities, like all other state activity, must be exercised

consistently with federal constitutional requirements as they apply to state action.
The Constitution created a government
dedicated to equal justice under law. The
Fourteenth Amendment embodied and emphasized that ideal. State support of segregated schools through any arrangement,
management, funds, or property cannot be
squared with the Amendment's command
that no State shall deny to any person
within its jurisdiction the equal protection
of the laws. The right of a student not to
be segregated on racial grounds in schools
so maintained is indeed so fundamental
and pervasive that it is embraced in the
concept of due process of law. *Bolling* v.
Sharpe, 347 U.S. 497. The basic decision
in Brown was unanimously reached by this
Court only after the case had been briefed
and twice argued and the issue had been
given the most serious consideration. Since
the first Brown opinion three new Justices
have come to the Court. They are at one
with the Justices still on the Court who
participated in that basic decision as to its
correctness, and that decision is now unanimously reaffirmed. The principles announced in that decision and the obedience
of the States to them, according to the command of the Constitution, are indispensable for the protection of the freedoms
guaranteed by our fundamental charter for
all of us. Our constitutional ideal of equal
justice under law is thus made a living
truth.

FRANKFURTER, J. While unreservedly participating with my brethren in our joint
opinion, I deem it appropriate also to deal

individually with the great issue here at
stake. . . .

We are now asked to hold that the illegal, forcible interference by the State of
Arkansas with the continuance of what the
constitution commands, and the consequences in disorder that it entrained,
should be recognized as justification for
undoing what the School Board had formulated, what the District Court in 1955
had directed to be carried out, and what
was in process of obedience.

No explanation that may be offered in
support of such a request can obscure the
inescapable meaning that law should bow
to force. To yield to such a claim would be
to enthrone official lawlessness, and lawlessness if not checked is the precursor of
anarchy. On the few tragic occasions in the
history of the nation, North and South,
when law was forcibly resisted or systematically evaded, it has signaled the break-
down of constitutional processes of government on which ultimately rest the liberties of all. Violent resistance to law cannot be made a legal reason for its suspension without loosening the fabric of our
society. . . .

Is there not the strongest reason for concluding that to accede to the board's request, on the basis of the circumstances
that gave rise to it, for a suspension of the
board's non-segregation plan, would be but
the beginning of a series of delays calculated to nullify this court's adamant
decisions in the Brown case that the
Constitution precludes compulsory segregation based on color in state-supported
schools? . . .

GOSS v. *BOARD OF EDUCATION*
373 U.S. 683 (1963)

MR. JUSTICE CLARK delivered the opinion
of the Court.

We granted certiorari . . . limited to
the question whether petitioners, Negro
school children seeking desegregation of

the public school systems of Knoxville,
Tennessee . . . and Davidson County, Tennessee, an area adjacent to Nashville . . .
are deprived of rights under the Fourteenth Amendment. The question centers

around . . . transfer provisions incorporated in formal desegregation plans adopted by the respective local school boards pursuant to court orders. . . . Under the overall desegregation plans . . . school districts would be rezoned without reference to race. However, by the terms of the transfer provisions, a student, upon request, would be permitted, solely on the basis of his own race and the racial composition of the school to which he has been assigned by virtue of rezoning, to transfer from such school, where he would be in the racial minority, back to his former segregated school where his race would be in the majority. The appropriate District Courts and the Court of Appeals approved the transfer plans. 301 F.2d 164, 301 F.2d 828. The transfer plans being based solely on racial factors which, under their terms, inevitably lead toward segregation of the students by race, we conclude that they run counter to the admonition of *Brown* v. *Board of Education of Topeka,* 349 U.S. 294, 301 (1955), wherein the District Courts were directed to "consider the adequacy of any plans" proposed by school authorities "to effectuate a . . . racially nondiscriminatory school system." . . . The transfer plans are essentially the same, each containing, in addition to the provisions at issue here, general provisions providing for transfers on a showing of "good cause." The crucial provision, however, present in somewhat the same form in each plan, is exemplified by § 6 of the Knoxville plan:

"6. The following will be regarded as some of the valid conditions to support requests for transfer:

"a. When a white student would otherwise be required to attend a school previously serving colored students only:

"b. When a colored student would otherwise be required to attend a school previously serving white students only:

"c. When a student would otherwise be required to attend a school where the majority of students of that school or in his or her grade are of a different race." . . .

It is readily apparent that the transfer system proposed lends itself to perpetuation of segregation. Indeed, the provisions can work only toward that end. While transfers are available to those who choose to attend school where their race is in the majority, there is no provision whereby a student might transfer upon request to a school in which his race is in a minority, unless he qualifies for a "good cause" transfer. As the Superintendent of Davidson County's schools put it, the effect of the racial transfer plan was "to permit a child [or his parents] to choose segregation outside of his zone but not to choose integration outside of his zone." . . . [I]f the transfer provisions were made available to all students regardless of their race and regardless as well of the racial composition of the school to which he requested transfer we would have an entirely different case. Pupils could then at their option (or that of their parents) choose, entirely free of any imposed racial considerations, to remain in the school of their zone or transfer to another.

Classifications based on race for purposes of transfers between public schools, as here, violate the Equal Protection Clause of the Fourteenth Amendment. As the Court said in *Steele* v. *Louisville & Nashville R. Co.,* 323 U.S. 192, 203, racial classifications are "obviously irrelevant and invidious." . . .

The alleged equality—which we view as only superficial—of enabling each race to transfer from a desegregated to a segregated school does not save the plans. Like arguments were made without success in *Brown, supra,* in support of the separate but equal educational program. Not only is race the factor upon which the transfer plans operate, but also the plans lack a provision whereby a student might with equal facility transfer from a segregated to a desegregated school. The obvious one-way operation of these two factors in combination underscores the purely racial character and purpose of the transfer provisions. . . .

In reaching this result we are not unmindful of the deep-rooted problems involved. Indeed, it was consideration for the multifarious local difficulties and "variety of obstacles" which might arise in this transition that led this Court eight years ago to frame its mandate in Brown in such language as "good faith compliance at the earliest practicable date" and "all deliberate speed." . . . Now, however, eight years after this decree was rendered and over nine years after the first Brown decision, the context in which we must in-terpret and apply this language to plans for desegregation has been significantly altered. . . . The transfer provisions here cannot be deemed to be reasonably de-signed to meet legitimate local problems, and therefore do not meet the requirements of Brown. . . .

Reversed and remanded.

NOTE: the 1963 Report of the United States Commission on Civil Rights (p. 65) indicates that nine years after the first *Brown* case less than one-half of one percent of Negro pupils in the nine southern states were enrolled in integrated schools.

In *Bell* v. *School City of Gary, Indiana,* 84 S. Ct. 1223 (1964), the Court refused to review a lower court decision upholding a neighborhood school system which resulted in *de facto* segregation since Negroes and whites tended to live in separate neighborhoods.

GRIFFIN v. PRINCE EDWARD COUNTY SCHOOL BOARD
84 S. Ct. 1226 (1964)

MR. JUSTICE BLACK delivered the opinion of the Court. . . .

II

In *County School Board of Prince Edward County* v. *Griffin,* 204 Va. 650, 133 S.E.2d 565 (1963), the Supreme Court of Appeals of Virginia upheld as valid under state law the closing of the Prince Edward County public schools, the state and county tuition grants for children who attend private schools, and the county's tax concessions for those who make contributions to private schools. The same opinion also held that each county had "an option to operate or not to operate public schools." 204 Va., at 671, 133 S.E.2d, at 580. We accept this case as a definitive and author-itative holding of Virginia law, binding on us, but we cannot accept the Virginia court's further holding, based largely on the Court of Appeals' opinion in this case, 322 F.2d 332, that closing the county's pub-lic schools under the circumstances of the case did not deny the colored school chil-dren of Prince Edward County equal pro-tection of the laws guaranteed by the Fed-eral Constitution.

Since 1959, all Virginia counties have had the benefits of public schools but one: Prince Edward. However, there is no rule that counties, as counties, must be treated alike; the Equal Protection Clause relates to equal protection of the laws "between persons as such rather than between areas." *Salsburg* v. *Maryland,* 346 U.S. 545, 551 (1954). Indeed, showing that different per-sons are treated differently is not enough, without more, to show a denial of equal protection. *Kotch* v. *Board of River Port Pilot Comm'rs,* 330 U.S. 552, 556 (1947). It is the circumstances of each case which govern. *Skinner* v. *Oklahoma ex rel. Wil-liamson,* 316 U.S. 535, 539–540 (1942).

Virginia law, as here applied, unques-tionably treats the school children of Prince Edward differently from the way it treats the school children of all other Virginia counties. Prince Edward children must go to a private school or none at all; all other Virginia children can go to public schools.

Closing Prince Edward's schools bears more heavily on Negro children in Prince Edward County since white children there have accredited private schools which they can attend, while colored children until very recently have had no available private schools, and even the school they now attend is a temporary expedient. Apart from this expedient, the result is that Prince Edward County school children, if they go to school in their own county, must go to racially segregated schools which, although designated as private, are beneficiaries of county and state support.

A State, of course, has a wide discretion in deciding whether laws shall operate statewide or shall operate only in certain counties, the legislature "having in mind the needs and desires of each." *Salsburg* v. *Maryland, supra*, 346 U.S., at 552, 74 S. Ct., at 284. A State may wish to suggest, as Maryland did in Salsburg, that there are reasons why one county ought not to be treated like another. 346 U.S., at 553–554. But the record in the present case could not be clearer that Prince Edward's public schools were closed and private schools operated in their place with state and county assistance, for one reason, and one reason only: to ensure, through measures taken by the county and the State, that white and colored children in Prince Edward County would not, under any circumstances, go to the same school. Whatever nonracial grounds might support a State's allowing a county to abandon public schools, the object must be a constitutional one, and grounds of race and opposition to desegregation do not qualify as constitutional.

In *Hall* v. *St. Helena Parish School Board*, 197 F.Supp. 649 (D.C.E.D.La.1961), a three-judge District Court invalidated a Louisiana statute which provided "a means by which public schools under desegregation orders may be changed to 'private' schools operated in the same way, in the same buildings, with the same furnishings, with the same money, and under the same supervision as the public schools." Id., at 651. In addition, that statute also provided

that where the public schools were "closed," the school board was "charged with responsibility for furnishing free lunches, transportation, and grants-in-aid to the children attending the 'private' schools." Ibid. We affirmed the District Court's judgment invalidating the Louisiana statute as a denial of equal protection. 368 U.S. 515 (1962). While the Louisiana plan and the Virginia plan worked in different ways, it is plain that both were created to accomplish the same thing: the perpetuation of racial segregation by closing public schools and operating only segregated schools supported directly or indirectly by state or county funds. See *Cooper* v. *Aaron*, 358 U.S. 1, 17 (1958). Either plan works to deny colored students equal protection of the laws. Accordingly, we agree with the District Court that closing the Prince Edward schools and meanwhile contributing to the support of the private segregated white schools that took their place denied petitioners the equal protection of the laws.

III

We come now to the question of the kind of decree necessary and appropriate to put an end to the racial discrimination practiced against these petitioners under authority of the Virginia laws. That relief needs to be quick and effective. The party defendants are the Board of Supervisors, School Board, Treasurer, and Division Superintendent of Schools of Prince Edward County, and the State Board of Education and the State Superintendent of Education. All of these have duties which relate directly or indirectly to the financing, supervision, or operation of the schools in Prince Edward County. The Board of Supervisors has the special responsibility to levy local taxes to operate public schools or to aid children attending the private schools now functioning there for white children. The District Court enjoined the county officials from paying county tuition grants or giving tax exemptions and from processing applications for state tuition grants so long as the county's public schools remained closed. We have no doubt of the power of the court to give this relief to enforce the discontinuance of the county's racially discriminatory practices. It has long been established that actions against a county can be maintained in United States courts in order to vindicate federally guaranteed rights. E.g., *Lincoln County* v. *Luning*, 133 U.S. 529 (1890); *Kennecott Copper Corp.* v. *State Tax Comm'n*, 327 U.S. 573, 579 (1946). The injunction against paying tuition grants and giving tax credits while public schools remain closed is appropriate and necessary since those grants and tax credits have been essential parts of the county's program, successful thus far, to deprive petitioners of the same advantages of a public school education enjoyed by children in every other part of Virginia. For the same reasons the District Court, may if necessary to prevent further racial discrimination, require the Supervisors to exercise the power that is theirs to levy taxes to raise funds adequate to reopen, operate, and maintain without racial discrimination a public school system in Prince Edward County like that operated in other counties in Virginia.

The District Court held that "the public schools of Prince Edward County may not be closed to avoid the effect of the law of the land as interpreted by the Supreme Court, while the Commonwealth of Virginia permits other public schools to remain open at the expense of the taxpayers." *Allen* v. *County School Board of Prince Edward County*, 207 F. Supp. 349, 355 (D.C.E.D. Va. 1962). At the same time the court gave notice that it would later consider an order to accomplish this purpose if the public schools were not reopened by September 7, 1962. That day has long passed, and the schools are still closed. On remand, therefore, the court may find it necessary to consider further such an order. An order of this kind is within the court's power if required to assure these petitioners that their constitutional rights will no longer be denied them. The time for mere "deliberate speed" has run out, and that phrase can no longer justify denying these Prince Edward County school children their constitutional rights to an education equal to that afforded by the public schools in the other parts of Virginia.

The judgment of the Court of Appeals is reversed, the judgment of the District Court is affirmed, and the cause is remanded to the District Court with directions to enter a decree which will guarantee that these petitioners will get the kind of education that is given in the State's public schools. And, if it becomes necessary to add new parties to accomplish this end, the District Court is free to do so. It is so ordered.

Judgment of Court of Appeals reversed, judgment of the District Court affirmed and cause remanded with directions.

MR. JUSTICE CLARK and MR. JUSTICE HARLAN, disagree with the holding that the federal courts are empowered to order the reopening of the public schools in Prince Edward County, but otherwise join in the Court's opinion.

NOTE: In *Watson* v. *City of Memphis*, 373 U.S. 526 (1963), a unanimous Court held that Memphis could not rely on the second *Brown* case to justify further delay in fully desegregating its public recreational facilities: "Given the extended time which has elapsed, it is far from clear that the mandate of the second *Brown* decision requiring that desegregation proceed with 'all deliberate speed' would today be fully satisfied by types of plans or programs for desegregation . . . which eight years ago might have been deemed sufficient. *Brown* never contemplated that the concept of 'deliberate speed' would countenance indefinite delay in elimination of racial barriers in schools, let alone other public facilities not involving the same physical problems or comparable conditions."

McLaughlin v. *Florida,* 85 S. Ct. 283 (1964), found "invidious discrimination" in a state statute prohibiting a white person and a Negro who are not married to each other from habitually occupying the same room in the nighttime. There was no corresponding prohibition with respect to couples of the same race.

A Louisiana statute required that in all elections the nomination papers and ballots shall designate the race of candidates. In *Anderson* v. *Martin* 84 S. Ct. 454 (1964), this was held invalid as a discrimination against Negroes.

Johnson v. *Virginia,* 373 U.S. 61 (1963), held invalid a contempt of court conviction of a Negro who refused to comply with segregated seating requirements in a courtroom: "Such a conviction cannot stand, for it is no longer open to question that a State may not constitutionally require segregation of public facilities."

Hamilton v. *Alabama,* 84 S. Ct. 982 (1964), reversed a contempt conviction of a Negro witness who refused in a trial court to answer questions for the reason indicated in the following exchange:

Q. Mary, I believe you were arrested. Who were you arrested by?
A. My name is Miss Hamilton. Please address me correctly.
Q. Who were you arrested by, Mary?
A. I will not answer until I am addressed correctly.

3. WHOSE DISCRIMINATION IS FORBIDDEN?

It is noteworthy that the old regime never questioned the *Strauder* holding which invalidates the conviction of a Negro by a court in which Negroes have been barred as potential jurymen. (Of course, it does not follow that every defendant is entitled to have members of his own race on the jury which tries him. *Cassell* v. *Texas,* 339 U.S. 282 [1950]. The point is simply that purposeful exclusion is invalid.) Moreover the old regime did strike down a law separating people on a racial basis for residential purposes. It is noteworthy that this was done not in the name of decency to the Negro, but to protect the property rights of a white owner who had contracted in violation of the zoning law to sell to a Negro. *Buchanan* v. *Warley,* 245 U.S. 60 (1917). Even this backhanded blow at Jim Crowism, however, was undermined when the Court permitted its circumvention by private restrictive covenants. *Corrigan* v. *Buckley,* 271 U.S. 323 (1926).

This brings us to a basic element in the Fourteenth and Fifteenth Amendments. Both literally prohibit only state—not private or individual—discriminatory action. Even the *Strauder* Court recognized this. Thus in the *Civil Rights Cases,* it was held that the Fourteenth Amendment did not outlaw discrimination by privately owned inns, theaters, and common carriers. This became the foundation for the evasion of *Buchanan* v. *Warley* by private covenant—notwithstanding the fact that the ultimate effectiveness of such restrictive agreements depends upon governmental (judicial) enforcement. Similarly the notion that a political party primary is a private affair permitted effective evasion of the Fifteenth Amendment's explicit guarantee of the right to vote—for in one-party states the winner in the primary is in effect elected. To keep Negroes from voting in the primary under such circumstances is to deprive them of any choice in the selection of elected officials. But, of course, the primary is an integral part of the state's electoral process! On this note of realism the new Court invalidated the white primary, the rise and fall of which are traced in *Rice* v. *Elmore*. It is also outlawed judicial, or governmental, enforcement of restrictive covenants. *Shelley* v. *Kraemer*. Finally, it has recognized that the Fourteenth Amendment applies to state officials who in the conduct of their duties, i.e., "under color of [state] law," mistreat a state prisoner, even though such "state action" is unauthorized, indeed forbidden, by state law. *Screws* v. *United States*. This and the *Shelley* case may be the first faint gleam of a general principle that failure of a state to bar at least some forms of private action—e.g., mob violence—constitutes "state action" within the meaning of the Fourteenth and Fifteenth Amendments.

Is the Fourteenth Amendment unusual in that it deals only with the powers of, and restrictions upon, government? Do you find any constitutional provisions which impose restrictions upon private persons? See Private Restraints on Utterance, Part Four, IV, above.

CIVIL RIGHTS CASES

109 U.S. 3 (1883)

These five cases tested the validity of the Civil Rights Act of 1875, which prohibited racial discrimination in inns, theaters, public conveyances, and similar private enterprises. Congress had passed the measure in view of the power given it in the final sections of the Thirteenth and the Fourteenth Amendments.

MR. JUSTICE BRADLEY delivered the opinion of the court. . . .

Has congress constitutional power to make such a law? Of course, no one will contend that the power to pass it was contained in the Constitution before the adoption of the last three amendments. The power is sought, first, in the Fourteenth Amendment, and the views and arguments of distinguished senators, advanced while the law was under consideration, claiming authority to pass it by virtue of that amendment, are the principal arguments adduced in favor of the power. We have carefully considered those arguments, as was due to the eminent ability of those who put them forward, and have felt, in all its force, the weight of authority which always invests a law that congress deems itself competent to pass. But the responsibility of an independent judgment is now thrown upon this court; and we are bound to exercise it according to the best lights we have.

The first section of the Fourteenth Amendment (which is the one relied on), after declaring who shall be citizens of the United States, and of the several States, is prohibitory in its character, and prohibitory upon the States. It delares that:

"No State shall make or enforce any law which shall abridge the privileges or immunities of citizens of the United States; nor shall any State deprive any person of life, liberty, or property without due process of law; nor deny to any person within its jurisdiction the equal protection of the laws."

It is State action of a particular character that is prohibited. Individual invasion of individual rights is not the subject-matter of the amendment. It has a deeper and broader scope. It nullifies and makes void all State legislation, and State action of every kind, which impairs the privileges and immunities of citizens of the United States, or which injures them in life, liberty or property without due process of law, or which denies to any of them the equal protection of the laws. It not only does this, but, in order that the national will, thus declared, may not be a mere *brutum fulmen*, the last section of the amendment invests Congress with power to enforce it by appropriate legislation. To enforce what? To enforce the prohibition. To adopt appropriate legislation for correcting the effects of such prohibited State laws and State acts, and thus to render them effectually null, void, and innocuous. This is the legislative power conferred upon Congress, and this is the whole of it. It does not invest Congress with power to legislate upon subjects which are within the domain of State legislation; but to provide modes of relief against State legislation, or State action, of the kind referred to. It does not authorize Congress to create a code of municipal law for the regulation of private rights; but to provide modes of redress against the operation of State laws, and the action of State officers executive or judicial, when these are subversive of the fundamental rights specified in the amendment. Positive rights and privileges are undoubtedly secured by the Fourteenth Amendment; but they are secured by way of prohibition against State laws and State proceedings affecting those rights and privileges, and by power given to Congress to legislate for the purpose of carrying such prohibition into effect: and such legislation must necessarily be predicated upon such supposed State laws or State proceedings, and be directed to the correction of their operation and effect. . . .

. . . Until some State law has been passed, or some State action through its officers or agents has been taken, adverse to the rights of citizens sought to be protected by the Fourteenth Amendment, no legislation of the United States under said amendment nor any proceeding under such legislation, can be called into activity: for the prohibitions of the amendment are against State laws and acts done under State authority. Of course, legislation may, and should be, provided in advance to meet the exigency when it arises; but it should be adapted to the mischief and wrong which the amendment was intended to provide against; and that is, State laws, or State action of some kind, adverse to the rights of the citizen secured by the amendment. Such legislation cannot properly cover the whole domain of rights appertaining to life, liberty and property, defining them and providing for their vindication. That would be to establish a code of municipal law regulative of all private rights between man and man in society. It would be to make Congress take the place of the State legislatures and to supersede them. It is absurd to affirm that, because the rights of life, liberty and property (which include all civil rights that men have), are by the amendment sought to be protected against invasion on the part of the State without due process of law, Congress may therefore provide due process of law for their vindication in every case; and that, because the denial by a State to any persons, of the equal protection of the laws, is prohibited by the amendment, therefore Congress may establish laws for their equal protection. In fine, the legislation which Congress is authorized to adopt in this behalf is not general legislation upon the rights of the citizen, but corrective legislation, that is, such as may be necessary and proper for counteracting such laws as the States may adopt or enforce, and which, by the amendment, they are prohibited from making or enforcing, or such acts and proceedings as the States may commit or take, and which, by the amendment, they are prohibited from committing or taking. It is not necessary for us to state, if we could, what legislation would be proper for Congress to adopt. It is sufficient for us to examine whether the law in question is of that character.

An inspection of the law shows that it makes no reference whatever to any supposed or apprehended violation of the Fourteenth Amendment on the part of the

States. It is not predicated on any such view. It proceeds *ex directo* to declare that certain acts committed by individuals shall be deemed offenses, and shall be prosecuted and punished by proceedings in the courts of the United States. It does not profess to be corrective of any constitutional wrong committed by the States; it does not make its operation to depend upon any such wrong committed. It applies equally to cases arising in States which have the justest laws respecting the personal rights of citizens, and whose authorities are ever ready to enforce such laws, as to those which arise in States that may have violated the prohibition of the amendment. In other words, it steps into the domain of local jurisprudence, and lays down rules for the conduct of individuals in society towards each other, and imposes sanctions for the enforcement of those rules, without referring in any manner to any supposed action of the State or its authorities.

If this legislation is appropriate for enforcing the prohibitions of the amendment, it is difficult to see where it is to stop. Why may not Congress with equal show of authority enact a code of laws for the enforcement and vindication of all rights of life, liberty, and property? If it is supposable that the States may deprive persons of life, liberty, and property without due process of law (and the amendment itself does not suppose this), why should not Congress proceed at once to prescribe due process of law for the protection of every one of these fundamental rights, in every possible case, as well as to prescribe equal privileges in inns, public conveyances, and theatres? The truth is, that the implication of a power to legislate in this manner is based upon the assumption that if the States are forbidden to legislate or act in a particular way on a particular subject, and power is conferred upon Congress to enforce the prohibition, this gives Congress power to legislate generally upon that subject, and not merely power to provide modes of redress against such State legislation or action. The assumption is certainly unsound. It is repugnant to the Tenth Amendment of the Constitution, which declares that powers not delegated to the United States by the Constitution, nor prohibited by it to the States, are reserved to the States respectively or to the people. . . .

In this connection it is proper to state that civil rights, such as are guaranteed by the Constitution against State aggression, cannot be impaired by the wrongful acts of individuals, unsupported by State authority in the shape of laws, customs, or judicial or executive proceedings. The wrongful act of an individual, unsupported by any such authority, is simply a private wrong, or a crime of that individual; an invasion of the rights of the injured party, it is true, whether they affect his person, his property, or his reputation; but if not sanctioned in some way by the State, or not done under State authority, his rights remain in full force, and may presumably be vindicated by resort to the laws of the State for redress. An individual cannot deprive a man of his right to vote, to hold property, to buy and sell, to sue in the courts, or to be a witness or a juror; he may, by force or fraud, interfere with the enjoyment of the right in a particular case; he may commit an assault against the person, or commit murder, or use ruffian violence at the polls, or slander the good name of a fellow-citizen; but, unless protected in these wrongful acts by some shield of State law or State authority, he cannot destroy or injure the right; he will only render himself amenable to satisfaction or punishment; and amenable therefore to the laws of the State where the wrongful acts are committed. Hence, in all those cases where the Constitution seeks to protect the rights of the citizen against discriminative and unjust laws of the State by prohibiting such laws, it is not individual offenses, but abrogation and denial of rights, which it denounces, and for which it clothes the Congress with power to provide a remedy. This abrogation and denial of rights, for which the States alone were or could be responsible, was the great seminal and fundamental wrong which was intended to be remedied. And the remedy to be provided must necessarily be predicated upon that wrong. It must assume that in the cases provided for, the evil or wrong actually committed rests upon some State law or State authority for its excuse and perpetration. . . .

But the power of Congress to adopt direct and primary, as distinguished from corrective legislation, on the subject in hand, is sought, in the second place, from the Thirteenth Amendment, which abolishes slavery. This amendment declares "that neither slavery, nor involuntary servitude, except as a punishment for crime, whereof the party shall have been duly convicted, shall exist within the United States, or any place subject to their jurisdiction;" and it gives Congress power to enforce the amendment by appropriate legislation. . . .

When a man has emerged from slavery, and by the aid of beneficent legislation has shaken off the inseparable concomitants of that state, there must be some stage in the progress of his elevation when he takes the rank of a mere citizen, and ceases to be the special favorite of the laws, and when his rights as a citizen, or a man, are to be protected in the ordinary modes by which other men's rights are protected. There were thousands of free colored people in this country before the abolition of slavery, enjoying all the essential rights of life, liberty and property the same as white citizens; yet no one, at that time, thought that it was any invasion of his personal status as a freeman because he was not admitted to all the privileges enjoyed by white citizens, or because he was subjected to discriminations in the enjoyment of accommodations in inns, public conveyances and places of amusement. Mere discriminations on account of race or color were not regarded as badges of slavery. If, since that time, the enjoyment of equal rights in all these respects has become established by constitutional enactment, it is not by force of the Thirteenth Amendment (which merely abolishes slavery), but by force of the Fourteenth and Fifteenth Amendments. . . .

MR. JUSTICE HARLAN dissenting. . . .

There seems to be no substantial difference between my brethren and myself as to the purpose of Congress; for, they say that the essence of the law is, not to declare broadly that all persons shall be entitled to the full and equal enjoyment of the accommodations, advantages, facilities, and privileges of inns, public conveyances, and theatres; but that such enjoyment shall not be subject to conditions applicable only to citizens of a particular race or color, or who had been in a previous condition of servitude. The effect of the statute, the court says, is, that colored citizens, whether formerly slaves or not, and citizens of other races, shall have the same accommodations and privileges in all inns, public conveyances, and places of amusement as are enjoyed by white persons; and *vice versa*.

The court adjudges, I think erroneously, that Congress is without power, under either the Thirteenth or Fourteenth Amendment, to establish such regulations, and that the first and second sections of the statute are, in all their parts, unconstitutional and void. . . .

Congress, has not, in these matters, entered the domain of State control and supervision. It does not, as I have said, assume to prescribe the general conditions and limitations under which inns, public conveyances, and places of public amusement, shall be conducted or managed. It simply declares, in effect, that since the nation has established universal freedom in this country, for all time, there shall be no discrimination, based merely upon race or color, in respect of the accommodations and advantages of public conveyances, inns, and places of public amusement.

I am of the opinion that such discrimination practised by corporations and individuals in the exercise of their public or quasi-public functions is a badge of servitude the imposition of which Congress may prevent under its power, by appropriate legislation, to enforce the Thirteenth Amendment; and, consequently, without reference to its enlarged power under the Fourteenth Amendment, the act of March

1, 1875, is not, in my judgment, repugnant to the Constitution. . . . The assumption that this amendment [the Fourteenth] consists wholly of prohibitions upon State laws and State proceedings in hostility to its provisions, is unauthorized by its language. The first clause of the first section—"All persons born or naturalized in the United States, and subject to the jurisdiction thereof, are citizens of the United States, and of the State wherein they reside"—is of a distinctly affirmative character. In its application to the colored race, previously liberated, it created and granted, as well citizenship of the United States, as citizenship of the State in which they respectively resided. It introduced all of that race, whose ancestors had been imported and sold as slaves, at once, into the political community known as the "People of the United States." They became, instantly, citizens of the United States, *and* of their respective States. Further, they were brought, by this supreme act of the nation, within the direct operation of that provision of the Constitution which declares that "the citizens of each State shall be entitled to all privileges and immunities of citizens in the several States." Art. 4, § 2.

The citizenship thus acquired, by that race, in virtue of an affirmative grant from the nation, may be protected, not alone by the judicial branch of the government, but by congressional legislation of a primary direct character; this, because the power of Congress is not restricted to the enforcement of prohibitions upon State laws or State action. It is, in terms distinct and positive, to enforce "the *provisions* of *this article*" of amendment; not simply those of a prohibitive character, but the provisions—*all* of the provisions—affirmative and prohibitive, of the amendment. It is, therefore, a grave misconception to suppose that the fifth section of the amendment has reference exclusively to express prohibitions upon State laws or State action. If any right was created by that amendment, the grant of power, through appropriate legislation, to enforce its provisions, authorizes Congress, by means of legislation,

operating throughout the entire Union, to guard, secure, and protect that right. . . .

It is said that any interpretation of the Fourteenth Amendment different from that adopted by the majority of the court, would imply that Congress had authority to enact a municipal code for all the States, covering every matter affecting the life, liberty, and property of the citizens of the several States. Not so. Prior to the adoption of that amendment the constitutions of the several States, without perhaps an exception, secured all *persons* against deprivation of life, liberty, or property, otherwise than by due process of law, and, in some form, recognized the right of all *persons* to the equal protection of the laws. Those rights, therefore, existed before that amendment was proposed or adopted, and were not created by it. If, by reason of that fact, it be assumed that protection in these rights of persons still rests primarily with the States, and that Congress may not interfere except to enforce, by means of corrective legislation, the prohibitions upon State laws or State proceedings inconsistent with those rights, it does not at all follow, that privileges which have been *granted by the nation,* may not be protected by primary legislation upon the part of Congress. The personal rights and immunities recognized in the prohibitive clauses of the amendment were, prior to its adoption, under the protection, primarily, of the States, while rights, created by or derived from the United States, have always been, and, in the nature of things, should always be, primarily, under the protection of the general government. Exemption from race discrimination in respect of the civil rights which are fundamental in *citizenship* in a republican government, is, as we have seen, a new right, created by the nation, with express power in Congress, by legislation, to enforce the constitutional provision from which it is derived. If, in some sense, such race discrimination is, within the letter of the last clause of the first section, a denial of that equal protection of the laws which is secured against State denial to all persons, whether citizens or not, it cannot be possible that a mere prohibition upon such State denial, or a prohibition upon State laws abridging the privileges and immunities of citizens of the United States, takes from the nation the power which it has uniformly exercised of protecting, by direct primary legislation, those privileges and immunities which existed under the Constitution before the adoption of the Fourteenth Amendment, or have been created by that amendment in behalf of those thereby made *citizens* of their respective States. . . .

But the court says that Congress did not, in the act of 1866, assume, under the authority given by the Thirteenth Amendment, to adjust what may be called the social rights of men and races in the community. I agree that government has nothing to do with social, as distinguished from technically legal, rights of individuals. No government ever has brought, or ever can bring, its people into social intercourse against their wishes. Whether one person will permit or maintain social relations with another is a matter with which government has no concern. I agree that if one citizen chooses not to hold social intercourse with another, he is not and cannot be made amenable to the law for his conduct in that regard; for even upon grounds of race, no legal right of a citizen is violated by the refusal of others to maintain merely social relations with him. What I affirm is that no State, nor the officers of any State, nor any corporation or individual wielding power under State authority for the public benefit or the public convenience, can, consistently either with

the freedom established by the fundamental law, or with that equality of civil rights which now belongs to every citizen, discriminate against freemen or citizens, in those rights, because of their race, or because they once labored under the disabilities of slavery imposed upon them as a race. The rights which Congress, by the act of 1875, endeavored to secure and protect are legal, not social rights. The right, for instance, of a colored citizen to use the accommodations of a public highway, upon the same terms as are permitted to white citizens, is no more a social right than his right, under the law, to use the public streets of a city or a town, or a turnpike road, or a public market, or a post office, or his right to sit in a public building with others, of whatever race, for the purpose of hearing the political questions of the day discussed. Scarcely a day passes without our seeing in this court-room citizens of the white and black races sitting side by side, watching the progress of our business. It would never occur to any one that the presence of a colored citizen in a courthouse, or court-room, was an invasion of the social rights of white persons who may frequent such places. And yet, such a suggestion would be quite as sound in law—I say it with all respect—as is the suggestion that the claim of a colored citizen to use, upon the same terms as is permitted to white citizens, the accommodations of public highways, or public inns, or places of public amusement, established under the license of the law, is an invasion of the social rights of the white race. . . .

RICE v. *ELMORE*

165 F. 2nd 387 (1947)

Certiorari denied, 333 U.S. 875 (1948).

JUDGE PARKER delivered the opinion of the Court: . . .

This is an appeal from a decree adjudg-

ing that Negroes are entitled to vote in Democratic primary elections in South Carolina and enjoining defendants, who conduct such elections, from denying to Negro electors the right to vote therein.

Plaintiff, who has brought this as a class suit in behalf of all Negro electors similarly situated, is a Negro duly qualified to vote under the Constitution and laws of the State of South Carolina. He has been denied the right to vote in the Democratic primary of that state by rules promulgated by the Democratic Party limiting the right to vote in the primary to white persons. The defendants are officials of the Democratic Party of South Carolina, who have charge of the primary in the county and precinct where plaintiff resides.

The only question presented by the appeal is the correctness of the declaration as to the right to vote contained in the decree appealed from and the validity of the injunction therein granted. Plaintiff contends that the decree should be upheld under the Fourteenth and Fifteenth Amendments to the Constitution and the provisions of the Civil Rights Acts . . . Defendants contend that, because there has been no statutory regulation of primaries in South Carolina since the repeal in 1944, 44 St. at Large, p. 2231, of the statutes relating thereto, the constitutional limitations on state action relied on by plaintiff have no application and that there is consequently no jurisdiction in the court to grant declaratory or injunctive relief. They argue that defendants in the action complained of were acting, not as state officials, but as members of the Democratic Party, which, they say, is a voluntary political association which can exercise unrestricted choice of membership. There is no dispute as to the facts, which are fully and fairly set forth in the opinion of the District Judge . . . They may be briefly summarized as follows:

For half a century or more the Democratic Party has absolutely controlled the choice of elective officers in the State of South Carolina. The real elections within that state have been contests within the Democratic Party, the general elections serving only to ratify and give legal validity to the party choice. So well has this been recognized that only a comparatively few

persons participate in the general elections. In the election of 1946, for instance, 290,223 votes were cast for Governor in the Democratic primary, only 26,326 in the general election.

In South Carolina, as in most other states of the Union, the primary had become an integral part of the election machinery recognized and regulated by law. Article II, section 10, of the State Constitution of 1895 directed that the Legislature provide by law for the regulation of party primary elections, and pursuant thereto a complete set of primary laws have been adopted and were in effect when the Supreme Court of the United States decided the case of *Smith* v. *Allwright*, 321 U.S. 649, holding that the right to vote in a primary election held under state law might not be denied on the ground of race or color. Immediately following this decision, the then Governor of South Carolina convened the state legislature and recommended that it repeal all laws with relation to primaries with the avowed purpose of preventing voting by Negroes in the Democratic primaries of the State. Pursuant to this recommendation, the primary laws of the state were repealed and the Democratic primary was conducted thereafter under rules prescribed by the Democratic Party. That the primary when conducted by the party fulfilled the same function in the election machinery of the state and was managed in practically the same way as when conducted under the state law, does not admit of doubt. With respect to this, the District Judge, after describing the procedure when the statutes regulating the primary were in effect, went on to say:

"In 1944 substantially the same process was gone through, although at that time and before the State Convention assembled, the statutes had been repealed by action of the General Assembly, heretofore set out. The State Convention that year adopted a complete new set of rules and regulations, these however embodying practically all of the provisions of the repealed statutes. Some minor changes were made but these amounted to very little more than the usual change of procedure in detail from year to year. . . .

"In 1946 substantially the same procedure was used in the organization of the Democratic Party and another set of rules adopted which were substantially the same as the 1944 rules, excepting that the voting age was lowered to 18 and party officials were allowed the option of using voting machines, and the rules relative to absentee voting were simplified . . ."

The question presented for our decision is whether, by permitting a party to take over a part of its election machinery, a state can avoid the provisions of the Constitution forbidding racial discrimination in elections and can deny to a part of the electorate, because of race and color, any effective voice in the government of the state. It seems perfectly clear that this question must be answered in the negative.

The fundamental error in defendant's position consists in the premise that a political party is a mere private aggregation of individuals, like a country club, and that the primary is a mere piece of party machinery. The party may, indeed, have been a mere private aggregation of individuals in the early days of the Republic, but with the passage of the years, political parties have become in effect state institutions, governmental agencies through which sovereign power is exercised by the people. Party primaries are of more recent growth. Originating in the closing years of the last century as a means of making parties more responsive to the popular will in the nomination of candidates for office, they had been adopted by 1917 in all except four of the states of the Union as a vital and integral part of the state election machinery . . . The relation of the primary to the election was well stated by Mr. Justice Pitney in his concurring opinion in *Newberry* v. *United States,* 256 U.S. 232, 285, where he said: "It seems to me too clear for discussion that primary elections and nominating conventions are so closely related to the final election, and their proper

regulation so essential to effective regulation of the latter, so vital to representative government that power to regulate them is within the general authority of Congress. It is matter of common knowledge that the great mass of the American electorate is grouped into political parties, to one or the other of which voters adhere with tenacity, due to their divergent views on questions of public policy, their interests, their environment, and various other influences, sentimental and historical. So strong with the great majority of voters are party associations, so potent the party slogan, so effective the party organization, that the likelihood of a candidate succeeding in an election without a party nomination is practically negligible. As a result, every voter comes to the polls on the day of the general election confined in his choice to those few candidates who have received party nominations, and constrained to consider their eligibility, in point of personal fitness, as affected by their party associations and their obligation to pursue more or less definite lines of policy, with which the voter may or may not agree. As a practical matter, the ultimate choice of the mass of voters is predetermined when the nominations have been made."

As primaries have become imbedded in the election machinery of the country, there has come gradually a recognition by the courts of the function they perform and the application to them of the laws relating to elections. In the *Newberry* case, *supra,* decided in 1921, the Supreme Court, by a bare majority, had held the Federal Corrupt Practices Act . . . not applicable to a primary election held for United States Senator under a law adopted prior to the Seventeenth Amendment. In *United States* v. *Classic,* 313 U.S. 299, decided in 1941, however, it was expressly held that a primary was an election within the meaning of article 1 section 4 of the Constitution and the court pointed out that the *Newberry* case could not be considered authority to the contrary. In *Nixon* v. *Herndon,* 273 U.S. 536, a Texas statute forbidding

Negroes to participate in Democratic primaries was held violative of the Fourteenth Amendment. Following that decision, the statute was repealed and a law enacted authorizing the Executive Committee of a political party to prescribe who might vote in its primaries, and under this the Democratic Executive Committee adopted a resolution limiting participation in the Democratic primary to white persons. The exclusion of Negroes from voting pursuant to this resolution was held violative of the Fourteenth Amendment, in *Nixon* v. *Condon,* 286 U.S. 73, the Court saying: "The test is not whether the members of the Executive Committee are the representatives of the state in the strict sense in which an agent is the representative of his principal. The test is whether they are to be classified as representatives of the state to such an extent and in such a sense that the great restraints of the Constitution set limits to their action." The Texas law was again amended to eliminate delegation of authority to the Executive Committee and thereupon the Democratic State Convention, without statutory authority for so doing, limited the right to participate in the Democratic primary to white persons. The exclusion of a Negro from voting in the Democratic primary pursuant to this action was held not violative of constitutional right in *Grovey* v. *Townsend,* 295 U.S. 45; but *Grovey* v. *Townsend* was expressly overruled a few years later in *Smith* v. *Allwright, supra,* 321 U.S. 649, where the Court said:

"When primaries become a part of the machinery for choosing officials, state and national, as they have here, the same tests to determine the character of discrimination or abridgment should be applied to the primary as are applied to the general election . . .

"The United States is a constitutional democracy. Its organic law grants to all citizens a right to participate in the choice of elected officials without restriction by any State because of race. This grant to the people of the opportunity for choice is not to be nullified by a State through

casting its electoral process in a form which permits a private organization to practice racial discrimination in the election. Constitutional rights would be of little value if they could be thus indirectly denied . . .

"The privilege of membership in a party may be, as this Court said in *Grovey* v. *Townsend,* 295 U.S. 45, 55, no concern of a state. But when, as here, that privilege is also the essential qualification for voting in a primary to select nominees for a general election, the state makes the action of the party the action of the state."

It is true, as defendants point out, that the primary involved in *Smith* v. *Allwright* was conducted under the provisions of state law and not merely under party rules, as is the case here, but we do not think this a controlling distinction. State law relating to the general election gives effect to what is done in the primary and makes it just as much a part of the election machinery of the state by which the people choose their offices as if it were regulated by law, as formerly. Elections in South Carolina remain a two step process whether the party primary be accounted a preliminary of the general election, or the general election be regarded as giving effect to what is done in the primary; and those who control the Democratic Party as well as the state government cannot by placing the first of the steps under officials of the party rather than of the state, absolve such officials from the limitations which the federal Constitution imposes. When these officials participate in what is a part of the state's election machinery, they are election officers of the state de facto if not de jure, and as such must observe the limitations of the Constitution. Having undertaken to perform an important function relating to the exercise of sovereignty by the people, they may not violate the fundamental principles laid down by the Constitution for its exercise . . . "We know of no reason why the state cannot create separate agencies to carry on its work in this manner, and when it does so, they become subject to the constitutional restraints imposed upon the state itself."

Even though the election laws of South Carolina be fair upon their face, yet if they be administered in such way as to result in persons being denied any real voice in government because of race and color, it is idle to say that the power of the state is not being used in violation of the Constitution . . .

It is pointed out in the case of *United States* v. *Classic, supra,* 313 U.S. 299, that the right to vote in the primary and to have one's vote counted is to be protected, not only where state law has made the primary an integral part of the procedure of choice, but also where in fact it effectively controls the choice, as is unquestionably true in South Carolina. The Court said in that case: "From time immemorial an election to public office has been in point of substance no more and no less than the expression by qualified electors of their choice of candidates. Long before the adoption of the Constitution the form and mode of that expression had changed from time to time. There is no historical warrant for supposing that the framers were under the illusion that the method of effecting the choice of the electors would never change or that if it did, the change was for that reason to be permitted to defeat the right of the people to choose representatives for Congress which the Constitution had guaranteed. The right to participate in the choice of representatives for Congress includes, as we have said, the right to cast a ballot and to have it counted at the general election whether for the successful candidate or not. Where the state law has made the primary an integral part of the procedure of choice, or where in fact the primary effectively controls the choice, the right of the elector to have his ballot counted at the primary, is likewise included in the right protected by Article I, section 2. And this right of participation is protected just as is the right to vote at the election, where the primary is by law made an integral part of the election machinery, whether the voter exercises his right in a party primary which invariably, sometimes or never determines the ultimate choice of the representative. Here,

even apart from the circumstance that the Louisiana primary is made by law an integral part of the procedure of choice, the right to choose a representative is in fact controlled by the primary because, as is alleged in the indictment, the choice of candidates at the Democratic primary determines the choice of the elected representative."

An essential feature of our form of government is the right of the citizen to participate in the governmental process. The political philosophy of the Declaration of Independence is that governments derive their just powers from the consent of the governed; and the right to a voice in the selection of officers of government on the part of all citizens is important, not only as a means of insuring that government shall have the strength of popular support, but also as a means of securing to the individual citizen proper consideration of his rights by those in power. The disfranchised can never speak with the same force as those who are able to vote. The Fourteenth and Fifteenth Amendments were written into the Constitution to insure to the Negro, who had recently been liberated from slavery, the equal protection of the laws and the right to full participation in the process of government. These amendments have had the effect of creating a federal basis of citizenship and of protecting the rights of individuals and minorities from many abuses of governmental power which were not contemplated at the time. Their primary purpose must not be lost sight of, however; and no election machinery can be upheld if its purpose or effect is to deny to the Negro, on account of his race or color, any effective voice in the government of his country or the state or community wherein he lives.

The use of the Democratic primary in connection with the general election in South Carolina provides, as has been stated, a two step election machinery for that state; and the denial to the Negro of the right to participate in the primary denies him all effective voice in the government of his country. There can be no question that such denial amounts to a denial of the constitutional rights of the Negro; and we think it equally clear that those who participate in the denial are exercising state power to that end, since the primary is used in connection with the general election in the selection of state officers. There can be no question, therefore, as to the jurisdiction of the court to grant injunctive relief . . . to redress the deprivation of civil rights.

There was no error and the judgment appealed from will be affirmed.

Affirmed.

NOTE: Abolition of the white primary does not mean that Negroes are free to vote. See *Report of the United States Commission on Civil Rights*, Vol. 1 (1961).

Opposition to federal enforcement of the right to vote is the counterpart of state measures designed to prevent the NAACP from supporting private litigation to enforce civil rights (see above). Behind both efforts is a common principle: the rights of the individual are of little value, if there is no effective means of enforcing them. Or as the ancient common law dictum puts it: without a remedy there is no right. The anti-NAACP measures may be summarized as follows:

1. Discriminatory use of existing laws to halt an organization's activity.
2. Bans on state employees' membership in specified organizations.
3. Laws requiring publication of the names of members of an organization, so that they will be exposed to economic and other oppression.
4. Laws requiring organizations to submit to registration requirements difficult if not impossible to fulfill.
5. Laws imposing on associations prohibitive or excessive license fees or taxes.
6. Laws prohibiting or burdening organized support of litigation to enforce particular rights.
7. Legislative investigations to harass an organization's leaders, sequester its records, expose its members or present its activities in an unfavorable light.
8. Laws creating "emergency" powers to halt organizational activity deemed harmful to the interests of the dominant group in the state.

SHELLEY v. KRAEMER

334 U.S. 1 (1948)

MR. CHIEF JUSTICE VINSON delivered the opinion of the Court:

These cases present for our consideration questions relating to the validity of court enforcement of private agreements, generally described as restrictive covenants, which have as their purpose the exclusion of persons of designated race or color from the ownership or occupancy of real property. Basic constitutional issues of obvious importance have been raised. . . .

It should be observed that these covenants do not seek to proscribe any particular use of the affected properties. Use of the properties for residential occupancy, as such, is not forbidden. The restrictions of these agreements, rather, are directed toward a designated class of persons and seek to determine who may and who may not own or make use of the properties for residential purposes. The excluded class is defined wholly in terms of race or color; "simply that and nothing more."

It cannot be doubted that among the

civil rights intended to be protected from discriminatory state action by the Fourteenth Amendment are the rights to acquire, enjoy, own, and dispose of property. Equality in the enjoyment of property rights was regarded by the framers of that Amendment as an essential pre-condition to the realization of other basic civil rights and liberties which the Amendment was intended to guarantee. Thus, § 1978 of the Revised Statutes, derived from § 1 of the Civil Rights Act of 1866 which was enacted by Congress while the Fourteenth Amendment was also under consideration, provides:

"All citizens of the United States shall have the same right, in every State and Territory, as is enjoyed by white citizens thereof to inherit, purchase, lease, sell, hold, and convey real and personal property."

This Court has given specific recognition to the same principle. *Buchanan* v. *Warley,* 245 U.S. 60 (1917).

It is likewise clear that restrictions on the right of occupancy of the sort sought to be created by the private agreements in these cases could not be squared with the requirements of the Fourteenth Amendment if imposed by state statute or local ordinance. [The discussion of *Buchanan* v. *Warley; Harmon* v. *Tyler,* 273 U.S. 668 (1927); and *Richmond* v. *Deans,* 281 U.S. 704 (1930), is here omitted.]

But the present cases, unlike those just discussed, do not involve action by state legislatures or city councils. Here the particular patterns of discrimination and the areas in which the restrictions are to operate, are determined, in the first instance, by the terms of agreements among private individuals. Participation of the State consists in the enforcement of the restrictions so defined. The crucial issue with which we are here confronted is whether this distinction removes these cases from the operation of the prohibitory provisions of the Fourteenth Amendment.

Since the decision of this Court in the *Civil Rights Cases,* 109 U.S. 3 (1883), the principle has become firmly embedded in our constitutional law that the action inhibited by the first section of the Fourteenth Amendment is only such action as may fairly be said to be that of the States. That Amendment erects no shield against merely private conduct, however discriminatory or wrongful.

We conclude, therefore, that the restrictive agreements standing alone cannot be regarded as violative of any rights guaranteed to petitioners by the Fourteenth Amendment. So long as the purposes of those agreements are effectuated by voluntary adherence to their terms, it would appear clear that there has been no action by the State and the provisions of the Amendment have not been violated. Cf. *Corrigan* v. *Buckley, supra.*

But here there was more. These are cases in which the purposes of the agreements were secured only by judicial enforcement by the state courts of the restrictive terms of the agreements. The respondents urge that judicial enforcement of private agreements does not amount to state action; or, in any event, the participation of the State is so attenuated in character as not to amount to state action within the meaning of the Fourteenth Amendment. Finally, it is suggested, even if the States in these cases may be deemed to have acted in the constitutional sense, their action did not deprive petitioners of rights guaranteed by the Fourteenth Amendment. We move to a consideration of these matters.

II

That the action of state courts and judicial officers in their official capacities is to be regarded as action of the State within the meaning of the Fourteenth Amendment, is a proposition which has long been established by decisions of this Court. [The compilation of precedents is here omitted.]

III

Against this background of judicial construction, extending over a period of some three-quarters of a century, we are called upon to consider whether enforcement by state courts of the restrictive agreements in these cases may be deemed to be the acts of those States; and, if so, whether that action has denied these petitioners the equal protection of the laws which the Amendment was intended to insure.

We have no doubt that there has been state action in these cases in the full and complete sense of the phrase. The undisputed facts disclose that petitioners were willing purchasers of properties upon which they desired to establish homes. The owners of the properties were willing sellers; and contracts of sale were accordingly consummated. It is clear that but for the active intervention of the state courts, supported by the full panoply of state power, petitioners would have been free to occupy the properties in question without restraint.

These are not cases, as has been suggested, in which the States have merely abstained from action, leaving private individuals free to impose such discriminations as they see fit. Rather, these are cases in which the States have made available to such individuals the full coercive power of government to deny to petitioners, on the grounds of race or color, the enjoyment of property rights in premises which petitioners are willing and financially able to acquire and which the grantors are willing to sell. The difference between judicial enforcement and non-enforcement of the restrictive covenants is the difference to petitioners between being denied rights of property available to other members of the community and being accorded full enjoyment of those rights on an equal footing.

The enforcement of the restrictive agreements by the state courts in these cases was directed pursuant to the common-law policy of the States as formulated by those courts in earlier decisions. In the *Missouri* case, enforcement of the covenant was directed in the first instance by the highest court of the State after the trial court had determined the agreement to be invalid for want of the requisite number of signatures. In the *Michigan* case, the order of enforcement by the trial court was affirmed by the highest state court. The judicial action in each case bears the clear and unmistakable imprimatur of the State. We have noted that previous decisions of this Court have established the proposition that judicial action is not immunized from the operation of the Fourteenth Amendment simply because it is taken pursuant to the state's common-law policy. Nor is the Amendment ineffective simply because the particular pattern of discrimination, which the State has enforced, was defined initially by the terms of a private agreement. State action, as that phrase is understood for the purposes of the Fourteenth Amendment, refers to exertions of state power in all forms. And when the effect of that action is to deny rights subject to the protection of the Fourteenth Amendment, it is the obligation of this Court to enforce the constitutional commands.

We hold that in granting judicial enforcement of the restrictive agreements in these cases, the States have denied petitioners the equal protection of the laws and that, therefore, the action of the state courts cannot stand. . . .

Respondents urge, however, that since the state courts stand ready to enforce restrictive covenants excluding white persons from the ownership or occupancy of property covered by such agreements, enforcement of covenants excluding colored persons may not be deemed a denial of equal protection of the laws to the colored persons who are thereby affected. This contention does not bear scrutiny. The parties have directed our attention to no case in which a court, state or federal, has been called upon to enforce a covenant excluding members of the white majority from ownership or occupancy of real property on grounds of race or color. But there are more fundamental considerations. The rights created by the first section of the Fourteenth Amendment are, by its terms, guaranteed to the individual. The rights established are personal rights. It is, therefore, no answer to these petitioners to say that the courts may also be induced to deny white persons rights of ownership and occupancy on grounds of race or color. Equal protection of the laws is not achieved

through indiscriminate imposition of inequalities. . . .

 Reversed.

Mr. Justice Reed, Mr. Justice Jackson, and Mr. Justice Rutledge took no part in the consideration or decision of these cases.

SCREWS v. UNITED STATES
325 U.S. 91 (1945)

Georgia police officers brutally beat a Negro, Robert Hall, whom they had arrested. Death resulted and the officers were indicted under Section 20 of the Federal Criminal Code (now 18 U.S.C., Sec. 242) which penalizes any person who "under color of any law . . . willfully subjects any inhabitant of any state . . . to the deprivation of any rights, privileges, or immunities secured or protected by the Constitution of the United States. . . ." At first the accused tried to justify their conduct by arguing that they had merely acted in self-defense and to prevent the escape of their prisoner. After being found guilty in a federal trial court, they argued on appeal that since their conduct had been illegal, they had not acted "under color of any law" within the meaning of the federal act, and also that the latter was unconstitutional because it was too vague and indefinite. Both arguments were rejected by the Supreme Court, though the case was sent back for retrial for other reasons. An excerpt from the chief opinion on the "under color of any law" problem is given below.

Mr. Justice Douglas announced the judgment of the Court and delivered the following opinion, in which The Chief Justice, Mr. Justice Black, and Mr. Justice Reed concurred: . . .

It is said, however, that petitioners did not act "under color of any law" within the meaning of § 20 of the Criminal Code. We disagree. We are of the view that petitioners acted under "color" of law in making the arrest of Robert Hall and in assaulting him. They were officers of the law who made the arrest. By their own admissions they assaulted Hall in order to protect themselves and to keep their prisoner from escaping. It was their duty under Georgia law to make the arrest effective. Hence, their conduct comes within the statute.

Some of the arguments which have been advanced in support of the contrary conclusion suggest that the question under § 20 is whether Congress has made it a federal offense for a state officer to violate the law of his State. But there is no warrant for treating the question in state law terms. The problem is not whether state

law has been violated but whether an inhabitant of a State has been deprived of a federal right by one who acts under "color of any law." He who acts under "color" of law may be a federal officer or a state officer. He may act under "color" of federal law or of state law. The statute does not come into play merely because the federal law or the state law under which the officer purports to act is violated. It is applicable when and only when someone is deprived of a federal right by that action. The fact that it is also a violation of state law does not make it any the less a federal offense punishable as such. Nor does its punishment by federal authority encroach on state authority or relieve the state from its responsibility for punishing state offenses.

We agree that when this statute is applied to the action of state officials, it should be construed so as to respect the proper balance between the States and the federal government in law enforcement. Violation of local law does not necessarily mean that federal rights have been invaded.

The fact that a prisoner is assaulted, injured, or even murdered by state officials does not necessarily mean that he is deprived of any right protected or secured by the Constitution or laws of the United States. Cf. *Logan* v. *United States,* 144 U.S. 263, dealing with assaults by federal officials. The Fourteenth Amendment did not alter the basic relations between the States and the national government. *United States* v. *Harris,* 106 U.S. 629; *In re Kemmler,* 136 U.S. 436, 448. Our national government is one of delegated powers alone. Under our federal system the administration of criminal justice rests with the States except as Congress, acting within the scope of those delegated powers, has created offenses against the United States. *Jerome* v. *United States,* 318 U.S. 101, 105. As stated in *United States* v. *Cruikshank,* 92 U.S. 542, 553–554, "It is no more the duty or within the power of the United States to punish for a conspiracy to falsely imprison or murder within a State, than it would be to punish for false imprisonment or murder itself." And see *United States* v. *Fox,* 95 U.S. 670, 672. It is only state action of a "particular character" that is prohibited by the Fourteenth Amendment and against which the Amendment authorized Congress to afford relief. *Civil Rights Cases,* 109 U.S. 3, 11, 13. Thus Congress in § 20 of the Criminal Code did not undertake to make all torts of state officials federal crimes. It brought within § 20 only specified acts done "under color" of law and then only those acts which deprived a person of some right secured by the Constitution or laws of the United States.

This section was before us in *United States* v. *Classic,* 313 U.S. 299, 326, where we said: "Misuse of power, possessed by virtue of state law and made possible only because the wrongdoer is clothed with the authority of state law, is action taken 'under color of' state law." In that case state election officials were charged with failure to count the votes as cast, alteration of the ballots, and false certification of the number of votes cast for the respective candidates. 313 U.S. pp. 308–309. We stated that those acts of the defendant's "were committed in the course of their performance of duties under the Louisiana statute requiring them to count the ballots, to record the result of the count, and to certify the result of the election." *Id.,* pp. 325–326. In the present case, as we have said, the defendants were officers of the law who had made an arrest and who by their own admissions made the assault in order to protect themselves and to keep the prisoner from escaping, i.e., to make the arrest effective. That was a duty they had under Georgia law. *United States* v. *Classic* is, therefore, indistinguishable from this case so far as "under color of" state law is concerned. In each officers of the State were performing official duties; in each the power which they were authorized to exercise was misused. We cannot draw a distinction between them unless we are to say that § 20 is not applicable to police officers. But the broad sweep of its language leaves no room for such an exception.

It is said that we should abandon the holding of the *Classic* case. It is suggested that the present problem was not clearly in focus in that case and that its holding was ill-advised. A reading of the opinion makes plain that the question was squarely involved and squarely met. It followed the rule announced in *Ex parte Virginia,* 100 U.S. 339, 346, that a state judge who in violation of state law discriminated against Negroes in the selection of juries violated the Act of March 1, 1875, 18 Stat. 336. It is true that that statute did not contain the words under "color" of law. But the Court in deciding what was state action within the meaning of the Fourteenth Amendment held that it was immaterial that the state officer exceeded the limits of his authority. ". . . as he acts in the name and for the State, and is clothed with the State's power, his act is that of the State. This must be so, or the constitutional prohibition has no meaning. Then the State has clothed one of its agents with power to annul or to evade it. (100 U.S. at p. 347.)"

And see *Virginia* v. *Rives,* 100 U.S. 313, 321. The *Classic* case recognized, without dissent, that the contrary view would defeat the great purpose which § 20 was designed to serve. Reference is made to statements of Senator Trumbull in his discussion of § 2 of the Civil Rights Act of 1866, 14 Stat. 27, and to statements of Senator Sherman concerning the 1870 Act as supporting the conclusion that "under color of any law" was designed to include only action taken by officials pursuant to state law. But those statements in their context are inconclusive on the precise problem involved in the *Classic* case and in the present case. We are not dealing here with a case where an officer not authorized to act nevertheless takes action. Here the state officers were authorized to make an arrest and to take such steps as were necessary to make the arrest effective. They acted without authority only in the sense that they used excessive force in making the arrest effective. It is clear that under "color" of law means under "pretense" of law. Thus acts of officers in the ambit of their personal pursuits are plainly excluded. Acts of officers who undertake to perform their official duties are included whether they hew to the line of their authority or overstep it. If, as suggested, the statute was designed to embrace only action which the State in fact authorized, the words "under color of any law" were hardly apt words to express the idea.

[MR. JUSTICE RUTLEDGE concurred in the result. JUSTICE MURPHY, dissenting, thought the conviction should have been sustained. JUSTICES ROBERTS, FRANKFURTER, and JACKSON in dissent responded as follows to the Court's position on "under color of any law":]

The Fourteenth Amendment prohibited a State from so acting as to deprive persons of new federal rights defined by it. Section 5 of the amendment specifically authorized enabling legislation to enforce that prohibition. Since a State can act only through its officers, Congress provided for the prosecution of any officer who deprives others of their guaranteed rights and denied such an officer the right to defend by claiming the authority of the State for his action. In short, Congress said that no State can empower an officer to commit acts which the Constitution forbade the State from authorizing, whether such unauthorized command be given for the State by its legislative or judicial voice, or by a custom contradicting the written law. See *Nashville, C. & St. L. R. Co.* v. *Browning,* 310 U.S. 362, 369. The present prosecution is not based on an officer's claim that that for which the United States seeks his punishment was commanded or authorized by the law of his State. On the contrary, the present prosecution is based on the theory that Congress made it a federal offense for a State officer to violate the explicit law of his State. We are asked to construe legislation which was intended to effectuate prohibitions against States for defiance of the Constitution, to be equally applicable where a State duly obeys the Constitution, but an officer flouts State law and is unquestionably subject to punishment by the State for his disobedience.

So to read § 20 disregards not merely the normal function of language to express ideas appropriately. It fails not merely to leave to the States the province of local crime enforcement, that the proper balance of political forces in our federalism requires. It does both, heedless of the Congressional purpose, clearly evinced even during the feverish Reconstruction days, to leave undisturbed the power and the duty of the States to enforce their criminal law by restricting federal authority to the punishment only of those persons who violate federal rights under claim of State authority and not by exerting federal authority against offenders of State authority. Such a distortion of federal power devised against recalcitrant State authority never entered the minds of the proponents of the legislation. . . .

It was assumed quite needlessly in the *Classic* case that the scope of § 20 was coextensive with the Fourteenth Amendment. Because the weight of the case was elsewhere, we did not pursue the difference between the power granted to Congress by that Amendment to bar "any State" from depriving persons of the newly created constitutional rights and the limited extent to which Congress exercised that power, in what is now § 20, by making it an offense for one acting "under color of any law" to deprive another of such constitutional rights. It may well be that Congress could, within the bounds of the Fourteenth Amendment, treat action taken by a State official even though in defiance of State law and not condoned by ultimate State authority as the action of "a State." It has never been satisfactorily explained how a State can be said to deprive a person of liberty or property without due process of law when the foundation of the claim is that a minor official has disobeyed the authentic command of his State. . . .

But assuming unreservedly that conduct such as that now before us, perpetrated by State officers in flagrant defiance of State law, may be attributed to the State under the Fourteenth Amendment, this does not make it action under "color of any law." Section 20 is much narrower than the power of Congress. Even though Congress might have swept within the federal criminal law any action that could be deemed within the vast reach of the Fourteenth Amendment, Congress did not do so. The presuppositions of our federal system, the pronouncements of the statesmen who shaped this legislation, and the normal meaning of language powerfully counsel against attributing to Congress intrusion into the sphere of criminal law traditionally and naturally reserved for the States alone. When due account is taken of the considerations that have heretofore controlled the political and legal relations between the States and the National Government, there is not the slightest warrant in the reason of things for torturing language plainly designed for nullifying a claim of acting under a State law that conflicts with the Constitution so as to apply to situations where State law is in conformity with the Constitution and local misconduct is in undisputed violation of that State law. In the absence of clear direction by Congress we should leave to the States the enforcement of their criminal law, and not relieve States of the responsibility for vindicating wrongdoing that is essentially local or weaken the habits of local law enforcement by tempting reliance on federal authority for an occasional unpleasant task of local enforcement.

QUAERE: Why in the federal legislation involved in the *Screws* case did Congress use the phrase "under color of any law"?

NOTE: On retrial, Screws was acquitted by a jury. Shortly thereafter he was elected to the state senate.

BURTON v. *WILMINGTON PARKING AUTHORITY*

365 U.S. 715 (1961)

MR. JUSTICE CLARK delivered the opinion of the Court.

In this action for declaratory and injunctive relief it is admitted that the Eagle Coffee Shoppe, Inc., a restaurant located within an off-street automobile parking building in Wilmington, Delaware, has refused to serve appellant food or drink solely because he is a Negro. The parking building is owned and operated by the Wilmington Parking Authority, an agency of the State of Delaware, and the restaurant is the Authority's lessee. Appellant claims that such refusal abridges his rights under the Equal Protection Clause of the Fourteenth Amendment to the United States Constitution. The Supreme Court of Delaware has held that Eagle was acting in "a purely private capacity" [157 A.2d 902] under its lease; that its action was not that of the Authority and was not, therefore, state action within the contemplation of the prohibitions contained in that Amendment. It also held that under 24 Del. Code § 1501, Eagle was a restaurant, not an inn, and that as such it "is not required [under Delaware law] to serve any and all persons entering its place of business." . . .

In this connection the Delaware Supreme Court seems to have placed controlling emphasis on its conclusion, as to the accuracy of which there is doubt, that only some 15% of the total cost of the facility was "advanced" from public funds; that the cost of the entire facility was allocated three-fifths to the space for commercial leasing and two-fifths to parking space; that anticipated revenue from parking was only some 30.5% of the total income, the balance of which was expected to be earned by the leasing; that the Authority had no original intent to place a restaurant in the building, it being only a happenstance resulting from the bidding; that Eagle expended considerable moneys on furnishings; that the restaurant's main and marked public entrance is on Ninth Street without any public entrance direct from the parking area; and that "the only connection Eagle has with the public facility . . . is the furnishing of the sum of $28,700 annually in the form of rent which is used by the Authority to defray a portion of the operating expense of an otherwise unprofitable enterprise." 157 A.2d 894, 901. While these factual considerations are indeed validly accountable aspects of the enterprise upon which the State has embarked, we cannot say that they lead inescapably to the conclusion that state action is not present. Their persuasiveness is diminished when evaluated in the context of other factors which must be acknowledged.

The land and building were publicly owned. As an entity, the building was dedicated to "public uses" in performance of the Authority's "essential governmental functions." 22 Del. Code, c. 5, §§ 501, 514. The costs of land acquisition, construction, and maintenance are defrayed entirely from donations by the City of Wilmington, from loans and revenue bonds and from the proceeds of rentals and parking services out of which the loans and bonds were payable. Assuming that the distinction would be significant, cf. *Derrington* v. *Plummer*, 5 Cir., 240 F.2d 922, 925, the commercially leased areas were not surplus state property, but constituted a physically and financially integral and, indeed indispensable part of the State's plan to operate its project as a self-sustaining unit. Upkeep and maintenance of the building, including necessary repairs, were responsibilities of the Authority and were payable out of public funds. It cannot be doubted that the peculiar relationship of the restaurant to the parking facility in which it is located confers on each an incidental variety of mutual benefits. Guests of the restaurant are afforded a convenient place to park their automobiles, even if they cannot enter the restaurant directly from the parking area. Similarly, its convenience for diners may well provide additional demand for the Authority's parking facilities. Should any improvements effected in the leasehold by Eagle become part of the realty, there is no possibility of increased taxes being passed on to it since the fee is held by a tax-exempt government agency. Neither can it be ignored, especially in view of Eagle's affirmative allegation that for it to serve Negroes would injure its business, that profits earned by discrimination not only contribute to, but are indispensable elements in the financial success of a governmental agency.

Addition of all these activities, obligations and responsibilities of the Authority, the benefits mutually conferred, together with the obvious fact that the restaurant is operated as an integral part of a public building devoted to a public parking service, indicates that degree of state participation and involvement in discriminatory action which it was the design of the Fourteenth Amendment to condemn. . . . Because readily applicable formulae may not be fashioned, the conclusions drawn from the facts and circumstances of this record are by no means declared universal truths on the basis of which every state leasing agreement is to be tested. . . .

The judgment of the Supreme Court of Delaware is reversed and the cause remanded for further proceedings consistent with this opinion.

Reversed and remanded.

MR. JUSTICE STEWART concurring. . . .

MR. JUSTICE HARLAN, whom MR. JUSTICE WHITTAKER joins, dissenting.

The Court's opinion, by a process of first undiscriminatingly throwing together various factual bits and pieces and then undermining the resulting structure by an equally vague disclaimer, seems to me to leave completely at sea just what it is in this record that satisfies the requirement of "state action."

I find it unnecessary, however, to inquire into the matter at this stage, for it seems to me apparent that before passing on the far-reaching constitutional questions that may, or may not, be lurking in this judgment, the case should first be sent back to the state court for clarification as to the precise basis of its decision. In deciding this case the Delaware Supreme Court, among other things, said:

"It [Eagle] acts as a restaurant keeper and, as such, is not required to serve any and all persons entering its place of business, any more than the operator of a bookstore, barber shop, or other retail business is required to sell its product to everyone. This is the common law, and the law of Delaware as restated in 24 Del. C., § 1501 with respect to restaurant keepers. . . . We, accordingly, hold that the operation of its

restaurant by Eagle does not fall within the scope of the prohibitions of the Fourteenth Amendment."

If in the context of this record this means, as my brother Stewart suggests, that the Delaware court construed this state statute "as authorizing discriminatory classification based exclusively on color," I would certainly agree, without more, that the enactment is offensive to the Fourteenth Amendment. It would then be quite unnecessary to reach the much broader questions dealt with in the Court's opinion. If, on the other hand, the state court meant no more than that under the statute, as at common law, Eagle was free to serve only those whom it pleased, then, and only then, would the question of "state action" be presented in full-blown form. . . .

MR. JUSTICE FRANKFURTER, dissenting. . . .

I certainly do not find the clarity that my brother Stewart finds in the views expressed by the Supreme Court of Delaware regarding 24 Del. Code § 1501. If I were forced to construe that court's construction, I should find the balance of considerations leading to the opposite conclusion from his, namely, that it was merely declaratory of the common law and did not give state sanction to refusing service to a person merely because he is colored. The Court takes no position regarding the statutory meaning which divides my brothers Harlan and Stewart. Clearly it does not take Mr. Justice Stewart's view of what the Supreme Court of Delaware decided. If it did, it would undoubtedly take his easy route to decision and not reach the same result by its much more circuitous route.

Since the pronouncement of the Supreme Court of Delaware thus lends itself to three views, none of which is patently irrational, why is not my brother Harlan's suggestion for solving this conflict the most appropriate solution? . . .

BELL v. MARYLAND

84 S. Ct. 1814 (1964)

Negro sit-ins had been convicted of criminal trespass. Pending review the state had adopted public accommodations laws. In an opinion by Mr. Justice Brennan, the Court remanded the cases to the state court for consideration of the effect of the new laws upon the convictions. Here again, as so often before, the Court avoided the basic Fourteenth Amendent issue raised by the sit-in and related cases. The following minority opinions suggest that the reason for avoidance is a basic multiple division among the Justices.

MR. JUSTICE DOUGLAS, with whom MR. JUSTICE GOLDBERG concurs as respects Parts II–V, reversing and directing dismissal of the indictment.

I

I reach the merits of this controversy. The issue is ripe for decision and petitioners, who have been convicted of asking for service in Hooper's restaurant, are entitled to an answer to their complaint here and now.

On this the last day of the Term, we studiously avoid decision of the basic issue of the right of public accommodation under the Fourteenth Amendment, remanding the case to the state court for reconsideration in light of an issue of state law.

This case was argued October 14 and 15, 1963—over eight months ago. The record of the case is simple, the constitutional guide lines well marked, the precedents marshalled. Though the Court is divided, the preparation of opinions laying bare the differences does not require even two months, let alone eight. Moreover, a majority reach the merits of the issue. Why then should a minority prevent a resolution of the differing views?

The laws relied on for vacating and remanding were enacted June 8, 1962, and March 29, 1963—long before oral argument. We did indeed not grant certiorari until June 10, 1963. Hence if we were really concerned with this state law question, we would have vacated and remanded for reconsideration in light of those laws on June 10, 1963. By now we would have

had an answer and been able to put our decision into the mainstream of the law at this critical hour. If the parties had been concerned, they too might have asked that we follow that course. Maryland adverted to the new law merely to show why certiorari should not be granted. At the argument and at our conferences we were not concerned with that question, the issue being deemed frivolous. Now it is resurrected to avoid facing the constitutional question.

The whole Nation has to face the issue; Congress is conscientiously considering it; some municipalities have had to make it their first order of concern; law enforcement officials are deeply implicated, north as well as south; the question is at the root of demonstrations, unrest, riots, and violence in various areas. The issue in other words consumes the public attention. Yet we stand mute, avoiding decision of the basic issue by an obvious pretense.

The clash between Negro customers and white restaurant owners is clear; each claims protection by the Constitution and tenders the Fourteenth Amendment as justification for his action. Yet we leave resolution of the conflict to others, when, if our voice were heard, the issues for the Congress and for the public would become clear and precise. The Court was created to sit in troubled times as well as in peaceful days. . . .

II

The issue in this case, according to those who would affirm, is whether a person's "personal prejudices" may dictate the way in which he uses his property and whether he can enlist the aid of the state to enforce those "personal prejudices." With all respect, that is not the real issue. The corporation that owns this restaurant did not refuse service to these Negroes because "it" did not like Negroes. The reason "it" refused service was because "it" thought "it" could make more money by running a segregated restaurant. . . .

Here, as in most of the sit-in cases before us, the refusal of service did not reflect "personal prejudices" but business reasons. Were we today to hold that segregated restaurants, whose racial policies were enforced by a State, violated the Equal Protection Clause, all restaurants would be on an equal footing and the reasons given in this and most of the companion cases for refusing service to Negroes would evaporate. Moreover, when corporate restaurateurs are involved, whose "personal prejudices" are being protected? The stockholders'? The directors'? The officers'? The managers'? The truth is, I think, that the corporate interest is in making money, not in protecting "personal prejudices."

III

I leave those questions to another part of this opinion and turn to an even more basic issue.

I now assume that the issue is the one stated by those who would affirm. The case in that posture deals with a relic of slavery —an institution that has cast a long shadow across the land, resulting today in a second-class citizenship in this area of public accommodations.

The Thirteenth, Fourteenth, and Fifteenth Amendments had "one pervading purpose . . . we mean the freedom of the slave race, the security and firm establishment of that freedom, and the protection of the newly-made freeman and citizen from the oppressions of those who had formerly exercised unlimited dominion over him." *Slaughter-House Cases*, 16 Wall. 36, 71.

Prior to those Amendments, Negroes were segregated and disallowed the use of public accommodations except and unless the owners chose to serve them. To affirm these judgments would remit those Negroes to their old status and allow the States to keep them there by the force of their police and their judiciary.

We deal here with public accommodations—with the right of people to eat and travel as they like and to use facilities whose only claim to existence is serving the public. . . .

When one citizen because of his race, creed, or color is denied the privilege of being treated as any other citizen in places of public accommodation, we have classes of citizenship, one being more degrading than the other. That is at war with the one class of citizenship created by the Thirteenth, Fourteenth, and Fifteenth Amendments.

As stated in *Ex parte Virginia*, 100 U.S. 339, 344–345, where a federal indictment against a state judge for discriminating against Negroes in the selection of jurors was upheld:

"One great purpose of these amendments was to raise the colored race from that condition of inferiority and servitude in which most of them had previously stood, into perfect equality of civil rights with all other persons within the jurisdiction of the States. They were intended to take away all possibility of oppression by law because of race or color. They were intended to be, what they really are, limitations of the power of the States and enlargements of the power of Congress."

IV

The problem in this case, and in the other sit-in cases before us, is presented as though it involved the situation of "a private operator conducting his own business on his own premises and exercising his own judgment" as to whom he will admit to the premises.

The property involved is not, however, a man's home or his yard or even his fields. Private property is involved, but it is property that is serving the public. As my Brother GOLDBERG says, it is a "civil" right, not a "social" right, with which we deal. Here it is a restaurant refusing service to a

Negro. But so far as principle and law are concerned it might just as well be a hospital refusing admission to a sick or injured Negro (cf. *Simkins* v. *Moses H. Cone Memorial Hospital*, 323 F.2d 959) or a drug store refusing antibiotics to a Negro, or a bus denying transportation to a Negro, or a telephone company refusing to install a telephone in a Negro's home.

The problem with which we deal has no relation to opening or closing the door of one's home. The home of course is the essence of privacy, in no way dedicated to public use, in no way extending an invitation to the public. Some businesses, like the classical country store where the owner lives overhead or in the rear, make the store an extension, so to speak, of the home. But such is not this case. The facts of these sit-in cases have little resemblance to any institution of property which we customarily associate with privacy. . . .

Apartheid, however, is barred by the common law as respects innkeepers and common carriers. There were, to be sure, criminal statutes that regulated the common callings. But the civil remedies were made by judges who had no written constitution. We, on the other hand, live under a constitution that proclaims equal protection under the law. Why then, even in the absence of a statute, should *apartheid* be given constitutional sanction in the restaurant field. That was the question I asked in *Lombard* v. *Louisiana*, 373 U.S. 267. I repeat it here. Constitutionally speaking, why should Hooper Food Co., Inc., or People's Drug Stores—or any other establishment that dispenses medicines or food—stand on a higher, more sanctified level than Greyhound Bus when it comes to a constitutional right to pick and choose its customers?

The debates on the Fourteenth Amendment show, as my Brother GOLDBERG points out, that one of its purposes was to grant the Negro "the rights and guarantees of the good old common law." *Post*, at 10. The duty of common carriers to carry all, regardless of race, creed, or color, was in part the product of the inventive genius of

judges. See *Lombard* v. *Louisiana*, 373 U.S., at 275–277. We should make that body of law the common law of the Thirteenth and Fourteenth Amendments so to speak. Restaurants in the modern setting are as essential to travelers as inns and carriers.

Are they not as much affected with a public interest? Is the right of a person to eat less basic than his right to travel, which we protected in *Edwards* v. *California*, 314 U.S. 160? Does not a right to travel in modern times shrink in value materially when there is no accompanying right to eat in public places?

The right of any person to travel *interstate* irrespective of race, creed, or color is protected by the Constitution. *Edwards* v. *California, supra*. Certainly his right to travel *intrastate* is as basic. Certainly his right to eat at public restaurants is as important in the modern setting as the right of mobility. In these times that right is, indeed, practically indispensable to travel either interstate or intrastate.

V

The requirement of Equal Protection, like the guarantee of Privileges and Immunities of citizenship, is a constitutional command directed to each State.

State judicial action is as clearly "state" action as state administrative action. Indeed, we held in *Shelley* v. *Kraemer*, 334 U.S. 1, 20, that "State action, as that phrase is understood for the purposes of the Fourteenth Amendment, refers to exertions of state power in all forms." . . .

The preferences involved in *Shelley* v. *Kraemer* and its companion cases were far more personal than the motivations of the corporate managers in the present case when they declined service to Negroes. Why should we refuse to let state courts enforce *apartheid* in residential areas of our cities but let state courts enforce *apartheid* in restaurants? It a court decree is state action in one case, it is in the other. Property rights, so heavily underscored, are equally involved in each case.

The customer in a restaurant is transitory; he comes and may never return. The colored family who buys the house next door is there for keeps—night and day. If "personal prejudices" are not to be the criterion in one case they should not be in the other. We should put these restaurant cases in line with *Shelley* v. *Kraemer,* holding that what the Fourteenth Amendment requires in restrictive covenant cases it also requires from restaurants.

Segregation of Negroes in the restaurants and lunch counters of parts of America is a relic of slavery. It is a badge of second-class citizenship. It is a denial of a privilege and immunity of national citizenship and of the Equal Protection guaranteed by the Fourteenth Amendment against abridgement by the states. When the state police, the state prosecutor, and the state courts unite to convict Negroes for renouncing that relic of slavery, the "state" violates the Fourteenth Amendment.

I would reverse these judgments of conviction outright, as these Negroes in asking for service in Hooper's restaurant were only demanding what was their constitutional right.

[Appendices I–V are here omitted.]

MR. JUSTICE GOLDBERG, with whom THE CHIEF JUSTICE joins, and with whom MR. JUSTICE DOUGLAS joins as to Parts II–V, concurring.

I

I join in the opinion and the judgment of the Court and would therefore have no occasion under ordinary circumstances to express my views on the underlying constitutional issue. Since, however, the dissent at length discusses this constitutional issue and reaches a conclusion with which I profoundly disagree, I am impelled to state the reasons for my conviction that the Constitution guarantees to all Americans the right to be treated as equal members of the community with respect to public accommodations. . . .

II

The Thirteenth, Fourteenth and Fifteenth Amendments do not permit Negroes to be considered as second-class citizens in any aspect of our public life. Under our Constitution distinctions sanctioned by law between citizens because of race, ancestry, color or religion "are by their very nature odious to a free people whose institutions are founded upon the doctrine of equality." *Hirabayashi* v. *United States,* 320 U.S. 81, 100. We make no racial distinctions between citizens in exacting from them the discharge of public responsibilities: The heaviest duties of citizenship—military service, taxation, obedience to laws—are imposed evenhandedly upon black and white. States may and do impose the burdens of state citizenship upon Negroes and the States in many ways benefit from the equal imposition of the duties of federal citizenship. Our fundamental law which insures such an equality of public burdens, in my view, similarly insures an equality of public benefits. This Court has repeatedly recognized and applied this fundamental principle to many aspects of community life.

III

Of course our constitutional duty is "to construe, not to rewrite or amend, the Constitution." *Post,* at . . . (dissenting opinion of Mr. Justice Black). Our sworn duty to construe the Constitution requires, however, that we read it to effectuate the intent and purposes of the Framers. We must, therefore, consider the history and circumstances indicating what the Civil War Amendments were in fact designed to achieve. . . .

V

In my view the historical evidence demonstrates that the traditional rights of access to places of public accommodation were quite familiar to Congressmen and to the general public who naturally assumed that the Fourteenth Amendment by its citizenship and equal protection clauses extended these traditional rights to Negroes. But even if the historical evidence were not as convincing as I believe it to be, the logic of *Brown* v. *Board of Education,* 347 U.S. 483, based as it was on the fundamental principle of constitutional interpretation proclaimed by Chief Justice Marshall, requires that petitioners' claim be sustained. In *Brown,* after stating that the available history was "inconclusive" on the specific issue of segregated public schools, the Court went on to say:

"In approaching this problem, we cannot turn the clock back to 1868 when the Amendment was adopted, or even to 1896 when *Plessy* v. *Ferguson* was written. We must consider public education in the light of its full development and its present place in American life throughout the Nation. Only in this way can it be determined if segregation in public schools deprives these plaintiffs of the equal protection of the laws." 347 U.S., at 492–493.

The dissent makes no effort to assess the status of places of public accommodation "in the light of" their "full development and . . . present place" in the life of American citizens. In failing to adhere to that approach the dissent ignores a pervasive principle of constitutional adjudication and departs from the ultimate logic of *Brown*. As Mr. Justice Holmes so aptly said:

"[W]hen we are dealing with words that also are a constituent act, like the Constitution of the United States, we must realize that they have called into life a being the development of which could not have been foreseen completely by the most gifted of its begetters. It was enough for them to realize or to hope that they had created an organism; it has taken a century and has cost their successors much sweat and blood to prove that they created a nation. The case before us must be considered in the light of our whole experience and not merely in that of what was said a hundred years ago." *Missouri* v. *Holland*, 252 U.S. 416, 433. . . .

MR. JUSTICE BLACK, with whom MR. JUSTICE HARLAN and MR. JUSTICE WHITE join, dissenting.

The case does not involve the constitutionality of any existing or proposed state or federal legislation requiring restaurant owners to serve people without regard to color. The crucial issue which the case does present but which the Court does not decide is whether the Fourteenth Amend-

ment, of itself, forbids a State to enforce its trespass laws to convict a person who comes into a privately owned restaurant, is told that because of his color he will not be served, and over the owner's protest refuses to leave. We dissent from the Court's refusal to decide that question. For reasons stated, we think that the question should be decided and that the Fourteenth Amendment does not forbid this application of a State's trespass laws. . . .

III

Section 1 of the Fourteenth Amendment provides in part:

"No State shall . . . deprive any person of life, liberty, or property, without due process of law; nor deny to any person within its jurisdiction the equal protection of the laws."

This section of the Amendment, unlike other sections, is a prohibition against certain conduct only when done by a State —"state action" as it has come to be known —and "erects no shield against merely private conduct, however discriminatory or wrongful." *Shelley* v. *Kraemer*, 334 U.S. 1, 13 (1948). This well-established interpretation of section 1 of the Amendment—which all the parties here, including the petitioners and the Solicitor General, accept— means that this section of the Amendment does not of itself, standing alone, in the absence of some cooperative state action or compulsion, forbid property holders, including restaurant owners, to ban people from entering or remaining upon their premises, even if the owners act out of racial prejudice. But "the prohibitions of the amendment extend to all action of the State denying equal protection of the laws" whether "by its legislative, its executive, or its judicial authorities." *Virginia* v. *Rives*, 100 U.S. 313, 318 (1880). The Amendment thus forbids all kinds of state action, by all state agencies and officers, that discriminate against persons on account of their race. It was this kind of state action that was held invalid in *Brown* v. *Board of Education*, 347 U.S. 483 (1954). *Peterson* v. *City of Greenville*, 373 U.S. 244 (1963), *Lombard* v. *Louisiana*, 373 U.S. 267 (1963), and *Grif-*

fin v. *County School Board*, 377 U.S. ——
(1964), and that this Court today holds invalid in *Robinson* v. *Florida, ante* p. ——.

Petitioners, but not the Solicitor General, contend that their conviction for trespass under the state statute was by itself the kind of discriminatory state action forbidden by the Fourteenth Amendment. This contention, on its face, has plausibility when considered along with general statements to the effect that under the Amendment forbidden "state action" may be that of the Judicial as well as of the Legislative or Executive Branches of Government. But a mechanical application of the Fourteenth Amendment to this case cannot survive analysis. The Amendment does not forbid a State to prosecute for crimes committed against a person or his property, however prejudiced or narrow the victim's views may be. Nor can whatever prejudice and bigotry the victim of a crime may have be automatically attributed to the State that prosecutes. Such a doctrine would not only be based on a fiction; it would also severely handicap a State's efforts to maintain a peaceful and orderly society. Our society has put its trust in a system of criminal laws to punish lawless conduct. To avert personal feuds and violent brawls it has led its people to believe and expect that wrongs against them will be vindicated in the courts. Instead of attempting to take the law into their own hands, people have been taught to call for police protection to protect their rights wherever possible. It would betray our whole plan for a tranquil and orderly society to say that a citizen, because of his personal prejudices, habits, attitudes, or beliefs, is cast outside the law's protection and cannot call for the aid of officers sworn to uphold the law and preserve the peace. The worst citizen no less than the best is entitled to equal protection of the laws of his State and of his Nation. None of our past cases justifies reading the Fourteenth Amendment in a way that might well penalize citizens who are law-abiding enough to call upon the law and its officers for protection instead of using their own physical strength or

dangerous weapons to preserve their rights.

In contending that the State's prosecution of petitioners for trespass is state action forbidden by the Fourteenth Amendment, petitioners rely chiefly on *Shelley* v. *Kraemer, supra.* That reliance is misplaced. *Shelley* held that the Fourteenth Amendment was violated by a State's enforcement of restrictive covenants providing that certain pieces of real estate should not be used or occupied by Negroes, orientals, or any other noncaucasians, either as owners or tenants, and that in case of use or occupancy by such proscribed classes, the title of any person so using or occupying it should be divested. Many briefs were filed in that case by the parties and by *amici curiae.* To support the holding that state enforcement of the agreements constituted prohibited state action even though the agreements were made by private persons to whom, if they act alone, the Amendment does not apply, two chief grounds were urged: (1) This type of agreement constituted a restraint on alienation of property, sometimes in perpetuity, which, if valid, was in reality the equivalent of and had the effect of state and municipal zoning laws, accomplishing the same kind of racial discrimination as if the State had passed a statute instead of leaving this objective to be accomplished by a system of private contracts, enforced by the State. See *Marsh* v. *Alabama*, 326 U.S. 501 (1946); *Terry* v. *Adams*, 345 U.S. 461 (1953); cf. *Yick Wo* v. *Hopkins*, 118 U.S. 356 (1886); *Nashville, C. & St. L.R. Co.* v. *Browning*, 310 U.S. 362 (1940). (2) Nearly all the briefs in *Shelley* which asked invalidation of the restrictive covenants iterated and reiterated that judicial enforcement of this system of covenants was forbidden state action because the right of a citizen to own, use, enjoy, occupy, and dispose of property is a federal right protected by the Civil Rights Acts of 1866 and 1870, validly passed pursuant to congressional power authorized by section 5 of the Fourteenth Amendment. This argument was buttressed by citation of many cases, some of which are referred to in this Court's opinion in *Buchanan* v.

Warley, 245 U.S. 60 (1917). In that case this Court, acting under the Fourteenth Amendment and the Civil Rights Acts of 1866 and 1870, struck down a city ordinance which zoned property on the basis of race, stating, 245 U.S., at 81, "The right which the ordinance annulled was the civil right of a white man to dispose of his property if he saw fit to do so to a person of color, and of a colored person to make such disposition to a white person." *Buchanan* v. *Warley* was heavily relied on by this Court in *Shelley* v. *Kraemer, supra,* where this statement from *Buchanan* was quoted: "The Fourteenth Amendment and these statutes [of 1866 and 1870] enacted in furtherance of its purpose operate to qualify and entitle a colored man to acquire property without state legislation discriminating against him solely because of color." 334 U.S., at 11–12. And the Court in *Shelley* went on to cite with approval two later decisions of this Court which, relying on *Buchanan* v. *Warley,* had invalidated other city ordinances.

It seems pretty clear that the reason judicial enforcement of the restrictive covenants in *Shelley* was deemed state action was, not merely the fact that a state court had acted, but rather that it had acted "to deny to petitioners, on the grounds of race or color, the enjoyment of property rights in premises which petitioners are willing and financially able to acquire and which the grantors are willing to sell." 334 U.S., at 19. In other words, this Court held that state enforcement of the covenants had the effect of denying to the parties their federally guaranteed right to own, occupy, enjoy, and use their property without regard to race or color. Thus, the line of cases from *Buchanan* through *Shelley* establishes these propositions: (1) When an owner of property is willing to sell and a would-be purchaser is willing to buy, then the Civil Rights Act of 1866, which gives all persons the same right to "inherit, lease, sell, hold, and convey" property, prohibits a State, whether through its legislature, executive, or judiciary, from preventing the sale on the grounds of the race or color of one of the

parties. *Shelley* v. *Kraemer, supra,* 334 U.S., at 19. (2) Once a person has become a property owner, then he acquires all the rights that go with ownership: "the free use, enjoyment, and disposal of a person's acquisitions without control or diminution save by the law of the land." *Buchanan* v. *Warley, supra,* 245 U.S., at 74. This means that the property owner may, in the absence of a valid statute forbidding it, sell his property to whom he pleases and admit to that property whom he will; so long as *both* parties are willing parties, then the principles stated in *Buchanan* and *Shelley* protect this right. But equally, when one party is unwilling, as when the property owner chooses *not* to sell to a particular person or *not* to admit that person, then, as this Court emphasized in *Buchanan,* he is entitled to rely on the guarantee of due process of law, that is, "law of the land," to protect his free use and enjoyment of property and to know that only by valid legislation, passed pursuant to some constitutional grant of power, can anyone disturb this free use. But petitioners here would have us hold that, despite the absence of any valid statute restricting the use of his property, the owner of Hooper's restaurant in Baltimore must not be accorded the same federally guaranteed right to occupy, enjoy, and use property given to the parties in *Buchanan* and *Shelley;* instead, petitioners would have us say that Hooper's federal right must be cut down and he be compelled—though no statute said he must—to allow people to force their way into his restaurant and remain there over his protest. We cannot subscribe to such a mutilating, one-sided interpretation of federal guarantees the very heart of which is equal treatment under law to all. We must never forget that the Fourteenth Amendment protects "life, liberty, or property" of all people generally, not just some people's "life," some people's "liberty," and some kinds of "property."

In concluding that mere judicial enforcement of the trespass law is not sufficient to impute to Maryland Hooper's refusal to serve Negroes, we are in accord with the

Solicitor General's views as we understand them. He takes it for granted "that the mere fact of State intervention through the courts or other public authority in order to provide sanctions for a private decision is not enough to implicate the State for the purposes of the Fourteenth Amendment. . . . Where the only State involvement is color-blind support for every property-owner's exercise of the normal right to choose his business visitors or social guests, proof that the particular property-owner was motivated by racial or religious prejudices is not enough to convict the State of denying equal protection of the laws."

The Solicitor General also says: "The preservation of a free and pluralistic society would seem to require substantial freedom for private choice in social, business and professional associations. Freedom of choice means the liberty to be wrong as well as right, to be mean as well as noble, to be vicious as well as kind. And even if that view were questioned, the philosophy of federalism leaves an area for choice to the States and their people, when the State is not otherwise involved, instead of vesting the only power of effective decision in the federal courts."

We, like the Solicitor General, reject the argument that the State's protection of Hooper's desire to choose customers on the basis of race by prosecuting trespassers is enough, standing alone, to deprive Hooper of his right to operate the property in his own way. But we disagree with the contention that there are other circumstances which, added to the State's prosecution for trespass, justify a finding of state action. There is no Maryland law, no municipal ordinance, and no official proclamation or action of any kind that shows the slightest state coercion of, or encouragement to, Hooper to bar Negroes from his restaurant. Neither the State, the city, nor any of their agencies has leased publicly owned property to Hooper. It is true that the State and city regulate the restaurants—but not by compelling restaurants to deny service to customers because of their race. License

fees are collected, but this licensing has no relationship to race. Under such circumstances, to hold that a State must be held to have participated in prejudicial conduct of its licensees is too big a jump for us to take. Businesses owned by private persons do not become agencies of the State because they are licensed; to hold that they do would be completely to negate all our private ownership concepts and practices.

Neither the parties nor the Solicitor General, at least with respect to Maryland, has been able to find the present existence of any state law or local ordinance, any state court or administrative ruling, or any other official state conduct which could possibly have had any coercive influence on Hooper's racial practices. Yet despite a complete absence of any sort of proof or even respectable speculation that Maryland in any way instigated or encouraged Hooper's refusal to serve Negroes, it is argued at length that Hooper's practice should be classified as "state action." This contention rests on a long narrative of historical events, both before and since the Civil War, to show that in Maryland, and indeed in the whole South, state laws and state actions have been a part of a pattern of racial segregation in the conduct of business, social, religious, and other activities. This pattern of segregation hardly needs historical references to prove it. The argument is made that the trespass conviction should be labeled "state action" because the "momentum" of Maryland's "past legislation" is still substantial in the realm of public accommodations. To that extent, the Solicitor General argues, "a State which has drawn a color line may not suddenly assert that it is color blind." We cannot accept such an *ex post facto* argument to hold the application here of Maryland's trespass law unconstitutional. Nor can we appreciate the fairness or justice of holding the present generation of Marylanders responsible for what their ancestors did in other days—even if we had the right to substitute our own ideas of what the Fourteenth Amendment ought to be for what it was written and adopted to achieve.

There is another objection to accepting this argument. If it were accepted, we would have one Fourteenth Amendment for the South and quite a different and more lenient one for the other parts of the country. Present "state action" in this area of constitutional rights would be governed by past history in the South—by present conduct in the North and West. Our Constitution was not written to be read that way, and we will not do it. . . .

[Omitted here is a lengthy response to Mr. Justice Goldberg's historical analysis of the meaning of the Fourteenth Amendment.]

We are admonished that in deciding this case we should remember that "it is *a constitution* we are expounding." We conclude as we do because we remember that it *is* a Constitution and that it is our duty "to bow with respectful submission to its provisions." And in recalling that it is a Constitution "intended to endure for ages to come," we also remember that the Founders wisely provided the means for that endurance: changes in the Constitution, when thought necessary, are to be proposed by Congress or conventions and ratified by the States. The Founders gave no such amending power to this Court. Cf. *Ex parte Virginia,* 100 U.S. 339, 345–346 (1880). Our duty is simply to interpret the Constitution, and in doing so the test of constitutionality is not whether a law is offensive to our conscience or to the "good old common law," but whether it is offensive to the Constitution. Confining ourselves to our constitutional duty to construe, not to rewrite or amend, the Constitution, we believe that section 1 of the Fourteenth Amendment does not bar Maryland from enforcing its trespass laws so long as it does so with impartiality.

This Court has done much in carrying out its solemn duty to protect people from unlawful discrimination. And it will, of course, continue to carry out this duty in the future as it has in the past. But the Fourteenth Amendment of itself does not compel either a black man or a white man running his own private business to trade with anyone else against his will. We do not believe that section 1 of the Fourteenth Amendment was written or designed to interfere with a storekeeper's right to choose his customers or with a property owner's right to choose his social or business associates, so long as he does not run counter to valid state or federal regulation. The case before us does not involve the power of the Congress to pass a law compelling privately owned businesses to refrain from discrimination on the basis of race and to trade with all if they trade with any. We express no views as to the power of Congress, acting under one or another provision of the Constitution, to prevent racial discrimination in the operation of privately owned businesses, nor upon any particular form of legislation to that end. Our sole conclusion is that section 1 of the Fourteenth Amendment, standing alone, does not prohibit privately owned restaurants from choosing their own customers. It does not destroy what has until very recently been universally recognized in this country as the unchallenged right of a man who owns a business to run the business in his own way so long as some valid regulatory statute does not tell him to do otherwise. . . .

We would affirm.

NOTE: The impasse caused by the deep differences among the Justices (as revealed in *Bell*) seems to have been largely "solved" in *Hamm* v. *City of Rockhill,* 85 S. Ct. 384 (1964). Hamm and others had been prosecuted for trespass in *peaceful,* lunch-counter "sit-ins." The Court held that no such prosecutions were permissible with respect to places of "public accommodation" covered by the federal Civil Rights Act of 1964. For Congress had in effect prohibited application of state trespass laws that would deprive any person of the rights granted under the new federal act. Moreover, the Court held that prosecutions (as in Hamm's case) begun before, but not concluded at the time of the passage of the 1964 Civil Rights Act, were abated. Such abatement was derived from the old principle that Congress must be presumed to have intended there should be no punishment when punishment could no longer further any legislative policy (the original policy having been repealed or invalidated by later legislation).

Justices Black, Stewart, Harlan, and White in separate dissenting opinions found, *inter alia*, that the abatement principle was not relevant to these cases.

VI. FREEDOM OF RELIGION

The First Amendment prohibits national legislation concerning "an establishment of religion" or interfering with "the free exercise thereof." Both propositions have been absorbed into the Fourteenth Amendment by virtue of the *Palko* rule. Each is plagued with difficulty. Does the restraint on "establishment" impose a complete "separation of church and state," or does it merely forbid preferred governmental treatment for one, or some, religions?

The "free exercise" provision presents another question. "Religion" is not a term of precise content. Its meaning for some is anything but religious for others. Precisely because there is such a variety of belief, things political and spiritual impinge upon each other endlessly. The injunction to render unto Caesar what belongs to Caesar recognizes, but does not solve, the difficulty. The first tolerant community in America attracted, and so had to face, a variety of unorthodox sects each claiming immunity from important civic obligations in the name of religious freedom. "To prevent such mistakes," said its founder, Roger Williams, "I shall at present only propose this case: There goes many a ship to sea, with many hundreds souls in one ship, whose weal and woe is common, and is a true picture of a commonwealth. . . . It hath fallen out sometimes, that both papists and protestants, Jews and Turks, may be embarked in one ship: upon which supposal I affirm, that all the liberty of conscience, that ever I pleaded for, turns upon these two hinges—that none of the papists, protestants, Jews, or Turks, be forced to come to the ship's prayers or worship, nor compelled from their own particular prayers or worship, if they practice any. I further add, that I never denied, that notwithstanding this liberty, the commander of this ship ought to command the ship's course, yea, and also command that justice, peace and sobriety, be kept and practiced, both among the seamen and all the passengers. If any of the seamen refuse to perform their services, or passengers to pay their freight; if any refuse to help, in person or purse, towards the common charges or defence; if any refuse to obey the common laws and orders of the ship, concerning their common peace or preservation; if any shall mutiny and rise up against their commanders and officers; if any should preach or write that there ought to be no commanders or officers, because all are equal in Christ, therefore no masters nor officers, no laws nor orders, nor corrections nor punishments;—I say, I never denied, but in such cases, whatever is pretended, the commander or commanders may judge, resist, compel and punish such transgressors, according to their deserts and merits. This if seriously and honestly minded, may, if it so please the Father of lights, let in some light to such as willingly shut not their eyes."

If Williams' analogy is neat, the rub comes in its application as in the cruel context of the *Barnette Flag Salute* case. Essentially the difficulty is that the First Amendment "embraces two concepts—freedom to believe and freedom to act. The first is absolute but, in the nature of things, the second cannot be." *Cantwell* v. *Connecticut,* 310 U.S. 296, 303–4 (1940). Thus Mormons have been penalized for practicing polygamy, *Reynolds* v. *United States,* 98 U.S. 145 (1878); conscientious pacifists for declining military training, *Hamilton* v. *Regents of the University of California,* 293 U.S. 245 (1934); and parents for permitting their children to violate child labor laws by the distribution of religious literature, *Prince* v. *Massachusetts,* 321 U.S. 158 (1944). On the other hand, peddling of church literature by adults is immune from general peddlers' license taxes, *Murdock* v. *Pennsylvania,* 319 U.S. 105 (1943); and from laws enacted to protect the privacy of householders, *Martin* v. *Struthers,* 319 U.S. 141 (1943). Let him who can, find a common denominator of principle in these decisions! The plain fact is that until 1937 fewer than a score of cases involving religious freedom reached the Supreme Court. (Recall the discretionary nature of the Court's reviewing authority—Part One, IV.) Since then cases have been numerous, but only time can provide adequate answers for such basic problems. This is the secret of constitutional, as of common, law. And this is what Holmes meant when he said that the life of the law is experience, not logic.

Davis v. *Beason,* 133 U.S. 333 (1890), is a convenient starting point. It involved the validity of an Act of the Idaho Territorial Legislature (in its application to Mormons) prohibiting polygamists from voting, and requiring an oath by every voter that he was not a member of an order that taught, counseled, or encouraged polygamy. Upholding this act, the Court observed:

The term "religion" has reference to one's views of his relations to his Creator, and to the obligations they impose of reverence for his being and character, and of obedience to his will. It is often confounded with the *cultus* or form of worship of a particular sect, but is distinguishable from the latter. The First Amendment to the Constitution, in declaring that Congress shall make no law respecting the establishment of religion, or forbidding the free exercise thereof, was intended to allow everyone under the jurisdiction of the United States to entertain such notions respecting his relations to his Maker and the duties they impose as may be approved by his judgment and conscience, and to exhibit his sentiments in such form of worship as he may think proper, not injurious to the equal rights of others, and to prohibit legislation for the support of any religious tenets, or the modes of worship of any sect . . . It was never intended or supposed that the Amendment could be invoked as a protection against legislation for the punishment of acts inimical to the peace, good order and morals of society.

PIERCE v. SOCIETY OF SISTERS
268 U.S. 510 (1925)

Appeals from decrees of the District Court of the United States for the District of Oregon.

Mr. Justice McReynolds delivered the opinion of the court:

These appeals [including *Pierce* v. *Hill Military Academy*] are from decrees, based upon undenied allegations, which granted preliminary orders restraining appellants from threatening or attempting to enforce [against the Society of Sisters and the Military Academy] the Compulsory Education Act adopted November 7, 1922, under the initiative provision of her Constitution by the voters of Oregon. Judicial Code, § 266. They present the same points of law; there are no controverted questions of fact. Rights said to be guaranteed by the Federal Constitution were specially set up, and appropriate prayers asked for their protection.

The challenged Act, effective September 1, 1926, requires every parent, guardian or other person having control or charge or custody of a child between eight and sixteen years to send him "to a public school for the period of time a public school shall be held during the current year" in the district where the child resides; and failure so to do is declared a misdemeanor. There are exemptions—not specially important here—for children who are not normal, or who have completed the eighth grade, or who reside at considerable distances from any public school, or who hold special permits from the County Superintendent. The manifest purpose is to compel general attendance at public schools by normal children, between eight and sixteen, who have not completed the eighth grade. And without doubt enforcement of the statute would seriously impair, perhaps destroy, the profitable features of appellees' business and

greatly diminish the value of their property. . . .

No question is raised concerning the power of the State reasonably to regulate all schools, to inspect, supervise and examine them, their teachers and pupils; to require that all children of proper age attend some school, that teachers shall be of good moral character and patriotic disposition, that certain studies plainly essential to good citizenship must be taught, and that nothing be taught which is manifestly inimical to the public welfare.

The inevitable practical result of enforcing the Act under consideration would be destruction of appellees' primary schools, and perhaps all other private primary schools for normal children within the State of Oregon. These parties are engaged in a kind of undertaking not inherently harmful, but long regarded as useful and meritorious. Certainly there is nothing in the present records to indicate that they have failed to discharge their obligations to patrons, students or the State. And there are no peculiar circumstances or present emergencies which demand extraordinary measures relative to primary education.

Under the doctrine of *Meyer* v. *Nebraska*, 262 U.S. 390, we think it entirely plain that the Act of 1922 unreasonably interferes with the liberty of parents and guardians to direct the upbringing and education of children under their control. As often heretofore pointed out, rights guaranteed by the Constitution may not be abridged by legislation which has no reasonable relation to some purpose within the competency of the State. The fundamental theory of liberty upon which all governments in this Union repose excludes any general power of the State to standardize its children by forcing them to accept instruction from public teachers only. The child is not the mere creature of the State; those who nurture him and direct his destiny have the right, coupled with the high duty, to recognize and prepare him for additional obligations.

These suits were not premature. The injury to appellees was present and very real, not a mere possibility in the remote future.

If no relief had been possible prior to the effective date of the Act, the injury would have become irreparable. Prevention of impending injury by unlawful action is a well recognized function of courts of equity.

The decrees below are
Affirmed.

WEST VIRGINIA BOARD OF EDUCATION v. BARNETTE
319 U.S. 624 (1943)

In *Minersville School District* v. *Gobitis,* 310 U.S. 586 (1940), Jehovah's Witnesses challenged a law requiring a brief flag salute ceremony as part of a public school curriculum. In their view the salute constituted a violation of the scriptural injunction against bowing down to graven images. Over the dissent of Mr. Justice Stone, the requirement was upheld on the ground that: "It is not our province to choose among competing considerations in the subtle process of securing effective loyalty to the traditional ideals of democracy, while respecting at the same time individual idiosyncrasies among a people so diversified in racial origins and religious allegiances. So to hold would in effect make us the school board for the country."

Some two years later the same issue arose on appeal in the *Barnette* case.

MR. JUSTICE JACKSON delivered the opinion of the Court: . . .

Appellees, citizens of the United States and of West Virginia, brought suit in the United States District Court for themselves and others similarly situated asking its injunction to restrain enforcement of these laws and regulations against Jehovah's Witnesses. The Witnesses are an unincorporated body teaching that the obligation imposed by law of God is superior to that of laws enacted by temporal government. Their religious beliefs include a literal version of Exodus, Chapter 20, verses 4 and 5, which says: "Thou shalt not make unto thee any graven image, or any likeness of anything that is in heaven above, or that is in the earth beneath, or that is in the water under the earth; thou shalt not bow down thyself to them nor serve them." They consider that the flag is an "image" within this command. For this reason they refuse to salute it. . . .

This case calls upon us to reconsider a precedent decision, as the Court throughout its history often has been required to do. Before turning to the *Gobitis* case, however, it is desirable to notice certain characteristics by which this controversy is distinguished.

The freedom asserted by these appellees does not bring them into collision with rights asserted by any other individual. It is such conflicts which most frequently require intervention of the State to determine where the rights of one end and those of another begin. But the refusal of these persons to participate in the ceremony does not interfere with or deny rights of others to do so. Nor is there any question in this case that their behavior is peaceable and orderly. The sole conflict is between authority and rights of the individual. The State asserts power to condition access to public education on making a prescribed sign and profession and at the same time to coerce attendance by punishing both parent and child. The latter stand on a right of self-determination in matters that touch individual opinion and personal attitude.

As the present Chief Justice said in dissent in the *Gobitis* case, the State may "require teaching by instruction and study of all in our history and in the structure and organization of our government, including the guaranties of civil liberty, which tend to inspire patriotism and love of country." 310 U.S. at 604. Here, however, we are dealing with a compulsion of students to declare a belief. They are not merely made acquainted with the flag salute so that they may be informed as to what it is or even what it means. The issue here is whether this slow and easily neglected route to aroused loyalties constitutionally may be short-cut by substituting a compulsory salute and slogan. . . .

There is no doubt that, in connection with the pledges, the flag salute is a form of utterance. Symbolism is a primitive but effective way of communicating ideas. . . .

It is also to be noted that the compulsory flag salute and pledge requires affirmation of a belief and an attitude of mind. It is not clear whether the regulation contemplates that pupils forego any contrary convictions of their own and become unwilling converts to the prescribed ceremony or whether it will be acceptable if they simulate assent by words without belief and by a gesture barren of meaning. It is now a commonplace that censorship or suppression of expression of opinion is tolerated by our Constitution only when the expression presents a clear and present danger of action of a kind the State is empowered to prevent and punish. It would seem that involuntary affirmation could be commanded only on even more immediate and urgent grounds than silence. But here the power of compulsion is invoked without any allegation that remaining passive during a flag salute ritual creates a clear and present danger that would justify an effort even to muffle expression. To sustain the compulsory flag salute we are required to say that a Bill of Rights which guards the individual's right to speak his

own mind, left it open to public authorities to compel him to utter what is not in his mind.

Whether the First Amendment to the Constitution will permit officials to order observance of ritual of this nature does not depend upon whether as a voluntary exercise we would think it to be good, bad or merely innocuous. . . .

Nor does the issue as we see it turn on one's possession of particular religious views or the sincerity with which they are held. While religion supplies appellees' motive for enduring the discomforts of making the issue in this case, many citizens who do not share these religious views hold such a compulsory rite to infringe constitutional liberty of the individual. It is not necessary to inquire whether non-conformist beliefs will exempt from the duty to salute unless we first find power to make the salute a legal duty.

The *Gobitis* decision, however, *assumed*, as did the argument in that case and in this, that power exists in the State to impose the flag salute discipline upon school children in general. The Court only examined and rejected a claim based on religious beliefs of immunity from an unquestioned general rule. The question which underlies the flag salute controversy is whether such a ceremony so touching matters of opinion and political attitude may be imposed upon the individual by official authority under powers committed to any political organization under our Constitution. . . .

In weighing arguments of the parties it is important to distinguish between the due process clause of the Fourteenth Amendment as an instrument for transmitting the principles of the First Amendment and those cases in which it is applied for its own sake. The test of legislation which collides with the Fourteenth Amendment because it also collides with the principles of the First, is much more definite than the test when only the Fourteenth is involved. Much of the vagueness of the due process clause disappears when the specific prohibitions of the First become its standard. The right of a State to regulate, for example, a public utility may well include, so far as the due process test is concerned, power to impose all of the restrictions which a legislature may have a "rational basis" for adopting. But freedoms of speech and of press, of assembly, and of worship may not be infringed on such slender grounds. They are susceptible of restriction only to prevent grave and immediate danger to interests which the State may lawfully protect. It is important to note that while it is the Fourteenth Amendment which bears directly upon the State it is the more specific limiting principles of the First Amendment that finally govern this case.

Nor does our duty to apply the Bill of Rights to assertions of official authority depend upon our possession of marked competence in the field where the invasion of rights occurs. True, the task of translating the majestic generalities of the Bill of Rights, conceived as part of the pattern of liberal government in the eighteenth century, into concrete restraints on officials dealing with the problems of the twentieth century, is one to disturb self-confidence. These principles grew in soil which also produced a philosophy that the individual was the center of society, that his liberty was attainable through mere absence of governmental restraints, and that government should be entrusted with few controls and only the mildest supervision over men's affairs. We must transplant these rights to a soil in which the laissez-faire concept or principle of non-interference has withered at least as to economic affairs, and social advancements are increasingly sought through closer integration of society and through expanded and strengthened governmental controls. These changed conditions often deprive precedents of reliability and cast us more than we would choose upon our own judgment. But we act in these matters not by authority of our competence but by force of our commissions. We cannot, because of modest estimates of our competence in such specialties as public education, withhold the judgment

that history authenticates as the function of this Court when liberty is infringed. . . .

The case is made difficult not because the principles of its decision are obscure but because the flag involved is our own. Nevertheless, we apply the limitations of the Constitution with no fear that freedom to be intellectually and spiritually diverse or even contrary will disintegrate the social organization. To believe that patriotism will not flourish if patriotic ceremonies are voluntary and spontaneous instead of a compulsory routine is to make an unflattering estimate of the appeal of our institutions to free minds. We can have intellectual individualism and the rich cultural diversities that we owe to exceptional minds only at the price of occasional eccentricity and abnormal attitudes. When they are so harmless to others or to the State as those we deal with here, the price is not too great. But freedom to differ is not limited to things that do not matter much. That would be a mere shadow of freedom. The test of its substance is the right to differ as to things that touch the heart of the existing order.

If there is any fixed star in our constitutional constellation, it is that no official, high or petty, can prescribe what shall be orthodox in politics, nationalism, religion, or other matters of opinion or force citizens to confess by word or act their faith therein. If there are any circumstances which permit an exception, they do not now occur to us.

We think the action of the local authorities in compelling the flag salute and pledge transcends constitutional limitations on their power and invades the sphere of intellect and spirit which it is the purpose of the First Amendment to our Constitution to reserve from all official control. . . .

The decision of this Court in *Minersville School District* v. *Gobitis* and the holdings of those few per curiam decisions which preceded and foreshadowed it are overruled, and the judgment enjoining enforcement of the West Virginia Regulation is affirmed.

Affirmed.

Mr. Justice Roberts and Mr. Justice Reed adhere to the views expressed by the Court in *Minersville School District* v. *Gobitis,* 310 U.S. 586, and are of the opinion that the judgment below should be reversed.

Mr. Justice Black and Mr. Justice Douglas, concurring ["explained" their change of view since the *Gobitis* case.]

Mr. Justice Frankfurter, dissenting.

One who belongs to the most vilified and persecuted minority in history is not likely to be insensible to the freedoms guaranteed by our Constitution. Were my purely personal attitude relevant I should wholeheartedly associate myself with the general libertarian views in the Court's opinion, representing as they do the thought and action of a lifetime. But as judges we are neither Jew nor Gentile, neither Catholic nor agnostic. We owe equal attachment to the Constitution and are equally bound by our judicial obligations whether we derive our citizenship from the earliest or the latest immigrants to these shores. As a member of this Court I am not justified in writing my private notions of policy into the Constitution, no matter how deeply I may cherish them or how mischievous I may deem their disregard. . . .

Under our constitutional system the legislature is charged solely with civil concerns of society. If the avowed or intrinsic legislative purpose is either to promote or to discourage some religious community or creed, it is clearly within the constitutional restrictions imposed on legislatures and cannot stand. But it by no means follows that legislative power is wanting whenever a general non-discriminatory civil regulation in fact touches conscientious scruples or religious beliefs of an individual or a group. . . .

Conscientious scruples, all would admit, cannot stand against every legislative compulsion to do positive acts in conflict with such scruples. We have been told that such compulsions override religious scruples only as to major concerns of the state. But the determination of what is major and what

is minor itself raises questions of policy. For the way in which men equally guided by reason appraise importance goes to the very heart of policy. Judges should be very diffident in setting their judgment against that of a state in determining what is and what is not a major concern, what means are appropriate to proper ends, and what is the total social cost in striking the balance of imponderables. . . .

The constitutional protection of religious freedom terminated disabilities, it did not create new privileges. It gave religious equality, not civil immunity. Its essence is freedom from conformity to religious dogma, not freedom from conformity to law because of religious dogma. Religious loyalties may be exercised without hindrance from the state, not the state may not exercise that which except by leave of religious loyalties is within the domain of temporal power. Otherwise each individual could set up his own censor against obedience to laws conscientiously deemed for the public good by those whose business it is to make laws.

The prohibition against any religious establishment by the government placed denominations on an equal footing—it assured freedom from support by the government to any mode of worship and the freedom of individuals to support any mode of worship. Any person may therefore believe or disbelieve what he pleases. He may practice what he will in his own house of worship or publicly within the limits of public order. But the lawmaking authority is not circumscribed by the variety of religious beliefs, otherwise the constitutional guaranty would be not a protection of the free exercise of religion but a denial of the exercise of legislation.

The essence of the religious freedom guaranteed by our Constitution is therefore this: no religion shall either receive the state's support or incur its hostility. Religion is outside the sphere of political government. This does not mean that all matters on which religious organizations or beliefs may pronounce are outside the sphere of government. Were this so, instead of the separation of church and state, there would be the subordination of the state on any matter deemed within the sovereignty of the religious conscience. Much that is the concern of temporal authority affects the spiritual interests of men. But it is not enough to strike down a non-discriminatory law that it may hurt or offend some dissident view. It would be too easy to cite numerous prohibitions and injunctions to which laws run counter if the variant interpretations of the Bible were made the tests of obedience to law. The validity of secular laws cannot be measured by their conformity to religious doctrines. It is only in a theocratic state that ecclesiastical doctrines measure legal right or wrong. . . .

The subjection of dissidents to the general requirement of saluting the flag, as a measure conducive to the training of children in good citizenship, is very far from being the first instance of exacting obedience to general laws that have offended deep religious scruples. Compulsory vaccination, see *Jacobson* v. *Massachusetts*, 197 U.S. 11, food inspection regulations, see *Shapiro* v. *Lyle*, D.C., 30 F.2d 971, the obligation to bear arms, see *Hamilton* v. *Regents*, 293 U.S. 245, 267, testimonial duties, see *Stansbury* v. *Marks*, 2 Dall. 213, compulsory medical treatment, see *People* v. *Vogelgesang*, 221 N.Y. 290, 116 N.E. 977 —these are but illustrations of conduct that has often been compelled in the enforcement of legislation of general applicability even though the religious consciences of particular individuals rebelled at the exaction. . . .

We are told that a flag salute is a doubtful substitute for adequate understanding of our institutions. The states that require such a school exercise do not have to justify it as the only means for promoting good citizenship in children, but merely as one of diverse means for accomplishing a worthy end. We may deem it a foolish measure, but the point is that this Court is not the organ of government to resolve doubts as to whether it will fulfill its purpose. Only if there be no doubt that any reasonable mind could entertain can we deny to the states the right to resolve doubts their way and not ours.

That which to the majority may seem essential for the welfare of the state may offend the consciences of a minority. But, so long as no inroads are made upon the actual exercise of religion by the minority, to deny the political power of the majority to enact laws concerned with civil matters, simply because they may offend the consciences of a minority, really means that the consciences of a minority are more sacred and more enshrined in the Constitution than the consciences of a majority.

We are told that symbolism is a dramatic but primitive way of communicating ideas. Symbolism is inescapable. Even the most sophisticated live by symbols. But it is not for this Court to make psychological judgments as to the effectiveness of a particular symbol in inculcating concededly indispensable feelings, particularly if the state happens to see fit to utilize the symbol that represents our heritage and our hopes. And surely only flippancy could be responsible for the suggestion that constitutional validity of a requirement to salute our flag implies equal validity of a requirement to salute a dictator. The significance of a symbol lies in what it represents. To reject the swastika does not imply rejection of the Cross. And so it bears repetition to say that it mocks reason and denies our whole history to find in the allowance of a requirement to salute our flag on fitting occasions the seeds of sanction for obeisance to a leader. To deny the power to employ educational symbols is to say that the state's educational system may not stimulate the imagination because this may lead to unwise stimulation.

The right of West Virginia to utilize the flag salute as part of its educational process is denied because, so it is argued, it cannot be justified as a means of meeting a "clear and present danger" to national unity. In passing it deserves to be noted that the four cases which unanimously sustained the power of states to utilize such an educational measure arose and were all decided before the present World War. But to measure the state's power to make such regulations as are here resisted by the imminence of national danger is wholly to misconceive the origin and purpose of the concept of "clear and present danger." To apply such a test is for the Court to assume, however unwittingly, a legislative responsibility that does not belong to it. To talk about "clear and present danger" as the touchstone of allowable educational policy by the states whenever school curricula may impinge upon the boundaries of individual conscience, is to take a felicitous phrase out of the context of the particular situation where it arose and for which it was adapted. Mr. Justice Holmes used the phrase "clear and present danger" in a case involving mere speech as a means by which alone to accomplish sedition in time of war. . . . He was not enunciating a formal rule that there can be no restriction upon speech and, still less, no compulsion where conscience balks, unless imminent danger would thereby be wrought "to our institutions or our government." . . .

Of course patriotism cannot be enforced by the flag salute. But neither can the liberal spirit be enforced by judicial invalidation of illiberal legislation. Our constant preoccupation with the constitutionality of legislation rather than with its wisdom tends to preoccupation of the American mind with a false value. The tendency of focusing attention on constitutionality is to make constitutionality synonymous with wisdom, to regard a law as all right if it is constitutional. Such an attitude is a great enemy of liberalism. Particularly in legislation affecting freedom of thought and freedom of speech much which should offend a free-spirited society is constitutional. Reliance for the most precious interests of civilization, therefore, must be found outside of their vindication in courts of law. Only a persistent positive translation of the faith of a free society into the convictions and habits and actions of a community is the ultimate reliance against unabated temptations to fetter the human spirit.

NOTE: At the end of the 1957–58 term the Supreme Court denied certiorari in *Harris* v. *City of New York*, 357 U.S. 907, and *Kissinger* v. *United States*, 356 U.S. 958. In the former a lower court had rejected a claim that the city was subsidizing a Roman Catholic university by allowing it to buy city land at less than cost. In the latter a lower court had rejected a claim that Federal law penalizing a farmer for exceeding his wheat quota violated his religious belief that he should use his land to realize its full fertility.

EVERSON v. BOARD OF EDUCATION

330 U.S. 1 (1947)

A New Jersey statute authorized local school boards to provide for transportation of children to and from school. Pursuant to this act the defendant in this case authorized reimbursement from public funds of money paid by parents for bus transportation of their children. Some of the money went to parents for the transportation of their children to and from Roman Catholic parochial schools. The validity of such expenditures was challenged by a taxpayer and sustained in the state courts.

Appeal from the Court of Errors and Appeals of New Jersey.

Mr. Justice Black delivered the opinion of the Court: . . .

The New Jersey statute is challenged as a "law respecting an establishment of religion." The First Amendment, as made applicable to the states by the Fourteenth, *Murdock* v. *Pennsylvania,* 319 U.S. 105, commands that a state "shall make no law respecting an establishment of religion, or prohibiting the free exercise thereof." . . . Whether this New Jersey law is one respecting an "establishment of religion" requires an understanding of the meaning of that language, particularly with respect to the imposition of taxes. Once again, therefore, it is not inappropriate briefly to review the background and environment of the period in which that constitutional language was fashioned and adopted.

A large proportion of the early settlers of this country came here from Europe to escape the bondage of laws which compelled them to support and attend government-favored churches. The centuries immediately before and contemporaneous with the colonization of America had been filled with turmoil, civil strife, and persecutions, generated in large part by established sects determined to maintain their absolute political and religious supremacy. With the power of government supporting them, at various times and places, Catholics had persecuted Protestants, Protestants had persecuted Catholics, Protestant sects had persecuted other Protestant sects, Catholics of one shade of belief had persecuted Catholics of another shade of belief, and all of these had from time to time persecuted Jews. In efforts to force loyalty to whatever religious group happened to be on top and in league with the government of a particular time and place, men and women had been fined, cast in jail, cruelly tortured, and killed. Among the offenses for which these punishments had been inflicted were such things as speaking disrespectfully of the views of ministers of government-estab-

lished churches, non-attendance at those churches, expressions of non-belief in their doctrines, and failure to pay taxes and tithes to support them.

These practices of the old world were transplanted to and began to thrive in the soil of the new America. The very charters granted by the English Crown to the individuals and companies designated to make the laws which would control the destinies of the colonials authorized these individuals and companies to erect religious establishments which all, whether believers or non-believers, would be required to support and attend. An exercise of this authority was accompanied by a repetition of many of the old-world practices and persecutions. Catholics found themselves hounded and proscribed because of their faith; Quakers who followed their conscience went to jail; Baptists were peculiarly obnoxious to certain dominant Protestant sects; men and women of varied faiths who happened to be in a minority in a particular locality were persecuted because they steadfastly persisted in worshipping God only as their own consciences dictated. And all of these dissenters were compelled to pay tithes and taxes to support government-sponsored churches whose ministers preached inflammatory sermons designed to strengthen and consolidate the established faith by generating a burning hatred against dissenters.

These practices became so commonplace as to shock the freedom-loving colonials into a feeling of abhorrence. The imposition of taxes to pay ministers' salaries and to build and maintain churches and church property aroused their indignation. It was these feelings which found expression in the First Amendment. No one locality and no one group throughout the Colonies can rightly be given entire credit for having aroused the sentiment that culminated in adoption of the Bill of Rights' provisions embracing religious liberty. But Virginia, where the established church had achieved a dominant influence in political affairs and where many excesses attracted wide public attention, provided a great stimulus and able leadership for the movement. The people there, as elsewhere, reached the conviction that individual religious liberty could be achieved best under a government which was stripped of all power to tax, to support, or otherwise to assist any or all religions, or to interfere with the beliefs of any religious individual or group. . . .

The meaning and scope of the First Amendment, preventing establishment of religion or prohibiting the free exercise thereof, in the light of its history and the evils it was designed forever to suppress, have been several times elaborated by the decisions of this Court prior to the application of the First Amendment to the states by the Fourteenth. The broad meaning given the Amendment by these earlier cases has been accepted by this Court in its decisions concerning an individual's religious freedom rendered since the Fourteenth Amendment was interpreted to make the prohibitions of the First applicable to state action abridging religious freedom. There is every reason to give the same application and broad interpretation to the "establishment of religion" clause. The interrelation of these complementary clauses was well summarized in a statement of the Court of Appeals of South Carolina, quoted with approval by this Court in *Watson* v. *Jones,* 13 Wall. 679, 730: "The structure of our government has, for the preservation of civil liberty, rescued the temporal institutions from religious interference. On the other hand, it has secured religious liberty from the invasion of the civil authority."

The "establishment of religion" clause of the First Amendment means at least this: Neither a state nor the Federal Government can set up a church. Neither can pass laws which aid one religion, aid all religions, or prefer one religion over another. Neither can force nor influence a person to go to or to remain away from church against his will or force him to profess a belief or disbelief in any religion. No person can be punished for entertaining or professing religious beliefs or disbeliefs, for church attendance or nonattendance. No tax in any amount, large or small, can

be levied to support any religious activities or institutions, whatever they may be called, or whatever form they may adopt to teach or practice religion. Neither a state nor the Federal Government can, openly or secretly, participate in the affairs of any religious organizations or groups and vice versa. In the words of Jefferson, the clause against establishment of religion by law was intended to erect "a wall of separation between church and State." *Reynolds* v. *United States, supra* [98 U.S. 164].

We must consider the New Jersey statute in accordance with the foregoing limitations imposed by the First Amendment. But we must not strike that state statute down if it is within the State's constitutional power even though it approaches the verge of that power. See *Interstate Ry.* v. *Massachusetts,* Holmes, J., *supra* at 85, 88. New Jersey cannot consistently with the "establishment of religion" clause of the First Amendment contribute tax-raised funds to the support of an institution which teaches the tenets and faith of any church. On the other hand, other language of the amendment commands that New Jersey cannot hamper its citizens in the free exercise of their own religion. Consequently, it cannot exclude individual Catholics, Lutherans, Mohammedans, Baptists, Jews, Methodists, Non-believers, Presbyterians, or the members of any other faith, *because of their faith, or lack of it,* from receiving the benefits of public welfare legislation. While we do not mean to intimate that a state could not provide transportation only to children attending public schools, we must be careful, in protecting the citizens of New Jersey against state-established churches, to be sure that we do not inadvertently prohibit New Jersey from extending its general state law benefits to all its citizens without regard to their religious belief.

Measured by these standards, we cannot say that the First Amendment prohibits New Jersey from spending tax-raised funds to pay the bus fares of parochial school pupils as a part of a general program under which it pays the fares of pupils attending public and other schools. It is undoubtedly true that children are helped to get to church schools. There is even a possibility that some of the children might not be sent to the church schools if the parents were compelled to pay their children's bus fares out of their own pockets when transportation to a public school would have been paid for by the State. The same possibility exists where the state requires a local transit company to provide reduced fares to school children including those attending parochial schools, or where a municipally owned transportation system undertakes to carry all school children free of charge. Moreover, state-paid policemen, detailed to protect children going to and from church schools from the very real hazards of traffic, would serve much the same purpose and accomplish much the same result as state provisions intended to guarantee free transportation of a kind which the state deems to be best for the school children's welfare. And parents might refuse to risk their children to the serious danger of traffic accidents going to and from parochial schools, the approaches to which were not protected by policemen. Similarly, parents might be reluctant to permit their children to attend schools which the state had cut off from such general government services as ordinary police and fire protection, connections for sewage disposal, public highways and sidewalks. Of course, cutting off church schools from these services, so separate and so indisputably marked off from the religious function, would make it far more difficult for the schools to operate. But such is obviously not the purpose of the First Amendment. That Amendment requires the state to be a neutral in its relations with groups of religious believers and non-believers; it does not require the state to be their adversary. State power is no more to be used so as to handicap religions than it is to favor them.

This Court has said that parents may, in the discharge of their duty under state compulsory education laws, send their children to a religious rather than a public school if the school meets the secular educational requirements which the state has power to impose. See *Pierce* v. *Society of Sisters*, 268 U.S. 510. It appears that these parochial schools meet New Jersey's requirements. The State contributes no money to the schools. It does not support them. Its legislation, as applied, does no more than provide a general program to help parents get their children, regardless of their religion, safely and expeditiously to and from accredited schools.

The First Amendment has erected a wall between church and state. That wall must be kept high and impregnable. We could not approve the slightest breach. New Jersey has not breached it here.

Affirmed.

MR. JUSTICE JACKSON, dissenting: . . .

There is no answer to the proposition, more fully expounded by Mr. Justice Rutledge, that the effect of the religious freedom amendment to our Constitution was to take every form of propagation of religion out of the realm of things which could directly be made public business and thereby be supported in whole or in part at taxpayers' expense. That is a difference which the Constitution sets up between religion and almost every other subject matter of legislation, a difference which goes to the very root of religious freedom and which the court is overlooking today.

This freedom was first in the Bill of Rights because it was first in the forefathers' minds; it was set forth in absolute terms, and its strength is its rigidity. It was intended not only to keep the states' hands out of religion, but to keep religion's hands off the state, and, above all, to keep bitter religious controversy out of public life by denying to every denomination any advantage from getting control of public policy or the public purse. . . .

MR. JUSTICE RUTLEDGE, with whom MR. JUSTICE FRANKFURTER, MR. JUSTICE JACKSON, and MR. JUSTICE BURTON agree, dissenting. [After an extensive historical analysis, he concluded:]

Two great drives are constantly in motion to abridge, in the name of education, the complete division of religion and civil authority which our forefathers made. One is to introduce religious education and observances into the public schools. The other, to obtain public funds for the aid and support of various private religious schools. See Johnson, *The Legal Status of Church-State Relationships in the United States* (1934); Thayer, *Religion in Public Education* (1947); Note (1941) 50 *Yale L.J.* 917. In my opinion both avenues were closed by the Constitution. Neither should be opened by this Court. The matter is not one of quantity, to be measured by the amount of money expended. Now as in Madison's day it is one of principle, to keep separate the separate spheres as the First Amendment drew them; to prevent the first experiment upon our liberties; and to keep the question from becoming entangled in corrosive precedents. We should not be less strict to keep strong and untarnished the one side of the shield of religious freedom than we have been of the other.

NOTE: In at least five post-*Everson* cases, state high courts have held that *state constitutions* bar public bus rides to parochial schools. See, for example, *Board of Education* v. *Antone*, 384 Pac. 2nd. 911 (Oklahoma 1963). Several other state decisions reach the same conclusion via statutory construction. No state supreme court decision seems to follow the *Everson* view of separation of church and state.

ZORACH v. CLAUSON

343 U.S. 306 (1952)

Appeal from the New York Court of Appeals.

MR. JUSTICE DOUGLAS delivered the opinion of the Court:

New York City has a program which permits its public schools to release students during the school day so that they may leave the school buildings and school grounds and go to religious centers for religious instruction or devotional exercises. A student is released on written request of his parents. Those not released stay in the classrooms. The churches make weekly reports to the schools, sending a list of children who have been released from public school but who have not reported for religious instruction.

This "released time" program involves neither religious instruction in public school classrooms nor the expenditure of public funds. All costs, including the application blanks, are paid by the religious organizations. The case is therefore unlike *Illinois ex rel. McCollum* v. *Board of Education*, 333 U.S. 203, which involved a "released time" program from Illinois. In that case the classrooms were turned over to religious instructors. We accordingly held that the program violated the First Amendment which (by reason of the Fourteenth Amendment) prohibits the states from establishing religion or prohibiting its free exercise.

Appellants, who are taxpayers and residents of New York City and whose children attend its public schools, challenge the present law, contending it is in essence not different from the one involved in the *McCollum* case. Their argument, stated elaborately in various ways, reduces itself to this: the weight and influence of the school is put behind a program for religious instruction; public school teachers police it, keeping tab on students who are released; the classroom activities come to a halt while the students who are released for religious instruction are on leave; the school is a crutch on which the churches are leaning for support in their religious training; without the cooperation of the chools this "released time" program, like he one in the *McCollum* case, would be futile and ineffective. . . .

Our problem reduces itself to whether New York by this system has either prohibited the "free exercise" of religion or has made a law "respecting an establishment of religion" within the meaning of the First Amendment.

It takes obtuse reasoning to inject any issue of the "free exercise" of religion into the present case. No one is forced to go to the religious classroom and no religious exercise or instruction is brought to the classrooms of the public schools. A student need not take religious instruction. He is left to his own desires as to the manner or time of his religious devotions, if any. . . .

Moreover, apart from that claim of coercion, we do not see how New York by this type of "released time" program has made a law respecting an establishment of religion within the meaning of the First Amendment. There is much talk of the separation of Church and State in the history of the Bill of Rights and in the decisions clustering around the First Amendment. See *Everson* v. *Board of Education.* . . . There cannot be the slightest doubt that the First Amendment reflects the philosophy that Church and State should be separated. And so far as interference with the "free exercise" of religion and an "establishment" of religion are concerned, the separation must be complete and unequivocal. The First Amendment within the scope of its coverage permits no exception; the prohibition is absolute. The First Amendment, however, does not say that in every and all respects there shall be a separation of Church and State. Rather, it studiously defines the manner, the specific ways, in which there shall be no concert or union or dependency one on the other. That is the common sense of the matter. Otherwise, the state and religion would be

aliens to each other—hostile, suspicious, and even unfriendly. Churches could not be required to pay even property taxes. Municipalities would not be permitted to render police or fire protection to religious groups. Policemen who helped parishioners into their places of worship would violate the Constitution. Prayers in our legislative halls; the appeals to the Almighty in the messages of the Chief Executive; the proclamations making Thanksgiving Day a holiday; "so help me God" in our courtroom oaths—these and all other references to the Almighty that run through our laws, our public rituals, our ceremonies would be flouting the First Amendment. A fastidious atheist or agnostic could even object to the supplication with which the Court opens each session: "God save the United States and this Honorable Court."

We would have to press the concept of separation of Church and State to these extremes to condemn the present law on constitutional grounds. . . .

We are a religious people whose institutions presuppose a Supreme Being. We guarantee the freedom to worship as one chooses. We make room for as wide a variety of beliefs and creeds as the spiritual needs of man deem necessary. We sponsor an attitude on the part of government that shows no partiality to any one group and that lets each flourish according to the zeal of its adherents and the appeal of its dogma. When the state encourages religious instruction or cooperates with religious authorities by adjusting the schedule of public events to sectarian needs, it follows the best of our traditions. For it then respects the religious nature of our people and accommodates the public service to their spiritual needs. To hold that it may not would be to find in the Constitution a requirement that the government show a callous indifference to religious groups. That would be preferring those who believe in no religion over those who do believe. Government may not finance religious groups nor undertake religious instruction nor blend secular and sectarian education nor use secular institutions to force one or some religion on any person. But we find no constitutional requirement which makes it necessary for government to be hostile to religion and to throw its weight against efforts to widen the effective scope of religious influence. The government must be neutral when it comes to competition between sects. It may not thrust any sect on any person. It may not make a religious observance compulsory. It may not coerce anyone to attend church, to observe a religious holiday, or to take religious instruction. But it can close its doors or suspend its operations as to those who want to repair to their religious sanctuary for worship or instruction. No more than that is undertaken here. . . .

Affirmed.

MR. JUSTICE BLACK, dissenting: . . .

I see no significant difference between the invalid Illinois system and that of New York here sustained. Except for the use of the school buildings in Illinois, there is no difference between the systems which I consider even worthy of mention. In the New York program, as in that of Illinois, the school authorities release some of the children on the condition that they attend the religious classes, get reports on whether they attend, and hold the other children in the school building until the religious hour is over. As we attempted to make categorically clear, the *McCollum* decision would have been the same if the religious classes had not been held in the school buildings. . . .

I am aware that our *McCollum* decision on separation of church and state has been subjected to a most searching examination throughout the country. Probably few opinions from this Court in recent years have attracted more attention or stirred wider debate. Our insistence on "a wall between Church and State which must be kept high and impregnable" has seemed to some a correct exposition of the philosophy and a true interpretation of the language of the First Amendment to which we should strictly adhere. With equal conviction and sincerity, others have thought

the *McCollum* decision fundamentally wrong and have pledged continuous warfare against it. . . .

The Court's validation of the New York system rests in part on its statement that Americans are "a religious people whose institutions presuppose a Supreme Being." This was at least as true when the First Amendment was adopted; and it was just as true when eight justices of this Court invalidated the released time system in *McCollum* on the premise that a state can no more "aid all religions" than it can aid one. It was precisely because eighteenth-century Americans were a religious people divided into many fighting sects that we were given the constitutional mandate to keep Church and State completely separate. . . .

Under our system of religious freedom, people have gone to their religious sanctuaries not because they feared the law but because they loved their God. The choice of all has been as free as the choice of those who answered the call to worship moved only by the music of the old Sunday morning church bells. The spiritual mind of man has thus been free to believe, disbelieve, or doubt, without repression, great or small, by the heavy hand of government. Statutes authorizing such repression have been stricken. Before today, our judicial opinions have refrained from drawing invidious distinctions between those who believe in no religion and those who do believe. The First Amendment has lost much if the religious follower and the atheist are no longer to be judicially regarded as entitled to equal justice under law.

State help to religion injects political and party prejudices into a holy field. It too often substitutes force for prayer, hate for love, and persecution for persuasion. Government should not be allowed, under cover of the soft euphemism of "co-operation," to steal into the sacred area of religious choice.

MR. JUSTICE FRANKFURTER, dissenting: . . .

The pith of the case is that formalized

religious instruction is substituted for other school activity which those who do not participate in the released-time program are compelled to attend. The school system is very much in operation during this kind of released time. If its doors are closed, they are closed upon those students who do not attend the religious instruction in order to keep them within the school. That is the very thing which raises the constitutional issue. It is not met by disregarding it. Failure to discuss this issue does not take it out of the case. . . .

The deeply divisive controversy aroused by the attempts to secure public school pupils for sectarian instruction would promptly end if the advocates of such instruction were content to have the school "close its doors or suspend operations"— that is, dismiss classes in their entirety, without discrimination—instead of seeking to use the public schools as the instrument for security of attendance at denominational classes. The unwillingness of the promoters of this movement to dispense with such use of the public schools betrays a surprising want of confidence in the inherent power of the various faiths to draw children to outside sectarian classes—an attitude that hardly reflects the faith of the greatest religious spirits.

Mr. Justice Jackson, dissenting:

This released time program is founded upon a use of the State's power of coercion, which, for me, determines its unconstitutionality. Stripped to its essentials, the plan has two stages, first, that the State compel each student to yield a large part of his time for public secular education and, second, that some of it be "released" to him on condition that he devote it to sectarian religious purposes.

No one suggests that the Constitution would permit the State directly to require this "released" time to be spent "under the control of a duly constituted religious body." This program accomplishes that forbidden result by indirection. If public education were taking so much of the pupils' time as to injure the public or the

student's welfare by encroaching upon their religious opportunity, simply shortening everyone's school day would facilitate voluntary and optional attendance at Church classes. But that suggestion is rejected upon the ground that if they are made free many students will not go to the Church. Hence, they must be deprived of freedom for this period, with Church attendance put to them as one of the two permissible ways of using it.

The greater effectiveness of this system over voluntary attendance after school hours is due to the truant officer who, if the youngster fails to go to the Church school, dogs him back to the public schoolroom. Here schooling is more or less suspended during the "released time" so the nonreligious attendance will not forge ahead of the churchgoing absentees. But it serves as a temporary jail for a pupil who will not go to Church. It takes more subtlety of mind than I possess to deny that this is governmental constraint in support of religion. It is as unconstitutional, in my view, when exerted by indirection as when exercised forth-rightly.

As one whose children, as a matter of free choice, have been sent to privately supported Church schools, I may challenge the Court's suggestion that opposition to this plan can only be antireligious, atheistic, or agnostic. My evangelistic brethren confuse an objection to compulsion with an objection to religion. It is possible to hold a faith with enough confidence to believe that what should be rendered to God does not need to be decided and collected by Caesar.

The day that this country ceases to be free for irreligion it will cease to be free for religion—except for the sect that can win political power. The same epithetical jurisprudence used by the Court today to beat down those who oppose pressuring children into some religion can devise as good epithets tomorrow against those who object to pressuring them into a favored religion. And, after all, if we concede to the State power and wisdom to single out "duly constituted religious" bodies as exclusive alternatives for compulsory secular instruction, it would be logical to also uphold the [State's] power and wisdom to choose the true faith among those "duly constituted." We start down a rough road when we begin to mix compulsory public education with compulsory godliness.

A number of Justices just short of a majority of the majority that promulgates today's passionate dialectics joined in answering them in *Illinois ex rel. McCollum v. Board of Education.* . . . The distinction attempted between that case and this is trivial, almost to the point of cynicism, magnifying its nonessential details and disparaging compulsion which was the underlying reason for invalidity. A reading of the Court's opinion in that case along with its opinion in this case will show such difference of overtones and undertones as to make clear that the *McCollum* case has passed like a storm in a teacup. The wall which the Court was professing to erect between Church and State has become even more warped and twisted than I expected. Today's judgment will be more interesting to students of psychology and of the judicial processes than to students of constitutional law.

ENGEL v. VITALE

370 U.S. 421 (1962)

Certiorari to the Court of Appeals of New York.

MR. JUSTICE BLACK delivered the opinion of the Court.

The respondent Board of Education of Union Free School District No. 9, New Hyde Park, New York . . . directed the School District's principal to cause the following prayer to be said aloud by each class in the presence of a teacher at the beginning of each school day:

"Almighty God, we acknowledge our dependence upon Thee, and we beg Thy blessings upon us, our parents, our teachers and our country."

This daily procedure was adopted on the recommendation of the State Board of Regents, a governmental agency created by the State Constitution to which the New York Legislature has granted broad supervisory, executive, and legislative powers over the State's public school system. These state officials composed the prayer which they recommended and published as a part of their "Statement on Moral and Spiritual Training in the Schools," saying: "We believe that this Statement will be subscribed to by all men and women of good will, and we call upon all of them to aid in giving life to our program." . . .

We think that by using its public school system to encourage recitation of the Regents' prayer, the State of New York has adopted a practice wholly inconsistent with the Establishment Clause. There can, of course, be no doubt that New York's program of daily classroom invocation of God's blessings as prescribed in the Regents' prayer is a religious activity. It is a solemn avowal of divine faith and supplication for the blessings of the Almighty. The nature of such a prayer has always been religious, none of the respondents has denied this and the trial court expressly so found. . . .

. . . [W]e think that the constitutional prohibition against laws respecting an establishment of religion must at least mean that in this country it is no part of the business of government to compose official prayers for any group of the American people to recite as a part of a religious program carried on by government.

It is a matter of history that this very practice of establishing governmentally composed prayers for religious services was one of the reasons which caused many of our early colonists to leave England and seek religious freedom in America. The Book of Common Prayer, which was created under governmental direction and which was approved by Acts of Parliament in 1548 and 1549, set out in minute detail the accepted form and content of prayer and other religious ceremonies to be used in the established, tax-supported Church of England. The controversies over the Book and what should be its content repeatedly threatened to disrupt the peace of that country as the accepted forms of prayer in the established church changed with the views of the particular ruler that happened to be in control at the time. . . .

It is an unfortunate fact of history that when some of the very groups which had most strenuously opposed the established Church of England found themselves sufficiently in control of colonial governments in this country to write their own prayers into law, they passed laws making their own religion the official religion of their respective colonies. . . .

By the time of the adoption of the Constitution, our history shows that there was a widespread awareness among many Americans of the dangers of a union of Church and State. These people knew, some of them from bitter personal experience, that one of the greatest dangers to the freedom of the individual to worship in his own way lay in the Government's placing its official stamp of approval upon one particular kind of prayer or one particular form of religious services. They knew the anguish, hardship and bitter strife that could come when zealous religious groups struggled with one another to obtain the Government's stamp of approval from each King, Queen, or Protector that came to temporary power. The Constitution was intended to avert a part of this danger by leaving the government of this country in the hands of the people rather than in the hands of any monarch. But this safeguard was not enough. Our Founders were no more willing to let the content of their prayers and their privilege of praying whenever they pleased be influenced by the ballot box than they were to let these vital matters of personal conscience depend upon the succession of monarchs. The First Amendment was added to the Constitution to stand as a guarantee that neither the power nor the prestige of the Federal Government would be used to control, support or influence the kinds of prayer the American people can say—that the people's religions must not be subjected to the pressures of government for change each time a new political administration is elected to office. Under that Amendment's prohibition against governmental establishment of religion, as reinforced by the provisions of the Fourteenth Amendment, government in this country, be it state or federal, is without power to prescribe by law any particular form of prayer which is to be used as an official prayer in carrying on any program of governmentally sponsored religious activity.

There can be no doubt that New York's state prayer program officially establishes the religious beliefs embodied in the Regents' prayer. . . . Neither the fact that the prayer may be denominationally neutral, nor the fact that its observance on the part of the students is voluntary can serve to free it from the limitations of the Establishment Clause, as it might from the Free Exercise Clause, of the First Amendment, both of which are operative against the States by virtue of the Fourteenth Amendment. Although these two clauses may in certain instances overlap, they forbid two quite different kinds of governmental encroachment upon religious freedom. The Establishment Clause, unlike the Free Exercise Clause, does not depend upon any showing of direct governmental compulsion and is violated by the enactment of laws which establish an official religion whether those laws operate directly to coerce nonobserving individuals or not. This is not to say, of course, that laws officially prescribing a particular form of religious worship do not involve coercion of such individuals. When the power, prestige and financial support of government is placed behind a particular religious belief, the indirect coercive pressure upon religious minorities to conform to the prevailing officially approved religion is plain. But the purposes underlying the Establishment Clause go much further than that. Its first and most immediate purpose rested on the belief that a union of government and religion tends to destroy government and to degrade religion. . . . Another purpose of the Establishment Clause rested upon an awareness of the historical fact that governmentally established religions and religious persecutions go hand in hand. . . . It was in large part to get completely away from this sort of systematic religious persecution that the Founders brought into being our Nation, our Constitution, and our Bill of Rights with its prohibition against any governmental establishment of religion. The New York laws officially prescribing the Regents' prayer are inconsistent with both the purposes of the Establishment Clause and with the Establishment Clause itself.

It has been argued that to apply the Constitution in such a way as to prohibit state laws respecting an establishment of religious services in public schools is to indicate a hostility toward religion or toward prayer. Nothing, of course, could be more wrong. The history of man is inseparable from the history of religion. And perhaps it is not too much to say that since the beginning of that history many people have devoutly believed that "More things are wrought by prayer than this world dreams of." It was doubtless largely due to men who believed this that there grew up a sentiment that caused men to leave the cross-currents of officially established state religions and religious persecution in Europe and come to this country filled with the hope that they could find a place in which they could pray when they pleased to the God of their faith in the language they chose. And there were men of this same faith in the power of prayer who led the fight for adoption of our Constitution and also for our Bill of Rights with the very guarantees of religious freedom that forbid the sort of governmental activity which New York has attempted here. These men knew that the First Amendment, which tried to put an end to governmental control of religion and of prayer, was not written to destroy either. They knew rather that it was written to quiet well-justified fears which nearly all of them felt arising out of an awareness that governments of the past had shackled men's tongues to make them speak only the religious thoughts that government wanted them to speak and to pray only to the God that government wanted them to pray to. It is neither sacrilegious nor antireligious to say that each separate government in this country should stay out of the business of writing or sanctioning official prayers and leave that purely religious function to the people themselves and to those the people choose to look to for religious guidance.[1]

It is true that New York's establishment of its Regents' prayer as an officially approved religious doctrine of that State does not amount to a total establishment of one particular religious sect to the exclusion of all others—that, indeed, the governmental endorsement of that prayer seems relatively insignificant when compared to the governmental encroachments upon religion which were commonplace 200 years ago. To those who may subscribe to the view that because the Regents' official prayer is so brief and general there can be no danger to religious freedom in its governmental establishment, however, it may be appropriate to say in the words of James Madison, the author of the First Amendment:

"[I]t is proper to take alarm at the first experiment on our liberties. . . . Who does not see that the same authority which can establish Christianity, in exclusion of all other Religions, may establish with the

1. There is of course nothing in the decision reached here that is inconsistent with the fact that school children and others are officially encouraged to express love for our country by reciting historical documents such as the Declaration of Independence which contain references to the Deity or by singing officially espoused anthems which include the composer's professions of faith in a Supreme Being, or with the fact that there are many manifestations in our public life of belief in God. Such patriotic or ceremonial occasions bear no true resemblance to the unquestioned religious exercise that the State of New York has sponsored in this instance.

same ease any particular sect of Christians, in exclusion of all other Sects? That the same authority which can force a citizen to contribute three pence only of his property for the support of any one establishment, may force him to conform to any other establishment in all cases whatsoever?"

The judgment of the Court of Appeals of New York is reversed and the cause remanded for further proceedings not inconsistent with this opinion.

Reversed and remanded.

MR. JUSTICE FRANKFURTER took no part in the decision of this case.

MR. JUSTICE WHITE took no part in the consideration or decision of this case.

MR. JUSTICE DOUGLAS, concurring.

. . . The point for decision is whether the Government can constitutionally finance a religious exercise. Our system at the federal and state levels is presently honeycombed with such financing.[2] Nevertheless, I think it is an unconstitutional undertaking whatever form it takes.

First, a word as to what this case does not involve.

Plainly, our Bill of Rights would not permit a State or the Federal Government to adopt an official prayer and penalize anyone who would not utter it. This, however, is not that case, for there is no element of compulsion or coercion in New York's regulation. . . .

. . . New York's prayer is of a character that does not involve any element of proselytizing as in the McCollum case.

The question presented by this case is therefore an extremely narrow one. It is whether New York oversteps the bounds when it finances a religious exercise.

What New York does on the opening of its public schools is what we do when we open court. Our Marshal has from the beginning announced the convening of the Court and then added "God save the United States and this honorable court." That utterance is a supplication, a prayer in which we, the judges, are free to join, but which we need not recite any more than the students need recite the New York prayer.

What New York does on the opening of its public schools is what each House of Congress does at the opening of each day's business.

. . . I cannot say that to authorize this prayer is to establish a religion in the strictly historic meaning of those words. A religion is not established in the usual sense merely by letting those who choose to do so say the prayer that the public school teacher leads. Yet once government finances a religious exercise it inserts a divisive influence into our communities. . . .

"We are a religious people whose institutions presuppose a Supreme Being." *Zorach v. Clauson,* 343 U.S. 306, 313. . . . The First Amendment leaves the Government

2. "There are many 'aids' to religion in this country at all levels of government. To mention but a few at the federal level, one might begin by observing that the very First Congress which wrote the First Amendment provided for chaplains in both Houses and in the armed services. There is compulsory chapel at the service academies, and religious services are held in federal hospitals and prisons. The President issues religious proclamations. The Bible is used for the administration of oaths. N. Y. A. and W. P. A. funds were available to parochial schools during the depression. Veterans receiving money under the 'G. I.' Bill of 1944 could attend denominational schools, to which payments were made directly by the government. During World War II, federal money was contributed to denominational schools for the training of nurses. The benefits of the National School Lunch Act are available to students in private as well as public schools. The Hospital Survey and Construction Act of 1946 specifically made money available to non-public hospitals. The slogan 'In God We Trust' is used by the Treasury Department, and Congress recently added God to the pledge of allegiance. There is Bible-reading in the schools of the District of Columbia, and religious instruction is given in the District's National Training School for Boys. Religious organizations are exempt from the federal income tax and are granted postal privileges. Up to defined limits . . . contributions to religious organizations are deductible for federal income tax purposes. . . . This list of federal 'aids' could easily be expanded, and of course there is a long list in each state." Fellman, *The Limits of Freedom* (1959), pp. 40–41.

in a position not of hostility to religion but of neutrality. The philosophy is that the atheist or agnostic—the nonbeliever—is entitled to go his own way. The philosophy is that if government interferes in matters spiritual, it will be a divisive force. The First Amendment teaches that a government neutral in the field of religion better serves all religious interests.

My problem today would be uncomplicated but for *Everson* v. *Board of Education*, 330 U.S. 1, 17. . . . The Everson case seems in retrospect to be out of line with the First Amendment. Its result is appealing, as it allows aid to be given to needy children. Yet by the same token, public funds could be used to satisfy other needs of children in parochial schools— lunches, books, and tuition being obvious examples. Mr. Justice Rutledge stated in dissent what I think is durable First Amendment philosophy. . . .

MR. JUSTICE STEWART, dissenting. . . .

. . . I cannot see how an "official religion" is established by letting those who want to say a prayer say it. On the contrary, I think that to deny the wish of these school children to join in reciting this prayer is to deny them the opportunity of sharing in the spiritual heritage of our Nation.

. . . I think that the Court's task, in this as in all areas of constitutional adjudication, is not responsibly aided by the uncritical invocation of metaphors like the "wall of separation," a phrase nowhere to be found in the Constitution. What is relevant to the issue here is not the history of an established church in sixteenth century England or in eighteenth century America, but the history of the religious traditions of our people, reflected in countless practices of the institutions and officials of our government.

At the opening of each day's Session of this Court we stand, while one of our officials invokes the protection of God. Since the days of John Marshall our Crier had said, "God save the United States and this Honorable Court." Both the Senate and

the House of Representatives open their daily Sessions with prayer. Each of our Presidents, from George Washington to John F. Kennedy, has upon assuming his Office asked the protection and help of God.

The Court today says that the state and federal governments are without constitutional power to prescribe any particular form of words to be recited by any group of the American people on any subject touching religion. The third stanza of "The Star-Spangled Banner," made our National Anthem by Act of Congress in 1931, contains these verses:

"Blest with vict'ry and peace, may the
    Heav'n rescued land
  Praise the Pow'r that hath made and
    preserved us a nation!
Then conquer we must, when our cause
    it is just,
  And this be our motto 'In God is our
    Trust.' "

In 1954 Congress added a phrase to the Pledge of Allegiance to the Flag so that it now contains the words "one Nation *under* God, indivisible, with liberty and justice for all." In 1952 Congress enacted legislation calling upon the President each year to proclaim a National Day of Prayer. Since 1865 the words "IN GOD WE TRUST" have been impressed on our coins.

Countless similar examples could be listed, but there is no need to belabor the obvious. It was all summed up by this Court just ten years ago in a single sentence: "We are a religious people whose institutions presuppose a Supreme Being." *Zorach* v. *Clauson*, 343 U.S. 306, 313.

I do not believe that this Court, or the Congress, or the President has by the actions and practices I have mentioned established an "official religion" in violation of the Constitution. And I do not believe the State of New York has done so in this case. What each has done has been to recognize and to follow the deeply entrenched and highly cherished spiritual traditions of our Nation. . . .

NOTE: *School District of Abington* v. *Schempp,* 373 U.S. (1963), and *Murray* v. *Curlett* 374, U.S. 203 (1963), applied the *Engel* principle to invalidate Bible reading in public schools. In each case children could be excused from the exercise upon requests of their parents or guardians. While this might be crucial in a "free exercise" case, the Court found it was not a saving grace in establishment cases. "The distinction between the two [Constitutional] clauses is apparent—a violation of the Free Exercise Clause is predicated on coercion while the Establishment Clause violation need not be so attended. . . . Nothing we have said here indicates that . . . study of the Bible or of religion, when presented objectively as part of a secular program of education, may not be effected consistent with the First Amendment. But the exercises here do not fall into those categories. They are religious exercises, required by the States in violation of the command of the First Amendment that the Government maintain strict neutrality, neither aiding nor opposing religion."

Mr. Justice Stewart, dissenting, thought the cases should be remanded for additional evidence, particularly "as to whether there would exist any coercion of any kind upon a student who did not want to participate." He thought that "religion and government must necessarily interact in countless ways" and that "there are areas in which a doctrinaire reading of the Establishment Clause leads to irreconcilable conflict with the Free Exercise Clause. . . . In the absence of coercion upon those who do not wish to participate . . . such [Bible reading] provisions cannot . . . be held to represent the type of support of religion barred by the Establishment Clause." Thus these cases present "a substantial Free Exercise claim on the part of those who affirmatively desire to have their children's school day open with the reading of passages from the Bible."

McGOWAN v. *MARYLAND*

366 U.S. 420 (1961)

Mr. CHIEF JUSTICE WARREN delivered the opinion of the Court.

The issues in this case concern the constitutional validity of Maryland criminal statutes, commonly known as Sunday Closing Laws or Sunday Blue Laws. These statutes, with exceptions to be noted hereafter, generally proscribe all labor, business and other commercial activities on Sunday. The questions presented are whether the classifications within the statutes bring about a denial of equal protection of the law, whether the laws are so vague as to fail to give reasonable notice of the forbidden conduct and therefore violate due process, and whether the statutes are laws respect-ing an establishment of religion or prohibiting the free exercise thereof.

Appellants are seven employees of a large discount department store located on a highway in Anne Arundel County, Maryland. They were indicted for the Sunday sale of a three-ring loose-leaf binder, a can of floor wax, a stapler and staples, and a toy submarine in violation of Md. Ann. Code, Art. 27, § 521. Generally, this section prohibited, throughout the State, the Sunday sale of all merchandise except the retail sale of tobacco products, confectioneries, milk, bread, fruits, gasoline, oils, greases, drugs and medicines, and newspapers and periodicals. Recently amended, this section

also now excepts from the general prohibition the retail sale in Anne Arundel County
of all foodstuffs, automobile and boating
accessories, flowers, toilet goods, hospital
supplies and souvenirs. It now further provides that any retail establishment in Anne
Arundel County which does not employ
more than one person other than the
owner may operate on Sunday. . . .

III

The final questions for decision are
whether the Maryland Sunday Closing
Laws conflict with the Federal Constitution's provisions for religious liberty. First,
appellants contend here that the statutes
applicable to Anne Arundel County violate
the constitutional guarantee of freedom of
religion in that the statutes' effect is to
prohibit the free exercise of religion in
contravention of the First Amendment,
made applicable to the States by the Fourteenth Amendment. But appellants allege
only economic injury to themselves; they
do not allege any infringement of their
own religious freedoms due to Sunday closing. In fact, the record is silent as to what
appellants' religious beliefs are. Since the
general rule is that "a litigant may only
assert his own constitutional rights or immunities," *United States* v. *Raines*, 362 U.S.
17, 22, we hold that appellants have no
standing to raise this contention. *Tileston*
v. *Ullman*, 318 U.S. 44, 46. Furthermore,
since appellants do not specifically allege
that the statutes infringe upon the religious
beliefs of the department store's present or
prospective patrons, we have no occasion
here to consider the standing question of
Pierce v. *Society of Sisters*, 268 U.S. 510,
535–536. Those persons whose religious
rights are allegedly impaired by the statutes
are not without effective ways to assert
these rights. Cf. *NAACP* v. *State of Alabama*, 357 U.S. 449, 459–460; *Barrows* v.
Jackson, 346 U.S. 249, 257. Appellants
present no weighty countervailing policies
here to cause an exception to our general
principles. See *United States* v. *Raines,
supra.*

Secondly, appellants contend that the
statutes violate the guarantee of separation
of church and state in that the statutes are
laws respecting an establishment of religion
contrary to the First Amendment, made
applicable to the states by the Fourteenth
Amendment. If the purpose of the "establishment" clause was only to insure protection for the "free exercise" of religion, then
what we have said above concerning appellant's standing to raise the "free exercise" contention would appear to be true
here. However, the writings of Madison,
who was the First Amendment's architect,
demonstrate that the establishment of a
religion was equally feared because of its
tendencies to political tyranny and subversion of civil authority. Thus, in *Everson* v.
Board of Education, supra, the Court permitted a district taxpayer to challenge, on
"establishment" grounds, a state statute
which authorized district boards of education to reimburse parents for fares paid for
the transportation of their children to both
public and Catholic schools. Appellants
here concededly have suffered direct economic injury, allegedly due to the imposition on them of the tenets of the Christian religion. We find that, in these circumstances, these appellants have standing
to complain that the statutes are laws respecting an establishment of religion.

The essence of appellant's "establishment" argument is that Sunday is the Sabbath day of the predominant Christian
sects; that the purpose of the enforced
stoppage of labor on that day is to facilitate
and encourage church attendance; that the
purpose of setting Sunday as a day of universal rest is to induce people with no
religion or people with marginal religious
beliefs to join the predominant Christian
sects; that the purpose of the atmosphere
of tranquility created by Sunday closing
is to aid the conduct of church services
and religious observance of the sacred day.
In substantiating their "establishment" argument, appellants rely on the wording of
the present Maryland statutes, on earlier
versions of the current Sunday laws and on
prior judicial characterizations of these laws
by the Maryland Court of Appeals. Although only the constitutionality of § 521,

the section under which appellants have been convicted, is immediately before us in this litigation, inquiry into the history of Sunday Closing Laws in our country, in addition to an examination of the Maryland Sunday closing statutes in their entirety and of their history, is relevant to the decision of whether the Maryland Sunday law in question is one respecting an establishment of religion. There is no dispute that the original laws which dealt with Sunday labor were motivated by religious forces. But what we must decide is whether present Sunday legislation, having undergone extensive changes from the earliest forms, still retains its religious character. . . .

Throughout this century and longer, both the federal and state governments have oriented their activities very largely toward improvement of the health, safety, recreation and general well-being of our citizens. Numerous laws affecting public health, safety factors in industry, laws affecting hours and conditions of labor of women and children, week-end diversion at parks and beaches, and cultural activities of various kinds, now point the way toward the good life for all. Sunday Closing Laws, like those before us, have become part and parcel of this great governmental concern wholly apart from their original purposes or connotations. The present purpose and effect of most of them is to provide a uniform day of rest for all citizens; the fact that this day is Sunday, a day of particular significance for the dominant Christian sects, does not bar the State from achieving its secular goals. To say that the States cannot prescribe Sunday as a day of rest for these purposes solely because centuries ago such laws had their genesis in religion would give a constitutional interpretation of hostility to the public welfare rather than one of mere separation of church and State. . . .

The distinctions between the statutes in the case before us and the state action in *People of State of Illinois ex rel. McCollum v. Board of Education, supra,* the only case in this Court finding a violation of the "establishment" Clause, lend further sub-

stantiation to our conclusion. In McCollum, state action permitted religious instruction in public school buildings during school hours and required students not attending the religious instruction to remain in their classrooms during that time. The Court found that this system had the effect of coercing the children to attend religious classes; no such coercion to attend church services is present in the situation at bar. In McCollum, the only alternative available to the nonattending students was to remain in their classrooms; the alternatives open to nonlaboring persons in the instant case are far more diverse. In McCollum, there was direct cooperation between state officials and religious ministers; no such direct participation exists under the Maryland laws. In McCollum, tax supported buildings were used to aid religion; in the instant case, no tax monies are being used in aid of religion.

Finally, we should make clear that this case deals only with the constitutionality of § 521 of the Maryland statute before us. We do not hold that Sunday legislation may not be a violation of the "Establishment" Clause if it can be demonstrated that its purpose—evidenced either on the face of the legislation, in conjunction with its legislative history, or in its operative effect—is to use the State's coercive power to aid religion.

Accordingly, the decision is affirmed.
Affirmed.

[*McGowan* was one of four Sunday Closing Law cases decided on the same day. *Braunfeld* v. *Brown,* 366 U.S. 599 (1961), and *Gallagher* v. *Crown Kosher Market,* 366 U.S. 617 (1961), raised, in addition to the Establishment problem, a problem in Free Exercise, because they involved Orthodox Jewish merchants who would have to give up their Sabbath or suffer economic disadvantage by having to close their businesses two days each week. Overriding this objection, the Court observed that "To strike, without the most critical scrutiny, legislation which imposes only an indirect burden on the exercise of religion, i.e., legislation which does not make unlawful the religious practice itself, would radically restrict the operating latitude of the legislature."

MR. JUSTICE FRANKFURTER, joined by his brother HARLAN, wrote an extensive concurring opinion covering all four cases.

MR. JUSTICE DOUGLAS' dissenting opinion which follows covers all four cases.]

MR. JUSTICE DOUGLAS, dissenting.

The question is not whether one day out of seven can be imposed by a State as a day of rest. The question is not whether Sunday can by force of custom and habit be retained as a day of rest. The question is whether a State can impose criminal sanctions on those who, unlike the Christian majority that makes up our society, worship on a different day or do not share the religious scruples of the majority.

If the "free exercise" of religion were subject to reasonable regulations, as it is under some constitutions, or if all laws "respecting the establishment of religion" were not proscribed, I could understand how rational men, representing a predominantly Christian civilization, might think these Sunday laws did not unreasonably interfere with any one's free exercise of religion and took no step toward a burdensome establishment of any religion.

But that is not the premise from which we start, as there is agreement that the fact that a State, and not the Federal Government, has promulgated these Sunday laws does not change the scope of the power asserted. For the classic view is that the First Amendment should be applied to the States with the same firmness as it is enforced against the Federal Government. . . .

It seems to me plain that by these laws the States compel one, under sanction of law, to refrain from work or recreation on Sunday because of the majority's religious views about that day. The State by law makes Sunday a symbol of respect or adherence. Refraining from works or recreation in deference to the majority's religious

feelings about Sunday is within every person's choice. By what authority can government compel it?

Cases are put where acts that are immoral by our standards but not by the standards of other religious groups are made criminal. That category of cases, until today, has been a very restricted one confined to polygamy (*Reynolds* v. *United States*, 98 U.S. 145, 25 L.Ed. 244) and other extreme situations. . . .

The Court balances the need of the people for rest, recreation, late-sleeping, family visiting and the like against the command of the First Amendment that no one need bow to the religious beliefs of another. There is in this realm no room for balancing. I see no place for it in the constitutional scheme. A legislature of Christians can no more make minorities conform to their weekly regime than a legislature of Moslems, or a legislature of Hindus. The religious regime of every group must be respected—unless it crosses the line of criminal conduct. But no one can be forced to come to a halt before it, or refrain from doing things that would offend it. That is my reading of the Establishment Clause and the Free Exercise Clause. Any other reading imports, I fear, an element common in other societies but foreign to us. Thus Nigeria in Article 23 of her Constitution, after guaranteeing religious freedom, adds, "Nothing in this section shall invalidate any law that is reasonably justified in a democratic society in the interest of defence, public safety, public order, public morality, or public health." And see Article 25 of the Indian Constitution. That may be a desirable provision. But when the Court adds it to our First Amendment, as it does today, we make a sharp break with the American ideal of religious liberty as enshrined in the First Amendment.

The State can of course require one day of rest a week: one day when every shop or factory is closed. Quite a few States make that requirement. Then the "day of rest" become purely and simply a health measure. But the Sunday laws operate differently. They force minorities to obey the majority's religious feelings of what is due and proper for a Christian community; they provide a coercive spur to the "weaker brethren," to those who are indifferent to the claims of a Sabbath through apathy or scruple. Can there be any doubt that Christians, now aligned vigorously in favor of these laws, would be as strongly opposed, if they were prosecuted under a Moslem law that forbade them from engaging in secular activities on days that violated Moslem scruples?

There is an "establishment" of religion in the constitutional sense if any practice of any religious group has the sanction of law behind it. There is an interference with the "free exercise" of religion if what in conscience one can do or omit doing is required because of the religious scruples of the community. Hence I would declare each of those laws unconstitutional as applied to the complaining parties, whether or not they are members of a sect which observes as their Sabbath a day other than Sunday.

When these laws are applied to Orthodox Jews, as they are in No. 11 and No. 67, or to Sabbatarians their vice is accentuated. If the Sunday laws are constitutional, Kosher markets are on a five-day week. Thus those laws put an economic penalty on those who observe Saturday rather than Sunday as the Sabbath. For the economic pressures on these minorities, created by the fact that our communities are predominantly Sunday-minded, there is no recourse. When, however, the State uses its coercive powers—here the criminal law—to compel minorities to observe a second Sabbath, not their own, the State undertakes to aid and "prefer one religion over another"—contrary to the command of the Constitution. See *Everson* v. *Board of Education, supra,* 330 U.S. 15.

In large measure the history of the religious clause of the First Amendment was a struggle to be free of economic sanctions for adherence to one's religion. *Everson* v. *Board of Education, supra,* 330 U.S. 11–14. A small tax was imposed in Virginia for religious education. Jefferson and Madison led the fight against the tax, Madison writing his famous Memorial and Remonstrance against that law. Id., 330 U.S. 12. As a result, the tax measure was defeated and instead Virginia's famous "Bill of Religious Liberty," written by Jefferson, was enacted. Id., 330 U.S. 12. That Act provided:

"That no man shall be compelled to frequent or support any religious worship, place, or ministry whatsoever, nor shall be enforced, restrained, molested, or burthened in his body or goods, nor shall otherwise suffer on account of his religious opinions or belief. . . ."

The reverse side of an "establishment" is a burden on the "free exercise" of religion. Receipt of funds from the state benefits the established church directly; laying an extra tax on nonmembers benefits the established church indirectly. Certainly the present Sunday laws place Orthodox Jews and Sabbatarians under extra burdens because of their religious opinions or beliefs. Requiring them to abstain from their trade or business on Sunday reduces their workweek to five days, unless they violate their religious scruples. This places them at a competitive disadvantage and penalizes them for adhering to their religious beliefs.

"The sanction imposed by the state for observing a day other than Sunday as holy time is certainly more serious economically than the imposition of a license tax for preaching," which we struck down in *Murdock* v. *Commonwealth of Pennsylvania,* 319 U.S. 105, and in *Follett* v. *Town of McCormick,* 321 U.S. 573. The special protection which Sunday laws give the dominant religious groups and the penalty they place on minorities whose holy day is Saturday constitute in my view state interference with the "free exercise" of religion.

[JUSTICES BRENNAN and STEWART also dissented in *Gallagher* and *Braunfeld*.]

SHERBERT v. VERNER

374 U.S. 398 (1963)

Appeal from the Supreme Court of South Carolina.

MR. JUSTICE BRENNAN delivered the opinion of the Court.

Appellant, a member of the Seventh-day Adventist Church was discharged by her South Carolina employer because she would not work on Saturday, the Sabbath Day of her faith. When she was unable to obtain other employment because from her conscientious scruples she would not take Saturday work, she filed a claim for unemployment compensation benefits under the South Carolina Unemployment Compensation Act. That law provides that, to be eligible for benefits, a claimant must be "able to work and is available for work;" and, further, that a claimant is ineligible for benefits "[i]f . . . he has failed, without good cause . . . to accept available suitable work when offered him by the employment office or the employer. . . ." The appellee Employment Security Commission, in administrative proceedings under the statute, found that appellant's restriction upon her availability for Saturday work brought her within the provision disqualifying for benefits insured workers who fail, without good cause, to accept "suitable work when offered . . . by the employment office or the employer. . . ." . . . The State Supreme Court held . . . that appellant's ineligibility infringed no constitutional liberties because such a construction of the statute "places no restriction upon the appellant's freedom of religion nor does it in any way prevent her in the exercise of her right and freedom to observe her religious beliefs in accordance with the dictates of her conscience." . . . We reverse the judgment of the South Carolina Supreme Court and remand for further proceedings not inconsistent with this opinion.

I

The door of the Free Exercise Clause stands tightly closed against any governmental regulation of religious *beliefs* as such, *Cantwell* v. *Connecticut*, 310 U.S. 296, 303. . . . On the other hand the Court has rejected challenges under the Free Exercise Clause to governmental regulation of certain overt acts prompted by religious beliefs or principles, for "even when the action is in accord with one's religious convictions, [it] is not totally free from legislative restrictions." *Braunfeld* v. *Brown*, 366 U.S. 599, 603. The conduct or actions so regulated have invariably posed some substantial threat to public safety, peace or order. . . .

Plainly enough, appellant's conscientious objection to Saturday work constitutes no conduct prompted by religious principles of a kind within the reach of state legislation. If, therefore, the decision of the South Carolina Supreme Court is to withstand appellant's constitutional challenge, it must be either because her disqualification as a beneficiary represents no infringement by the State of her constitutional rights of free exercise; or because any incidental burden on the free exercise of appellant's religion may be justified by a "compelling state interest in the regulation of a subject within the State's constitutional power to regulate. . . ." *NAACP* v. *Button*, 371 U.S. 415, 438.

II

We turn first to the question whether the disqualification for benefits imposes any burden on the free exercise of appellant's religion. We think it is clear that it does. In a sense the consequences of such a disqualification to religious principles and practices may be only an indirect result of welfare legislation within the State's general competence to enact; it is true that no criminal sanctions directly compel appellant to work a six-day week. But this is only the beginning, not the end of our inquiry. . . . Here not only is it apparent that appellant's declared ineligibility for benefits derives solely from the practice of her religion, but the pressure upon her to forego that practice is unmistakable. The ruling forces her to choose between following the precepts of her religion and forfeiting benefits, on the one hand, and abandoning one of the precepts of her religion in order to accept work, on the other hand. Governmental imposition of such a choice puts the same kind of burden upon the free exercise of religion as would a fine imposed against appellant for her Saturday worship.

Nor may the South Carolina court's construction of the statute be saved from constitutional infirmity on the ground that unemployment compensation benefits are not appellant's "right" but merely a "privilege." It is too late in the day to doubt that the liberties of religion and expression may be infringed by the denial or placing of conditions upon a benefit or privilege. . . .

III

We must next consider whether some compelling state interest enforced in the eligibility provisions of the South Carolina statute justifies the substantial infringement of appellant's First Amendment right. It is basic that no showing merely of a rational relationship to some colorable state interest would suffice; in this highly sensitive constitutional area, "[o]nly the gravest abuses, endangering paramount interests, give occasion for permissible limitation," *Thomas* v. *Collins*, 323 U.S. 516, 530. No such abuse or danger has been advanced in the present case. The appellees suggest no more than a possibility that the filing of fraudulent claims by unscrupulous claimants feigning religious objections to Saturday work might not only dilute the unemployment compensation fund but also hinder the scheduling by employers of necessary Saturday work. But that possibility is not apposite here because no such objection appears to have been made before the South Carolina

Supreme Court, and we are unwilling to assess the importance of an asserted state interest without the views of the state court. Nor, if the contention had been made below, would the record appear to sustain it; there is no proof whatever to warrant such fears of malingering or deceit as those which the respondents now advance. Even if consideration of such evidence is not foreclosed by the prohibition against judicial inquiry into the truth or falsity of religious beliefs, *United States* v. *Ballard*, 322 U.S. 78,—a question as to which we intimate no view since it is not before us— it is highly doubtful whether such evidence would be sufficient to warrant a substantial infringement of religious liberties. For even if the possibility of spurious claims did threaten to dilute the fund and disrupt the scheduling of work, it would plainly be incumbent upon the appellees to demonstrate that no alternative forms of regulation would combat such abuses without infringing First Amendment rights. . . .

In these respects, then, the state interest asserted in the present case is wholly dissimilar to the interests which were found to justify the less direct burden upon religious practices in *Braunfeld* v. *Brown*, *supra*. The Court recognized that the Sunday closing law which that decision sustained undoubtedly served "to make the practice of [the Orthodox Jewish merchants'] religious beliefs more expensive," 366 U.S., at 605. But the statute was nevertheless saved by a countervailing factor which finds no equivalent in the instant case—a strong state interest in providing one uniform day of rest for all workers. That secular objective could be achieved, the Court found, only by declaring Sunday to be that day of rest. Requiring exemptions for Sabbatarians, while theoretically possible, appeared to present an administrative problem of such magnitude, or afford the exempted class so great a competitive advantage that such a requirement would have rendered the entire statutory scheme unworkable. In the present case no such justifications underlie the determination of the state court that appellant's religion makes her ineligible to receive benefits.

IV

In holding as we do, plainly we are not fostering the "establishment" of the Seventh-day Adventist religion in South Carolina, for the extension of unemployment benefits to Sabbatarians in common with Sunday worshippers reflects nothing more than the governmental obligation of neutrality in the face of religious differences, and does not represent that involvement of religious with secular institutions which it is the object of the Establishment Clause to forestall. . . . Our holding today is only that South Carolina may not constitutionally apply the eligibility provisions so as to constrain a worker to abandon his religious convictions respecting the day of rest. . . .

Reversed and remanded.

MR. JUSTICE DOUGLAS, concurring.

The case we have for decision seems to me to be of small dimensions, though profoundly important. . . .

Some have thought that a majority of a community can, through state action, compel a minority to observe their particular religious scruples so long as the majority's rule can be said to perform some valid secular function. That was the essence of the Court's decision in the Sunday Blue Law Cases, . . . a ruling from which I then dissented . . . and still dissent. . . .

That ruling of the Court travels part of the distance that South Carolina asks us to go now. She asks us to hold that when it comes to a day of rest a Sabbatarian must conform with the scruples of the majority in order to obtain unemployment benefits.

The result turns not on the degree of injury, which may indeed be nonexistent by ordinary standards. The harm is the interference with the individual's scruples or conscience—an important area of privacy which the First Amendment fences off from government. . . .

This case is resolvable not in terms of what an individual can demand of government, but solely in terms of what government may not do to an individual in violation of his religious scruples. The fact that government cannot exact from me a surrender of one iota of my religious scruples does not, of course, mean that I can demand of government a sum of money, the better to exercise them. For the Free Exercise Clause is written in terms of what the government cannot do to the individual, not in terms of what the individual can exact from the government.

Those considerations, however, are not relevant here. If appellant is otherwise qualified for unemployment benefits, payments will be made to her not as a Seventh-day Adventist, but as an unemployed worker. Conceivably these payments will indirectly benefit her church, but no more so than does the salary of any public employee. Thus, this case does not involve the problems of direct or indirect state assistance to a religious organization—matters relevant to the Establishment Clause, not in issue here.

MR. JUSTICE STEWART, concurring.

Although fully agreeing with the result which the Court reaches in this case, I cannot join in the Court's opinion. This case presents a double-barreled dilemma, which in all candor I think the Court's opinion has not succeeded in papering over. The dilemma ought to be resolved.

I

. . . I am convinced that no liberty is more essential to the continued vitality of the free society which our Constitution guarantees than is the religious liberty protected by the Free Exercise Clause explicit in the First Amendment and imbedded in the Fourteenth. And I regret that on occasion, and specifically in *Braunfeld* v. *Brown, supra,* the Court has shown what has seemed to me a distressing insensitivity to the appropriate demands of this constitutional guarantee. By contrast I think that the Court's approach to the Establishment Clause has on occasion, and specifically in Engel, Schempp and Murray, been not only insensitive, but positively wooden, and that the Court has accorded to the Establishment Clause a meaning which neither the words, the history, nor the intention of the authors of that specific constitutional provision even remotely suggests.

But my views as to the correctness of the Court's decisions in these cases are beside the point here. The point is that the decisions are on the books. And the result is that there are many situations where legitimate claims under the Free Exercise Clause will run into head-on collision with the Court's insensitive and sterile construction of the Establishment Clause. The controversy now before us is clearly such a case. . . .

South Carolina would deny unemployment benefits to a mother unavailable for work on Saturdays because she was unable to get a babysitter. Thus, we do not have before us a situation where a State provides unemployment compensation generally, and singles out for disqualification only those persons who are unavailable for work on religious grounds. This is not, in short, a scheme which operates so as to discriminate against religion as such. But the Court nevertheless holds that the State must prefer a religious over a secular ground for being unavailable for work. . . .

Yet in cases decided under the Establishment Clause the Court has decreed otherwise. It has decreed that government must blind itself to the differing religious beliefs and traditions of the people. With all respect, I think it is the Court's duty to face up to the dilemma posed by the conflict between the Free Exercise Clause of the Constitution and the Establishment Clause as interpreted by the Court. It is a duty, I submit, which we owe to the people, the States, and the Nation, and a duty which we owe to ourselves. For so long as the resounding but fallacious fundamentalist rhetoric of some of our Establishment Clause opinions remains on our books, to be disregarded at will as in the present case, or to be undiscriminatingly invoked as in the Schempp case, . . . so long will the possibility of consistent and perceptive decision in this most difficult and delicate area of constitutional law be impeded and

impaired. And so long, I fear, will the guarantee of true religious freedom in our pluralistic society be uncertain and insecure.

II

My second difference with the Court's opinion is that I cannot agree that today's decision can stand consistently with *Braunfeld* v. *Brown, supra.* The Court says that there was a "less direct burden upon religious practices" in that case than in this. With all respect, I think the Court is mistaken, simply as a matter of fact. . . .

The impact upon the appellant's religious freedom in the present case is considerably less onerous. We deal here not with a criminal statute, but with the particularized administration of South Carolina's Unemployment Compensation Act. Even upon the unlikely assumption that the appellant could not find suitable non-Saturday employment, the appellant at worst would be denied a maximum of 22 weeks of compensation payments. I agree with the Court that the possibility of that denial is enough to infringe upon the appellant's constitutional rights to the free exercise of her religion. But it is clear to me that in order to reach this conclusion the court must explicitly reject the reasoning of *Braunfeld* v. *Brown.* I think the Braunfeld case was wrongly decided and should be overruled, and accordingly I concur in the result reached by the Court in the case before us.

MR. JUSTICE HARLAN, whom MR. JUSTICE WHITE joins, dissenting. . . .

. . . What the Court is holding is that if the State chooses to condition unemployment compensation on the applicant's availability for work, it is constitutionally compelled to *carve out an exception*—and to provide benefits—for those whose unavailability is due to their religious convictions. Such a holding has particular significance in two respects.

First, despite the Court's protestations to the contrary, the decision necessarily overrules *Braunfeld* v. *Brown.* . . . The secular purpose of the statute before us today is

even clearer than that involved in Braunfeld. And just as in Braunfeld—where exceptions to the Sunday closing laws for
Sabbatarians would have been inconsistent
with the purpose to achieve a uniform day
of rest and would have required case-by-case
inquiry into religious beliefs—so here, an
exception to the rules of eligibility based
on religious convictions would necessitate
judicial examination of those convictions
and would be at odds with the limited
purpose of the statute to smooth out the
economy during periods of industrial in-
stability. Finally, the indirect financial burden of the present law is far less than that
involved in Braunfeld. . . . Clearly, any
difference between this case and Braunfeld
cut against the present appellant.

Second, the implications of the present
decision are far more troublesome than its
apparently narrow dimensions would indicate at first glance. The meaning of today's holding, as already noted, is that the
State must furnish unemployment benefits
to one who is unavailable for work if the
unavailability stems from the exercise of
religious convictions. The State, in other
words, must *single out* for financial assistance those whose behavior is religiously
motivated, even though it denies such assistance to others whose identical behavior
(in this case, inability to work on Saturdays) is not religiously motivated.

It has been suggested that such singling
out of religious conduct for special treatment may violate the constitutional limitations on state action. See Kurland, *Of*

Church and State and The Supreme Court,
29 *U. of Chi. L. Rev.* 1; cf. *Cammarano* v.
United States, 358 U.S. 498, 515 (concurring
opinion). My own view, however, is that
at least under the circumstances of this
case it would be a permissible accommodation of religion for the State, if it *chose* to
do so, to create an exception to its eligibility
requirements for persons like the appellant.
The constitutional obligation of "neutrality" . . . is not so narrow a channel that
the slightest deviation from an absolutely
straight course leads to condemnation.
There are too many instances in which no
such course can be charted, too many areas
in which the pervasive activities of the State
justify some special provision for religion
to prevent it from being submerged by an
all-embracing secularism. . . .

For very much the same reasons, however, I cannot subscribe to the conclusion
that the State is constitutionally *compelled*
to carve out an exception to its general rule
of eligibility in the present case. Those
situations in which the Constitution may
require special treatment on account of
religion are, in my view, few and far between, and this view is amply supported by
the course of constitutional litigation in
this area. . . . Such compulsion in the present case is particularly inappropriate in
light of the indirect, remote, and insubstantial effect of the decision below on the
exercise of appellant's religion and in light
of the direct financial assistance to religion
that today's decision requires. . . .

NOTE: *Torcaso* v. *Watkins,* 367 U.S. 488 (1961), invalidated, as an invasion of
"freedom of belief and religion," a Maryland law requiring a "declaration of
belief in the existence of God" by those who hold public office.

VII. CITIZENSHIP AND ALIENAGE

Dred Scott v. *Sandford,* 19 Howard 393 (1857), held that Negroes "are not included, and were not intended to be included, under the word 'citizens' in the

Constitution, and can, therefore, claim none of the rights and privileges which that instrument provides for and secures to citizens of the United States." This was "reversed" by Section 1 of the Fourteenth Amendment which, as the Court said in *United States* v. *Wong Kim Ark,* 169 U.S. 469 (1898),

contemplates two sources of citizenship and only two: birth and naturalization. Citizenship by naturalization can only be acquired by naturalization under the authority and in the forms of law. But citizenship by birth is established by the mere fact of birth under the circumstances defined in the Constitution. Every person born in the United States [even of alien parents] and subject to the jurisdiction thereof, becomes at once a citizen of the United States, and needs no naturalization. A person born out of the jurisdiction of the United States can only become a citizen by being naturalized, either by treaty, as in the case of the annexation of foreign territory, or by authority of Congress, exercised either by declaring certain classes of persons to be citizens, as in the enactments conferring citizenship upon foreign-born children of citizens, or by enabling foreigners individually to become citizens by proceedings in the judicial tribunals, as in the ordinary provisions of the naturalization acts.

However acquired, citizenship may be forfeited by such voluntary conduct as Congress may proscribe in the exercise of its power to deal with foreign relations. *Perez* v. *Brownell.* But in the exercise of its military powers Congress is more restricted. *Trop* v. *Dulles.*

It is settled that naturalized citizens may lose citizenship obtained by fraud, though there is controversy as to the degree of proof required in such cases. *Knauer* v. *United States,* 328 U.S. 654 (1946); *Baumgartner* v. *United States,* 322 U.S. 665 (1944). In this respect the status of a naturalized citizen is less secure than that of a citizen by birth. Perhaps the only other constitutional difference between the two is that which springs from the Article II, Section 1 provision with respect to eligibility for the presidency. *Schneider* v. *Rusk,* 84 S. Ct. 1187 (1964), held invalid that part of the 1952 Act which expatriates naturalized citizens who reside continuously for three years in the countries of their birth. The basis of the decision was: (a) mere administrative convenience, i.e., easing of the burden of protecting "nominal" United States citizens abroad, did not justify interference with the "most precious right" of citizenship; and (b), the Act unjustifiably discriminated against naturalized citizens—native-born citizens being free to reside abroad indefinitely without loss of citizenship. Justices Clark, Harlan, and White dissented.

A more tantalizing problem concerns the distinction between the constitutional rights and privileges of the citizen and those of the alien. Of course, the Bill of Rights covers all persons within the jurisdiction of the United States regardless of citizenship. This is also true of the Civil War amendments, excepting that provision of the Fourteenth which secures the "privileges and immunities" of citizens of the United States from state interference. But as we have seen (Part Four, I) the privileges and immunities clause has been narrowly construed. It follows that apart from eligibility for Congress and the presidency, there is little or no difference in the constitutional status of citizens and non-citizens with this major exception: the alien is subject to deportation at any time for any reason, as *Galvan* v. *Press* suggests. Some older decisions permit discrimination against aliens with respect to economic privileges, but later cases indicate that these may have lost their vitality. *Takahashi* v. *Fish and Game Commission.*

PEREZ v. *BROWNELL*

356 U.S. 44 (1958)

(This case appears above at p. 172.)

TROP v. *DULLES*

356 U.S. 86 (1958)

(This case appears above at p. 175.)

KENNEDY v. *MENDOZA-MARTINEZ,*

372 U.S. 144 (1963)

(See note on this case above at p. 176.)

GALVAN v. *PRESS*

347 U.S. 522 (1954)

Galvan had entered the United States in 1918 at the age of seven, and had lived there continuously for thirty-two years when his deportation as an alien was ordered on the ground that he had been a Communist Party member from 1944 to 1946. He had an American wife, to whom he had been married for sixteen years, and four children, all born in the United States. Membership in the Communist Party *regardless of knowledge of the Party's purposes* had been made a specific ground for deportation by the Internal Security Act of 1950, some four years after Galvan had ceased to be a member. In a habeas corpus proceeding he challenged the validity of the Act as applied to him. The essence of Mr. Justice Frankfurter's opinion for the Court sustaining the deportation order was that:

The power of Congress over the admission of aliens and their right to remain is necessarily very broad, touching as it does basic aspects of national sovereignty, more particularly our foreign relations and the national security. Nevertheless, considering what it means to deport an alien who legally became part of the American community, and the extent to which, since he is a "person," an alien has the same protection for his life, liberty and property under the due process clause as is afforded to a citizen, deportation without permitting the alien to prove that he was unaware of the Communist Party's advocacy of violence strikes one with a sense of harsh incongruity. If due process bars Congress from enactments that shock the sense of fair play—which is the essence of due process— one is entitled to ask whether it is not beyond the power of Congress to deport an alien who was duped into joining the Communist Party, particularly when his conduct antedated the enactment of the legislation under which his deportation is sought. And this because deportation may, as this Court has said in *Ng Fung Ho* v. *White,* 259 U.S. 276, 284, deprive a man "of all that makes life worth living"; and, as it has said in *Fong Haw Tan* v. *Phelan,* 333 U.S. 6, 10; "deportation is a drastic measure and at times the equivalent of banishment or exile."

In light of the expansion of the concept of substantive due process as a limitation upon all powers of Congress, even the war power, see *Hamilton* v. *Kentucky Distilleries Co.,* 251 U.S. 146, 155, much could be said for the view, were we writing on a clean slate, that the due process clause qualifies the scope of political discretion heretofore recognized as belonging to Congress in regulating the entry and deportation of aliens. And since the intrinsic consequences of deportation are so close to punishment for crime, it might fairly be said also that the ex post facto clause, even though applicable only to punitive legislation, should be applied to deportation.

But the slate is not clean. As to the extent of the power of Congress under review, there is not merely "a page of history," *New York Trust Co.* v. *Eisner,* 256 U.S. 345, 349, but a whole volume. Policies pertaining to the entry of aliens and their right to remain here are peculiarly concerned with the political conduct of government. In the enforcement of these policies, the executive branch of the government must respect the procedural safeguards of due process. The *Japanese Immigrant Case,* 189 U.S. 86, 101; *Wong Yang Sung* v. *McGrath,* 339 U.S. 33, 49. But that the formulation of these policies is entrusted exclusively to Congress has become about as firmly imbedded in the legislative and judicial tissues of our body politic as any aspect of our government. And whatever might have been said at an earlier date for applying the ex post facto clause, it has been the unbroken rule of this Court that it has no application to deportation.

MR. JUSTICE REED concurred in the judgment of the Court.

[JUSTICES BLACK and DOUGLAS dissented. What follows is from the latter's opinion:]

As MR. JUSTICE BLACK states in his dissent, the only charge against this alien is an act that was lawful when done. I agree that there is, therefore, no constitutional basis for deportation, if aliens, as well as citizens, are to be the beneficiaries of due process of law. . . . I cannot agree that because a man was once a Communist, he always must carry the curse. . . .

HARISIADES v. *SHAUGHNESSY*

342 U.S. 580 (1952)

MR. JUSTICE DOUGLAS, with whom MR. JUSTICE BLACK concurs, dissenting. . . .

The view that the power of Congress to deport aliens is absolute and may be exercised for any reason which Congress deems appropriate rests on *Fong Yue Ting* v. *United States,* 149 U.S. 698, decided in 1893 by a six-to-three vote. That decision seems to me to be inconsistent with the philosophy of constitutional law which we have developed for the protection of resident aliens. We have long held that a resi-

dent alien is a "person" within the meaning
of the Fifth and the Fourteenth Amendments. He therefore may not be deprived
either by the national government or by
any state of life, liberty or property without
due process of law. Nor may he be denied
the equal protection of the laws. A state
was not allowed to exclude an alien from
the laundry business because he was a
Chinese, nor discharge him from employment because he was not a citizen, nor
deprive him of the right to fish because he
was a Japanese ineligible for citizenship. An
alien's property (provided he is not an
enemy alien) may not be taken without just
compensation. He is entitled to habeas corpus to test the legality of his restraint, to
the protection of the Fifth and Sixth
Amendments in criminal trials, and to the
right of free speech as guaranteed by the
First Amendment.

The right to be immune from arbitrary
decrees of banishment certainly may be
more important to "liberty" than the civil
rights which all aliens enjoy when they
reside here. Unless they are free from arbitrary banishment, the "liberty" they enjoy
while they live here is indeed illusory.
Banishment is punishment in the practical
sense. It may deprive a man and his family
of all that makes life worth while. Those
who have their roots here have an important stake in this country. Their plans for
themselves and their hopes for their children all depend on their right to stay. If
they are uprooted and sent to lands no
longer known to them, no longer hos-
pitable, they become displaced, homeless
people condemned to bitterness and
despair.

This drastic step may at times be necessary in order to protect the national interest. There may be occasions when the
continued presence of an alien, no matter
how long he may have been here, would be
hostile to the safety of welfare of the nation
due to the nature of his conduct. But unless
such condition is shown, I would stay the
hand of the government and let those to
whom we have extended our hospitality
and who have become members of our
communities remain here and enjoy the
life and liberty which the Constitution
guarantees. . . .

TAKAHASHI v. *FISH & GAME COMMISSION*
334 U.S. 410 (1948)

Certiorari to the Supreme Court of California.

MR. JUSTICE BLACK delivered the opinion
of the Court.

The respondent, Torao Takahashi, born
in Japan, came to this country and became
a resident of California in 1907. Federal
laws, based on distinctions of "color and
race," *Toyota* v. *United States*, 268 U.S.
402, 411–412, have permitted Japanese and
certain other non-white racial groups to
enter and reside in the country, but have
made them ineligible for United States citizenship. The question presented is whether
California can, consistently with the Federal Constitution and laws passed pursuant
to it, use this federally created racial ineligibility for citizenship as a basis for barring Takahashi from earning his living as
a commercial fisherman in the ocean waters
off the coast of California.

Prior to 1943 California issued commercial fishing licenses to all qualified persons
without regard to alienage or ineligibility
to citizenship. From 1915 to 1942 Takahashi, under annual commercial fishing
licenses issued by the State, fished in ocean
waters off the California coast, apparently
both within and without the three-mile
coastal belt, and brought his fresh fish
ashore for sale. In 1942, while this country

was at war with Japan, Takahashi and other California residents of Japanese ancestry were evacuated from the State under military orders. See *Korematsu* v. *United States,* 323 U.S. 214. In 1943, during the period of war and evacuation, an amendment to the California Fish and Game Code was adopted prohibiting issuance of a license to any "alien Japanese." Cal. Stats. 1943, ch. 1100. In 1945, the state code was again amended by striking the 1943 provision for fear that it might be "declared unconstitutional" because directed only "against alien Japanese"; the new amendment banned issuance of licenses to any "person ineligible to citizenship," which classification included Japanese. Cal. Stats. 1945, ch. 181. Because of this state provision barring issuance of commercial fishing licenses to persons ineligible for citizenship under federal law, Takahashi, who met all other state requirements, was denied a license by the California Fish and Game Commission upon his return to California in 1945.

Takahashi brought this action for mandamus in the Superior Court of Los Angeles County, California, to compel the Commission to issue a license to him. The court granted the petition for mandamus. It held that lawful alien inhabitants of California, despite their ineligibility to citizenship, were entitled to engage in the vocation of commercial fishing on the high seas beyond the three-mile belt on the same terms as other lawful state inhabitants, and that the California code provision denying them this right violated the equal protection of the Fourteenth Amendment. The State Supreme Court, three judges dissenting, reversed, holding that California had a proprietary interest in fish in the ocean waters within three miles of the shore, and that this interest justified the State in barring all aliens in general and aliens ineligible to citizenship in particular from catching fish within or without the three-mile coastal belt and bringing them to California for commercial purposes. 30 Cal.2d 719, 185 P.2d 805. To review this question of im-

portance in the fields of federal-state relationship and of constitutionally protected individual equality and liberty, we granted certiorari.

We may well begin our consideration of the principles to be applied in this case by a summary of this Court's holding in *Truax* v. *Raich,* 239 U.S. 33, not deemed controlling by the majority of the California Supreme Court, but regarded by the dissenters as requiring the invalidation of the California law. That case involved an attack upon an Arizona law which required all Arizona employers of more than five workers to hire not less than eighty (80) percent qualified electors or native-born citizens of the United States. Raich, an alien who worked as a cook in a restaurant which had more than five employees, was about to lose his job solely because of the state law's coercive effect on the restaurant owner. This Court, in upholding Raich's contention that the Arizona law was invalid, declared that Raich, having been lawfully admitted into the country under federal law, had a federal privilege to enter and abide in "any State in the Union" and thereafter under the Fourteenth Amendment to enjoy the equal protection of the laws of the state in which he abided; that this privilege to enter in and abide in any state carried with it the "right to work for a living in the common occupations of the community," a denial of which right would make of the Amendment "a barren form of words." In answer to a contention that Arizona's restriction upon the employment of aliens was "reasonable" and therefore permissible, this Court declared:

"It must also be said that reasonable classification implies action consistent with the legitimate interests of the State, and it will not be disputed that these cannot be so broadly conceived as to bring them into hostility to exclusive Federal power. The authority to control immigration—to admit or exclude aliens—is vested solely in the Federal Government. *Fong Yue Ting* v. *United States,* 149 U.S. 698, 713. The assertion of an authority to deny to aliens the opportunity of earning a livelihood when lawfully admitted to the State would be tantamount to the assertion of the right to deny them entrance and abode, for in ordinary cases they cannot live where they cannot work. And, if such a policy were permissible, the practical result would be that those lawfully admitted to the country under the authority of the acts of Congress, instead of enjoying in a substantial sense and in their full scope the privileges conferred by the admission, would be segregated in such of the States as choose to offer hospitality. (*Truax* v. *Raich, supra* at 42.)"

Had the *Truax* decision said nothing further than what is quoted above, its reasoning, if followed, would seem to require invalidation of this California code provision barring aliens from the occupation of fishing as inconsistent with federal law, which is constitutionally declared to be "the supreme Law of the Land." However, the Court there went on to note that it had on occasion sustained state legislation that did not apply alike to citizens and non-citizens, the ground for the distinction being that such laws were necessary to protect special interests either of the state or of its citizens as such. The *Truax* opinion pointed out that the Arizona law, aimed as it was against employment of aliens in *all* vocations, failed to show "special public interest with respect to any particular business . . . that could possibly be deemed to support the enactment." The Court noted that it had previously upheld various state laws which restricted the privilege of planting oysters in the tidewater rivers of a state to citizens of that state, and which denied to aliens within a state the privilege of possessing a rifle and of shooting game within that state; it also referred to decisions recognizing a state's broad powers, in the absence of overriding treaties, to restrict the devolution of real property to non-aliens.

California now urges, and the State Supreme Court held, that the California fishing provision here challenged falls within the rationale of the "special public interest"

cases distinguished in the *Truax* opinion, and thus that the state's ban upon commercial fishing by aliens ineligible to citizenship is valid. The contention is this: California owns the fish within three miles of its coast as a trustee for all California citizens as distinguished from its non-citizen inhabitants; as such trustee-owner, it has complete power to bar any or all aliens from fishing in the three-mile belt as a means of conserving the supply of fish; since migratory fish caught while swimming in the three-mile belt are indistinguishable from those caught while swimming in the adjacent high seas, the State, in order to enforce its three-mile control, can also regulate the catching and delivery to its coast of fish caught beyond the three-mile belt under this Court's decision in *Bayside Fish Co.* v. *Gentry,* 297 U.S. 422. Its law denying fishing licenses to aliens ineligible for citizenship, so the state's contention goes, tends to reduce the number of commercial fisherman and therefore is a proper fish conservation measure; in the exercise of its power to decide what groups will be denied licenses, the State has a right, if not a duty, to bar first of all aliens, who have no community interest in the fish owned by the State. Finally, the legislature's denial of licenses to those aliens who are "ineligible to citizenship" is defended as a reasonable classification, on the ground that California has simply followed the Federal Government's lead in adopting that classification from the naturalization laws.

First. The state's contention that its law was passed solely as a fish conservation measure is vigorously denied. The petitioner argues that it was the outgrowth of racial antagonism directed solely against the Japanese, and that for this reason alone it cannot stand. See *Korematsu* v. *United States, supra,* at 216; *Kotch* v. *Board of River Pilot Comm'rs,* 330 U.S. 552, 556; *Yick Wo* v. *Hopkins,* 118 U.S. 356; *In re Ah Chong,* 2 F. 733, 737. We find it unnecessary to resolve this controversy concerning the motives that prompted enactment of the legislation. Accordingly, for purposes of our decision we may assume that the code provision was passed to conserve fish in the California coastal waters, or to protect California citizens engaged in commercial fishing from competition by Japanese aliens, or for both reasons.

Second. It does not follow, as California seems to argue, that because the United States regulates immigration and naturalization in part on the basis of race and color classifications, a state can adopt one or more of the same classifications to prevent lawfully admitted aliens within its borders from earning a living in the same way that other state inhabitants earn their living. The Federal Government has broad constitutional powers in determining what aliens shall be admitted to the United States, the period they may remain, regulation of their conduct before naturalization, and the terms and conditions of their naturalization. See *Hines* v. *Davidowitz,* 312 U.S. 52, 66. Under the Constitution the states are granted no such powers; they can neither add to nor take from the conditions lawfully imposed by Congress upon admission, naturalization and residence of aliens in the United States or the several states. State laws which impose discriminatory burdens upon the entrance or residence of aliens lawfully within the United States conflict with this constitutionally derived federal power to regulate immigration, and have accordingly been held invalid. Moreover, Congress, in the enactment of a comprehensive legislative plan for the nation-wide control and regulation of immigration and naturalization, has broadly provided:

"All persons within the jurisdiction of the United States shall have the same right in every State and Territory to make and enforce contracts, to sue, be parties, give evidence, and to the full and equal benefit of all laws and proceedings for the security of persons and property as is enjoyed by white citizens, and shall be subject to like punishment, pains, penalties, taxes, licenses, and exactions of every kind, and to no other. (16 Stat. 140, 144, 8 U.S.C. § 41.)"

The protection of this section has been held to extend to aliens as well as to citizens. Consequently the section and the Fourteenth Amendment on which it rests in part protect "all persons" against state legislation bearing unequally upon them either because of alienage or color. See *Hurd* v. *Hodge,* 334 U.S. 24. The Fourteenth Amendment and the laws adopted under its authority thus embody a general policy that all persons lawfully in this country shall abide "in any state" on an equality of legal privileges with all citizens under non-discriminatory laws.

All of the foregoing emphasizes the tenuousness of the state's claim that it has power to single out and ban its lawful alien inhabitants, and particularly certain racial and color groups within this class of inhabitants, from following a vocation simply because Congress has put some such groups in special classifications in exercise of its broad and wholly distinguishable powers over immigration and naturalization. The state's law here cannot be supported in the employment of this legislative authority because of policies adopted by Congress in the exercise of its power to treat separately and differently with aliens from countries composed of peoples of many diverse cultures, races, and colors. For these reasons the power of a state to apply its laws exclusively to its alien inhabitants as a class is confined within narrow limits.

Third. We are unable to find that the "special public interest" on which California relies provides support for this state ban on Takahashi's commercial fishing. As before pointed out, California's claim of "special public interest" is that its citizens are the collective owners of fish swimming in the three-mile belt. It is true that this Court did long ago say that the citizens of a state collectively own "the tide-waters . . . and the fish in them, so far as they are capable of ownership while running." *McCready* v. *Virginia,* 94 U.S. 391, 394. Cf. *United States* v. *California* 332 U.S. 19, 38; *Toomer* v. *Witsell, ante,* p. 385. The *McCready* case upheld a Virginia law which prohibited citizens of other states from planting oysters in a Virginia tidewater river. Though the *McCready* case has been often distinguished, its rationale has been relied on in other cases, including *Greer* v. *Connecticut*, 161 U.S. 519. That decision, where only the commerce clause was involved, sustained a state law that, in order to restrict the use of game to the people of the state, prohibited the out-of-state transportation of game killed within the state. On the other hand, where Louisiana laws declared that the state owned all shrimp within the waters of the state, but permitted ultimate sale and shipment of shrimp for consumption outside that state's boundaries, Louisiana was denied power under the commerce clause to require the local processing of shrimp taken from Louisiana marshes as a prerequisite to out-of-state transportation. *Foster Packing Co.* v. *Haydel*, 278 U.S. 1. In the absence of overriding federal treaties, this Court sustained a state law barring aliens from hunting wild game in the interest of conserving game for citizens of the state against due process and equal protection challenges. *Patsone* v. *Pennsylvania*, 232 U.S. 138. Later, however, the Federal Migratory Bird Treaty Act of 1918, 40 Stat. 755, was sustained as within federal power despite the claim of Missouri of ownership of birds within its boundaries based on prior statements as to state ownership of game and fish in the *Greer* case. *Missouri* v. *Holland*, 252 U.S. 416. The Court was of opinion that "To put the claim of the State upon title is to lean upon a slender reed." P. 434. We think that same statement is equally applicable here. To whatever extent the fish in the three-mile belt off California may be "capable of ownership" by California, we think that "ownership" is inadequate to justify California in excluding any or all aliens who are lawful residents of the State from making a living by fishing in the ocean off its shores while permitting all others to do so.

This leaves for consideration the argument that this law should be upheld on authority of those cases which have sustained state laws barring aliens ineligible to citizenship from land ownership. Assuming the continued validity of those cases,

we think they could not in any event be controlling here. They rested solely upon the power of states to control the devolution and ownership of land within their borders, a power long exercised and supported on reasons peculiar to real property. They cannot be extended to cover this case.

The judgment is reversed and remanded for proceedings not inconsistent with this opinion.

Reversed.

[MR. JUSTICE MURPHY and MR. JUSTICE RUTLEDGE, concurring, argued that the statutory provision in question was "the direct outgrowth of antagonism toward persons of Japanese ancestry."]

MR. JUSTICE REED, dissenting.

The reasons which lead me to conclude that the judgment of the Supreme Court of California should be affirmed may be briefly stated. As fishing rights have been treated traditionally as a natural resource, in the absence of federal regulation, California as a sovereign state has power to regulate the taking and handling of fish in the waters bordering its shores. It is, I think, one of the natural resources of the state that may be preserved from exploitation by aliens. The ground for this power in the absence of any exercise of federal authority is California's authority over its fisheries.

The right to fish is analogous to the right to own land, a privilege which a state may deny to aliens as to land within its borders. *Terrace* v. *Thompson*, 263 U.S. 197. It is closely akin to the right to hunt, a privilege from which a state may bar aliens, if reasonably deemed advantageous to its citizens. A state's power has even been held to extend to the exclusion of aliens from the operation of pool and billiard halls when a city deemed them not as well qualified as citizens for the conduct of a business thought to have harmful tendencies. *Clarke* v. *Deckebach*, 274 U.S. 392.

The Federal Government has not pursued a policy of equal treatment of aliens and citizens. Citizens have rights superior to those of aliens in the ownership of land

and in exploiting natural resources. Perhaps Congress as a matter of immigration policy may require that states open every door of opportunity in America to all resident aliens, but until Congress so determines as to fisheries, I do not feel that the judicial arm of the Government should require the states to admit all aliens to this privilege.

Certainly *Truax* v. *Raich,* 239 U.S. 33, upon which the majority opinion appears to rely in holding that the California statute denies equal protection in attempting to classify aliens by putting restrictions on their right to land fish, is not an authority for such a decision. The power of a state to discriminate against aliens on public works and the exploitation of natural resources was recognized in that case. And, at the very time that it was under consideration, this Court also had before it *Heim* v. *McCall,* 239 U.S. 175. In that case, Heim attacked the constitutionality of a New York Statute which provided that "In the construction of public works by the State or a municipality, or by persons contracting with the state or such municipality, only citizens of the United States shall be employed; and in all cases where laborers are employed on any such public works, preference shall be given citizens of the State of New York."

A unanimous court held that the statute, which was attacked on the ground that it denied aliens their rights under the privileges and immunities, due process, and equal protection clauses of the Constitution, was a constitutional exercise of state power as applied to the construction of New York City subways by private contractors. The Constitution that permits the bar of aliens from public works surely must permit their bar from state fishing rights. A state has power to exclude from enjoyment of its natural resources those who are unwilling or unable to become citizens.

If aliens, as I think they can, may be excluded by a state from fishing privileges, I see no reason why the classification established by California excluding only aliens ineligible to citizenship is prohibited by the Constitution. *Terrace* v. *Thompson,* 263 U.S. 197, 220. Whatever we may think of the wisdom of California's statute, we should intervene only when we conclude the state statute passes constitutional limits.

MR. JUSTICE JACKSON joins in this dissent.

NOTE: In *Fujii* v. *California,* 38 Cal. 2nd. 718 (1952), the Supreme Court of California held the state Alien Land Law invalid by virtue of the equal protection clause of the Fourteenth Amendment. The "law" in question, barring aliens ineligible for citizenship from owning land, is referred to at the end of the Court's opinion in *Takahashi.*

VIII. THE SUFFRAGE

In *Minor* v. *Happersett,* 21 Wallace 162 (1875), a suit was brought against a registration officer for refusing to register a female citizen. The law of her state confined suffrage to males. Plaintiff's claim was based on the privileges and immunities clause of the Fourteenth Amendment. The Court observed that the provision in question did not add to the privileges of citizenship, but merely gave an additional guarantee for those a citizen already had: "Certainly, if the courts can consider any question settled, this is one. For nearly ninety years the people have acted upon the idea that the Constitution, when it conferred citizenship, did not necessarily confer the right of suffrage. If uniform practice, long continued, can settle the construction of so important an instrument as the Constitution of the United States confessedly is, most certainly it has been done here. Our province is to decide what the law is, not to declare what it should be." See the Nineteenth Amendment.

BREEDLOVE v. SHUTTLES

302 U.S. 277 (1937)

In this case appellant, a white male citizen of Georgia, had been denied a vote for failure to pay a poll tax.

Mr. Justice Butler delivered the opinion of the Court: . . .

A Georgia statute provides that there shall be levied and collected each year from every inhabitant of the State between the ages of 21 and 60 a poll tax of one dollar, but that the tax shall not be demanded from the blind or from females who do not register for voting. Georgia Code, 1933, § 92–108. The state constitution declares that to entitle a person to register and vote at any election he shall have paid all poll taxes that he may have had opportunity to pay agreeably to law. Art. II, § I, par. III; Code, § 2–603. . . .

Levy by the poll has long been a familiar form of taxation, much used in some countries and to a considerable extent here, at first in the Colonies and later in the States. . . .

Payment as a prerequisite is not required for the purpose of denying or abridging the privilege of voting. It does not limit the tax to electors; aliens are not there permitted to vote, but the tax is laid upon them, if within the defined class. It is not laid upon persons of 60 or more years old, whether electors or not. Exaction of payment before registration undoubtedly serves to aid collection from electors desiring to vote, but that use of the State's power is not prevented by the Federal Constitution. Cf. *Mangano Co.* v. *Hamilton,* 292 U.S. 40, 44.

Affirmed.

NOTE: See the Twenty-fourth Amendment.

LASSITER v. NORTHAMPTON COUNTY BOARD OF ELECTIONS

360 U.S. 45 (1959)

Mr. Justice Douglas delivered the opinion of the Court. . . .

The states have long been held to have broad powers to determine the conditions under which the right of suffrage may be exercised . . . absent of course the discrimination which the Constitution condemns. Article I § 2 of the Constitution in its provision for the election of members of the House of Representatives and the Seventeenth Amendment in its provision for the election of Senators provide that officials will be chosen "by the people." Each provision goes on to state that "The electors in each State shall have the qualifications requisite for electors of the most numerous branch of the State legislatures." So while the right of suffrage is established and guaranteed by the Constitution (*Ex parte Yarbrough*, 110 U.S. 651, 663–665; *Smith* v. *Allwright*, 321 U.S. 649, 661–662) it is subject to the imposition of state standards which are not discriminatory and which do not contravene any restriction that Congress acting pursuant to its constitutional powers, has imposed. See *United States* v. *Classic*, 313 U.S. 299, 315. While § 2 of the Fourteenth Amendment, which provides for apportionment of Representatives among the States according to their respective numbers counting the whole number of persons in each State (except Indians not taxed), speaks of "the right to vote," the right protected "refers to the right to vote as established by the laws and constitution of the state." *McPherson* v. *Blacker*, 146 U.S. 1, 39.

We do not suggest that any standards which a State desires to adopt may be required of voters. But there is wide scope for exercise of its jurisdiction. Residence requirements, age, previous criminal record (*Davis* v. *Beason*, 133 U.S. 333, 345–347) are obvious examples indicating factors which a State may take into consideration in determining the qualifications of voters. The ability to read and write likewise has some relation to standards designed to promote intelligent use of the ballot. Literacy and illiteracy are neutral on race, creed, color, and sex, as reports around the world show. Literacy and intelligence are obviously not synonymous. Illiterate people may be intelligent voters. Yet in our society where newspapers, periodicals, books, and other printed matter canvass and debate campaign issues, a State might conclude that only those who are literate should exercise the franchise. Cf. *Franklin* v. *Harper*, 205 Ga. 779, 55 S.E.2d 221, appeal dismissed 339 U.S. 946. It was said last century in Massachusetts that a literacy test was designed to insure an "independent and intelligent" exercise of the right of suffrage. *Stone* v. *Smith*, 159 Mass. 413–414, 34 N.E. 521. North Carolina agrees. We do not sit in judgment on the wisdom of that policy. We cannot say, however, that it is not an allowable one measured by constitutional standards.

Of course a literacy test, fair on its face, may be employed to perpetuate that discrimination which the Fifteenth Amendment was designed to uproot. No such influence is charged here. On the other hand, a literacy test may be unconstitutional on its face. In *Davis* v. *Schnell*, D.C., 81 F. Supp. 872, 873, affirmed 336 U.S. 933, the test was the citizen's ability to "understand and explain" an article of the Federal Constitution. The legislative setting of that provision and the great discretion it vested in the registrar made clear that a literacy requirement was merely a device to make racial discrimination easy. We cannot make the same inference here. The present requirement, applicable to members of all races, is that the prospective voter "be able to read and write any section of the Constitution of North Carolina in the English language." That seems to us to be one fair way of determining whether a person is literate, not a calculated scheme to lay springes for the citizens. Certainly we cannot condemn it on its face as a device unrelated to the desire of North Carolina to raise the standards for people of all races who cast the ballot.

Affirmed.

RICE v. ELMORE

165 F.2d 387 (1947)

(This case appears above at p. 54.)

GOMILLION v. LIGHTFOOT
364 U.S. 339 (1960)

(See references to this case in *Baker* v. *Carr*, above, at p. 20.)

BAKER v. CARR
369 U.S. 186 (1962)

(This case appears above at p. 20.)

NOTE: *Gray* v. *Sanders*, 372 U.S. 368 (1963), invalidated the Georgia county unit system "which in end result weights the rural vote more heavily than the urban vote and weights some small rural counties heavier than other larger rural counties" *all in the same, i.e. statewide, constitutency.* Thus, as the Court emphasized, this has nothing to do "with the composition of the state or federal legislature." The essence of the decision was simply that within the same voting district "all who participate in the election are to have an equal vote."

Mr. Justice Harlan in dissent rejected the Court's view that the electoral college approach was irrelevant: "One need not close his eyes to the circumstance that the Electoral College was born in compromise . . . in order to agree with the court below that 'it could hardly be said that such a system used in a state among its counties could be termed invidious.' " Disproportionate vote weighting, he thought, could not alone prove unconstitutionality. "At the core of Georgia's diffusion of voting strength . . . is the rural-urban problem. . . . Given the undeniably powerful influence of a state governor on law and policy making, I do not see how it can be deemed irrational for a State to conclude that a candidate for such office should not be one whose choice lies with the numerically superior electoral strength of urban voters"—thus assuring a predominantly "city point of view."

WESBERRY v. SANDERS
84 S. Ct. 526 (1964)

The plaintiffs, qualified voters in the Fifth Congressional District of Georgia, sued to invalidate a state districting law of 1931. The basis of their complaint was that: (1) the Fifth District was more than twice as large in population as some other congressional districts in Georgia; and (2) these disparities deprived plaintiffs and others of a Federal right to have their votes for Congressmen given the same weight as the votes of other Georgians.

MR. JUSTICE BLACK delivered the opinion of the court.

[As in *Baker* v. *Carr*, the court began by rejecting *Colegrove* v. *Green* on which the lower court had erroneously relied in dismissing the present case.]

We hold that, construed in its historical context, the command of Art. I, § 2, that Representatives be chosen "by the People of the several States" means that as nearly as is practicable one man's vote in a congressional election is to be worth as much as another's. This rule is followed automatically, of course, when Representatives are chosen as a group on a statewide basis, as was a widespread practice in the first 50 years of our Nation's history. It would be extraordinary to suggest that in such statewide elections the votes of inhabitants of some parts of a State, for example, Georgia's thinly populated Ninth District, could be weighed at two or three times the value of the votes of people living in more populous parts of the State, for example, the Fifth District around Atlanta. Cf. *Gray* v. *Sanders*, 372 U.S. 368. We do not believe that the Framers of the Constitution intended to permit the same vote-diluting discrimination to be accomplished through the device of districts containing widely varied numbers of inhabitants. To say that a vote is worth more in one district than in another would not only run counter to our fundamental ideas of democratic government, it would cast aside the principle of a House of Representatives elected "by the People," a principle tenaciously fought for and established at the Constitutional Convention. The history of the Constitution, particularly that part of it relating to the adoption of Art. I, § 2, reveals that those who framed the Constitution meant that, no matter what the mechanics of an election, whether statewide or by districts, it was population which was to be the basis of the House of Representatives.

During the Revolutionary War the rebelling colonies were loosely allied in the Continental Congress, a body with authority to do little more than pass resolutions and issue requests for men and supplies. Before the war ended the Congress had proposed and secured the ratification by the States of a somewhat closer association under the Articles of Confederation. Though the Articles established a central government for the United States, as the former colonies were even then called, the States retained most of their sovereignty, like independent nations bound together only by treaties. There were no separate judicial or executive branches: only a Congress consisting of a single house. Like the members of an ancient Greek league, each State, without regard to size or population, was given only one vote in that house. It soon became clear that the Confederation was without adequate power to collect needed revenues or to enforce the rules its Congress adopted. Far-sighted men felt that a closer union was necessary if the States were to be saved from foreign and domestic dangers.

The result was the Constitutional Convention of 1787, called for "the sole and express purpose of revising the Articles of Confederation. . . ." When the Convention met in May, this modest purpose was soon abandoned for the greater challenge of creating a new and closer form of government that was possible under the Confederation. Soon after the Convention assembled, Edmund Randolph of Virginia presented a plan not merely to amend the Articles of Confederation but to create an entirely new National Government with a National Executive, National Judiciary, and a National Legislature of two Houses, one house to be elected by "the people," the second house to be elected by the first.

The question of how the legislature should be constituted precipitated the most bitter controversy of the Convention. One principle was uppermost in the minds of many delegates: that, no matter where he lived, each voter should have a voice equal with that of every other in electing members of Congress. In support of this principle, George Mason of Virginia "argued strongly for an election of the larger branch by the people. It was to be the grand depository of the democratic principle of the Govt."

James Madison agreed, saying "If the power is not immediately derived from the people, in proportion to their numbers, we may make a paper confederacy, but that will be all." Repeatedly, delegates rose to make the same point: that it would be unfair, unjust, and contrary to common sense to give a small number of people as many Senators or Representatives as were allowed to much larger groups—in short, as James Wilson of Pennsylvania put it, "equal numbers of people ought to have an equal no. of representatives . . ." and representatives "of different districts ought clearly to hold the same proportion to each other, as their respective constituents hold to each other."

Some delegates opposed election by the people. The sharpest objection arose out of the fear on the part of small States like Delaware that if population were to be the only basis of representation the populous States like Virginia would elect a large enough number of representatives to wield overwhelming power in the National Government. Arguing that the Convention had no authority to depart from the plan of the Articles of Confederation which gave each State an equal vote in the National Congress, William Paterson of New Jersey said, "If the sovereignty of the States is to be maintained, the Representatives must be drawn immediately from the States, not from the people: and we have no power to vary the idea of equal sovereignty." To this end he proposed a single legislative chamber in which each State, as in the Confederation, was to have an equal vote. A number of delegates supported this plan.

The delegates who wanted every man's vote to count alike were sharp in their criticism of giving each State, regardless of population, the same voice in the national legislature. Madison entreated the Convention "to renounce a principle wch. was confessedly unjust," and Rufus King of Massachusetts "was prepared for any event, rather than sit down under a Govt. founded in a vicious principle of representation and

which must be as shortlived as it would be unjust."

The dispute came near ending the Convention without a Constitution. Both sides seemed for a time to be hopelessly obstinate. Some delegations threatened to withdraw from the Convention if they did not get their way. Seeing the controversy growing sharper and emotions rising, the wise and highly respected Benjamin Franklin arose and pleaded with the delegates on both sides to "part with some of their demands, in order that they may join in some accommodating proposition." At last those who supported representation of the people in both houses and those who supported it in neither were brought together, some expressing the fear that if they did not reconcile their differences, "some foreign sword will probably do the work for us." The deadlock was finally broken when a majority of the States agreed to what has been called the Great Compromise, based on a proposal which had been repeatedly advanced by Roger Sherman and other delegates from Connecticut. It provided on the one hand that each State, including little Delaware and Rhode Island, was to have two Senators. As a further guarantee that these Senators would be considered state emissaries, they were to be elected by the state legislatures, Art. I, § 3, and it was specially provided in Article V that no State should ever be deprived of its equal representation in the Senate. The other side of the compromise was that, as provided in Art. I, § 2, members of the House of Representatives should be chosen "by the People of the several States" and should be "apportioned among the several States . . . according to their respective Numbers." While those who wanted both houses to represent the people had yielded on the Senate, they had not yielded on the House of Representatives. William Samuel Johnson of Connecticut had summed it up well: "in *one* branch the *people,* ought to be represented; in the *other,* the *States.*"

The debates at the Convention make at least one fact abundantly clear: that when the delegates agreed that the House should represent "people" they intended that in allocating Congressmen the number assigned to each State should be determined solely by the number of the State's inhabitants. The Constitution embodied Edmund Randolph's proposal for a periodic census to ensure "fair representation of the people," an idea endorsed by Mason as assuring that "numbers of inhabitants" should always be the measure of representation in the House of Representatives. The Convention also overwhelmingly agreed to a resolution offered by Randolph to base future apportionment squarely on numbers and to delete any reference to wealth. And the delegates defeated a motion made by Elbridge Gerry to limit the number of Representatives from newer Western States so that it would never exceed the number from the original States.

It would defeat the principle solemnly embodied in the Great Compromise—equal representation in the House of equal numbers of people—for us to hold that, within the States, legislatures may draw the lines of congressional districts in such a way as to give some voters a greater voice in choosing a Congressman than others. The House of Representatives, the Convention agreed, was to represent the people as individuals, and on a basis of complete equality for each voter. The delegates were quite aware of what Madison called the "vicious representation" in Great Britain whereby "rotten boroughs" with few inhabitants were represented in Parliament on or almost on a par with cities of greater population. Wilson urged that people must be represented as individuals, so that America would escape the evils of the English system under which one man could send two members to Parliament to represent the borough of Old Sarum while London's million people sent but four. The delegates referred to rotten borough apportionments in some of the state legislatures as the kind of objectionable governmental action that the Constitution should not tolerate in the election of congressional representatives.

Madison in *The Federalist* described the system of division of States into congressional districts, the method which he and others assumed States probably would adopt: "The city of Philadelphia is supposed to contain between fifty and sixty thousand souls. It will therefore form nearly two districts for the choice of Fœderal Representatives." "[N]umbers," he said, not only are a suitable way to represent wealth but in any event "are the only proper scale of representation." In the state conventions, speakers urging ratification of the Constitution emphasized the theme of equal representation in the House which had permeated the debates in Philadelphia. Charles Cotesworth Pinckney told the South Carolina Convention, "the House of Representatives will be elected immediately by the people, and represent them and their personal rights individually . . ." Speakers at the ratifying conventions emphasized that the House of Representatives was meant to be free of the malapportionment then existing in some of the state legislatures—such as those of Connecticut, Rhode Island, and South Carolina—and argued that the power given Congress in Art. I, § 4, was meant to be used to vindicate the people's right to equality of representation in the House. Congress' power, said John Steele at the North Carolina convention, was not to be used to allow Congress to create rotten boroughs; in answer to another delegate's suggestion that Congress might use its power to favor people living near the seacoast, Steele said that Congress "most probably" would "lay the State off into districts," and if it made laws "inconsistent with the Constitution, independent judges will not uphold them, nor will the people obey them."

Soon after the Constitution was adopted, James Wilson of Pennsylvania, by then an Associate Justice of this Court, gave a series of lectures at Philadelphia in which, drawing on his experience as one of the most active members of the Constitutional Convention, he said:

"[A]ll elections ought to be equal. Elections are equal, when a given number of citizens, in one part of the state, choose as many representatives, as are chosen by the same number of citizens, in any other part of the state. In this manner, the proportion of the representatives and of the constituents will remain invariably the same."

It is in the light of such history that we must construe Art. I, § 2, of the Constitution, which, carrying out the ideas of Madison and those of like views, provides that Representatives shall be chosen "by the People of the several States" and shall be "apportioned among the several States . . . according to their respective Numbers." It is not surprising that our Court has held that this Article gives persons qualified to vote a constitutional right to vote and to have their votes counted. *United States* v. *Mosley*, 238 U.S. 383; *Ex parte Yarbrough*, 110 U.S. 651. Not only can this right to vote not be denied outright, it cannot, consistently with Article I, be destroyed by alteration of ballots, see *United States* v. *Classic*, 313 U.S. 299, or diluted by stuffing of the ballot box, see *United States* v. *Saylor*, 322 U.S. 385. No right is more precious in a free country than that of having a voice in the election of those who make the laws under which, as good citizens, we must live. Other rights, even the most basic, are illusory if the right to vote is undermined. Our Constitution leaves no room for classification of people in a way that unnecessarily abridges this right. In urging the people to adopt the Constitution, Madison said in No. 57 of *The Federalist:*

"Who are to be the electors of the Fœderal Representatives? Not the rich more than the poor; not the learned more than the ignorant; not the haughty heirs of distinguished names, more than the humble sons of obscure and unpropitious fortune. The electors are to be the great body of the people of the United States. . . ."

Readers surely could have fairly taken this to mean, "one person, one vote." Cf. *Gray* v. *Sanders*, 372 U.S. 368, 381.

While it may not be possible to draw congressional districts with mathematical precision, that is no excuse for ignoring our

Constitution's plain objective of making equal representation for equal numbers of people the fundamental goal for the House of Representatives. That is the high standard of justice and common sense which the Founders set for us.

Reversed and remanded.

[JUSTICES CLARK and STEWART agreed that congressional districting is subject to judicial scrutiny, but concurred in the dissenting view on the merits.]

MR. JUSTICE HARLAN, dissenting. . . .

Before coming to grips with the [court's] reasoning, . . . it is important to have firmly in mind the provisions of Article I [Sections 2, 4, 5] of the Constitution which control this case. . . .

As will be shown, these constitutional provisions and their "historical context," *ante,* p. . . . , establish:

1. that congressional Representatives are to be apportioned among the several States largely, but not entirely, according to population;

2. that the States have plenary power to select their allotted Representatives in accordance with any method of popular election they please, subject only to the supervisory power of Congress; and

3. that the supervisory power of Congress is exclusive.

In short, in the absence of legislation providing for equal districts by the Georgia Legislature or by Congress, these appellants have no right to the judicial relief which they seek. It goes without saying that it is beyond the province of this Court to decide whether equally populated districts is the preferable method for electing Representatives, whether state legislatures would have acted more fairly or wisely had they adopted such a method, or whether Congress has been derelict in not requiring state legislatures to follow that course. Once it is clear that there is no *constitutional* right at stake, that ends the case.

II

Disclaiming all reliance on other provisions of the Constitution, in particular those of the Fourteenth Amendment on which the appellants relied below and in this Court, the Court holds that the provision in Art. I, § 2, for election of Representatives "by the People" *means* that congressional districts are to be "as nearly as is practicable" equal in population, *ante*, p. 530. Stripped of rhetoric and a "historical context," *ante*, p. . . . , which bears little resemblance to the evidence found in the pages of history, see *infra*, p. ——, the Court's opinion supports its holding only with the bland assertion that "the principle of a House of Representatives elected 'by the People'" would be "cast aside" if "a vote is worth more in one district than in another," *ante* p. 530, *i.e.*, if congressional districts within a State, each electing a single Representative, are not equal in population. The fact is, however, that Georgia's 10 Representatives *are* elected "by the People" of Georgia, just as Representatives from other States are elected "by the People of the several States." This is all that the Constitution requires.

Although the Court finds necessity for its artificial construction of Article I in the undoubted importance of the right to vote, that right is not involved in this case. All of the appellants do vote. The Court's talk about "debasement" and "dilution" of the vote is a model of circular reasoning, in which the premises of the argument feed on the conclusion. Moreover, by focusing exclusively on numbers in disregard of the area and shape of a congressional district as well as party affiliations within the district, the Court deals in abstractions which will be recognized even by the politically unsophisticated to have little relevance to the realities of political life.

In any event, the very sentence of Art. I, § 2, on which the Court exclusively relies confers the right to vote for Representatives only on those whom *the State* has found qualified to vote for members of "the most numerous Branch of the State Legislature." *Supra*, p. . . . . So far as Article I is concerned, it is within the State's power to confer that right only on persons of wealth or of a particular sex or, if the State chose, living in specified areas of the State. Were

Georgia to find the residents of the Fifth District unqualified to vote for Representatives to the State House of Representatives, they could not vote for Representatives to Congress, according to the express words of Art. I, § 2. Other provisions of the Constitution would, of course, be relevant, *but so far as Art. I, § 2, is concerned,* the disqualification would be within Georgia's power. How can it be, then, that this very same sentence prevents Georgia from apportioning its Representatives as it chooses? The truth is that it does not.

The Court purports to find support for its position in the third paragraph of Art. I, § 2, which provides for the apportionment of Representatives among the States. The appearance of support in that section derives from the Court's confusion of two issues: direct election of Representatives within the States and the apportionment of Representatives among the States. Those issues are distinct, and were separately treated in the Constitution. The fallacy of the Court's reasoning in this regard is illustrated by its slide, obscured by intervening discussion (see *ante* p. ——), from the intention of the delegates at the Philadelphia Convention "that in allocating Congressmen the number assigned to each State should be determined solely by the number of the State's inhabitants," *ante*, p. . . . , to a "principle solemnly embodied in the Great Compromise—equal representation in the House of equal numbers of people," *ante*, p. 533. The delegates did have the former intention and made clear provision for it. Although many, perhaps most, of them also believed generally—but assuredly not in the precise, formalistic way of the majority of the Court—that within the States representation should be based on population, they did not surreptitiously slip their belief into the Constitution in the phrase "by the People," to be discovered 175 years later like a Shakespearian anagram.

Far from supporting the Court, the apportionment of Representatives among the States shows how blindly the Court has marched to its decision. Representatives were to be apportioned among the States on the basis of free population plus three-fifths of the slave population. Since no slave voted, the inclusion of three-fifths of their number in the basis of apportionment gave the favored States representation far in excess of their voting population. If, then, slaves were intended to be without representation, Article I did exactly what the Court now says is prohibited: it "weighted" the vote of voters in the slave States. Alternatively, it might have been thought that Representatives elected by free men of a State would speak also for the slaves. But since the slaves added to the representation only of their own State, Representatives from the slave States could have been thought to speak only for the slaves of their own States, indicating both that the Convention believed it possible for a Representative elected by one group to speak for another nonvoting group and that Representatives were in large degrees still thought of as speaking for the whole population *of a State*.

There is a further basis for demonstrating the hollowness of the Court's assertion that Article I requires "one man's vote in a congressional election . . . to be worth as much as another's," *ante*, p. 530. Nothing that the Court does today will disturb the fact that although in 1960 the population of an average congressional district was 410,481, the States of Alaska, Nevada, and Wyoming each have a Representative in Congress, although their respective populations are 226,167, 285,278, and 330,066. In entire disregard of population, Art. I, § 2, guarantees each of these States and every other State "at Least one Representative." It is whimsical to assert in the face of this guarantee that an absolute principle of "equal representation in the House of equal numbers of people" is "solemnly embodied" in Article I. All that there is is a provision which bases representation in the House, generally but not entirely, on the population of the States. The provision for representation of *each State* in the House of Representatives is not a mere exception to the principle framed by the majority; it

shows that no such principle is to be found.

Finally in this array of hurdles to its decision which the Court surmounts only by knocking them down is § 4 of Art. I which states simply:

"The Times, Places and *Manner* of holding elections for Senators and Representatives, shall be prescribed in each State by the Legislature thereof; but the Congress may at any time by Law make or alter such Regulations, except as to the Places of chusing Senators." (Emphasis added.)

The delegates were well aware of the problem of "rotten boroughs" as material cited by the Court, *ante*, p. 534, and hereafter makes plain. It cannot be supposed that delegates to the Convention would have labored to establish a principle of equal representation only to bury it, one would have thought beyond discovery, in § 2, and omit all mention of it from § 4, which deals explicitly with the conduct of elections. Section 4 states without qualification that the state legislatures shall prescribe regulations for the conduct of elections for Representatives and, equally without qualification, that Congress may make or alter such regulations. There is nothing to indicate any limitations whatsoever on this grant of plenary initial and supervisory power. The Court's holding is, of course, derogatory not only of the power of the state legislatures but also of the power of Congress, both theoretically and as they have actually exercised their power. See *infra*, pp. —, —. It freezes upon both, for no reason other than that it seems wise to the majority of the present Court, a particular political theory for the selection of Representatives.

III

There is dubious propriety in turning to the "historical context" of constitutional provisions which speak so consistently and plainly. But, as one might expect when the Constitution itself is free from ambiguity, the surrounding history makes what is already clear even clearer.

As the Court repeatedly emphasizes, delegates to the Philadelphia Convention frequently expressed their view that representation should be based on population. There were also, however, many statements favoring limited monarchy and property qualification for suffrage and expressions of disapproval for unrestricted democracy. Such expressions prove as little on one side of this case as they do on the other. Whatever the dominant political philosophy at the Convention, one thing seems clear: it is in the last degree unlikely that most or even many of the delegates would have subscribed to the principle of "one person, one vote," *ante*, p. —. Moreover, the statements approving population-based representation were focused on the problem of how representation should be apportioned among the States in the House of Representatives. The Great Compromise concerned representation *of the States* in the Congress. In all of the discussion surrounding the basis of representation of the House and all of the discussion whether Representatives should be elected by the legislatures or the people of the States, there is nothing which suggests even remotely that the delegates had in mind the problem of districting within a State.

The subject of districting within the States is discussed explicitly with reference to the provisions of Art. I, § 4, which the Court so pointedly neglects. The Court states: "The delegates referred to rotten borough apportionments in some of the state legislatures as the kind of objectionable governmental action that the Constitution should not tolerate in the election of congressional representative." *Ante*, p. . . . . The remarks of Madison cited by the Court are as follows:

"The necessity of a Genl. Govt. supposes that the State Legislatures will sometimes fail or refuse to consult the common interest at the expense of their local conveniency or prejudices. The policy of referring the appointment of the House of Representatives to the people and not to the Legislatures of the States, supposes that the result will be somewhat influenced by the mode. This view of the question seems to decide that the Legislatures of the States ought not to have the uncontrouled right

of regulating the times places & manner of holding elections. These were words of great latitude. It was impossible to foresee all the abuses that might be made of the discretionary power. Whether the electors should vote by ballot or viva voce, should assemble at this place or that place; should be divided into districts or all meet at one place, shd all vote for all the representatives; or all in a district vote for a number allotted to the district; *these & many other points would depend on the Legislatures* and might materially affect the appointments. Whenever the State Legislatures had a favorite measure to carry, they would take care so to mould their regulations as to favor the candidates they wished to succeed. Besides, the inequality of the Representation in the Legislatures of particular States, would produce a like inequality in their representation in the Natl. Legislature, as it was presumable that the Counties having the power in the former case would secure it to themselves in the latter. *What danger could there be in giving a controuling power to the Natl. Legislature?*" (Emphasis added.)

These remarks of Madison were in response to a proposal to strike out the provision for congressional supervisory power over the regulation of elections in Art. I, § 4. Supported by others at the Convention, and not contradicted in any respect, they indicate as clearly as may be that the Convention understood the state legislatures to have plenary power over the conduct of elections for Representatives, including the power to district well or badly, subject only to the supervisory power of Congress. How, then, can the Court hold that Art. I, § 2, prevents the state legislatures from districting as they choose? If the Court were correct, Madison's remarks would have been pointless. One would expect, at the very least, some reference to Art. I, § 2, as a limiting factor on the States. This is the "historical context" which the Convention debates provide.

Materials supplementary to the debates are as unequivocal. In the ratifying conventions, there was no suggestion that the provisions of Art. I, § 2, restricted the power of the States to prescribe the conduct of elections conferred on them by Art. I, § 4. None of the Court's references to the ratification debates supports the view that the provision for election of Representatives "by the People" was intended to have any application to the apportionment of Representatives within the States; in each instance, the cited passage merely repeats what the Constitution itself provides: that Representatives were to be elected by the people of the States.

In sharp contrast to this unanimous silence on the issue of this case, when Art. I, § 2, was being discussed, there are repeated references to apportionment and related problems affecting the States' selection of Representatives in connection with Art. I, § 4. The debates in the ratifying conventions, as clearly as Madison's statement at the Philadelphia Convention, *supra*, pp. 542, 543, indicate that under § 4, the state legislatures, subject only to the ultimate control of Congress, could district as they choose.

[Here MR. JUSTICE HARLAN quotes extensively from several state ratifying conventions.]

In *The Federalist*, No. 59, Hamilton discussed the provision of § 4 for regulation of elections. He justified Congress' power with the "plain proposition, that *every government ought to contain in itself the means of its own preservation.*" Further on, he said:

"It will not be alledged that an election law could have been framed and inserted into the Constitution, which would have been always applicable to every probable change in the situation of the country; and it will therefore not be denied that a discretionary power over elections ought to exist somewhere. *It will, I presume, be as readily conceded, that there were only three ways, in which this power could have been reasonably modified and disposed, that it must either have been lodged wholly in the National Legislature, or wholly in the State Legislatures, or primarily in the latter, and*

ultimately in the former. The last mode has with reason been preferred by the Convention. They have submitted the regulation of elections for the Fœderal Government in the first instance to the local administrations; which in ordinary cases, and when no improper views prevail, may be both more convenient and more satisfactory; but they have reserved to the national authority a right to interpose, *whenever, extraordinary circumstances might render that interposition necessary to its safety.*" (Emphasis added.)

Thus, in the number of *The Federalist* which does discuss the regulation of elections, the view is unequivocally stated that the state legislatures have plenary power over the conduct of congressional elections subject only to such regulations as Congress itself might provide.

The upshot of all this is that the language of Art. I, §§ 2 and 4, the surrounding text, and the relevant history are all in strong and consistent direct contradiction of the Court's holding. The constitutional scheme vests in the States plenary power to regulate the conduct of elections for Representatives, and, in order to protect the Federal Government, provides for congressional supervision of the States' exercise of their power. Within this scheme, the appellants do not have the right which they assert, in the absence of provision for equal districts by the Georgia legislature or the Congress. The constitutional right which the Court creates is manufactured out of whole cloth.

IV

The unstated premise of the Court's conclusion quite obviously is that the Congress has not dealt, and the Court believes it will not deal, with the problem of congressional apportionment in accordance with what the Court believes to be sound political principles. Laying aside for the moment the validity of such a consideration as a factor in constitutional interpretation, it becomes relevant to examine the history of congressional action under Art. I, § 4. This history reveals that the

Court is not simply undertaking to exercise a power which the Constitution reserves to the Congress; it is also overruling congressional judgment.

Congress exercised its power to regulate elections for the House of Representatives for the first time in 1842, when it provided that Representatives from States "entitled to more than one Representative" should be elected by districts of contiguous territory, "no one district electing more than one Representative." The requirement was later dropped, and reinstated. In 1872, Congress required that Representatives "be elected by districts composed of contiguous territory, and containing as nearly as practicable an equal number of inhabitants, . . . no one district electing more than one Representative." This provision for equal districts which the Court exactly duplicates in effect, was carried forward in each subsequent apportionment statute through 1911. There was no reapportionment following the 1920 census. The provision for equally populated districts was dropped in 1929, and has not been revived, although the 1929 provisions for apportionment have twice been amended and, in 1941, were made generally applicable to subsequent censuses and apportionments.

The legislative history of the 1929 Act is carefully reviewed in *Wood* v. *Broom,* 287 U.S. 1. As there stated:

"It was manifestly the intention of the Congress not to re-enact the provision as to compactness, contiguity, and equality in population with respect to the districts to be created pursuant to the reapportionment under the act of 1929.

"This appears from the terms of the act, and its legislative history shows that the omission was deliberate. The question was up, and considered." 287 U.S., at 7.

Although there is little discussion of the reasons for omitting the requirement of equally populated districts, the fact that such a provision was included in the bill as it was presented to the House, and was deleted by the House after debate and notice of intention to do so, leaves no doubt that the omission was deliberate. The likely explanation for the omission is suggested by a remark on the floor of the House that "the States ought to have their own way of making up their apportionment when they know the number of Congressmen they are going to have."

Debates over apportionment in subsequent Congresses are generally unhelpful to explain the continued rejection of such a requirement; there are some intimations that the feeling that districting was a matter exclusively for the States persisted. Bills which would have imposed on the States a requirement of equally or nearly equally populated districts were regularly introduced in the House. None of them became law.

For a period of about 50 years, therefore, Congress, by repeated legislative act, imposed on the States the requirement that congressional districts be equal in population. (This, of course, is the very requirement which the Court now declares to have been constitutionally required of the States all along without implementing legislation.) Subsequently, after giving express attention to the problem, Congress eliminated that requirement, with the intention of permitting the States to find their own solutions. Since then, despite repeated efforts to obtain congressional action again, Congress has continued to leave the problem and its solution to the States. It cannot be contended, therefore, that the Court's decision today fills a gap left by the Congress. On the contrary, the Court substitutes its own judgment for that of the Congress.

V

The extent to which the Court departs from accepted principles of adjudication is further evidenced by the irrelevance to today's issue of the cases on which the Court relies. . . .

[Here the Justice examines the cases in question.]

REYNOLDS v. *SIMS*

84 S. Ct. 1362 (1964)

Mr. Chief Justice Warren delivered the opinion of the Court. . . .

III

A predominant consideration in determining whether a State's legislative apportionment scheme constitutes an invidious discrimination violative of rights asserted under the Equal Protection Clause is that the rights allegedly impaired are individual and personal in nature. As stated by the Court in *United States* v. *Bathgate*, 246 U.S. 220, 227, "the right to vote is personal. . . ." While the result of a court decision in a state legislative apportionment controversy may be to require the restructuring of the geographical distribution of seats in a state legislature, the judicial focus must be concentrated upon ascertaining whether there has been any discrimination against certain of the State's citizens which constitutes an impermissible impairment of their constitutionally protected right to vote. Like *Skinner* v. *Oklahoma*, 316 U.S. 535, such a case "touches a sensitive and important area of human rights," and "involves one of the basic civil rights of man," presenting questions of alleged "invidious discriminations . . . against groups or types of individuals in violation of the constitutional guaranty of just and equal laws." 316 U.S., at 536, 541. Undoubtedly, the right of suffrage is a fundamental matter in a free and democratic society. Especially since the right to exercise the franchise in a free and unimpaired manner is preservative of other basic civil and political rights, any alleged infringement of the right of citizens to vote must be carefully and meticulously scrutinized. Almost a century ago, in *Yick Wo* v. *Hopkins*, 118 U.S. 356, the Court referred to "the political franchise of voting" as "a fundamental political right, because preservative of all rights." 118 U.S., at 370.

Legislators represent people, not trees or acres. Legislators are elected by voters, not farms or cities or economic interests. As long as ours is a representative form of government, and our legislatures are those instruments of government elected directly by and directly representative of the people, the right to elect legislators in a free and unimpaired fashion is a bedrock of our political system. It could hardly be gainsaid that a constitutional claim had been asserted by an allegation that certain otherwise qualified voters had been entirely prohibited from voting for members of their state legislature. And, if a State should provide that the votes of citizens in one part of the State should be given two times, or five times, or 10 times the weight of votes of citizens in another part of the State, it could hardly be contended that the right to vote of those residing in the disfavored areas had not been effectively diluted. It would appear extraordinary to suggest that a state could be constitutionally permitted to enact a law providing that certain of the state's voters could vote two, five, or 10 times for their legislative representatives, while voters living elsewhere could vote only once. And it is inconceivable that a state law to the effect that, in counting votes for legislators, the votes of citizens in one part of the State would be multiplied by two, five, or 10, while the votes of persons in another area would be counted only at face value, could be constitutionally sustainable. Of course, the effect of state legislative districting schemes which give the same number of representatives to unequal numbers of constituents is identical. Overweighting and overvaluation of the votes of those living here has the certain effect of dilution and undervaluation of the votes of those living there. The resulting discrimination against those individual voters living in disfavored areas is easily demonstrable mathematically. Their right to vote is simply not the same right to vote as that of those living in a favored part of the State. Two, five, or 10 of them must vote before the effect of their voting is equivalent to that of their favored neighbor. Weighting the votes of citizens differently, by any method or means, merely because of where they happen to reside, hardly seems justifiable. One must be ever aware that the Constitution forbids "sophisticated as well as simple-minded modes of discrimination." *Lane* v. *Wilson,* 307 U.S. 268, 275. *Gomillion* v. *Lightfoot,* 364 U.S. 339, 342. As we stated in *Wesberry* v. *Sanders, supra:*

"We do not believe that the Framers of the Constitution intended to permit the same vote-diluting discrimination to be accomplished through the device of districts containing widely varied numbers of inhabitants. To say that a vote is worth more in one district than in another would . . . run counter to our fundamental ideas of democratic government. . . ."

State legislatures are, historically, the fountainhead of representative government in this country. A number of them have their roots in colonial times, and substantially antedate the creation of our Nation and our Federal Government. In fact, the first formal stirrings of American political independence are to be found, in large part, in the views and actions of several of the colonial legislative bodies. With the birth of our National Government, and the adoption and ratification of the Federal Constitution, state legislatures retained a most important place in our Nation's governmental structure. But representative government is in essence self-government through the medium of elected representatives of the people, and each and every citizen has an inalienable right to full and effective participation in the political processes of his State's legislative bodies. Most citizens can achieve this participation only as qualified voters through the election of legislators to represent them. Full and effective participation by all citizens in state

government requires, therefore, that each citizen has an equally effective voice in the election of members of his state legislature. Modern and viable state government needs, and the Constitution demands, no less.

Logically, in a society ostensibly grounded on representative government, it would seem reasonable that a majority of the people of a State could elect a majority of that State's legislators. To conclude differently, and to sanction minority control of state legislative bodies, would appear to deny majority rights in a way that far surpasses any possible denial of minority rights that might otherwise be thought to result. Since legislatures are responsible for enacting laws by which all citizens are to be governed, they should be bodies which are collectively responsive to the popular will. And the concept of equal protection has been traditionally viewed as requiring the uniform treatment of persons standing in the same relation to the governmental action questioned or challenged. With respect to the allocation of legislative representation, all voters, as citizens of a State, stand in the same relation regardless of where they live. Any suggested criteria for the differentiation of citizens are insufficient to justify any discrimination, as to the weight of their votes, unless relevant to the permissible purposes of legislative apportionment. Since the achieving of fair and effective representation for all citizens is concededly the basic aim of legislative apportionment, we conclude that the Equal Protection Clause guarantees the opportunity for equal participation by all voters in the election of state legislators. Diluting the weight of votes because of place of residence impairs basic constitutional rights under the Fourteenth Amendment just as much as invidious discriminations based upon factors such as race, *Brown* v. *Board of Education,* 347 U.S. 483, or economic status, *Griffin* v. *Illinois,* 351 U.S. 12, *Douglas* v. *California,* 372 U.S. 353. Our constitutional system amply provides for the protection of minorities by means other than giving them majority control of state legislatures. And the democratic ideals of equality and majority rule, which have served this Nation so well in the past, are hardly of any less significance for the present and the future.

We are told that the matter of apportioning representation in a state legislature is a complex and many-faceted one. We are advised that States can rationally consider factors other than population in apportioning legislative representation. We are admonished not to restrict the power of the States to impose differing views as to political philosophy on their citizens. We are cautioned about the dangers of entering into political thickets and mathematical quagmires. Our answer is this: a denial of constitutionally protected rights demands judicial protection; our oath and our office require no less of us. As stated in *Gomillion* v. *Lightfoot, supra:*

"When a State exercises power wholly within the domain of state interest, it is insulated from federal judicial review. But such insulation is not carried over when state power is used as an instrument for circumventing a federally protected right."

To the extent that a citizen's right to vote is debased, he is that much less a citizen. The fact that an individual lives here or there is not a legitimate reason for overweighting or diluting the efficacy of his vote. The complexions of societies and civilizations change, often with amazing rapidity. A nation once primarily rural in character becomes predominantly urban. Representation schemes once fair and equitable become archaic and outdated. But the basic principle of representative government remains, and must remain, unchanged—the weight of a citizen's vote cannot be made to depend on where he lives. Population is, of necessity, the starting point for consideration and the controlling criterion for judgment in legislative apportionment controversies. A citizen, a qualified voter, is no more nor less so because he lives in the city or on the farm. This is the clear and strong command of our Constitution's Equal Protection Clause. This is an essential part of the concept of a government of laws and not men. This is at the heart of Lincoln's vision of "government of the people, by the people, [and] for the people." The Equal Protection Clause demands no less than substantially equal state legislative representation for all citizens, of all places as well as of all races.

IV

We hold that, as a basic constitutional standard, the Equal Protection Clause requires that the seats in both houses of a bicameral state legislature must be apportioned on a population basis. Simply stated, an individual's right to vote for state legislators is unconstitutionally impaired when its weight is in a substantial fashion diluted when compared with votes of citizens living in other parts of the State. Since, under neither the existing apportionment provisions nor under either of the proposed plans was either of the houses of the Alabama Legislature apportioned on a population basis, the District Court correctly held that all three of these schemes were constitutionally invalid. Furthermore, the existing apportionment, and also to a lesser extent the apportionment under the Crawford-Webb Act, presented little more than crazy quilts, completely lacking in rationality, and could be found invalid on that basis alone. Although the District Court presumably found the apportionment of the Alabama House of Representatives under the 67-Senator Amendment to be acceptable, we conclude that the deviations from a strict population basis are too egregious to permit us to find that that body, under this proposed plan, was apportioned sufficiently on a population basis so as to permit the arrangement to be constitutionally sustained. Although about 43% of the State's total population would be required to comprise districts which could elect a majority in that body, only 39 of the 106 House seats were actually to be distributed on a population basis, as each of Alabama's 67 counties was given at least one representative, and population-variance ratios of close to 5-to-1 would have existed. While mathematical nicety is not a constitutional requisite, one could hardly conclude that the Alabama House, under the proposed constitutional amendment, had been apportioned sufficiently on a population basis to be sustainable under the requirements of the Equal Protection Clause. And none of the other apportionments of seats in either of the bodies of the Alabama Legislature, under the three plans considered by the District Court, came nearly as close to approaching the required constitutional standard as did that of the House of Representatives under the 67-Senator Amendment.

Legislative apportionment in Alabama is signally illustrative and symptomatic of the seriousness of this problem in a number of the States. At the time this litigation was commenced, there had been no reapportionment of seats in the Alabama Legislature for over 60 years. Legislative inaction, coupled with the unavailability of any political or judicial remedy, had resulted, with the passage of years, in the perpetuated scheme becoming little more than an irrational anachronism. Consistent failure by the Alabama Legislature to comply with state constitutional requirements as to the frequency of reapportionment and the bases of legislative representation resulted in a minority strangle hold on the State Legislature. Inequality of representation in one house added to the inequality in the other. With the crazy-quilt existing apportionment virtually conceded to be invalid, the Alabama Legislature offered two proposed plans for consideration by the District Court, neither of which was to be effective until 1966 and neither of which provided for the apportionment of even one of the two houses on a population basis. We find that the court below did not err in holding that neither of these proposed reapportionment schemes, considered as a whole, "meets the necessary constitutional requirements." And we conclude that the District Court acted properly in considering these two proposed plans, although neither was to become effective until the 1966 election and the proposed constitutional amendment was scheduled to be submitted to the State's voters in November 1962. Consideration by the court below of the two proposed

plans was clearly necessary in determining whether the Alabama Legislature had acted effectively to correct the admittedly existing malapportionment, and in ascertaining what sort of judicial relief, if any, should be afforded.

V

Since neither of the houses of the Alabama Legislature, under any of the three plans considered by the District Court, was apportioned on a population basis, we would be justified in proceeding no further. However, one of the proposed plans, that contained in the so-called 67-Senator Amendment, at least superficially resembles the scheme of legislative representation followed in the Federal Congress. Under this plan, each of Alabama's 67 counties is allotted one senator, and no counties are given more than one Senate seat. Arguably, this is analogous to the allocation of two Senate seats, in the Federal Congress, to each of the 50 States, regardless of population. Seats in the Alabama House, under the proposed constitutional amendment, are distributed by giving each of the 67 counties at least one, with the remaining 39 seats being allotted among the more populous counties on a population basis. This scheme, at least at first glance, appears to resemble that prescribed for the Federal House of Representatives, where the 435 seats are distributed among the States on a population basis, although each State, regardless of its population, is given at least one Congressman. Thus, although there are substantial differences in underlying rationale and result, the 67-Senator Amendment, as proposed by the Alabama Legislature, at least arguably presents for consideration a scheme analogous to that used for apportioning seats in Congress.

Much has been written since our decision in *Baker* v. *Carr* about the applicability of the so-called federal analogy to state legislative apportionment arrangements. After considering the matter, the court below concluded that no conceivable analogy could be drawn between the federal scheme and the apportionment of seats in the Alabama Legislature under the proposed constitutional amendment. We agree with the District Court, and find the federal analogy inapposite and irrelevant to state legislative districting schemes. Attempted reliance on the federal analogy appears often to be little more than an after-the-fact rationalization offered in defense of maladjusted state apportionment arrangements. The original constitutions of 36 of our States provided that representation in both houses of the state legislatures would be based completely, or predominantly, on population. And the Founding Fathers clearly had no intention of establishing a pattern or model for the apportionment of seats in state legislatures when the system of representation in the Federal Congress was adopted. Demonstrative of this is the fact that the Northwest Ordinance, adopted in the same year, 1787, as the Federal Constitution, provided for the apportionment of seats in territorial legislatures solely on the basis of population.

The system of representation in the two Houses of the Federal Congress is one ingrained in our Constitution, as part of the law of the land. It is one conceived out of compromise and concession indispensable to the establishment of our federal republic. Arising from unique historical circumstances, it is based on the consideration that in establishing our type of federalism a group of formerly independent States bound themselves together under one national government. Admittedly, the original 13 States surrendered some of their sovereignty in agreeing to join together "to form a more perfect Union." But at the heart of our constitutional system remains the concept of separate and distinct governmental entities which have delegated some, but not all, of their formerly held powers to the single national government. The fact that almost three-fourths of our present States were never in fact independently sovereign does not detract from our view that the so-called federal analogy is inapplicable as a sustaining precedent for state legislative apportionments. The developing history and growth of our republic cannot cloud the fact that, at the time of the inception of the system of representation in the Federal Congress, a compromise between the larger and smaller States on this matter averted a deadlock in the constitutional convention which had threatened to abort the birth of our Nation. In rejecting an asserted analogy to the federal electoral college in *Gray* v. *Sanders, supra,* we stated:

"We think the analogies to the electoral college, to districting and redistricting, and to other phases of the problems of representation in state or federal legislatures or conventions are inapposite. The inclusion of the electoral college in the Constitution, as the result of specific historical concerns, validated the collegiate principle despite its inherent numerical inequality, but implied nothing about the use of an analogous system by a State in a statewide election. No such specific accommodation of the latter was ever undertaken, and therefore no validation of its numerical inequality ensued."

Political subdivisions of States—counties, cities, or whatever—never were and never have been considered as sovereign entities. Rather, they have been traditionally regarded as subordinate governmental instrumentalities created by the State to assist in the carrying out of state governmental functions. As stated by the Court in *Hunter* v. *City of Pittsburgh,* 207 U.S. 161, 178, these governmental units are "created as convenient agencies for exercising such of the governmental powers of the State as may be entrusted to them," and the "number, nature and duration of the powers conferred upon [them] . . . and the territory over which they shall be exercised rests in the absolute discretion of the State." The relationship of the States to the Federal Government could hardly be less analogous.

Thus, we conclude that the plan contained in the 67-Senator Amendment for apportioning seats in the Alabama Legislature cannot be sustained by recourse to the so-called federal analogy. Nor can any other inequitable state legislative apportionment scheme be justified on such an asserted basis.

This does not necessarily mean that such a plan is irrational or involves something other than a "republican form of government." We conclude simply that such a plan is impermissible for the States under the Equal Protection Clause, since perforce resulting, in virtually every case, in submergence of the equal-population principle in at least one house of a state legislature.

Since we find the so-called federal analogy inapposite to a consideration of the constitutional validity of state legislative apportionment schemes, we necessarily hold that the Equal Protection Clause requires both houses of a state legislature to be apportioned on a population basis. The right of a citizen to equal representation and to have his vote weighted equally with those of all other citizens in the election of members of one house of a bicameral state legislature would amount to little if States could effectively submerge the equal-population principle in the apportionment of seats in the other house. If such a scheme were permissible, an individual citizen's ability to exercise an effective voice in the only instrument of state government directly representative of the people might be almost as effectively thwarted as if neither house were apportioned on a population basis. Deadlock between the two bodies might result in compromise and concession on some issues. But in all too many cases the more probable result would be frustration of the majority will through minority veto in the house not apportioned on a population basis, stemming directly from the failure to accord adequate overall legislative representation to all of the State's citizens on a nondiscriminatory basis. In summary, we can perceive no constitutional difference, with respect to the geographical distribution of state legislative representation, between the two houses of a bicameral state legislature.

We do not believe that the concept of bicameralism is rendered anachronistic and meaningless when the predominant basis of representation in the two state legislative bodies is required to be the same —population. A prime reason for bicameralism, modernly considered, is to insure mature and deliberate consideration of, and to prevent precipitate action on, proposed legislative measures. Simply because the controlling criterion for apportioning representation is required to be the same in both houses does not mean that there will be no differences in the composition and complexion of the two bodies. Different constituencies can be represented in the two houses. One body could be composed of single-member districts while the other could have at least some multimember districts. The length of terms of the legislators in the separate bodies could differ. The numerical size of the two bodies could be made to differ, even significantly, and the geographical size of districts from which legislators are elected could also be made to differ. And apportionment in one house could be arranged so as to balance off minor inequities in the representation of certain areas in the other house. In summary, these and other factors could be, and are presently in many States, utilized to engender differing complexions and collective attitudes in the two bodies of a state legislature, although both are apportioned substantially on a population basis.

VI

By holding that as a federal constitutional requisite both houses of a state legislature must be apportioned on a population basis, we mean that the Equal Protection Clause requires that a State make an honest and good faith effort to construct districts, in both houses of its legislature, as nearly of equal population as is practicable. We realize that it is a practical impossibility to arrange legislative districts so that each one has an identical number of residents, or citizens, or voters. Mathematical exactness or precision is hardly a workable constitutional requirement.

In *Wesberry* v. *Sanders, supra,* the Court stated that congressional representation must be based on population as nearly as is practicable. In implementing the basic constitutional principle of representative government as enunciated by the Court in *Wesberry*—equality of population among districts—some distinctions may well be made between congressional and state legislative representation. Since, almost invariably, there is a significantly larger number of seats in state legislative bodies to be distributed within a State than congressional seats, it may be feasible to use political subdivision lines to a greater extent in establishing state legislative districts than in congressional districting while still affording adequate representation to all parts of the State. To do so would be constitutionally valid, so long as the resulting apportionment was one based substantially on population and the equal-population principle was not diluted in any significant way. Somewhat more flexibility may therefore be constitutionally permissible with respect to state legislative apportionment than in congressional districting. Lower courts can and assuredly will work out more concrete and specific standards for evaluating state legislative apportionment schemes in the context of actual litigation. For the present, we deem it expedient not to attempt to spell out any precise constitutional tests. What is marginally permissible in one State may be unsatisfactory in another, depending on the particular circumstances of the case. Developing a body of doctrine on a case-by-case basis appears to us to provide the most satisfactory means of arriving at detailed constitutional requirements in the area of state legislative apportionment. Cf. *Slaughter-House Cases*, 16 Wal. 36, 78–79. Thus, we proceed to state here only a few rather general considerations which appear to us to be relevant.

A State may legitimately desire to maintain the integrity of various political subdivisions, insofar as possible, and provide for compact districts of contiguous territory in designing a legislative apportionment scheme. Valid considerations may underlie such aims. Indiscriminate districting, without any regard for political subdivision or natural or historical boundary lines, may be little more than an open invitation to partisan gerrymandering. Single-member districts may be the rule in one State, while

another State might desire to achieve some flexibility by creating multimember or floterial districts. Whatever the means of accomplishment, the overriding objective must be substantial equality of population among the various districts, so that the vote of any citizen is approximately equal in weight to that of any other citizen in the State.

History indicates, however, that many States have deviated, to a greater or lesser degree, from the equal-population principle in the apportionment of seats in at least one house of their legislatures. So long as the divergences from a strict population standard are based on legitimate considerations incident to the effectuation of a rational state policy, some deviations from the equal-population principle are constitutionally permissible with respect to the apportionment of seats in either or both of the two houses of a bicameral state legislature. But neither history alone, nor economic or other sorts of group interests, are permissible factors in attempting to justify disparities from population-based representation. Citizens, not history or economic interests, cast votes. Considerations of area alone provide an insufficient justification for deviations from the equal-population principle. Again, people, not land or trees or pastures, vote. Modern developments and improvements in transportation and communications make rather hollow, in the mid 1960's, most claims that deviations from population-based representation can validly be based solely on geographical considerations. Arguments for allowing such deviations in order to insure effective representation for sparsely settled areas and to prevent legislative districts from becoming so large that the availability of access of citizens to their representatives is impaired are today, for the most part, unconvincing.

A consideration that appears to be of more substance in justifying some deviations from population-based representation in state legislatures is that of insuring some voice to political subdivisions, as political subdivisions. Several factors make more than insubstantial claims that a State can rationally consider according political subdivisions some independent representation in at least one body of the state legislature, as long as the basic standard of equality of population among districts is maintained. Local governmental entities are frequently charged with various responsibilities incident to the operation of state government. In many States much of the legislature's activity involves the enactment of so-called local legislation, ...ected only to the concerns of particular political subdivisions. And a State may legitimately desire to construct districts along political subdivision lines to deter the possibilities of gerrymandering. However, permitting deviations from population-based representation does not mean that each local governmental unit or political subdivision can be given separate representation, regardless of population. Carried too far, a scheme of giving at least one seat in one house to each political subdivision (for example, to each county) could easily result, in many States, in a total subversion of the equal-population principle in that legislative body.

This would be especially true in a State where the number of counties is large and many of them are sparsely populated, and the number of seats in the legislative body being apportioned does not significantly exceed the number of counties. Such a result, we conclude, would be constitutionally impermissible. And careful judicial scrutiny must of course be given, in evaluating state apportionment schemes, to the character as well as the degree of deviations from a strict population basis. But if, even as a result of a clearly rational state policy of according some legislative representation to political subdivisions, population is submerged as the controlling consideration in the apportionment of seats in the particular legislative body, then the right of all of the State's citizens to cast an effective and adequately weighted vote would be unconstitutionally impaired.

VII

One of the arguments frequently offered as a basis for upholding a State's legislative apportionment arrangement, despite substantial disparities from a population basis in either or both houses, is grounded on congressional approval, incident to admitting States into the Union, of state apportionment plans containing deviations from the equal-population principle. Proponents of this argument contend that congressional approval of such schemes, despite their disparities from population-based representation, indicate that such arrangements are plainly sufficient as establishing a "republican form of government." As we stated in *Baker* v. *Carr,* some questions raised under the Guaranty Clause are nonjusticiable, where "political" in nature and where there is a clear absence of judicially manageable standards. Nevertheless, it is not inconsistent with this view to hold that, despite congressional approval of state legislative apportionment plans at the time of admission into the Union, even though deviating from the equal-population principle here enunciated, the Equal Protection Clause can and does require more. And an apportionment scheme in which both houses are based on population can hardly be considered as failing to satisfy the Guaranty Clause requirement. Congress presumably does not assume, in admitting States into the Union, to pass on all constitutional questions relating to the character of state governmental organization. In any event, congressional approval, however well-considered, could hardly validate an unconstitutional state legislative apportionment. Congress simply lacks the constitutional power to insulate States from attack with respect to alleged deprivations of individual constitutional rights.

VIII

That the Equal Protection Clause requires that both houses of a state legislature be apportioned on a population basis does not mean that States cannot adopt some reasonable plan for periodic revision of their apportionment schemes. Decennial reapportionment appears to be a rational approach to readjustment of legislative representation in order to take into account population shifts and growth. Reallocation of legislative seats every 10 years coincides with the prescribed practice in 41 of the States, often honored more in the breach than the observance, however. Illustratively, the Alabama Constitution requires decennial reapportionment, yet the last reapportionment of the Alabama Legislature, when this suit was brought, was in 1901. Limitations on the frequency of reapportionment are justified by the need for stability and continuity in the organization of the legislative system, although undoubtedly reapportioning no more frequently than every 10 years leads to some imbalance in the population of districts toward the end of the decennial period and also to the development of resistance to change on the part of some incumbent legislators. In substance we do not regard the Equal Protection Clause as requiring daily, monthly, annual or biennial reapportionment, so long as a State has a reasonably conceived plan for periodic readjustment of legislative representation. While we do not intend to indicate that decennial reapportionment is a constitutional requisite, compliance with such an approach would clearly meet the minimal requirements for maintaining a reasonably current scheme of legislative representation. And we do not mean to intimate that more frequent reapportionment would not be constitutionally permissible or practicably desirable. But if reapportionment were accomplished with less frequency, it would assuredly be constitutionally suspect.

IX

Although general provisions of the Alabama Constitution provide that the apportionment of seats in both houses of the Alabama Legislature should be on a population basis, other more detailed provisions clearly make compliance with both sets of requirements impossible. With respect to the operation of the Equal Protection Clause, it makes no difference whether a State's apportionment scheme is embodied in its constitution or in statutory provisions. In those States where the alleged malapportionment has resulted from noncompliance with state constitutional provisions which, if complied with, would result in

an apportionment valid under the Equal Protection Clause, the judicial task of providing effective relief would appear to be rather simple. We agree with the view of the District Court that state constitutional provisions should be deemed violative of the Federal Constitution only when validly asserted constitutional rights could not otherwise be protected and effectuated. Clearly, courts should attempt to accommodate the relief ordered to the apportionment provisions of state constitutions insofar as is possible. But it is also quite clear that a state legislative apportionment scheme is no less violative of the Federal Constitution when it is based on state constitutional provisions which have been consistently complied with than when resulting from a noncompliance with state constitutional requirements. When there is an unavoidable conflict between the Federal and State Constitution, the Supremacy Clause of course controls.

X

We do not consider here the difficult question of the proper remedial devices which federal courts should utilize in state legislative apportionment cases. Remedial technique in this new and developing area of the law will probably often differ with the circumstances of the challenged apportionment and a variety of local conditions. It is enough to say now that, once a State's legislative apportionment scheme has been found to be unconstitutional, it would be the unusual case in which a court would be justified in not taking appropriate action to insure that no further elections are conducted under the invalid plan. However, under certain circumstances, such as where an impending election is imminent and a State's election machinery is already in progress, equitable considerations might justify a court in withholding the granting of immediately effective relief in a legislative apportionment case, even though the existing apportionment scheme was found invalid. In awarding or withholding immediate relief, a court is entitled to and should consider the proximity of a forthcoming election and the mechanics and complexities of state election laws, and should act and rely upon general equitable principles. With respect to the timing of relief, a court can reasonably endeavor to avoid a disruption of the election process which might result from requiring precipitate changes that could make unreasonable or embarrassing demands on a State in adjusting to the requirements of the court's decree. As stated by Mr. Justice Douglas, in concurring in *Baker* v. *Carr*, "any relief accorded can be fashioned in the light of well-known principles of equity."

We feel that the District Court in this case acted in a most proper and commendable manner. It initially acted wisely in declining to stay the impending primary election in Alabama, and properly refrained from acting further until the Alabama Legislature had been given an opportunity to remedy the admitted discrepancies in the State's legislative apportionment scheme, while initially stating some of its views to provide guidelines for legislative action. And it correctly recognized that legislative reapportionment is primarily a matter for legislative consideration and determination, and that judicial relief becomes appropriate only when a legislature fails to reapportion according to federal constitutional requisites in a timely fashion after having had an adequate opportunity to do so. Additionally, the court below acted with proper judicial restraint, after the Alabama Legislature had failed to act effectively in remedying the constitutional deficiencies in the State's legislative apportionment scheme, in ordering its own temporary reapportionment plan into effect, at a time sufficiently early to permit the holding of elections pursuant to that plan without great difficulty, and in prescribing a plan admittedly provisional in purpose so as not to usurp the primary responsibility for reapportionment which rests with the legislature.

We find, therefore, that the action taken by the District Court in this case, in ordering into effect a reapportionment of both houses of the Alabama Legislature for purposes of the 1962 primary and general elections, by using the best parts of the two proposed plans which it had found, as a whole, to be invalid, was an appropriate and well-considered exercise of judicial power. Admittedly, the lower court's ordered plan was intended only as a temporary and provisional measure and the District Court correctly indicated that the plan was invalid as a permanent apportionment. In retaining jurisdiction while deferring a hearing on the issuance of a final injunction in order to give the provisionally reapportioned legislature an opportunity to act effectively, the court below proceeded in a proper fashion. Since the District Court evinced its realization that its ordered reapportionment could not be sustained as the basis for conducting the 1966 election of Alabama legislators, and avowedly intends to take some further action should the reapportioned Alabama Legislature fail to enact a constitutionally valid, permanent apportionment scheme in the interim, we affirm the judgment below and remand the cases for further proceedings consistent with the views stated in this opinion.

It is so ordered.

MR. JUSTICE CLARK, concurring in the reversal.

The Court goes much beyond the necessities of this case in laying down a new "equal population" principle for state legislative apportionment. This principle seems to be an offshoot of *Gray* v. *Sanders*, 372 U.S. 368, 381 (1963), i.e., "one person, one vote," modified by the "nearly as is practicable" admonition of *Wesberry* v. *Sanders*, 376 U.S. 1, 8 (1964). Whether "nearly as is practicable" means "one person, one vote" qualified by "approximately equal" or "some deviations" or by the impossibility of "mathematical nicety" is not clear from the majority's use of these vague and meaningless phrases. But whatever the standard, the Court applies it to each house of the State Legislature.

It seems to me that all that the Court need say in this case is that each plan considered by the trial court is "a crazy quilt," clearly revealing invidious discrimination in each house of the Legislature and therefore violative of the Equal Protective Clause. See my concurring opinion in *Baker* v. *Carr*, 369 U.S. 186, 253–258 (1962).

I, therefore, do not reach the question of the so-called "federal analogy." But in my view, if one house of the State Legislature meets the population standard, representation in the other house might include some departure from it so as to take into account, on a rational basis, other factors in order to afford some representation to the various elements of the State. See my dissenting opinion in *Lucas* v. *The Forty-Fourth General Assembly of Colorado*, ⸺ U.S. ⸺, decided this date.

MR. JUSTICE STEWART.

In this case all of the parties have agreed with the District Court's finding that legislative inaction for some 60 years in the face of growth and shifts in population has converted Alabama's legislative apportionment plan enacted in 1901 into one completely lacking in rationality. Accordingly, for the reasons stated in my dissenting opinion in *Lucas* v. *The Forty-Fourth General Assembly of the State of Colorado, ante*, p. ⸺, I would affirm the judgment of the District Court holding that this apportionment violated the Equal Protection Clause.

I also agree with the Court that it was proper for the District Court, in framing a remedy, to adhere as closely as practicable to the apportionments approved by the representatives of the people of Alabama, and to afford the State of Alabama full opportunity, consistent with the requirements of the Federal Constitution, to devise its own system of legislative apportionment.

MR. JUSTICE HARLAN dissenting. [This opinion applies to eight cases from six states all decided on June 15, 1964. Three of the cases are referred to in the note hereafter].

In these cases the Court holds that seats in the legislatures of six States are apportioned in ways that violate the Federal Constitution. Under the Court's ruling it is bound to follow that the legislatures in all but a few of the other 44 States will meet the same fate. These decisions, with *Wesberry* v. *Sanders*, 376 U.S. 1, involving congressional districting by the States, and *Gray* v. *Sanders*, 372 U.S. 368, relating to elections for statewide office, have the effect of placing basic aspects of state political systems under the pervasive overlordship of the federal judiciary. Once again, I must register my protest.

PRELIMINARY STATEMENT

Today's holding is that the Equal Protection Clause of the Fourteenth Amendment requires every State to structure its legislature so that all the members of each house represent substantially the same number of people; other factors may be given play only to the extent that they do not significantly encroach on this basic "population" principle. Whatever may be thought of this holding as a piece of political ideology—and even on that score the political history and practices of this country from its earliest beginnings leave wide room for debate (see the dissenting opinion of Frankfurter, J., in *Baker* v. *Carr*, 369 U.S. 186, 266, 301–323)—I think it demonstrable that the Fourteenth Amendment does not impose this political tenet on the States or authorize this Court to do so.

The Court's constitutional discussion, found in its opinion in the Alabama cases (Nos. 23, 27, 41, *ante*, p. ⸺) and more particularly at pages 26–33 thereof, is remarkable (as, indeed, is that found in the separate opinions of my Brothers Stewart and Clark, *ante*, pp. ⸺, ⸺) for its failure to address itself at all to the Fourteenth Amendment as a whole or to the legislative history of the Amendment pertinent to the matter at hand. Stripped of aphorisms, the Court's argument boils down to the assertion that petitioners' right to vote has been invidiously "debased" or "diluted" by systems of apportionment which entitle them to vote for fewer legislators than other voters, an assertion which is tied to the Equal Protection Clause only by the constitutionally frail tautology that "equal" means "equal."

Had the Court paused to probe more deeply into the matter, it would have found that the Equal Protection Clause was never intended to inhibit the States in choosing any democratic method they pleased for the apportionment of their legislatures. This is shown by the language of the Fourteenth Amendment taken as a whole, by the understanding of those who proposed and ratified it, and by the political practices of the States at the time the Amendment was adopted. It is confirmed by numerous state and congressional actions since the adoption of the Fourteenth Amendment, and by the common understanding of the Amendment as evidenced by subsequent constitutional amendments and decisions of this Court before *Baker* v. *Carr, supra,* made an abrupt break with the past in 1962.

The failure of the Court to consider any of these matters cannot be excused or explained by any concept of "developing" constitutionalism. It is meaningless to speak of constitutional "development" when both the language and history of the controlling provisions of the Constitution are wholly ignored. Since it can, I think, be shown beyond doubt that state legislative apportionments, as such, are wholly free of constitutional limitations, save such as may be imposed by the Republican Form of Government Clause (Const., Art. IV, § 4), the Court's action now bringing them within the purview of the Fourteenth Amendment amounts to nothing less than an exercise of the amending power by this Court.

So far as the Federal Constitution is concerned, the complaints in these cases should all have been dismissed below for failure to state a cause of action, because what has been alleged or proved shows no violation of any constitutional right. . . .

I

A. *The Language of the Fourteenth Amendment*

The Court relies exclusively on that portion of § 1 of the Fourteenth Amendment which provides that no State shall "deny to any person within its jurisdiction the equal protection of the laws," and disregards entirely the significance of § 2, which reads:

"Representatives shall be apportioned among the several States according to their respective numbers, counting the whole number of persons in each State, excluding Indians not taxed. *But when the right to vote at any election for* the choice of electors for President and Vice President of the United States, Representatives in Congress, *the Executive and Judicial officers of a State, or the members of the Legislature thereof, is denied* to any of the male inhabitants of such State, being twenty-one years of age, and citizens of the United States, *or in any way abridged,* except for participation in rebellion, or other crime, the basis of representation therein shall be reduced in the proportion which the number of such male citizens shall bear to the whole number of male citizens twenty-one years of age in such State." (Emphasis added.)

The Amendment is a single text. It was introduced and discussed as such in the Reconstruction Committee,[1] which reported it to the Congress. It was discussed as a unit in Congress and proposed as a unit to the States,[2] which ratified it as a unit. A proposal to split up the Amendment and submit each section to the States as a separate amendment was rejected by the Senate.[3] Whatever one might take to be the application to these cases of the Equal Protection Clause if it stood alone, I am unable to understand the Court's utter disregard of the second section which expressly recognizes the States' power to deny "or in any way" abridge the right of

1. See the Journal of the Committee, reprinted in Kendrick, The Journal of the Joint Committee of Fifteen on Reconstruction (1914), 83–117.

2. See the debates in Congress, Cong. Globe, 39th Cong., 1st Sess., 2459–3149, *passim* (1886) (hereafter Globe).

3. Globe 3040.

their inhabitants to vote for "the members of the [State] Legislature," and its express provision of a remedy for such denial or abridgement. The comprehensive scope of the second section and its particular reference to the state legislatures precludes the suggestion that the first section was intended to have the result reached by the Court today. If indeed the words of the Fourteenth Amendment speak for themselves, as the majority's disregard of history seems to imply, they speak as clearly as may be against the construction which the majority puts on them. But we are not limited to the language of the Amendment itself.

B. *Proposal and Ratification of the Amendment*

The history of the adoption of the Fourteenth Amendment provides conclusive evidence that neither those who proposed nor those who ratified the Amendment believed that the Equal Protection Clause limited the power of the States to apportion their legislatures as they saw fit. Moreover, the history demonstrates that the intention to leave this power undisturbed was deliberate and was widely believed to be essential to the adoption of the Amendment.

(i) *Proposal of the amendment in Congress.*—A resolution proposing what became the Fourteenth Amendment was reported to both houses of Congress by the Reconstruction Committee of Fifteen on April 30, 1866.[4] The first two sections of the proposed amendment read:

"SEC. 1. No State shall make or enforce any law which shall abridge the privileges or immunities of citizens of the United States; nor shall any State deprive any person of life, liberty, or property without due

process of law; nor deny to any person within its jurisdiction the equal protection of the laws.

"SEC. 2. Representatives shall be apportioned among the several States which may be included within this Union, according to their respective numbers, counting the whole number of persons in each State, excluding Indians not taxed. But whenever, in any State, the elective franchise shall be denied to any portion of its male citizens not less than twenty-one years of age, or in any way abridged except for participation in rebellion or other crime, the basis of representation in such State shall be reduced in the proportion which the number of such male citizens shall bear to the whole number of male citizens not less than twenty-one years of age." [5]

In the House, Thaddeus Stevens introduced debate on the resolution on May 8. In his opening remarks, Stevens explained why he supported the resolution although it fell "far short" of his wishes:

"I believe it is all that can be obtained in the present state of public opinion. Not only Congress but the several States are to be consulted. Upon a careful survey of the whole ground, we did not believe that nineteen of the loyal States could be induced to ratify any proposition more stringent than this." [6]

In explanation of this belief, he asked the House to remember "that three months since, and more, the committee reported and the House adopted a proposed amendment fixing the basis of representation in such way as would surely have secured the enfranchisement of every citizen at no distant period," but that proposal had been rejected by the Senate.[7]

---

4. Globe 2265, 2286.

5. As reported in the House. Globe 2286. For prior versions of the Amendment in the Reconstruction Committee, see Kendrick, *op. cit., supra,* note 7, 83–117. The work of the Reconstruction Committee is discussed in Kendrick, *supra,* and Flack, The Adoption of the Fourteenth Amendment (1908), 55–139, *passim.*

6. Globe 2459.

7. *Ibid.* Stevens was referring to a proposed amendment to the Constitution which provided that "whenever the elective franchise shall be denied or abridged in any State on account of race or color, all persons therein of such race or color shall be excluded from the basis of representation." Globe 535. It passed the House, *id.,* at 538, but did not muster the necessary two-thirds vote in the Senate, *id.,* at 1289.

He then explained the impact of the first section of the proposed Amendment, particularly the Equal Protection Clause.

"This amendment . . . allows Congress to correct the unjust legislation of the States, so far that the law which operates upon one man shall operate *equally* upon all. Whatever law punishes a white man for a crime shall punish the black man precisely in the same way and to the same degree. Whatever law protects the white man shall afford 'equal' protection to the black man. Whatever means of redress is afforded to one shall be afforded to all. Whatever law allows the white man to testify in court shall allow the man of color to do the same. These are great advantages over their present codes. Now different degrees of punishment are inflicted, not on account of the magnitude of the crime, but according to the color of the skin. Now color disqualifies a man from testifying in courts, or being tried in the same way as white men. I need not enumerate these partial and oppressive laws. Unless the Constitution should restrain them those States will all, I fear, keep up this discrimination, and crush to death the hated freedmen." [8]

He turned next to the second section, which he said he considered "the most important in the article." [9] Its effect, he said, was to fix "the basis of representation in Congress." [10] In unmistakable terms, he recognized the power of a State to withhold the right to vote:

"If any State shall exclude any of her adult male citizens from the elective franchise, or abridge that right, she shall forfeit her right to representation in the same proportion. The effect of this provision will be either to compel the States to grant universal suffrage or so to shear them of

their power as to keep them forever in a hopeless minority in the national Government, both legislative and executive." [11]

Closing his discussion of the second section, he noted his dislike for the fact that it allowed "the States to discriminate [with respect to the right to vote] among the same class, and receive proportionate credit in representation." [12]

Toward the end of the debate three days later, Mr. Bingham, the author of the first section in the Reconstruction Committee and its leading proponent,[13] concluded his discussion of it with the following:

"Allow me, Mr. Speaker, in passing, to say that this amendment takes from no State any right that ever pertained to it. No State ever had the right, under the forms of law or otherwise, to deny to any freeman the equal protection of the laws or to abridge the privileges or immunities of any citizen of the Republic, although many of them have assumed and exercised the power, and that without remedy. *The amendment does not give, as the second section shows, the power to Congress of regulating suffrage in the several States.*" [14] (Emphasis added.)

He immediately continued:

"*The second section excludes the conclusion that by the first section suffrage is subjected to congressional law;* save, indeed, with this exception, that as the right in the people of each State to a republican government and to choose their Representatives in Congress is one of the guarantees of the Constitution, by this amendment a remedy might be given directly for a case supposed by Madison, where treason might change a State government from a republican to a despotic government, and thereby deny suffrage to the people." [15] (Emphasis added.)

8. Globe 2459.

9. *Ibid.*

10. *Ibid.*

11. *Ibid.*

12. Globe 2460.

13. Kendrick, *op. cit., supra,* note 7, 87, 106; Flack, *op. cit., supra,* note 11, 60–68, 71.

14. Globe 2542.

15. *Ibid.* It is evident from the context of the reference to a republican government that Bingham did not regard limitations on the right to vote or the denial of the vote to specified categories of individuals as violating the guarantee of a republican form of government.

He stated at another point in his remarks:

"To be sure we all agree, and the great body of the people of this country agree, and the committee thus far in reporting measures of reconstruction agree, that *the exercise of the elective franchise, though it be one of the privileges of a citizen of the Republic, is exclusively under the control of the States.*" [16] (Emphasis added.)

In the three days of debate which separate the opening and closing remarks, both made by members of the Reconstruction Committee, every speaker on the resolution, with a single doubtful exception,[17] assumed without question that, as Mr. Bingham said, *supra*, "the second section excludes the conclusion that by the first section suffrage is subjected to congressional law." The assumption was neither inadvertent nor silent. Much of the debate concerned the change in the basis of representation effected by the second section, and the speakers stated repeatedly, in express terms or by unmistakable implication, that the States retained the power to regulate suffrage within their borders. Attached as Appendix A hereto are some of those statements. The resolution was adopted by the House without change on May 10.[18]

Debate in the Senate began on May 23, and followed the same pattern. Speaking for the Senate Chairman of the Reconstruction Committee, who was ill, Senator Howard, also a member of the Committee, explained the meaning of the Equal Protection Clause as follows:

"The last two clauses of the first section of the amendment disable a State from depriving not merely a citizen of the United States, but any person, whoever he may be, of life, liberty, or property without due process of law, or from denying to him the equal protection of the laws of the State. This abolishes all class legislation in the States and does away with the injustice of subjecting one caste of persons to a code not applicable to another. It prohibits the hanging of a black man for a crime for which the white man is not to be hanged. It protects the black man in his fundamental rights as a citizen with the same shield which it throws over the white man. Is it not time, Mr. President, that we extend to the black man, I had almost called it the poor privilege of the equal protection of the law? . . .

"But, sir, the first section of the proposed amendment does not give to either of these classes the right of voting. The right of suffrage is not, in law, one of the privileges or immunities thus secured by the Constitution. It is merely the creature of law. It has always been regarded in this country as the result of positive local law, not regarded as one of those fundamental rights lying at the basis of all society and without which a people cannot exist except as slaves, subject to a depotism [*sic*]." [19] (Emphasis added.)

Discussing the second section, he expressed his regret that it did "not recognize the authority of the United States over the question of suffrage in the several States at all. . . ." [20] He justified the limited purpose of the Amendment in this regard as follows:

"But, sir, it is not the question here what will we do; it is not the question what you, or I, or half a dozen other members of the Senate may prefer in respect to colored suffrage; it is not entirely the question what measure we can pass through the two Houses; but the question really is, what will the Legislatures of the various States to whom these amendments are to be submitted do in the premises; what is it likely

---

16. *Ibid.*

17. Representative Rogers, who voted against the resolution, Globe 2545, suggested that the right to vote might be covered by the Privileges and Immunities Clause. Globe 2538. But immediately thereafter he discussed the possibility that the southern States might "refuse to allow the negroes to vote." *Ibid.*

18. Globe 2545.

19. Globe 2766.

20. *Ibid.*

will meet the general approbation of the people who are to elect the Legislatures, three fourths of whom must ratify our propositions before they have the force of constitutional provisions? . . .

"The committee were of opinion that the States are not yet prepared to sanction so fundamental a change as would be the concession of the right of suffrage to the colored race. We may as well state it plainly and fairly, so that there shall be no misunderstanding on the subject. It was our opinion that three fourths of the States of this Union could not be induced to vote to grant the right of suffrage, even in any degree under any restriction, to the colored race. . . .

"The second section leaves the right to regulate the elective franchise still with the States, and does not meddle with that right." [21] (Emphasis added.)

There was not in the Senate, as there had been in the House, a closing speech in explanation of the Amendment. But because the Senate considered, and finally adopted, several changes in the first and second sections, even more attention was given to the problem of voting rights there than had been given in the House. In the Senate, it was fully understood by everyone that neither the first nor the second section interfered with the right of the States to regulate the elective franchise. Attached as Appendix B hereto are representative statements from the debates to that effect. After having changed the proposed amendment to the form in which it was adopted, the Senate passed the resolution on June 8, 1866.[22] As changed, it passed in the House on June 13.[23]

(ii) *Ratification by the "loyal" States.*— Reports of the debates in the state legislatures on the ratification of the Fourteenth Amendment are not generally available.[24] There is, however, compelling indirect evidence. Of the 23 loyal States which ratified the Amendment before 1870, five had constitutional provisions for apportionment of at least one house of their respective legislatures which wholly disregarded the spread of population.[25] Ten more had constitutional provisions which gave primary emphasis to population, but which applied also other principles, such as partial ratios and recognition of political subdivisions, which were intended to favor sparsely settled areas.[26] Can it be seriously contended that the legislatures of these States, almost two-thirds of those concerned, would have ratified an amendment which

---

21. *Ibid.*

22. Globe 3042.

23. Globe 3149.

24. Such evidence as there is, mostly committee reports and messages to the legislatures from Governors of the States, is to the same effect as the evidence from the debates in the Congress. See Ark. House J. 288 (1866–1867); Fla. Sen. J. 8–10 (1866); Ind. House J. 47–48, 50–51 (1867); Mass. Legis. Doc., House Doc. No. 149, 4–14, 16–17, 23, 24, 25–26 (1867); Mo. Sen. J. 14 (1867); N. J. Sen. J. 7 (Extra Sess. 1866); N. C. Sen. J. 96–97, 98–99 (1866–1867); Tenn. House J. 12–15 (1865–1866); Tenn. Sen. J. 8 (Extra Sess. 1866); Va. House J. & Doc., Doc. No. 1, 35 (1866–1867); Wis. Sen. J. 33, 101–103 (1867). Contra, S. C. House J. 34 (1866); Tex. Sen. J. 422 (1866 App.).

For an account of the proceedings in the state legislatures and citations to the proceedings, see Fairman, "Does the Fourteenth Amendment Incorporate the Bill of Rights?" 2 Stan. L. Rev. 5, 81–126 (1949).

25. Conn. Const., 1818, Art. Third, § 3 (towns); N. H. Const., 1792, Part Second, § XXVI (direct taxes paid); N. J. Const., 1844, Art. IV, § II, cl. 1 (counties); R. I. Const., 1842, Art. VI, § 1 (towns and cities); Vt. Const., 1793, c. II, § 7. (towns).

In none of these States was the other House apportioned strictly according to population. Conn. Const., 1818, Amend. II; N. H. Const., 1792, Pt. Second, §§ IX–XI; N. J. Const., 1844, Art. IV, § III, cl. 1; R. I. Const., 1842, Art. V, § 1; Vt. Const., 1793, Amend. 23.

26. Iowa Const., 1857, Art. III, § 35; Kan. Const., 1859, Art 2, § 2, Art. 10, § 1; Me. Const., 1819, Art. IV–Pt. First, § 3; Mich. Const., 1850, Art. IV, § 3; Mo. Const., 1865, Art. IV, § 2; N. Y. Const., 1846, Art. III, § 5; Ohio Const., 1851, Art. XI, §§ 2–5; Pa. Const., 1838, Art. I, §§ 4, 6, 7, as amended; Tenn. Const., 1834, Art. II, § 5; W. Va. Const., 1861–1863, Art. IV, § 9.

might render their own States' constitutions unconstitutional?

Nor were these state constitutional provisions merely theoretical. In New Jersey, for example, Cape May County, with a population of 8,349, and Ocean County, with a population of 13,628, each elected one State Senator, as did Essex and Hudson Counties, with populations of 143,839 and 129,067, respectively.[27] In the House, each county was entitled to one representative, which left 39 seats to be apportioned according to population.[28] Since there were 12 counties besides the two already mentioned which had populations over 30,000,[29] it is evident that there were serious disproportions in the House also. In New York, each of the 60 counties except Hamilton County was entitled to one of the 128 seats in the Assembly.[30] This left 69 seats to be dis-

tributed among counties the populations of which ranged from 15,420 to 942,292.[31] With seven more counties having populations over 100,000 and 13 others having populations over 50,000,[32] the disproportion in the Assembly was necessarily large. In Vermont, after each county had been allocated one Senator, there were 16 seats remaining to be distributed among the larger counties.[33] The smallest county had a population of 4,082; the largest had a population of 40,651 and there were 10 other counties with populations over 20,000.[34]

(iii) *Ratification by the "reconstructed" States.*—Each of the 10 "reconstructed" States was required to ratify the Fourteenth Amendment before it was readmitted to the Union.[35] The Constitution of each was scrutinized in Congress.[36] Debates over re-

27. Ninth Census of the United States, Statistics of Population (1872) (hereafter Census), 49. The population figures, here and hereafter, are for the year 1870, which presumably best reflect the figures for the years 1866–1870. Only the figures for 1860 were available at that time, of course, and they would have been used by anyone interested in population statistics. See, *e.g.*, Globe 3028 (remarks of Senator Johnson).

The method of apportionment is contained in N. J. Const., 1844, Art. IV, §II, cl. 1.

28. N. J. Const., 1844, Art. IV, § III, cl. 1. Census 49.

29. *Ibid.*

30. N. Y. Const., 1846, Art. III, §§ 2, 5. Census 50–51.

31. *Ibid.*

32. *Ibid.*

33. There were 14 counties, Census 67, each of which was entitled to at least one out of a total of 30 seats. Vt. Const., 1793, Amend. 23.

34. Census 67.

35. Act of Mar. 2, 1867, § 5, 14 Stat. 429. See also Act of June 25, 1868, 15 Stat. 73, declaring that the States of North Carolina, South Carolina, Louisiana, Georgia, Alabama, and Florida, would be admitted to representation in Congress when their legislatures had ratified the Fourteenth Amendment. Other conditions were also imposed, including a requirement that Georgia nullify certain provisions of its Constitution. *Ibid.* Arkansas, which had already ratified the Fourteenth Amendment, was readmitted by Act of June 22, 1868, 15 Stat. 72. Virginia was readmitted by Act of Jan. 26, 1870, 16 Stat. 62; Mississippi by Act of Feb. 23, 1870, 16 Stat. 67; and Texas by Act of Mar. 30, 1870, 16 Stat. 80. Georgia was not finally readmitted until later, by Act of July 15, 1870, 16 Stat. 363.

36. Discussing the bill which eventuated in the Act of June 25, 1868, see note 41, *supra*. Thaddeus Stevens said:

"Now, sir, what is the particular question we are considering? Five or six States have had submitted to them the question of forming constitutions for their own government. They have voluntarily formed such constitutions, under the direction of the Government of the United States. . . . They have sent us their constitutions. Those constitutions have been printed and laid before us. We have looked at them; we have pronounced them republican in form; and all we propose to require is that they shall remain so forever. Subject to this requirement, we are willing to admit them into the Union." Cong. Globe, 40th Cong., 2d Sess., 2465 (1868). See also the remarks of Mr. Butler, *infra*. p. 19–20.

The close attention given the various Constitutions is attested by the Act of June 25, 1868, which conditioned Georgia's readmission on the deletion of "the first and third subdivisions of section seventeen of the fifth article of the constitution of said State, except the proviso to the first subdivision. . . ." 15 Stat. 73. The sections involved are printed in Sen. Ex. Doc. No. 57, 40th Cong., 2d Sesss, 14–15.

Compare *United States* v. *Florida*, 363 U.S. 121, 124–127.

admission were extensive.[37] In at least one instance, the problem of state legislative apportionment was expressly called to the attention of Congress. Objecting to the inclusion of Florida in the Act of June 25, 1868, Mr. Farnsworth stated on the floor of the House:

"I might refer to the apportionment of representatives. By this constitution representatives in the Legislatures of Florida are apportioned in such a manner as to give to the sparsely-populated portions of the State the control of the Legislature. The sparsely-populated parts of the State are those where there are very few negroes, the parts inhabited by the white rebels, the men who, coming in from Georgia, Alabama, and other States, control the fortunes of their several counties. By this constitution every county in that State is entitled to a representative. There are in that State counties that have not thirty registered voters; yet, under this constitution, every one of those counties is entitled to a representative in the Legislature; while the populous counties are entitled to only one representative each, with an additional representative for every thousand inhabitants." [38]

The response of Mr. Butler is particularly illuminating:

"All these arguments, all these statements, all the provisions of this constitution have been submitted to the Judiciary Committee of the Senate, and they have found the constitution republican and proper. This constitution has been submitted to the Senate, and they have found it republican and proper. It has been submitted to your own Committee on Reconstruction, and they have found it republican and proper, and have reported it to this House." [39]

The Constitutions of six of the 10 States contained provisions departing substantially from the method of apportionment now held to be required by the Amendment. And, as in the North, the departures were as real in fact as in theory. In North Carolina, 90 of the 120 representatives were apportioned among the counties without regard to population, leaving 30 seats to be distributed by numbers. Since there were seven counties with populations under 5,000 and 26 counties with populations over 15,000, the disproportions must have been widespread and substantial. In South Carolina, Charleston, with a population of 88,863, elected two Senators; each of the other counties, with populations ranging from 10,269 to 42,486 elected one Senator. In Florida, each of the 39 counties was entitled to elect one Representative; no county was entitled to more than four. These principles applied to Dade County with a population of 85 and to Alachua County and Leon County, with populations of 17,328 and 15,236, respectively.

It is incredible that Congress would have exacted ratification of the Fourteenth Amendment as the price of readmission, would have studied the State Constitutions for compliance with the Amendment, and would then have disregarded violations of it.

The facts recited above show beyond any possible doubt:

(1) that Congress, with full awareness of and attention to the possibility that the States would not afford full equality in voting rights to all their citizens, nevertheless deliberately chose not to interfere with the States' plenary power in this regard when it proposed the Fourteenth Amendment;

(2) that Congress did not include in the Fourteenth Amendment restrictions on the States' power to control voting rights because it believed that if such restrictions were included, the Amendment would not be adopted.

(3) that at least a substantial majority, if not all, of the States which ratified the Fourteenth Amendment did not consider that in so doing, they were accepting limitations on their freedom, never before ques-

---

37. See, *e.g.*, Cong. Globe, 40th Cong., 2d Sess., 2412–2413, 2858–2860, 2861–2871, 2895–2900, 2901–2904, 2927–2935, 2963–2970, 2998–3022, 3023–3029 (1868).

38. Cong. Globe, 40th Cong., 2d Sess., 3090–3091 (1868).

39. *Id.*, at 3092.

tioned, to regulate voting rights as they chose.

Even if one were to accept the majority's belief that it is proper entirely to disregard the unmistakable implications of the second section of the Amendment in construing the first section, one is confounded by its disregard of all this history. There is here none of the difficulty which may attend the application of basic principles to situations not contemplated or understood when the principles were framed. The problems which concern the Court now were problems when the Amendment was adopted. By the deliberate choice of those responsible for the Amendment, it left those problems untouched.

C. *After 1868*

The years following 1868, far from indicating a developing awareness of the applicability of the Fourteenth Amendment to problems of apportionment, demonstrate precisely the reverse: that the States retained and exercised the power independently to apportion their legislatures. In its Constitutions of 1875 and 1901, Alabama carried forward earlier provisions guaranteeing each county at least one representative and fixing an upper limit to the number of seats in the House. Florida's Constitution of 1885 continued the guarantee of one representative for each county and reduced the maximum number of representatives per county from four to three. Georgia, in 1877, continued to favor the smaller counties. Louisiana, in 1879, guaranteed each parish at least one representative in the House. In 1890, Mississippi guaranteed each county one representative, established a maximum number of representatives, and provided that specified groups of counties should each have approximately one-third of the seats in the House, whatever the spread of population. Missouri's Constitution of 1875 gave each county one representative and otherwise favored less populous areas. Montana's original Constitution of 1889 apportioned the State Senate by counties. In 1877, New Hampshire amended its Constitution's provisions for apportionment, but continued

to favor sparsely settled areas in the House and to apportion seats in the Senate according to direct taxes paid; the same was true of New Hampshire's Constitution of 1902.

In 1894, New York adopted a Constitution the peculiar apportionment provisions of which were obviously intended to prevent representation according to population: no county was allowed to have more than one-third of all the senators, no two counties which were adjoining or "separated only by public waters" could have more than one-half of all the senators, and whenever any county became entitled to more than three senators, the total number of senators was increased, thus preserving to the small counties their original number of seats. In addition, each county except Hamilton was guaranteed a seat in the Assembly. The North Carolina Constitution of 1876 gave each county at least one representative and fixed the maximum number of representatives for the whole House. Oklahoma's Constitution at the time of its admission to the Union (1907) favored small counties by the use of partial ratios and a maximum number of seats in the House; in addition, no county was permitted to "take part" in the election of more than seven representatives. Pennsylvania, in 1873, continued to guarantee each county one representative in the House. The same was true of South Carolina's Constitution of 1895, which provided also that each county should elect one and only one Senator. Utah's original Constitution of 1895 assured each county of one representative in the House. Wyoming, when it entered the Union in 1889, guaranteed each county at least one senator and one representative.

D. *Today*

Since the Court now invalidates the legislative apportionments in six States, and has so far upheld the apportionment in none, it is scarcely necessary to comment on the situation in the States today, which is, of course, as fully contrary to the Court's decision as is the record of every prior period in this Nation's history. As of 1961, the

Constitutions of all but 11 States, roughly 20% of the total, recognized bases of apportionment other than geographic spread of population, and to some extent favored sparsely populated areas by a variety of devices, ranging from straight area representation or guaranteed minimum area representation to complicated schemes of the kind exemplified by the provisions of New York's Constitution of 1894, still in effect until struck down by the Court today in No. 20, *post,* p. ——. Since Tennessee, which was the subject of *Baker* v. *Carr,* and Virginia, scrutinized and disapproved today in No. 69, *post,* p. ——, are among the 11 States whose own Constitutions are sound from the standpoint of the Federal Constitution as construed today, it is evident that the actual practice of the States is even more uniformly than their theory opposed to the Court's view of what is constitutionally permissible.

E. *Other Factors*

In this summary of what the majority ignores, note should be taken of the Fifteenth and Nineteenth Amendments. The former prohibited the States from denying or abridging the right to vote "on account of race, color, or previous condition of servitude." The latter, certified as part of the Constitution in 1920, added sex to the prohibited classifications. In *Minor* v. *Happersett,* 21 Wall. 162, this Court considered the claim that the right of women to vote was protected by the Privileges and Immunities Clause of the Fourteenth Amendment. The Court's discussion there of the significance of the Fifteenth Amendment is fully applicable here with respect to the Nineteenth Amendment as well.

"And still again, after the adoption of the fourteenth amendment, it was deemed necessary to adopt a fifteenth, as follows: 'The right of citizens of the United States to vote shall not be denied or abridged by the United States, or by any State, on account of race, color, or previous condition of servitude.' The fourteenth amendment had already provided that no State should make or enforce any law which should abridge the privileges or immunities of citizens of the United States. If suffrage was one of these privileges or immunities, why amend the Constitution to prevent its being denied on account of race, &c.? Nothing is more evident than that the greater must include the less, and if all were already protected why go through with the form of amending the Constitution to protect a part?" *Id.,* at 175.

In the present case, we can go still further. If constitutional amendment was the only means by which all men and, later, women, could be guaranteed the right to vote at all, even for *federal* officers, how can it be that the far less obvious right to a particular kind of apportionment of *state* legislatures—a right to which is opposed a far more plausible conflicting interest of the State than the interest which opposes the general right to vote—can be conferred by judicial construction of the Fourteenth Amendment? Yet, unless one takes the highly implausible view that the Fourteenth Amendment controls methods of apportionment but leaves the right to vote itself unprotected, the conclusion is inescapable that the Court has, for purposes of these cases, relegated the Fifteenth and Nineteenth Amendments to the same limbo of constitutional anachronisms to which the second section of the Fourteenth Amendment has been assigned.

Mention should be made finally of the decisions of this Court which are disregarded or, more accurately, silently overruled today. *Minor* v. *Happersett, supra,* in which the Court held that the Fourteenth Amendment did *not* confer the right to vote on anyone, has already been noted. Other cases are more directly in point. In *Colegrove* v. *Barrett,* 330 U.S. 804, this Court dismissed "for want of a substantial federal question" an appeal from the dismissal of a complaint alleging that the Illinois legislative apportionment resulted in "gross inequality in voting power" and "gross and arbitrary and atrocious discrimination in voting" which denied the plaintiffs equal protection of the laws. In *Remmey* v. *Smith,* 102 F. Supp. 708 (D.C.E.D. Pa.), a three-judge District Court dismissed a complaint alleging that the apportionment of the Pennsylvania Legislature deprived the plaintiffs of "constitutional rights guaranteed to them by the Fourteenth Amendment." *Id.,* at 709. The District Court stated that it was aware that the plaintiffs' allegations were "notoriously true" and that "the practical disenfranchisement of qualified electors in certain of the election districts in Philadelphia County is a matter of common knowledge." *Id.,* at 710. This Court dismissed the appeal "for the want of a substantial federal question." 342 U.S. 916.

In *Kidd* v. *McCanless,* 292 S.W.2d 40, the Supreme Court of Tennessee dismissed an action for a declaratory judgment that the Tennessee Apportionment Act of 1901 was unconstitutional. The complaint alleged that "a minority of approximately 37% of the voting population of the State now elects and controls 20 of the 33 members of the Senate; that a minority of 40% of the voting population of the State now controls 63 of the 99 members of the House of Representatives." *Id.,* at 42. Without dissent, this Court granted the motion to dismiss the appeal. 352 U.S. 920. In *Radford* v. *Gary,* 145 F. Supp. 541 (D.C.W.D. Okla.), a three-judge District Court was convened to consider "the complaint of the plaintiff to the effect that the existing apportionment statutes of the State of Oklahoma violate the plain mandate of the Oklahoma Constitution and operate to deprive him of the equal protection of the laws guaranteed by the Fourteenth Amendment to the Constitution of the United States." *Id.,* at 542. The plaintiff alleged that he was a resident and voter in the most populous county of the State, which had about 15% of the total population of the State but only about 2% of the seats in the State Senate and less than 4% of the seats in the House. The complaint recited the unwillingness or inability of the branches of the state government to provide relief and alleged that there was no state remedy available. The District Court granted a motion to dismiss. This Court affirmed without dissent. 352 U.S. 991.

Each of these recent cases is distinguished on some ground or other in *Baker* v. *Carr.* See 369 U.S., at 235–236. Their summary dispositions prevent consideration whether these after-the-fact distinctions are real or imaginary. The fact remains, however, that between 1947 and 1957, four cases raising issues precisely the same as those decided today were presented to the Court. Three were dismissed because the issues presented were thought insubstantial and in the fourth the lower court's dismissal was affirmed.

I have tried to make the catalogue complete, yet to keep it within the manageable limits of a judicial opinion. In my judgment, today's decisions are refuted by the language of the Amendment which they construe and by the inference fairly to be drawn from subsequently enacted Amendments. They are unequivocally refuted by history and by consistent theory and practice from the time of the adoption of the Fourteenth Amendment until today.

II

The Court's elaboration of its new "constitutional" doctrine indicates how far—and how unwisely—it has strayed from the appropriate bounds of its authority. The consequence of today's decision is that in all but the handful of States which may already satisfy the new requirements the local District Court or, it may be, the state courts, are given blanket authority and the constitutional duty to supervise apportionment of the State Legislatures. It is difficult to imagine a more intolerable and inappropriate interference by the judiciary with the independent legislatures of the States. . . .

It should by now be obvious that these cases do not mark the end of reapportionment problems in the courts. Predictions once made that the courts would never have to face the problem of actually working out an apportionment have proved false. This Court, however, continues to avoid the consequences of its decisions, simply assuring us that the lower courts "can and . . . will work out more concrete and specific standards," *ante*, p. 43. Deeming it "expedient" not to spell out "precise constitutional tests," the Court contents itself with stating "only a few rather general considerations." *Ibid.*

Generalities cannot obscure the cold truth that cases of this type are not amenable to the development of judicial standards. No set of standards can guide a court which has to decide how many legislative districts a State shall have, or what the shape of the districts shall be, or where to draw a particular district line. No judicially manageable standard can determine whether a State should have single-member districts or multimember districts or some combination of both. No such standard can control the balance between keeping up with population shifts and having stable districts. In all these respects, the courts will be called upon to make particular decisions with respect to which a principle of equally populated districts will be of no assistance whatsoever. Quite obviously, there are limitless possibilities for districting consistent with such a principle. Nor can these problems be avoided by judicial reliance on legislative judgments so far as possible. Reshaping or combining one or two districts, or modifying just a few district lines, is no less a matter of choosing among many possible solutions, with varying political consequences, than reapportionment broadside.

The Court ignores all this, saying only that "what is marginally permissible in one State may be unsatisfactory in another, depending on the particular circumstances of the case," *ante*, p. 43. It is well to remember that the product of today's decisions will not be readjustment of a few districts in a few States which most glaringly depart from the principle of equally populated districts. It will be a redetermination, extensive in many cases, of legislative districts in all but a few States.

Although the Court—necessarily, as I believe—provides only generalities in elaboration of its main thesis, its opinion nevertheless fully demonstrates how far removed these problems are from fields of judicial competence. Recognizing that "indiscriminate districting" is an invitation to "partisan gerrymandering," *ante*, pp. 43–44, the Court nevertheless excludes virtually every basis for the formation of electoral districts other than "indiscriminate districting." In one or another of today's opinions, the Court declares it unconstitutional for a State to give effective consideration to any of the following in establishing legislative districts:

(1) history;

(2) "economic or other sorts of group interests";

(3) area;

(4) geographical considerations;

(5) a desire "to insure effective representation for sparsely settled areas";

(6) "availability of access of citizens to their representatives";

(7) theories of bicameralism (except those approved by the Court);

(8) occupation;

(9) "an attempt to balance urban and rural power."

(10) the preference of a majority of voters in the State.

So far as presently appears, the *only* factor which a State may consider, apart from numbers, is political subdivisions. But even "a clearly rational state policy" recognizing this factor is unconstitutional if "population is submerged as the controlling consideration. . . ."

I know of no principle of logic or practical or theoretical politics, still less any constitutional principle, which establishes all or any of these exclusions. Certain it is that the Court's opinion does not establish them. So far as the Court says anything at all on this score, it says only that "legislators represent people, not trees or acres," *ante*, p. 27; that "citizens, not history or economic interests, cast votes," *ante*, p. 45; that "people, not land or trees or pastures, vote," *ibid.* All this may be conceded. But it is surely equally obvious, and, in the context of elections, more meaningful to note that people are not ciphers and that legislators can represent their electors only by speaking for their interests—economic, social, political—many of which do reflect the place where the electors live. The Court does not establish, or indeed even attempt to make a case for the proposition that conflicting interests within a State can only be adjusted by disregarding them when voters are grouped for purposes of representation.

CONCLUSION

. . . Finally, these decisions give support to a current mistaken view of the Constitution and the constitutional function of this Court. This view, in a nutshell, is that every major social ill in this country can find its cure in some constitutional "principle," and that this Court should "take the lead" in promoting reform when other branches of government fail to act. The Constitution is not a panacea for every blot upon the public welfare, nor should this Court, ordained as a judicial body, be thought of as a general haven for reform movements. The Constitution is an instrument of government, fundamental to which is the premise that in a diffusion of governmental authority lies the greatest promise that this Nation will realize liberty for all its citizens. This Court, limited in function in accordance with that premise, does not serve its high purpose when it exceeds its authority, even to satisfy justified impatience with the slow workings of the political process. For when, in the name of constitutional interpretation, the Court *adds* something to the Constitution that was deliberately excluded from it, the Court in reality substitutes its view of what should be so for the amending process. . . .

NOTE: In companion cases decided contemporaneously with *Reynolds,* the Court held: (1), a trial court may consider the immediacy of the 1964 New York elections in determining whether to permit them under the existing invalid apportionment scheme (*WMCA* v. *Lomenzo*); (2), Colorado malapportionment is not made constitutionally valid either by voters' approval or by the possibility of change by majority rule through the initiative process (*Lucas* v. *Forty-Fourth General Assembly of Colorado*); (3), failure of Maryland legislature to reapportion before the 1966 election would require trial court to bar elections under existing, or any other, unconstitutional scheme (*Maryland Committee for Fair Representation* v. *Tawes*).

GOVERNOR EARL WARREN ON REDISTRICTING

Some sixteen years before the *Reynolds* decision, California was considering a proposal to apportion the state senate in accordance with population. In a speech at Merced, California on October 29, 1948 Governor Warren (then the Republican candidate for the vice-presidency of the United States) made the following remarks:

Many California counties are far more important in the life of the State than their population bears to the entire population of the State. It is for this reason that I have never been in favor of restricting the representation in the senate to a strictly population basis.

It is the same reason that the Founding Fathers of our country gave balanced representation to the States of the Union—equal representation in one house and proportionate representation based on population in the other.

Moves have been made to upset the balanced representation in our State, even though it has served us well and is strictly in accord with American tradition and the pattern of our National Government.

There was a time when California was completely dominated by boss rule. The liberal election laws and legislative reapportionment of the system have liberated us from such domination. Any weakening of the laws would invite a return to boss rule which we are now happily rid of.

Our State has made almost unbelievable progress under our present system of legislative representation. I believe we should keep it.

WMCA, INC. v. *LOMENZO*

84 S. Ct. 1418 (1964)

LUCAS v. *FOURTY-FOURTH GENERAL ASSEMBLY OF COLORADO*

84 S. Ct. 1472 (1964)

In these cases the Court found New York's and Colorado's legislative apportionment schemes not based substantially on population—and hence unconstitutional. Mr. Justice Harlan's dissent in *Sims* covers these cases.

MR. JUSTICE STEWART, whom MR. JUSTICE CLARK joins, dissenting. . . .

Simply stated, the question is to what degree, if at all, the Equal Protection Clause of the Fourteenth Amendment limits each sovereign State's freedom to establish appropriate electoral constituencies from which representatives to the State's bicameral legislative assembly are to be chosen. The Court's answer is a blunt one, and, I think, woefully wrong. The Equal Protection Clause, says the Court, "requires that the seats in both houses of a bicameral state legislature must be apportioned on a population basis."

After searching carefully through the Court's opinions in these and their companion cases, I have been able to find but two reasons offered in support of this rule. First, says the Court, it is "established that the fundamental principle of representative government in this country is one of equal representation for equal numbers of people. . . ." With all respect, I think that this is not correct, simply as a matter of fact. It has been unanswerably demonstrated before now that this "was not the colonial system, it was not the system chosen for the national government by the

Constitution, it was not the system exclusively or even predominantly practiced by the States at the time of adoption of the Fourteenth Amendment, it is not predominantly practiced by the States today." Secondly, says the Court, unless legislative districts are equal in population, voters in the more populous districts will suffer a "debasement" amounting to a constitutional injury. As the Court explains it, "To the extent that a citizen's right to vote is debased, he is that much less a citizen." We are not told how or why the vote of a person in a more populated legislative district is "debased," or how or why he is less a citizen, nor is the proposition self-evident. I find it impossible to understand how or why a voter in California, for instance, either feels or is less a citizen than a voter in Nevada, simply because, despite their population disparities, each of those States is represented by two United States Senators.

To put the matter plainly, there is nothing in all the history of this Court's decisions which supports this constitutional rule. The Court's draconian pronouncement, which makes unconstitutional the legislatures of most of the 50 States, finds no support in the words of the Constitution, in any prior decision of this Court, or in the 175-year political history of our Federal Union. With all respect, I am convinced these decisions mark a long step backward into that unhappy era when a majority of the members of this Court were thought by many to have convinced themselves and each other that the demands of the Constitution were to be measured not by what it says, but by their own notions of wise political theory. The rule announced today is at odds with long-established principles of constitutional adjudication under the Equal Protection Clause, and it stifles values of local individuality and initiative vital to the character of the Federal Union which it was the genius of our Constitution to create.

I

What the Court has done is to convert a particular political philosophy into a constitutional rule, binding upon each of the 50 States, from Maine to Hawaii, from Alaska to Texas, without regard and without respect for the many individualized and differentiated characteristics of each State, characteristics stemming from each State's distinct history, distinct geography, distinct distribution of population, and distinct political heritage. My own understanding of the various theories of representative government is that no one theory has ever commanded unanimous assent among political scientists, historians, or others who have considered the problem. But even if it were thought that the rule announced today by the Court is, as a matter of political theory, the most desirable general rule which can be devised as a basis for the make-up of the representative assembly of a typical State, I could not join in the fabrication of a constitutional mandate which imports and forever freezes one theory of political thought into our Constitution, and forever denies to every State any opportunity for enlightened and progressive innovation in the design of its democratic institutions, so as to accommodate within a system of representative government the interests and aspirations of diverse groups of people,

without subjecting any group or class to absolute domination by a geographically concentrated or highly organized majority.

Representative government is a process of accommodating group interests through democratic institutional arrangements. Its function is to channel the numerous opinions, interests, and abilities of the people of a State into the making of the State's public policy. Appropriate legislative apportionment, therefore, should ideally be designed to insure effective representation in the State's legislature, in cooperation with other organs of political power, of the various groups and interests making up the electorate. In practice, of course, this ideal is approximated in the particular apportionment system of any State by a realistic accommodation of the diverse and often conflicting political forces operating within the State.

I do not pretend to any specialized knowledge of the myriad of individual characteristics of the several States, beyond the records in the cases before us today. But I do know enough to be aware that a system of legislative apportionment which might be best for South Dakota, might be unwise for Hawaii with its many islands, or Michigan with its Northern Peninsula. I do know enough to realize that Montana with its vast distances is not Rhode Island with its heavy concentrations of people. I do know enough to be aware of the great variations among the several States in their historic manner of distributing legislative power—of the Governors' Councils in New England, of the broad powers of initiative and referendum retained in some States by the people, of the legislative power which some States give to their Governors, by the right of veto or otherwise, of the widely autonomous home rule which many States give to their cities. The Court today declines to give any recognition to these considerations and countless others, tangible and intangible, in holding unconstitutional the particular systems of legislative apportionment which these States have chosen. Instead, the Court says that the requirements of the Equal Protection Clause can be met in any State only by the uncritical, simplistic, and heavy-handed application of sixth-grade arithmetic.

But legislators do not represent faceless numbers. They represent people, or, more accurately, a majority of the voters in their districts—people with identifiable needs and interests which require legislative representation, and which can often be related to the geographical areas in which these people live. The very fact of geographic districting, the constitutional validity of which the Court does not question, carries with it an acceptance of the idea of legislative representation of regional needs and interests. Yet if geographical residence is irrelevant, as the Court suggests, and the goal is solely that of equally "weighted" votes, I do not understand why the Court's constitutional rule does not require the abolition of districts and the holding of all elections at large.[1]

The fact is, of course, that population factors must often to some degree be subordinated in devising a legislative apportionment plan which is to achieve the important goal of ensuring a fair, effective, and balanced representation of the regional, social, and economic interests within a State. And the further fact is that throughout our history the apportionments of State Legislatures have reflected the strongly felt American tradition that the public interest is composed of many diverse interests, and that in the long run it can better be expressed by a medley of component voices than by the majority's monolithic command. What constitutes a rational plan reasonably designed to achieve this objective will vary from State to State, since each State is unique, in terms of topography,

geography, demography, history, heterogeneity and concentration of population, variety of social and economic interests, and in the operation and interrelation of its political institutions. But so long as a State's apportionment plan reasonably achieves, in the light of the State's own characteristics, effective and balanced representation of all substantial interests, without sacrificing the principle of effective majority rule, that plan cannot be considered irrational.

II

This brings me to what I consider to be the proper constitutional standards to be applied in these cases. Quite simply, I think the cases should be decided by application of accepted principles of constitutional adjudication under the Equal Protection Clause. A recent expression by the Court of these principles will serve as a generalized compendium:

"[T]he Fourteenth Amendment permits the States a wide scope of discretion in enacting laws which affect some groups of citizens differently than others. The constitutional safeguard is offended only if the classification rests on grounds wholly irrelevant to the achievement of the State's objective. State legislatures are presumed to have acted within their constitutional power despite the fact that, in practice, their laws result in some inequality. A statutory discrimination will not be set aside if any state of facts reasonably may be conceived to justify it." *McGowan* v. *Maryland*, 366 U.S. 420, 425–426.

These principles reflect an understanding respect for the unique values inherent in the Federal Union of States established by our Constitution. They reflect, too, a wise perception of this Court's role in that con-

---

1. Even with legislative districts of exactly equal voter population, 26% of the electorate (a bare majority of the voters in a bare majority of the districts) can, as a matter of the kind of theoretical mathematics embraced by the Court, elect a majority of the legislature under our simple majority electoral system. Thus, the Court's constitutional rule permits minority rule.

Students of the mechanics of voting systems tell us that if all that matters is that votes count equally, the best vote-counting electoral system is proportional representation in state-wide elections. See, e.g., *Lakeman and Lambert, supra,* n. 10. It is just because electoral systems are intended to serve functions other than satisfying mathematical theories, however, that the system of proportional representation has not been widely adopted. *Ibid.*

stitutional system. The point was never better made than by Mr. Justice Brandeis, dissenting in *New State Ice Co.* v. *Liebmann,* 285 U.S. 262, 280. The final paragraph of that classic dissent is worth repeating here:

"To stay experimentation in things social and economic is a grave responsibility. Denial of the right to experiment may be fraught with serious consequences to the nation. It is one of the happy incidents of the federal system that a single courageous state may, if its citizens choose, serve as a laboratory; and try novel social and economic experiments without risk to the rest of the country. This Court has the power to prevent an experiment. We may strike down the statute which embodies it on the ground that, in our opinion, the measure is arbitrary, capricious or unreasonable. . . . But, in the exercise of this high power, we must be ever on our guard, lest we erect our prejudices into legal principles. If we would guide by the light of reason we must let our minds be bold." 285 U.S., at 311.

That cases such as the ones now before us were to be decided under these accepted Equal Protection Clauses standards was the clear import of what was said on this score in *Baker* v. *Carr,* 369 U.S. 186, 226:

"Nor need the appellants, in order to succeed in this action, ask the Court to enter upon policy determinations for which judicially manageable standards are lacking. Judicial standards under the Equal Protection Clause are well developed and familiar, and it has been open to courts since the enactment of the Fourteenth Amendment to determine, if on the particular facts they must, that a discrimination reflects *no* policy, but simply arbitrary and capricious action."

It is to be remembered that the Court in *Baker* v. *Carr* did not question what had been said only a few years earlier in *MacDougall* v. *Green,* 335 U.S. 281, 284:

"It would be strange indeed, and doctrinaire, for this Court, applying such broad constitutional concepts as due process and equal protection of the laws, to deny a

State the power to assure a proper diffusion of political initiative as between its thinly populated counties and those having concentrated masses, in view of the fact that the latter have practical opportunities for exerting their political weight at the polls not available to the former. The Constitution—a practical instrument of government—makes no such demands on the States."

Moving from the general to the specific, I think that the Equal Protection Clause demands but two basic attributes of any plan of state legislative apportionment. First, it demands that, in the light of the State's own characteristics and needs, the plan must be a rational one. Secondly, it demands that the plan must be such as not to permit the systematic frustration of the will of a majority of the electorate of the State. I think it is apparent that any plan of legislative apportionment which could be shown to reflect no policy, but simply arbitrary and capricious action or inaction, and that any plan which could be shown systematically to prevent ultimate effective majority rule, would be invalid under accepted Equal Protection Clause standards. But, beyond this, I think there is nothing in the Federal Constitution to prevent a State from choosing any electoral legislative structure it thinks best suited to the interests, temper, and customs of its people. In the light of these standards, I turn to the Colorado and New York plans of legislative apportionment.

III

COLORADO

The Colorado plan creates a General Assembly composed of a Senate of 39 members and a House of 65 members. The State is divided into 65 equal population representative districts, with one representative to be elected from each district, and 39 senatorial districts, 14 of which include more than one county. In the Colorado House, the majority unquestionably rules supreme, with the population factor untempered by other considerations. In the Senate rural minorities do not have effective control, and therefore do not have even a veto power over the will of the urban majorities. It is true that, as a matter of theoretical arithmetic, a minority of 36% of the voters could elect a majority of the Senate, but this percentage has no real meaning in terms of the legislative process.[2] Under the Colorado plan, no possible combination of Colorado senators from rural districts, even assuming *arguendo* that they would vote as a bloc, could control the Senate. To arrive at the 36% figure, one must include with the rural districts a substantial number of urban districts, districts with substantially dissimilar interests. There is absolutely no reason to assume that this theoretical majority would ever vote together on any issue so as to thwart the wishes of the majority of the voters of Colorado. Indeed, when we eschew the world of numbers, and look to the real world of effective representation, the simple fact of the matter is that Colorado's three metropolitan areas, Denver, Pueblo, and Colorado Springs, elect a majority of the Senate.

The State of Colorado is not an economically or geographically homogeneous unit. The Continental Divide crosses the State in a meandering line from north to south, and Colorado's 104,247 square miles of area are almost equally divided between high plains in the east and rugged mountains in the west. The State's population is highly concentrated in the urbanized eastern edge of the foothills, while farther to the east lies that agricultural area of Colorado which is a part of the Great Plains. The area lying to the west of the Continental Divide is largely mountainous, with two-thirds of the population living in communities of less than 2,500 inhabitants or on farms. Livestock raising, mining and tourism are the dominant occupations. This area is further subdivided by a series of mountain ranges containing some of the highest peaks in the United States, isolating communities and making transportation from point to point difficult, and in some places during the winter months almost impossible. The fourth distinct region of the State is the South Central region, in which is located the most economically depressed area in the State. A scarcity of water makes a state-wide water policy a necessity, with each region affected differently by the problem.

The District Court found that the people living in each of these four regions have interests unifying themselves and differentiating them from those in other regions. Given these underlying facts, certainly it was not irrational to conclude that effective representation of the interests of the residents of each of these regions was unlikely to be achieved if the rule of equal population districts were mechanically imposed; that planned departures from a strict per capita standard of representation were a desirable way of assuring some representation of distinct localities whose needs and problems might have passed unnoticed if districts had been drawn solely on a per capita basis; a desirable way of assuring that districts should be small enough in area, in a mountainous State like Colorado, where accessibility is affected by configuration as well as compactness of districts, to enable each senator to have firsthand knowledge of his entire district and to maintain close contact with his constituents; and a desirable way of avoiding the drawing of district lines which would submerge the needs and wishes of a portion of the electorate by grouping them in districts with larger numbers of voters with wholly different interests.

2. The theoretical figure is arrived at by placing the legislative districts for each house in rank order of population, and by counting down the smallest population end of the list a sufficient distance to accumulate the minimum population which could elect a majority of the house in question. It is a meaningless abstraction as applied to a multimembered body because the factors of political party alignment and interest representation make such theoretical bloc voting a practical impossibility. For example, 31,000,000 people in the 26 least populous States representing only 17% of United States population have 52% of the Senators in the United States Senate. But no one contends that this bloc controls the Senate's legislative process.

It is clear from the record that if per capita representation were the rule in both houses of the Colorado Legislature, counties having small populations would have to be merged with larger counties having totally dissimilar interests. Their representatives would not only be unfamiliar with the problems of the smaller county, but the interests of the smaller counties might well be totally submerged to the interests of the larger counties with which they are joined. Since representatives representing conflicting interests might well pay greater attention to the views of the majority, the minority interest could be denied any effective representation at all. Its votes would not be merely "diluted," an injury which the Court considers of constitutional dimensions, but rendered totally nugatory.

The findings of the District Court speak for themselves:

"The heterogeneous characteristics of Colorado justify geographic districting for the election of the members of one chamber of the legislature. In no other way may representation be afforded to insular minorities. Without such districting the metropolitan areas could theoretically, and no doubt practically, dominate both chambers of the legislature. . . .

"The realities of topographic conditions with their resulting effect on population may not be ignored. For an example, if [the rule of equal population districts] was to be accepted, Colorado would have one senator for approximately every 45,000 persons. Two contiguous Western Region senatorial districts, Nos. 29 and 37, have a combined population of 51,675 persons inhabiting an area of 20,514 square miles. The division of this area into two districts does not offend any constitutional provisions. Rather, it is a wise recognition of the practicalities of life. . . .

"We are convinced that the apportionment of the Senate by Amendment No. 7 recognizes population as a prime, but not controlling, factor and gives effect to such important considerations as geography, compactness and contiguity of territory, accessibility, observance of natural boundaries, conformity to historical divisions such as county lines and prior representation districts, and 'a proper diffusion of political initiative as between a state's thinly populated counties and those having concentrated masses.' " 219 F. Supp., at 932.

From 1954 until the adoption of Amendment 7 in 1962, the issue of apportionment had been the subject of intense public debate. The present apportionment was proposed and supported by many of Colorado's leading citizens. The factual data underlying the apportionment were prepared by the wholly independent Denver Research Institute of the University of Denver. Finally, the apportionment was adopted by a popular referendum in which not only a 2–1 majority of all the voters in Colorado, but a majority in each county, including those urban counties allegedly discriminated against, voted for the present plan in preference to an alternative proposal providing for equal representation per capita in both legislative houses. As the District Court said:

"The contention that the voters have discriminated against themselves appalls rather than convinces. Difficult as it may be at times to understand mass behavior of human beings, a proper recognition of the judicial function precludes a court from holding that the free choice of the voters between two conflicting theories of apportionment is irrational or the result arbitrary." Ibid.

The present apportionment, adopted overwhelmingly by the people in a 1962 popular referendum as a state constitutional amendment, is entirely rational, and the amendment by its terms provides for keeping the apportionment current.[3] Thus the majority has consciously chosen to protect the minority's interests, and under the

3. Within the last 12 years, the people of Michigan, California, Washington, and Nebraska (unicameral legislature) have expressed their will in popular referenda in favor of apportionment plans departing from the Court's rule. See *Dixon*, 38 Notre Dame Lawyer, *supra,* at 383–385.

liberal initiative provisions of the Colorado Constitution, it retains the power to reverse its decision to do so. Therefore, there can be no question of frustration of the basic principle of majority rule.

IV

NEW YORK

"Constitutional statecraft often involves a degree of protection from minorities which limits the principle of majority rule. Perfect numerical equality in voting rights would be achieved if an entire State legislature were elected at large but the danger is too great that the remote and less populated sections would be neglected or that, in the event of a conflict between two parts of the State, the more populous region would elect the entire legislature and in its councils the minority would never be heard.

"Due recognition of geographic and other minority interests is also a comprehensible reason for reducing the weight of votes in great cities. If seventy percent of a State's population lived in a single city and the remainder was scattered over wide country areas and small towns, it might be reasonable to give the city voters somewhat smaller representation than that to which they would be entitled by a strictly numerical apportionment in order to reduce the danger of total neglect of the needs and wishes of rural areas."

The above two paragraphs are from the brief which the United States filed in *Baker v. Carr*, 369 U.S. 186, 82 S.Ct. 691.[4] It would be difficult to find words more aptly to describe the State of New York, or more clearly to justify the system of legislative apportionment which that State has chosen.

Legislative apportionment in New York follows a formula which is written into the New York Constitution and which has been a part of its fundamental law since 1894.

The apportionment is not a crazy quilt; it is rational, it is applied systematically, and it is kept reasonably current. The formula reflects a policy which accords major emphasis to population, some emphasis to region and community, and a reasonable limitation upon massive over-centralization of power. In order to effectuate this policy, the apportionment formula provides that each county shall have at least one representative in the Assembly, that the smaller counties shall have somewhat greater representation in the legislature than representation based solely on numbers would accord, and that some limits be placed on the representation of the largest counties in order to prevent one megalopolis from completely dominating the legislature.

New York is not unique in considering factors other than population in its apportionment formula. Indeed, the inclusion of such other considerations is more the rule than the exception throughout the states. Two-thirds of the States have given effect to factors other than population in apportioning representation in both houses of their legislatures, and over four-fifths of the States give effect to nonpopulation factors in at least one house. The typical restrictions are those like New York's affording minimal representation to certain political subdivisions, or prohibiting districts composed of parts of two or more counties, or requiring districts to be composed of contiguous and compact territory, or fixing the membership of the legislative body. All of these factors tend to place practical limitations on apportionment according to population, even if the basic underlying system is one of equal population districts for representation in one or both houses of the legislature.

That these are rational policy considerations can be seen from even a cursory ex-

4. Brief for the United States as *amicus curiae* on reargument, No. 6, 1961 Term, pp. 29–30. The Solicitor General, appearing as *amicus* in the present cases, declined to urge this Court to adopt the rule of per capita equality in both houses, stating that "[s]uch an interpretation would press the Equal Protection Clause to an extreme, as applied to State legislative apportionment, would require radical changes in three-quarters of the State governments, and would eliminate the opportunities for local variation." Brief for the United States as *amicus curiae*, No. 508, 1963 Term, p. 32.

amination of New York's political makeup. In New York many of the interests which a citizen may wish to assert through the legislative process are interests which touch on his relation to the government of his county as well as to that of the State, and consequently these interests are often peculiar to the citizens of one county. As the District Court found, counties have been an integral part of New York's governmental structure since early colonial times, and the many functions performed by the counties today reflect both the historic gravitation toward the county as the central unit of political activity and the realistic fact that the county is usually the most efficient and practical unit for carrying out many governmental programs.

A policy guaranteeing minimum representation to each county is certainly rational, particularly in a State like New York. It prevents less densely populated counties from being merged into multicounty districts where they would receive no effective representation at all. Further, it may be only by individual county representation that the needs and interests of all the areas of the State can be brought to the attention of the legislative body. The rationality of individual county representation becomes particularly apparent in States where legislative action applicable only to one or more particular counties is the permissible tradition.

Despite the rationality of according at least one representative to each county, it is clear that such a system of representation, coupled with a provision fixing the maximum number of members in the legislative body—a necessity if the body is to remain small enough for manageably effective action—has the result of creating some population disparities among districts. But since the disparity flows from the effectuation of a rational state policy, the mere existence of the disparity itself can hardly be considered an invidious discrimination.

In addition to ensuring minimum representation to each county, the New York apportionment formula, by allocating somewhat greater representation to the smaller counties while placing limitations on the representation of the largest counties, is clearly designed to protect against overcentralization of power. To understand fully the practical importance of this consideration in New York, one must look to its unique characteristics. New York is one of the few States in which the central cities can elect a majority of representatives to the legislature. As the District Court found, the 10 most populous counties in the State control both houses of the legislature under the existing apportionment system. Each of these counties is heavily urban; each is in a metropolitan area. Together they contain 73.5% of the citizen population, and are represented by 65.5% of the seats in the Senate and 62% of the seats in the Assembly. Moreover, the nine counties comprising one metropolitan area—New York City, Nassau, Rockland, Suffolk and Westchester—contain 63.2% of the total citizen population and elect a clear majority of both houses of the legislature under the existing system which the Court today holds invalid. Obviously, therefore, the existing system of apportionment clearly guarantees effective majority representation and control in the State Legislature.

But this is not the whole story. New York City, with its seven million people and a budget larger than that of the State, has, by virtue of its concentration of population, homogeneity of interest, and political cohesiveness, acquired an institutional power and political influence of its own hardly measurable simply by counting the number of its representatives in the legislature. Elihu Root, a delegate to the New York Constitutional Convention of 1894, which formulated the basic structure of the present apportionment plan, made this very point at that time:

"The question is whether thirty separate centers of 38,606 each scattered over the country are to be compared upon the basis of absolute numerical equality with one center of thirty times 38,606 in one city, with all the multiplications of power that comes from representing a single interest, standing together on all measures against a scattered and disunited representation from the thirty widely separated single centers of 38,606. Thirty men from one place owing their allegiance to one political organization representing the interest of one community, voting together, acting together solidly; why they are worth double the scattered elements of power coming from hundreds of miles apart." 3 Revised Record of the New York State Constitutional Convention of 1894, p. 1215.

Surely it is not irrational for the State of New York to be justifiably concerned about balancing such a concentration of political power, and certainly there is nothing in our Federal Constitution which prevents a State from reasonably translating such a concern into its apportionment formula. See *MacDougall* v. *Green*, 335 U.S. 281, 69 S. Ct. 1.

The State of New York is large in area and diverse in interests. The Hudson and Mohawk Valleys, the farm communities along the southern belt, the many suburban areas throughout the State, the upstate urban and industrial centers, the Thousand Islands, the Finger Lakes, the Berkshire Hills, the Adirondacks—the people of all these and many other areas, with their aspirations and their interests, just as surely belong to the State as does the giant metropolis which is New York City. What the State has done is to adopt a plan of legislative apportionment which is designed in a rational way to ensure that minority voices may be heard, but that the will of the majority shall prevail.

V

In the allocation of representation in their State Legislatures, Colorado and New York have adopted completely rational plans which reflect an informed response to their particularized characteristics and needs. The plans are quite different, just as Colorado and New York are quite different. But each State, while clearly ensuring that in its legislative councils the will of the majority of the electorate shall rule, has sought to provide that no identifiable minority shall be completely silenced or engulfed. The Court today holds uncon-

stitutional the considered governmental choices of these two Sovereign States. By contrast, I believe that what each State has achieved fully comports with the letter and the spirit of our constitutional traditions.

I would affirm the judgments in both cases.

MR. JUSTICE CLARK, dissenting.

While I join my Brother Stewart's opinion, it is well that additional observations be recorded with reference to the Colorado case.

The parties concede that the Colorado House of Representatives is now apportioned "as nearly equal in population as may be." The Court does not disturb this stipulation though it seems to accept it in niggardly fashion. The fact that 45.1% of the State's population resides in the area which selects a majority of the House indicates rather conclusively that the apportionment comes within the test laid down in *Reynolds* v. *Sims*, 377 U.S. ——: " 'one person, one vote,' " that is, "approximately equal" or " 'as nearly as is practicable' " with only "some deviations. . . ." Indeed, the Colorado House is within 4.9% of being perfect. Moreover, the fact that the apportionment follows political subdivision lines to some extent is also a teaching of *Reynolds* v. *Sims, supra.* But the Court strikes down Colorado's apportionment, which was adopted by the majority vote of every political subdivision in the State, because the Senate's majority is elected by 33.2% of the population, a much higher percentage than that which elects a majority of the Senate of the United States.

I would refuse to interfere with this apportionment for several reasons. First, Colorado enjoys the initiative and referendum system which it often utilizes and which, indeed, produced the present apportionment. As a result of the action of the Legislature and the use of initiative and referendum, the State Assembly has been reapportioned eight times since 1881. This indicates the complete awareness of the people of Colorado to apportionment problems and their continuing efforts to solve them. The courts should not interfere in such a situation. See my concurring opinion in *Baker* v. *Carr*, 369 U.S. 186, 258–259 (1962). Next, as my Brother Stewart has pointed out, there are rational and most persuasive reasons for some deviations in the representation in the Colorado Assembly. The State has mountainous areas which divide it into four regions, some parts of which are almost impenetrable. There are also some depressed areas, diversified industry and varied climate, as well as enormous recreational regions and difficulties in transportation. These factors give rise to problems indigenous to Colorado, which only its people can intelligently solve. This they have done in the present apportionment.

Finally, I cannot agree to the arbitrary application of the "one man, one vote" principle for both houses of a State Legislature. In my view, if one house is fairly apportioned by population (as is admitted here) then the people should have some latitude in providing, on a rational basis, for representation in the other house. The Court seems to approve the federal arrangement of two Senators from each State on the ground that it was a compromise reached by the framers of our Constitution and is a part of the fabric of our national charter. But what the Court overlooks is that Colorado, by an overwhelming vote, has likewise written the organization of its legislative body into its Constitution, and our dual federalism requires that we give

it recognition. After all, the Equal Protection Clause is not an algebraic formula. Equal protection does not rest on whether the practice assailed "results in some inequality" but rather on whether "any state of facts reasonably can be conceived that would sustain it"; and one who attacks it must show "that it does not rest upon any reasonable basis, but is essentially arbitrary." Mr. Justice Van Devanter in *Lindsley* v. *Natural Carbonic Gas Co.*, 220 U.S. 61, 78–79 (1911). Certainly Colorado's arrangement is not arbitrary. On the contrary, it rests on reasonable grounds which, as I have pointed out, are peculiar to that State. It is argued that the Colorado apportionment would lead only to a legislative stalemate between the two houses, but the experience of the Congress completely refutes this argument. Now in its 176th year, the federal plan has worked well. It is further said that in any event Colorado's apportionment would substitute compromise for the legislative process. But most legislation is the product of compromise between the various forces acting for and against its enactment.

In striking down Colorado's plan of apportionment, the Court, I believe, is exceeding its powers under the Equal Protection Clause; it is invading the valid functioning of the procedures of the States, and thereby commits a grievous error which will do irreparable damage to our federal-state relationship. I dissent.

SELECTED READINGS

G. Abernathy, *The Right of Assembly and Association* (1961)

"The Adamson Case: A Study in Constitutional Technique," 58 *Yale Law Journal* 268 (1949)

A. Barth, *Government by Investigation* (1947)

W. S. Bernard (ed), *American Immigration Policy: A Reappraisal* (1950)

W. Berns, *Freedom, Virtue, and the First Amendment* (1957)

A. Bickel, "The Original Understanding and the Segregation Decision," 69 *Harvard Law Review* 1 (1955)

D. E. Boles, *The Bible, Religion, and the Public Schools* (1963)

D. B. Bonsal, *The Federal Loyalty-Security Program: Report of the Special Committee of the Association of the Bar of the City of New York* (1956)

E. Bontecou, *The Federal Loyalty-Security Program* (1953)

E. M. Borchard and E. R. Lutz, *Convicting the Innocent* (1932)

R. S. Brown, *Loyalty and Security* (1958)

Z. Chafee, *Free Speech in the United States* (1948)

H. W. Chase, "Improving Congressional Investigations: A No-Progress Report," 30 *Temple Law Quarterly* 126 (1957)

T. I. Cook, *Democratic Rights versus Communist Activity* (1954)

S. Dash, R. F. Schwartz, and R. E. Knowlton, *The Eavesdroppers* (1959)

T. I. Emerson and D. Haber, *Political and Civil Rights in the United States* (1964)

S. J. Ervin, "Literacy Tests for Voters: A Case Study in Federalism," 27 *Law and Contemporary Problems* 481 (1962)

C. Fairman, "Does the Fourteenth Amendment Incorporate the Bill of Rights," 2 *Stanford Law Review* 5 (1949)

D. Fellman, *The Limits of Freedom* (1954)

D. Fellman, *The Defendant's Rights* (1958)

D. Fellman, *The Constitutional Right of Association* (1963)

"A Forum on the Interrogation of the Accused," 49 *Cornell Law Quarterly* 382 (1964)

L. G. Forer, "A Free Press and a Fair Trial," 39 *American Bar Association Journal* 800, 843 (1953)

C. Gordon and H. Rosenfield, *Immigration Law and Procedure* (1959)

J. R. Green, "The Bill of Rights, the Fourteenth Amendment, and the Supreme Court," 46 *Michigan Law Review* 869 (1948)

J. Greenberg, *Race Relations and American Law* (1959)

E. N. Griswold, *The Fifth Amendment Today* (1955)

R. W. Haney, *Comstockery in America* (1960)

L. Henkin, "*Shelley* v. *Kraemer*: Notes for a Revised Opinion," 110 *University of Pennsylvania Law Review* 871 (1957)

J. Hetherington, "State Economic Regulation and Substantive Due Process of Law," 53 *Northwestern University Law Review* 13, 226 (1958)

W. E. Hocking, *Freedom of the Press: A Framework of Principle* (1947)

S. Hook, *The Paradoxes of Freedom* (1962)

R. A. Horn, *Groups and the Constitution* (1956)

J. B. James, *The Framing of the Fourteenth Amendment* (1956)

S. H. Kadish, "Methodology and Criteria in Due Process Adjudication: A Survey and Criticism," 66 *Yale Law Journal* 319 (1958)

Y. Kamisar, "On the Tactics of Police Oriented Critics of the Courts," 49 *Cornell Law Quarterly* 436 (1964)

J. Kerwin, *Catholic Viewpoint on Church and State* (1960)

M. R. Konvitz, *The Alien and the Asiatic in American Law* (1947)

M. R. Konvitz, *A Century of Civil Rights* (1961)

P. B. Kurland, "Of Church and State and the Supreme Court," 29 *University of Chicago Law Review* 1 (1961)

L. Levy, *Legacy of Suppression* (1960)

T. P. Lewis, "The Meaning of State Action," 60 *Columbia Law Review* 1083 (1960)

W. B. Lockhart and R. C. McClure, "Obscenity Censorship: The Core Constitutional Issue—What Is Obscene," 7 *Utah Law Review* 289 (1961)

D. O. McGovney, *The American Suffrage Medley* (1949)

B. Marshall, "Federal Protection of Negro Voting Rights," 27 *Law and Contemporary Problems* 455 (1962)

A. Meiklejohn, *Political Freedom: The Constitutional Powers of the People* (1960)

W. Mendelson, *Discrimination* (1962)

C. B. Nutting, "Is the First Amendment Obsolete?" 30 *George Washington Law Review* 167 (1961)

A. Pekelis, *Law and Social Action* (1950)

J. Peltason, *58 Lonely Men* (1961)

L. Pfeffer, *Church, State and Freedom* (1953)

D. Pollitt, "Timid Lawyers and Neglected Clients," *Harper's Magazine,* vol. 229 (August 1964)

Report of the Attorney General's Committee on Poverty and the Administration of Federal Criminal Justice (1963)

D. Reisman, "Democracy and Defamation: Control of Group Libel," 42 *Columbia Law Review* 727 (1942)

S. H. Rifkind, "When the Press Collides with Justice," 34 *Journal of the American Judicature Society* 46 (1950)

E. V. Rostow, *The Sovereign Prerogative* (1962)

R. A. Rutland, *The Birth of the Bill of Rights, 1776–1791* (1955)

T. Taylor, *Grand Inquest: The Story of Congressional Investigations* (1955)

United States Commission on Civil Rights, *Report* (1961)

United States Commission on Civil Rights, *Freedom to the Free* (1963)

C. E. Voss, *Caucasians Only* (1959)

B. F. Wright, *The Contract Clause of the Constitution* (1938)

Appendix I | THE CONSTITUTION OF THE UNITED STATES

WE THE PEOPLE of the United States, in Order to form a more perfect Union, establish Justice, insure domestic Tranquility, provide for the common defence, promote the general Welfare, and secure the Blessings of Liberty to ourselves and our Posterity, do ordain and establish this CONSTITUTION for the United States of America.

ARTICLE I

SECTION 1. All legislative Powers herein granted shall be vested in a Congress of the United States, which shall consist of a Senate and House of Representatives.

SECTION 2. 1.[1] The House of Representatives shall be composed of Members chosen every second Year by the People of the several States, and the Electors in each State shall have the Qualifications requisite for Electors of the most numerous Branch of the State Legislature.

2. No Person shall be a Representative who shall not have attained to the Age of twenty five Years, and been seven Years a Citizen of the United States, and who shall not, when elected, be an Inhabitant of that State in which he shall be chosen.

3. Representatives and direct Taxes shall be apportioned among the several States which may be included within this Union, according to their respective Numbers, which shall be determined by adding to the whole Number of free Persons, including those bound to Service for a Term of Years, and excluding Indians not taxed, three fifths of all other Persons. [See Amendment XIV.] The actual Enumeration shall be made within three Years after the first Meeting of the Congress of the United States, and within every subsequent Term in ten Years, in such Manner as they shall by Law direct. The Number of Representatives shall not exceed one for every thirty Thousand, but each State shall have

[1] The separate paragraphs (or subsections) of each Section are not numbered in the Constitution. Numbers have been added here to facilitate class discussion.

at Least one Representative; and until such enumeration shall be made, the State of New Hampshire shall be entitled to chuse three, Massachusetts eight, Rhode-Island and Providence Plantations one, Connecticut five, New-York six, New Jersey four, Pennsylvania eight, Delaware one, Maryland six, Virginia ten, North Carolina five, South Carolina five, and Georgia three.

4. When vacancies happen in the Representation from any State, the Executive Authority thereof shall issue Writs of Election to fill such Vacancies.

5. The House of Representatives shall chuse their Speaker and other Officers; and shall have the sole Power of Impeachment.

SECTION 3. 1. The Senate of the United States shall be composed of two Senators from each State, chosen by the Legislature thereof, for six Years; and each Senator shall have one Vote. [See Amendment XVII.]

2. Immediately after they shall be assembled in Consequence of the first Election, they shall be divided as equally as may be into three Classes. The Seats of the Senators of the first Class shall be vacated at the Expiration of the second Year, of the second Class at the Expiration of the fourth Year, and of the third Class at the Expiration of the sixth Year, so that one third may be chosen every second Year; and if Vacancies happen by Resignation, or otherwise, during the Recess of the Legislature of any State, the Executive thereof may make temporary Appointments until the next Meeting of the Legislature, which shall then fill such Vacancies.

3. No Person shall be a Senator who shall not have attained to the Age of thirty Years, and been nine Years a Citizen of the United States, and who shall not, when elected, be an Inhabitant of that State for which he shall be chosen.

4. The Vice President of the United States shall be President of the Senate, but shall have no Vote, unless they be equally divided.

5. The Senate shall chuse their other Officers, and also a President pro tempore, in the Absence of the Vice President, or when he shall exercise the Office of President of the United States.

6. The Senate shall have the sole Power to try all Impeachments. When sitting for that Purpose, they shall be on Oath or Affirmation. When the President of the United States is tried, the Chief Justice shall preside: And no Person shall be convicted without the Concurrence of two thirds of the Members present.

7. Judgment in Cases of Impeachment shall not extend further than to removal from Office, and disqualification to hold and enjoy any Office of honor, Trust or Profit under the United States: but the Party convicted shall nevertheless be liable and subject to Indictment, Trial, Judgment and Punishment, according to Law.

SECTION 4. 1. The Times, Places and Manner of holding Elections for Senators and Representatives, shall be prescribed in each State by the Legislature thereof; but the Congress may at any time by Law make or alter such Regulations, except as to the Places of chusing Senators.

2. The Congress shall assemble at least once in every Year, and such Meeting shall be on the first Monday in December, unless they shall by Law appoint a different Day. [See Amendment XX.]

SECTION 5. 1. Each House shall be the Judge of the Elections, Returns and Qualifications of its own Members, and a Majority of each shall constitute a Quorum to do Business; but a smaller Number may adjourn from day to day, and may be authorized to compel the attendance of absent Members, in such Manner, and under such Penalties as each House may provide.

2. Each House may determine the Rules of its Proceedings, punish its Members for Disorderly Behaviour, and, with the Concurrence of two thirds expel a Member.

3. Each House shall keep a Journal of its Proceedings, and from time to time publish the same, excepting such Parts as may in their Judgment require Secrecy; and the Yeas and Nays of the Members of either House on any question shall, at the Desire of one fifth of those Present, be entered on the Journal.

4. Neither House, during the Session of Congress, shall, without the Consent of the other, adjourn for more than three days, nor to any other Place than that in which the two Houses shall be sitting.

SECTION 6. 1. The Senators and Representatives shall receive a Compensation for their Services, to be ascertained by Law, and paid out of the Treasury of the United States. They shall in all Cases, except Treason, Felony and Breach of the Peace, be privileged from Arrest during their Attendance at the Session of their respective Houses, and in going to and returning from the same; and for any Speech or Debate in either House, they shall not be questioned in any other Place.

2. No Senator or Representative shall, during the Time for which he was elected, be appointed to any civil Office under the Authority of the United States, which shall have been created, or the Emoluments whereof shall have been encreased during such time; and no Person holding any Office under the United States, shall be a member of either House during his Continuance in Office.

SECTION 7. 1. All Bills for raising Revenue shall originate in the House of Representatives; but the Senate may propose or concur with Amendments as on other Bills.

2. Every Bill which shall have passed the House of Representatives and the Senate, shall, before it becomes a Law, be presented to the President of the United States; If he approve he shall sign it, but if not he shall return it, with his Objections to that House in which it shall have originated, who shall enter the Objections at large on their Journal, and proceed to reconsider it. If after such Reconsideration two thirds of that House shall agree to pass the Bill, it shall be sent, together with the Objections, to the other House, by which it shall likewise be reconsidered, and if approved by two thirds of that House, it shall become a Law. But in all such Cases the Votes of both Houses shall be determined by Yeas and Nays, and the Names of the Persons voting for and against the Bill shall be entered on the Journal of each House respectively. If any Bill shall not be returned by the President within ten Days (Sundays excepted) after it shall have been presented to him, the same shall be a Law, in like Manner as if he had

signed it, unless the Congress by their Adjournment prevent its Return, in which Case it shall not be a Law.

3. Every Order, Resolution, or Vote to which the Concurrence of the Senate and House of Representatives may be necessary (except on a question of Adjournment) shall be presented to the President of the United States; and before the same shall take Effect, shall be approved by him, or being disapproved by him, shall be repassed by two thirds of the Senate and House of Representatives, according to the Rules and Limitations prescribed in the Case of a Bill.

SECTION 8. The Congress shall have Power 1. To lay and collect Taxes, Duties, Imposts and Excises, to pay the Debts and provide for the common Defence and general Welfare of the United States; but all Duties, Imposts and Excises shall be uniform throughout the United States;

2. To borrow Money on the credit of the United States;

3. To regulate Commerce with foreign Nations, and among the several States, and with the Indian Tribes;

4. To establish a uniform Rule of Naturalization, and uniform Laws on the subject of Bankruptcies throughout the United States;

5. To coin Money, regulate the Value thereof, and of foreign Coin, and fix the Standard of Weights and Measures;

6. To provide for the Punishment of counterfeiting the Securities and current Coin of the United States;

7. To establish Post Offices and post Roads;

8. To promote the Progress of Science and useful Arts, by securing for limited Times to Authors and Inventors the exclusive Right to their respective Writings and Discoveries;

9. To constitute Tribunals inferior to the supreme Court;

10. To define and punish Piracies and Felonies committed on the high Seas, and Offences against the Law of Nations;

11. To declare War, grant Letters of Marque and Reprisal, and make Rules concerning Captures on Land and Water;

12. To raise and support Armies, but no Appropriation of Money to that Use shall be for a longer Term than two Years;

13. To provide and maintain a Navy;

14. To make Rules for the Government and Regulation of the land and naval Forces;

15. To provide for calling forth the Militia to execute the Laws of the Union, suppress Insurrections and repel Invasions;

16. To provide for organizing, arming, and disciplining, the Militia, and for governing such Part of them as may be employed in the Service of the United States, reserving to the States respectively, the Appointment of the Officers, and the Authority of training the Militia according to the discipline prescribed by Congress;

17. To exercise exclusive Legislation in all Cases whatsoever, over such District (not exceeding ten Miles square) as may, by Cession of particular States, and the Acceptance of Congress, become the Seat of the Government of the United States, and to exercise like Authority over all Places purchased by the Consent

of the Legislature of the State in which the same shall be, for the Erection of Forts, Magazines, Arsenals, dock-Yards, and other needful Buildings;—And

18. To make all Laws which shall be necessary and proper for carrying into Execution the foregoing Powers, and all other Powers vested by this Constitution in the Government of the United States, or in any Department or Officer thereof.

SECTION 9. 1. The Migration or Importation of such Persons as any of the States now existing shall think proper to admit, shall not be prohibited by the Congress prior to the Year one thousand eight hundred and eight, but a Tax or duty may be imposed on such Importation, not exceeding ten dollars for each Person.

2. The Privilege of the Writ of Habeas Corpus shall not be suspended, unless when in Cases of Rebellion or Invasion the public Safety may require it.

3. No Bill of Attainder or ex post facto Law shall be passed.

4. No Capitation, or other direct, Tax shall be laid, unless in Proportion to the Census or Enumeration herein before directed to be taken. [See Amendment XVI.]

5. No Tax or Duty shall be laid on Articles exported from any State.

6. No Preference shall be given by any Regulation of Commerce or Revenue to the Ports of one State over those of another: nor shall Vessels bound to, or from, one State, be obliged to enter, clear, or pay Duties in another.

7. No Money shall be drawn from the Treasury, but in Consequence of Appropriations made by Law; and a regular Statement and Account of the Receipts and Expenditures of all public Money shall be published from time to time.

8. No Title of Nobility shall be granted by the United States: And no Person holding any Office of Profit or Trust under them, shall, without the Consent of the Congress, accept of any present, Emolument, Office, or Title, of any kind whatever, from any King, Prince, or foreign State.

SECTION 10. 1. No State shall enter into any Treaty, Alliance, or Confederation; grant Letters of Marque and Reprisal; coin Money; emit Bills of Credit; make any Thing but gold and silver Coin a Tender in Payment of Debts; pass any Bill of Attainder, ex post facto Law, or Law impairing the Obligation of Contracts, or grant any Title of Nobility.

2. No State shall, without the Consent of the Congress, lay any Imposts or Duties on Imports or Exports, except what may be absolutely necessary for executing its inspection Laws: and the net Produce of all Duties and Imposts, laid by any State on Imports or Exports, shall be for the Use of the Treasury of the United States; and all such Laws shall be subject to the Revision and Controul of the Congress.

3. No State shall, without the Consent of Congress, lay any Duty of Tonnage, keep Troops, or Ships of War in time of Peace, enter into any Agreement or Compact with another State, or with a foreign Power, or engage in War, unless actually invaded, or in such imminent Danger as will not admit of delay.

ARTICLE II

SECTION 1. 1. The executive Power shall be vested in a President of the United States of America. He shall hold his Office during the Term of four Years, and, together with the Vice President, chosen for the same Term, be elected, as follows

2. Each State shall appoint, in such Manner as the Legislature thereof may direct, a Number of Electors, equal to the whole Number of Senators and Representatives to which the State may be entiled in the Congress: but no Senator or Representative, or Person holding an Office of Trust or Profit under the United States, shall be appointed an Elector.

3. The Electors shall meet in their respective States, and vote by Ballot for two Persons, of whom one at least shall not be an Inhabitant of the same State with themselves. And they shall make a List of all the Persons voted for, and of the Number of Votes for each; which List they shall sign and certify, and transmit sealed to the Seat of the Government of the United States, directed to the President of the Senate. The President of the Senate shall, in the Presence of the Senate and House of Representatives, open all the Certificates, and the Votes shall then be counted. The Person having the greatest Number of Votes shall be the President, if such Number be a Majority of the whole Number of Electors appointed; and if there be more than one who have such Majority, and have an equal Number of Votes, then the House of Representatives shall immediately chuse by Ballot one of them for President; and if no Person have a Majority, then from the five highest on the List the said House shall in like Manner chuse the President. But in chusing the President, the Votes shall be taken by States, the Representation from each State having one Vote; A quorum for this Purpose shall consist of a Member or Members from two thirds of the States, and a Majority of all the States shall be necessary to a Choice. In every Case, after the Choice of the President, the Person having the greatest Number of Votes of the Electors shall be the Vice President. But if there should remain two or more who have equal Votes, the Senate shall chuse from them by Ballot the Vice President. [See Amendments XII and XX.]

4. The Congress may determine the Time of chusing the Electors, and the Day on which they shall give their Votes; which Day shall be the same throughout the United States.

5. No Person except a natural born Citizen, or a Citizen of the United States, at the time of the Adoption of this Constitution, shall be eligible to the Office of President; neither shall any Person be eligible to that Office who shall not have attained to the Age of thirty five Years, and been fourteen Years a Resident within the United States.

6. In Case of the Removal of the President from Office, or of his Death, Resignation, or Inability to discharge the Powers and Duties of the said Office, the Same shall devolve on the Vice President, and the Congress may by Law provide for the Case of Removal, Death, Resignation, or Inability, both of the President and Vice President, declaring what Officer shall then act as President, and such Officer shall act accordingly, until the Disability be removed, or a President shall be elected. [See Amendment XX.]

7. The President shall, at stated Times, receive for his Services, a Compensation, which shall neither be encreased nor diminished during the Period for which he shall have been elected, and he shall not receive within that Period any other Emolument from the United States, or any of them.

8. Before he enter on the Execution of his Office, he shall take the following Oath or Affirmation:—"I do solemnly swear (or affirm) that I will faithfully execute the Office of President of the United States, and will to the best of my Ability, preserve, protect and defend the Constitution of the United States."

SECTION 2. 1. The President shall be Commander in Chief of the Army and Navy of the United States, and of the Militia of the several States, when called into the actual service of the United States; he may require the Opinion, in writing, of the principal Officer in each of the executive Departments, upon any Subject relating to the Duties of their respective Officers, and he shall have Power to grant Reprieves and Pardons for Offences against the United States, except in Cases of Impeachment.

2. He shall have Power, by and with the Advice and Consent of the Senate, to make Treaties, provided two thirds of the Senators present concur; and he shall nominate, and by and with the Advice and Consent of the Senate, shall appoint Ambassadors, other public Ministers and Consuls, Judges of the supreme Court, and all other Officers of the United States, whose Appointments are not herein otherwise provided for, and which shall be established by Law: but the Congress may by Law vest the Appointment of such inferior Officers, as they think proper, in the President alone, in the Courts of Law, or in the Heads of Departments.

3. The President shall have Power to fill up all Vacancies that may happen during the Recess of the Senate, by granting Commissions which shall expire at the End of their next Session.

SECTION 3. He shall from time to time give to the Congress Information of the State of the Union, and recommend to their Consideration such Measures as he shall judge necessary and expedient; he may, on extraordinary Occasions, convene both Houses, or either of them, and in Case of Disagreement between them, with Respect to the Time of Adjournment, he may adjourn them to such Time as he shall think proper; he shall receive Ambassadors and other public Ministers; he shall take Care that the Laws be faithfully executed, and shall Commission all the Officers of the United States.

SECTION 4. The President, Vice President and all civil Officers of the United States, shall be removed from Office on Impeachment for, and Conviction of, Treason, Bribery, or other high Crimes and Misdemeanors.

ARTICLE III

SECTION 1. The judicial Power of the United States, shall be vested in one supreme Court, and in such inferior Courts as the Congress may from time to time ordain and establish. The Judges, both of the supreme and inferior Courts, shall hold their Offices during good Behaviour, and shall, at stated Times, receive for their Services, a Compensation, which shall not be diminished during their Continuance in Office.

SECTION 2. 1. The judicial Power shall extend to all Cases, in Law and Equity, arising under this Constitution, the Laws of the United States, and Treaties made, or which shall be made, under their Authority;—to all Cases affecting Ambassadors, other public Ministers and Consuls;—to all Cases of admiralty and maritime Jurisdiction;—to Controversies to which the United States shall be a Party;—to Controversies between two or more States;—between a State and Citizens of another State; [See Amendment XI.]—between Citizens of different States,—between Citizens of the same State claiming Lands under Grants of different States, and between a State, or the Citizens thereof, and foreign States, Citizens or Subjects.

2. In all Cases affecting Ambassadors, other public Ministers and Consuls, and those in which a State shall be Party, the supreme Court shall have original Jurisdiction. In all the other Cases before mentioned, the supreme Court shall have appellate Jurisdiction, both as to Law and Fact, with such Exceptions, and under such Regulations as the Congress shall make.

3. The Trial of all Crimes, except in Cases of Impeachment, shall be by Jury; and such Trial shall be held in the State where the said Crimes shall have been committed; but when not committed within any State, the Trial shall be at such Place or Places as the Congress may by Law have directed.

SECTION 3. 1. Treason against the United States, shall consist only in levying War against them, or in adhering to their Enemies, giving them Aid and Comfort. No Person shall be convicted of Treason unless on the Testimony of two Witnesses to the same overt Act, or on Confession in open Court.

2. The Congress shall have Power to declare the Punishment of Treason, but no Attainder of Treason shall work Corruption of Blood, or Forfeiture except during the Life of the Person attainted.

ARTICLE IV

SECTION 1. Full Faith and Credit shall be given in each State to the public Acts, Records, and judicial Proceedings of every other State. And the Congress may by general Laws prescribe the Manner in which such Act, Records and Proceedings shall be proved, and the Effect thereof.

SECTION 2. 1. The Citizens of each State shall be entitled to all Privileges and Immunities of Citizens in the several States.

2. A Person charged in any State with Treason, Felony, or other Crime, who shall flee from Justice, and be found in another State, shall on Demand of the executive Authority of the State from which he fled, be delivered up, to be removed to the State having Jurisdiction of the Crime.

3. No Person held to Service or Labour in one State, under the Laws thereof, escaping into another, shall, in Consequence of any Law or Regulation therein, be discharged from such Service or Labour, but shall be delivered up on Claim of the Party to whom such Service or Labour may be due.

SECTION 3. 1. New States may be admitted by the Congress into this Union; but no new State shall be formed or erected within the Jurisdiction of any other

State; nor any State be formed by the Junction of two or more States, or Parts of States, without the Consent of the Legislatures of the States concerned as well as of the Congress.

2. The Congress shall have Power to dispose of and make all needful Rules and Regulations respecting the Territory or other Property belonging to the United States; and nothing in this Constitution shall be so construed as to Prejudice any Claims of the United States, or of any particular State.

SECTION 4. The United States shall guarantee to every State in this Union a Republican Form of Government, and shall protect each of them against Invasion; and on Application of the Legislature, or of the Executive (when the Legislature cannot be convened) against domestic Violence.

ARTICLE V

The Congress, whenever two thirds of both Houses shall deem it necessary, shall propose Amendments to this Constitution, or, on the Application of the Legislatures of two thirds of the several States, shall call a Convention for proposing Amendments, which, in either Case, shall be valid to all Intents and Purposes, as Part of this Constitution, when ratified by the Legislatures of three fourths of the several States, or by Conventions in three fourths thereof, as the one or the other Mode of Ratification may be proposed by the Congress; Provided that no Amendment which may be made prior to the Year One thousand eight hundred and eight shall in any Manner affect the first and fourth Clauses in the Ninth Section of the first Article; and that no State, without its Consent, shall be deprived of its equal Suffrage in the Senate.

ARTICLE VI

1. All Debts contracted and Engagements entered into, before the Adoption of this Constitution, shall be as valid against the United States under this Constitution, as under the Confederation.

2. This Constitution, and the Laws of the United States which shall be made in Pursuance thereof; and all Treaties made, or which shall be made, under the Authority of the United States, shall be the supreme Law of the Land; and the Judges in every State shall be bound thereby, any Thing in the Constitution or Laws of Any State to the Contrary notwithstanding.

3. The Senators and Representatives before mentioned, and the Members of the several State Legislatures, and all executive and judicial Officers, both of the United States and of the several States, shall be bound by Oath or Affirmation, to support this Constitution; but no religious Test shall ever be required as a Qualification to any Office or public Trust under the United States.

ARTICLE VII

The Ratification of the Conventions of nine States, shall be sufficient for the Establishment of this Constitution between the States so ratifying the Same.

AMENDMENTS

ARTICLE I

Congress shall make no law respecting an establishment of religion, or prohibiting the free exercise thereof; or abridging the freedom of speech, or of the press; or the right of the people peaceably to assemble, and to petition the Government for a redress of grievances.

ARTICLE II

A well regulated Militia, being necessary to the security of a free State, the right of the people to keep and bear Arms, shall not be infringed.

ARTICLE III

No Soldier shall, in time of peace be quartered in any house, without the consent of the Owner, nor in time of war, but in a manner to be prescribed by law.

ARTICLE IV

The right of the people to be secure in their persons, houses, papers, and effects, against unreasonable searches and seizures, shall not be violated, and no Warrants shall issue, but upon probable cause, supported by Oath or affirmation, and particularly describing the place to be searched, and the persons or things to be seized.

ARTICLE V

No person shall be held to answer for a capital, or otherwise infamous crime, unless on a presentment or indicted of a Grand Jury, except in cases arising in the land or naval forces, or in the Militia, when in actual service in time of War or public danger; nor shall any person be subject for the same offence to be twice put in jeopardy of life or limb; nor shall be compelled in any criminal case to be a witness against himself, nor be deprived of life, liberty, or property, without due process of law; nor shall private property be taken for public use, without just compensation.

ARTICLE VI

In all criminal prosecutions the accused shall enjoy the right to a speedy and public trial, by an impartial jury of the State and district wherein the crime shall have been committed, which district shall have been previously ascertained by law, and to be informed of the nature and cause of the accusation; to be confronted with the witnesses against him; to have compulsory process for obtaining witnesses in his favor, and to have the Assistance of Counsel for his defence.

ARTICLE VII

In suits at common law, where the value in controversy shall exceed twenty dollars, the right of trial by jury shall be preserved, and no fact tried by a jury shall be otherwise re-examined in any Court of the United States, than according to the rules of the common law.

ARTICLE VIII

Excessive bail shall not be required, nor excessive fines imposed, nor cruel and unusual punishments inflicted.

ARTICLE IX

The enumeration in the Constitution, of certain rights, shall not be construed to deny or disparage others retained by the people.

ARTICLE X

The powers not delegated to the United States by the Constitution, nor prohibited by it to the States, are reserved to the States respectively, or to the people.
[The first ten Amendments were adopted in 1791.]

ARTICLE XI

The Judicial power of the United States shall not be construed to extend to any suit in law or equity, commenced or prosecuted against one of the United States by Citizens of another State, or by Citizens or Subjects of any Foreign State. [Adopted 1798.]

ARTICLE XII

The Electors shall meet in their respective states, and vote by ballot for President and Vice-President, one of whom, at least, shall not be an inhabitant of the same state with themselves; they shall name in their ballots the person voted for as President, and in distinct ballots the person voted for as Vice-President, and they shall make distinct lists of all persons voted for as President, and of all persons voted for as Vice-President, and of the number of votes for each, which lists they shall sign and certify, and transmit sealed to the seat of the government of the United States, directed to the President of the Senate;— The President of the Senate shall, in the presence of the Senate and House of Representatives, open all the certificates and the votes shall then be counted;— The person having the greatest number of votes for President, shall be the President, if such number be a majority of the whole number of Electors appointed; and if no person have such majority, then from the persons having the highest numbers not exceeding three on the list of those voted for as President, the House of Representatives shall choose immediately, by ballot, the President. But in choosing the President, the votes shall be taken by the states, the representation from each state having one vote; a quorum for this purpose shall consist of a member or members from two-thirds of the states, and a majority of all the states shall be necessary to a choice. And if the House of Representatives shall not choose a President whenever the right of choice shall devolve upon them, before the fourth day of March next following, then the Vice-President shall act as President, as in the case of the death or other constitutional disability of the President.—The person having the greatest number of votes as Vice-President, shall be the Vice-President, if such number be a majority of the whole number of Electors appointed, and if no person have a majority, then from the two highest numbers on the list, the Senate shall choose the Vice-President; a quorum for the purpose shall consist of two-thirds of the whole number of Senators, and a majority of the whole number shall be necessary to a choice. But no person constitutionally ineligible to the office of President shall be eligible to that of Vice-President of the United States. [Adopted 1804.]

ARTICLE XIII

SECTION 1. Neither slavery nor involuntary servitude, except as a punishment for crime whereof the party shall have been duly convicted, shall exist within the United States, or any place subject to their jurisdiction.

SECTION 2. Congress shall have power to enforce this article by appropriate legislation. [Adopted 1865.]

ARTICLE XIV

SECTION 1. All persons born or naturalized in the United States, and subject to the jurisdiction thereof, are citizens of the United States and of the State wherein they reside. No State shall make or enforce any law which shall abridge the privileges or immunities of citizens of the United States; nor shall any State deprive any person of life, liberty, or property, without due process of law; nor deny to any person within its jurisdiction the equal protection of the laws.

SECTION 2. Representatives shall be apportioned among the several States according to their respective numbers, counting the whole number of persons in each State, excluding Indians not taxed. But when the right to vote at any election for the choice of electors for President and Vice President of the United States, Representatives in Congress, the Executive and Judicial officers of a State, or the members of the Legislature thereof, is denied to any of the male inhabitants of such State, being twenty-one years of age, and citizens of the United States, or in any way abridged, except for participation in rebellion, or other crime, the basis of representation therein shall be reduced in the proportion which the number of such male citizens shall bear to the whole number of male citizens twenty-one years of age in such State.

SECTION 3. No person shall be a Senator or Representative in Congress, or elector of President and Vice President, or hold any office, civil or military, under the

United States, or under any State, who, having previously taken an oath, as a member of Congress, or as an officer of the United States, or as a member of any State legislature, or as an executive or judicial officer of any State, to support the Constitution of the United States, shall have engaged in insurrection or rebellion against the same, or given aid or comfort to the enemies thereof. But Congress may by a vote of two-thirds of each House, remove such disability.

SECTION 4. The validity of the public debt of the United States, authorized by law, including debts incurred for payment of pensions and bounties for services in suppressing insurrection or rebellion, shall not be questioned. But neither the United States nor any State shall assume or pay any debt or obligation incurred in aid of insurrection or rebellion against the United States, or any claim for the loss or emancipation of any slave; but all such debts, obligations and claims shall be held illegal and void.

SECTION 5. The Congress shall have power to enforce, by appropriate legislation, the provisions of this article. [Adopted 1868.]

ARTICLE XV

SECTION 1. The right of citizens of the United States to vote shall not be denied or abridged by the United States or by any State on account of race, color, or previous condition of servitude.

SECTION 2. The Congress shall have power to enforce this article of appropriate legislation. [Adopted 1870.]

ARTICLE XVI

The Congress shall have power to lay and collect taxes on incomes, from whatever source derived, without apportionment among the several States, and without regard to any census or enumeration. [Adopted 1913.]

ARTICLE XVII

The Senate of the United States shall be composed of two Senators from each State, elected by the people thereof, for six years; and each Senator shall have one vote. The electors in each State shall have the qualifications requisite for electors of the most numerous branch of the State legislatures.

When vacancies happen in the representation of any State in the Senate, the executive authority of such State shall issue writs of election to fill such vacancies: *Provided*, That the legislature of any State may empower the executive thereof to make temporary appointments until the people fill the vacancies by election as the legislature may direct.

This amendment shall not be so construed as to affect the election or term of any Senator chosen before it becomes valid as part of the Constitution. [Adopted 1913.]

ARTICLE XVIII

SECTION 1. After one year from the ratification of this article the manufacture, sale, or transportation of intoxicating liquors within, the importation thereof into, or the exportation thereof from the United States and all territory subject to the judisdiction thereof for beverage purposes is hereby prohibited.

SECTION 2. The Congress and the several States shall have concurrent power to enforce this article by appropriate legislation.

SECTION 3. This article shall be inoperative unless it shall have been ratified as an amendment to the Constitution by the legislatures of the several States, as provided in the Constitution, within seven years from the date of the submission hereof to the States by the Congress. [Adopted 1919.]

ARTICLE XIX

The right of citizens of the United States to vote shall not be denied or abridged by the United States or by any State on account of sex.

Congress shall have power to enforce this article by appropriate legislation. [Adopted 1920.]

ARTICLE XX

SECTION 1. The terms of the President and Vice President shall end at noon on the 20th day of January, and the terms of Senators and Representatives at noon on the 3d day of January, of the years in which such terms would have ended if this article had not been ratified; and the terms of their successors shall then begin.

SECTION 2. The Congress shall assemble at least once in every year, and such meeting shall begin at noon on the 3d day of January, unless they shall by law appoint a different day.

SECTION 3. If, at the time fixed for the beginning of the term of the President, the President elect shall have died, the Vice President elect shall become President. If a President shall not have been chosen before the time fixed for the beginning of his term, or if the President elect shall have failed to qualify, then the Vice President elect shall act as President until a President shall have qualified; and the Congress may by law provide for the case wherein neither a President elect nor a Vice President elect shall have qualified, declaring who shall then act as President, or the manner in which one who is to act shall be selected, and such person shall act accordingly until a President or Vice President shall have qualified.

SECTION 4. The Congress may by law provide for the case of the death of any of the persons from whom the House of Representatives may choose a President whenever the right of choice shall have devolved upon them, and for the case of the death of any of the persons from whom the Senate may choose a Vice President whenever the right of choice shall have devolved upon them.

SECTION 5. Sections 1 and 2 shall take effect on the 15th day of October following the ratification of this article.

SECTION 6. This article shall be inoperative unless it shall have been ratified as an amendment to the Constitution by the legislatures of three-fourths of the several States within seven years from the date of its submission. [Adopted 1933.]

ARTICLE XXI

SECTION 1. The eighteenth article of amendment to the Constitution of the United States is hereby repealed.

SECTION 2. The transportation or importation into any State, Territory, or possession of the United States for delivery or use therein of intoxicating liquors, in violation of the laws thereof, is hereby prohibited.

SECTION 3. This article shall be inoperative unless it shall have been ratified as an amendment to the Constitution by conventions in the several States, as provided in the Constitution, within seven years from the date of the submission hereof to the States by the Congress. [Adopted 1933.]

ARTICLE XXII

SECTION 1. No person shall be elected to the office of the President more than twice, and no person who has held the office of President, or acted as President, for more than two years of a term to which some other person was elected President shall be elected to the office of the President more than once. But this Article shall not apply to any person holding the office of President when this Article was proposed by the Congress, and shall not prevent any person who may be holding the office of President, or acting as President, during the term within which this Article becomes operative from holding the office of President, or acting as President during the remainder of such term.

SECTION 2. This Article shall be inoperative unless it shall have been ratified as an amendment to the Constitution by the legislatures of three-fourths of the several States within seven years from the date of its submission to the States by the Congress. [Adopted 1951.]

ARTICLE XXIII

SECTION 1. The District constituting the seat of Government of the United States shall appoint in such manner as the Congress may direct:
A number of electors of President and Vice President equal to the whole

number of Senators and Representatives in Congress to which the District would be entitled if it were a State, but in no event more than the least populous state; they shall be in addition to those appointed by the states, but they shall be considered, for the purposes of the election of President and Vice President, to be electors appointed by a state; and they shall meet in the District and perform such duties as provided by the twelfth article of amendment.

SECTION 2. The Congress shall have power to enforce this article by appropriate legislation. [Adopted 1961.]

ARTICLE XXIV

SECTION 1. The right of citizens of the United States to vote in any primary or other election for President or Vice President, for electors for President or Vice President, or for Senator or Representative in Congress, shall not be denied or abridged by the United States or any State by reason of failure to pay any poll tax or other tax.

SECTION 2. The Congress shall have power to enforce this article by appropriate legislation. [Adopted 1964.]

Appendix II | JUSTICES OF THE SUPREME COURT

Justices of the Supreme Court of the United States, their terms of service, political affiliation (F., Federalist; R., Republican; D., Democrat; W., Whig; Ind., Independent), residence at time of appointment, and the Presidents who appointed them. The names of the Chief Justices are indicated by italics. The letter preceding the name of each Justice is used to identify the line of succession for each "seat" on the bench. Thus, "seat" A was held first by Chief Justice Jay, next by Chief Justice Rutledge, then by Chief Justice Ellsworth, etc.

Appointed by
President Washington (1789–1797)
Federalist from Virginia

A. *John Jay* (1789–1795) F., N.Y.
B. John Rutledge (1789–1791) F., S.C.
C. William Cushing (1789–1810) F., Mass.
D. James Wilson (1789–1798) F., Pa.
E. John Blair (1789–1796) F., Va.
F. James Iredell (1790–1799) F., N.C.
B. Thomas Johnson (1791–1793) F., Md.
B. William Paterson (1793–1806) F., N.J.
A. *John Rutledge* (1795) F., S.C.
E. Samuel Chase (1796–1811) F., Md.
A. *Oliver Ellsworth* (1796–1800) F., Conn.

Appointed by
President Adams (1797–1801)
Federalist from Massachusetts

D. Bushrod Washington (1789–1829) F., Va.
F. Alfred Moore (1799–1804) F., N.C.
A. *John Marshall* (1801–1835) F., Va.

Appointed by
President Jefferson (1801–1809)
Republican from Virginia

F. William Johnson (1804–1834) R., S.C.
B. Brockholst Livingston (1806–1823) R., N.Y.
G. Thomas Todd (1807–1826) R., Ky.

Appointed by
President Madison (1809–1817)
Republican from Virginia

E. Gabriel Duval (1811–1835) R., Md.
C. Joseph Story (1811–1845) R., Mass.

Appointed by
President Monroe (1817–1825)
Republican from Virginia

B. Smith Thompson (1823–1843) R., N.Y.

Appointed by
President Adams (1825–1829)
Republican from Massachusetts

G. Robert Trimble (1826–1828) R., Ky.

Appointed by
President Jackson (1829–1837)
Democrat from Tennessee

G. John McLean (1829–1861) D. (later R.), Ohio
D. Henry Baldwin (1830–1844) D., Pa.
F. James M. Wayne (1835–1867) D., Ga.
A. *Roger B. Taney* (1836–1864) D., Md.
E. Philip P. Barbour (1836–1841) D., Va.

Appointed by
President Van Buren (1837–1841)
Democrat from New York

H. John Catron (1837–1865) D., Tenn.

I. John McKinley (1837–1852) D., Ky.
E. Peter V. Daniel (1841–1860) D., Va.

Appointed by
President Tyler (1841–1845)
Whig from Virginia

B. Samuel Nelson (1845–1872) D., N.Y.

Appointed by
President Polk (1845–1849)
Democrat from Tennessee

C. Levi Woodbury (1845–1851) D., N.H.
D. Robert C. Grier (1846–1870) D., Pa.

Appointed by
President Fillmore (1850–1853)
Whig from New York

C. Benjamin R. Curtis (1851–1857) W., Mass.

Appointed by
President Pierce (1853–1857)
Democrat from New Hampshire

I. John A. Campbell (1853–1861) D., Ala.

Appointed by
President Buchanan (1857–1861)
Democrat from Pennsylvania

C. Nathan Clifford (1858–1881) D., Me.

Appointed by
President Lincoln (1861–1865)
Republican from Illinois

G. Noah H. Swayne (1862–1881) R., Ohio
E. Samuel F. Miller (1862–1890) R., Iowa
I. David Davis (1862–1877) R. (Later D.), Ill.
J. Stephen J. Field (1863–1897) D., Cal.
A. *Salmon P. Chase* (1864–1873) R., Ohio

Appointed by
President Grant (1869–1877)
Republican from Illinois

D. William Strong (1870–1880) R., Pa.
F. Joseph P. Bradley (1870–1892) R., N.J.
B. Ward Hunt (1872–1882) R., N.Y.
A. *Morrison R. Waite* (1874–1888) R., Ohio

Appointed by
President Hayes (1877–1881)
Republican from Ohio

I. John Marshall Harlan (1877–1911) R., Ky.
D. William B. Woods (1880–1887) R., Ga.

Appointed by
President Garfield (Mar.–Sept. 1881)
Republican from Ohio

G. Stanley Matthews (1881–1889) R., Ohio

Appointed by
President Arthur (1881–1885)
Republican from New York

C. Horace Gray (1881–1902) R., Mass.
B. Samuel Blatchford (1882–1893) R., N.Y.

Appointed by
President Cleveland (1885–1889)
Democrat from New York

D. Lucius Q. C. Lamar (1888–1893) D., Miss.
A. *Melville W. Fuller* (1888–1910) D., Ill.

Appointed by
President Harrison (1889–1893)
Republican from Indiana

G. David J. Brewer (1889–1910) R., Kans.
E. Henry B. Brown (1890–1906) R., Mich.
F. George Shiras (1892–1903) R., Pa.
D. Howell E. Jackson (1893–1895) D., Tenn.

Appointed by
President Cleveland (1893–1897)
Democrat from New York

B. Edward D. White (1894–1910) D., La.
D. Rufus W. Peckham (1895–1909) D., N.Y.

Appointed by
President McKinley (1897–1901)
Republican from Ohio

J. Joseph McKenna (1898–1925) R., Cal.
or
H.

Appointed by
President Roosevelt (1901–1909)
Republican from New York

C. Oliver Wendell Holmes (1902–1932) R., Mass.
F. William R. Day (1903–1922) R., Ohio
E. William H. Moody (1906–1910) R., Mass.

Appointed by
President Taft (1909–1913)
Republican from Ohio

D. Horace H. Lurton (1909–1914) D., Tenn.
G. Charles E. Hughes (1910–1916) R., N.Y.
A. *Edward D. White* (1910–1921)
Promoted from associate justiceship
B. Willis Van Devanter (1910–1937) R., Wyo.
E. Joseph R. Lamar (1910–1916) D., Ga.
I. Mahlon Pitney (1912–1922) R., N.J.

Appointed by
President Wilson (1913–1921)
Democrat from New Jersey

D. James C. McReynolds (1914–1941) D., Tenn.
E. Louis D. Brandeis (1916–1939) D., Mass.
G. John H. Clarke (1916–1922) D., Ohio

Appointed by
President Harding (1921–1923)
Republican from Ohio

A. William H. Taft (1921–1930) R., Conn.
G. George Sutherland (1922–1938) R., Utah
F. Pierce Butler (1922–1939) D., Minn.
I. Edward T. Sanford (1923–1930) R., Tenn.

Appointed by
President Coolidge (1923–1929)
Republican from Massachusetts

H. Harlan F. Stone (1925–1941) R., N.Y.

Appointed by
President Hoover (1929–1933)
Republican from California

A. *Charles E. Hughes* (1930–1941) R., N.Y.
I. Owen J. Roberts (1930–1945) R., Pa.
C. Benjamin N. Cardozo (1932–1938) D., N.Y.

Appointed by
President Roosevelt (1933–1945)
Democrat from New York

B. Hugo L. Black (1937–   ) D., Ala.
G. Stanley F. Reed (1938–1957) D., Ky.
C. Felix Frankfurter (1939–1965) Ind., Mass.
E. William O. Douglas (1939–1962) D., Conn.
F. Frank Murphy (1940–1949) D., Mich.
D. James F. Byrnes (1941–1942) D., S.C.
A. *Harlan F. Stone* (1941–1946)
Promoted from associate justiceship

H. Robert H. Jackson (1941–1954) D., N.Y.
D. Wiley B. Rutledge (1943–1949) D., Iowa

Appointed by
President Truman (1945–1953)
Democrat from Missouri

I. Harold H. Burton (1945–1958) R., Ohio
A. *Fred M. Vinson* (1946–1953) D., Ky.
F. Tom C. Clark (1949–   ) D., Tex.
D. Sherman Minton (1949–1956) D., Ind.

Appointed by
President Eisenhower (1953–1961)
Republican from New York

A. *Earl Warren* (1953–   ) R., Cal.
H. John M. Harlan (1955–   ) R., N.Y.
D. William J. Brennan (1956–   ) D., N.J.
G. Charles E. Whittaker (1957–1962) R., Mo.
I. Potter Stewart (1958–   ) R., Ohio

Appointed by
President Kennedy (1961–1963)
Democrat from Massachusetts

C. Arthur J. Goldberg (1962–   ) D., Ill.
G. Byron R. White (1962–   ) D., Colo.

Appendix III | LIST OF CASES BY HISTORICAL PERIODS

I. The Marshall Court (1801–1835)

Marbury v. *Madison* (1803), 5
Dartmouth College v. *Woodward* (1819), 242
McCulloch v. *Maryland* (1819), 185
Cohens v. *Virginia* (1821), 41
Gibbons v. *Ogden* (1824), 85
Brown v. *Maryland* (1827), 211

II. The Taney Court (1836–1864)

Cooley v. *Board of Wardens* (1851), 196
Dred Scott v. *Sandford* (1857), 516
Ex parte Merryman (1861), 70
The Prize Cases (1863), 56
Ex parte Milligan (1866), 166

III. The Court Under Chase and Waite (1864–1888)

Ex parte Milligan (1866), 166
The Daniel Ball (1871), 91
The Slaughter House Cases (1873), 245
Munn v. *Illinois* (1877), 252
Pensacola Telegraph Co. v. *Western Union* (1878), 92
Civil Rights Cases (1883), 536
Hurtado v. *California* (1884), 278
Juilliard v. *Greenman* (1884), 191

IV. The Court Under Fuller (1888–1910)

Pollock v. *Farmers' Loan & Trust Co.* (1895), 129
United States v. *E. C. Knight* (1895), 97
Plessy v. *Ferguson* (1896), 519
Lochner v. *New York* (1905), 256

Galveston, Harrisburg, & San Antonio Ry. v. *Texas* (1908), 216

V. The Court Under White and Taft (1910–1930)

Muskrat v. *United States* (1911), 10
The Shreveport Case (1914), 100
Masses Publishing Co. v. *Patten* (1917), 387
Hammer v. *Dagenhart* (1918), 102
Schenck v. *United States* (1919), 388
Johnson v. *Maryland* (1920), 225
Missouri v. *Holland* (1920), 179
Bailey v. *Drexel Furniture Co.* (1922), 133
Moore v. *Dempsey* (1923), 306
Gitlow v. *New York* (1925), 392
Pierce v. *Society of Sisters* (1925), 566
Weaver v. *Palmer Bros. Co.* (1926), 261
DiSanto v. *Pennsylvania* (1927), 208
McGrain v. *Daugherty* (1927), 427
Tumey v. *Ohio* (1927), 305
Whitney v. *California* (1927), 390

VI. The Hughes Court—First Phase (1930–1936)

Federal Radio Commission v. *General Electric* (1930), 54
Near v. *Minnesota* (1931), 413
Federal Radio Commission v. *Nelson Bros. Co.* (1933), 55
Nebbia v. *New York* (1934), 262
Mooney v. *Holohan* (1935), 380
Ashwander v. *Tennessee* (1936), 9
United States v. *Butler* (1936), 149
United States v. *California* (1936), 128

Index of Cases

Index of Cases

The principal cases reproduced in this book and the page numbers on which they begin are in **boldface** type. The cases that are mentioned in the text and in the comments, notes, and quaeres, and their page numbers, are in lightface type.